06

The Greenwood Library of
AMERICAN WAR REPORTING

The Greenwood Library of
AMERICAN WAR REPORTING

| VOLUME 3 | The Civil War, North and South |

The Civil War North, Amy Reynolds
The Civil War South, Debra Reddin van Tuyll

David A. Copeland, General Editor

Greenwood Press
Westport, Connecticut • London

Library of Congress Cataloging-in-Publication Data

The Greenwood library of American war reporting / David A. Copeland, general editor.
  v. cm.
    Consists chiefly of contemporary first-person and news accounts.
    Includes bibliographical references and index.
    Contents: v. 1. The French and Indian War & the Revolutionary War—v. 2. The War of 1812
& the Mexican-American War—v. 3. The Civil War, north and south—v. 4. The Indian wars
& the Spanish-American War—v. 5. World War I & World War II, the European Theater—v.
6. World War II, the Asian Theater & the Korean War—v. 7. The Vietnam War & post-Vietnam
conflicts—v. 8. The Iraq wars and the War on Terror & index.
    ISBN 0–313–33435–8 (set : alk. paper)—ISBN 0–313–32885–4 (v. 1 : alk. paper)—
ISBN 0–313–32931–1 (v. 2 : alk. paper)—ISBN 0–313–32941–9 (v. 3 : alk. paper)—ISBN
0–313–32990–7 (v. 4 : alk. paper)—ISBN 0–313–32888–9 (v. 5 : alk. paper)—ISBN
0–313–32942–7 (v. 6 : alk. paper)—ISBN 0–313–32930–3 (v. 7 : alk. paper)—ISBN
0–313–32933–8 (v. 8 : alk. paper)
    1. Military history, Modern—Sources.   2. United States—History, Military—Sources.
3. United States—Armed Forces—History—Sources.   I. Copeland, David A., 1951–   .
II. Greenwood Press (Westport, Conn.)
    D5.G84   2005
    973—dc22   2005010122

British Library Cataloguing in Publication Data is available.

Library of Congress Catalog Card Number: 2005010122
ISBN: 0–313–33435–8 (set)
        0–313–32885–4 (vol. 1)
        0–313–32931–1 (vol. 2)
        0–313–32941–9 (vol. 3)
        0–313–32990–7 (vol. 4)
        0–313–32888–9 (vol. 5)
        0–313–32942–7 (vol. 6)
        0–313–32930–3 (vol. 7)
        0–313–32933–8 (vol. 8)

First published in 2005

Greenwood Press, 88 Post Road West, Westport, CT 06881
An imprint of Greenwood Publishing Group, Inc.
www.greenwood.com

Printed in the United States of America

The paper used in this book complies with the
Permanent Paper Standard issued by the National
Information Standards Organization (Z39.48–1984).

10 9 8 7 6 5 4 3 2 1

THE GREENWOOD LIBRARY OF AMERICAN WAR REPORTING

Volume 1
The French and Indian War & The Revolutionary War
David A. Copeland and Carol Sue Humphrey

Volume 2
The War of 1812 & The Mexican-American War
David A. Copeland, Carol Sue Humphrey, and Ralph Frasca

Volume 3
The Civil War, North and South
Amy Reynolds and Debra Reddin van Tuyll

Volume 4
The Indian Wars & The Spanish-American War
John M. Coward and W. Joseph Campbell

Volume 5
World War I & World War II, The European Theater
Ross F. Collins and Patrick S. Washburn

Volume 6
World War II, The Asian Theater & The Korean War
Bradley Hamm, Donald L. Shaw, and Douglass K. Daniel

Volume 7
The Vietnam War & Post-Vietnam Conflicts
Russell J. Cook and Shannon E. Martin

Volume 8
The Iraq Wars and the War on Terror & Index
Brooke Barnett

CONTENTS

Set Foreword   xxvii

Reader's Guide to the Documents   xxix

I NORTHERN NEWSPAPERS DURING THE CIVIL WAR   1

Timeline   3

Introduction   7

1 Settling Kansas   19

3 December 1857, Gamaliel Bailey: Governor Walker's Position
on the Lecompton Constitution   23

10 December 1857, Gamaliel Bailey: Tense Situation in Kansas—
Citizens of Territory Remaining Calm   23

11 January 1858, Henry Raymond: Editorial Writer Declares
President Should Respect Outcome of Kansas Election, Expects
Defeat of Lecompton Constitution   24

23 January 1858, Henry Raymond: Political Significance of
Defeat of Lecompton Constitution in Kansas   25

4 February 1858, Henry Raymond: How President Buchanan
Proposes to Keep the Peace in Kansas   25

4 February 1858, *St. Louis Republican*: Proslavery Kansan
Criticizes Republican Lies and General Calhoun's Secrecy   26

29 March 1858, *Adams County Sentinel & General Advertiser*:
What They Say in Kansas—The Political Divide between the
Free State and Proslavery Movements   27

31 January 1861, *Philadelphia Inquirer*: Kansas Enters Union
as Free State   28

2 The Case of *Dred Scott,* 1857   31

7 March 1857, *New York Daily Times*: Decision of Supreme Court
in *Dred Scott* Case   33

16 July 1857, *New York Daily Times*: What the *Dred Scott* Case
Decided and Did Not Decide   34

11 March 1857, *New York Daily Times*: Southern Reaction to *Dred
Scott* Decision   35

9 March 1857, Henry Raymond: Editorial Writer Predicts *Dred
Scott* Decision Will Spur Creation of Antislavery Party   35

7 March 1857, David N. White: Editorial—Voters, Not Courts,
Will Decide Slavery Issue   36

12 March 1857, Joseph Medill: Editorial—Condemning the *Dred
Scott* Decision   37

11 March 1857, Thurlow Weed: Political Implications of *Dred
Scott* Decision   37

16 March 1857, *Kentucky Journal*: How the *Dred Scott* Decision
Will Affect Slavery in the Western Territories   38

18 March 1857, *New Hampshire Patriot & State Gazette*: Dangers
of Black Republican Opposition to *Dred Scott* Decision   39

12 March 1857, John W. Forney: Editorial—Country Should
Respect *Dred Scott* Decision   41

15 March 1857, W. S.: Letter Writer Describes Importance of
Dred Scott Decision for Northern Opponents of Slavery   41

18 April 1857, Mary Ann Carey Shadd: Description of
Philadelphia Meetings Protesting *Dred Scott* Decision   42

18 April 1857, Sydney Howard Gay: Editorial—*Dred Scott*
Decision Violates Basic Principles of American Freedom   43

3 John Brown and Harper's Ferry, 1859   47

18 October 1859, *New York Times*: First News of Raid on Harper's
Ferry   48

18 October 1859, Charles C. Fulton: Origins of Harper's Ferry
Conspiracy   49

20 October 1859, Q.: Particulars of Harper's Ferry Rebellion   49

19 October 1859, Henry Raymond: John Brown and the
Virginia Insurrection   50

20 October 1859, Thurlow Weed: Editorial—Refuting
Democratic Claims That Republicans Encourage Insurrections   51

22 October 1859, Joseph Medill: Editorial—Responsibility of
Democratic Party and *Dred Scott* Decision for Harper's Ferry
Uprising   51

26 October 1859, *New Hampshire Patriot & State Gazette*:
Editorial—Republicans Who Supported Violence in Kansas
Responsible for Harper's Ferry Affair   53

29 October 1859, John McLean: Editorial—Republican
Agitation in Kansas Leads to Harper's Ferry Violence   54

25 November 1859, American Anti-Slavery Society: Trial and
Likely Execution of Captain John Brown   54

3 December 1859, *New York Tribune*: Execution of John Brown   55

9 December 1859, John Brown: Last Words of John Brown—
"I Die Alone"   55

2 December 1859, Joseph Medill: Republican Editorial on John
Brown's Execution   56

3 December 1859, John McLean: Democratic Editorial on John
Brown's Execution   56

3 December 1859, David N. White: Editorial—Regrettable
Necessity of John Brown's Execution   56

4 Abraham Lincoln Elected President, 6 November 1860   59

29 October 1860, *Baltimore Sun*: Report of Preparations in
Virginia to Protect State in Event of Lincoln's Election   62

6 November 1860, A. S. Abell: Vote for Lincoln Risks Southern
Secession   63

6 November 1860, *Chicago Tribune*: Douglas Vote Pointless
Given Southern Refusal to Support Democratic Nominee   63

7 November 1860, Henry Raymond: Newspapers Serve Intense
Public Interest in Current Election   64

7 November 1860, *Chicago Tribune*: "Victory! Victory!"—
Republican Newspaper Reports Lincoln's Election   64

9 November 1860, A. S. Abell: Election of Lincoln Exhibits
Northern Hostility toward South   65

8 November 1860, *Boston Daily Advertiser*: Excerpts from Other
Newspapers—What Is Being Said of Election Result   66

9 November 1860, *Baltimore Sun*: News of Southern Reaction to
Lincoln's Election   66

10 November 1860, *Baltimore Sun*: Economic Consequences of
Republican Victory   67

10 November 1860, *Baltimore Sun*: Growing Likelihood of
Southern Secession   67

16 November 1860, William Lloyd Garrison: Despite Secession
Threat, North Should Not Submit to Southern Demands   68

5 Southern Secession, 1860–1861 71

7 November 1860, *Baltimore Sun*: South Carolina Preparations for
Possible Lincoln Election 72

7 November 1860, *Baltimore Sun*: Meeting of South Carolina
Officials 73

31 December 1860, *Illinois State Journal*: Northern Newspaper
Views South Carolina Secession as "All Rant" 73

20 December 1860, Charles Hale: How South Carolinians View
the North 73

21 December 1860, A. S. Abell: Secession of South Carolina 74

11 January 1861, *Philadelphia Inquirer*: South Carolina's War
against the United States 75

4 January 1861, William Lloyd Garrison: Disunion Means
Abolition of Slavery 75

10 January 1861, *Philadelphia Inquirer*: Another Star Lost—
Secession of Mississippi 75

11 January 1861, A Man of Influence: Private Letter from
Mississippi Explores Economic Consequences of State's Secession 76

14 January 1861, J. McGowan, Captain: Mood in Florida and
Alabama after Both States Secede 76

12 January 1861, Thomas N. Day: Growing Likelihood of War 77

1 February 1861, William Harding: Secession of Louisiana
Closes Mississippi River to North 77

7 February 1861, *Philadelphia Inquirer*: Secession of Texas—
Seventh Star Gone 78

20 February 1861, William Harding: Editorial—Jefferson Davis
on the Cotton Confederacy 78

15 January 1861, Joseph Medill: Republican Editor Demands
Democratic Papers Cease Encouraging Secession by
Misrepresenting Republican Positions 79

8 February 1861, Uriah J. Jones: Democratic Editor Blames
Republicans for Causing Secession by Refusing to Compromise
with South 80

14 January 1861, Thomas N. Day: Mr. Seward's Speech—
Southern Refusal to Accept Defeat Makes War Likely 80

12 April 1861, *The Liberator*: Let Seceding States Go—They
Will Fail 81

11 April 1861, Thomas N. Day: Progress of Secession—
Growing Tension over Status of Federal Property in the South 82

6 War Begins—The Attack on Fort Sumter, 12 April 1861 85

4 March 1861, *Philadelphia Inquirer*: Attack on Fort Sumter Is
Imminent 86

13 April 1861, *Philadelphia Inquirer*: "War! War!! War!!!"—First
Report of Attack on Fort Sumter   87

13 April 1861, Joseph Medill: War Inaugurated!   88

16 April 1861, David N. White: Unconfirmed Report of Attack
on Fort Sumter   89

15 April 1861, Charles Hale: President Buchanan's Mishandling
of Sumter Crisis   89

18 April 1861, A. S. Abell: Must There Be War over Fort Sumter?   90

16 April 1861, Uriah J. Jones: The Duty before Us to Restore the
Union   90

16 April 1861, David N. White: Southern Aggression at Fort
Sumter Unifies North   90

16 April 1861, Thomas N. Day: Effect of War News in Connecticut   91

13 April 1861, William Harding: The War Commenced   91

13 April 1861, Thomas N. Day: The Fight to Save the Union   91

15 April 1861, William Harding: Attack on Sumter—Its Unifying
Effect throughout the Union   92

July 1861, *Harper's New Monthly Magazine*: British Reaction to
the American War   93

7 Union Call for Volunteers, April 1861   95

15 April 1861, Thomas N. Day: Editorial—Volunteer and Support
the Union Cause   98

15 April 1861, *Philadelphia Inquirer*: Editorial—Support for
Lincoln's Call for Volunteers   98

17 April 1861, William Harding: Pennsylvania Men Eager to
Volunteer—State Will Likely Exceed Quota   99

16 April 1861, Charles Hale: Massachusetts Forms Two Regiments
in One Day   99

16 April 1861, *Chicago Tribune*: States of Northwest Quickly
Forming Regiments   99

17 April 1861, David N. White: Border State Concern over
Virginia's Secession   100

17 April 1861, *Philadelphia Inquirer*: Effect of President's
Proclamation in the South   100

17 April 1861, A. S. Abell: Southern Reaction to Lincoln's Call for
Volunteers   101

July 1861, *Harper's New Monthly Magazine*: President's Call for
Volunteers Highly Effective   101

8 First Battle of Bull Run, 21 July 1861   103

17 July 1861, *New York Evening Post*: Assessment of Union
Commanders Scott and McDowell   107

17 July 1861, *Chicago Daily Tribune*: Battle in Washington
Area Imminent ... 107

19 July 1861, Uriah H. Painter: Early Reports of Encounter on
16 July ... 108

22 July 1861, *Baltimore Sun*: First Report of Battle at Bull Run ... 108

22 July 1861, *Hartford Daily Courant*: War Correspondent's
Description of Contest at Bull Run ... 109

21 July 1861, William Harding: Erroneous Early Report of
Union Victory at Bull Run ... 109

22 July 1861, Uriah J. Painter: "Great Slaughter and Brilliant
Victory"—Another Erroneous Report of Union Triumph ... 110

22 July 1861, A. S. Abell: Editorial Calls for Calm in Baltimore
after Union Defeat at Bull Run ... 110

24 July 1861, Uriah J. Jones: Defeat at Bull Run Strengthens
Fighting Spirit in Union ... 111

23 July 1861, William Harding: Responsibility of Press for
Forcing Unprepared Army to Fight at Bull Run ... 112

26 July 1861, William Lloyd Garrison: Government Forces
Defeated at Bull Run ... 112

24 July 1861, William Harding: Repulse at Manassas and the
Influence of the Press ... 113

26 July 1861, Thomas N. Day: The Sad Battle—Somebody
Blundered ... 114

24 July 1861, Charles Hale: "Pushed Too Quickly"—
Responsibility of Press for Promoting the Premature Campaign ... 115

23 July 1861, David N. White: Size of the Armies at Manassas
Junction ... 115

25 July 1861, Charles Hale: Impact of Loss at Bull Run in
Europe ... 116

9 Battle of Shiloh, 6–7 April 1862 ... 119

9 April 1862, *Hartford Daily Courant*: Early and Inaccurate
Report of Fighting in Tennessee ... 121

10 April 1862, *Cincinnati Times*: Account of Battle at Shiloh ... 122

10 April 1862, William Harding: Account of Glorious Union
Victory at Pittsburg Landing (Shiloh) ... 123

10 April 1862, Charles Hale: Shiloh Won by Hard-Fighting
Union Troops in Tennessee ... 124

10 April 1862, *Hartford Daily Courant*: Confederate General
Johnston Dead—Union Victory Complete ... 125

14 April 1862, *Hartford Daily Courant*: Confederate Accounts
of Battle at Pittsburg Landing (Shiloh) ... 125

18 April 1862, Charles Hale: Summary of General Grant's
Report of Battle at Pittsburg Landing (Shiloh)—Union Troops
Surprised   126

31 May 1862, P.G.T. Beauregard: Confederate General's Official
Report on Shiloh   127

14 April 1862, *Baltimore Sun*: "The Scene at Midnight"—The
Horrible Battle of Shiloh   128

21 April 1862, *St. Louis Republican*: Eyewitness Account of
Shiloh   129

17 April 1862, Manton Marble: Who Was Responsible for Not
Detecting Confederate Attack at Shiloh?   129

3 May 1862, U. S. Grant: Union Command at Shiloh Responds
to Criticism   130

15 April 1862, William Harding: Capture and Escape of Our War
Correspondent at Pittsburg Landing   131

10 Union Capture of New Orleans, April 1862   133

27 April 1862, Thomas N. Day: New Orleans in Union
Possession—Rebels Destroy Large Amount of Property   135

28 April 1862, William Harding: Account of Capture of
New Orleans   135

10 May 1862, Thomas N. Day: Account of New Orleans
Campaign   135

9 May 1862, Theodorus Bailey: Capture of New Orleans—Small
Loss of Life for Union but Large Economic Loss for Rebels   137

30 April 1862, Charles Hale: Significance of Capture of New
Orleans   137

29 April 1862, Thomas N. Day: Capture of New Orleans Cuts off
Confederate Line of Retreat from Mississippi   138

1 May 1862, Thomas N. Day: Trade at New Orleans   138

29 April 1862, William Harding: New Orleans—Importance of
Capture Abroad and at Home   139

11 Union Capture of Memphis, June 1862   141

1 May 1862, *Hartford Daily Courant*: Confederate Despair at Loss
of New Orleans, Fears of Union Advances along Middle
Mississippi   142

3 May 1862, *Hartford Daily Courant*: Rebels Fear Attack on
Memphis, Prepare to Burn City   143

7 June 1862, William Harding: Difficulty of Obtaining News from
Mississippi Valley   143

12 June 1862, William Harding: Account of River Fight before
Memphis   144

12 June 1862, Thomas N. Day: Condition of Newly Captured
Memphis   145

10 June 1862, Charles Hale: No Threat from Citizens of
Captured Memphis   146

16 June 1862, William Harding: Memphis—Reconquered
Southern Cities and Their Mobs   146

12 Second Battle of Bull Run, 28–30 August 1862   149

1 September 1862, A. S. Abell: War Department Reports on
Second Battle at Bull Run   151

29 August 1862, *Hartford Daily Courant*: Reports of Rebel
Seizure of Manassas Junction   152

29 August 1862, George Smalley: Rebel Raid on Manassas
Junction   152

30 August 1862, Thomas N. Day: Situation at Manassas   153

3 September 1862, Thomas N. Day: Likely Implications of
Recent Action at Bull Run   153

2 September 1862, John W. Forney: Prospects Poor for Rebel
Invasion of North   154

2 September 1862, James M. Winchell: Analysis of
Confederate and Union Leadership at Second Bull Run   154

4 September 1862, Uriah J. Jones: More Volunteers Needed to
Defend Union   155

1 September 1862, Charles Hale: Not Time for Citizens to
Criticize Union's Civil and Military Leaders   155

13 Battle of Antietam, 17 September 1862   157

7 September 1862, John W. Forney: Pennsylvania Concerned
about Lee's Northward March   159

8 September 1862, Uriah J. Jones: Likelihood of Battle in
Maryland   160

22 September 1862, George Smalley: Report on Battle in
Maryland   160

23 September 1862, *Adams Sentinel & General Advertiser*:
Report of Initial Encounters at Antietam   161

20 September 1862, Associated Press: Letter from Antietam
Battlefield   162

17 September 1862, Thomas N. Day: Union Victory in
Maryland; Northern Press Too Anxious to Assault Richmond   163

19 September 1862, Thomas N. Day: Significance of Union
Victory at Antietam   163

20 September 1862, Associated Press: Condition of Lee's Army
after Battle of Sharpsburg (Antietam)   164

23 September 1862, Charles Hale: Significance of Antietam
and State of Affairs in Virginia   165

14 Emancipation Proclamation, September 1862   167

23 September 1862, Abraham Lincoln: Emancipation
Proclamation   168

23 September 1862, *Baltimore Sun*: Summary of President's
Proclamation   169

25 September 1862, *New York Times*: Wide Support for
Proclamation—President Serenaded in Washington   169

24 September 1862, Charles Hale: Proclamation Makes No
Change in War Aims   170

24 September 1862, Thomas N. Day: "Year of Jubilee Has
Come"—Slavery Rightfully Recognized as Root Cause of War   170

23 September 1862, Henry Raymond: Beneficial Effects of
President's Proclamation on War Effort   171

28 September 1862, Henry Raymond: President's Proclamation
Will Overthrow Southern Economy   171

1 October 1862, *New York Times*: Southerners Expected
Proclamation from Republican President   172

1 January 1863, R. J. Haldeman: Proclamation Takes Effect—
Slaves Given License to Revolt   173

25 September 1862, Thomas N. Day: Political Lines Drawn
around Proclamation   173

23 September 1862, John Forney: War Democrats on the
Proclamation   174

23 September 1862, D. M. Stone: Initial Democratic Response to
President's Proclamation   174

23 September 1862, *Philadelphia Evening Journal*: Another
Democratic Assessment of the President's Proclamation   174

23 September 1862, William W. Seaton: Comparison of Lincoln's
Proclamation with General Hunter's Suppressed Edict of
Emancipation   175

26 September 1862, R. J. Haldeman: Protest against the
President's Proclamation   175

3 October 1862, William Lloyd Garrison: Praise for Lincoln;
Condemnation for Opposition Democratic Press   176

15 Battle of Fredericksburg, 13 December 1862   179

14 December 1862, *New York Herald*: Account of Battle of
Fredericksburg   180

17 December 1862, *New York Herald*: No Reason for
Discouragement Concerning Recent Battle at Fredericksburg   180

15 December 1862, A. S. Abell: Actions of General Franklin at
Fredericksburg   181

17 December 1862, J.: Detailed Account of Battle of
Fredericksburg   181

18 December 1862, D. M. Stone: Blame for Defeat Rests with
Administration   183

18 December 1862, *Providence Journal*: No Reason for Despair
at News of Recent Battle   184

19 December 1862, Thomas N. Day: Severe Union Losses at
Fredericksburg   184

20 December 1862, William Harding: Changes in the Lincoln
Cabinet and Administration   185

19 December 1862, Charles C. Fulton: Changes in Lincoln
Cabinet   185

19 December 1862, Samuel Bowles: Effects from Fredericksburg   185

27 December 1862, R. J. Haldeman: "Fredericksburg
Massacre"—Democratic Criticism of Lincoln for Union Loss   186

16 Battle of Chancellorsville, 1–6 May 1863   189

6 May 1863, *Washington Republican*: Early Reports of Battle at
Chancellorsville   191

6 May 1863, *Washington Star*: Report on Fighting at
Chancellorsville   192

6 May 1863, Charles Hale: Difficulty of Obtaining Information
from General Hooker's Army   192

5 May 1863, L. L. Crounse: Battles on the Rappahannock—
Hooker's Position   192

13 May 1863, *New York Times*: Account of Battle at
Wilderness Church   193

8 May 1863, Charles Hale: Union Can Not Sustain Continued
Defeat in Eastern Theater   193

22 May 1863, An Intelligent Gentleman: Significance of Battle
of Chancellorsville   194

17 May 1863, A Union Soldier: Soldier's Account of Battle of
Chancellorsville   195

13 May 1863, *Boston Daily Advertiser*: Report of Death of
Stonewall Jackson   196

14 May 1863, Henry Raymond: Account of Death of Stonewall
Jackson   196

17 Battle of Gettysburg, 1–3 July 1863   199

25 June 1863, *Washington Republican*: Lee's Whole Army
Reported Moving on Pennsylvania   202

27 June 1863, R. J. Haldeman: The Threatened Confederate
Invasion of Pennsylvania   203

7 July 1863, *Adams County Sentinel & General Advertiser*:
Account of Battle at Gettysburg   203

6 July 1863, R. J. Haldeman: The Situation in Pennsylvania   204

7 July 1863, *Adams County Sentinel & General Advertiser*:
Local Gettysburg Newspaper Apologizes for Temporary
Suspension of Publication Caused by Battle   206

14 July 1863, *Adams County Sentinel & General Advertiser*:
The Sentinel Junior—Local Gettysburg Newspaper Reduced in
Size by Paper Shortage Caused by Battle   206

14 July 1863, *Adams County Sentinel & General Advertiser*:
Destruction of Property Caused by Battle of Gettysburg   206

4 July 1863, A Gentleman: Account of Horrendous Confederate
Losses at Gettysburg   207

5 July 1863, Frank Chapman: Summary of Confederate Rout at
Gettysburg   207

9 July 1863, *Hartford Daily Courant*: Estimates of Dead and
Wounded at Gettysburg   208

13 July 1863, Sam Wilkeson: Inhumanity and Poltroonery of
Rebel Surgeons at Gettysburg   208

6 July 1863, Charles Hale: Editorial—Invasion of North Halted,
but Was Government Unprepared for Rebel Advance?   209

18 Battle of Vicksburg, 1–4 July 1863   211

8 July 1863, Official Report: Fall of Vicksburg   213

13 July 1863, Official Report: Details of Confederate Surrender at
Vicksburg   213

9 July 1863, Thomas N. Day: Significant and Hopeful Successes
at Gettysburg and Vicksburg   216

19 New York Draft Riots, July 1863   217

13 July 1863, Henry Raymond: Editorial—Conscription Is a
Great Benefit   218

14 July 1863, *New York Times*: "Crush the Mob!"—New York
Newspapers Demand Restoration of Order   219

14 July 1863, Henry Raymond: The Mob and the Press—Rioters
Target Newspaper Offices   220

15 July 1863, Henry Raymond: Rival Newspapers Unite to
Denounce Mob Violence   220

16 July 1863, Thomas N. Day: Riot Report from Outside New
York   221

15 July 1863, *Boston Daily Advertiser*: Riot in Boston   221

20 War Prisoners and the Fort Pillow Massacre, 12 April 1864   223

20 November 1863, R. J. Haldeman: Cruelty to War Prisoners   225

19 November 1863, *New York Herald*: Rebels Responsible for
End of Prisoner Exchanges   225

27 November 1863, *Washington Chronicle*: Account of Prison
Conditions in Richmond   225

22 April 1864, William Lloyd Garrison: The Fort Pillow
Murders   226

6 May 1864, *Hartford Daily Courant*: Account of Rebel
Atrocities at Fort Pillow   226

7 May 1864, Thomas N. Day: The Fort Pillow Massacre   228

20 April 1864, *St. Louis Democrat*: Butchery of Black Union
Soldiers at Fort Pillow   228

10 May 1864, *Salem Observer*: Suggested Retaliation for
Massacre at Fort Pillow   229

2 May 1864, Henry Raymond: How to Deal with Fort Pillow
Butchers   229

10 May 1864, By a Connecticut Woman: Letter Writer
Suggests Proper Retaliation for Fort Pillow Massacre   230

3 May 1864, *Baltimore American*: Sad Condition of Released
Union Prisoners   230

27 December 1864, Henry Raymond: What Can Be Done for
Union Prisoners?   230

21 Grant's Overland Campaign, 1864   233

5 May 1864, Thomas N. Day: Mystification of Rebels—Grant
Keeps Military Plans Secret   235

13 May 1864, Charles Hale: Praise for Grant   235

9 May 1864, Thomas N. Day: Fall of Richmond Is Near   236

11 May 1864, Thomas N. Day: Account of Fighting in The
Wilderness   237

10 May 1864, *Hartford Daily Courant*: Union Victory in The
Wilderness   237

14 May 1864, Charles Hale: Report of Grant's Campaign in
The Wilderness   238

6 June 1864, *Boston Daily Advertiser*: Account of Fighting at
Cold Harbor   239

6 June 1864, Henry Raymond: Rebel Resolve at Cold Harbor   240

11 June 1864, Edward Crapsey: A Flag of Truce—The
Proceedings under It   240

17 June 1864, Henry J. Winser: Account of Grant's
Abandonment of His Position at Cold Harbor   240

22 Battle of Atlanta, July–September 1864   243

24 May 1864, Henry Raymond: The Campaign in Georgia   245

20 July 1864, *New York Times*: General Sherman's Army
Approaches Atlanta   246

22 July 1864, Henry Raymond: Union Indebtedness to
Confederate General Bragg   247

27 July 1864, Thomas N. Day: General Sherman's
Success at Atlanta   247

5 September 1864, *Hartford Daily Courant*: Northern Cities
Celebrate Fall of Atlanta   248

23 Sherman's March, November–December 1864   251

6 December 1864, Thomas N. Day: Dodging Sherman's Army   253

20 December 1864, Charles Hale: War-Weary Georgia—Sherman's
Army Faces Little Resistance in State   253

26 December 1864, Thomas N. Day: Capture of Savannah   254

27 December 1864, Charles Hale: Magnificent Achievement of
General Sherman—Fall of Confederacy Imminent   254

8 April 1865, Huguenot: Account of General Sherman's
Campaign in the Carolinas   254

24 Presidential Election of 1864   257

9 June 1864, Charles Hale: Lincoln Wins Republican
Nomination—Support for President Widespread   258

18 November 1864, William Lloyd Garrison: Lincoln's Reelection
Indicates Northern Support for Abolition of Slavery   259

6 March 1865, Thomas N. Day: Inauguration of President Lincoln—
Comparison of 1861 and 1865   259

25 Petersburg and Richmond Campaigns, 1865   263

6 April 1865, Thomas N. Day: Account of Battles around
Petersburg on 1 April   264

6 April 1865, *New York Times*: Condition of Petersburg after
Rebel Evacuation   265

4 April 1865, *Adams County Sentinel & General Advertiser*:
Report on Fall of Richmond   266

5 April 1865, Manton Marble: Report of Jefferson Davis' Flight
from Richmond   266

4 April 1865, Charles Hale: Fall of Richmond   266

5 April 1865, Charles Hale: Editorial Predicts End of Confederacy
Little More Than a Week Away   267

8 April 1865, Thomas N. Day: Fall of Richmond Signals End of
Rebellion   267

4 April 1865, Charles Hale: People of Boston Foresee End to
War   268

5 April 1865, Henry Raymond: Completeness of the National
Victory at Petersburg and Richmond   268

26 Confederate Surrender at Appomattox Courthouse, 9 April 1865   271

8 April 1865, Henry Raymond: The Rout of Lee's Army   272

9 April 1865, *New York Times*: The Pursuit of Lee's Army   273

10 April 1865, *New York Times*: Rejoicing at End of War; Last
Exchanges between Lee and Grant   273

10 April 1865, Thomas N. Day: Surrender of Lee's Army   274

10 April 1865, R. J. Haldeman: Surrender of General Lee   275

12 April 1865, Thomas N. Day: Peace and Fraternity   275

22 April 1865, Charles Hale: Thanks to God for
Restoration Peace   276

Selected Bibliography   279

**II SOUTHERN NEWSPAPERS DURING
THE CIVIL WAR**   283

Timeline   285

Introduction   295

27 The 1860 Presidential Election and Secession   323

3 November 1860, George Kendall or Francis Lumsden: States
Moving toward Secession If Lincoln Elected   325

4 November 1860, George Kendall or Francis Lumsden: Editorial—
What Is the True Issue in This Election?   326

7 November 1860, S. B. Crafton: Editorial—Lincoln's Election
Makes Outlook Gloomy for Union   328

21 December 1860, *New Orleans Picayune*: Form and Manner of
South Carolina Secession Ordinance   329

21 December 1860, Robert Barnwell Rhett, Jr.: Rejoicing at
South Carolina's Decision to Secede   329

18 January 1861, John Harvey: Southern Constitutional
Argument for Secession   330

1 February 1861, Tiber: Correspondent Predicts the Coming
of War   331

5 February 1861, George Kendall or Francis Lumsden: Account
of Montgomery Convention   332

6 February 1861, George Kendall or Francis Lumsden: Border
State Conferences Seek Compromise   334

10 February 1861, George Kendall or Francis Lumsden: Jefferson Davis and Alexander Stephens Chosen as President and Vice President of Confederacy   336

31 March 1861, Tiber: Fate of Fort Sumter and the Coming of War   336

12 April 1861, Special Report to the *Picayune*: Confederate Cabinet Awaits Washington's Response to Its Peace Commissioners   337

28 Reporting the War, 1861   339

31 December 1860, Robert Barnwell Rhett, Jr.: Move of Federal Troops to Fort Sumter May Encourage Progress of Southern Secession   341

2 April 1861, Tiber: Report on Crittenden Compromise Proposals   342

9 April 1861, Robert Barnwell Rhett, Jr.: Lincoln's Decision to Resupply Fort Sumter Is Declaration of War   344

16 April 1861, Your Correspondent: Report of Fighting at Fort Sumter—Start of War Likely   345

12 April 1861, By Telegraph: South Carolinians Open Fire on Fort Sumter   345

13 April 1861, *New Orleans Picayune*: Fort Sumter Surrenders   346

14 April 1861, George Kendall or Francis Lumsden: Account of Fall of Fort Sumter   348

15 April 1861, *New Orleans Picayune*: War Proclamation by Lincoln   349

16 April 1861, *New Orleans Picayune*: Major Anderson Permitted to Depart Fort Sumter   351

23 July 1861, *Memphis Appeal*: Report of Confederate Victory at Manassas   352

23 July 1861, Benjamin F. Dill or John McClanahan: Great Victory at Manassas   353

28 July 1861, John R. Thompson: Rejoicing over Victory at Manassas Tempered by Wait for Word about Loved Ones   353

30 July 1861, Benjamin F. Dill or John McClanahan: Consequences of Manassas—Much Work Still to Be Done   356

19 August 1861, Peter W. Alexander: Description of Manassas Battlefield   357

5 September 1861, Joan: Army Hospitals—What Louisiana Is Doing for Its Wounded Soldiers   360

7 September 1861, Felix G. de Fontaine: Military Rumors in Richmond; South Carolina Needs to Provide for Its Wounded Soldiers   362

1 October 1861, Peter W. Alexander: Camp Life in Virginia   363

16 October 1861, James R. Sneed: Supplies for Soldiers in
Virginia—Outrageous Mismanagement   365

19 November 1861, Joan: Correspondent's Last Letter
from Virginia   366

29 Reporting the War, 1862   369

7 February 1862, Benjamin F. Dill or John McClanahan:
Report of Fall of Fort Henry   372

18 February 1862, Benjamin F. Dill or John McClanahan:
Serious Consequences of Loss of Cumberland Forts   373

8, 10 April 1862, Robert Ette: Reports of Battle of Shiloh   375

7 May 1862, Henry Timrod: Army at Corinth—Situation in
Northern Mississippi   378

6 May 1862, Samuel Chester Reid, Jr.: Letter from Corinth—
Beauregard's Rousing Speech to His Troops   379

27 April 1862, By Telegraph: Account of Bombardment of
Fort Jackson   381

27 April 1862, George Kendall or Francis Lumsden: New
Orleans Must Endure Yankee Occupation   382

7 October 1862, Albert J. Street: Account of Battle at Corinth   383

14 October 1862, Clint: Account of Recent Fighting in
Mississippi   384

18 October 1862, John Forsyth: Account of Battle of Perryville   385

9 June 1862, Dr. George W. Bagby: Battle of Seven Pines   388

27 June 1862, Dr. George W. Bagby: Account of Fighting during
Seven Days Battles   390

3 July 1862, Charleston Mercury: Summary of Recent Battles
before Richmond   391

7 July 1862, G. B. Cuthbert: Latest Reports from Richmond—
Lee Drives McClellan from City   396

29 May 1862, Dr. George W. Bagby: News of McClellan's
Advance on Richmond, Jackson's Operations in Shenandoah
Valley   397

18 June 1862, Charleston Mercury: Achievements of Stonewall
Jackson in Shenandoah Valley Campaign   398

9 September 1862, Peter W. Alexander: Account of Second
Battle of Manassas   402

1 October 1862, Peter W. Alexander: Account of Lee's Retreat
from Sharpsburg (Antietam)   406

3 October 1862, Peter W. Alexander: Our Army, Its Great
Deeds, Its Trials, Its Sufferings, and Its Perils in the Future   408

22 October 1862, James R. Sneed and George W. Randolph:
Clothing for the Soldiers   409

22 October 1862, Peter W. Alexander: What the Government
Has Done and Is Doing for Sick, Wounded and Destitute Soldiers 410

24, 23 December 1862, Peter W. Alexander: Accounts of Battle
at Fredericksburg 413

15 December 1862, *Richmond Examiner*: Battle of
Fredericksburg—Another Confederate Victory 415

30 Reporting the War, 1863 419

2 January 1863, Joseph Clisby: Summary of Victory at
Murfreesboro 422

10 April 1863, Peter W. Alexander: Union Attack on
Charleston Repulsed 424

12 July 1863, *Savannah Republican*: Account of Unsuccessful
Union Attack on Battery Wagner, Morris' Island 425

13 July 1863, James R. Sneed: Account of Recent Fighting in
Charleston Harbor 426

8 July 1863, *Augusta Constitutionalist*: Military Situation at
Vicksburg 430

9 July 1863, *Savannah Republican*: Editorial—Who Is Responsible
for Fall of Vicksburg? 431

22 September 1863, Isham G. Harris and Others: Account of
Battle of Chickamauga 434

22 September 1863, CPA Reporters: Reports from Chickamauga
Battlefield 435

2 November 1863, Felix G. de Fontaine: News of Union Activity
at Chattanooga 435

26 November 1863, Samuel Chester Reid, Jr.: Reports of Fighting
at Lookout Mountain 437

26 November 1863, *Memphis Appeal*: Rout of Bragg's Forces 438

1 December 1863, Benjamin F. Dill or John McClanahan:
Consequences of Defeat at Lookout Mountain 439

1 May 1863, *Richmond Examiner*: News of Advance of Hooker's
Army 441

6 May 1863, Robert E. Lee/*Richmond Examiner*: Commanding
General's Report on Battle of Chancellorsville; Stonewall
Jackson Wounded 442

11 May 1863, *Richmond Examiner*: Account of Battle of
Chancellorsville 443

11 May 1863, John M. Daniel: Death of Stonewall Jackson 444

7 July 1863, James R. Sneed: First Reports of Battle at Gettysburg 446

14 July 1863, Peter W. Alexander: Account of Fighting at
Gettysburg 447

11 September 1863, Peter W. Alexander: Reflections on
Fighting in 1863   447

31 Reporting the War, 1864   451

9 May 1864, Waverly: State of General Johnston's Army   455

25 May 1864, Waverly: State of Morale in Atlanta   457

21 June 1864, Special: Confederate Preparations at
Kennesaw Mountain   458

1 July 1864, Captain Matthews: Account of Truce to Bury
Dead at Kennesaw Mountain   458

31 July 1864, Telegraph and Felix G. de Fontaine: Reports of
Fighting around Atlanta   459

9 August 1864, Confederate: Report on the Defense of Atlanta   461

5 September 1864, *Charleston Mercury*: Fall of Atlanta   462

7 September 1864, *Charleston Mercury*: Evacuation of Atlanta   463

6 October 1864, Dr. George W. Bagby: General Hood Marches
North from Atlanta   464

30 November 1864, Observer: Account of Battle of
Griswoldville   466

11 December 1864, *The Mississippian*: Effects of Sherman's
March through Georgia   467

12 December 1864, Richard Orme, Jr. or Sr.: Atlanta after
Sherman's Occupation   468

20 December 1864, Henry Lynden Flash: Sherman's Campaign
against Savannah   469

28 December 1864, Henry Lynden Flash: Fall of Savannah   470

18 November 1864, Henry Lynden Flash: Hood's Campaign in
Tennessee   471

16 December 1864, Henry Lynden Flash: Account of
Battle of Franklin   472

10 January 1865, John Bell Hood: Commanding General's
Report on Battle of Franklin   473

10 May 1864, John R. Thompson: Start of Wilderness
Campaign; Political News from Richmond   476

14 May 1864, Benjamin F. Dill or John McClanahan: The War
Can Be Won   477

1 June 1864, Peter W. Alexander: Battle of The Wilderness   478

16 June 1864, Peter W. Alexander: Account of Battle of Cold
Harbor   482

3 August 1864, *Macon Telegraph*: Battle of the Crater   484

16 September 1864, Dr. George W. Bagby: News from
Petersburg   485

27 September 1864, Dr. George W. Bagby: Account of Fighting
in Shenandoah Valley   486

28 September 1864, John M. Daniel: Fall Campaign in
Richmond   486

32 Reporting the War, 1865   489

18 February 1865, *Augusta Constitutionalist*: Opposing Sherman in
South Carolina   492

23 February 1865, Dr. Nagle: Sherman's Advance into North
Carolina   493

25 February 1865, *Augusta Constitutionalist*: Evacuation of
Charleston   493

1 March 1865, William W. Holden: Union Advance on
Wilmington   494

23 March 1865, Dr. Nagle: General Johnston's Battle Near
Bentonville; Occupied Savannah   495

28 March 1865, Refugee: Evacuation of Fayetteville   496

5 January 1865, Larkin: Letter from Richmond   498

28 March 1865, *Augusta Constitutionalist*: Battle in Front of
Petersburg   499

31 March 1865, *Augusta Constitutionalist*: Sheridan's Raid in
Shenandoah Valley   499

1 April 1865, *Augusta Constitutionalist*: Report of Fighting
around Petersburg   500

3 April 1865, *Richmond Examiner*: News of Union Breakthrough
at Petersburg   500

11 April 1865, *Augusta Constitutionalist*: Latest from Lee's Army   501

14 April 1865, *Augusta Constitutionalist*: Evacuation of
Richmond   501

19 April 1865, Cartouche: Terrible Battle of Petersburg   502

23 April 1865, *Augusta Constitutionalist*: Capitulation of Lee's
Army   503

27 April 1865, *Augusta Chronicle and Sentinel*: Death of
Lincoln Reported   505

3 June 1865, Andrew Johnson: President Johnson's Amnesty
Proclamation   506

**33 The Confederate Home Front: Women and Slaves,
Sacrifice and Valor**   509

1 November 1860, J.C.C. Featherstone or James A. Hoyt: "The
Wheel of Life"—Six Articles on Nineteenth-Century Social
Thought and Values   510

4 January 1861, D. A. Hobbie or B. H. Thrasher:
Editorial—The Place of Women   511

31 May 1861, C. E. Haynes: Southern Women as Nurses   512

2 August 1861, John Harvey: How Southern
Women Support the Confederate War Effort   513

7 September 1861, Joan: Female Correspondent Describes
Women's War Work   513

25 December 1861, Southron: Tribute to the Women of the
South   515

5 March 1863, *Richmond Dispatch*: Account of Southern
Women Outwitting Yankees   516

20 March 1863, *Edgefield Advertiser*: Useful Advice for
Women—A Substitute for Bread   516

29 June 1863, James R. Sneed: Career of a Female Volunteer   517

13 April 1863, James R. Sneed: Georgia Women Riot against
Shortages   518

14 May 1864, *Memphis Appeal*: Patriotic Females Maintain
Telegraph Communication in Georgia   518

4 January 1861, D. A. Hobbie or B. H. Thrasher: Story of
Yankees Outwitted by a Slave   519

4 May 1861, James R. Sneed: Dedication of First African
Baptist Church of Savannah   519

11 June 1861, James R. Sneed: Our Free Colored Population   520

31 July 1861, D. A. Hobbie or B. H. Thrasher: Maintaining
Control of Slaves While the Men Are Away at War   520

3 May 1863, Henry Cleveland: Treatment of Slaves and Free
Blacks—May Day Party for Black "Elites"   521

28 October 1864, Ruth Raymond: Conversations with My
Female Friends—The Likely Consequences of the War for
Southern Women   521

Selected Bibliography   525

Set Index can be found in Volume 8.

SET FOREWORD

Few events that involve humankind affect people more than war. Ask anyone who remembers World War II, Vietnam, or the events of 11 September 2001. Ask anyone who has a direct connection with conflict in Korea, Bosnia, or Iraq if these experiences have changed their lives. Because of the far-reaching effects of war, we want to know as much about it as possible. For that information, we turn to media. "This is the first line of history," veteran CBS anchor Walter Cronkite said of the relationship between media and war.

The Greenwood Library of American War Reporting provides the "first line of history" as its 8 volumes use primary sources to reconstruct the events of America's major military conflicts and present them to readers. Each volume gives readers the information that contemporaries of the conflicts experienced. The words, the images, and the emotions of the time are captured in these volumes from the front lines to the home front. The set begins with the French and Indian War and ends with the conflicts that have encompassed the nation since 9/11. In between, one finds some of the most important events in the history of the United States—events that in many cases continue to shape the nation. Besides the books containing the French and Indian War (combined in Volume 1 with the Revolutionary War) and post-9/11 America (Volume 8), the set includes volumes on the War of 1812 and the Mexican American War (Volume 2), the Civil War (Volume 3, which includes sections on both the North and the South), the Spanish-American War (Volume 4), World War I, World War II (Volumes 4 and 5, with sections on the European and Asian theaters), the Korean War (Volume 5), and the war in Vietnam (Volume 7). Other parts of this set tackle less obvious conflicts that, nonetheless, affected the nation. Volume 4 also covers the Indian wars of the nineteenth century. Volume 7 takes readers inside the "little wars" that have plagued the nation from the end of the Vietnam War to the tragic events of 11 September 2001. In addition to the primary documentation and images, each volume provides readers with a comprehensive overview of its respective wars and/or conflicts and a bibliography of sources.

The ability of media to deliver the impact of war is always powerful. It only changes with the advancement and development of technology. For Americans in 1755, the words that described the massacre of General William Braddock's forces in the Pennsylvania backcountry were just as powerful to the people of that era as the television images that riveted Americans during four days of nonstop television coverage after the attacks on the World Trade Center and the Pentagon in 2001. Media have the power to bring war to us. As a reviewer in the *New-York Times* of 20 October 1862 said of Matthew Brady's photographs of the horrific Battle of Antietam: "Mr. Brady has done something to bring home to us the terrible reality and earnestness of war. If he has not brought bodies and laid them on our dooryard and along our streets, he has done something very like it."

The Greenwood Library of American War Reporting offers readers a chance to experience war as those who lived through those conflicts did. Some of the wars are removed from us by centuries, and the language and images from them will, at times, seem odd to us. For the people of that time, the language conveyed powerful images. Other wars and conflicts will be chillingly familiar to readers because they still remember them. The imagery and language of those wars will evoke emotions and thoughts that may be similar, yet each will be unique. These volumes also demonstrate to us the power of media in our lives and the lives of those Americans who lived before us. Truly, as Walter Cronkite said, media reports are the first line of our history, and, as the *Times* correspondent said nearly a century and a half ago, they bring the events of war to our doorsteps and into our living rooms.

READER'S GUIDE TO THE DOCUMENTS

BATTLES AND CAMPAIGNS—EASTERN THEATER

Chapter 8

17 July 1861, *New York Evening Post*: Assessment of Union Commanders Scott and McDowell

17 July 1861, *Chicago Daily Tribune*: Battle in Washington Area Imminent

19 July 1861, Uriah H. Painter: Early Reports of Encounter on 16 July

22 July 1861, *Baltimore Sun*: First Report of Battle at Bull Run

22 July 1861, *Hartford Daily Courant*: War Correspondent's Description of Contest at Bull Run

21 July 1861, William Harding: Erroneous Early Report of Union Victory at Bull Run

22 July 1861, Uriah J. Painter: "Great Slaughter and Brilliant Victory"—Another Erroneous Report of Union Triumph

22 July 1861, A. S. Abell: Editorial Calls for Calm in Baltimore after Union Defeat at Bull Run

24 July 1861, Uriah J. Jones: Defeat at Bull Run Strengthens Fighting Spirit in Union

23 July 1861, William Harding: Responsibility of Press for Forcing Unprepared Army to Fight at Bull Run

26 July 1861, William Lloyd Garrison: Government Forces Defeated at Bull Run

24 July 1861, William Harding: Repulse at Manassas and the Influence of the Press

26 July 1861, Thomas N. Day: The Sad Battle—Somebody Blundered

24 July 1861, Charles Hale: "Pushed Too Quickly"—Responsibility of Press for Promoting the Premature Campaign

23 July 1861, David N. White: Size of the Armies at Manassas Junction

25 July 1861, Charles Hale: Impact of Loss at Bull Run in Europe

Chapter 12

1 September 1862, A. S. Abell: War Department Reports on Second Battle at Bull Run

29 August 1862, *Hartford Daily Courant*: Reports of Rebel Seizure of Manassas Junction

29 August 1862, George Smalley: Rebel Raid on Manassas Junction

30 August 1862, Thomas N. Day: Situation at Manassas

3 September 1862, Thomas N. Day: Likely Implications of Recent Action at Bull Run

2 September 1862, John W. Forney: Prospects Poor for Rebel Invasion of North

2 September 1862, James M. Winchell: Analysis of Confederate and Union Leadership at Second Bull Run

4 September 1862, Uriah J. Jones: More Volunteers Needed to Defend Union

1 September 1862, Charles Hale: Not Time for Citizens to Criticize Union's Civil and Military Leaders

Chapter 13

7 September 1862, John W. Forney: Pennsylvania Concerned about Lee's Northward March

8 September 1862, Uriah J. Jones: Likelihood of Battle in Maryland

22 September 1862, George Smalley: Report on Battle in Maryland

23 September 1862, *Adams Sentinel & General Advertiser*: Report of Initial Encounters at Antietam

20 September 1862, Associated Press: Letter from Antietam Battlefield

17 September 1862, Thomas N. Day: Union Victory in Maryland; Northern Press Too Anxious to Assault Richmond

19 September 1862, Thomas N. Day: Significance of Union Victory at Antietam

20 September 1862, Associated Press: Condition of Lee's Army after Battle of Sharpsburg (Antietam)

23 September 1862, Charles Hale: Significance of Antietam and State of Affairs in Virginia

Chapter 15

14 December 1862, *New York Herald*: Account of Battle of Fredericksburg

17 December 1862, *New York Herald*: No Reason for Discouragement Concerning Recent Battle at Fredericksburg

15 December 1862, A. S. Abell: Actions of General Franklin at Fredericksburg

17 December 1862, J.: Detailed Account of Battle of Fredericksburg

18 December 1862, D. M. Stone: Blame for Defeat Rests with Administration

18 December 1862, *Providence Journal*: No Reason for Despair at News of Recent Battle

19 December 1862, Thomas N. Day: Severe Union Losses at Fredericksburg

20 December 1862, William Harding: Changes in the Lincoln Cabinet and Administration

19 December 1862, Charles C. Fulton: Changes in Lincoln Cabinet

19 December 1862, Samuel Bowles: Effects from Fredericksburg

27 December 1862, R. J. Haldeman: "Fredericksburg Massacre"—Democratic Criticism of Lincoln for Union Loss

Chapter 16

6 May 1863, *Washington Republican*: Early Reports of Battle at Chancellorsville

6 May 1863, *Washington Star*: Report on Fighting at Chancellorsville

6 May 1863, Charles Hale: Difficulty of Obtaining Information from General Hooker's Army

5 May 1863, L. L. Crounse: Battles on the Rappahannock—Hooker's Position

13 May 1863, *New York Times*: Account of Battle at Wilderness Church

8 May 1863, Charles Hale: Union Can Not Sustain Continued Defeat in Eastern Theater

22 May 1863, An Intelligent Gentleman: Significance of Battle at Chancellorsville

17 May 1863, A Union Soldier: Soldier's Account of Battle of Chancellorsville

13 May 1863, *Boston Daily Advertiser*: Report of Death of Stonewall Jackson

14 May 1863, Henry Raymond: Account of Death of Stonewall Jackson

Chapter 17

25 June 1863, *Washington Republican*: Lee's Whole Army Reported Moving on Pennsylvania

27 June 1863, R. J. Haldeman: The Threatened Confederate Invasion of Pennsylvania

7 July 1863, *Adams County Sentinel & General Advertiser*: Account of Battle at Gettysburg

6 July 1863, R. J. Haldeman: The Situation in Pennsylvania

7 July 1863, *Adams County Sentinel & General Advertiser*: Local Gettysburg Newspaper Apologizes for Temporary Suspension of Publication Caused by Battle

14 July 1863, *Adams County Sentinel & General Advertiser*: The Sentinel Junior—Local Gettysburg Newspaper Reduced in Size by Paper Shortage Caused by Battle

14 July 1863, *Adams County Sentinel & General Advertiser*: Destruction of Property Caused by Battle of Gettysburg

4 July 1863, A Gentleman: Account of Horrendous Confederate Losses at Gettysburg

5 July 1863, Frank Chapman: Summary of Confederate Rout at Gettysburg

9 July 1863, *Hartford Daily Courant*: Estimates of Dead and Wounded at Gettysburg

13 July 1863, Sam Wilkeson: Inhumanity and Poltroonery of Rebel Surgeons at Gettysburg

6 July 1863, Charles Hale: Editorial—Invasion of North Halted, but Was Government Unprepared for Rebel Advance?

Chapter 18

9 July 1863, Thomas N. Day: Significant and Hopeful Successes at Gettysburg and Vicksburg

Chapter 21

5 May 1864, Thomas N. Day: Mystification of Rebels—Grant Keeps Military Plans Secret

13 May 1864, Charles Hale: Praise for Grant

9 May 1864, Thomas N. Day: Fall of Richmond Is Near

11 May 1864, Thomas N. Day: Account of Fighting in The Wilderness

10 May 1864, *Hartford Daily Courant*: Union Victory in The Wilderness

14 May 1864, Charles Hale: Report of Grant's Campaign in The Wilderness

6 June 1864, *Boston Daily Advertiser*: Account of Fighting at Cold Harbor

6 June 1864, Henry Raymond: Rebel Resolve at Cold Harbor

11 June 1864, Edward Crapsey: A Flag of Truce—The Proceedings under It

17 June 1864, Henry J. Winser: Account of Grant's Abandonment of His Position at Cold Harbor

Chapter 26

8 April 1865, Henry Raymond: The Rout of Lee's Army

9 April 1865, *New York Times*: The Pursuit of Lee's Army

10 April 1865, *New York Times*: Rejoicing at End of War; Last Exchanges between Lee and Grant

10 April 1865, Thomas N. Day: Surrender of Lee's Army

10 April 1865, R. J. Haldeman: Surrender of General Lee

12 April 1865, Thomas N. Day: Peace and Fraternity

22 April 1865, Charles Hale: Thanks to God for Restoration Peace

Chapter 28

31 December 1860, Robert Barnwell Rhett, Jr.: Move of Federal Troops to Fort Sumter May Encourage Progress of Southern Secession

2 April 1861, Tiber: Report on Crittenden Compromise Proposals

9 April 1861, Robert Barnwell Rhett, Jr.: Lincoln's Decision to Resupply Fort Sumter Is Declaration of War

16 April 1861, Your Correspondent: Report of Fighting at Fort Sumter—Start of War Likely

12 April 1861, By Telegraph: South Carolinians Open Fire on Fort Sumter

13 April 1861, *New Orleans Picayune*: Fort Sumter Surrenders

14 April 1861, George Kendall or Francis Lumsden: Account of Fall of Fort Sumter

15 April 1861, *New Orleans Picayune*: War Proclamation by Lincoln

16 April 1861, *New Orleans Picayune*: Major Anderson Permitted to Depart Fort Sumter

23 July 1861, *Memphis Appeal*: Report of Confederate Victory at Manassas

23 July 1861, Benjamin F. Dill or John McClanahan: Great Victory at Manassas

28 July 1861, John R. Thompson: Rejoicing over Victory at Manassas Tempered by Wait for Word about Loved Ones

30 July 1861, Benjamin F. Dill or John McClanahan: Consequences of Manassas—Much Work Still to Be Done

19 August 1861, Peter W. Alexander: Description of Manassas Battlefield

5 September 1861, Joan: Army Hospitals—What Louisiana Is Doing for Its Wounded Soldiers

7 September 1861, Felix G. de Fontaine: Military Rumors in Richmond; South Carolina Needs to Provide for Its Wounded Soldiers

1 October 1861, Peter W. Alexander: Camp Life in Virginia

16 October 1861, James R. Sneed: Supplies for Soldiers in Virginia—Outrageous Mismanagement

19 November 1861, Joan: Correspondent's Last Letter from Virginia

Chapter 29

9 June 1862, Dr. George W. Bagby: Battle of Seven Pines

27 June 1862, Dr. George W. Bagby: Account of Fighting during Seven Days Battles

3 July 1862, *Charleston Mercury*: Summary of Recent Battles before Richmond

7 July 1862, G. B. Cuthbert: Latest Reports from Richmond—Lee Drives McClellan from City

29 May 1862, Dr. George W. Bagby: News of McClellan's Advance on Richmond, Jackson's Operations in Shenandoah Valley

18 June 1862, *Charleston Mercury*: Achievements of Stonewall Jackson in Shenandoah Valley Campaign

9 September 1862, Peter W. Alexander: Account of Second Battle of Manassas

1 October 1862, Peter W. Alexander: Account of Lee's Retreat from Sharpsburg (Antietam)

24, 23 December 1862, Peter W. Alexander: Accounts of Battle at Fredericksburg

15 December 1862, *Richmond Examiner*: Battle of Fredericksburg—Another Confederate Victory

Chapter 30

10 April 1863, Peter W. Alexander: Union Attack on Charleston Repulsed

12 July 1863, *Savannah Republican*: Account of Unsuccessful Union Attack on Battery Wagner, Morris' Island

13 July 1863, James R. Sneed: Account of Recent Fighting in Charleston Harbor

1 May 1863, *Richmond Examiner*: News of Advance of Hooker's Army

6 May 1863, Robert E. Lee/*Richmond Examiner*: Commanding General's Report on Battle of Chancellorsville; Stonewall Jackson Wounded

11 May 1863, *Richmond Examiner*: Account of Battle of Chancellorsville

11 May 1863, John M. Daniel: Death of Stonewall Jackson

7 July 1863, James R. Sneed: First Reports of Battle at Gettysburg

14 July 1863, Peter W. Alexander: Account of Fighting at Gettysburg

Chapter 31

10 May 1864, John R. Thompson: Start of Wilderness Campaign; Political News from Richmond

14 May 1864, Benjamin F. Dill or John McClanahan: The War Can Be Won

1 June 1864, Peter W. Alexander: Battle of The Wilderness

16 June 1864, Peter W. Alexander: Account of Battle of Cold Harbor

3 August 1864, *Macon Telegraph*: Battle of the Crater

16 September 1864, Dr. George W. Bagby: News from Petersburg

27 September 1864, Dr. George W. Bagby: Account of Fighting in Shenandoah Valley

28 September 1864, John M. Daniel: Fall Campaign in Richmond

Chapter 32

18 February 1865, *Augusta Constitutionalist*: Opposing Sherman in South Carolina

23 February 1865, Dr. Nagle: Sherman's Advance into North Carolina

25 February 1865, *Augusta Constitutionalist*: Evacuation of Charleston

1 March 1865, William W. Holden: Union Advance on Wilmington

23 March 1865, Dr. Nagle: General Johnston's Battle Near Bentonville; Occupied Savannah

28 March 1865, Refugee: Evacuation of Fayetteville

5 January 1865, Larkin: Letter from Richmond

28 March 1865, *Augusta Constitutionalist*: Battle in Front of Petersburg

31 March 1865, *Augusta Constitutionalist*: Sheridan's Raid in Shenandoah Valley

1 April 1865, *Augusta Constitutionalist*: Report of Fighting around Petersburg

3 April 1865, *Richmond Examiner*: News of Union Breakthrough at Petersburg

11 April 1865, *Augusta Constitutionalist*: Latest from Lee's Army

14 April 1865, *Augusta Constitutionalist*: Evacuation of Richmond

19 April 1865, Cartouche: Terrible Battle of Petersburg

23 April 1865, *Augusta Constitutionalist*: Capitulation of Lee's Army

27 April 1865, *Augusta Chronicle and Sentinel*: Death of Lincoln Reported

3 June 1865, Andrew Johnson: President Johnson's Amnesty Proclamation

BATTLES AND CAMPAIGNS—WESTERN THEATER

Chapter 9

9 April 1862, *Hartford Daily Courant*: Early and Inaccurate Report of Fighting in Tennessee

10 April 1862, *Cincinnati Times*: Account of Battle at Shiloh

10 April 1862, William Harding: Account of Glorious Union Victory at Pittsburg Landing (Shiloh)

10 April 1862, Charles Hale: Shiloh Won by Hard-Fighting Union Troops in Tennessee

10 April 1862, *Hartford Daily Courant*: Confederate General Johnston Dead—Union Victory Complete

14 April 1862, *Hartford Daily Courant*: Confederate Accounts of Battle at Pittsburg Landing (Shiloh)

18 April 1862, Charles Hale: Summary of General Grant's Report of Battle at Pittsburg Landing (Shiloh)—Union Troops Surprised

31 May 1862, P.G.T. Beauregard: Confederate General's Official Report on Shiloh

14 April 1862, *Baltimore Sun*: "The Scene at Midnight"—The Horrible Battle of Shiloh

21 April 1862, *St. Louis Republican*: Eyewitness Account of Shiloh

17 April 1862, Manton Marble: Who Was Responsible for Not Detecting Confederate Attack at Shiloh?

3 May 1862, U. S. Grant: Union Command at Shiloh Responds to Criticism

15 April 1862, William Harding: Capture and Escape of Our War Correspondent at Pittsburg Landing

Chapter 22

24 May 1864, Henry Raymond: The Campaign in Georgia

20 July 1864, *New York Times*: General Sherman's Army Approaches Atlanta

22 July 1864, Henry Raymond: Union Indebtedness to Confederate General Bragg

27 July 1864, Thomas N. Day: General Sherman's Success at Atlanta

5 September 1864, *Hartford Daily Courant*: Northern Cities Celebrate Fall of Atlanta

Chapter 23

6 December 1864, Thomas N. Day: Dodging Sherman's Army

20 December 1864, Charles Hale: War-Weary Georgia—Sherman's Army Faces Little Resistance in State

26 December 1864, Thomas N. Day: Capture of Savannah

27 December 1864, Charles Hale: Magnificent Achievement of General Sherman—Fall of Confederacy Imminent

8 April 1865, Huguenot: Account of General Sherman's Campaign in the Carolinas

Chapter 25

6 April 1865, Thomas N. Day: Account of Battles around Petersburg on 1 April

6 April 1865, *New York Times*: Condition of Petersburg after Rebel Evacuation

4 April 1865, *Adams County Sentinel & General Advertiser*: Report on Fall of Richmond

5 April 1865, Manton Marble: Report of Jefferson Davis' Flight from Richmond

4 April 1865, Charles Hale: Fall of Richmond

5 April 1865, Charles Hale: Editorial Predicts End of Confederacy Little More Than a Week Away

8 April 1865, Thomas N. Day: Fall of Richmond Signals End of Rebellion

4 April 1865, Charles Hale: People of Boston Foresee End to War

5 April 1865, Henry Raymond: Completeness of the National Victory at Petersburg and Richmond

Chapter 29

7 February 1862, Benjamin F. Dill or John McClanahan: Report of Fall of Fort Henry

18 February 1862, Benjamin F. Dill or John McClanahan: Serious Consequences of Loss of Cumberland Forts

8, 10 April 1862, Robert Ette: Reports of Battle of Shiloh

7 May 1862, Henry Timrod: Army at Corinth—Situation in Northern Mississippi

6 May 1862, Samuel Chester Reid, Jr.: Letter from Corinth—Beauregard's Rousing Speech to His Troops

27 April 1862, By Telegraph: Account of Bombardment of Fort Jackson

27 April 1862, George Kendall or Francis Lumsden: New Orleans Must Endure Yankee Occupation

7 October 1862, Albert J. Street: Account of Battle at Corinth

14 October 1862, Clint: Account of Recent Fighting in Mississippi

18 October 1862, John Forsyth: Account of Battle of Perryville

Chapter 30

2 January 1863, Joseph Clisby: Summary of Victory at Murfreesboro

8 July 1863, *Augusta Constitutionalist*: Military Situation at Vicksburg

9 July 1863, *Savannah Republican*: Editorial—Who Is Responsible for Fall of Vicksburg?

22 September 1863, Isham G. Harris and Others: Account of Battle of Chickamauga

22 September 1863, CPA Reporters: Reports from Chickamauga Battlefield

2 November 1863, Felix G. de Fontaine: News of Union Activity at Chattanooga

26 November 1863, Samuel Chester Reid, Jr.: Reports of Fighting at Lookout Mountain

26 November 1863, *Memphis Appeal*: Rout of Bragg's Forces

1 December 1863, Benjamin F. Dill or John McClanahan: Consequences of Defeat at Lookout Mountain

Chapter 31

9 May 1864, Waverly: State of General Johnston's Army

25 May 1864, Waverly: State of Morale in Atlanta

21 June 1864, Special: Confederate Preparations at Kennesaw Mountain

1 July 1864, Captain Matthews: Account of Truce to Bury Dead at Kennesaw Mountain

31 July 1864, Telegraph and Felix G. de Fontaine: Reports of Fighting around Atlanta

9 August 1864, Confederate: Report on the Defense of Atlanta

5 September 1864, *Charleston Mercury*: Fall of Atlanta

7 September 1864, *Charleston Mercury*: Evacuation of Atlanta

6 October 1864, Dr. George W. Bagby: General Hood Marches North from Atlanta

30 November 1864, Observer: Account of Battle of Griswoldville

11 December 1864, *The Mississippian*: Effects of Sherman's March through Georgia

12 December 1864, Richard Orme, Jr. or Sr.: Atlanta after Sherman's Occupation

20 December 1864, Henry Lynden Flash: Sherman's Campaign against Savannah

28 December 1864, Henry Lynden Flash: Fall of Savannah

18 November 1864, Henry Lynden Flash: Hood's Campaign in Tennessee

16 December 1864, Henry Lynden Flash: Account of Battle of Franklin

10 January 1865, John Bell Hood: Commanding General's Report on Battle of Franklin

CITIES AND FORTS

Chapter 6

4 March 1861, *Philadelphia Inquirer*: Attack on Fort Sumter Is Imminent

13 April 1861, *Philadelphia Inquirer*: "War! War!! War!!!"—First Report of Attack on Fort Sumter

13 April 1861, Joseph Medill: War Inaugurated!

16 April 1861, David N. White: Unconfirmed Report of Attack on Fort Sumter

15 April 1861, Charles Hale: President Buchanan's Mishandling of Sumter Crisis

18 April 1861, A. S. Abell: Must There Be War over Fort Sumter?

16 April 1861, Uriah J. Jones: The Duty before Us to Restore the Union

16 April 1861, David N. White: Southern Aggression at Fort Sumter Unifies North

16 April 1861, Thomas N. Day: Effect of War News in Connecticut

13 April 1861, William Harding: The War Commenced

13 April 1861, Thomas N. Day: The Fight to Save the Union

15 April 1861, William Harding: Attack on Sumter—Its Unifying Effect throughout the Union

July 1861, *Harper's New Monthly Magazine*: British Reaction to the American War

Chapter 10

27 April 1862, Thomas N. Day: New Orleans in Union Possession—Rebels Destroy Large Amount of Property

28 April 1862, William Harding: Account of Capture of New Orleans

10 May 1862, Thomas N. Day: Account of New Orleans Campaign

9 May 1862, Theodorus Bailey: Capture of New Orleans—Small Loss of Life for Union but Large Economic Loss for Rebels

30 April 1862, Charles Hale: Significance of Capture of New Orleans

29 April 1862, Thomas N. Day: Capture of New Orleans Cuts off Confederate Line of Retreat from Mississippi

1 May 1862, Thomas N. Day: Trade at New Orleans

29 April 1862, William Harding: New Orleans—Importance of Capture Abroad and at Home

Chapter 11

1 May 1862, *Hartford Daily Courant*: Confederate Despair at Loss of New Orleans, Fears of Union Advances along Middle Mississippi

3 May 1862, *Hartford Daily Courant*: Rebels Fear Attack on Memphis, Prepare to Burn City

7 June 1862, William Harding: Difficulty of Obtaining News from Mississippi Valley

12 June 1862, William Harding: Account of River Fight before Memphis

12 June 1862, Thomas N. Day: Condition of Newly Captured Memphis

10 June 1862, Charles Hale: No Threat from Citizens of Captured Memphis

16 June 1862, William Harding: Memphis—Reconquered Southern Cities and Their Mobs

Chapter 18

8 July 1863, Official Report: Fall of Vicksburg

13 July 1863, Official Report: Details of Confederate Surrender at Vicksburg

9 July 1863, Thomas N. Day: Significant and Hopeful Successes at Gettysburg and Vicksburg

Chapter 19

13 July 1863, Henry Raymond: Editorial—Conscription Is a Great Benefit

14 July 1863, *New York Times*: "Crush the Mob!"—New York Newspapers Demand Restoration of Order

14 July 1863, Henry Raymond: The Mob and the Press—Rioters Target Newspaper Offices

15 July 1863, Henry Raymond: Rival Newspapers Unite to Denounce Mob Violence

16 July 1863, Thomas N. Day: Riot Report from Outside New York

15 July 1863, *Boston Daily Advertiser*: Riot in Boston

Chapter 20

20 November 1863, R. J. Haldeman: Cruelty to War Prisoners

19 November 1863, *New York Herald*: Rebels Responsible for End of Prisoner Exchanges

27 November 1863, *Washington Chronicle*: Account of Prison Conditions in Richmond

22 April 1864, William Lloyd Garrison: The Fort Pillow Murders

6 May 1864, *Hartford Daily Courant*: Account of Rebel Atrocities at Fort Pillow

7 May 1864, Thomas N. Day: The Fort Pillow Massacre

20 April 1864, *St. Louis Democrat*: Butchery of Black Union Soldiers at Fort Pillow

10 May 1864, *Salem Observer*: Suggested Retaliation for Massacre at Fort Pillow

2 May 1864, Henry Raymond: How to Deal with Fort Pillow Butchers

10 May 1864, By a Connecticut Woman: Letter Writer Suggests Proper Retaliation for Fort Pillow Massacre

3 May 1864, *Baltimore American*: Sad Condition of Released Union Prisoners

27 December 1864, Henry Raymond: What Can Be Done for Union Prisoners?

Chapter 22

24 May 1864, Henry Raymond: The Campaign in Georgia

20 July 1864, *New York Times*: General Sherman's Army Approaches Atlanta

22 July 1864, Henry Raymond: Union Indebtedness to Confederate General Bragg

27 July 1864, Thomas N. Day: General Sherman's Success at Atlanta

5 September 1864, *Hartford Daily Courant*: Northern Cities Celebrate Fall of Atlanta

Chapter 23

26 December 1864, Thomas N. Day: Capture of Savannah

Chapter 25

6 April 1865, Thomas N. Day: Account of Battles around Petersburg on 1 April

6 April 1865, *New York Times*: Condition of Petersburg after Rebel Evacuation

4 April 1865, *Adams County Sentinel & General Advertiser*: Report on Fall of Richmond

5 April 1865, Manton Marble: Report of Jefferson Davis' Flight from Richmond

4 April 1865, Charles Hale: Fall of Richmond

5 April 1865, Charles Hale: Editorial Predicts End of Confederacy Little More Than a Week Away

8 April, Thomas N. Day: Fall of Richmond Signals End of Rebellion

4 April 1865, Charles Hale: People of Boston Foresee End to War

5 April 1865, Henry Raymond: Completeness of the National Victory at Petersburg and Richmond

Chapter 29

7 February 1862, Benjamin F. Dill or John McClanahan: Report of Fall of Fort Henry

18 February 1862, Benjamin F. Dill or John McClanahan: Serious Consequences of Loss of Cumberland Forts

27 April 1862, By Telegraph: Account of Bombardment of Fort Jackson

27 April 1862, George Kendall or Francis Lumsden: New Orleans Must Endure Yankee Occupation

Chapter 30

10 April 1863, Peter W. Alexander: Union Attack on Charleston Repulsed

12 July 1863, *Savannah Republican*: Account of Unsuccessful Union Attack on Battery Wagner, Morris' Island

13 July 1863, James R. Sneed: Account of Recent Fighting in Charleston Harbor

2 November 1863, Felix G. de Fontaine: News of Union Activity at Chattanooga

Chapter 31

25 May 1864, Waverly: State of Morale in Atlanta

31 July 1864, Telegraph and Felix G. de Fontaine: Reports of Fighting around Atlanta

9 August 1864, Confederate: Report on the Defense of Atlanta

5 September 1864, *Charleston Mercury*: Fall of Atlanta

7 September 1864, *Charleston Mercury*: Evacuation of Atlanta

6 October 1864, Dr. George W. Bagby: General Hood Marches North from Atlanta

12 December 1864, Richard Orme, Jr. or Sr.: Atlanta after Sherman's Occupation

20 December 1864, Henry Lynden Flash: Sherman's Campaign against Savannah

28 December 1864, Henry Lynden Flash: Fall of Savannah

CONFEDERACY AND SECESSION

Chapter 5

7 November 1860, *Baltimore Sun*: South Carolina Preparations for Possible Lincoln Election

7 November 1860, *Baltimore Sun*: Meeting of South Carolina Officials

31 December 1860, *Illinois State Journal*: Northern Newspaper Views South Carolina Secession as "All Rant"

20 December 1860, Charles Hale: How South Carolinians View the North

21 December 1860, A. S. Abell: Secession of South Carolina

11 January 1861, *Philadelphia Inquirer*: South Carolina's War against the United States

4 January 1861, William Lloyd Garrison: Disunion Means Abolition of Slavery

10 January 1861, *Philadelphia Inquirer*: Another Star Lost—Secession of Mississippi

11 January 1861, A Man of Influence: Private Letter from Mississippi Explores Economic Consequences of State's Secession

14 January 1861, J. McGowan, Captain: Mood in Florida and Alabama after Both States Secede

12 January 1861, Thomas N. Day: Growing Likelihood of War

1 February 1861, William Harding: Secession of Louisiana Closes Mississippi River to North

7 February 1861, *Philadelphia Inquirer*: Secession of Texas—Seventh Star Gone

20 February 1861, William Harding: Editorial—Jefferson Davis on the Cotton Confederacy

15 January 1861, Joseph Medill: Republican Editor Demands Democratic Papers Cease Encouraging Secession by Misrepresenting Republican Positions

8 February 1861, Uriah J. Jones: Democratic Editor Blames Republicans for Causing Secession by Refusing to Compromise with South

14 January 1861, Thomas N. Day: Mr. Seward's Speech—Southern Refusal to Accept Defeat Makes War Likely

12 April 1861, *The Liberator*: Let Seceding States Go—They Will Fail

11 April 1861, Thomas N. Day: Progress of Secession—Growing Tension over Status of Federal Property in the South

Chapter 7

17 April 1861, David N. White: Border State Concern over Virginia's Secession

Chapter 25

4 April 1865, *Adams County Sentinel & General Advertiser*: Report on Fall of Richmond

5 April 1865, Manton Marble: Report of Jefferson Davis' Flight from Richmond

4 April 1865, Charles Hale: Fall of Richmond

5 April 1865, Charles Hale: Editorial Predicts End of Confederacy Little More Than a Week Away

8 April 1865, Thomas N. Day: Fall of Richmond Signals End of Rebellion

4 April 1865, Charles Hale: People of Boston Foresee End to War

5 April 1865, Henry Raymond: Completeness of the National Victory at Petersburg and Richmond

Chapter 26

8 April 1865, Henry Raymond: The Rout of Lee's Army

9 April 1865, *New York Times*: The Pursuit of Lee's Army

10 April 1865, *New York Times*: Rejoicing at End of War; Last Exchanges between Lee and Grant

10 April 1865, Thomas N. Day: Surrender of Lee's Army

10 April 1865, R. J. Haldeman: Surrender of General Lee

12 April 1865, Thomas N. Day: Peace and Fraternity

22 April 1865, Charles Hale: Thanks to God for Restoration Peace

Chapter 27

3 November 1860, George Kendall or Francis Lumsden: States Moving toward Secession If Lincoln Elected

4 November 1860, George Kendall or Francis Lumsden: Editorial—What Is the True Issue in This Election?

7 November 1860, S. B. Crafton: Editorial—Lincoln's Election Makes Outlook Gloomy for Union

21 December 1860, *New Orleans Picayune*: Form and Manner of South Carolina Secession Ordinance

21 December 1860, Robert Barnwell Rhett, Jr.: Rejoicing at South Carolina's Decision to Secede

18 January 1861, John Harvey: Southern Constitutional Argument for Secession

1 February 1861, Tiber: Correspondent Predicts the Coming of War

5 February 1861, George Kendall or Francis Lumsden: Account of Montgomery Convention

6 February 1861, George Kendall or Francis Lumsden: Border State Conferences Seek Compromise

10 February 1861, George Kendall or Francis Lumsden: Jefferson Davis and Alexander Stephens Chosen as President and Vice President of Confederacy

31 March 1861, Tiber: Fate of Fort Sumter and the Coming of War

12 April 1861, Special Report to the *Picayune*: Confederate Cabinet Awaits Washington's Response to Its Peace Commissioners

DAILY LIFE/HOME FRONT

Chapter 19

13 July 1863, Henry Raymond: Editorial—Conscription Is a Great Benefit

14 July 1863, *New York Times*: "Crush the Mob!"—New York Newspapers Demand Restoration of Order

14 July 1863, Henry Raymond: The Mob and the Press—Rioters Target Newspaper Offices

15 July 1863, Henry Raymond: Rival Newspapers Unite to Denounce Mob Violence

16 July 1863, Thomas N. Day: Riot Report from Outside New York

15 July 1863, *Boston Daily Advertiser*: Riot in Boston

Chapter 29

3 October 1862, Peter W. Alexander: Our Army, Its Great Deeds, Its Trials, Its Sufferings, and Its Perils in the Future

22 October 1862, James R. Sneed and George W. Randolph: Clothing for the Soldiers

22 October 1862, Peter W. Alexander: What the Government Has Done and Is Doing for Sick, Wounded and Destitute Soldiers

Chapter 33

1 November 1860, J.C.C. Featherstone or James A. Hoyt: "The Wheel of Life"—Six Articles on Nineteenth-Century Social Thought and Values

4 January 1861, D. A. Hobbie or B. H. Thrasher: Editorial—The Place of Women

31 May 1861, C. E. Haynes: Southern Women as Nurses

2 August 1861, John Harvey: How Southern Women Support the Confederate War Effort

7 September 1861, Joan: Female Correspondent Describes Women's War Work

25 December 1861, Southron: Tribute to the Women of the South

5 March 1863, *Richmond Dispatch*: Account of Southern Women Outwitting Yankees

20 March 1863, *Edgefield Advertiser*: Useful Advice for Women—A Substitute for Bread

29 June 1863, James R. Sneed: Career of a Female Volunteer

13 April 1863, James R. Sneed: Georgia Women Riot against Shortages

14 May 1864, *Memphis Appeal*: Patriotic Females Maintain Telegraph Communication in Georgia

4 January 1861, D. A. Hobbie or B. H. Thrasher: Story of Yankees Outwitted by a Slave

4 May 1861, James R. Sneed: Dedication of First African Baptist Church of Savannah

11 June 1861, James R. Sneed: Our Free Colored Population

31 July 1861, D. A. Hobbie or B. H. Thrasher: Maintaining Control of Slaves While the Men Are Away at War

3 May 1863, Henry Cleveland: Treatment of Slaves and Free Blacks—May Day Party for Black "Elites"

28 October 1864, Ruth Raymond: Conversations with My Female Friends—The Likely Consequences of the War for Southern Women

NEWSPAPERS AND CORRESPONDENTS

Chapter 8

23 July 1861, William Harding: Responsibility of Press for Forcing Unprepared Army to Fight at Bull Run

26 July 1861, Thomas N. Day: The Sad Battle—Somebody Blundered

24 July 1861, Charles Hale: "Pushed Too Quickly"—Responsibility of Press for Promoting the Premature Campaign

Chapter 9

17 April 1862, Manton Marble: Who Was Responsible for Not Detecting Confederate Attack at Shiloh?

3 May 1862, U. S. Grant: Union Command at Shiloh Responds to Criticism

15 April 1862, William Harding: Capture and Escape of Our War Correspondent at Pittsburg Landing

Chapter 11

7 June 1862, William Harding: Difficulty of Obtaining News from Mississippi Valley

Chapter 16

6 May 1863, Charles Hale: Difficulty of Obtaining Information from General Hooker's Army

Chapter 17

7 July 1863, *Adams County Sentinel & General Advertiser*: Local Gettysburg Newspaper Apologizes for Temporary Suspension of Publication Caused by Battle

14 July 1863, *Adams County Sentinel & General Advertiser*: The Sentinel Junior—Local Gettysburg Newspaper Reduced in Size by Paper Shortage Caused by Battle

14 July 1863, *Adams County Sentinel & General Advertiser*: Destruction of Property Caused by Battle of Gettysburg

6 July 1863, Charles Hale: Editorial—Invasion of North Halted, but Was Government Unprepared for Rebel Advance?

Chapter 19

14 July 1863, *New York Times*: "Crush the Mob!"—New York Newspapers Demand Restoration of Order

14 July 1863, Henry Raymond: The Mob and the Press—Rioters Target Newspaper Offices

15 July 1863, Henry Raymond: Rival Newspapers Unite to Denounce Mob Violence

Chapter 28

5 September 1861, Joan: Army Hospitals—What Louisiana Is Doing for Its Wounded Soldiers

7 September 1861, Felix G. de Fontaine: Military Rumors in Richmond; South Carolina Needs to Provide for Its Wounded Soldiers

1 October 1861, Peter W. Alexander: Camp Life in Virginia

16 October 1861, James R. Sneed: Supplies for Soldiers in Virginia—Outrageous Mismanagement

19 November 1861, Joan: Correspondent's Last Letter from Virginia

Chapter 29

3 October 1862, Peter W. Alexander: Our Army, Its Great Deeds, Its Trials, Its Sufferings, and Its Perils in the Future

22 October 1862, James R. Sneed and George W. Randolph: Clothing for the Soldiers

22 October 1862, Peter W. Alexander: What the Government Has Done and Is Doing for Sick, Wounded and Destitute Soldiers

Chapter 30

11 September 1863, Peter W. Alexander: Reflections on Fighting in 1863

Chapter 31

14 May 1864, Benjamin F. Dill or John McClanahan: The War Can Be Won

POLITICS AND ELECTIONS

Chapter 1

3 December 1857, Gamaliel Bailey: Governor Walker's Position on the Lecompton Constitution

10 December 1857, Gamaliel Bailey: Tense Situation in Kansas—Citizens of Territory Remaining Calm

11 January 1858, Henry Raymond: Editorial Writer Declares President Should Respect Outcome of Kansas Election, Expects Defeat of Lecompton Constitution

23 January 1858, Henry Raymond: Political Significance of Defeat of Lecompton Constitution in Kansas

4 February 1858, Henry Raymond: How President Buchanan Proposes to Keep the Peace in Kansas

4 February 1858, *St. Louis Republican*: Proslavery Kansan Criticizes Republican Lies and General Calhoun's Secrecy

29 March 1858, *Adams County Sentinel & General Advertiser*: What They Say in Kansas—The Political Divide between the Free State and Proslavery Movements

31 January 1861, *Philadelphia Inquirer*: Kansas Enters Union as Free State

Chapter 2

7 March 1857, *New York Daily Times*: Decision of Supreme Court in *Dred Scott* Case

16 July 1857, *New York Daily Times*: What the *Dred Scott* Case Decided and Did Not Decide

11 March 1857, *New York Daily Times*: Southern Reaction to *Dred Scott* Decision

9 March 1857, Henry Raymond: Editorial Writer Predicts *Dred Scott* Decision Will Spur Creation of Antislavery Party

7 March 1857, David N. White: Editorial—Voters, Not Courts, Will Decide Slavery Issue

12 March 1857, Joseph Medill: Editorial—Condemning the *Dred Scott* Decision

11 March 1857, Thurlow Weed: Political Implications of *Dred Scott* Decision

16 March 1857, *Kentucky Journal*: How the *Dred Scott* Decision Will Affect Slavery in the Western Territories

18 March 1857, *New Hampshire Patriot & State Gazette*: Dangers of Black Republican Opposition to *Dred Scott* Decision

12 March 1857, John W. Forney: Editorial—Country Should Respect *Dred Scott* Decision

15 March 1857, W. S.: Letter Writer Describes Importance of *Dred Scott* Decision for Northern Opponents of Slavery

18 April 1857, Mary Ann Carey Shadd: Description of Philadelphia Meetings Protesting *Dred Scott* Decision

18 April 1857, Sydney Howard Gay: Editorial— *Dred Scott* Decision Violates Basic Principles of American Freedom

Chapter 3

18 October 1859, *New York Times*: First News of Raid on Harper's Ferry

18 October 1859, Charles C. Fulton: Origins of Harper's Ferry Conspiracy

20 October 1859, Q.: Particulars of Harper's Ferry Rebellion

19 October 1859, Henry Raymond: John Brown and the Virginia Insurrection

20 October 1859, Thurlow Weed: Editorial—Refuting Democratic Claims That Republicans Encourage Insurrections

22 October 1859, Joseph Medill: Editorial—Responsibility of Democratic Party and *Dred Scott* Decision for Harper's Ferry Uprising

26 October 1859, *New Hampshire Patriot & State Gazette*: Editorial—Republicans Who Supported Violence in Kansas Responsible for Harper's Ferry Affair

29 October 1859, John McLean: Editorial—Republican Agitation in Kansas Leads to Harper's Ferry Violence

25 November 1859, American Anti-Slavery Society: Trial and Likely Execution of Captain John Brown

3 December 1859, *New York Tribune*: Execution of John Brown

9 December 1859, John Brown: Last Words of John Brown—"I Die Alone"

2 December 1859, Joseph Medill: Republican Editorial on John Brown's Execution

3 December 1859, John McLean: Democratic Editorial on John Brown's Execution

3 December 1859, David N. White: Editorial—Regrettable Necessity of John Brown's Execution

Chapter 4

29 October 1860, *Baltimore Sun*: Report of Preparations in Virginia to Protect State in Event of Lincoln's Election

6 November 1860, A. S. Abell: Vote for Lincoln Risks Southern Secession

6 November 1860, *Chicago Tribune*: Douglas Vote Pointless Given Southern Refusal to Support Democratic Nominee

7 November 1860, Henry Raymond: Newspapers Serve Intense Public Interest in Current Election

7 November 1860, *Chicago Tribune*: "Victory! Victory!"—Republican Newspaper Reports Lincoln's Election

9 November 1860, A. S. Abell: Election of Lincoln Exhibits Northern Hostility toward South

8 November 1860, *Boston Daily Advertiser*: Excerpts from Other Newspapers—What Is Being Said of Election Result

9 November 1860, *Baltimore Sun*: News of Southern Reaction to Lincoln's Election

10 November 1860, *Baltimore Sun*: Economic Consequences of Republican Victory

10 November 1860, *Baltimore Sun*: Growing Likelihood of Southern Secession

16 November 1860, William Lloyd Garrison: Despite Secession Threat, North Should Not Submit to Southern Demands

Chapter 5

7 November 1860, *Baltimore Sun*: South Carolina Preparations for Possible Lincoln Election

15 January 1861, Joseph Medill: Republican Editor Demands Democratic Papers Cease Encouraging Secession by Misrepresenting Republican Positions

8 February 1861, Uriah J. Jones: Democratic Editor Blames Republicans for Causing Secession by Refusing to Compromise with South

Chapter 7

15 April 1861, Thomas N. Day: Editorial—Volunteer and Support the Union Cause

15 April 1861, *Philadelphia Inquirer*: Editorial—Support for Lincoln's Call for Volunteers

17 April 1861, William Harding: Pennsylvania Men Eager to Volunteer—State Will Likely Exceed Quota

16 April 1861, Charles Hale: Massachusetts Forms Two Regiments in One Day

16 April 1861, *Chicago Tribune*: States of Northwest Quickly Forming Regiments

17 April 1861, David N. White: Border State Concern over Virginia's Secession

17 April 1861, *Philadelphia Inquirer*: Effect of President's Proclamation in the South

17 April 1861, A. S. Abell: Southern Reaction to Lincoln's Call for Volunteers

July 1861, *Harper's New Monthly Magazine*: President's Call for Volunteers Highly Effective

Chapter 14

23 September 1862, Abraham Lincoln: Emancipation Proclamation

23 September 1862, *Baltimore Sun*: Summary of President's Proclamation

25 September 1862, *New York Times*: Wide Support for Proclamation—President Serenaded in Washington

24 September 1862, Charles Hale: Proclamation Makes No Change in War Aims

24 September 1862, Thomas N. Day: "Year of Jubilee Has Come"—Slavery Rightfully Recognized as Root Cause of War

23 September 1862, Henry Raymond: Beneficial Effects of President's Proclamation on War Effort

28 September 1862, Henry Raymond: President's Proclamation Will Overthrow Southern Economy

1 October 1862, *New York Times*: Southerners Expected Proclamation from Republican President

1 January 1863, R. J. Haldeman: Proclamation Takes Effect—Slaves Given License to Revolt

25 September 1862, Thomas N. Day: Political Lines Drawn around Proclamation

23 September 1862, John Forney: War Democrats on the Proclamation

23 September 1862, D. M. Stone: Initial Democratic Response to President's Proclamation

23 September 1862, *Philadelphia Evening Journal*: Another Democratic Assessment of the President's Proclamation

23 September 1862, William W. Seaton: Comparison of Lincoln's Proclamation with General Hunter's Suppressed Edict of Emancipation

26 September 1862, R. J. Haldeman: Protest against the President's Proclamation

3 October 1862, William Lloyd Garrison: Praise for Lincoln; Condemnation for Opposition Democratic Press

Chapter 15

20 December 1862, William Harding: Changes in the Lincoln Cabinet and Administration

19 December 1862, Charles C. Fulton: Changes in Lincoln Cabinet

19 December 1862, Samuel Bowles: Effects from Fredericksburg

27 December 1862, R. J. Haldeman: "Fredericksburg Massacre"—Democratic Criticism of Lincoln for Union Loss

Chapter 17

6 July 1863, Charles Hale: Editorial—Invasion of North Halted, but Was Government Unprepared for Rebel Advance?

Chapter 20

20 November 1863, R. J. Haldeman: Cruelty to War Prisoners

19 November 1863, *New York Herald*: Rebels Responsible for End of Prisoner Exchanges

27 November 1863, *Washington Chronicle*: Account of Prison Conditions in Richmond

3 May 1864, *Baltimore American*: Sad Condition of Released Union Prisoners

27 December 1864, Henry Raymond: What Can Be Done for Union Prisoners?

Chapter 24

9 June 1864, Charles Hale: Lincoln Wins Republican Nomination—Support for President Widespread

18 November 1864, William Lloyd Garrison: Lincoln's Reelection Indicates Northern Support for Abolition of Slavery

6 March 1865, Thomas N. Day: Inauguration of President Lincoln—Comparison of 1861 and 1865

Chapter 27

3 November 1860, George Kendall or Francis Lumsden: States Moving toward Secession If Lincoln Elected

4 November 1860, George Kendall or Francis Lumsden: Editorial—What Is the True Issue in This Election?

7 November 1860, S. B. Crafton: Editorial—Lincoln's Election Makes Outlook Gloomy for Union

21 December 1860, *New Orleans Picayune*: Form and Manner of South Carolina Secession Ordinance

21 December 1860, Robert Barnwell Rhett, Jr.: Rejoicing at South Carolina's Decision to Secede

18 January 1861, John Harvey: Southern Constitutional Argument for Secession

1 February 1861, Tiber: Correspondent Predicts the Coming of War

5 February 1861, George Kendall or Francis Lumsden: Account of Montgomery Convention

6 February 1861, George Kendall or Francis Lumsden: Border State Conferences Seek Compromise

10 February 1861, George Kendall or Francis Lumsden: Jefferson Davis and Alexander Stephens Chosen as President and Vice President of Confederacy

31 March 1861, Tiber: Fate of Fort Sumter and the Coming of War

12 April 1861, Special Report to the *Picayune*: Confederate Cabinet Awaits Washington's Response to Its Peace Commissioners

PRESIDENTS AND GENERALS

Chapter 1

11 January 1858, Henry Raymond: Editorial Writer Declares President Should Respect Outcome of Kansas Election, Expects Defeat of Lecompton Constitution

4 February 1858, Henry Raymond: How President Buchanan Proposes to Keep the Peace in Kansas

4 February 1858, *St. Louis Republican*: Proslavery Kansan Criticizes Republican Lies and General Calhoun's Secrecy

Chapter 4

29 October 1860, *Baltimore Sun*: Report of Preparations in Virginia to Protect State in Event of Lincoln's Election

6 November 1860, A. S. Abell: Vote for Lincoln Risks Southern Secession

6 November 1860, *Chicago Tribune*: Douglas Vote Pointless Given Southern Refusal to Support Democratic Nominee

7 November 1860, Henry Raymond: Newspapers Serve Intense Public Interest in Current Election

7 November 1860, *Chicago Tribune*: "Victory! Victory!"—Republican Newspaper Reports Lincoln's Election

9 November 1860, A. S. Abell: Election of Lincoln Exhibits Northern Hostility toward South

8 November 1860, *Boston Daily Advertiser*: Excerpts from Other Newspapers—What Is Being Said of Election Result

9 November 1860, *Baltimore Sun*: News of Southern Reaction to Lincoln's Election

10 November 1860, *Baltimore Sun*: Economic Consequences of Republican Victory

10 November 1860, *Baltimore Sun*: Growing Likelihood of Southern Secession

16 November 1860, William Lloyd Garrison: Despite Secession Threat, North Should Not Submit to Southern Demands

Chapter 5

7 November 1860, *Baltimore Sun*: South Carolina Preparations for Possible Lincoln Election

Chapter 6

15 April 1861, Charles Hale: President Buchanan's Mishandling of Sumter Crisis

Chapter 7

15 April 1861, *Philadelphia Inquirer*: Editorial—Support for Lincoln's Call for Volunteers

17 April 1861, *Philadelphia Inquirer*: Effect of President's Proclamation in the South

17 April 1861, A. S. Abell: Southern Reaction to Lincoln's Call for Volunteers

July 1861, *Harper's New Monthly Magazine*: President's Call for Volunteers Highly Effective

Chapter 8

17 July 1861, *New York Evening Post*: Assessment of Union Commanders Scott and McDowell

Chapter 9

10 April 1862, *Hartford Daily Courant*: Confederate General Johnston Dead—Union Victory Complete

18 April 1862, Charles Hale: Summary of General Grant's Report of Battle at Pittsburg Landing (Shiloh)—Union Troops Surprised

31 May 1862, P.G.T. Beauregard: Confederate General's Official Report on Shiloh

17 April 1862, Manton Marble: Who Was Responsible for Not Detecting Confederate Attack at Shiloh?

3 May 1862, U. S. Grant: Union Command at Shiloh Responds to Criticism

Chapter 12

1 September 1862, Charles Hale: Not Time for Citizens to Criticize Union's Civil and Military Leaders

Chapter 14

23 September 1862, Abraham Lincoln: Emancipation Proclamation

23 September 1862, *Baltimore Sun*: Summary of President's Proclamation

25 September 1862, *New York Times*: Wide Support for Proclamation—President Serenaded in Washington

23 September 1862, Henry Raymond: Beneficial Effects of President's Proclamation on War Effort

28 September 1862, Henry Raymond: President's Proclamation Will Overthrow Southern Economy

1 October 1862, *New York Times*: Southerners Expected Proclamation from Republican President

23 September 1862, D. M. Stone: Initial Democratic Response to President's Proclamation

23 September 1862, *Philadelphia Evening Journal*: Another Democratic Assessment of the President's Proclamation

23 September 1862, William W. Seaton: Comparison of Lincoln's Proclamation with General Hunter's Suppressed Edict of Emancipation

26 September 1862, R. J. Haldeman: Protest against the President's Proclamation

3 October 1862, William Lloyd Garrison: Praise for Lincoln; Condemnation for Opposition Democratic Press

Chapter 15

15 December 1862, A. S. Abell: Actions of General Franklin at Fredericksburg

20 December 1862, William Harding: Changes in the Lincoln Cabinet and Administration

19 December 1862, Charles C. Fulton: Changes in Lincoln Cabinet

27 December 1862, R. J. Haldeman: "Fredericksburg Massacre"—Democratic Criticism of Lincoln for Union Loss

Chapter 16

13 May 1863, *Boston Daily Advertiser*: Report of Death of Stonewall Jackson

14 May 1863, Henry Raymond: Account of Death of Stonewall Jackson

Chapter 21

13 May 1864, Charles Hale: Praise for Grant

14 May 1864, Charles Hale: Report of Grant's Campaign in The Wilderness

17 June 1864, Henry J. Winser: Account of Grant's Abandonment of His Position at Cold Harbor

Chapter 22

20 July 1864, *New York Times*: General Sherman's Army Approaches Atlanta

22 July 1864, Henry Raymond: Union Indebtedness to Confederate General Bragg

27 July 1864, Thomas N. Day: General Sherman's Success at Atlanta

Chapter 23

6 December 1864, Thomas N. Day: Dodging Sherman's Army

20 December 1864, Charles Hale: War-Weary Georgia—Sherman's Army Faces Little Resistance in State

27 December 1864, Charles Hale: Magnificent Achievement of General Sherman—Fall of Confederacy Imminent

8 April 1865, Huguenot: Account of General Sherman's Campaign in the Carolinas

Chapter 24

9 June 1864, Charles Hale: Lincoln Wins Republican Nomination—Support for President Widespread

18 November 1864, William Lloyd Garrison: Lincoln's Reelection Indicates Northern Support for Abolition of Slavery

6 March 1865, Thomas N. Day: Inauguration of President Lincoln—Comparison of 1861 and 1865

Chapter 25

5 April 1865, Manton Marble: Report of Jefferson Davis' Flight from Richmond

Chapter 26

8 April 1865, Henry Raymond: The Rout of Lee's Army

9 April 1865, *New York Times*: The Pursuit of Lee's Army

10 April 1865, *New York Times*: Rejoicing at End of War; Last Exchanges between Lee and Grant

10 April 1865, Thomas N. Day: Surrender of Lee's Army

10 April 1865, R. J. Haldeman: Surrender of General Lee

Chapter 27

3 November 1860, George Kendall or Francis Lumsden: States Moving toward Secession If Lincoln Elected

4 November 1860, George Kendall or Francis Lumsden: Editorial—What Is the True Issue in This Election?

7 November 1860, S. B. Crafton: Editorial—Lincoln's Election Makes Outlook Gloomy for Union

21 December 1860, *New Orleans Picayune*: Form and Manner of South Carolina Secession Ordinance

21 December 1860, Robert Barnwell Rhett, Jr.: Rejoicing at South Carolina's Decision to Secede

18 January 1861, John Harvey: Southern Constitutional Argument for Secession

1 February 1861, Tiber: Correspondent Predicts the Coming of War

5 February 1861, George Kendall or Francis Lumsden: Account of Montgomery Convention

6 February 1861, George Kendall or Francis Lumsden: Border State Conferences Seek Compromise

10 February 1861, George Kendall or Francis Lumsden: Jefferson Davis and Alexander Stephens Chosen as President and Vice President of Confederacy

31 March 1861, Tiber: Fate of Fort Sumter and the Coming of War

12 April 1861, Special Report to the *Picayune*: Confederate Cabinet Awaits Washington's Response to Its Peace Commissioners

Chapter 28

9 April 1861, Robert Barnwell Rhett, Jr.: Lincoln's Decision to Resupply Fort Sumter Is Declaration of War

15 April 1861, *New Orleans Picayune*: War Proclamation by Lincoln

16 April 1861, *New Orleans Picayune*: Major Anderson Permitted to Depart Fort Sumter

Chapter 29

7 July 1862, G. B. Cuthbert: Latest Reports from Richmond—Lee Drives McClellan from City

29 May 1862, Dr. George W. Bagby: News of McClellan's Advance on Richmond, Jackson's Operations in Shenandoah Valley

18 June 1862, *Charleston Mercury*: Achievements of Stonewall Jackson in Shenandoah Valley Campaign

1 October 1862, Peter W. Alexander: Account of Lee's Retreat from Sharpsburg (Antietam)

Chapter 30

1 May 1863, *Richmond Examiner*: News of Advance of Hooker's Army

6 May 1863, Robert E. Lee/*Richmond Examiner*: Commanding General's Report on Battle of Chancellorsville; Stonewall Jackson Wounded

11 May 1863, John M. Daniel: Death of Stonewall Jackson

Chapter 31

9 May 1864, Waverly: State of General Johnston's Army

6 October 1864, Dr. George W. Bagby: General Hood Marches North from Atlanta

11 December 1864, *The Mississippian*: Effects of Sherman's March through Georgia

12 December 1864, Richard Orme, Jr. or Sr.: Atlanta after Sherman's Occupation

20 December 1864, Henry Lynden Flash: Sherman's Campaign against Savannah

18 November 1864, Henry Lynden Flash: Hood's Campaign in Tennessee

10 January 1865, John Bell Hood: Commanding General's Report on Battle of Franklin

Chapter 32

23 March 1865, Dr. Nagle: General Johnston's Battle Near Bentonville; Occupied Savannah

27 April 1865, *Augusta Chronicle and Sentinel*: Death of Lincoln Reported

3 June 1865, Andrew Johnson: President Johnson's Amnesty Proclamation

SLAVERY AND SECTIONALISM

Chapter 1

3 December 1857, Gamaliel Bailey: Governor Walker's Position on the Lecompton Constitution

10 December 1857, Gamaliel Bailey: Tense Situation in Kansas—Citizens of Territory Remaining Calm

11 January 1858, Henry Raymond: Editorial Writer Declares President Should Respect Outcome of Kansas Election, Expects Defeat of Lecompton Constitution

23 January 1858, Henry Raymond: Political Significance of Defeat of Lecompton Constitution in Kansas

4 February 1858, Henry Raymond: How President Buchanan Proposes to Keep the Peace in Kansas

4 February 1858, *St. Louis Republican*: Proslavery Kansan Criticizes Republican Lies and General Calhoun's Secrecy

29 March 1858, *Adams County Sentinel & General Advertiser*: What They Say in Kansas—The Political Divide between the Free State and Proslavery Movements

31 January 1861, *Philadelphia Inquirer*: Kansas Enters Union as Free State

Chapter 2

7 March 1857, *New York Daily Times*: Decision of Supreme Court in *Dred Scott* Case

16 July 1857, *New York Daily Times*: What the *Dred Scott* Case Decided and Did Not Decide

11 March 1857, *New York Daily Times*: Southern Reaction to *Dred Scott* Decision

9 March 1857, Henry Raymond: Editorial Writer Predicts *Dred Scott* Decision Will Spur Creation of Antislavery Party

7 March 1857, David N. White: Editorial—Voters, Not Courts, Will Decide Slavery Issue

12 March 1857, Joseph Medill: Editorial—Condemning the *Dred Scott* Decision

11 March 1857, Thurlow Weed: Political Implications of *Dred Scott* Decision

16 March 1857, *Kentucky Journal*: How the *Dred Scott* Decision Will Affect Slavery in the Western Territories

18 March 1857, *New Hampshire Patriot & State Gazette*: Dangers of Black Republican Opposition to *Dred Scott* Decision

12 March 1857, John W. Forney: Editorial—Country Should Respect *Dred Scott* Decision

15 March 1857, W. S.: Letter Writer Describes Importance of *Dred Scott* Decision for Northern Opponents of Slavery

18 April 1857, Mary Ann Carey Shadd: Description of Philadelphia Meetings Protesting *Dred Scott* Decision

18 April 1857, Sydney Howard Gay: Editorial—*Dred Scott* Decision Violates Basic Principles of American Freedom

Chapter 3

18 October 1859, *New York Times*: First News of Raid on Harper's Ferry

18 October 1859, Charles C. Fulton: Origins of Harper's Ferry Conspiracy

20 October 1859, Q.: Particulars of Harper's Ferry Rebellion

19 October 1859, Henry Raymond: John Brown and the Virginia Insurrection

20 October 1859, Thurlow Weed: Editorial—Refuting Democratic Claims That Republicans Encourage Insurrections

22 October 1859, Joseph Medill: Editorial—Responsibility of Democratic Party and *Dred Scott* Decision for Harper's Ferry Uprising

26 October 1859, *New Hampshire Patriot & State Gazette*: Editorial—Republicans Who Supported Violence in Kansas Responsible for Harper's Ferry Affair

29 October 1859, John McLean: Editorial—Republican Agitation in Kansas Leads to Harper's Ferry Violence

25 November 1859, American Anti-Slavery Society: Trial and Likely Execution of Captain John Brown

3 December 1859, *New York Tribune*: Execution of John Brown

9 December 1859, John Brown: Last Words of John Brown—"I Die Alone"

2 December 1859, Joseph Medill: Republican Editorial on John Brown's Execution

3 December 1859, John McLean: Democratic Editorial on John Brown's Execution

3 December 1859, David N. White: Editorial—Regrettable Necessity of John Brown's Execution

Chapter 5

4 January 1861, William Lloyd Garrison: Disunion Means Abolition of Slavery

Chapter 14

23 September 1862, Abraham Lincoln: Emancipation Proclamation

23 September 1862, *Baltimore Sun*: Summary of President's Proclamation

25 September 1862, *New York Times*: Wide Support for Proclamation—President Serenaded in Washington

24 September 1862, Charles Hale: Proclamation Makes No Change in War Aims

24 September 1862, Thomas N. Day: "Year of Jubilee Has Come"—Slavery Rightfully Recognized as Root Cause of War

23 September 1862, Henry Raymond: Beneficial Effects of President's Proclamation on War Effort

28 September 1862, Henry Raymond: President's Proclamation Will Overthrow Southern Economy

1 October 1862, *New York Times*: Southerners Expected Proclamation from Republican President

1 January 1863, R. J. Haldeman: Proclamation Takes Effect—Slaves Given License to Revolt

25 September 1862, Thomas N. Day: Political Lines Drawn around Proclamation

23 September 1862, John Forney: War Democrats on the Proclamation

23 September 1862, D. M. Stone: Initial Democratic Response to President's Proclamation

23 September 1862, *Philadelphia Evening Journal*: Another Democratic Assessment of the President's Proclamation

23 September 1862, William W. Seaton: Comparison of Lincoln's Proclamation with General Hunter's Suppressed Edict of Emancipation

26 September 1862, R. J. Haldeman: Protest against the President's Proclamation

3 October 1862, William Lloyd Garrison: Praise for Lincoln; Condemnation for Opposition Democratic Press

Chapter 33

4 January 1861, D. A. Hobbie or B. H. Thrasher: Story of Yankees Outwitted by a Slave

31 July 1861, D. A. Hobbie or B. H. Thrasher: Maintaining Control of Slaves While the Men Are Away at War

3 May 1863, Henry Cleveland: Treatment of Slaves and Free Blacks—May Day Party for Black "Elites"

I

NORTHERN NEWSPAPERS DURING THE CIVIL WAR

Amy Reynolds

TIMELINE

1820

3 March   Congress passes the Missouri Compromise.

1850

September   Congress passes the Compromise of 1850.

1854

30 May   Congress passes the Kansas-Nebraska Act, which establishes the territories of Kansas and Nebraska, repeals the Missouri Compromise, and renews tension between anti- and proslavery factions.

1857

4 March   Democrat James Buchanan is inaugurated as the fifteenth president of the United States.

6 March   The U.S. Supreme Court decides the case of *Dred Scott v. John F. A. Sanford* and rules that blacks are not citizens.

1859

16 October   John Brown leads his raid on Harper's Ferry, Virginia.

2 December   John Brown is executed.

1860

6 November   Republican Abraham Lincoln is elected as the sixteenth president of the United States.

20 December South Carolina secedes from the Union.

1861

9 January   Mississippi secedes from the Union.

10 January	Florida secedes from the Union.
11 January	Alabama secedes from the Union.
19 January	Georgia secedes from the Union.
26 January	Louisiana secedes from the Union.
1 February	The Texas Convention votes to secede but does not actually do so until 2 March.
4 February	Delegates from the seceding states meet in Montgomery, Alabama, to form a provisional Confederate government.
8 February	The Montgomery Convention adopts the Provisional Confederate Constitution.
9 February	The Montgomery Convention selects former U.S. Mississippi senator Jefferson Davis as its provisional president.
18 February	Davis and provisional vice president Alexander Stephens are inaugurated in front of the Alabama state capitol building.
4 March	Lincoln is inaugurated as the sixteenth president of the United States.
11 March	The Montgomery Convention unanimously adopts the Constitution of the Confederate States of America, which is very similar to the U.S. Constitution except for the fact that it specifically protects slavery.
12 April	South Carolina forces in Charleston begin to attack Fort Sumter.
13 April	Fort Sumter surrenders.
15 April	President Lincoln issues a call for 75,000 volunteers to put down the Southern rebellion.
17 April	Virginia secedes from the Union.
6 May	Arkansas secedes from the Union.
20 May	North Carolina secedes from the Union.
1 June	Confederate capital moved from Montgomery, Alabama to Richmound, Virginia.
8 June	Tennessee secedes from the Union.
21 July	Battle of Bull Run (First).
September	Union troops capture Paducah, Kentucky; Lexington, Missouri, surrenders to the Confederates.
21 October	Battle of Ball's Bluff in Virginia (Confederate victory).
6 November	Jefferson Davis elected regular president of the Confederacy.

1862

February	Battles in Tennessee, North Carolina, and New Mexico territory. Fort Donelson, Tennessee, surrenders to the Union. Jefferson Davis is inaugurated as regular president of the Confederacy.
March	Battles in Arkansas, Virginia, New Mexico territory, Missouri, and North Carolina. The Union captures New Madrid, Missouri, and New Bern, North Carolina.

6 April	Battle of Shiloh.
7 April	Island No. 10 on the Mississippi River falls to the Union.
25 April	New Orleans falls to the Union; Fort Macon, North Carolina, captured by the Union.
4 May	Union forces occupy Yorktown, Virginia (began siege of the city on 5 April).
6 June	Battle of Memphis.
25 June	Battle of the Seven Days (in Virginia) began; ended on 1 July with Union forces driven away from Richmond.
29–30 August	Second Battle of Bull Run.
17 September	Battle of Antietam.
22 September	Lincoln issues Emancipation Proclamation.
13 December	Battle of Fredericksburg.

1863

1 January	Lincoln's Emancipation Proclamation takes effect.
May	General Ulysses Grant begins his Vicksburg Campaign.
1–6 May	Battle of Chancellorsville.
10 May	Confederate General Stonewall Jackson dies from pneumonia after being accidentally shot by his own men, causing the amputation of his arm.
1–3 July	Battle of Gettysburg.
4 July	Vicksburg surrenders to the Union.
13–16 July	New York City Draft Riots.
19–20 September	Battle of Chickamauga, Georgia (Confederate victory).
19 November	War memorial dedication at Gettysburg; Lincoln gives his "Gettysburg Address."
23–25 November	Battle of Chattanooga (Union victory).

1864

12 April	Fort Pillow massacre.
5 May	Battle of The Wilderness opens Grant's Overland Campaign.
7 May	General William T. Sherman begins his Atlanta Campaign.
8 May	Battle of Spotsylvania.
1–3 June	Battle of Cold Harbor; end of Grant's Overland Campaign.
15 June	Union assault of Petersburg begins.
27 June	Battle of Kennesaw Mountain, outside Atlanta.
22 July	Battle of Atlanta (Confederate victory).
30 July	Battle of the Crater at Petersburg.
2 September	Atlanta occupied by Union troops.

8 November	Lincoln reelected president of the United States; Andrew Johnson becomes his vice president.
15 November	Sherman begins his March to the Sea.
15–16 December	Battle of Nashville (Union victory).
22 December	Sherman captures Savannah, Georgia.

1865

1 February	Sherman begins his march through the Carolinas.
4 March	President Lincoln inaugurated.
2 April	Petersburg falls to the Union.
3 April	Richmond occupied by Union troops.
9 April	Confederate General Robert E. Lee surrenders to General Grant at Appomattox Courthouse, effectively ending the war.
12 April	Mobile, Alabama, surrenders to Union forces.
14–15 April	President Abraham Lincoln shot at Ford's Theatre by John Wilkes Booth; Lincoln dies the next day. On 15 April, Andrew Johnson is sworn in as president.
26 April	Confederate General Joseph Johnston surrenders to General Sherman in North Carolina.
26 April	Union troops find John Wilkes Booth hiding in a barn near Port Royal, Virginia, where he dies from a gunshot wound.
10 May	Union forces capture Confederate President Jefferson Davis near Irwinville, Georgia; President Andrew Johnson declares that the war is officially ended.
23 June	Last Confederate army surrenders.
7 July	Four conspirators in Lincoln's assassination are executed.
18 December	Thirteenth Amendment, which abolishes slavery, is ratified.

INTRODUCTION

In 1850, more than a decade before the Civil War started, the literacy rate in the United States was 89 percent. The growth of newspapers in the country was rapid—between 1825 and 1860 the number quadrupled. On the eve of the Civil War nearly 2,500 newspapers were published in the United States, twice as many in the North as the South. The papers in the North had four times the circulation of the Southern papers. Of the thousands of papers published, about 375 were published daily. Almost 300 of those daily papers were published in the North. The city of New York alone supported seventeen daily newspapers, several of which were widely circulated in Washington, D.C., which had three daily newspapers when the war began. Richmond, Virginia, the city that would become the capital of the Confederate States of America, supported four dailies. Citizens of the United States learned about the Civil War mostly through newspaper accounts. And most of the accounts of the war came from special correspondents. Northern newspapers had about 350 war correspondents; about 150 war correspondents worked for Southern papers.[1]

As historians study the vast number of newspaper accounts of the Civil War—total wartime journalistic output has been estimated at more than 100 million words—they must understand the context in which the reporting and writing emerged. That includes sensitivity to the social and political climate of the time. In 1860, the United States had a population of more than 31 million people. Two-thirds of them lived in the North. Blacks, both free and slave, comprised about 14 percent of the total population, but 95 percent of them lived in the South and were slaves. In South Carolina alone, slaves comprised 57 percent of the state's population. In Mississippi the slave population also exceeded 50 percent. Fifteen states permitted slavery in 1860—Missouri, Kentucky, Delaware, and Maryland in the North, and Texas, Arkansas, Louisiana, Mississippi, Tennessee, Alabama, Georgia, Florida, North Carolina, South Carolina, and Virginia in the South. Of the fifteen slave states, only Delaware had more free blacks than slaves, and Maryland had a free black population that was almost equal to its slave population.

Another demographic difference between the North and South was urbanization. By 1860 about 26 percent of Northerners lived in towns or cities; only 10 percent of Southerners lived in these more urban areas. New York was the largest city in the country, with a population of 813,699. Brooklyn, which is today part of New York City, was considered a separate city until 1898, and it ranked as the North's third largest city, with a population of 266,661. Philadelphia was the second largest city, with 566,529 residents. Baltimore (212,418) and Boston (177,840) were fourth and fifth, respectively. In the South, New Orleans was the largest city, with a population of 168,675. There were no other cities larger than 50,000 in the South in 1860, and only three of the twenty-five largest cities in the country would end up in the Confederacy—New Orleans, Charleston, South Carolina (population 40,522), and Richmond (37,910).[2]

Between 1800 and 1860 the U.S. economy grew rapidly. The development of strong transportation systems helped spur economic growth and was responsible for some of the shift away from agricultural work in the North. The railroad system, which was developed in the 1830s, boasted 2,818 miles of track in 1840. By 1860 there were 30,626 miles of railroad tracks across the country, and two-thirds of those tracks were in the North. In 1860, 45 percent of workers in the United States held nonagricultural jobs. In the North, only 40 percent of its workforce was employed in agriculture. Innovations in farming techniques and production created more efficient agricultural systems and the rise of factories; businesses and railroads provided attractive employment opportunities that drew workers away from farms. In the South, agriculture continued to be the primary source of employment—80 percent of the workforce (including slaves) remained in agriculture.

In the South, the primary "cash" crops were cotton, tobacco, rice, and sugar. During the 1850s cotton prices soared, and many Southern planters began devoting more and more land to raise cotton. They also added sugar and tobacco to their fields but consequently reduced their production of food staples like corn. The investment in cotton was an expensive one in the South because the price of slaves increased along with the price of cotton. Many Southern planters relied on slave labor to make a profit, while the North had reduced its reliance on labor and turned to more efficient and productive machinery.

While many Southerners were investing in slaves to produce more cotton, Northerners were investing in manufacturing companies, banks, insurance companies, steamships, and railroads—the more modern aspects of economic development. The South's failure to invest in manufacturing was not because of Southern poverty. Per capita, Southern whites were almost twice as rich as Northern whites—the average Southern white adult was worth $3,978, compared to the average Northern white adult who was worth, on average, $2,040. Although nonslave Southerners only represented 30 percent of the U.S. free population, that 30 percent included more than 60 percent of the country's wealthiest individuals.[3]

Historians have offered several reasons for the slow industrialization of the South. Some blame the South's dependence on slave labor; others argue that Southern wealth was too heavily invested in slaves and land[4] so that money was not available for investment in other things. Some historians suggest that the slow industrial growth was tied to the cultural value of agriculture in the South. In the tradition of Thomas Jefferson as the ideal of the Southern gentleman farmer, many Southerners defended the plantation slave system and condemned what they called the "wage slavery" of the industrialized North. Equally important to the understanding of the South's economic choices is that the majority of Southern whites accepted the idea of white supremacy and believed it was necessary to keep blacks subordinate. That is, "racial subordination went hand-in-hand with plantation-based agriculture."[5]

Slaves also represented the most important privately held property in the South. In 1860 nearly 400,000 individuals owned slaves in the United States. Slave owners were members of between 25 and 30 percent of all Southern white families, but because the head of the household was typically the slave owner and because typically all other family members had access to and used the slaves, historians have noted that the slaveholding class was actually much larger than U.S. Census figures suggest. Half of all slave owners had five or fewer slaves. The state of Virginia had the most slave owners (52,128) in 1860, but more than 70 percent of them owned less than ten slaves. South Carolina had about half the number of slaveholders as Virginia but had twice as many plantations with fifty or more slaves. And the primary cotton-producing states of Alabama, Georgia, Mississippi, Louisiana, and South Carolina clearly had the largest concentrations of large slave plantations. For more than 200 years slavery was not just economical; it was also entrenched in the social culture of the South, and the distinction between the black and white races was central to the order of Southern society.[6]

It is in this social context one must consider the politics of the country leading up to and including the Civil War. The Democratic Party, the oldest continuous party in the United States at the time, had achieved national membership by 1800 and was a dominant political force in the country under President Andrew Jackson, who was elected to the office in 1828 and held it for two terms. The Democratic Party favored limited government, but the party became divided on the issue of slavery as discussion of expanding slavery into U.S. territories became more intense and public. By the 1860s the party was split between those who believed in popular sovereignty and those who believed slavery should be protected in the territories. The concept of popular sovereignty was most commonly associated with Illinois Senator Stephen A. Douglas, the chairman of the committee on territories during most of the discussions about slavery in the territories. Popular sovereignty simply meant that questions of slavery should be left to territorial settlers themselves for resolution.

After Andrew Jackson left the presidency in 1837, the Democrats and the Whigs controlled that office until the 1860 election of Republican Abraham Lincoln. The Whig Party, which took its name from the British political party that opposed undue royal authority and privilege in England, formed in 1834 to mount opposition against Jackson and the powerful Democratic Party. The party stood for many different principles, most notably states' rights, but the one unifying force behind its effectiveness was the party's opposition to the Democrats. The Whigs successfully elected William Henry Harrison, then Zachary Taylor, as president in 1840 and 1848, respectively. In 1852, when the Democratic Party successfully elected Franklin Pierce, the Whig Party fell apart, mostly because its membership was also divided on the slavery question. Former Whigs joined the American, Republican, and Democratic Parties.

The American Party—also called the Know-Nothings because of their standard response, "I know nothing," when asked about their organization's members or activities—came about primarily in response to the millions of immigrants who came to the United States during the 1840s and 1850s. Members of the American Party were generally antiforeign and anti-Catholic and pushed for tightening requirements for citizenship, allowing only native-born Americans to hold public office and in general supporting measures that would ensure the dominance of Anglo-Saxon Protestant culture. In 1854 the Know-Nothings won victories in Massachusetts, New York, Pennsylvania, and Delaware, but by 1855 the party fell apart because it too was split over the slavery issue.[7]

The Republican Party formed in 1854 as a coalition of former Whigs, antislavery Democrats, Know-Nothings, and Free Soilers. The Free Soil Party had emerged in 1848 after the Mexican War. That party opposed the extension of slavery into the western territories and promoted a homesteading law. Its members were a mix of radical Democrats from New York, antislavery Whigs, and former members of the abolitionist Liberty Party.

The Republicans adopted policies that favored business, high tariffs, social reforms, and internal improvements and appealed almost exclusively to people in the North. The party opposed the expansion of slavery in the territories but believed that the federal government did not have the authority to affect slavery in the Southern states. Most Republicans believed that the institution of slavery was protected by the Constitution, but they also believed that if the expansion of slavery was eliminated, the institution would eventually die. Some radical Republican activists opposed slavery and supported racial equality, but the vast majority of Republicans were not abolitionists or supporters of black rights. The radicals who did support racial equality were often called "Black Republicans."

In 1856 Republican candidate John Fremont lost the presidential election to Democrat James Buchanan. But the Republicans were successful in electing Abraham Lincoln to office in 1860, which was one of the direct triggers of the Civil War. About 6 weeks after Lincoln was elected, South Carolina seceded from the Union and paved the way for the formation of the Confederate States of America.[8]

As the social, economic, and political landscape of the country changed rapidly between about 1830 and 1860, so did the press. When Andrew Jackson took office in 1828, newspapers were sold by subscription to a small number of people, mostly men who had an interest in either political or commercial information. By the time Abraham Lincoln took office, major newspapers were readily available to the general public in urban centers, cities, and small towns. The process of printing was driven by the steam-powered rotary press, which allowed larger metropolitan newspapers to produce thousands of copies per hour. And as transportation expanded, newspapers had a better ability to distribute their copy beyond their home locations.[9]

The development of the telegraph in the 1840s helped revolutionize the newspaper industry. Newspapers encouraged the development of the telegraph—the first telegraph line in the United States was an experimental line between Washington, D.C., and Baltimore that was used by the *Baltimore Sun*. The *Sun*'s early use of the technology encouraged wider acceptance of telegraphic communication, although early on people were skeptical about its promise. The *New York Herald*, the *New York Tribune*, the *New York Sun*, and the *Philadelphia Public Ledger* were among the first newspapers to make full use of telegraphic services. By using the telegraph, newspapers could carry nearly instantaneous reports of news and events happening all over the country and world.[10]

According to historians, by the 1850s newspapers had truly become "mass media."

> The three characteristics of mass media were in place and accelerating: availability of steam-driven presses for reproduction, growing railroad networks for distribution, and rapid development of near-instantaneous communication via telegraph lines for gathering and disseminating the most important news. Together they added up to newspapers that had more outreach and the power to portray—and distort—events and to amplify, often exacerbate, political arguments.[11]

The technological advances in the newspaper industry also allowed papers to provide audiences with a lot of information for a small price—typically a penny or two. The so-called penny press emerged in the early 1830s and is credited to Benjamin Day, a young printer in New York City who sold his small paper, the *New York Sun*, on the streets of New York for a penny. Day's model of the cheap, popular newspaper was adopted by enterprising publishers in major cities across the country, and the penny press flourished. Many historians have connected the rise of "Jacksonian democracy" and the Democratic Party in the 1830s to the rise of the penny press. The widely read and available newspapers played a significant role in informing the poorer classes, and a significant number of the cheap penny papers were staunch supporters of Jackson and the Democratic Party.[12]

Many of America's newspapers were the creations of political parties and their leaders, and through the early nineteenth century most important newspapers were largely political and partisan. In the 1840s, *New York Tribune* editor Horace Greeley, an abolitionist, was one of the most politically active editors in the country. But Greeley was not alone in using his press to express a specific political point of view. According to the 1860 census, 80 percent of U.S. newspapers at that time were classified as "political in their character."

By the 1850s editors did worry less about pleasing politicians than they had in their earlier years, but their content still tended to be one-sided in favor of their chosen political party. The significance of the newspaper to the public and in influencing and perhaps forming political public opinion was clear to some publishers at the time. In 1845 *New York Herald* publisher James Gordon Bennett suggested that journalism's

> sphere of action will be widened. It will, in fact, be more influential than ever. The public mind will be stimulated to greater activity by the rapid circulation of news. The swift communication of tidings of great events, will awake in the masses of the community a keener interest in public affairs. Thus the intellectual, philosophic and original journalist will have a greater, more excited and thoughtful audience than ever.

Bennett was right—by the 1860s, all newspapers' annual circulation nationwide had reached nearly 888 million copies. The newspaper had emerged as an important force in American politics since so many people now got their information from newspapers.[13]

In 1860 nearly 2,500 newspapers were published in the United States, twice as many in the North as the South. Citizens of the United States learned about the

Civil War mostly through newspaper accounts. The job of a "reporter" was a relatively new one. As the newspaper industry grew, so did the profession of journalism. Historically, printers and politicians wrote much of what appeared in a newspaper. Newspaper correspondents as we think of them today existed since President Jackson's administration, but those correspondents were considered to be "high caste," people who could rub elbows with important politicians in Washington. It was the telegraph that practically propelled the newspaper industry to begin to consider the role of the correspondent differently and to consider employing people in this capacity. "The notion that a reporter on the end of a wire to a distant and newsworthy spot was a profitable investment quickly took root in the minds of those editors whose establishments were fortunate enough to afford expenses of a novel kind." By 1850, Greeley's *New York Tribune* had employed three regular correspondents in Washington, D.C., and had signed agreements for two residents of California and one each in Philadelphia, Baltimore, and Boston to wire periodic letters to the paper. The newspaper also had four agents in European capitals, two in Canada, and one each in Mexico, Cuba, and Central America. By 1858 New York City's newspapers had formed a local Associated Press in an effort to lower their costs associated with correspondents and telegraph wires.[14]

Most large daily papers in the North began employing special telegraphic correspondents as news of the start of the war spread in April 1861. Some saw it as the only way to ensure the integrity and "rightness" of the information they were receiving from a distant location. The Republican *Chicago Daily Tribune* noted for its readers,

> Our full and intensely interesting special dispatch from Washington comes from our special telegraphic correspondent, whose position is such that he cannot be deceived as to the intentions of the President and his Cabinet. We offer it to our readers as the summary of the present plans of the Cabinet, and as conclusive of the scope and aim of Republican policy.
>
> In connection with this matter, we may be permitted to say that dissatisfaction with the meagerness of the information brought us by the arrangement of the associated Press, and with the unreliability of that dished up by the sensational papers of the metropolis, we have determined to incur the great expense of a special correspondent at the seat of government and daily special dispatches copious enough to give our readers a correct idea of all passing events which have a bearing upon the great issues now presented to the people of the West. We need not say that the expense of all this is heavy; but we rely upon the friendship and generosity of our friends to make us whole. For them we labor.[15]

Although there is not much biographical data that exists on correspondents in the nineteenth century, there are many collective historical accounts of the reporters and correspondents who covered the Civil War, including some highlights from their writings.[16] Of the 350 or so correspondents who covered the war for the North, there is some biographical data available for about a fifth of them. Four of five had previous newspaper experience, and more than half had been born in cities. Their average age was "late twenties," and the overwhelming majority were white men.[17] In general, few of these reporters wrote under their full names. Some used initials; some used nicknames; but most stories written by correspondents during the Civil War were published unsigned and without any byline or specific reporter credit by name. Small weekly newspapers, which did not employ correspondents, typically clipped news from big-city papers and put it under a heading generally called "The latest news" or something similar. They did write their own editorials, but the news on their pages came directly from the large papers and not from correspondents.

The Northern newspapers that covered the Civil War ran the political spectrum from radical Republican to Democrat. Some of the best-known radical Republican papers were the *New York Tribune*, the *Chicago Tribune*, and the *Philadelphia Inquirer*. Major moderate Republican papers were the *New York Times*, the *Cincinnati Commercial*, and the *Boston Journal*. The *Chicago Times*, the *Cincinnati Enquirer*, and the *New York World* were some of the most staunchly Democratic papers of the time. Sometimes a paper's political affiliation was given away in its name, but that could also be misleading as in the case of the *St. Louis Republican*, which was a Democratic paper. Conversely, the *St. Louis Democrat* was a Republican publication. Nearly all of the newspapers in the South were Democratic, particularly after the secession movement began in December 1860. A few Southern papers before the war were Whig, which at the time showed some sympathy toward the Republican Party.

As one can imagine, the mix of partisan reporting and telegraph speed to deliver information led to a significant amount of "bad" news. Journalists of this time did not follow any professional code of responsibility or ethics. Reporting was very much a trade, and those who practiced it only had rudimentary notions of fairness, accuracy, and balance. A newspaper's political perspective was quite apparent on its pages. And often the speed with which reporters were sending the news resulted in the publication of errors, rumors, military propaganda, and political propaganda. Often it was hard for a reader to discern the truth of information that came quickly from the Civil War battlefield. There are numerous examples in this part, particularly in Chapters 8 through 26, of the speculative reporting that caused a great deal of confusion in sorting out Union victories and losses as the war raged on.

Some of the difficulty the war correspondents and editors faced in distributing accurate news came about not only as a result of political and technological pressures but also because of the challenges inherent in covering a war. Soon after the federal loss at the first Battle of Bull Run in July 1861, which is detailed in Chapter 8, the government decided it needed better control of the press. Although most Northern newspapers, politics aside, rallied around the federal government in its fight to put down the Southern rebellion, there were a few newspapers in the North that remained sympathetic to the South and its new government. During the summer of 1861 the federal government suppressed some of these Northern papers. On 18 August 1861, federal troops took possession of the Savannah, Missouri, *Northwest Democrat*, and on 22 August 1861, U.S. marshals seized paper, type, and other materials from the *Philadelphia Christian Observer*. The *Philadelphia Press* reported that the government saved the paper from a public assault: "The indignation of the people against this sheet [is] . . . a matter of which the authorities were cognizant."[18]

Later in August and September 1861, U.S. postal privileges were denied to several papers including the *New York Daily News*, the *New York Evening Day Book*, the *New York Journal of Commerce*, *Freeman's Journal*, the *Brooklyn Eagle*, and the *Baltimore Exchange*. In the case of the *Baltimore Exchange*, the editor was also arrested along with a number of members of the Maryland legislature, the Baltimore city legislature, and the editor of the *Baltimore South*, all under orders from the War Department.

The War Department was trying to keep citizens in the slaveholding Border States calm and to keep them from rioting over war-related issues as they had in April and May 1861 after President Lincoln issued a call for volunteers to fight for the Union. F. Key Howard, the editor of the *Exchange*, was a Southern sympathizer, and he refused to keep his opinions to himself, writing in his paper the day after his arrest that a newspaper had a right to discuss and condemn government policy.[19]

The federal government believed it was controlling sedition (actions or words intended to incite rebellion against the government) in its actions against the press. It was particularly sensitive to what it saw as acts of sedition since the South was considered to be actively in rebellion against the Union. The federal government did not recognize the right of a state to secede from the federal Union, and by extension it did not recognize the Confederacy's right to exist. But by the end of 1861 the federal government had for the most part stopped trying to shut down or punish newspapers that opposed the war. This was partially because the number of opposition papers had significantly diminished. There were a few isolated incidents in 1862 of papers being banned from the U.S. mail "for giving comfort and aid to the enemy and for advocating the overthrow of the government," and the *Baltimore South* was suppressed for a second time and its editor arrested in February 1862.

On 17 July 1862, Congress passed what became known as the "treason" act, which targeted individuals who gave comfort and aid to the enemy "through the expression of disloyal statements." Some government officials believed that newspaper editors could be considered individuals and charged a few editors under the law. For example, the editor of the *Harrisburg Patriot & Union* (Harrisburg, Pa.) was arrested on 6 August 1862 for publishing antirecruiting posters. This kind of arrest was rare, and in the end, no cases brought against an editor actually resulted in a conviction. Still, these government actions actually fueled the efforts of editors who did not support the Union cause. A few weeks after his arrest, the editor of the *Patriot & Union* wrote a warning to government leaders in his paper. "Learn that your attempt to stifle free discussion, to stop the tongue and the pen by imprisonment, or even death, will but recoil upon your own heads," he wrote. "It is but adding more fuel to the already raging fire—an act of incendiarism of which none but the hopelessly insane or desperately wicked would be guilty. Be rational, if you can; and, in the lucid interval, which may Heaven grant you, repeal the iniquitous order, and cease to play the despot."[20]

There were a few acts of government aggression against newspapers in 1863—federal soldiers destroyed the offices of the Columbus, Ohio, *Crisis* in March, and in May the Department of Missouri prohibited the sale or distribution of four newspapers, including the *Chicago Times*. Union General Ambrose Burnside also suppressed the *Chicago Times* and banned the *New York World* from the Department of Ohio because of "repeated expressions of disloyal and incendiary statements [designed to] exert a pernicious and treasonable influence."[21]

Newspaper editors were not the only press representatives who had to confront and try to work around issues of government censorship. The war correspondents themselves had a difficult time reporting from the battlefields and from the nation's capital because of government concerns about the information that was appearing in the press that was critical of Union military leaders, that might tip off the Confederacy as to federal troop locations and battle strategies, and that might influence public opinion about the effectiveness of the Union war plan.

In the spring of 1862, after the devastating human loss at the Battle of Shiloh, which was generally considered a Union victory, general-in-chief of the Union army Henry Halleck ordered all federal commanders to remove all newspaper reporters from their armies. As Chapter 12 (which focuses on the second Battle of Bull Run in August 1862) notes, the fighting at the second Battle of Bull Run was not well reported in the North largely because it came on the heels of Halleck's order. That order also had consequences for the coverage of the Battle of Antietam that followed a few weeks later. Most of the Northern press reports of the actual battle of Antietam came from one man—*New York Tribune* reporter George Smalley who, wearing a blue Union uniform, slipped in to join Union General Joseph Hooker's division. Smalley's report of the fighting was supposed to be wired to the *Tribune* office in New York but was instead sent to the War Department in Washington, where it was approved and eventually distributed and reprinted in nearly 1,400 newspapers nationwide.[22]

Government control and censorship of war information that was sent over the telegraph wires began as early as February 1862. On 3 February 1862, Congress gave the president the power to take possession of the telegraph and railroad lines in the United States whenever he deemed it necessary to protect public safety. When Edwin Stanton was sworn in as secretary of war on 25 February 1862, the "Act of February 3" was implemented immediately. Some newspapers took note of this in their papers, but few challenged the validity of it, instead suggesting that as a result of

certain newspapers having flagrantly persisted in the publication of military details in violation of the rules and articles of war and the orders of the War Department, thereby endangering the safety of our armies and the success of military operations, the Secretary of War has ordered the enforcement of the penalties, and a special court-martial to be assembled at Washington for the trial and punishment of the offenders.[23]

Soon after Stanton took office the *Hartford Daily Courant* published a notice to the country's postmasters from the postmaster general that read:

The Secretary of War now regulates the transmission of information by telegraph affecting the conduct of the war. In order to prevent the communication of such information to the rebels, it is also thought necessary by the Secretary of War to put restrictions on the publishing of facts of this character, however derived, and the aid of this department is requested for this purpose. You will, therefore, notify publishers not to publish any fact which has been excluded from the telegraph and that a disregard of this order will subject the paper to be excluded from the mails.[24]

By the end of 1862, Secretary Stanton made efforts to tighten further the censorship of the telegraph wires to try to keep sensitive information from the Confederate forces. Although reporters argued that the enemy already knew everything that they did because camps on both sides were teeming with spies, the truth was that the press could move information more quickly than the spies could, so often the press did end up inadvertently tipping the other side's hand. Stanton had dispatched censors to the battlefields, many of whom had no firm or consistent guidelines to follow, and often they would alter or suppress reporters' dispatches at will. In an effort to get around the censors, journalists trying to cover the Battle of Chancellorsville in May

1863 resorted to creating codes and ciphers to evade the field censors. But despite the issues with field censors, reporters could avoid the censorship of the telegraph wires if they sent their reports via mail, messenger, or personal delivery. The obvious end result of this was a delay in the delivery of the actual news, which is evidenced in some of the Northern press coverage of battles that are generally detailed in Chapters 15 through 26.

In addition to navigating the censors on the battlefield, the effectiveness of field reporters also had much to do with the general in command. For example, in May 1864 the Northern press actively covered the battles that comprised General Grant's Overland Campaign in Virginia. General Grant, who was now the Union general-in-chief, was much less antagonistic to the press than General Halleck and generally "trusted the gentlemen of the press to do the right thing," and "until someone demonstrated otherwise," he left reporters alone. Union General George Meade disliked reporters and did not trust them after several erroneous reports about him and his conduct in battle were reported; General George B. McClellan generally liked the press, and the press liked him. General William T. Sherman, who commanded the federal forces in the West, had an actively antagonistic view of the press. He did not do much to help the press produce reports about him or his military campaigns. His long history of dealing with reporters, which began primarily at the Battle of Shiloh in April 1862, left him believing that correspondents were "gossips" and that they were "tempted to prophesy events and state facts which, to an enemy, reveal a purpose in time to guard against it. Moreover, they are always bound to see the facts colored by the partisan or political character of their own patrons, and thus bring army officers into the political controversies of the day."[25]

This part highlights the fruits of the labors of the Northern press editors and correspondents of the Civil War. The first five chapters detail important events that helped lead to the Civil War and highlight how the partisan press weighed in on social and political issues significant to the future of the country. The remaining chapters are mostly about the Northern press coverage of the major Civil War battles, although some focus on important nonbattle events such as Lincoln's Emancipation Proclamation, the New York Draft Riots of 1863, and the election of 1864. This part is arranged chronologically and contains articles and editorials from forty-three different newspapers from a variety of political and geographical perspectives and from a variety of writers (black and white, male and female, young and old).[26] Most of the newspapers are from the larger influential metropolitan areas in the North, but smaller papers are represented as well, such as the weekly *Adams County Sentinel & General Advertiser*, which was the newspaper published in the village of Gettysburg, Pennsylvania, during the Civil War.

NOTES

1. Brayton Harris, *Blue & Gray in Black & White* (Washington, D.C.: Brassey's, 1999), 9.

2. Margaret E. Wagner, Gary W. Gallagher, and Paul Finkelman (Eds.), *The Library of Congress Civil War Desk Reference* (New York: Simon & Schuster, 2002), 69–72. Information comes from the 1860 U.S. Census.

3. Ibid., 73–76.

4. The prewar South was geographically more than 300,000 square miles larger than the North.

5. Wagner, Gallagher, and Finkelman, *Civil War Desk Reference*, 76.

6. Ibid., 81.

7. See Charles Granville Hamilton, *Lincoln and the Know Nothing Movement* (Washington, D.C.: Public Affairs Press, 1954).

8. Wagner, Gallagher, and Finkelman, *Civil War Desk Reference*, 123.

9. Lorman Ratner and Dwight L. Teeter, Jr., *Fanatics and Fire-eaters: Newspapers and the Coming of the Civil War* (Urbana: University of Illinois Press, 2003), 7–8.

10. Michael Schudson, *Discovering the News: A Social History of American Newspapers* (New York: Basic Books, 1978), 34.

11. Ratner and Teeter, *Fanatics and Fire-eaters*, 8.

12. Mitchell Stephens, *A History of the News* (Ft. Worth, Tex.: Harcourt Brace, 1997), 189–194.

13. Ratner and Teeter, *Fanatics and Fire-eaters*, 20.

14. Bernard A. Weisberger, *Reporters for the Union* (Boston: Little, Brown, 1953), 20–21.

15. "Our Dispatches," *Chicago Daily Tribune*, 12 April, 1861.

16. See, for example, J. Cutler Andrews, *The North Reports the Civil War* (Pittsburgh: University of Pittsburgh Press, 1955); Andrews, *The South Reports the Civil War* (Princeton, N.J.: Princeton University Press, 1970); Bernard A. Weisberger, *Reporters for the Union* (Boston: Little, Brown, 1953); Emmet Crozier, *Yankee Reporters, 1861–1865* (New York: Oxford University Press, 1956); James M. Perry, *A Bohemian Brigade: The Civil War Correspondents—Mostly Rough, Sometimes Ready* (New York: John Wiley and Sons, 2000); Harris, *Blue & Gray*.

17. There is at least one known black correspondent, Thomas Morris Chester of the *Philadelphia Press*. Three women are known to have reported war events from Washington.

18. *Philadelphia Press*, 23 August 1861.

19. Harris, *Blue & Gray*, 97.

20. "Freedom of the Press," *Harrisburg Patriot & Union*, 30 August 1862.

21. Harris, *Blue & Gray*, 106.

22. Ibid., 171–183.

23. "Publication of Military Details in Violation of the Articles of War," *Hartford Daily Courant*, 25 March 1862.

24. "Papers to Be Excluded from the Mails for the Improper Publication of Army Movements," *Hartford Daily Courant*, 25 March 1862.

25. William T. Sherman, *Memoirs of General William T. Sherman*, 2nd ed., rev. (New York: D. A. Appleton and Co., 1875), 2:408.

26. The vast majority of the articles and editorials reprinted in this book were originally unsigned, as previously noted in this introduction—that is, no byline or credit appeared with the story. But when the author of an article, report, or editorial is known, his or her name appears in this text even if it was not published with the original work. If a story appeared without a byline and the author is not known, the story will be noted as "An Anonymous Report."

1

SETTLING KANSAS

Kansas became a state on 26 January 1861, three months before the start of the Civil War. But the events that led to Kansas's statehood served as early warnings about the bloody war to come. In 1854, the Kansas-Nebraska Act became law. It established Kansas and Nebraska as territories. Territorial development west of Missouri had proven difficult, leading up to the 1854 act because of the slavery question. As settlers moved west, enough people lived in the lands north and west of Missouri to justify the organization of a territory there. But, as a result of the Missouri Compromise, any territory in this geographic location would have to be free of slavery. The slave question, which dominated the debate about Missouri's entry into the Union as a state between 1818 and 1820, had resurfaced in debate about the establishment of the Kansas and Nebraska Territories.

In 1818 Missouri Territory petitioned Congress for admission to the Union as a state. Its settlers were primarily from the South, and most people expected Missouri to enter the Union as a slave state. At the time, nearly 2,000 slaves lived in Missouri. Vigorous and heated debate about the status of slavery in Missouri ensued by officials and newspapers in the North and South and was not resolved until the Missouri Compromise was signed in 1820.

After Alabama entered the Union as a state in December 1819, the Union consisted of eleven free and eleven slave states. The free states controlled the House of Representatives because they had larger populations. But in the Senate the balance of power between the free and slave states was equal. Both sides had a vested interest in Missouri's status as either a free or slave state because it would shift the balance of power.

In February 1819 James Tallmadge, a representative from New York, proposed an amendment to Missouri's statehood request that would ban slavery in Missouri. Some of the Northern concern about allowing Missouri to enter the Union as a slave state had to do with the territory's geographic location. Tallmadge noted,

> When I had the honor to submit to this House the amendment now under consideration, I accompanied it with a declaration, that it was intended to confine its operation to the newly acquired territory across the Mississippi [River]; and I then expressly declared that I would in no manner intermeddle with the slaveholding States, nor attempt manumission in any one of the original States in the Union.[1]

Despite those remarks, Southern representatives did think that Tallmadge's amendment would interfere with questions of slavery in the slaveholding states. Tallmadge's amendment sparked intense debate on the question and foreshadowed events to come in the discussions surrounding the establishment of the Kansas Territory. In his remarks to the House after proposing his amendment, Tallmadge said, "Sir, if a dissolution of the Union must take place, let it be so! If civil war, which gentlemen so much threaten must come, I can only say, let it come!"[2]

The amendment passed the House but not the Senate. The bitter debate over slavery in Missouri continued, and in January 1820, when the House passed a bill to admit Maine into the Union as a state, Speaker of the House Henry Clay helped usher in a solution to the divide over what was often called "the Missouri Question." It was clear that Maine, which at the time was a part of Massachusetts, would enter the Union as a free state. Clay warned the Northern congressmen that Southern congressmen would likely reject Maine's petition for statehood if Missouri were not admitted to the Union as a slave state.

Clay encouraged both Northern and Southern representatives to pass a compromise bill that Illinois Senator Jesse Thomas had authored. Thomas's bill called for the admission of Missouri to the Union as a slave state and the admission of Maine as a free state; and it drew a line of demarcation through the Louisiana Purchase territory located at the southern boundary of Missouri that would determine the slave status of future statehood requests. It established that territory north of the line would be admitted as free states and that territory south of the line would be admitted as slave states.[3] On 3 March 1820 Congress passed the Missouri Compromise, and in August 1821 Missouri officially became a state.

By the 1850s, nearly thirty years after the passage of the Missouri Compromise, many Southerners viewed the legislation as unequal and unjust and believed it would ultimately lead to the end of slavery because it limited the ability of western territories to become slave states. When the Kansas and Nebraska Act was debated in Congress in 1853–1854, the same issues that surrounded Missouri's statehood petition resurfaced. Between the time Missouri became a state and the debate over the Kansas Territory started, Arkansas (slave), Michigan (free), Florida (slave), Texas (slave), Iowa (free), Wisconsin (free), and California (free) became states.

In the debates over California's admission to the Union in 1850, the balance of power question emerged again. California's entry as a free state would give the free states a sixteen-to-fifteen edge in the makeup of the country and in the Senate. The slave states had no more territory in which to expand south and looked west for the possibility of gaining new territories.[4]

Senator Henry Clay, of Kentucky, the former Speaker of the House who helped secure the passage of the Missouri Compromise, offered a solution. He proposed five measures that would attempt to balance Northern and Southern interests. These five bills are commonly called the Compromise Measures of 1850. The Compromise of

1850 primarily focused on the question of slavery in the land acquired from Mexico after the Mexican War. As part of the Compromise Measures of 1850, California was admitted into the Union as a free state. Land east of California was divided into the new territories of New Mexico and Utah (geographically today this land is New Mexico and Arizona). New Mexico and Utah Territory were open to settlement by both slaveholders and antislavery settlers. This contradicted the Missouri Compromise of 1820. The Compromise of 1850 also called for the abolition of the slave trade in the District of Columbia; it gave Texas (already a slaveholding state in the Union) $10 million in settlement claims to adjoining territory; and it included passage of the Fugitive Slave law of 1850, which called for the return of runaway slaves to their masters.

What also emerged from the Compromise of 1850 was the concept of popular sovereignty, which was most commonly associated with Senator Stephen A. Douglas, the chairman of the committee on territories at the time the questions about establishing the Kansas Territory emerged. *Popular sovereignty* simply meant that questions of slavery should be left to territorial settlers themselves for resolution. Douglas was an advocate of popular sovereignty. As debates about the creation of a Kansas Territory continued in late 1853, Douglas introduced the Kansas-Nebraska Bill. The Kansas-Nebraska Bill divided the single proposed Kansas Territory into two territories, Kansas and Nebraska, and stipulated that the settlers of each territory should decide the slavery question under the principle of popular sovereignty. The bill passed, and President Franklin Pierce signed it into law. The result of the passage of the Kansas-Nebraska Act was that the Kansas Territory was thrown open for settlement. The side that got there first with the most settlers would win, so both pro- and antislavery factions flooded the state. The passage of the act also repealed the demarcation line created by the Missouri Compromise.[5]

As a result of the passage of the Kansas-Nebraska Act, tension between the North and South intensified. Politically, the act is credited with the creation of the Republican Party, which collected dissatisfied members of the Whig Party, antislavery Democrats, and members of the Free Soil and Know-Nothing Parties. The Know-Nothing Party had emerged in the 1850s and was a champion of the rights of American-born Protestants. They were fearful of the impact of surging immigration.[6]

Violence also came to Kansas as a result of the Kansas-Nebraska Act. The clashes that took place between proslavery factions and abolitionists who fought to gain control over the state by flooding it with settlers resulted in what has been commonly called "Bleeding Kansas." Between 1854 and 1861 nearly 200 people died as a result of the violence in Kansas that ensued after it was opened for settlement. Early Kansas settler Thomas Gladstone wrote in 1857, "Murder and cold-blooded assassination were of almost daily occurrence at the time of my visit." Newspaper accounts of the struggle to gain control of the territory were sensational, and both North and South stretched the truth of the level of atrocity that occurred in Kansas during these years.[7]

Captain John Brown, who gained infamy in leading an insurrection at Harper's Ferry, Virginia, in 1859 (see Chapter 3) in the name of abolishing slavery, was perhaps the most famous leader of political violence in the territory. Brown, an abolitionist, became best known for leading the Pottawatomie Massacre in Kansas on

25 May 1856. Along with four of his sons, one son-in-law, and two other Kansas settlers, Brown raided proslavery settlers on Mosquito and Pottawatomie Creek, killing five men.[8]

In 1857, the issue of Kansas's status as a future free or slave state received a great deal of attention in the national press. In September 1857 proslavery advocates created what would later become known as the Lecompton Constitution. It was named after the small town of Lecompton, Kansas, where it was created. The Lecompton Constitution called for Kansas to be admitted to the Union as a slave state. On 20 December 1857, voters in the Kansas Territory were asked to ratify the Lecompton Constitution, which only gave them a choice between limited or unlimited slavery. Free state advocates refused to participate in the ratification vote because the only options in the Lecompton Constitution included some form of slavery.[9]

The Lecompton Constitution was ratified by voters in Kansas and subsequently sent to Congress. Congress then had to decide whether to accept the Lecompton Constitution and admit Kansas to the Union as a slave state. A few weeks after the Lecompton Constitution vote, Kansas held elections for its government officers as well as a second election regarding the acceptance or rejection of the Lecompton Constitution. The second election on the Lecompton Constitution came about owing to claims of election fraud at the 20 December election. General John Calhoun, the president of the Lecompton Constitution and a staunch proslavery advocate, oversaw the December election.

In the elections of 4 January 1858, the free state advocates clearly won and sent a message to the federal Congress that the majority will of the people of Kansas was in opposition to slavery. The Lecompton Constitution was rejected by a majority of Kansans, and a significant number of free state advocates were elected to the future state legislature.[10]

Despite this, President James Buchanan still urged Congress to admit Kansas as a slave state under the Lecompton Constitution.[11] His efforts were not successful, and in a third election on the Lecompton Constitution in August 1858, Kansas voters decisively rejected the controversial constitution. Kansas was eventually admitted to the Union as a free state in 1861.

It was clear in the press coverage of Kansas in 1857 and 1858 that the pro- and antislavery struggle over Kansas's statehood would foreshadow debates to come. The fighting in and about Kansas is considered by many historians to be the first significant event that directly contributed to the national debate over slavery and states' rights that led to Abraham Lincoln's election in 1860. Chapter 4 details Lincoln's election win and how it led to Southern secession and ultimately Civil War. Chapter 2 (about the *Dred Scott* decision by the Supreme Court) and Chapter 3 (about John Brown, of Kansas, and his murderous insurrection at Harper's Ferry) detail two other pivotal events that even further divided the country in the years leading up to the war.

The articles below highlight the politicization of settling Kansas, from debates about the legitimacy of the Lecompton Constitution to the admission of Kansas as the thirty-fourth state in 1861. They shed light on how deeply divided the country was on the questions of both states' rights and slavery. They also show a Northern press proclivity toward generally supporting free state ideals, even though Democrats and Republicans were divided on these issues.

GAMALIEL BAILEY: GOVERNOR WALKER'S POSITION ON THE LECOMPTON CONSTITUTION

The National Era, *a black-run newspaper edited in Washington, D.C., by Gamaliel Bailey, echoed the sentiments of many in the North who argued that the voters of Kansas should decide the slavery question. The paper opposed President Buchanan's appeal to Congress to admit Kansas to the Union as a state under the Lecompton Constitution. This article focuses on Kansas's territorial governor Robert J. Walker and whether he will keep his promise to fight in Washington against the Lecompton Constitution. Walker, a friend of Buchanan's, was appointed as territorial governor by Buchanan. This article was written two weeks before the election to ratify the Lecompton Constitution. Its ratification was a foregone conclusion.*

National Era, 3 December 1857 (Washington, D.C.)

The newspapers and their correspondents give Governor Walker three positions in reference to the work of the Constitutional Convention of Kansas. One class represents him as friendly to the proposed Constitution, and indeed prompting the lenders in their work. Another set of editors and letter-writers are equally sure that the Governor is upon the fence about the constitution difficulties; while still another class represent him to be in sympathy with the Free State men, and freely condemning the bogus Convention, and its unfair reference of a Constitution to the people. In this class we must reckon the author of the subjoined letter, which appears in the columns of the N.Y. Times:

"LEAVENWORTH CITY, Nov. 10, 1857. There is a general feeling of disgust and contempt on the part of the people, as far as I have heard an expression of opinion, at the juggling manner in which the Constitution is attempted to be passed, without a fair expression of the will of the people. Gov. Walker is at present in the city, and quite unwell. Though confined to the house, he receives visitors, and talks very freely on the matters pertaining to the elections and the Constitution. He denounces in round terms the rascality of the Convention just adjourned, and says that the trick shall not be taken by those minority men who composed that Convention;

and unless the Constitution is fairly submitted to the people of the Territory, whether 'for' or 'against' the Constitution, he will oppose it, both in his private and official character. He acknowledges that he did not understand the true nature of the political aspect of the parties on his arrival; but that he now sees wherein the people have suffered, how they have suffered, and from what causes. . . ."

If this letter-writer is to be believed, Gov. Walker will use his influence here against the acceptance of the Constitution of Kansas. But a half dozen other letter-writers and journalists affirm that Governor Walker is hand-in-glove with the members of the Constitutional Convention. The truth will soon be known; Congress will come together next Monday, and its members will soon have an opportunity to take their positions upon this question. At present, the Northern Democracy is sadly divided upon it. Col. Forney, the *Chicago Times*, Mr. Douglas's organ, and many other able Democratic journals, condemn the action of the Constitutional Convention, while the South generally condemns Mr. Walker, and is barely satisfied with the reference of the Slavery clause of the proposed Constitution of Kansas. To the people, "Signs of a storm" are in the sky, as the almanac makers say.

GAMALIEL BAILEY: TENSE SITUATION IN KANSAS—CITIZENS OF TERRITORY REMAINING CALM

One week after the above article appeared, the National Era *acknowledged the tension that existed in Kansas and praised the citizens of the territory for remaining peaceful. This article appeared ten days before the scheduled election to ratify the Lecompton Constitution. The election gave voters the choice between limited and unlimited slavery in Kansas. Free state men in the state refused to participate in the election because only these two options were presented.*

National Era, 10 December 1857 (Washington, D.C.)

The People of Kansas thus far are acting wisely. They seem cool, but determined. We do not believe they will injure their cause by violence. The time for the last resort has not

yet come. They have the numerical force; they have the Territorial Government; it is not certain that Congress will accept the Lecompton Constitution; the probabilities on the whole are against it: at all events, it cannot be forced through both Houses until after the first of January, the time fixed for the meeting of the new Kansas Legislature. The Free State men, therefore, have every reason to be calm, hopeful, and resolute. They will not vote at the election ordered on the 20th December; nor do we believe that they will resort to any violent measures to prevent it; but, we trust that they will appoint Committees of Vigilance at all the polls, and be out in full force, to take notice exactly of what is done, and to expose what ever fraudulent transactions may be attempted. The Legislature which will meet in January will of course take instant measures for apprising Congress of the will of the People, and proceed to prepare for the vindication of the People's rights. If Congress should reject the Lecompton Constitution, well and good. If not—if it should accept it, and the attempt be then made to cram it down the throats of the majority of the People of the Territory, we do not know what course the Legislature might adopt; but we do not believe that majority would submit to any such outrage, and no American who reverse the patriots of 1776 could condemn their resistance. The doctrines of passive obedience and non-resistance are fit only for slaves.

HENRY RAYMOND: EDITORIAL WRITER DECLARES PRESIDENT SHOULD RESPECT OUTCOME OF KANSAS ELECTION, EXPECTS DEFEAT OF LECOMPTON CONSTITUTION

The following New York Times *editorial gives a good overview of the context in which the Kansas elections took place following the ratification of the Lecompton Constitution. It also calls on the president to honor the outcome, which it is clear the writer thinks will be in opposition to the Lecompton Constitution.*

New York Times, 11 January 1858

We shall soon have returns of the election held in Kansas on Monday last. All parties in Washington seem to be waiting for news of the result, before taking any decisive action upon the admission of the State. The election was upon the Lecompton Constitution, and for State officers under it. It was ordered by the Territorial Legislature and was held under the direct supervision of the Governor appointed by the President. Its legality had been recognized by the Administration; the Secretary of State had instructed the Governor to protect the polls and guarantee a full and fair chance to vote; and Gen. DENVER issued a Proclamation carrying out what he declares to be the "anxious desire of the President that the approaching election shall be fairly held, and that every one shall have free access to the polls, without being subjected to violence or intimidation."

The main point decided by this election was whether a majority of the People of Kansas were *for*, or *against* the Lecompton Constitution. The vote was direct and conclusive. Every inhabitant of the Territory had a right to vote,—and it was his duty to vote,—upon this question at that election. If any man or any party staid away from the polls it was his own fault, and he has no right to complain of the result. If the majority of the votes cast at that election were *for* the Lecompton Constitution, then it is the plain duty of Congress to admit the State with that Constitution, the Slavery clause included. And if, on the contrary, a majority of votes shall prove to have been on the other side,—*against* the Constitution,—Congress cannot adopt it without the grossest interference in the affairs of Kansas, and a manifest violation of the spirit of the Federal Constitution. New States are to be *admitted* to the Union,—which can only be upon application of their inhabitants. They cannot be *forced* in, against the expressed will of a majority, without the grossest outrage and wrong.

It is becoming a matter of considerable interest to know what course the President will pursue when the returns of this election shall be received. . . .

We shall soon know the issue of the contest. If Mr. BUCHANAN yields gracefully and promptly to the popular will as expressed at the Kansas election on the 4th, he may retain for his Administration the confidence and support of the Democratic Party. If he persists in ignoring it, and forcing upon Congress the Lecompton Constitution against the will of the majority, nothing can save him from sudden and disastrous shipwreck.

HENRY RAYMOND: POLITICAL SIGNIFICANCE OF DEFEAT OF LECOMPTON CONSTITUTION IN KANSAS

In this article the election results are known and suggest that the free state forces in Kansas are the majority. Henry Raymond, the editor of the New York Times, *notes the political significance of the outcome of the 4 January election.*

New York Times, 23 January 1858

The Kansas question is substantially settled. The points that remain to be adjusted may have importance and interest upon grounds of principle, but so far as practical results are concerned, they are of very little consequence. Congress may adopt or reject the Lecompton Constitution, —may admit or exclude Kansas under the instrument; —it can in neither case seriously or permanently affect the State or the character of its political institutions. The PEOPLE of Kansas are now in possession of their rightful sovereignty: —they can mold their institutions to suit themselves; —and neither Congress nor the Federal Executive can much longer postpone a result which dispassionate men have for a long time seen to be inevitable.

In October last the Free-State men elected a majority of the Territorial Legislature, which will have full legislative

authority if Kansas is *not* admitted into the Union under the Lecompton Constitution. On the 4th of January the same party elected the State Legislature, for which provision is made in the Lecompton instrument, and which will have supreme control if Kansas should be admitted and become a sovereign State. In either event, therefore, the Free-State party has political possession of the Territory. It has a two third majority in each branch of both Legislature, and is thus entirely independent even of the Governor. In either event, therefore, —upon the admission or rejection of the Lecompton Constitution, —it has only to order a new Convention, and frame a new Constitution, which shall embody the sentiments and represent the interests of the people of Kansas.

HENRY RAYMOND: HOW PRESIDENT BUCHANAN PROPOSES TO KEEP THE PEACE IN KANSAS

Within a month of the January elections, President Buchanan spoke publicly about the Kansas situation and focused his attention on the need for peace in the territory. The political struggles in Kansas, as previously noted, led to widespread violence. The height of that violence occurred in 1856, but many, including the president, had concerns that peace would not prevail in Kansas until the statehood question was settled. The Kansas election issue was somewhat complicated after the fact because of allegations of election fraud by General Calhoun, who conducted the elections as president of the Lecompton Constitution.

New York Times, 4 February 1858

The President's Lecompton Message is a prayer for peace. He dwells with touching tenderness upon the necessity of restoring quiet to Kansas and peace to the country. He even makes a personal appeal upon the subject, saying that his "public life will terminate in a brief period," and that he has "no other object of earthly ambition than to leave his country in a peaceful and prosperous condition and to live in the affections and respect of his countrymen." This, though a little too much in the style of "pity the sorrows of a poor old man," is creditable to Mr. BUCHANAN's heart, and will not be without effect upon the sympathy of the public. Certainly, the whole country concurs with the President in desiring peace for Kansas. But we suspect it differs from him in regard to the best method of attaining that most desirable object. . . .

Let us, without attempting any argument upon its justice or propriety, trace the probable consequences of the policy upon which Mr. BUCHANAN relies for "restoring peace" to Kansas.

Suppose Kansas is admitted as a State under the Lecompton Constitution. A State government will at once come into operation. The officers of that government were elected on the 4th of January. A majority of the legal votes cast are known to have elected the Free-State officers and a Free-State majority in each branch of the Legislature. But the Lecompton Constitution authorizes General CALHOUN (who oversaw the election) to decide upon the returns and give certificates to the officers elected. He has already declared his purpose to give certificates to the Pro-Slavery Governor and other State officers, and to a majority of Pro-Slavery men in both branches of the Legislature. That he will do so, in utter and flagrant defiance of facts,—by the admission of returns which he knows to be false, no one doubts. The people of Kansas know it perfectly well. *Four-fifths* of them are opposed, resolutely and immovably, against being thus governed by fraud and will beyond all question prevent the Pro-Slavery Legislature and State officers from assuming official functions and wielding official power. The Pro-Slavery Governor will apply to the President for troops to suppress "domestic insurrection" in the State of Kansas.

Up to this point there can be no reasonable doubt of the course that will be pursued. Unless Mr. BUCHANAN is willfully blind, he cannot believe that the people of Kansas will permit this Legislature to assemble and elect CALHOUN and CATO to be United States Senators for six years, and thus consummate the fraud which is now in progress. *They will resist.* They will drive them out of the Territory, and the Pro-Slavery Governor, who is falsely declared to be elected for this very purpose, will apply to the President for troops to guard the fraudulent State Legislature, while it performs the work for which it has been created.

Mr. BUCHANAN, in his Message, professes a determination to *withdraw* the troops upon admission of Kansas. The profession is disingenuous and intended to deceive. We happen to know that the contingency to which we have referred has been contemplated and discussed at Washington, and that Mr. BUCHANAN has declared *that he will protect the Calhoun, Pro-Slavery State Legislature with troops of the United States.* This is the "peace" to which the President looks forward. This is the manner in which he expects the clouds now impending over the Union to be "dissipated!" . . .

[President Buchanan, in his efforts to] disarm [the Free State men's] active hostility [toward the Lecompton Constitution, gave them] *the solemn promise that the Constitution which the Convention might frame should be submitted to their vote.* He made this promise, through is [sic] officers in

the Territory, over and over again. He was thoroughly committed to it by every engagement which can commit a man of honor. *Yet he violated his pledge.* He forfeited that promise by which the acquiescence of the people of Kansas had been secured. And he now pleads a "mental reservation" in excuse of his conspicuous and unparalleled violation of good faith. "When I instructed GOV. WALKER in general terms," says the President in his Special Message, "in favor of submitting the Constitution to the people, I had no object in view except the all-absorbing subject of Slavery. In what manner the people of Kansas might regulate their *other* concerns, was not the subject which attracted my attention." A man inclined to deal fairly and honorably with a great community, upon a great question of this sort, would have been more anxious to meet the expectations of those who had put their confidence in his word, than to reduce his promise to the lowest possible terms which casuistry could construe into a fulfillment. The President of a great nation, speaking on behalf of the Government, should accord to equivocate. If the people of Kansas understood him to promise that the whole Constitution should be submitted,—as they certainly did,—MR. BUCHANAN should in honor and good faith have fulfilled their expectations. He prefers to cheat them of their promised rights upon the ground that, when he *said* the whole, he only *meant* a part. There is nothing in Jesuitism worse than this.

Nothing, in our mind, is more certain than the forcing of Kansas into the Union, against the will of its inhabitants, will involve that State in civil war;—that President BUCHANAN will attempt the subjugation of the people of the State by the Federal Army;—and that the determined, active conspicuous Disunionists of the South,—in and out of Congress,—will do everything in their power to make the contest so general as to enable them to carry into effect the scheme of separation which they have in view. And this is the manner in which Mr. BUCHANAN proposes to restore peace to Kansas, and to the whole country!

AN ANONYMOUS REPORT: PROSLAVERY KANSAN CRITICIZES REPUBLICAN LIES AND GENERAL CALHOUN'S SECRECY

As previously noted, many people voiced concerns about election fraud, and most of those concerns centered on General John Calhoun, who was in charge of the Kansas elections. The following article comes from the St. Louis Republican, *which was (despite its name) a Democratic, proslavery paper. This is a letter from a proslavery Kansas Territory resident who has election concerns, mostly about Republican misrepresentation of the election results and Calhoun's lack of public disclosure of the results.*

St. Louis Republican, 4 February 1858

ATCHISON, K.T. In relation to the Lecompton Constitution, you may rest assured that a majority of the Free-State men in the Territory are now willing to see Kansas admitted as a State under that instrument, either with or without Slavery; provided, the first and any subsequent Legislature shall have the power of calling a new Convention to alter or amend it. I have conversed with many of their most intelligent men on the subject, and they now think this the most certain plan of getting rid of the public disturbers. The State once organized, very soon the good men of all parties will unite to put an end to the Laneites, Danites, &c.

The reports which have been circulated in regard to the result of the election on the 4th ult., have created some distrust, and dissatisfaction in the ranks of both parties, and without intending to impute anything improper to Gen. Calhoun, I must say the matter has been managed awkwardly, and given our enemies an opportunity of manufacturing some capital. The returns of the election had to be made to Gen. C., and he invited the President of the Council and Speaker of the House of Representatives to be present at the opening of the returns. They attended, and they published the success of the Free-State ticket.

Gen. C. published nothing, but very soon those claiming to be his friends publish the election of the Democratic ticket, and ever since we have had it first one way and then the other, without hearing anything from Gen. Calhoun, and he has left for Washington without making the result public.

All this is seized upon by designing men of the Free-State Party, and paraded about as evidence of trickery and fraud, and many of the Democrats are dissatisfied and think the matter ought to have been made public.

Honest men of all parties want a fair game played, and don't like too much secrecy and mystery about political matters. I very much regret that the General did not publish the result before he left, as the omission will prejudice him and us, when I feel well satisfied that he intended no wrong to any one—Constitution or no Constitution—Election Returns or no Election Returns—State or Territory—Nigger or no Nigger; we of Atchison, are too busy building railroads and hotels, grading streets and making farms—in a word, we are too much engaged in building up our town and improving our country to let worthless demagogues make tools of us to accomplish their political tricks.

AN ANONYMOUS REPORT: WHAT THEY SAY IN KANSAS—THE POLITICAL DIVIDE BETWEEN THE FREE STATE AND PROSLAVERY MOVEMENTS

The Kansas Territory was filled with newspapers that supported both the free state movement as well as the proslavery movement. The following article, from the self-proclaimed independent Elwood Advertiser *in Kansas, shows how strongly Kansans felt about the political issues in their state, and it gives some indication of the depth of the divide over questions of state sovereignty as well as slavery. This article was reprinted in the* Adams County Sentinel & General Advertiser *(Gettysburg, Pa.).*

Adams County Sentinel & General Advertiser, 29 March 1858 (Gettysburg, Pa.)

Many Eastern papers are discussing the events likely to arise if Kansas is admitted under the Lecompton Constitution. Our paper is, and has been, independent, and what we have to say on this subject is in no spirit of bragging or threatening; we only express what we believe to be—from our knowledge of the Squatters in Kansas—the result in case that swindle should pass.

The people of this Territory will *never* live under that Constitution, and all the power of the Federal Government cannot *force* it upon them. The whole army of the United States does not number 15,000 men, and not over six or seven thousand can be brought into the field against us; of these one-third would desert before they would fight the freemen of Kansas. To oppose this force, we have upwards of 13,000 men, intelligent citizens, who love their liberty better than life. Should the Governor call for aid from Missouri, or some

other slaveholding State, we should instantly receive assistance from the free States, and thus inaugurate a civil war, which would end in a dissolution of the Union. If the Democratic Party and President Buchanan like the picture, they have but to carry out the line of policy already commenced.

If the certificates of election are granted to the Free State men, and they do their *duty*, we shall have no trouble; but if Calhoun gives them to the Pro-Slavery candidates, they can never hold their offices on the soil of Kansas. Should Jack Henderson and Calhoun then dare to enter Kansas, they would be strung higher than Haman. Nor is this all. We *know* that in ten days after any attempt to set in motion a Pro Slavery State Government, not a single prominent or obnoxious Pro-Slavery man would be left in the whole Territory; while the officials of every grade would receive lessons in the Terpsichorian art of dancing or nothing. Let none be so foolish as to think that any session of the Legislature could be held, even under the gun of Fort Leavenworth. Pass the Lecompton Constitution, grant certificates to Marshall & Co., and a majority of the Pro-Slavery Legislators, and Calhoun, Henderson, *et. id. omnegenus*, become outlaws, whose deaths, if caught on Kansas soil, would pay the penalty of their past villainy and treachery; nor would Cate, Lecompte, Emory, Clarkson, Sheriff Jones, or the remaining prominent Pro-Slavery ultraists, be *slighted* (!) in the universal attention paid that ilk.

Gentlemen, one word—we advocate peace and mildness; we disapprove of violence so long as it can possibly be avoided; we do not wish to see you suffering in property or person, but we caution you, if you value your lives, the moment the Lecompton Constitution passes (provided Calhoun declares your ticket elected) that you had better bid adieu to Kansas. We don't charge you anything for this ad-

vice, but offer it freely, for your benefit and your peace. Moderate Pro Slavery men, who have never wronged their neighbors, and have been oppressive in their day of power, are in *no danger*.

Ye supporters of the President's Lecompton policy, read this and ponder it; we have not written this article for effect nor to frighten anyone; neither do we in publishing it, yield our neutrality in the political arena, but as the watchman startles the sleeping citizen with the cry of fire, that they may save themselves and property so we as watchers of the signs of the times, have herein declared our firm conviction of the result, and given a friendly warning to those we deem endangered. Do not slight our caution; we are no alarmists, but write words of truth and soberness, gleaned from an intimate acquaintance with the ins and outs of Kansas politics.

Let Lecomptonites, in and out of Kansas, beware—pause and take another look before you leap.

AN ANONYMOUS REPORT: KANSAS ENTERS UNION AS FREE STATE

The Lecompton Constitution did not pass the federal Congress. By 1860, affairs in Kansas were no longer front-page news. But Kansas's admission to the Union as a free state in early 1861 did garner some attention in the press. Kansas's admission was bittersweet—by the time Kansas had officially become a state, South Carolina, Mississippi, Florida, Alabama, Georgia, and Louisiana had seceded from the Union.

Philadelphia Inquirer, 31 January 1861

The President signed the Kansas bill yesterday, and the Territory so long the source and the subject of political troubles, has come forth as a State. Her career since the Territorial organization in 1854, has been a "seven years' war;" now let us anticipate for her a long reign of peace and prosperity. An act of Congress provides that on the fourth day of July succeeding the admission of a new State, an additional star

shall be added to the national flag. On this occasion, however, when stars are falling from the blue field of the standard, it appears that the authorities intend to observe the law regulating the stars in the flag, before the specified day arrives, for our dispatches inform us that the flags on the public buildings in that city will bear to-day a thirty-fourth star, for Kansas.

NOTES

1. "Admission of Missouri," *Annals of Congress*, House of Representatives, 15th Cong., 2nd ses., February 1819, 1203–1204.

2. Ibid.

3. Roger L. Ransom, *Conflict and Compromise* (New York: Cambridge University Press, 1989), 35.

4. Alice Nichol, *Bleeding Kansas* (New York: Oxford University Press, 1954), 7.

5. Ibid., 8.

6. Charles Granville Hamilton, *Lincoln and the Know Nothing Movement* (Washington, D.C.: Public Affairs Press, 1954), 3.

7. Dale E. Watts, "How Bloody Was Bleeding Kansas? Political Killings in Kansas Territory, 1854–1861," *Kansas History* 18 (Summer 1995): 116–129.

8. James C. Malin, "Identification of the Stranger at the Pottawatomie Massacre," *Kansas Historical Quarterly* 9, no. 1 (February 1940): 3–12.

9. "The Lecompton Constitution—History of the Plan of Submission," *Philadelphia Press*, 3 December 1857.

10. "The Kansas Question—The Contest Over," *New York Times*, 23 January 1858.

11. "How President Buchanan Proposes to Keep the Peace," *New York Times*, 4 February 1858.

FURTHER READINGS

Goodrich, Thomas. *War to the Knife: Bleeding Kansas, 1854–1861*. Mechanicsburg, Pa.: Stackpole Books, 1998.

Nichol, Alice. *Bleeding Kansas*. New York: Oxford University Press, 1954.

Watts, Dale E. "How Bloody Was Bleeding Kansas? Political Killings in Kansas Territory, 1854–1861." *Kansas History* 18 (Summer 1995): 116–129.

Wolff, Gerald W. *The Kansas-Nebraska Bill: Party, Section, and the Coming of the Civil War*. New York: Revisionist Press, 1977.

2

THE CASE OF *DRED SCOTT*, 1857

As debate about the status of Kansas continued through 1857 and 1858, attention to all questions involving slavery and the rights of individual states either to embrace or abolish slavery intensified. In February and March of 1857, as Congress still considered whether to admit Kansas as a state under the Lecompton Constitution, the U.S. Supreme Court was also considering the question of slavery in the case *Scott v. Sandford*.[1]

Dred Scott was born a slave in 1799 in Virginia, owned by the family of Peter Blow. The Blow family moved to St. Louis in 1830 and sold Scott to an army doctor named John Emerson. Scott remained Emerson's slave until Emerson died in 1843. Between 1830 and Emerson's death in 1843, Scott moved with Emerson to the neighboring state of Illinois, then to the Wisconsin Territory. Both Illinois and Wisconsin prohibited slavery—Wisconsin's slavery prohibition was part of the Missouri Compromise since it was located north of the Missouri Compromise demarcation line.

While in Wisconsin, Scott met and married Harriet Robinson, a slave whose ownership was transferred to Emerson after Dred and Harriet married. After a transfer to the South—first back to St. Louis, then to Louisiana, Emerson married Irene Sanford. Emerson kept his slaves in Wisconsin for nearly a year after his transfer; but in 1842 he summoned them back to St. Louis where he had once again returned. Emerson died in St. Louis in 1843, and ownership of the Scotts transferred to his wife. Irene Emerson hired out the entire Scott family (Dred and Harriet had two daughters) to work for other families.[2] During this time Scott offered to buy his freedom from Mrs. Emerson for $300. She refused. After this, Dred and Harriet Scott decided to try to gain their freedom in court.

In April 1846 Harriet and Dred Scott sued Mrs. Emerson in a St. Louis Circuit Court. They argued that their residence in a free state (Illinois) and then a free territory (Wisconsin) had ended their bondage. In the first of many rulings in this case, the

St. Louis court rejected the Scott's case but allowed them to file it again with the same court. The second time around a St. Louis jury heard the case and decided that the Scotts did deserve to be free because of the time they lived in Illinois and Wisconsin.

Mrs. Emerson appealed the decision to the Missouri Supreme Court—in that appeal the lawyers on both sides agreed that the case should proceed based only on Dred Scott's case, with the findings applied equally to his wife. The Missouri Supreme Court decided that the St. Louis jury was wrong, and it held that the Scotts were still slaves.

In 1853, with the support of antislavery lawyers, Dred Scott decided to try his case again in federal instead of Missouri court. The defendant in the federal case was not Mrs. Emerson but rather her brother, John Sanford, who had assumed responsibility for handling the Emerson estate. Sanford was a resident of New York. The federal court in St. Louis agreed to hear the case because of the diversity of state citizenship involved. In 1854 the federal court (the Circuit Court of Missouri, located in St. Louis) held that Scott was still a slave. Scott appealed to the Supreme Court.[3]

Until Scott's case came before the Supreme Court, it had not attracted much public attention. But by early 1856 when Congress had renewed the debate over slavery in the territories, many people on both sides of the issue believed the Supreme Court would be the most appropriate place for resolution on this issue.[4] The Supreme Court heard arguments in the case in 1856 and 1857.

In the Supreme Court, the arguments in the *Dred Scott* case focused on two key questions: Are slaves citizens? Does Congress have the power (through the Missouri Compromise specifically) to decide issues of slavery in the territories? Most Northern newspapers carried articles about the arguments before the Supreme Court in the case, and many were quick to point out that of the nine Supreme Court justices hearing the case, five came from the South—including three former slaveholders. Also, seven of the nine justices had been appointed by a proslavery president.[5]

In the end, the Supreme Court held that slaves were not citizens under the Constitution but rather property. Chief Justice Roger Taney, a Southerner and a publicly proslavery judge, wrote in his majority opinion that blacks "whose ancestors . . . were sold as slaves" were not entitled to rights of a federal citizen and therefore had no standing to even bring a claim to the U.S. Supreme Court.[6] Taney's majority opinion further stated that the U.S. Congress did not have the authority to prohibit slavery in the territories, and it declared the Missouri Compromise unconstitutional.

Two justices, John McLean of Ohio and Benjamin Curtis of Massachusetts, vigorously dissented from the majority. Both argued in favor of upholding the Missouri Compromise and of emancipating Scott. The text of their dissents was released immediately, while Chief Justice Taney withheld the text of the majority opinion until late May. The only record of the majority opinion prior to that was from the press who published the outcome of the case based on the Court's reading of the decision.[7]

Despite this delay in the full publication of the decision, Chief Justice Taney's majority opinion had immediate impact. One historian has noted that Taney's words "burned like fire on the pages of city and rural newspapers, widening the gulf that separated the factions in American political life and inflaming the passions of a nation that stood on the threshold of civil war."[8]

The reaction to the *Dred Scott* decision was strong, particularly among Northern

Republican newspapers that argued that the Supreme Court's despicable ruling would result in the eventual transfer of federal power from the Democratic Party to the Republicans. They suggested that the only way to eliminate slavery was to elect officials who were not sympathetic to the Southern system of slavery or swayed by its influence. Republican newspapers had a bit more ammunition for their articles and editorials since they had the full text of the Curtis and McLean dissents from which to quote and summarize, but they did not have the full majority opinion.

Northern democratic newspapers generally suggested that the Supreme Court's decision had now given the appropriate clarity to the slavery issues that had been plaguing the country. They supported the sentiment offered by recently inaugurated Democratic President James Buchanan, who said in his 4 March 1857 inaugural address,

> A difference of opinion has arisen in regard to the point of time when the people of a Territory shall decide this question [of slavery] for themselves. This is, happily, a matter of but little practical importance. Besides, it is a judicial question, which legitimately belongs to the Supreme Court of the United States, before whom it is now pending, and will, it is understood, be speedily and finally settled. To their decision, in common with all good citizens, I shall cheerfully submit, whatever this may be.[9]

Historians have noted that Buchanan, prior to his inaugural address, spoke with Chief Justice Taney and knew the outcome of the case a few days before it was officially issued.[10]

Southern papers, of course, applauded the decision. Their enthusiasm toward the Court's decision did not go unnoticed by Northern papers. Many reprinted in their papers what Southern editors were writing about the subject. One such short article appears below. The other articles and editorials represent the general coverage of the actual decision and the editorial response to the decision by both Democratic and Republican newspapers in the North. The common theme to these writings is the impact this decision will have on national politics. Like the Kansas issue, the outcome of the *Dred Scott* case clearly widened the divide between anti- and proslavery advocates and created even more momentum toward a resolution that would become hotly contested politically and would eventually turn bloody.[11]

AN ANONYMOUS REPORT: DECISION OF SUPREME COURT IN *DRED SCOTT* CASE

The New York Daily Times *offered its readers a clear summary of the Supreme Court's decision and provided information about how the Court delivered the opinion to the public.*

New York Daily Times, 7 March 1857

IMPORTANT FROM WASHINGTON

Decision of the Supreme Court in the Dred Scott Case

The Ordinance of 1787 and the Missouri Compromise Declared Unconstitutional

WASHINGTON, Friday, March 6. The opinion of the Supreme Court in the DRED SCOTT case was delivered by Chief Justice TANEY. It was a full and elaborate statement of the views of the Court. They have decided the following important points:

First—Negroes, whether slaves or free, that is, men of the African race, are not citizens of the United States by the Constitution.

Second—The Ordinance of 1787 had no independent constitutional force or legal effect subsequently to the adoption of the Constitution and could not operate of itself to confer freedom or citizenship within the Northwest Territory on negroes not citizens by the Constitution.

Third—The provisions of the Act of 1820, commonly called the Missouri Compromise, in so far as it undertook to exclude negro slavery from, and communicate freedom and citizenship to, negroes in the northern part of the Louisiana cession, was a Legislative act exceeding the powers of Congress, and VOID, and of no legal effect to that end.

In deciding these main points, the Supreme Court determined the following incidental points:

First—The expression "territory and other property" of the Union, in the Constitution, applies "in terms" only to such territory as the Union possessed at the time of the adoption of the Constitution.

Second—The rights of citizens of the United States emigrating into any Federal territory, and the power of the Federal Government there depend on the general provisions of the Constitution, which defines in this, as in all other respects, the powers of Congress.

Third—As Congress does not possess power itself to make enactments relative to the persons or property of citizens of the United States, in a Federal territory, other than such as the Constitution confers, so it cannot constitutionally delegate any such powers to a Territorial Government, organized by it under the Constitution.

Fourth—The legal condition of a slave in the State of Missouri is not affected by the temporary sojourn of such slave in any other Sate, but on his return his condition still depends on the laws of Missouri.

As the plaintiff was not a citizen of Missouri, he, therefore, could not sue in the Courts of the United States. The suit must be dismissed for want of jurisdiction.

The delivery of this opinion occupied about three hours, and was listened to with profound attention by a crowded Courtroom. Among the auditors were gentlemen of eminent legal ability, and a due proportion of ladies.

Judge NELSON stated the merits of the case. The question was whether or not the removal of SCOTT from Missouri with his master to Illinois, with a view to temporary residence there, worked his emancipation. He maintained that the question depended wholly on the law of Missouri, and for that reason the judgment of the Court below should be affirmed.

Judge CATRON believed the Supreme Court has jurisdiction to decide the merits of the case. He argued that Congress could not do directly what it could not do indirectly. If it could exclude one species of property, it could exclude another. With regard to the Territories ceded, Congress could govern them only with the restrictions of the States which ceded them; and the Missouri act of 1820 violated the leading features of the Constitution, and was therefore void. He concurred with his brother Judges, that SCOTT is a slave, and was so when this suit was brought.

Several other judges are to deliver their views tomorrow.

AN ANONYMOUS REPORT: WHAT THE *DRED SCOTT* CASE DECIDED AND DID NOT DECIDE

This account provides a more detailed legal analysis of the Dred Scott *case that comes from the* Boston Law Reporter. *It appeared in the* New York Daily Times *several months after the decision was announced.*

New York Daily Times, 16 July 1857

The *Boston Law Reporter* for June contains a very able and thorough review of the Dred Scott "Decision," which will enable the reader to know what the Supreme Court has decided in that important case, far more readily and clearly than he can learn from the official report itself. In fact, the review has done just what the reporter, Mr. Howard, in a long and confused head-notes, attempted, but failed to accomplish.

Those, also, who desire to understand, not merely the points which the so-called decision really decided, but what it did not decide, will do well to consult the *Law Reporter's* article, the authorship of which is ascribed to Horace Gray, Jr., and John Lowell, two well-known legal gentlemen of Boston. The result of their investigation of the decision is briefly stated, as follows:

"*First*—As to the question, 'Can a negro be a citizen of the United States?' It has been commonly supposed that the Court decided this question in the negative. This is a mistake. From the form in which it was presented it was very doubtful whether it was before the Court for a decision. Four of the nine Judges thought that it was; these were the Chief Justice, and Justices Wayne and Daniel, who answer the question in the negative, and Justice Curtis, who answers it in the affirmative. Of the Judges who gave no opinion on the point, one (Judge McLean) declares that if he answered the question at all it would be in the affirmative; Justice Catron, when Chief Justice of the Supreme Court of Tennessee, gave an opinion directly involving an affirmative answer to the question; the three other judges give no clue to their opinions. On this question, then, the Court stands thus: Three in the affirmative, three in the negative, and three silent.

"*Secondly*—Was the Missouri Compromise Constitutional? It is a perfectly well-settled principle of the Supreme Court, and one that has been often laid down from its bench, that no part of an opinion of the Court is to be regarded as of authority as a precedent which was not necessary to the determination of the question before it. Anything beyond this is merely the expression of the individual opinion of the Judge; and it has been well said that 'if general dicta are to be considered as establishing the law, nothing is yet settled or can long be settled.' Bearing this in mind, let us look at the facts of the case. Scott was a slave in Missouri; was taken by his master to Illinois, and thence into a Territory of the United States, where Slavery was prohibited by the Missouri compromise; and thence back to Missouri. The opinion of the Court is placed upon the ground that the laws of Missouri are to decide whether Scott is or is not a slave, now that he has returned thither. If this be so, what matters it whether the compromise was valid or invalid? In other words, whether Scott was free when in Illinois, or in the Territory, or whether he continued to be a slave all the time? And if the Court goes out of its way to give an opinion on this point, could a plainer instance be found of an opinion on a point not necessary to the determination of the rights of the parties?

The Court, then, has not decided that the Missouri Compromise was unconstitutional.

Thirdly—This case is often spoken of as deciding that a master may take his slave to a free State and there hold him there as a slave. This is a simple mistake; there is no such point decided. But

Fourthly—The doctrine is here established that, if a slave be taken by his master to a free State, and does not *there* claim his liberty, but consents to return with his master to a slave State, he may be held as a slave there, if the higher court or that State considers him still to be a slave. In other words, the Dred Scott case does not decide that a negro is a slave in a free State because he *was* a slave in the State from which he was brought; nor, that a slave carried from a slave to a free State and brought back, is free because he might have claimed his freedom in the free State; nor, that he is necessarily a slave after his return; but leaves his freedom or slavery to be settled by the laws of the slave State to which he returned with his master."

AN ANONYMOUS REPORT: SOUTHERN REACTION TO *DRED SCOTT* DECISION

This short New York Daily Times *article reprints part of a Charleston (S.C.)* Mercury's *editorial about slavery and suggests how the news of the outcome of the* Dred Scott *case will be received in the South.*

New York Daily Times, 11 March 1857

The last thing we should anticipate from our Southern brethren would be a self-reproach that they had not been true to themselves. But such is the opinion of the Charleston *Mercury*. That paper says:

"If we ever save ourselves—if we ever establish firmly the institution of Slavery beyond question at the South—it will be by acting independently of both these allies. The Slavery party at the North has gone down for the want of efficient support at the South."

"If we ever establish the institution of Slavery beyond question at the South," is decidedly good. The *Mercury* will probably feel assured that Slavery is tolerably well established at the South, and everywhere else also, when it hears of the decision of the Supreme Court in the Dred Scott case.

HENRY RAYMOND: EDITORIAL WRITER PREDICTS *DRED SCOTT* DECISION WILL SPUR CREATION OF ANTISLAVERY PARTY

The New York Daily Times *editorial on the* Dred Scott *decision suggests that the effect of the decision will be the creation of an Abolition Party. The paper suggests that this decision will do more to stimulate the growth and power of such a party than any other event that has yet occurred with regard to slavery. The paper was right.*

New York Daily Times, 9 March 1857

Twenty years ago South Carolina denied the paramount authority of the Supreme Court of the United States, and flew to arms to resist it; while Massachusetts took the lead in asserting the absolute, unqualified duty of every citizen and every state to yield implicit obedience to its decisions upon all questions of Constitutional law. To-day the position of these two States, and of the sections which they represent, is likely to be reversed. South Carolina will become the champion of federal supremacy, and Massachusetts will assert the doctrine of State Rights. And this change of position illustrates the fact, to which it is due, that *interests* and not *reason*, rules over and regulates the action of States as well as of individuals. South Carolina resisted the Federal Government in 1832 because her interests were menaced by its action. She asserts its supremacy in 1857 because it has become the champion and proctor of her institutions and her property.

The decision of the Supreme Court in the case of DRED SCOTT completes the nationalization of Slavery. Slavery is no longer a local institution,—the creature of local law,—dependent for its existence and protection upon State sovereignty and State legislation. It is incorporated into the Constitution of the United States. Its tenure is the tenure of all property, and the Constitution protects and preserves it, to the same extent and upon the same principles, as it protects any other property of any kind whatever. This is the fundamental position which the Supreme Court has just asserted, and upon which all its decisions in this case rest. Congress cannot exclude Slavery from Federal territory, because the *right* to slaves is the right to *property*, and cannot be divested. For those same reasons the people of the Territory cannot exclude slavery from their own domain;—and when the time for the next step comes, we shall have it in the logical sequence, that *no State Government has a right to deprive any citizen of property, which the Constitution of the United States protects him in holding.*

It is not too much to say that this decision revolutionizes the Federal Government, and changes entirely the relation which Slavery has hitherto held towards it. Slavery is no longer local: it is national. The Federal Government is no longer held aloof from it, as a thing wholly and exclusively out of its jurisdiction:—it is brought directly within its sphere and put immediately under its protection. The doctrine of State Rights, so long its friend, is now its foe.

That this decision is to produce the most profound impression upon the public judgment is certain. Its first effect will be to paralyze and astound the public mind. Familiar as our people have become to the advancement of Slavery towards supremacy in our Government, they have not believed that it could obtain so absolute a seat in the supreme council of the Republic at so early a day. The decision will be accepted and obeyed as law. There will be no wide or loud protest against it. The public peace will not be disturbed,—the public ear will not be vexed,—by clamorous outcries or noisy denunciations of the Court and its decree. But the doctrine it has promulgated will sink deep into the public heart, and germinate there as the seed of discontent and contest and disaster thereafter. They mistake the temper of the men of this Republic, who believe that they will ever accept Slavery as the fixed and permanent law of the American Union. They have trusted to time,—to the progress of civilization, to the melioration of legal codes,—to climate, to population, to established metes and bounds, to old covenants and compacts and the advancement of Christian principle, for ultimate deliverance. They will strive still to cling to such of these as violence and wrong have left untouched. But this last decision leaves little to hope and everything to fear. And the people will begin to ask why, if Slavery is *national*, the nation should not assume the custody and control of it:—why it should be constitutional for the Federal Government to protect, and not to remove, it;—why, if its extension is synonymous with its existence, both should not be ended altogether.

Apparent peace will follow the action of the Supreme Court. The partisans of its conduct and its doctrine will proclaim it to be the end of controversy upon this subject, and the immediate result will seem to confirm their hopes. But it has laid the only solid foundation which has ever yet existed for an Abolition party; and it will do more to stimulate the growth, to build up the power and consolidate the action of such a party, than has been done by any other event since the Declaration of Independence.

DAVID N. WHITE: EDITORIAL—VOTERS, NOT COURTS, WILL DECIDE SLAVERY ISSUE

In this editorial about the Dred Scott *case the author focuses on the "recent dicta" of the Court. In legal terms the word* dicta *(also called* obiter dicta*) refers to opinion voiced by a judge or judges that has only incidental bearing on a case in question and is therefore not binding. Like the* New York Daily Times *editorial, this one also suggests that the slavery question will be resolved in upcoming elections. The* Pittsburgh Gazette*, which was the first newspaper published west of the Allegheny Mountains (it began publishing in 1786), was an influential abolitionist-friendly newspaper in the region, and its editor, David N. White, helped create the Republican Party in the Pittsburgh area.*

Pittsburgh Gazette, 7 March 1857

We do not know how other persons may feel in view of the recent *dicta* of the Supreme Court in the case of Dred Scott, an abstract of which was published in our telegraphic column on Saturday morning, but it appears to us that the almost diabolical spirit it evinces in going out of the way to Freedom at the expense of Slavery, ought to be sufficient to arouse to indignation the coolest and most torpid of northern men. The decision is a fitting crown to the aborted tyranny which has just submerged with [*president*] Pierce; an iron clasp, well forged to link the dead with the living administration. It comes pat upon the recent inaugural, "rounds and caps it to the tyrant's eye" and just fills up the cup of inequity.

What matter is it that this decision upsets those we have on record? New lights have arisen with the progress of revolving years, and Story and Marshall, Jefferson, Madison, and Monroe hide their twinkling lights before the full-orbed glory of Douglas, Pierce and Davis. The Supreme Court has aimed a blow at State Sovereignty which is baser and more iniquitous than any thing we had before conceived of. The State of Illinois for example, under this decision in her legislative capacity, has no power to enact such a law as can make a slave coming there with the consent of his master a

freeman! The decision that the Court has no jurisdiction in this case make all the other remarks from the bench touching the ordinance of 1787, and the compromise of 1820, mere *obiter dicta*, it is true, but the fact that the Court has gone out of its way to say what it has, shows its animus, and trumpets to the four corners of the earth the eager alacrity with which it echoes the mouthings of demagogues like Pierce and Douglas. We may henceforth throw to the winds the reasoning of Story and the decisions of Marshall, so far as this court is concerned, and submit to seeing the government surrendered, bound hand and foot to the same power which has given Kansas over to blood and desolation, elevated a weak old man to the executive chair, given the Treasury, the Post Office, the Army, the Navy and the Department of the Interior to be its willing servants and exhilarated and energized by its success, pressed on to the Supreme Court, made that the echo of its will and left no place for hope to rest upon, but the virtue of the masses of the people, to which we must henceforth appeal. Let them come in their might and at the ballot box root up the rotten fabric to its foundations which four years of misrule has served so much to weaken, and which the four years to come will doubtless not improve or strengthen.

JOSEPH MEDILL: EDITORIAL—CONDEMNING THE *DRED SCOTT* DECISION

The Chicago Daily Tribune *also considered the Court's ruling to be filled with dicta and in this untitled editorial excerpt strongly condemns the decision.*

Chicago Daily Tribune, 12 March 1857

We must confess we are shocked at the violence and servility of the Judicial Revolution caused by the decision of the Supreme Court of the United States. We scarcely know how to express our detestation of its inhuman dicta or fathom the

wicked consequences which may flow from it. . . . To say or suppose, that a Free People can respect or will obey a decision so fraught with disastrous consequences to the People and their Liberties, is to dream of impossibilities.

THURLOW WEED: POLITICAL IMPLICATIONS OF *DRED SCOTT* DECISION

This editorial from the Albany Evening Journal *(Albany, N.Y.) explores the political implications of the decision from a Republican perspective and largely echoes the* New York Daily Times *and* Pittsburgh Gazette *sentiments about how this decision will impact the controlling Democratic Party. Republicans were the strongest antislavery advocates of the existing political parties at the time, but not all Republicans were staunch abolitionists.*

Albany Evening Journal, 11 March 1857

The Oligarchy who breed men and women for the market and make unceasing war on free labor, laid broad the foundations of their conspiracy against Liberty, in the convention

which nominated Buchanan for the Presidency. They planned to inaugurate on the 4th of March, 1857, a Federal combination of influences in behalf of Slavery, that should include the

Executive power, the Legislative power and the Judicial power of the Republic. Through the patronage of the President they calculated upon corrupting and enlisting an army of ambitious and energetic spirits in the Free States. Through the 35th Congress they counted surely on legislation that should expand Slavery and contract Freedom. Through the Supreme Court of the United States they reckoned, with audacious cunning, on a conquest of all the subordinate courts of Law in the law-abiding North—on a conquest of the vast body of Northern lawyers trained by their profession to yield obedience and respect to the final decisions of the judiciary, and educated all of them into a veneration of that high court over which Marshall presided and in which Story was a justice—counted on a conquest of the great body of the Northern people, through their habit of submission to law and to public authority. To this end the appeal of the case of Dred Scott had been prepared. Its decision was certain and ready long and long ago. But its influence was wanted for the inauguration of the new pro-slavery administration of James Buchanan. So the formal delay of a re-argument was gone through with. The case was ready again for decision and publicity. But a Republican House of Representatives was in session. The horrible wrong inflicted through the person of Dred Scott upon half a million of free colored citizens, and the great crime against Freedom and Humanity enveloped in the denial of this black man's petition for his unquestionable rights, would inevitably have fired them to indignation and protest. Their denunciation of the Supreme Court was to be avoided by all means, and their hostility to the legislation necessary to the South and to the incoming Administration, was especially to be avoided. So the decision was withheld till Congress adjourned. Then it came.

The army of "Democratic" applicants for office came with it, and of course came under it as a yoke, as was anticipated. The army of the present "Democratic" incumbents of office, hopeful of reappointment, accept the decision as the highest expression of law and equity. Editorial slaves din into the shocked ear of the public their lying sophistries to persuade that a decision which nationalizes Human Bondage, and disfranchises citizens of African descent, is a sacred one. But in vain is it all. The People stand angry and implacable in front of this giant judicial iniquity. No shaking of old ermines, nor fluttering of moth-eaten silk gowns, nor invocation of the shades of Marshall, Jay, Ellsworth and Story—no extent of snivel and cant about the purity of the Federal Judiciary, and the obligation to put up with false law and falser equity, will avail at all to persuade the people of the Free States that Slavery has unrestricted rights in the Public Domain, and neither Freedom nor Congress has any opposing rights therein—that people of African descent can not be citizens of the United States—and that men and women can lawfully be held in slavery on Free Soil. No, the People will from the hour of this Dred decision, unintermittingly roll back this mixed Conspiracy, till through a recovered and reorganized Federal Judiciary and a republicanized Executive, they can administer justice and good government in the whole nation.

AN ANONYMOUS REPORT: HOW THE *DRED SCOTT* DECISION WILL AFFECT SLAVERY IN THE WESTERN TERRITORIES

The Kentucky Journal's *interpretation of the outcome of the* Dred Scott *case is also steeped in politics. This commentary focuses less on outrage about the decision and more on the practical implications for the Republican and Democratic Parties as well as on slavery questions as they arise in the territories now that the Missouri Compromise was found to be unconstitutional.*

Kentucky Journal, 16 March 1857 (Louisville)

We publish to-day abstracts of the opinions of the Judges of the Supreme Court of the United States in the case of Dred Scott against Sanford. The importance of this decision in the highest legal tribunal established under our Federal Constitution is a sufficient reason for devoting to it so much of the space in our columns. The questions upon which these opinions have been rendered are among those which have shaken our Union from centre to circumference, and threatened imminently its dissolution. The points adjudicated are more strictly political than legal, and affect materially the *status* of political parties throughout the confederacy.

The Court, by Taney, Chief Justice, decided that the case was not within the jurisdiction of the Court, as the plaintiff was not a citizen, and had no right to sue in a Federal Court. This decision was concurred in by Judges Campbell, Catron, Wayne, Daniels, Nelson, and Grier. The opinion of the Court was delivered by Chief Justice Taney. Judges Nelson and Catron delivered separate opinions concurring in the decision, but arriving at it by a somewhat different course of reasoning. Judges McLean and Curtis delivered opinions dissenting, in conclusion and in detail, from the opinion of the majority of the Court.

The principal points in this decision are that a negro cannot, under the *Constitution*, become a *citizen* of the United

States, that the power given to Congress to make all needful rules and regulations respecting the Territory or other property of the United States, referred exclusively to the Territory which belonged to the United States at the time of the adoption of the Constitution and can have no influence on Territory subsequently acquired; that the ordinance of 1787 was a compact between confederated colonies which was set aside by the adoption of the *Constitution*, and that by the provisions of the *Constitution* neither Congress nor a Territorial Legislature organized by authority of an act of Congress, has any right to prohibit slavery in the Territories, and that consequently the Missouri Compromise act of 1820, and the squatter sovereignty feature of the Kansas-Nebraska act are void for unconstitutionality.

In a strictly legal sense perhaps all of these questions were not properly before the court for adjudication, and all, except the decision that the court had no jurisdiction over the case of Dred Scott against Sanford, because Dred was not a citizen of the United States, may be considered as mere dicta and not strictly decisions of the court; but for all practical purposes they are equivalent to regular decisions upon adjudicated cases, as they indicate clearly what would be the decision of the court in any case directly presenting the questions which in this are simply incidental. However different this decision may be from the views entertained by a large portion of the people of the United States, it must be regarded as an authoritative exposition of constitutional law, emanating from the highest legal tribunal in the country, to whose decisions the people and the Government are bound to yield obedience and respect.

The importance of the decision is greatly enhanced by its immediate effect upon two of the great political parties of the country. At a single blow it shatters and destroys the platform of the Republican party. It annihilates the issue which was made paramount in the recent Presidential election, and takes away from the Democratic party all the advantages of its advocacy of popular sovereignty in the Territories. It leaves both of these great parties all abroad,

without a single plank of their late platforms upon which to rest.

In the recent election, while the Republicans demanded the *restoration* of the Missouri compromise, the Democratic party strongly advocated the popular sovereignty doctrine incorporated in the Nebraska-Kansas act. They made this popular sovereignty doctrine the chief, and, in fact, the only, plank in their platform. They made it the paramount issue of the canvass [*sic*]. They eulogised it as "more ancient than free government itself," and contended most justly that the only truly constitutional method of disposing of the question of slavery in the Territories was to allow the people of the Territories themselves, while in a territorial condition, to decide whether they would establish or prohibit slavery therein. In the Inaugural address of Mr. Buchanan, delivered, we believe, only the day before the decision in this Dred Scott case was tendered, the Democratic President elect greatly eulogised this squatter sovereignty doctrine, "that the will of the majority shall govern the settlement of the question of domestic slavery in the Territories," and frankly admitted that it was upon this doctrine that the Democratic party had succeeded in the last election.

The voice of the President elect, admitting the position of the Democratic party in favor of squatter sovereignty, had hardly ceased to be echoed from the walls of the Capitol when this decision of the Supreme Court pronounced the new favorite doctrine of the Democracy unconstitutional. It has therefore become necessary for the formation of a new platform. What this will be has already been foreshadowed in the action of the Democrats in the United States Senate in reference to Bigg's amendment to the Minnesota bill, and the significant declaration in the inaugural address of Mr. Buchanan that "it is the imperative and indispensable duty of the Government to secure to every *resident inhabitant* the free and independent expression of his opinions by his vote." The alien suffrage and States' rights doctrine will be made the cardinal principles of the Democratic and Republican parties, and they will seek to avoid annihilation by a fusion of their failing fortunes.

AN ANONYMOUS REPORT: DANGERS OF BLACK REPUBLICAN OPPOSITION TO *DRED SCOTT* DECISION

The Democratic New Hampshire Patriot & State Gazette *used the* Dred Scott *decision to discredit Republicans and suggest that it is the antislavery constituencies who will ultimately destroy the Union. The paper says resistance to this Supreme Court decision is resistance to the Union itself.*

New Hampshire Patriot & State Gazette, 18 March 1857 (Concord)

We give in this paper an abstract of the decision of the U.S. Supreme Court in the Dred Scott case, in which it is solemnly adjudged and decided, by the highest judicial tribunal of the Union, that the Missouri Compromise was unconstitutional, and that Congress has no constitutional power

or authority to legislate upon the subject of slavery in the Territories. It will be seen that other incidental questions were decided in this case, but this is the one of the most political importance, and interest. It utterly demolishes the whole black republican platform and stamps it as directly antagonistical to the constitution. This is the end of the matter, so far as argument and voting and legislation are concerned. The constitution is the supreme law; the Supreme Court is the authorized interpreter of the constitution; the construction which that tribunal puts upon that instrument is, for all practical purposes, the constitution itself, and therefore their decision must be fully and freely acquiesced in by all good citizens. That decision is now the supreme law of the land; it is practically the constitution itself, being the meaning and intent of that instrument as officially interpreted and declared by the tribunal authorized to interpret it, and from whose decision there is no appeal. Resistance to that decision is, therefore, resistance to the constitution—to the government—to the Union itself. It cannot be made legally, rightfully, peacefully, or with the least chance or hope of success. That decision must be carried into effect—that interpretation must be acquiesced in and acted upon, *or else it must be resisted by force.* There is no other alternative. It is the law, the constitution, and will be respected and acted upon by the constituted authorities, no matter to what party they belong nor what their private views may be in regard to it. It cannot be evaded; if Congress and the President should undertake to resist it, the effort would be futile. In a word, we repeat, nothing but force, open rebellion, can successfully oppose the practical application and enforcement of the decision of the court in this case.

But what is the course and talk of the black republican organs upon this subject? Why, one would suppose, from their talk, that the decision of the highest judicial tribunal of the Union is of no binding force! The N.Y. Tribune even declares that their decision in this case is entitled to "no more weight than would be the judgment of a majority in a Washington bar-room," and other black papers declare the judges to be "scoundrels," and Benedict Arnolds, and the black press and pulpit unite in reviling the court and denouncing their decision!

Now this only goes to prove, what we have heretofore alleged, that the black republican creed and purposes are at war with the constitution, are treasonable, and contemplate the overthrow of the Union. It only goes to show that their leaders stand precisely upon Garrison's platform, and that the road to the attainment of their objects lies over the ruins of the constitution and the Union. There is no escape from this; they preach resistance to law, to the supreme law—resistance to what is authoritatively adjudged to be the constitution. Such resistance, if carried into practical effect, would be treason; and all who preach it, preach treason, and all who seek to make a practical thing of it, seek to overthrow the constitution. This is the sum and substance of the matter; and all patriotic citizens—all who have a regard for the continued existence, peace and prosperity of the country, will [*unreadable*] constitution, and to the government which is bound to respect and enforce it.

This decision effects a legal and constitutional settlement of the sectional issue which has so long agitated the country and endangered the very existence of the government. Of course, no one expects it will stop the mouths or check the efforts of the professional agitators; for, as Daniel Webster well and truly said in his Buffalo speech in 1851, "their livelihood consists in agitating; their freehold, their copyhold, their capital, their all in all, depend on the excitement of the public mind." These men will agitate still; the noise and rant and howl of interested fanaticism will still resound. But it will be without substantial foundation, without plausible object, and with the palpable certainty that no good can come from it, but that it is an agitation and a warfare against the constitution itself. With this fact before the eyes of all men, such agitation must be up-hill work, however industriously it may be prosecuted.

The Washington *Union,* in view of this decision, well and truly says that "the Democratic party is now enjoying the greatest triumph—not merely that they have elected their candidates and secured four more years of party ascendancy in the executive branch of the government, but that their victory has been won on the most momentous issue that ever divided the public mind, and that political triumph has been confirmed and endorsed by the highest judicial tribunal known to the constitution."

If the sectional question be not now settled, then we may despair of the republic. We believe it is settled, and that henceforth sectionalism will cease to be a dangerous element in our political contests. No issue was ever more directly and squarely made than that on which Mr. Buchanan was elected. The result was an unmistakable popular judgment against sectionalism, and in favor of a broad, conservative, constitutional nationalism. The questions involved in the canvass could not have been more fairly and directly made and maintained, and if the success of the democratic nominees did not settle those questions as fully as a popular decision could settle any question, then it is idle to rely on popular elections as tests of political principles.

There was but one thing needed to give to the result in the Presidential contest the force of an absolute and final settlement of the sectional issue. That thing was the judgment of the Supreme Court in confirmation of the Democratic doctrines which had received the popular endorsement. The decision in the Dred Scott case has furnished the closing and clinching confirmation needed, and henceforth sectional fanaticism cannot maintain its warfare without arraying itself distinctly against the constitution. The people have decided that sectional agitation must cease, and the highest judicial authority has declared that the people have decided in accordance with the constitution.

Whoever now seeks to revive sectionalism, arrays himself against the constitution, and consequently, against the Union. Of course, it is to be expected that fanaticism will rave and clamor against the decision of the Supreme Court. But fanaticism ceases to be a formidable enemy when it seeks to measure strength with the Union-loving spirit of the people, sustained and confirmed by the great arbiter of constitutional questions. Fanaticism becomes powerless against such a combination, and hence we may smile at the madness with which the organs of black republicanism assail the late decision of the Supreme Court. It is the last dying fit of fanatical sectionalism. It will have the effect of fixing public attention upon the reckless wickedness which has heretofore impelled the sectional agitators to force the republic to the very verge of disruption.

We feel, therefore, that the danger is for the present over; that sectionalism is virtually dead—that it has been crushed out by the popular verdict in the presidential election; and that the decision of the Supreme Court had left nothing vital in republicanism, and has placed the Democratic party beyond and above all competition as the constitutional, national, Union party of the country. Mr. Buchanan takes the helm under these auspicious circumstances, and his acts thus far give token of a successful and prosperous administration.

JOHN W. FORNEY: EDITORIAL—COUNTRY SHOULD RESPECT *DRED SCOTT* DECISION

The Democratic Washington Daily Union *in Washington, D.C., quoted above in the* Patriot *editorial, not only promoted the Democratic Party in its writings about the case but also urged the country to unite and respect the decision issued by the highest court in the nation. This editorial appeared untitled and was written by John W. Forney, the* Daily Union's *editor. Later in 1857 Forney left the* Daily Union *to start the* Philadelphia Press. *Forney switched political parties between 1857 and 1860 and the* Philadelphia Press *reflected this shift, so it is known historically as a Republican newspaper despite Forney's early Democratic leanings.*[12]

Washington Daily Union, 12 March 1857 (Washington, D.C.)

We cherish a most ardent and confident expectation that this decision will meet a proper reception from the great mass of our intelligent countrymen; that it will be regarded with soberness and not with passion; and that it will thereby exert a mighty influence in diffusing sound opinions and

restoring harmony and fraternal concord throughout the country. . . . It would be fortunate, indeed, if the opinion of that court on this important subject could receive the candid and respectful acquiescence which it merits.

W. S.: LETTER WRITER DESCRIBES IMPORTANCE OF *DRED SCOTT* DECISION FOR NORTHERN OPPONENTS OF SLAVERY

This letter to the editor of the black-run newspaper the Provincial Freeman *gives additional insight to how significant the outcome of the* Dred Scott *case was for those who opposed slavery in the North.*

Provincial Freeman, 15 March 1857 (Chatham, Canada West)

To the Editor of the Provincial Freeman:

DEAR FRIENDS: You who have "fled for refuge," or emigrated for freedom to Canada, are I presume very anxious to learn how "our people" view the decision of the Supreme Court, in the case of Dred Scott &c.

With much pains, in my walks in this city, I have endeavored to ascertain their opinions on the subject, and will report them for what they are worth. Of course quite a diversity of opinion and sentiment prevails—though this decision is precisely in keeping with the pro-slavery usages and policy of this

Government, and hence just what might have been expected, nevertheless, its influence has been more discouraging and prostrating to the hopes of the colored man, than any preceding act of tyranny ever perpetrated upon him by this nation.

From the interested, or all hands, the anxious inquiry is made as to the source from whence to look for redress, or reversal of this atrocious decision; also to how it will effect our brethren in the Eastern States, where they have the right of suffrage &c. Some occupying the ground, that we are hopelessly doomed; some that only those of "African descent whose ancestors were of pure African blood and were brought into this country and sold as slaves," are included in the decision, or excluded from citizenship. Some affect to believe that they are "glad" of it; that it will work ultimately to the advantage of those aimed to be ostracize &c. The hope of this class rests on the foundation that "the darkest hour is just before the break of day" and that great evils must be consummated that good may come. Vain hope!

A leading (colored) Rev. gentlemen of this city on being asked what he thought of the decision, replied: "first rate, That pleases me precisely." And he added that he hoped that this "administration, would re-open the African Slave Trade, and import one hundred and fifty thousand natives, annually." Next that all the barriers prohibiting slave holders from bringing their slaves into the Free states, would be removed, and finally that the white, mechanics &c., would be reduced to slavery; on the fulfillment of which he fancied emancipation would come. How would a prayer in keeping with such hopes sound from Bethel Church? From one of her leading Ministers?

Some turn to Canada as a land of hope, in this trying hour. Others oppose because they apprehend that prejudice is about as virulent there as it is here: besides, with some the duty to stay here and fifth it out seems paramount.

Mr. Wear, a distinguished leader amongst us very emphatically assumes the position that not a free man (!) can be spared, even if all the attractions of Heaven could be found elsewhere; and the facilities in reaching such a place as favourable as they are in going to Canada. To many the idea that we must endure . . . may seem consistent, manly and noble; to my own mind however, viewing us with our hands tied, filling menial avocations, and made drudge horses of for the whites, generally, while in the eye of the nation, and the decision of the detestable Chief Justice Taney, we are "unfit associates for the white race, socially or politically;" as "having no rights which white men were bound to respect," and as "never being thought of or spoken of except as property." I confess I see but a faint prospect of any very great change for the better, at least in the present generation. Therefore I am not of the number any longer to subscribe to the above "staying" &c. doctrine; and verily hope never to again as long as this abominable decision and pro-slavery constitution remains.

Of course if in taking a retrospective view of the free colored people in the Northern States, we could find them lively interested in their own cause, sustaining and establishing anti-slavery Presses and Advocates; vigorously contending for their rights; encouraging talent and genius amongst one another, it would then seem imperative duty to submit to existing circumstances.

But what are the facts in the case? Suppose I come directly home to this state, Pennsylvania, containing the largest number of colored inhabitants, the most wealth and intelligence perhaps of any northern state in the Union, and how are we fighting it out? Out of the 30,000 inhabitants of Philadelphia, how many support anti-slavery papers, whether published by white or colored? I am confident, not four hundred.

How many signatures have been procured this winter to send into the Legislature for the right of suffrage? Certainly not three hundred. Two public meetings were held here in the early part of the winter to interest the people on the suffrage question, but both meetings contained less than forty persons; and although a committee of ten were appointed to agitate &c., I have yet to learn whether a single name has reached the Legislature, from this city, up to this hour.

To turn to our Library Companies and Literary Institutions, what do we find, but prostration and desertion! How few intelligent and respectable young men give them their support and countenance! How.

How very rarely are to be seen in the Anti-Slavery prints of the Country, elaborate productions on our rights or destiny from colored minds of Pennsylvania! It is hard to have to acknowledge these truths and it is with shame I do it; but concealment will avail us nothing. Indeed it is impossible to keep an intelligent public ignorant, while the question of the black-man is being so universally viewed. That there is another side to this picture I am aware of, and that the crushing tyranny to which we have been subjected is irrationally adduced as the chief cause of our delinquencies is also obvious; but that so many intelligent industrious and professedly liberty loving men amongst us should disregard a country whose laws proscribe no color; where all the immunities and privileges are as sacred to the black man as to the white, as in Canada for instance is, I confess a mystery that I cannot fathom. Here robbed of all our rights, experience teaches how slowly we have progressed; there in possession of all our rights—and citizens of the most powerful nation on earth, and as "fine a country for the poor man as the Sun ever shone upon," what would hinder us from rising?

MARY ANN CAREY SHADD: DESCRIPTION OF PHILADELPHIA MEETINGS PROTESTING *DRED SCOTT* DECISION

Soon after the Supreme Court decision in the Dred Scott *case, many cities and organizations, outraged by the outcome of the case, gathered to challenge the ruling in various forms. Here the* Provincial Freeman, *a black-run newspaper published in Canada, reports on a meeting in Philadelphia and suggests that opponents of the decision consider leaving the United States. This account was written by Mary Ann Carey Shadd, the paper's editor. She was the first African American woman to edit a weekly newspaper in North America. The* Provincial Freeman *was written for displaced Americans living in Canada.*

Provincial Freeman, 18 April 1857 (Chatham, Canada West)

We beg to call attention to the proceedings of a meeting held in Philadelphia lately, to express condemnation of the Dred Scott decision, &c. Mrs. Mott, Messrs. Still, Remon, Purvis, McKimm and many others, white and colored participated.

THE resolutions are strong and pointed, but why not go farther? This is not the time for strong words only; when all realize the yoke so forcibly as now why not act? Protests are well enough in their way, but to be of effect, they must point to determined action. Do the Purvises, Remonds, and others, who took part in the meeting intend to stay in the U. States? If so, the resolutions amount to nothing, if not why not say so friends? Your national ship is rotten sinking, why not leave it, and why not say so boldly, manfully?

Canada is a good country,—we have British freedom and an abundance of it,—equal political rights of course, and if you covet it, social intercourse with those in your position in life. We here give you facts. If Canada should be distasteful, British Europe, or the Isles, may be more to your mind; at all events, leave that slavery-cursed republic. Another meeting of respectable free and independent colored citizens was held previously, as they claim to believe in the United States Constitution, we shall wait with patience to see what it will do for them. We hope, however, that they too, will look at facts instead of everlastingly theorising.

SYDNEY HOWARD GAY: EDITORIAL— *DRED SCOTT* DECISION VIOLATES BASIC PRINCIPLES OF AMERICAN FREEDOM

The antislavery press was vocal about its opposition to the Dred Scott *ruling. In this commentary on the case the editor of the* National Anti-Slavery Standard *writes that the Court decision violates basic principles of freedom, liberty, and democracy.*

National Anti-Slavery Standard, 18 April 1857 (New York City)

IN commenting upon the decision of the Supreme Court in the Dred Scott case, we referred to the rule of our Southern masters, one never varied from, to test always the obedience of the North, either when she really complains that her burden was greater than she could bear, or when the load laid upon her patient shoulders is so heavy that she might be expected to complain. In other and homelier words the South always proves her pudding according to the proverb. It may be a very good pudding, according to the proverb. It may be a very good pudding, fair to look upon, round as a ball, unbroken as a globe, smooth as glass, and smoking hot—but the proof, after all is in the eating thereof; the good maker is not deceived by the outside; a fair seeming does not satisfy her; she must plunge into its depths for the evidence she needs; she eats the pudding, and thus proves it. Do not accuse us of treating a serious matter lightly. Proverbs are epitomes of the wisdom of ages, and some times one of these pithy sentences illustrates more completely than columns can do the wisdom of an action which is universally in accordance with it.

The Dred Scott case is decided; the Supreme Court makes

the law of the land, so far as they could, in a decision of this case, the monstrous doctrine which Judge Kane was the first to promulgate, and profess to be governed by in the seat of a Judge. We at the North, have had our say about it: Tribunes have blustered; the Journals have sneered; the Couriers have solemnly argued; one class has thundered in indignant words; another has protested in meek humility; a third has given apprehensive warning of trouble to come; all are moved. It is desirable to know, say the overseers, just what these "niggers" mean; are they moved even to the point of seizing the whip which is laid on their backs? Let us see.

We beg the intelligent reader to consider for five minutes the character of the decision of the Supreme Court; how it ignores all history; how it sets all law at defiance; how it outrages common sense; how it scorns human pretences; how it tramples upon the plainest principles of the Christian religion; how it laughs at liberty; how it scoffs at democracy; and how it scouts all Northern pretension to freedom of thought, or freedom of act, or freedom of conscience. And consider then that the March in which all this was done has counted out but little more than half its thirty-one days ere, under the very eyes, and within the reach of the very hands of some hundreds of thousands of grown men, to whose faces all these things have been said, there appeared first in Boston a slavehunter, in search of a man who had lived there for years, a respectable, a thrifty, an honourable man—the free citizen of a free State, who helped to make Governors and Mayors and other officials, more or less worthy—who paid taxes, and, probably, supported the preaching of the Gospel like any other well-to do and respectable citizen—a man like any other man who goes daily down State street, or on Sundays into the broad aisle of the Rev. Dr. Adams's Church—but who this slave hunter was to take, if he found him, back to the South to drag out his weary life hereafter as a mere chattel slave.

Boston stands where it did eighty years ago, and the tide into which her people once threw a cargo of tea still rolls into her harbour. Have they thrown a man into it this time? Not at all. In all probability the slave hunter has the best rooms in the Revere House—it may be, like Daniel Webster, is entertained only for the honour done by his presence; perhaps he has dined with Judge Loring, and Edward Everett invited to meet him; perhaps asked to say grace over parson Adams's breakfast table, or to lead in prayer in any Bible Class or Sunday School where his hungry soul might lead him to seek a meal of spiritual cold victuals. And how is it with the man whom he seeks? The Vigilance Committee, as the best thing they can do, and notwithstanding the Personal Liberty Law of Massachusetts hurry him off as fast as steam can carry him, to where British Law and Lord Palmerston's Government will give him a refuge. If the slavehunter had got hold of him, he would have been taken back to Virginia as sure as there is a monument on Bunker's Hill.

Nor is this all. A scoundrel of the same sort was prowling about this city nearly all last week, in search of two fugitives. The particular villain who is known, of all our policemen, for his past services in the perpetration of wickedness of this sort, was seen during the day—he knew too well to go there in the evening—lurking about, in company with a white fellow, in those streets where the colored people congregate. The pair were slave-hunting here in New York, one of them sent, at this particular moment, to test our obedience to the powers that be, and also show us the precise measure of our opposition to the decision of the Supreme Court.

If the two poor wretches had been found, does any body think that New York would have raised her hand in anger, or bowed head in humiliation? Not a bit of it. The quantity of bough in this particular pudding, which the mistress has just proved, has as many ounces to the pound as ever.

NOTES

1. Sanford's name was misspelled in the original Court document to read "Sandford."

2. *Dred Scott v. John F. A. Sandford*, 60 U.S. 393 (1857).

3. Ibid.

4. Lisa Cozzens, "A Hard Shove for a 'Nation on the Brink': The Impact of Dred Scott" (Department of Alfa-informatica, University of Groningen, Netherlands, 2003), http://www.let.rug.nl/-usa/E/dred_scott/scottxx.htm.

5. "The Declaration of the Supreme Court in the Case of Dred Scott," *New York Daily Times*, 10 March 1857.

6. *Scott v. Sandford* (1857), 406.

7. Stanley Kutler, *The Dred Scott Decision: Law or Politics?* (Boston: Houghton Mifflin, 1967), 46–48.

8. Kenneth C. Kaufman, *Dred Scott's Advocate: A Biography of Roswell M. Field* (Columbia: University of Missouri Press, 1996), 2.

9. Kutler, *The Dred Scott Decision*, 4–5.

10. Ibid.

11. After Dred Scott's case was resolved by the U.S. Supreme Court, he remained a slave for several months. The children of Peter Blow, Scott's first owner, had paid Scott's legal fees throughout his court battles, and a few months after the Supreme Court decision, they bought Dred and Harriet Scott and their two children and set them free. Nine months after gaining his freedom, Dred Scott died of tuberculosis.

12. In 1868, Forney switched political loyalties again and returned to the Democratic Party.

FURTHER READINGS

Cozzens, Lisa. "A Hard Shove for a 'Nation on the Brink': The Impact of Dred Scott." Department of Alfa-informatica, University of Groningen, Netherlands, 2003: http://www.let.rug.nl/-usa/E/dred_scott/scottxx.htm.

Kaufman, Kenneth C. *Dred Scott's Advocate: A Biography of Roswell M. Field.* Columbia: University of Missouri Press, 1996.

Kutler, Stanley. *The Dred Scott Decision: Law or Politics?* Boston: Houghton Mifflin, 1967.

3

JOHN BROWN AND HARPER'S FERRY, 1859

Early in the morning on 16 October 1859, Captain John Brown set into motion a plan he had devised nearly two years earlier—a plan that involved the creation of a base in the mountains of Virginia to assist runaway slaves and launch attacks on Southern slaveholders. Brown, a militant abolitionist, started to raise funds for his plan in 1857 and wanted to launch an assault on Harper's Ferry as early as spring 1858. His strategy changed, however, after one of his followers made Brown's plan public. Even before Brown's name was publicly associated with a plan for insurrection, he was quite well known and feared by most Southerners.

Brown was infamous for his efforts to rid Kansas of proslavery influences as the political fight over its slave status began in 1854 (see Chapter 1). He was best known in Kansas for leading the Pottawatomie Massacre on 25 May 1856. Along with four of his sons, one son-in-law, and two other Kansas settlers, Brown raided proslavery settlers on Mosquito and Pottawatomie Creek, killing five men.[1] Brown had a national reputation as an abolitionist fanatic who advocated violence as a means to put an end to slavery. He had backed his violent words with action in Kansas.

After Brown's intentions in Virginia were made public, he went into hiding for a year; but during the summer of 1859, he reemerged and rented a farm in Maryland across the Potomac River from Harper's Ferry under an assumed name and began to revive his plan. Brown and a group of men he had recruited, including two of his sons and more than a dozen free blacks, would cross the Potomac and capture the federal armory and arsenal in Harper's Ferry, hold some of the prominent townspeople hostage, and try to incite local slaves to insurrection. For months Brown and a few of his men watched the daily operations of Harper's Ferry, its residents, and the government buildings that Brown and his followers wanted to occupy. On 16 October 1859, Brown's raid on Harper's Ferry began.[2]

The night before, Brown and his men had crossed the Potomac River and marched in heavy rains to get to the town. At around 4:00 A.M. on 16 October,

Brown and his men cut the telegraph wires, secured the train bridge leading into the town, and made their assault. First, they captured the federal armory. They then moved on to Hall's Rifle Works, a privately owned factory next to the arsenal that supplied weapons to the government.[3] Brown and his men rounded up several prominent citizens of the town to hold hostage at the armory. One of the hostages was Colonel Lewis Washington, a descendant of the first U.S. president.[4]

Brown and his men had hoped they could stir the area slaves to rebellion, but no slaves came forth. They hoped to be joined by more abolitionists in the states of Maryland and Virginia, but no reinforcements arrived. And as the assault continued, the local militia rallied and was able to hold Brown and his men at bay in the armory. The federal government called in the marines and soldiers under the leadership of Colonel Robert E. Lee (who would later become a prominent Confederate general). Before the federal troops arrived, eight of Brown's twenty-two-man "army" had been killed, including one of his sons. Once the federal troops took over, the insurrection quickly ended.[5]

In the end, ten of Brown's men were killed—including both his sons—seven were captured and five escaped. Brown was seriously injured in the raid; he suffered two bayonette wounds and multiple cuts and was taken to a hospital in Charlestown, Virginia.[6] Afterward, Brown and the other captured insurgents faced trial in Virginia and were quickly convicted. Brown was sentenced to be hanged—and on 2 December 1859 he was executed in Charlestown, Virginia, before a large crowd.

Brown's raid on Harper's Ferry continued to move the country toward civil war. As is seen below in the various editorials from different political perspectives, Southerners and proslavery Democrats used the event to associate Brown and militant forms of abolition with the Republican Party as a whole. To them, Brown was an example of how dangerous fanatical abolitionists could be. This further heightened Southern fears about their future, should a Republican be elected to high office. Republicans, on the other hand, showed sympathy toward Brown because many believed that it was the evil institution of slavery that drove him to his madness. Virtually no Republicans advocated violent means to end slavery, but they did argue that the lack of the Democratic federal government's response to put an end to or significantly challenge slavery might encourage some people to take matters into their own hands.

While Brown's raid was condemned by nearly every newspaper in the North, the strong division of feeling about what should happen to Brown after his raid is what highlighted the strong political divisions that continued to fracture the country when it came to the question of slavery.

The first few articles below provide some short examples of how the press covered the actual Harper's Ferry insurrection. The remaining articles and editorials focus on Brown's execution, responsibility for the condition of the country, and still more indications that the nation was headed for civil war.

AN ANONYMOUS REPORT: FIRST NEWS OF RAID ON HARPER'S FERRY

This excerpt is the first to have appeared in the New York Times *about the news coming from Harper's Ferry. Much of the information is not accurate and shows how quickly rumors about the raid had spread even though much of the information was spotty.*

New York Times, 18 October 1859

A threatening insurrection has broken out at Harper's Ferry, for which no sufficient reason has, as yet, been assigned. A band, said to be composed of negroes and white men, numbering two hundred and fifty, on Saturday night seized the bridge and took possession of the Government arsenal, which is located at Harper's Ferry. The express train, going east, was twice fired into and the assistant baggage-master is said to have been killed, while one of the baggage-masters, in attempting to cross the bridge, was seized by the insurgents and put in confinement. The streets of the town had been barricaded and were said to be in the possession of the originators of the revolt. Government troops had been sent on from Washington to quell the disturbance, and those in the immediate neighborhood had also been called out. Some considered the movement as originating with the Abolitionists, while others looked upon it as an attempt to get possession of the funds in the Government pay-house, a large amount having been recently deposited there.

CHARLES C. FULTON: ORIGINS OF HARPER'S FERRY CONSPIRACY

Most of the initial accounts of the Harper's Ferry rebellion contained little information beyond the who, what, when, and where of the story, with one exception. The Baltimore American *editor wrote about the origins of the conspiracy only one day after it occurred. Here is an excerpt from that article.*

Baltimore American, 18 October 1859

The principle [*sic*] originator of this short but bloody insurrection was, undoubtedly, Capt. John Brown, whose connection with scenes of violence in the Border warfare in Kansas then made his name familiarly notorious throughout the whole country. Brown made his first appearance in Harper's Ferry more than a year ago, accompanied by his two sons—all three of them assuming the name of Smith. He inquired about land in the vicinity, and made investigations as to the probability of finding ores there, and for some time boarded at Sandy Point, a mile east of the Ferry. After an absence of some months the elder Brown reappeared in the vicinity, and rented or leased a farm on the Maryland side, about four miles from the Ferry. They bought a large number of picks and spades, and this confirmed the belief that they intended to mine for ores. They were frequently seen in and about Harper's Ferry, but no suspicion seems to have existed that "Bill Smith" was Capt. Brown, or that he intended embarking any movement so desperate or extraordinary. Yet the development of the plot leaves no doubt that his visit to the Ferry and his lease on the farm were all parts of his preparations for insurrection which he supposed would be successful in exterminating Slavery in Maryland and Western Virginia.

Q.: PARTICULARS OF HARPER'S FERRY REBELLION

The following excerpts come from a New York Times *correspondent who reported from Harper's Ferry the day after the rebellion began.*

New York Times, 20 October 1859

THE HARPER'S FERRY REBELLION

Northern Abolitionists Apparently Implicated

Revelations of Captain Brown

From the Special Correspondent of the New York Times.
HARPER'S FERRY, Tuesday, October 18—P.M.

The excitement is subsiding into astonishment at the insane undertaking of the insurgents.

Many erroneous reports are flying over the country relative to the purpose of the fanatics, and the extent of their organization. I have sought information from reliable sources, and am able to give the reader of the TIMES an accurate account of the whole affair.

The name of JOHN BROWN is not unknown to the American public. It was he who became the scourge of Southern Kansas, and with his band of outlaws pillaged Kickapoo City. Since then he has not been heard from until now, when he turns up in a new quarter, but at his old game—not appreciating, however, the difference between an unprotected frontier village and a town in Virginia. . . .

To MR. MILLS, Master of the Armory, who was captured and kept in custody by BROWN, this ringleader said:

"We are all Abolitionists from the North; we come to take and release your slaves; our organization is large and must succeed; I suffered much in Kansas, and expect to suffer here in the cause of human freedom; Slaveholders I regard as robbers and murderers and I have sworn to abolish Slavery, and liberate my fellow man."

Such are the purposes declared by Brown himself to one of his prisoners. To your correspondent he stated, after his capture, that it was no part of his purpose to seize the public arms. He had arms and ammunition enough, furnished by the Massachusetts Emigrant Aid Society. He only intended to make the first demonstration at this point, when he expected to receive a rapid increase of allies from Abolitionists everywhere settled through Maryland and Virginia, sufficient to take possession of both States, with all of the negroes they could capture.

I asked if he did not expect to encounter the Federal troops.

"Not if I had followed up my plans. I intended to remain here but a few hours, but a lenient feeling towards the citizens led me into a parley with them as to compromise, and by prevarication on their part I was delayed until attacked and then in self-defence was forced to entrench myself." . . .

MR. WASHINGTON, who was confined with the other prisoners in the engine house and all of whom, it was feared, would be shot in the *mele*, reports that all the insurgents wished to surrender but BROWN; that he never quailed, but exhibited a coolness and courage seldom equaled. He ordered and arranged port-holes drilled in the wall with as much composure as if it had been an ordinary transaction of every-day business. During the firing he never faltered. He also says the prisoners were treated by BROWN with great consideration and kindness. . . .

Captain Brown had nearly $350 about him when wounded. His money is now in the Paymaster's strong box. He fell under two bayonet wounds—one in the groin and one in the breast—and four sabre-cuts on the head. During the fight he was supposed to be dead, or, doubtless, he would have been shot. He was not touched by a ball, and will probably recover.

It is not true that the Government funds were touched or the Pay-office interfered with.

Brown says he has no regrets to express, or apology to offer for his conduct. . . .

Gov. Wise, with two companies of troops, and Mr. Ould, United States District-Attorney for the District of Columbia, reached here a few moments ago. It is apprehended that Gov. Wise will try to hand the prisoners over to the State authorities for prosecution. Mr. Ould will take the necessary steps for their trial in the Federal Court of Virginia.

One white insurgent and one negro are now in Jefferson Jail. Five of them—four white and one black—were shot one mile above Harper's Ferry, and their bodies thrown into the Shenandoah (River). . . .

Too much praise cannot be awarded the managers of the Baltimore and Ohio Railroad, for the efficient manner in which they managed their trains and track, and prevented confusion or accident. Their magnificent bridge over the Potomac remains unhurt.

HENRY RAYMOND: JOHN BROWN AND THE VIRGINIA INSURRECTION

In likely anticipation of the political war of words to come, this New York Times *editorial identifies Brown as the leader of the Harper's Ferry insurrection and suggests that there is no connection between him and any political movement of the time.*

New York Times, 19 October 1859

The insurrection at Harper's Ferry, which startled the public yesterday morning, though sufficiently alarming at the outset, proves to have been but a short-lived affair. It was very speedily crushed by the formidable military forces brought against it from Washington, Baltimore, and Virginia—but, unhappily, not without serious loss of life. The parties actively engaged in it seem never to have numbered over fifty or sixty, though ten times that number were before the close of the affair induced or coerced into an apparent support of the movement. So far as appears, it was not the result of any combination among the slaves themselves, but was merely the explosion of a clumsy plot concocted by a single man, JOHN BROWN, of Kansas notoriety, with the aid of his two sons and one or two other accomplices. . . .

There seems to be no reason for believing that the plot had any extensive ramifications, or that any further danger is to be apprehended. Yet the affair can scarcely fail to startle the public mind in Virginia, and it may have the same effect as Brown's movements had in Missouri, and increase, largely and rapidly, the transfer of slaves from Virginia to the more Southern States. Every such outbreak, from whatever causes it may spring, quickens the public sense of the insecurity of slave property on the borders of the slaveholding States, and so tends to the removal southward of that frontier.

As a matter of course, the violent partisan prints will seek to make the most of the affair. But we see no reason for supposing that it had any connection whatever with any political movement, or that any party can with justice be held responsible for it. It seems to have been the work of a single man,—smarting under a sense of personal wrong, and insanely seeking to avenge them upon a whole community. He will probably pay the penalty of his rash insanity with his life, and leave, we trust, no inheritors of his passion or his fate.

THURLOW WEED: EDITORIAL—REFUTING DEMOCRATIC CLAIMS THAT REPUBLICANS ENCOURAGE INSURRECTIONS

In this editorial, in a Republican newspaper, the writer takes issue with the Democratic Party's claim that the new Republican Party is responsible for acts like those committed by John Brown at Harper's Ferry. Instead, this writer says that the Republican Party is devoted to only legal, peaceful, and constitutional measures to end slavery.

Albany Evening Journal, 20 October 1859

Yet its Democratic opponents have perniciously insisted that it was an Abolition Party, seeking to liberate the Slaves by fire and sword; have trumpeted this lie through their newspapers, shouted it in their public meetings, inserted it in their resolutions, reiterated it in their conversation, at home and abroad, in the streets, at the table and by the fireside, until ignorant, uneducated negro slaves at the South, having it thus dinned daily into their ears, by their masters, have come to believe it! . . . If there is now, as they assert, any wide spread conspiracy among the Slaves, Slaveholders themselves are its creators and fomenters. They madly and blindly endanger the safety of their own homes by their persistent political falsehoods!

Nor is it the blacks alone whom the Democratic Party encourages to deeds of violence. Within the past few years it has lent its sanction to lawless enterprises of every sort, Border Invasions, Filibuster Expeditions, Lynch Law to suppress discussion, brutality and bloodshed among Congressmen, violence at Elections, &c., thus ministering to the vilest passions, encouraging contempt for law, and resort to the bludgeon, the pistol and the bowie-knife. Here are the madman Brown, and his crazy crew, endangering the lives and property of innocent people by an insane outbreak. But who made Brown a madman by murdering his sons? Who taught that crazy crew to band together with arms in their hands, as the most effective way to accomplish political purposes? The Border Ruffians of Kansas and the Democratic Administration at Washington!

The classic fable relates that he who went out and sowed dragon's teeth suddenly found himself surrounded by a crop of armed men. Buchanan and Pierce have been sowing dragon's teeth seven years. Their encouragement of lawlessness and violence is hurrying one locality after another into scenes of anarchy, for which the only sure, speedy and permanent cure is the peaceful transfer, at the next election, of the reins of Government, from the imbecile hands that hold them, into the grasp of men who neither deal in mob violence themselves, nor will permit it to be attempted by others.

JOSEPH MEDILL: EDITORIAL—RESPONSIBILITY OF DEMOCRATIC PARTY AND *DRED SCOTT* DECISION FOR HARPER'S FERRY UPRISING

The following editorial, like the one above, is also from a Republican newspaper and shows how Republicans clearly assigned blame for Harper's Ferry on the Democratic Party. This editorial also shows how many people made connections between Harper's Ferry, the Dred Scott *decision, and other events that may have directly led to the Harper's Ferry massacre. It also moves beyond simple political criticisms to attack the institution of slavery itself and foreshadow events to come if slavery is not soon abolished.*

Chicago Daily Tribune, 22 October 1859

The late insurrection in Virginia, which has meant shivers of fear to the inmost fibre of every white man, woman and child in that State, and which will produce a panic throughout all slaveholding communities, is probably but the beginning of a series of like endeavors, which will horrify the country, if the present policy of the bogus Democratic party is pursued for another ten or twenty years. With the madness and recklessness of men bent upon their certain destruction, those engaged in promoting the slaveholding interest are filling the land with their clamor for more negroes, are weakening the defences of the institution by spreading it over an indefinite area, and are opposing with deadly bitterness every attempt of the humane and philanthropic to ward off the dangers which they are accumulating upon their heads. In all this they are assisted by the bogus Democratic Party. Utterly blind to or regardless of the impending crisis, they have, by their repeated outrages upon the rights and sensibilities of the North, by their breaches of solemn compacts, in the Kansas-Nebraska bill, by their mode of enforcing the Fugitive Slave Law, by their Kansas policy, by their Dred Scot decisions, and by their attempted revival of the infamous Slave-Trade, alienated their most powerful friends of the North, and have put to work bands of reckless and bloody men, like Brown and his confederates, who will shrink at nothing, stop at nothing in the gratification of their instincts of fanaticism and revenge. While all this has been going on, in spite of all repressive measures—the lash, the thumbscrew, the faggot and the blood-hounds—exercised without mercy, the slaves themselves have been steadily improving in intelligence and dangerous acquirements. A sense of their own degraded and oppressed condition is stealing upon them; men qualified by large admixtures of white blood in their veins, and by a preparatory schooling in tyranny and vice to be their leaders, are springing up; fugitives that have tasted in the Northern States or in Canada, the sweets of liberty, and who have learned the full hatefulness and atrocity of Slavery, are making their way back to the plantations for the instruction of their old companions; white men, who, like the leaders of the late revolt, have been goaded to insanity by the outrages perpetrated upon them by pro-slavery men at the outposts and in the citadel of the institution, are, we believe, busy with their nefarious schemes for the promotion of murder; and among the enslaved themselves we are told there is a growing spirit of insubordination that needs only an opportunity to break out into the fearful excesses which marked the revolution at St. Domingo. These things point to contingencies which no sane man can contemplate without a thrill of horror. They suggest scenes which we pray may never be enacted, terrible retribution which should be left to God alone. But if such a picture may be drawn, when the slave population numbers barely four millions and a half, what may we not fear, if the rule of the Democracy continues uninterrupted and the accompanying slave-breeding, slavery-extending, slave-whipping and slave-burning go on for twenty or fifty years more. At the end of this century—a period of only forty years, or half the time of our national existence—

the slaves of the United States will number *thirteen and a half millions*—a population four and a half times larger than that which fought the battles of the American Revolution and overpowered the most warlike and puissant nation of the earth! These people—these millions of "things without any rights which white men are bound to respect"—will not be "niggers" pure and simple. The work of amalgamation is going on. At this date, there is at least one mulatto for each democratic voter in all the South; and the well known propensities of those who fill the air with their cries in reprobation of the debasement of the white blood will continue the bleaching process which has been so inauspiciously commenced. Out of the thirteen millions, three millions will be the possessors of an Anglo-Saxon lineage on either the father's or the mother's side. In every one of them, the capabilities for all in the way of hate and revenge in which either Africans or Europeans ever indulge, will be fully developed!

We ask, if, in view of facts like these which come home fortified by the lessons of history and experience, it is not time for a reversal of the policy of the country on this everlasting Slavery question? Shall we encourage the Democracy in their attempt to re-open the Slave Trade, and thus add new and more fearful dangers to those which are incident to the presence of the servile race already within our borders? Shall we permit the taunts and opprobrious epithets which are hurled at the Republican party to prevent the doing all that may be done for the restriction of the institution within the area which it already curses? Shall we not put the policy of the false and fallen Democracy behind us, and by the encouragement of Emancipation in Kentucky, Missouri, Virginia, Maryland, and Delaware, and the deportation of the freed men to Liberia, Hayti, Central America and Jamaica, rescue the border slave States from the fate which threatens their Southern neighbors? Shall we not, by the work of educating and Christianizing the blacks everywhere, from Maine to Texas, prepare them for that life of independence for which their struggles will never cease? Shall we not as patriots, warned by the insurrections past, and those more terrible which loom up in the future, do whatever in us lies, for the riddance of the country, of that volcanic element, which, neglected, will carry arson, rape and murder wherever it breaks out in wrath? Let us unite in the endeavor to restore the old and safe policy of the country when the revolutionary patriots ruled it—patriots who foresaw the dangers which the late outbreak has made fearfully apparent. The Democratic policy is exploded. It is the policy of propagandism, which can have but one end, and that will be the bloodiest succession of tragedies that the world ever knew. The rights of humanity cannot always be disregarded. It is time for this nation to begin its preparations for retribution. Permit the Democracy to rule, and this Harper's Ferry blood is but the few falling drops which presage the burst.

AN ANONYMOUS REPORT: EDITORIAL—REPUBLICANS WHO SUPPORTED VIOLENCE IN KANSAS RESPONSIBLE FOR HARPER'S FERRY AFFAIR

This editorial, from a Democratic newspaper, also highlights the connections between the events in Kansas and the insurrection at Harper's Ferry. While this author is critical of the Republican Party, he is careful not to blame all Republicans for the violence but rather those who "applauded" and "instigated" violence in the Kansas Territory.

New Hampshire Patriot & State Gazette, 26 October 1859 (Concord)

The public mind throughout the country, during the past week, has been much agitated by the most deplorable events at Harper's Ferry, Va., an account of which we give in another part of this paper. The circumstances were of a nature to strongly attract public attention. A quiet community, in the night time, was startled by an insurrection in its very midst. The suddenness of the alarm, with the uncertainty of the nature and extent of the danger, at first paralyzed the people for any resistance, and the insurgents, being fully armed, gained possession of the place. But after a bloody conflict, resulting in the loss of twenty-one lives in all, the insurrection was quelled and order returned.

In this atrocious affair there were peculiar features to excite alarm, not only in the community where it occurred, but also throughout the country. Although the proposed object of it was the release of the slaves, yet it now clearly appears that they had no part in it. In fact, one of the first victims was a colored man, shot by the insurgents because he refused to join them. The chief actors, and by far the greater number, were white men. Neither was it a sudden outbreak, occasioned by some occurrence of the moment; but it was in pursuance of a plan deliberately considered and formed by men elsewhere, who had gone to that place for the very purpose of making preparations and carrying it into execution. These are the circumstances which render this insurrection of more than ordinary importance and deserving reflection.

Notwithstanding the melancholy result in the loss of so many lives, these events will not be without advantage to the country, if they shall serve to recall the public mind from prejudice and excitement to a clear and honest consideration of the dangerous tendencies of the pernicious doctrines which, during a few years past, have been so zealously taught and advocated by political leaders and partisan preachers here at the North. It is not a long time since not only on the stump, but even from the pulpit, "Sharpe's rifles" were recommended and applauded as the proper and best means for the relief of "bleeding Kansas." We then denounced those principles as deserving the severest condemnation, not more, certainly, on account of the circumstances of the particular case to which they were applied, than for their dangerous and fatal tendencies, if ever admitted as proper in practice. We could not admit violence or force as, in any case, a necessary or proper recourse, in this country, for the establishment of any political principles, or for relief from political evils. But we did not then expect so soon to see so striking a proof and illustration of the correctness of our views, as is now offered by these tragical events at Harper's Ferry. They are the natural and perfect fruit of the seed sown in Kansas. The instigator and leader at Harper's Ferry was Capt. John Brown of Kansas notoriety; his confederates here were his associates there, and the arms used were the very same "Sharpe's rifles" furnished for use in Kansas. It seems appropriate that it should have been so, and we may add, almost providential that these circumstances should thus concur to connect and identify the one transaction with the other. Gerrit Smith, in his letter to Brown enclosing funds to aid him in carrying into execution his nefarious schemes at Harper's Ferry, very truly and correctly calls it "Kansas work." It was, in principle, the same.

Those black republicans who have heretofore been so loud in their applause and instigation of the work of violence and bloodshed in Kansas, now seek to relieve themselves from the unfavorable consequences in the public mind of their recent "Kansas work" on another field, by stigmatizing Brown and his associates as fools and maniacs. It is true that extreme folly and madness are apparent in this Harper's Ferry affair; but that folly and madness were not so much error on their part with regard to the principle of the "Kansas work," as in the hopeless circumstances for success under which they undertook to carry it into practice. But in what position does this new view by these defenders of black republicanism, place that party? If Brown and his confederates were fools and madmen at Harper's Ferry, may they not have been such in Kansas also? And if so, who shall say how much of the wrong in that unfortunate territory is justly to be charged against those who were the instigators of these fools and madmen, and who placed in their hands the weapons for violence and bloodshed! . . .

Let us not be misunderstood. We do not intend to charge all the members of the black republican party as being responsible for this deplorable affair at Harper's Ferry. On the contrary, we know that most of them will denounce it in as strong terms as we do, and as it deserves. But we ask them to consider whether, if not the fair and natural consequence, it is not at least the probable effect of the principles and doctrine of arms and violence advocated by the black republican leaders for the relief of Kansas, and of the doctrine of "irrepressible conflict" which they are now urged to make the sum and substance of their political faith. For if such be their view of it, we know the people of this State will not support a party from whose principles or acts results so fatal, not only to the peace but even to the continuance of the Union, are in any degree likely to follow.

JOHN McLEAN: EDITORIAL—REPUBLICAN AGITATION IN KANSAS LEADS TO HARPER'S FERRY VIOLENCE

This editorial, also from a Democratic newspaper, links the Republicans to the Harper's Ferry incident and shows how the political debates about settling Kansas had implications for assigning the blame at Harper's Ferry.

Cincinnati Enquirer, 29 October 1859

During the Kansas Troubles of 1855, 1856 and 1857 the Republicans insisted that the Democratic party of the Union was responsible for every excess and every outrage that was committed in that Territory by excited and infuriated pro-slavery men. The "Kansas outrages" were their real political staple, and by it they came near electing a President in 1856. The Democrats contended that they had nothing to do with them, and were not responsible in any sense. But the Republicans insisted that the act of every pro-slavery man was the act of the Democratic party. Now, when an Abolitionist, who has graduated in the Kansas school, organizes a band for the fomenting of a slave insurrection in the South, and makes a murderous attack upon Harper's Ferry, and when it has been proven that he was backed up and sustained by money and arms obtained from Abolitionists and Republicans of the North, the latter think it very unjust that the whole organization should be held responsible for the conduct of Brown's band, which was imbued with their ideas, and which was seeking to carry them out. They don't like to have the same responsibility forced upon them that they put upon the Democrats about Kansas.

AMERICAN ANTI-SLAVERY SOCIETY: TRIAL AND LIKELY EXECUTION OF CAPTAIN JOHN BROWN

William Lloyd Garrison's abolitionist newspaper The Liberator *covered the Harper's Ferry insurrection thoroughly and widely reported the abolitionist response to Brown's death sentence. The passage below highlights the response made by the American Anti-Slavery Society to Brown's trial in Virginia and its assumed outcome—his execution.*

The Liberator, 25 November 1859 (Boston)

At a meeting of the Executive Committee of the American Anti-Slavery Society, held in Boston, Nov. 1st, the following Resolution was adopted: —

Resolved, That it is recommended to the friends of impartial freedom throughout the Free States, in case of the execution of Capt. John Brown, now on trial for his life in Virginia, to observe that tragical event ON THE DAY OF ITS OCCURRENCE, in such manner as by them may be deemed most appropriate in their various localities—whether by public meetings and addresses, the adoption of resolutions, private conferences, or any other justifiable mode of action—for the furtherance of the Anti-Slavery cause, and renewedly to consecrate themselves to the patriotic and Christian work of effecting the abolition of that most dangerous, unnatural, cruel and impious system of slavery, which is the fruitful source of all our sectional heart-burnings and conflicts, which powerfully and increasingly tends to promote servile insurrection and civil war, which cannot be more truly or more comprehensively described than as THE SUM OF ALL VILLANIEL, which is a burning disgrace and fearful curse to the whole country, and by the speedy extinction of which, alone, can the land be saved from violence, blood, and utter demoralization.

This recommendation has been widely copied by the press, and is favorably regarded in all directions. The Committee leaves the mode and hour of observance to local choice. It will be observed that their appeal is not to abolitionists in special, but to all who profess to deplore the existence of slavery, the great source of all our national troubles, perils and threatening judgments. The object of it is to make a strong moral demonstration that shall powerfully impress the South, and to gather up and concentrate the feelings and sympathies engendered by the occasion into a live thunderbolt, to be hurled with divine assistance at the head of the Colossal Iniquity of the land.

It is probable that a public meeting will be held in Boston on the evening of Dec. 2d, with reference to the tragic event of the day. Should the necessary arrangements be made, due notice will be given in the daily papers of the city.

In whatever form that event may be observed, it is suggested that contributions should then be taken up for the benefit of the suffering family of Capt. Brown and those of his slaughtered sons and associates, unless previously made.

AN ANONYMOUS REPORT: EXECUTION OF JOHN BROWN

The following account, written by a New York Tribune *reporter, offered firsthand observations of the last minutes of John Brown's life. The article appeared untitled.*

New York Tribune, 3 December 1859

The scaffold is approached. He alights from the wagon and ascends to the platform, which last sustains Old John Brown alive. There is no faltering in his step, but firmly and erect he stands amid the almost breathless lines of soldiery that surround him. With a graceful motion of his pinioned right arm, he takes the slouched hat from his head, and carelessly casts it upon the platform by his side. The cap is drawn over his eyes, and the rope adjusted about his neck. John Brown is ready to meet his God.

But what next? The military have yet to go through some senseless evolutions, and near ten minutes elapse before Gen. Taliaferro's chivalrous hosts are in their proper position, during which time John Brown stands with the cap drawn over his head, and the hangman's knot under his ear.

Each moment seems an hour, and some of the people, unable to restrain an expression of their sense of the outrage murmur "Shame!" "Shame!"

At last, the Virginia troops are arranged *a la mode.*

"Capt. Brown, you are not standing on the drop—will you come forward?" said the Sheriff.

"I can't see gentlemen," was the reply; "you must lead me."

The Sheriff led his prisoner forward to the centre of the drop.

"Shall I give you a handkerchief, and let you drop it as a signal?" inquired the Sheriff.

"No, I am ready at any time; but don't keep me waiting needlessly," was the reply.

A moment after, the Sheriff springs the latch—the drop falls—and the body of John Brown is suspended between heaven and earth. A few convulsive twitchings of the arms are observed. These cease after a moment. John Brown is dead.

The majesty of Virginia law and the executions of Virginia vengeance are now satisfied—but time alone will tell whether Virginia peace will be conserved by it.

The surgeon says he died easily—that the neck was not dislocated, but the spinal column was ruptured, and that his death was probably instantaneous. What is unusual in executions, (so I am informed, for this is the first I've ever witnessed) his legs were not drawn up by convulsive twitchings.

The body remained suspended about 38 minutes, and was then taken down and placed in the coffin.

JOHN BROWN: LAST WORDS OF JOHN BROWN—"I DIE ALONE"

Garrison's Liberator *printed Brown's last words in the paper's extensive coverage of his execution in an untitled article.*

The Liberator, 9 December 1859 (Boston)

The last words of Brown were understood to be:—"I die alone responsible for my own operations, and ask for no sympathy. I am satisfied in my own belief—but desire no other man to believe as I do, unless his conscience and philosophy approve. I am singly responsible for my own acts, good or bad. If right or wrong, the consequence rests only upon myself."

JOSEPH MEDILL: REPUBLICAN EDITORIAL ON JOHN BROWN'S EXECUTION

The following excerpts from two articles, the first from the Republican Chicago Daily Tribune, *the second from the Democratic* Cincinnati Enquirer, *show that both agree that John Brown should have been executed for the Harper's Ferry massacre.*

Chicago Daily Tribune, 2 December 1859

John Brown dies to-day! As Republicans, maintaining as we do, that neither individuals nor parties in the North have a right to interfere with slavery where it exists under the sanction of positive law in the States, we cannot say that he suffers unlawfully. The man's heroism which is as sublime as that of a martyr, his constancy to his convictions, his suffering, the disgraceful incidents of his trial, the poltroonery of those who will lead him forth to death, have excited throughout all the North strong feeling of sympathy in his behalf, but no where, within our knowledge, is the opinion entertained that he should not be held answerable, for the legal consequence of his act. As long as we are a part of the Union, consenting to the bond by which the States are bound together, supporting the constitution and the laws, and using the language and entertaining the sentiments of loyalty, we cannot join in the execration of the extreme penalty which the unfortunate and infatuated old man will suffer. We may question the wisdom of the method by which he is punished—may believe that Virginia would have added to her honor and confounded her enemies, by an act of clemency toward him and his associates—may condemn in unmeasured terms the cowardice and blood-thirstiness which her people have displayed—but when we question the right of a Sovereign State to inflict a penalty for so glaring and fatal an infraction of her laws, we are advocating disunion in its most objectionable form. For that we are not prepared. We would be glad to avert the axe which hangs over the old man's head, if persuasion and entreaty would do it; but we see no way under Heaven by which, doing our duty as law-abiding citizens, we could counsel the use of force for his rescue, or by which we could join in a crusade against those by whom he has been legally though hastily, and because hastily, shamefully, condemned!

JOHN McLEAN: DEMOCRATIC EDITORIAL ON JOHN BROWN'S EXECUTION

Cincinnati Enquirer, 3 December 1859

We rejoice that old BROWN has been hung. He was not only a murderer of innocent persons, but he attempted one of the greatest crimes against society—the stirring up of a servile and civil war. He has paid the penalty for his crimes, and we hope his fate may be a warning to all who might have felt inclined to imitate his aggressive conduct.

DAVID N. WHITE: EDITORIAL—REGRETTABLE NECESSITY OF JOHN BROWN'S EXECUTION

The following untitled editorial about John Brown's execution, from a Republican paper, shows that many Republicans who condemned Brown's actions at Harper's Ferry also considered him a hero. The insurrection that Brown led further showed how strongly people felt about the issue of slavery; it was not uncommon for Republicans and abolitionists to blame the system of slavery itself for Brown's actions, as seen in this editorial.

Pittsburgh Gazette, 3 December 1859

The immolation of John Brown was, in short, in accordance with the philosophy of slavery—*a necessity*. He had dared to act on the conviction of his life, and these settled principles of his were the only ones which such a man could entertain. He was too brave to have thought differently from what he did, and the same noble impulses which inculcated a love of Freedom and Right, impelled him constantly and irresistibly to the practical development of his theory. He has failed, according to the popular mode of calculating failure and success; but that his life and tragic death must of necessity constitute a failure, is a point too broad and high to be disposed of in this summary manner. We cannot but disapprove his mad and folly-stricken act, but the unselfishness of the deed; his moderation, when victorious, over the town which he captured; his spartan courage in defending himself and his fellows, and his sublime contempt of death while overborne and made the manacled tenant of a prison; his stern integrity in scorning the technicalities of the law, and his manliness *in all things*, will not be quickly forgotten; but rather a contemplation of this heroic old man's character will irresistibly compel thinking men to ask themselves whether it is John Brown, of Osawatomie, or the system of slavery which has failed in this conflict.

The execution of the old man at Charlestown yesterday, was a plain admission on the part of Slavery that they dare not spare a brave man's life, and that magnanimity is impossible to a system based on wrong and upheld by violence. History will do justice to the institution of Slavery and its uncompromising foe alike, when both are gone; and, in the meantime, the comparison which this affair provokes between the two, which none can clearly foresee, but enough of which is now plainly visible to change the popular judgment. Slavery in all the plenitude of its triumph and power is a failure; and old John Brown of Osawatomie has succeeded—Sampson-like—in dragging down the pillars of Slavery in his fall, and his victory is complete! While millions of prayers went up for the old martyr yesterday, so millions of curses were uttered against the hellish system which so mercilessly and ferociously cried out for his blood. Every heart in which a free spirit throbbed gave utterance to its pent-up agony in contemplating the enormities of this bloody institution—this sum of all villainies—in the dispensations of its power and the exactions of its bloody code.

NOTES

1. James C. Malin, "Identification of the Stranger at the Pottawatomie Massacre," *Kansas Historical Quarterly* 9, no. 1 (February 1940): 3–12.

2. Truman Nelson, *The Old Man John Brown at Harper's Ferry* (New York: Holt, Rinehart and Winston, 1973), 11–24.

3. "The Negro Insurrection: Origin and Objects of the Plot. Storming and Capturing of the Armory," *New York Times*, 19 October 1859.

4. Thomas Goodrich, *War to the Knife: Bleeding Kansas, 1854–1861* (Mechanicsburg, Pa.: Stackpole Books, 1998), 227.

5. "The Insurrection at Harper's Ferry," *New York Times*, 21 October 1859; "The Harper's Ferry Rebellion," *New York Times*, 20 October 1859.

6. "The Harper's Ferry Rebellion."

FURTHER READINGS

Finkelman, Paul. *His Soul Goes Marching On: Responses to John Brown and the Harper's Ferry Raid*. Charlottesville: University Press of Virginia, 1995.

Goodrich, Thomas. *War to the Knife: Bleeding Kansas, 1854–1861*. Mechanicsburg, Pa.: Stackpole Books, 1998.

Nelson, Truman. *The Old Man John Brown at Harper's Ferry*. New York: Holt, Rinehart and Winston, 1973.

4

ABRAHAM LINCOLN ELECTED PRESIDENT, 6 NOVEMBER 1860

Six months after John Brown was executed in Virginia for the raid on Harper's Ferry, the Republican convention was held in Chicago. Senator William Seward of New York, who was closely associated with the abolitionist movement, was not able to secure enough support to become the Republican presidential nominee. Republican Party leaders feared that his close association with the abolitionists would earn him the label of a radical and that would kill his chances of becoming president. After Seward's nomination was defeated, attention turned to Abraham Lincoln, an attorney in Illinois who gained national attention when he ran against and debated Illinois Senator Stephen Douglas in 1858. During those statewide political debates, Lincoln earned national newspaper attention even though he eventually lost to Douglas. Prior to his unsuccessful run for the U.S. Senate, Lincoln's only prior political experience at the federal level was as a member of the U.S. House of Representatives from Illinois. Lincoln was elected as a representative of the Whig Party but lost his bid for reelection in 1849, mostly because he had opposed the Mexican War. After that, Lincoln returned to Springfield, Illinois, to practice law.

Republican Party leaders considered Lincoln a moderate. And despite the national attention that he earned in 1858 in running against Douglas, not much was known about Lincoln's views on slavery. He secured the Republican presidential nomination at the Chicago Convention on 16 May 1860.

The Democratic Party, which convened in Charleston, South Carolina, in late April, was in a state of confusion. After fifty-seven ballots that did not produce a consensus candidate, the Democrats decided to reassemble in Baltimore six weeks later. Much of the difficulty the party faced in choosing a nominee had to do with divisions between Northern and Southern Democrats. The Northern Democrats wanted to elect Illinois Senator Stephen Douglas, but Southern Democrats opposed Douglas because he was instrumental in the defeat of the Lecompton Constitution (see Chapter 1). When the Democrats reconvened in Baltimore, the division was still strong. Eventually, as a result of the divisions between the Northern and Southern party constituencies, many of the delegates of the lower South walked out. This secured Douglas as the party nominee.

Upset by this outcome, the Southern Democrats held another convention of their own in Baltimore ten days later, and John Breckinridge of Kentucky emerged as their candidate. Breckinridge was President James Buchanan's vice president. He would run on a platform that focused on protecting the rights of slaveholders, which included allowing for the expansion of slavery into the territories and called for the repeal of state laws that contradicted the federal Fugitive Slave Law. The state laws typically granted escaped slaves their freedom, while the federal Fugitive Slave Law required escaped slaves to be returned to their masters.

Douglas's position on slave issues was not that different from Breckinridge's, but it placed the issue of slavery in the territories in the hands of the U.S. Supreme Court (based on its *Dred Scott* decision) and noted the divisions in the party in its platform: "Inasmuch as difference of opinion exists in the Democratic party as to the nature and extent of the powers of a Territorial Legislature and as to the powers and duties of Congress, under the Constitution of the United States, over the institution of slavery within the Territories, Resolved, that the Democratic party will abide by the decision of the Supreme Court of the United States upon these questions of Constitutional law." Douglas also supported enforcement of the Fugitive Slave Law.[1]

Lincoln's primary departure from the Democrats involved the issue of slavery in the territories—he opposed the expansion of slavery into the territories.

Later, John Bell of Tennessee also emerged as a candidate for the Constitutional Union Party. That party consisted of old members of the Whig Party who believed the Republican Party was becoming too influenced by radical factions. They formed the Constitutional Union Party and chose Bell as their candidate because he was a Southerner who supported slavery but who, like Lincoln, opposed its expansion into the territories. Bell was the secretary of war under Presidents Harrison and Tyler. The Constitutional Union Party refused to issue a platform for the 1860 election.

Lincoln's Democratic opponents, by fighting among themselves, largely ensured his victory in the fall election. This was often observed in the Democratic newspapers, particularly as the election drew close. By early November the *St. Paul Pioneer and Democrat*, which had staunchly supported Douglas, realized that Breckinridge would carry the South and that the only way to prevent an expansion of slavery and to reinforce Northern supremacy was to vote for Lincoln instead of Douglas.

The canvas is reduced, by indications which are prophetic both in their tenor and force, to a contest between Lincoln and a Free Code on the one hand, and Breckinridge and a Slave Code on the other. This is a result which all who cherish the peace and harmony of the Union must deplore; but, deplorable or not, it is a plain fact, which cannot be gainsaid or obliterated, and which should, therefore, be looked at and acted upon as such, frankly and manfully. And being a fact, the voice of the North, in the expression of its sentiments at the polls, will neither be feeble nor uncertain. A million majority will show the fidelity of the Northern masses to the instincts of their section, when these are appealed to by an issue which cannot be avoided or delayed.[2]

From May 1860 through December when South Carolina seceded from the Union, newspapers North and South spent a great deal of time detailing Lincoln's views on a variety of issues and painting a picture of Lincoln's character. The accounts of Lincoln's positions varied greatly. Republican newspapers generally asserted that Lincoln was a man who valued the sanctity of the Union above all and that he respected Southerners' rights to hold slaves in their own states. He opposed the expansion of slavery into the territories. Southern newspapers generally described Lincoln as a black Republican bent on eliminating slavery and disrespecting states' rights. Many Southern papers suggested that if Lincoln were elected, secession was the only option for them in response. Democratic papers in the North also warned of Southern secession if Lincoln were elected and supported the Southern idea that slaves would be incited to rebellion under a Republican administration. The Republican response was to dismiss threats of secession since the South had threatened it before.[3] A few Republican editors in trying to predict a worst-case scenario suggested that if secession did occur, it would only be by South Carolina and Mississippi and that no other Southern states would follow their lead.

Amid threats of secession and early predictions of a Lincoln victory, on 6 November 1860 the country finally voted. The results appeared in papers across the country, including the *New York Times*. The *Times'* headline declared "Astounding Triumph of Republicanism," then offered the following account of the election results:

The canvas for the Presidency of the United States terminated last evening, in all the States of the Union, under the revised regulation of Congress, passed in 1845, and the result, by the vote of New York, is placed beyond question at once. It elects ABRAHAM LINCOLN of Illinois, President, and HANNIBAL HAMLIN, of Maine, Vice-President of the United States, *for four years, from the 4th of March next, directly by the People*. These Republican candidates having a clear majority of the 303 Electoral votes of the 33 States, over all three of the opposing tickets. They receive, including MR. LINCOLN'S own State, from which the returns have not yet come, in the

New-England States	41
New-York	35
Pennsylvania	27
New-Jersey	7
And the Northwest	<u>61</u>
Total Electoral for LINCOLN	171

Being 19 over the required majority, without wasting the returns from the two Pacific States of Oregon and California.

The election, so far as the City and State of New-York are concerned, will probably stand, hereafter as one of the most remarkable in the political contests of the country; marked, as it is, by far the heaviest popular vote ever cast in the City, and by the sweeping and almost uniform Republican majorities in the country.

The State of Pennsylvania, which virtually decided her preference in October, has again thrown an overwhelming majority for the Republican candidates. And New-Jersey, after a sharp contest has, as usual in nearly all the Presidential elections, taken her place on the same side. The New-England majorities run up by tens of thousands.[4]

Lincoln had clearly won the presidency without obtaining a single Southern state electoral vote, but the Democrats retained control of Congress. Immediately after the results of the election were announced, the secession talk began with furor. As expected, South Carolina led the Southern states in realizing this threat on 20 December (which is detailed in Chapter 5). Both before and after South Carolina seceded, some Democratic newspapers both North and South, like the *Washington Intelligencer* in the District of Columbia and the *Memphis Appeal*, urged Southern citizens to give Lincoln a chance before moving toward secession.

The newspaper accounts that appear below provide some examples of Northern Democratic and Republican appeals to the public both before and after the election. They represent the most common views expressed in the politically divided Northern newspapers at the time.

AN ANONYMOUS REPORT: REPORT OF PREPARATIONS IN VIRGINIA TO PROTECT STATE IN EVENT OF LINCOLN'S ELECTION

Before the election the level of concern about a Lincoln victory was high in the South, as seen in this report of preemptive actions taken in Virginia.

Baltimore Sun, 29 October 1860

It has already been stated that at a democratic meeting held in Princess Anne county, Va., last week, resolutions of an important character were offered by Ex-Governor Wise and adopted with enthusiasm. The resolutions referred to are preceded by a long preamble. After reviewing the history of the progress and acts of the anti-slavery party at the North, the following conclusions are arrived at as the sense of the meeting:

1st. The election of Abraham Lincoln to the Presidency will be an open and official avowal by a popular majority of the North and of the nation that the past aggressions of black republicanism are right.

2d. That they are to be persisted in with great aggravation for the future.

3d. That the slave States shall not govern themselves in respect to their own property in their own limits, but that, whilst territories are to be allowed to prohibit slavery in their limits, the States will not be permitted to protect it in peace in theirs.

4th. That the slave States and their citizens are to be coerced to submission. And such aggression as this amounts to *actual war*. It is proclaimed already, and awaits only the election for the power and the means to coerce submission.

The election will give it both. —And it is the worse for coming all the panoply of a mere *form* of right. The *form* is the *election*—and the *election* will be *constitutional*. —that is to be the pore out of which the courage of resistance is to ooze. The form of the election may be constitutional, but its intent and purpose is our invasion and a violent infraction of the constitution. No matter what may be the form, the substance is aggression—the aggression is to us vital! If we submit to it, we are at once subjugated, and if we intend to resist, it is time we were prepared for the conflict, which we cannot repress but may repel. In view of these issues we deliberately resolve: . . .

That the moment the election returns are made known and it is ascertained that Abraham Lincoln is elected President of the United States, the general council of this county shall select one delegate from each district to meet such delegates as may be appointed by other counties to assemble in convention at Richmond, to determine upon measures for protecting our own safety and honor as a people for defending the constitution of the United States, for saving our rights in the Union, and for obtaining the sanction of the sovereign State of Virginia.

A. S. ABELL: VOTE FOR LINCOLN RISKS SOUTHERN SECESSION

The following article not only urges the citizens of Baltimore to vote but also suggests that if they choose to vote for Lincoln, then they may be giving the South just cause for secession. Maryland was a slave state, and the Baltimore Sun *was a Democratic paper.*

Baltimore Sun, 6 November 1860

It only remains for us this morning to urge upon every citizen the importance of depositing his vote to-day and with a judicious selection of the candidates for whom that vote is given. It is a duty we owe to ourselves, and to that section of territory with which we are identified, to act in defense of its rights and institutions. This is not sectionalism. When an attack becomes sectional the defense is in degree *necessarily so*—not from choice, but because the section assailed has no choice. The South is not the aggressor in the startling crisis which may be evoked this day, and whatever her citizens may do in their extremity will be done only in self-defense. There is no spirit of disunion or of secession in the South; the action of the North is to provoke the necessity for secession as an inevitably defensive measure, or to humiliate the South by submission to an avowed adversary. We trust that such an alternative may not be presented, and that the crisis we have so much cause to apprehend may be averted.

Pending the issue let us all bear in mind the vast and incalculable importance of the stake. The destruction of this Union is an act so momentous, and involves a calamity so deplorable, that the deed which provokes it will be the most fearful and heinous public crime we can conceive of. The wretches guilty of such a deed deserve to suffer the penalty of an ignominious death as traitors to their country and to humanity. Its consequences, far-reaching, may entail disaster, oppression, strike and anarchy utterly beyond conception, throughout the land and into remote posterity. The progress of Christianity, civilization, science and art may be arrested entirely for a cycle of years, or at least retarded, and society demoralized proportionately for a lengthened period. None can foresee the consequences or anticipate the evils which a blind and furious fanaticism may evoke, while the history of the past teaches us how terrible they have been and may be again.

But whatever may be the issue of this day, it behooves us all to act wisely and prudently; not to encounter fanaticism with fanaticism, or to mock the usurper and destroyer with a hasty ruin as the empty honor of his conquest. A burning Moscow may challenge our admiration as the device of a semi-civilized race, by which to thwart and blast the successes of a proud, daring, all-conquering invader. But we have a civilization to vindicate; an honorable reputation to maintain; a proud and chivalric self-respect to asset in the name and behalf of Southern rights and institutions. Let us in all things, then, meet the issue with a calm and dignified self-reliance; and in so doing, whatsoever may be required at our hands, we shall be prepared to do it well, energetically, bravely and efficiently.

In the duty we have to perform to-day, we expect, confidently, under the wholesome discipline of an active and impartial police, the universal prevalence of peace and good order. There is no reason why it should not be so. —Every legal voter should be free to deposit this vote unmolested, and no man should be suffered to poll an illegal vote. But the exercising of the right or resistance to the wrong may be done decently and in order. There will be some brawlers and braggarts and bullies ready for anything like disorder; but the police will, doubtless, deal promptly and effectively with these. The numbers of precincts offers ample accommodations for all, and every legal voter will have the opportunity to deposit his vote without conflict with his neighbor. So let us do our duty, and leave the immediate result to be shaped in the cool and deliberate counsels of the future.

AN ANONYMOUS REPORT: DOUGLAS VOTE POINTLESS GIVEN SOUTHERN REFUSAL TO SUPPORT DEMOCRATIC NOMINEE

The Republican Chicago Tribune *also urged its readers to vote and contended, like many papers did closer to the election, that a vote for Democrat Stephen Douglas would be a throwaway vote, given the strong division in the Democratic Party and the Southern intentions to vote for Breckinridge.*

Chicago Tribune, 6 November 1860

Abraham Lincoln and Stephen A. Douglas are both Illinoisans, and both candidates for the Presidency. The Republicans and the Douglas Democracy have conferred a high honor upon our State. It is now apparent to all intelligent men that DOUGLAS CANNOT BE ELECTED AND THAT LINCOLN CAN. We ask Douglas men not to be so foolish as to throw away their votes. VOTE FOR LINCOLN, AND DO YOUR BEST TO SECURE AN ILLINOIS PRESIDENT. Make it the proud boast of Illinois that our youthful State has furnished a ruler for this might nation.

HENRY RAYMOND: NEWSPAPERS SERVE INTENSE PUBLIC INTEREST IN CURRENT ELECTION

The following New York Times *column gives a glimpse of how widely and intensely the public watched the election of 1860 and notes the importance of the newspaper to the process of reporting the results.*

New York Times, 7 November 1860

If any one doubted last evening that the telegraph wires were big with the fate of this glorious Union, a walk in the vicinity of the different newspaper offices would have speedily convinced him to the contrary. Such crowds as were gathered around the doors of the TIMES, *Tribune* and *Herald* are only to be seen on these quadrennial occasions of the country's salvation or destruction. Even our mundane neighbor suffered from a temporary deluge of humanity, and crowds rushed to read the latest entries in the Day Book. The publication offices were soon filled; "happy thou," thought the crowd outside, who have gained admittance to the inner mysteries. . . . Anxious to see as well as to hear, the outside crowd flattened their noses painfully against the panes—one would have imagined that they thought to smell out the returns. They climbed on each others shoulders and stood on each other's heads in a vain attempt to peer in at the second story windows. Curiosity, apprehension, exultation— these and all other emotions, were as plainly stamped on each individual countenance as the Eagle on a quarter. . . . These emotions found expression whenever returns came in from a Ward or a County. There were cheers and groans and huzzas and hisses. And until the night had grown old and morning was born, the clamorous crowd demanded more news and later intelligence. They demanded to know the fate of the Union before daybreak, and many of them learnt it before they went home. But it is questionable whether the majority of them would find out during the coming Presidential term whether the country were saved or lost, if it were not for the information supplied by their party newspaper.

AN ANONYMOUS REPORT: "VICTORY! VICTORY!"—REPUBLICAN NEWSPAPER REPORTS LINCOLN'S ELECTION

The day after the election the Republican Chicago Tribune *carried this short news item next to articles with headlines such as "Honest Old Abe Elected" and "Republicanism Triumphant over Fraud, Fusion, Cotton, Disunion and Treason."*

Chicago Tribune, 7 November 1860

The Republic renews its ancient glories. The great ideas which led to the Revolution—which first found utterance in the Declaration of Independence, and which were afterwards embodied in practical form in the Federal Constitution, still live in the hearts of the American people. The maxims of Jefferson, of Franklin, of Adams, of Madison, of Clay and of Jackson, survive. The patriotism which guided their every act has been transmitted to the present generation. There is hope yet for freedom, for honesty, for purity. Let distrust and apprehension be banished forever. Let the patriot fan the flame which ascends now from the Altar of his country's freedom. Let the people shout. The battle has been fought and the victory won. Hail! All hail!!

We have not time at the late hour at which our paper goes to press to speak in detail. It is enough to say that the triumph is a glorious one—that Abraham Lincoln is President elect of this great Republic. And let all the people say Amen!

A. S. ABELL: ELECTION OF LINCOLN EXHIBITS NORTHERN HOSTILITY TOWARD SOUTH

The Democratic Baltimore Sun *offers sympathy for the Southern states in the result of the presidential election. This editorial suggests that the North clearly showed its hostility toward the South and the federal Constitution by voting Lincoln into the presidency.*

Baltimore Sun, 9 November 1860

This is the theme of every tongue just now, and yet a most unwelcome one to use. No man, however, with any degree of intelligence, has observed the steady progress of northern fanaticism during the past ten or twelve years without the conviction that such an event as we now contemplate in its fulfillment was inevitable. Eight years ago, when Mr. Pierce was elected, we could scarcely realize the possibility of a republican and sectional President; yet the inevitable thing was then apparent, when Mr. Buchanan overcame Fremont, the danger was more palpable and near; but we took scarcely the full measure of it, because it was not so imminent as it has been of late. When the election was over, however, even then men breathed freer, as with a great sense of relief.

As the day of the late election drew near, it was with a painful conviction upon all men's minds throughout the South, that the sectional sentiment of the North would triumph in the election of the candidate selected as its representative; and the result has proved the reality of that conviction. The fact is now beyond peradventure. And an exclusively sectional candidate has been elected to the chief magistracy of the country. He is expected to take the reins of government and rule with an authority over the people of sovereign States, who reject his principles and avowed policy as in direct conflict with their constitutions, rights, their institutions, their interests, their equality in the general confederacy, their honor, dignity, and self-respect.

In the very flush of such an offensive triumph as this, when in her perplexity the South is at a loss what to do for her own safety, she is taunted with the purpose of treason, and her citizens who talk of escaping from consequences which they believe threaten her integrity, are already branded as traitors by the minions of this newly fledged and unhallowed power. The treason is not with the South. In her federal compact she was supposed to be secure in constitutional rights and the perfect equality of the States. But she is taught by bitter experience, under the exercise of a mere popular majority in one section of the Union, that she may be reduced and subjugated at will.

It is in this extremity, her obvious duty to consider wisely, temperately and fearlessly the crisis of the hour, and to act decidedly and harmoniously. The treachery which assails her is not of her provoking. She has mediated no wrong against the North, has devised no aggression, and sanctified no crusade against her fellow-citizens. The North has originated, nursed, cherished, and finally invested with the powers of government the hostile spirit of disloyalty to the constitution. And the issue thus presented to the acceptance of the South, while it denies the right to escape from her avowed adversary, and stigmatizes such a purpose as treason, leaves her no alternative but submission.

Under all these circumstances, and which we are by no means disposed to consider in all their odiousness of character, the South needs the utmost measure of forbearance, and of such devotion to the Union as she has never in all her trials been required to exercise before, to govern and guide her in this emergency. The act of deliberate secession, and which has been ascribed to her as a thing of choice, will be, should the necessity ever occur, most repugnant to her. And it was to avert an apparent necessity which threatened her that the man, who of all others has been stigmatized as the embodiment of secession, has within the past month or two traversed the North and made appeal after appeal to the reason, intelligence and patriotism of his fellow-citizens there; but, unfortunately, so far as the result is indicative, without avail.

We can but insist, therefore, at such a crisis as this, upon common decency in the treatment of the States and people occupying so anomalous a position as the South must do, in the Union or out of it. In the Union she must remain for a time, at least, subject to a power she can neither recognize civilly, socially nor politically. And in all that time, with an uncertain future before her, must live on the hope of her emancipation from the most odious thralldom that could be inflicted upon her. Out of the Union she could only exist burdened with regret as an unwilling separatist, having chosen an undesirable political independence because her first choice has been rudely and offensively denied to her, with an equality of the rights and honors of confederation.

AN ANONYMOUS REPORT: EXCERPTS FROM OTHER NEWSPAPERS—WHAT IS BEING SAID OF ELECTION RESULT

Two days after the election, the Republican Boston Daily Advertiser *printed the following excerpts about the results from three New York newspapers, the Republican* New York Times *and* New York Herald *and the Democratic* Journal of Commerce.

Boston Daily Advertiser, 8 November 1860

The New York Times of yesterday, announcing Lincoln's election, remarks upon it as follows:—

"This election will inaugurate a marked and most important change in the administration of the government. The policy of extending slavery, and increasing its political power, will now be checked. The slave interest will no longer impose its claims and its law upon the federal government. The Constitution will no longer be regarded as a mere instrument for fortifying and increasing slavery. The African slave trade will not be reopened, and more vigorous and effective measures will be taken for its suppression. But above all, we shall have established at Washington a rule of honesty and patriotism, in place of the corruption, imbecility and intrigue which have controlled our public councils for the last few years. It is quite time we had a change in these respects. The republicans now have it in their power to lay the basis for the most useful, popular and permanent administration the country has seen for a long time. But they must not conceal from themselves the obstacles which they will be compelled to encounter." The New York Herald briefly notices the event in the following remarks, the quiet, not to my hopeful tone of which is in strong contrast to the violent declaration and dismal prophecies of that paper on the morning before:—

"We have neither space nor time this morning to comment at length upon this great and momentous revolution in our political affairs. The conservatives, who still believe in the strength of the Union, will be comforted with the assurance of an anti-republican majority in both houses of Congress. . . . Upon the Congressional issue the city of New York has dis-

charged her duty handsomely. We refer the reader to our copious details upon the subject, elsewhere in this paper. We begin with this day a new epoch in the political history of the United States. The republican party have crossed the Rubicon. Are our anxieties at an end, or are our troubles only about to begin? We cannot answer until we shall have heard from the Legislature of South Carolina touching the test question of Lincoln's election."

The Journal of Commerce also surrenders very quietly and with a hopeful allusion to the sea-going qualities of the ship of state. Elsewhere we are glad to record the very handsome acknowledgement by that paper that its friends were beaten in a "fair fight:"—

"We have met the enemy, and we are theirs. Such at least are the unmistakable indications. The splendid democratic-union majority of 29,000 in this city has doubtless been overbourne by the avalanche of black republicanism from the middle, Western and Northern parts of the State; and if so, we have nothing to do but to submit, with the best grace we can. The vote of the Empire State, added to those of other States which may be considered for sure for Lincoln, make it all but certain that he will be our next President. We regret it deeply—profoundly; not so much on our own account, as because of the dangers it will bring upon the country. Heaven grant that she may survive them all. She has rode out many a storm, and may ride out this. One consolation remains to us as conservative men, viz, that we have both Houses of Congress. This will check any wayward fancies that may seize the Executive, under the pressure of his abolition advisers or otherwise. Let us hope for the best."

AN ANONYMOUS REPORT: NEWS OF SOUTHERN REACTION TO LINCOLN'S ELECTION

Just days after it was clear that Lincoln had won the election, Northern newspapers were filled with reports from the Southern papers about the heightened state of affairs in the slave states.

Baltimore Sun, 9 November 1860

The election of Lincoln, as has already been announced by telegraph, has created a profound sensation all through the South. "Minute Men" are forming in several of the slave States. In Charleston they are equipping a "volunteer rifle corps" of one hundred young men, who are being

instructed in Hardie's tactics. They will tender their services to the Governor for any emergency. The feeling displayed in the city of Columbia, the capital of North Carolina, on Monday night before election, has already been briefly referred to.

AN ANONYMOUS REPORT: ECONOMIC CONSEQUENCES OF REPUBLICAN VICTORY

This article includes part of a story that appeared in a Rochester, New York, newspaper and focuses on the immediate, perceived economic impact of Lincoln's election win.

Baltimore Sun, 10 November 1860

The journals are still so absorbed in the perilous crisis through which the country is passing, that they can attract attention to nothing else. All acknowledge the secession passion is raging wilder. Even the blind republican journals now see and own up at last. Two hundred million dollars, it is calculated, is already the cost of Lincoln's election, in the fall in the value of flour, wheat, cotton, wool, corn, State securities, railroad and bank stocks, real estate and other property. The Rochester (N.Y.) Union says:

"The recent decline in wool has affected many parties in this country, who held large stocks, and among them were some of our own citizens. The decline is said to be fully ten cents per pound, and forced sales would reduce it to fifteen cents, no insignificant proportion of first cost. The indications are not favorable for an improvement. The eastern manufactories are now stopping, and many of them will not operate for six months to come, or only on limited time. The impression appears to be that wool holders must submit to a decline of about 25 per cent, on the cost of the article when it was taken in from the growers. The decline will hurt many who hold large stocks."

AN ANONYMOUS REPORT: GROWING LIKELIHOOD OF SOUTHERN SECESSION

This article offers readers a glimpse of the secession rhetoric that dominated the postelection discussion. It was clear to a majority of Northern newspaper editors that secession was becoming inevitable after Lincoln won the 1860 election.

Baltimore Sun, 10 November 1860

Our Southern exchanges continue to teem with accounts of the excitement produced at Lincoln's election, the speeches of prominent men, and the various incidents accompanying an uneasy and painful state of the public mind. At the serenade given the Hon. W. W. Boyce, a member of Congress from South Carolina, in that State, on Wednesday evening, he spoke as follows:

Fellow-Citizens:—I thank you for this manifestation of your kindness. I attribute it to the deep interest that you take in the present condition of our public affairs; and, indeed, the condition of our country is such as to demand the earnest consideration of every lover of his country. In all human probability, our enemies, the black republican party, has now at this moment elected the President of the United States. From this fact arises the greatest question which the people of South Carolina can probably be called upon to decide: one which I hope we will consider and determine among ourselves in a spirit of fraternal kindness, and with a due allowance for the opinions of all, whatever these opinions may be. —My judgment is that the South cannot submit to that election, because Lincoln is the *nominee of a sectional party*—a party confined altogether to the Northern States. And it was not such a union as this that our ancestors entered into. It was not into a union where one section dominated over another that Washington, Madison, Rutledge and other great men of the South entered; but if there were no other objections, this alone would be sufficient:—*Why should we continue in a Union where we are about to be subordinate to another section?*

WILLIAM LLOYD GARRISON: DESPITE SECESSION THREAT, NORTH SHOULD NOT SUBMIT TO SOUTHERN DEMANDS

William Lloyd Garrison's abolitionist newspaper encouraged Republicans not to cave to Southern demands under threats of secession. By using quotes from Lincoln he tries to illustrate that Southern perceptions of Lincoln are not only wrong but, he thinks, crazy. Garrison says the Southern states intentionally misrepresented Lincoln's political platform to bully the North into submitting to Southern demands.

The Liberator, 16 November 1860 (Boston)

The election of the Republican candidate, Abraham Lincoln, to the Presidency of the United States, has operated upon the whole slaveholding South in a manner indicative of the torments of the damned. The brutal dastards and bloody-minded tyrants, who have so long ruled the country with impunity, are now furiously foaming at the mouth, gnawing their tongues for pain, indulging in the most horrid blasphemies, uttering the wildest threats, and avowing the most treasonable designs. Their passions, "set on fire of hell," are leading them into every kind of excess, and they are inspired by a demoniacal phrenzy. To the South is strikingly applicable, at this hour, the language of the Revelator:—"Babylon is fallen, is fallen, and is become the habitation of devils, and the hold of every foul spirit, and a cage of every unclean and hateful bird. Her sins have reached unto heaven, and God hath remembered her inequities. In the cup which she hath filled, fill to her double. In her is found the blood of prophets and of saints. How much she hath glorified herself, and lived deliciously, so much torment and sorrow give her. Therefore shall her plagues come in one day, death and mourning, and famine; and she shall be utterly burned with fire; for strong is the Lord God who judgeth her." So much for dealing in "slaves and souls of men," trampling upon all human rights, defying God and his eternal law, and giving unlimited indulgence to ever sensual and devilish inclination! "Rejoice over her, thou heaven, and ye holy apostles and prophets; for God hath judged the great whore, which did corrupt the earth with her fornication, and hath avenged the blood of his servants at her hand."

Never has the truth of the ancient proverb, "Whom the gods intend to destroy, they first make mad," been more signally illustrated than in the present condition of the Southern slaveholders. They are insane from their fears, their guilty forebodings, their lust of power and rule, their hatred of free institutions, their consciousness of merited judgments; so that they may be properly classed with the inmates of a lunatic asylum. Their dread of Mr. Lincoln, of his administration, of the Republican party, demonstrates their insanity. In vain does Mr. Lincoln tell them, "I do not now, nor ever did, stand in favor of the unconditional repeal of the Fugitive Slave Law"—"I do not now, nor ever did, stand pledged against he [*sic*] admission of any more Slave States into the Union"—"I do not stand pledged to the abolition of slavery in the District of Columbia"—"I do not stand pledged to the prohibition of the slave trade between the different States"—"they rave just as fiercely as though he were another John Brown, armed for Southern invasion and universal emancipation! In vain does the Republican party present but one point of antagonism to slavery—to wit, no more territorial expansion—and exhibit the utmost cautiousness not to give offence in any other direction—and make itself hoarse in uttering professions of loyalty to the Constitution and the Union—still, they protest that its designs are infernal, and for them there is "sleep no more"! Are not these the signs of a demented people?

Nevertheless, there is "method" in their madness. In their wildest paroxyams, they know precisely how far to proceed. Will they secede from the Union? Will they jump into the Atlantic? Will they conflagrate their own dwellings, cut their own throats, and enable their slaves to rise in successful insurrection? Perhaps they will—probably they will not! By their bullying and raving, they have many times frightened the North into a base submission of their demands and they expect to do it again. Will they succeed?

NOTES

1. Donald Bruce Johnson, *National Party Platforms*, vol. 1, *1840–1956*, rev. ed. (Urbana: University of Illinois Press, 1978), 30–31.

2. *St. Paul Pioneer and Democrat*, 2 November 1860.

3. Lorman Ratner and Dwight L. Teeter, Jr., *Fanatics and Fire-eaters: Newspapers and the Coming of the Civil War* (Urbana: University of Illinois Press, 2003).

4. "Astounding Triumph of Republicanism," *New York Times*, 7 November 1860.

FURTHER READINGS

Donald, David H. *Lincoln*. New York: Simon & Schuster, 1996.

Lincoln, Abraham. *Abraham Lincoln: Speeches and Writings, 1859–1865*. Ed. Donald E. Fehrenbacher. New York: Library of America, 1989.

Nicolay, John G., and Hay, John (Eds.). *Complete Works of Abraham Lincoln*. Vol. 9. New York: F. D. Tandy Co., 1905.

Stephenson, Nathaniel W. *Abraham Lincoln and the Union: A Chronicle of the Embattled North*. New Haven, Conn.: Yale University Press, 1921.

5

SOUTHERN SECESSION, 1860–1861

Less than a week after news of Lincoln's win, the South Carolina legislature unanimously voted to hold a state convention to consider the question of secession. On 5 December 1860, President James Buchanan, who would not turn over his office to Lincoln until 4 March 1861, gave his annual message to Congress and announced that all of the federal officers in the state of South Carolina had resigned. According to accounts of the president's message in the *Baltimore Sun*: "The President does not recognize the right of secession, but as revolution; at the same time he recognizes no authority in the constitution to make war upon or coerce a State with a view to compel her to remain in the Union." The article continues:

> The President comments upon the legislation of Northern States, hostile to the rights of the South, and thinks that the South demands only justice in asking the repeal of such legislation. Should the repeal of these offensive laws be refused, the President thinks that such refusal would constitute a willful hostility to Southern rights, and justify the withdrawal of the Southern States, after having exhausted all constitutional means of redress. The election of Mr. Lincoln and the present aspect of republicanism is not deemed sufficient cause for secession; the President thinks the South should wait the overt act.
>
> Such legislation is recommended to Congress with a view to the amendment of the constitution on the subject of slavery as the President confidently believes would lead to a final adjustment of this vexed issue, and the restoration of peace and union.[1]

The president's call fit the general Democratic perspective on secession—that the antagonistic North should follow federal law and stop antagonizing the slave states and that the South should give Lincoln a chance and not secede prematurely. The Republican perspective discouraged any Northern concessions to the South and suggested that states such as South Carolina had been waiting for the right time to secede. Many Republicans viewed the action of secession as an act of war; nearly all of them considered it treason against the Union. Most Republicans did not think the Constitution gave a state the right to secede.

As debate about the issue raged for weeks after the election, it was clear by early December that South Carolina would secede. On 20 December 1860 a resolution for secession was approved, and South Carolina was out of the Union. By January 1861 Mississippi, Florida, Alabama, Georgia, and Louisiana followed suit. On 9 February, delegates from the seceded states formed the Confederate States of America and chose Jefferson Davis, the U.S. senator from Mississippi, to become the Confederate president. Davis was inaugurated on 18 February 1861.

Lincoln assumed the office of the U.S. president on 4 March 1861. Between the inauguration of Davis and the inauguration of Lincoln, Texas seceded and joined the Confederacy. In the months to come, four other states would leave the Union: Virginia in April, Arkansas and North Carolina in May, and Tennessee in June.

Northern press coverage of the secession movements, beginning immediately after the 1860 election, focused on the Democratic and Republican positions on the issue. South Carolina received the most attention and criticism from the Northern press, particularly the Republican papers, for taking the lead in "disunion." Nearly every newspaper, no matter what its political affiliation, correctly predicted that the country was headed for civil war. On 12 April 1861 that prediction came true when South Carolina militiamen fired on the federal Fort Sumter in Charleston and initiated the war.

AN ANONYMOUS REPORT: SOUTH CAROLINA PREPARATIONS FOR POSSIBLE LINCOLN ELECTION

These two articles from the Baltimore Sun, *which appeared back to back, show how South Carolina began preparing for secession even before Lincoln was elected. Both of these stories appeared one day before the election, which was held on 6 November 1860.*

Baltimore Sun, 7 November 1860

Meeting of the Legislature—Message of the Governor—Immediate Secession Recommended in Case of Lincoln's Election—Ten Thousand Volunteers to Be Enrolled—Fifty Thousand Georgians Pledged to Assist South Carolina, &c.

COLUMBIA, S.C., November 5, 1860. —The Legislature met to-day. There is an evident disposition to act instead of talk. The Legislature organized, and received the Governor's message. Therein he suggests that the Legislature should, in view of the threatening aspect of affairs, remain in session, and take action to prepare the State for the crisis. He earnestly recommends, in case Lincoln is elected, an immediate call of a convention to determine the mode and measure of redress. He says he, individually, considers secession the only alternative left; that the indications show the secession of South Carolina would in-

stantly bring about that of the entire South; and that if the general government attempts coercion, our solemn duty is to meet force by force; and he promises to carry out the convention's decision during the remainder of his term, regardless of hazard. He recommends military reorganization, and that every man between the ages of eighteen and forty-five, should be armed by the State with the most efficient weapons of modern warfare. He recommends raising immediately ten thousand volunteers, to be in readiness at the shortest notice, with other preparations. We may, says the Governor, trust our cause to the keeping of the Supreme Disposer of events. . . .

There is the greatest enthusiasm for a Southern confederacy here. Every hat has a cockade, and all minds are resolved to fight.

AN ANONYMOUS REPORT: MEETING OF SOUTH CAROLINA OFFICIALS

This report appeared untitled.

Baltimore Sun, 7 November 1860

COLUMBIA, Nov. 5.—12 P.M.—A caucus was held to-night, at which it was ascertained that a large majority of the Legislature are for immediate secession by State action.

An immense crowd assembled this evening at the Congress House and serenaded Senator Chesnut. He spoke long and eloquently declaring the last hope of the Union gone and resistance unavoidable. The speech was enthusiastically received, because Mr. Chesnut was hitherto uncommitted.

It is rumored that Senator Hammond will follow suit.

Messrs. Benham, Rhett, ex-Governor Adams and others spoke also in the same strain.

AN ANONYMOUS REPORT: NORTHERN NEWSPAPER VIEWS SOUTH CAROLINA SECESSION AS "ALL RANT"

In Lincoln's hometown of Springfield, Illinois, one newspaper had the following thought on South Carolina's secession, which it printed in this untitled commentary.

Illlinois State Journal, 31 December 1860 (Springfield)

South Carolina has, and the other cotton States are about to pass seceding resolutions, professedly because they cannot get their rights in this Union. We are told by some Southern men, and a great many Northern ones, that the North has behaved so badly that the cotton States cannot live with us. Now, this is all rant. The Personal Liberty bills and the violation of the Fugitive Slave law have about as much to do with this cotton stampede as the banking laws of Canada, or the violation of a city ordinance in Springfield.

They make the slavery question the pretext, but not the cause for disunion. They do not want to leave the Union because the laws protecting slavery are not numerous enough, or strong enough, or are not faithfully enforced. They want to build up a great Southern Confederacy, "resting," as they say, "on the solid substratum of African slavery." To Southern statesmen, the picture of such a confederacy is one of beauty and grandeur. They seem to imagine that their progress is retarded by their connection with free communities, and that once released from the clogs of free society, they will outstrip all the nations of the earth in the race of progress.

CHARLES HALE: HOW SOUTH CAROLINIANS VIEW THE NORTH

The excerpts from this untitled editorial in the Boston Daily Advertiser, *which appeared the same day that South Carolina seceded, suggests that South Carolinians believe the North to be ruled by fanatics who want slavery abolished. It highlights comments from a Charleston, South Carolina, judge who says that South Carolina had been interested in secession for a while but was waiting to do so until it became clear to the other Southern states that the entire North was headed down the path of abolition.*

Boston Daily Advertiser, 20 December 1860

It is really so seldom that any coherent account is given of what the original secessionists think and want, that any fresh light thrown upon their opinions and sentiments never fails to excite our interest. Articles in the *Charleston Mercury*, speeches from Mr. Rhett or from Messrs. Iverson and Wigfall, and addresses like that of Hon. Howell Cobb, are either too wild or too indefinite. We look with a curiosity which is seldom gratified, for a distinct statement from some clear headed and cool secessionist of what he really believes about the North, and fears from it. Judge Magrath of Charleston is such a man, and in his letter in reply to Mr. Richard Lathers of New York, he gives us such a statement. This statement displays such an utter misconception of the state of things here, and of the principles of our people, as would be ludicrous, were it not for the painful reflection that is honestly believed, not only by the respected man who makes it, but by a large part of the people of his State and of adjoining States.

Of course, Judge Magrath believes that the North is ruled by fanaticism, and that we are all abolitionists together, leaving out the minority who sympathize with his State. South Carolina, he says, has long been aware of the tendencies of this government; she has waited for years for the circumstances to arise which should bring her neighbors to an agreement with herself, and these are now furnished by the result of the late election, when the fanatical spirit finally triumphed at the North. He refers to no specific act or design of injustice, past or to come; it is a prevailing spirit and an accepted theory of property and morals at the North, which in his judgment makes us no longer safe company. The South he declares has forborne with this and has endured its attacks, but the danger is now too great to longer be incurred. This fanatical spirit, in his opinion, has an influence extending far beyond the slavery question; he thinks it more dangerous to the North than to the South, for the later can place herself beyond its reach, while the former is governed by it. And it is interesting to see that all Judge Magrath regrets at this moment, are for his northern friends. They are yet to feel the power of fanaticism, and, he says, "we deeply sympathize with you when that power will be exercised upon you and against you in all the plentitude of agrarian violence and atheistic cruelty." The reigning spirit, he declares,

undertakes to decide a question of property, to determine a matter of private right, and therefore, he thinks, "the failure of the attempt which was made to stem the tide of abolition sentiment, is chiefly regretted because of the desolating influences it must exercise within the limits of those States where it prevails, upon the persons and property, the life and liberty of those who within those limits may become the object of its wrath."

How monstrous does all this seem when it is read in the light of what all intelligent men here *know* to be the fact! Here we know that the influence which carried the late election was not one which aimed at the disturbance of any chartered right; the people of these States questioned no man's right to security in his own State in the enjoyment of what its laws make property; they did not undertake to deal with any existing or future rights, but simply to pass upon the question whether a certain form of society should be extended into territory where it does not now exist. It was no question of any man's right to hold slaves, but a question whether he should carry them into the territories or keep them in the slaveholding States. No issue was ever passed upon at a popular election in a spirit more free from fanaticism, with a more sedulous avoidance of all questions beyond that immediately in hand, or upon principles which more carefully guarded existing rights. And yet this is to Judge Magrath the evidence of an agrarian spirit which is threatening the very groundwork even of our own society as well as that of the South.

A. S. ABELL: SECESSION OF SOUTH CAROLINA

The following Baltimore Sun *editorial discusses the implications of South Carolina's decision to secede. The* Baltimore Sun *had been sensitive to the Southern states' concerns, but as hostilities between the North and South grew as the war approached, the* Baltimore Sun *became less sympathetic to the Southern cause. Maryland was a slave state at the time. This editorial does not clearly show support for either side—North or South—but it does indicate how many people saw South Carolina's secession as the "beginning of the end" of the Union.*

Baltimore Sun, 21 December 1860

It will be seen by the report of proceedings of the "Sovereign Convention" of South Carolina that the ordinance of secession was yesterday passed by a unanimous vote. It amply reveals the act by which State originally entered into Federal Union with the other twelve States constituting the United States of America.

The event has been generally anticipated by our readers, and the act itself only fulfills general expectation. It has a significance, however, which is impossible to regard without deep emotion; and unless there is an instant return to the obligations of the constitution and the equality of the rights of the States, this secession of South Carolina is the beginning of the end.

The fact that this "Sovereign Convention" has been

elected directly by the people; that none but delegates pledged to secession were chosen, and no others entered the canvass; that upon assembling the act of secession is promptly adopted so soon as it is presented, and that by a unanimous vote, shows the deep and settled purpose with which the State resents the indignity of sectional lawlessness to which she has been exposed.

This act of South Carolina will unquestionably impart a quickening impulse to other Southern States, and there remains no hope now but in an unconditional return to the constitution, and an ample recognition of the rights of the South by the people of the North of the restoration of the Union—AS IT WAS.

AN ANONYMOUS REPORT: SOUTH CAROLINA'S WAR AGAINST THE UNITED STATES

In building a public case against the seceding states, the Philadelphia Inquirer, *like many Republican papers, made great effort to report on acts of what they perceived to be Southern state aggressions. The article below offers some foreshadowing of how the civil war would actually begin. Major Anderson, who was in charge of the Union's Fort Sumter in Charleston, South Carolina, was at the center of attention as early as January 1861. In April 1861 the attack on Fort Sumter by the Confederates would officially begin the war. At the time this article was written, only South Carolina, Mississippi, Alabama, and Florida had seceded.*

Philadelphia Inquirer, 11 January 1861

The following are the conquests, &c., of South Carolina, achieved in ten days.—

1st. Castle Pinckney; taken by storm.

2d. Fort Moultrie; taken.

3d. The U.S. Arsenal in Charleston; seized.

4th. The U.S. Custom House and Post Office in Charleston; seized.

5th. The U.S. Revenue cutter brig *Aiken*; taken.

6th. New fortifications raised on Sullivan's Island and Johnson's Island.

7th. Major ANDERSON besieged in Fort Sumter.

8th. One thousand negro slaves brought into service raising fortifications to capture Major ANDERSON.

9th. The commander of the slaver *Bonita* taken violently from the custody of the authority of the United States.

To this we may add the seize of the United States forts in Georgia and the firing into the *Star of the West*.

Is this "peaceful constitutional secession?" Or is it *armed rebellion against the United States.*

WILLIAM LLOYD GARRISON: DISUNION MEANS ABOLITION OF SLAVERY

The excerpt, written by prominent abolitionist William Lloyd Garrison, suggests that South Carolina's secession will bring disunion and that will in turn lead to the abolition of slavery.

The Liberator, 4 January 1861 (Boston)

At last, the "covenant with death" is annulled. At least, by the action of South Carolina, and ere long, by all the slaveholding States—for their doom is one. "The dissolution of the Union is the abolition of slavery," said Mr. ARNOLD, of Tennessee, in the United States House of Representatives, a few years ago. Hail the approaching jubilee, ye millions who are wearing the galling chains of slavery, for, assuredly, the day of your redemption draws nigh, bringing liberty to you and salvation to the whole land!

AN ANONYMOUS REPORT: ANOTHER STAR LOST—SECESSION OF MISSISSIPPI

The following report in the Philadelphia Inquirer *comes after Mississippi's state convention voted to secede from the Union on 9 January 1861. Mississippi was quickly followed by Florida (10 January) and Alabama (11 January).*

Philadelphia Inquirer, 10 January 1861

GENERAL REJOICING

JACKSON, Miss., Jan. 9.—The State Convention to-day passed an ordinance declaring the immediate secession of Mississippi from the Federal Union. It was adopted by a vote of 81 yeas to 15 nays.

A number of public and private buildings are illuminated to-night, salutes are being fired, and fireworks displayed, and other manifestations of rejoicing exhibited.

A resolution was adopted amid much applause, inviting the delegates from South Carolina and Alabama to occupy seats on the floor of the Convention.

All efforts to postpone action on the ordinance of immediate secession were voted down.

The fifteen opposing votes will sign the ordinance to-morrow, making it unanimous.

The Convention was in secret session this morning.

There is a grand display of fireworks at the Capitol to-night, in honor of the event. The excitement is intense.

A MAN OF INFLUENCE: PRIVATE LETTER FROM MISSISSIPPI EXPLORES ECONOMIC CONSEQUENCES OF STATE'S SECESSION

The Philadelphia Inquirer *printed the following letter from a Mississippi resident the next day, and it suggests the economic impact of the state's decision to secede.*

Philadelphia Inquirer, 11 January 1861

The writer is a man of influence, and could command some of the most honorable offices in the State. He says:—

"I have great dread of the consequences of this secession movement. The 4th of March fills me with apprehension. Surely these things ought not to be. But who is there now to mount the whirlwind and direct the storm? We have no CLAY or WEBSTER, or Gen. JACKSON now. Owls and bats fill the high places once consecrated to eagles. *Mississippi was never in a worse condition than now for any violent action; she has no spare resources, no credit, and worse, nothing to eat.* Much suffering is inevitable: I know many families who have no corn, nor anything to buy it with; and none have enough to carry them through to the next crop. No debts are being paid, and consternation marks the countenance of all thinking men. Our taxes are already high, and are obliged to be increased one hundred fold to support the new Government about to be inaugurated."

J. McGOWAN, CAPTAIN: MOOD IN FLORIDA AND ALABAMA AFTER BOTH STATES SECEDE

These two news items, received via the telegraph, give a brief report of the mood in Alabama's and Florida's capital cities the day after each state voted to secede from the Union (Alabama seceded on 11 January, Florida on 10 January). The author is a U.S. ship captain (of the Brooklyn*) who watched the events unfold.*

Hartford Daily Courant, 14 January 1861 (Hartford, Conn.)

THE CRISIS
THE VERY LATEST NEWS

Arrival of the Brooklyn at Charleston!
Her Mission One of Peace

Messengers Sent to Washington by Major Anderson and South Carolina

MOBILE, Jan. 12.—The secession of the State has caused great rejoicing here. One hundred guns are being fired in honor of the event. Impromptu speeches are being made in all the prominent buildings. To-night the city will be illuminated and there will be a military parade. One hundred thousand dollars have been subscribed by the citizens for the defence of Mobile.

TALLAHASSE, Jan. 11.—The ordinance of secession was signed to-day in the eastern portico of the Capitol, amid the firing of cannon and the cheers and enthusiasm of the people. Hon. T. Butler King of Georgia, made a speech on the occasion, which was loudly cheered. . . .

As it was now strong ebb-tide, and the water having fallen some three feet, we proceeded with caution and crossed the bar safely at 8:50 A.M., and continued on our course for this port, where we arrived this morning after a boisterous passage:

A steamer from Charleston followed us for about three hours, watching our movements.

In justice to the officers and crew of each department of the ship, I must add that their behavior while under the fire of the battery reflected the great credit on them.

Mr. Brewer, the New York pilot, was of very great assistance to me, in helping to pilot the ship over Charleston Bar, and up and down the channel.

THOMAS N. DAY: GROWING LIKELIHOOD OF WAR

This editorial in the Hartford Daily Courant *appeared after Alabama and Florida seceded and suggests that war may be inevitable.*

Hartford Daily Courant, *12 January 1861 (Hartford, Conn.)*

It is becoming palpable to all eyes that the efforts of well-meaning men at Washington, to settle the national differences by compromises and concessions, are futile and premature. The South is not in a mood to be placated by any concessions the North can honestly offer; and it is evident that nothing that time and experience can bring the maddened and ignorant masses of Southern whites to anything like common sense. Nature's way is harsh and stern. Inex-

orable and careless of immediate consequences, from the first beginnings of history to the present day, the records show that the course of Providence has been to let men settle their difference by an appeal to the sword; the weakest foes to the wall, and the pluckiest and strongest carry the day. So it has been heretofore, and so we have every reason to think it will be now.

WILLIAM HARDING: SECESSION OF LOUISIANA CLOSES MISSISSIPPI RIVER TO NORTH

This editorial was written before the seceding states officially formed the Confederate States of America. It appears nearly a week after Louisiana became the sixth state to secede from the Union.

Philadelphia Inquirer, *1 February 1861*

The so-called "right of secession" is clearly a pretext put forward by men who were pre-determined to establish a Southern Confederacy, regardless of all other considerations. In the case of Louisiana, for instance, no fair-minded man can for a moment believe that her Ordinance of Secession was the exercise of a moral and political "right." That ordinance declared as follows:—

"That the ordinance passed by this State on the 22d of November 1817, whereby the Constitution of the United States, and the amendments of said Constitution were adopted, and all the laws and ordinances by which Louisiana became a member of the Federal Union; be and the same are hereby repealed and abrogated."

Now glance at the history of Louisiana. On the 20th of February, 1811, Congress passed an act enabling the people resident on the purchased territory of New Orleans to organize a State. Section 3 of that act, after providing for a Convention of the people to frame a Constitution, adds:—

"Said Convention shall proclaim by ordinance, *irrevocable without the consent of the United States,* that the people inhabiting thee said Territory do agree and declare that the River Mississippi and the navigable rivers and waters leading into the same, or into the Gulf of Mexico, shall be common highways and forever free, as well as to the inhabitants of the said State, or to the other citizens of the United States."

AN ANONYMOUS REPORT: SECESSION OF TEXAS—SEVENTH STAR GONE

Although Texas did not formally secede until 2 March 1861, this short report about how Texas officials voted on secession in early February clearly indicated where Texas' loyalties would lie. By the time Texas seceded, South Carolina, Mississippi, Florida, Alabama, Georgia, and Louisiana had left the Union, and Jefferson Davis had already become the president of the Confederacy.

Philadelphia Inquirer, 7 February 1861

NEW ORLEANS, Feb. 6.—Advices to the 5th inst. have been received from Galveston. The Convention passed the Ordinance of Secession on the 1st instant—yeas 166, nays 7. The Governor, Legislature, Supreme Judges and Commissioners are there remain as at present. The ordinance is to be voted on for the 23d instant, and, if adopted, will go into effect on the 2d of March.

Governor HOUSTON recognizes the Convention, and that the people have declared their attachment to the South and a desire to join the Southern Confederacy; but if none is formed, he will cast his lot with the Republic of Texas.

The secession news from, Florida, Georgia, Alabama, Mississippi, and Louisiana has created much excitement in Northern Texas.

WILLIAM HARDING: EDITORIAL—JEFFERSON DAVIS ON THE COTTON CONFEDERACY

The following editorial was written after Jefferson Davis, who was elected president of the Confederate States of America, gave his inaugural address in Montgomery, Alabama, the new Confederate capital.

Philadelphia Inquirer, 20 February 1861

The so-called President of the pretended Government, formed by the Seceded States, is a personage, as we have before stated, with good reputation for ability and more claims to respect for prudence and reason than most of the Southern politicians of his school. In his Inaugural Address, speaking to the world upon the great event of the age, it was to be expected that he would try and that he, if any one, would be able to show, what were the real reasons for the separation, and what were the present plans and future prospects of his insurgent constituency, respecting both domestic and foreign policy. Let us see what a case he, the chosen one of treason's chosen, has made out for its excuse and its successes.

MR. DAVIS'S first statement, after the usual personal prelude, is that the objects of the old Union were to establish justice, insure domestic tranquility, provide for the common defence, promote the general welfare, and secure the blessings of liberty; and that because these ends were not attained, through the fault of the North, the Gulf States have taken their present course. . . .

MR. DAVIS, your secession business reeks with corruption and wickedness, so you need'nt brag about observing the rights of "property;" and as to those of "person," it would be a slightly insane act for any non-traitor to go among your law-abiding constituents just now, even with the most innocent purposes. Tar and feathers would be the lightest token of welcome.

The speaker goes on to boast and brag about fighting, and about there being no domestic trouble arising out of the late act, and other such nonsense; and then makes what he considers the greatest hit of the whole—stating that the pride of his Confederation is the prevailing "homogeneity"—Whatever MR. DAVIS means by this big word, it's hard to tell. If that the whites in the Gulf States came from the same nation and blood, it is very absurd, for there is no district wherein the descent is more varied. Neither can he mean that there is much "homogeneity" between the whites and the about equal numbers of blacks—nor that there is much sameness of interest between the many poor whites and the comparatively small class of slaveholders. If he means anything, it is that cotton is the great, almost the sole product of his new realm. Now, it shows very little knowledge of political economy for his excellency to congratulate himself upon what is a serious evil. A nation is prosperous for the variety of its productions, and from the multifarious adaptability of its resources, not from the fact that but one article is raised for export, not for home use, and that its people know but one art, the cultivation of a particular plant. There is to be a rivalry for the Confederation in the cotton production; there may be great fluctuations in its demand and price, and they may be cut off from any market. What, then, becomes of "homogeneity?" There will be a famine and howling in the new empire. It is not, and never can be, independent. If shut off from the world it would soon be like a scorpion in a ring of fire, and sting it-self to death in horrible social convulsions. So much for "ho-mogeneity."

On the whole, the production of the selected Chief of the Confederation has shown no cause for secession, no excuse for anything, no plans or policy, and no common sense. The speech is emphatically Buncombe, except what is puerility, and laughable error, except what is a sad presage of danger-ous insanity.

JOSEPH MEDILL: REPUBLICAN EDITOR DEMANDS DEMOCRATIC PAPERS CEASE ENCOURAGING SECESSION BY MISREPRESENTING REPUBLICAN POSITIONS

The Republican Chicago Tribune *squarely blamed the Democratic newspapers in the North for fueling the secession spirit in the South and for leading the country to war. In this strongly worded editorial, it calls on the Democratic papers to correct Southern misconceptions that the Republican Party is bent on violating states rights and putting an end to slavery. It specifically takes issue with the charge that prominent abolitionists William Lloyd Garrison and Wendell Phillips are leaders in the Republican Party or that Republicans in any way supported the tactics of John Brown (referred to below as Os-awatomie Brown) of Harper's Ferry fame (see Chapter 3).*

Chicago Tribune, 15 January 1861

The most painful part of this miserable secession busi-ness, is the attitude of certain of the professedly Democratic journals of the North. Having, by their baseless, careless, senseless, witless misrepresentations of purposes and policy of the Republican party been more largely instrumental than any other agency whatever in poisoning the public mind, stir-ring up the baser passions and exciting the sectional hate of the South, they are now calling upon the Republicans to make "great concessions" and thereby confess that all they have charged is true—that negro equality has been a part of the Republican platform—that interference with Slavery in the States has been a fundamental article in our party creed, and that invasion and revolution for the propagation of Re-publican doctrines, for the punishment of all who deny them, are abandoned upon compulsion alone. If not this, what do these demands for concession mean? No, gentlemen, this will not do. The dispute will not be adjusted upon a lasting basis, by the nostrums that you would employ. The first and indis-pensable pre-requisite for the attainment of peace is that YOU STOP LYING! Go now honestly and zealously at work to correct the falsehoods that you have scattered abroad. Tell the people of the South that you have played an unmanly part; that your talk about Republican intentions and Repub-lican agencies was for partisan effect at home; that your alle-gations that Phillips and Garrison are the leaders of the party and Osawatomie Brown its evangel, were slanders, and that you knew them to be such when you said it; that your inter-pretation of the "irrepressible conflict" was knowingly wicked and treasonable; that your theories regarding Lin-coln's intentions were never sincerely entertained; and that in all the management of the two last Presidential campaigns you never told the truth when a lie could be invented. Do *that*, and at the same time declare that Republican policy contemplates no interference with State institutions; no avoidance of the constitutional rights of any section; that it looks only to obedience to the Constitution and the laws; that Mr. Lincoln is a wise, moderate, conservative and patriotic man; that the rights of the South will be safe in his hands, and that under his rule the country may have prosperity and peace, and if your many gross falsehoods have not ruined your reputation for veracity, the harmony of the jarring sections will be restored.

We make no unreasonable demand. We require nothing that the danger of the situation does not suggest. We ask for nothing but justice to the Republican party and the Presi-dent whom it has elevated to power; and until that demand is complied with, that justice rendered, and the Southern people are made to know that their confidence has been abused, that their property is not to be wrested out of their hands, that their wives are not to be given up to the lust of slaves in revolt, that their children are not to be brained against the door-posts of their homes, and that all their rights under the Constitution are to be assuredly respected, discontent will not cease, and revolutionary effort will not be arrested.

Let the so-called Democratic papers begin. There is little time left them to effect the change which will save the shed-ding of blood. Their stories—idle tales at home, which not even the ignorant believe—are the causes of Southern hate and fear; and the preparations for a fight show how widely they have been believed. There is no time to lose. Let the *Chicago Times* lead off!

URIAH J. JONES: DEMOCRATIC EDITOR BLAMES REPUBLICANS FOR CAUSING SECESSION BY REFUSING TO COMPROMISE WITH SOUTH

The following editorial in the Democratic Harrisburg Patriot & Union *blames the Republican Party for the secession difficulties. It suggests, as the previous* Chicago Tribune *editorial critically points out, that if the Republican Party made some concessions regarding states' rights, then the country might not be headed for civil war.*

Harrisburg Patriot & Union, 8 February 1861 (Harrisburg, Pa.)

Our national difficulties could be settled in twenty-four hours if the Republicans would agree to abide by the Constitution of the United States in all its provisions, as interpreted by the Supreme Court. The most ultra Southern States ask nothing more than this. We hear a great deal of bluster about the exorbitant demands of the South. Republicans tell us that it would be degrading to the North to yield to them; and yet, these demands embrace nothing more than the South is entitled to under a judicial construction of the Constitution.

The first demand of the South is, that the provision of the Constitution requiring the return of fugitives from labor shall be faithfully executed, and that all State laws which embarrass, conflict with, retard, or obstruct the peaceful enforcement of the fugitive slave law shall be repealed. There is nothing unreasonable in this demand. The South has a right to its runaway slaves, and the North has no right to protect them from capture. There can be no appeal in such cases from the Constitution to public opinion. No matter how deep the sympathies of Northern men may be in behalf of fugitives from bondage—no matter how great their reluctance to witness the return of runaway negroes, they have no right to array public sentiment against law. No excuse will avail to avoid the execution of a direct and plain provision of the Constitution. Many Northern States have been grossly culpable in the enactment of laws which increase the dangers and difficulties in the way of the capture of fugitive slaves, or render their return next to impossible. The South demands that these laws shall be repealed—that masters shall meet with no difficulty in re-taking their fugitive property, and that the

provision of the Constitution, made in their behalf, shall be executed to the very letter. Is this an unjust exaction? Would it be a humiliating concession for the North to acknowledge the binding force of the Constitution and the laws passed in pursuance thereof?

The second demand of the South is in reference to the territories. The Supreme Court of the United States having decided that slaves are property, and that the citizens of Southern States have the right to take such property into the common territories and hold it there until excluded by the authority of a State Constitution, the Southern States, interested in slave property, ask that this decision be respected and enforced as all other decisions of the Supreme Court are respected and enforced. This is the sum and substance of their demands. They don't require anything more than the highest judicial authority in the country has pronounced their right. They only demand that the Constitution, as authoritatively expounded by the Court, shall be respected.— While that decision stands, it is the right of the South to enjoy all the benefits which it confers. Congress has not power to destroy this right; and yet, because they insist upon it, the Southern States are accused of exacting degrading terms from the North.

If the Northern majority are required to recede from the position that Congress may and should exclude slavery from the territories, it is their own fault. They had no business to assume the right to exercise power not warranted by the Constitution. If it is humiliating to abandon an unjust and illegal claim, they must suffer this mortification; for the obligations of law are more imperative than the decrees of party.

THOMAS N. DAY: MR. SEWARD'S SPEECH—SOUTHERN REFUSAL TO ACCEPT DEFEAT MAKES WAR LIKELY

This editorial from the Hartford Daily Courant *chastises the Southern states for being poor losers in the 1860 election and suggests that war between the Union and the disloyal Southern states is impending.*

Hartford Daily Courant, 14 January 1861 (Hartford, Conn.)

THE SOUTH does not, as yet, begin to understand the intensity of the indignation which the North feels, and *under which it will soon begin to act*, at the conduct of the South in breaking up the hopes of our national existence. To be a member of the freest confederacy on earth; to have our strength, our intelligence, and our prosperity commensurate with our freedom, has been the desire of the North. The people looked with pride on our national power—with exultation at the brilliant prospects of our future—and their deep seated indignation at the folly which has sacrificed all this, is not realized, at present, at the South. They will feel it and will realize it, if a hot headed Southern invasion touches Washington. The indignation that pervades our whole community is intensified by the knowledge, that all the evils the South pretends to dread are fanciful merely. She can put her finger on no wrong suffered or reasonably anticipated. She breaks up the Union, simply because she did not carry the last election! Such meanness from men who talk loudly of chivalry, is characteristic, but disgusting to truly honorable men. Throw politics to the dogs; and ask the next sporting man you meet whether it is honorable to go into a convention; then go into an election; do your best for your candidate; and cast your votes for him, fairly and fully; and after all, *bolt* if he is not elected! The voice of all the world, civilized or barbarous, will scorn the meanness of the seceding States.

AN ANONYMOUS REPORT: LET SECEDING STATES GO—THEY WILL FAIL

Garrison reprinted this article from the Democratic Boston Evening Gazette *just days before the war started at Fort Sumter in Charleston, South Carolina. It provides a fact-based argument for allowing the Southern states to try their own government instead of going to war because, the author argues, there is no way for the Confederacy to succeed. It largely ignores the slavery issue, since to many Northern Democrats the fundamental issue involved in the separation of the states had to do with the protection of states' rights. They had little interest in resolving the slavery issue.*

The Liberator, 12 April 1861 (Boston)

Statistics are very ugly things. The importance attached to "Secession" diminishes as we look at the ugly figures which authentic documents supply.

The bank capital of the seven States of the Southern Confederacy is $61,349,488. The bank capital of Massachusetts is $64,519,200. The S.C. want a fifteen million loan, and Mississippi is one of the States which pledges her faith to pay it, when there is not a bank of issue of sufficient account in the whole State to receive mention in statistical documents. The aggregate debt of the Confederacy is $31,915,103.

The population of the seven departed States is 2,703,646 free and 2,350,677 slave making a total of 5,054,323. The white population of New York alone is 3,851,563, which exceeds that of "Secession" over a million, and combined with the population of Pennsylvania, which is 2,924,501, these two States show a front of a million and a half freemen above the united-free and enslaved of the South.

The receipts for carrying the mails one year in the Southern Confederacy were $829,582, and the expense $3,082,960, a loss to the Treasury of $2,253,378. In the five New England states, the receipts during the same year were $1,224,280, and the expenses $1,156,721, leaving a surplus of over fifty thousand dollars. The sooner we stop the mails, the more profitable it will be.

We see no easier or more politic method of making these United States one and truly inseparable than by acknowledging the Southern Confederacy. Let the seven States take care of themselves if they can. Let them have their forts and their revenue peaceably, and they will find that setting up on their own book is the most disastrous job they ever undertook. The heavy direct taxation which is sure to follow will touch the pockets of the wealthy, time will assuage the imaginary wrongs which the North is charged with, and we shall see the reign of reason bring with it a reconstruction of our Government through the medium of a National Convention.

It is very easy to talk about pluck and bloodshed, but there is nothing to be obtained by war which cannot be accomplished by conciliatory measures. It is not a foreign enemy we are contending against, but men who have been our friends, who differing from us upon a vital principle, have sought a rash method to relieve themselves from evils which it pleased politicians, for selfish ends, to so magnify, that by subtlety and design they precipitated the South into a revolution. We at the North do not believe that a fair expression of opinion has yet been made by the Conservative men of the South, and many, we think the majority, are opposed to the adoption of measures that would certainly induce them to espouse the cause of their State, or they would be less than men. The attempt to stigmatize such a course as the effect of fear is ridiculous when we consider that the wisest diplomacy is that which prevents suffering, and accomplishes a result without loss of human life. The surrender of the forts is not a matter of any weight whatever, and must inevitably follow a recognition of the Southern Confederacy. We require the cooperation of the Border States, and we believe Mr. Lincoln will retain them.

It is not to be expected that this trouble will be settled in a day, for it will require many months to convince the seceding States that they are not so well off as they were before. They love the Almighty Dollar just as well where the Palmetto (the Confederate flag) waves and the magnolia blooms, as where pine, granite and ice are marketable commodities. When they find the dollar clipped by taxes on imports and exports, when they see that increased competition increases the cost of all the necessaries of life, we have strong faith that they will do just as we Yankees would do, arrive at the conclusion that the style of conducting things was not exactly the style conducive to comfort and happiness.

THOMAS N. DAY: PROGRESS OF SECESSION—GROWING TENSION OVER STATUS OF FEDERAL PROPERTY IN THE SOUTH

One of the topics for discussion after the Confederacy was formed was whether Confederate troops would leave Union property in the South unmolested. At the center of this issue was the existence of Union forts and other military outposts in the South. As early as January 1861, Northern papers reported that signs of aggression against Union forts and military officers were seen in Charleston, South Carolina. The following editorial highlights the building tension between the North and South on this issue. It was published a few days before the Civil War officially started when Southern troops assaulted Fort Sumter in Charleston, South Carolina.

Hartford Daily Courant, 11 April 1861 (Hartford, Conn.)

The recent advices from the South show that most important events are at hand. The air is filled with warlike rumors, and the thunder of cannon, "peal on peal afar," may at any moment burst upon our ears. It is not the time for us calmly to ask, who is responsible for all of this. The time will come when the historian, tracing events step by step without prejudice or partiality, shall adjudge to all parties their proper measures of merit and guilt, and determine who shall bear the infamy of overthrowing this great Republic. History will make known who are the traitors and parricides, and who the patriots and heroes and for her solemn verdict we may wait. But our work is to act. Such cries as these do not brook long meditation. Where do we stand? To what labors do truth, right and duty call us in this fearful trial?

We believe that the attempt of Government to supply the garrisons of Fort Sumter and Pickens with food, peaceably if it may, forcibly if it must, will meet the ready and hearty support of the great body of our citizens. And why should it not? Are not these forts the property of the Union? Are they not garrisoned by the soldiers of the Union? What right have the Seceded States to make the holding . . . of these forts a cause of war? What just claims have they upon them? None. They are the joint property of all the States. If hereafter the Union shall choose to give them, by treaty, into the hands of the respective States in which they lie, well; but to take them by violence from the Union is robbery—is civil war.

It is necessary that this matter should be clearly understood. The Seceded States are now, and have been for months, not threatening merely, but actually waging civil war against the Union. They have with violence seized upon the property of the Federal Government, they have with large bodies of armed men invaded its fortresses, driven out its troops and pulled down the national flag. They have pillaged mints, taken possession of custom houses, turned sick soldiers out of their hospitals and surprised revenue cutters lying at anchor. If acts like these do not constitute war, what does? But more than this. The Federal Government sends a vessel to one of its fortresses; this vessel is fired upon. Bearing the flag of the Union, she is forced to turn and flee ignominiously away. Is not this war? But more than this. For months around these two forts, yet in possession of the Union, armed men have been steadily gathering. Skillful officers have been engaged in erecting batteries and preparing every possible means of assault. Hostile troops have environed them round, in the one case forbidding all communication between the fort and the government to which it belongs; and in the other, permitting it only under a flag of truce. Is not this war? Two beleaguered fortresses surrounded by armies whose leaders openly proclaim that they delay the attack only that they may make resistance impossible; is not this war? Yes, it is war. The Seceded States have for months been in open, undisguised war against the Union.

With a forbearance to which history furnishes no parallel, the Federal Government has not employed force to resist these aggressions. It has seen its fortresses invaded, its property plundered, its flag dishonored, and yet has done nothing. It has seen its vessels fired upon in open day and yet no shot has been returned. It has seen hostile troops in larger and larger numbers surrounding the two forts that yet remain unassaulted, and beneath their walls and within the range of their guns, busily engaged from week to week in preparation to attack and destroy them, and yet not a solitary gun has been fired. The world looked and wondered. Was if forbearance, or was it conscious weakness? Well might European statesmen think that the Federal Government had ceased to exist, that the Union was a total and helpless wreck. It seemed as if it had lost all power even for self-defence. Insults and outrages which, in other lands, would have aroused a nation to put forth its strength to the utmost to avenge them, were here received with an apathy that betokened national decay and approaching death. Was this the pitiable end of the Great Republic?

Is it not high time that this forbearance of the Government should cease? It was well-meant, but it has accomplished little. The Seceded States thought because it did nothing, that it dared do nothing and could do nothing. With each hour of forbearance their arrogant demands have increased. So long already at open war with the Union, and resisted, they think no power of resistance remains. Yesterday it was the mints, the custom houses they demanded; to-day it is the fortresses, to-morrow it will be the Capitol. This state of things must come to an end. It must be decided once for all whether the forts built by the money and garrisoned by the soldiers of the Union, shall remain in the possession of the Union. It must be decided whether hordes of lawless men can without provocation fire upon the flag of the Union. It must be decided whether this Republic has any claim to be reckoned among the great powers of the world, able to protect itself from insult and invasion, whether from without or within, or is only a large carcass without life, breeding all slimy reptiles within its own entrails, and furnishing a feast to all the kingly vultures far and near. It is not a question of national prosperity, it is a question of national existence. Shall this nation live or shall it die? A drop of Prussic acid does not more certainly bring physical death, than the principle of secession brings demoralization, discord, war and anarchy. Once adopted and the Union would not be worth preserving, nor could it be preserved.

Here then we stand. The Administration has wisely determined not to give up the fortresses now held by them for the welfare of the nation. In this determination we do not question that the body of the citizens of the Union will uphold them. In reinforcing these forts the Federal Government does not begin civil war. That began months ago. If the Seceded States shall have the hardihood and madness to continue their aggressions, they must take the consequences.

NOTE

1. When the president refers to hostile Northern Legislation, he is talking about the laws in many free states, called Personal Liberty Bills, that directly contradicted the federal fugitive slave laws that required escaped slaves to be returned to their masters. The Personal Liberty Bills gave escaped slaves their freedom. From "The President's Message," *Baltimore Sun*, 5 December 1860.

FURTHER READINGS

Dew, Charles B. *Apostles of Disunion: Southern Secession Commissioners and the Causes of the Civil War*. Charlottesville: University Press of Virginia, 2002.

Faust, Patricia L. (Ed.). *Historical Times Illustrated Encyclopedia of the Civil War*. New York: Harper & Row, 1986.

Paquette, Robert Louis; Ferleger, Louis A.; and Ferleger, Lou. *Slavery, Secession and Southern History*. Charlottesville: University Press of Virginia, 2000.

Rhodes, James Ford. *History of the Civil War, 1861–1865*. New York: Macmillan, 1917.

6

WAR BEGINS—THE ATTACK ON FORT SUMTER, 12 APRIL 1861

The Confederate attack on Fort Sumter in Charleston Harbor in South Carolina started the Civil War on 12 April 1861. Although it was apparent to many as early as January 1861 that war was forthcoming, the events that directly led to the Fort Sumter attack began to take shape more clearly after Lincoln's inauguration on 4 March.[1]

When Lincoln assumed the presidency, seven states had seceded and the Confederacy had already formed. One of the first significant issues that faced Confederate President Jefferson Davis was whether he should allow foreign troops on Southern soil. Because the U.S. government no longer controlled the Confederate states, Union troops were not welcome, and their presence posed a problem for Davis. President Lincoln also had concerns about the presence of the Union troops in the Confederate states. If Lincoln removed the troops, he would, by default, be recognizing the legitimacy of the Confederacy as its own country. But if the troops remained, they were certain to be attacked.

In his inaugural address, Lincoln asked the country for reconciliation but would not offer any compromises to the South. One of Lincoln's primary objectives was to keep the remaining slaveholding states in the Union. If he could not persuade the seceded states to return to the Union and if more states joined the Confederacy, Lincoln would have to consider whether force should be used to thwart the rebellion against the government. When the issue of the presence of federal troops within the Confederate borders arose, it was becoming more apparent that if armed conflict occurred, it would likely begin in connection with this issue.

By the end of March, it was clear to Jefferson Davis that the federal troops needed to leave the Confederate states; but Davis also believed that the U.S. government would not willingly remove them. Lincoln was unwilling to escalate the conflict, and he refused to reinforce the garrison at Fort Sumter, which had become the first target of this specific disagreement. Lincoln also refused to remove the troops from Fort

Sumter and tried, unsuccessfully, to resupply them with food and other rations.[2] This set the stage for the Fort Sumter conflict.

The formal attack on Fort Sumter began at 4:30 A.M. on 12 April 1861. The *New York Times* correspondent describes the event as he saw it from a nearby pier:

> The first shot was fired from the Five-mortar Battery on James' Island, followed in quick succession by the iron Battery at Cumming's Point, the Floating Battery, Fort Moultrie, and the one at Mount Pleasant. . . . [About 30 minutes later] the first gun was fired from Fort Sumter, directed at Steven's Point, and soon the conflict became general on either side.[3]

General Pierre Gustav Tautant Beauregard of Louisiana led the Confederate forces; the Union forces inside Fort Sumter were led by Major Robert Anderson. Most eyewitnesses who described the morning blasts called it a "truly grand . . . pyrotechnic display," and according to an *Associated Press* reporter, "The terrific fighting reached an awful climax at 10 o'clock at night. . . . Nearly all night long the streets were thronged with people full of excitement and enthusiasm. The housetops, the Battery, the wharves, the shipping, in fact, every available place was taken possession of by the multitude."[4] The battle ended thirty-four hours after it started when Major Anderson waived the white flag and surrendered the fort. No one on either side died as a result of the fighting.

The impact of the Fort Sumter attack in the North was profound. According to historians Ratner and Teeter, "Examining newspaper accounts of the crisis before the attack and then after it, it is evident that the Fort Sumter incident represented for the people of both regions a passing of the point of no return in the march away from reconciliation and toward civil war."[5]

The differences seen in the Democratic and Republican papers prior to the Fort Sumter attack were substantial, as previously noted. On the slavery and states' rights issues raised in Kansas, the *Dred Scott* case, the Harper's Ferry incident, and the election and subsequent secession movement, the divisions between the two political parties played out publicly. This political division continued up to the point of the Fort Sumter attack. Once shots had actually been fired against the Union, nearly every Northern Democratic paper shifted its rhetoric and offered loyal support to the Union in fighting the Southern rebellion. Democrats still placed blame for the conflict on Republican ideals and actions and often criticized Republican as well as abolitionist rhetoric, but it was clear that once war commenced, the North was unified.

The articles that appear in this chapter highlight this process of unification after the fighting commenced and also provide some examples of the early dispatches that appeared as the conflict unfolded.

AN ANONYMOUS REPORT: ATTACK ON FORT SUMTER IS IMMINENT

Beginning in January 1861, many predicted the war would begin in Charleston, South Carolina, because of the tension between the South Carolinians and the Union forts that existed there. Accounts like

the one below from the Philadelphia Inquirer *appeared commonly in newspapers during March 1861,*
more than a month before the first shots were fired.

Philadelphia Inquirer, 4 March 1861

IMPORTANT—FORT SUMTER TO BE ATTACKED BY NIGHT

Despatches From Major Anderson

The War Department has received important dispatches from MAJOR ANDERSON. The gallant officer, in a letter to SECRETARY HOLT, denies the truth of the report that Jefferson Davis had exchanged visits with him. He has had no communication whatever with the President of the Confederate States. He is satisfied that Fort Sumter will be attacked, and he can clearly discern with the naked eye to the arrangements for the assault, which he believes will be at night, and will be of the most determined character. The fortification is only now entirely completed, the reports to that effect before being untrue. The utmost ingenuity of himself and brother officers have been employed to strengthen every part and to provide means for resisting the attack, which, in his opinion, is certain to come.

AN ANONYMOUS REPORT: "WAR! WAR!! WAR!!!"—FIRST REPORT OF ATTACK ON FORT SUMTER

The headline of this news story says it all: "WAR! WAR!! WAR!!!" In this first account of what happened in Charleston on 12 April 1861, details are lacking. It typically took a few days for correspondents to get good information, even though they could fairly quickly deliver their news via the telegraph.

Philadelphia Inquirer, 13 April 1861

WAR! WAR!! WAR!!!

HIGHLY IMPORTANT FROM CHARLESTON

Correspondence between General Beauregard and the Confederate Secretary of War.
The Rebels Open Fire on Fort Sumter.

MAJOR ANDERSON REPLIES

Two Guns Silenced in Sumter.

AN EMBRASURE MADE IN THE WALLS OF SUMTER

Only Two Rebels Reported Wounded.
The Firing Ceased for the Night, to Commence in the Morning.

THREE STEAMERS OFF THE BAR

Surveillance of the Telegraph Lines.

CHARLESTON, April 12—The fight has commenced. This is all I can say at present.

SECOND DESPATCH.

CHARLESTON, April 12—The ball has been opened at last, and war is inaugurated.

The batteries on Sullivan's Island, Morris Island and other points, opened on Fort Sumter at 4 o'clock this morning.

Fort Sumter returned the fire, and a brisk cannonading has been kept up.

No information has been received from the seaward yet.

The militia are under arms, and the whole of our population are on the streets.

Every available space facing the harbor is filled with anxious spectators. . . .

THIRD DESPATCH.

CHARLESTON, April 12—*(Received in Philadelphia 9:30 P.M.)*—The firing has continued all day without intermission.

Two of Fort Sumter's guns have been silenced.

It is reported that a breach has been made in the southeast wall of Fort Sumter.

The answer made by Major Anderson to Gen. Beauregard's demand was, that he would surrender when his supplies were exhausted, if he was not reinforced.

Not a casualty has as yet happened to any of our men (the Carolinians).

Of the nineteen batteries in position, only seven have opened on Fort Sumter. The remainder are held in reserve for the expected fleet [*which would deliver Union supplies to the Fort*].

Two thousand men reached the city this morning, and embarked for Morris Island and other points in that neighborhood. . . .

FOURTH DESPATCH.

CHARLESTON, April 12—*(Received in Philadelphia at 10:30 P.M.)*—The bombardment of Fort Sumter still continues.

The Floating battery and Stephens battery are operating freely.

Fort Sumter continues to return the fire.

It is reported that three war vessels are outside the bar.

FIFTH DESPATCH.

CHARLESTON, April 12—The fighting has ceased for the night, to be renewed at daylight in the morning, unless an attempt be made in the meantime to reinforce Fort Sumter, to repel which ample arrangements have been made.

The Seceders worked their guns admirably well.

Only two were wounded during the day.

The Pawnee, Harriet Lane, and a third war steamer, are reported off the bar.

Fresh troops are arriving here by every train.

SIXTH DESPATCH.

CHARLESTON, April 12—(Received in Philadelphia, April 13th, at 2 o'clock A.M.)—The bombardment of Fort Sumter is still going on, every twenty minutes, from the mortars.

It is supposed that Major Anderson is resting his men for the night, as he has ceased to reply.

Three vessels of war are reported outside, but they cannot get in. The sea is rough.

Nobody on the Carolina side has been hurt by this day's engagement.

The floating battery works well.

Every inlet is well guarded.

There are lively times on the Palmetto coast.

THE LATEST

SEVENTH DESPATCH.

CHARLESTON, April 13—12:30 A.M.—It will be utterly impossible to reinforce Fort Sumter tonight, as a storm is raging, and the sea is very rough.

The mortar batteries will be kept playing on Fort Sumter all night.

JOSEPH MEDILL: WAR INAUGURATED!

The initial predictions of Fort Sumter's fate by the Chicago Tribune *were not optimistic; this front-page column did not contain the typical telegraph dispatches because, according to the paper, "At the moment when we most need the special dispatches for which we bargained on Tuesday last, they fail to come, being probably suspended, as Jeff Davis ought to be, on the poles somewhere between here and Washington. We regret the miscarriage, and hope to have it occur no more." But the column did offer a quick synopsis of events and assigned blame for the war to the previous Democratic presidents who allowed slavery to continue in the country.*

Chicago Tribune, 13 April 1861

By the act of a handful of ingrates and traitors, war is inaugurated in this heretofore happy and peaceful Republic! While we write, the bombardment of Sumter is going on; and the blood of the few gallant defenders of the glorious old flag which yet, we hope, floats over that fortress, is being poured out for their fidelity to the Constitution as it is, and the Union as our fathers made it!

The people know the cause of the fratricidal strife. The party, which, in the interest of a barbarous institution, has governed the country for the last forty years, was beaten in the November elections. The verdict of the people which does not touch a single one of the rights of any man, guaranteed by the fundamental law, forbids the extension of that barbarous institution into national territory as yet uncursed by its blighting presence. This is the cause of the rebellion which months of effort has ripened into the bloody strife this day commenced! This and nothing else—this determination of a meager minority to rule a powerful majority—this

deification of Human Slavery as the guiding principle and polar star of a free people—are the dragon's teeth which, sown in a pestilent soil, have produced armed men.

While we write, the issue of the conflict, which is yet going on, is doubtful. Major Anderson contends against fearful odds. His men are few and weary of prolonged confinement, and perhaps awed by the portentous preparations of the enemy. The fleet has not come to his aid. Only the *Harriet Lane* is in the offing. The accounts of the fray are from the traitors, in whose hands the telegraph is. They represent that a breach has been made in the walls of the fortress, and that two of its great guns have been already dismounted. Tomorrow will tell us more; meanwhile we pray that treason may have its reward.

The duty of the Government from this moment is plain. The resources of the Republic must be put forth with no grudging or tardy hand. The strife must be short—the war quick, sharp and decisive. Whatever ample means, courageous men and universal patriotism can do must be done at once. Our fathers fought seven long years that the Constitution might be framed. We, their descendants, can afford any sacrifices, any exertion, that their labor may be preserved to the world for the blessing of mankind. Now, men of the North, for the struggle!

DAVID N. WHITE: UNCONFIRMED REPORT OF ATTACK ON FORT SUMTER

Much of the reporting of the battles that occurred during the Civil War came in waves that included unconfirmed rumors and cloudy details. Often papers acknowledged how difficult it was to discern truth from the reports coming over the telegraph wires. An example of one of these kinds of stories appears below.

Pittsburgh Daily Gazette, 16 April 1861

From Friday afternoon until Sunday afternoon our community was kept in most perplexing anxiety and excitement by the extravagant and often contradictory and absurd accounts of the bombardment of Fort Sumter. At last, however, the fact had to be admitted that it had fallen into the hands of the rebels. This general fact is all that is reliable; for the details respecting the fire in the fort, the damage done to the walls, and many other stories of the same kind are so manifestly absurd as to be entitled to no consideration. For authentic details we must wait for official and epistolary reports. In the meantime it is but just that judgment should be suspended upon the conduct of Major Anderson, in yielding before a breach was made or a man killed. He may have had good reasons for doing what he did.

CHARLES HALE: PRESIDENT BUCHANAN'S MISHANDLING OF SUMTER CRISIS

This untitled account of the Fort Sumter surrender criticizes the actions taken (or not taken) by President Buchanan in his last days in office. The writer suggests that Buchanan faces some of the blame for the loss of the fort. President Buchanan handled the secession crisis between the times of Lincoln's election on 6 November 1860, through Lincoln's inauguration on 4 March 1861.

Boston Daily Advertiser, 15 April 1861

The sad news with which our columns are loaded this morning, will excite the most profound feelings in the bosom of every American citizen. The first long and weary scene in the drama of secession is at last ended by the forced surrender of Fort Sumter. Seven thousand men in arms, provided with all the engines and munitions of modern warfare, which twenty weeks of active effort could supply them, have prevailed against this solitary and isolated post, insufficiently garrisoned and poorly supplied, in which Major Anderson and his little band, numbering altogether less than one hundred, have been imprisoned,—the tale is no marvel. We do not envy the people of Charleston their jubilation and their bell-ringings. We join with them, too, in their happiness that no blood has been shed. It would have been hard indeed had Anderson and his gallant little band been doomed to pay with the sacrifice of their heroic lives the penalty for President Buchanan's imbecility. It has long been evident that he miserable policy of passive sympathy for treason which that functionary pursued, had lost Fort Sumter to the government. However great the desire of the present administration to maintain the lawful authority of the United States, it could not effect an impossibility. The seceders had been allowed too much time to strengthen their position. The batteries upon Cumming's Point and Morris Island ought to have been destroyed before they were made, and this could and doubtless would have been done, had not Major Anderson received contrary orders from the last administration. He was obliged to hold his hands, doing nothing to prevent the elevation of the most powerful enginery of war over against the hapless Sumter, to which no reinforcement either or men or of munitions was allowed. It is the belief of the best military authorities that no walls of masonry whatever can be made strong enough to withstand modern artillery. Sumter could claim no exemption from the common condition, except by virtue of its peculiar position; and whatever advantage it might possess on this score was more than lost by the extraordinary immunity enjoyed by its antagonists in prosecuting their works without let or hindrance during the easy leisure of weeks and months of forbearant delay.

A. S. ABELL: MUST THERE BE WAR OVER FORT SUMTER?

Despite their vast political differences prior to the start of the war, Democratic and Republican newspapers shared their concern about what war now meant for the country. Some Democratic papers, like the Baltimore Sun, *still held out hope for peace, suggesting that the aggressions toward Fort Sumter were not enough to trigger war.*

Baltimore Sun, 18 April 1861

The importance and magnitude of the theme of this inquiry are beyond all calculation. It seems almost a waste of words to attempt to prove this.—But the guilt, the folly, the fratricidal, suicidal character of such a war as seems to be at this moment pending, surpasses all comprehension. Let us, therefore, consider, with an earnest purpose to arrive at a peaceful solution of the question we propose—must there be war?

We say at once, and decidedly, there is no necessity for war—if war should come it is without necessity or justification. The Sumter business is no sufficient cause for war; and though we may easily account for all the wild excitement it has created North and South, we may just as certainly assure ourselves that it will subside and the fact itself be properly esteemed, by the sober second through of the people.

URIAH J. JONES: THE DUTY BEFORE US TO RESTORE THE UNION

The Democratic editors of the Harrisburg Patriot & Union *came to a different conclusion than the editors of the* Sun *about the significance of the Fort Sumter attack and the necessity for war. This is a good example of the unification effect the attack had.*

Harrisburg Patriot & Union, 16 April 1861 (Harrisburg, Pa.)

[*Fort Sumter*] is now in the possession of those who have not only thrown off their allegiance to the Government, but have audaciously assailed its troops and trampled upon its flag. Professing anxiety for peace, the authorities of the Confederate States have taken the initiative in war—and much as we deprecate a civil conflict, far as we would go in the way of compromise to avert bloodshed, deeply as we condemn the defiant attitude of the Republican party towards the South, we are not prepared to countenance or submit to such an indignity to the authority and the flag of our country. The issue is upon us. We do not seek to avoid it. We have done our full duty in behalf of peace. Since war has been forced upon us, and since the Government has resolved to wipe out the insult offered to the stars and stripes, it is our duty to stand by it, whatever may be the consequences, and regardless of the

opinions we may entertain as to the causes which have produced this lamentable condition of affairs. . . .

Time makes all things even. The secession movement has reached a point of audacity where it must be humbled, in order that we may live side by side as neighbors in peace. Further forbearance would only invite future aggressions. Peace must be received by the seceded States as a gift—not extorted by violence. We have no idea that war will restore the Union, but it will establish respect for its defied authority. And after this is accomplished: after the Confederate Government learns to respect the power of the United States; after the people have united to rescue the country from anarchy, they may turn their attention to the Abolition agitators who have contributed in a very great degree to bring about this conflict, and drive them from power by the peaceful means at their command.

DAVID N. WHITE: SOUTHERN AGGRESSION AT FORT SUMTER UNIFIES NORTH

The excerpt that appears below also reinforces the point that the South's aggression toward the Union at Fort Sumter had a unifying effect on the North.

Pittsburgh Daily Gazette, 16 April 1861

No act on the part of the Secessionists has been more reckless, mad and ill-advised than the attack upon a weak and exhausted garrison, for it possesses at once all the abhorred attributes of meanness, cowardice, barbarity and treason. It has had the effect of exasperating the people, and awakening a sentiment of national patriotism which, like a deluge, overwhelms and obliterates all party lines. Democrats and Republicans are now brethren of one faith, and that is devotion to their common country—one platform, and that is the Constitution—one banner, and that is their country's flag. With irrepressible ardor the young men of the country are pressing into the service of the nation, while the treasures of the wealthy will be thrown open to supply its wants. Never before was there such a putting forth of power as we now behold.

THOMAS N. DAY: EFFECT OF WAR NEWS IN CONNECTICUT

The Republican newspaper in Hartford offers its perspective on the effect the attack on Fort Sumter had in the state of Connecticut.

Hartford Daily Courant, 16 April 1861 (Hartford, Conn.)

The news of the events at Charleston created a perfect torrent of indignation in the little but loyal State of Connecticut. The sympathizers with treason were so few that they considered silence the better policy, and but little was heard from them.

In New Haven, Sunday, a custom-house flunkey gave expression of sympathy with treason, and found the boot trade so lively that he quieted down; Jeff. Davis was hung in effigy; and the organist in the George street M.E. Church played the national airs, and the choir sung the national ode, "America," joined by the congregation.

In Norwich, among men of all parties there was but one feeling, and that, of loyalty and patriotism. Party differences seem to have been forgotten, and party lines obliterated. "Our citizens in this crisis, says the *Bulletin*, with but few dishonorable exceptions, know no party but their country; no line but that between loyalty and rebellion; no difference but between patriots and traitors." There was but one man in the town to give expression of sympathy with the rebels. The people of Norwich will take care of *him*. Norwich gave Benedict Arnold to the country, and she wiped out *that* stain long ago.

WILLIAM HARDING: THE WAR COMMENCED

This short excerpt echoes the sentiment that there is no longer neutral ground on which to stand when it comes to questions of secession and the future of the Union.

Philadelphia Inquirer, 13 April 1861

The treason commenced in secession on the 23rd of December last, has thus been consummated in levying actual war against the United States. There is no longer any neutral ground for the sympathizers with the Confederacy. The first shot fired yesterday upon the fortress bearing the flag of the United States, makes every man who gives that act the slightest countenance a traitor in the heart, if not in law. Palliation of this wanton proceeding is giving "aid and comfort to the enemies of the country," in the meanest, most despicable way. The prayers of the loyal people of the Union will be with the brave soldiers who are defending its honor and its rights against such fearful odds.

THOMAS N. DAY: THE FIGHT TO SAVE THE UNION

The following two articles, both contained in Republican papers, are illustrative of the effect the Fort Sumter attack had on Northern men's willingness to fight for the Union. Stories like these appeared in articles and editorials in papers across the North.

Hartford Daily Courant, 13 April 1861 (Hartford, Conn.)

The awful fact that CIVIL WAR has begun in bloody earnest seems to be only too well authenticated. Our telegraphic columns tell the sad story, so far as it has come to hand. The South Carolinians took the initiative. Let it be forever remembered, that the greatest crime committed since the crucifixion of our Savior, was wantonly and willfully committed on behalf of African Slavery! Anderson was doing nobody any harm, when the batteries of the South were opened upon him in anticipation of the arrival of the American fleet. The unarmed steamer loaded with provisions had not even crossed the bar: no hostile fleet had appeared in the offing; no shot had been fired or threatened by the forces of the United States, when the wanton bombardment of Fort Sumter was commenced. Slavery has sown the wind; it will soon reap the whirlwind. The heavy southeasterly storm that has been raging for three days past, off the South Carolina coast, may prevent our fleet from reaching the rendezvous at the appointed time; but that it will reach Charleston, and will redeem the insulted honor of our country, who can doubt? This causeless attack upon Sumter will be avenged! The loyal heart of the nation will pant for retribution, and every drop of blood shed at Sumter will be amply atoned for hereafter. Let the South remember that they who live by the sword are sure to die by the sword; and that any temporary advantage that the fortune of war may give them, though pleasant to their palate for the moment, will prove bitterer than wormwood and gall in their bellies. Let not him who putteth on his armor boast himself like one who putteth it off; but may we all, sobered by the grim reality of internal war, gird up our energies and quit ourselves like men. It is sweet to die for one's country; and never had mortal a better cause than that which now summons all who feel themselves to be men, to rally around the flag of our fathers. Men of Connecticut! To ARMS!! You must be counted for or against the government: which shall it be? Descendants of those who marched under the banner of George Washington, which shall it be? . . . Sons of the old Charter Oak State, on which side do you enlist?

WILLIAM HARDING: ATTACK ON SUMTER—ITS UNIFYING EFFECT THROUGHOUT THE UNION

The editorial below offers similar thoughts to the one published in the Hartford Courant *above.*

Philadelphia Inquirer, 15 April 1861

Our despatches from all parts of the country show great readiness on the part of the people to volunteer instantly in support of the Government. The Governor of Rhode Island has offered his own services at the head of a force of several thousand men. Twenty-five thousand men, it is understood, are ready to go from New York to Washington at once, and the Seventh Regiment are by this time probably on their way to the Federal Capital. GOVERNOR CURTIN [*of Pennsylvania*] has telegraphed to the Railroad Company for the accommodations requisite to transport five thousand men immediately, and at least one hundred thousand men can be furnished by Pennsylvania, should the exigency demand it. Massachusetts has promised to furnish six thousand men at twelve hours' notice. The HON. JOHN SHERMAN has just left Washington to proceed to Ohio, to make arrangements for the transportation of ten thousand troops. In Connecticut, the volunteers are organizing at New Haven, Norwich, and elsewhere, to proceed at once to Washington, if needed. In our own Stat, besides the troops tendered by GOVERNOR CURTIN, above mentioned, we understand that GENERAL SHALL of this city, had tendered two thousand volunteers ready for service, at twelve hours' notice.

In the Borough of Easton, a meeting was held on Saturday evening, and resolutions were passed to raise, equip and sustain volunteer companies. Three thousand dollars were instantly subscribed for this purpose, and one hundred men volunteered on the spot.

A similar meeting was held at Lancaster, and a large amount of money subscribed.

In Baltimore the Union feeling is rampant. A Secessionist, wearing a cockade, was chased through the streets on Saturday. Enlisting of recruits for the Southern Confederacy has been suspended and the American flag is universally displayed throughout the city and in the harbor. A gentleman has informed us that on Friday evening, when the American flag was introduced during the performances at the theatre, it was greeted with tremendous applause.

On receipt of the news from Charleston at Chicago the excitement was immense. All party lines were obliterated, and a determination was expressed to support the Government to the last extremity. At Detroit an impromptu meeting of influential citizens, members of the bar and others, was held, and resolutions adopted, denouncing in the strongest terms the action of the rebellious party at the South, who call themselves the Confederate States, and pledging themselves to support the Government.

In view of this feeling of patriotism which is pervading the various communities throughout the North, we would suggest that a Mass Meeting of the citizens of Philadelphia be held at an early moment, for the purpose of expressing to the country their determination to adhere to and support the General Government.

AN ANONYMOUS REPORT: BRITISH REACTION TO THE AMERICAN WAR

Many publications devoted space to Europe's thoughts about the war. As Harper's New Monthly Magazine *reports, on 14 May 1861 England issued a royal proclamation that forbid British participation in the American Civil War and argued for the protection of British sea vessels that might come in contact with Union navy ships charged to control the Southern coast.*

Harper's New Monthly Magazine, July 1861 (New York City)

The attitude to be assumed by the Great Powers of Europe in relation to the American war is of high importance. That of England is indicated by the Royal proclamation, issued on the 14th of May, which says that, "Whereas hostilities have unhappily commenced between the United States of America and certain States styling themselves the Confederate States of America, and whereas we being at peace with the Government of the United States, have declared our royal determination to maintain a strict neutrality in the contest between the said contending parties, we therefore have thought fit to issue this our royal proclamation." The proclamation then goes on to forbid all British subjects from taking part in any way in the contest, by enlisting in the army or navy of either party; by fitting out or arming any vessel; by breaking any lawfully established blockade; by carrying to either troops or any articles contraband of war. All subjects violating any of the provisions of this proclamation are warned that they will incur the penalties provided by law, and will moreover do so at their own peril, forfeiting any protection from any liabilities or penal consequences.—This proclamation, taken in connection with the explanations of the Ministers and the speeches in Parliament, has an unfriendly aspect toward the United States, recognizing, as it does, the Confederate States, as belligerents, and, by implication, entitled equally to the right of carrying prizes into the ports of Great Britain.—In the House of Commons, Lord John Russell said that the character of belligerency was not so much a principle as a fact; that a certain amount of force and consistency acquired by any mass of population engaged in war entitled them to be treated as a belligerent. A power or a community which was at war with another, and which covered the sea with its cruisers, must either be acknowledged as a belligerent or dealt with as a pirate. The Government had come to the opinion that the Southern Confederacy, according to those principles which were considered just, must be treated as a belligerent. . . .

—The French Government has not yet defined its position.

NOTES

1. It was not only secession that indicated early signs of war. On 9 January 1861, South Carolinians fired upon the *Star of the West*, a merchant steamer sending supplies and troops to Fort Sumter in Charleston Habor. Major Anderson, the Union commander at Fort Sumter, did not open his batteries and return fire. A few days later a truce was secured between Major Anderson and the South Carolina governor, but relations were far from cordial.

2. Richard W. Current, *Lincoln and the First Shot* (Philadelphia: J. B. Lippincott, 1963).

3. "A Reliable Account of the Commencement of Hostilities," *New York Times*, 17 April 1861.

4. "Details of the Taking of Sumter," *New York Times*, 16 April 1861.

5. Lorman A. Ratner and Dwight L. Teeter, Jr., *Fanatics and Fire-eaters: Newspapers and the Coming of the Civil War* (Urbana, Ill.: University of Chicago Press, 2003), 103.

FURTHER READINGS

Current, Richard W. *Lincoln and the First Shot*. Philadelphia: J. B. Lippincott, 1963.

Detzer, David. *Allegiance: Fort Sumter, Charleston, and the Beginning of the Civil War*. Orlando, Fla.: Harcourt, 2001.

Faust, Patricia L. (Ed.). *Historical Times Illustrated Encyclopedia of the Civil War*. New York: Harper & Row, 1986.

7

UNION CALL FOR VOLUNTEERS, APRIL 1861

Nearly six weeks before the war officially started, Confederate President Jefferson Davis, based out of the then-Confederate capital city of Montgomery, Alabama, began formally assembling the Confederate army. The United States was also working to bolster the strength of its troops prior to the outbreak of the war—mostly by making continual calls for volunteers.

The *Philadelphia Inquirer* noted, just days before the attack on Fort Sumter, that the volunteer militia troops in Washington were excited and ready to defend the public buildings in the capital as needed. "They have nobly responded to the call made upon them, and have come forward in large numbers to be mustered into service," the paper wrote.[1]

Before the start of the war, the Union army numbered 16,000 officers and men. Once the war began on 12 April 1861, more than 300 of those men left the Union to join the Confederate army.[2] It was clear that the Union needed more troops as war got under way. On 15 April 1861, three days after the Confederacy fired its first shots on Fort Sumter, President Abraham Lincoln issued the following proclamation:

Whereas, The laws of the United States have been for some time past, and are now, opposed, and the execution thereof obstructed in the States of South Carolina, Georgia, Alabama, Florida, Mississippi, Louisiana and Texas by combinations too powerful to be suppressed by the ordinary course of judicial proceedings, or by the powers vested in the Marshals by laws,

Now therefore, I, ABRAHAM LINCOLN, President of the United States, by virtue of the power in me vested by the Constitution and the laws, have thought fit to call forth, and hereby do call forth, the militia of the several States of the Union, to the aggregate number of seventy-five thousand, in order to suppress the said combinations and to cause the laws to be duly executed. The details for this object will be immediately communicated to the State authorities through the War Department.

I appeal to all loyal citizens to favor, facilitate and aid this effort to maintain the honor, the integrity and the existence of our National Union, and the perpetuity of the popular Government, and to redress the wrongs already long enough endured.

I deem it proper to say that the first service assigned to the forces hereby called forth will probably be to repossess the forts, places and property which have been seized from the Union, and in every event the utmost care will be observed, consistently with the objects aforesaid, to avoid any devastation, any destruction of or interference with property, or any disturbance of peaceful citizens in any part of the country.

And I hereby command the persons composing the combinations aforesaid, to disperse and retire peaceably to their respective abodes within twenty days from this date.

Deeming that the present condition of public affairs presents an extraordinary occasion, I do hereby, in virtue of the power in me vested by the Constitution, convene both Houses of Congress. The Senators and Representatives are therefore summoned to assemble at their respective chambers at twelve o'clock, noon, on Thursday the 4th of July next, then and there to consider and determine such measures as, in their wisdom, the public safety and interest may seem to demand.

In witness whereof, I have hereunto set my hand and cause the seal of the United States to be affixed.

Done at the City of Washington, this 15th day of April, in the year of our Lord, one thousand eight hundred and sixty-one, and of the independence of the United States, the eighty-fifth.

(Signed)   ABRAHAM LINCOLN.

By the President.

WM. II. SEWARD, Secretary of State[3]

Public response to Lincoln's call in the North was overwhelming: "People responded to this call with wild enthusiasm. Crowds took to the streets in every city, town and hamlet. Militiamen mustered, patriotic rallies were held, speeches made and bonfires lit."[4] Lincoln's call for 75,000 additional troops was a prominent feature in the day's news both North and South, often appearing next to or with stories about the surrender of Fort Sumter.

The following day, the War Department issued a call to all of the state governors for troops and provided the breakdown of where the 75,000 men would come from. Most newspapers printed a copy of the War Department call, which was as follows:

SIR—Under the act of Congress for the calling out of the militia to execute the laws of the Union, suppress insurrection, repel invasions, etc., approved February 28th, 1795, I have the honor to request your Excellency to cause to be immediately detached from the militia of your State the quota designated in the table below, to serve as infantry or riflemen for a period of three months, unless sooner discharged.

Your Excellency will please communicate to me the time at which your quota will be expected at its rendezvous, as it will be met as soon as practicable by an officer or officers to muster it into the service and pay of the United States. At the same time the oath of fidelity to the United States will be administered to every officer and man.

The mustering officers will be instructed to receive no man under the rank of commissioned officer whose years are apparently over forty-five or under eighteen, or who is not in physical strength or vigor.

The quota for each State is as follows:——

Maine, New Hampshire, Vermont, Rhode Island, Connecticut, Delaware, Arkansas, Michigan, Wisconsin, Iowa and Minnesota, one regiment each.

Massachusetts, North Carolina and Tennessee, two regiments each.

New York, seventeen regiments.

Pennsylvania, sixteen regiments.

Ohio, thirteen regiments.

New Jersey, Maryland, Kentucky and Missouri, four regiments each.

Illinois and Indiana, six regiments each.

Virginia, three regiments.

It is ordered that each regiment shall consist in the aggregate officers and men, of 780. The total thus to be called out is 73,391. The remainder, to constitute the 75,000 under the President's proclamation will be composed of troops in the District of Columbia.[5]

As a result of the call for troops and the confirmation that war with the South had begun, Virginia, North Carolina, Arkansas, and Tennessee all refused to send troops to the North. All four states would eventually join the Confederacy, beginning with Virginia the day after the War Department call appeared on 16 April. Arkansas seceded on 6 May, followed by North Carolina on 20 May and Tennessee on 8 June. Kentucky and Missouri were also unwilling to send men to Washington to fight for the Union, but in the end, both states—while sympathetic to the South—were also respectful of the power of the federal government. They decided not to participate in the war on either side.

Lincoln's call for troops was well received in all other Union states at the time. Although Pennsylvania was only asked to supply sixteen regiments, it provided twenty-five; Ohio offered twenty-two instead of the requested thirteen. Most men sought to join the Union army because of the pay—this led to a disproportionate number of poor and unemployed men joining the service. Free blacks also tried to respond to Lincoln's call but were not accepted as soldiers. They were, however, given jobs as army cooks, waiters, and camp attendants.

Democratic and Republican Northern newspapers, which became largely unified after the attack on Fort Sumter, promoted the call for volunteers to serve in the Union army. Most actively assisted the government in its efforts to recruit men to fight in the war, and many encouraged citizens to engage in assisting the Union cause in other ways as well. For example, a few newspapers actively encouraged women to support the war effort by making army clothing or helping prepare medical supplies.

"The movements among the ladies in different Wards have become quite active," the *Philadelphia Inquirer* wrote.

They show no lack of patriotism. . . . A lady who corresponded suggests as follows:— "The troops now rallying for the defence of their country and their flag will not be likely to report, as from Charleston, 'Nobody was hurt.' Some instruction from those who know as to what will be needed, how to prepare, and where to send such preparations seem important to A LADY. The female pupils of Zane street Grammar School are at work making bandages and lint for the army, and will also furnish, to the extent of their means, the volunteers with towels, combs, &c., &c."[6]

The articles below generally reflect this kind of supportive appeal, but a few also provide some perspective on how the South received the news of Lincoln's proclamation. There is also some discussion about the impact of the call for volunteers and

Virginia's decision to secede and join the Confederacy only two days after Lincoln is-sued his proclamation.

Lincoln, of course, was not the only president trying to strengthen his army in readiness for the conflict ahead. Soon after, Jefferson Davis also issued a call for soldiers—he sought 82,000 men to fight for the South.

THOMAS N. DAY: EDITORIAL——VOLUNTEER AND SUPPORT THE UNION CAUSE

Most of the Northern papers reacted favorably to Lincoln's call for 75,000 volunteers and encouraged their readers to support the Union cause in whatever way possible. What follow are two excerpts from pa-pers that made clear appeals to their readers along those lines.

Hartford Daily Courant, 15 April 1861 (Hartford, Conn.)

The two great facts we announce this morning are, that Major Anderson has surrendered Fort Sumter to the Confed-erate States, and that the President of the United States has issued to-day a call for seventy-five thousand volunteers and an extra session of Congress, to convene on a day that has heretofore been memorable—the Fourth of July. . . .

Every man and every woman can do something for the cause by exerting good influences; those who have pecuniary means should hold them at their country's disposal; and those who have only stout hearts and vigorous constitutions should volunteer for the fight. Connecticut is a small state, and not as rich as some others; but we have passed creditably through all the wars America has ever been engaged in, from the old French war to the present day, and we may reasonably hope to give a fair account of ourselves if the shock of inter-nal warfare is bound up in our destiny.

AN ANONYMOUS REPORT: EDITORIAL——SUPPORT FOR LINCOLN'S CALL FOR VOLUNTEERS

Here is how the Philadelphia Inquirer *supported the call for troops. As previously noted, it is supportive in much the same way that the Hartford newspaper was.*

Philadelphia Inquirer, 15 April 1861

There are about three hundred and fifty thousand citi-zens of Pennsylvania liable to be called upon to perform military duty. The equipments of the State to furnish this army of men are as follows, according to the last annual re-port of the Adjutant General of the State:—69 six powder cannon, 32,080 muskets and accoutrements, 4703 rifles and accoutrements, 2809 cavalry swords and sabers, 3149 pistols and holsters, 575 tents. It must be borne in mind that many of these arms are behind the age, and unfit to en-able soldiers to cope with the improved weapons with which the men now arrayed against the Government are so liber-ally provided.

To show that our citizens are preparing themselves for the conflict, we copy the following placard, which was posted around the streets on Saturday:—

"Volunteers! Volunteers!! Volunteers!! Young men de-sirous of rallying round the Standard of the Union, and will-ing to maintain its time-honored folds unsullied over the ramparts of Fort Sumter, will enroll themselves immediately in the new volunteer Light Artillery Regiment, now rapidly filling up, and ready to march upon the receipt of orders from the Governor. Muster Rolls open every day and evening, at Military Hall, Third Street, near Green. By order of Captain J. BRADY, Acting Major."

At an early hour on that evening, a large crowd was collected.

WILLIAM HARDING: PENNSYLVANIA MEN EAGER TO VOLUNTEER—STATE WILL LIKELY EXCEED QUOTA

As early as two days after Lincoln issued his proclamation men in Pennsylvania were lining up to fight. This account in the Philadelphia Inquirer *correctly noted that the state would supply more men than requested.*

Philadelphia Inquirer, 17 April 1861

Pennsylvania is thoroughly aroused. Everywhere throughout her borders her brave sons are gathering in defence of the Union, and in vindication of the insulted honor of our country's flag. The President asks this commonwealth for twelve thousand five hundred men. From present appearances there will be enrolled and ready for orders before the close of this week, more than twice the number required. Already regiments and companies are on the march to Harrisburg, and some are actually in camp in that city. The several counties are rivaling each other for the palm in the matter of prompt response to the call of the Executive. . . . The warlike spirit of the old Pennsylvania line is living and breathing again in their patriot sons.

CHARLES HALE: MASSACHUSETTS FORMS TWO REGIMENTS IN ONE DAY

Massachusetts also quickly responded to the call, having assembled its two regiments for the Union in one day, as described in this untitled report.

Boston Daily Advertiser, 16 April 1861

The President's requisition upon the governor of Massachusetts for two regiments, amounting together to 1500 men, came to hand yesterday, and received such speedy attention that it is expected the men will begin to gather in this city to-day and be ready very shortly to go forward to Washington. There is a strong feeling that the government now must put forth a *strong arm* and crush treason and disloyalty before our liberties are lost forever. There is no doubt that the other states will respond with equal zeal; and very shortly the President will be provided with an army of 75,000 men against which the seceders will find it harder to contend than with the little garrison of Sumter.

AN ANONYMOUS REPORT: STATES OF NORTHWEST QUICKLY FORMING REGIMENTS

Although it did not respond as quickly as Massachusetts and Pennsylvania, the Chicago Tribune *notes that Illinois would soon assemble its regiments and contribute effectively to the Union cause. At the time, Illinois, Wisconsin, Indiana, and Michigan made up what many called the Northwest area of the country.*

Chicago Tribune, 16 April 1861

Massachusetts, New York, Pennsylvania, Ohio, Indiana, Michigan and Wisconsin are coming up to the work in the true spirit. Regiments from the Western States will be on the march in a few days. Governor Yates [of Illinois] has issued his proclamation convening the Legislature, and Illinois will respond next as becomes the Empire State of the fighting Northwest.

DAVID N. WHITE: BORDER STATE CONCERN OVER VIRGINIA'S SECESSION

This article highlights the concerns of people living in what were called the "Border States" at the time of Virginia's secession. The Border States were those that bordered Confederate states. Of all the papers in the North, the ones in the Border States were obviously most concerned about the impact of Virginia secession on the security of the nation's capital in Washington, D.C., and the role that their respective states would play in protecting the Union and its seat of government.

Pittsburgh Daily Gazette, 17 April 1861

Pennsylvania has a great duty to perform. She is a border State. The threatening condition of things in Virginia, right upon her own confines, renders it of the highest importance that she should prepare herself for the worst. The aggressive policy of the Montgomery government has been boldly announced by the head of the War Department there, who threatens to take Washington City [*D.C.*], and even to invade the North. That this is no idle boast may be seen at a glance. There is now at Charleston a victorious army of ten thousand troops, with vast accumulations of artillery and munitions of war, and Fort Sumter being captured there is nothing to engage the attention of General Beauregard. There is a railway connection direct from Charleston to Washington and in three days the whole of that army, with all its baggage, artillery and stores, could be at the Potomac. With the present state of feeling in Virginia there cannot be a doubt that this force could be immediately doubled by accessions from that State.

In truth we are altogether taken at a disadvantage. We did not expect war with the South and are totally unprepared for it, while on the other hand the whole time of the Montgomery government has been occupied in arming its adherents, gathering men and munitions of war, and preparing the hearts of the people for a struggle. Now that the decision has been made between peace or war, all hesitation ought to end. It is our imperative duty to arm at once, and to do it generally, and to the fullest extent. We want everything; and it seems an enormous task to set about improvising an army without officers and arms or military stores. Nothing however, is impossible to American energy.

AN ANONYMOUS REPORT: EFFECT OF PRESIDENT'S PROCLAMATION IN THE SOUTH

Several papers included in their coverage snapshots of the South's reaction to Lincoln's proclamation. The following comes from the Republican Philadelphia newspaper.

Philadelphia Inquirer, 17 April 1861

RICHMOND, April 15—The Proclamation of the president is received with general execration. The public mind is fearfully excited, and the Secessionists declare that nothing could be more favorable to their cause than the conduct of the President. Our military men would sooner die than to respond to such a call.

WILMINGTON, N.C., April 15—The President's proclamation is received here with perfect contempt and indignation.

Union men openly denounce the cause of the Administration. The greatest possible unanimity prevails.

There were great rejoicings here on Saturday at the reception of the news of the reduction of Fort Sumter.

KENTUCKY WAVERING

LOUISVILLE, April 15—The recent news considerably paralyzes our people, and they have not yet recovered from its startling effect.

Companies are enlisting for the service of the Southern Confederacy. Several will start tomorrow.

Our citizens generally deplore the existing state of affairs.

Alexandria, Va., April 15—The publication of Mr. Lincoln's Proclamation has greatly increased the secession feeling. Business of all kinds is completely suspended, and merchants are solely engaged in discussing the probability of a prolonged and sanguinary civil war. The impression is that the Virginia Convention will instantaneously pass an Ordinance of Secession, or call a Border State Convention.

A. S. ABELL: SOUTHERN REACTION TO LINCOLN'S CALL FOR VOLUNTEERS

Here is how the Democratic Baltimore Sun *described the South's reaction to the call for troops.*

Baltimore Sun, 17 April 1861

Mr. Lincoln's call for 75,000 volunteers is the main topic of discussion at the South. Some denounce its severity, and other indulge in ridicule. . . .

The Richmond [*Virginia*] Dispatch urges that the people of the various counties and neighborhoods of Virginia and Maryland, especially upon the rivers and such points as are most easy of access by an enemy, should at once proceed to adopt some organization for immediate defense. Earthworks, it says, might be cast up at assailable points, and positions taken upon the principal routes of travel, to prevent it a sudden incursion of one of the Northern hordes into the very heart of the Border States.

The Wilmington (N.C.) Journal urges the Governor of that State to convene the Legislature immediately. The Wilmington Herald says:

"Although the 'Old North State' has been slow to move, she will be quick to strike a death blow at any that may attempt to cross her soil or use her property in subjugating the South. With open arms and extended hands we welcome all Northern hirelings to a hospitable grave that may enter our midst for that purpose."

AN ANONYMOUS REPORT: PRESIDENT'S CALL FOR VOLUNTEERS HIGHLY EFFECTIVE

This article in Harper's New Monthly Magazine *suggests that Lincoln's call for volunteers, right after the attack on Fort Sumter, was an effective plea.*

Harper's New Monthly Magazine, July 1861 (New York City)

War-like preparations, upon both sides, have been carried on with the utmost vigor. At this date there are fully a quarter of a million of soldiers enrolled and in the pay of the United States. Of these about one half are in the immediate vicinity of the seat of war in Virginia, and the remainder are distributed throughout various camps, in such a manner that they can be brought into immediate service. The contributions of money by States, towns, and individuals, have been on a large scale. . . .

—Governor Hicks [*of Maryland*], who had before declined to comply with the requisition of the President for a quota of troops, now issued a proclamation stating that the requisition had been made in the spirit of and in pursuance of the law; and as he had received satisfactory assurance that the troops called for would be detailed to serve only within the State, or for the defense of the capital, he therefore called upon the loyal citizens of the State to volunteer to the extent of four regiments for the term of three months subject to the orders of the Commander-in-chief of the army of the United States.

NOTES

1. "The Troops in Washington," *Philadelphia Inquirer,* 12 April 1861.

2. W. J. Wood, *Civil War Generalship: The Art of Command* (Cambridge, Mass.: Da Capo Press, 2000).

3. Lincoln's proclamation was printed in nearly every Northern newspaper; this copy comes from the *Philadelphia Inquirer,* 15 April 1861.

4. Curt Johnson and Mark McLaughlin, *Civil War Battles* (New York: Crown Publishers, 1977), 33.

5. "Requisition for Volunteers," *Philadelphia Inquirer,* 16 April 1861.

6. "Promptness and Patriotism," *Philadelphia Inquirer,* 23 April 1861.

FURTHER READINGS

Johnson, Curt, and McLaughlin, Mark. *Civil War Battles*. New York: Crown Publishers, 1977.

Stephenson, Nathaniel W. *Abraham Lincoln and the Union: A Chronicle of the Embattled North*. New Haven, Conn.: Yale University Press, 1921.

Wood, W. J. *Civil War Generalship: The Art of Command*. Cambridge, Mass.: Da Capo Press, 2000.

8

FIRST BATTLE OF BULL RUN, 21 JULY 1861

Although President Lincoln's call for volunteers was hugely successful, Washington, D.C., was basically defenseless at the time of the call. Fears ran high in the city because of Virginia's secession and the uncertain status of Maryland, a slave state with strong secession sympathies. Soon after its secession on 17 April, Virginia troops quickly seized the Harper's Ferry Arsenal and the Norfolk Navy Yard, both of which had been damaged by retreating Union forces; the Virginians also cut the Baltimore & Ohio Railroad, which was Washington's only rail communication with the West. Secessionist riots in Baltimore led to attacks on some of the volunteers trying to get to Washington to defend the capital and fight for the Union. For a few days, rail, telegraph, and mail communications with the rest of the North were suspended, and the residents of Washington were unaware of the overwhelmingly positive response to Lincoln's call. They did not know that thousands of Union soldiers were on their way to the capital.[1]

Within a week, however, the situation in Washington shifted. On 25 April two regiments—one from New York, the other from Massachusetts—arrived under the direction of Brigadier General Benjamin Butler, who had outsmarted the Baltimore mobs and found a way to Washington via Annapolis and a feeder line of the Baltimore & Ohio Railroad. Within a month of Butler's arrival in the capital, he was able to "clear the northern approaches" to it, and afterward troops streamed into the city by the thousands.[2] Maryland quickly decided to remain in the Union, even though the decision was a difficult one. Just a week earlier the *Baltimore Sun* posed the question that was on the minds of most Maryland residents:

We, in Baltimore, are peculiarly concerned about the issue of this contest, and it becomes us to look upon it rather as it may be a year hence, or in all the future than as it is now. . . . The Union, honored by the name of Washington, is now assailed and insulted as the name and memory of that great man is at this day, by the very same people. . . . It is time for us to consider whether we can unite with them in such a work of destruction. If we do, we must assuredly share the fate richly merited by those who would destroy this Union.[3]

Troops continued to amass in Washington, D.C., and under the leadership of Major-General Irvin McDowell, the first plan of Southern invasion was drafted. Although McDowell did not support such an early offensive against the South, he was ordered by President Lincoln to move in July before the three-month enlistment terms of the volunteer militia expired. McDowell's general charge was to break the Confederacy's defensive positions near the Potomac River in northern Virginia and the lower Shenandoah Valley, specifically at Manassas Junction and Harper's Ferry.[4]

At the same time, Confederate General Robert E. Lee, who was a Union colonel until Virginia seceded, had been drafting defensive plans for the South.[5] On 1 June the Confederate capital was moved from Montgomery, Alabama, to Richmond, Virginia, and defense of the capital city became a priority. Much of Lee's thinking about war plans focused on defense since Southern leaders believed that the longer the Confederacy existed the better its chances were in gaining eventual recognition as a separate nation.[6]

The Confederate troops at Harper's Ferry and Manassas were charged with protecting the most direct route to Richmond. The Union leaders wanted to capture Richmond quickly for politically strategic rather than militaristic reasons—they believed that the political consequences of the fall of the Confederate capital would have a catastrophic effect on the South's credibility abroad and its ability to support itself as a nation.

On 24 June, in compliance with orders from General Winfield Scott, McDowell submitted his war plan. He estimated that the Confederate forces at Manassas Junction numbered 25,000 and that he would need at least 40,000 men to defeat the Southerners. McDowell continued to express concern about the early offensive mostly because his troops were "too green" for battle. To compensate for this, he wrote in his battle report,

> I think it of great consequence that, as for the most part our regiments are exceedingly raw and the best of them, with few exceptions, not over steady in line, they be organized into as many small fixed brigades as the number of regular colonels will admit . . . so that the men may have as fair a chance as the nature of things and the comparative inexperience of most will allow.[7]

McDowell's basic plan was to overwhelm Confederate General P. T. Beauregard at Manassas Junction, while Union General Robert Patterson would pin down the Confederate forces under the command of General Joseph Johnston at Harper's Ferry in the Shenandoah Valley. Patterson's efforts would be crucial to Union success in this battle since McDowell outnumbered Beauregard's forces three to two if Beauregard were not able to get support from Johnston's men. But if Patterson could not keep Johnston's troops away from the fighting at Manassas, the Confederates would outnumber the federal troops and gain the edge.

McDowell launched his offensive on 16 July when his troops began their 20-mile march to Centreville. Once there, General Daniel Tyler's advance guard moved down to Bull Run Creek to check out the Confederate defenses and became involved in an early skirmish. It was reported in the *Philadelphia Inquirer* as follows:

> About two P.M. the advance of General Tyler's Division, consisting of the Wisconsin, Connecticut, and Thirteenth New York Regiments, were going through the woods, four miles from Manassas, on Bull's Run, when a masked battery opened upon them with fearful destruction. The men took behind the trees, and kept up the fire for more than an hour. The Rebel troops consisted of seven regiments of South Carolina and Alabama troops.
>
> Reinforcements were sent for, and the balance of the division came up with the artillery, but owing to the intervention of trees it could not be used with much effect. The 14,000 men fought until four o'clock, when we captured their battery, and then fell back for help. The loss is very heavy on both sides. A Chaplain is reported as killed, and a number of officers.
>
> Both sides fought with a fierceness, determination and coolness never before surpassed. We have not been able to secure any names of our killed and wounded. Before night, Tyler was no doubt reinforced, and we are now waiting for further particulars.[8]

McDowell's concern about the "rawness" of his troops was confirmed in the early fighting at Bull Run and had a demoralizing effect on the rest of the Union troops. Also problematic for the Union was the fact that General Beauregard knew of the Union advance toward Manassas. He immediately called for reinforcements, which he received from General Johnston in the Valley. General Patterson had not contained Johnston as planned because his troops had drifted away from the Confederate army's main body as a result of miscommunication over the telegraph lines. The stage had been set for Union disaster.

Because General Johnston outranked General Beauregard, he assumed command of the impending battle at Manassas Junction. He approved Beauregard's plan to attack the Union left forces via the country roads that converged on Centreville. In the meantime, General McDowell spent two days having his officers scout the Confederate line at Bull Run and decided to attack the far left of the Confederate line. On 21 July the Union attack began—General Tyler managed successfully to trick the Confederates into thinking the fight would be at Blackburn's Ford near Bull Run by virtue of a false attack. He diverted Confederate troops successfully, allowing Union Colonel Ambrose Burnside and the Rhode Island brigade to advance on the Confederate extreme left. The Union troops overwhelmed the Confederate brigades and eventually broke up the Confederate line. Rebel troops ran down into a nearby valley while Union troops continued to fire on them. The Confederates knew that if they lost the Henry plateau, where their troops had fled, they would be defeated at Manassas.[9]

General McDowell's troops had convincingly won the morning phase of the battle. To ensure a complete victory, they only needed to pursue the fleeing Confederate forces. But, largely due to the inexperience of the troops, the Union brigades disintegrated, and a lack of organization and complete confusion allowed the Confederate forces time to regroup. Under the leadership of General Thomas Jackson, the Confederates formed a concave line that stretched nearly 330 yards between Manassas-Sudley Road and Robinson House near Bull Run. Jackson's men were in position when the fragmented, disorganized Union troops trailed back over the plateau. Inspired by Jackson, Confederate General B. E. Bee called to his troops to join Jackson's line: "Form! Form! There stands Jackson like a stone wall! Rally behind the Virginians." The troops of Confederate Generals Bee, Bartow, and Evans did rally with Jackson's—then General Beauregard and Johnston's troops were led into the line.[10]

McDowell's attack on the reformed Confederate line began at 1:00 P.M. Four brigades commanded by Generals Sherman, Porter, Franklin, and Wilcox charged the rebel forces. Charge and countercharge continued on both sides across the plateau. Sensing the upper hand, McDowell ordered two batteries to the front to take a new southern position. For nearly an hour that position did no good for the Union; then at about 3:00 P.M. one of Jackson's Virginia regiments advanced on the two newly positioned batteries. Because they wore blue militia uniforms, the color of the Union, Jackson's men were mistaken for Union troops. The Union batteries did not fire on them. Soon after, the Virginia militia leveled 400 muskets and opened fire, immediately killing fifty-four Union men and 104 horses. The Union troops counterattacked, but by 4:00 P.M. the army began to disintegrate. Exhausted, a majority of the Union troops began to straggle away before the next Confederate attack. When the Confederate attack finally came, fear and panic took over, and the Union retreat turned into a disorderly rout.

The battle ended with the flight of the Union soldiers. McDowell's army was shattered but reorganized in Washington, D.C., days later under new command (General George B. McClellan). The Confederate army was too tired to advance beyond Centreville after the fighting. The Confederate soldiers fortified a camp there and waited for more Union movement. In the end, 460 Union men were killed, 1,124 were wounded, and 1,312 were captured or missing, for a total loss of 2,896. The Confederates suffered less, with 387 killed, 1,582 wounded, and thirteen captured or missing, for a total loss of 1,982. Both sides were in virtually the same positions they had occupied before the battle.[11] The significance of the battle for the North was that it recognized the war would not be quickly ended. Soon after the battle, Congress voted to raise an army of a half million long-term volunteers.

The Northern press covered the Battle at Bull Run with great interest. Coverage started well before the fighting with accounts of battle preparations. The reports from the battlefield reflected the events as they happened in sequential order, which led to premature declarations of a Union victory based on General McDowell's early success. After the battle had concluded and it was clear that the Confederacy had fared better and won a moral victory at the very least, Northern papers took to their editorial pages to bolster support for the Union army.

Most press accounts correctly identified the inexperience of the troops as the primary reason for the loss at Bull Run, but other theories emerged as well. Some editors mistakenly charged that it was the fault of a few fellow Northern newspaper editors who engaged in rhetoric about taking Richmond before the troops were ready. They argued that these editors' "on to Richmond" mentality led to the defeat at Bull Run. In fact, this strategy to try to take Richmond quickly was created by the president and his military officers, and there is no indication that the press influenced this decision. As previously noted, McDowell had opposed such a strategy as early as May because of his inexperienced troops. Still, he was ordered to take the young troops into battle, and the result was Union defeat in the first significant battle of the war.

AN ANONYMOUS REPORT: ASSESSMENT OF UNION COMMANDERS SCOTT AND McDOWELL

This article provides a general analysis of the strength of the Union army commanders, specifically Generals Scott and McDowell, and largely dismisses the rebel army leaders, including General Robert E. Lee, as Union troops headed toward what would later be called the Battle of Bull Run.

New York Evening Post, 17 July 1861

The time has at last come when the Commander-in-Chief thinks it prudent to order his grand army to take up the line of march towards the headquarters of rebellion. Fifty thousand men left Washington yesterday to proceed towards Fairfax and Manassas Junction.

This is a formidable array of force; but General Scott does not disguise from himself his difficulties or his dangers; he observed to a friend yesterday, as he was about to visit the Virginia side of the Potomac, before giving the final order for departure, "This is no child's play; our troops have been honorably eager to move, but they will find that they have work before them." Nevertheless, while the Commander-in-Chief properly appreciates the magnitude of his task, and endeavors to impress upon the minds of all who are co-operating with him, the importance of what they undertake, he does not despair in the least of the ultimate result. On the other hand, we have reason to know, that Gen. Scott, who is fully informed of the operations and strength of the rebels, relies with confidence upon the wisdom of his own combinations and the sufficiency of his troops. He has taken his own time, he knows what he is about, and he believes

that apart from the discipline and drill of his men, the enthusiasm of a good cause will carry them triumphant forward until the end.

General Scott is assisted by officers worthy of his own exalted reputation. An impression has gone abroad that the rebels carted off with them in their revolt a surplus of the best army officers. A few good men they did appropriate, of inferior rank, and not of the higher grades. Beauregard, Lee, Johnston and Magruder, we are told by competent military authority; though excellent artillerists and engineers, are not qualified to command vast masses of men. Impelled by the genius of Scott, they would be serviceable subordinates, but left to themselves, they will be found deficient. Not one of them is equal to [*Union General*] McClellan, whose brilliant exploits at the West are now in every mouth. Gen. McDowell, who leads the advance from Arlington, is superior to any of them in military knowledge, in dash, in energy, and in any solid military quality. [*Union officers*] Lynn, Burnside, Doubleday, and many others, might be cited in the same application. If they do not bag Jeff. Davis in less than a month, then we are mistaken.

AN ANONYMOUS REPORT: BATTLE IN WASHINGTON AREA IMMINENT

This article focused on the supplies headed to the area and offered a general prediction that there would be an upcoming battle near Washington, D.C.

Chicago Daily Tribune, 17 July 1861

**THE LATEST NEWS
ACTIVITY AT WASHINGTON
ALL READY TO ADVANCE
A BATTLE IN PREPARATION**

From Washington

(Special Dispatch to the Chicago Tribune)
Washington, July 16, 1861.

About five hundred horses per day, for army uses have

been received at the Quartermaster's Department during the last week. Some hundreds of army ambulances have been sent across the Potomac within a few days. A good many people refuse to believe that the long-deferred "forward movement" is about to take place, notwithstanding these extraordinary ocular demonstrations. The majority however, are less incredulous.

URIAH H. PAINTER: EARLY REPORTS OF ENCOUNTER ON 16 JULY

The two following news briefs are an example of the first, early reports of fighting that appeared in the Northern newspapers. These accounts discuss the 16 July conflict five days prior to the Battle of Bull Run.

Philadelphia Inquirer, 19 July 1861

The report at the War Department says, that the Rebel battery was not taken, and that the fight is over for to-night; the South Carolina troops having retreated. Our men will not follow them until morning. Four of our men were killed and three wounded. During the fight our artillery was brought to bear on a barn up the river bank; and at the first shot fired, out ran a company of Rebels with a battery.

They fired into our ranks, and at each fire they would cheer. Their loss is heavy, from our shells. General TYLER thinks it was the rear of their retreating army with whom we had the engagement. Want of baggage wagons compels them to move slow, and if we only had a few regiments of cavalry we could cut off their retreat.

AN ANONYMOUS REPORT: FIRST REPORT OF BATTLE AT BULL RUN

This account gives an early picture of the fighting at the 21 July Battle of Bull Run and offers some prediction about the outcome.

Baltimore Sun, 22 July 1861

STIRRING WAR NEWS

Another Severe Battle at Bull's Run.
Bull's Run Battery Silenced.
Confederates Driven Back to Manassas.

**GREAT SLAUGHTER ON BOTH SIDE
THREE MASKED BATTERIES TAKEN
COL. CAMERON AND COL. SLOCUM REPORTED
KILLED**

Col. Hunter Mortally Wounded.
Operations of Gen. Mile's Command.

HIGHLY INTERESTING DETAILS

We received last night the subjoined highly important news from the seat of war, giving accounts of a terrible battle at Bull's Run, with great loss of life.

Among the federal officers reported to be killed are Col. Cameron, of the New York 79th regiment, and Col. Slocum, of the 97th N.Y. regiment of volunteers.

Col. David Hunter, of the Third U.S. Cavalry, and acting Major-Gen. McDowell's army, is reported to be mortally wounded.

[Special Dispatch to the Baltimore Sun.]

Great Battle and Loss of Life

WASHINGTON, July 21—8 P.M.—An official dispatch from the Major-General McDowell, received at the War Department at 5 o'clock this afternoon announces that the battle at Bull's run was recommenced at 7 o'clock this morning, and lasted until 4 o'clock this afternoon.

The result of the battle was the capture of the Bull's Run battery, and the driving of the Confederates back to Manassas Junction, with terrible slaughter.

The Federal troops also suffered severely in killed and wounded.

There are various exciting rumors afloat here—one that the Federal army have taken three other Confederate batteries.

Cannonading was distinctly heard to-day at Arlington Heights, and in Washington.

A large portion of both armies are reported to have participated in the battle. The artillery, however, did the principal part of the fighting.

[SECOND SPECIAL DISPATCH.]

WASHINGTON, July 24, 9 P.M.—The city is in a state of intense excitement and filled with rumors from the field of battle, of continued fighting and the taking of Manassas Junction. I cannot, however, trace these rumors to any reliable source.

An immense number of ambulances and wagons, and about 8,000 troops were dispatched from this city to day to the scene of hostilities.

AN ANONYMOUS REPORT: WAR CORRESPONDENT'S DESCRIPTION OF CONTEST AT BULL RUN

Many of the accounts of battles in the Civil War read a bit like modern-day sports "play by play." This article is an example of how war correspondents often dissected the fighting of a battle and how they detailed the regiments and individuals involved.

Hartford Daily Courant, 22 July 1861 (Hartford, Conn.)

A DESCRIPTION OF THE CONTEST

RUMORS OF THE DEAD AND WOUNDED

The Order of Battle

WASHINGTON, July 21. Many unauthenticated rumors prevail which serve to confuse the truth. The smoke of battle could be seen in Washington. A number of members of Congress, and even ladies, went to the neighborhood of Bull's Run to witness the battle. The conflict was desperate, lasting over nine hours.

The programme as previously stated was carried out until the troops met with a succession of masked batteries, which were attacked with vigor and success. Our troops advanced as follows: Col. Richardson, who distinguished himself in the previous engagement, proceeded on the left with four regiments of the fourth brigade, to hold the battery still on the Warrenton road and in the vicinity of the place where the last battle was fought.

Schenck's and Sherman's commands of Tyler's brigade advanced by the Warrenton road, while Heiutzelmann's and Hunter's divisions took the fork of Warrenton road to move between Bull Run and Manassas Junction.

Keyes' brigade remained at Centerville. Information was received by Tyler's command of the existence of the enemies battery commanding the road. Our troops then formed in the order of battle array. The 2nd N.Y. and the 1st Ohio on the left, the 2nd Ohio and 2nd Wisconsin, the 79th, 13th and 69th New York on the right. Col. Miles' division followed in the rear.

The 1st range gun was fired by Sherman's battery at 10 minutes of seven. The rebels did not return his shot until one hour and a half afterwards, when another battle became general. Col. Hunter's movement to gain the rear of the enemy was almost a success. The enemy's position was opened upon by several of Carlisle's howitzers followed by slight skirmishing.

The rebels rapidly received re-enforcements from Manassas after the attack opened. The battle consisted in a succession of fires from masked batteries which opened in every direction. When one was silenced its place was supplied by two, and in the daring charges of our infantry in unmasking them, the 2nd Ohio and the 2nd New York were marched by flank through the woods by a new-made road within a mile of the main road, when they came on a battery of eight guns with four regiments flanked in rear. Our men were immediately ordered to lie down on either side of the road in order to allow the artillery to pass through and attack the work, when this battery opened upon us and killed, the third round, Lieut. Dempsey of the New York 2nd.

Our troops were kept for fifteen or twenty minutes under a galling fire, not being able to exchange shots with the enemy, although within a stone's throw of their batteries. They succeeded in retiring with their battery.

The most gallant charge of the day was made by the 13th, 69th and 79th New York, who rushed upon one battery, firing as they proceeded, with perfect *éclat* and attacking it with the bayonet's point. Their yell of triumph seemed to carry all before it. They found the rebels had abandoned the battery and only taken one gun, but this success was acquired only by a severe loss of life, in which the 69th most severely suffered, and it was reported that Lieut. Col. Nugent was among the first killed.

WILLIAM HARDING: ERRONEOUS EARLY REPORT OF UNION VICTORY AT BULL RUN

Some early reports that appeared in Northern newspapers jumped the gun and declared victory for the federal government based on the Union army's success early that morning; later it was clear that the South emerged as the winner of the Battle of Bull Run.

Philadelphia Inquirer, 21 July 1861

Many a patriotic heart, that has been depressed by the temporary check to the advance of the Grand Army of the Union, will swell with pride and exultation this morning over the grand triumph of yesterday. The strong position held by the Rebels at the Bull's Run crossing, has been carried by General McDOWELL's column, and THE TRAITORS HAVE BEEN DRIVEN BACK UPON MANASSAS JUNCTION. By the time this reaches the public, the Junction itself may have fallen before the irresistible sweep of the soldiers of the nation.

The battle is reported to have been in progress all of Sunday, and every inch of ground appears to have been stubbornly contested until five o'clock, when the batteries at Bull's Run were carried. On both sides the fighting was fierce, and the slaughter fearful; but treason, thank heaven! has gone down before loyalty and right. Those who remember that, when the Union troops were checked by the galling fire

from the concealed battery on Thursday last, the Rebels cheered lustily at every shot, may now imagine the thrilling shouts that went up from the patriot ranks as the rebellious "stars and bars" made way for the victorious Stars and Stripes.

We do not of course, go into particulars, as every one will read carefully and dwell with gratification upon every line of the news as it appears under the proper head. The great feature of this victory—greater than the mere successful storming of the enemy's entrenchments—is, that it establishes the *morale* of the forces of the Government. It shows that new as they are, and fresh from the pursuits of peaceful life, they are yet true to the instincts of the warlike races from which they spring; that they are equal to any ordeal they are likely to meet in this war; and it enforces and establishes the *prestige* of invincibility inaugurated by General McCLELLAN's grand career in Western Virginia.

URIAH J. PAINTER: "GREAT SLAUGHTER AND BRILLIANT VICTORY"—ANOTHER ERRONEOUS REPORT OF UNION TRIUMPH

The following news item also incorrectly gave the Union credit for an early victory.

Philadelphia Inquirer, 22 July 1861

FROM OUR SPECIAL REPORTER
THE BATTLE AT BULL'S RUN
GREAT SLAUGHTER AND BRILLIANT VICTORY

This has indeed been a glorious day for the Union. From morning till night the battle has been progressing, and on both sides have the troops shown their courage and fearless impetuosity. Hundreds on both sides have been slain and now

sleep in death on the gory field of battle. The slaughter was indeed terrific, and the sight appalling to one unaccustomed to the horrors of war. General McDOWELL telegraphed at five o'clock this afternoon, that he had taken the batteries at Bull Run. A complete victory has been gained over the Rebels at this place, and they are now in full retreat towards Manassas, with our troops following them closely. The firing was so heavy that it has been heard in Washington for an hour past.

A. S. ABELL: EDITORIAL CALLS FOR CALM IN BALTIMORE AFTER UNION DEFEAT AT BULL RUN

In light of the federal government's newfound defeat at Bull Run, this article urges citizens in nearby Baltimore to remain calm and peaceful. Given the riots that occurred in Baltimore in April, the citizens there remained on edge. Despite a tenuous allegiance to the Union, a majority of residents in the state still sympathized with the South.

Baltimore Sun, 22 July 1861

Our columns this morning are occupied to a great extent with such details of the recent conflict between the Federal and Confederate troops as are accessible to us and our correspondents. There will of course be some repetition, probable discrepancies, and occasional facts or surmises that may not

be verified, but in the main we apprehend the statements contained in our reports will be as usual accurate, reliable and ample as care and attentive supervision can make them.

The result of the conflict, which seems to have been very desperate and bloody, is such as could scarcely have been expected by either the general government, the South or its friends and sympathizers. The troops of the Federal army seem to have appeared before Manassas in great strength, and to have made considerable advances with success; and in view of the losses they have sustained must have encountered the Confederate forces with sustained resistance and valor. But from some cause, whether the vigor of the Confederate defense, an attack by an overwhelming force, or the conclusion after hours of hard fighting that the assault was hopeless and desperate, the Federal troops seem to have fallen into despair, and, under a general panic, retreated from the fatal scene of their first great endeavor.

The nature of the retreat is presented in detail by our correspondents, with as much particularity as the case admits of. It seems to have been a most disastrous affair to the government forces, and there is scarcely a doubt that the Confederate loss is correspondingly heavy. The loss of government property, consisting of artillery, wagons, arms, stores and ammunition must have been enormous, all of which has fallen into the hands of the Confederates.

The exact status and relation of the opposing forces can scarcely be estimated in the confusion of the hour, and it is not possible to conjecture what the next move will be. Certainly on the part of the federal government the aggressive will not be assumed at an early day. Whether Beauregard is in a condition to improve his advantages and assume the offensive a few hours will probably determine, as, if such is his purpose, he will not suffer the retreating army to employ time in maturing its defenses. We do not think from the present aspect of the case that such an attack is probable.

We have heretofore intimated the propriety of abstaining from needless and unprofitable demonstrations under the excitement which plainly agitates the people of Baltimore. Our citizens ought to understand by this time the position in which they are placed with respect to the overwhelming power of the government, and to exercise such self-control as will obviate collision, which if carried to any general extent could only be disastrous. —Moreover, with our political relation to the general government, we are bound by every principle of honor and self-respect to maintain peaceful relations with it until in the progress of this unhappy controversy our position shall be definitely determined. While we deplore this civil war, and profoundly regret the carnage which involves American citizens of the North or the South, we cannot despair of such an early adjustment of the controversy as will be more becoming to a civilized people than the frenzied arbitrameni of the battlefield. Let us then wait the issue patiently, decently, and with the trusting confidence of true men that the right shall prevail with or without the terrible issue of war.

URIAH J. JONES: DEFEAT AT BULL RUN STRENGTHENS FIGHTING SPIRIT IN UNION

One of the responses to the Union defeat at Bull Run was to stir up and encourage even more fighting spirit in the North.

Harrisburg Daily Patriot & Union, 24 July 1861 (Harrisburg, Pa.)

The events of the last thirty-six hours seem to us much more like a vague, undefined dream than the stern reality, which weighs us down with almost unutterable grief. On the clear stillness of Sabbath night the bells rang forth a merry peal, and the hearts of the people leaped with joy, because victory was ours. —Yesterday, while a park of artillery was firing a salvo, and while friend was congratulating friend upon the triumphs, real and imaginary, gained by our army in Virginia, the lightning flashed a different tale across the wires. We feel in no mood to speculate upon the result— "Sufficient unto the day is the evil thereof."

If any one had predicted such a catastrophe in the North two days ago, he would with great propriety have been set down as a madman.—Indeed so unable were people to realize the real extent of the disaster that for hours yesterday many doubted the truth of the dispatches received. When at last the facts were palpable, there was not only an intense excitement, but a feeling of patriotic ardor that rose superior to all the humiliation inspired by the defeat.

Animated by one common feeling, the masses are ready by thousands and tens of thousands to rally and fill up the broken and diminished ranks of the army, and to-day Pennsylvania is prepared to furnish fifty thousand men to the place of those who have fallen in defence of the Stars and Stripes.

The defeat at Manassas has awed but not conquered us. The shrieks of the wounded and the groans of the dying—the wail of the widow and the tears of the orphan will arouse the entire united North, who *will* "strike until "the last foe expires." The lion of the Nation has been aroused, and he will soon enter the arena in his might.

WILLIAM HARDING: RESPONSIBILITY OF PRESS FOR FORCING UNPREPARED ARMY TO FIGHT AT BULL RUN

This article suggests that the Confederate army entered the Battle of Bull Run with a decided advantage. It also criticizes the writings of some journalists and editors who encouraged the federal troops to move forward and take the Confederate capital city of Richmond prematurely. This article is particularly critical of Horace Greeley, the publisher of the New York Tribune, *who is mentioned by name in passing.*

Philadelphia Inquirer, 23 July 1861

Yesterday a great sorrow overspread this city and the country like a shroud. The army of the Union, in which was centered the pride, the prayers and the hopes of the people of the Free States, was reported to have been repulsed, beaten and scattered in the great battle on Sunday, of which we all had such high hopes of signal victory. That such a calamity can have happened is almost too stunning in its immensity to be realized even now. When the history of the conflict comes to be written by the dispassionate historian, the causes of our defeat may be summed up briefly in a few words. Masked batteries—inexperienced officers—the unaccountable and unobstructed escape of JOHNSTON'S column from the upper Potomac—and the wild and fanatical clamor of the *Tribune* and its allies for an unseasonable advance—these are the pernicious influences that did the fatal work. . . .

No proper appreciation of the battle, or of the stupendous odds against our army, can be had without reference to the advantages possessed by the Rebels. They were upon ground of their own choice—in a position which they had occupied for months. They chose it after thorough examination—were acquainted with the whole face of the country, knew every hill, knoll, gorge, defile, road and pass. At every point where it was possible for the Union troops to pass, there was a concealed battery. The woods, roads, hills, deep cuts and thickets fairly bristled with them. To attempt to pass was running a gauntlet of the most formidable ar-

tillery for miles and miles. Yet, against this terrible array our men charged in the most fearless manner; but it was not in the power of man to go through them by sheer fighting. It was a field in which strategy was more wanted than it ever was in any battle in history; but this was the only element that was lacking.

We cannot but think that it was the plan of the General-in-Chief to drive the Rebels from the Junction mainly by military maneuvre, and not by throwing his men into the jaws of such a terrible fire. But his policy seems to have been overruled through the influence of the senseless clamors of a set of pestilent political editors in New York and elsewhere, who rung the changes upon the catchwords, "On to Richmond," "The people cry for an advance," &c., &c., regardless of the condition of the army or the ability of its separated divisions to co-operate, until a forward movement was precipitated and the country humiliated by defeat.

This disgrace must be wiped out; this defeat must be retrieved by a victory, before which this of the Rebels will pale. But to achieve this great result, our troops must have Generals who know how to deal with masked batteries—who are able to estimate the numerical force of the enemy and the strength of his position—and, above all, these Generals must be protected from the GREELEYS, and other mischief-makers of that ilk, who are responsible for much of our present trouble.

WILLIAM LLOYD GARRISON: GOVERNMENT FORCES DEFEATED AT BULL RUN

William Lloyd Garrison's abolitionist newspaper The Liberator *did not devote many pages to reports on specific battles with a few exceptions. One exception was this article about the Union defeat at Bull Run.*

The Liberator, 26 July 1861 (Boston)

On Sunday last—("there are no Sabbaths in Revolutionary times," said Mr. Webster, or some one else)—the first general engagement with the rebel army took place at Bull's Run, not far from Manassas Junction, in Virginia—the result being the defeat of the Government forces with great loss of life on both sides. This . . . though wholly unexpected, is not

surprising, in view of the great disparity between the contending parties—the rebels having immense superiority in point of numbers, and every advantage in choice of position, with masked batteries in all directions. There was evidently no lack of courage or determination on the part of the Northern troops; but in such circumstances, every step of the way openly exposed to the murderous fire of concealed enemies, the most desperate valor is unavailing, especially when there is great inequality of forces. It is true, a panic at last look place in their ranks, and a disastrous retreat followed; but not until nine hours of almost incessant conflict, passed under the hottest fire.

It is evident that, cost what it might in the sequel, Jefferson Davis and his generals saw the vast importance of gaining the first victory in a general engagement in order to inspirit the rank and file of their own army, and to affect European sentiment favorably to a recognition of the independence of the confederate States, if not with the expectation of disheartening the Government at Washington; and so they brought nearly their whole immense force into action, and decided the fortunes of the day by one tremendous, if not absolutely exhaustive effort. —An invading army inevitably labors under great embarrassments from lack of that familiar knowledge of localities, which is worth a host of men to the invaded, who know precisely where to decoy, to mine, to ambuscade, to plant their secret batteries, to choose the most available position of defence and attack; often making it a massacre rather than a conflict. Under such disadvantages will the Northern soldiers labor every inch of the way; and no amount of valor can overcome these, unless accompanied by a greatly preponderating numerical force. From the responses already made, that force will be speedily obtained,

for the power of the North has scarcely yet been touched; and then a very different result may be confidently looked for, though not without the most sanguinary encounters.

But—at the best—what a horrid spectacle is presented to the world of a powerful nation rent with civil feuds, and millions of its people stimulated to. the highest degree of hostility to each other! What desolate households—what wide-spread bereavements—what wailings of widows and orphans—what heaps of the dead, the dying, and the mutilated! And all this because of SLAVERY—accursed SLAVERY!

We predicted that the most demoniacal acts would be perpetrated upon the Northern soldiers falling under the power of the Southern Sepoys; and already we hear of the wounded on the battle-field thrust through and through with bowie-knives and bayonets, and otherwise mangled—in some instances their bodies quartered, and in others their heads cut off, and made the foot-balls of their fiendish enemies. Atrocities like these, and in every conceivable shape, may be expected in every encounter where the day shall be won by these debased and dastardly minions of the Slave Power. It is sickening to think of what is to come; for the struggle is evidently to be more protracted, and more formidable, than any have yet anticipated, unless it be cut short by a quick and an annihilating blow at the whole slave system—the sole cause of all this complication of horrors.

WILLIAM HARDING: REPULSE AT MANASSAS AND THE INFLUENCE OF THE PRESS

The Philadelphia Inquirer *took issue with the* New York Tribune *for its alleged influence connected with the premature Union advance on Manassas. It had previously criticized the paper and its publisher, Horace Greeley, for too aggressively promoting a Union assault on the Confederate capital city of Richmond.*

Philadelphia Inquirer, 24 July 1861

Anxiety about the great disaster of Sunday last almost exclusively occupies the public mind. Details are eagerly sought after and caught up, and especially those which give reason to believe that the calamity was after all not so great as it appeared to be at first. As the confusion which followed the battle is gradually dispelled, there appears to be good ground for hope that the reported casualties are happily diminishing, both in number and in importance.

Public opinion, however, is settling down into consistency, and almost into unanimity, as to the parties and the causes to be charged with the responsibility of the disaster at Manassas. Inexperienced officers, incomplete organization, and

premature action are the causes believed to be at the bottom of our most unlooked-for defeat, and for these the parties that are almost universally blamed are, the Secretary of War, who is held to be unequal to his position, and the clamorous mischief-makers of the New York *Tribune*, who have been fairly howling for a forward movement, without regard to the condition of the army, and reckless of the cost of life, and of the peril to the country.

Upon these points it is our purpose to speak fully and freely, and, we hope, dispassionately, but the facts are not yet sufficiently clear, and the smoke of the battle still obscures the truth.

THOMAS N. DAY: THE SAD BATTLE—SOMEBODY BLUNDERED

The Hartford Daily Courant *offers an elaborate analysis of what may have caused the loss at Bull Run and also, in passing, criticizes the* New York Tribune.

Hartford Daily Courant, 26 July 1861 (Hartford, Conn.)

No more plausible theory of the causes which demoralized McDowell's division last Sunday, than the following has yet been made public:

General McDowell, with an army which, including the reserves at Centerville, did not number more than 40,000 actually attacked the rebels at Manassas Gap, where Beauregard has been for months preparing his fortifications, and where he had lined the hills with elaborate and carefully-constructed entrenchments, behind which were rifled cannon of large caliber properly manned and supported by an army which subsequent information leads me to estimate at nearly 100,000 men. Behind these batteries the Southern troops fought. They were constructed in a manner calculated to deceive the most experienced eye. The breastworks were in the shape of a gently sloping hill, neatly sodded, with here and there a tree left growing to more thoroughly deceive our troops as to their existence. Their line of batteries covered two or three miles. The whole region seemed literally to be one masked battery. What appeared to be a natural delivery would in a moment bellow forth a most fearful charge of grape-shot, shell, and canister; and from every clump of bushes or shrubbery the terrible messengers of death would come at the most unexpected moment.

I mention this in order that you may more properly understand the details of this great battle, and more properly appreciate the gallantry of our men. Notwithstanding they had slept on their arms, and had marched ten miles to the place of engagement, they rushed into the contest weary, wanting food and water; they drove the enemy from battery and battery; slowly and slowly pushing them from their position. From nine o'clock till three the battle was a victory; and, if at three o'clock there had been ten thousand fresh men to assist them; if Gen. Patterson had only come from Martinsburg, or McClellan over the Blue Ridge from Western Virginia, or if even Miles' division of reserves could have been marched from Centerville, we could have driven them from the field and won the day. Our men were weary, and in many cases inefficiently commanded. The enemy were being constantly reinforced. So rapidly did they arrive, that many of their knapsacks on their shoulders, and I could distinctly see with a strong spy-glass even from the hills beyond Centerville, regiment after regiment of the rebels coming from the neighboring districts and passing over the roads to Manassas. In many cases the colors of their flags could be easily distinguished.

The causes of our defeat appear to be these: A premature advance on the enemy without a sufficient force, which may be attributed to the clamors of politicians, and newspapers like the New York *Tribune*; the negligence of Gen. Patterson in not intercepting the Gen. Johnston at Winchester, and preventing him from joining Beauregard at Manassas; the want of efficient force of artillery to answer their masked batteries; the inefficiency of many of the officers; the want of proper discipline among the volunteers, and the general panic which seized upon our forces in the latter part of the action.

I have heard many stories of the bravery of some regiments and the inefficiency of others. But if we can make any such distinction, it is with the officers, who commanded, and not with the men, who obeyed. The material of our army is of an extraordinary character, and this disastrous battle has shown it; for character, and this disastrous battle has shown it; for the men who could fight double there numbers behind masked batteries for ten hours, in a country where water could not be found, under the torrid rays of a Southern summer sun, and make that fight a victory until their endurance had been overtasked and the ranks of the enemy had been filled up by fresh men, are capable of anything which may be demanded of the soldier. And this is the story of the battle of Manassas; this is the substance of every rumor—the logical result from every fact the contest furnishes.

The general panic took place about five o'clock in the afternoon. There are a number of stories told as to the apparent reason for the precipitate flight of our troops; but without stopping to relate them, or even to consider their manifest absurdity, I would simply say that it was caused by their utter exhaustion, and the terrible fire of masked batteries, which were taken by them, again and again, at the point of the bayonet, only to find when taken, that others would open them. The reinforcements vastly strengthened the enemy, their fire was increased, and, before that fire, our men retreated. If they had been properly commanded, they might have retreated in good order, like the regulars, under Major Sykes; but this, and the want of experience, gave rise to a panic, which soon swept everything before it, and carried our army like a tumultuous mob, from Manassas to Washington.

CHARLES HALE: "PUSHED TOO QUICKLY"—RESPONSIBILITY OF PRESS FOR PROMOTING THE PREMATURE CAMPAIGN

This untitled editorial echoes many of the sentiments in the two previous articles and provides a more significant critique of the press and its involvement in military affairs.

Boston Daily Advertiser, 24 July 1861

We have been reluctant to believe the reports which have been circulated from time to time, that the advance of our forces upon Manassas was undertaken prematurely in consequence of the clamors of a portion of the press, and of some equally unwise and indiscreet politicians. We have been unable to believe that General Scott could be moved by the folly of outside critics to forego the conclusions of his own experienced judgment, nor could we believe that either the President or his advisers could have been guilty of the absurdity of insisting, that an educated and consummate soldier should follow the advice of unmilitary critics. It has seemed to us more natural to believe that the old general, who in the long run will be held mainly responsible for our good or ill success in this campaign, was left, as he ought to be, to follow his own plans, in supreme disregard of the absurd projects insolently and officiously thrust upon his notice by men who have never seen a battle and will never fight in one.

We are still disposed to adhere to this belief and to attribute our reverse of Sunday, partly to the failure of Patterson to carry out his part of the grand scheme and prevent Johnston from turning the scale in favor of the rebel army, and partly to one of those unforeseen and inevitable chances which may at any moment, even in the hour of substantial victory, overwhelm the best laid plans. But we cannot help seeing that there is also some reason for now believing that our force was pushed forward from the Potomac more rapidly than General Scott approved. There are reports of the interference by members of Congress, aided by insensate clamors from the press; the President is said to have been told that the People demanded action and that the army must march; a pretended public opinion, created by the efforts of a few journalists, is said to have been brought to bear in the highest quarters and to have weighed more than the counsels of the gray-haired veteran, whose task it is to repair the mischief done by such impertinent meddlers. We cannot believe these reports to be true, but they are widely in circulation, and they raise a question which must be answered.

It is due to the country that the exact truth of this matter should be known. If a great military plan, affecting the welfare of the nation, has been hastened to its ruin by the noisy interference of men who may be able to estimate the vote at the next election, but who are guiltless of all military knowledge,—the country has a right to know the fact and to have the names of those who have wrought this mischief. If the case be as it is represented, the popular opinion which has been fraudulently invoked in this matter will soon settle the cases of those who have made it the cloak for their own presumptuous and ignorant folly. If any man, whether journalist or member of Congress, has undertaken to settle the time and manner for our military movements and to carry out his own ideas by personal influence, by operating on the minds of the troops, or by urging any great popular demand for his particular plan, let it be know, and there will be such a demonstration of *real* popular opinion, as will free the Commander-in-Chief's office, the departments, and the Executive Mansion from intrusive advisers, for the remainder of the war. For the people do demand one thing. Smarting under a misfortune, the cause of which they as yet apprehend but dimly, they demand today that the great business which is in hand should be left henceforward exclusively to those who understand and are responsible for its management, and that all others should stand aloof.

DAVID N. WHITE: SIZE OF THE ARMIES AT MANASSAS JUNCTION

Many articles, including a few on previous pages, suggested a rebel numbers advantage. In truth, both sides commanded similarly sized armies. The Union was 35,000 strong, with only 18,572 who engaged in the battle. The Confederacy had 32,500 men, of which only 18,053 engaged in the fighting. Both sides had forty-nine pieces of artillery.[12] This article focuses on the issue of troop strength and puts a positive spin on the outcome.

Pittsburgh Gazette, 23 July 1861

Since the smoke of the battle has in some degree cleared away, and we can get a wider and clearer view of things, the aspect is far more cheerful and satisfactory than it was yesterday. We shall not criticize the conduct of Gen. Scott in sending 40,000 men to fight with 50,000 strongly entrenched. We think he was not aware of the number of men or the strength of the fortifications at Manassas Junction, but be that as it may, the victory on our side would still have been complete had Gen. Patterson kept Gen. Johnston in play until the fight at Manassas was over.

In the battle on Sunday the secession forces were decidedly worsted and on Monday the weary men were set at it again, having had but little sleep or food, while they had to contend against continued accessions of fresh troops, especially Johnston's division, who were brought by railroad from the mountains while others poured in by railroad from the direction of Richmond. No men ever fought more brave than did ours on that occasion; but long continued labor and excitement wore out their nervous energy, and caused that panic which astonished and grieved us all. In this way the thing can be easily accounted for—in psychological principles. It is said that Sherman's battery, having exhausted its ammunitions, started back to replenish and that the movement was misconstrued by the other troops as a retreat and the panic having thence communicated to the teamsters, everything conspired to lead to a general stampede. Still, we now know that the rout was not as disorderly as was at first reported.

Nothing has occurred to weaken our confidence in the bravery of our troops. Already are these overtasked and unfortunate men pleading to be led back that they may have an opportunity to wipe out what they feel to be a stigma, but which when all the circumstances are considered is no dishonor. . . . Let no unkind reflection, therefore, be made upon that precipitate retreat for too much fighting had made those brave men weak. The effect of that terrible conflict upon the country has been very good. On Monday, when the most gloomy and disheartening news was coming hourly over the telegraph, we had in this city several companies of new recruits only partially filled; but that day they filled up with increasing rapidity. On Tuesday morning two regiments, the 8th and 11th, left this city for the seat of war in the highest spirits. Colonel Black leaves to-day, we believe, with his new regiment, and many of the Home Guards are ready to go if needed. This reverse, like the bombardment of Sumter, only served to exhibit the indomitable energy of the American people, and although the war may be rendered more fierce and protracted by this partial triumph of the rebels, still their ultimate discomfiture is none the less certain, and the cause of all this trouble is only the more likely to be rooted out.

CHARLES HALE: IMPACT OF LOSS AT BULL RUN IN EUROPE

In this untitled editorial, the author expresses concern about the impact of the Union loss at Bull Run on European perceptions of the North's ability to win the war. Part of the concern centers on the South's appeal to Europe to buy its cotton. Prior to the Battle of Bull Run, Northern ships created a blockade of Southern ports, inhibiting the rebels' ability to export cotton to Europe. This writer is concerned that if Europe believes the North can not win the war, then it might resist the Union blockade and try to resume the cotton trade with the South, despite European efforts to remain neutral and not become involved in the war in any way. As previously noted, much of the Union strategy involved in trying to take Richmond early was to undermine the credibility and legitimacy of the Confederacy abroad.

Boston Daily Advertiser, 25 July 1861

No one who has observed the manner in which the press has met the disaster in Virginia, or has had occasion to note very extensively the prevailing tone of public opinion, can have any fear as to the courage and resolution with which the country will seek to repair its misfortunes. The elastic spirit of the people is not only undaunted, but is wrought up to higher exertions; there is a universal sentiment that the field lost on Saturday must be retrieved, and a universal determination that this defeat shall not go to the world as the statement of what Northern troops can do. The fall of Manassas Junction is now a point of honor which engage the feelings of the whole North, and no demand which the government can make upon the resources of the country or upon the courage of our citizens for that end would be refused. The military results of the defeat are not important, except as it delays the final approach to Richmond and inspires the enemy with fresh courage by reviving their fading belief in the cowardice and weakness of northern troops. And as we now see the only political result of the reverse, in this part of the country, is to increase the general determination to leave our cause set right in the sight of the world; of the political result in the border states there is yet hardly ground for speaking.

We cannot but feel that the political effect of the defeat upon our foreign relations is that which is most to be considered, and which demands the most active measures of pre-caution. When the army marched out of Washington, public confidence in the real neutrality of Europe was fast reviving and with good reason. It was felt that the general government was making such an exhibition of strength as must, even to the most prejudiced eyes, show that the success of the rebels was extremely doubtful; we were believed to be on the eve of important successes, which would show to all the world that the rebels had a failing cause. The rebels themselves, so far as could be judged from such of their journals as chanced to stray hither, were beginning to lose heart as to the success of their arms, and to rely more and more upon their cotton. The enormous bribe, however, which this crop offers to the leading European powers to interfere in this contest, directly or indirectly, and especially to resist our blockade, was felt on all hands to be at least suspended and held in abeyance, while the government was apparently closing in upon an antagonist of inferior strength. There was general confidence that foreign powers who had seen this nation collect and organize its strength with such rapidity, after the national power was believed by them to be dead, would see, before the cotton year should begin, such a test of strength between the parties as should dispel all doubts of the actual and early supremacy of the general government.

Reviewing the position of affairs today, we do not indeed find any substantial reason which should lead any foreign power to a different policy from that which it would have adopted last week. But we do find that the national arms are under a cloud. We can explain our failure in the march upon Manassas, but the news of defeat will outrun the explanation and be remembered when that is forgotten. While we are approaching the most critical period perhaps of the whole struggle, the season when the cotton crop comes in and when Europe must decide once for all what to do with its millions of operatives, we find that we are thrown back for weeks in our campaign, and that the decisive success for which we looked is not to be so early as we had planned.

We have thus noticed this effect of our misfortune of Sunday, because it appears to us at present to be the only really important result from which we have much to apprehend, and because, so far from a fair view of this being in any way a discouragement to our people, it seems to us to be, on the contrary, an incentive to the most strenuous and instant exertion. What we have to fear is not that we shall be beaten in the sight of Europe, but that Europe shall fall into the mistake of supposing that we are going to be beaten, and shape its policy accordingly. The people of the loyal States know that they are strongest, from the superiority of material resources, as well as from a solid national character, and the pursuit of a just cause. They now have only to fear lest Europe may relapse into the mistaken expectations of April and May, at the time when it is fast becoming all important that correct views should prevail. This danger, however, may be counteracted by instant and efficient action, which, shall carry abroad a speedy contradiction of the unfavorable impression which yesterday's steamer must carry out. We have not lost so much but that energy and a courageous spirit may retrieve it as speedily as it has been lost.

NOTES

1. Curt Johnson and Mark McLaughlin, *Civil War Battles* (New York: Crown Publishers, 1977).

2. Ibid., 33.

3. "Must There Be War?" *Baltimore Sun*, 18 April 1861.

4. Johnson and McLaughlin, *Civil War Battles*, 33.

5. Lee, a native Virginian, chose to fight with his state, which is how he became a Confederate general.

6. Ned Bradford (Ed.), *Battles and Leaders of the Civil War* (New York: Appleton-Century-Crofts, 1956), 28; Johnson and McLaughlin, *Civil War Battles*, 33.

7. Bradford, *Battles and Leaders*, 29.

8. *Philadelphia Inquirer*, 19 July 1861.

9. *Baltimore Sun*, 22 July 1861.

10. Johnson and McLaughlin, *Civil War Battles*, 37. This famous incident is also where General Thomas Jackson picked up the nickname "Stonewall," which stuck with him. Jackson died from a battle wound in 1863 (see Chapter 16).

11. Ibid., 39.

12. Ibid.

FURTHER READINGS

Bradford, Ned (Ed.). *Battles and Leaders of the Civil War*. New York: Appleton-Century-Crofts, 1956.

Davis, William H. *Battle at Bull Run: A History of the First Major Campaign of the Civil War*. Baton Rouge: Louisiana State University Press, 1981.

Johnson, Curt, and McLaughlin, Mark. *Civil War Battles*. New York: Crown Publishers, 1977.

9

BATTLE OF SHILOH, 6–7 APRIL 1862

Five days after the federal loss at Bull Run, General George McClellan assumed leadership of McDowell's army, called the Union Army of the Potomac. McClellan replaced officers, laid out new camps, and staged reviews to boost the morale of the Union troops. He was eventually promoted to general-in-chief of all the federal forces, and as such McClellan devised a strategic war plan that had three basic points of attack on the Confederacy—one in Virginia, one in Kentucky and Tennessee that would secure that area, then one that would allow the federal troops to advance from their Kentucky and Tennessee positions toward the heart of the Confederacy in Mississippi, Alabama, and Georgia. As the troops advanced south, the Union navy would clear the Mississippi and surround the Confederacy by sea, choking off its supplies.

In September 1861, General Ulysses S. Grant successfully captured Paducah, Kentucky. By the end of 1861 the Union army was 700,000 strong. Grant was one of the U.S. generals fighting on the western front along the Mississippi River and was based out of Cairo, Illinois. His success continued in February 1862 when he captured Forts Henry and Donelson in northwestern Tennessee.

Meanwhile, also in February 1862, Confederate General Albert Johnston was creating a defensive line that stretched nearly 300 miles from the Mississippi River at its most western point to Cumberland Gap on the Virginia border on the east to thwart federal attempts to move further south. Johnston had 45,000 troops scattered along this line, and their main objective was to defend the major invasion routes from the north and to protect the Confederate heartland.[1]

By March, Johnston had concentrated most of his troops at Corinth, Mississippi, an important rail town because it was located at the juncture of the Mobile & Ohio and Memphis & Charleston Railroads. Corinth was also a good base from which to defend the Memphis & Ohio line, which was the South's only adequate line of communication between the Atlantic Coast and the Mississippi River. Johnston amassed

60,000 troops at Corinth. His second in command was General Pierre G. T. Beauregard.[2]

While Johnston was building and organizing his forces at Corinth, General Grant transported his army into southwest Tennessee and joined General William T. Sherman at Pittsburg Landing. Pittsburg Landing was chosen by Sherman as a campsite because it was a transfer point for goods shipped from the Tennessee River to Corinth, 22 miles to the southwest. Eventually Grant established his campsite at Savannah, Tennessee, a river town 8 miles north of Pittsburgh Landing. Grant's camp was called "Camp Shiloh" because it was located near Shiloh Church, a tiny log meetinghouse that was about 2.5 miles from the landing. During most of March the federal army was conducting raids against the railroad and gathering forces to mount an attack on Corinth.[3]

By early April 1862, Generals Prentiss, Stuart, Grant, Sherman, McClernand, Wallace, and Hurlburt had federal troops established in and around the Pittsburg Landing/Camp Shiloh area. Confederate General Johnston knew of the federal troop presence at Shiloh. Upon hearing that Major General Don Carlos Buell's troops were also heading for Shiloh, he was urged by General Beauregard to take the offensive and attack the Union army there before they could strike Corinth. On 6 April 1862, that attack happened, to the complete surprise of the federals.

Johnston's plan was to overwhelm Grant's troops by surprise attack before Buell's troops arrived as reinforcements. Specifically, the Confederates wanted to cut off a line of retreat to the Tennessee River and force Grant back to a location called Owl Creek, where they assumed he would be forced to surrender. Surprise was the key element to Johnston's plan, and the day before the attack Confederate Generals Bragg and Beauregard suggested that Johnston call off the attack because Union and Confederate troops had engaged in some minor skirmishes in the area just the day before. They worried that the Union army already knew of their presence.

Johnston refused to call off the attack. At about 5:00 A.M. on 6 April, federal troops discovered the Confederate soldiers in a nearby field, and a skirmish ensued, followed by the federals falling back. About ninety minutes later, General Johnston maneuvered eight of his Confederate brigades toward General Prentiss's camps and routed the Union army there.[4]

Heavy fighting ensued, and throughout the day on 6 April both sides fought fiercely. While Johnston had some brigades attacking General Prentiss's men, he also had five brigades attacking General Sherman's division. Sherman's troops suffered heavy casualties and fell back to join General McClernand's division. The Confederates continued to assault the two units that comprised the Union's right flank and drove them back.

While Sherman, Prentiss, and McClernand were fighting losing battles, Generals Wallace and Hurlburt moved their divisions to the front of the line and threatened Johnston's right flank. In response, Johnston ordered Confederate Generals Chalmers, Jackson, and Breckinridge to attack the Union left flank, but the federal troops under the leadership of General Stuart managed to hold their position. Later in the day, between 1:00 and 4:00 P.M., Johnston ordered another assault on the federal left flank, and he was killed in the fight. General Beauregard assumed command of the Confederates. By the time night fell, the federal troops had been beaten back toward

Pittsburg Landing and Shiloh Church. Federal gunboats on the Tennessee River fired into the captured federal camps much of the night. And General Sherman received support from General Wallace's troops at Shiloh Church in preparation for the next day's battle.

The next morning, at about 7:00 A.M., the federal troops under General Wallace began to drive the Confederates back. Generals Grant and Buell advanced, too, and after another day of intense back-and-forth fighting, by 4:00 P.M. the Confederates retired from the field, and the federals reclaimed their position and bivouacs.[5]

In the end, both sides suffered terrible losses. The Union troops saw 1,754 men killed, 8,308 wounded, and 2,885 captured or missing, for a total of 12,947 casualties. The Confederate troops fared only slightly better, with 1,728 killed, 8,012 wounded, and 959 captured or missing, for a total of 10,699 casualties.[6]

Early reports of the battle highlighted the devastating loss on both sides. This brief article in the *Baltimore Sun* notes, "The fight, it appears, lasted two days, and resulted in the success of the Federal arms. The accounts show it to have been one of the most desperate and bloody engagements of modern times. The losses on both sides are probably exaggerated, but doubtless they are very large."[7]

Similar to the coverage of Bull Run, the press focus was on recounting the details of the battle and in continuing to promote the Union cause. Because Shiloh represented the bloodiest battle of the war up to this point, many of these articles highlight this. As was common in early reports of Civil War battles, these accounts are also filled with some bad information. For example, Confederate General Beauregard was not seriously injured in the fighting; rather, a captain who assisted Beauregard sustained a serious arm injury. Early reports also suggested that federal General Wallace had been killed, but Wallace was only injured.

Many Northern reports also emphasized a federal win in the contest at Shiloh. A few criticized the Union commanders for not seeing the attack coming. In many ways, the battle was a draw—both lost nearly equal amounts of men, and neither gained an advantage in location. But the perception that the North had won did have some merit since the South lost its opportunity to reestablish strategic balance in the West. As a result of the losses at Shiloh the Confederate leaders virtually abandoned the Mississippi Basin. This left Chattanooga vulnerable and led to the eventual Union capture of Corinth, Island No. 10 on the Mississippi River, New Orleans, and Memphis.

AN ANONYMOUS REPORT: EARLY AND INACCURATE REPORT OF FIGHTING IN TENNESSEE

This early report of the battle is not accurate in its assessment that the federals won the first day of fighting on 6 April. The latest dispatch contained in this report is the most correct in noting that the federal lines were driven back in that first day of fighting. It was common for early battle reports to appear as this one does below with large headlines and sketchy and often incorrect information.

Hartford Daily Courant, 9 April 1862 (Hartford, Conn.)

THE LATEST NEWS
BY TELEGRAPH

From Gen. McClellan's Command

No Extraordinary Progress

One More Union Victory.
Great Battle in Tennessee.
The Rebels under Beauregard attack General Grant.

A DESPERATE FIGHT ALL DAY
REPULSE OF THE REBELS

Gen. Grant in Pursuit

WASHINGTON, April 8.— . . . The following message was received by the Secretary of War this evening: "On the 6th inst. the rebels in overwhelming numbers attacked our forces at Pittsburg landing; the battle lasted from morning till late in the afternoon, and resulted in the complete defeat of the rebels, with heavy loss on both sides. Gen Grant is following up the enemy. Gen Buell has arrived in Tennessee; two divisions of his army were in the battle.

CHICAGO, April 8.—A private dispatch received in this city to-night, from one of Gen Grant's staff, says:

"We have fought and won the hardest battle ever fought on this continent."

The dispatch is dated Pittsburg Landing, 6th.

ST. LOUIS, April 8.— . . . To-night, Gen. Halleck said that Gen. Beauregard, with an immense army, advanced from Corinth and attacked the combined forces of Gens. Grant and Buell. The battle began at daybreak yesterday, and continued till late in the afternoon, with terrible loss on both sides. We have gained a complete victory and driven the enemy back within his fortifications. He also announced his departure for the field to-morrow morning.

LOUISVILLE, April 8.—The Nashville *Patriot* of this morning says a gentleman who left the neighborhood of the rebel army of the west, last Thursday, says: Gen. Beauregard left Corinth that day for Pardy, Tenn., and Gen. Johnston left for Pardy the same day. It was expected they would bring up a battle, Friday or Saturday, if their march was not impeded by the rain.

Further advices from New Madrid report that Gen. Pope has taken 3000 prisoners at Tipton in their retreat.

A special to the Chicago Times says that 480 prisoners including 7 officers, 30 pieces of artillery. The rebels had become perfectly demoralized and refused to obey orders. There was no confidence felt in the commanding officer.

CAIRO, April 8.—Information was received here, tonight, that on the 6th the rebel forces under Gen. Beauregard attacked our forces Gen. Grant. The battle lasted all day. Our lines were driven in by the attack.

But as our reserves were brought into action the lost ground was regained, and the rebels repulsed with great slaughter. Our loss is very heavy. No particulars known.

AN ANONYMOUS REPORT: ACCOUNT OF BATTLE AT SHILOH

The following report comes from a war correspondent who witnessed the battle firsthand. Its focus is on the engagement aspects of the fighting.

Cincinnati Times, 10 April 1862

Our forces were stationed in the form of a semi-circle, the right resting on a point north of Crump's Landing, our sentry being in front of the main road to Corinth, and our left extending to the river in the direction of Hamburg, four miles north of Pittsburg Landing. At 2 o'clock on the morning of the 6th, 4,000 men of Gen. Prentiss' division were attacked by the enemy half a mile in advance of our lines. Our men fell back on the 25th Missouri safely, pursued by the enemy. The advance of the rebels reached Col. Peabody's regiment just as the long roll was called, and the men were falling into line. Resistance was short, and they retreated under a falling fire till they reached the lines of the 2d division.

At 6 o'clock the attack had become general. Along our whole front the enemy, in large numbers, drove in the pickets of Gen. Sherman's division, and fell on the 4th, 50th and 72d Ohio. These troops were never before in action, and being so unexpectedly attacked, made as able resistance as possible, but were, in common with the forces of Gen. Prentiss, forced to seek the support of the troops immediately in the rear. At 10 o'clock the entire line on both sides was fully engaged. The roar of cannon and musketry was without interruption, from the main centre to a point extending halfways down the left wing. The rebels made a desperate charge on the 14th Ohio battery, which, not being sufficiently supported by infantry, fell into their hands. Another severe fight occurred for the possession of the 5th Ohio battery, and three of its guns were taken by the enemy. By 11 o'clock a number of regimental commanders had fallen and in some cases not a single field-officer remained. Yet the fighting continued with an earnestness on both sides, which showed the contest was for death or victory. Foot by foot the ground was contested, and the rebels, finding it impossible to drive back our centre, made vigorous efforts on our left, under Gen. Hurlburt. Fronting its line, however, were the 44th, 57th and 77th Ohio, and 5th Ohio cavalry of General Sherman Livingston. For nearly two hours the battle blazed fiercely, and while it was the hottest the Tyler passed up the river and pouring in broadsides from her immense guns, greatly aiding in forcing the enemy back. Up to 3 o'clock every effort to break our lines failed. They had been unable to drive in our main column, or our left. They now made another attempt at our centre, endeavoring to rout us before reinforcements should arrive. At 5 o'clock they retired a half a mile, but suddenly turned upon our left, but were driven off by the terrible discharges from the Tyler and Lexington. In the meanwhile Gen. Wallace, who had taken a circuitous route from Crump's Landing, appeared suddenly on the enemy's right. Under these circumstances they fell back to an advantageous position on the main road to Corinth. After several hours of watchfulness and anxiety Gen. Buell's advance appeared on the river bank opposite, and were greeted with cheer after cheer. All night long steamers were engaged in ferrying Buell's army across and at daylight it appeared evident that the rebels also had been reinforced.

They opened the battle at 7 o'clock, at the Corinth road, and in half an hour it extended along the whole line. They were met by our reinforcements and the still unwearied soldiers of yesterday with an unexpected energy. The rebels were handled with masterly generalship; leaving one point and suddenly returning to it again, and then again directed their attack at some unexpected quarter; but our fire was as steady as clock work, and the rebels were soon convinced that their task was hopeless. Further reinforcements came up and took position in the main center under Gen. Wallace. Gens. Grant, Buell, Nelson, Sherman and Crittenden were everywhere present directing the movements for a new stroke on the rebels. Suddenly both wings of our army were turned upon the enemy, intending to drive them into an extensive ravine. At the same time a powerful battery stationed in the open field poured volley after volley of canister into the rebel ranks. Our fire increased in energy, while the rebels' slackened and fell slowly back.

They retreated in excellent order, fighting at all advantageous points, but they were closely pursued by all the divisions of our lines, a galling fire being kept up upon their ear. They were in full retreat for Corinth, pursued by our forces.

The number of forces engaged is estimated at 70,000 on each side.

CAIRO, April 10—An arrival from Pittsburg Landing says that the rebels in making the first attack on Sunday morning, carried the Stars and Stripes and wore the Federal uniform.

Gen. Bragg is reported to have been killed. Johnson, Provisional Governor of Kentucky, is wounded and taken prisoner.

It is stated that Gen. Prentiss escaped in the confusion of the rebel retreat, on the second day.

Our loss is 7,000. This is the estimate of the military commanders who were in the engagement. Of this number about 2,000 were taken prisoners. The balance are killed and wounded in the usual proportion.

Gen. Wallace was reported dead, as it was thought impossible that he could live. He was alive on Wednesday, and improving. He was shot in the back of the ear, the bullet coming out of his nose.

A special to the Chicago *Tribune* says that Gen. Prentiss had no artillery with him when he was attacked on the retreat Sunday afternoon. Thousands of our men took refuge under the bank, and utterly refused to fight any longer. In fact, they could not, officers and men were in such inextricable confusion. The gunboats Tyler and Lexington opened fire, and thus prevented a defeat. They kept it up during the night, and one shell set the woods on fire, burning the dead rebels.

About midnight, the rebels attempted to erect a battery near our siege-guns, but were prevented by the gun boats.

Our informants persist in estimating our loss on Sunday at 3000 killed and 5000 wounded.

During the night the rebels were reinforced by Gens. Van Dorn and Price from Ark., with a very large force.

Gen. Buell is reported to have taken Corinth with its immense stores of arms and ammunition.

The rebel troops were mostly from Texas, Miss., La., Ga. and Ala.

Our informants say they could not ride through the field where lay the rebel dead, they were so thick.

Gen. McClernand's division fought with great gallantry for the most part, but the 53d Ohio were ordered to the rear in disgrace for refusing to fight.

Our informants state that John C. Breckenridge is taken prisoner. They saw him pass the general headquarters.

WILLIAM HARDING: ACCOUNT OF GLORIOUS UNION VICTORY AT PITTSBURG LANDING (SHILOH)

This is another example of the early reporting that came from Shiloh and Pittsburg Landing. Most Northern papers called this the Battle of Pittsburg Landing. Today it is more commonly known as the Battle of Shiloh, but many also still call this the Battle of Pittsburg Landing.[8] This account erroneously reports Beauregard's injury and the death of General Wallace.

Philadelphia Inquirer, 10 April 1862

To those who have learned sagacity by the experience of this war, there was evidently something in the Rebel despatch which came from Norfolk, *via* Mobile, of a great battle near Corinth, and which was generally pronounced a *canard*, designed to keep up the sinking spirits of their troops.

But the true version of the story has now reached us, and we are able to present our readers with a connected summary of the principal events in the giant battle fought at Pittsburg Landing on Sunday and Monday last—not less remarkable for the bravery of our troops and the admirable conduct of our Generals, than for the great results which must ensue from it.

The concentration of the Rebel army at Corinth seems to have been determined upon several grounds. It is at the junction of two important railroads—the Memphis and Charleston and the Mobile and Ohio; it communicates directly with Memphis; it covers New Orleans; it offers great facilities for the transportation and collection of supplies; it is near the frontiers of Tennessee, Alabama and Mississippi; and the hilly nature of the surrounding country renders works of defence easy of construction. Here the rebel generals had concentrated an army of from seventy to eighty thousand men; and here it seemed their determination to await the attack of GRANT and BUELL, in the hope that, behind their entrenchments, they could defeat the Union Generals, and perhaps retrieve the fortunes of war.

But finding GRANT'S command, of MCCLERNAND'S, SHERMAN'S and HURLBURT'S Divisions, at Pittsburg Landing, the temptation was very strong to march upon them and overpower them, and, if possible, drive them into the river before BUELL'S expected reinforcements could arrive. To this end,

the Rebel General, JOHNSTON, moved forward in two heavy columns, each about thirty thousand strong, the left one directed upon Purdy, a small town on the Corinth and Columbus Railroad, and the other on Hamburg, a village a short distance towards the Northeast. Between these two lay Pittsburg Landing, on the Tennessee; and thus their plans were laid to enclose GRANT'S Army on both flanks, and make a Western Ball's Bluff. Their generalship was excellent, as their fighting was afterwards proved to be, yet both were defeated, and their fortunes are ten times as desperate as before. . . .

This battle will be long remembered by the casualties which occurred and the dangers to which Generals were exposed. Gen. A. S. JOHNSTON is said to be killed; BEAUREGARD to be badly wounded—an arm shot off; and, on our side, SHERMAN had two horses killed and was wounded in the hand, while MCCLERNAND and HURLBURT each received balls through the clothes. General W. H. WALLACE was killed, as were also a number of acting Brigadiers. GRANT and SMITH were both wounded, although they seemed to bear a charmed life, moving, through both days, amid showers of shot and shell.

The loss of JOHNSTON and BEAUREGARD would, in itself, were there not far greater disasters, be sufficient to make the Rebels despair.

Such seem to be the features in outline of the bloodiest battle ever fought in America. Elsewhere we treat of its probable results.

At a late hour last night we learned, by telegraph, that the victorious Union forces occupied the town of Corinth, while the panic-stricken Rebels are fleeing before our cavalry, some distance beyond.

CHARLES HALE: SHILOH WON BY HARD-FIGHTING UNION TROOPS IN TENNESSEE

This untitled account focuses on the bravery of the Union army in Tennessee, and it promotes the Union troops fighting in Virginia under General McClellan as well.

Boston Daily Advertiser, 10 April 1862

Making every allowance for the exaggeration of excited informants, it is clear that the battle of Sunday and Monday on the Tennessee River was most severely contested, and that it was won by sheer hard fighting. The nature of the contest makes it certain that this must have been so. The rebel generals, finding that our forces under Grant were speedily to be joined by Buell's formidable column, determined to overwhelm the corps immediately before them by a general attack in greatly superior numbers. Nobly did the men thus assailed at disadvantage sustain themselves. Fighting inch by inch

against a powerful enemy, who on this field showed himself brave and resolute, they wore away the day in a desperate resistance, giving way slowly before a tide which they could not stem. It was on both sides a fight against time,—on our side of men struggling to hold out until the arrival of relief known to be at hand, on the other of men who knew that their last hope of success was slipping away with every hour of delay. The efforts of men who fight thus are no boy's play. Such a struggle is the death grapple, when all that fierce determination and stubborn valor can do on either side is done.

The critical moment, however, when an attack of this sort might have resulted in a partial success, had passed. The stern courage of our gallant troops sustained them through Sunday's conflict, and that night the tide turned. The next morning saw the Union forces in a position to give battle on equal terms, and both sides eager to retrieve whatever they had lost or failed to accomplish on the previous day. It may easily be credited that, as the telegraph informs us, this was the most fiercely contested battle as it was the longest in respect to the numbers of men engaged, ever witnessed on this continent. The destinies of the republic in large measure depended upon the day; and the soldiers who won the field fought with a full consciousness of the great interests dependent upon their courage and strength. To enthusiasm and bravery and endurance such as patriot soldiers bring in aid of the cause of their country, is this grand victory due. This noble success, achieved by the strong arms and stout hearts of western troops, gives new interest to the prospect of a similar achievement on the part of our forces in Virginia. The attack now in progress under General McClellan will not close without giving to our soldiers from the east some opportunity for giving as solemn testimony to their devotion and bravery, as was given by their western brethren on the Tennessee. Severe as will be the price paid by New England and the Middle States for the result of the approaching struggle, they will pay it cheerfully, and will be proud to emulate the heroism of the West. They will rejoice at the opportunity to conquer the respect of the South, and to secure that of the West, for the manly qualities which characterize the sons of what has usually been deemed the section least qualified for military affairs.

AN ANONYMOUS REPORT: CONFEDERATE GENERAL JOHNSTON DEAD—UNION VICTORY COMPLETE

One of the most significant losses to the Confederate army at Shiloh was the death of General Albert Johnston. Johnston's death was not immediately reported to the Confederate troops because of its predicted demoralizing effect.

Hartford Daily Courant, 10 April 1862 (Hartford, Conn.)

**THE LATEST NEWS
BY TELEGRAPH**

Later from the Great Battle.

OUR VICTORY COMPLETE

Our Loss 6000 Killed and Missing

Pursuit of the Flying Rebels.
Corinth in Our Possession.
DEATH OF GEN. JOHNSTON

CAIRO, April 9.—Further advices from Pittsburg Landing give the following about the battle: "The enemy attacked our forces at 4 o'clock Sunday morning, the brigades of Gen. Sherman and Prentiss being first engaged. The attack was successful, and our entire force was driven back to the river, where the advance of the enemy was checked by the fire of the gunboats. Our force was then increased by the arrival of Gen. Grant with the troops from Savannah, and inspirited by the report of the arrival of General Buell's armies. Our loss this day was heavy, and besides the killed and wounded, embraced our camp equipage and 36 field-guns.

The next morning our forces, amounting to 80,000, resumed the offensive, and by 2 o'clock P.M. had taken our camp and batteries together with some forty of the enemy's guns, and a number of prisoners, and the enemy were in full retreat, pursued by our victorious forces. Our casualties were numerous, and include Gen. Grant, wounded in the ankle, slightly; Gen. W. H. Wallace, killed; Gen. Smith, severely wounded; Col. Hall, 16th Ill., killed; Col. Logan, 32d Ill., wounded severely; Col. Davis, 51st Ill., wounded severely; Major Hunter, 32d Ill., killed; Col. Peabody, 25th Ill., severely wounded. Our killed wounded and missing are not less than 5,000.

WASHINGTON, April 9.—The following was received at the war department this evening: "General A. Sidney Johnston's body was left on the battlefield and is in our possession. Also the bodies of a large number of other prominent rebel officers."

AN ANONYMOUS REPORT: CONFEDERATE ACCOUNTS OF BATTLE AT PITTSBURG LANDING (SHILOH)

This article from the Hartford Daily Courant *provides information of the Confederate accounts of the battle. Often Northern papers relied cautiously on Southern newspaper accounts of battles when they did not have any other sources of information.*

Hartford Daily Courant, 14 April 1862 (Hartford, Conn.)

BALTIMORE, April 11.—The gunboat "Reliance" has arrived with the schooner "Hartford," captured off Wycomico river. Found aboard, the Richmond *Whig* of the 8th, containing dispatches in reference to the battle at Pittsburg, all dated the 6th, and giving the following account of Sunday's fight only:

THE BATTLE OF SHILOH, APRIL 5, via Corinth and Chattanooga.

Gen. S. Cooper, Adjt. Gen.—We this morning attacked the enemy in a strong position in front of Pittsburg, and after a severe battle of ten hours gained a complete victory, driving the enemy from every position. Loss on both sides heavy, including our commander-in-chief, Albert Sidney Johnston, who fell gallantly leading his troops into the thickest of the fight. P.G.T. Beauregard, Gen. Commanding.

FIRST DISPATCH

MOBILE, April 7.—Specials to the *Advertiser and Register*, dated Corinth yesterday afternoon, say the battle continued fast and furious, the enemy stubbornly resisting their fate while the Southerners continued to press upon them with resistless determination, slowly—but surely forcing them back. Our loss is heavy but our men are in good spirits and are thoroughly warmed up to the work in hand.

All fight well, but the Alabama, Mississippi and Louisiana troops display great gallantry. The 21st Alabama covered themselves with glory. This regiment captured two batteries. The 1st Louisiana regiment of regulars took a battery. Gen. Bushrod, one of the Fort Donelson prisoners who subsequently escaped, is wounded.

Sunday Night—The enemy are in full retreat and the confederates in hot pursuit. I write from the enemy's camp and on federal paper. Large numbers of prisoners have been taken, and we expect to capture the greater part of the federal army. We are driving them back on the river and shall kill or capture the entire army.

The battle is still raging with great fury. We have captured Gen. Prentiss and a large number of officers. Gen. Albert Sydney Johnston fell at half past 2 o'clock. One of his legs was torn by a shell and a Minnie ball struck him in the body. He died while gallantly and steadily leading our victorious troops.

Gen. Beauregard now commands the army. He says this is a second Manassas fight. Gen. Buell was not in time to take part in the action. Gen. Grant was in command of the federals.

SECOND DISPATCH

Gen. Prentiss was captured. He says they have thirty-five thousand men on the field and eighteen batteries nearly all of which have been captured. Gen. Buell had a portion of his force at Duck Creek. We have the enemy's camp and all their ammunition stores, &c. The battle was a very severe one, and the loss on both sides is heavy. The fight is still going on. Gen. Polk is in the advance. Gens. Prentiss, Grant, Sherman, McClernand, Wallace and Smith commanded the federals. Gen. Smith was sick. Two thousand prisoners have been taken and sent to our rear. It is reported here that our forces are fighting Buell to-day, (Monday). Gen. Clark and Col. Brown of Mississippi and Col. Richards of Missouri, were wounded. The federals have been driven to the river and are attempting to cross in transports. Many prisoners are still being brought in. There is no account in the paper of Monday's battle, in which the rebels were so completely routed.

CHARLES HALE: SUMMARY OF GENERAL GRANT'S REPORT OF BATTLE AT PITTSBURG LANDING (SHILOH)—UNION TROOPS SURPRISED

This article provides a summary of General Grant's account of the battle and suggests that the federal troops should have seen the attack coming.

Boston Daily Advertiser, 18 April 1862

General Grant's report on the battle at Pittsburg Landing clears up very few of the doubtful points respecting the enemy's surprise of our troops. This might be accounted for in part by the report which is given by several authorities, that General Grant himself did not appear on the field until about noon on Sunday. This circumstance reminds one strongly of a similar absence on his part reported at Fort Donelson.

The truth is that there was somewhere a shameful disregard of all ordinary rules of prudence or of military art; and while we do not charge this upon General Grant, it nevertheless must subject him to the gravest suspicions, that he should give no hint in his report of any short-coming on the part of any one, where negligence and inefficiency are so clearly apparent.

An officer of Halleck's staff, who had his information from an aide of Grant, writes an account in the New York Evening Post, in which he says that it is understood that Beauregard made his advance on Friday before the battle to a point within a few miles of General Grant's position. He formed in battle array, and on Saturday night resumed the march, coming upon our forces at daybreak and completely surprising them. That the enemy should have passed at least one whole day at appoint not over half a day's march from our camp, would seem incredible.

P.G.T. BEAUREGARD: CONFEDERATE GENERAL'S OFFICIAL REPORT ON SHILOH

The following article focuses on the Confederate General Beauregard's account of the battle.

Baltimore Sun, 31 May 1862

Gen. Beauregard's official report of the battle of Shiloh (dated April 11th) has been received at New York. We make the subjoined extracts:

THE DESIGN OF ATTACK

It was then determined to assume the offensive and strike a sudden blow at the enemy in position under Gen. Grant, on the west bank of the Tennessee, at Pittsburg and in the direction of Savannah, before he was reinforced by the army under General Buell, then know to be advancing for that purpose by rapid marches from Nashville via Columbia. About the same time Gen. Johnston was advised that such an operation conformed to the expectations of the President.

By a rapid and vigorous attack on General Grant, it was expected he would be beaten back into his transports and the river, or captured in time to enable us to profit by the victory, and remove to the rear all the stores and munitions that would fall into our hands in such an event, before the arrival of Gen. Buell's army on the scene. It was never contemplated, however, to retain the position thus gained, and abandon Corinth, the strategic point of the campaign.

THE FIRST DAY'S ENGAGEMENT AND ITS RESULTS

Thirty minutes after five o'clock A.M., our lines and columns were in motion, all animated evidently by a promising spirit. The front line was engaged at once, but advanced steadily, followed in due order with equal resolution and steadiness by the other lines which were brought successively into action with rare skill, judgment and gallantry, by the several corps commanders, as the enemy made a stand with his masses rallied for the struggle for his encampments. Like an Alpine avalanche our troops moved forward, despite the determined resistance of the enemy, until after six o'clock P.M., when we were in possession of all encampments between Owl and Lick Creeks, but one. Nearly all of his field artillery, about thirty flags, colors and standards, over 3,000 prisoners, including a division commander, (Gen. Prentiss,) and several brigade commanders, thousands of small arms,

an immense supply of subsistence, forage and munitions of war, and a large amount of means of transportation—all the substantial fruits of a complete victory—such, indeed, as rarely have followed the most successful battles; for never was an army so well provided as that of our enemy.

The remnant of his army had been driven in utter disorder to the immediate vicinity of Pittsburg, under the shelter of the heavy guns of his iron-clad gunboats, and we remained undisputed masters of his well-selected; admirably provided cantonments, after over twelve hours of obstinate conflict with his forces, who had been beaten from them and the contiguous covert, but only by a sustained onset of all the men we could bring into action.

Our loss was heavy. Our commander-in-chief, General A. S. Johnston, fell mortally wounded, and died on the field at 2:30 P.M., after having shown the highest qualities of the commander, and a personal intrepidity that inspired all around him, and gave resistless impulsion to his columns at critical moments.

THE SECOND DAY'S CONFLICT

About six o'clock on the afternoon of the 7th of April, however, a hot fire of musketry and artillery opened from the enemy's quarter on our advanced line, assured me of the junction of his forces, and soon, the battle raged with a fury which satisfied me I was attacked by a largely superior force. But from the onset our troops, notwithstanding their fatigue and losses from the battle of the day before, exhibited the most cheering, veteran-like steadiness. On the right and centre the enemy was repulsed in every attempt he made with his heavy column in that quarter of the field; on the left, however, and nearest to the point of arrival of his reinforcements, he drove forward line after line of his fresh troops, which were met with a resolution and courage of which our country may be proudly hopeful.

Again and again our troops were brought to the charge, invariably to drive back their foe.—But hour by hour thus opposed to an enemy constantly reinforced, our ranks were perceptibly thinned under the unceasing, withering fire of the enemy, and by twelve meridian, eighteen hours of hard fighting had sensibly exhausted a large number, my last reserves had necessarily been disposed of, and the enemy was evidently receiving fresh reinforcements after each repulse; accordingly, about 1 P.M., I determined to withdraw from so unequal a conflict, securing such of the day before as was then practicable.

A VICTORY CLAIMED

To give more in detail the operations of the two battles, resulting from the movements on Pittsburg than now attempted, must have delayed this report for weeks, and interfered materially with the important duties of my position; but I may be permitted to say that not only did the obstinate conflict for twelve hours on Sunday leave the Confederate army masters of the battle-field, and our adversary beaten, but we left the field on the next day only after eight hours' incessant battle with a superior army of fresh troops, whom we had repulsed in every attack on our lines—so repulsed and crippled, indeed, as to leave it unable to take the field for the campaign for which it was collected and equipped at such enormous expense, and with such profusion of all the appliances of war.

These successful events were not achieved, however, as before said, without severe loss—a loss not to be measured by the number of the slain and wounded, but by the high social and personal worth of so large a number of those who were killed or disabled, including the commander of the forces, whose high qualities will be greatly missed in the momentous campaign impending.

LAGGARDS AND COWARDS

From this agreeable duty I turn to one in the highest degree unpleasant—one due, however, to the brave men under me, as a contrast to the behavior of most of the army who fought so heroically. I allude to the fact that some of the officers, non-commissioned officers and men abandoned their colors early on the first day to pillage the captured encampments; others retired shamefully from the field on both days, while the thunder of cannon and other roar and rattle of musketry told them that their brothers were being slaughtered by the fresh legions of the enemy. I have ordered the names of the most conspicuous upon this roll of laggards and cowards to be published in orders.

THE LOSSES

It remains to state that our loss in the two days in the killed outright was 1,728, wounded 8,012, missing 959, making an aggregate of casualties of 10,699.

This sad list tells in simple language of the stout fight made by our countrymen in front of the rude long chapel at Shiloh, especially when it is known that on Monday, from exhaustion and other causes, not twenty thousand men on our side could be brought into action.

Of the losses of the enemy I have no exact knowledge. Their newspapers report it as very heavy. Unquestionably it was greater, even in proportion, than our own, on both days, for it was apparent to all that their dead left on the field outnumbered ours two to one.

AN ANONYMOUS REPORT: "THE SCENE AT MIDNIGHT"—THE HORRIBLE BATTLE OF SHILOH

The following excerpt comes from a Cincinnati Times *correspondent who witnessed the two days of fighting in what later became called the Battle of Shiloh. He writes below about the terrible suffering of soldiers on both sides of the conflict. This correspondent's report was reprinted in the* Baltimore Sun.

Baltimore Sun, 14 April 1862

As I sit to-night, writing this epistle, the dead and the wounded are all around me. The knife of the surgeon is busy at work, and amputated legs and arms lie scattered in every direction. The cries of the suffering victim, and the groans of those who patiently await for medical attendance, are most distressing to any one who has any sympathy with his fellow man. All day long they have been coming in, and they are placed upon the decks and within the cabins of the steamers, and wherever else they can find a resting place. I hope my eyes may never again look upon such sights. Men with their entrails protruding, others with broken arms and legs, others with bullets in their breasts or shoulders, and one poor retch

I found whose eyes had been entirely shot away. All kinds of conceivable wounds are to be seen, in all parts of the body, and from all variety of weapons.

It is midnight, and beside the cries of distress, all is silent, save the hourly discharge of a broadside from the gunboats, sending heavy shell into the vicinity of the enemy's camps. I should judge that they are having a rather sleepless night, under the circumstances. The rain is beginning to fall heavily and mercilessly on the poor wounded who are exposed to its peltings. Every particle of sheltered space is occupied by them, and yet there are hundreds who have no protection from the storm.

AN ANONYMOUS REPORT: EYEWITNESS ACCOUNT OF SHILOH

This unsigned account, from the St. Louis Republican's *correspondent (which was actually a Democratic paper), gives another firsthand account of the high human cost.*

St. Louis Republican, 21 April 1862

THE GREAT BATTLE AT SHILOH

Painful Scenes—An Army of Sextons—The Dead and Wounded.

On Thursday it was impossible to move without caution, as dead men were lying thickly everywhere for miles—sometimes a dozen in a space of as many feet. No such scene was ever before witnessed in America. The opponents lay as they had fallen, often the bodies of one heaped upon those of the other. Wounded men, mangled horses, crushed bodies, extended so interminably it was impossible to pass through them, and the visitor would finally be compelled to turn and retrace his steps.

Rains had soaked the ground and covered it with pools of water, and sometimes the wounded could be seen crawling on to the dead and lying there to keep off from the damp earth. Many had died in that position, and not a few of the deaths were caused by exposure. Physicians were busy, laboring nobly but instruments became blunted and useless, and surgeons dropped with fatigue at their posts before a fiftieth part of the work had been done.

Numbers were drowned by being unable to crawl away from the positions where they had fallen, and in which the water rapidly collected. Your city readers can form some idea of the carnage by picturing a walk as far as from St. Louis to the Fair Grounds among dead and dying, stretched away out of sight on either side. The woods, far beyond our picket guards, are being now explored, and hundreds of injured, abandoned by the enemy on their retreat, brought in. Every house between here and Corinth is a hospital. We visited several of them and found the floors covered with poor wretches, lying in pools of blood, their arms or legs torn off. Days passed without any nourishment, and in half the cases death outstripped the physicians, and was coming to their relief. Certainly a greater scene of wide-spread misery never existed. The first day or two the air was filled with groans, sobs and phrenzied curses, but now the sufferers are quiet; not from cessation of pain, but mere exhaustion.

We frequently, a little to one side, where first the ambulances, afterwards the dead carts, had failed to find them, came across the bodies of men who had bled to death.—Around them the grass was stained with blood, and often their hands was grasped convulsively on a few leaves, with which they had endeavored to stop the life-tide, until growing fainter and fainter, they had given up in despair and laid back to die.—One poor fellow, a boy, who could not have been over fourteen, was lying against a tree, a knife in his hand, with which he had carved the letters John Dan——. The N was but partially finished, when death had compelled him to give up the gloomy task of carving his own epitaph. The terrible destruction caused by cannon balls was evidenced in the sight of three bodies mangled by the same shot.—The latter, a twelve-pounder, had struck a fourth man, while he was evidently in a stooping posture, hitting immediately on the top of the head, and driving the fragments of skull downward into the body, the shot remaining half hidden between the shoulders. I saw in three houses near our outer pickets, and two miles from the battle-ground, four wounded rebel captains, and thirty or forty privates. Beauregard, as he retreated, bore back with him his wounded, leaving them in houses, barns and fence corners by the way. It is thus they are strewn over so great a space. One of the officers was being carried to a wagon as we stopped, and in the height of delirium waved an arm above his head cheering imaginary companies on to attack.

It will be a week before all can be collected and taken care of, as the further out our pickets go, the thicker they find them. Now the battle is over, it becomes a subject of wonder that the loss on both sides was not even greater. For two days the bullets flew without cessation, and passed like a storm of destruction through the woods and camp. We were unable to find, over the entire area of hundreds of acres, where the sternest firing took place, a single tree that was not scarred.— Some had thirty or forty bullets imbedded in them, while shot and shell had covered the ground with limbs and trunks.

MANTON MARBLE: WHO WAS RESPONSIBLE FOR NOT DETECTING CONFEDERATE ATTACK AT SHILOH?

The editor of the New York World *offers the following analysis of the battle, which focused on assigning blame for the Confederate attack and subsequent Union losses in this untitled piece. His estimates of*

Grant's forces are greatly inflated. A total of 66,800 officers were in the area, but Grant only had command of 48,894, of which 12,000 were considered noncombatants.[9]

New York World, 17 April 1862

It is a matter pressed with a great deal of persistency, who is to blame for the surprise, and the consequent disorder which attended it. The testimony is not unanimous on this point, but there are some points on which the best informed persons agree as far as I can learn. It is conceded that although the army has been landed several weeks, there had been no systematic brining of troops, nor were the brigades of divisions together. One brigade of Gen. Sherman's division was next to Gen. Prentiss's for instance, on the left, while the remaining three were on the right and separated from the first by a wide space filled by McClernand's division. The brigades of this division had no superior officer to command them on Sunday, and suffered very severely, the brigade commanders acting as they best could.

It is notorious, too, that the most ordinary duties of an army in the field were neglected. It will sound strangely to the military ear to learn that a thoroughly organized system of pickets was posted beyond the camp lines when in the very face of the enemy. Equally strange is the admission that no regular reconnaissance was made for some days previous to the battle. Yet there is grave reason to believe such are the facts! "The words of an intelligent eyewitness are:— 'We had no outer line of pickets. It had not been the practice during our stay in camp. The ordinary pickets around the tents were not always very perfect. There were two or three reconnaissances in as many weeks, but none of which I could hear a day or two previous to the battle.' It furthermore appears, as I am well assured, that the loosest system of guard had been adopted. One man, it is confidently asserted, went in and out of the pines every day, going with a bag of grist to the mill in the morning and as regularly returned at night! Another gentleman informs me that a rebel scouting party ventured up within full view of the parade ground while a brigade was being reviewed, and that no notice was taken of it!

These facts may be disproved, possibly, but the testimony is meanwhile too strong to repudiate.

It cannot be pleaded that either officers or men had not been experienced in camp duty. If months of field service had not taught them how to station a guard or beware of a surprise we may despair of learning them war or winning when they command.

Neither will it do to complain of the smallness of our force. Gen Grant's force alone, without reckoning-upon the reinforcements of Gen. Buell, amounted, by all accounts, to sixty-five thousand effective men. Twenty-five steamers lay at the landings, and every facility for rapid transportation. These could have been used to ferry over the entire army in a day, if it had been decided to attack upon a junction with Buell. None of these considerations seem to have had any weight with a great general, pointed to this attack. The matter was discussed at messes, of all grades; the danger foreseen, and yet no action taken. An easygoing, blind and fatal confidence seems to have pervaded the minds of those upon whom the responsibilities rested, which well-nigh proved fatal to our army, and which nothing but the most superhuman heroism could excuse. The common maxims of military science were ignored, no counsel asked or given, and we appear to have drifted into a most terrible struggle without plan, purpose or harmony.

U. S. GRANT: UNION COMMAND AT SHILOH RESPONDS TO CRITICISM

The following excerpt gives Grant's response to criticisms like the one above from the New York World. *It is based on a summary of a letter sent from General Grant to the* Cincinnati Commercial.

Hartford Daily Courant, 3 May 1862 (Hartford, Conn.)

LETTER FROM GENERAL GRANT

HIS DEFENCE

KILLED AND WOUNDED

CINCINNATI, May 2.—The *Commercial* gives and extract of a letter from General Grant in reply to a letter informing him of the motive of the criticism of his management of the battle of Pittsburg. Gen Grant says, "I will go on to do my duty to the very best of my ability, without praise—and do all I can to bring the war to a speedy close. I am not an aspirant for anything at the close of the war. There is one thing I feel well assured of, that is I have confidence in every brave man in my command. Those who showed the white feather will do all in their power to distract public attention from themselves. I had perhaps a dozen officers arrested for cowardice on the first day's fight. These men are necessarily my enemies. As to the talk about a surprise here, nothing could be more false. If the enemy had sent up word when and where they would attack us, we could not have been better prepared. Skirmishing had been going on for two days between our reconnoitering parties and the enemy's advance. I did not believe, however, they intended to make a determined attack, but were simply making a reconnaissance in force. My headquarters were at Savannah, but I usually spent the day at Pittsburgh. Troops were constantly arriving to be arraigned into brigades and divisions, and were all ordered to report at Savannah, making it necessary to keep an officer and some men there. I was also looking for Gen Buell to arrive—it was important that I should have every arrangement complete for his speedy transit to this side of the river."

The *Commercial's* correspondence with General Mitchell's army, gives the following explanation of the manner in which Gen Beauregard's dispatch was taken at Huntsville. The wires were broken at a point beyond Huntsville, and was being prepared by the operator there to be forwarded by locomotive to Chattanooga and there repeated by telegraph to Richmond, when Gen Mitchell surprised the town and instantly seized the telegraph office. General Mitchell himself solved the cipher after several hours of hard study. There is no doubt of the genuiness [*sic*] of the dispatch. Beauregard lost not less than 20,000 men killed, wounded and prisoners, and the sick and used up and panic stricken, during his movements from Corinth upon Pittsburgh.

The official list of our killed and wounded at Pittsburgh Landing, according to the Commercial is killed, 1375; wounded, 1882, and 4044 missing. Total 7301.

WILLIAM HARDING: CAPTURE AND ESCAPE OF OUR WAR CORRESPONDENT AT PITTSBURG LANDING

War correspondents knew they faced great dangers by covering the battles so closely. This article is an account of what happened to the Philadelphia Inquirer's *correspondent Henry Bentley at the battle.*

Philadelphia Inquirer, 15 April 1862

For some days prior to Sunday last, we had serious apprehensions that our correspondent with General GRANT's army, Mr. Henry Bentley, had either been killed or captured in the battle of Pittsburg Landing. His last letter was written, "Five miles inland from Pittsburg Landing, on the road to Corinth," and was dated the day before the battle. He had attached himself to Col. PEABODY's twenty-fifth Missouri Regiment which was in the advance with Gen. PRENTISS' division, so badly cut up early in the morning of the first day's fight. Taking this in connection with the fact that he, so admirably prompt with his despatches heretofore, was entirely silent, we had sad forebodings that he had met with some disaster in the fearful slaughter of his regiment and division.

The event has shown that he was both unfortunate and fortunate. As we learn by the despatch published yesterday, he was at breakfast with Colonel PEABODY and Major POWELL, of the Twenty-fifth Missouri, at the moment of the surprise by BEAUREGARD's advancing columns, and of these three, the two officers were killed and our correspondent was taken prisoner. Subsequently Mr. BENTLEY eluded the vigilance of his captors, and after being robbed by the Rebels of everything but his pantaloons and boots, escaped, and is now on the way to Philadelphia with the despatches containing his observations from the Rebel side of the battlefield. These will be most important and interesting additions to the literature of that great battle.

What led us the more readily to fear that our correspondent was captured or killed, was his known daring on several former occasions during the war. It was he that first leaped over the entrenchments at Roanoke Island and hauled down the Rebel flag; and it was he, also, that was with the advance at Columbus, his account of the capture of which stronghold being the first to reach not only the people of the Atlantic cities, but also those of Europe, where it was published in the London *Times*.

Sympathizing with him in his misfortune, we congratulate him thus in advance upon his lucky escape from the military prisons of Secessia.

NOTES

1. Curt Johnson and Mark McLaughlin, *Civil War Battles* (New York: Crown Publishers, 1977).

2. "The Glorious Victory at Pittsburg Landing," *Philadelphia Inquirer*, 10 April 1862.

3. Johnson and McLaughlin, *Civil War Battles*, 44.

4. James M. McPherson (Ed.), *The Atlas of the Civil War* (New York: Macmillan, 1994).

5. Ibid.

6. Johnson and McLaughlin, *Civil War Battles*, 49.

7. "Exciting Intelligence from Tennessee," *Baltimore Sun*, 10 April 1862.

8. The *New York Times* briefly commented on the battle name in an 18 April 1862 article: "We learn from General Beauregard's letter to Gen. Grant, asking leave to bury his dead, that the field which our brave fellows fought so stoutly and won so nobly should be called Shiloh and not Pittsburg Landing. We willingly accept the name. For Shiloh means deliverance; and on that field of Shiloh we believe that the deliverance of our country was really accomplished."

9. Johnson and McLaughlin, *Civil War Battles*, 49.

FURTHER READINGS

Daniel, Larry J. *Shiloh: The Battle That Changed the Civil War*. New York: Simon & Schuster, 1998.

Faust, Patricia L. (Ed.). *Historical Times Illustrated Encyclopedia of the Civil War*. New York: Harper & Row, 1986.

Johnson, Curt, and McLaughlin, Mark. *Civil War Battles*. New York: Crown Publishers, 1977.

McDonough, James L. *Shiloh: In Hell before Night*. Knoxville: University of Tennessee Press, 1977.

10

UNION CAPTURE OF NEW ORLEANS, APRIL 1862

Since the beginning of the war, the U.S. government understood the importance of controlling the Mississippi River. By controlling the Mississippi River, the North would cut the Confederate states into two and would be able to block the delivery of western supplies to the East. New Orleans was one of the chief commercial cities in the South, serving as the main distribution point for cotton, sugar, and slaves.

According to a profile of the city that appeared in the *Baltimore Sun* a few days after the federal troops occupied the city, New Orleans had a population of 174,488, including 14,479 slaves. The paper noted, "The population of New Orleans has long been remarkable for the diversity of its elements. About one-half of the whites are of foreign birth, and among these the French and Spanish are predominant. There is also a large number of northerners."

The *Sun* discussed New Orleans' importance as a shipping city and also noted its significant railroads and notable buildings.

> Among the notable buildings are the branch mint of the United States—which the Confederates seized a year ago—the Custom House, one of the most massive structures in America, but not yet completed, the Cathedral of St. Louis and sixty other churches, the St. Charles Hotel, which cost $500,000; the hospital, banks, benevolent institutions and four theatres. On Jackson square is a bronze equestrian statue of General Jackson, by Clark Mills.[1]

The city's primary defenses were Fort Jackson and Fort St. Phillips, located on opposite sides of the Mississippi River about 75 miles south of New Orleans. President Lincoln, General George McClelland, and other military leaders decided that the best way to capture New Orleans was to get an armed fleet past the two forts, then navigate the river up to the city, which would be at their mercy. Later they added to the plan the reduction of the two forts by a mortar flotilla before the federal armed fleet would pass through.[2]

Admiral David Farragut commanded the Union navy fleet that would conquer New Orleans in April 1862. His fleet consisted of six ships and twelve gunboats, while Commander David Porter joined him with a mortar flotilla of nineteen schooners and six armed steamships for guard and towing service. They began their bombardment of Fort Jackson on 18 April, and after two days the Union fleet had not exacted enough damage to force a Confederate surrender. Against the opinion of Commander Porter, Farragut decided to revert to the original plan of running past the forts and heading toward the defenseless city.

On 21 April Farragut sent a force to remove an obstruction—a chain that crossed the river and was strongly moored and supported by eight hulks—opposite Fort Jackson. By 23 April Farragut was ready to try to maneuver his fleet past the forts. At 2:00 A.M. on 24 April he gave the signal to begin the operation. Commander Porter had continued his bombardment of the forts the past few days; and his shelling continued as Farragut's fleet advanced. After some fierce fighting and after having his flagship the *Hartford* run ashore and set aflame by a fire-raft, Farragut managed to assemble thirteen of his fleet above the forts. Four were missing, but only one had been sunk. Farragut proceeded up the river to New Orleans. As Farragut advanced toward the city, he observed ships filled with burning cotton bales and other destroyed property, a sign of the panic that had gripped the city upon advanced indication and rumors that the federal troops were headed to New Orleans.[3]

On 25 April he reached the Chalmette batteries 3 miles below the city and vigorously attacked them. He was successful within thirty minutes; then he anchored off New Orleans. "The levee," Farragut later wrote, "was one scene of desolation; ships, steamers, cotton, coal, etc., were all in one common blaze."[4] As Farragut had predicted, the Union's ability to bypass Forts Jackson and St. Phillips compelled the evacuation of New Orleans by Confederate forces and secured its capture. On 29 April, Forts Jackson and St. Phillips also fell. General Benjamin Butler, the Massachusetts leader who first arrived in Washington, D.C., and helped secure that city in April 1861, commanded the troops that accompanied Farragut. Butler became the military governor of the city and stayed there until December 1862.

The capture of New Orleans was significant in many ways but mostly because it convinced some European leaders, most notably French Emperor Napoleon III, to refrain from declared intentions to recognize the Confederate states and open trade in violation of the federal blockade of Southern ports. The success in New Orleans also greatly lifted Union spirits after the great loss of life at Shiloh. One early report of the capture of New Orleans in the *Hartford Daily Courant* noted, "This news will greatly inspire our troops."[5]

Most of the newspaper accounts played up the naval battle and called the capture of New Orleans one of the most important events of the war up to that point for these reasons and because it secured Union control of the lower Mississippi. Once Memphis fell in June (see Chapter 11), only Vicksburg, Mississippi, and Port Hudson, Louisiana, remained in Confederate control along the Mississippi River.

THOMAS N. DAY: NEW ORLEANS IN UNION POSSESSION—REBELS DESTROY LARGE AMOUNT OF PROPERTY

In this short confirmation of the seizure of New Orleans, the Hartford newspaper takes a shot at England, given its failed attempt to capture the Crescent City during the War of 1812.

Hartford Daily Courant, 27 April 1862 (Hartford, Conn.)

WASHINGTON, April 27—The news of the fall of New Orleans excites general joy. The news is deemed to be of the utmost importance. What Old England failed to do with all her power, has been accomplished by New England. The manner in which the successes at Forts Jackson and Phillip were followed up is highly commended. In 30 hours our brave men consummated their victory, and appeared before the great city of the Southwest to receive its submission. This is but a foretaste of the Southwestern operations. No mention is made by the rebels of iron clad "Turtles" and "Rams" that were to annihilate the Yankee fleet, which leads to the suspicion that the common estimate of the rebel motive power from their own misrepresentation has been a mistake. It is pretty clear that on this occasion they could not stop to conceal the truth.

WILLIAM HARDING: ACCOUNT OF CAPTURE OF NEW ORLEANS

This article from the Philadelphia Inquirer *focuses on General Butler's troops rather than on the naval aspects of the seizure of the city.*

Philadelphia Inquirer, 28 April 1862

Despatches [*sic*] received at Washington, yesterday, from Generals WOOL and McDOWELL, convey the important and exhilarating information that the City of New Orleans has fallen into the possession of the Union troops, and is once again under the dominion of the United States Government. The Petersburg *Express*, of Saturday last, and the Richmond *Examiner*, of the same day, announce that at an early hour on Thursday morning our troops passed Fort Jackson *en route* for New Orleans. The advance created the most intense excitement and consternation, and business was entirely suspended. The torch of the incendiary was applied to all the cotton in the city and vicinity, and such of the steamboats as were not required for the transportation of ammunition and coin were also destroyed.

The information, although emanating from Rebel sources, and without detail, can doubtless be relied upon. Our latest authentic advices from Ship Island (April 6th) inform us that General BUTLER was, at that time, busily at work preparing his forces for the advance upon New Orleans. As usual with such large expeditions, some mistakes had been made in regard to supplies, which were being rectified with all possible alacrity.

The force under General BUTLER was about fifteen thousand strong. He was also accompanied by the mortar-fleet, under command of Commander DAVID D. PORTER, United States Navy, comprising thirty vessels and two thousand men.

One by one are the cities of the South being compelled to acknowledge the supremacy of the United States Government; and the capture of no locality in the Rebel realm could tend so much to demoralize their army, and to show them the utter hopelessness of success, as that of the "Crescent City."

THOMAS N. DAY: ACCOUNT OF NEW ORLEANS CAMPAIGN

This account from the Hartford Daily Courant *gives a good overview of the New Orleans campaign from the start of the fighting at the forts. It also details the federal military plan and strategy involved.*

Hartford Daily Courant, 10 May 1862 (Hartford, Conn.)

The naval battle at New Orleans was attended by all the paraphernalia of the grand old sea-fights whose recital stirs the blood and captivates the imagination. Added to the traditional bravery of the American sailor, the skill of the commanders, and the ordinary incidents of marine warfare, were the ingenious devices of the enemy for defending themselves of overwhelming our fleet, and the new and more terrible enginery of war, which science and ingenuity have of late contributed to the military art. Twenty loud-mouthed mortars sent their screeching shells into the enemy's forts at the rate of four every minute for six days. Gunboats whirled shot and shell from their rifled cannon into the solid stone. An unintermittent shower of iron meteors tore up the walls and barracks of the beleaguered fortresses.

Months of labor had been expended upon the defenses of New Orleans. Beyond the formidable forts on both sides of the river, beyond tier upon tier of battery, beyond rebel gunboat and "ram" and "turtle," the Crescent City reposed in fancied security. No Union force was strong enough, no Union fleet was large enough to break through, no Yankee enterprise of Hessian valor could ever overcome the mighty barrier which commanded the waters of the lower Mississippi. Stretched across from shore to shore at the lower fort lay an iron chain whose huge bulk would, by mere passivity, render every attempt at passage impossible. Fire rafts had been prepared to be set afloat and carried by the current down the stream, and thus consume the fleet of the "invading foe." But all devices were intended "weak inventions of the enemy."

After six days of mortar firing, com. Farragut determined to run the gauntlet of the forts with his steam sloops and his gunboats. The burden and head of the day and night had fallen upon the brave and enduring men of the mortar fleet. Wearied with their innocent labors, stunned by the ever-jarring reports of the bellowing armament, the signal was given for them to retire down the river, thus placing them out of the reach of any mischief-seeking rebel gunboat, while the hitherto inactive fleet of steam vessels was ordered to run past the enemy's fortifications and take them in the rear. And they had well earned their immunity from further duty. They had proved themselves heroes, and to the mortar fleet is due much of the success of the attack upon New Orleans. These sailor boys with true Yankee ingenuity, on their first arrival went on shore, and cutting down branches enough from the woods which fringed the river, brought them on board the mortar schooners, and trimmed the vessels throughout with the green foliage, thus completely baffling the enemy who were unable to distinguish the floating arbors from the bushes on the bank. And so from shady bowers would leap the deathful bomb, screaming its notes of warning, and leafy alcoves became the sources of hideous destruction.

At three o'clock on the morning of the 24th, the fleet under the command of Com. Farragut got under way. The formidable chain across the river had been successfully severed three nights previous, and the hulks which bore it floated harmlessly away. The mortars, in order to divert the enemy, concentrated their fire upon the forts, and the night was ablaze with their constant passage through the air. But from above the forts, a light is seen. A lurid glare is thrown upon the scene for miles around; a heavy smoke, blacker than the night, ascends from the burning mass. To the lookers on in the fleet, the flame comes nearer and brighter, and it is soon apparent that the blazing object is moving. All hands are alert throughout the fleet, as it becomes known that it is a fire raft. They spring into their boats; buckets and axes are taken with them; from one ship after another they put off toward their flaming adversary. Unmindful that it may contain materials which will blow them into eternity, they boldly approach, and with the stroke of the axe and the deluge of water, soon render it harmless, although part of it eludes them and sets on fire the "Hartford." The flames are quickly subdued, and the steamers dash up the river. They are soon discovered, and upon them are hurled the largest missiles that the rebels possess. With but little damage they pass the fiery gauntlet and plunge in amongst the rebel vessels that lies in the stream, which scatter like frightened sheep, with the celebrated "ram" at their head. Eleven of them are soon sunk or burned. The wooded Mississippi utterly oblivious of iron plate, rushes at the Manassas and by mere momentum half drowns the monster, and then turning, completes its destruction by a tremendous broadside, the water gushing in through a hundred wounds. The Union gunboat Varuna and the rebel gunboat Webster engage in close conflict and both sink grappling each other.

The Federal fleet being now in their rear, the rebel vessels destroyed the supplies cut off from New Orleans, there is nothing left for the two forts but to surrender, and they are given up. Valiant Farragut steams up to the Crescent City, demands submission, and thus triumphantly completes a gloriously fought battle. The minute history of this affair will shed new luster upon the thickly clustering glories of the American Navy.

THEODORUS BAILEY: CAPTURE OF NEW ORLEANS—SMALL LOSS OF LIFE FOR UNION BUT LARGE ECONOMIC LOSS FOR REBELS

This report on the capture of New Orleans appeared nearly two weeks after the city was occupied by federal troops. It reports on the small loss of life in the conflict and tells of the large losses in cotton and shipping at the hands of the rebels.

New York Times, 9 May 1862

THE LATEST NEWS
BY TELEGRAPH
THE CAPTURE OF NEW ORLEANS

Our Loss, 36 killed, 123 Wounded

The Enemy's Loss, 1000 to 1500

FORTRESS MONROE, May 8—To the Hon. Gideon Welles, Secretary of the Navy: I have the honor to announce that, under the providence of God which smiles upon a just cause, the squadron under flag officer Farragut has been vouchsafed a glorious victory and triumph in the capture of the city of New Orleans, Forts Jackson, St. Philip, Livingston and Pike, the batteries below and above New Orleans, as well as the total destruction of the enemy's gunboats, steam-rums, floating batteries, iron clad, fire-rafts, and obstructive booms and chains. The enemy with their own hands destroyed from eight to ten million dollars worth of cotton and shipping. Our loss is 36 killed and 123 wounded. The enemy lost from 1000 to 1500, besides several hundred prisoners. The way is clear and the rebel defenses destroyed from the Gulf to Baton Rouge, and probably to Memphis.—Our flag waves triumphantly over them all. I am bearer of dispatches. THEODORUS BAILEY, Captain of the gunboat Cayuga.

CHARLES HALE: SIGNIFICANCE OF CAPTURE OF NEW ORLEANS

This untitled article recounts for its Northern readers the reasons that the fall of New Orleans was significant. It also predicts "speedy" Union control of the entire Mississippi River. That did not actually occur until the fall of Vicksburg, Mississippi, in July 1863.

Boston Daily Advertiser, 30 April 1862

The capture of New Orleans, of which there can scarcely remain a reasonable doubt, is beyond question one of the great events of the war. It is an event which will demonstrate to the world the progress which the Union forces are making. When it is announced that some Columbus or Bowling Green or Huntsville has been taken, although the fact may be of capital importance for the campaign, the chances are that the foreign reader never before heard of the captured positions,—at least that he knows them only as positions recently talked of as among the rebel defences. But when it is said New Orleans is taken, the world knows that that means the fall of the greatest city of the South, the unlocking of the Mississippi, and a lodgment in a State which is now thoroughly identified with the rebellion. The actual progress may not be greater than in other cases, but it is measured by something of which all the world knows the value.

We shall not be suspected, however, of underrating the substantial value of the capture of the great seaport of the gulf and the outlet of the Mississippi valley. It seals the issue of the war in the southwest, we apprehend, and will give us the speedy control of the whole course of the great river, the upper stream and the mouth of which are now in our possession. It will give us a vast storehouse of supplies, and will deprive the rebels of one of their chief workshops. It will prove to both parties that what we are now seeing is indeed the decisive struggle, and not a mere series of temporary reverses which have taken over the rebel arms.

We especially rejoice at the capture of New Orleans, however, from a recollection of the many and steadfast friends whom the Union has had there in other days. It is the city where more than anywhere else we may hope to find a little of the old leaven remaining,—enough we trust to leaven the whole in good time. No loyal man can ever forget the [intensity] with which secession was opposed there, the dishonest tricks by which it was felt necessary to overcome the unwilling spirit of the majority, or the almost mad persistency with which at least one public journal, the True Delta, continued its opposition to the last. It is not credible that all this devotion and loyalty has faded away. It is not to be believed that in the city, which never ceased to honor Andrew Jackson and Henry clay for their steady support of the Union, and which has so many ties of northern kindred and of ancient friendship, the love of country and of Union is yet extinct. No State in our judgment, unless it be Tennessee and North Carolina, offers so good a field as Louisiana for the development of genuine Union sentiment, if judicious measures are taken to call it forth. . . . As little as possible, we trust, will be left to the harsh and peremptory procedure of military power, and the return to regular civil administration will, we hope, be made as easy and as early as possible. It is a superb field for practical, firm and conciliatory statesmanship; and we have the fullest confidence in the skill and discernment with which it will be improved by the national executive.

THOMAS N. DAY: CAPTURE OF NEW ORLEANS CUTS OFF CONFEDERATE LINE OF RETREAT FROM MISSISSIPPI

One reason the fall of New Orleans is significant, according to this account, is that it cuts off an avenue of retreat for Confederate forces in Corinth, who had not yet been defeated by federal troops at this point. It also addresses issues regarding continuing U.S. control of the city.

Hartford Daily Courant, 29 April 1862 (Hartford, Conn.)

The seizure of New Orleans will influence the results of the [*military*] campaign more than may appear, perhaps, at first. It practically cuts off all avenue of retreat for Beauregard and his army, should they be defeated in battle, and affords us a point from which he may be attacked in the rear. It opens up the Mississippi river so that Memphis can be assailed by our gunboats from the South. It affords us opportunities for penetrating Louisiana by means of gunboats in Red river, and Arkansas through Arkansas river. It is the great export city of the South. Through it the bulk of the cotton and sugar crops have reached their consumers. It renders further blockade of the Mississippi unnecessary. It is perfectly easy to hold. The whole city is lower than the surface of the water, which is kept from overflowing by artificial levees. Should our troops be compelled to evacuate it, our gunboats could prevent the enemy from occupying, either by shelling it or laying it under water by cutting the dykes.

The Population of New Orleans is about 175,000, according to the last census, but this has been much diminished by the flight of the Union men and the drafts for the rebel army. Previous to the fall of Fort Sumter, New Orleans might really be esteemed a loyal city. The commercial interests, especially, were adverse to secession, but they could not resist the pressure brought to bear, and the city was swept into the vortex of treason, and its press muzzled or dragooned into the support of Jeff. Davis. Every report that has come thence has represented the Union sentiment as strong, though kept under by military despotism. It will not be so difficult a matter, we opine, to enlist a large Union force among the inhabitants. The city is doomed to immediate destruction or gradual decay unless it shall become reasonable and submissive.

It will probably be a week or ten days before we have any knowledge of its capture through our own sources of information, but the rebel account does not as far as we can see, admit of a doubt in respect to its veraciousness.

It is rejoicing to the loyal heart to reflect that the Stars and Stripes now probably float over custom-house, and post-office, and mint, and all other public buildings which grace and adorn the Crescent City.

THOMAS N. DAY: TRADE AT NEW ORLEANS

This editorial provides an analysis of the impact of the capture of New Orleans from the economic trade perspective. It encourages the federal government to lift its blockade of the city now that it is in U.S. control.

Hartford Daily Courant, 1 May 1862 (Hartford, Conn.)

Although New Orleans is not yet taken formal possession of, it will, without doubt, be soon held by a strong army under Gen. Butler. The rebels are, already, deeply lamenting its loss, and well they may, for it cuts off the produce of the fertile fields of Texas, and may result in starving the Southwest into submission.

The question will now arise, Shall it be permitted to resume its enormous foreign and domestic trade. The Federal Government has thus far steadily refused to break any portion of the established blockade in case of any port that has come into our possession, by allowing it commercial facilities, but the seizures of ports and harbors have hitherto been of comparatively to little importance that the advantages accruing from such permission could not compensate for the equivocal attitude in which the Federal Government would be placed, in respect to the law of blockade, by such an act. But if, by a resumption of business, New Orleans could be at once fixed in its present inclinations to loyalty, the effect would be happy.

Nor in this case could England, at least, object, for the grand motive of England's to interfere in our struggle would be removed. There is good reason to believe that the rebel stories in regard to their immense destruction of property are either extravagantly exaggerated or wholly false. A gentleman who has long been a resident of New Orleans, and who was familiar with the condition of the city up to January last, writes to the New York *Times* in regard to these stories that they are the results of wishes not to be gratified. He states that as to the burning of 15,000 bales of cotton, which were in New Orleans on the 15th of January, it would be utterly impossible, without destroying at least one third of the entire city, for the cotton is stored in presses located in thickly-settled neighborhoods scattered every where within the municipal borders. The citizens are not mad enough to permit it. Nor would they permit the numerous steamers to be burned, for, scattered as they are along the levee, the flames from them would involve the destruction of a large part of the city. Nor do the later reports thence allude to this wholesale conflagration.

If we assume, therefore, that the vast stores of cotton, sugar and tobacco which through the strict embargo during the last year of the magnificent commerce of the Crescent City have accumulated in its storehouses and on its wharves, a trade might be revived which . . . would establish the Government firmly in the rebellious city, while its prosperity would be an object of envy and consequently a stimulating example to its sister cities on the Southern coast.

WILLIAM HARDING: NEW ORLEANS—IMPORTANCE OF CAPTURE ABROAD AND AT HOME

This article highlights the importance of the capture of New Orleans in the context of relations with Europe.

Philadelphia Inquirer, 29 April 1862

Assuming that the Rebel account of the fall of New Orleans is true, this event is, in every aspect, by far the most important of the war. Reeling, as the rebellion has been under the fast following and victorious blows administered by the Union armies, since the advent of the present year, this terrible stroke must so far stager it as to leave nothing more necessary but the final *coup de grace* in Virginia. Its crushing force must tell powerfully against the Rebel cause, both abroad and at home. In England it will present itself in this aspect. The city which, in its infancy, repelled and routed a well appointed and powerful British army, is now captured with ease, when it is vastly more populous, immensely more powerful, and infinitely better protected by fortifications against attack from any quarter, and captured, too, by a mere fragment of the naval and forces of the United States. There could be no more signal exemplification of the power of the uprisen Union. Or, if even the malignant hostility of the London *Times* cheapens the triumph by an allegation that New Orleans was not defended, what better illustration can there be to foreign powers of the utter absence of the Revolutionary spirit among the people of that city.

In France, too, the capture of New Orleans must be regarded as a fatal and almost finishing blow to the Rebellion. There the people of the Crescent City are regarded as, in large part, their own children; and, if the spirit of resistance was at all general and genuine, it would have shown itself in a defence of their city, characterized by their own fiery and impetuous valor. But, so far as we can judge, no such brilliant effort to repel their assailants is likely to be exhibited to the eyes of the French, or of any other people. Will not this argue, conclusively either that the Government is powerful enough to overcome even such resistance as people of the French blood are able to make, or that these people permit their city to be restored to the Union without an earnest fight, *because they have no heart in the war?* On the one hand or the other, the conclusion is inevitable—that the Rebellion is certain to be put down, and the common sense of the French must recognize and accept the fact.

But the fall of New Orleans must be an impressive event abroad for other reasons. Not only in the two countries we have named, but in all commercial States, it is known as the great seat of commerce in the South. Charleston is known, Savannah is known, and Mobile is known, but New Orleans stands out in the sight of the world in conspicuous pre-eminence. It is the second commercial city of the United States, and the greatest exporting mart of the Western world. While New York is the acknowledged gate of entrance of the vast importing trade of the country, New Orleans is the equally admitted great portal of exit for the hundreds of millions of our products heretofore sent out annually to the European world. The capture of such a city by the Union forces must, therefore, have a moral effect that will outweigh a dozen victories upon hard-fought fields in less conspicuous and important places. Hence, we may fairly date the downfall of the Rebel cause in Europe from the day when the restoration of New Orleans to the Union is made known beyond the Atlantic.

NOTES

1. "The City of New Orleans," *Baltimore Sun*, 29 April 1862.
2. James Ford Rhodes, *History of the Civil War, 1861–1865* (New York: Macmillan, 1917), 119.
3. Ibid., 123.
4. Ibid.
5. "The News," *Hartford Daily Courant*, 28 April 1862.

FURTHER READINGS

Faust, Patricia L. (Ed.). *Historical Times Illustrated Encyclopedia of the Civil War*. New York: Harper & Row, 1986.

Rhodes, James Ford. *History of the Civil War, 1861–1865*. New York: Macmillan, 1917.

Wagner, Margaret E.; Gallagher, Gary W.; and Finkelman, Paul (Eds.). *The Library of Congress Civil War Desk Reference*. New York: Simon & Schuster, 2002.

11

UNION CAPTURE OF MEMPHIS, JUNE 1862

The Union success at Shiloh, combined with additional federal advances down the Mississippi River in March, set the stage for a series of important federal advances into the Confederacy. As noted in Chapter 9, Confederate leaders virtually abandoned the Mississippi Basin after the loss at Shiloh. This left many of the Mississippi River towns vulnerable to Union occupation. Immediately following the battle at Shiloh, Union Major-General Henry Halleck advanced on Corinth, Mississippi. It took Halleck three weeks to travel 5 miles and gain position to lay siege to the town. Halleck began preliminary bombardment, and on the evening of 30 May Confederate General Pierre G. T. Beauregard evacuated Corinth and withdrew his troops to Tupelo, Mississippi. The federals had gained control of Corinth.

As Halleck and many other Union generals converged on Pittsburg Landing in March and April of 1862, Brigadier General John Pope and Flag Officer Andrew Foote focused their attention on gaining control of Island No. 10 on the Mississippi River near New Madrid, Missouri, where General Beauregard had sent troops to serve as the Confederate strongpoint for defending the Mississippi River.

On 3 March 1862, Union forces marched through swamps with their supplies and artillery to begin their attack on the city of New Madrid. Confederate Brigadier General John McCown defended the Confederate positions and launched a sortie against the federal troops. He also bombarded the federals with heavy artillery, but he was not able to discourage the Union soldiers. By 13 March, McCown realized he could not defend New Madrid, and he evacuated Confederate troops and gunboats to Island No. 10. A day later Brigadier General Pope realized New Madrid had been deserted and occupied it. Foote arrived a day after that on 15 March along with a U.S. Navy flotilla and anchored upstream from Island No. 10. About three weeks later the U.S. ironclad *Carondelet* passed the Island No. 10 batteries and anchored outside New Madrid. Three days later, on 6 April, the Confederates suffered their losses at Shiloh, and the Union forces retained control of Pittsburg Landing on the banks of the Tennessee River. It was clear to the Confederate commanders that their Tennessee River escape route had been cut off, and Brigadier General William Mackall, who had replaced McCown, surrendered Island No. 10 on 7 April. Practically, this opened up the Mississippi River to the Union down to Fort Pillow, Tennessee.

The Union's attention was now turned to Memphis. According to a description of the city in the *Baltimore Sun*:

> The city is the most populous and important on the river between St. Louis and New Orleans, and it is said occupies the only eligible site for a commercial depot from the mouth of the Ohio river to Vicksburg, a distance of six hundred and fifty miles. The bluff on which it stands is elevated thirty feet above the highest water mark. An esplanade, several feet wide, extends along the bluff in front of the town, and is bordered with large warehouses. About ten years ago the United States government established a naval depot at Memphis, the river being deep enough to float the largest ships from the city to its mouth. The quantity of cotton annually shipped from the place has been estimated at one hundred and fifty thousand bales. A large fleet of steamboats, owned in the city, has been engaged in the carrying trade of the Mississippi and its tributaries. Memphis is the western terminus of the Charleston and Memphis railroad, and also of a railroad from Nashville. The population is estimated at sixteen thousand.[1]

On 25 April, Commander David Farragut secured Union control of New Orleans. That left only Memphis, Vicksburg, Mississippi, and Fort Hudson, Louisiana, in Confederate control. A Confederate defense fleet commanded by Captain James Montgomery and Brigadier General Jeff Thompson was based out of Memphis after 10 May. On 4 June, after General Beauregard learned that General Halleck had secured Corinth, he ordered Confederate troops out of Fort Pillow and Memphis. As the Union forces approached the city, only Thompson's troops and Montgomery's fleet remained to defend the city.

On 6 June 1862, U.S. Flag Officer Charles Davis and Colonel Charles Ellet began a naval attack on the city. Within ninety minutes, the Union fleet captured or sank all but one of the Confederate vessels. According to the *Baltimore Sun*, "Their crews endeavored to escape to the shores, but were mostly captured. Soon after the engagement the mayor formally surrendered the city and a Federal officer took military possession."[2]

Much like the enthusiasm that came with the news of the capture of New Orleans, Northern newspapers also reported the successful capture of Memphis with great enthusiasm.

AN ANONYMOUS REPORT: CONFEDERATE DESPAIR AT LOSS OF NEW ORLEANS, FEARS OF UNION ADVANCES ALONG MIDDLE MISSISSIPPI

This report, which appeared after New Orleans was captured but before either Corinth or Memphis fell (30 May and 6 June, respectively), discusses general Confederate concerns in Memphis and provides some of the news coming from Corinth. It also briefly mentions concern about the Confederate conscription law that was the first military draft instituted in the South.

Hartford Daily Courant, 1 May 1862 (Hartford, Conn.)

SOUTHERN NEWS

The Rebels in Despair
Beauregard has 80,000 Men

No Hope of Resisting Halleck, who they suppose has
200,000 Men

CAIRO, April 30.—A refugee from Memphis says Humboldt [*Tennessee*] is occupied by a small rebel force, who are engaged in throwing up defensive works. He brings Memphis papers of 26th inst. They contain little matter of interest further than a confirmation of the fall of New Orleans.

The [*Memphis*] *Avalanche* grumbles that the rebel authorities suppress the details in regard to affairs, and says nothing but the bare fact of the surrender is known.

The same paper says the Southern people are fast losing all confidence in their river defenses, and it is generally admitted that the federal army can be no longer successfully resisted, and also intimates a lack of confidence by advising its patrons to invest whatever money they have in real estate while purchases can be made with the money now in circulation,—chiefly rebel treasury notes.

The conscription law is rigidly enforced, and Union men are secreting themselves or flying to avoid its operations. This refugee says that merchants of avowed secession proclivities are removing their goods to places of concealment and security, and large numbers of families are moving away daily. The idea of burning the town is abandoned in consequence of the determined opposition of property holders.

It is currently reported in Memphis that Beauregard has over 80,000 men at Corinth, and no hope of successfully resisting Halleck, who is believed to have 200,000.

AN ANONYMOUS REPORT: REBELS FEAR ATTACK ON MEMPHIS, PREPARE TO BURN CITY

In a follow-up story two days later in the Hartford Daily Courant *the panic that was beginning to creep into Memphis is evident. Although this brief article suggests that citizens would burn the city, that did not actually occur.*

Hartford Daily Courant, 3 May 1862 (Hartford, Conn.)

CAIRO, May 2—The news from Pittsburg Landing is of the highest importance, but its transmission over the wires is prohibited. The latest news from the fleet says it was generally believed that a simultaneous attack would be made by the fleet before the close of the week.

Memphis papers of the 29th say a meeting held the night before decided to burn the city, in case of approach of the federal fleet. Editorials frequently call on the people to reinforce Price as the only means of hope and salvation to the city.

Gen. Yates left tonight for Pittsburg with the hospital steamer and a very large quantity of sanitary stares. The river is stationary and 8 inches higher than ever before known.

WILLIAM HARDING: DIFFICULTY OF OBTAINING NEWS FROM MISSISSIPPI VALLEY

This article expresses the frustration some editors felt in trying to determine the authentic nature of telegrams coming from Cairo, Illinois, regarding the status of the war in the Southwest. Fort Wright is located in northern Kentucky near Cincinnati and was built to protect the area from the Confederacy.

Philadelphia Inquirer, 7 June 1862

We have a chronic distrust of telegrams from "Cairo." The reporters and correspondents there are by no manner of means what a truthful man would call "reliable gentlemen." Yesterday the public were informed from General HALLECK'S Headquarters, that a refugee reported the surrender of Memphis and Fort Wright on the previous Friday, but other advices, dated Chicago, announced a fight pending between DAVIS' flotilla and Fort Wright, as late as Wednesday last.

Another despatch [*sic*] gave news from Memphis to Monday last, at which time the mouthing orators of that blusterous city had resolved never to surrender *voluntarily*. (This is the opposite of FALLSTAFFS doughty refusal to give a reason upon "compulsion.") All these despatches, although variously dated, there is reason to believe, had their origin at Cairo. Such things have happened time and again during the war in the Southwest. Hence the chronic distrust we mention, for all telegrams dated from the damp little town at the confluence of the Ohio and Mississippi.

Nevertheless, we have faith in the particular despatch we publish this morning, which announces that Fort Wright is at last in possession of the Union forces, and that the fleet has passed down to Memphis. There are good reasons why this should be true. The flight of BEAUREGARD'S from Corinth; the breaking up and capture of at least a portion of his army; HALLECK'S possession of all the railroads in the rear of Fort Wright,

Fort Randolph and Memphis, are calculated to make these localities very unwholesome—not to say unsafe—places of residence for Rebel armies. They could stay there no longer, except in extreme danger, and therefore we believe they have fled.

Assuming this intelligence to be true, there will only remain to be disposed of, the batteries at Vicksburg, where FARRAGUT and Davis must shortly meet to shake hands, and congratulate the nation over the enfranchised Mississippi. In that free condition "long may it wave."

WILLIAM HARDING: ACCOUNT OF RIVER FIGHT BEFORE MEMPHIS

This article highlights the dramatic success of the Union navy in the battle for Memphis.

Philadelphia Inquirer, 12 June 1862

Last Friday morning, between the hours of five-and-a-half and seven, in the full sunlight, on the broad breast of the Mississippi, and beneath the eyes of the crowded and expectant population of Memphis, a conflict occurred between the National and Rebel flotillas, the close of which saw the latter destroyed, and left Loyalty sole master of all the Western waters.

The Rebel force lies opposite lower Memphis, close to the Arkansas shore, and numbers eight gun-boats—the first six named after the Rebel Generals, *Van Dorn, Beauregard, Bragg, Price, Lovell, Thompson,* and the other two called *Sumter* and *Little Rebel.* Six of these are river-boats; one, the *Bragg,* is a stout ocean steamer, and the *Little Rebel* is a powerful tug, formerly employed at New Orleans. They are all plated, though partially and poorly, are furnished with strong prows, to act as rams, and are moved by powerful engines. Hugging the Tennessee shore lies the Federal flotilla, of five plated gun-boats, the *Benton, Louisville, Cairo, St. Louis* and *Carondelet,* with four rams, the *Queen of the West, Monarch, Lancaster* and *Switzerland,* which are nothing but old tow-boats, made a little stronger in the ribs, and "nosed" with iron prows. Of these, the *Lancaster* and *Switzerland* were scarcely in the fight.

Thus the Rebels have somewhat the advantage in number of men and boats, the Loyalists in guns, besides the strength of their cause. But the Rebels, having long and confidently boasted of coming triumph, open the fight by firing several rounds at the *Benton,* which returns the compliment. While the shots of nearly all the boats are now flying freely to and fro, the *Queen,* followed by the *Monarch,* steams furiously down upon the *Beauregard,* aiming to dash in his ribs because of his hated namesake. *Beauregard,* the "Artful Dodger," slips dextrously aside, and she goes, crash! against the *Price,* seeming almost to shatter both to pieces. *Beauregard* now bears down on her, hitting her wheel-house and silencing her engine, but, alas! then runs upon the *Price,* his own partner,

rending her side and tearing away her whole wheel. Thus, victim alike to friend and foe, she cries *enough!* and floats down stream with the *Queen,* both of them crippled and fast going under. The *Monarch,* indignant at this slaughter of his *Queen,* bears down fiercely on *Beauregard,* who, being also pierced with many balls, hoists the white flag, transfers his men to the *Little Rebel,* and drifts helplessly ashore.

Meanwhile, the Union gun-boats discharge their iron hail with sure aim and deadly effect, while the Rebels, apparently disconcerted by the onset of the Rams, fire wildly or at least seem to hit nothing. The *Lovell* is raked and riddled with balls from the *Benton* and our other boats, and soon meets with a fate that shocks us, Rebel though she be. Her boilers explode; she fills fast; her mangled and scalded crew raise their arms in despair, and shriek in agony; the few, who can be, are saved by the *Benton;* but most of them—these praying, and those cursing—go down with the boat in sixteen fathom water; and with the boat in sixteen fathom water; and with the whirlpool that briefly yawns above them, all trace of both is smoothed away forever!

This combat, so strangely one-sided *in its results*—for our boats lost no men, and excepting the *Queen,* received no damage—we cannot here trace further. Our readers know that all the other Rebel boats were sunk, burned up, blown up, or run ashore, except the fleet *Van Dorn,* which ran down stream, and probably is now skulking in some creek, scared and helpless as MOSES in the bulrushes. But we will add two or three remarks. First:—As between the gun-boats and the rams—which latter some have foolishly derided—honors seem even, and they both showed power and efficiency for their purpose. Next:—This conflict is likely to deepen, in England, the wonder that has grown chronic over our naval achievements. They will see that the vessels of both parties to this desperate affair were, in large part, extemporized—comparatively made from nothing. They will see, again, that our Rebels, *being Americans*, are no mean foes in any respect, yet we always beat them. They are fearless, but our courage conquers theirs. They are active and ingenious, but their activity and inventions are always over-matched by ours.

THOMAS N. DAY: CONDITION OF NEWLY CAPTURED MEMPHIS

This report, offered six days after Memphis fell, suggested a happy state of affairs in the city among the people. But it also documents the economic problems Southern cities already faced with inflated prices and increasingly worthless Confederate money.

Hartford Daily Courant, 12 June 1862 (Hartford, Conn.)

Correspondents report favorably the state of feeling in Memphis. The city has been under such infernal despotism for the last year that any change seems to them desirable. There has been no opposition or angry demonstration, the rebel flags have been quietly taken down, and in some cases the act has been cheered. But one man was heard during the entire first day to speak disrespectfully, the better class remaining in doors or quietly minding their own business on the streets. Says one correspondent: "I have not seen, nor do I see, the sullen, angry faces that one met for months at St. Louis and Baltimore. On the contrary, every one looks calm or pleased, and conveys, physiognomically, the idea of satisfaction with the new order of things.

The men in office under the "Confederate" Government were for the most part devoid of principle, honesty, or character, and so rendered an odious law doubly odious. Bribery of all kinds was the rule, and corruption crept into every nook and corner of the administration and executive affairs.

For six months Memphis has been like a graveyard, and business has been a mere pretense, and commerce a shallow make-believe. The Overton House, built especially for a hotel, has long been occupied as a military hospital, and the Gayoso, Worsham and Commercial have been nearly as free from guests as if they were plague-infected. The proprietors have not pretended to keep hotel, because they could not purchase the needful supplies.

The *Argus* and the *Avalanche* are the only daily journals in the city, (the *Appeal* having been removed to Grenada, Miss.), and they are in a most embarrassed state of finances at present, and have been suffering from the same cause for many months. The *Appeal* was prospering greatly, and proved very profitable as a Conservative Democratic paper up to the time of the rebellion; but since then it has been steadily and rapidly losing money.

The *Avalanche* was a violent Pro-Slavery journal from the beginning, and an extreme advocate of Southern State Rights, and so continued until some six months ago, when it became rather conservative, owing to causes mentioned in a previous letter. Dr. Jeptha Fowlkes is the chief proprietor and controller of the *Avalanche*, and there is little doubt it will advocate the Union before many weeks.

The *Argus* had a brilliant prospect for a new journal, and was doing remarkably well until Tennessee was carried out of the Union. Since then it has grown very sickly, and experienced no little difficulty in surviving on half sheets of wrapping-paper.

Provisions are very scarce and high. Confederate shin-plasters abound, but are much discredited. "Lincoln's Green-Backs" were at once sought for. A dinner costs a dollar in scrip; a pair of common sewed boots, twenty dollars; a glass of liquor, twenty-five cents; sugar, eight cents a pound and flour twenty dollars a barrel.

The [*New York*] *World's* correspondent says:

"From our day's wanderings among the people of Memphis, we doubt not that the happiest feeling will be restored immediately. Even the well known secessionists of the city are already gently backing down from their former high pretensions. We heard two of the solid men conversing as follows:

"Well, Mr. ———, what do you think of it now?" "Well," replied the other, "I suppose they will not hurt us, at any rate. It's a relief to know the thing is over, I don't think they will hurt us much, anyhow."

There is a manifest anxiety to trade, but the greater portion of them have nothing but worthless paper money. It will be a long season of suffering for the masses, whose little all has been swept away by the rapacity of these incendiaries."

There is every reason to believe, however, that trade will at once set in with St. Louis and Cincinnati and thus restore the city, by its quiet influences, to order and decency, if not to loyalty. With the fall of Memphis the rebels lost complete control of the Mississippi and they can never regain it.

CHARLES HALE: NO THREAT FROM CITIZENS OF CAPTURED MEMPHIS

The Boston Daily Advertiser *offers a different perspective on the people of Memphis. This writer draws a distinction between the threats that came from Memphis compared to the actual behavior of its citizens once the federal troops captured the city in this untitled report.*

Boston Daily Advertiser, 10 June 1862

It seems to be a general rule with the rebels, that when they threaten the most they do the least; and when they most vehemently protest against the very thought of surrender, they are nearest the act itself. Probably no city in the South, except Charleston, has hectored more ferociously than Memphis. An early convert to secession, what has not that city threatened to do? One of the very earliest phenomena of the war was the raising of a company there, bearing the name of "Avengers" or some other truculent title, every man a walking arsenal, clothed in red and black, the colors of death,— and sworn neither to give nor take quarter. But to what a tame conclusion has all this savage preparation led! On Friday of the week before last a public meeting in Memphis resolved for the hundredth time never to surrender the city; on Friday of last week the citizens all came out early in the morning to witness a naval engagement, at the conclusion of which the city surrendered to the control of the United government as quietly as a brood of chickens seeks the protection of the mother's wings,—and then all went composedly home to breakfast, we suppose, with the reflection that under the new order of things coffee will soon enliven that meal once more.

Memphis having failed so completely to perform its promises, it may be safely concluded, we think, that rebel brag and menace is something which it is unnecessary to take into account quite as much as has been the practice. From the very beginning of the war, the country has responded with the boasts and threats of these men who so coolly do that which they have declared to be worse than death itself. Gasconade of the more ferocious sort has become a sort of idiomatic peculiarity with them,—an habitual style of speech, which is to be taken into account and allowed for, precisely as we abate something from the declarations of one addicted to exaggeration. It shows itself throughout the Southern press, and in the words of every rebel general or orator. A resort to boasting to vehement appeals to honor, to professions of devotion, and to threats of terrible deeds to be performed hereafter, is the rule.

It might be an interesting subject for speculation, to inquire to what this is due, and whether it is not originally the effect to be expected from an institution, which habituates men to the assumption of a style of speech which will terrify, when it does so otherwise control, a race of inferiors. And it would be interesting too to note the extent to which this habit of speech has been fostered by the constant and successful assertion of political supremacy,—in holding which, threats and what is commonly known as "bluff" have played so important a part. At present, however, it is enough to observe that there appears to be very little behind all this threatening talk. The men who talk so wildly and resolve so desperately, at the end act very much as ordinary men act under the same circumstances. They resolve never to "surrender voluntarily," but that does not prevent a surrender "by the force of circumstances,"—to use the language of the Mayor of Memphis.

WILLIAM HARDING: MEMPHIS—RECONQUERED SOUTHERN CITIES AND THEIR MOBS

The Philadelphia Inquirer *offers a third perspective on the state of affairs in the city after the federal troops assumed control.*

Philadelphia Inquirer, 16 June 1862

"Memphis is as quiet as a Northern city." Such was the welcome news sent lately from a Rebel town but just before a pest and a terror to itself and to the country. On the very last day prior to its occupation by our troops, it had to call out the Home Guard to quell the riotous soldiers, who were shooting now at dogs, now at men, on the streets and sidewalks. The slaughter of the former is not recorded; of the latter they killed several industrious citizens. The papers spoke, also, of various other shooting affairs, of late occurrence, but which, fearful, perhaps, of vengeance, they said it was best not to locate or particularize. How many lives this pleasant pistol-practice may have cost, is left to conjecture. The same general state of things existed in New Orleans before its capture by our forces, as Richmond journals have for months asserted that there, too, violence is "the order of the day." But the two former towns are now "as quiet as a Northern city." Of course. In this civil war ours is the civilized and civilizing party. Order, peace, security march with our armies, and wherever these may triumph, there those will pitch their tents. The above is the bright and cheering obverse of the picture.

But it has, also, a reverse of dark and dangerous aspect. In New Orleans, and yet more in Memphis and elsewhere, the citizens, though rejoiced at the reign of order and security, are yet few and slow to pronounce for the Union. Whence this delay? From the dread of sudden mob-violence, and yet more from the reign of private terrorism. They fear violence or death in out-of-the-way places, even when our troops are near at hand, and if these be, from any cause, withdrawn, they are threatened with general destruction. On the very day that our troops took Memphis unopposed, the brutal cowards, who would not fight for their city, were yet brave enough to beat almost to death some poor, defenceless men, whose loyalty had made spontaneous utterance.

What is the cure for these evils? Instant and unsparing rigor. The strong policy of General BUTLER [*in New Orleans*]

our Government should adopt at once and everywhere. Traitorous assassins and murderous ruffians must be smitten down without hesitation and without exception. Small were the use to have expended so much of treasure, and toil and blood in reducing the Rebel States to a mere nominal allegiance, while our friends are still to be "terrorized," silenced, humbled, oppressed, outraged, murdered. If instant punishment is not enforced in each Rebel region as fast as we reclaim it, we shall only have changed very bad into a great deal worse. We shall have drawn out a few loyalists only to expose them to destruction, and forced thousands to act with the Rebels through simple terror. We shall have opened a vast theatre to be crowded with crimes and horrors. Unsparing severity exercised at once upon these ruffian mobs may save to the country thousands of lives, release the Government from a trooping crowd of troubles, and avert from its Southern adherents long years of fear and affliction. Let, then, our Government smite down all Rebel ruffianism with the iron hand, and stamp out its detested life with the armed heel. So may we soon hear that, not alone Memphis and New Orleans, but all the reconquered towns in Secessia are "as quiet and as *secure* as a Northern city."

NOTES

1. "The War News," *Baltimore Sun*, 9 June 1862.
2. Ibid.

FURTHER READINGS

Faust, Patricia L. (Ed.). *Historical Times Illustrated Encyclopedia of the Civil War*. New York: Harper & Row, 1986.

Rhodes, James Ford. *History of the Civil War, 1861–1865*. New York: Macmillan, 1917.

Wagner, Margaret E.; Gallagher, Gary W.; and Finkelman, Paul (Eds.). *The Library of Congress Civil War Desk Reference*. New York: Simon & Schuster, 2002.

12

SECOND BATTLE OF BULL RUN, 28–30 AUGUST 1862

The late spring and early summer of 1862 saw important Union victories in the West, including the capture of New Orleans and Memphis. But success in the East was more elusive, particularly toward the end of the summer. The Union did not fare well in three different campaigns fought mostly in Virginia—Confederate General Thomas "Stonewall" Jackson's Valley Campaign, Union General George McClellan's Peninsula Campaign, and Major General John Pope's Northern Virginia Campaign (for the Union).

By June, General Jackson had ended his successful campaign for the Confederacy and had gained control of the upper and middle parts of the Shenandoah Valley. That freed up his army to reinforce General Robert E. Lee in Richmond.

The threat that Jackson's forces in the Shenandoah Valley posed to Washington caused President Abraham Lincoln great concern and resulted in the redirection of a substantial number of Union reinforcements to the Valley early in Jackson's campaign. These troops came from General McClellan's Army of the Potomac, which was preparing for an attack against the Confederate capital in Richmond. McClellan's army, still 100,000 men strong after sending troops to the Valley, was unsuccessful in its efforts to capture Richmond, mostly because McClellan was outmaneuvered and bluffed into defeat by General Lee during the Seven Days Campaign fought the last week in June. The Seven Days Campaign, which consisted of six battles, turned for McClellan and the Union at the Battle of Gaines' Mill, when Confederate forces drove the federals to retreat back across the James River and convinced McClellan to give up his plans to continue to advance to Richmond because he feared (wrongly) that he was outnumbered. McClellan later suggested that Lincoln's redirection of his men to the Valley cost him the Virginia Peninsula Campaign.[1]

General Pope's Northern Virginia Campaign began in July near the Rapidan River in Virginia; General Lee sent General Jackson to that area to defend against General

Pope's advances. Pope's most significant loss came on familiar ground, at Bull Run near Manassas where federal troops suffered their first meaningful defeat at the hands of the Confederate soldiers in July 1861 (see Chapter 8).[2] The second Bull Run, however, was not the first battle in the Northern Virginia Campaign. On 9 August 1862, General Jackson's troops and Union Major General Nathaniel Banks's corps fought at Cedar Mountain. Although the federal troops gained an early advantage, a Confederate counterattack led by General A. P. Hill managed to repulse the Union troops. This battle clearly showed that the front lines of the fighting had shifted from the Peninsula to northern Virginia. This campaign had started, and it was clear to both Generals Lee and McClellan that they needed to send their men to Jackson and Pope as reinforcements.

General Lee sent Confederate General James Longstreet's corps to attend to the Rappahannock River line, while Jackson's men were to cut through the Shenandoah Valley and come out behind the Union forces at Manassas Junction and capture the Union supplies at Pope's base there. McClellan's men, as well as the troops under Union Major General Ambrose Burnside, joined Pope's men to form a line that ran from the left bank of the Rappahannock River north and west into the Shenandoah Valley.

A few days before the fighting at Manassas that would later become known as the Second Battle of Bull Run, the *New York Times* discussed the strategic implications of the federals moving back to Manassas to fight: "Manassas is now, as it was when in rebel hands, one of the strongest natural positions in Virginia. . . . If Pope fell back to Manassas and if he succeeded in drawing the rebel army there, it will not be merely for the purpose of challenging the rebels to battle on that historic ground."[3]

Pope did fall back to Manassas, but not before Jackson had arrived and taken advantage of the "natural positions" the *Times* had pointed out in its article. On 28 August, to draw Pope's forces into battle, Jackson ordered an attack on a federal column that had passed across his Confederate front at Brawner's Farm, where the fighting at the first Battle of Bull Run took place. The fighting lasted for several hours and ended in a stalemate. Pope believed he had trapped General Jackson and concentrated all of his forces on this one area, including the reinforcements he had received from General McClellan's army. He planned to crush the rebel forces the next morning, unaware that Jackson had been reinforced by General Longstreet's men, who had arrived opposite his left flank. In essence, the Confederate troops of Jackson and Longstreet formed a "V." General Pope's troops were unknowingly stuck in the middle.[4]

When General Pope attacked General Jackson on the morning of 30 August, two days after Jackson had engaged him in battle, he buried himself and his men deeper into the Confederate "V." When Longstreet's wing of 28,000 men joined the attack, it was the largest, simultaneous mass assault of the war. The Union's left flank was crushed, and the army was driven back to Bull Run. Pope and his troops retreated to Centreville, taking the same route the defeated federal troops took at the first Battle of Bull Run.

On 1 September, General Jackson headed to Chantilly in Fairfax County with the intent of cutting off the Union retreat from Bull Run. Recognizing his troops were still in danger at Centreville, General Pope ordered a full retreat to Washington.

The second Battle of Bull Run resulted in 13,830 federal and 8,350 Confederate casualties; the skirmishes at Chantilly caused 1,300 more Union and 800 more rebel deaths. Just as with the first Battle of Bull Run, press accounts of the fighting began with reports of a Union victory that ended with the realization of another federal loss. Fears about rebel invasions of Washington ran high. Much of the reporting of the second Bull Run came secondhand since General Henry Halleck, the general in chief of the Union army, had ordered all federal commanders to remove newspaper reporters from their ranks after the Battle of Shiloh in April. This impeded the flow of information greatly.[5]

General McClellan, who had been removed by President Lincoln as the head of the Army of the Potomac after the disappointing Peninsula Campaign, resumed his command after the second Battle of Bull Run and worked to rebuild the federal troops' confidence, replace equipment, and restore discipline to the Union army. Some of the discussion about the Union cause in the press focused on the shift in command and the need to provide adequate leadership in the military "not only to drive back and annihilate the present rebel army, but to extinguish at short notice the whole Southern Confederacy."[6]

The press predictions about Confederate attention turning toward Maryland and perhaps invasions of Washington from the North were not that far from the mark. As a result of the federal withdrawal to Washington, Confederate General Lee turned his attention to a new campaign, the northern and western invasion of Maryland, which began in early September.

A. S. ABELL: WAR DEPARTMENT REPORTS ON SECOND BATTLE AT BULL RUN

This account of the battle comes directly from the federal War Department and consists of information from General Pope in the field. It puts the Union retreat to Centreville in a positive light, suggesting that the troops there are ready for more battle. In truth, the same day this article appeared Pope's troops were headed back toward Washington under pressure from General Jackson's men.

Baltimore Sun, 1 September 1862

The intelligence from the seat of war in Virginia is highly important. Since our last issue information has been received of desperate fighting within hearing of the capital. A battle was fought on Friday on the field of Bull Run, bearing towards Gainesville and Haymarket on the Manassas Gap railroad. Of this engagement we have the official account of Gen. Pope, who states that the Federal army engaged the combined forces of the Confederates at daylight, the battle raging until after dark, when the Southern army—which had been acting on the defensive all day—retired from the field, but remained still in the front.—The Federal loss in killed and wounded is estimated at eight thousand while that of the Confederates is believed to be double as many. The Federal army is said to have made great, captured prisoners, but the General was not able to report the number. At the close of the battle the Federal troops were much too exhausted to pursue or harass their enemy, but it was expected that before the next morning reinforcements would arrive and the engagement be renewed.

These are the important statements of Gen. Pope's dispatch, which is dated at an early hour on Saturday morning at the headquarters on the field of battle, and the information of subsequent movements of the hostile armies is received through the press agency. The dispatch from this source is dated Washington, yesterday, and states that the expected reinforcements did not reach Gen. Pope, and that the Confederates, largely strengthened by fresh troops, assumed the offensive on Saturday morning and attacked the Federal army, which boldly met the assault and a severe battle followed, the advantage all going with the Confederates. Gen. Pope fell back to Centreville, where he was joined by the troops marching to his relief. The position of the Federal army at Centreville is said to be a very strong one, having railroad communication with Washington.—Centreville is eight miles from Gainesville, four from Bull Run and eighteen from Washington. Large quantities of hospital supplies have been sent from Washington to the battle field, and many of the medical officers of the army and private physicians have proceeded to the same locality. The advices received in Washington indicated that there was but little, if any, fighting yesterday. The Federal army is well-concentrated and the soldiers in good condition.

AN ANONYMOUS REPORT: REPORTS OF REBEL SEIZURE OF MANASSAS JUNCTION

Some Northern newspapers had trouble getting access to information about the fighting at Manassas so they relied on the accounts in other newspapers, particularly those close to the fighting. This is an example of a compilation of press reports that appeared in a Hartford, Connecticut, newspaper.

Hartford Daily Courant, 29 August 1862 (Hartford, Conn.)

ANOTHER REBEL RAID—MANASSAS JUNCTION TAKEN!

Artillery Captured—Cars Seized

The Washington *Intelligencer* of Thursday publishes an account of a rebel raid on Manassas, and adds the following: "A dispatch received at the Commissary General's office from an officer at Alexandria: 'Capt. Musser's son is here. He says that his father is either killed or taken prisoner and that our stores are destroyed. I have two trains but cannot get out as the road it probably destroyed. They are fighting at Manassas now. A great many troops are going out to regulate matters.' The foregoing dispatch is dated 12 o'clock, noon, yesterday.

The New York *Express* prints the following—"The value of quartermaster's stores captured by the rebels at Manassas Junction was half a million dollars. This is officially stated. The rebels were still in possession of Manassas Junction Wednesday morning. It is said the rebels had with them flying artillery, and that they used it against a railway train arriving from Alexandria. There can be no doubt but that the rebels have destroyed all the buildings, public and private, the station houses and storehouses, and it is said that they have burnt the railroad bridge over Bull Run; but this is denied. Meantime, the Capital is without communication with the army by rail or telegraph.

The Washington *Star* of Wednesday states that the attack was probably made by a portion of the same force that attacked Catlett's Station, and is variously estimated at from 500 to 2000 cavalry.

The Federal guard at Manassas is said to have consisted of the Twelfth Pennsylvania Cavalry (very green troops), two companies of infantry and a battery of artillery.

The skedaddling men bringing the news to Centreville and Fairfax, were of the cavalry, and represent that most of the infantry and artillery were captured and that the latter turned immediately against us in the skirmish. It appears that the Federal wagon trains there at the time had sufficient warning to enable them to move back to Centreville without loss. Four trains of empty cars on the sideling at Manassas are understood to have fallen into the hands of the masquerading party.

As soon as information of this affair reached Washington from Fairfax Station, a considerable force was dispatched by rail under Gen. Sturgie, to punish the darting marauders, but the probability is that they hurried off when they had completed the work of destruction, and our troops will not catch them.

The *Star* thinks that the rebels have retreated to Gordonsville, and that these attacks are made by a small force left behind to distract attention and prevent pursuit.

A correspondent of the Philadelphia *Press* says it was at Catlett's Station that the four trains were captured. Another train with sick and wounded soldiers put back to Manassas Junction and ran into some cars there, smashing them up and injuring several.

GEORGE SMALLEY: REBEL RAID ON MANASSAS JUNCTION

This is an early report of the battle that appeared in the New York Tribune; *even though this report comes before the real Union defeat is reported, it shows how worried many Northerners were about a rebel victory at Manassas.*

New York Tribune, 29 August 1862

A messenger just arrived states that the rebels are still in possession of Manassas Junction! That they have destroyed all the buildings, public and private, the stationhouses and storehouses and *have burnt the railway bridge over Bull Run!* That bridge is *six miles this side* of Manassas Junction; it is a structure of considerable length and expense. Its destruction cuts off railway communication between the Capital and the Army. No trains will leave Alexandria to-day.

I have received no further particulars. . . . It is not easy to see what excuse is to be offered for this [*rebel*] success. . . . But such a success, one might expect, would put a General on his guard against its repetition. Here we have it again, on a larger scale, still bolder in its plan, and more sudden and complete in execution. There is a very brilliant field indeed for future explanation. Meantime, the Capital is without communication with the army by rail or telegraph, and the War Department received its dispatch this noon by a special messenger.

THOMAS N. DAY: SITUATION AT MANASSAS

This article is meant to calm the fears of some Northerners who believed the Confederate forces were headed to Washington, D.C. It also notes that if the rebels did successfully take Washington, it would be sufficient evidence in Europe of the legitimacy of the Confederacy.

Hartford Daily Courant, 30 August 1862 (Hartford, Conn.)

Some good people thought it the thing, yesterday, to get panicky, because the rebels were said to be advancing 30,000 strong on Washington! And to have crossed the Rappahannock in force, with the deliberate intention of burning our Capitol. We trust they will persevere. The Richmond *Whig* says it is a military as well as a political necessity that Washington should be laid in ashes; when the Confederates have done that, Europe will recognize them as a nation, and their independence will be achieved! Very well; if the combined armies of Pope and McClellan are not strong enough to drive back the rebels under Gen. Ewell, it is time the confederacy was acknowledged. As Senator Hale says, "Nothing has equaled the energy of the rebels, except the weakness with which we have opposed them." The time has come for our army in Virginia to show its metal, and this inroad of Gen. Ewell must be met by a similar dash and energy or a blur will settle upon somebody's military reputation.

There is not the slightest reason for anxiety about Washington; and it is to be hoped that our generals will see in this imprudence of the rebels, in crossing the Rappahannock, their opportunity for closing in upon them, and cutting up the force which has ventured into such a position. As we suffered at Ball's Bluff for such imprudence, so it is hoped the rebels will be made on this occasion to regret that they ventured north of the Rappahannock. We look for glorious news from Pope's and McClellan's forces; they must capture or disperse all the rebels in their vicinity. And our latest advices indicate that there is a fair prospect of their succeeding.

THOMAS N. DAY: LIKELY IMPLICATIONS OF RECENT ACTION AT BULL RUN

The following account of the effect of the second Bull Run battle suggests that the rebels could not, or at least should not, consider an attack into Maryland because of their losses at Manassas. But that is exactly what the Confederate army was about to do. These early reports of the fighting at Bull Run did not clearly convey to Northern readers the heavier loss that the Union troops sustained in the fighting.

Hartford Daily Courant, 3 September 1862 (Hartford, Conn.)

The aggressive is now the game of the rebels. Immediately after the Bull Run panic of last year there was a general cry throughout the South that Washington must be laid in ashes, and even Philadelphia, New York, and Boston were not spared in the imaginations of the more enthusiastic. But the good sense of Jefferson Davis fought stoutly against any movements of the kind. Now, however, it seems that the opposition of Davis has been withdrawn and overcome, and the rebels are bent upon sacking and burning the northern cities. Cincinnati is threatened, and Washington will be captured if a determined and persistent effort of the rebels can bring it about. Prisoners captures in the recent battles agree that Washington is the goal for which the rebels are struggling. Colonels and generals, for weeks past, have encouraged their faltering men by holding out the possibility of taking Washington, and the certainty that it should be handed over to indiscriminate plunder, whenever taken. As for provisions, the prisoners now in Washington say that Jackson has captured enough prisoners at Warrenton, laid in for the federal armies, to supply the whole rebel force for a month. Having possession of all the ground in the rear, and being among friends the rebels can get their supplies now direct from Warrenton.

As to the effect of the late battles, there can be little doubt. The plan of capturing Washington, via Maryland, by a round about march will have to be, if it is not already, abandoned; and the inertness of the rebels, as to attacking our forces at Centreville, show that his strength has been materially weakened by his losses in recent battles.

JOHN W. FORNEY: PROSPECTS POOR FOR REBEL INVASION OF NORTH

This untitled report also suggests that a Southern invasion of the North, or an attack on Washington, would be futile.

Philadelphia Press, 2 September 1862

That we have succeeded in thwarting Jackson's two well-laid plans of entering Maryland with a large force is certain, and that we have caused him immense loss cannot be doubted, but we have not done with him yet for a moment; we must move on him before he is in condition to advance again at all, if possible. We must be up and doing immediately. We think it probable that Jackson's forces have been entirely cut up and demoralized, and that he will retreat for the purpose of reorganizing his army, or regaining a fresh one, which can be obtained, it is thought at Gordonsville. To sum up the results of the late battles, it would appear that we have done the enemy great damage, and that our victorious retreats and repulses all tend to show the great advantages we have gained, and perhaps the battles of the past week will prove of a more decisive character than we at present anticipate. It is gratifying to announce that the Commander-in-Chief is confident, and that he is perfectly satisfied with the plans suggested in a council of war held at Centreville yesterday, between Generals Pope, McDowell, Sigel, Banks, Heintzelman, Kearney, Hooker, Porter, Reno, Cox, Sumner and Sturgis. The prospect before us it promising, and we believe Pope will advance upon the enemy soon again.

JAMES M. WINCHELL: ANALYSIS OF CONFEDERATE AND UNION LEADERSHIP AT SECOND BULL RUN

The New York Times *had a correspondent in Washington who provided the following analysis of the Confederate and Union leadership at the second Bull Run. His analysis appeared with a detailed account of the battle that came from another* Times *field correspondent (who signed his account "Whit"); because General Halleck had removed reporters from the troops, it was less common to see field reports this soon after Shiloh.*

New York Times, 2 September 1862

That the greatest battle of the war has been raging for several days past in the vicinity of Manassas, is now known in Washington, although the information is not allowed to go over the wires. That this fight, up to the present time, has *not* resulted in a success to the National arms, is also now known. The same mail that carries this will convey to you an account of this fearful contest, by one of your special correspondents in the field, and hence I shall not attempt any account in detail; but I will give a few observations from this point of view, and the conclusions to which the intelligent public here has arrived in regard to the present "situation."

When Jackson threw himself with a comparatively small force, in the rear of Pope, he executed one of those bold inspirations of genius whose very audacity almost insures success. Pope's retreat had been a feat of such astonishing rapidity that he may almost be excused for not conceiving it to be possible for Jackson to thus overtake and flank him. At the same time, Jackson's daring subjected him to a terrible risk but promised brilliant rewards. The risk, thanks to his prompt reinforcement by Lee and Longstreet, he has survived, and the rewards he has realized in the capture of immense stores, giving the rebels a welcome supply of ordinance stores and ammunition, as well as of provisions, of which, in consequence of their rapid march, they were destitute.

Had our military leaders, however, possessed the boldness and promptitude of Jackson, he would inevitably have fallen a sacrifice to his enterprise and courage. Probably he estimated all the chances, as in his raid in the Shenandoah Valley, and the fact shows that his estimate was correct. . . .

I think confidence is lost in Gen. Pope. To-night an officer of some prominence, who was in the fight, announces, after visiting the War Office, that to-morrow morning will see a new Commander in the field. Whom it can be I can only guess.

URIAH J. JONES: MORE VOLUNTEERS NEEDED TO DEFEND UNION

One response to the Union losses in Virginia coupled with the fear of a Confederate attack into the North was to call on more volunteers to defend the Union. Pennsylvania papers were particularly eager to drum up corps to protect the state since it was more vulnerable as a Border State.

Harrisburg Patriot & Union, 4 September 1862 (Harrisburg, Pa.)

Men of Pennsylvania—true men, who love your country and would preserve her institutions—it is perhaps needless to say to you that now, this very hour, your country needs your help, wants your services on the field of battle, and expects every loyal son to do his duty. O, by every sacred tie that binds you to the past, by every hope of present safety and a glorious future, we conjure you hang not back in this hour of gloom and of peril. The rebel banner waves almost in sight of Washington—our veteran regiments, worn by the toils of war, and thinned by the bullets of the enemy, call upon you to come to their assistance and aid them in routing and driving back the foe. Gallant young men of the old Keystone, your brothers are bathing daily the soil of Virginia with their blood, and they call upon you to imitate their glorious example. You will not refuse—you dare not now hold back: honor, patriotism forbid. Your country and your brethren in this field call upon you to come—to hasten; and surely you cannot be insensible to the magnitude and energy of the call.

The rebels are in earnest now. They do not intend to let an opportunity slip that will give them a single advantage. They are fighting desperate battles, for it is their last opportunity to give us pitched battles in great force. They must save Virginia or all is lost to them. Young men of Pennsylvania, it is your duty to prevent their success, by rushing into the army, by swelling its numbers, and opposing your breasts to the foes. Death is glorious in such a cause, and he who seeks an immortal name, should court rather than shun it. Go, then, in God's and in your country's name! Go where the foe stands thickest and the death wages most deadly; go where duty, honor, patriotism call you, and go quickly; for now time is precious, and your place is not at home in the lap of indolence and ease, but under the banner of your courage in the field of strife. Let it not be said that in the most dangerous day of the Republic our stalwart young men had to be forced into the ranks to fight the battles of self-preservation. Our State has a history in the past that is honorable; we must make an honorable history for the future.—Give, therefore, one more profound and earnest response to the call of the President and go forth quickly to the rescue of your friends and brothers and to the crushing out of rebellion. Go! Your country will honor, and may God bless you.

CHARLES HALE: NOT TIME FOR CITIZENS TO CRITICIZE UNION'S CIVIL AND MILITARY LEADERS

This article in a Republican Boston newspaper encourages Northerners to refrain from criticizing the federal government and military leadership at this moment in the war.

Boston Daily Advertiser, 1 September 1862

The news received yesterday and this morning from the seat of war is of a very different character from what we had been led to expect. The rebels have struck their great blow at last, and it proves to be both skillfully devised and fiercely dealt. They have clutched at the very throat of the nation; they have projected a movement which shall bring them before the Capital itself, and have undertaken its execution with far more success, in the earlier stages at least, than we had hoped. It now remains for soldiers whom we know to be brave, and generals whom we believe to be skillful, to defeat the combinations of the enemy, and to repel his fierce assault. Such is the utter desperation of his present effort that a decisive repulse is now likely to prove his complete destruction.

The exigency, however, calls upon every man now if ever to work for his country. It is folly now to spend our time in angry accusations of any for their share of the real or supposed responsibility for the reverses of the last few days. It is puerile to stop to indulge in gloomy anticipation of the future or regretful reviews of the past. Work, instant and hearty, is what the country now demands of all her sons. We are to keep up a cheerful hope to trust in our own right arms, to distract ourselves by no needless forebodings, but to stand by our government and rescue our nation. Even from the desperate struggles of the rebels we may learn what men can do when in earnest or less awake when patriotism calls upon us, than they who obey the call of a most foul treason.

NOTES

1. Curt Johnson and Mark McLaughlin, *Civil War Battles* (New York: Crown Publishers, 1977), 63.

2. "The Repulse at Manassas," *Philadelphia Inquirer*, 24 July 1861.

3. "The Lines of the Rappahannock," *New York Times*, 25 August 1862.

4. Johnson and McLaughlin, *Civil War Battles*, 63.

5. Brayton Harris, *Blue & Gray in Black & White* (Washington, D.C.: Brasseys, 1999), 171.

6. "The Battles Near Washington," *New York Times*, 1 September 1862.

FURTHER READINGS

Faust, Patricia L. (Ed.). *Historical Times Illustrated Encyclopedia of the Civil War*. New York: Harper & Row, 1986.

Harris, Brayton. *Blue & Gray in Black & White*. Washington, D.C.: Brassey's, 1999.

Hennessey, John J. *Return to Bull Run: The Campaign and Battle of Second Manassas*. Norman: University of Oklahoma Press, 1999.

Johnson, Curt, and McLaughlin, Mark. *Civil War Battles*. New York: Crown Publishers, 1977.

13

BATTLE OF ANTIETAM, 17 SEPTEMBER 1862

It did not take long for the Northern press to hear of Confederate General Robert E. Lee's troops advancing into Maryland. The Confederates crossed the Potomac into Maryland on 5 September. Initially, Northern papers thought the reports of the rebel invasion were rumors. The *New York Times* wrote on 5 September, "An instance of more recent date is notable in the rumor of Stonewall Jackson advancing upon Maryland by way of Edward's Ferry—a rumor calculated to produce the profoundest alarm in the North, and no doubt designed to weaken the force in front of Washington by causing the dispatch of two or three divisions to defeat the pretended movement of the rebels."[1]

The paper soon corrected the report of rumors by noting that "a farmer from the neighborhood of Poolesville, Md., who is known to be thoroughly loyal" reported seeing a rebel cavalry regiment crossing the Potomac.[2] The *Philadelphia Evening Bulletin* also reported on the rebel's attempted movements into the state via the Virginia town of Leesburgh: "A large number of them, it is apprehended, are proceeding up the river, being already in some force about Leesburgh, and in larger force between there and the Chain Bridge, as if intending to make a demonstration at the ferry opposite Poolesville."[3]

By 7 September, the Confederate army was concentrated in Frederick, Maryland. The newspapers reported General Thomas "Stonewall" Jackson's invasion of the city and noted, "Discipline was very strict, [rebel] guards being posted at all the liquor shops, and private property being rigidly respected. The rebels have possession of the Baltimore and Ohio Railroad at that point, and have torn up the track and destroyed the culverts in several places east of Frederick. They have also cut the telegraph wires."[4]

The day after invading Frederick, General Lee issued an address to the people of Maryland. Lee told residents of the state that Southerners had "watched with the deepest sympathy the wrongs and outrages that have been inflicted upon the citizens of the Commonwealth allied to the States of the South by the strongest social, political and commercial ties." Lee continued by suggesting the North had denied Maryland citizens their rights under the Constitution for having spoken out against the federal government and opposing Union aggression against the South:

> Believing that the people of Maryland possess a spirit too lofty to submit to such a government, the people of the South have long wished to aid you in throwing off this foreign yoke, to enable you again to enjoy the inalienable rights of freemen, and restore independence and sovereignty to your State. In obedience to this wish, our army has come among you, and is prepared to assist you, with the power of its arms, in regaining the rights of which you have been despoiled.[5]

Lee had hoped to convince Maryland citizens to join the Confederate cause. But his address went unanswered, and his plan of Northern invasion continued without Maryland reinforcements or newly converted troops. Lee remained in Frederick for more than a week to finalize his plan to advance north into Pennsylvania. He believed he had a lead on the federal army since General George McClellan was still revamping his forces in Washington after General John Pope's devastating loss at the second battle at Bull Run. While at Frederick, Lee crafted his "Special Order 191," which involved the separation of his army into five major parts. Three columns, one of which included General Jackson's division, were to converge on Harper's Ferry, Virginia, and trap the Union garrison there. Meanwhile, General James Longstreet's troops, as well as artillery and baggage, were to move north toward Pennsylvania in preparation of an advance into the state. General Daniel Harvey (D. H.) Hill's troops would secure a position along the South Mountain to cover Longstreet's troops and to prevent a Union escape from Harper's Ferry. Finally, General Jeb Stuart's cavalry would be split among all the columns to screen and survey the troops.

Lee's plan was set into motion on 12 September when the Confederate troops left Frederick. Unbeknownst to General Lee, one copy of his "Special Order 191" was accidentally left behind. Lee also did not realize that the Union troops had organized swiftly under General McClellan—the same day the Confederates left Frederick, the Union troops arrived. When they did, two men of the 27th Indiana Infantry who were resting in a field that had just been used as Lee's headquarters found three cigars wrapped in paper. As they unwrapped the cigars to smoke them, they discovered that the wrapping around one of the cigars was the lost copy of Lee's Special Order 191. It was quickly given to General McClellan, who realized the significance of what the infantrymen had found.[6]

As General McClellan moved to catch General Lee, the Confederate plan had fallen behind schedule, and General Lee learned the fate of his lost Special Order 191. He directed General Longstreet to fall back to Boonsboro and join General Hill's troops at the South Mountain. On the morning of 14 September, General Hill was looking across the valley from atop Turner's Gap, and he saw the Union army moving forward like a blue tide. On 17 September, General McClellan's army confronted Lee's forces at Sharpsburg, Maryland. The battle of Antietam had officially begun.

On 17 September, Union General Joseph Hooker mounted a strong assault on General Lee's left flank that would start the single bloodiest day in American military history. Most of the fighting occurred near Antietam Creek at a cornfield in front of

Dunker's Church. By the end of the day, Union General Ambrose Burnside's troops joined the action, as did Confederate General A. P. Hill's division, which had arrived from Harper's Ferry. Although the Confederate forces were outnumbered two to one, General Lee committed all of his forces to the fighting and was able to lock the federal troops to a standstill. General McClellan had sent in only three-fourths of his army, which enabled Lee's corps in their efforts.

On the night of 17 September, both armies consolidated their lines; and despite crippling casualties on both sides, fighting continued the next day. Eventually General McClellan did not continue his assaults on the Confederate forces, and during the night of 18 September, General Lee ordered his army to retreat back across the Potomac into the Shenandoah Valley.

More than 27,940 combined troops were dead, injured, or missing. Although the losses were fairly even on both sides, the Battle of Antietam was considered a federal victory, mostly because it thwarted Lee's forward momentum toward Pennsylvania and further depleted the shrinking Confederate army. It was not a strong or decisive victory, however; and after that battle, President Lincoln permanently relieved General McClellan of his duty. Some historians have suggested that if McClellan had fought Lee at Antietam with his full federal army, the Union might have secured a decisive victory and perhaps even won the war at that time.

The Northern press did not widely report General McClellan's removal after the battle. In fact, the Northern press was still facing difficulties in reporting the war at all, beyond information released directly from the federal government. As noted in Chapter 12, the second Battle of Bull Run was not well reported in the North since it came on the heels of General Henry Halleck's order to remove journalists from the battlefields after Shiloh. Most of the Northern press reports of the actual battle at Antietam came from *New York Tribune* reporter George Smalley, who, wearing a blue Union uniform, slipped in to join General Hooker's division. Smalley's report of the fighting was supposed to be wired to the *Tribune* office in New York but was instead sent to the War Department in Washington, where it was eventually distributed and reprinted in nearly 1,400 newspapers nationwide.[7] A summary of Smalley's report appears below, as do various accounts of the battle and its significance to the war effort in 1862, nearly eighteen months after the war had commenced.

JOHN W. FORNEY: PENNSYLVANIA CONCERNED ABOUT LEE'S NORTHWARD MARCH

John Forney's Philadelphia Press *showed some of the concerns in Pennsylvania about the Confederate advance, even though they did not realize that rebel troops were already in control of Frederick when this article was published. Most in Pennsylvania did not know early on that their state was where Lee had been directing his troops.*

Philadelphia Press, 7 September 1862

The people are much disturbed at the recent retrograde movement of our armies in Virginia, and the near approach of a desperate and wicked enemy to our homes. We can assure them that no apprehension need be felt until the rebels cross the Potomac in force, which we believe to be an impossibility under existing circumstances. General Stonewall Jackson is moving towards the Potomac, it is thought to a point near Harper's Ferry, where he will offer heavy battle, and endeavor to draw our troops from below on the Maryland shore; Longstreet will, in the meantime, force his way over the river into Maryland, with the main body of the rebel army, move rapidly upon Annapolis Junction and the Relay House, take possession of Baltimore, and force the Government to surrender the national capital and all the troops around it. Such is the rebel plan, it is said, and stupendous as it may appear, we believe they will make a strong effort to carry out the scheme. It will be their last and greatest act of impudence that our Government has submitted to during this outrageously impertinent rebellion. The chivalry hope by this move to humble us in the dust and force us to sue for peace upon any terms, to take the capital, scatter our army, steal our wealth, inaugurate Jefferson Davis as President of the United States, claim foreign recognition instantly, make us the rebels, and turn things upside down, generally. But if they should not succeed in carrying out this grand design, they will march off with whatever spoils they may be allowed to secure, and General Lee will exclaim with Captain Bobadil, "I was panic-struck, certainly." We have not been in the habit of criticising the work of our Government, or its generals, of late, or tinkering their plans, but we would like to make a suggestion touching our future movements: Let an able fighting general head a portion of the army, and move upon the enemy, attacking him in flank and rear, and thereby save the capital, stir up the enthusiasm of the people, thwart the enemy in his designs, and perhaps send his army flying in every direction, disorganized and demoralized, never again to concentrate in the vicinity of Washington. It will be by such advances and attacks that the rebel army will be destroyed, and peace restored to our bleeding country.

URIAH J. JONES: LIKELIHOOD OF BATTLE IN MARYLAND

After learning that the Confederate army had approached Maryland, newspapers began to speculate about the location of an impending conflict.

Harrisburg Patriot & Union, 8 September 1862 (Harrisburg, Pa.)

It is now certain that the rebel army has crossed the Potomac and occupies the Virginia side, and that Gen. McClellan, with the army of the Potomac, on Sunday evening were on the Maryland side. That the enemy intend to resist the passage of the Union troops appears evident from the position he has assumed, and the formidable force he keeps massed ready for action. But the river will be crossed, when we do not know, nor where, nor at what sacrifice; but it will be crossed; and we may expect to hear, before many days have passed, of another bloody battle. Until then let us be patient. Our troops require some rest: it is necessary for them before being again put in motion, and surely we are not so impatient for "blood and carnage" that we cannot wait for it contentedly another week. Let us hope that victory again waits our arms, and that "the end draweth nigh."

GEORGE SMALLEY: REPORT ON BATTLE IN MARYLAND

The Baltimore Sun *was one of the hundreds of papers that reprinted all or part of Smalley's report of the battle at Antietam. Their summary of Smalley's account appears below.*

Baltimore Sun, 22 September 1862

WAR IN MARYLAND

DETAILED ACCOUNT OF THE GREAT BATTLE OF SHARPSBURG GRAPHIC AND INTERESTING PARTICULARS TERRIFIC ENCOUNTER HEROISM AND DESPERATION

The correspondent of the New York Tribune gives a detailed account of the battle of Wednesday, the 17th inst., which he terms "the greatest fight since Waterloo, and contested all over the field with an obstinacy equal even to Waterloo." It appears, from his statement, that Tuesday was spent chiefly in deploying forces and gaining positions. After the day was over, Gen. Hooker remarked: "We are through for to-night, but to-morrow we fight the battle that will decide the fate of the Republic."

THE REBEL ATTACK

In another moment a rebel battle line appears on the brow of the ridge above them, moves swiftly down in the most perfect order, and though met by incessant discharges of musketry, of which we plainly see the flashes, does not fire a gun. White spaces show where men are falling, but they close up instantly, and still the line advances. The brigades of Burnside are in heavy column; they will not give way before a bayonet charge in line. The rebels think twice before they dash into these hostile masses. There is a halt, the rebel left gives way and scatters over the field, the rest stand fast and fire. More infantry comes up Burnside is outnumbered, flanked, compelled to yield the hill he took so bravely. His position is no longer one of attack; he defends himself with unfaltering firmness, but he sends to McClellan for help. McClellan's for the last half hour has seldom been turned away from the left.

He sees clearly enough that Burnside is pressed—needs no messenger to tell that. His face grows darker with anxious thought. Looking down in the valley where 15,000 troops are lying, he turns a half-questioning look on Fitz John Porter, who stands by his side, gravely scanning the field. They are Porter's troops below, are fresh, and only impatient to share in this fight. But Porter slowly shakes his head, and one may believe that the same thought is passing through the minds of both generals: "They are the only reserves of the army; they cannot be spared."

McClellan remounts his horse, and with Porter and a dozen officers of his staff rides away to the left in Burnside's direction. Sykes meets them on the road—a good soldier, whose opinion is worth taking. The three generals talk briefly together. It is easy to see that the moment has come when everything may turn on one order given or withheld, when the history of the battle is only to be written in thoughts and purposes and words of the general.

BURNSIDE ASKES REINFORCEMENTS

Burnside's messenger rode up: His message is, "I want troops and guns. If you do not send them I cannot hold my position for half an hour." McClellan's only answer for the moment is a glance at the western sky. Then he turns and speaks very slowly: "Tell General Burnside that this is the battle of the war. He must hold his ground till dark at any cost."

"I will send him Miller's battery. I can do nothing more. I have no infantry." Then as the messenger was riding away he called him back. "Tell him if he cannot hold his ground, then the bridge, to the last man!—always the bridge! If the bridge is lost, all is lost."

The sun is already down; not half an hour of daylight is left. Till Burnside's message came it had seemed plain to every one that the battle could not be finished to-day. None suspected how near was the peril of defeat, of sudden attack on exhausted forces—how vital to the safety of the army and the nation was fifteen thousand waiting troops of Fitz John Porter in the hollow. But the rebels halted instead of pushing on; their vindictive cannonade died away as the light faded. Before it was quite dark the battle was over. Only a solitary gun of Burnside's thundered against the enemy, and presently this also ceased, and the field was still.

THE GREAT PERIL

The peril came every near, but it has passed, and, in spite of the peril, at the close the day was partly a success—not a victory, but an advantage had been gained. Hooker, Sumner and Franklin held all the ground they had gained, and Burnside still held the bridge and his position beyond.

It is hard to estimate losses on a field of such extent, but I think ours cannot be less than six thousand killed and wounded—it may be much greater. Prisoners have been taken from the enemy. I hear of a regiment captured entire, but I doubt it.

AN ANONYMOUS REPORT: REPORT OF INITIAL ENCOUNTERS AT ANTIETAM

This battle summary highlights the second day of fighting in the cornfield near Dunker Church.

Adams Sentinel & General Advertiser, 23 September 1862 (Gettysburg, Pa.)

WEDNESDAY EVENING, Sept 17—9, P.M.—This has been an eventful day in the history of the rebellion. A battle has taken place, in which the Army of the Potomac has again been victorious, and which exceeded in extent any battle herefore fought on this continent.

At the dawn of the day the battle was renewed on the centre and right by Generals Hooker and Sumner, who, after a sharp contest of two hours, drove the enemy about one mile. The Rebels rallied stoutly, and with terrible loss, regained most of the ground. At this time, the fearless and indomitable General Hooker received a shot in the ankle, and was carried from the field. The command of his troops now devolved upon General Sumner. General Richardson, commanding a Division, was severely wounded at the same time.

General Sumner determined to retake the lost ground, and ordered the troops to advance, which they did with a will, driving the Rebels before them with great slaughter. They not only retook the ground, but drove them a quarter of a mile beyond.—In this action General Mansfield was shot in the lungs, and died soon after—He was at the head of his troops with sword waving over his head cheering on his men at the time he received his wound.

During this time the troops under Generals Burnside and Porter had not been idle. They drove the enemy from the line of Antietam creek, on the main road to Sharpsburg, built a bridge, the old one having been burnt, and occupied the opposite bank. The loss here was considerable.

The troops now held both banks of the creek. To get possession of the ridge of hills on the right and left hand sides of the road from which the Rebels were thundering away with artillery, was a task not so easily accomplished. General Sykes' brigade, with the assistance of General Sumner, crossed the ridge on the right hand side after considerable trouble and loss, the Rebels running in all directions.

It was now five o'clock, and all the enemy's positions had been carried except the one on the left hand side of the road. To perform this duty Gen. Burnside was assigned. The artillery opened and the infantry advanced, and the point was carried at a charge. They were, however, forced to retire before a largely superior force. Knowing that if they lost this ridge, a complete rout of their army would be the result, they fought with great desperation.

Darkness now overtook the two armies and hostilities ceased as though by mutual consent. The battle lasted from five o'clock in the morning in the morning till seven o'clock at night without a moment's cessation.

ASSOCIATED PRESS: LETTER FROM ANTIETAM BATTLEFIELD

This Associated Press account of the battle comes from a correspondent who managed to join Smalley after the fighting had ended.

Associated Press, 20 September 1862

BATTLE-FIELD OF ANTIETAM. Sept. 20.

Yesterday our lines advanced towards the enemy, when the discovery was made that the entire rebel army had retreated during the night, leaving their pickets along the entire line, so as to prevent us from gaining a knowledge of their movements until they had accomplished their purpose. Those left behind to perform this duty generally surrendered as soon as our skirmishers appeared.

It seems, from statements of residents of Sharpsburg and vicinity, that rebel reinforcements were expected on Friday, but they did not arrive, and consequently it was decided to cross the river, as they were in no condition to stand another such battle as that of the 17th instant. So they commenced leaving at dark on Thursday night, and the rear of the line passed through Sharpsburg just before daylight yesterday morning. They crossed the river at different points in the vicinity of Sharpsburg, as there are several fords within two miles of that place, although the contrary has been represented. Our cavalry started in pursuit as soon as the retreat was known, but beyond capturing a few hundred stragglers they succeeded in inflicting on the enemy little injury.

About a mile from the river quite a contest took place between a part of Porter's corps, which were in the advance, and the enemy for the possession of two guns, which they seemed unable to move fast enough. They were finally compelled to abandon them, one of which they spiked. Their trains have all got off, notwithstanding it is said their horses were completely worn out. They seem to have taken a position on the other side of the Potomac, but they did not reply to our guns this afternoon, with the exception of three or four shots.

An attempt was made to cross and flank them, but they were in too good a position to be attacked with success.

A Union man named Hughes came in from Williamsport this afternoon and reports a large force of the enemy had crossed this morning at that place, but could not say how many. For fear he might be caught he left in haste, and therefore did not count them. He said at least two thousand infantry were on this side, and the column was still coming over, the rear not being visible. According to another report, it was only a small party sent over to forage the country and harass the inhabitants.

The retreat of an army so large as that of the rebels, in the face of one like our own, was certainly creditable to its commanders, especially when it is considered they met with but slight loss while it was being consummated. One thing, however, was in their favor, which was they had the Antietam in their front about half the length of their line, over which our troops could cross only at one point. It was at this bridge Pleasanton's cavalry made such a splendid dash across in the face of a fire from several batteries planted to sweep it from different points, and which rained a perfect shower of shell upon it while our troops were crossing, most of which, fortunately, did not explode.

As soon as the cavalry crossed they were followed by Sykes' Regulars, in support of three batteries—Tidball's Gibson's and Robinson's—which, after getting into position, silenced the rebels at this point, and relieved Sumner's corps from a fire under which they would have otherwise been compelled to fall back.

Some of the most desperate fighting ever recorded in history took place on this field.—In passing over the ground today, the evidence was manifest where the most deadly contests occurred—the dead lying thick and in rows where they had fallen on the enemy's centre. Three lines of battle had been formed from a point west of the Hagerstown turn-pike, across the road and several fields, to near the Boons-boro' turnpike, a distance of about half a mile; and these lines were almost as distinct as when the living mass still found them, the dead lying so close as to be nearly within reach of one another's hands along the entire distance; while in many places they laid one upon another.

THOMAS N. DAY: UNION VICTORY IN MARYLAND; NORTHERN PRESS TOO ANXIOUS TO ASSAULT RICHMOND

In these back-to-back news items, the Republican Hartford Daily Courant *cheers the Union victory in Maryland and criticizes those in the Northern press who are too anxious to return to fight at Richmond after the recent Union losses there.*

Hartford Daily Courant, 17 September 1862 (Hartford, Conn.)

This morning's telegraphic news will send a thrill of joy throughout the nation. It will gladden the hearts of all loyal men, and cause the disloyal to tremble with dismay as they realize their impending doom. We have the glorious words, *"the rebel army in Maryland will be captured or annihilated this night"*. The large rebel army which entered Maryland a few days since in triumph, yesterday was fleeing for its life, to escape the clutches of an advancing army, led by the gallant McClellan. A nation's gratitude will be poured out upon the gallant army which has achieved this great and glorious tri-umph.

The newspaper generals of the irrepressible kind, are out again in full chorus, with the "on to Richmond" cry. They want to have the army of the North press upon the rebels and anni-hilate them. Of course, so we all do; but the question is a *military* question, not a political question, and should be left to the most competent military man we have, to decide. If editors, in their cosy chairs are the best judges of what it is competent and possible for the army to do, then of course, their advice should be followed. But men who can remember as far back as the first battle of Bull Run, will have more confidence in the judgment of the generals in the field, than in all the dogmatic scolding that editors utterly innocent of military knowledge can improvise. It is of course, the simplest principle in war-fare, that a beaten foe is to be followed up relentlessly and pressed with all possible celerity; but we prefer to rely on Gen. Halleck's or Gen McClellan's judgment as to what is practica-ble, rather than risk everything on [*publishers*] General Horace Greeley's or Rev. Ward Beecher's views of propriety. The pub-lic must remember that ours is a vast country in geographical area; and that modes of action which are successful in Europe, are demonstrated to be inefficacious in this country. Let us all support the patriotic Lincoln, who has the best of advisers at his elbow, and make some allowance, for what is getting to be conceded, the very big and tough job he has undertaken.

THOMAS N. DAY: SIGNIFICANCE OF UNION VICTORY AT ANTIETAM

This editorial offers some analysis of the significance of the Union victory at Antietam, which was as much symbolic as strategic.

Hartford Daily Courant, 19 September 1862 (Hartford, Conn.)

The long agony of doubt is over, and our side is victorious. Glory to God in the Highest for the result! It breaks the back of rebeldom, and opens a door of deliverance for the op-pressed. Our forces have nothing now to fear; they have met the trained troops of the South, splendidly led by their most skilful officers, and they have whipped them thoroughly. The long course of privation, of exposure, of semi-starvation, of reckless roamings, by day and by night, month in and month out, had made the Southern army under General Lee, sol-diers every inch of them. They had forgotten the tender hu-manities of civilized life, and become so absorbed in their ex-citing and laborious life, that it seemed like exposing lambs to wolves to send the fresh levies of the North to compete with the brown savages, which the Southerners have become. But, under the skillful guidance of McClellan, seconded by fighting generals inferior to none in the world, the Southern army that dared to defy the force of our Government on Northern soil has been most effectually used up. What can there be for us more to fear? There were no gunboats in this Maryland business; the army has, for once at least, done something without the aid of our navy. The insolent boast of the South, so often repeated both here and in Europe, that the Southern soldier can whip three Northern soldiers, must now be taken for what it is worth. Again we say, the back of rebeldom is broken, and our generals can "enter Richmond" about as soon as they choose to try. It is most fortunate that there is an army of Virginia, as well as an army of the Potomac, already in existence, and daily swelling; and whenever the advance may be ordered, there will be no backing out. This time the job will be done sure.

Let us give thanks to Almighty God, for what has been gained. While we were getting, yesterday, the most exciting tidings of triumph, the Southerners must have been overwhelmed with despondency; and yet, it was the day set apart by Jeff. Davis for a solemn Thanksgiving for victory! What mockery, to exult on the surface, while at the core, ground with and fear! It seems as if offended deity had brought about results in such a way as to rebuke the South, for its conceit, in claiming as it has heretofore most strenuously insisted, that the smiles of Providence were lavished on the Confederacy. What does it think of this frown upon the very day appointed for thanksgiving? Let the men of the North quit themselves like men: pour in the volunteers, or the drafted men, if the volunteers do not come; and from this auspicious dawn, we shall go on conquering and to conquer, until the star of Peace returns, and the Union is once more entire.

Our telegraph columns furnish some of the particulars of the fight of Tuesday, and of the terrible battle and carnage of Wednesday. Our loss is estimated as 10,000 in killed and wounded, and the rebels as much more. It is terrible to contemplate.—There was no fighting yesterday, but the dreadful strife is to be renewed to-day, and our troops are confident of a complete victory. The rebels are making a desperate resistance. We have nothing further relative to Harper's Ferry, or the capture of rebel generals.

ASSOCIATED PRESS: CONDITION OF LEE'S ARMY AFTER BATTLE OF SHARPSBURG (ANTIETAM)

Once the news of the rebel defeat spread through the North, attention was focused on the fate of General Lee and his troops, as suggested in this article.

Baltimore Sun, 20 September 1862

BY TELEGRAPHY

For the Baltimore Sun.
[From the Agents of the Associated Press.]

THE BATTLE OF SHARPSBURG

Fearful Slaughter of the Rebels
Rebel Loss 18,000 or 20,000

GENERAL STARK KILLED

[Correspondence of the Associated Press.]
HEADQUARTERS ARMY OF POTOMAC,
Saturday, September 20, 1862

The rebel army has succeeded in making its escape from Maryland. They commenced to leave about dusk on Thursday evening and by daylight yesterday morning were all over, except a small rear guard. They saved all their transportation, and carried off all their wounded but about three hundred.

Between three hundred and four hundred rebels stragglers were taken during the day by General Pleasanton's cavalry brigade, who took the advance in the pursuit of the rebel army.

Every house in Sharpsburg was struck by our shells. Two were burned, and also a large barn located in the centre of the town.

The citizens who remained escaped injury by staying in their cellars. One child was killed. Two rebels, while cooking their supper on Tuesday, were killed by one of our shots passing through the kitchen of the house in which they were.

The name given to this battle is the "Battle of Antietam."

After our forces occupied the whole field the rebel loss was found to be far greater—particularly in killed—than was at first supposed.

Fully 2,500 dead were found lying on the field of battle, while a larger number had been removed the day before by their friends. Their loss in killed and wounded will not come far from 18,000 to 20,000.

CHARLES HALE: SIGNIFICANCE OF ANTIETAM AND STATE OF AFFAIRS IN VIRGINIA

This untitled article addresses the significance of the battle and discusses the present state of affairs in Virginia according to the press there. It also critiques the Confederacy's decision to invade Maryland, given the outcome of the campaign.

Boston Daily Advertiser, 23 September 1862

Somewhat to the chagrin of the loyal people of these States, as it must be confessed, the rebels have escaped from what was certainly a most dangerous trap in Maryland. The folly of a subordinate officer, opening Harper's Ferry to them, has given them the opportunity for the concentration necessary for their retreat. Their enterprise, however, had failed of every important object. It failed to make any impression upon the security of Washington, of Baltimore, of Philadelphia, or any other of our cities. It failed to effect anything for the rebel cause in Maryland, and seems, in fact, if we may trust the common account, to have proved to be a stimulus rather than otherwise to the Union feeling throughout that State. And as for the supplies which it was fancied were to be secured by this grand foraging expedition as some termed it, we apprehend that, except the captures made at Harper's Ferry, very little booty has been taken out of the Potomac valley. The stay has been too short, the retreat too rapid to allow the collection and removal of any considerable amount of supplies.

The rebels have therefore very little for which to thank the policy which sent them into Maryland. The progress of their retreat is not likely to develop any new subject for congratulation. The Richmond papers informed us before this movement began that Virginia was bare of supplies. Except the Shenandoah valley that State is a desert. One hundred years must pass, according to one of these papers, before Virginia can regain her old position. Grain and provisions have been consumed by contending armies, crops have been destroyed and agriculture broken up, until the State has become too poor to subsist an army. If then these facts afforded any reason, as was alleged, for the advance into Maryland they render the retreat upon Virginia the worst of calamities. It would apparently have been infinitely better to wear away the time in defensive warfare, than to throw two great armies once

more upon the soil of a State which is already exhausted and suffering. And especially a forced and hasty retreat, in the face of an enemy elated by victory and backed by powerful reinforcements, would seem under such circumstances to be a disaster of fearful weight.

But although we believe there is yet cause to hope that the invasion of Maryland will cost the rebels the greater part of their army, through disorganization if not by actual battle, we apprehend that the moral advantages gained by the government are after all, perhaps, the most important consequences of the movement. and those of worst import to the enemy. For example, it would have been better for them never to have crossed the Potomac, never to have crossed the Rappahannock even, rather than to furnish an occasion for the reestablishment of McClellan at the head of our army, and especially for the thorough vindication of his military capacity and his superior fitness for the leading position which has followed. It is of course hazardous to conjecture what would have been in a supposed case, but there is at least reason to believe, that it is to the vigorous onset made by the rebels themselves that we owe the sudden fall of Generals Pope and McDowell, and the discovery that McClellan's name alone has the power to keep alive the confidence of the army, and that he more than any other has the abilities needed to carry our arms forward to a durable triumph. It was something worse than the loss of a pitched battle for the rebels, when they forced the removal of the cloud which misfortune and reckless personal enmity had thrown over his name. They did that which reaches far beyond the present moment or the fate of their present campaign. They gave to our general an assured place of confidence of the country and to our army a new life and hope which will carry the power of the Union forward with an impetus which the declining strength of the rebellion can no longer resist.

NOTES

1. "Editorial Article No. 1," *New York Times*, 5 September 1862.

2. "The Rebels Attempting to Invade the North," *New York Times*, 5 September 1862.

3. *Philadelphia Evening Bulletin*, 5 September 1862.

4. "The Rebel Army of Invasion under Jackson in Maryland," *New York Times*, 7 September 1862.

5. John Esten Cooke, *Virginia: A History of the People* (Boston: Houghton Mifflin, 1884).

6. Curt Johnson and Mark McLaughlin, *Civil War Battles* (New York: Crown Publishers, 1977), 64.

7. Brayton Harris, *Blue & Gray in Black & White* (Washington, D.C.: Brasseys, 1999), 183.

FURTHER READINGS

Faust, Patricia L. (Ed.). *Historical Times Illustrated Encyclopedia of the Civil War*. New York: Harper & Row, 1986.

Harris, Brayton. *Blue & Gray in Black & White*. Washington, D.C.: Brasseys, 1999.

Johnson, Curt, and McLaughlin, Mark. *Civil War Battles*. New York: Crown Publishers, 1977.

Sears, Stephen W. *Landscape Turned Red: The Battle of Antietam*. New York: Mariner Books, 2003.

Top left: New York newspaper correspondents' row in Richmond, Virginia. New York correspondents often used the telegraph offices in cities like Richmond to send their stories back to their papers. (Courtesy of the Library of Congress)

Top right: Mathew Brady, one of the most celebrated Civil War photographers. He hired a corps of photographers to work with him to bring images of the war to the public. The *New York Times* said Brady brought "home to us the terrible reality and earnestness of war." Few newspapers published photographs during this time; rather, photos were typically made available directly to the public. This photograph of Brady was taken in 1875. (Courtesy of the Library of Congress)

Middle right: A newspaper vendor's cart in a Virginia camp in 1863. (Courtesy of the Library of Congress)

Below: A group of unidentified men sitting at the tent and wagon of the *New York Herald* in Bealeton, Virginia, in 1863. (Courtesy of the Library of Congress)

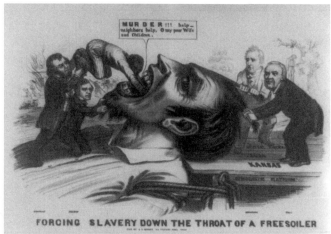

Left: This wood engraving appeared on the front page of *Frank Leslie's Illustrated Newspaper* in June 1857. The top image is of Eliza and Lizzie, Dred and Harriet's children. Dred Scott is pictured on the left, Harriet on the right. (Courtesy of the Library of Congress)

Above: In this 1856 political drawing, artist John Magee suggests that the Democrats are to blame for violence against antislavery Kansas settlers after passage of the Kansas–Nebraska Act. A bearded "freesoiler" is bound to the "Democratic Platform" and restrained by two small figures: presidential nominee James Buchanan and Democratic Senator Lewis Cass. Democratic Senator Stephen A. Douglas and President Franklin Pierce are also shown as tiny figures. "The freesoiler's head rests on a platform marked 'Kansas,' 'Cuba,' and 'Central America,' probably referring to Democratic ambitions for the extension of slavery," according to the Library of Congress archives. (Courtesy of the Library of Congress)

Above: This wood engraving by Arthur Berghaus shows John Brown riding atop his coffin to his execution. The illustration appeared in *Frank Leslie's Illustrated Newspaper* in December 1859. (Courtesy of the Library of Congress)

Right: An 1859 portrait of John Brown, shown holding the *New York Tribune*. Brown had a national reputation as an abolitionist fanatic who advocated violence as a means to put an end to slavery—for that reason, he attracted a lot of attention in the Northern pre-Civil War press. (Courtesy of the Library of Congress)

Top: This is a nonpartisan satirical image that parodied all four candidates in the 1860 presidential election. Lincoln (far left) and Douglas are on the left, Breckinridge is in the center and John Bell is on the right. (Courtesy of the Library of Congress)

Bottom right: Abraham Lincoln. (Courtesy of the Library of Congress)

Bottom left: An artist's rendering of the first reading of the Emancipation Proclamation before Lincoln's cabinet. (Courtesy of the Library of Congress)

A photo of the Confederate flag flying over Fort Sumter after it was captured. The formal attack on Fort Sumter began at 4:30 A.M. on 12 April, 1861. General Pierre Gustav Tautant Beauregard of Louisiana led the Confederate forces; the Union forces inside Fort Sumter were led by Major Robert Anderson. Most eyewitnesses who described the morning blasts called it a "truly grand...pyrotechnic display," and according to an Associated Press reporter, "The terrific fighting reached an awful climax at 10 o'clock at night...Nearly all night long the streets were thronged with people full of excitement and enthusiasm. The house-tops, the Battery, the wharves, the shipping, in fact, every available place was taken possession of by the multitude." The battle ended thirty four hours after it started when Major Anderson waived the white flag and surrendered the fort. No one on either side died as a result of the fighting. (Courtesy of the Library of Congress)

Confederate General Pierre Gustave Toutant Beauregard. Beauregard, nicknamed "The Little Napoleon," captured Fort Sumter at the start of the war and led Confederate forces in many major battles, including the first Bull Run and Shiloh, where he drafted the attack orders and took command after Confederate General Albert Johnston was mortally wounded on the battlefield. Beauregard also managed to thwart the early Union attempts to capture Petersburg in 1864. He spent the final days of the war as second in command under General Joseph E. Johnston in North Carolina. (Courtesy of the Library of Congress)

This is an interior view of Fort Sumter taken in 1864 by a Confederate photographer. (Courtesy of the Library of Congress)

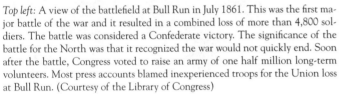

Top left: A view of the battlefield at Bull Run in July 1861. This was the first major battle of the war and it resulted in a combined loss of more than 4,800 soldiers. The battle was considered a Confederate victory. The significance of the battle for the North was that it recognized the war would not quickly end. Soon after the battle, Congress voted to raise an army of one half million long-term volunteers. Most press accounts blamed inexperienced troops for the Union loss at Bull Run. (Courtesy of the Library of Congress)

Top right: Major General Irvin McDowell, who commanded the Union troops at the Battle of Bull Run. McDowell's army was shattered at Bull Run, but reorganized in Washington, D.C. days later under the new command of General George B. McClellan. In March 1862 McDowell was sent to protect Washington, D.C. from possible attack after Confederate Major Stonewall Jackson's successful Shenandoah Valley campaign struck fear in those living in the nation's capital. (Courtesy of the Library of Congress)

Bottom right: This image shows two photographers having lunch in the Bull Run area before the second battle commenced. (Courtesy of the Library of Congress)

Bottom left: Rebel soldiers building fortifications at Manassas five months before it became the scene of the second Bull Run. (Courtesy of the Library of Congress)

Top left: General Benjamin Butler became the military governor of New Orleans and stayed in the city through the end of 1862. (Courtesy of the Library of Congress)

Top right: Vice Admiral David Farragut commanded the Union navy fleet that conquered New Orleans in April 1862. The capture of New Orleans was significant in many ways—it convinced some European leaders, most notably French Emperor Napoleon III, to refrain from declared intentions to recognize the Confederate states and open trade in violation of the federal blockade of Southern ports. The success in New Orleans also lifted Union spirits after the great loss of life at Shiloh. (Courtesy of the Library of Congress)

Bottom left: Union General Henry Halleck, nicknamed "Old Brains" for his ability to think and plan, was Ulysses S. Grant's superior in the West early in the war. He became general-in-chief of the Union army and moved to Washington in 1862. After the devastating human loss at the Battle of Shiloh, which was generally considered a Union victory, Halleck ordered all federal commanders to remove all newspaper reporters from their armies. Grant would replace Halleck in March 1864, but Halleck stayed on as chief of staff. (Courtesy of the Library of Congress)

Above: Photo taken by Mathew Brady of a monument erected on the battlefield of Shiloh in 1863. Brady was one of the most celebrated photographers of the war. As a reviewer in the *New York Times* of 20 October, 1862, said of his photographs of the horrific Battle of Antietam: "Mr. Brady has done something to bring home to us the terrible reality and earnestness of war. If he has not brought bodies and laid them on our dooryard and along our streets, he has done something very like it." (Courtesy of the Library of Congress)

Right: President Abraham Lincoln and General George B. Mc-Clellan in the general's tent at Antietam after the battle. (Courtesy of the Library of Congress)

Dead Confederate soldiers on the Hagerstown road at the Battle of Antietam. (Courtesy of the Library of Congress)

Union soldiers filling canteens at Fredericksburg. In December 1862 Union forces suffered terrible casualties at the hands of entrenched Confederate forces at Prospect Hill and Marie's Heights. After several days of fighting General Ambrose Burnside called off the federal attacks and crossed back over the Rappahannock thus ending the battle. The federal losses were significant compared to the Confederates: 12,600 Union men killed compared to 5,300 Confederates'. (Courtesy of the Library of Congress)

Confederate General Thomas "Stonewall" Jackson. (Courtesy of the Library of Congress)

Wounded soldiers in the field after the Battle of Chancellorsville. The death toll at Chancellorsville was significant: the federal forces lost 17,000 men, while the Confederates suffered a loss of 14,000. Many historians have considered the battle at Chancellorsville to be General Robert E. Lee's greatest victory for the South. Although the Confederates won the battle at Chancellorsville, they lost a greater percentage of their men than the federals and they also lost General Thomas "Stonewall" Jackson. He was seriously wounded in the fighting and later had his left arm amputated. Jackson died of pneumonia on 10 May, 1863 while recovering from the amputation. (Courtesy of the Library of Congress)

Top left: Alfred R. Waud, an artist for *Harper's Weekly*, sketches on the battlefield at Gettysburg, July 1863. (Courtesy of the Library of Congress)

Top right: Union General George Meade's Gettysburg headquarters on Cemetery Ridge. Meade's victory for the Union at Gettysburg cannot be understated. It was the first time the Union forces defeated Confederate General Robert E. Lee's Army of Northern Virginia in a significant battle; it changed Northern public sentiment about the ability of the North to win the war; it jump-started a series of Union victories that would lead to more support of the Republican administration and the eventual re-election of President Lincoln more than a year later; and it exacted a devastating moral and human loss to the Confederate military, which was struggling to increase its strength with shrinking numbers of available Confederate men. The Battle of Gettysburg was the northern-most battlefield in the entire four year conflict and it would become the site of President Lincoln's famous Gettysburg Address (in November 1863) at a ceremony to honor the fallen federal soldiers of the battle. (Courtesy of the Library of Congress)

Bottom right: Four dead soldiers in the woods near Little Round Top. During the second day of fighting at Gettysburg, Union General Joshua L. Chamberlain and his troops from Maine were surrounded by the rebel forces at their position on Little Round Top. Nearly out of ammunition, Chamberlain ordered his men to fix bayonettes, and while the right side of his line held straight, he ordered his left to head down the hillside. The attack took the rebel forces by surprise and the front ranks dropped their weapons and ran. Some previously unaccounted-for men from Chamberlain's Maine Company B suddenly rose and fired at the fleeing Confederate forces. Chamberlain captured 400 rebel soldiers that day and held Little Round Top. On the third day of fighting, July 3, the federal forces gained decisive advantage in the battle that led to their ultimate victory at Gettysburg. (Courtesy of the Library of Congress)

Left: The levee and steamboats at Vicksburg, Mississippi, in 1864. Beginning in October 1862, Union General Ulysses S. Grant made several unsuccessful attempts to capture Vicksburg; one of two remaining Confederate strongholds on the Mississippi River. On 22 May, 1863 the siege of the city began and for forty eight days General Grant pounded the city by land while the Union navy attacked the city from the river. On 4 July, 1863, the same day that Confederate General Robert E. Lee retreated from Gettysburg, General John Pemberton surrendered Vicksburg to General Grant. Grant's campaign against Vicksburg has been called one of the most brilliant military campaigns of the war. (Courtesy of the Library of Congress)

Above: Historians credit this print to Henry L. Stephens and they suspect that the drawing was commissioned by the *New York Tribune.* In this image, New York Governor Horatio Seymour is trying to quiet the angry mob. He gave a speech, famously called the "My Friends" speech on the steps of New York City Hall during the draft riots in 1863. Horace Greeley, the *Tribune's* editor, was a vocal critic of Seymour. (Courtesy of the Library of Congress)

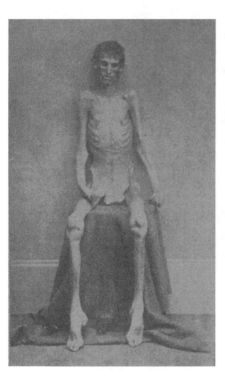

Left: A recently released Union prisoner. War prison facilities on both sides lacked proper sanitation, food, shelter, and clothing. Historians have noted that neither side intentionally mistreated its prisoners; rather, Americans had never been faced with what to do with hundreds of men in captivity and were ill-prepared to handle the thousands of prisoners the war produced for each side. Although exact figures are not known, historians estimate that 56,000 men died in Civil War prisons. The leading cause of death was disease. There were more than 150 prisons established during the war and all were filled beyond capacity. (Courtesy of the Library of Congress)

Above: This 1862 image shows Union soldiers guarding Confederate prisoners at a Union prison camp. The rebel soldiers were captured in the Shenandoah Valley. (Courtesy of the Library of Congress)

Top left: Wounded Union soldiers from the Battle of The Wilderness. General Ulysses S. Grant's first campaign against Confederate General Robert E. Lee in the East was called the Overland Campaign and it opened with a 5 May 1864 battle in The Wilderness, an area known to both sides from the Battle of Chancellorsville. The Battle of The Wilderness lasted for two bloody days—the federal forces lost 17,666 men, while the Confederate losses totaled 7,750. (Courtesy of the Library of Congress)

Top right: General William T. Sherman, pictured here on the right leaning on the breach of a gun at Federal Fort No. 7 in Atlanta, after he captured the city in 1864. His staff also appears in the photo, taken by George N. Barnard, the official photographer of the Chief Engineer's Office. (Courtesy of the Library of Congress)

Right: General William T. Sherman was a key Union general in the West and one of General Grant's most trusted allies throughout the war. Nearly two months after he captured Atlanta, Sherman marched to Savannah, then through the Carolinas, in what became his most celebrated military action in the Civil War, "Sherman's March." Sherman's troops exacted more than one million dollars in damage throughout Georgia and the Carolinas and freed thousands of slaves. (Courtesy of the Library of Congress)

Above: Federal soldiers at the captured Fort McAllister. Sherman stormed Fort McAllister on 13 December 1864, before moving on to Savannah. (Courtesy of the Library of Congress)

Right: Federal picket post at Atlanta, shortly before the battle of 22 July, 1864. Although the federal forces did not take the city in the July 22 battle, they exacted a lot of damage to the Confederates who lost 8,500 men. General William T. Serman finally captured the important Southern city when Confederate General John Hood evacuated. On his way out, Hood's rebels set fire to train cars filled with ammunition and set off explosions that seriously damaged the inner city. (Courtesy of the Library of Congress)

Top left: Portrait of Major General George B. McClellan, 1864 Democratic presidential candidate. His wife, Ellen Mary Marcy, is also in the image. (Courtesy of the Library of Congress)

Top right: Lincoln taking the oath at his second inauguration, 4 March 1865. (Courtesy of the Library of Congress)

Bottom left: Ruins of Richmond & Petersburg Railroad Depot, April 1865. (Courtesy of the Library of Congress)

Middle left: Union telegraph operators at military headquarters in Petersburg, Virginia, in 1864. (Courtesy of the Library of Congress)

Above: Union soldiers in front of Appomattox Courthouse, Virginia On 9 April 1865, after a series of exchanges between Generals Grant and Lee, the two met at Wilbur McLean's home in the village of Appomattox Courthouse to agree on the terms of Lee's surrender. On 12 April 1865 a formal surrender ceremony took place, four years to the day after South Carolina militia began its assault on Fort Sumter, initiating the war. (Courtesy of the Library of Congress)

Left: Union general Ulysses S. Grant. (Courtesy of the Library of Congress)

14

EMANCIPATION PROCLAMATION, SEPTEMBER 1862

Following the Battle of Antietam, the Union cause for winning the Civil War would officially and dramatically change. On 22 September 1862, President Abraham Lincoln issued a preliminary Emancipation Proclamation that declared all slaves residing in territory in rebellion against the federal government would be free as of 1 January 1863. Although President Lincoln was known to condemn the system of slavery, he had consistently said the reason for the Civil War was the restoration of the Union. But as the Union army continued to struggle, Lincoln realized that emancipation was not only the morally right thing to do but also a military necessity. After Lincoln issued his Emancipation Proclamation, the Civil War's focus shifted from bringing about the restoration of the Union to bringing about an end to slavery.

The Union's perceived victory at Antietam gave Lincoln the perfect opportunity to announce his Proclamation, which American historians have called one of the most significant proclamations issued by an American president since the formation of the country. Lincoln read his Proclamation to his cabinet on 22 September, and the next day it was printed in newspapers across the country.

In reality, the Emancipation Proclamation freed few people. It did not apply to the slaves in the Border States who were fighting with the federal government, and it did not affect slaves in Southern areas already under Union control. What the Emancipation Proclamation practically did was redefine the cause of the war—it confirmed for the world that at the end of the contest if the Union prevailed, slavery would come to an end. Although Lincoln's Emancipation Proclamation became effective on 1 January 1863, it did not practically abolish slavery. Slavery was formally abolished with the passage of the Thirteenth Amendment to the Constitution on 18 December 1865, nearly 6 months after the war ended.

To this point in the war, the Northern press had been mostly united in supporting the Union cause for victory. Upon the announcement of Lincoln's Proclamation, new divisions arose between political factions. The Peace Democrats, who formed in late 1860 as a result of the secession crisis, generally supported war to save the Union but thought that Republicans had largely provoked the South into the conflict. Peace Democrats did not trust the federal government, and many were states' rights advocates. Some were sympathetic to the South, and others were pacifists who opposed war in all forms. The party, which came to be called the Copperheads because they wore the copper penny with its head of Liberty as a peace button, was such a mix of factions, principles, and interests that it was hard to identify as one specific group.[1]

In the Northern press, it was clear that Republicans supported the president's Proclamation, as did the War Democrats. The Copperheads/Peace Democrats, who were often attacked in the Republican presses, generally opposed the Emancipation Proclamation because it changed the purpose of the war, and it directly interfered with states' rights. As seen below, the response to the president's Proclamation was mixed, very much along party lines. Although the "Democratic" response is somewhat mixed based on the Peace and War Democratic divisions, it is clear in the articles which Democratic papers supported a war fought to end slavery and which did not.

ABRAHAM LINCOLN: EMANCIPATION PROCLAMATION

The Proclamation in full was printed in nearly every Northern newspaper the day after Lincoln announced it to his cabinet.[2]

New York Times, 23 September 1862

Whereas, on the twenty-second day of September, in the year of our Lord one thousand eight hundred and sixty-two, a proclamation was issued by the President of the United States, containing, among other things, the following, to wit:

"That on the first day of January, in the year of our Lord one thousand eight hundred and sixty-three, all persons held as slaves within any State, or designated part of a State, the people whereof shall then be in rebellion against the United States, shall be then, thenceforward, and forever free; and the Executive Government of the United States, including the military and naval authority thereof, will recognize and maintain the freedom of such persons, and will do no act or acts to repress such persons, or any of them, in any efforts they may make for their actual freedom."

"That the Executive will, on the first day of January aforesaid, by proclamation, designate the States and parts of States, if any, in which the people thereof respectively shall then be in rebellion against the United States; and the fact that any State, or the people thereof, shall on that day be in good faith represented in the Congress of the United States by members chosen thereto at elections wherein a majority of the qualified voters of such State shall have participated, shall in the absence of strong countervailing testimony be

deemed conclusive evidence that such State and the people thereof are not then in rebellion against the United States."

Now, therefore, I, Abraham Lincoln, President of the United States, by virtue of the power in me vested as commander-in-chief of the army and navy of the United States, in time of actual armed rebellion against the authority and government of the United States, and as a fit and necessary war measure for suppressing said rebellion, do, on this first day of January, in the year of our Lord one thousand eight hundred and sixty-three, and in accordance with my purpose so to do, publicly proclaimed for the full period of 100 days from the day first above mentioned, order and designate as the States and parts of States wherein the people thereof, respectively, are this day in rebellion against the United States, the following, to wit:

Arkansas, Texas, Louisiana (except the parishes of St. Bernard, Plaquemines, Jefferson, St. John, St. Charles, St. James, Ascension, Assumption, Terre Bonne, Lafourche, St. Mary, St. Martin, and Orleans, including the city of New Orleans), Mississippi, Alabama, Florida, Georgia, South Carolina, North Carolina, and Virginia (except the forty-eight counties designated as West Virginia, and also the counties of Berkeley, Accomac, Northampton, Elizabeth City, York,

Princess Anne, and Norfolk, including the cities of Norfolk and Portsmouth), and which excepted parts are for the present left precisely as if this proclamation were not issued.

And by virtue of the power and for the purpose aforesaid, I do order and declare that all persons held as slaves within said designated States and parts of States are, and henceforward shall be, free; and that the Executive Government of the United States, including the military and naval authorities thereof, will recognize and maintain the freedom of said persons.

And I hereby enjoin upon the people so declared to be free to abstain from all violence, unless in necessary self-defense; and I recommend to them that, in all cases where allowed, they labor faithfully for reasonable wages.

And I further declare and make known that such persons of suitable condition will be received into the armed service of the United States to garrison forts, positions, stations, and other places, and to man vessels of all sorts in said service.

And upon this act, sincerely believed to be an act of justice, warranted by the Constitution upon military necessity, I invoke the considerate judgment of mankind and the gracious favor of Almighty God."

AN ANONYMOUS REPORT: SUMMARY OF PRESIDENT'S PROCLAMATION

Some Northern newspapers offered short summaries of the president's Proclamation, like this news item in the Baltimore Sun. *Maryland was a slaveholding Union Border State, so it was not immediately affected by the Proclamation.*

Baltimore Sun, 23 September 1862

The President of the United States has issued a proclamation declaring that the war shall be prosecuted for the purpose of restoring the constitutional relations between the United States and each of the States wherein such relations are now suspended or disturbed. As one of the means to reach this end, the Executive gives notice that he will, on the 1st day of January, 1863, by proclamation, designate the States, and parts of States, wherein the people are in rebellion, and declare the persons held as slaves in the same to be thenceforward and forever free; and that the government will recognize and maintain the freedom of such persons, and will do no act to repress them in any efforts which they may make to obtain their actual freedom. The Executive also gives notice that he will, at the coming session of Congress, again recommend the adoption of a practical measure tendering pecuniary aid to the free acceptance or rejection of all slave States whose people may not then be in rebellion against the United States, and which States may then have voluntarily adopted, or thereafter may adopt, immediate or gradual abolishment of slavery within their respective limits. —The President states that he will, in due time, recommend that all citizens of the United States who shall have remained loyal thereto throughout the rebellion, shall—when constitutional relations are restored between the government and their States—be compensated for all losses by acts of the United States, including the loss of slaves.

AN ANONYMOUS REPORT: WIDE SUPPORT FOR PROCLAMATION—PRESIDENT SERENADED IN WASHINGTON

This Washington dispatch to the New York Times *tells of overwhelming public support in Washington for the president's Proclamation.*

New York Times, 25 September 1862

The city was enlivened last evening by a serenade to the President, in token of satisfaction with his proclamation. The crowd formed with a band of music at the National Hotel, and marched with continually increasing numbers to the White House, and arriving at which place it had swelled to a small army. After the preliminary music, calls were made for the President, who obediently appeared at a window over the front entrance, and addressed them very briefly.

. . . The crowd was large and very enthusiastic, vociferously cheering all loyal and Anti-Slavery sentiments.

CHARLES HALE: PROCLAMATION MAKES NO CHANGE IN WAR AIMS

In this untitled commentary, the Republican Boston Daily Advertiser *defends Lincoln's Proclamation and suggests that it would only have been issued if deemed necessary by the president.*

Boston Daily Advertiser, 24 September 1862

The final act of emancipation is still deferred, and is simply threatened to those who at a certain period shall prove to be contumacious in their resistance. We find in all this no sign of any disposition to change the issues or the purposes of the war. On the other hand we find ample proof that the President has striven to postpone, as far as his judgment would permit, the actual occurrence of that dire extremity, upon which the rebels madly rushed, when they turned their parricidal hands against their country.

It seems therefore that if emancipation comes, —it will be because the Commander-in-Chief has decided this to be the only means of securing a speedy close of the war. And what have men of all parties been saying for months past, but that upon this and the other great issues of the conflict the President's judgment should be relied upon, and that the President should have the general support of the people? Many even of the most diverse political sentiments, have kept constantly in view the possible occurrence of a state of things, in which the government might reluctantly feel itself compelled

to resort to this expedient, and have expressly excepted [*sic*] such a case of adjudged necessity, in their opposition to the radical influences which have sought to precipitate the question rashly and injuriously. The case contemplated as possible has at last come; the President has passed upon it, and in this proclamation we have his decision. Now therefore is the time to redeem the multiplied pledges of confidence in his judgment of deference to his decision, and of support to himself in such action as he deems necessary for the success of the war.

This proclamation, like most of the documents with which the President occasionally startles the country, has a very shrewd adaptation to the condition of politics in the loyal States, as well as to the necessities of the war. The question of emancipation, so long as it remained open, was a source of constantly increasing dissensions, fomented by the mutual suspicions of ulterior purposes, entertained by the friends and opponents of the policy. The President has now decided the question once for all.

THOMAS N. DAY: "YEAR OF JUBILEE HAS COME"—SLAVERY RIGHTFULLY RECOGNIZED AS ROOT CAUSE OF WAR

The Republican Hartford Daily Courant's *response is much more enthusiastically supportive of the Proclamation than the Boston paper. It suggests that slavery has always been at the root of the problems between the North and South and that it is time to have the slavery issue work in favor of the Union.*

Hartford Daily Courant, 24 September 1862 (Hartford, Conn.)

We rejoice, most heartily, that the axe is laid to the root of the tree. The proclamation meets our views, both in what it does and in what it omits to do. Its limitations show that President Lincoln means to preserve good faith toward the loyal border slave States. So long as they are loyal, their slaves are safe; let them become rebellious, and the terms of the proclamation will reach them, like their sisters in revolt. It should be remembered that some sixty days ago, the President issued his proclamation, based on the confiscation act, whereby the property of all persons found in rebellion after sixty days of grace had expired should be confiscated to public uses. The time was up, September 22d, 1862, and the President took the opportunity, indirectly, to remind the rebels of that fact, while he gave them a further admonition of

what was impending on the 1st of January, 1863, a little more than 90 days from date.

The President calls the attention of all his officers in the navy or the army, to the acts of Congress prohibiting any army or naval officer from returning a fugitive slave; and declaring all slaves of rebels, escaping, captured, or deserting into the lines of the United States, to be FREE; and all slaves within places then occupied by forces of the United States to be free; and forbidding the return of any slave in any case, unless his owner could prove his loyalty.

We all know slavery to be the root of our present difficulties; and most men have ceased to expect any great progress until we bring over that element which has worked so powerfully against us, to cooperate with us. At least, let the experiment be tried; the mouths of the ultra abolitionists will be closed. Their favorite panacea has been, or is to be administered; and if it does not work to a charm, let them at least, be less virulent in their attacks upon the man and the cabinet, which we believe is doing all in their own power to bring things to a happy conclusion.

HENRY RAYMOND: BENEFICIAL EFFECTS OF PRESIDENT'S PROCLAMATION ON WAR EFFORT

The Republican New York Times *offered two opinion pieces about the Proclamation during the first week it was reported in the newspaper. The first one calls the Proclamation the "most important and far-reaching document" issued since the formation of the U.S. government. The second one argues that slaves will overwhelmingly respond to the president's Proclamation and in cities like Charleston, South Carolina, they will peacefully seek their immediate freedom. The editorial also suggests that freedom for slaves will devastate the Southern economy.*

New York Times, 23 September 1862

There has been no more important and far-reaching document ever issued since the foundation of this Government than the proclamation of President LINCOLN concerning Slavery and slaves, published this morning. . . .

The wisdom of the step taken—we refer at present to that clause in the document which declares free the slaves of rebel States after the 1st of January—is unquestionable; its necessity, indisputable. It has been declared time and again by President LINCOLN that as soon as this step became a necessity, he should adopt it. Its adoption now is not a confession that the military means of suppressing the great rebellion have proved a failure; but simply that there is a point at which any other legitimate appliances that can be called in, shall also be availed of. Slavery is an element of strength to the rebels if left untouched; it will assuredly prove an element of weakness—it may be of total destruction—to

them and their cause, when we make such use of it and its victims as lies in our power.

From now till the 1st of January—the day when this proclamation will take effect—is little over three months. What may happen between now and then, in the progress of the war, it is hard to say. We earnestly hope, however, that by that time, the rebellion will be put down by the military hand, and that the terrible element of slave-insurrection, may not be invoked. If, by that day, the rebel army be overthrown, and their Capital captured; and, if the slaveholding rebels still prove malignant, irrepressible, and, as in the Southwest, disorganizers and marauders, then let that which Vice-President STEPHENS called the corner-stone of the Southern Confederacy be knocked from under it, and see whether the whole fabric of rebellion will not necessarily tumble to the ground.

HENRY RAYMOND: PRESIDENT'S PROCLAMATION WILL OVERTHROW SOUTHERN ECONOMY

This is the Times' *second editorial on the Proclamation.*

New York Times, 28 September 1862

The Proclamation of Emancipation by President LINCOLN, looking at its possible economical and moral results in the future, is undoubtedly one of the great events of the century. Still, it should be remembered that it has been given out, especially as a military measure, with the authority indeed of Congress, but by the Commander-in-Chief of the armies and navy of the United States, for the purpose of putting down the rebellion. It is not pretended to be justified by the Constitution, except as a means of self-preservation, even as war itself on the part of the General Government is justified. It is a war measure, overriding

State laws and personal rights, striking right at the heart and strength of this atrocious rebellion. It belongs to the same category with the orders of the Government to bombard rebellious cities or to take the lives of rebellious citizens, or with the measures establishing military governments over States in armed resistance to the National authority. It finds its technical and legal justification in "military necessity." Its moral justification will be found in the approval of mankind and the increasing voice of admiration through all future history. But what, regarding it as a military measure, will be its peculiar effects?

This war has corrected several wide-spread errors in regard to the race this proclamation is designed especially to affect. We discover that the slaves are by no means so inclined for insurrections or bloody acts of violence as was formerly supposed. They are evidently a remarkably good-natured, mild, forgiving folk, who would far rather run away than attempt any doubtful or perilous venture of insurrection or warfare. We find, too, that, despite all Southern ideal pictures, they are most earnestly desirous of liberty, and have very little attachment for their masters. It is evident, also, that there is much more understanding among them of the questions at issue in this war, and a far more rapid and secret diffusing of intelligence and news through the plantations than was ever dreamed of at the North.

On the 1st of January next, in the States then in rebellion, the slaves will probably generally understand that if they can escape from rebel jurisdiction anywhere within our lines they are free. Should we hold at that time—as we may reasonably expect—Savannah, Mobile, and Charleston, an immense population of this ignorant peasantry will have abandoned their masters' estates and have placed themselves within reach of our protection.

The agriculture of the South will have been almost disorganized; a general sense of insecurity will pervade the rural districts; men who would have enlisted, will prefer to remain for the protection of their homes from dangers, which are all the more terrible from being imaginary; regiments will be obliged to return to guard against this insurrectionary population. Soon, it is probable that the Southern masters, finding themselves losing their property, will resort to cruel preventive measures, which may call out the very outbreaks they were designed to discourage.

A natural result of these large gatherings of able-bodied men within our lines—our own numbers becoming diminished from sickness and battle—will be the arming them for their own protection and for use, as a kind of *Sepoys* in our armies. This result will be postponed as long as possible, both from dislike of the negro and from dread thus of throwing away the scabbard against the sough. But the logic of events, if the rebellion continue, must force it upon us. The burden of the draft, the devilish spirit of the insurrection, the necessity of protecting these refugees in our lines, and the military duty of weakening the enemy, will all compel it. Then all the devil in the fierce passions of the South will be aroused, and in reprisal they will endeavor to make the war a death-struggle, without mercy or any consideration of humanity.

The punishment for it will be terrible and awful, and will involve nothing less than the utter extermination of the slaveholding aristocracy of the Cotton States, and an entire reorganization of society.

How much wiser, how much healthier for the vast future, would be a rational return by the Cotton States to their allegiance, and an acceptance of the wise proposition of the President, affirmed by Congress, organizing a gradual emancipation. The stand now on the verge of an abyss whose depth and horrors no human eye can measure. With them is the choice, whether to return, or to take the fatal leap.

AN ANONYMOUS REPORT: SOUTHERNERS EXPECTED PROCLAMATION FROM REPUBLICAN PRESIDENT

This brief in the New York Times *suggests that the Proclamation had no meaningful effect on Southerners who expected such a Proclamation from a black Republican administration.*

New York Times, 1 October 1862

NEWS FROM WASHINGTON
OUR SPECIAL WASHINGTON DISPATCHES
WASHINGTON, Tuesday, Sept. 30.
EFFECT OF THE PRESIDENT'S PROCLAMATION.

Recent advices from a TIMES' special correspondent, who has had extended opportunities to converse with the residents of Fairfax, Loudon, Prince William and Farquier counties, Virginia, in regard to the recent emancipation proclamation of President LINCOLN, are to the effect that the slaveholders in the above-named counties manifest remarkable indifference to the prospect of emancipation; that the proclamation creates no excitement whatever, it being what prominent Secessionists and those most interested have long expected. Instead of exasperating slaveholders, it has had the effect of compelling them to realize that at last the Government is in earnest about crushing the rebellion.

R. J. HALDEMAN: PROCLAMATION TAKES EFFECT—SLAVES GIVEN LICENSE TO REVOLT

On 1 January 1863, the day the Emancipation Proclamation took effect, the Democratic Harrisburg[3] paper suggested that the federal government had formally given slaves license to revolt and cause harm to their masters, should they desire to be free.

Harrisburg Patriot & Union, 1 January 1863 (Harrisburg, Pa.)

When the President tells [*the slave*] that neither the Army nor the Navy shall be used against him in any efforts he may make to secure his freedom, what is it but saying to him in so many words: "Who would be free *himself must strike the blow!*" The President knows that a mere proclamation of freedom, without a clause for the encouragement of insurrection, would be a nullity, for which he would be laughed at by the world—therefore he makes it, as he believes, effective, by saying to the slave:—"Arise, slay and eat," make your arm bare for slaughter, hew your way to freedom with the sword, the axe, the knife, whatever you can grasp; hew it through fire and slaughter; my soldiers shall not interfere to check your progress to liberty. Such will be the tenor and design of the proclamation with which the President intends to usher in the New Year. Hallelujah! Let Abolitiondom rejoice—there is blood enough, horror enough in prospect, under this proclamation, to gratify the most hellish instincts of the most rabid radicals. Let the Abolitionists, therefore, make merry. New Year's day will, indeed, be a day of rejoicing to them, in which we cannot participate. We hail its dawn in sorrow, and shall mourn at its close. It is a dark day in our history, one which will consign to eternal infamy the name of Abraham Lincoln and all his advisers and abettors in the act by which he has signalized its advent. More than the mere act itself, it is the fanatical spirit which prompted it, the *animus* of the man that we deplore, condemn and abhor.

THOMAS N. DAY: POLITICAL LINES DRAWN AROUND PROCLAMATION

This article, written by a Republican newspaper, provides a look ahead toward the politicking that unfolded after Lincoln announced the Emancipation Proclamation. Horatio Seymour was the Democratic governor of New York at this time.

Hartford Daily Courant, 25 September 1862 (Hartford, Conn.)

The President's proclamation is to be seized by the Democratic party all over the North, judging from various bits of evidence that have come to our knowledge, as the basis of an anti-administration party. The Buchanan democrats are about to come out and declare their hostility to all emancipation schemes. The hollow truce that has nominally existed since the fall of Sumter, is to be formally abandoned; and the men who love slavery more than they do their country's cause, are about to take open and avowed opposition grounds. The speeches made in New York by the friends of Horatio Seymour, have no doubt on that point as to the plan in New York State; and what we saw at the late town meeting for the choice of assessors, and what we hear in the streets as to the intentions of prominent democrats in this city, lead us to believe that we shall soon have a political opposition party in full blast in this city. That men have a right to their political sentiments, and to the expression thereof in all proper places and modes, cannot be denied, even in war times. The more vital are the issues discussed, the more important it is that they be discussed freely, and just as frankly on the one side as the other. Come on then, we say, to our political opponents; if you think the country will not sustain Lincoln's proclamation, try the issue, and let us see the result. Truth fears not discussion, even in war time. Only let there be discretion in the mode.

JOHN FORNEY: WAR DEMOCRATS ON THE PROCLAMATION

John Forney's Philadelphia Press, *which started as a Democratic organ in 1857, became a supporter of Lincoln when the war started in 1861. Democrats who supported the war were often called "War Democrats." That designation was even more significant after the Emancipation Proclamation was issued. The article above refers to the early buzz about the formation of the Peace Democrats as an official alternative party. This article reflects the War Democrats' take on the Emancipation Proclamation.*

Philadelphia Press, 23 September 1862

The President turns a new leaf, and, at the head of the page, writes—*Emancipation*. He has written emancipation, and there it will last forever a tribute to his own wise statesmanship and the fortitude of the American people. The patience and self-denial we have manifested from the beginning, in fighting this war with smaller weapons, while the great engine of death still remained in the arsenal, must forever be a wonder. But we have as yet been patient and self-denying before, let us be active, vigilant, and unrelenting now. If any one ever dreamed that out of this chaos of war and destruction peace might suddenly come as a compromise, or by submission, let him dismiss it from his brain like an idle dream as it was. This proclamation of the President ends the rebellion. It will not do so to-day, or even to-morrow, but it will end it in a very short time, and in a very summary manner. We are now putting the axe to the root; heretofore we have contended ourselves with trimming the boughs, and breaking the branches, forgetting that new life was constantly oozing from the soil. It does not come as a wild exhibition of despair, nor as a mere effort to rouse a drooping public sentiment or rally beaten and disheartened columns. It is the manifestation of Northern power; it is the result of overwhelming victories. We have shown the rebels that the sword is potent with us; we have shown them that, without going beyond the mere voluntary offerings of life and treasure, we have laid their conscript Confederacy at our feet, and now we propose to crush where we have conquered, and to take away the life of the great criminal who has been indicted and convicted at the bar of Christian civilization.

D. M. STONE: INITIAL DEMOCRACTIC RESPONSE TO PRESIDENT'S PROCLAMATION

The following excerpt provides a sample of the initial Democratic response to the president's Proclamation.

New York Journal of Commerce, 23 September 1862

Mr. Lincoln has yielded to the radical pressure, and issued a proclamation. It is, on the whole, a curious document. We have no inclination to-day to discuss its wisdom or the probabilities of the effect it will produce in rebeldom. We have only anticipations of evil from it, and we regard it, as will an immense majority of the people of the North, with profound regret.

AN ANONYMOUS REPORT: ANOTHER DEMOCRATIC ASSESSMENT OF THE PRESIDENT'S PROCLAMATION

Philadelphia Evening Journal, 23 September 1862

The gravity of this proclamation will strike every one. It has been forced upon the nation by the Abolitionists of the North. It inaugurates an overwhelming revolution in the system of labor in a vast and important agricultural section of the country, which will, if the rebels persist in their course, suddenly emancipate three or four millions of human beings, and throw them, in the fullness of their helplessness and ignorance, upon their own resources and the wisdom of the white race to properly regulate and care for them in their new condition of life. But the importance of this great social revolution will not be confined to the section where the black race now forms the chief laboring element. It will have an influence on the labor of the North and West. It will, to a certain extent, bring the black labor of the South in competition with the white labor on the extensive grain farms of the West, unless the existing stringent laws of some of the Western States, confining the negro to his present geographical position, are adopted in all the other free States.

WILLIAM W. SEATON: COMPARISON OF LINCOLN'S PROCLAMATION WITH GENERAL HUNTER'S SUPPRESSED EDICT OF EMANCIPATION

This response to Lincoln's September Emancipation Proclamation compares it to the emancipation proclamation issued by Union Major General David Hunter in May 1862. Hunter declared that all slaves in South Carolina, Georgia, and Florida were free because "[s]lavery and martial law in a free country are altogether incompatible; the persons in these three States—Georgia, Florida and South Carolina—heretofore held as slaves, are therefore declared forever free."[4] On 19 May 1862, President Lincoln issued a proclamation that nullified Hunter's edict of emancipation and urged the slaveholding Border States of Kentucky, Missouri, Maryland, and Delaware to embrace gradual, compensated emancipation.

National Intelligencer, 23 September 1862 (Washington, D.C.)

The reader will find in another part of to-day's *Intelligencer* a proclamation of the President of the United States, declaring prospectively the emancipation of slaves in the insurgent States on the 1st of January next, unless in the meantime the people of these States shall so far return to their constitutional relations as to send Representatives to Congress.

With our well-known and oft-repeated views respecting the inutility of such proclamations, it can hardly be necessary for us to say that, where we expect no good, we shall be only too happy to find that no harm has been done by the present declaration of the Executive.

This new proclamation with regard to the contingent emancipation of slaves in the insurgent States not being self-enforcing any more than the proclamation of General Hunter in regard to the immediate emancipation of slaves in the States of South Carolina, Georgia and Florida, the only difference between the two papers resides in the signatures respectively attached to them. And as, in themselves considered, they are likely to prove equally void of practical effect, we are not without the suspicion that the President has taken this method to convince the only class of persons likely to be pleased with this proclamation of the utter fallacy of the hopes they have founded upon it. This opinion, we may add, derives confirmation from the fact that he suspends *for some months* the enforcement of so much of his declaration as denounces the emancipation of slaves in punishment for contumacy on the part of the insurgent States, while he gives immediate force and effect, so far as force and effect result from proclamations, to the regulations prescribed by the new article of war and the provisions of the confiscation act in the matter of slaves. On any other theory than this the proclamation may be said to open issues too tremendous, and to be fraught with consequences too undeveloped, to admit of calculation or forecast by any intelligence we can command.

R. J. HALDEMAN: PROTEST AGAINST THE PRESIDENT'S PROCLAMATION

The Democratic Harrisburg, Pennsylvania, newspaper formally printed a protest to the Proclamation, noting that it will increase bloodshed and invades the individual rights of U.S. citizens.

Harrisburg Patriot & Union, 26 September 1862 (Harrisburg, Pa.)

We enter our most solemn protest of the Proclamation of Abraham Lincoln, President of the United States, bearing date the 24th of September, A.D. 1862, as in violation of the Constitution, and as not warranted by the circumstances, if it were clearly in accordance with the Constitution. We protest against it as an invasion of individual rights, as a blow at the personal liberty of the citizen, at the liberty of speech and of the press. We protest against it as an act of despotism unwarranted and uncalled for, arresting the administration of the civil law, and subjecting us to military arrest, trial and punishment. In the name of the Constitution and of civil Liberty, in the name of Reason and of Justice, in the name of Peace which it threatens, and Blood which it invites, we most solemnly and fervently protest against it.

WILLIAM LLOYD GARRISON: PRAISE FOR LINCOLN; CONDEMNATION FOR OPPOSITION DEMOCRATIC PRESS

William Lloyd Garrison, in his abolitionist newspaper, not only applauds President Lincoln's Proclamation but also denounces the Democratic press response to the edict.

The Liberator, 3 October 1862 (Boston)

Probably the President has little time, and perhaps less inclination, to read the newspapers of the day; so that he may not have been aware of the fact,—by no means a creditable one,—that, until his recent proclamation concerning the abolition of slavery in the Rebel States, every semi-seditious, rancorously pro-slavery, and thoroughly "satanic" journal in the Free States was hugely delighted with his policy, and praised him as a model of disinterested patriotism and statesman-like sagacity. It was a bad sign, and furnished conclusive evidence that he was lacking in clear discernment and true wisdom, in the management of the war. We congratulate him that he no longer lies under this injurious imputation. His emancipation proclamation has . . . [*transformed*] every pseudo-loyal toad it has touched into a semi-rebellious devil without disguise. The papers that were loudest in his praise, and that counseled the most absolute reliance upon his prudence and fidelity to his high trust, (such, for example, as the New York *Herald*, *Express*, *Journal of Commerce*, and *World*, and *Boston Post* and *Courier*,) and that hotly resented any criticism upon his official acts as indicative of a purely factious spirit, are now denouncing him in language and spirit essentially treasonable, and representing him as equally weak and fanatical. Read the articles we have grouped together in the "Refuge of Oppression," this week, as samples! It is nothing with these desperate journals, that the war has already lasted eighteen months, and little been done in crippling the rebellion; nothing, that a hundred thousand lives have already been sacrificed, and the nation is bleeding at every pore; nothing, that the debt already incurred by the war is of frightful magnitude; nothing, that the rebellion is avowedly for slaveholding purposes, and uses the entire slave population within its grasp to achieve success; nothing, that the President has tried in every way, by long forbearance and generous overtures, but in vain, to terminate the struggle without decreeing emancipation as a military necessity and a governmental right they are for preserving slavery at whatever expense of blood and treasure to the North, and though thereby the Union should remain dismembered forever! And now see how menacing is their tone, and how bullying their attitude, at this perilous crisis, toward the President and the Government! If this is not giving "aid and comfort to the enemy," then words have lost their significance. Fort Warren and Fort Lafayette have had no inmates more deserving of incarceration than the editors and proprietors of the journals we have referred to.

NOTES

1. Nathaniel W. Stephenson, *Abraham Lincoln and the Union: A Chronicle of the Embattled North* (New Haven, Conn.: Yale University Press, 1921).

2. John G. Nicolay and John Hay (Eds.), *Complete Works of Abraham Lincoln* (New York: F. D. Tandy Co., 1905), 9:161.

3. R. J. Haldeman became editor of the Harrisburg newspaper in November 1862, replacing Uriah J. Jones after the paper was sold to O. Barrett and T. G. Pomeroy.

4. Major General David Hunter, *General Orders No. 11*, 9 May 1862.

FURTHER READINGS

Guelzo, Allen C. *Lincoln's Emancipation Proclamation: The End of Slavery in America*. New York: Simon & Schuster, 2004.

Lincoln, Abraham. *Abraham Lincoln: Speeches and Writings, 1859–1865*. Ed. Donald E. Fehrenbacher. New York: Library of America, 1989.

Nicolay, John G, and Hay, John (Eds.). *Complete Works of Abraham Lincoln*. Vol. 9. New York: F. D. Tandy Co., 1905.

Stephenson, Nathaniel W. *Abraham Lincoln and the Union: A Chronicle of the Embattled North*. New Haven, Conn.: Yale University Press, 1921.

15

BATTLE OF FREDERICKSBURG, 13 DECEMBER 1862

The year 1862 proved to be a bloody one for both the Union and the Confederacy. The Union had fared particularly poorly in the East despite the spring victories in the West. The eastern losing streak continued as the year came to a close.

In November, General Ambrose Burnside inherited General George McClellan's Union command. Within two days, Burnside created a new Union strategy that involved marching quickly across the country to Fredericksburg, Virginia, a key Confederate transportation link on the Rappahannock River. Burnside believed that if he could capture Fredericksburg, he would secure for the federal troops a direct road to Richmond as well as secure a supply line to Washington. The president approved Burnside's plan, and the federal troops began marching toward Fredericksburg on 17 November.[1]

In November, Confederate General Robert E. Lee was at a decided disadvantage in defending Fredericksburg. Lee had divided the 78,000 remaining Confederate troops who had retreated from Maryland. General Thomas "Stonewall" Jackson's men were positioned in the Shenandoah Valley, while General James Longstreet's troops had been sent to Culpepper, Virginia, to stave off a federal attack there.[2] He had not anticipated Burnside's shift toward Fredericksburg, leaving the city virtually defenseless.

Lee benefited, however, from the difficulties that the federal troops faced in crossing the Rappahannock River. Because civilian bridges across the river had been destroyed earlier in the war, Burnside had to reconstruct a path across the Rappahannock. Bad weather, miscommunication, and army bureaucracy delayed this process and gave Lee's Confederate army time to get to Fredericksburg to defend the city.

On 19 November, Longstreet's men arrived at Fredericksburg and became entrenched on the heights behind the town where they awaited Burnside's assault. On 11 December, Union engineers under Confederate fire finally had laid five pontoon bridges across the Rappahannock. On 12 December, the federal army crossed the river, and the next day Burnside mounted frontal assaults on the city at two key points—Prospect Hill and Marye's Heights—that resulted in terrible Union casualties. Briefly on 13 December, a Union division under the command of General George Meade managed to penetrate General Jackson's line but was eventually driven back by a counterattack. On 15 December, General Burnside called off the federal attacks and crossed back over the Rappahannock, thus ending the battle.[3]

The federal losses were significant compared to the Confederates: 12,600 Union men killed compared to 5,300 Confederates. The loss in Fredericksburg, followed by a couple of additional failures in January 1863, led to Burnside's removal. General Joseph Hooker replaced him. Although the Confederate troops won decisively in Fredericksburg on the battlefield, it proved to be a difficult fight because Lee had trouble replenishing troops and supplies after the fighting. Although the Fredericksburg loss was discouraging to the North, the Union armies did not face the same shortages of manpower or supplies as the Confederacy. Practically, the loss simply postponed a federal advance toward Richmond.

The Northern press reported the battle in much the way it had reported the other losses suffered in Virginia in 1862. The press commentary generally focused on keeping Northern public spirits up by not overplaying the significance of the loss to the Union. Some Northern newspaper editors also analyzed the federal government's military plans as a result of the series of Union defeats.

AN ANONYMOUS REPORT: ACCOUNT OF BATTLE OF FREDERICKSBURG

The correspondent for the New York Herald *offered the following introduction to his account of the fighting in Fredericksburg.*

New York Herald, 14 December 1862

FREDERICKSBURG, Va., Dec. 14—The battle yesterday was one of the most severely and desperately contested of the whole war. It raged fiercely throughout the entire day, and even after darkness had shrouded the field it was kept up with a determination on both sides which seemed as though it was likely to last until one army or the other had become so exhausted as to be unable to maintain the fight any longer.

AN ANONYMOUS REPORT: NO REASON FOR DISCOURAGEMENT CONCERNING RECENT BATTLE AT FREDERICKSBURG

This untitled New York Herald *excerpt below is an example of a report that tried to put a positive spin on the battle, going so far as not to declare the fighting a Confederate victory. It was too soon to know the outcome of the battle when this report was published.*

New York Herald, 17 December 1862

It is evident that the whole of Burnside's available forces were engaged and that part of them were so severely handled as to be unfit to recommence the battle on Sunday morning. Hooker, whose two corps acting as reserves came latest into action, and Franklin, who had a partial success on the left, were probably in fighting condition next morning; but Sumner's Grand Division, especially Couch's corps, was exhausted by its efforts, and sorely in need of rest. Burnside waits, therefore, to collect and refresh his halting columns.

There is no reason for discouragement in this result, notwithstanding the attempts of the semi secession journals to magnify it into a defeat. The rebels had ample time to entrench themselves in a naturally strong position, and, of course, improved it. The first effort to dislodge them has failed. When Burnside is ready he will try again.

A. S. ABELL: ACTIONS OF GENERAL FRANKLIN AT FREDERICKSBURG

This early report of the battle tells a little of the efforts of Union General William Franklin. Franklin was responsible for sending General Meade to spearhead the attack against General Jackson, which briefly penetrated the Confederate line.

Baltimore Sun, 15 December 1862

Since our last issue stirring news has been received from the seat of war on the Rappahannock. At an early hour on Saturday morning artillery firing was commenced by the Confederates, and responded to by the heavy guns on the Federal side. Towards noon the infantry of the two armies became engaged, and the Federal centre twice attempted to storm the Confederate position on the first ridge of hills behind Fredericksburg, but were compelled to retire by the terrible fire brought to bear upon them. Late in the afternoon another advance was made and the firing kept up until after night came on, and as the dispatches state the Federal dead were left on

the field, it is to be presumed that they were again unsuccessful. During the engagement at this point the carnage must have been dreadful on both sides, as the Federals alone lost two generals killed and four wounded. The battle did not cease with night, the Confederates keeping up an artillery fire upon the town until eight o'clock, the place being occupied by heavy masses of Federal troops. On the left the Federal army was more successful, as it is stated that General Franklin, after hard fighting all day, succeeded in causing the Confederates to fall back a mile, with heavy loss in killed and wounded, and five hundred taken prisoners.

J.: DETAILED ACCOUNT OF BATTLE OF FREDERICKSBURG

This lengthy and detailed account of the fighting at Fredericksburg comes from a New York Times *correspondent. He tells of the terrible Union loss, particularly to General Otho French's division.*

New York Times, 17 December 1862

THE BATTLE OF FREDERICKSBURG

Full and Reliable Details from Our Special Correspondent. PHILLIPS HOUSE, HEADQUARTERS OF GEN. SUMNER, OPPOSITE FREDERICKSBURGH, VA., Saturday—Midnight, Dec. 12, 1862.

The battle of Fredericksburgh, which has been raging since 10 o'clock this morning, without a moment's pause, was closed by darkness to-night.

In its duration, its intensity, if not, also, in the losses it has occasioned, it caps the climax of the whole series of the battles of the campaign. The Nation will stand aghast at the terrible price which has been paid for its life when the realities of the battle-field of Fredericksburgh are spread before it.

Unhappily, like many of our engagements, though serving

to illustrate the splendid valor of our troops, it has failed to accomplish the object sought. The sequel alone can tell whether the work of to-day is to be the prelude to a glorious victory or an ignominious defeat. But the result thus far leaves with a loss of from ten to fifteen thousand men, and absolutely nothing gained. Along the whole line the rebels hold their own. Again and again we have hurled forward our masses on their position. At each time the hammer was broken on the anvil!

I have no heart, in the mood which the events of to-day have inspired, to write other than a bald record of facts. Whatever there was in the battle scene of picturesque or sublime—and viewed merely as a spectacle a great battle displays these qualities in a way that no manifestation of natural forces or of human energy ever can—must shrink and shrivel before the awful earnestness of the issue. Of course at this moment it is impossible to give more than the most general impressions;—the phenomena of a battle are too multifarious and complicated for the resources of any one observer; and the man does not live who can reproduce with life and truth the reality of even the smallest engagement.

The theatre of operations to-day extended from Fredericksburgh on the right and down the south side of the Rappahannock for two miles. The accompanying diagram, together with a brief description, may serve to make the account a little clearer. Immediately behind the town of Fredericksburgh, the land forms a plateau, or smooth field, running back for about a third of a mile. It then rises for forty or fifty yards, forming a ridge of ground, which runs along to the left for about a quarter of a mile, where it abuts at Hazel Dell, a ravine formed by the Hazel River, which empties into the Rappahannock, west of the town. At the foot of the ridge runs the telegraph road, flanked by a stone wall. This eminence was studded with rebel batteries. To the right, along up the river, the ridge prolongs itself to opposite Falmouth, and beyond; and here, too, batteries were planted on every advantageous position. Back of the first ridge is another plateau, and then a second terrace of wooded hills, where a second line of fortifications were placed. Between the rear of the town and the first ridge, a canal runs right and left, and empties into the river some distance above Falmouth.

This plain, of a third of a mile deep, between the suburbs of Fredericksburgh and the first ridge of hills, was the theatre of operations of the Right Grand Division of the army, under Major-Gen. SUMNER. On this narrow theatre our brave troops surged wind swept, forward and backward, in the tide of battle, for ten long hours.

A word now on the scene of operations of the Left Grand Division.

From the lower part of the town the ridge on which it is built slopes abruptly down to a comparatively level or undulating country, which stretches for some miles down the Rappahannock. About a couple of miles back of the river it rises into a wooded slope. At a point a mile and a half below Fredericksburgh, two pontoons had been thrown across on Thursday morning, and on Friday the whole of the Left Grand Division, under the command of Maj.-Gen. FRANKLIN, had marched over the river. Daylight of Saturday found the force drawn up in battle array on this broad plain skirting the Rappahannock.

The battle-ground, though very marshy in some places, presented a fine field for military evolutions. The turnpike leading to Fredericksburgh runs about one-half of a mile from and nearly parallel to the river. Beyond is the railroad, and still further beyond, the woody range of hills in which the enemy were strongly entrenched. About a mile and a half from Fredericksburgh, nearly on the river edge, is situated A. N. BARNORD'S stone mansion, after the English style.

The line of battle as it appeared in the morning, was as follows: The Sixth Army Corps, under Gen. SMITH, (FRANKLIN'S old force,) on the right, composed of three divisions, namely: Gen. NEWTON, on extreme right and rear; Gen. BURKE, on the centre and Gen. HOWE, on the left.

The First Army Corps, Gen. REYNOLDS', extending still further to the left, drawn up in the following order: Gen. GIBBONS' division on the right, connecting with Gen. HOWE'S; Gen. MEADE'S, centre, and Gen. DOUBLEDAY, left, fronting to the southward and resting nearly on the river. This constituted the order in which our forces were drawn up, there being three distinct lines of battle.

Opposed to our right under GEN. SUMNER, was the rebel left, under command of Gen. LONGSTREET. Opposed to our left, under Gen. FRANKLIN, was the rebel right, under Gen. JACKSON. Gen. LEE, Generalisimo of the Southern army, was in person in command of the Confederate forces during the whole day.

The plan of Gen. BURNSIDE, agreed upon in Council of War, was to endeavor to pierce the rebel centre. Early on the morning of Saturday the order was given that SUMNER'S left, composed of the ninth Army Corps, under command of Gen. WILCOX, should be extended until it reached FRANKLIN'S right—thus forming a continuous line of battle along the river for two miles, the left resting on Fredericksburgh. The left wing, comprising the whole of FRANKLIN'S command, (fifty thousand men,) should then be swung round, as on a pivot formed by SUMNER'S extreme right, resting on Fredericksburgh. If successful in this maneuver, FRANKLIN would divide the rebel lines, take possession of the railroad, (the line of retreat,) and come in on the flank of the rebel works back of Fredericksburgh. While this movement was being developed a division was to be sent up from Gen. SUMNER'S command, by the plank road, to storm the ridge. If there should be any failure in this, it was hoped the cooperation of FRANKLIN would presently make success certain. HOOKER'S corps was destined to act as a reserve.

The dawn of Saturday found the forces distributed as thus indicated. It was a fine Virginia morning—mild and balmy as a September day, though the mist and fog of a late Indian Summer hung over the field of battle. About 8 o'clock, the Phillips House (the headquarters of Gen. SUMNER, about a mile from the river on the north side, and where, by the kind hospitality of the large-hearted old soldier, I had been staying for some time during a spell of camp-fever) was the scene of a numerous assemblage of officers. Gen. BURNSIDE and Gen. HOOKER joined Gen. SUMNER here, and the balcony and grounds in front were presently filled with officers and Aides.

It was with alarm and pain I found a general want of confidence and gloomy forebodings among some men whose sound judgment I had learned to trust. The plan of attacking the rebel stronghold directly in front would, it was feared, prove a most hazardous enterprise, and one of which there is no successful example in military history. It was doubted that the cooperation of the right and left, according to the programme, would admit of practical executions, and things were generally at loose ends. "The chess-board," said NAPOLEON at Wagram, "is dreadfully confused; there is but I that see through it!"

About 11½ o'clock I crossed the Rappahannock on the upper pontoon bridge, and passed through the town of Fredericksburgh, along the main street. At this time brisk skirmishing was going on in the outskirts of the town, the rebel sharpshooters stubbornly consisting every inch of the ground as our skirmishers advanced. Caroline, or Mainstreet, was occupied by Gen. KIMBALL'S, Gen. FERRARO'S, and Acting Gen. ZOOK'S Brigade, with portions of HANCOCK'S Division; that latter, with his artillery, lined the bank of the river in the neighborhood of the middle crossing, which is just below the railroad bridge. Other troops from the corps of Gens. WILCOCK and COUCH occupied the other streets of the town nearer the line of advance. Our batteries replied across the river, covering the advance of our forces.

In the meantime FRANKLIN had been for a couple of hours briskly engaged with the enemy on the left. The force in Fredericksburgh had driven the rebels out of the suburbs of the town and rested their column on the canal. The time had now come to attempt and advance on the rebel position.

The orders were to move rapidly; charge up the hill and take the batteries at the point of the bayonet. Orders easy to give, but, ah! how hard of execution!

Look at the position to be stormed.

There is a bare plateau of third of a mile, which the storming party will have to cross. In doing so they will be exposed to the fire, first, of the enemy's sharpshooters, posted behind a stone wall running along the base of the ridge—of a double row of rifle-pits on the rise of the crest—of the heavy batteries behind strong field-works that stud the top of the hill—of a powerful infantry force now lying concealed behind these—of a plunging fire from the batteries on the lower range—of a double enfilading fire from "cannon to right of them, cannon to left of them." Sebastopol was not half as strong.

The line of battle was formed by COUCH'S Corps, (the Second,) composed of the Divisions of FRENCH, HANCOCK and HOWARD, the left of the line abutting on STURGIS' Division of WILCOX'S Corps, (the Ninth.) The first advanced was FRENCH'S, composed of the brigades of KIMBALL, MORRIS and WEBER, supported by HANCOCK'S Division, consisting of the Brigades of CALDWELL, ZOOK and MEAGHER.

Forming his men under cover of a small knoll in the rear of the town, skirmishers were deployed to the left toward Hazel Dell; STURGIS, supporting at the same time, moved up, and rested on a point on the railroad.

The moment they exposed themselves on the railroad, forth burst the deadly hail. From the rifle-pits came the murderously-aimed missiles; from the batteries, tier above tier, on the terraces, shot planes of fire; from the enfilading cannon, distributed on the arc of a circle two miles in extent, came cross showers of shot and shell.

Imagine, if you can, for my resources are unequal to the task of telling you, the situation of that gallant but doomed division.

Across the plain for a while they swept under this fatal fire. They were literally mowed down. The bursting shells make great gaps in their ranks; but these are presently filled by the "closing up" of the line. For fifteen immortal minutes at least they remain under this fiery surge. Onward they press, though their ranks grow fearfully thin. They have passed over a greater part of the interval and have almost reached the base of the hill, when brigade after brigade of rebels rise up on the crest and pour in fresh volleys of musketry at short range. To those who, through the glass, looked on, it was a parlous sight indeed. Flesh and blood could not endure it. They fell back shattered and broken, amid shouts and yells from the enemy.

Gen. FRENCH'S Division went into the fight six thousand strong; late at night he told me he could count but fifteen hundred!

D. M. STONE: BLAME FOR DEFEAT RESTS WITH ADMINISTRATION

In this untitled excerpt, the New York Journal of Commerce *suggests that the defeat in Fredericksburg should not be blamed on General Burnside, who had recently taken over as head of the Army of the Potomac. Rather, the paper indirectly places blame on Lincoln's administration for its flawed war plan.*

New York Journal of Commerce, 18 December 1862

First and foremost, let it be known that the gallant Burnside is not responsible, his brave corps commanders are not responsible, his noble army, almost an army of martyrs, is not responsible for the awful disaster. Ordered peremptorily to cross the river, they but obeyed as soldiers obey, even to death, and went over the fatal stream to sacrifice. We have

lying before us as we write, a private letter from as gallant an officer as ever led a column into battle, written the night before the crossing of the Rappahannock, in which he says: "I expect to be sacrificed to-morrow. Good-bye—and if to morrow night finds me dead, remember me kindly as a soldier who meant to do his duty."

AN ANONYMOUS REPORT: NO REASON FOR DESPAIR AT NEWS OF RECENT BATTLE

Other papers echoed this sentiment and showed great confidence in Burnside even as news of the retreat began to surface. This untitled article is one such example.

Providence Journal, 18 December 1862 (Providence, R.I.)

But there is no reason for despairing. We have, as we believe, a much larger force in and near Virginia than the rebels. Because we have failed in one attempt to drive the rebels from their strong works, we need not conclude that success is unattainable. . . . Burnside is entirely master of the ground he occupies. The enemy dare not assail him. They are forced to the defensive by their interior strength. He will yet find a way to give them that punishment which they would quickly get if they were to meet him in a fair field. If he had defeated them, the strength of the rebellion would have been broken. But his failure to conquer them does not by any means prove his inability to do it before the campaign is closed.

THOMAS N. DAY: SEVERE UNION LOSSES AT FREDERICKSBURG

This article highlights the devastating Union losses at Fredericksburg but also suggests that Burnside was not responsible for the carnage.

Hartford Daily Courant, 19 December 1862 (Hartford, Conn.)

The past week has been one of the most eventful and saddening in the whole history of the war. Having crossed the Rappahannock in safety, the Army of the Potomac advanced, Saturday last, upon the intrenchments behind Fredericksburg. They were mowed down with terrible slaughter. Several brigades were almost annihilated.

The enemy enjoying every advantage of position, added strong artificial to the natural defences of their lines. The revel cannon were planted behind strong earth-works. On the low ground in front, behind the shelter of a stone wall, their infantry awaited the approach of our columns. At this point General French's division was ordered to advance with fixed bayonets, and carry the intrenchments by assault. When they came within easy range of the rebel infantry, there were surprised by the most destructive volleys of musketry. The rebel sharp-shooters, taking deliberate aim, poured a constant stream of lead into our devoted lines. At the same time sixty pieces of artillery hurled upon them a storm of grape and canister, raking them in front and upon both flanks. Out of 7,000 men which Gen. French led into the engagement, scarcely one-sixth of the number had reported to him two days afterward. Many of the residue perhaps are held as prisoners. But there is too much reason to fear that the larger number of the absent will never return.

The rebel infantry were so disposed on the low ground before their batteries, that they were perfectly protected from their own artillery in the rear, while the federal cannon could not be brought to bear upon them without at the same time slaughtering our own infantry who were moving to the assault. Completely sheltered, they accomplished their horrible work with impunity.

Gen. Hancock afterward fought on the same ground and with hardly less loss. Gen. Howard came to his support but was repulsed. Thus in the corps of Gen. Couch, containing the divisions of French, Hancock and Howard, and numbering all about twenty thousand men, the loss will fall little short of ten thousand.

On the night of the 15th, the army re-crossed the river without the loss of a man or a gun. The attempt was extremely perilous, but was accomplished with singular good fortune. A heavy storm of wind and rain prevailing at the time, greatly facilitated the movement by shielding the troops from the observation of the enemy. Every precaution was taken to conceal the step, and the rebels only discovered it when too late to take advantage of it. Gen. Burnside deserves great credit for the skill with which he conducted the retreat. The army is now encamped on the north bank of the Rappahannock.

WILLIAM HARDING: CHANGES IN THE LINCOLN CABINET AND ADMINISTRATION

After the devastating loss at Fredericksburg, President Lincoln made some administrative changes in his cabinet. Soon after the Battle of Fredericksburg, Secretary of State William Seward resigned, and many newspapers speculated that resignation came because of the loss at Fredericksburg. Many also predicted more changes in both the military and the administration were to come. This untitled article discusses these issues and suggests that the changes are needed.

Philadelphia Inquirer, 20 December 1862

Since the disaster at Fredericksburgh the feeling has grown strong, almost universal, that there must be a change in the Cabinet and policy before the war can be prosecuted further. It finally took shape by a number of Republican Senators waiting upon the President last night and urging the reconstruction of his Cabinet. On being informed of the intention of the Senators, Secretary Seward and his son, the Assistant Secretary, tendered their resignations. They have not yet been accepted, but it is highly probable they will be, and that Secretary Blair [*Postmaster General*] will follow suit, and Gen. Halleck will be removed. Secretary [*of War*] Stanton still retains the confidence of the President.

CHARLES C. FULTON: CHANGES IN LINCOLN CABINET

This editorial echoes the sentiments articulated by the editor of the Inquirer *and discusses changes Lincoln should make in his cabinet.*

Baltimore American, 19 December 1862

Political circles in Washington are to-day in a complete whirl of excitement over the resignation of Secretary Seward and the expected complete explosion of President Lincoln's Cabinet. No two people agree in relation to the facts in the case, and nobody appears to be able to say what is the exact upshot of the complications, into the midst of which the Administration has been thrown by the great blunder and disaster before Fredericksburg.

The facts, as near as they can now be got at, are these—a caucus of the Republican Senators was held on Wednesday evening. The holding of the caucus was generally known, but amid the excitement existing in relation to military events, it attracted less attention than is usually given to such movements, and the secret of its proceedings was kept with an unusual degree of secrecy. Not a whisper was heard until this morning, when it was suddenly announced that Secretary Seward had peremptorily and definitely resigned the portfolio of the State Department, asking to be relieved at the earliest moment. It then appeared that at the caucus held on Monday night a resolution was proposed . . . declaring, or rather intimating that the Republican Senators lacked confidence in Secretary Seward and in delicate, yet definite terms, requesting the President to dispense with his services. The resolution was discussed and several amendments proposed, but no decisive vote taken. It appeared from the discussion that the caucus was nearly equally divided, though on a test vote it was probable the resolution would have had a majority of one or two votes in its favor.

. . . Mr. Seward, it has been known here for some time, has been anxious to be relieved, and his friends have predicted his resignation as a very probable event. As the chief adviser of the president, his position has not been a pleasant one, though his personal relations with Mr. Lincoln are of the most cordial kind. He has, however, been pursued with bitter animosity by [*some of the press*], and has been held responsible for measures which he was powerless to prevent.

SAMUEL BOWLES: EFFECTS FROM FREDERICKSBURG

This untitled commentary highlights the significance of the Fredericksburg battle and suggests that Union soldiers are being sacrificed by the federal government.

Springfield Republican, 19 December 1862 (Springfield, Mass.)

The unexpected and stunning reverse suffered by our army at Fredericksburg, has excited the most profound feeling throughout the country. The Cabinet was in session on the subject on Tuesday; the Republican Senators were in caucus several hours over it, and it was the absorbing topic in all circles. It is felt to be one of the worst defeats of the whole war in many of its aspects. It produces no alarm, but much indignation and discouragement. The universal feeling is that if our volunteers are to be thus uselessly sacrificed and our strength wasted, no superiority of men and means can ensure final success.

R. J. HALDEMAN: "FREDERICKSBURG MASSACRE" — DEMOCRATIC CRITICISM OF LINCOLN FOR UNION LOSS

This elaborate report in the Harrisburg Democratic paper focuses on the Senate investigation of the causes of the Fredericksburg loss and directly attacks President Lincoln even though the Senate report refrains "from censuring anybody."

Harrisburg Patriot & Union, 27 December 1862 (Harrisburg, Pa.)

We give up most of our space to-day to the report of the committee appointed by the U.S. Senate to investigate the causes of the recent massacre and defeat at Fredericksburg. The report will be found quite interesting, and although of great length, we have no doubt will be generally read; at least it ought to be read by every one who is desirous to keep himself posted in matters relating to the war and the manner in which it is being conducted. The committee refrain from censuring anybody, and the presumption is that the upshot of the whole business will be an official declaration, "No-body to blame." Already General Lincoln has advanced the opinion, in an address to the army, that the "attempt *was not an error*, nor the failure other than an *accident*;" although it is perfectly clear that a few more such "attempts" and "failures," even if they should occur without "error," and from "accident" alone, will inflict a blow upon the army from which it will never recover, and place the city of Washington, in spite of its fortifications, at the mercy of the rebels. Such an opinion having been expressed by the President, however, it may be fairly presumed that he will act upon it, and that no greater precaution will be taken hereafter than heretofore, in guarding against such fearful accidents, by which thousands of valuable lives are uselessly sacrificed, the bosom of the nation torn with anguish, and the army discouraged, embittered and disorganized.

But our convictions after a perusal of the testimony, are different from those of the President. We do not see things as he does, and must, therefore, dissent from the opinion he has expressed. We are strongly impressed with the idea that the bloody and unsuccessful result of the battle of Fredericksburg is attributable far more to "error" than to "accident." The error, in the first place, is in the adoption of the Fredericksburg route; in the second place, in not sending a co-operating force up the York or James rivers to make a diversion in that direction, and thus weaken the strength of Lee at Fredericksburg, after that line had been determined upon. On whom should the responsibility of these grave errors rest? Burnside magnanimously assumes the whole responsibility for the first; the administration is accountable for the second. The President, the War Secretary, or the General-in chief, one or all of them must answer to the country for this blunder. They may unite in taking the responsibility, and so lighten the burden; but united or separate they must bear it. But beyond all this, there are still other, and very grave errors, intimately connected with the Fredericksburg disaster, for which the administration is undoubtedly accountable. The error of withdrawing McClellan from the James river, where he was within twenty-five miles of Richmond, and, subsequently, after he had gained the splendid victories of South Mountain and Antietam, with Pope's defeated and disorganized army, removing him from command and supplying his place with a general who ingenuously acknowledged his incompetency, and expressed his conviction that McClellan was better qualified than any other to lead that army, "if matters could be so arranged as to remove their [*the President and Secretary of War's*] objection to him." These are errors overlooked by the investigating committee, and probably not thought of by the President, when he wrote his address, but they are remembered by the people and by the army. . . .

[*The attack on Fredericksburg*] was a rash experiment, made without judgment or military skill; and, under the same commander and the same influences, we may look for similar and perhaps even more serious "accidents" very soon after the Army of the Potomac is again set in motion.

NOTES

1. Report of Major General Ambrose E. Burnside, U.S. Army, commanding Army of the Potomac, Battle of Fredericksburg, 17 December 1862.

2. "The Battle of Saturday," *New York Times*, 15 December 1862.

3. James M. McPherson (Ed.), *The Atlas of the Civil War* (New York: Macmillan, 1994).

FURTHER READINGS

Ingram, W. Scott. *The Battle of Fredericksburg.* Woodbridge, Conn.: Blackbirch Press, 2002.

McPherson, James M. (Ed.). *The Atlas of the Civil War.* New York: Macmillan, 1994.

O'Reilly, Francis Augustin. *The Fredericksburg Campaign: Winter War on the Rappahannock.* Baton Rouge: Louisiana State University Press, 2002.

Wagner, Margaret E.; Gallagher, Gary W.; and Finkelman, Paul (Eds.). *The Library of Congress Civil War Desk Reference.* New York: Simon & Schuster, 2002.

16

BATTLE OF CHANCELLORSVILLE, 1–6 MAY 1863

When General Joseph Hooker took over command of the Union army from General Ambrose Burnside in January 1863, he quickly reformed military camp conditions, making life more sanitary and healthy for federal soldiers. He also revamped the federal intelligence system that had not been working, and he added a modern cavalry arm. In a fairly short time, Hooker managed to create a system under which he could gain accurate knowledge of the numbers of Confederate troops facing him. His cavalry changes included the collection of 12,000 "horse-soldiers" from all the detached headquarters guards, pickets, and riders that had previously been parceled out to individual generals. Although the cavalry arm was inexperienced, it was greatly improved and modernized. Previously, the federal forces had little cavalry success compared to the Confederates. Hooker's Army of the Potomac now numbered 130,000 with 400 guns.[1]

Facing Hooker's strong, well-supplied, and reenergized forces was Lee's embattled Army of Northern Virginia, which had been reduced to 60,000 men. The Confederate soldiers were not well fed, their uniforms were falling off their backs, and their equipment was falling apart. But the rebel forces still had confidence, mostly because the federal forces had not been able to beat them in Virginia. The Confederate forces focused much of their attention on digging and improving the trench system that General James Longstreet and the Confederate engineers had established for 25 miles from Port Royal, Virginia, to the upper fords of the Rapidan River. The Confederate forces also reorganized their artillery to give them better advantage even though they did not have as much firepower as the federal forces.[2]

By April, General Hooker had decided to strike at the Confederate forces while a substantial number were detached under General Longstreet to the Suffolk, Virginia, area. Hooker left a significant number of federal troops at Fredericksburg to try to contain General Robert E. Lee's men to the hills, where the Confederates had soundly defeated General Ambrose Burnside in the Battle of Fredericksburg that past December. A separate Union force was dispatched west to cross the Rappahannock and Rapidan Rivers to try to converge on Fredericksburg from that direction. Hooker planned to have his newly formed cavalry open the campaign by raiding General Lee's line of communication with Richmond, causing a Confederate retreat from the city. Hooker believed the Union troops could then defeat the rebels as they tried to escape the city from the west.

The stage for the Battle of Chancellorsville was set on 27 April when Hooker's forces crossed the Rappahannock and Rapidan Rivers. On 29 April, the federals crossed Kelly's Ford, and the army secured Getmanna and Ely's fords. The Union cavalry column that had split from the army and pushed west reunited with the army at Chancellorsville, Virginia. General Lee responded to the news of the presence of the Union troops by sending General Richard Anderson's division to investigate. After General Anderson found the federals gaining strength in numbers in the woods around Chancellorsville, he had his men begin building an earthworks at nearby Zoan Church. General Thomas "Stonewall" Jackson arrived on 1 May to help Anderson's division block the federal advance to Fredericksburg.

On 1 May, Hooker's army of 115,000 men converged on Chancellorsville. Although General Lee's forces were outnumbered two to one, he did not retreat from Fredericksburg. With half his forces meeting Hooker's advance from Chancellorsville, the remaining forces stayed in Fredericksburg to guard the city. Although Hooker had passed through Chancellorsville and was pushing toward Fredericksburg, he pulled his troops back to an area known as "The Wilderness," upon sensing the Confederate movement. Hooker took up a defensive line in The Wilderness while General Lee further divided his troops. Two divisions were to focus Hooker's attention while General Jackson would march the bulk of the Confederate army across the front of the federal line to position it against the Union's right flank. Jackson completed the dangerous march on 2 May, and to the surprise of the federals, Jackson's men attacked them two hours before dusk. Jackson's troops routed the federal forces in their camps, but by 9:00 P.M. the darkness, coupled with confusion along the Confederate line, stopped the fighting. Jackson, who was riding in front of the Confederate lines to reorganize and regroup them, was accidentally shot by his own men during the chaos. He had been seriously wounded and later had to have his left arm amputated. The injury would eventually prove fatal.

The next day, 3 May, Confederate General J.E.B. Stuart assumed Jackson's command and initiated an attack on both wings of the Union army while trying to reconnect with General Lee's forces. They finally broke the federal line at Chancellorsville, which caused General Hooker to withdraw about a mile north of the Chancellor House. As the rebel forces were mounting a final attack on the federal troops at Chancellorsville, General Lee was diverted by a message from Confederate General Jubal Early at Fredericksburg. On 4 May, General Lee managed to block the federal attack on Fredericksburg and set out to return to Chancellorsville. On 6 May, General Hooker and his forces retreated across the Rappahannock River before Lee could attack again.[3]

By repeatedly dividing his forces and outmaneuvering General Hooker, General Lee and his massively outnumbered Confederate forces drove the federal troops from the battlefield. The death toll at Chancellorsville was significant: The federal forces lost 17,000 men, while the Confederates suffered a loss of 14,000. Many historians have considered the Battle at Chancellorsville to be General Lee's greatest victory.[4]

Although the Confederates won the Battle of Chancellorsville, they not only lost a greater percentage of their men than the federals, but they also lost General Jackson. Jackson died of pneumonia on 10 May while recovering from the amputation of his left arm.

The Northern press did not give the Battle of Chancellorsville as much significant coverage as some of the other battles in Virginia, mostly because Secretary of War Edwin Stanton had made a special effort in late 1862 to tighten the censorship of the telegraph wires to try to keep sensitive information from the Confederate forces. Although reporters argued that the enemy already knew everything that they did because camps on both sides were teeming with spies, the truth was that the press could move information more quickly than the spies could; so often the press did end up inadvertently tipping the other side's hand. Stanton had dispatched field censors who had no firm or consistent guidelines to follow, and often they would alter or suppress reporters' dispatches at will. Journalists trying to cover the Battle of Chancellorsville resorted to creating codes and ciphers to evade the field censors. For example, *New York Times* correspondent L. L. Crounse developed his own code that included the phrase "will send you 12 pages tonight," which actually meant "Hooker will fight today."[5]

Despite the issues with field censors, reporters could avoid the censorship of the telegraph wires if they sent their reports via mail, messenger, or personal delivery. The obvious end result of this was a delay in the delivery of the actual news, which is seen in some of the excerpts that appear below.

AN ANONYMOUS REPORT: EARLY REPORTS OF BATTLE AT CHANCELLORSVILLE

Early reports from Chancellorsville reflected well on the federal troops and General Hooker. The lack of immediate information caused many Northern newspapers to assume that the battle was going well for the federal troops, as seen in this untitled news brief.

Washington Republican, 6 May 1863 (Washington, D.C.)

Our latest advices from the battlefields on the south side of the Rappahannock are up to last night.

Correspondents who were at Chancellorsville last night, state that Gen. Hooker has captured over eight thousand prisoners, and a large number of guns and rebel standards. Among the guns captured are ten belonging to the famous Washington Battery, of Louisiana.

Yesterday Gen. Hooker accomplished several very important movements, forcing Lee's whole army back more than two miles from the point it occupied, inflicting upon the rebels great loss in killed, wounded, and captured.

A dispatch was received this morning at headquarters from Gen. Stahl, stating that in addition to the telegraph report of yesterday in regard to the fight at Warrenton Junction, the rebels were completely routed and scattered in all directions. Their [*the rebel*] loss is very heavy in killed, and the road from Warrenton Junction to Warrenton is strewn with their dead. . . .

All has been quiet along the lines to-day. Major Steele is better to-day. Our loss is two killed and five officers and ten privates wounded. We also captured forty horses.

AN ANONYMOUS REPORT: REPORT ON FIGHTING AT CHANCELLORSVILLE

This untitled report offers few details but was typical of some reports on the war at this time because of Secretary of War Stanton's tightened censorship of the telegraph wires.

Washington Star, 6 May 1863 (Washington, D.C.)

The fighting yesterday afternoon, as heard from Falmouth, was mostly musketry. The cannonading ceased about 10 o'clock A.M., but the musketry was continued through the day.

The number of prisoners on both sides, thus far, is believed to be about equal. Our greatest loss [*in prisoners*] was in the Eleventh Army Corps—Howard's, late Sigel's.

The country where Hooker is now operating is undulated wooded and broken, fully as rough as the Bull Run country, though not cut up by any large courses.

No information from Gen. Hooker himself, or from any officer in his army, has reached Washington in the last 48 hours by telegraph, though the wires between here and Gen. H's headquarters are working well, and he is certainly busy enough in sending almost momentary messages between his different camps and corps, having wires communicating with all of them.

It is known here that there was no fighting of importance yesterday; and, further, that he held his ground previously won throughout yesterday, except in a few unimportant points.

A noticeable feature of the present fighting is, we are told, in the few stragglers seen. At the time of Sedgwick's crossing to Fredericksburgh every man went, and the *élan* of the army, as a whole, was of the same satisfactory sort.

CHARLES HALE: DIFFICULTY OF OBTAINING INFORMATION FROM GENERAL HOOKER'S ARMY

This untitled report more accurately reflects the state of affairs at the Battle of Chancellorsville. It also notes that the government control of information about the fighting caused problems receiving information about the battle.

Boston Daily Advertiser, 6 May 1863

The accounts from General Hooker's army show the position of the affairs to be extremely critical. On the right near Chancellorsville a terrific battle raged on Saturday and Sunday, the rebels under Jackson making a desperate attempt to turn our []ight. Jackson's attack was at first successful in consequence of the rout of Howard's corps and some artillery was lost; but Berry's corps checked the movement, General Berry himself falling. Another fierce attack was made by the rebels on Sunday and handsomely repulsed by our forces, with heavy loss to the enemy. Near Fredericksburg, the heights were carried by General Sedgwick in front and Gens. Gibbon and Newton advancing from the direction of Bowling Green, artillery and prisoners being captured. A correspondent of the New York Post states that the battle was renewed on Monday morning, and that the enemy fought with desperate courage, and appeared to be as strong in numbers as our own forces. It is also stated that the line of railroad over the Massaponax and Mattapony creeks south of Fredericksburg had been broken, and the retreat of the enemy thus cut off. Large numbers of rebel prisoners, including Maj.-Gen. Evans and a Brigadier-General whose name was not learned, had been brought to Washington and lodged in the Old Capitol prison. The censorship on the telegraph is rigid, and no dispatches relating to army movements are allowed to leave Washington.

L. L. CROUNSE: BATTLES ON THE RAPPAHANNOCK—HOOKER'S POSITION

The following is an example of the reporting that New York Times *correspondent L. L. Crounse produced during the Battle of Chancellorsville. His reports were accompanied by reports from a second* Times *correspondent who was also on the battlefield.*

New York Times, 5 May 1863

Two of our correspondents with GEN. HOOKER'S army, arrived in the City yesterday, bringing the latest intelligence from the field of battle. MR. SWINTON left GEN. HOOKER'S headquarters at 6 o'clock on Sunday morning and reached this City at 6 o'clock yesterday morning: MR. CROUNSE left at 9 o'clock on Sunday evening and arrived a 10 o'clock last night. We have from them, therefore, very full and complete reports of everything that has happened on the Rappahannock down to a late hour on Sunday night.

GEN. HOOKER had thrown his army across the Rappahannock, taken a position on the left of the rebel intrenchments at Fredericksburgh thus compelling the enemy to leave. HOOKER himself had chosen, and had fought two of the severest and bloodiest battles of the war, without attaining any absolutely decisive result, but achieving such successes as render the enemy's defeat or withdrawal nearly certain.

Recovering himself with masterly promptitude from what was well nigh a crushing disaster on Saturday night, when JACKSON succeeded in turning our right wing and routing the Eleventh corps, the battle was renewed on Sunday, and though not absolutely decisive, yet has put him decidedly on the winning side.

This battle is to the rebels by far the bloodiest they have yet had, while our sacrifice is much less. We have taken *four thousand* prisoners with a loss on our side of not a tenth of that number.

The result of Sunday's operations on the left is still more brilliant. The powerfully defended heights in the rear of Fredericksburgh, the attempt to take which cost us so dearly last December, have, by the movement on Chancellorsville, been turned, and after being gallantly assailed by SEDGWICK'S corps, are now ours.

The rebel army is now, therefore, between two columns, separated but by an interval of five miles—the one a hundred thousand strong, the other twenty thousand. It will be strange if, between the upper and the nether millstone, the accursed thing is not ground to atoms.

AN ANONYMOUS REPORT: ACCOUNT OF BATTLE AT WILDERNESS CHURCH

This short and belated news item in the New York Times, *which actually comes from information contained in a Richmond, Virginia, newspaper, begins to hint at the high number of casualties on both sides. Many papers had to reprint Southern accounts of the battle because of the federal government's reluctance to let war information quickly leave Washington.*

New York Times, 13 May 1863

We have received a copy of the Richmond *Dispatch* extra of the 6th, which says the fight on Sunday at Wilderness Church was one of the bloodiest of the war. It claims that the Confederates had taken at that date 5,000 prisoners, including Brig.-Gen. HAYS of COUCH'S corps, and his Aid-de-Camp, Capt. ECHOLS. It also claims that they captured five batteries of field artillery.

Among the rebel officers killed besides Gen. PAXTON, were Col. WALKER of the Tenth Virginia. The *Dispatch* says: "The country will lament the misfortune with has befallen our army in the severe wounding of Lieut.-Gen. JACKSON, who lost his left arm."

As showing the severity of the contest, the *Dispatch* says that the Forty-fourth Virginia regiment went into the late fight at Chancellorsville 175 strong, and lost all but 61.

CHARLES HALE: UNION CAN NOT SUSTAIN CONTINUED DEFEAT IN EASTERN THEATER

This untitled article offers the familiar tone of defeat, but it is heavier this time around. The writer recognizes that the Union cannot continue to lose battles in the East and urges decisive action by the federal government to fix perceptions of the Union army at home and abroad.

Boston Daily Advertiser, 8 May 1863

It is saying very little to say that the result of General Hooker's passage of the Rappahannock, which it is our painful duty to record this morning, is a bitter disappointment.

The means provided for the work were more ample than the country has ever before applied to any military undertaking; the movement appeared to have been well matured and its preliminary steps well executed, and there was reason to hope everything, both from the troops and from their general. But it pleased providence to send us reverse instead of victory, and to defer yet again the day when a Union army shall enter the capital of the rebel confederacy. The nation had hoped for a different reward for its labors, and had thought its efforts deserving of better success. It now remains, however, once more to essay such efforts as shall deserve and secure the victory.

It does not appear to us possible as yet to fairly review this brief campaign and ascertain the cause of its failure. Our intelligence of its course is still disjointed and of uncertain authenticity. We are as unable to subscribe to the views of those who hastily assume the incompetency of the general, as to the opinion which as hastily finds the enemy's force to have been in overwhelming superiority. The case is one where the materials for correct judgment are still wanting to a great extent, and we do not envy those who have the faculty of passing upon it at this stage, and of turning their invective against the man on whom all hopes centered a few hours ago. We hold, and not now for the first time, that some faith is due to an officer in the moment of reverse, as well as when he is sweeping on in the full tied of success and hope, and we reject, in this case as much as in another, the judgment which is passed in advance of the evidence, or upon a narrow view of the evidence.

With the question of generalship then, and what may be connected with it, we have nothing to do at present it is for the government to satisfy itself and the country upon that point. But we may assume to speak with more confidence of what the public mind now requires of the government in other respects. The situation is not one for trifling, whether we look at home or abroad. The country needs upon the heels of this misfortune some signal proof by its government, of resolution, of confidence in itself, and of real power in dealing with a serious condition of affairs. Semi-official announcements like that made a day or two ago by a Washington paper, upon "high authority," that "even if the enemy" have been successful it will amount to nothing "at all," are never rated as anything better than worthless, by the good sense of the people, and least of all will they answer now. The country requires some positive and vigorous action such as distinctly recognizes all the possibilities of our position and prepares to meet them,—some positive and tangible pledge of determination, of courage and of hope, of resolution never to abandon the purpose for which we strive to accomplish, and to use promptly and with energy the immense resources of the loyal States.

We need not seek far for such a pledge as this of which we speak, which shall inspire the hope of the nation and establish its position against every effect of this temporary reverse, at home or abroad. Let the government today order a levy by conscription of five hundred thousand men, let it fill every regiment in the service to the maximum with the men thus raised, thus powerfully reinforcing all its armies, let it establish heavy reserves, which we have never yet had in proportion to the magnitude of our operations and let it then proceed to organize a regular system for supplying the drain which a campaign makes upon our armies, and it will have counteracted, by these measures the effects of this unfortunate reverse upon public feeling at home and abroad. The number of men which we have named is immense, but whoever surveys the field and considers the number of those who are to leave the army in a few months, and whose places must be filled in advance, will not find it excessive. Let the preparation be made now. Let the country be told by an act, showing confidence and resolution, that it may have suffered a check but not a defeat of its main purpose. Let the rebels have warning in the midst of their triumph that it is to be short lived, and that the nation will never cease to uphold this righteous cause with all its strength. Let Europe also learn, at the moment when it hears of our reverse, that the government is not cast down, does not falter, or hesitate to lay its hand on the resources which the country offers, or slacken its efforts, and that peace is farther off in the hour of our national adversity than in the hour of our triumph.

With vigorous and prompt action such as we have suggested, the effects of our present misfortunes may be speedily removed, and we shall indeed hold a stronger position than ever. The blood that has been spent ineffectually in our past efforts cannot be recovered, but if we at last succeed, the nation will count the cost as light in comparison with the gain. Massachusetts has left many of her sons on the fields which lie between Washington and Richmond; but she will hereafter reckon the glorious sacrifice as the noblest page in all her history, if it is accepted as a pledge binding the government to use her patriotic offerings until they win for us the final victory for the Union.

AN INTELLIGENT GENTLEMAN: SIGNIFICANCE OF BATTLE OF CHANCELLORSVILLE

This article provides an account of the impact of the battle from a captured Union man. Receiving information from people involved in the conflicts who were not reporters was one way the press tried to get around the censorship issue.

Washington Republican, 22 May 1863 (Washington, D.C.)

We have reliable information from a highly intelligent gentleman, who was captured at Chancellorsville, and who is directly from the south side of the Rappahannock, in rebeldom, to the following effect:

The enemy claims that he has, altogether, eight thousand three hundred of our men captured, which includes the wounded left upon the field. This number embraces one thousand and six *wounded* men belonging to the Eleventh army corps, *all of whom were doing well day before yesterday.* At least one hundred and fifty men of that corps were killed on the field, or have since died of their wounds.

According to the rolls two thousand and six hundred men are missing from the Eleventh army corps since the battle. After deducting the number named above, as killed and wounded, from the total missing, it will appear that one thousand four hundred and forty-four were captured by the surprise resulting from the rear movement of Jackson.

The rebel officials acknowledge that they lost altogether in killed, wounded and missing, about 10,000 men. They do not hesitate to say that the battles at Chancellorsville and in Fredericksburgh, under Hooker and Sedgwick, were the severest and most expensive that the Confederacy has yet experienced in the war.

Gen. Lee expressed himself to his officers, very freely, that Hooker was a much abler man than he [*Lee*] supposed. He said he did not think Hooker could handle so many men so well as he did. Lee don't hesitate to tell his officers that Hooker is a man to be feared and watched closely.

Gen. Lee also expressed his wonder that Hooker was shrewd enough to return, with his army, to the north side of the Rappahannock.

Our informant says that the leading rebels acknowledged to him that Lee was expecting reinforcements to enable him to get between Hooker and the river, with the intention of cutting off his supplies, by destroying all the ferries and pontoon bridges, with the hope of starving him out.

Jackson's death was a most terrible blow to the rebels.

Our soldiers, who are prisoners of the enemy, are suffering greatly for the want of food, although they do not hesitate to say that they shared equally with the rebel soldiers, so far as they could judge.

Our informant says he was frequently asked when he thought the war would end. He replied that some of our people thought it might end in twenty years, some thought ten, but for himself he was of the opinion that five years might see its termination. This kind of logic was anything but pleasant.

A UNION SOLDIER: SOLDIER'S ACCOUNT OF BATTLE OF CHANCELLORSVILLE

This account of the battle comes from a Union soldier in Hooker's Army of the Potomac and gives an account of the fighting on 2–3 May.

New York Times, 17 May 1863

THE BATTLE OF CHANCELLORSVILLE

Interesting Letter from a Soldier

Headquarters Hancock's Division.
Camp Near Falmouth, May 11, 1863.

Our men felt in the best of spirits and full of confidence in their leader and cause. About 2 o'clock on Saturday afternoon the enemy came out and made his attack on our right. His bold and dashing movements plainly bespoke his determination to break through our lines. Their fire was murderous, but they got from us no doubt more than they bargained for. Our lines of infantry sent tremendous volleys into them, while our batteries were constantly throwing grape, cannister and shell. Still, nothing daunted, on they came, line after line, column after column. Our centre and left never wavered, but our right was held by the Eleventh corps, (GEN. SIGEL'S old command,) commanded by GEN. HOWARD. At this point the enemy made a most determined attack, and unfortunately broke through the line. Things now looked very "dubious," for the whole corps fell back and ran, nearly causing the destruction of the whole army. It was a most critical time.

Regiments and brigades could be seen running in the utmost confusion. To rally them was impossible, but through the exertions of GEN. HOWARD and some other brave officers, a general stampede was prevented. Their position was immediately taken by the Second corps, commanded by MAJ.-GEN. COUCH, and the ground they lost was partly gained again, but the enemy had succeeded in getting into and holding the rifle pits which the Eleventh Corp had so ingloriously deserted. The fight, however, still raged fiercely. Running headlong through the woods could be seen whole regiments and skedaddlers by the thousand. Teams, pack mules, droves of bullocks, ambulances, &c., all rushed madly on. A number of cavalry were, however, ordered back, who thoroughly scoured the weeds and drove every skedaddler to his regiment. Toward evening matters became more quiet, although the fighting did not cease before midnight. Up to this late hour the enemy would at times "charge" on our rifle-pits and our batteries, and do their utmost to drive us from them. Their fighting was of the most desperate character. At daybreak on Sunday morning every one was up and preparing for another great fight. Generals and commanding officers were all on the move, mounting their horses, giving orders preparatory to the battle. But very little time however, elapsed, before anything was in readiness. About 5 o'clock, the artillery and musketry reopened. The enemy formed *en masse*, and strove to break through our right. The firing of artillery and musketry at this point was almost deafening. We had five lines of infantry and three of artillery, each line well intrenched. Column after column poured in their deadly missiles, while our men obstinately held their position, sending into the midst of their assailants showers of shot, shell and canister. For some two hours our men held out against overwhelming numbers and a most terrific fire, and although we had to fall back, our lines still stood firm. As the enemy was not able to accomplish his aim, he moved to our left centre, and then made another attempt to turn our left flank. At this point their attack was the most determined, but not enough to gain their end, for our men fought like heroes and repulsed them. Our batteries suffered not a little. Some were taken and retaken. Others were so disabled by the enemy's fire that our infantry had to lay down their arms, and rush in and draw the pieces out by hand under a most galling fire. Other batteries had their caissons blown up, horses killed and many of the officers and most of the men disabled or killed. A large red brick house stood in the front and on the cross roads where our line of battle was formed, which was used as the headquarters of GEN. HOOKER, but afterward as a hospital. This they shelled and unfortunately set it on fire causing a fearful scene. However, we succeeded in removing our own men. The wounded rebels made piteous cries for help, but we were obliged to take care of our own men first. After five hours' desperate fighting there was a lull in the contest.

AN ANONYMOUS REPORT: REPORT OF DEATH OF STONEWALL JACKSON

The Northern press understood the significance of the death of General Jackson to the Southern military. This excerpt represents the way that most Northern papers reported his death—briefly but prominently.

Boston Daily Advertiser, 13 May 1863

HEADQUARTERS ARMY OF THE POTOMAC, May 12.—The Richmond papers of yesterday announced the death of Stonewall Jackson on Sunday afternoon from the effects of his recent amputation and pneumonia. His burial was fixed for today. The military band in Fredericksburg have been performing dirges a greater portion of the afternoon. He was accidentally shot by his own men.

HENRY RAYMOND: ACCOUNT OF DEATH OF STONEWALL JACKSON

This editorial provides greater detail about Jackson and his importance to the Confederacy.

New York Times, 14 May 1863

In the death of STONEWALL JACKSON the rebels have unquestionably lost by far their greatest military leader, in the peculiar style of strategy which has made his name famous. Immediately after the secession of Virginia he appeared on the scene, and ever since then he has been one of the foremost figures. He was the leader in the first hostile act of the Secessionists of Virginia—the march upon Harper's Ferry. In the first great action of the war, the battle of Manassas Plains, he took part, and one of his characteristic personal and military qualities, expressed in his title of "Stonewall," here first appeared. In every great battle fought since that time by the main rebel army, and in many minor affairs, he has been a leading actor—in the Peninsular battles, where he was the first to attack our right; in the second battle of Manassas; at the battle of Antietam; at the battle of Fredericksburgh, and lastly at the battle of Chancellorsville, on the 3d, in which engagement he received his death-wound—inflicted accidentally, it is said, by one of his own men. His campaign up and down the Shenandoah Valley, in the Spring of last year, and his series of engagements with GENS. BANKS and FREMONT, were only inferior in importance to the six or seven first-class battles in which he played his part. In each of the battles in which he acted subordinately, he was generally assigned to the peculiar and critical duties of opening the assault, making a dashing movement upon the flank or rear, or seizing and holding a point which might be called the key of the situation.

In a short letter, written by him about a year ago, in reply to the accusation of having written a piece of sentimental poetry, he denied the poetical imputation, and said that the only ambition of his life was to serve the South, and "give a practical illustration of war." These rules seem to have been celerity of movement, concentration of force, and rapid, persistent and heavy blows on his adversary's most vulnerable point;—while the body with which he operated he kept in an extraordinary state of mobility. The numerical strength of that force seems to have varied from the twelve or fifteen thousand he commanded in the Shenandoah Valley to the forty thousand he was usually credited with in the great actions.

The traits of STONEWALL JACKSON'S personal character are nearly as familiar to the public as his military feats. He was a man of narrow mind, but of tremendous will and indomitable purpose; and he flung the great energy of his nature into all that he undertook. He was strictly moral and fanatically religious; and the fact that he was a ruling elder in the Presbyterian Church shows that he stood well with his brethren. He was an acute political speculator and an ardent devotee of the Southern State Rights school. Like GEN. LEE himself, he was, however, a theoretical Unionist up to the very date of Virginia's secession; and, like LEE, he is said to have struggled long in deciding between his duty to his country and his devotion to Virginia; and it was only when his own State drew the sword, that he at last determined to follow her fortunes. He was but 37 years of age at the time of his death—was a graduate of West Point, an actor in the Mexican war, and at the time of the breaking out of secession, was a Professor in the Military Institute in Lexington, Va. His death is a tremendous and irreparable loss to the secession cause, as no other rebel like character has been developed during the war. He will figure in history as one of the ablest of modern military leaders; and it will only be the brand of *traitor* on his brow that will consign him to infamy, as it has brought him to an untimely grave.

NOTES

1. Curt Johnson and Mark McLaughlin, *Civil War Battles* (New York: Crown Publishers, 1977), 73.
2. Ibid., 73–74.
3. James M. McPherson (Ed.), *The Atlas of the Civil War* (New York: Macmillan, 1994).
4. Ibid.
5. Brayton Harris, *Blue & Gray in Black & White* (Washington, D.C.: Brasseys, 1999), 151.

FURTHER READINGS

Harris, Brayton. *Blue & Gray in Black & White*. Washington, D.C.: Brasseys, 1999.

Johnson, Curt, and McLaughlin, Mark. *Civil War Battles*. New York: Crown Publishers, 1977.

Robertson, James I., Jr. *Stonewall Jackson, the Man, the Soldier, the Legend*. New York: Macmillan, 1997.

Sears, Stephen W. *Chancellorsville*. New York: Houghton Mifflin, 1998.

17

BATTLE OF GETTYSBURG, 1–3 JULY 1863

After the Battle of Chancellorsville, morale in the Union Army of the Potomac was at perhaps its lowest point. The large federal army had yet to beat the Confederate Army of Northern Virginia in any significant battle, and it seemed as if after each major loss, the troops were handed a new general who led them into greater defeat.

Conversely, the Confederate army's morale was high. The rebel troops were beginning to think they were unbeatable, and they grew stronger as General Robert E. Lee added General James Longstreet's Carolina troops to their ranks to increase their numbers. Not long after Chancellorsville, the rebel forces in northern Virginia numbered between 70,000 and 75,000, mostly veterans of the war. One of the biggest obstacles General Lee faced in recovering from Chancellorsville was finding a replacement for General Thomas "Stonewall" Jackson, whom many called Lee's alter ego. Lee knew that without a trusted general like Jackson in the field who shared his style of warfare, he would have to be everywhere at once if he wanted to be sure that his battle plans were carried out correctly. Although Longstreet was a trusted and consistent veteran general, his style was decidedly different than Lee's. He was much more focused on defense than offense.[1]

After the victory at Chancellorsville, General Lee and Confederate President Jefferson Davis created a plan for Northern invasion. Lee had hoped that such an attack would fuel the Northern peace movement, which gained steam after Lincoln's Emancipation Proclamation, or would, at the very least, disrupt the Union war effort. Davis had been particularly concerned about the war in the West where Union General Ulysses S. Grant had been for months working toward capturing Vicksburg, Mississippi, the last Confederate stronghold on the Mississippi River. Davis hoped a Northern invasion would result in Grant being pulled out of the West and sent to help defend the North. That did not happen—the battle for Vicksburg occurred at the same time as the Battle of Gettysburg and is detailed in the next chapter.

To aid Lee with the rebel's Northern invasion were Generals Longstreet, A. P. Hill, and Dick Ewell; General J.E.B. Stuart would command the Confederate cavalry. The focus of the Confederate offensive was Pennsylvania. What would eventually become known as the Gettysburg Campaign officially began on 9 June at Brandy Station in Virginia, near Culpeper, where Lee had amassed his infantry in preparation for the advance into Pennsylvania. The rebel cavalry was camped at Brandy Station, and at dawn on 9 June, they were attacked by the Union cavalry corps under General Alfred Pleasonton. The fighting lasted all day and was the largest cavalry battle of the war. In the end, neither side gained any ground. The federal cavalry gained strength and confidence after the fight, but it never discovered the rebel forces in nearby Culpeper.

After the fighting at Brandy Station, General Lee ordered the Confederate troops to clear the lower Shenandoah Valley of Union opposition, which led to a battle at Winchester, Virginia, in which the rebels opened the door for Lee's second invasion of the North.[2] On 13 June, the same day the fighting began in Winchester, General Joseph Hooker ordered his federal troops north. After the Confederate victory at Winchester, the rebel forces moved unchecked into the Cumberland Valley of Pennsylvania. General Lee agreed to a plan by General Stuart to take the Confederate cavalry across the Blue Ridge Mountains to cut across the rear of the federal forces. A series of battles followed in mid-June in Loudon County, Virginia, which borders the Blue Ridge Mountains. Stuart had mixed success in those battles, but ultimately his arrival in Gettysburg was delayed because of the fighting and detours he had to face because of an increasingly confident and aggressive Union cavalry that was patrolling the region.

On 27 June, when the Union army was at Frederick, Maryland, and heading north to meet the rebel forces in Pennsylvania, a courier from Washington arrived to tell General Hooker that he had been relieved of his command and that General George Meade would lead the federal forces that comprised the Army of the Potomac into battle. On 28 June, Confederate Generals Longstreet and Hill and their corps arrived at Chambersburg in Pennsylvania, while General Ewell's corps had crossed the Blue Ridge Mountains and had arrived in York and Carlisle, Pennsylvania, and were preparing to attack Harrisburg.[3]

Citizens in Harrisburg were aware of the approaching rebel troops as early as a week before they arrived in Carlisle. According to the *Harrisburg Patriot & Union*,

> The situation is becoming unpleasant, but as the danger becomes more apparent, and the rebel forces approach nearer and nearer, we are pleased to say that, generally, our citizens appear to be more calm than they were when all was rumor and uncertainty. At this hour, 3 p.m. Saturday afternoon, we have no information that is at all reliable as to the numerical strength of the invaders. Some place it as high as 10,000 and others believe it exceeds 20,000. Our own opinion is that it is not half 10,000—indeed we question whether there is at any one point a rebel force of 2,000 men. —But be that as it may, we have evidence that they are within 25 miles of Harrisburg, and that some skirmishing, resulting in casualties to our troops, has occurred.[4]

The same day that Confederate forces arrived in Carlisle and York, General Lee learned of Hooker's dismissal and the presence of the Union troops at Frederick. Lee decided to move his entire army east of the mountains for battle. At the same time, Meade continued to march the Union forces north, and by 30 June, both sides were converging on the small town of Gettysburg in Adams County, Pennsylvania. The four-day battle would become the bloodiest of the war, and it would serve as a turning point for the Union.

The Battle of Gettysburg began at 5:30 in the morning on 1 July 1863 when shots were exchanged over Marsh Creek. The Confederate forces converged on the town from the west and the north and drove the Union troops back through the streets to Cemetery Hill, where fighting raged most of the day. At the end of the day, the Union had held the high ground. And because General Stuart's cavalry had not arrived to aid Lee, he did not have good information about Union troop locations. Still, Lee wanted to take the offensive the next morning and focused the Confederate attacks on two hills known as Big and Little Round Tops as well as on Cemetery and Culp's Hills. After reinforcements had arrived overnight for both sides, the morning of 2 July saw 65,000 Confederate troops facing 85,000 Union troops.[5]

General Longstreet's rebel corps spent the day attacking the Union left flank at the round tops with much of the fighting occurring in a peach orchard nearby; General Hill's division attacked the Union right at Culp's Hill and Cemetery Hill. By the end of the day, the Union left and right held. In perhaps the most dramatic battle of the afternoon, Union General Joshua L. Chamberlain and his troops from Maine were surrounded by the rebel forces at their position on Little Round Top. Nearly out of ammunition, Chamberlain ordered his men to fix bayonettes, and while the right side of his line held straight, he ordered his left to head down the hillside. The attack took the rebel forces by surprise, and the front ranks dropped their weapons and ran. Some previously unaccounted for men from Chamberlain's Maine Company B suddenly rose and fired at the fleeing Confederate forces. Chamberlain captured 400 rebel soldiers that day and held Little Round Top.

On the third day of fighting, 3 July, the federal forces would gain decisive advantage in the battle that would lead to their victory at Gettysburg. The day began badly for the Confederate troops—General Ewell's men were driven back from Culp's Hill; General Stuart, whose cavalry had finally arrived, was held off by the Union cavalry at its rear; and Confederate success was dependent upon General Longstreet's attack on the Union center at Cemetery Ridge.

General Meade saw the attack coming and was prepared for the fight. After two hours of an explosive exchange that began with a Confederate artillery barrage to try to soften the Union defenses, the Union guns went silent. General Lee chose General George Pickett to lead the Confederate infantry assault that would follow, and the result was devastating. In what has become famously known as Pickett's Charge, three divisions of Confederate men marched forward to assault the Union center. Although they momentarily pierced the federal line, the Union artillery reopened its fire from Little Round Top and Cemetery Hill and shot down most of the thousands of advancing rebel troops.[6]

On 4 July, General Lee began to withdraw his army toward Williamsport on the Potomac River. The battle was effectively over. The federal troops lost about 23,000 men; the Confederate losses were estimated at 28,000. The victory for the Union at Gettysburg cannot be understated. It was the first time the Union forces defeated Lee's Army of Northern Virginia in a significant battle; it changed Northern public sentiment about the ability of the North to win the war; it jump-started a series of Union victories that would lead to more support of the Republican administration and the eventual reelection of President Lincoln more than a year later; and it exacted a devastating moral and human loss to the Confederate military, which was struggling to increase its strength with shrinking numbers of available Confederate men. The Battle of Gettysburg would also mark the northernmost battlefield in the entire four-year conflict and would become the site of President Lincoln's famous Gettysburg Address (in November 1863) at a ceremony to honor the fallen federal soldiers of the battle.

The Northern press devoted pages to the coverage and subsequent discussion of the battle. Coverage began in June when many Northern towns in Pennsylvania and Maryland reacted with panic to the news that rebel forces were advancing on their soil.

Reporting of the actual battle was complicated by the fact that General Stuart's cavalry had cut the telegraph line in numerous places as he advanced toward Gettysburg. Some reports of the conflict originated in Baltimore where reporters rode to file their stories of the first day's battle.[7]

Perhaps one of the most compelling personal stories that came from a reporter at the battle was written by *New York Times* correspondent Sam Wilkeson. He wrote his report of the fighting next to the shallow grave of his nineteen-year-old son who was killed at Gettysburg. "Who can write the history of a battle whose eyes are immovably fastened upon a central figure of transcendingly absorbing interest—the dead body of an oldest born, crushed by a shell in a position where a battery should never have been sent, and abandoned to death in a building where surgeons dared not to stay?"[8]

The articles below include a variety of accounts of the battle that range from the first notification of the rebel troops on Northern soil to the impact of the battle on the small town of Gettysburg from its local newspaper the *Adams County Sentinel & General Advertiser*, a weekly paper that did not publish on 1 July as scheduled because of the first day's fighting.

AN ANONYMOUS REPORT: LEE'S WHOLE ARMY REPORTED MOVING ON PENNSYLVANIA

The following article provides an example of how the Northern press reported on the rebel presence in Pennsylvania and Maryland.

Washington Republican, 25 June 1863 (Washington, D.C.)

A gentleman arrived here this morning who left Hagerstown at six o'clock yesterday (Wednesday) morning. He saw Ewell's forces, comprising the left wing of Lee's army, pass through that place. The head of the column entered Hagerstown on Tuesday morning and moved directly through to Pennsylvania. The rear of the column, understood to belong to Ewell, did not pass through the place until that night. This force was estimated to be from 20,000 to 25,000 strong.

The troops did very little damage, besides seizing all the horses they could find.

Our informant says when he left Hagerstown yesterday morning it was understood that Longstreet, in command of the right wing of Lee's army, was then crossing the Potomac below Williamsport.

The main body of Gen A. P. Hill's forces, comprising the centre of Lee's army, was understood yesterday to be somewhere between Winchester and Martinsburg, moving towards the river.

To-day, we have no doubt, from all the information we have gathered, that the whole of Ewell's column is in Pennsylvania, not from Chambersburg.

The gentlemen who saw Ewell's troops says they had with them a very large number of wagons. From this fact they intend to gather all the supplies they can find.

R. J. HALDEMAN: THE THREATENED CONFEDERATE INVASION OF PENNSYLVANIA

The readers of the Harrisburg Patriot & Union *were particularly interested in the Confederate troop movements, since many correctly believed that Harrisburg was Lee's target.*

Harrisburg Patriot & Union, 27 June 1863 (Harrisburg, Pa.)

Whether it grows out of the almost universal scare which seems to have overtaken our people, or from the wand of a proper organization by the heads of departments, we are left without any reliable information in reference to the invading forces apparently so near to us. The rumor of one hour, always said to have come from a reliable source, is almost sure to be contradicted by the next. The messages to the Governor received by telegraph seem no more reliable than the rumors upon the street. The Government at Washington has established a censorship over messages sent over the wires to the Associated Press, and yet they are alike contradictory with news received from other quarters. We are therefore left in a sea of doubt, without either rudder or compass. This vagueness and uncertainty serves largely to increase the alarm all along our borders : every marauding band of rebels, no matter how small in number, is looked upon as the advance guard or scouting party of an immense army immediately in their rear, and our alarmed militia and citizens fly in terror, not from the realities they see but from the phantom army their imaginations picture in the "dark beyond." In some quarters this fear has become a regular panic, and will no doubt produce a much greater loss to the border counties and the State than the damage we shall sustain at the hands of the rebels. If, instead of establishing a censorship over the press, the Governments, National and State, would organize a reliable line of scouts, and furnish the press with an accurate statement of the condition of affairs to lay before the people, all this trouble and anxiety would be avoided, and, knowing the direction from which they were menaced and the extent of the danger, they would prepare manfully to meet it. Mankind are so constituted that they can readily nerve themselves to meet real and present dangers, while

they may be entirely unnerved by a vaguely portentous future.

FRIDAY, June 26.—2 P.M.—Yesterday evening at 8 o'clock we were assured by telegraph from Carlisle that there were no rebels in that vicinity, nor had there been more than six or eight hundred seen at a time at any one place, this side of the borough of Chambersburg, and yet at 10 o'clock the same evening we had a message from Washington that three grand divisions of Lee's army were in Maryland and Pennsylvania, marching rapidly towards Harrisburg and probably Philadelphia. This morning the operator at Carlisle informed us that Gen. Knipe had fallen back with his forces five miles this side of Carlisle, and rebels in large force were about taking possession of town. This afternoon he has mustered courage enough to return to Carlisle, and now informs us that there are no enemies in Carlisle nor have they been nearer than seven miles, and then only in small force.

In this state of things we are left only to conjecture, and theories are as wild and various as the rumors. *Seventeen* regiments have been sent to our aid from New York, four or five from New Jersey, and some twenty or thirty thousand of our State militia have been enrolled. These forces have been divided and sent to various parts of the State to protect our railroad and valleys penetrating into the interior, while but a comparatively small force has been sent down the Cumberland valley, from which direction the enemy are said to be advancing. From these facts we may naturally conclude that the hypothesis upon which our State authorities and the Commander of this department is acting, is that the rebels intend to divide into small bands, and endeavor to cut our railroads, burn our bridges, destroy public property, &c., and not to advance upon Harrisburg.

AN ANONYMOUS REPORT: ACCOUNT OF BATTLE AT GETTYSBURG

The following detailed account of the battle is from the local Gettysburg newspaper.

Adams County Sentinel & General Advertiser, 7 July 1863 (Gettysburg, Pa.)

In our last, which was issued two weeks ago, we spoke of the possibility of the invaders visiting our own neighborhood, and a great battle being fought before they would be allowed to return to Virginia—Little, it must be confessed, did we realize what we then included in that possibility. The fortnight

past has developed from it a *terrible*, and yet *glorious* reality.

Terrible in the desolation of our homes, our fair farms and friendly firesides, the slaughter of thousands, and the mangling of tens of thousands of our fellow men, our friends, and many of them our kindred, our fathers, our brothers, our husbands, our lovers, our sons. *Terrible* in the din, the dread, the dire destruction of war in its most appalling form.

Glorious in the fruits gathered, the vindication of truth, the triumph of right, the victory achieved for Liberty, Justice, the Union and good Government.

On Friday, the 26th, a hostile force consisting of Cavalry, came to our town, going up to York and Carlisle. They remained all night, taking what they wanted, robbing the stores and dwellings of food and valuables, and leaving what was of no use to themselves. The surrender of the place, with $5,000 in gold and silver, and other supplies of which they were in need were haughtily demanded and manfully refused. Saturday these passed on East, and left us a little time in which to digest what they had furnished in the room of what they stolen.

On Tuesday, the 30th the advance of Lee's main army appeared on Seminary hill from the direction of Chambersburg. At the same time Gen. Buford, of the Potomac Army, appeared on the opposite side of the town with a body of cavalry. It now became painfully evident that our own beautiful village was to be the scene of a terrible conflict. Thus rested things, each party gathering his strength and arranging his plans, until Wednesday the 1st inst., when the Eleventh Corps, supported by the First, passed southwest of the town to M'Pherson's farm where began the fight. Gen. Reynolds, who led the First corps, fell before the battle had fairly commenced, being killed by a sharpshooter. At 3 P.M. our forces were obliged to retire to Cemetery Hill, which they did in good order. —It was not, however, with out first capturing the rebel General Archer, and his entire brigade, who remain in our hands. At 4 P.M. of Thursday the fight was renewed, the enemy now being the advancing and attacking party. The roar of artillery and musketry was terrific from that time until dark, when as if by mutual consent, the wearied and battle-worn ceased the conflict. But it was only to open again on the following morning with still more dreadful and terrible ferocity. This was the decisive day. Each had brought to the work his entire force. Along the whole line, extending from Wolf Hill on our right, to a point east of the Emmittsburg road,

about a mile from town, on the left the battle raged with a desperation and to an extent unknown in the previous history of the war. The enemy had determined to crush our lines, break through and possess the Baltimore Pike. To accomplish this, whole brigades charged repeatedly our batteries, only to be mown down, captured, or driven back in confusion, but they fell back only to rally and rush again with maddened fury into the red jaws of death. Thus raged the battle with fearful carnage until 4 P.M., when the enemy withdrew and retired, *weaker by twenty five to thirty thousand than when the battle began.* Many brave officers and brave and noble men have fallen, but praised be God, not on our side in vain. It is the universal testimony of those engaged that "Antietam, Fredericksburg and Chancellorsville were skirmishes as compared with this." We have captured about 15,000 to 20,000 prisoners, including those sent in by Pleasanton who pursued the enemy in his retreat. Large supply and ammunition trains have also been captured numbering in all several hundreds. Several guns have also fallen into our hands.

Our own loss is frightful to contemplate, but much less than that of the enemy in killed and wounded, and comparatively none in prisoners.

The enemy is terribly punished for his reckless villainy in thus attempting to make the North the future battle ground. Nor is this all; with French and Pleasanton to intercept the retreat, and Couch and Meade to pursue, the providential rise of the Potomac, the destruction of the rebel pontoons, which we are informed is accomplished there is scarcely a possibility that the rebels can escape. Thus we hope, upon our own soil, and at our own houses has been given the death blow to the rebellion.

One feature of this invasion has been peculiarly gratifying to every lover of the Union. Those who have been notorious sympathisers with the enemy, have been required to give tangible and practical evidence of their sympathy. They have been by great odds the heaviest sufferers. Truly there is a God in Heaven.

Instead of mourning and repining at our misfortunes let us Thank God and take courage.

R. J. HALDEMAN: THE SITUATION IN PENNSYLVANIA

Prior to its lengthy account of the Battle of Gettysburg that appears below, the Harrisburg Patriot & Union *tried to put some context to the fighting in Pennsylvania. The Democratic paper had soundly denounced Lincoln's Emancipation Proclamation, but it continued to support the Union war effort, particularly after Lee's invasion into the Cumberland Valley of Pennsylvania.*

Harrisburg Patriot & Union, 6 July 1863 (Harrisburg, Pa.)

Those who live far from the scenes of war, have no conception of war. To them it is simply sound, while to us, who are under its very breath, it is emphatically sense. For many

days past the extensive and fertile valley of the Cumberland has been the scene of sanguinary struggles between two immense conflicting armies of tried veterans in war, and every boom of the cannon, every sharp detonation of musketry has sent a thrill to the hearts of those upon the immediate borders of the strife which those who are out of reach of the sight and sound of the conflict cannot imagine.

We begin to-day—Sunday afternoon—to breathe more freely. . . . Tidings are coming in of an encouraging nature.

Without being able to go into particulars, we may state generally that Gen. Meade has well managed the campaign, and has at this time got Gen. Lee into a position from which escape, without terrible loss, seems to be impossible.

It seems to us that this conflict in the valley, whether the result of strategy or necessity on the part of Gen. Lee, or those still higher in authority directing the movements of the Confederate armies, is "the beginning of the end" of the war. Looking at it in this light, bloody as has been the struggle, we hail it with joy, and look forward with renewed hopes and fervent desires for the dawning of that day which shall give us a peace based upon a restored Union and an unimpaired and overruling Constitution, securing liberty and equal rights to all.

Excepting the mad fanatics who have plunged us into this terrible war to carry out an unsound and impracticable idea, and the men who, through court favor, are plundering the nation, the universal voice of the people is for peace, unity and the old fraternal relations.

War longer pursued for African emancipation is sheer madness, because years of strife, of bloodshed and devastation cannot accomplish the object, nor is it desirable if it could be accomplished. The condition of the African is best as it was before this war between brethren of the same race and color commenced. The time may come—in God's own providence it will probably come—when that condition may be favorably changed, but no device, no plot or plan of man can change the decrees of Heaven or hasten the period by one moment. While the corpses of our countrymen, slain in battle, are thickly strewn over fields almost within sight of our capital, for God and humanity's sake let us awake to serious reflections and sound ideas. Let us throw fanatics and fanaticism to the winds, and by judicious and Christian measures end this strife which is destroying the life of the nation.

Having at length gained a military advantage over the rebellion; having, as we believe, Gen. Lee cooped and the Confederate administration paralysed, let us be both just and generous, and while we press the war as vigorously as ever, let us hold out to the Southern people the olive branch, asking from them no other condition than a return to the old order of things.

As we understand at this hour—five o'clock p.m. Sunday— Gen. Meade occupies a decidedly advantageous position on a line stretching from Hanover beyond Gettysburg, towards Chambersburg. Rumor has it that the enemy are endeavoring to retreat in a north-westerly direction on the Cove Mountain road, perhaps intending to strike for Hancock or some other point in Maryland. But if the news we subjoin is true, and we believe it to be so, it will be only by something nearly like a miracle that any considerable portion of the rebel army can escape. Let us thank God and take courage, humbly imploring our Creator to give us wisdom in these trying times to use whatever of victory may be vouchsafed to us to the best advantage to the interest of the nation and the universal freedom of our distinctive race.

Up to this writing the following embraces all the news we have:

ARMY OF THE POTOMAC, July 8, 8:35 P.M.—The enemy opened at one o'clock p.m., with one hundred and fifty guns concentrated on our left and centre, and fought three hours. —He then assaulted our entire lines, and was handsomely repulsed, with a very severe loss in dead and wounded, and leaving 8,000 prisoners in our hands. Brig. Gen. Armistead and many general officers were killed and captured.

The enemy left many dead and wounded in- our hands. Our losses are considerable.

Maj. Gen. Hancock and Brig. Gen. Gibbons are wounded.

Gen. Meade pursued the enemy and found them in force on his left.

All is quiet now.

Our cavalry is doing great things and the army is in fine spirits.

HANOVER, July 4—5 P.M. —There has been no fighting up to this time to-day. Last evening we drove the enemy back to Gettysburg. Our lines this morning extend eight miles around Gettysburg; our batteries being on the hills looking on the town from the South. We occupy Round Top Ridge, commanding the Chambersburg turnpike, and have cut off all the lines of retreat. Our forces occupy the strongest possible position. A flank movement on our left is impossible.

At about 8 o'clock last night the Florida Brigade of General Longstreet's division, with Brigadier General in command, advanced to within our lines and gave themselves up with their colors.

A bearer of dispatches from Jeff. Davis to Gen Lee has been captured. The dispatches order Gen. Lee particularly to retreat on Richmond; he states the movement into Pennsylvania was totally against his wishes.

. . . We have captured at least eight thousand prisoners.

ADDRESS OF PRESIDENT LINCOLN

WASHINGTON. July 4.—10 A.M.—The President announces to the country that the news from the Army of the Potomac up to 10 A.M., of the 3d, is such as to cover the army with the highest honor, to promise a great success to the cause of the Union and to claim the condolence of all for the many gallant fallen; and that for this he especially desires that, on this day He whose will, not ours, should ever be done, be everywhere remembered, and reverenced with the profoundest gratitude. . . .

STILL LATER—IMPORTANT IF TRUE

The rumor is current on the streets, said to rest upon dispatches received by Gov. Curtin and Gen. Couch, that the army of Gen. Meade to-day captured 25,000 prisoners and 118 pieces of artillery. This, if true to the extent represented, would seem to settle the question as to the fate of the rebel army in the valley, and possible as to the longer continuance of the war. We can only account for the capture of so many men and so much artillery on the supposition that they were out of ammunition or tired of the war. The rumor seems to be well founded, and we see no reason why we should not credit it. The fortune of war seems once more to be on our side, and, our rulers acting wisely, we may reasonably hope to see the conflict brought to a speedy conclusion.

HALF PAST 10 o'CLOCK, P.M.—We have just heard officially that although there is no confirmation of the above rumor, yet it has been received in such form by the authorities as to render it nearly reliable. It has come in telegram from Baltimore, and this telegram is backed by intelligence from a respectable source in Cumberland county. We have reason, therefore, to believe it correct.

AN ANONYMOUS REPORT: LOCAL GETTYSBURG NEWSPAPER APOLOGIZES FOR TEMPORARY SUSPENSION OF PUBLICATION CAUSED BY BATTLE

The Battle of Gettysburg temporarily halted publication of the town's weekly newspaper, the Adams County Sentinel & General Advertiser, *as noted in this apology to subscribers.*

Adams County Sentinel & General Advertiser, 7 July 1863 (Gettysburg, Pa.)

We need scarcely apologize to our readers for not making our usual visit to their homes last week. Those only, who, with respect to surroundings, pursued the even tenor of their way, and met and discharged their accustomed duties, may consistently find fault. These we apprehend, will be few. But yet we owe, in the room of the Sentinel for the last week, this statement of our reason for its non-appearance. The unusual interest of the present number owing to the glorious news contained therein, will more than make amends.

AN ANONYMOUS REPORT: THE SENTINEL JUNIOR—LOCAL GETTYSBURG NEWSPAPER REDUCED IN SIZE BY PAPER SHORTAGE CAUSED BY BATTLE

The Sentinel & General Advertiser *was also affected in weeks to come, as observed in the following brief note that appeared in several editions of the paper after the battle.*

Adams County Sentinel & General Advertiser, 14 July 1863 (Gettysburg, Pa.)

Some of our farmers have had half their crops gathered for them in consequence of the invasion. At least they are saved the trouble of gathering them. Some, indeed do not escape with half. The Sentinel field also bears only half the usual amount of fruit. The sword of war has at least succeeded in clipping off one half of our sheet. But only temporarily. The supply of paper on hand is very small, and we find it absolutely impossible to obtain more at present. Upon the principle that "half a loaf is better than no bread" we offer what we have, and promise as soon as possible to expand again to our wonted dimensions.

AN ANONYMOUS REPORT: DESTRUCTION OF PROPERTY CAUSED BY BATTLE OF GETTYSBURG

Obviously, the Gettysburg newspaper was not alone in being negatively affected by the battle. The following article briefly highlights some of the loss of property to local individuals.

Adams County Sentinel & General Advertiser, 14 July 1863 (Gettysburg, Pa.)

The people of Adams county have nearly all suffered more or less from both armies, but those in the immediate vicinity of the battle field have lost the heaviest—some indeed have lost all. We regret to learn that the house and barn of Mr. Wm. Bliss with all their contents were totally destroyed. He has lost his stock and everything else. The house and barn occupied by Mr. Wm. Comfort, (the old McLean property) were also destroyed.—The house and barn of Mr. Alexander Currens were both burned. The barns of Messrs. John Herbst and Alexander Cobean were destroyed and probably many others that have not come to our knowledge.

A GENTLEMAN: ACCOUNT OF HORRENDOUS CONFEDERATE LOSSES AT GETTYSBURG

Northern newspapers and their readers relished the accounts of the devastating Confederate loss, particularly given the brazenness of the Southerners to advance so far north into Union territory. The Hartford paper, in the account that follows, acknowledged to its readers that the source of its information was "a gentleman holding an official position which enables him to obtain the earliest and most reliable news."

Hartford Daily Courant, 4 July 1863 (Hartford, Conn.)

SUNDAY, July 5.—A private dispatch received from Baltimore this morning states that a messenger reached that place at midnight last night, having left the battle-field at midnight last night, having left the battle-field at a late hour on the evening of the 4th. From it we should infer that there was no engagement yesterday.

After the battle of Friday, General Hill sent a flag of truce to General Meade asking the privilege of burying his dead, and removing the wounded; to which General Meade replied that he would take care of the wounded, the dead would take care of themselves.

A reconnaissance showed that the rebels were retreating to the mountains. Pleasanton's cavalry were immediately dispatched, a strong reserve following, which sent the whole rebel army skedaddling.

We have captured from 12,000 to 20,000 prisoners, and the battle-field shows a loss to the enemy in the engagement of Friday of 20,000 to 30,000.

General Meade had been heavily reinforced from various sources.

From high official sources we are assured that this is the most terribly contested engagement and signal success of the war.

The rebel pontoon bridges across the Potomac at Williamsport have been captured with the guards, and thus, it is said, General Lee's retreat is cut off.

At 11 o'clock Sunday, three thousand of the prisoners captured by General Meade were marched through the streets of Baltimore on their way to secure quarters.

FRANK CHAPMAN: SUMMARY OF CONFEDERATE ROUT AT GETTYSBURG

The following excerpt from the New York Herald *shows the kind of quick, untitled summary that was sent over the telegraph wires from Baltimore to provide news of the outcome of the battle. The* Herald *reporter is said to have handed the telegraph operator a copy of his pocket Bible to transmit to New York as he saw the* New York Tribune *correspondent headed to the same telegraph office. He wanted to tie up the telegraph line to prevent the competition, the* Tribune, *from getting a timely report.*[9]

New York Herald, 5 July 1863

NEW YORK, July 5.—The greatest and most glorious battle of the war. The rebels completely routed. Longstreet and Hill wounded and in our hands. The fighting yesterday was beyond all parallel. The enemy attempted to turn both our flanks, and afterwards attacked our center, but were repulsed on all hands. He then made a general attack along the whole line, but was defeated terribly. The victory of the Union army is complete. The enemy is in full retreat, and is being pursued by the Union troops.

AN ANONYMOUS REPORT: ESTIMATES OF DEAD AND WOUNDED AT GETTYSBURG

Early estimates of the casualties were low; many of the wounded eventually died, which elevated the final death counts after the battle, helping to explain the numbers in this untitled article.

Hartford Daily Courant, 9 July 1863 (Hartford, Conn.)

The Union wounded, during the three days fighting at Gettysburg, are estimated at the Surgeon-General's office at 12,000. Five thousand are to be sent to Philadelphia, 5,000 to New York, 1,000 will go to Baltimore, and 1,000 will remain in the improvised hospitals at Gettysburg. About 5,000 of this number still remain in the houses at Gettysburg, and are receiving the best of treatment. Those too much injured for transportation will not be removed from Gettysburg, Between 3,000 and 4,000 rebel wounded were left in our possession. Most of them are badly wounded, having been taken away by Lee's army.

A dispatch from Hanover, Tuesday, says: "Our scouts out on the Chambersburg Pike brought to Gettysburg about 2,500 more rebel prisoners today. From the great numbers of the prisoners constantly brought in, it is evident the rebels desire to be captured. Large numbers of rebel dead and wounded are daily discovered lying about the fields where they were abandoned. Cannonading has been heard at intervals throughout the day in the direction of Hagerstown."

SAM WILKESON: INHUMANITY AND POLTROONERY OF REBEL SURGEONS AT GETTYSBURG

The New York Times *reporter whose son perished in the battle reported that the Confederate doctors abandoned their wounded on the battlefield.*

New York Times, 13 July 1863

The infamy and cowardice of the rebel Surgeons in deserting the men of their army wounded at the battle of Gettysburgh is without parallel in the war. In every battle in which fortune has been adverse to our arms, and our wounded have been temporarily left within the rebel lines, the brave and self-denying Surgeons of the regiments have either remained with the fallen, or have immediately applied for passes within the rebel lines that they might be cared for. But the rebels left lying on the field many thousands of their wounded—DR. VELLUM reports the number at ten thousand—and left with them neither Surgeons, stores nor nurses, but literally abandoned them to their fate. These men complained bitterly of the cruelty of their Surgeons in thus forsaking them, but bore up patiently under their sufferings for many days until they could be attended to by some of our

own Surgeons, most of whom had at once to hasten forward with their own regiments to the other fields. We published yesterday a thrilling letter from the battle-field, written on Thursday last, six days after the close of the contest, which stated that there were hundreds of the rebel wounded not then reached, —that hundreds of them it had been found impossible even to cover and that they lay in the woods with broken limbs and torn bodies, drenched in the rain, some having even been drowned in the floods which rose around them. Of course everything possible was being done for them, and doctors, wound-dressers and nurses were arriving. We were not prepared for, and could not have foreseen, the flight of all the rebel Surgeons. It will be long remembered to their disgrace, both by the unfortunate rebels and the whole country.

CHARLES HALE: EDITORIAL—INVASION OF NORTH HALTED, BUT WAS GOVERNMENT UNPREPARED FOR REBEL ADVANCE?

Although the Boston Daily Advertiser *suggests that fears no longer remain about a Southern assault on Baltimore or Washington, in this untitled report the perception that the federal government was unprepared for the rebel invasion of Pennsylvania is some cause for concern.*

Boston Daily Advertiser, 6 July 1863

The sanguinary struggle of last week has ended all fears of a serious attack by Lee upon Baltimore and Washington. That attack, as our readers know, was not feared upon its own account. If properly provided for and met, it promised to our forces the opportunity of meeting the enemy upon terms more favorable than could be obtained otherwise, and the chance of fighting a decisive battle, instead of a battle of uncertain consequence like most of those which have decimated our army. It was not felt to be any misfortune that the enemy should find his second Antietam when far advanced into Pennsylvania instead of being close to the Potomac. The desperation which could drive the rebel leader to such a course was to be welcomed rather than deprecated by all loyal minds.

That the alarm occasioned by the advance into Pennsylvania exceeded the trepidation which necessarily precedes a decisive contest is due more to the certain assurance that the government had not provided carefully for such an issue, and that our own forces had not carefully kept pace with the movement. There is unfortunately but too much reason to believe that the enemy's bold push took our own authorities unawares, that he had the start by some days, that the forces upon which we could rely were neither strong nor well concentrated, and in short that disaster as well as success might be the result of an event which had been looked forward to with a certain sort of content. To these causes for fear and doubt the sudden change of command, made at the most critical moment, and entailing new dangers as well as leading to new hopes, unquestionably add increased weight in many minds.

NOTES

1. Curt Johnson and Mark McLaughlin, *Civil War Battles* (New York: Crown Publishers, 1977), 85.

2. The first was in Maryland in September 1862 that resulted in the loss at Antietam (see Chapter 13).

3. James M. McPherson (Ed.), *The Atlas of the Civil War* (New York: Macmillan, 1994).

4. "The Situation," *Harrisburg Patriot & Union,* 20 June 1863.

5. Johnson and McLaughlin, *Civil War Battles,* 87.

6. McPherson, *Atlas of the Civil War.*

7. Brayton Harris, *Blue & Gray in Black & White* (Washington, D.C.: Brasseys, 1999), 278.

8. "Details from Our Special Correspondent," *New York Times,* 6 July 1863.

9. Harris, *Blue & Gray,* 279.

FURTHER READINGS

Gottfried, Bradley M. *Brigades of Gettysburg: The Union and Confederate Brigades at the Battle of Gettysburg.* Cambridge, Mass.: Da Capo Press, 2002.

Johnson, Curt, and McLaughlin, Mark. *Civil War Battles.* New York: Crown Publishers, 1977.

Luvaas, Jay. *Guide to the Battle of Gettysburg.* Lawrence: University Press of Kansas, 1994.

Wagner, Margaret E.; Gallagher, Gary W.; and Finkelman, Paul (Eds.). *The Library of Congress Civil War Desk Reference.* New York: Simon & Schuster, 2002.

18

BATTLE OF VICKSBURG, 1–4 JULY 1863

As the Battle of Gettysburg raged in the East on 1–4 July, General Ulysses S. Grant's lengthy campaign to take Vicksburg, Mississippi, had entered its final stage. Beginning in October 1862, General Grant made several unsuccessful attempts to capture Vicksburg, one of two remaining Confederate strongholds on the Mississippi River (the other was Port Hudson, Louisiana).

In December 1862, soon after Union forces in the East were suffering from the loss at the Battle of Fredericksburg, General Grant suffered a loss at Chickasaw Bayou in Mississippi when General William Sherman's troops were not able to penetrate the Confederacy's northeast defenses of Vicksburg. Grant finally realized that he would not be able to capture the city by direct approach. In January 1863 General Grant continued his operations against Vicksburg and reorganized his forces under the leadership of Generals Sherman, John McClernand, Stephen Hurlburt, and James B. McPherson. Rear Admiral David Porter's fleet would provide naval support for Grant's new Vicksburg Campaign, which began in the spring of 1863.

In April, Grant's Army of the Tennessee began its southward march along the west side of the Mississippi River in Louisiana, building bridges and roads along the way. They would eventually rendezvous with the federal navy fleet, which on 16 April began a run past the Vicksburg batteries to head toward the Louisiana shore south of Vicksburg. Porter only lost one vessel in the successful run. Grant's plan next called for the Union fleet to bombard Grand Gulf, Mississippi, to secure an area for federal troops to land. The Confederate troops prevailed at Grand Gulf—on 29 April Grant was forced to abandon the landing there and continue his march south.[1]

After receiving advice from a local slave, Grant chose to begin his Mississippi invasion at Bruinsburg. In the early morning hours of 30 April, federal regiments successfully stepped onto Mississippi soil and officially began the invasion of Vicksburg. The landing at Bruinsburg was unopposed by Confederate forces and constituted the largest amphibious operation in American history until the Allied invasion of

Normandy during World War II. Generals McClernand's and McPherson's corps were ferried east across the Mississippi from Hard Times, Louisiana, and General Sherman was sent word to follow McPherson's route south.

On 1 May, the federal troops captured the town of Port Gibson. Sherman's troops joined the Union forces on 8 May, and on 14 May the federal army captured Jackson, Mississippi, after fighting Confederate General Joseph E. Johnston, who had headed to Jackson to oppose the Union troops. In the victory at Jackson, General Grant managed to cut General Johnston off from General John Pemberton, who was in command of the Confederate forces at Vicksburg. General Sherman's troops burned part of the town and cut off railroad connections with Vicksburg.[2]

Approaching Vicksburg from the east and northeast, the troops of Generals McClernand, McPherson, and Sherman neared the city's defenses. On 22 May the siege of the city began, and for 48 days General Grant pounded the city by land while the Union Navy attacked the city from the river. On 4 July 1863, the same day that Confederate General Robert E. Lee retreated from Gettysburg, General Pemberton surrendered Vicksburg to General Grant.

Grant's campaign against Vicksburg has been called one of the most brilliant military campaigns of the war. Grant's success in the West was greatly overshadowed in the Northern press by the accounts of the Battle of Gettysburg, but Northerners understood the significance of the capture of the city. As noted in the *Hartford Daily Courant*:

> Vicksburg has fallen. . . . The town with its garrison, guns and stores are now in General Grant's possession. The rebel power in the valley of the Mississippi is totally broken. The capture of Port Hudson [Louisiana] will speedily follow as the inevitable consequence of this victory. The States in revolt are cut in twain, never to be reunited except under the Government of the Union. The importance of the result cannot be overestimated. Jeff. Davis saw it, when in public speeches last autumn he openly staked the establishment of the Confederacy upon the defense of Vicksburg. This surrender in connection with the defeat of Lee [at Gettysburg], will give the stunning blow to rebel hopes. The news has been received throughout the North with the wildest demonstrations of rejoicing.[3]

The paper was correct about Port Hudson—it did surrender to federal forces on 9 July.

Of course, the symbolism of the victories of Gettysburg and Vicksburg on the Fourth of July did not go unnoticed by the North. Many of the press accounts of the Independence Day celebrations included mention of the important federal wins. Grant's successes in the West ultimately led to his appointment as general-in-chief of the Union armies. He was nicknamed "Unconditional Surrender" when he forced the surrender of Fort Donelson in Tennessee in February 1862. As the Civil War was coming to an end in April 1865, the *New York Times* noted, "Three rebel armies have surrendered to Gen. Grant . . . [and] he is the only one of our Generals who has ever induced a rebel army to surrender."[4] The three articles below focus on the details of the surrender of Vicksburg and on the significance the Northern press assigned to the victory.

OFFICIAL REPORT: FALL OF VICKSBURG

Like most of the reports about the surrender of Vicksburg, this one was based on official federal government dispatches that came from Washington and from the U.S. military post at Cairo, Illinois.

Hartford Daily Courant, 8 July 1863 (Hartford, Conn.)

VICKSBURG IS OURS!

Official Dispatch from Admiral Porter
An "Unconditional Surrender!"

WASHINGTON, July 7—1 P.M.—The following dispatch has just been received:

U.S. Mississippi Squadron,
Flagship Black Hawk, 4 July 1863

To HON. GIDEON WELLES, Secretary of the Navy:—*Sir*: I have the honor to inform you that Vicksburg surrendered to the United States forces on the fourth of July.

Very respectfully
Your obedient servant,

(Signed) D.D. PORTER,
Acting Rear Admiral.

Cairo, Ill., July 7—The dispatch boat has just arrived here from Vicksburg. She left at 10 o'clock Sunday morning.

The passengers announce that General Pemberton sent a flag of truce on the morning of the 4th of July and offered to surrender if his men were allowed to march out.

Gen. Grant is reported to have replied that "No man should leave except as prisoner of war." Gen. Pemberton then, after consultation with his commanders, unconditionally surrendered.

This news is perfectly reliable.

OFFICIAL REPORT: DETAILS OF CONFEDERATE SURRENDER AT VICKSBURG

This New York Times *article about the Confederate surrender comes from federal government reports. The paper reprinted for its readers the complete exchanges between Grant and Pemberton that led up to the surrender.*

New York Times, 13 July 1863

THE FALL OF VICKSBURGH

Full Official Details of the Surrender

The Communications Which Passed Between Gens. Pemberton and Grant

WASHINGTON, Sunday, July 12.

The following has been received at the War Department:
NEAR VICKSBURGH, Saturday, July 4.

Vicksburgh has been capitulated. Yesterday GEN. GRANT received the following letter:

GEN. PEMBERTON TO GEN. GRANT
HEADQUARTERS, VICKSBURGH, July 3.
Maj.-Gen. Grant, Commanding United States Forces:
GENERAL: I have the honor to propose to you an armistice for—hours, with a view to arranging terms for the capitulation of Vicksburgh. To this end, if agreeable to you, I will appoint three Commissioners to meet a like number to be named by yourself, at such place and hour to-day as you may find convenient. I make this proposition to save the further

effusion of blood, which must otherwise be shed to a frightful extent, feeling myself fully able to maintain my position for a yet indefinite period. This communication will be handed you under flag of truce by Maj.-Gen. JAMES BOWEN.

Very respectfully, your obedient servant,

J. C. PEMBERTON.

To this Gen. Grant replied as follows:

GEN. GRANT TO GEN. PEMBERTON
HEADQUARTERS, DEPARTMENT OF TENNESSEE,
IN THE FIELD, NEAR VICKSBURGH, JULY 3, 1863
Lieut.-Gen. J. C. Pemberton, Commanding Confederate Forces, &c.:
GENERAL: Your note of this date, just received, proposes an armistice of several hours for the purpose of arranging terms of capitulation through commissioners to be appointed, &c. The effusion of blood you propose stopping by this course, can be ended at any time you may choose, by an unconditional surrender of the city and garrison. Men who have

shown so much endurance and courage as those now in Vicksburgh, will always challenge the respect of an adversary, and, I can assure you, will be treated with all the respect due them as prisoners of war. I do not favor the proposition of appointing commissioners to arrange terms of capitulation, because I have no other terms than those indicated above.

I am, General, very respectfully,
Your obedient servant,
U. S. GRANT, Maj.-Gen.

GEN. BOWEN, the bearer of GEN. PEMBERTON'S letter, was received by GEN. A. J. SMITH. He expressed a strong desire to converse with GEN. GRANT, and accordingly, while GEN. GRANT declining this, requested GEN. SMITH to say that if GEN. PEMBERTON desired to see him an interview would be granted between the lines, in MCPHERSON'S front, at any hour in the afternoon which GEN. PEMBERTON might appoint. A message was sent back to GEN. SMITH, appointing 3 o'clock as the hour. GEN. GRANT was there with his Staff, and with GENS. ORD, MCPHERSON, LOGAN and A. J. SMITH. GEN. PEMBERTON came late, attended by GEN. BOWEN and COL. MONTGOMERY. He was much excited, and impertinent in his answers to GEN. GRANT. The conversation was held apart between GEN. PEMBERTON and his officers, and GEN. GRANT, MCPHERSON and A. J. SMITH. The rebels insisted on being paroled, and allowed to march beyond our lines, officers and men, all with eight days' rations drawn from their own stores, the officers to retain their private property and body servants. GEN. GRANT heard what they had to say, and left them at the end of an hour and half, saying the he would send in his ultimatum, in writing, to which GEN. PEMBERTON promised to reply before night, hostilities to cease in the meantime.

GEN. GRANT then conferred at his headquarters with his corps and division commanders, and sent the following letter to GEN. PEMBERTON, by the hand of GEN. LOGAN, and LIEUT.-COL. WILSON:

GEN. GRANT'S ULTIMATUM.
HEADQUARTERS, DEPARTMENT OF TENNESSEE,
NEAR VICKSBURGH, JULY 3, 1863
Lieut.-Gen. J. C. Pemberton, Commanding Confederate Forces, Vicksburgh, Miss.:
GENERAL: In conformity with the agreement of this afternoon, I will submit the following proposition for the surrender of Vicksburgh, public stores, &c. On your accepted the terms proposed, I will march in one division as a guard and take possession at 8 A.M. to-morrow. As soon as paroles can be made out and signed by the officers and men, you will be allowed to march out of our lines, the officers taking with them their regimental clothing, and Staff, Field and cavalry officers one horse each. The rank and file will be allowed all their clothing, but no other property. If these conditions are accepted, any amount of rations you may deem necessary can be taken from the stores you now have, and also the necessary cooking utensils for preparing them, thirty wagons

also, counting two horse or mule teams as one. You will be allowed to transport such articles as cannot be carried along. The same conditions will be allowed to all sick and wounded officers and privates as fast as they become able to travel. The paroles for these latter must be signed, however, whilst officers are present authorized to sign the roll of prisoners.

I am, General, very respectfully,
Your obedient servant,
U. S. GRANT, MAJOR-GENERAL

The officers who received this letter stated that it would be impossible to answer it by night, and it was not till a little before peep of day that the proposed reply was furnished.

PEMBERTON'S REPLY
HEADQUARTERS, VICKSBURGH, July 3.
Maj.-Gen. Grant, Commanding United States Forces:
GENERAL: I have the honor to acknowledge the receipt of your communication of this date proposing terms for the surrender of this garrison and post. In the main your terms are accepted, but in justice both to the honor and spirit of my troops manifested in the defence of Vicksburgh, I have the honor to submit the following amendments, which, if acceded to by you, will perfect the agreement between us. At 10 o'clock to-morrow I propose to evacuate the works in and around Vicksburgh, and to surrender the city and garrison under my command by marching out with my colors and arms and stacking them in front of my present lines, after which you will take possession; officers to retain their side arms and personal property, and the rights and property of citizens to be respected.

I am, General, yours very respectfully,
J. C. PEMBERTON,
Lieutenant-General.

To this Gen. Grant immediately replied as follows:

Not Satisfactory.
HEADQUARTERS, DEPARTMENT OF TENNESSEE,
BEFORE VICKSBURGH, JULY 3, 1863
Lieut.-Gen. J. C. Pemberton, commanding forces in Vicksburgh:
GENERAL: I have the honor to acknowledge your communication of the 3d of July. The amendments proposed by you cannot be acceded to in full. It will be necessary to furnish every officer and man with a parole, signed by himself, which, with the completion of the rolls of prisoners, will necessarily take some time. Again, I can make no stipulation with regard to the treatment of citizens and their private property. While I do not propose to cause any of them undue annoyance or loss, I cannot consent to leave myself under restraint by stipulation. The property which officers can be allowed to take with them will be as stated in the proposition of last evening; that is, that officers will be allowed their private baggage and side-arms, and mounted officers one horse each. If you mean by your proposi-

tion for each brigade to march to the front of the lines now occupied by it, and stack their arms at 10 o'clock A.M., and then return to the inside, and remain as prisoners until properly paroled, I will make no objections to it. Should no modification be made of your acceptance of my terms by 9 o'clock A.M., I shall regard them as having been rejected and act accordingly. Should these terms be accepted, white flags will be displayed along your lines to prevent such of my troops as may not have been notified, from firing upon your men.

I am, General, very respectfully,
Your obedient servant,

U. S. GRANT, MAJOR-GENERAL

To this the subjoined answer has this moment been received:

ALL RIGHT.

HEADQUARTERS, VICKSBURGH, July 4, 1863.

Maj.-Gen. Grant, Commanding U.S. Forces, &c.:

GENERAL: I have the honor to acknowledge the receipt of your communication of this date, and in reply to say that the terms proposed by you are accepted. Very respectfully, your obedient servant,

J. C. PEMBERTON, *Lieutenant General.*

All preparations for occupying the town are completed. In an hour it will be in our possession.

THE SURRENDER CONSUMMATED.

The following dispatch has been received at the War Department:

VICKSBURGH, Miss., July 5—11 P.M.

The surrender was quietly consummated yesterday morning, at the appointed hour of 10 o'clock. The rebel troops marched out and stacked arms in front of their works, while GEN. PEMBERTON appeared for a moment with his Staff upon the parapet of the central front. The occupation of the place by our force was directed by GEN. MCPHERSON, who had been appointed to the command here, GEN. LOGAN being assigned to the command of the post under him. The divisions of GENS. LOGAN, J. E. SMITH, and HERRON now garrison the line of fortifications, and furnish guards for the interior of the city. No troops remain outside. Everything is quiet here. GEN. GRANT entered the city at 11 o'clock, and was received by GEN. PEMBERTON with more marked impatience than at the former interview. He bore it like a philosopher, and in reply treated GEN.

PEMBERTON with even greater courtesy and dignity than before.

Of the number of prisoners we have, as yet, no precise information. MAJ. LUCKETT, GEN. PEMBERTON'S Chief of Engineers reported it unofficially, yesterday, at 27,000. To-day when the rebel Brigadier brought in their requisition for food, which they did, notwithstanding GEN. PEMBERTON'S clause in the capitulation that he should draw eight day's supplies from his own stores, the aggregate of men for whom they thus drew rations was a little over 30,000. GEN. MCPHERSON issued to them five rations per man—all they are to have. No citizens have yet applied for the rations.

The paroling is being pushed with all possible rapidity, and will doubtless be completed by close of day after to-morrow. Among the officers already paroled are nineteen Generals, with their Staffs, including one Lieutenant and four Major-Generals. Large numbers of the men express a warm desire to take the oath of allegiance, and it is certain that their officers will find it difficult to march them to their camps east of the Tombigbee. They have 5,400 men on the sick list. Of these, 2,500 must be left behind here.

Their losses during the siege is estimated by JUDGE HAMILTON, an intelligent citizen of the place, at 6,000, GEN. PEMBERTON having complained that the thirty wagons agreed upon in the capitulation were not enough. GEN. GRANT has told him to take fifty.

The universal testimony of the rebel officers is that their conscripts have been worthless to them.

The official return of the field artillery surrendered makes it 100, including many French, Spanish and Austrian guns. No report of coast and siege guns has been made. The number is from 30 to 50. Neither do we yet know what quantity of ammunition the rebels had remaining; but some of their officers say they had only twenty rounds per man and per cannon.

CAPT. COMSTOCK, GEN. GRANT'S Chief Engineer, to-day visited the fortifications. He reports them as simple field works, but of considerable strength from the natural conformation of the ground. With one single exception, the forts are all open at the gorge.

The buildings of the town are much less damaged than we expected.

There is a considerable supply of railroad carriages here, with one or two exceptions, in working condition. Orders have been given instantly to put the railroad in repair as far as the Big Black, and it will be ready to supply them with transportation before to-morrow night.

THOMAS N. DAY: SIGNIFICANT AND HOPEFUL SUCCESSES AT GETTYSBURG AND VICKSBURG

This short editorial in the Hartford Daily Courant *highlights the battle successes at Gettysburg and Vicksburg and shows the newfound optimism about the ultimate success of the Union cause in winning the war.*

Hartford Daily Courant, 9 July 1863 (Hartford, Conn.)

The Fourth of July was a glorious day for the Republic, and a day of culminating disasters to its enemies. One short week has changed the whole aspect of the war, raising the American people from the depths of despondency to the topmost altitude of rejoicing. With shouts of defiance and yells of demoniac exultation, Lee's army crossed the Potomac for the avowed purpose of capturing the capital of the nation, and of occupying for the residue of the war its richest and most populous districts. By tightening the clutch of the invader upon the throat of Pennsylvania—by threatening to carry rapine and desolation even to the doors of our metropolis, they expected to extort for the Government an ignominious peace. The first of the month found that army coiled up among the mountains of Pennsylvania for the fateful spring at Washington, Baltimore and Philadelphia. Its ranks were full, its spirits jubilant, and it leaders confident of easy and overwhelming victories. The sun of the Fourth looked down upon that army shattered, routed, fleeing in terror along the same roads by which it had recently advanced in insolence of triumph. The main pillar of the Confederacy was broken. The fabric hence one week before hurled was defiance at the power of the Republic, was shorn of its choicest strength, and tottering helplessly on ruined foundations.

In the far Southwest the same day witnessed the consummation of another series of triumphs, not less glorious for the Union, or less disastrous to the rebels. A few weeks since the bold advance of Gen. Grant into the heart of Mississippi, his swift marches, frequent battles, and splendid victories, once more restored the waning prestige of the federal arms. But when he struck the impregnable defenses of Vicksburg, our enthusiasm was cooled by the delay of hopes. While feeling sure of ultimate success, the popular mind looked forward to an indefinite postponement of the time. The news of victory came at length almost unexpectedly. It is no wonder, considering the splendor of the triumph and the magnitude of its results, that the whole land, with one impulse, gave way to tumultuous beginnings.

NOTES

1. Patricia L. Faust (Ed.), *Historical Times Illustrated Encyclopedia of the Civil War* (New York: Harper & Row, 1986), 781–784.
2. Ibid., 783.
3. "The Surrender at Vicksburg," *Hartford Daily Courant*, 9 July 1863.
4. "Rebel Surrenders," *New York Times*, 11 April 1865.

FURTHER READINGS

Arnold, James R. *Grant Wins the War: Decision at Vicksburg*. New York: John Wiley and Sons, 1997.

Faust, Patricia L. (Ed.). *Historical Times Illustrated Encyclopedia of the Civil War*. New York: Harper & Row, 1986.

Foote, Shelby. *The Beleaguered City: The Vicksburg Campaign December 1862–July 1863*. New York: Modern Library, 1995.

Johnson, Curt, and McLaughlin, Mark. *Civil War Battles*. New York: Crown Publishers, 1977.

19

NEW YORK DRAFT RIOTS, JULY 1863

The Civil War was the first U.S. war in which a draft of soldiers was instituted. As Chapter 7 noted, as soon as the war began in April 1861, President Abraham Lincoln issued a call for 75,000 Union volunteers. Confederate President Jefferson Davis also requested volunteers in early 1861. Before fighting began at the first Battle of Bull Run, both sides saw experienced numbers of civilians enlisting in their armies. But as the war continued through 1861 and early 1862, the number of volunteers was not enough to sustain the growing number of casualties, particularly in the South.

The Confederate states instituted a draft in April 1862 for men between the ages of eighteen and thirty-five. It required 3 years of service to the Confederacy and allowed men of certain professions to opt out of service. The South, with its smaller population, had a much greater need for a draft. Before the war had ended, it had enlarged its pool of draftees to those between the ages of seventeen and fifty.

The North did not begin a draft until 1863. The 37th Congress passed the Enrollment Act of 1863, which subjected men between the ages of twenty and forty-five to a draft that would begin to enroll citizens on 1 July of that year. The act allowed exemptions for men who were physically or mentally impaired, the only son of a widow, the son of infirm parents, or a widower with dependent children. The act also allowed men to avoid the draft by paying $300 to a substitute who was willing to serve in their place. The act divided the United States into enrollment districts that matched existing congressional districts.[1]

There was general opposition to the drafts in both the North and the South, and although the drafts themselves did not produce a sufficient number of soldiers for either side, the threat of being drafted led many people to hire volunteers for army service. The enrollment process ran smoothly in the North with one significant exception—on 13 July 1863, when the first draft lists were published in New York City, four days of violent rioting ensued.

As the *New York Times* reported the day after the riots started,

> The initiation of the draft on Saturday in the Ninth Congressional District was characterized by so much order and good feeling as to well-nigh dispel the forebodings of tumult and violence which many entertained in connection with the enforcement of the conscription in this city. Very few, then, were prepared for the riotous demonstrations which yesterday, from 10 in the morning until late at night, prevailed almost unchecked in our streets.[2]

Hundreds of people were injured or killed in the several days of rioting that ensued—estimates have ranged from seventy to 1,000. Angry mobs caused nearly $1.5 million in property damage, and President Lincoln had to call in federal troops, many of whom had just finished fighting the Battle of Gettysburg, to finally put down the riots.

The New York riots received national attention and even sparked a smaller riot in Boston. Rioters generally objected to the unfairness of the draft, since poorer men could not buy their way out of service. The initial riot began at the hands of recent Irish immigrants who opposed being subjected to the draft and who largely targeted blacks with their violent responses. Most of the general press coverage outside of New York briefly observed the fact that the rioting had occurred. It then reported on the calmness and order that surrounded the draft processes in their locales. The New York newspapers reported the incidents heavily. A few examples appear below, including one report on the Boston rioting from one of the newspapers in that city.

HENRY RAYMOND: EDITORIAL—CONSCRIPTION IS A GREAT BENEFIT

This editorial provides context to the draft question. The writer clearly favors the draft and suggests that if the draft effort is successful, it will give the United States "a respect, both at home and abroad, far beyond any ever accorded to it before. It will be a new and priceless security against all future rebellion and wanton foreign attack."

New York Times, 13 July 1863

The National Enrollment Act, the enforcement of which was commenced in this City on Saturday, will be carried into execution until the quota of the State of New-York and of every State in the Union shall be raised and in the field. It may not be necessary that a man of those drafted shall ever go into line of battle during this war. Yet it is a national blessing that the Conscription has been imposed. It is a matter of prime concern that it should now be settled, once and for all, whether this Government is or is not strong enough to *compel* military service in its defence. More than any other one thing, this will determine our durability as a Republic and our formidableness as a nation. Once establish that not only the property, but the personal military service of every able-bodied citizen is at the command of the national authorities, constitutionally exercised, and both successful rebellion and

successful invasion are at once made impossible for all time to come. From that time it will be set down as a known fact that the United States is the most solidly based Government on the face of the earth.

The standing reproach against the Republican form of government hitherto has been, that its superior freedom was obtained at the expense of its security. It has been deemed a very comfortable sort of Government for fair weather, but quite unfit for a storm. A Federal Republic, made up like ours, of distinct States, has been considered particularly weak. Every philosophical writer who has treated of our institutions, has put his finger upon the weakness of the central authority as the special reason for doubting their perpetuity. DE TOCQUEVILLE himself, much as he admired our constitutional system, did not hesitate to say, "It appears to me unquestionable that if any portion of the Union seriously desired to separate itself from the other States, *they would not be able*, nor indeed would the attempt, to prevent it;" and to illustrate the helplessness of the federal authority, he cites from a letter of JEFFERSON'S to LAFAYETTE the statement that, "during the war of 1812, four of the Eastern States were only attached to the Union like so many inanimate bodies to living men." Everybody knows that one of the chief embarrassments of that war was the unwillingness of some of the State authorities to surrender the control of their military forces to the Federal Executive. Another of these embarrassments was the great difficulty of keeping the armies up to the necessary figure, notwithstanding extraordinary bounties for the encouragement of enlistments. The Secretary of War, at that period, in his strait for soldiers, proposed a Conscription system, but it was deemed by Congress dangerous and impracticable, and hardly obtained a hearing.

In fact, up to the last year the popular mind had scarcely bethought itself for a moment that the power of an unlimited Conscription was, with the sanction of Congress, one of the living powers of the Government in time of war. The general notion was that Conscription was a feature that belonged exclusively to despotic governments, and that the American reliance could only be upon volunteered effort, as prompted by patriotic feeling or pecuniary inducements. It was not until the second year of this terrible rebellion that the public mind began seriously to question whether it would answer to depend entirely upon these precarious stimulants; and even then it began to question only in a whisper. Even the boldest shrank; for they well understood how quickly the factious enemies of the Government would seize upon the old hated word *Conscription*, and do their best with it to make the war itself odious. But as the war lingered on without result, the Government gradually braced itself up to the responsibility of demanding, under the mild name of a National Enrollment bill, what was in reality nothing less than a Conscription law on the European model. Congress, after deliberation, framed and passed such a law. The great practical question now to be determined is whether such a law can be sustained or not; in other words, whether this American Republic has or has not the plenary power for its own defence which is possessed by a European monarchy.

For a time after that act was passed, the chiefs of faction were free in their threats that any attempt to carry it out should be resisted by force and arms. In some few localities they succeeded in working up popular passion against its first processes, even to a fighting pitch; but it was very quickly made apparent that the people at large would never sustain any such resort to violence, and that it was worse than idle to contend thus with the Government. Since then, the talk of these factionalists on the platform and in their newspaper organs has been that the appeal shall be carried to the ballot-box. They flatter themselves that, by working diligently upon the basest motives and meanest prejudices, they can secure popular majorities that will force a repeal of the measure, or at least defer the Government from carrying it out to its complete execution.

Well, let them do their worst. We want it determined whether the majority of the American people can be induced by any such influences to abandon the cause of their country. So far as the Government itself is concerned, we have no fear that it will fail to do its duty. Every day adds new evidence that it means to go straight on to the complete enforcement of the act. The world will now have a better chance to judge than ever before what the real strength of this Republic is. And unless we greatly mistake, it will be seen that an overwhelming majority of the people will stand by the Government in this exercise of the mightiest of its powers; and will show a proud satisfaction in demonstrating that freemen are as capable as subjects and serfs of abiding any needful requirements for the national safety. No people on the face of the earth have such reason to submit to the extremest sacrifices for the salvation of their Government; and, if conscription be necessary to replenish its struggling armies, no population, we undertake to say, has ever endured it with more patience or cheerfulness than the American people will now do. The Government is the people's Government, and the people will never consent that their Government shall suffer in a critical hour for the want of a power which is not grudged even the worst Government when its existence is threatened. When it is once understood that our national authority has the right, under the Constitution, to every dollar and every right arm in the country for its protection, and that the great people recognize and stand by that right, thenceforward for all time to come this Republic will command a respect, both at home and abroad, far beyond any ever accorded to it before. It will be a new and priceless security against all future rebellion and wanton foreign attack.

AN ANONYMOUS REPORT: "CRUSH THE MOB!"—NEW YORK NEWSPAPERS DEMAND RESTORATION OF ORDER

The following short passage represents the typical plea for order that New York City newspapers carried in an effort to help restore peace in the city.

New York Times, 14 July 1863

MAYOR OPDYKE has called for volunteer policemen—to serve for the special and temporary purpose of putting down the mob which threatened yesterday to burn and plunder the City. *Let no man be deaf to this appeal!* No man can afford to neglect it. No man, whatever his calling or condition in life, can afford to live in a City where the law is powerless, and where mobs of reckless ruffians can plunder dwellings and burn whole blocks of buildings with impunity. Let the mob which raged yesterday in our streets with so little real restraint, obtain the upper hand for a day or two longer, and no one can predict or imagine the extent to the injury they may inflict, or the weight of the blow they may strike at our peace and prosperity. This mob must be crushed at once. Every day's—every hour's delay—is big with evil. Let every citizen come promptly forward and give his personal aid to so good and indispensable a work.

HENRY RAYMOND: THE MOB AND THE PRESS——RIOTERS TARGET NEWSPAPER OFFICES

The mob violence that ensued as a result of the start of the draft in New York City also targeted the press. In the article that follows, the New York Times *offers support to the* New York Tribune, *a paper that became victim to mob violence. The passage shows the* Times' *devotion to free press ideals.*

New York Times, 14 July 1863

The mob last evening broke the windows and demolished the furniture in the counting-room of the *Tribune*, and attempted to crown their infamous and fiendish ruffianism by setting the building on fire. The prompt arrival and vigorous action of a body of Police interrupted their proceedings, and deprived them of the pleasure of being as brutal as they had hoped and expected to be.

We have not always agreed with our neighbor on political topics, and have not deemed it wise on grounds of the public welfare to make Slavery and the negro so prominent in these discussions as the *Tribune* has done. But that is a matter concerning which judgments and tastes may differ. It is intolerable that a mob should undertake by violence and destruction of property to dictate topics for public discussion, or to control the sentiments and utterances of the public Press. When such an issue is forced upon journalists, they must make it their common cause.

We regret that the *Tribune* should have suffered in such a shape even the trifling loss which last night's mob inflicted upon them. They had the aid of some among our *employes* in protecting their property, and shall have it again whenever the invidious favor of the mob shall again release us from the necessity of defending our own.

HENRY RAYMOND: RIVAL NEWSPAPERS UNITE TO DENOUNCE MOB VIOLENCE

Broad-based support for the press is reinforced in the second article in which the Times *praises New York City newspapers for working together to denounce the mob mentality that had temporarily gripped the city.*

New York Times, 15 July 1863

As a general thing, the Press of the City, without distinction of party, dealt in terms of just denunciation with the cowardly and ferocious mob which made our streets hideous with the most revolting crimes day before yesterday. The *Daily News*, which denounces the conscription with unjust and what seems to us unpatriotic severity, reminds the men who resort to violence against it that they are only disgracing themselves, and bringing ruin upon the very cause they profess to serve. The *World*, with still more emphatic and mischievous denunciation of the draft, brands, in the sharpest terms, the resort to mob law as a remedy, and declares that "no Government can tolerate it for an instant." The *Journal of Commerce* calls upon every citizen to stand by the laws and the constituted authorities of the City, State, Nation.

There can be but one sentiment in such an emergency as this, and we rejoice that the unanimous voice of the Press and the public is in favor of the prompt and effective suppression of the mob spirit which has burst out with such sudden and destructive fury. Let the mob be put down, and then we can remedy whatever evils may demand attention.

THOMAS N. DAY: RIOT REPORT FROM OUTSIDE NEW YORK

This excerpt from the Hartford Daily Courant *is an example of the typical attention the riots received in cities beyond New York.*

Hartford Daily Courant, *16 July 1863 (Hartford, Conn.)*

Late advices indicate that the riot in New York is nearly over. So far as it is based on opposition to the Conscription Law, it may be pronounced substantially at an end. In some quarters of the city gangs of thieves are busily engaged in plunder. They pillage Democrats and Republicans indiscriminately, aiming solely at booty. Pickpockets, too, are improving the opportunity to prosecute their trade with vigor. The police and military force have been successful in all attacks on the rioters. In a few hours more complete tranquility will unquestionably be restored. The guilty parties are known, as they will soon find, to their lasting sorrow.

AN ANONYMOUS REPORT: RIOT IN BOSTON

The Boston papers, like the papers in New York, devoted substantial attention to coverage of the riots there. No federal troops were needed to control the Boston mobs, which were much smaller and less destructive than those in New York.

Boston Daily Advertiser, *15 July 1863*

**RIOT AT THE NORTH END
ATTACK ON A PROVOST MARSHAL'S OFFICER**

Assault on the Cooper St. Armory

The Rioters Fired Upon and Several Killed

THE RIOT QUELLED BY THE MILITARY

Boston witnessed a scene of riot yesterday which will not soon be forgotten, either on account of the reckless boldness of its instigators or the prompt and efficient measures which subdued it. The news received the previous day from New York greatly excited the public mind, and jolted many hot-headed persons to intemperate and treasonable language. On Monday night the North End was in a dangerous state of ferment, and the police predicted an attack at daybreak. The disaffected parties held several meetings on that night, as they have since boasted. During yesterday forenoon all was quiet but police precautions were taken against an attack.... Everything proceeded quietly until half-past 12 o'clock [*when a small group of men physically attacked two police officers*].

... On the appearance of [*additional*] police the cry of "Kill them," was raised, and while Officer Curtis Trask of the 2d Station was attempting to arrest one of the leaders one of the ruffians stopped behind him and struck at his face with a knife, making a flesh wound on his right cheek. Police officer Winship of the Second Station having been detailed with Trask and two others to go to the scene of the disturbance was set upon by the crowd as soon as he arrived there and badly beaten, and it was only through the exertions of the housekeepers in the neighborhood that he was saved from more severe injury. Word being sent to the station house for more aid, ten or a dozen officers soon arrived on the spot, but the trouble by this time was nearly over in this particular locality.

A large crowd, one-half of whom was composed of women and children, assembled in front of Station One on Hanover street after the above scenes, and made some disturbance but did no material damage. For about forty rods the street was completely blockaded. A rush was inside for a negro near No. 201, but without success....

THE EVENING RIOT

At nightfall everybody but the police and military authorities thought the disgraceful scenes were ended and even the authorities justly indulged in such a hope. Yet every possible precaution had been taken to check any further outbreak and secure the peace of the city.... By dark at least a thousand men were under arms to keep the peace. Shortly after seven o'clock the low grumblings of an approaching storm were heard in various localities in the North End. Knots of men began to collect on Endicot, Hanover, and Prince streets, and well disposed citizens took good care to keep out of their way, but instead of retiring to their homes like good citizens, collected on the outskirts of the disaffected portions of the city to witness the course of events and thus increased the crowd and the labors of the police.

... At the various armories the men only waited the word to start. Meanwhile the rioters were enacting the fiercest scenes at the North End. A large and boisterous crowd had assembled in front of the Light Artillery Armory in Cooper street; wherein waited Capt. Jones with a loaded piece. At the same instant showers of bricks and other missiles fell upon the armory, hurled by the mob below and from the roofs of the neighboring houses. The windows were smashed and the missiles fell thick and fast about the men within. It was at this time that Lieut. Sawin of the Battery, was knocked down senseless by a brick. It is stated that he was thrown in the gutter and actually trampled upon by women, a large number of whom was in the crowd, and added to its fury by their demoniac yells. The fierceness of the assault drove nearly all the men from the positions in the armory. Now was the criti-

cal time. The mob seemed to be gaining the upper hand, and with the gun once in their possession the direful results could not be predicted. Capt. Jones's gallant little band were sore pressed indeed. A man yet stood at the gun. Capt. Jones ordered him to fire; and,—not a blank cartridge,—but a good round of canister burst into the close ranks of the rioters. Several fell; some were at once borne away dead and some wounded, whose names we shall probably never learn. Other casualties are monitored below. This timely and soldier-like order of Capt. Jones turned the tide against the rioters. The men now used their small arms freely and the rabble was now glad to disperse, having received additional losses.

NOTES

1. Michael T. Meier, "Civil War Draft Records: Exemptions and Enrollments," *Prologue* 26 (Winter 1994): 1.
2. "The Mob in New York," *New York Times*, 14 July 1863.

FURTHER READINGS

Cook, Adrian. *The Armies of the Streets: The New York City Draft Riots.* Lexington: University of Kentucky Press, 1974.

Meier, Michael T. "Civil War Draft Records: Exemptions and Enrollments." *Prologue* 26 (Winter 1994): 1–3.

Wagner, Margaret E.; Gallagher, Gary W.; and Finkelman, Paul (Eds.). *The Library of Congress Civil War Desk Reference.* New York: Simon & Schuster, 2002.

WAR PRISONERS AND THE FORT PILLOW MASSACRE, 12 APRIL 1864

By 1862 both the Union and the Confederacy recognized the growing problem of prisoners of war. Both sides used former jails, penitentiaries, fortifications, altered buildings, enclosures around tents and stockades, and enclosures around barracks to contain their growing number of prisoners. In July 1862, both sides agreed on a formal system of prisoner exchange. But within a year the system broke down, partially because the Confederacy refused to parole or exchange black prisoners.[1]

The general problem with the war prison facilities on both sides was a lack of proper sanitation, food, shelter, and clothing. Historians have noted that neither side intentionally mistreated its prisoners; rather, Americans had never before been faced with what to do with hundreds of men in captivity and were ill prepared to handle the thousands of prisoners the war would produce for each side. Although exact figures are not known, historians estimate that 56,000 men died in Civil War prisons. The leading cause of death was disease. There were more than 150 prisons established during the war, and all were filled beyond capacity.

In the North the most infamous war prison was in Elmira, New York, where there was a nearly 25 percent mortality rate. In the South, the enclosure stockade prison at Andersonville, Georgia, was considered the worst. By the end of the war, 13,000 men died at Andersonville, which equaled 29 percent of those housed in the Georgia facility.[2]

The majority of the press gave little attention to the broader prison issue. Instead, Northern newspapers briefly reported on early prisoner exchanges and criticized the bad treatment of federal prisoners without noting the equally bad conditions that existed for the Confederate men in Union prison facilities. The one prison-related issue that received the most attention in the Northern press came after the rebel massacre at Fort Pillow, Tennessee. Although the Fort Pillow incident was not specifically a prison issue, it was related because it highlighted the Confederacy's view of the Union's black soldiers, their white commanders, and how to handle their capture and treatment after battle.

On 12 April 1864, Confederate General Nathan Bedford Forrest attacked Fort Pillow while on an expedition into west Tennessee and Kentucky. Fort Pillow was in the possession of the Union but had previously been a Confederate-built earthen fortification that overlooked the Mississippi River about 40 miles north of Memphis. Stationed at Fort Pillow were nearly 300 white troops and 262 black troops, all under the command of Major Lionel Booth. Forrest's cavalry attacked the fort with 2,500 men and killed Booth. Major William Bradford took over the Union command and continued to try to thwart the rebel attack, to no avail. After Forrest demanded unconditional surrender, Bradford refused, and the fighting resumed.

According to the correspondent from the *St. Louis Democrat*, who was on board a steamer that landed at Fort Pillow under a flag of truce after the fight, the rebels then

charged with great boldness down the declivity, and faced without blanching a murderous fire from the guns and small arms of the fort, and crowded into the ravine where they were sheltered from fire by the steep bank which had been thus left by some unaccountable neglect or ignorance. Here the rebels organized for a final charge upon the fort, after sending a flag of truce with a demand of surrender, which was refused. The approach from the ravine was up through a deep, narrow gully, and the steep embankments of the fort. The last charge was made about 4 P.M., by the whole rebel force, and was successful after a most desperate and gallant defence.[3]

He added:

By the uniform and voluntary testimony of the rebel officers, as well as the survivors of the fight, the negro artillery regiments fought with the bravery and coolness of veterans and served the guns with skill and precision. They did not falter nor flinch until at the last charge, when it was evident they would be overpowered, they broke and fled towards the river, and here commenced the most barbarous and cruel outrage that ever the fiendishness of rebels have perpetrated during the war.

After the rebels were in undisputed possession of the fort and the survivors had surrendered, they commenced the indiscriminate butchery of all the Federal soldiery. The colored soldiers threw down their guns and raised their arms in a token of surrender, but not the least attention was paid to it.[4]

The report that the Confederate soldiers murdered the black federal troops after they surrendered outraged Union citizens. Nearly a year prior to the Fort Pillow massacre, the Confederates denounced the Union's recruitment of black soldiers and said that if they were captured, they would be returned to their masters and that their white commanders would be treated more harshly when captured. This is when the federal government quit cooperating with the prison exchanges for all practical purposes. But after the massacre, General Ulysses S. Grant and President Abraham Lincoln formally ended the prison exchanges. The end of the prison exchanges created dramatically worse conditions for prisoners of war on both sides because the prisons would continue to grow larger.

Although the Northern press would devote a large amount of attention to the Fort Pillow massacre, a few months after the devastating event, few newspapers continued to monitor issues related to prisoners of war and the treatment of captured troops. News accounts did appear that suggested the awful conditions Union men faced in Confederate prisons, but only a handful of newspapers devoted much space to these stories, and they appeared sporadically.

R. J. HALDEMAN: CRUELTY TO WAR PRISONERS

This short article draws some attention to the issue in late 1863, after the prisoner exchanges had ended but before the Fort Pillow massacre, and takes direct aim at the conditions for federal prisoners in Richmond.

Harrisburg Patriot & Union, 20 November 1863 (Harrisburg, Pa.)

It appears by the latest intelligence from the rebel Capital that, while the Confederate Government are unable to feed our thousands of prisoners held at Richmond, they are also determined that we shall not provide for them. We hope there may be some mistake in the intelligence which has reached us to this effect . . . gives us to understand that our prisoners are suffering and are doomed to suffer at Richmond unless relieved by the capture of the place. If that is the only way to relieve them, the whole military force of the Government should be thrown upon Richmond as soon as possible and it should be captured without delay. It is grievous to reflect that 18,000 of our fellow-citizens of the northern States are now languishing for want of food and clothing in the prisons of Richmond. Let Richmond be taken, and taken without delay, if it be true that these poor fellows are there and doomed to suffer because the Confederate authorities cannot provide for their necessities, and will not permit the Government or people of the North to do it.

AN ANONYMOUS REPORT: REBELS RESPONSIBLE FOR END OF PRISONER EXCHANGES

The New York Herald *offered the following untitled assessment of conditions at Richmond and blamed the Confederates for putting an end to the prisoner exchanges.*

New York Herald, 19 November 1863

A telegram from Fortress Monroe informs us that the steamer which left there last Saturday, carrying clothing and provisions to the Union prisoners at Richmond has been obliged to return with her cargo, since the rebel authorities refuse to permit Colonel Irving, who had charge of the steamer, to convey the supplies to the rebel capital. The war began with the refusal of rebels to allow us to relieve the starving garrison of Fort Sumter. It ought to end with this rebel refusal to allow us to relieve our poor starving prisoners at Richmond. We cannot relieve but we can release them. The rebels will not exchange them, and, with barbarous brutality, they will neither feed these poor prisoners themselves nor permit us to supply them with food. This announcement must be made the signal for a new crusade, the object of which is the immediate capture of the rebel capital.

AN ANONYMOUS REPORT: ACCOUNT OF PRISON CONDITIONS IN RICHMOND

This account of prison conditions in Richmond comes from a report issued by federal doctors who visited Union soldiers held captive there in late 1863.

Washington Chronicle, 27 November 1863 (Washington, D.C.)

RETURN OF SURGEONS FROM RICHMOND

Interesting Narrative of their Experiences—Short Rations—Their Money Taken Away from Them—The Belle Isle Prisoners Starving.

The Surgeon states that the *outhouse* provided for the use of the officers directly communicated with the room they occupied, and the condition of it (a room only eight feet square) was of the most disgusting filthy character. The water furnished them was the muddy water of the James River, and the supply was at all times most deficient, so much so, that it was difficult to procure enough for cooking and drinking purposes, let alone that needed for the cleanliness of their persons.

When these Surgeons entered the prison their rations consisted of one pound of beef a day, (bones and all,) and sixteen ounces of bread. The beef they were obliged to cook for themselves. Ten stoves were allowed for some three hundred and fifty men, one hundred and fifty of them in the story over where the officers were confined. In the matter of rations, the Surgeons both state that the prisoners began to notice a deficiency after the middle of last month. Then the article of fresh beef was missing, making its appearance only about once every four days. One *pound of corn bread* was furnished them each day, with the usual accompaniment of one *sweet potato*. They were treated with the greatest contempt on every occasion—dogs could hardly be treated worse. From the hearsay of these gentlemen, they supposed that about 10,000 prisoners are yet confined at Richmond, some 6,300 of them at Belle Island. The treatment of the prisoners at Belle Island is described to be of the most inhuman character.

WILLIAM LLOYD GARRISON: THE FORT PILLOW MURDERS

The massacre at Fort Pillow received a good amount of attention in the Northern press. It served as a strong rallying cry against slavery. Northern abolitionists and those who generally opposed slavery as an institution considered the massacre an example of the kind of cruelties toward blacks that were a direct result of the teachings and practice of slavery.

The Liberator, 22 April 1864 (Boston)

Gen. Sherman telegraphs from somewhere in the South-West that after the capture last week of Fort Pillow, near Columbus, by Forrest's raiding rebel force, *three hundred of our colored soldiers*, whom their commander had surrendered as prisoners of war, including those who had been wounded in the defence, *were butchered in cold blood by their captors.* The Cairo correspondent of the Associated Press adds that five of them were buried alive! Four of these were among the wounded; while the fifth was compelled to help dig the pits, and *then tumbled in and covered up.* The correspondent adds that Gen. Chalmers gave notice that no quarter was henceforth to be given to "*home-made* Yankees"—that is, to Southern Unionists, white or black. The correspondent of the *St. Louis Union* telegraphs that of three hundred and fifty colored soldiers who were engaged in the defence, but fifty-six are left alive, and that every one of their (white) officers was killed. Also, that the rebels went over the field the morning after the fight, and killed every wounded negro who was not already dead. Many of our wounded, he adds, were shot in the hospital, which was finally burned. Gen. Chalmers told the *Union's* correspondent that he had endeavored to stop this butchery of prisoners, but that *it was contrary to the policy of his Government to spare negro soldiers or their* (white) *officers, and that he considered that policy right.* Another rebel officer observed that *our white troops would have been protected from butchery, if they had not been found fighting side by side with negroes.*

AN ANONYMOUS REPORT: ACCOUNT OF REBEL ATROCITIES AT FORT PILLOW

The following account from the Republican Hartford, Connecticut, newspaper provides graphic details about the alleged offenses of the Confederate forces at Fort Pillow. The information in the article below comes from a federal government investigation into the incident.

Hartford Daily Courant, 6 May 1864

Immediately after the 2d flag of truce retired, the rebels made a rush from the positions they had so treacherously gained, and obtained possession of the fort, raising the cry of "No quarter." But little opportunity was allowed for resistance. Our troops, white and black, threw down their arms and sought to escape by running down the steep bluff near the fort, and secreting themselves behind the trees and logs, in the bushes, and under the brush, some even jumping into the river leaving only their heads above water. Then followed a scene of cruelty and murder without parallel in civilized warfare, which needed but the tomahawk and scalping knife to exceed the worst atrocities even committed by savages.

The rebels commenced an indiscriminate slaughter, sparing neither age nor sex, white nor black soldiers, or civilians. The officers and men seemed to vie with each other in the devilish work. Men, women, and children, wherever found, were deliberately shot down, beaten and hacked with sabres. Some of the children, not more than ten years old, were forced to stand up and face their murderers while being shot.

The sick and wounded were butchered without mercy, the rebels even entering the hospital buildings and dragging them out to be shot or killing them as they lay there unable to offer the least resistance. All over the hill side the work of murdering was going on. Numbers of our men were collected together in lines or groups, and shot. Some were shot while in the river, while others on the bank were shot and their bodies kicked in to the water, many of them still living, but unable to make exertions to save themselves from drowning.

Some of the rebels stood upon the top of the hill, at a short distance from its side, and called to our soldiers to come up to them, and as they approached shot them down in cold blood, and if their guns or pistols missed fire, forcing them to stand there until they were again prepared to fire. All around were heard cries of "no quarter;" "no quarter." "Kill the damn niggers." "Shoot them down." All who asked for mercy were answered by the most cruel taunts and sneers. Some were spared for a time, only to be murdered under circumstances of greater cruelty. One white soldier, who was wounded in the leg, so as to be unable to walk, was made to stand up while his tormentors shot him. Others who were wounded and unable to stand were held up and again shot. One negro who had been ordered by a rebel officer to hold his horse, was killed by him because he remonstrated. Another, a mere child, whom an officer had taken up behind him on his horse, was seen by Chalmers, who at once ordered him to put him down and shoot him, which was done.

The huts and tents in which many of the wounded had sought shelter, were set on fire, both that night and the next morning, while the wounded were still in them, those only escaping who were able to get themselves out, or who could prevail on others less injured to help them out, and even some of these trying to escape the flames, were met and shot down and had their brains beaten out.

One man was deliberately fastened down to the floor of a tent, face upward, by nails driven through his clothing and into the boards under him, so that he could not possibly escape, and then the tent was set on fire. Another was nailed to the side of a building outside the fort, and then the building set on fire and burned. The charred remains of five or six bodies were afterwards found, all but one so much disfigured and consumed by the flames that they could not be identified, and the identification of that one is not absolutely certain, although there can hardly be a doubt it was the body of Lieut. Albertson, quartermaster of the 13th Virginia cavalry and a native of Tennessee.

Several witnesses who saw the remains, and who were personally acquainted with him, testified that it is their firm belief that it was his body that was thus treated. These deeds of murder and cruelty closed when night came on only to be renewed the next morning, when the demons carefully sought among the dead lying about in the fort, for the wounded, and those they found were deliberately shot. Some of the dead and wounded were found the day of the massacre by the men from some of our gunboats, who were permitted to go on shore and collect the wounded and bury the dead.

The rebels themselves had made a pretense of burying a great many, but they had merely thrown them in the trenches and ditches about the fort, or the little holes and ravines on the hill side, covering them but partially with earth. Portions of heads, faces, hands and feet were found protruding through the earth, in every direction, and even when your committee visited the spot two weeks after, although parties of men had been sent on shore, from time to time, to bury the bodies unburied and re-bury the other, and were even then engaged in the same work, we found the evidences of the murder still most painfully. We saw bodies still unburied at some distance from the fort, of some sick men, who had been met fleeing from the hospital, and beaten down and murdered, and other bodies left where they had fallen. We could still see the hands and faces, white and black, protruding out of the ground whose graves had not been reached by those engaged in re-intering the victims, and though a great deal of rain had fallen within the two weeks, the ground on the side and at the foot of the bluff where the most of the murders had been committed, was still discolored by the blood of our brave but unfortunate men, and the logs and trees showed too plainly the evidences of the atrocities perpetuated there.

Many other instances of equally atrocious cruelty might be enumerated, but your committee feel compelled to refrain from giving here more of the heartsickening details. Of the men, from 300 to 400 are known to have been killed at Fort Pillow, of whom at least 300 were murdered in cold blood, after the fort was in possession of the rebels, and our men had thrown down their arms and ceased to offer resistance.

THOMAS N. DAY: THE FORT PILLOW MASSACRE

In a follow-up article about the massacre, the Hartford Daily Courant *criticizes the federal officers who visited Fort Pillow soon after the incident.*

Hartford Daily Courant, 7 May 1864 (Hartford, Conn.)

The report of the committee on the conduct of the war, fully confirms the newspaper statements relative to the civilities extended by a number of federal officers to the cutthroat Chalmers and a party of his associates, immediately after the massacre at Fort Pillow. On the morning following the capture, the gunboats Silver Cloud and New Era, and the transport Platte Valley, landed under flag of truce to recover the wounded and bury the dead. A number of rebel officers, Chalmers among them, went down to the landing, and some went on board the boats.—Several federal army officers on board the Platte Valley were ostentatious in the display of attentions to an enemy whose hands were hardly washed from the blood of their butchered comrades. Amid abundant and sickening evidences of the massacre, men clad in the federal uniform and decorated with badges of federal authority, were so lost to decency and shame, as to welcome the murderers of their associates to the sacred rights of hospitality. No instance of similar character has heretofore disgraced the history of the American people. The committee were unable to learn the names of the offenders.—They give the assurance, however, that no efforts will be spared to hunt them out and bring them to punishment. Nothing less than their dismissal and irretrievable disgrace, will satisfy either justice or the country. The facts connected with the massacre are now presented to the world stamped with official seal.—They stand forth in all their bloody and pitiless atrocity—melancholy proofs of the brutifying tendencies of slavery. It is to a bastard government waging war by such methods and sanctioning such atrocities, that the dainty aristocrats of England and France have proffered profusion of sympathy.

[*Confederate President Jefferson*] Davis, more than once, has appealed to high heaven to witness the justice of his cause. Let characteristic outgrowths of the two systems, today grappling in fierce combat, pronounce judgment between them. Where the Union arms have triumphed, the victors have fed the hungry and clothed the naked among the vanquished. For many months thousands of bitter enemies of the government have drawn their daily bread from its generous storehouses. The damning guilt that blackens the ruins of Fort Pillow, speaks for slavery. That is the kind of justice and humanity upon which the rebels would build their empire.

AN ANONYMOUS REPORT: BUTCHERY OF BLACK UNION SOLDIERS AT FORT PILLOW

This is additional information that appeared in the St. Louis Democrat *reporter's account of the capture of Fort Pillow and the "butchery" of the Union's black soldiers that followed.*

St. Louis Democrat, 20 April 1864

Dr. Fitch, surgeon of the fort, was taken prisoner, and through the influence of some rebel surgeons was released on his parole and came up with us. He confirms, from his own personal observation, the butchery of our soldiers by the rebels. He informed me that after the fort was taken the soldiers ran down the bluff to the river, throwing away their arms, holding up their hands, and crying out that they surrendered, but the rebels continued to fire on them from the bluff without the least regard to their cries. Dr Fitch says he saw twenty white soldiers paraded in line on the bank of the river, and when in line the rebels fired upon and killed all but one, who ran to the river and hid under a log, and in that condition was fired at a number of times and wounded. He says Major Bradford also ran down to the river, and after he told them he had surrendered, more than fifty shots were fired at him.

AN ANONYMOUS REPORT: SUGGESTED RETALIATION FOR MASSACRE AT FORT PILLOW

After the news of the massacre was spread in the North, citizens and editors across the country sought retribution for the Confederate atrocities. In this article from the Salem Observer, *the writer urges a form of retaliation that is more civilized than the "barbarism" witnessed at Fort Pillow.*

Salem Observer, 10 May 1864 (Salem, Mass.)

President Lincoln has promised that retaliation must follow the act of the rebels in the massacre at Fort Pillow. Every fair-minded man must concede that retaliation for such barbarities would be an act of justice, but there are many grave objections in the way of it. It must be remembered that the perpetrators stand low in the scale of civilization. They illustrate too truly the "barbarism of Slavery," and their acts of barbarism are not to be imitated. Our civilization, our self-respect, our position in the eyes of the world, prevent us from retaliation in *kind*. Other modes may possibly be resorted to, which though they may not possibly be so effectual, will be more in consonance with an enlightened age and country.

Such retaliation in kind, would bring counter retaliation and the cold blooded slaughter would be terrible in the eyes of the world. The nations of the old world would find justification in an attempt to prevent it, as they did at the time of the cruelties of the Turks to the Greeks. Let me give them no pretext for intervention.

We are willing to leave the whole matter to the wisdom and sagacity of our President. Perhaps he may deem it best for the black troops to be their own avengers in any future successes we may gain. Whatever he may decide to do of severity will be approved by the loyal men of the republic.

HENRY RAYMOND: HOW TO DEAL WITH FORT PILLOW BUTCHERS

The New York Times *suggests a retaliatory approach but one that deals specifically with the troops under Confederate General Forrest who committed the terrible acts at Fort Pillow and not randomly against innocent rebel soldiers.*

New York Times, 2 May 1864

We hear every day accounts from Tennessee, of [*Union Colonel*] GRIERSON having captured parties of FORREST's men. If they are true, and there is no reason to doubt them, he must have in his hands by this time nearly two hundred, if not more. It will not, or certainly ought not to be difficult for an active and vigilant officer such as he is to pick up three hundred and sixty of them, considering that they are all given to drink, and that as they are mostly occupied in plundering, they must scatter and straggle a good deal. Now if this is the case, does it not furnish a ready solution of our difficulty about retaliation for the Fort Pillow affair? It would certainly be very hard for us either to counsel or to witness the execution in cold blood of this number of Confederate prisoners who have had no share in this bloody deed. The butchery of a large number of men for a crime of which, though technically answerable for

it, they are not really guilty, is something no Christian man at the North likes to face, if it can possibly be avoided. We have not got down to the confederate level yet, and have no love of bloodshed for its own sake. But we doubt very much if there is anybody amongst us, or in any part of the civilized world, who would not hear with intense satisfaction that three hundred and sixty of FORREST's butchers had been strung up as fast as they were caught. They are the very who have done the deed, and the only men who, if simple justice was always attainable, ought to be made to suffer for it. We are satisfied, therefore, that if Col. GRIERSON will hang on the nearest tree every prisoner who falls into his hands, who shall proved to have belonged to FORREST's gang, he will relieve the Government from great embarrassment, set a valuable and striking example, and give satisfaction to the Northern public.

BY A CONNECTICUT WOMAN: LETTER WRITER SUGGESTS PROPER RETALIATION FOR FORT PILLOW MASSACRE

This suggestion of how to deal with the Fort Pillow massacre was sent to the New York Independent *by a reader from New Haven, Connecticut.*

New York Independent, 10 May 1864

We cannot pass over the Fort Pillow massacre in silence. As regards the cruelty to our soldiers and the insult to our government, we need not notice it; because deeds like this are always a greater injury to those who commit, than to those who suffer them. But this bloody act is another expression, on the part of the rebels, of their determination never to recognize the negroes as men, whatever uniform they may wear—always and everywhere to deny to them the rights of humanity. Now we have an answer that we can make to this. The Legislature of Connecticut will assemble soon. Let it respond to butchery on the Mississippi, by giving to black men the right of suffrage, and making them citizens. And let every other State, which has not yet yielded to the claims of justice, make the same response. Let the Government at Washington, that shrinks from a bloody retaliation, make answer by securing the abolition of slavery and the recognition of the black man as the equal, before the law, of the white. Such a response would make a deeper impression upon the rebels, than the execution of three hundred prisoners of war. By retaliating in kind, we should declare the black patriot to be the equal of the white traitor. But by making the black man a citizen, we should declare him to be *our* equal, to whom we restore rights which we have wrongfully withheld. Such a response would be a greater protection to the black soldier; for the rebels, whatever may be their policy, would feel a greater respect for him if he were a citizen of the government which he serves, and not a mere hired soldier, sent for the purpose of saving the white citizen from the perils of war. It would be a greater encouragement to him; for it would assure him that, wherever he could help to carry our flag, there he would be recognized as a man. It would do infinitely greater damage to the rebel cause; for it would be a blow aimed at its very corner-stone.

We must remember that, while we deny to these blacks the rights of men, we share in the guilt of those who slaughter them like cattle. The Government at Washington must remember that while it recognizes black men *only* as contrabands, it lends its sanction to Jefferson Davis in his treatment of them; it is not guiltless of the blood of our soldiers slain at Fort Pillow, nor will the most scrupulous retaliation of itself, suffice to wash away the stain.

AN ANONYMOUS REPORT: SAD CONDITION OF RELEASED UNION PRISONERS

This is an example of the typical amount of attention paid to the prison condition issue following the Fort Pillow massacre.

Baltimore American, 3 May 1864

BALTIMORE, Tuesday, May 3.—The flag-of-truce steamer *New-York* arrived at the Naval Academy wharf yesterday morning, from City Point, with 34 paroled officers and 364 men. Such was the condition of the latter that every man of them were admitted to the hospital. One hundred and fifty of them had to be carried from the boats on stretchers and cars. Their looks and words abundantly show that their miserable condition has been produced by starvation, and many are undoubtedly past the reach of medicine or nourishment. Among the officers is Col. Rose, of the Seventy-seventh Pennsylvania Regiment, who was the chief-engineer of the tunnel by which so many of our officers escaped in February last, he having been recaptured.

HENRY RAYMOND: WHAT CAN BE DONE FOR UNION PRISONERS?

The New York Times *devoted more space to the problem than many papers and provides a good overview of the history and context of the problem. The following article appeared about five months before the war ended and suggested that the public wanted the federal government to take some action regarding the issue.*

New York Times, 27 December 1864

It is worse than useless to disguise or ignore the fact that the condition of Union prisoners in rebel hands is exciting the profoundest feeling in the public mind, and that the action of the Government upon the subject is not regarded with satisfaction. This feeling is perfectly natural and not unreasonable. So far as the public has been informed of the action of the Government, that action does not seem adequate to the awful emergencies of the case. And while the whole subject is surrounded with difficulties, it is felt that nothing but absolute necessity—no question of etiquette, no fear of embarrassing concessions, no question of policy and expediency merely, should lead the Government to permit 40,000 of our soldiers to perish by starvation and exposure at the hands of their Southern captors.

How stands the case? We are at war with a people that have been half barbarized by slavery. The destructive influences of slavery upon the moral nature of masters, that JEFFERSON so vividly depicted in that memorable passage of his "Notes on Virginia," have wrought themselves fully out in the present Southern generation. The virus of the institution has been transmitted from father to son with an ever-growing rankness, until now it has eaten out every atom of the higher nature originally brought from European civilization. It has gradually converted the breed into a race like the Asiatic. They have a certain friendly complaisance, indeed a certain gentlemanly polish, well observed until their will is crossed; then flashes out the savage. What BONAPARTE said of the Russian is truer of the Southerner—a scratch will show the Cossack.

A civilized people is always at a disadvantage in conducting a war with a barbarous race like this. There is a civilized mode of warfare which all civilized nations recognize as binding, when engaged in the last awful appeal to arms. Its requirements are as definite as those of any part of international law. In all the modern wars between civilized nations they have been closely conformed to, with only here and there a casual exception quickly rectified. Military law ordinarily works smoothly and easily. But when a civilized nation wars with a barbarous one, there is sure to be trouble in this regard. Barbarous care nothing for civilized usages. They know no law but their own passions and will. They will not fight under civilized restraints, while their adversaries find it almost morally impossible to fight otherwise. Thus the warfare is made very unequal, and constantly subjects the civilized power to the most difficult dilemma, whether to submit to the worst outrage or also to act the savage.

Our Government undertook, at an early period of this war, to establish with the rebellion the civilized cartel in reference to the exchange of prisoners. The cartel recognizes the military *parole d'honneur*. But it was soon found that the rebellion had

not honor enough to keep true to any such parole. Thousands of the prisoners taken at Vicksburgh and elsewhere, and put on parole, were soon back again in the rebel ranks, fighting us with as much fury as ever, though not exchanged. There was no alternative but to stop paroling, and either to exchange prisoners, man for man, or not to exchange at all. The first of these two plans was tried; but immediately came the barbaric assumption of the rebels that prisoners of African descent were not men and should be permanently held by them as slaves. Of course our Government could not so barbarize itself as to agree to this. It felt that if exchanges could be effected only on that condition, they must cease altogether, that each side must retain its prisoners, treating them as the laws of civilization prescribe. But the Southern barbarians would not so treat our prisoners. While their soldiers in our hands were placed in salubrious and comfortable camps, were given wholesome and abundant rations and had every needful medical attention, our soldiers in their hands were driven into pestilential corrals, left exposed, without the least shelter, to all kinds of weather; were fed on food, generally repulsive, and always miserably scant, and had no medical care whatever. In this way, thousands of our soldiers, strong, when first taken, as any men in the land, have been brought to the grave. We have talked of the Cawnpore massacre by the Sepoys, of the atrocities of the Sarawak pirates, of the deeds done with the tomahawk and scalping-knife of North American Indians, but in no known part of the world, for the last century, has there been such fiendish cruelty as has been practiced upon our prisoners by these Southern rebels. Its peculiar nefariousness lies in the fact that it has been so cold-blooded. The fire of passion has had nothing to do with it. It has been kept up steadily, month after month. The difference between this conduct and that of the other savages, has been the difference between murdering inch by inch and murdering by one fell stroke.

But what shall be done? Are we to wait for these people to change their disposition? Absurd. They cannot change it, or, if at all, only from bad to worse. In the beginning, they could content themselves with maltreating the dead—with converting arm-bones into pipes, and skulls into drinking-cups. But, as the war went on, their savagery grew. It became sweeter to them to torture the living than to insult the dead. The barbarian spirit, left to itself, never improves.

Shall we try to check it by wholesale retaliation? It is useless to talk of that. There is too much Christian civilization here in the North to tolerate it. No argument or persuasion can make the Northern people consent that forty thousand human beings shall be systematically frozen and starved to death within the sound of their church-bells. There are moral impossibilities; this is one of them.

And yet, perhaps, considering the humane end to be gained, a limited extent of retaliation might be permitted. The true way is to try this. The rebel authorities in their extreme want of more soldiers, have said that they would exchange white prisoner for white prisoner. By this plan we should get out of their clutches all of our white prisoners, as we have a far larger number of theirs. Surely, it is better thus to save a portion of our prisoners, than to leave all, white and black, alike to perish. The present policy does the black man no good, and yet destroys the white man. Probably the true policy is to save the white man by exchange, and to protect the black man by retaliation. The rebels won't exchange by wholesale; we can't retaliate by the wholesale. Our course is to exchange so far as we can, and let retaliation take care of the rest. The rebels have one or two thousand of our black soldiers in their hands. Take a similar number of rebel prisoners, visit upon them the rigors which our colored soldiers are experiencing at the hands of the rebels. We believe that Northern civilization can by an effort, nerve itself up to that severity, in the reasonable hope that the rebels would soon conclude that it was not worth while to visit cruelties upon the blacks which had to be so rigorously paid for by their whites. Barbarians, though they cannot feel, can calculate. The rebel authorities probably can be reached in this way, so that in the end they will consent to a regular civilized system of exchanges, and conform to it tolerably well, through motives of self-interest. We think, at all events, that the experiment should be tried.

NOTES

1. Congress authorized black troops in 1862, but it was a year before the first blacks began to serve in the field as soldiers under white officers.

2. Yancey Hall, "Civil War Prison Camps Claimed Thousands," *National Geographic News* (July 2003), http://news.nationalgeographic.com/news/2003/07/0701_030701_civilwar prisons.html.

3. "The Capture of Fort Pillow," *St. Louis Democrat*, 20 April 1864.

4. Ibid.

FURTHER READINGS

Genoways, Ted, and Genoways, Hugh H. *A Perfect Picture of Hell: Eyewitness Accounts from Civil War Prisoners from the 12th Iowa.* Iowa City: University of Iowa Press, 2001.

Smith, John David. *Black Soldiers in Blue: African American Troops in the Civil War Era.* Chapel Hill: University of North Carolina Press, 2002.

Wagner, Margaret E.; Gallagher, Gary W.; and Finkelman, Paul (Eds.). *The Library of Congress Civil War Desk Reference.* New York: Simon & Schuster, 2002.

21

GRANT'S OVERLAND CAMPAIGN, 1864

In the winter of 1863, General Ulysses S. Grant became the commander of the entire Union army. He replaced General Henry Halleck, who remained with the Union army as Grant's chief-of-staff. Grant chose to make his headquarters with General George Meade, the head of the Army of the Potomac who had successfully defeated Confederate General Robert E. Lee at Gettysburg. As general-in-chief, Halleck was mostly desk bound in Washington. Grant did not want to leave the battlefield, so when he joined General Meade, he assumed command of his troops as well. The Army of the Potomac was quickly nicknamed "Grant's army." General William T. Sherman took over Grant's position as the head of the Union forces in the West.

Grant's first campaign against Lee in the East was formally called the Overland Campaign (sometimes called The Wilderness Campaign), and it opened with a May 1864 battle in The Wilderness, an area known to both sides from the Battle of Chancellorsville. Grant's battle plan was fairly straightforward—he would crush the rebel forces with his superior advantage of men and supplies. When Grant first assumed command of the entire Union army, he managed to break through the red tape that had kept a significant number of federal soldiers from the front. By simplifying the deployment process and better utilizing the available federal resources, Grant managed to ensure that a steady supply of field reinforcements would be available for the federal forces that would fight in the Overland Campaign. He knew his army was larger, and his reserves deeper, than General Lee's.[1]

After Grant organized his armies, his overall plan involved connecting the Union's forces in the East and West to overwhelm the Confederacy. He instructed General Sherman to overpower Confederate General Joseph E. Johnston and get as far into the Confederate heartland as possible while exacting terrible damage. This led to Sherman's successful campaign to Atlanta (see Chapter 22) and eventually to his famous "march" to Savannah, Georgia, at the end of 1864 (see Chapter 23).

Sherman embarked on his Atlanta Campaign while Grant was preparing the Overland Campaign.

While Sherman was busy in the South, Grant's forces would directly challenge Lee's army in the East. Grant reportedly told General Meade that "wherever Lee's army goes, you will go also," so that the federal forces could keep pressure on Lee and prevent the rebel troops from uniting its east and west forces. Complementing these two main efforts were some smaller offensives that included Union General Benjamin Butler's advance against Richmond and General Franz Sigel's move through the Shenandoah Valley toward Staunton and the lines of the Virginia & Tennessee Railroads. Butler's and Sigel's forces were to cut rail communications to General Lee so that he would not be able to receive reinforcements from smaller, secondary Confederate forces in those areas.[2]

Grant's Overland Campaign against Lee began on 4 May; the first battle began on 5 May at The Wilderness and lasted for two days. The battle was bloody—the federal forces lost 17,666 men, while the Confederate losses totaled 7,750. The battle was tactically a draw, and unlike the Union generals that came before him, Grant did not retreat. After the fighting ended at The Wilderness, Grant's forces moved on to their next encounter with the rebels at Spotsylvania Court House. The battle lasted for two weeks, beginning the day after the fighting at The Wilderness. Once again, losses on both sides were heavy—Grant lost about 18,000 men, Lee about 12,000—and Grant continued to move toward Richmond on 21 May, after he disengaged his forces at Spotsylvania. If Lee's objective had been to keep federal forces out of central Virginia, he was losing; but by delaying Grant's forces for two weeks at Spotsylvania, Lee managed to give other Confederate forces time to successfully resist the Union efforts of Butler and Sigel.

On 23 May the fighting resumed near the North Anna River where the federal forces were not able to breach Lee's defensive line. For the next eight days, fighting would continue in various locations until on 1 June Union General Philip Sheridan and his cavalry managed to seize the vital crossroads at Old Cold Harbor, only 10 miles from Richmond. Both sides converged on the area, and Lee's forces spent the entire day of 2 June constructing a strong line of fortifications.

The battle began on 3 June when Generals Grant and Meade attacked in a series of frontal assaults. The federal forces were slaughtered, suffering nearly 7,000 casualties, compared to the Confederates' 1,500. For ten days the two sides dug in, and on 14 June Grant decided to shift his plan of attack. By 15 June all of the federal forces headed south of the James River to threaten Petersburg (see Chapter 25). Cold Harbor was a decisive victory for the Confederates, but because Lee's forces lacked the strength to take any initiative, they had to wait for the next federal attack.

Although Grant did not manage to get to Richmond in this campaign because of the blunders by Butler and Sigel and his own error in charging the Confederates at Cold Harbor, it was largely considered a success. It exacted a terrible loss of life on both sides, but the federal forces could recover; the Confederates increasingly could not.

The press actively covered the battles that comprised the Overland Campaign. General Grant was much less antagonistic to the press than General Halleck and generally "trusted the gentlemen of the press to do the right thing, unless and until someone demonstrated otherwise"; he left reporters alone. He did agree to the expulsion of a *New York Times* correspondent who was caught eavesdropping on Generals Grant and Meade on 6 May, but the blame for that expulsion was publicly and unfairly placed on General Meade who had for months been complaining about inaccuracies in Northern newspaper reports about him and the war.[3]

Much of Meade's trouble with the press included the fact that General Grant was quite popular among Northern reporters and the Northern public because of his success in the West and because of his laissez-faire approach with the press. When he arrived in Washington in early 1864 to assume his new position as general-in-chief, the unassuming Grant received warm welcomes and embarrassingly public displays of gratitude, which reportedly made Grant uncomfortable.

THOMAS N. DAY: MYSTIFICATION OF REBELS—GRANT KEEPS MILITARY PLANS SECRET

Although Grant did not exclude reporters from battlefields, he took precautions to keep military plans secret. This article highlights the military secrecy that preceded the Overland Campaign and applauds General Grant for it.

Hartford Daily Courant, 5 May 1864 (Hartford, Conn.)

In one important particular the spring campaign of 1864 presents a remarkable contrast to all that have preceded. Heretofore the plans of the federal commanders have been known and openly discussed in Washington, in the newspapers, and of course in Richmond. Now nothing is divulged and no questions are asked. Whatever information is communicated to the public relative to the movements of troops, is gleaned from Southern newspapers. Even these, usually so well posted through rebel spies, are at a loss to conjecture where and how Gen Grant intends to strike his first blow. In face of the vast concentration of strength on the north bank of the Rapidan, some of the Richmond journals insist that this preparation is an ostentatious feint, that the real campaign is to be opened in Georgia, and that Atlanta is the objective point. In Virginia the rebels are puzzled to divine whether Gen. Grant purposes to assail Lee's fortifications in front, or to flank his position above or below, or to remain stationary in his present encampment till columns advancing on Richmond from other quarters open the campaign by a blow in the rear. They are equally uncertain as to the destination of Burnside, and the route to be taken by the army at Fortress Monroe under Gen Smith. The secrecy which Gen. Grant has been able to maintain is an omen of good import. Although our accounts from the army of the Potomac are few and brief, it is the centre of intense activity. For many weeks it has been gaining rapidly in strength and discipline, and when it starts will advance with a momentum never attained by it before.

CHARLES HALE: PRAISE FOR GRANT

This untitled article, published during the fighting at Spotsylvania, gives a glimpse of why the North liked Grant so much. He was considered trustworthy, deliberate, and cool by this writer. Continual editorials and reports like these bolstered Grant's reputation in the North.

Boston Daily Advertiser, 13 May 1864

Stripped of all the inevitable exaggerations, before which even "Solferino and Waterloo "pale," the last few days have amply justified the predictions of those who looked for the heaviest fighting of the war this spring. From the moment of the great movement across the Rapidan, incessant marching and fighting have been the order of the day,—fighting of a desperate and bloody sort, a series of battles some of which will rank in the first class, fought between armies as large as those with which Napoleon usually operated, and each contesting the ground with a tenacity which is a worthy subject of national pride, whether shown on the one side or the other. The seven days' battles on the Peninsula, hitherto our most

striking example of continuous fighting, will now take a secondary place beside this tremendous struggle, in which entire armies come into line day after day, to renew the contests
which shattered their ranks in the last encounter. And military history in the old world will present few examples of protracted struggles of such extraordinary fierceness. It is the
wrestling of giants, at which the continent quivers and by
which the fate of a nation is to be wrought out.

Of the general results of this appalling struggle, the language of General Grant quoted by the Secretary of War
doubtless gives a just and cool estimate, as well as a most advantageous impression of the man who makes it. Having
"ended the sixth day of very heavy fighting," he says, "the result to this time is much in our favor. Our losses have been
heavy," but I "think the loss of the enemy must be greater."
In these few words we get out of the atmosphere of bravado
and exaggeration which dictates so many of the unofficial accounts. We hear nothing of a "race for Richmond," nothing of
having "crushed" Lee, or of "perfectly bewildering" him,
nothing of "routing" the rebel army, all of which has been
made so stale by repetition in campaign after campaign. We
have the sound professional judgment of a man who has an
immense personal stake in correctly judging of every step of
the contest, that the general result is much in our favor. He
does not pretend that he has not found a foe worthy of his
steel, nor that the edge of battle does not sometimes waver
ominously, nor that he has not hard fighting still to do before
his enemy can be fairly said to have been crushed and deci-

sively defeated. He will say neither more nor less than that
the general result is good. The opinion is cool, deliberate and
trustworthy.

Undoubtedly this result falls short of what most of us had
been led to anticipate. The enemy has been found in apparently stronger force than had been expected, and the prepon-
derance on our own side is less decisive than was expected.
Instead of the easy victory which was hoped for, we are having the sequel of the great contests of the Peninsula, of Antietam and Gettysburg. But after all, with an enemy filled with
all the energy that desperation can give, and maddened at the
thought of failing to foil us as he has done heretofore, our
army has steadily gained ground. It takes no steps backward,
but after every fight pushes the enemy still harder, over-
matching his endurance by persevering energy, and advancing by slow but well marked degrees to the great object of its
efforts,—his destruction. If the success is less rapid than was
hoped, it is still substantial, encouraging and honorable.

The duty of all patriots then is epitomized in that sturdy
resolution of the Lieutenant-General, "to fight it out on this
line if it takes all summer. That is the spirit undismayed and
resolute, that admits of no possibility of defeat or change of
purpose. If it is to be a struggle of endurance, we must be
ready to endure to the end, shaken from our equilibrium neither by depression nor elation confident of the result, generous to the errors of our leaders, trusting their will and tried
capacity, and above all confiding in that supreme justice
which will not let our cause fail of success.

THOMAS N. DAY: FALL OF RICHMOND IS NEAR

*This early enthusiasm for the Union attack in Virginia refocuses attention on Richmond. Once again,
the North jumped the gun on assuming that Richmond was about to fall.*

Hartford Daily Courant, 9 May 1864 (Hartford, Conn.)

The intelligence this morning from all quarters is of the
most cheering character. The clouds that for three long and
wearisome years have overhung the Republic, are dissolving.
Gens. Grant, Butler and Sherman, advanced simultaneously
last week, and each one thus far has achieved brilliant and
substantial success. The army of the Potomac having crossed
the Rapidan without serious opposition, encountered the enemy on Thursday. Lee massed his troops and made a desperate effort to get between our forces and the fords of the river.
In this he was completely foiled. On Friday General Grant renewed the contest, making a furious attack upon the enemy
in full strength. Lee was driven three miles, leaving his dead
and wounded on the field.

Richmond is threatened on the south also, General Butler
having effected a landing at City Point, advanced directly on
Petersburg. The rebel army operating in the quarter was se-

verely repulsed. Having set fire to Petersburg, the routed column retired northward toward Richmond. General Butler
now has possession of the Southern approaches to the rebel
capital. The railroad line leading southwest has also been cut
in several places. Richmond is thus completely isolated from
the rest of the confederacy. Not a barrel of provisions can be
carried into the city, and none of the military stores and machinery accumulated there can be removed to a place of
safety. Our gunboats and monitors are above the bar at Harrison's Landing, ready to co-operate with the land forces.

General Grant will push his pursuit rapidly. Lee will be allowed no opportunity to slip away so as to concentrate all his
strength against Butler. The pursuit will be as rapid as the
flight. In a few days we may reasonably hope to see the rebel
capital closely invented. It must soon fall from starvation.
The plan of the campaign contemplates the capture of the

entire rebel army, with all its munitions, equipments and stores. At the same time Gens. Couch, Sigel and Averill, are moving down the Shenandoah valley, while Hooker's corps is aiming at a vulnerable point in the Old Dominion. Not less than three hundred thousand men are closing in from different directions upon Richmond. A few days more of such work will give its death wound to the rebellion.

THOMAS N. DAY: ACCOUNT OF FIGHTING IN THE WILDERNESS

This article discusses the fighting at The Wilderness on 7 May, the last day of the battle there. It incorrectly implies that only Lee had formally withdrawn from the battle. Actually, both sides withdrew to refocus their efforts and continue fighting at Spotsylvania.

Hartford Daily Courant, 11 May 1864 (Hartford, Conn.)

In the battle of Friday, as well as of the day before, the enemy were the attacking party. Lee hoped by sudden and unexpected attacks, in overwhelming numbers, to crush our advance before our reserves could come up. On more than one previous occasion this system of tactics had proved eminently successful, but in this instance it failed. The dense wood in which the battle was fought, gave Lee a great advantage, enabling him to mass his troops unobserved, to disguise their preliminary movements, and to hurl them without warning upon different positions of our line.

On Friday, the battle lasted fourteen hours. Early in the morning Gen. Grant's forces were in position and ready to take the initiative, but were forestalled by the enemy. A quarter before five o'clock, Ewell attacked Sedgwick on the right, and Longstreet attacked Hancock on the left simultaneously. In both quarters the enemy were repulsed. An hour later, Gen Hancock's corps advanced, speedily driving the enemy from their works, forcing them back a considerable distance and capturing several hundred prisoners. A little before nine o'clock, our right advanced to attack the enemy, but were stopped by a marsh intervening between them and the fortified ridge on which the rebels were posted. Frustrated by this natural impediment, they returned to their former ground. At eleven o'clock, the enemy advanced on the centers, commanded by Warren, and on the right Sedgwick repulses them. Warren, sends forward two divisions from the left of the centre, which crowd the enemy for some distance before them, but are finally driven back in confusion. While attempting to rally these troops, Gen. Wadsworth is killed. The rebels are brought to a halt by our entrenched line, and in turn driven back.

Till 5 P.M. there was little further fighting. At half past 5, Hancock on the left is attacked with great energy. A portion of his line is forced and thrown into confusion. Rallying they make a furious charge upon Longstreet's column, one federal brigade taking it on the flank, and a second time repulse it with great slaughter. No further demonstrations were made against our left.

Meanwhile perfect quietude prevailed along our center and right. Just before dark, however, they fell with great violence upon our extreme right, overwhelming two brigades. General Seymour, late from Florida, and General Shaler were captured, though great credit is awarded to both for their gallantry. Through the exertions of General Sedgwick and his officers, the enemy were held at bay and prevented from reaping any advantage from their preliminary success in this attack. The tow brigades which fled in panic, had just been assigned to the sixth corps from Milroy's division. While stationed in the Shenandoah valley, the entire command of Milroy was more famous for blundering than for fighting qualities. Little else could have been expected from troops trained under such regimen.

The fighting of Friday was very severe, and on the whole the balance of success rested with the federal arms. The enemy lost heavily. During the night Lee hastily withdrew—thus affording good evidence of his inability to renew the contest on the following day.

AN ANONYMOUS REPORT: UNION VICTORY IN THE WILDERNESS

This article suggests a Union victory at The Wilderness. It also notes the death of Union General James Wadsworth. Union General Alexander Hays was also killed.

Hartford Daily Courant, 10 May 1864 (Hartford, Conn.)

THE GREAT VICTORY!

Official Confirmation
Desperate Fighting

WASHINGTON, May 9—10:45 A.M.—To Major General John A. Dix. New York—We have this morning intelligence by scouts direct from the army as late as Saturday evening, but no official reports. The general results may be stated as success to our arms. The fighting on Friday was on both sides the most desperate known in modern times. I deeply regret to say that the country will have to mourn the death of that accomplished soldier, Brigadier General Wadsworth, who was struck in the forehead by a ball at the head of his command, while leading them against one of the enemy's strongest positions. His remains are in our hands in charge of Colonel Sharpe.

CHARLES HALE: REPORT OF GRANT'S CAMPAIGN IN THE WILDERNESS

This article in the Boston Daily Advertiser *shows how effective Grant's campaign strategy was after the Battle of The Wilderness when troops were heading for Spotsylvania Court House.*

Boston Daily Advertiser, 14 May 1864

The news from General Grant, of which we present full details this morning from our special correspondent and from other sources, is of the most gratifying character. It appears that no fighting of importance took place on Wednesday, but that on Thursday the contest was renewed, and one of the most fearful battles of the whole desperate series was fought. General Hancock's corps made a little after daylight one of those brilliant charges for which his name has become famous, storming the centre of the rebel line, capturing their entrenchments and taking prisoners by the suddenness of his assault the entire division of General Edward Johnson, with a large number of pieces of artillery. A little later General Wright's corps also moved upon the rebel works, and also made valuable captures. Still later in the day General Warren's corps made a charge upon the rebel right, but was repulsed with a heavy loss, estimated at two thousand men. The battle was not renewed during the day for reasons given in our despatch, but a general advance was ordered to take place yesterday morning. The rebel commander, however, warned by the terrible losses he had suffered on the preceding day, withdrew his army during the night, and was retreating southward. Notwithstanding the difficulties of pursuit through roads made marshes by the storm and by men worn out with a week of fighting, our army was following up the rebels closely. Our captures of prisoners during the campaign are now estimated at 12,000, and of cannon in Thursday's battle at not much less than forty.

A general view of the military situation at all points of the wide field on which operations are now going on, develops much which is encouraging to the friends of the Union cause, and very little which need occasion them misgiving. The principal one of our armies under the personal supervision of the Lieutenant-General, after eight days of continuous fighting, the most desperate and bloody in the whole record of the war, is now pressing close on the retreat of its crippled and defeated adversary. After triumphantly repelling for several days the most furious and determined assaults, it has during the present week itself assumed the offensive,—and as the result we see an entire rebel division captured with its major-general, brigade commanders and subordinate officers, its thirty or forty pieces of artillery, and several thousand prisoners of the flower of Lee's army. We see also the rebel commander tacitly acknowledging the severity of the losses which his army has sustained in the great battles of Tuesday and Thursday by abandoning the position which he has been striving to defend, and falling back towards Richmond before General Grant's advancing columns. Even the road of his retreat, however, is not left open to him. While our infantry and artillery have been pouring deadly volleys into the ranks of the rebels at Spotsylvania Court House, our cavalry have been busy in their rear, destroying large amounts of trains and supplies, and tearing up miles of the track of the railroad connecting the rebel army with the capital which it is defending.

The auxillary army which is playing the part next in importance to the force of General Meade in the combined movement against Richmond, under command of General Butler, is moving on the south bank of the James river. It has secured itself a fortified base in the peninsula of Bermuda Hundreds, a position admirably qualified for defence, and at last accounts, which come up to Thursday of this week, was moving westward in the direction of the railroad between Petersburg and Richmond. This line of rebel communication was already severed by our cavalry advance several days ago, and it is understood that the forces of Beauregard, which were hurrying to the defence of Richmond were severed in the transit by the sudden interruption of the road. A strong cavalry force under General Kautz sent out last week with a roving commission, has not yet been heard from, and will probably make its next report from North Carolina, after having done an effective work is the destruction of the railroad lines south of Petersburg. The Army of the Potomac has a co-operating force on its right as well as on its left, which is doubtless doing equally well the work assigned to it. A strong column commanded by General Sigel began its march down the Shenandoah Valley some time before the advanced pickets of the grand army crossed the Rapidan. The operations of this force have not been announced from day to day, but the public confidence in the character of its commander and of the regiments which compose it begets an assurance that its record will be a creditable one. A despatch was received at General Grant's headquarters on Thursday announcing that General Sigel had reached a point twenty-six miles below Charlottesville without meeting any rebel force of importance, and had destroyed the railroad communication between that point and Lynchburg, and also the track of the railroad leading to Gordonsville. These successes, if confirmed, will be a most important element in contributing to the triumphant conclusion of the campaign in Virginia.

AN ANONYMOUS REPORT: ACCOUNT OF FIGHTING AT COLD HARBOR

This account of the early fighting at the Battle of Cold Harbor mistakenly calls the location Coal Harbor. The report was pieced together from various sources and several correspondents and gives a glimpse of how the federal forces were mowed down in their early advances against the rebels.

Boston Daily Advertiser, 6 June 1864

FROM THE ARMY OF THE POTOMAC
THE FIGHTING ON WEDNESDAY AND FRIDAY
RUMORS FROM RICHMOND

Another correspondent with the 18th army corps says of the fight at Coal Harbor:—"The enemy were in heavy force between Coal Harbor and Gaines Mills, strongly intrenched on the edge of a dense wood. They had rifle pits and earthworks thrown up at half-past four, and the troops were in three lines of battle at five, when skirmishing commenced. A battery of 20 pounders opened fire on the rebels. At half-past five an order was received for both the 6th and 7th corps to charge the rebel works in front. Brook's and Deven's divisions pushed through the woods and poured like a tornado over the open field. The rebels opened with grape, canister and a heavy musketry fire, and the first line was badly cut up. The second mingled with it and almost immediately after a wild, inspiring cheer rang out above every other sound as the rebels were driven pell-mell from their works and through the woods.

"The rebels were rallied behind their reserves and attempted to recapture their last position. They rushed forward but were received with no close and murderous a fire of artillery and musketry, that they broke and fled in confusion. Again and again they rallied to the charge, but only returned to greater slaughter.

The same correspondent says 510 rebel soldiers belonging to the 16th and 18th Georgia Volunteers came into our lines at daybreak on the 2d. They say they are tired of fighting, and don't want any more of it. They advised our men to go in and fight it out, as this was the last fight for Richmond, and we could take it this time. They represent the rebel army as becoming each day more and more demoralized with constant reverses." The Herald's Fortress Monroe despatch of June 3d says Kautz was to have started on an important mission on the night of the 2d. Its destination was a point of most vital importance to the enemy and will assist Grant materially. A northern machinist from Richmond reports Lee to have fallen back into the Richmond intrenchments on the 1st. The Mayor of Richmond has been placed in Castle Thunder for proposing to surrender the city instead of burning it as was proposed. Every man and boy, and even foreign subjects, were pressed into the service.

The rebel papers complain of [*General*] Joe Johnston [*facing Sherman in Atlanta*], and say he is whipped.

Lee is sick and confined to his bed in Richmond. Grant has kept him so busy for the past month that he has had to succumb to great fatigue.

A Coal Harbor despatch of the 3d to the Herald says:—"A general attack was ordered along the whole line this morning, resulting in the fiercest fight of the campaign. The left of Hancock's corps, after a desperate resistance, turned the enemy's left, carrying a portion of their main line, capturing guns, colors and many prisoners, but unfortunately were unable to hold the ground or bring off the guns. The battle still rages with the promise of a bloody day."

A Fortress Monroe despatch of the 3d to the Herald says a despatch was received from Baldy Smith to the effect that the rebels attacked his forces with three columns, but were driven off after a desperate fight. Smith is reported to have captured 600 rebels. Heavy firing was going on and Grant was pursuing the enemy at every point.

HENRY RAYMOND: REBEL RESOLVE AT COLD HARBOR

Early signs of the rebels' strength and lack of willingness to surrender at Cold Harbor are shown in this short excerpt from the New York Times.

New York Times, 6 June 1864

The fighting in these various affairs [*at Cold Harbor*] must have been more severe than might appear to some readers of the dispatches; for the Adjutant-General reports the loss in killed, wounded and missing, during the three days' operation around Cold Harbor, at as high a number as seven thousand five hundred.

There have been quite a number of these heavy blows given and taken by both armies during the last week. In every one of them, we believe, the rebels have been forced to give way, while we have steadily been acquiring new ground and better positions. They have demonstrated, however, that LEE holds his main line strongly and persistently, even though he be not prepared to fall upon GRANT with his whole army. The contest for Richmond bids fair to be prolonged and desperate.

EDWARD CRAPSEY: A FLAG OF TRUCE—THE PROCEEDINGS UNDER IT

One sign that the fighting was about to come to an end came in this excerpt from the Philadelphia Inquirer, *which reported a brief truce.*

Philadelphia Inquirer, 11 June 1864

COLD HARBOR, Tuesday, June 7—Night. The most interesting event of to-day was a truce of two hours, between six and eight o'clock this evening, for the purpose of burying the dead and getting off wounded, if any should be found on the ground between our own and rebel lines. Flags of truce had been exchanged for the purpose of making negotiations on this subject yesterday, but up to last night nothing had been effected. . . .

Although it has been comparatively quiet for two or three days past, it was a strange and unusual thing to hear for two hours no sound of war.

HENRY J. WINSER: ACCOUNT OF GRANT'S ABANDONMENT OF HIS POSITION AT COLD HARBOR

This New York Times *article tells of Grant's abandonment of Cold Harbor to head to Petersburg. Grant's evacuation was completed on 15 June.*

New York Times, 17 June 1864

The Evacuation of the Position at Cold Harbor—The Movement of the Eighteenth Corps—The Enemy do Not Interfere—His Suspicions Awakened.
From Our Special Correspondent

WHITE HOUSE, Va., Monday, June 13, 1864. The Army of the Potomac is again on the move. That it was about to retire from the position in front of Cold Harbor has been evident for some days to the most superficial observer. The immense trains of forage, ammunition, commissariat, and other supplies began two days since to pass to the rear, and their thousands of wheels plowing through the soft and dry roads have covered the country with a pall of gray dust, hiding everything and choking everybody. . . . The prospect is now that operations will be conducted from a base on the James River.

It has been fully understood that GEN. GRANT was determined not to waste the lives of our brave army uselessly in further assaulting the formidable works of the enemy near Cold Harbor, against which the army "butted" with a terrible shock on the 1st and 3rd inst, and there has been patient waiting for the developments of time.

Yesterday the word came to move. . . . The enemy must have had a shrewd suspicion that GRANT intended to change his base. For several nights past there has been a very perceptible diminution of his camp fires, and other indications that his lines at Cold Harbor were materially weakened.

NOTES

1. Curt Johnson and Mark McLaughlin, *Civil War Battles* (New York: Crown Publishers, 1977), 107–108.

2. Ibid., 108.

3. Brayton Harris, *Blue & Gray in Black & White* (Washington, D.C.: Brasseys, 1999), 285.

FURTHER READINGS

Gallagher, Gary W. *The Wilderness Campaign*. Chapel Hill: University of North Carolina Press, 1997.

Grant, Ulysses S. *Personal Memoirs: Ulysses S. Grant*. Introduction by Geoffrey Perrett. New York: Modern Library, 1999.

Harris, Brayton. *Blue & Gray in Black & White*. Washington, D.C.: Brasseys, 1999.

Johnson, Curt, and McLaughlin, Mark. *Civil War Battles*. New York: Crown Publishers, 1977.

22

BATTLE OF ATLANTA, JULY—SEPTEMBER 1864

As noted in the last chapter, when Union General-in-Chief Ulysses S. Grant reorganized the federal armies, he put General William T. Sherman in charge of the federal forces fighting in the West. His overall battle plan to win the war involved connecting the Union's forces in the East and West to overwhelm the Confederacy. So while Grant pursued his Overland Campaign in the East, General Sherman was instructed to overwhelm Confederate General Joseph E. Johnston and get as far into the Confederate heartland as possible while exacting terrible damage. Sherman's primary target was Atlanta, and he began his march to capture the Southern city in early May.

Atlanta was important to the Confederacy for many reasons. The state of Georgia produced the most cotton of any Southern state, and cotton was the primary cash crop of the South. Georgia was second only to Virginia in the number of rails that ran across the state, and Atlanta was the crossroads of the state's four main railroads. Atlanta's railroad functions helped keep the Confederacy afloat—it sent iron to arm the river fleets, it distributed food to the rebel armies in Virginia and Tennessee, and it sent reinforcements in the form of Georgia troops.[1]

After a strong federal victory at Chattanooga, Tennessee, in November 1863, federal troops established a base there from which Sherman's march to Atlanta would begin. Chattanooga was about 100 miles northwest of Atlanta. After the loss of Chattanooga the Confederate forces retreated about 25 miles south to Dalton, Georgia. In December 1863, General Joseph E. Johnston took over command of the rebel forces, which were in a bad state. Morale was low, and reportedly hundreds of men were deserting from the army every week. When Johnston assumed command, he restored morale by granting furloughs for men to go home and rest with their families; he held mock battles to help bring the army back to fighting shape; he offered amnesty for deserters who returned to the army; and he gathered fresh fruits and vegetables from the area to help improve the diet of the troops. By the spring of 1864, Johnston's troops were ready for battle. They numbered 62,000, including 2,000 cavalry.[2]

Sherman's troops were much stronger. Before the start of the Atlanta Campaign, General Sherman had three primary armies of about twenty infantry supervised by Generals George Thomas, John Schofield, and James McPherson. His men numbered 106,000 including four cavalry divisions and more than 250 field guns. Under orders from Grant to begin his campaign in coordination with the Overland Campaign, General Sherman began his march to Atlanta on 7 May 1864.[3]

Sherman's first target was Dalton, Georgia, where General Johnston had set up his primary defensive position. By 9 May, after Sherman, McPherson, Schofield, Thomas, and the Union cavalry had descended on Dalton from all directions (and fought several actions around an area called Rocky Face Ridge), Johnston withdrew from Dalton without a decisive engagement. Reinforced by Confederate General Leonidas Polk, the rebel defensive position was now set up in Resaca, Georgia. Fighting ensued at Resaca from 13 May to 16 May, and Johnston eventually withdrew further south after Sherman threatened an envelopment similar to the one he completed at Dalton.

By continually changing the direction of his approaches to attack Johnston and by successfully turning the Confederate lines, Sherman continued to defeat the rebel forces in skirmishes and move rapidly toward Atlanta. After successfully marching through Rome, Adairsville, Kingston, and Dallas, Sherman's troops had now arrived at Pine Hill, which was about 25 miles from Atlanta.[4] On 14 June, Confederate General Polk was killed in the fighting there. By the end of June, General Johnston had taken up defensive position at Kennesaw Mountain, which was challenged by Sherman on 27 June. Sherman launched a full frontal assault, believing that Johnston had stretched his line too thin, but was repulsed, suffering one of the few significant Union losses in the campaign. Sherman did not advance past this area until early July.

On 17 July, after suffering many publicly reported losses at the hands of General Sherman, General Johnston was relieved of command and replaced by General John B. Hood. After more fighting outside of Atlanta and after suffering heavy losses in the Battle of Peach Tree Creek, Hood withdrew the Confederate forces into the city of Atlanta to defend it. Sherman mistakenly read Hood's retreat as an abandonment of the city and ordered General McPherson's troops into the city from the south and east. On 22 July the Battle of Atlanta ensued, and McPherson was killed. Although the federal forces did not take the city and suffered a loss of 3,700, the damage to the Confederates was worse, having lost 8,500.[5] July ended with General Hood holding Atlanta with 37,000 infantry, reinforced by 5,000 Georgia state militiamen. Sherman's troops now numbered 85,000 and had only one strong cavalry division remaining. Because of McPherson's death, Sherman had to reorganize his command.

Both sides maneuvered throughout August. After a series of battles around important railroad locations where the Union troops managed to sever the rail lines in and out of the city, and after the culmination of months of devastating troop losses, General Hood finally evacuated Atlanta. On his way out, his rebels set fire to train cars filled with ammunition and set off explosions that seriously damaged the inner city. Hood and the rebel forces then relocated to Lovejoy's Station, where Sherman's troops pursued them. After a few days of fighting, Sherman realized the Confederate defensive concentration was too strong, and the federal forces returned to Atlanta on 4 September. Sherman's army occupied Atlanta for two months and began preparations for its march to Savannah, Georgia, commonly called "Sherman's March" (see

Chapter 23). After that, the army began its march northward through the Carolinas.

The significance of the capture of Atlanta was great. As the *New York Times* reported,

> Four months of constant and vigorous campaigning, a contested march of full two hundred miles, ten pitched battles, and two score of lesser engagements by night and day make up the price we paid for Atlanta. It is worth them all; for our highest estimate will not outreach the magnitude of the solid fact. Considering simply the military results of Sherman's campaign, in the first place, it has worsted and nearly destroyed the second army of the Confederacy. Fifty thousand men have dropped from the thinned ranks of that army [since Dalton]. . . . Next, Atlanta is ours. . . . But the downfall of Atlanta does not mean the occupation of that city alone. It includes the assured possession of contiguous and valuable cities and regions—of Rome, Rossville, and Marietta—where are manufactured guns, ammunition, cotton, and woolen clothing in abundance. In one word, Atlanta is at the centre of a network of towns and villages which have furnished forth half its war material to the entire Confederacy, from the Rappahannock [in Virginia] to the Rio Grande [in Texas]. This valuable region is now all ours.[6]

The press was generally favorable to Sherman's campaign, with the exception of the short stagnant period between the end of July and the capture of the city in September. Some of the editorial coverage of the Atlanta Campaign was purely political. Republican newspapers wanted the campaign to succeed because it would help President Lincoln's reelection campaign. Consequently, Democratic newspapers knew that if the campaign were perceived as a failure, it would help the chances of their candidate, former Union Army of the Potomac General George McClellan. Although all papers reported evenly about the battles, usually based on reports that came from western correspondents (particularly those who wrote for papers in Cincinnati, Chicago, and St. Louis), their editorial responses to the campaign's success prior to the September occupation of the city did vary.

General Sherman did not do much to help the press produce reports about him or his campaigns. His long history of dealing with reporters began primarily at the Battle of Shiloh. It left him believing that correspondents were "gossips" and that they were "tempted to prophesy events and state facts which, to an enemy, reveal a purpose in time to guard against it. Moreover, they are always bound to see the facts colored by the partisan or political character of their own patrons, and thus bring army officers into the political controversies of the day."[7]

The examples of the reporting of Sherman's Atlanta Campaign and subsequent capture of the city that appear below are not overtly political. But all come from Republican newspapers, and all work to make the significance of Sherman's campaign clear to Northern readers. It would be Sherman's success in Atlanta that would eventually help President Lincoln win a second term in office (see Chapter 24).

HENRY RAYMOND: THE CAMPAIGN IN GEORGIA

This early report of Sherman's successful march gives the reader context and background about Georgia and its significance to the Confederacy. It recognizes the importance of providing public awareness of the significance of Sherman's campaign since Grant's Overland Campaign was receiving the lion's share of press attention in the North during the month of May.

New York Times, 24 May 1864

In the absorbing interest of the campaign in Virginia, the public are almost overlooking a brilliant advance of the Union armies toward a point which last year we should have considered equal in importance to Richmond itself—Atlanta. It is well understood that Gen. SHERMAN began his movement from Chattanooga with a force so imposing and of such excellent fighting quality that nothing in the Southwestern rebel States could be expected to withstand it for a week. The positions held by the different portions of JOHNSTON'S army were exceedingly strong, being often mountain passes where every advantage of nature was on their side. But the great superiority of number with SHERMAN enabled him to make flank movements with as heavy force as he kept in front of the enemy, and he has thus succeeded in turning all their positions in the mountains, and has now reached that part of the uplands of Georgia, where the country is open and rolling, and not so easily defended by small bodies of men.

On Friday he was at Etowah River, within forty-five miles of Atlanta; in a few days he will probably attack the fortified positions which the enemy have been constructing with such care around that important strategic point. He will undoubtedly capture Atlanta, though after severe fighting, and thus hold the most valuable workshops, and the most vital railroad connection in the whole South. Nothing could more effectually cut the Confederacy in two, though the rebels will still have a roundabout connection between Alabama and

Virginia, by a more southerly route. To occupy Atlanta would be, in effect, to occupy Georgia, the richest of the rebel States, the want of whose supplies, as has been acknowledged by the Richmond Enquirer, would break up their great armies in Virginia. No other State is materially so important for the Confederacy, and the weakness, as well as the desperation, of the rebel leaders, is shown in nothing than in their thus giving up Georgia to force the Army out of Virginia. With Georgia occupied and *raided* over by our troops, even a doubtful campaign in Virginia would, by the Autumn, leave LEE'S army broken up, through want of supplies. There is another important element of this Georgia campaign which has not been much considered. All the most valuable negro population of the Confederate States is believed to be now concentrated in Georgia and South Carolina. It is supposed that two millions of slaves have been sent to these two States, to be far from Northern depredations and from all inducements to run away. These must represent 800,000 or 400,000 fighting men. When SHERMAN breaks into these communities there will be an exodus into his lines from the whole country around, such as has not been seen since the beginning of the war. If he has the arms he can at once equip a vast body of fresh regiments who will be able to do excellent service in guarding his immense lines of communications, leaving his veterans for distant and more important movements.

AN ANONYMOUS REPORT: GENERAL SHERMAN'S ARMY APPROACHES ATLANTA

The report below of Sherman's approach to Atlanta is based on War Department dispatches as well as news from the Atlanta newspapers. It was common for newspapers in the North to use Southern newspapers to glean information when they did not have correspondents in the area.

New York Times, 20 July 1864

**GEN. SHERMAN'S ARMY
THE ADVANCE UPON ATLANTA
THE WHOLE ARMY IN MOTION
NO RESISTANCE BY JOHNSTON**

The Rebels Getting Into the Defences of the City

Special Dispatch to the New-York Times.

Gen. SHERMAN'S dispatches to the War Department convey the gratifying intelligence that, having previously passed the Chattahoochee, his whole army yesterday advanced five miles south of the river and crossed Peach Tree Creek. This movement, for which was opposed only a very feeble resis-

tance by JOHNSTON, necessarily forces the rebels into the defences of Atlanta; and though it does not bring that city absolutely under siege, yet it lays it under artillery fire. The Atlanta papers have lately acknowledged that if JOHNSTON cannot hold the Union forces in check along the Chattahoochee, he cannot anywhere below it.

The capture of Atlanta and the formation of a base of operation there, thus completely severing rebel communication between the eastern and western zones, would be a victory of more real and far more substantial importance than even a great success in Virginia; although the concentration of the two chief armies of the opposing forces in front of Richmond has given to operations in that theatre an importance not justified by any military or material considerations involved.

The probability that the rebels will be compelled to abandon Atlanta, adds increased likelihood to the theory that LEE will endeavor to draw reinforcements from Georgia; but it is fully expected that any efforts in this direction will be frustrated by speedy operations before Petersburgh that will bring the rebel calculations to naught.

HENRY RAYMOND: UNION INDEBTEDNESS TO CONFEDERATE GENERAL BRAGG

Many in the North were quite happy to hear of General Johnston's removal from the head of the Confederate forces that Sherman was facing. Although General Hood replaced him, General Braxton Bragg was also a major figure in the Confederate leadership in the region. This article shows how much the Northern press "liked" General Bragg, particularly after the federals successfully captured Chattanooga while maneuvering against him.

New York Times, 22 July 1864

The most encouraging piece of news which has reached us with regard to SHERMAN'S position in Georgia, is that Gen. BRAGG has gone to Atlanta to exercise a personal supervision over the movements of the rebel army. This only is sufficient to remove all doubts as to the ultimate success of SHERMAN'S operations. There are not many Generals to whom the Union cause is more deeply indebted than to Gen. BRAGG, and the assistance which he has rendered it is all the more creditable to him, as his sympathies must of course be altogether on the rebel side. No matter how this war may end, no true Unionist an ever forget the valuable cooperation which Gen. ROSECRANS received from him in TENNESSEE, during the retreat from Murfreesboro; and it was, in fact, in no small degree to the masterly combinations of the Confederate leader that we got into Chattanooga without firing a shot. If we were indebted to him for no other service than this, the burden of our obligations would be great; but he did not stop here. Finding our army was in great straits at Chattanooga for supplies, he generously let us have Lookout Valley, and believing that LONGSTREET'S presence on Missionary Ridge was probably embarrassing us, he dispatched that officious and turbulent personage to Knoxville, and left himself for Dalton, when requested to do so by Gen. GRANT. There has, in short, not been a single stage in this excellent man's career since this war began, in which he has not afforded us valuable facilities for the accomplishment of the great work which our armies have before them.

We consider, therefore, the arrival of such an old and tried friend at Atlanta as a happy omen. We may feel satisfied that if he begins to "supervise" there, he will, before many days, "supervise" the city, if not the garrison, into Gen. SHERMAN'S hands.

THOMAS N. DAY: GENERAL SHERMAN'S SUCCESS AT ATLANTA

Although this report jumps the gun on Sherman's capture of Atlanta, which did not occur until September, it gives its readers a good overview of everything Sherman accomplished through the end of July and once again notes the importance of the city to the Confederacy.

Hartford Daily Courant, 27 July 1864 (Hartford, Conn.)

General Sherman has reached Atlanta, fought a great battle, and won a great victory with the outer line of intrenchments that gird the city. He has pushed his columns over the ravines and through the passes between Chattanooga and Atlanta, with a fixity of purpose, and inflexibility of will and fertility of resource that mark him as one of the first military leaders of the age. Johnston, next to Lee, the pet general of South, at the head of a large army, operating in a country that offered numerous and apparently almost impregnable lines of defense, has been driven back by hard fighting and skillful maneuvers from two-thirds of the district that furnished the sinews of war to the confederacy.

General Sherman plunged into hostile territory depending for supplies upon a single thread railway, stretching back hundreds of miles to his secondary base. So exact were his calculations, and so thorough his arrangements, that his lines have never been broken for a day. Johnston, shorn of military renown, now gives place to a successor. Hood exhibits more enterprise, but it will only devour his army the sooner. One of his first acts was to storm a line of federal intrenchments where he lost in the proportion of three to one. Governor Brown appeals frantically to the exempts of the State. He might as well call spirits from the vastly deep. They will not rise at his bidding. The old men of Georgia are too prudent to be led willingly to indiscriminate slaughter.

Where will Hood retreat to? General Rosseau has cut the communications between Atlanta and Montgomery, leaving open only the line to Macon. If he falls back, and retreat seems to be the only alternative, he gives up not only the manufacturing but also the agricultural districts of the State. In ordinary times, the inhabitants of lower Georgia drew a large share of their supplies from the "up country." Now the barren and arid plains of the low country are packed with negroes and refugees. It cannot support the numbers that swarm there already.

Baring the line of railway from Montgomery to Macon, the eastern half of the confederacy is cleft in twain. That road is poorly built and will not bear hard usage. Sherman can disable it any day by raiding parties.

With the food growing regions cut off, Richmond is threatened with famine. Davis made great exertions to store there a large quantity of provisions, in anticipation of a siege. But with a large army and the inhabitants of the city to be fed, the stock must diminish very rapidly. The confederacy is in a bad way.

AN ANONYMOUS REPORT: NORTHERN CITIES CELEBRATE FALL OF ATLANTA

The significance of the fall of Atlanta was well understood in the Union after months of coverage that gave readers some sense of how important Georgia was to Jefferson Davis and General Robert E. Lee. Below is an accounting of how many Northern cities celebrated the news of Atlanta's fall.

Hartford Daily Courant, 5 September 1864

There was great rejoicing everywhere on Saturday by the friends of the Union, and by those who are determined to put down the rebellion, over the glorious victory won by Sherman at Atlanta. We give a synopsis of dispatches received Saturday:

Saratoga.—Bells were rung and 100 guns were fired.
Rochester.—200 guns fired; bonfires, torch light procession and speeches; streets filled with immense throngs.
Buffalo.—Flags displayed, guns fired, bonfires, speeches, &c.
Troy.—100 guns fired.

Oswego.—100 guns fired.
Boston.—100 guns fired. Also at Lynn, Belfast, Me., and many other localities in New England.
New York City.—Flags generally hoisted throughout the city, except on the City Hall, and other city buildings, where they were hoisted on the receipt of the Chicago nominations [*of Republican Abraham Lincoln for President*].
Newark, N.J.—Great rejoicing, flags flying and a salute of 100 guns fired.
Albany.—100 guns were fired by the Union men of Albany, and also 100 guns fired by order of the Adjutant General.

NOTES

1. "The Fall of Atlanta," *New York Times*, 5 September 1864.

2. Curt Johnson and Mark McLaughlin, *Civil War Battles* (New York: Crown Publishers, 1977), 117.

3. Ibid.

4. "General Sherman's Army, Occupation of Rome and Kinston," *New York Times*, 20 May 1864.

5. "Before Atlanta, Partial Occupation of the City," *National Republican* (Washington, D.C.), 24 July 1864.

6. "The Fall of Atlanta."

7. William T. Sherman, *Memoirs of General William T. Sherman*, 2nd ed., rev. (New York: D. A. Appleton and Co., 1875), 2:408.

FURTHER READINGS

Bailey, Ronald H. *Battles for Atlanta*. New York: Time-Life Books, 1986.

Bradford, Ned (Ed.). *Battles and Leaders of the Civil War*. New York: Appleton-Century-Crofts, 1956.

Johnson, Curt, and McLaughlin, Mark. *Civil War Battles*. New York: Crown Publishers, 1977.

Sherman, William T. *Memoirs of General William T. Sherman*. Vol. 2. 2nd ed., rev. New York: D. A. Appleton and Co., 1875.

23

SHERMAN'S MARCH, NOVEMBER–DECEMBER 1864

Nearly two months after General William T. Sherman captured Atlanta he marched from the city and headed for Savannah, in what would become his most celebrated military action in the Civil War. "Sherman's March," as it was known in both the North and South, commenced after Sherman ordered his troops to burn all of the military resources in Atlanta. He collected about 50,000 veteran army men to lead the charge east and left enough troops in Atlanta to "watch" Confederate General John Hood. Sherman's plan was to steal supplies and food, carve a path of destruction through the fruitful Georgia countryside, which "had hitherto escaped the ravages of war," and capture the city of Savannah on the Atlantic Ocean. Along the way, the press suggested that Sherman would free the thousands of slaves who lived in this region, which stretched about 290 miles.[1]

About ten days after Sherman began his march to Savannah, his plan was clear to those in the North, and the specifics of it appeared in newspapers. Northern reporters had no fear that they were tipping the South of Sherman's plan because they believed it would be impossible for the rebels to mount a challenge. In its details of Sherman's plan, the *Hartford Daily Courant* reported that

> General Sherman started with five corps of veteran infantry, commanded by experienced officers, and nine thousand picked cavalry. . . . He carries rations for thirty days, and expects to obtain an indefinite quantity of supplies from the country through which he moves. The railroad from Atlanta to Chattanooga, one hundred and thirty eight miles, was destroyed so effectually that it cannot be repaired by the rebels during the continuance of the war. . . . The rear corps is also destroying the road between Atlanta and Macon. . . . On the road between Atlanta and Augusta, the road will share the same fate.
>
> After demolishing the rebel factories at Macon, and along different lines of communication, Sherman's forces will rendezvous at Augusta or Millen, the point where the road from Augusta taps the main road from Macon to Savannah. His subsequent move-

ments are conjectural. The capture of Savannah will open the river to navigation as far as Augusta, which can then be easily held as a base for operations against the interior of South Carolina.

Sherman's campaign will effectually bisect the eastern half of rebeldom without the necessity of holding it. Alabama will be severed for South Carolina by a march of twenty days. For a distance of three hundred miles, neither troops, food, or forage can be transported by rail. The Mississippi [River], patrolled by gunboats, is a barrier hardly more insuperable. Virginia will be supported only by North and South Carolina, with powerful armies operating on her borders. The enemy have carried on the manufacture of war munitions, since the abandonment of Atlanta, chiefly at Macon, Augusta, Columbia. These resources will now be lost to them.[2]

Sherman reached Savannah on 10 December and claimed the city on 21 December 1864, after about 10,000 Confederate troops evacuated to avoid capture.

Sherman did not remain in Savannah for long—by February his troops were on the move again, this time headed to South and North Carolina to continue to destroy the Southern countryside, to capture key cities, and ultimately to meet up with General Ulysses S. Grant's forces in Virginia to help fight against General Robert E. Lee. Sherman encouraged his troops to demolish not only military but also civilian resources along the way to demoralize the South and to help end the war more quickly. Sherman's troops exacted the harshest damage to citizens in South Carolina since the federal forces largely blamed that state and its citizens for starting the war. On 17 February 1865, Sherman's troops captured Columbia, South Carolina, and soon after the city was burned to the ground.[3]

After the capture of Columbia, the Confederate troops finally attempted to stop Sherman's forces; General Joseph Johnston, who had faced Sherman as he marched to Atlanta, was given control of all remaining rebel troops in North Carolina. Although Johnston was not ultimately successful, he was able to slow Sherman's progress and beat back a federal attack at Bentonville, North Carolina.

Sherman eventually reached Raleigh, North Carolina, and planned to continue on to Virginia when he received news of General Lee's surrender on 9 April (see Chapter 26). On 26 April 1865, Johnston's Confederate army, which had been fighting Sherman through North Carolina, formally surrendered at Durham Station. Since they began their march at Atlanta, Sherman's troops exacted more than a million dollars in damage. About 25,000 slaves fled to Sherman's army through the duration of the Savannah and Carolina Campaigns. During "Sherman's March" to Savannah, the press reported that he gathered up 7,000 slaves, 1,200 cattle and "so many horses, mules and wagons to embarrass him."[4]

Sherman's March and his continuing raids through the Carolinas were not continual front-page news—the struggles in Petersburg and Richmond continued to dominate the news through much of early 1865 (see Chapter 25). But the captures of Savannah and Columbia were prominently covered, and many newspapers used their editorial columns to praise Sherman and his foray through the South. Many reprinted articles from Southern newspapers that detailed the damage that Sherman's men caused, and most hailed Sherman as one of the most important Union military leaders of the war.

THOMAS N. DAY: DODGING SHERMAN'S ARMY

The following report from the Hartford Daily Courant *highlights the success of Sherman's March to Savannah in its early stages based on reports from Southern newspapers.*

Hartford Daily Courant, 6 December 1864

A writer in the Augusta *Chronicle* gives a lengthy account of his journey home, after the closing of the Georgia Legislature. He wanted to be near enough to see and far enough to keep out of the way. In the first he succeeded very well, finding the Yankees everywhere, at every turn. He says on many of the plantations the buildings were destroyed and the cattle killed. Of the loss of Hon. Joshua Hill,[5] he says:

"His loss was greater than that of any other planter in this section. Besides the cotton several thousand bushels of corn, potatoes, several hundred of wheat, and much other valuable property, with every horse and mule, and many negroes are gone. No farm on the road to this place and as far as we can hear towards Atlanta escaped their brutal ravages. They ravaged the country below here to the Oconee river. The roads were strewn with the debris of their progress. Dead horses, cows, sheep, hogs, chickens, corn, wheat, cotton, books, paper, broken vessels, coffee mills, and fragments of nearly every species of property that adorned the beautiful farms of this country, strew the wayside—monuments of the meanness and rapacity of the people who boast that they are not robbers and do not interfere with private property."

According to this account, many negroes have been "enticed" away from home, so that many families of wealth have not a servant left.

"There was no provocation for any of these acts of violence, for everybody treated them civilly and offered them all they wanted to eat. Their excuse is that they cannot control their men. Many of them, including their officers, behave civilly, and my humble domicile escaped any serious depredations. Those citizens who remained at home and watched their premises lost but little save horses, food and stock."

CHARLES HALE: WAR-WEARY GEORGIA—SHERMAN'S ARMY FACES LITTLE RESISTANCE IN STATE

This untitled article details the lack of resistance Sherman's troops faced as they marched through Georgia in December 1864. Much of the reason for the lack of resistance was because virtually no men remained at home during this time. All available healthy men in the South were fighting the war as Confederate soldiers.

Boston Daily Advertiser, 20 December 1864

In General Sherman's letter of the 13th from Ossabaw Sound one hint is let fall, which strikes us as having not a little significance. Describing his march, the General says, "we were not at all molested by guerillas." Now, as our readers will remember, the rebel authorities had made every effort to have the people of the country oppose Sherman's march by all possible means. The people were urged to harass our forces night and day, to cut off straggling parties, to prevent the collection of supplies, and by all the expedients of partisan warfare to make that resistance which there was no regularly organized force to make. And the circumstances were such as to render this method of operation promising. A long march had been undertaken through the heart of the rebel country, by a force which was obliged to forage as it went, which could not long delay to look for missing parties, or to call assailants to account. That with circumstances favoring and their own leaders urging hostilities, the people of Georgia should have permitted Sherman to pass "not at all molested by guerillas" is a matter for explanation. We must say that in our judgment it is not overstating the argument, if we infer from this fact that the people of the districts through which Sherman passed have little heart for the contest. They may have been enthusiastic in their support of the war heretofore; but they now prefer, it would seem, to occupy a position resembling neutrality at least, rather than undertake active resistance when the war is brought to their very doors. It is not long since we called attention to the plain hints given by some of the rebel papers, that a spirit of submission was prevalent in Georgia, and that that great State could not be relied upon for any vigorous and steady resistance. We infer from General Sherman's remark, that the forebodings of the more zealous rebels have been justified, and that, as they intimated, a considerable part of the people of Georgia are sick of the war.

THOMAS N. DAY: CAPTURE OF SAVANNAH

The fall of Savannah was noticed in most Northern newspapers. This account gives a good estimate of the supplies the federal army captured.

Hartford Daily Courant, 26 December 1864 (Hartford, Conn.)

On Thursday last at 7 p.m., General Sherman's army entered the city of Savannah in triumph. Tuesday night General Hardee, with the garrison succeeded in crossing the river into South Carolina. Before leaving he blew up the navy yard and ironclads, but left everything else undisturbed. One hundred and fifty heavy guns, large quantities of ammunition, twenty-five thousand bales of cotton, thirteen locomotives, one hundred and ninety cars, three steamers, and a large amount of the material of war are among the captures. The inhabitants, numbering about twenty thousand, are quiet and well disposed. Our steamers have passed up to the wharves. The city that was one of the most violent in urging on secession, after three years and a half of costly and fruitless sacrifice, again reposes beneath the flag which it tried in vain to disclaim and dishonor.

Savannah, lying within an hour's sail of the ocean, has been captured at last by an army which had marched through more than seven hundred miles of hostile territory. This history of war presents few if any parallels.

CHARLES HALE: MAGNIFICENT ACHIEVEMENT OF GENERAL SHERMAN—FALL OF CONFEDERACY IMMINENT

The Boston Daily Advertiser's *untitled editorial on the fall of Savannah noted the timing of the capture and elevated General Sherman to a position among great leaders. It also correctly notes the significance of Sherman's achievements in Georgia and predicts the fall of the Confederacy.*

Boston Daily Advertiser, 27 December 1864

There are no gifts left to be made by our generals like that of Vicksburg and the command of the Mississippi River, which Grant made to the nation one Fourth of July; but of what is left General Sherman gave to the country for Christmas one of the best. He gave us the fourth city in population of the South, with ample supplies and armament, and also the definite and triumphant conclusion of the first act of his most dramatic scheme of strategy. He has rounded off and finished a great chapter in the story of the downfall of the rebellion. We can afford to wait in patient ignorance to learn what new chapter he will open.

This magnificent achievement establishes General Sherman's right to a place in the front rank of our commanders. While this undertaking was still unfinished it remained to be settled whether his daring genius had not at last attempted an impossible flight. But in this case, as in his earlier exploits, it has proved that his most reckless movements are reckless in appearance only, and are based on the careful calculation of a master of military science. Tested by success, none of our generals stands higher than he; indeed, if we measure the cost at which success is attained, who stands so high? "There is not a general now alive in Europe," says the London Spectator, "who, if Sherman succeeds, will not recognize the addition of one more name to the short list of first-class leaders of armies." The success, which was still held doubtful when these words were written, has been gloriously won; and the gallant general has achieved the highest reward of personal fame which the profession of arms can offer on this continent, and by the same stroke has established the final success of his country, and insured the restoration of its unity and peace and the countless blessings flowing from these.

HUGUENOT: ACCOUNT OF GENERAL SHERMAN'S CAMPAIGN IN THE CAROLINAS

By 1865, most war correspondents were concentrated in Virginia. This article comes from a New York Times *correspondent who was marching with Sherman, and it provides a good overview of the campaign in the Carolinas, particularly the later efforts in North Carolina.*

New York Times, 8 April 1865

GEN. SHERMAN'S CAMPAIGN

Review of the March through the Carolinas—Statistics of the Campaign.

From Our Own Correspondent.

GOLDSBORO, N.C., Thursday, March 29, 1865. A few days' leisure after the successful termination of a campaign always induces reflection upon its effects—the magnitude of its consequences. The . . . narrative evolved at the first opportunity to relate experience gives way to calculation as to substantial results derived, the precise extent to which the enemy's resources have been weakened and our own cause strengthened. It is the object of the present letter to estimate the fruits of the campaign, and to indulge in a few curious calculations illustrative of its history.

STRENGTH AND EQUIPMENT OF THE ARMY

It is next to an impossibility to state in exact figures the numerical strength of SHERMAN's army; but competent judges estimate the forces, in round numbers, to have been, on leaving Savannah, sixty thousand infantry, five thousand cavalry, and five thousand artillerymen, pontoniers, engineers, &c. One hundred guns were about the amount of cannon at the service of Gen. SHERMAN. Each of the four corps had with it a wagon and ambulance train of about one thousand vehicles; the cavalry three hundred, and pontoniers and engineers two hundred more—making, in all, a train for the entire army of not less than four thousand five hundred vehicles. Army transportation, in moving, generally occupies a length of road in the proportion of one hundred wagons per mile. Gen. SHERMAN's train, upon his moderate estimate, would fill a road forty-five miles in length.

The transportation was divided in four parts; each moved with its command on a separate road, thus avoiding the difficulty of campaigning with so great an encumbrance as a baggage and supply train nearly fifty miles in length. The extent of country, front and rear, occupied by each column in moving through the country, was commensurate with the length of train.

EXTENT AND DURATION OF THE CAMPAIGN

When we consider the duration of time that the army remained independent of its base, and the distance traveled, Gen. SHERMAN's campaign through the Carolinas stands as prominent among the most wonderful tests of armies recorded in history.

The right wing left its communication with Beaufort, S.C., Jan. 19, and marching nearly, if not quite, five hundred miles, arrived at Goldsboro, N.C., March 25, thus being away from a base for the space of sixty-four days.

The left wing abandoned their base at Sister's Ferry, S.C., Feb. 4, and reached Goldsboro, March 25, after an interim of fifty days.

MANNER OF SUBSISTING

During all this period, excepting fifteen days, for which rations were carried in the wagons, the corps subsisted upon the country through which they passed. In order to accomplish this, each regiment, brigade, or separate command, organized foraging parties which, under command of energetic officers, scoured the country on the flanks and on by-roads, gathering in supplies of forage, flour, meal chickens, bacon, &c., with which the rich plantations of Carolina abounded.

Fayetteville, on Cape Fear River, was made the means of landing a limited amount of rations for the army; but it was insufficient to supply its demands for one day. No actual base was reached until the corps arrived at Goldsboro.

TOWNS VISITED

The following-named districts and towns were entered. Everything found in them which could benefit the rebel cause was taken or destroyed.

Beaufort District—Beaufort.
Barnwell—The towns of Barnwell, Midway, Bamburgh, Blackville and Aiken, all wealthy communities of from 1,000 to 2,000 people—were visited by portions of the right and left wings.
Orangeburgh—Orangeburgh; population 1,500.
Lexington—Lexington; population 800.
Richland—In this district, Columbia, the capital of South Carolina, is located. Prior to its occupation by SHERMAN's army it contained 20,000 inhabitants. Before the war its population was not quite 12,000.
Kershaw—Contains Camden—the scene of a battle during the revolution—containing a population of about 3,000.

NOTES

1. "Sherman's New Campaign," *Hartford Daily Courant*, 11 November 1864.
2. "Sherman's Campaign," *Hartford Daily Courant*, 22 November 1864.
3. Historians note that the origins of the Columbia fire are unknown. Some suggest that the federal forces likely started the fire but that the fire was not ordered by General Sherman. Others say the fire spread to the city from burning cotton that had been intentionally set on fire by fleeing Confederate forces.
4. "General Sherman," *Hartford Daily Courant*, 21 December 1864.

5. Ironically, Joshua Hill was a pro-Unionist in Georgia who was elected to Congress in 1856. He was an outspoken opponent of secession and resigned his seat in 1861 rather than withdraw Georgia from the Union with the other members of the Georgia delegation.

FURTHER READINGS

Davis, Burke. *Sherman's March*. New York: Vintage Books, 1988.

Glatthaar, Joseph T. *The March to the Sea and Beyond: Sherman's Troops in the Savannah and Carolinas Campaigns*. Baton Rouge: Louisiana State University Press, 1995.

Johnson, Curt, and McLaughlin, Mark. *Civil War Battles*. New York: Crown Publishers, 1977.

Sherman, William T. *Memoirs of General William T. Sherman*. Vol. 2. 2nd ed., rev. New York: D. A. Appleton and Co., 1875.

24

PRESIDENTIAL ELECTION OF 1864

The election of 1864 is one of the most important presidential elections in the history of the United States. Had Abraham Lincoln not been reelected and the Democrats honored their campaign platform, the war would have quickly ended, and the Confederacy would have been recognized as a sovereign nation.

Early in 1864 it was not clear that Lincoln would even secure the Republican nomination. The radical arm of the party was not satisfied with Lincoln's war policies and later would nominate John Fremont, one of Lincoln's most celebrated generals early in the war, as their choice for president. Fremont had focused Union attention on the role emancipation should play in the North's war policy before Lincoln issued the Emancipation Proclamation and was popular among radical Republicans.

Moderate Republicans refused to support anyone but Lincoln and unanimously named him the Republican nominee at the party convention in June. Senator Andrew Johnson, a Tennessee Democrat and the only congressman from a secessionist state to remain loyal to the Union, was nominated as Lincoln's vice president.

The Democrats nominated General George B. McClellan, who had been Lincoln's head of the Army of the Potomac after the loss at the first Battle of Bull Run in July 1861. He was replaced in March 1862 only to return again after the loss at the second Battle of Bull Run. McClellan finally relinquished command for good in November 1862. The Democrats nominated McClellan with the hopes that his popularity among soldiers and his victory at Antietam would help him carry the election. The Democrats ran on a peace platform, calling for an immediate end to the war that they called four years of failure. The Democratic slogan was "The Constitution as it is, The Union as it was."[1] McClellan, however, did not support the Democratic platform—he favored continuing the war and would not denounce the conflict in which he led troops into battle. He still believed the Union could be victorious over the Confederacy.[2]

By the early summer of 1864, Lincoln's chances for reelection did not look good. General Ulysses S. Grant's army had stalled at Petersburg after sustaining heavy casualties in his Overland Campaign, and General William Sherman had stalled before Atlanta. In July 1864, Washington, D.C., was briefly threatened by Confederate General Jubal Early, who had been conducting raids in the Shenandoah Valley. The Republican *New York Times* observed, "The Democrats everywhere are very confident of victory in the pending Presidential canvas. Their exultation may be premature but it is sincere. They evidently believe they are going to win."[3]

But in September the war outlook improved, as did Lincoln's chances for reelection. Sherman captured Atlanta, and General Philip Sheridan, under orders from General Grant, put an end to General Early's raids and destroyed the rebel stronghold in the Shenandoah Valley. Fremont dropped out of the election, which caused the Republican Party to unite behind Lincoln. Early reports of Sheridan's success were discounted by the Democratic presses, who could feel the election tide turning. "Intelligent readers will doubtless analyze for themselves the series of ante-election victories which may now be expected by telegraph," wrote the Democratic *Boston Courier*.[4]

When the election was held on 8 November, Lincoln would win all but three states—Kentucky, Delaware, and New Jersey. He earned 212 electoral votes to McClellan's 21, and in the popular vote Lincoln beat McClellan with 2,206,938 votes, compared to 1,803,787 votes. Lincoln also carried the soldier vote.

The Northern press was very active in covering the election and the campaign that led up to it. Republican papers devoted their pages to the promotion of Lincoln, and Democratic papers promoted McClellan. By October it seemed clear that Lincoln would win the election, but active campaigning continued until election day. As the *New York Times* wrote a little more than a week before the election:

> One man says, "It's all right. McClellan hasn't a chance. He won't make a show at all;" and so takes it easy. *That is just the way to elect McClellan.* . . . The national existence is threatened by many wealthy, powerful and determined enemies. It is true that the best men of the Democratic party have left it, and that its vital principle, namely, its patriotism, is gone; but its *organization* remains, by means of which it once won many victories, and elected three Presidents who should never have been chosen."[5]

The following articles represent the Republican perspective on three points in the election process: Lincoln's nomination, his election, and his inaugural address in March 1865.

CHARLES HALE: LINCOLN WINS REPUBLICAN NOMINATION—SUPPORT FOR PRESIDENT WIDESPREAD

The Republican Boston Daily Advertiser, *in its notice about Lincoln's nomination as the Republican candidate for president, offers a few highlights from his first term and observes that had the election been held in early 1863, Lincoln might not have even secured his party's nomination. Now, the writer suggests, Lincoln's support runs far deeper than just the Republican Party.*

Boston Daily Advertiser, 9 June 1864

The nomination for the Presidency, made yesterday at Baltimore, we believe to be the formal record of the settled wish of a great majority of the supporters of the Union, whether in distinct political association with the republican party or not. The choice of Mr. Lincoln for his own successor is one that had been made with singular deliberation and alterations of feeling. It was almost the universal expression two years ago, when he had but fairly completed his first year of office, that there should be no change at the end of his term. The early part of 1863, a season long to be remembered for the thick gloom which overspread both political and military affairs, brought with it such a degree of dissatisfaction with the President, that at that time his very nomination might have been difficult, to say nothing of his election. But from the summer of last year, a period marked both by renewed hope in the conduct of the war and by a fuller sense of the dangerous character of the opposition, the public appreciation of Mr. Lincoln's services and qualities and the general approval of his course have steadily increased. At the moment, as the observation of anybody can tell him, the feeling partakes of the character of enthusiasm,—no mean compliment to the political leader who had had to conduct a nation's affairs during three years of war.

We speak of the judgment passed by the public upon Mr. Lincoln's official career as singularly deliberate, because the course of its formation exhibits so clearly the balancing and revision of opinions. The country early discovered and admired his sagacity, his patience, his caution and his firm hold upon the great objects of this contest. In a period of depression it constructed his caution into irresolution; and forgot that the most sagacious counsels may not at once command success. But these hasty judgments were reversed, as time and events vindicated the wisdom of the President's action; and while it may be that no two persons would agree in their estimates of every part of his career, the great majority now feel that upon the whole, Abraham Lincoln is the man for the time. This is the point upon which the public mind has settled after such vicissitudes as we have noted; this is the result of three years experience, and it is a result which does honor to the sound sense and discernment of our people.

WILLIAM LLOYD GARRISON: LINCOLN'S REELECTION INDICATES NORTHERN SUPPORT FOR ABOLITION OF SLAVERY

William Lloyd Garrison's abolitionist newspaper was overjoyed by Lincoln's sound victory and suggests that the win shows how great Northern confidence was in Lincoln to put an end to slavery.

The Liberator, 18 November 1864 (Boston)

Through all the loyal States there is felt the deepest joy, mingled with solemn thanksgiving, at the overwhelmingly triumphant result of the late Presidential struggle—an almost unanimous vote of those States for the re-election of ABRAHAM LINCOLN! This joy does not find expression in noisy exultation or pompous display, but is marked by profound sobriety of mind and true dignity of demeanor—the elements entering into it being of the highest and purest character. Never was there a political conflict so momentous in its bearings, not only upon the nation's welfare, but upon the liberties of mankind; never one that so challenged and absorbed the earnest interest of the civilized world; never one that so divided the good from the bad, the humane from the brutal, the law-abiding from the disorderly, the truly patriotic from the pseudo loyal, the liberty-loving from the liberty-hating, the thoroughly enlightened from the fearfully ignorant and debased, the hosts of freedom from the powers of despotism; never one so remarkable for the appeals made to the understanding and conscience, to virtue and honor, to personal accountability and divine authority, to patriotism and piety, to all that is highest and noblest in the soul, on the one hand—or for the appeals made to the worst prejudices, the most selfish considerations, the basest passions, the wildest delusions, the most inflammable emotions, and the wickedest purposes on the other.

THOMAS N. DAY: INAUGURATION OF PRESIDENT LINCOLN—COMPARISON OF 1861 AND 1865

This article compares Lincoln's first inauguration in 1861 to his inauguration in 1865 and traces some of the obstacles he faced during his first term in office.

Hartford Daily Courant, 6 March 1865 (Hartford, Conn.)

On Saturday last, the first Presidential term of Abraham Lincoln came to a close, and at 12 o'clock, noon, he again took the oath of office, were inaugurated, and commenced a second term, being the only President who has had a second inauguration since that of General Jackson, thirty-two years ago. . . . Four years ago the President, who had been constitutionally elected, was threatened with assassination. The Democratic party was his bitter enemy, and threatened to defy his authority; in fact, the Southern wing of the party, cheered on by their northern allies, did revolt, and refused to submit to the laws and the constitution. The whole country labored under the most intense excitement. The President elect was obliged to enter Washington in disguise to escape assassination; threats were uttered that he should never be allowed to enter upon the duties of his office, and it was necessary to assemble troops to preserve the peace on that memorable day, the 4th of March, 1861. Mr. Lincoln took the oath of office under circumstances calculated to appall and dismay any many realizing the weighty responsibility which must rest upon the Chief Magistrate at such a crisis in the nation's affairs. Buchanan, weak and vacillating, if not corrupt, who had been surrounded by advisers, a majority of whom were traitors and some of them actually engaged in robbing the nation of its property to be used for the destruction of the Union, refused to do anything, or to allow General Scott to take any measures to interfere with the designs of traitors and rebels, so that at the close of his administration the gulf states were ripe for the revolt which they soon inaugurated.

It was under these circumstances that Mr. Lincoln took the oath of office, and declared his determination to "hold, occupy, and possess the property and places belonging to the United States, including all its forts and arsenals."

President Lincoln commenced his official term with a spirit of forebearance and conciliation which showed that he had resolved that by no act of his should the people, or any portion of them, have any excuse for revolt. . . . Since that day the trials of this nation have been such as have been experienced by scarcely any civilized people. We have carried on a war of greater magnitude than ever before witnessed in any country; but, knowing our cause to be just, and learning at fearful cost our strength as a nation, we have held and are determined to hold on, until the authority of the government is acknowledged in every State in the Union, and the laws obeyed in every one of the States which ever have been a part of the Union. We have not only learned the value of the Union, but we have been taught our strength, financially and morally; we have learned that we are a powerful people—one to be feared and respected by all nations. We have been led through terrible war to look upon slavery as the cause of the rebellion, and as a curse to the nation which must, and shall be removed. . . .

This nation has passed through a mighty struggle. It has seen many dark and gloomy days, when it seemed as if all was lost—as if God had forsaken us, and we were to be given over to destruction—but the dark days have passed, and we are now permitted to behold the rainbow of hope encircling the horizon. We congratulate the President upon the auspicious signs of the times at the commencement of his second term—signs which lead us to believe the nation will soon be at peace, having its authority fully restored and acknowledged. . . .

We commend to our readers Mr. Lincoln's inaugural address. . . . His sublime and confiding trust in God and his Providences, forms a marked feature, and his honest desire to be the instrument in carrying out the purpose of the Almighty, will be pleasing to a religious people, who will most heartily join with him in his closing sentence, which is as follows:

"With malice toward no man, with charity to all, with firmness in the right, as God gives us to see the right, let us strive to finish the work we are in, to bind up the nation's wound, to care for him who shall have borne the battle, and for his widow and his orphans, to do all which may achieve and cherish a just and lasting peace among ourselves and with all nations."

NOTES

1. Margaret E. Wagner, Gary W. Gallagher, and Paul Finkelman (Eds.), *The Library of Congress Civil War Desk Reference* (New York: Simon & Schuster, 2002), 165.

2. "Did He Accept the Platform?" *New York Times*, 12 September 1862.

3. "The Presidential Election," *New York Times*, 10 August 1864.

4. Brayton Harris, *Blue & Gray in Black & White* (Washington, D.C.: Brasseys, 1999), 295.

5. "Current Delusions and Their Dangers," *New York Times*, 29 October 1864.

FURTHER READINGS

Harris, Brayton. *Blue & Gray in Black & White*. Washington, D.C.: Brasseys, 1999.

Long, David E. *The Jewel of Liberty: Abraham Lincoln's Re-Election and the End of Slavery*. Mechanicsville, Pa.: Stackpole Books, 1994.

Wagner, Margaret E.; Gallagher, Gary W.; and Finkelman, Paul (Eds.). *The Library of Congress Civil War Desk Reference*. New York: Simon & Schuster, 2002.

Waugh, John C. *Reelecting Lincoln: The Battle for the 1864 Presidency*. Cambridge, Mass.: Da Capo Press, 1997.

25

PETERSBURG AND RICHMOND CAMPAIGNS, 1865

When Petersburg and Richmond fell, on 2 April and 3 April 1865, respectively, the Northern press reported it as one event. It *was* one event in the sense that the capture of these two Virginia cities meant that the end of the war was very close. Less than a week after the fall of Petersburg and the capture of Richmond, Confederate General Robert E. Lee surrendered to Union General Ulysses S. Grant, and the war was effectively over (see Chapter 26).

The campaign for Petersburg began in June 1864 after General Grant's loss at Cold Harbor, part of the Overland Campaign (see Chapter 21). Grant's troops arrived in Petersburg in June after the bloody fighting at Cold Harbor, and on 15 June 1864, they began a cautious attack on the Confederate forces at Petersburg. Confederate General Pierre G. T. Beauregard was in charge of the Southern troops.

The campaign to capture Petersburg would become the longest sustained operation of the Civil War, lasting for ten months. Petersburg was important as a vital railroad center and because of its location along the James River. In early June 1864, General Lee told another Confederate general that if Grant succeeded in crossing the James River, then both Richmond and Petersburg would fall. The Confederates dug in to protect Petersburg even though in the first fighting their troops only numbered 5,400 to Grant's 48,000.[1]

The Confederate forces were able to beat back Grant's initial assaults between 15 June and 18 June, and afterward both sides dug in for the lengthy siege. Both sides created elaborate trenchworks that created long lulls in the campaign, and both sides attempted to gain advantage through pursuing selected actions. Between June and August, the federal troops worked to sever the railroad lines into the city to cut off Confederate supplies. Although his first attempt failed, the second attempt by General Grant succeeded. By 21 August, the Confederate forces had to maneuver around Union troops to move supplies.

In July 1864 in what became known as the Battle of the Crater, Colonel Henry Pleasants suggested that the federals tunnel under the Confederate lines and set off a huge powder charge that would blow a gap in the lines. Under the supervision of General Ambrose Burnside, some coal miners in Pleasant's division put the plan into action. On 27 July, four days after the miners finished digging a 511-foot tunnel, the Union troops put 8,000 pounds of gunpowder in the tunnel and set it off. The blast killed nearly 300 Confederates and created a 170-foot-long crater (30 feet deep). The Union plan went awry when the forces who were supposed to charge the stunned Confederates did so by advancing directly into the crater. The Confederates quickly recovered from the blast and fired down into the crater on the Union forces there, specifically targeting the black troops. The Union suffered 3,798 casualties to the Confederate's 1,500. Burnside and two of his subordinates were later found by a military court of inquiry to be responsible for the heavy federal loss.[2]

Grant renewed his attacks on the Confederates at Petersburg in February and March of 1865. His ultimate plan was gradually to extend the federal lines around Petersburg and force Lee to do the same. The end result would be that Lee's line and his resources would be stretched so thin that they would eventually break. That is exactly what happened, most notably at the Battle of Five Forks. Under the command of Generals Phil Sheridan and Gouverneur Warren, the Union forces attacked the left flank of the outnumbered Confederates and were able to capture the rear of Confederate General George Pickett's division, about 1,000 men. The victory at Five Forks allowed Grant to launch an all-out assault on Petersburg and finally force Lee's withdrawal on 2 April. Confederate General A. P. Hill was killed in the fighting that occurred the night before the evacuation. The day after the fall of Petersburg the federal forces marched into Richmond. Lee had ordered the evacuation of both cities after the federal victory at Five Forks; the Confederate leadership and the remaining gold in the treasury were put on a train and sent south to Danville, Virginia. The retreating Confederates set fire to much of the city—the fire eventually spread to an arsenal, setting off large explosions that caused significant damage.[3]

Richmond, the Confederate capital city, had been a target of the Union since the war began. When the Union troops arrived on 3 April, they hoisted the U.S. flag above the city. On 4 April, 1865, Abraham Lincoln toured the capital with his son, and according to Northern press reports, he was received by the people "with enthusiastic expressions of joy."[4] The same day from Danville, Virginia, Jefferson Davis pledged to continue fighting and said the Confederacy would not make peace with the federal invaders.

General Lee had retreated across the Appomattox River and was headed westward, hoping eventually to turn south and connect with the forces of General Joseph Johnston. This set up the standoff at Appomattox Courthouse that would lead to Lee's surrender and the end of the war.

THOMAS N. DAY: ACCOUNT OF BATTLES AROUND PETERSBURG ON 1 APRIL

The following account details the fighting that occurred on 1 April when a small number of rebel soldiers under General A. P. Hill led a last-ditch effort from Fort Gregg to keep the federal forces out of Petersburg.

Hartford Daily Courant, 6 April 1865 (Hartford, Conn.)

Correspondents of the metropolitan press furnish detailed accounts of the fighting which resulted in the capture of Petersburg and Richmond, and in the overthrow of Lee's army.

According to the plan previously arranged, the 8th and 9th, with portions of the 24th; 25th, and 2d corps, assaulted the rebel lines on the east and south of Petersburg, at daylight on Sunday morning. Notwithstanding the secrecy of the preparations, the enemy discovered the movement, and opened a terrific fire upon our troops. Under cover of darkness, the men formed and moved to the assault in the face of a fierce but irregular and ineffective fire. After a short struggle the 9th corps carried the lines east of Petersburg, including most of the formidable salients. Wilcox's division, resting on the Appomattox, was now furiously assailed and driven back to its old position. The divisions . . . further to the left held the positions they had captured despite the efforts to dislodge them. Many charges and counter-charges were made, the works finally remaining in our hands.

The 6th corps carried all the rebel lines in front of them, and sweeping westward, cut the South Side railroad, capturing two thousand prisoners, twenty guns, and many other trophies. The fire of batteries and musketry was unavailing to stop their progress. These operations cut the rebel army in twain. On the left, Sheridan was crushing everything before him, and shouts of victory rose along the line.

The enemy were being rapidly doubled up and ground between the mill-stones, when night threw over them its friendly screen. They did not neglect the opportunity, but hurried from the field, leaving cannon, muskets, tents, implements, etc., to fall into our hands. Thousands were added to the number of prisoners. The rebel Gen. A. P. Hill was killed.

During these engagements the rebel losses in killed and wounded, are estimated at fifteen thousand, and in prisoners at twenty-five thousand. Over two hundred pieces of artillery, with immense quantities of stores and small arms, were also captured.

When the national troops marched into Petersburg, at four o'clock Monday morning, they found the fortifications, cannon and camps, as they had been used while the rebels had possession of them, showing the hasty character of the flight. Warehouses filled with all manner of army stores, wagons, horses and mules without number, were also found.

For a short time now the Davis government will need a capital on wheels to meet its necessities.

AN ANONYMOUS REPORT: CONDITION OF PETERSBURG AFTER REBEL EVACUATION

A New York Times *correspondent offers this report of the status of the city of Petersburg after the rebel forces evacuated.*

New York Times, 6 April 1865

FROM PETERSBURGH

Particulars of the Occupation of the City—Large Quantities of Tobacco Burned by the Rebels.
PETERSBURGH, Monday, April 3.

The Army of the Potomac has been in and out of Petersburgh this morning, merely making a flying visit. The rebels commenced evacuating last night at 10 o'clock, and by 3 o'clock this morning were across the river, having burned about $1,000,000 worth of tobacco, the Southside Railroad Dept, and the bridges across the Appomattox. Our troops charged the inner line of works at daylight, taking a picket line of some five hundred men prisoners.

The troops, on entering the city, behaved most admirably—not more than half a dozen being entered by them and those mostly containing tobacco, cigars, liquor, etc. The Provost Guard soon arrived and established order.

For more than a month past the rebel troops have been receiving less rations than ever before, only just enough being brought to last from day to day. The citizens say they have suffered much, but it is well to take such stories with a good deal of allowance. The rebels managed to get away with all their artillery, excepting one or two old columbiads, and a few heavy mortars which they could not transport readily.

A large number of men deserted and hid away in town until our troops entered, when they made their appearance and were taken into custody. It is believed they retreated toward Lynchburgh or Danville, but they will have to make good time if they elude the pursuit of our army, now flushed with victory, and willing to travel at any rate and any distance to head them off.

The city presents a very cleanly and respectable appearance, and there are many residences here that would do no discredit to Fifth-avenue. Many of the houses in the lower part of the city have been badly injured by the shot and shell thrown from our batteries last Summer, and since that time most of the houses located there have been vacated.

The report of Gen. A. P. Hill's death is confirmed by the citizens here, some of whom saw his body.

AN ANONYMOUS REPORT: REPORT ON FALL OF RICHMOND

The small village of Gettysburg, where the bloodiest battle of the Civil War was fought in 1863, received the news of the fall of the two cities from its weekly newspaper the Adams County Sentinel & General Advertiser. *The paper notes that the city was rejoicing.*

Adams County Sentinel & General Advertiser, 4 April 1865 (Gettysburg, Pa.)

GLORIOUS NEWS!
PETERSBURG & RICHMOND CAPTURED!
TWELVE THOUSAND PRISONERS AND FIFTY CANNON TAKEN!

A telegraphic despatch yesterday says, that Petersburg was captured, with all its garrison, guns, &c.

Another official despatch from General Weitzell, dated 11 yesterday, was also received. He says:—"We took Richmond at 8:15 this morning. I have captured many guns. The enemy left in great haste. The City is on fire in one part, and I am making every effort to put it out.—The people received us with enthusiastic expressions of joy. Gen. Grant started early this morning with his army towards the Danville road to cut off Lee's retreating army, if possible. President Lincoln has gone to the front."

Twelve thousand prisoners and fifty pieces of artillery are already taken, and Grant is pushing on after Lee, who is in full retreat. The President is at the front, and telegraphed regularly to the Secretary of War.

Our town was quite jubilant last evening over the glorious intelligence. The flags, the ringing of bells, the firing-of salutes, bonfires, and the cheering of the crowds, were evidences of the general rejoicing. We shall be now daily in receipt of stirring news.

MANTON MARBLE: REPORT OF JEFFERSON DAVIS' FLIGHT FROM RICHMOND

A New York newspaper offered the following untitled story about how Confederate President Jefferson Davis received the news from Lee to evacuate.

New York World, 5 April 1865

It is stated here that Jeff. Davis and his family, and the other rebel officers with their families, did not leave Richmond until early Monday morning. Had Gen. Weitzel's troops made for the railroad depot after they entered the city, the whole party might have been captured. It is also stated that when Davis received Lee's dispatch at ten o'clock, on Saturday night, announcing the turning of his right wing by Sheridan, and his purpose to retreat upon Danville, the rebel president would not believe it was genuine, and charged the messenger with playing an April fool trick upon him.

CHARLES HALE: FALL OF RICHMOND

Although the news of the fall of Petersburg was greatly celebrated, the news of Richmond's capture was even more glorious to those in the North. This untitled editorial appeared before the press received news of the official fall of the Confederate capital city.

Boston Daily Advertiser, 4 April 1865

Whatever great events the war may still have in store for us, none of them will so fill the heart of the country as the fall of Richmond, or hold the same place in the public sentiment with that long-deferred victory. Even the return of peace is not likely to bring any one moment when the hope and sus-pense of years are so brought to their climax and culminate in sudden triumph; for peace is likely to return by a gradual subsidence, at no point in which we can say that here the war closes. Richmond, however, with its outwork Petersburg, have fallen at the instant when the interest of the contest was at its height, after three days in which giants wrestled for the mastery, and at the close of which the rebel commander found himself thrown back, broken and exhausted, from the line which was the key of his position. In these days the burning anxiety of many past campaigns was revived and re-enforced the hopes of the present; and with the crowning victory the recollections of years of brave effort, baffled but still renewed, throng the mind and fill the measure of our joy and gratitude.

CHARLES HALE: EDITORIAL PREDICTS END OF CONFEDERACY LITTLE MORE THAN A WEEK AWAY

This untitled editorial guesses about Lee's next move and suggests that the Confederacy only has days left before it is finished. The author offers hope that the rebels will surrender without additional blood-shed.

Boston Daily Advertiser, 5 April 1865

Although we are still favored with but little authentic information of the condition in which Lee extricated his army from Petersburg, such details as reach us increase the probability that he now has with him little more than the wreck of the once proud Army of Northern Virginia. The struggle which ensued when General Grant, penetrating the enemy's designs, anticipated his retirement by a decisive attack, is now seen to have been even fiercer and more destructive than it was made to appear in the earlier despatches. It cost Lee heavily in killed and wounded; his loss in prisoners was beyond any previous experience in the history of that army; and the method of the attack, the crushing in and sweeping away of his right, followed by a retreat which every man knew was the abandonment of all Eastern Virginia, was disorganizing, destructive of the *morale* of his force, and peculiarly adapted to destroy its cohesion. It would seem from the accounts thus far received that the last ten days of his stay in Petersburg can hardly have cost him less than one-third of a force which was sadly shorn of its strength to begin with. His retreat under such circumstances, cannot have been orderly; we have General Grant's authority for the statement that the country is filled with Lee's strugglers,—men who are tired of the vain contest and would gladly find themselves at home again; abandoned artillery and destroyed trains are reported to mark his path; and in short all the accounts point, not indeed to a rout, but to a disastrous retreat, which when well pushed may yet become a rout.

In what direction this retreat will be directed is the engrossing question which the hours now passing are to determine, a question hardly inferior in importance to that of the reduction of the rebel position. Lee's effort is doubtless to fall back upon Danville, and there to unite his remaining force with the army of Johnston, and by their united strength to make head for a time against our generals, in the hope perhaps that a well-delivered blow at Sherman or Grant singly may save the rebel cause from instant ruin. But neither Lee nor Johnston can carry out his share of this scheme of concentration unmolested. Aside from some hints that Grant may have been beforehand with the enemy in this scheme, and that the cavalry struck the Danville road as soon as the course of events at Petersburg was known, it is certain that Lee is closely pursued by our forces upon a line which would seem to be parallel with his retreat, and that their effort to crowd him more and more to the north has some promise of success. Probably in the present position of affairs General Grant would ask for nothing better than to direct Lee's retreat upon Lynchburg. Meantime also we know of Johnston, that if he projects a retreat upon Danville, he has Sherman to deal with, a General never slack in his work, and who is acting upon fresh consultation with Grant. The last few days have brought us no news except from Virginia; but we have little doubt that it will prove that they have been eventful days in North Carolina also.

The question of the hour is then, how long,—we may almost say how many days,—the enemy are to have an organized army in the Atlantic States. The time must be short, unless the most significant indications for once deceive all hopes. And this question of an organized military power being settled, there is no ground for apprehension that the rebel leaders will succeed in inducing the Southern people to court their own utter ruin, by a desultory, sullen and hopeless resistance of lawful authority.

THOMAS N. DAY: FALL OF RICHMOND SIGNALS END OF REBELLION

The fall of Richmond led to predictions of the end of the war that would come true very soon.

Hartford Daily Courant, 8 April 1865 (Hartford, Conn.)

With the fall of Richmond commenced the death rattle of the rebellion. Good news comes to us from our armies in such rapid succession, that one chorus of victory hardly dies away before another fills the air. Yesterday afternoon the surrender of Lee's whole army was announced in a dispatch from Philadelphia; but this was premature as shortly after it was qualified by the following:

PHILADELPHIA, April 7.—Jay Cooke has a second dispatch from Washington, stating that the report that Gen. Robert E. Lee is taken is contradicted; it is Fitz Hugh Lee. *We have the army, however, except small fragments, whose capture, with Lee Sheridan reports inevitable.*

Glory enough for great rejoicing was written in this intelligence, and in many cities bells were rung, and common fired, amid the wildest demonstration of joy. Last night no army news was received, but look out soon for stirring announcements.

CHARLES HALE: PEOPLE OF BOSTON FORESEE END TO WAR

The fall of Richmond led people in Boston to conclude the war would soon end.

Boston Daily Advertiser, 4 April 1865

Our city was electrified with joy yesterday by the reception of an official announcement of the event so long hoped for, the fall of Richmond. Though it was an event long expected, often promised, and even announced, the news came at last with great suddenness. Few doubted, after the victory of Sunday, that Petersburg would be abandoned, but it is thought that there were few who did not receive the information yesterday, that the Union flag waved over both cities, with surprise mingled with their delight. The rejoicings of the loyal people in this and in other cities and towns will be found to occupy much of our space today. It was a biter pill for the proud braggarts who were compelled to leave their boasted capital, to have not only the hated "Yankees," occupy it, but that the first Union troops to take possession of it should be of the race whom they have so despised and oppressed. We shall probably hear today from General Grant and of the fate of the army of Lee, of which he was at the last accounts in pursuit, and also of the extent of the fire spoken of in Richmond.

HENRY RAYMOND: COMPLETENESS OF THE NATIONAL VICTORY AT PETERSBURG AND RICHMOND

The New York Times *offers a good overview of how devastating the victories at Petersburg and Richmond were to the Confederacy and Lee's forces.*

New York Times, 5 April 1865

The material losses inflicted upon the rebel army around Petersburgh, in men, in the equipments and munitions of war, not less than in position, have not yet been so computed that their overwhelming weight can be made at once appreciable. A careful comparison of different data gave LEE, three months ago, an army of 85,000 men. Within that period there is superabundant evidence to prove to us that this force, so formidable in numbers, and, peradventure, scarcely less formidable in its tough experience, had lost full 15,000 men. We should clearly be under, rather than over the actual number, if we set down LEE'S losses, in killed and wounded, in the five day's engagements, at 10,000 more. And putting together all the returns of captured prisoners already received, we are unable, by the most moderate computation to reduce their aggregate below 25,000. These deductions alone bring the relics of the rebel army of Virginia down to 85,000 men, without including the gangs of stragglers from that fugitive band, met with at every furlong of GRANT and SHERIDAN'S pursuit. If LEE to-day has even 30,000 in his immediate command he must have found material for conscription in the line of his inglorious fight. And each succeeding sunrise can but witness not only the decline of his army in bulk, but its rapid and irreclaimable demoralization as well.

The captures of guns in the storming of the right of LEE'S Petersburgh intrenchments and in the great field engagements, large as these are, represent—by accumulated testimony from every quarter of the field lately held by LEE—but a mere fraction of the war material sacrificed in the rebel flight. Not only are the lines of retreat strewed in all directions with abandoned arms of every variety and calibre, but so overwhelmingly sudden was the swoop of our cavalry around and behind the right wing of LEE'S army, which gave GRANT the first signal and assurance of his victory, that there was not time left to the enemy to either use or destroy the railroad plant concentrated in Richmond, all of which was essential war material to the rebels only three days ago. Not only have we reported on the authority of SHERIDAN—as the first experience of his pursuit of the rebels—that "the majority of the arms that were left in the hands of LEE'S army are now scattered between Richmond and where his troops now are;" and that "the line of retreat is marked with artillery, ammunition, burned or charred wagons, caissons and ambulances."—but the rolling stock of DAVIS' late military roads seems to have been abandoned as an utterly useless provision hereafter in the regular warfare on which the remaining rebel forces has fallen back.

With these material losses may be computed the loss of the best military position alike for offensive and defensive operations that remained to the Confederacy. To the value set upon that position, the countless battlefields of Virginia, from Loudon Heights to the Rappahannock, the Chickahominy, and the Appomattox, bear grim proofs which permit neither of cavil or dispute. In that death-grapple of Sunday, around and beyond the forts at Petersburgh, the position thus cherished, thus clung to in the very agony of his desperate and hopeless situation, was abandoned by LEE, never to be retaken, till a more recreant race than ours shall control the power, and assume to uphold the honor of this Republic.

Yet, vast even almost beyond compute as are these immediate and palpable losses of the insurgent force, they cannot compare, in any rebel estimate to-day, with the overwhelming disaster which has overtaken the Confederacy as a political power. In the fall of Richmond every junction it had exercised as a political combination ceased thenceforth and for all time. As an *organic* force it passed out of existence, and lapsed incontinently into a mere insurrection. The flight of DAVIS from Richmond put an everlasting period to the relationship of his administration to every single one of the States that adhered to his political system. His spurious machinery of legislation became thereafter a by-word for history. His Executive Departments resolved themselves into visions of thing spurious that *had been* but *should be* no more. His conscription appliances, his taxing agencies, his money-printing apparatus, his foreign relations—Heaven help them!—his postal system, his military tribunals, and his libel of a Constitution—all passed away like the spectral creations of some ugly dream. And what passed among the friendly crowd of on-lookers, but the other day, for the dignity and circumstances of an organized and permanently established power, was blown in a night to the winds by the hot breath of the avenging destroyer.

Were LEE'S armed bands, from the James to the Red River, twice as numerous and many times more faithful to the Confederacy than they, what compensation could it be for this utter demolition of the political structure in which the fortunes of the leading rebel gang had been staked? At best, these bands could but provide for their own sustenance and for escape from the immediate and the condign punishment of the prime actors in this murderous league. At most they could play the *role* of bandit or guerrillas for a term which would be altogether in the power of the supreme government to limit, with less exertion, probably, than has been expended on a single one out of a store of campaigns that have marked the past history of the war. With the disappearance, then, of all that gave cohesion and political vitality to this wretched Confederacy, goes all that made it formidable at home, or gave it informal recognition abroad.

NOTES

1. Margaret E. Wagner, Gary W. Gallagher, and Paul Finkelman (Eds.), *The Library of Congress Civil War Desk Reference* (New York: Simon & Schuster, 2002), 311.

2. Ibid., 312.

3. "Richmond: The Occupation of the Late Rebel Capital by Our Forces," *New York Times*, 6 April 1865.

4. "Richmond and Victory," *New York Times*, 4 April 1865.

FURTHER READINGS

Bradford, Ned (Ed.). *Battles and Leaders of the Civil War*. New York: Appleton-Century-Crofts, 1956.

Johnson, Curt, and McLaughlin, Mark. *Civil War Battles*. New York: Crown Publishers, 1977.

Kinard, Jeff. *The Battle of the Crater*. New York: Ryan Place Publishers, 1995.

Wagner, Margaret E., Gallagher, Gary W., and Finkelman, Paul (Eds.). *The Library of Congress Civil War Desk Reference*. New York: Simon & Schuster, 2002.

26

CONFEDERATE SURRENDER AT APPOMATTOX COURTHOUSE, 9 APRIL 1865

After the evacuation of Petersburg and Richmond, Confederate General Robert E. Lee began leading his army to a rendezvous with General Joseph E. Johnston's forces. Johnston's troops were retreating as Union General William Sherman advanced through North Carolina. Lee hoped that once the two Confederate armies were unified, they could make a stand against the converging armies of Ulysses S. Grant in Virginia and General Sherman.

Lee traveled along the Richmond & Danville railroad line, which was still operating as a supply line for the South. He was headed for Lynchburg, Virginia. The closely pursuing federal army managed to cut the railroad to Lynchburg, and on 6 April, along a tributary of the Appomattox River, three engagements between Lee's forces and Union forces occurred that resulted in the capture of about 8,000 Confederate troops. The loss of nearly a quarter of Lee's army gave Grant's forces a three-to-one advantage over the rebels. On 7 April, Grant sent a message to Lee calling for his surrender. Grant's message noted the "hopelessness of further resistance" on the part of Lee's army, to which Lee replied that he did not think the situation was hopeless. Still, he asked for Grant's terms for surrender. Two days later, on 9 April 1865, after a series of exchanges between the two generals, they met at Wilbur McLean's home in the village of Appomattox Courthouse to agree on the terms of surrender. On 12 April 1865, a formal surrender ceremony took place, four years to the day after the South Carolina militia initiated the war with the assault on Fort Sumter (see Chapter 6).[1]

The Northern press smelled Union victory once Petersburg and Richmond fell. Their coverage of events between the fall of Richmond and Lee's surrender focused on Lee's retreat and the Battle of Sayler's Creek, where the large number of retreating Confederate forces were captured. When the news of Lee's surrender finally arrived, it was expected, but as the *New York Times* noted in an article two days after the event,

The excitement was equaled only by that which followed the attack upon Fort Sumter; the surrender of Lee and his army was anticipated, looked for, and to a great extent discounted in advance. The utter demoralization of the rebel army, the increased esprit of our own forces, the vigorous pursuit of the Union troops and the prophecy of Gen. Grant had prepared us for the great news which, on Sunday night, was flashed across the wires to an expectant public. Despite this, however, the errand of the mercurial newsboys was successful; with their arms full of extras they rushed up town and over to the neighboring cities, shouting the glad tidings as they ran, so that before the morning papers disclosed the fact, the great mass of the people were aware that Lee and his armed men no longer stood in the pathway of the Army of the Potomac. . . . The dispatch characteristic of [War] Secretary Stanton settled every doubt and the wildest delirium of joy seized everybody and held possession for the night.[2]

Editorials and articles about Northern celebrations abounded—many schools and businesses were closed so that "general jollification" could take place among citizens. Northern newspapers chronicled the events. "In all the cities and towns of the land, it has been a jubilee of the most enthusiastic character; and the country has probably never witnessed more heart felt rejoicing," wrote the editor of the small *Adams County Sentinel & General Advertiser*, published in Gettysburg.[3] The articles below provide some examples of the coverage of Lee's retreat as well as short editorial comments about the end of the war and the celebrations that came with Lee's surrender.

Although the surrender of Lee did effectively put an end to the physical fighting, significant events continued throughout 1865. Just two days after the surrender ceremony at Appomattox Courthouse, President Abraham Lincoln was shot by an assassin and died the next day. Andrew Johnson became the seventeenth president of the United States on 15 April 1865. The war did not officially end until Confederate President Jefferson Davis was captured by Union forces in Georgia on 10 May. The institution of slavery was finally abolished on 18 December 1865 when the Thirteenth Amendment to the Constitution was ratified. It read, "Neither slavery nor involuntary servitude, except as punishment for crime whereof the party shall have been duly convicted, shall exist within the United States, or any place subject to their jurisdiction. Congress shall have power to enforce this article by appropriate legislation."[4]

HENRY RAYMOND: THE ROUT OF LEE'S ARMY

This short column in the New York Times *details the day-by-day blows to Lee's Army of Northern Virginia. It suggests that his best course of action is surrender, which he did 1 day after this article was published. The Thursday struggle that is referred to in this story was often called "Black Thursday" in the South since the capture of so many of Lee's men near Sayler's Creek helped lead to his surrender.*

New York Times, 8 April 1865

The official telegrams to-day give abundant indication that Lieut.-Gen. GRANT is still engaged with tremendous vigor in the work of demolishing the army of LEE. Three corps of our infantry, with the cavalry under Gen. SHERIDAN, were actively and immediately operating against him, on Thursday, near Amelia court-house; and two of these corps, the Second and Sixth, under Gens. HUMPHREY and WRIGHT, succeeded in forcing LEE to action, the result of which was the rout of the enemy, the capture of EWELL, and other general officers, and many prisoners and guns.

There can be no doubt, from the statements officially made by the officers immediately in command, that the army of Gen. LEE, so long the bulwark of the Confederacy, is virtually crushed; and that he can neither have men nor guns enough to effect anything more brilliant than a rabble rout. We had yesterday a telegraphic report that LEE and all the army left to him had surrendered. This was premature; but the event is one which seems to be hourly expected by those whose position gives them the best opportunities of knowing the circumstances and prospects. It would be a graceful week. He was disastrously defeated on Sunday, abandoned Richmond on Monday, spent Tuesday and Wednesday in flight, was routed on Thursday, was at his wit's end what to do on Friday, which difficulty he can solve by surrendering to-day.

AN ANONYMOUS REPORT: THE PURSUIT OF LEE'S ARMY

This brief article offers readers a glimpse of the aggressiveness with which Grant's forces pursued Lee and his men. It confirms the fact that Lee would not be able to meet up successfully with General Johnston's forces fighting in and fleeing from North Carolina.

New York Times, 9 April 1865

Mr. STANTON'S brief telegram, of yesterday, gives us news from Gen. GRANT up to noon. He was then at Farmville, sixteen miles west of Burkesville Station. This position puts beyond the possibility of doubt the fact, that LEE is completely shut out from North Carolina, and, in fact, from the whole South. Consequently he turns northwesterly, and hastens toward Lynchburgh. Our pursuit is so vigorous that Gen. GRANT is very sanguine that the rebel leader will very soon be driven to a surrender. He cannot be unaware that both THOMAS and SCHOFIELD—the former from East Tennessee and the latter from the Shenandoah Valley—are rapidly nearing Lynchburg, and may be on hand to bid him welcome. We have no direct news from SHERMAN, but it is pretty certain that he is looking after JOHNSTON, and probably moving rapidly toward the grand theatre in which GRANT is doing his great work.

AN ANONYMOUS REPORT: REJOICING AT END OF WAR; LAST EXCHANGES BETWEEN LEE AND GRANT

The New York Times *published the official dispatches related to the surrender, including all of the preliminary correspondence between Generals Grant and Lee, followed by reports of the celebrations that were had in cities across the North. What appears below is an excerpt that contains the last two exchanges between Grant and Lee as well as the reports of the "rejoicings."*

New York Times, 10 April 1865

HANG OUT YOUR BANNERS
UNION VICTORY! PEACE!
Surrender of General Lee and His Whole Army. . . .

The Preliminary Correspondence

. . . GENERAL [*Grant*]: I received, at a late hour, your note of to-day, in answer to mine of yesterday.

I did not intend to propose the surrender of the Army of Northern Virginia, but *to ask the terms* of your proposition. To be frank, I do not think the emergency has arisen to call for the surrender.

But as *the restoration of peace should be the sole object of all,* I desire to know whether your proposal would tend to that end. I cannot, therefore, meet you with a view to surrender the Army of Northern Virginia, but *as far as your proposition may affect the Confederate States forces under my command, and tend to the restoration of peace,* I should be pleased to meet you at 10 A.M. to-morrow, on the old stage road to Richmond, between the picket lines of the two armies.

Very respectfully, your obedient servant, R. E. LEE, General C.S.A.

. . . GENERAL [*Lee*]: Your note of yesterday is received. As I have no authority to treat on the subject of peace, the meeting proposed for 10 A.M. to-day could lead to no good. I will state, however, General, that *I am equally anxious for peace with yourself*; and the whole North entertain the same feeling. *The terms upon which peace can be had are well understood.*

By the South laying down their arms, they will hasten that most desirable event, save thousands of human lives and hundreds of millions of property not yet destroyed.

Sincerely hoping that all our difficulties may be settled without the loss of another life, I subscribe myself,

Very respectfully, Your Obedient Servant, ULYSSES S. GRANT, Lieutenant-General United States Army.

Rejoicings

WILMINGTON, Del., Sunday, April 9.

Wilmington is in an uproar and blaze of glory, rejoicing over the greatest of victories yet achieved by our arms. Guns are firing, bells are ringing, and a large procession is proceeding through the streets. Such an excitement was never before witnessed in this city.

ALBANY, Monday, April 10—1 A.M.

There is great rejoicing here over the news of the surrender of Gen. LEE and his army.

The news was received at about 10 P.M., and about midnight State and Pearl streets were filled with people anxiously awaiting the particulars.

The bells are ringing, cannon firing, while the multitude are indulging in fireworks.

The Governor was called up and briefly addressed the throng around his residence.

The State House and many private residences are illuminated.

PHILADELPHIA, April 9.

The glorious announcement of LEE'S surrender was received here about nine o'clock. It was telegraphed to all sections of the city, and was announced in the several churches. *The Ledger* office was illuminated in five minutes. The bell of Independence Hall was rung by order of the Mayor. The firemen immediately assembled and blocked up the street. Salutes were fired, and the whistles of the steam-engines and the cheers of the assembled multitudes made the whole city ring.

WORCESTER, Mass., Sunday, April 9.

The news of the surrender of LEE and his army created an intense excitement here to-night. The bells were rung, guns were fired, bonfires kindled, the fire companies turned out, and many stores and buildings were illuminated.

PITTSBURGH, Pa., Sunday, April 9.

The news to-night brought nearly the entire population into the streets. The recruiting booths were turned into bonfires, salutes were fired, speeches were made, and bands played.

TRENTON, N.J., Sunday, April 9.

The glorious news was received here with cheering and ringing of bells. The people are turning out en mass to receive and rejoice over the glad tidings.

PROVIDENCE, R.I., Sunday, April 9—Midnight.

Bells are ringing, cannon are firing, and the citizens are rejoicing over the news of Lee's surrender. A large bonfire is burning on Waybosset bridge.

THOMAS N. DAY: SURRENDER OF LEE'S ARMY

The following editorial account of the surrender in the Hartford Daily Courant *shows no deference to the South, still calling them enemies of the Republic. It predicts that Johnston's troops are next to surrender.*

Hartford Daily Courant, 10 April 1865 (Hartford, Conn.)

God be praised. Lee's army has surrendered. The rebellion is crushed. Justice and Liberty are vindicated. The Republic triumphs over its enemies, emerging from a four years' conflict stronger than ever before. The heroism of the loyal North is crowned at last by a triumph which sweeps treason and slavery out of existence together. The victories at Richmond, the hurried evacuation of the city, and the swift pursuit gave the country confidence that Lee's army would either be captured or annihilated. Sunday afternoon Lee surrendered the remnants of the forces under his command, officers and men to be paroled, not to serve against the United States until regularly exchanged. The only body of troops left to the confederacy east of the Mississippi is the army of Johnston in North Carolina, with its record of defeats. It is hemmed in on both sides, and must share the fate of the Army of Northern Virginia. Peace, Union and rejoicings are the order of the day.

R. J. HALDEMAN: SURRENDER OF GENERAL LEE

Despite their differences throughout the war, Democratic and Republican papers united in their celebration of the Republic on the news of Lee's surrender. This account comes from the Democratic Harrisburg Patriot & Union. *The commentary ends by urging the country's elected officials to engage in "wise statesmanship" as the country is restored.*

Harrisburg Patriot & Union, 10 April 1865 (Harrisburg, Pa.)

The glorious news by telegraph last night has electrified the whole country, and caused a throb of joy in the great popular heart. Peace already seems to be stretching her radiant wings over the boundaries of the Old Union in all its geographic integrity. The surrender of the Army of Northern Virginia will probably bring about the disintegration of the Old Dominion from the thralldom of rebellion and its speedy restoration of the Federal Union. The grand Army of the Potomac, under the victorious Grant, will now be thrown with resistless force among the small remaining detachments of the rebel army south of Virginia so there can remain no other course for the rebel leaders but submission, self-expatriation in Mexico, or a resort to desultory guerrilla warfare.

The demonstrations of joy and gladness with which this great victory of our Northern sons was received all over the North indicate more clearly than words how devoted are our people to peace and how earnestly and unceasingly they have yearned for the hour of victory and the end of war. God grant that peace and prosperity may soon follow the heroic achievements of the army of the North. It now only remains for those in authority to exercise wisdom in finishing up what Northern bravery and genius have so nearly accomplished. It is in their power now to restore the Union in all its wonted integrity, and to put the nation again upon the road to prosperity. Will they do it? It is, also, in their power to protract the strife and leave to coming generations a heritage of anarchy and disruption. If ever there is a period more requiring wisdom and all the virtues, it is the hour of victory. Let, therefore, all good men, while rejoicing in the glad tidings of the hour, pray that wise statesmanship may govern in the executive councils.

THOMAS N. DAY: PEACE AND FRATERNITY

In this editorial celebrating the end of the war the writer praises the Union for defending principles related to self-governance. The writer laments the terrible loss the South has endured in fighting in the name of slavery.

Hartford Daily Courant, 12 April 1865 (Hartford, Conn.)

In all quarters of the country, the people gave themselves up, on Monday, to unrestrained rejoicings. All eyes were opened to see that the Republic was safe and its destiny secure. In a night the doubts of the faithless and the fears of the timorous had given way. The nation had realized its strength, and caught a glimpse of the grandeur that awaits it in the future. It was a day of thanksgiving to God and of forgiveness to enemies. The noble sentiments expressed in the letters of General Grant to General Lee met a response in every generous heart. They cared not to look to the bad men or wicked councils which had caused so much sorrow and bloodshed. With a magnanimity worthy of the heroism which had defended the gates to the temple of Liberty through four years of murderous war, our people recalled their thoughts from projects of revenge, to turn them forward to sweeter pictures of Union, peace and fraternity.

The North has not waged this war so persistently from enmity to the South, but from devotion to the country and to the eternal principles upon which the foundations of its government are planted. They believe in the capacity of man for self-government, and in that faith have shrunk from no extremity of sacrifice. Through all the vicissitudes of the struggle, the mass of the people have never faltered in meeting the demands of the emergency, and have never distrusted the certainty of final triumph. Having accomplished this—having disarmed the power of the rebellion, they can find no place for low thoughts of revenge. They pity the miserable leaders and miserable dupes of the South rather than desire to add to the overwhelming burden of their sorrows. They commenced the war to perpetuate slavery. What have they accomplished? The institution is smitten to the dust, and the chains of the bondman are broken forever. Their male population is cut off, and their wealth squandered. Railroads are decayed; commerce swallowed up; factories in ashes, and nearly all the monuments of past industry in ruins. The bare fields, intersected by rickety fences, and dotted here and there with melancholy habitations, are about all that remain of the former splendor of the South. The attempt to secede leaves their section without men and without means. Surely their punishment has been heavy. What remains may well be left to the Great Judge.

Once more the *eagles* of the Republic wave triumphantly over every bay and inlet along three thousand miles of coast. Over all our domain may they continue to wave in increasing splendor and widening beneficence till the regeneration of mankind is complete.

CHARLES HALE: THANKS TO GOD FOR RESTORATION PEACE

This untitled editorial focuses on the justness of the Union cause for fighting the war. It suggests that the final achievement of peace is a blessing from God.

Boston Daily Advertiser, 22 April 1865

The sensation of relief and victory is expressed without words. There is no orator in the land who would venture to speak the nation's gratitude.

That our difficulties may be settled without the loss of another life;—

That this restoration of peace may be immediate;—

That it is the first wish of the highest officers of both armies;—

That the thanks of the country will be given to its soldiers for all time;—

And that thanks are to be poured out to Almighty God for this great victory; such were the wishes and prayers which spontaneously expressed themselves in those brief despatches of Sunday,—by which peace was secured, and by which it was acknowledged. To throw out everywhere the national flag, of which the lustre is regained,—to leave everywhere daily routine for the expression of joy and thanksgiving,—to salute strangers and friends alike with the cry of congratulation,—was the natural tribute of the people.

Four years ago this morning we were obliged to say in this place, "We do not seek to pierce the gloom which now seems to overspread the future." Four years of that future, as they have unrolled themselves, have shown many another crisis, of agony more acute, but none of gloom so depressing as settled on us all in that week of uncertainty. This day is the anniversary of the humiliating correspondence between General Beauregard and Major Anderson, in which he demanded the surrender of Fort Sumter as a foregone necessity. Tomorrow is the anniversary of the day on which he opened his fire. Those four years have called upon the nation to show its steadfast endurance. They have called for that loyalty to institutions which does not seek to pierce the gloom of the future. They have bidden the nation stand firm on the eternal principles of its government, and trust God to give, it victory when for

victory the time had come. Through that gloom, and through all the crises of agony, or flushes of hope, which at one moment or another varied it, the nation has stood firm, and at last the end has come.

That end is, of course, a beginning. It may be to this nation a beginning of peace such as nations only card when they have shown themselves fit for war. It may be the beginning of such a peace for centuries as came to the Roman Empire when, at the end of civil war, Augustus closed the gates which had so long stood open. The one gulf which yawned in the way of our national prosperity is closed. It had to be filled with our choicest treasures. It has cost us our bravest and our best. But they were ready for the sacrifice. We have known that none were ready for the sacrifice. The sacrifice has been made, and that curse is removed from the land. The nation understands its power, and the success of its power. The North understands the South; the South understands the North. The West understands the East; the East understands the West. The people understand that they can have free institutions if they are willing to die for them. They understand that they do not deserve them unless they are willing to die for them. And every public man understands that in the people of this country there is a determination which cannot be maneuvered with or managed, that the substantial principles of American liberty shall go down unimpaired to all time.

Such are the moral advantages of the victory. They make a nation so strong that war in its future is wholly unnecessary,—it seems hardly possible. This nation is just,—it can be as generous as it is just. It has no entangling foreign alliances. It need have no petty foreign jealousies. God has shown it His mercy in a thousand ways, and now that He blesses it with Peace, it has His promise that Peace shall lead in every other angel of His kingdom.

NOTES

1. Margaret E. Wagner, Gary W. Gallagher, and Paul Finkelman (Eds.), *The Library of Congress Civil War Desk Reference* (New York: Simon & Schuster, 2002), 326.

2. "The Quiet and Reverent Gratitude of the People," *New York Times*, 11 April 1865.

3. *Adams County Sentinel & General Advertiser*, 11 April 1865.

4. U.S. Constitution, Thirteenth Amendment (ratified 18 December 1865).

FURTHER READINGS

Blount, Roy, Jr. *Robert E. Lee*. New York: Viking Books, 2003.

Bradford, Ned (Ed.). *Battles and Leaders of the Civil War*. New York: Appleton-Century-Crofts, 1956.

Grant, Ulysses S. *Personal Memoirs: Ulysses S. Grant*. Introduction by Geoffrey Parrett. New York: Modern Library, 1999.

Marvel, William. *Lee's Last Retreat: The Flight to Appomattox*. Chapel Hill: University of North Carolina Press, 2002.

———. *A Place Called Appomattox*. Chapel Hill: University of North Carolina Press, 2000.

Wagner, Margaret E.; Gallagher, Gary W.; and Finkelman, Paul (Eds.). *The Library of Congress Civil War Desk Reference*. New York: Simon & Schuster, 2002.

SELECTED BIBLIOGRAPHY

"Admission of Missouri." *Annals of Congress*. House of Representatives. 15th Cong., 2nd sess., February 1819.

Andrews, J. Cutler. *The North Reports the Civil War*. Pittsburgh: University of Pittsburgh Press, 1955.

————. *The South Reports the Civil War*. Princeton, N.J.: Princeton University Press, 1970.

Arnold, James R. *Grant Wins the War: Decision at Vicksburg*. New York: John Wiley and Sons, 1997.

Bailey, Ronald H. *Battles for Atlanta*. New York: Time-Life Books, 1986.

Blount, Roy, Jr. *Robert E. Lee*. New York: Viking Books, 2003.

Bradford, Ned (Ed.). *Battles and Leaders of the Civil War*. New York: Appleton-Century-Crofts, 1956.

Cook, Adrian. *The Armies of the Streets: The New York City Draft Riots*. Lexington: University of Kentucky Press, 1974.

Cooke, John Esten. *Virginia: A History of the People*. Boston: Houghton Mifflin, 1884.

Cozzens, Lisa. "A Hard Shove for a 'Nation on the Brink': The Impact of Dred Scott." Department of Alfa-informatica, University of Groningen, Netherlands, 2003. http:// www. let.rug.nl/-usa/E/dred_scott/scottxx.htm.

Crozier, Emmet. *Yankee Reporters, 1861–1865*. New York: Oxford University Press, 1956.

Current, Richard W. *Lincoln and the First Shot*. Philadelphia: J. B. Lippincott, 1963.

Daniel, Larry J. *Shiloh: The Battle That Changed the Civil War*. New York: Simon & Schuster, 1998.

Davis, Burke. *Sherman's March*. New York: Vintage Books, 1988.

Davis, William H. *Battle at Bull Run: A History of the First Major Campaign of the Civil War*. Baton Rouge: Louisiana State University Press, 1981.

Detzer, David. *Allegiance: Fort Sumter, Charleston, and the Beginning of the Civil War*. Orlando, Fla.: Harcourt, 2001.

Dew, Charles B. *Apostles of Disunion: Southern Secession Commissioners and the Causes of the Civil War*. Charlottesville: University Press of Virginia, 2002.

Donald, David H. *Lincoln*. New York: Simon & Schuster, 1996.

Faust, Patricia L. (Ed.). *Historical Times Illustrated Encyclopedia of the Civil War*. New York: Harper & Row, 1986.

Finkelman, Paul. *His Soul Goes Marching On: Responses to John Brown and the Harper's Ferry Raid*. Charlottesville: University Press of Virginia, 1995.

Foote, Shelby. *The Beleaguered City: The Vicksburg Campaign December 1862–July 1863*. New York: Modern Library, 1995.

Gallagher, Gary W. *The Wilderness Campaign*. Chapel Hill: University of North Carolina Press, 1997.

Genoways, Ted, and Genoways, Hugh H. *A Perfect Picture of Hell: Eyewitness Accounts from Civil War Prisoners from the 12th Iowa*. Iowa City: University of Iowa Press, 2001.

Glatthaar, Joseph T. *The March to the Sea and Beyond: Sherman's Troops in the Savannah and Carolinas Campaigns*. Baton Rouge: Louisiana State University Press, 1995.

Goodrich, Thomas. *War to the Knife: Bleeding Kansas, 1854–1861*. Mechanicsburg, Pa.: Stackpole Books, 1998.

Gottfried, Bradley M. *Brigades of Gettysburg: The Union and Confederate Brigades at the Battle of Gettysburg*. Cambridge, Mass.: Da Capo Press, 2002.

Grant, Ulysses S. *Personal Memoirs: Ulysses S. Grant*. Introduction by Geoffrey Perrett. New York: Modern Library, 1999.

Guelzo, Allen C. *Lincoln's Emancipation Proclamation: The End of Slavery in America*. New York: Simon & Schuster, 2004.

Hall, Yancey. "Civil War Prison Camps Claimed Thousands." *National Geographic News* (July 2003). http://news.nationalgeographic.com/news/2003/07/0701_030701_civilwarprisons.html.

Hamilton, Charles Granville. *Lincoln and the Know Nothing Movement*. Washington, D.C.: Public Affairs Press, 1954.

Harris, Brayton. *Blue & Gray in Black & White*. Washington, D.C.: Brassey's, 1999.

Hennessey, John J. *Return to Bull Run: The Campaign and Battle of Second Manassas*. Norman: University of Oklahoma Press, 1999.

Hunter, Maj. Gen. David. *General Orders No. 11*, 9 May 1862.

Ingram, W. Scott. *The Battle of Fredericksburg*. Woodbridge, Conn.: Blackbirch Press, 2002.

Johnson, Curt, and McLaughlin, Mark. *Civil War Battles*. New York: Crown Publishers, 1977.

Johnson, Donald Bruce. *National Party Platforms*. Vol. 1, *1840–1956*. Rev. ed. Urbana: University of Illinois Press, 1978.

Kaufman, Kenneth C. *Dred Scott's Advocate: A Biography of Roswell M. Field*. Columbia: University of Missouri Press, 1996.

Kinard, Jeff. *The Battle of the Crater*. New York: Ryan Place Publishers, 1995.

Kutler, Stanley. *The Dred Scott Decision: Law or Politics?* Boston: Houghton Mifflin, 1967.

Lincoln, Abraham. *Abraham Lincoln: Speeches and Writings, 1859–1865*. Ed. Donald E. Fehrenbacher. New York: Library of America, 1989.

Long, David E. *The Jewel of Liberty: Abraham Lincoln's Re-Election and the End of Slavery*. Mechanicsburg, Pa.: Stackpole Books, 1994.

Luvaas, Jay. *Guide to the Battle of Gettysburg*. Lawrence: University Press of Kansas, 1994.

Malin, James C. "Identification of the Stranger at the Pottawatomie Massacre." *Kansas Historical Quarterly* 9, no. 1 (February 1940): 3–12.

Marvel, William. *Lee's Last Retreat: The Flight to Appomattox*. Chapel Hill: University of North Carolina Press, 2002.

———. *A Place Called Appomattox*. Chapel Hill: University of North Carolina Press, 2000.

McDonough, James L. *Shiloh: In Hell before Night*. Knoxville: University of Tennessee Press, 1977.

McPherson, James M. (Ed.). *The Atlas of the Civil War*. New York: Macmillan, 1994.

Meier, Michael T. "Civil War Draft Records: Exemptions and Enrollments." *Prologue* 26 (Winter 1994): 1–3.

Nelson, Truman. *The Old Man John Brown at Harper's Ferry*. New York: Holt, Rinehart and Winston, 1973.

Nichol, Alice. *Bleeding Kansas*. New York: Oxford University Press, 1954.

Nicolay, John G., and Hay, John (Eds.). *Complete Works of Abraham Lincoln*. Vol. 9. New York: F. D. Tandy Co., 1905.

O'Reilly, Francis Augustin. *The Fredericksburg Campaign: Winter War on the Rappahannock*. Baton Rouge: Louisiana State University Press, 2002.

Paquette, Robert Louis; Ferleger, Louis A.; and Ferleger, Lou. *Slavery, Secession and Southern History*. Charlottesville: University Press of Virginia, 2000.

Perry, James M. *A Bohemian Brigade: The Civil War Correspondents—Mostly Rough, Sometimes Ready*. New York: John Wiley and Sons, 2000.

Ransom, Roger L. *Conflict and Compromise*. New York: Cambridge University Press, 1989.

Ratner, Lorman, and Teeter, Dwight L., Jr. *Fanatics and Fire-eaters: Newspapers and the Coming of the Civil War*. Urbana: University of Illinois Press, 2003.

Report of Maj. Gen. Ambrose E. Burnside, U.S. Army, Commanding Army of the Potomac, Battle of Fredericksburg. 17 December 1862.

Rhodes, James Ford. *History of the Civil War, 1861–1865*. New York: Macmillan, 1917.

Robertson, James I., Jr. *Stonewall Jackson, the Man, the Soldier, the Legend*. New York: Macmillan, 1997.

Schudson, Michael. *Discovering the News: A Social History of American Newspapers*. New York: Basic Books, 1978.

Sears, Stephen W. *Chancellorsville*. New York: Houghton Mifflin, 1998.

———. *Landscape Turned Red: The Battle of Antietam*. New York: Mariner Books, 2003.

Sherman, William T. *Memoirs of General William T. Sherman*. Vol. 2. 2nd ed., rev. New York: D. A. Appleton and Co., 1875.

Smith, John David. *Black Soldiers in Blue: African American Troops in the Civil War Era*. Chapel Hill: University of North Carolina Press, 2002.

Stephens, Mitchell. *A History of the News*. Ft. Worth, Tex.: Harcourt Brace, 1997.

Stephenson, Nathaniel W. *Abraham Lincoln and the Union: A Chronicle of the Embattled North*. New Haven, Conn.: Yale University Press, 1921.

Wagner, Margaret E.; Gallagher, Gary W.; and Finkelman, Paul (Eds.). *The Library of Congress Civil War Desk Reference*. New York: Simon & Schuster, 2002.

Waugh, John C. *Reelecting Lincoln: The Battle for the 1864 Presidency*. Cambridge, Mass.: Da Capo Press, 1997.

Watts, Dale E. "How Bloody Was Bleeding Kansas? Political Killings in Kansas Territory, 1854–1861." *Kansas History* 18 (Summer 1995): 116–129.

Weisberger, Bernard A. *Reporters for the Union*. Boston: Little, Brown, 1953.

Wolff, Gerald W. *The Kansas-Nebraska Bill: Party, Section, and the Coming of the Civil War*. New York: Revisionist Press, 1977.

Wood, W. J. *Civil War Generalship: The Art of Command*. Cambridge, Mass.: Da Capo Press, 2000.

THE NORTHERN PRESS

Adams County Sentinel & General Advertiser (Gettysburg, Pa.)

Albany Evening Journal

Associated Press

Baltimore American

Baltimore Sun

Boston Daily Advertiser
Boston Journal
Chicago Daily Tribune/Chicago Tribune
Chicago Times
Cincinnati Commercial
Cincinnati Enquirer
Cincinnati Times
Crisis
Harper's New Monthly Magazine (New York City)
Harrisburg Patriot & Union/Harrisburg Daily Patriot & Union (Harrisburg, Pa.)
Hartford Daily Courant (Hartford, Conn.)
Illinois State Journal (Springfield)
Journal of Commerce
Kentucky Journal (Louisville)
The Liberator (Boston)
Memphis Appeal
National Anti-Slavery Standard (New York City)
National Era (Washington, D.C.)
National Intelligencer/Washington Intelligencer (Washington, D.C.)
National Republican (Washington, D.C.)
New Hampshire Patriot/State Gazette (Concord)
New York Evening Post
New York Herald
New York Independent
New York Journal of Commerce
New York Sun
New York Times/New York Daily Times
New York Tribune
New York World
Northwest Democrat
Philadelphia Christian Observer
Philadelphia Evening Bulletin
Philadelphia Evening Journal
Philadelphia Inquirer
Philadelphia Press
Philadelphia Public Ledger
Pittsburgh Gazette/Pittsburgh Daily Gazette
Providence Journal (Providence, R.I.)
Provincial Freeman (Chatham, Canada West)
Salem Observer (Salem, Mass.)
Springfield Republican (Springfield, Mass.)
St. Louis Democrat
St. Louis Republican
St. Paul Pioneer and Democrat (St. Paul, Minn.)
Washington Chronicle (Washington, D.C.)
Washington Daily Union (Washington, D.C.)
Washington Intelligencer (Washington, D.C.)
Washington Republican (Washington, D.C.)
Washington Star (Washington, D.C.)

II

SOUTHERN NEWSPAPERS DURING THE CIVIL WAR

Debra Reddin van Tuyll

TIMELINE

1860

6 November	Lincoln is elected president.
20 December	South Carolina secedes from the Union.
26 December	Major Robert Anderson moves his force from Fort Moultrie in Charleston Harbor to Fort Sumter, which he believes can be more easily defended with a small force. Southerners see this as a hostile move.

1861

9 January	Mississippi secedes; South Carolina batteries commit the first act of war by firing on the *Star of the West* to prevent it from bringing reinforcements to Fort Sumter.
10 January	Florida secedes.
11 January	Alabama secedes.
19 January	Georgia secedes.
26 January	Louisiana secedes.
29 January	Kansas is admitted to the Union.
1 February	Texas secedes.
8 February	Delegates from the six seceded states form the Confederate Congress in Montgomery and begin work on a provisional Constitution for the newly formed Confederate States of America (CSA).
9 February	Mississippian Jefferson Davis is elected president of the Confederate States of America with Georgian Alexander H. Stephens as his vice president. Davis is not in Montgomery; he is at his plantation in Mississippi when he receives word of his election.

15 February	Davis appoints a peace commission to negotiate with Union leaders. They are unsuccessful.
18 February	Davis and Stephens are inaugurated in Montgomery.
4 March	Abraham Lincoln is inaugurated president of the United States.
6 March	Davis calls for 100,000 volunteers to serve for 1 year in the Confederate army. By mid-April, the South had 35,000 men in the military, about twice the existing U.S. force of 16,367.
10 April	General Pierre Gustav Toutant Beauregard receives and carries out the order to demand the surrender of Fort Sumter. Major Anderson refuses.
12–14 April	Confederate batteries begin shelling Fort Sumter, which is garrisoned by eighty-three men, seven officers, and seventy-six enlisted.
13 April	Major Anderson officially surrenders.
14 April	Federal troops evacuate Fort Sumter.
15 April	Lincoln calls for 75,000 men to volunteer for three months of military service.
17 April	Virginia secedes.
19 April	Lincoln proclaims a blockade of Southern ports. Union troops from Massachusetts are attacked by a pro-Confederate street mob, and two soldiers are killed.
20 April	Norfolk Navy Yard is captured by the Virginia militia for the Confederacy.
3 May	Lincoln calls for volunteers for three years and orders the size of the regular army increased.
6 May	Arkansas secedes.
20 May	North Carolina secedes.
24 May	Kentucky declares its neutrality. Virginia militia occupy Alexandria.
1 June	Battle of Boonville, Missouri. Union General Nathaniel F. Lyon drives pro-South militia toward Arkansas. They are reinforced by Arkansas militia and try to retake Missouri for the Confederacy. Lyon's force wins.
3 June	First skirmish of the war at Philippi, Virginia. Major General G. B. McClellan clears the town of Confederate troops.
10 June	Confederate troops defeat Union troops at Big Bethel, Virginia.
11 June	Federal troops defeat Confederate troops at Romney, Virginia.
17 June	Federal troops defeat Confederate troops at Boonville, Missouri.
3 July	Lincoln organizes the Department of the West and places General John C. Frémont in command.
5 July	Confederate troops defeat Union troops at Cartage, Missouri.

11 July	Union troops defeat Confederate troops at Rich Mountain, Virginia.
19 July	38,000 Union soldiers move out from Washington to attack Confederate forces of 20,000 near Manassas, Virginia.
21 July	First Battle of Manassas. This is the first major battle of the war. Confederates rout the Union and chase them almost all the way back to Washington, D.C.
1 August	General George B. McClellan is given command of the Army of the Potomac.
2 August	Battle of Dug Spring, Missouri, a Union victory.
6 August	Union Brigadier General Ulysses S. Grant attempts to occupy Paducah, Kentucky, but is forestalled by Confederate forces under Major General Leonidas Polk.
10 August	Skirmish at Wilson's Creek, Missouri, a Confederate victory.
20 August	Confederates capture Union garrison at Lexington, Missouri.
28–29 August	Fighting at Hattaras Inlet, North Carolina, a Union victory.
12–13 September	Battle of Cheat Mountain. Lee is repulsed by Union troops in his attempt to recover western Virginia.
21 October	Fighting at Balls Bluff, Virginia, a Confederate victory.
31 October	General Winfield Scott, a hero of the Mexican-American War of the 1850s, retires. He is succeeded by McClellan as general-in-chief of the U.S. Armies.
7 November	Port Royal, South Carolina, falls to Union forces.
8 November	The *Trent* Affair. Charles Wilkes, captain of the USS *San Jacinto*, stopped the British packet *Trent* in the Bahamas and forcibly removed two Confederate representatives who were on their way to England to negotiate for recognition. The action nearly led to war with Great Britain, but American diplomatic efforts were able to smooth out the disagreement.

1862

19 January	Battle of Mill Springs, Kentucky, a Union victory.
27 January	Lincoln issues General War Order No. 1 authorizing a unified and aggressive attack on the Confederacy.
6 February	Fort Henry in Tennessee falls to the Union army.
8 February	Roanoke Island, North Carolina, falls to the Union.
16 February	Fort Donelson in Tennessee falls to the Union army after three days of hard fighting. Nearly 15,000 Confederate troops are captured with Fort Donelson.
17 February	CSA provisional congress is terminated. Permanent Congress of the Confederate States is organized.
18 February	Davis and Stephens are inaugurated as president and vice president of the Confederate States of America. They will serve six-year terms, as specified in the Confederate Constitution.

24 February	Nashville, Tennessee, surrenders to the Union.
26 February	Union troops occupy Nashville.
7–8 March	Battle of Pea Ridge, Arkansas. This Union victory gives the United States control of Missouri.
8 March	Peninsular Campaign begins after Lincoln reorganizes the Army of Virginia and relieves McClellan of supreme command. McClellan, who has angered the president with his refusal to act against the Confederates, is given command of the Army of the Potomac and ordered to attack Richmond. Battle of Hampton Roads, Virginia, begins.
9 March	CSS *Virginia* and USS *Monitor* battle at Hampton Roads. Results were inconclusive.
14 March	Battle of New Madrid, Missouri, a Union victory.
23 March	Stonewall Jackson is defeated at Kernstown, Virginia, the first action in the Shenandoah Valley.
6–7 April	Battle of Shiloh, Union victory. Confederate General Albert Sydney Johnson is killed.
10–11 April	Fort Pulaski near Savannah is surrendered to the Union.
15 April	Battle of Peralta, New Mexico, a Union victory.
16 April	Confederate Congress approves draft for men eighteen to thirty-five, with certain exemptions that include journalists, blacksmiths, overseers, and others.
24 April	Federal fleet gets past forts near New Orleans.
25 April	Union captures New Orleans.
1 May	Union forces officially occupy New Orleans.
4 May	Union occupies Yorktown, Virginia, after Confederate withdrawal on 3 May.
5 May	Battle of Williamsburg, Virginia, a Union victory.
8 May	Battle of McDowell, Virginia, a Confederate victory.
9 May	Union advances on Richmond; Confederates abandon Norfolk; Pensacola naval yard evacuated by Confederates.
12 May	Union occupies Baton Rouge, Louisiana.
23 May	Confederates recapture Front Royal, Virginia.
25 May	Confederates run Union troops out of Winchester, Virginia.
26 May	Bombardment of Vicksburg begins; skirmish at Hanover Court House, Virginia.
27 May	Confederates evacuate Corinth, Mississippi.
31 May	Battle of Seven Pines (Fair Oaks) begins.
1 June	Robert E. Lee is appointed to command the Army of Northern Virginia after Joseph E. Johnston is wounded.
4 June	Confederates evacuate Fort Pillow in Tennessee.

6 June	Gunboat battle in front of Memphis. City surrenders and is occupied.
8–9 June	Confederates defeat Union troops at Battle of Cross Keys and Port Republic, Virginia.
25 June	Seven Days Battles begin, resulting in Union retreat. Battles continue through 1 July. On 2 July, Confederates withdraw to Richmond, ending the Peninsular Campaign. Battles fought in this period at Mechanicsville (26–27 June); Gaines's Mill (27 June); Savage's Station (29 June); Frayser's Farm (30 June); and Malvern Hill (1 July).
26 June	Battle of Mechanicsville, Virginia.
27 June	Battle of Gaines's Mill, Virginia.
29–30 June	Battles of Peach Orchard, Savage State, White Oak Swamp, Glendale-Frayser's Farm in Virginia.
1 July	Battle of Malvern Hill, Virginia.
13 July	Battle of Murfeesboro, Tennessee.
22 July	Confederate and Union government agree to a general exchange of prisoners.
24 July	Union gunboats abandon contest at Vicksburg.
9 August	Battle of Cedar Mountain, Virginia, a Confederate victory
29–30 August	Second Battle of Manassas begins and lasts until 1 September, a Confederate victory.
30 August	Battle of Richmond, Kentucky, a Confederate victory.
31 August	Battle of Chantilly, Virginia.
4 September	Army of Northern Virginia crosses the Potomac in an invasion of Maryland.
7 September	McClellan follows Lee into Maryland.
12 September	McClellan reaches Frederick, where his advance guard finds a copy of an order Lee had written that detailed Confederate troop placements and movements.
14 September	Battle of South Mountain, Maryland.
14–15 September	Harper's Ferry falls to the Confederates, along with 12,000 Union soldiers and many supplies.
17 September	Battle of Antietam Creek near Sharpsburg, Maryland. Federals and Confederates clash in the single bloodiest day of the Civil War. More than 2,000 Union soldiers died, and 9,500 were wounded. On the Confederate side, 2,700 men lost their lives, and 9,000 were wounded. The result is inconclusive, though Lee's retreat back into Virginia allowed McClellan to claim victory. The contest had a profoundly bad result for the Confederates; the French and English decided to forestall their decisions on official recognition of the Confederacy, and it gave Lincoln

the justification to announce his Preliminary Emancipation Proclamation, which announced all slaves in areas rebelling against the United States would be freed on 1 January 1863.

19 September	Confederates defeated at Iuka, Mississippi.
20 September	Battle of Shepherdstown, Virginia.
22 September	Lincoln announces the Preliminary Emancipation Proclamation.
23 September	Battle of Sabine Pass.
25 September	General Beauregard assumes command of the army on the coast near Charleston.
3–4 October	Battle of Corinth, Mississippi.
8 October	Battle of Perryville, Kentucky.
9 October	Union occupies Galveston, Texas.
10 October	Confederate cavalry commander General J.E.B. Stuart makes a raiding expedition into Pennsylvania.
7 November	General Ambrose E. Burnside is appointed commander of the Army of the Potomac, replacing McClellan.
7 December	Battle of Prairie Grove, Arkansas. Union gains control of northern Arkansas.
11 December	Burnside crosses the Rappahannock at Fredericksburg. Lee did not contest the crossing.
13 December	Battle of Fredericksburg, a Confederate victory. The Union army lost 12,000 men in this four-day battle.
29 December	Murfreesboro Stones River Campaign, a Confederate victory.
30 December	Lincoln issues the Emancipation Proclamation.
31 December	Battle of Murfreesboro (Stones River), Tennessee; concludes 2 January 1863.

1863

1 January	Emancipation Proclamation freed slaves in the rebelling states. Major General John B. Magruder recaptures Galveston.
2 January	Battle of Stones River.
14 March	Admiral Farragut steams past Port Hudson on the Mississippi.
7 April	Federal gunboats attack Fort Sumter and begin the siege of Charleston Harbor.
1 May	Union forces, led by Ulysses S. Grant, defeat Confederate forces at Port Gibson, Mississippi, in the opening move toward Vicksburg.
1–6 May	Battle of Chancellorsville.
2 May	Battle of Chancellorsville begins. It will continue through 6 May. The Confederates force Hooker to withdraw across the Rappahannock River, but the victory is costly for the South in terms of the number of men killed or wounded.
3 May	Second Battle of Fredericksburg.

10 May	Stonewall Jackson dies of pneumonia following the amputation of his arm after the Battle of Chancellorsville. Jackson had been shot accidentally by two of his men.
16 May	Battle of Champion's Hill, Mississippi.
19 May	Siege of Vicksburg begins.
3 June	Lee's Army of Northern Virginia begins its second invasion of the North.
9 June	Battle of Brandy Station.
13 June	Second Battle of Winchester. Army of Northern Virginia defeats Union forces at Winchester, Virginia, and then continue North on their march into Maryland and Pennsylvania.
15–24 June	Lee crosses the Potomac with 76,000 men.
1–3 July	Battle of Gettysburg. This Confederate defeat puts an end to Southern hopes for recognition by England and France.
4 July	Vicksburg surrenders. Pemberton turns 30,000 Confederate soldiers over to Grant after a six-week-long siege.
4–14 July	Lee's army retreats from Maryland to Virginia.
9 July	Port Hudson, Louisiana, surrenders to federal troops.
10–11 July	Fighting at Battery Wagner in Charleston Harbor.
16 July	Major General William T. Sherman leads federal troops in an attack on Jackson, Mississippi, that leaves the city devastated.
17 August	Bombardment of Fort Sumter begins and continues for 6 days. The fort's garrison holds out.
6 September	Union troops occupy Fort Wagner near Charleston.
9 September	Federals enter Chattanooga.
19–20 September	Confederates, led by General Braxton Bragg, win the Battle of Chickamauga. Federals retreat into Chattanooga.
24 November	Battle of Lookout Mountain begins. Federal forces put Confederates away from Chattanooga and deeper into Georgia. Sets the stage for Sherman's Atlanta Campaign the following spring.
25 November	Battle of Missionary Ridge.

1864

20 February	Battle of Olustee.
22 February	Battle of Okolona, Mississippi, a Confederate victory.
28 February	First day of the Kilpatrick-Dahlgren Raid, which continued until 2 March. Union Major General Judson Kilpatrick headed toward Richmond with 4,500 horsemen. Possibly forged papers regarding the plan, found on the body of Colonel Ulric Dahlgren, indicated Kilpatrick intended to burn the city and assassinate Jefferson Davis and his cabinet. Mead disavowed any knowledge of the plan.
18 April	Confederate troops recapture Fort Pillow.

4 May	Sherman begins his Atlanta Campaign that culminates in his famed March to the Sea the following fall. Grant crosses the Rapidan to begin implementation of his planned Wilderness Campaign.
5–6 May	Battle of The Wilderness in Virginia. Lee is driven back.
8–18 May	Battle of Spotsylvania, a Confederate victory.
11 May	Battle of Yellow Tavern.
13–15 May	Battle of Resaca, Georgia, a Confederate defeat.
15 May	Battles of Drewry's Bluff and New Market.
23–31 May	North Anna and Haw's Shop.
3–12 June	Cold Harbor Campaign, Virginia, a Confederate victory. Grant loses more than 7,000 men in twenty minutes on 3 June. This is Lee's last clear victory of the war.
10 June	Battle of Brice's Cross Roads, Mississippi.
11–12 June	Battle of Trevilian Station, Virginia.
15–18 June	Battle of Petersburg, Virginia.
18 June	Grant begins siege of Petersburg, Virginia.
25 June	Battle of Missionary Ridge, Tennessee.
27 June	Battle of Kennesaw Mountain, a Confederate victory.
9 July	Battle of Monocacy, Maryland.
12 July	Confederate forces are repulsed after reaching the outskirts of Washington, D.C.
14–15 July	Battle of Tupelo, Mississippi, a Confederate defeat.
20 July	Battle of Peachtree Creek, Georgia.
22–28 July	Battle of Atlanta, a Confederate defeat.
28 July	Battle of Ezra Church, a Confederate defeat.
30 July	Battle of the Crater in Virginia, a Confederate victory.
5 August	Battle of Mobile Bay, a Confederate defeat.
27–31 August	Fall of Atlanta.
1 September	Confederates evacuate Atlanta.
2 September	Sherman captures Atlanta.
4 September	Sherman orders civilians out of Atlanta.
19 September	Third Battle of Winchester, Virginia, a Confederate defeat.
22 September	Battle of Fisher's Hill, Virginia, a Confederate defeat.
23 September	Jefferson Davis travels to Macon, Georgia, to speak to the Atlanta refugees there. He reveals that two-thirds of the Confederate army are missing from the ranks. The *Macon Telegraph* reports this story, and Sherman reads it. Fort Morgan, Alabama, the last defense for Mobile Bay, falls. The port of Mobile is closed, but the city is not captured.
19 October	Battle of Cedar Creek, Virginia. Sheridan runs Confederates from the Shenandoah Valley.

23 October	Battle of Westport, Missouri, a Confederate defeat.
15 November	Sherman burns Atlanta and leaves it behind as he embarks with two columns on his infamous March to the Sea.
22 November	Battle of Griswoldville, Georgia, a Confederate defeat.
30 November	Battle of Franklin, Tennessee. Five Confederate generals killed.
4 December	Battle of Waynesboro, Georgia, a Confederate defeat.
13 December	Sherman captures Fort McAllister, exposing Savannah.
15–16 December	Battle of Nashville, a Confederate defeat.
22 December	Sherman captures Savannah.

1865

17 February	Sherman's troops burn Columbia, South Carolina.
18 February	Fort Sumter is abandoned. Federals seize Charleston.
22 February	Fall of Wilmington, North Carolina.
2 March	Battle of Waynesboro, a Confederate defeat.
13 March	Confederate Congress approves drafting slaves into the army, with the promise of freedom for good military service.
19–20 March	Battle of Bentonville, North Carolina, a Confederate defeat.
24 March	Battle of Fort Steadman in Virginia, a Confederate defeat.
29–31 March	Battle of Dinwiddie Court House in Virginia.
1 April	Battle of Five Forks, near Petersburg, Virginia.
2 April	Confederate Congress evacuates Richmond. Petersburg, Virginia, falls after a ten-month siege. Wilson's cavalry assaults earthworks near Selma, Alabama, in the Battle of Selma, a Confederate defeat.
6–7 April	Battle at Sayler's Creek, Virginia, a Confederate defeat.
9 April	Battle of Appomattox, a Confederate defeat. Lee surrenders at Appomattox Courthouse, Virginia.
14 April	John Wilkes Booth assassinates President Lincoln.
26 April	General Joseph Johnston surrenders to Sherman at Durham, North Carolina; Confederate cabinet meets for the last time at Charlotte, North Carolina. Davis intends to flee west to meet up with Kirby Smith and his troops, but he will be captured in a few days near Washington, Georgia.
10 May	Wilson captures Jefferson Davis near Washington, Georgia.
13 May	Last battle of the war is fought, the Battle of Pamito Ranch near Brownsville, Texas.
26 May	Kirby Smith surrenders his troops.
29 May	President Andrew Johnson issues his Proclamation of Amnesty, officially ending the Civil War.

INTRODUCTION

THE BEST HISTORY OF THE WAR—The best history of the present war that has been, or ever will be, written is already penned. It will be found in the newspapers of the Confederacy. Any man who has a complete file of any good newspaper that has been published uninterruptedly during the War, has the best and most complete history of the revolution that will ever be written. He owns an invaluable piece of property, which will serve to teach his children not only the great events that occurred in the progress of this unparalleled war, but to afford them a narrative more intensely interesting than any romance that was ever written. And yet how little importance is attached to a newspaper by many people. It is read and thrown away as lightly as a squeezed orange.

—*The Western Democrat*
Charlotte, North Carolina
28 March 1865

The story of the Southern press in the Civil War did not begin at 4:30 A.M. on 12 April 1861 when Virginia newspaper editor Edmund Ruffin fired the first shot at Fort Sumter.[1] Nor did it begin some two months previously when leading men of the six seceded states gathered in Montgomery to form a new government, complete with a Constitution, a Congress, and a chief executive. The story did not even really begin with the presidential election of 1860, though for the sake of convenience, that is where this work will start. In truth, the story of the Southern press in the Civil War began at least a decade prior to 1860—and perhaps as much as thirty years before.

For the better part of the period 1832 to 1860, a number of Southern newspapers did their best to foment secession sentiment. In the early part of America's national history, the country's two regions had more commonalities than differences, but this began to change in the 1820s as the debate heated up between Southern slaveholders and Northern abolitionists. Sectional tensions developed over issues such as nullification and the westward expansion of slavery. The underlying issue involved property rights. Slaves were, by law, property, and Southerners did not believe anyone should have the right to tell them where they could or could not take their belongings. Usually, the arguments were framed more in terms of protecting Southern rights, or states' rights, but there was a subtle threat of secession, should Southern rights not be protected within the Union.

Journalists were the leading spokesmen for the parties debating these issues. Most antebellum newspapermen, even in the South, were pro-union, but those few determined voices of the fire-eaters could keep the idea of secession at the forefront of public thought. Fire-eaters were men like Robert Barnwell Rhett, a prominent Charleston journalist, politician, and disciple of John C. Calhoun. Rhett and other fire-eaters worked feverishly throughout the antebellum period for Southern rights and threatened secession if their rights were not upheld. The Charleston editor, though, had an advantage other fire-eaters did not: the *Charleston Mercury*. Rhett used his well-known newspaper to pound away mercilessly with demands for states' rights and Southern independence.

The radical fire-eating perspective was not the only one represented by Southern newspapers in the antebellum period, nor was it the position of most journalists or citizens. Opposing opinions ranged from staunch unionism, that is, the idea that the states should stay together in one country, no matter what, to a perspective described as "cooperationist." The cooperationists were a group of Southerners who did not rule out secession entirely but who believed that secession should be a last resort. For example, most fire-eaters believed the election of a Republican president was sufficient justification for secession since that party supported abolition of slavery. Cooperationists did not agree. They argued that the president alone cannot affect U.S. policy or law. It would take a Republican president and a Republican Congress to outlaw slavery, so even after Lincoln was elected in 1860, cooperationists were not ready to secede. They believed secession would be justified only if Lincoln took some action against the South. Further, cooperationists believed that any steps to dissolve the Union should be taken in concert by all the cotton states rather than by separate state action.[2] Most Southern newspapers initially advocated positions that were closer to the cooperationists or unionists than the fire-eaters. Much of that initial editorial caution began to fade and eventually move toward support for secession following the confrontation over Fort Sumter and Lincoln's call for 75,000 volunteers to put down the rebellion.

A LITTLE BACKGROUND

The nineteenth-century Southern press has sometimes been treated as an anomaly in American journalism history. Some scholars have viewed it as a poor relation of mainstream American journalism, a sort of out-of-step, slightly eccentric (some have considered it extremely eccentric), red-headed third cousin twice removed. This opinion has been based on the fact that Southern newspapers were predominantly published in small towns and therefore were not as sophisticated as the North's major metropolitan newspapers like the *New York Herald* or the *New York*

Times. It is true that the antebellum Southern press served mostly rural communities with widely dispersed readers. Southern newspapers were not as quick to pick up on some journalistic innovations as the North's metropolitan press was. The first local reporter in Charleston, South Carolina, was not hired until the late 1850s, some thirty years after the rise of the "penny press" made reporters a commonality at newspapers in large cities like New York and Baltimore. Such newspapers did exist, in limited numbers, in larger Southern cities such as New Orleans and Savannah, but they were not widespread.

The antebellum Southern press also has been viewed as backward because of its support for slavery. Some have speculated the South's newspapers took a proslavery stance because they were forced to by the planter elite who would broker no criticism of the "peculiar institution," but such criticism overlooks the fact that many Southern journalists were slave owners themselves. Further, Southern newspapermen were overwhelmingly born and reared in the South. Nearly 33 percent of Southern journalists owned slaves, a higher rate of ownership than the Southern population in general.[3] They were products of a culture that did not question the "rightness" of slave owning. Perhaps some editors were prohibited from criticizing slavery by social constraints, but many others would never have even thought to question the South's peculiar institution. As the example of Elijah Lovejoy's murder illustrated, even in the North, it was not always safe for a journalist to espouse abolitionist sentiments.

In most ways, Southern newspapers were typical of those in other regions of the United States. Some were good in that they provided strong news and editorial content for their readers, and some were little more than advertising sheets. Primarily, the South's press was built on the community newspaper model with an orientation toward printing political, agricultural, and business news, supplemented by feature material including short stories and poetry. Most Southern newspapers had at least occasional content designed specifically for female and young readers. The primary exception here was commercial newspapers like the *Charleston Courier*. Such newspapers were devoted to business and politics and covered little else until the war actually began. Most Southern newspapers, as the 1860 presidential election approached, ran four pages. Pages one and four were usually devoted to advertising with some editorial content—this would change dramatically during the Civil War when news made a permanent shift to the front page—and pages two and three were reserved for editorial and new matter. A few newspapers, the *New Orleans Picayune*, for one, printed eight pages daily and even more on Sundays. Newspapers were hand-delivered in town by carriers, some of whom were black, and by mail or train in outlying areas. Newsboys would become a standard during the Civil War, but readers had to be careful of them: They tended to be extortionists who would demand a higher price for the newspaper than the 25¢ face price.

Southerners, like Northerners, had long been huge consumers of newspapers. Newspapers were the only source of information, besides letters and personal communications, of what was going on in other American communities and on the national level. When the antebellum period's many national debates finally burst into war in April 1861, demand for newspapers rose at an almost exponential rate. The *Augusta Chronicle and Sentinel* (Augusta, Ga.) received seventy-five new subscriptions each week during the spring of 1861.[4] The day after Fort Sumter fell, a bidding war errupted in the Confederate capital over a single copy of the *Charleston Mercury* that reported the battle.[5] Demand for news grew throughout the war. North Carolinian Cornelia Phillips Spencer wrote in her diary that people in her community, many of whom had never subscribed to a newspaper other than their local weekly, had come to see the Richmond dailies as indispensible. Any sort of news was welcome, according to Spencer, but most welcome of all was news about the military. There was considerable "general anxiety to have the latest news, and above all from the army," she wrote.[6] Newspapers were seen "irreplacable media for the transmission of social ideas."[7] During the Civil War, this influence redoubled. Newspaper editors were aware of their impact. The *Augusta Chronicle and Sentinel* declared in a 25 June 1861 editorial: "The CHRONICLE AND SENTINEL, we are proud to think, is considered by many people almost second in importance to meat and bread." The *Athens Southern Watchman* (Athens, Ga.) editor was also convinced of the importance of newspapers. He argued that only the Confederate army was of greater importance than newspapers in the South's struggle for independence.[8]

As the Civil War began, Southerners were moderately well supplied with newspapers, though not in the numbers available to urban residents in the North. When Frenchman Alexis de Tocqueville visited the United States in the 1830s to study the progress of democracy here, he commented, "There is scarcely a hamlet which has not its newspaper."[9] This was not as true in the South, even in 1860, as it was in the more populated North. In the South, there were still large expanses where there was not even so much as a hamlet, much less one with its own newspaper. The tiny villages in the swamplands of southern Georgia, for example, were devoid of newspapers on the eve of the Civil War. In total the United States had some 4,051 newspapers and periodicals in circulation in 1860.[10] Of those 4,051 newspapers and periodicals, fewer than a quarter (842, or 21 percent) were being published in the eleven states that would become the Confederate States of America.[11] Some newspapers and periodicals appeared weekly, some daily, some twice weekly, some three times weekly.

Newspaper readership in the South was extensive among the white population, though circulations for individual journals were typically lower than in the North. This was due to population differences between the two regions, as well as differences in Southern and Northern economic and social life and, to some extent, literacy rates. Of the 31.4 million Americans in 1860, only 9.1 million of them lived in the South. Nearly half that number were blacks, who, whether free or slave, typically would not have had the education or the economic ability to afford newspapers. Southern newspapers, then, had a potential readership of only about 5.4 million, while in the North the potential readership was greater than 25 million.[12] Population, though, was only one influence on newspaper circulation. Regional lifestyle differences also accounted for some of the disparity. The South was rural and agarian with few large cities and a small industrial base. In the North, immigration and urbanization were spurring the growth of cities and of businesses and manufacturing industries. Larger towns and greater population density meant more advertisers, more potential subscribers with greater diversity in their backgrounds, and the need for more and more diverse newspapers.

Readership would also have been accounted for, in part, by literacy rates. Some scholars have speculated that high illiteracy rates may have been part of the reason for the lower newspaper readership rate in the South. While illiteracy was higher in the South than in the North, the difference may not have been as great as has been speculated.[13]

Most studies of circulations of nineteenth-century newspapers deal with per capita circulation, that is, how many subscribers did a newspaper have compared to how many copies it printed, rather than readership. Readership is the actual number of people who see the paper, not just those who pay for a copy. As many as twenty people other than the subscriber may have read, or heard read, each individual copy of a newspaper. From the Revolutionary War period on, American men would gather in taverns and coffee houses on publication day or at post offices on mail day to read the latest newspapers aloud to whomever was in hearing distance.[14] Still, it is difficult to establish conclusively how many readers a newspaper had since, for the most part, subscriber lists have not survived. Most Southerners, as far as can be determined using 1860 census data, and if Cornelia Phillips Spencer is to be believed, would have subscribed to their local weeklies most of the time, and they would have supplemented these with an occasional daily paper.[15]

Despite the strong increase in subscriptions at the beginning of the war, many Southern newspapers, especially weeklies, closed their doors during the conflict. Usually, the cause was either that their owners decided to join the Confederate army or, in many cases, that there was just not enough business to provide sufficient advertising or people on their subscription list were not paying regularly for their newspapers. Some newspapers adopted the practice of demanding cash up front for newspapers. A few optimists braved the business difficulties inherent in news operations and started newspapers during the war, but newspaper doors were more likely to close than to open from 1861 to 1865.

THE ROLE OF THE PRESS IN CONFEDERATE SOCIETY

The Confederate press had multiple roles and responsibilities. Most of those roles and responsibilities were similar to what they had been prior to secession; however, the "mix" of those purposes changed. On the business side, Southern newspapers continued to be economic machines that either produced or—almost as often—consumed wealth. They provided jobs and produced a consumer good. They provided a place for other businesses to advertise their products or services. On the editorial side, Confederate newspapers still provided editorial commentary to help readers contextualize news and form their own opinions of the day's issues. They provided entertainment and educational content for readers, including materials mothers could use in teaching their children to read. The Southern press continued to provide news—in a more or less timely fashion—and this was by far its most important editorial function in the Civil War. This was a big change from the antebellum period when the Southern press's role as a political commentator dominated.

The news imperative won out over political commentary for several reasons. First, Confederate politicians worked hard to downplay politics in the Southern republic. Historian George Rable, for good reason, subtitled his book about the Confederacy "A Revolution against Politics." Confederates, as Rable observed, were fearful of the effects of partisan politics. Had not partisan politics already brought about disunion? To eliminate partisan bickering and related problems, Confederates early on decided to discard the party ephemera and to create a partyless political system in which voters were encouraged to select the best man for the job rather than voting by party.[16]

The change in the Southern political system from party to partyless brought changes in the role and work of the region's press. In the antebellum period, Southerners had lived and died by politics, and that was also true—literally—for the many Southern newspapers that served as party organs. Southern editors were often ranking party officials, and they used their newspapers to accomplish party goals like getting candidates elected, spreading the party's platform, or making sure other party members were carrying out their responsibilities. It was a symbiotic relationship since elected party officials would make sure supportive newspapers received government printing contracts and would often also find government jobs for party editors.

Party politics were especially important in the antebellum South because Southerners saw politics as their one means of protecting the institution of slavery. From the Nullification Crisis of 1832 on through the other sectional crises of the antebellum period, politics gave antebellum Southerners a means by which to aggitate for legislation, to enforce that legislation once passed, to debate and argue over issues, and to find compromises that would keep the hot-headed, radically conservative Southern fire-eaters from leading their region out of the Union. The 1860 election of Lincoln, a sectional candidate and one from an abolitionist party to boot, was sufficient evidence for some Southerners that American politics could no longer protect slavery. Both the region and its labor system, they believed, would be safer outside the Union in an independent nation where partisan politics would no longer be a threat.

Changing reader tastes also contributed to the altered role of the Confederate press. Even before Fort Sumter fell, Southern boys were donning Confederate gray and butternut uniforms and marching off to Virginia to fight for the independence of their new country and glory for themselves. The mothers and sweethearts left behind had only two ways of knowing how their loved ones were faring: letters home and newspapers. Southern readers wanted news. The Confederate people were no longer worried about arcane political debates. Secession, expansion of slavery to the territories, states' rights, and the other antebellum political debates were, for all intents and purposes, settled. Secession was a done deal. Slavery could expand to whatever territory the new Southern republic could acquire either through conquest or admission of other states. States' rights and slavery were protected by the new Confederate Constitution. Southerners did not want to read an editor's ideas on those issues any more. They wanted to read about what was happening to their loved ones in faraway Virginia or Mississippi or Tennessee. They wanted to know what was happening at the front and how the war was affecting their local boys.[17]

CONFEDERATE NEWS GATHERING: PRACTICES, STANDARDS, AND REGULATIONS

American journalism historians generally have looked to the elite metropolitan press in places like New York, Boston, Washington, D.C., or Chicago to identify the press standards and norms of a period, but that approach does not work for the Confederate press. At the beginning of the war, the South had only one metropolitan area that could come anywhere near to comparing with New York City, and that was New Orleans. However, New Orleans fell to the Union in April 1862, thereby depriving the South of any vestige of elite metropolitan journalism. Tennessee's major cities, Nashville and Memphis, which might have vied for a position on the list of important newspaper towns, lost out, too, because they also fell in the spring and summer of 1862. The majority of the newspapers that made up the Confederate press, even the more prominent ones, had as much in common with the community press as they did with the metropolitan press. A major community newspaper trait probably the majority of Confederate newspapers had in common with the community press was impecunity, that is, a lack of money. While a metropolitan New York newspaper like Horace Greeley's *New York Herald* could afford to field scores of correspondents to cover the war, most Confederate newspapers did not have the $5,000 per month it could cost to put a single paid correspondent in the field. That meant Southern newspapers had to be innovative and resourceful in getting the stories their readers wanted to read. Southern editors used a combination of new and old techniques, and they made good use of new communications technologies such as the telegraph and railroad to speed up the dissemination of information.

One of the tried-and-true methods of news gathering that continued to be effective during the Civil War was the exchanges. Nineteenth-century postal law allowed newspapers to send for free one copy of each edition to other newspaper editors, and the common practice was for editors who received exchange newspapers to cut stories out of them for use in their own journals. Many an amusing editorial spat resulted when a rival newspaper did not give credit to the appropriate exchange. Considerable amounts of battlefront news circulated through all kinds of Southern newspapers via exchanges, especially stories by the South's most prominent war correspondents, the *Savannah Republican*'s Peter W. Alexander and the *Charleston Courier*'s and *Columbia South Carolinian*'s Felix G. de Fontaine.

Editors who could not afford to hire full-time journalist-correspondents had other means of attaining news as well. It was very common for newspapers to arrange for local soldiers to write letters from their posts. "Notwithstanding the hard times, we shall inform our friends of what the enemy is doing, and be sure that, as a Sentinel on the walls, we shall Chronicle all the glorious deeds of our brave soldiers," wrote the editor of the *Augusta Chronicle and Sentinel* on 27 April 1861. Quite often, soldier-correspondents were journalists who had left their newspaper work to join the army. W. P. Price and C. M. McJunkin, editor and assistant editor of the *Greenville Southern Enterprise* (Greenville, S.C.), both reported for the newspaper after they joined the army, as did Hugh Wilson, an editor of the *Abbeville Press* (Abbeville, S.C.). In February 1865, when the *Anderson Intelligencer* (Anderson, S.C.) started up again after a four-year hiatus, the paper announced that Major W. W. Humphreys of the Army of Northern Virginia would be supplying war correspondence for the paper. Humphreys, along with the rest of the *Intelligencer*'s staff, had joined the Confederate army in 1861, prompting the paper's closing. However, his partner had been invalided out of the army in the winter of 1864 and decided to start the paper up again with Humphreys as his Virginia war correspondent.[18]

After its founding in 1863, the Confederate Press Association (CPA), a cooperative news service, provided war news for the South's dailies and weeklies. The Confederate Press Association had twenty-seven permanent correspondents in the field and six "occasional" reporters who would sometimes report on local news for the wire service's forty-plus members. Members received a limited amount of copy, though, only 3,500 words of news each week.[19] The Press Association was based in Atlanta, and its correspondents provided news to subscribing newspapers from 1863 until virtually the end of the war. A CPA correspondent was filing stories by telegraph almost daily as Joseph E. Johnston's Army of Tennessee did its level best to block Sherman's invasion into North Carolina. The press organization also functioned as a trade association and worked out agreements with Southern commanders for access to military information and the Southern Congress for copyrights on news stories.

The best war reporting, though, came from the paid correspondents who were on the spot on behalf of a newspaper (or the CPA) and could provide eyewitness accounts of the conflict. The *Charleston Courier* had several full-time correspondents in Virginia for much of the war and a number of others who provided them with periodic stories. The two daily Augusta, Georgia, newspapers, the *Constitutionalist* and the *Chronicle and Sentinel*, shared a Richmond correspondent, Salem Dutcher, from 1862 on. A number of journalists covered Sherman's March to the Sea in 1864, including "Personne," "Rover," and "Kentuckian" for the *Augusta Chronicle and Sentinel* and "Observer" for the *Constitutionalist*.

These glamorous correspondents wrote under romantic noms de guerre, or pseudonyms, like Hermes, Quel Qu'un, and Bohemian, or sometimes under silly names like Grape or Mint Julep.[20] Regardless of how they signed their dispatches, the South's war correspondents were widely known and respected, and readers eagerly awaited their dispatches. The two best Southern war correspondents have already been mentioned, Peter W. Alexander of the *Savannah Republican* and Felix G. de Fontaine of the *Charleston Courier*. Alexander was particularly important because of his use of advocacy journalism techniques to get shoes, clothing, and other supplies sent to the front for Georgians serving in the Army of Northern Virginia in 1862.

Alexander and de Fontaine were both extraordinary writers who had a real knack for describing the battles they witnessed in such precise terms that readers could not help but visualize the action themselves. The two men, though, came from very different backgrounds. Alexander, who wrote under his initials rather than a pseudonym, was a lawyer and a politician from Georgia who had been an editor at the *Savannah Republican* for a while before the war. De Fontaine, "Personne" to his Southern readers, was the son of a former French aristocrat who had grown up in New York and who came South just as the war was starting to cover the siege of Fort Sumter. He had come to cover the Fort Sumter story for the *New York Herald*, but he ended up staying and becoming a correspondent for the *Courier*. Both men, though, were devoted to telling the stories of the Confederate armies in the field.

A handful of women provided correspondence for Southern newspapers, though their work focused on issues other than the battles themselves. Typically, the female correspondents wrote about hospital affairs, the treatment of wounded soldiers, or the politics of the war, or they provided descriptive accounts of camp life. The longest-lived correspondence by a female writer was that provided by "Joan," a South Carolina woman whose son was serving in Virginia. When she traveled to Virginia to be near him, she wrote about her experiences for the *Charleston Courier*. Joan wrote at least one letter and often more virtually daily from mid-July 1861 to the end of August 1861. Her correspondence was far more frequent than that of the male correspondents, though in September, her stories were conspicuously absent for several days while she moved from Richmond to an army camp near Leesville, Virginia, to be nearer her son. She wrote less frequently that fall but continued on through mid-November 1861 when her last dispatch appeared in the *Courier*. Joan's dispatches almost always ran on the front page, often paired with those of Personne's or Sumter's, the *Courier*'s other Virginia correspondents. The only time a Joan dispatch was consigned to an inside page was on 12 August 1861 when news of a major fire in Charleston took up the front page.

Joan wrote mostly about the politics of the war, life in the Confederate capital, and the military hospitals in Richmond. The hospitals were her particular passion. For example, Joan advocated each state setting up hospitals for its own soldiers. She wrote approvingly about Alabama, Mississippi, and Louisiana when those states did so. She was also a master at setting a scene so that a reader could imagine a place quite vividly. In October, Joan wrote from Fairfax, Virginia, about a sunny autumn day's cool winds and how lovely a seat by a fire felt on such a day when children were "busy running to the chestnut trees, which are shedding their abundant crop, and are sought for almost as eagerly by soldiers as by children; in this land where luxuries are unheard of."[21]

Occasionally, newspaper editors themselves donned the role of war correspondent. The editors of the two Savannah newspapers, William T. Thompson of the *Daily Morning News* and James R. Sneed of the *Republican*, traveled together to Charleston to cover the shelling of Fort Sumter. After 1863, "Personne," de Fontaine, was editor of his own newspaper, the *South Carolinian* of Columbia, South Carolina, but he still struck off across Georgia to cover Sherman's Georgia campaign. An advantage of having editors in the field rather than correspondents was the greater clout they carried with military officials. An editor could hobnob with higher officials and often obtain better information.[22]

Covering the war was not an easy job for either a correspondent or an editor. Correspondents traveled with or behind armies—depending on the particular commander's sentiments about journalists. If the unit they were covering moved out at 2:00 A.M. on a rainy morning, the correspondent moved with it. The Confederate government provided at least subsistence food for its army much of the time, but correspondents had to scrounge their own meals. One of the issues J. S. Thrasher, superintendent of the Confederate Press Association, undertook was to try to arrange for his correspondents to buy food from military units. Since the Confederacy was having a hard time feeding its soldiers, Thrasher's requests fell on deaf ears.[23]

Correspondents were in just as much danger of capture, disease, or injury as the soldiers they wrote about, and several Confederate correspondents did die while on the job. John Linebaugh of the *Memphis Appeal*, for example, drowned while traveling from Richmond to Tennessee to cover John Bell Hood's invasion of that state. A correspondent for the *Augusta Chronicle and Sentinel* came near to being captured by Union troops while covering Sherman's campaign through Georgia in the fall of 1864. The correspondent was on the road from Eatonton to Madison, relying on Confederate pickets to call out the alarm if Northern troops approached. About 3:00 P.M., the correspondent wrote, "A scout came dashing down the road at a Gilpin speed, crying 'to the woods,' 'to the woods,' and we wooded." The correspondent reported that he waited several hours in the rain and then decided to risk going to the road to see what was happening. "We had not traveled a hundred yards," he wrote, "before a party of cerulean clad equestrians came dashing up, and in a very polite and insinuating manner briefly requested us to halt. The request was accompanied with most significant cocking of carbines and pistols, which, brought to a horizontal attitude in one's front are very persuasive, especially to an unarmed civilian, and we halted." The Union officers questioned the correspondent about the countryside and any Confederate troops that might be nearby before letting him go.[24]

Correspondents had to deal with fatigue and illness, just like the troops did. Once battles were over, correspondents would telegraph short articles about the fighting and then stay up late at night writing a longer version of their stories that could be either mailed back to their newspapers or hand-carried by a courier. Such long days of arduous and physically demanding labor moving through rough terrain from one section of the battlefield to another left journalists susceptible to camp diseases and other illnesses. Ivy W. Duggan, a popular soldier-correspondent for the Sandersville, Georgia, *Central Georgian* was hospitalized three times in the first year of the war for camp diseases he contracted. The *Central Georgian* editor commented, "Mr. Duggan's patriotism is greater than his strength." A correspondent for the *Carolina Spartan*, "L," contracted typhoid fever and was unable to work for nearly a month.[25]

Despite the challenges of their work, Southern war correspondents were not well paid. Henry Timrod, who would become the unofficial poet laureate of the Confederacy, received $6 a day plus traveling expenses for the reporting he did from the Army of the West for the *Charleston Mercury*. This fee would have been in addition to his military pay, but still was quite meager. The Southern Associated Press, a predecessor of the Confederate Press Association, as well as the Richmond newspapers, were paying their correspondents in Fredericksburg, Virginia, $100 a month in 1863.

Despite the hardships and low pay, the South's correspondents worked with amazing dedication to gather the news and get it back to their newspapers so that eagerly awaiting readers could know what was happening at the front. Because of reader demand, Southern newspapers adopted another innovation: placing news, rather than advertising, on the front page. The use of news on the front page was a major change.

Confederate newspapers emphasized war news not only by placement but also by quantity. War news dominated most front pages. The *Savannah Daily Morning News* devoted 59 percent of its content to war news in a two-week period just before and just after the fall of Fort Sumter. During the Battle of Chancellorsville, 2 May to 14 May 1863, the *Daily Morning News* ran 106 war stories, or about 81 percent of its content during that period. As hostilities escalated, so did the paper's war coverage.[26] Greater coverage was possible in part, too, because of the decline in advertising as the war took its toll on Southern businesses. There was more room available for news.

War news, though, was not the only news Confederate newspapers offered, nor should it have been. While the war certainly dominated the short existence of the Confederate States of America and the lives of its people, everyday life continued as well. Once the war began, there were profound differences in the quality of that everyday life, especially for women who had to keep their homes, farms, and plantations running in the absence of their menfolk. Still, even after the war began, people got married, had babies, died, held benefit concerts, ran for election, gawked at two-headed calves, committed murders, visited restaurants, and earned livings.[27] These stories, too, were told by Confederate newspapers and often made for lively reading.

Another common, though perhaps unexpected, source of news for Southern newspapers was Northern newspapers. Southern and Northern newspapers had exchanges prior to secession, and some of those continued, to some degree, even during the war. Newspapers crossed the lines, both officially and unofficially, and Southern editors published the content of those from the North with great relish, often commenting negatively on the Yankee editor's interpretation of events. The exchanges of Northern newspapers were aided in large measure by the Confederate Signal Bureau, a division of the Confederate Secret Service that regularly received mail from Washington, D.C. In fact, during one six-month stretch, the Signal Bureau got Washington and Baltimore papers within a day of publication and New York papers within two days. Northern papers were so regularly received that the *Charleston Courier* was able to complain on 15 July 1862 that the Yankee papers did not have much news in them. The Confederate Press Association was another source of Northern news. At its first board meeting, members agreed to hire an agent and provide him with the funding needed to get the latest Northern newspapers through the lines. Unfortunately, the minutes of that meeting do not indicate whether the funding was for bribes or subscriptions.[28]

Transmission of their stories back to their newspapers was a perennial problem for Confederate correspondents. Shortly after telegraph service ended between Washington, D.C., and Richmond, Virginia, on 1 June 1861, Confederate President Jefferson Davis took control of the telegraph lines for military use. The Southern press responded immediately. A. D. Banks, a member of the Richmond press corps, approached Secretary of War Leroy Walker to gain permission for journalists to use the telegraph lines.[29] Eventually, the restrictions on the telegraph were eased somewhat, but local military commanders were known to block access if they believed a dispatch would be harmful to the army, and military censors would refuse to send telegraphs they believed would be harmful to the cause. There were no restrictions, though, on putting that same information in a letter and mailing it back to the newspaper, but that, of course, slowed the delivery of the news. The Confederate post office was never particularly efficient, a problem compounded when mail had to cross through or be delivered to battle areas. In fact, later in the war, Confederate mail service got so bad that some editors resorted to sending their newspapers by Southern Express, a freight company, even thought that meant they had to pay the freight services as well as postage. Early on, Confederate Postmaster General John Regan had decided that newspapers should be considered mailable matter rather than manufactured products. That meant that they had to be mailed rather than shipped by a freight service, and that meant more revenue for the Confederate post office, which was required by law to be self-supporting.

Gathering and delivering news was not the only concern Confederate editors had about their product. They also had to ensure it met certain professional standards. Those standards were perhaps rudimentary, compared to those by which later American news organizations would function. Further, nineteenth-century journalism was highly individualistic, and so although it is possible to see the earliest seeds of professional standards being planted in this period, certainly there were few moves to bring about any sort of widespread adherence to a set of standards. However, as early as 1837, editors were gathering at professional meetings and discussing how "to do" journalism and how to punish infractions, usually on a state-by-state basis. That year, a group of North Carolina editors meeting in Raleigh approved a series of resolutions that specified journalism's best practices. Those practices emphasized the public service aspects of journalism. According to these resolutions, journalists were supposed to advocate for morality, national liberty, and social order; they were supposed to promote the arts, science, and industry; and further, newspapers were supposed to be incorruptible champions of the Constitution and of American laws. According to the resolution those editors adopted in Raleigh, North Carolina, editors who did not live up to these standards faced a truly draconian punishment: banishment from the exchanges. Since exhange newspapers were one of the primary news sources available to antebellum editors, this was indeed a serious threat.[30]

Public service was high on the list of press standards beyond North Carolina, too. William King, a Charleston printer who rose to the editorial ranks at the *Charleston Courier*, discussed nineteenth-century press standards in his history of the journalism of that city. In his small book, King wrote that the press had "a high mission to perform and responsible duties to discharge." These duties precluded, for example, using personal attacks in an editorial debate with another editor. Such invective, King wrote, diverted a newspaper from its proper public service–oriented mission.[31]

During the Civil War, journalistic standards and practices continued to evolve. In the South, the evolution was spurred to some degree by rules and regulations of the Confederate Press Association. Press Association Superintendent Thrasher set certain standards for his correspondents. However, because the CPA was a mutual news-gathering service as well as a wire service and a trade association, its standards trickled down to local writers whose copy had to be suitable for adding to the news service's offerings. Thrasher's rules required that Press Association dispatches be objective and fact-based. He also required dispatches to be timely, and he added a competitive aspect to Southern news gathering by reminding his correspondents that they were not to be beaten on stories. "I shall expect from you, and the superior facilities opened to you for procuring intelligence, that you will be seldom, if ever, beaten," Thrasher wrote to a new hire, a Mr. Wagner, in a letter of instruction.[32] Local journalists were at least exposed to the ideas of objectivity, accuracy, competitiveness, use of facts, and timeliness because of their association with the wire service.

The news values promulgated by Thrasher and the Confederate Press Association fit well with what audiences wanted and expected from their newspapers. Readers wanted truthful, accurate, and timely newspaper reports, despite the problems with and breakdowns of the Southern communications infrastructure—telegraph, mail, and railroads—that developed during the Civil War. Truth telling and accuracy were enormously demanding standards for war correspondents whose view of a battle often was limited to a narrow field of action, just like that of the soldiers fighting the battles and the generals commanding them. Most of the better and more accurate stories about the military action of the Civil War were actually those "recap" stories written a few weeks after the battle was over when correspondents had a chance to walk the battlefield and to interview participants. De Fontaine, Personne of the *Charleston Courier*, described reporting the war as being caught in an Odyssian struggle between

Scylla and Charybdis—the desire to print rumor so as to get information out and prudently holding back until the rumor could be confirmed.[33] While truth telling and accuracy may have been important professional values, they were not always adhered to. Confederate journalists, like their Northern counterparts, were known to take bribes for "revising" their stories to make some particular officer's battle performance sound better than it had been. Southern newspapers also published stories of Yankee atrocities as a kind of propaganda to steel their readers' resolve to support the war. For example, the *Atlanta Intelligencer* reported on 16 October 1863 that the Union troops had found a way to poison flesh with gunshot wounds.[34]

Fairness was another important news value of which Confederate journalists also had at least a rudimentary understanding. Several newspapers, for example, would not accept unsigned letters to the editor for publication. Pen names were common in those days, both for letter writers and for regular reporters and correspondents, but editors of these newspapers wanted to know the real names of letter writers, especially those who were writing in to support or recommend political candidates. Such policies were not always adequate protection for newspapers, though. Two months after the *Augusta Chronicle and Sentinel* adopted its no-unsigned-letters policy, it was victimized by a hoax when someone sent in a wedding announcement for Mr. George C. Conner of Atlanta and a woman from Tennessee. After being informed of the error, the *Chronicle and Sentinel* ran a terse correction. The article, the paper admitted, had been "a pure fabrication of some wicked jester." The paper added its apologies for the mistake: "We regret that we should have been made a party to a transaction so dishonorable; and we make this public statement and correction."[35]

While the Civil War certainly had an influence on the evolution of journalistic standards and ethics, American journalists, both Southern and Northern, were still a long way from having a systematized system of ethics and professional practices. In the South, most editors followed their own ideas about what were the right and wrong ways to practice journalism. Dr. Robert Gibbes, a physician and former college professor who was also editor and owner of the *Columbia South Carolinian* until early 1864, had firm ideas about his editorial responsibilities and policies. Gibbes believed newspapers should be dignified, patriotic, and conservative. Like William L. King, Gibbes believed newspaper editors should take the moral high ground and avoid condescending to name-calling with their adversaries. Gibbes was not, however, averse to giving fair reply when another newspaper started a hot debate with him. For Gibbes, though, the overarching journalistic imperative was independence, that is, espousing principles that grew from the editor's own convictions—based, of course, on sound "Southern policy." Editorial independence was desirable, but not so much as to rattle the ship of state, Gibbes believed. He was not always consistent on that point, either. A few years before the Civil War began, Gibbes sued the mayor of Columbia for access to city council meetings. The mayor had given preference to the newspaper of his political party with regard to access to minutes and to meetings. Gibbes certainly rocked the Columbia ship of state when he won his lawsuit.[36]

Despite their penchants for independence, Confederate journalists were fairly consistent in determining what was newsworthy, and their news values were not that much different from those of journalists today. An article from the 27 September 1861 *Augusta Chronicle and Sentinel* provides a useful illustration:

> Is there anybody around who feels like kicking up a muss and getting his name in the papers? Reader, if you see any person who conversed with another man who told him he had been reliably informed that Mr. Whatshisname had met with a severe accident from which he would probably recover—send us word. Locals are scarce as hens-teeth. A wormy chinquepin for the first item.

"Kicking up a muss," or doing something out of the ordinary, was news, and people who did unusual things made the news. Accidents, the example the *Chronicle and Sentinel* editor used, were something out of the ordinary; most people went through their days without having accidents. Of course, the editor did not want to wish an ill fate on anyone, so he specified that "Mr. Whatshisname" should not have been injured severely. Perhaps a slight injury, though, would make the story just ever so much more interesting to the reader. Further, it was specifically local news the editor wanted and for which he was willing to pay a wormy chinquepin.[37] One further and final insight regarding news values can be gleaned from this example. Note that the editor has asked specifically for a source who had been "reliably informed." This harkens back to the value of accuracy and is an example of the few clues that exist to the nature of nineteenth-century press standards.

During the Civil War, journalists were not the only group to have interests in and concerns about their standards and practices. So did the Confederate government and military. Military leaders were concerned about the spread of news from battlefields and camps because of what could happen, should sensitive information fall into the hands of the enemy. If a newspaper correspondent wrote too much about a general's plans for a campaign or the location of troops, he could be giving the enemy just the intelligence they needed to foil the plans. These fears were bolstered by the fact that the speed of news transmission in the United States had increased by more than 50 percent from 1820 to 1860. By 1860, the average newspaper article would be picked up by other newspapers within one to three days of publication. Because newspapers circulated pretty freely across enemy lines for most of the war, publication of military news, especially numbers and locations of troops and generals, posed significant risks; newspapers could reach enemy generals as quickly as they could friendly ones.[38] For the most part, Confederate newspapers and correspondents tried to handle information responsibly. A number of authors have called the Confederate press's caution about publishing "self-censorship," and while that moniker applies to some extent, Southern journalists generally held back information out of a desire to aid the national cause, not fear of punishment, the usual foundation of self-censorship. Even hard-line press libertarians like *Augusta Chronicle and Sentinel* editor Nathan Morse supported caution with the publication of military secrets. Morse wrote, "A man who happens to own a printing press should not be allowed to print sentiments intended to aid the enemy." The one primary naysayer to the idea of restraining publication to benefit the military was the *Charleston Mercury*. Its editors believed the public had a complete right to know everything possible about the Confederate military and its work since the public was supplying the men and the money to fight the war.[39]

Of course, military leaders would have liked to have had greater legal control of the Confederate press, but for the most part there was virtually no government censorship of Southern newspapers. In fact, it would have been virtually impossible for the

Confederacy to sanction official censorship of the press because of the justification it had used for secession: its desire to correct the constitutional errors of the North. A country that had gone into revolution because it believed it understood the Constitution better could not then turn around and violate a key provision. In fact, the Confederate government used its lack of censorship as a point of pride to distinguish it and its firmer grasp of the ideals of liberty from the North where Lincoln was not above suppressing the Copperhead press in great numbers. After General Robert E. Lee complained to the War Department about a dispatch in the *Richmond Dispatch*, Secretary of War George W. Randolph informed the Confederate commander that his intention was to conclude the war without the suppression of a single newspaper. That is not to imply, however, that the War Department prohibited military censorship entirely, and even Randolph himself was certainly not above threatening to censor. In response to Lee's complaint, Randolph sent a copy of the general's letter to all Richmond newspapers with a notation that he hoped it would not become necessary for him to seek legislation giving him the power to censor newspapers. Randolph's reluctance to censor, despite his threat, did not mean that military authorities were without any means of controlling what information flowed from their armies. Commanding officers were empowered, for example, to restrict press access to army camps, and many took advantage of that power. They found other means as well. Confederate military leaders responded to the possible risks of newspaper publication by imposing certain restrictions, though the Southern Congress was quick to rebuke generals who went too far in their attempts to censor the press.[40]

The Civil War was the first time in American history that government had had to consider how to regulate press publication of war information. In the country's three previous major wars, the Revolutionary War, the War of 1812, and the Mexican-American War, news moved too slowly to threaten military security. By the time newspapers could get military information into print, the battlefield situation had changed, and the reportage had no impact on the outcome.[41] By the Civil War, though, news-gathering, production, and dissemination technologies were sufficiently sophisticated and fast that military or government control was sometimes warranted. The problem was compounded in the Civil War by the fact that each side's newspapers were being published in close proximity to the other. Northern generals received Southern newspapers almost as quickly as Southern generals did.[42]

The first Confederate Secretary of War Leroy Walker was the first official to broach the topic of press censorship, but he did so in the form of a request rather than a legal regulation. Scarcely had the fighting begun when Walker asked the press not to report on unit size, number of weapons, condition of the troops, or possible military movements. The most any Confederate secretary of war would do to control the press was write letters and, on occasion, make a veiled threat about what might happen to newspapers, should he have to intervene. For the most part, though, these reminders from the War Department were sufficient to keep most Southern editors in line. When self-restraint failed, military commanders, however, were often reluctant to rely on self-censorship by the press. They were quick to act against reporters.[43]

In early 1861, Confederate General Joseph Johnston expelled all the reporters from his command after Secretary of War Judah Benjamin reminded him of his power to do so. Johnston had written the secretary of war regarding the conduct of *Richmond*

Dispatch reporter William G. Shepardson, known to readers as "Bohemian." The reporter had included in one of his stories the locations of the winter headquarters for several units in Virginia. Benjamin agreed that the publication was egregious, but he wrote Johnston that he had no power to take any action against Bohemian. The war secretary accused Johnston of being too lenient with reporters covering his command and of not enforcing the powers that military law gave Johnston to control journalists. The Southern press responded at its spring 1862 convention by appointing a committee of three distinguished journalists to write and circulate to all Southern newspapers a series of articles critical of the general.[44]

Major General Earl Van Dorn, commander of the military district of Southern Mississippi and Eastern Louisiana, got the harshest reprimand from the Confederate government for interfering with press liberties. Van Dorn published an order that declared martial law in his district and ordered the arrest of any journalist who published troop movements or anything that would impair public confidence in the military or government. Under Van Dorn's order, the penalty for communicating with the enemy was death. The biggest issue regarding Van Dorn's order was the imposition of martial law, an action that only the president was authorized to take. The order provoked a lively debate in the Confederate Congress and brought the general a rebuke from the secretary of war. Congress went further and adopted a resolution to restrain military commanders from unconstitutionally exercising military powers. Van Dorn bowed to public pressure and revoked his order.[45]

The Southern government did take affirmative steps to limit use of the telegraph lines by journalists, but they were only partially successful. In May 1861, the Confederate Congress authorized Jefferson Davis to seize the lines and to appoint censors—the resolution used the word *agents*, but the proposed function of those "agents" was clear. The measure also outlawed any transmission of military information that would endanger the success of or otherwise hinder military operations. Dispatches the telegraph agents might decline to transmit could, however, still be sent back to the home office by mail or courier. And often sensitive dispatches got sent by telegraph anyway. Despite the law adopted by the Confederate Congress, telegraphic news was only sporadically subject to "the blue pencil of any censor." Whether a dispatch would be censored depended as much on the zeal of the telegraph operator on duty as anything else.

Toward the end of the war, the issue of conscription got caught up with press censorship, and the result was a huge controversy that threatened to topple the Davis presidency. Confederate editors, along with several other types of essential workers, had been exempt from the draft since the first conscription law passed in 1862. By the fall of 1864, though, the Confederate army's numbers had been ravaged by desertions, deaths, and injuries. In a September speech at Macon, Georgia, President Davis revealed that the army was desperate for manpower. To solve the manpower shortage, Davis would propose in November that Congress repeal most of the exemptions, including that of newspaper editors. The journalists, though, were suspicious of Davis's proposal. Many believed Davis did not desire to fill the ranks of the army but to get rid of those editors who were becoming increasingly critical of the way the president was running the country and the military. They were suspicious because a second aspect of the president's proposal gave him and the secretary of war the power to detail—that is, assign—any new recruits as they saw fit. Davis was aware that the country would need newspapers, and he proposed to assign some of the newly drafted editors to continue their editorial work while sending others to fight. Editors were not spread evenly throughout the Confederacy, Davis argued. If he had the power to send some to fight and some to the homefront, he could swell the ranks of the army while ensuring the Confederate press continued to operate.[46]

Editors did not accept Davis's explanation. Most believed he would keep friendly editors at home and send opposition editors to the front as a means of silencing criticism, and a handful of Confederate congressmen agreed with the editors. All over the Confederacy, journalists declared open season on the president. They raised the banner of the constitutional guarantee of free speech in defiance of Davis's proposal. A number of newspapers started running the full text of Article 9, Section 1 of the Confederate Constitution (its counterpart, the First Amendment to the U.S. Constitution, is better known, but they say exactly the same thing), and others called Davis every unpleasant name they could devise and urged opposition to the proposal. One newspaper even went so far as to proclaim that if the South had to be ruled by a despot, its editors would prefer Lincoln.[47] Tennessee Congressman Henry S. Foote introduced a resolution to express the Congress's displeasure with the president's proposal, and the resolution passed, though in slightly altered form. It read in part, "It is the sense of this House that the exemption of one editor to each newspaper under the conditions now required by law is as narrow a margin for exemption from that class as is expedient, and that the existing law on the subject of such exemption requires no amendment."[48]

In all probability, President Davis was not trying to influence press criticism with his proposal, which did also extend to other exempt classes of workers. A greater possibility was that Davis was trying to gain control of the state militias so he could incorporate those units into the Confederate armies. Some historians believe that the idea to propose changes to the conscription law did not originate with Davis at all but with his secretary of war, Judah Benjamin. They believe Benjamin's purpose was to move toward establishing a dictatorship in the Confederacy with Davis at its head.[49]

Confederate journalists retained considerable freedom to speak and publish what they saw fit during the Civil War. Some constraints were applied, but more often by the military than the Confederate government. In almost every instance when Congress considered legislation regarding freedom of the press, it voted to protect the rights of journalists. Two historians of the Georgia press, Griffith and Talmadge, wrote, "For all its mistakes and near-sightedness, it was a free press—possibly the freest that ever published during a national emergency." These historians may be overstating the case; certainly, they were writing before the Vietnam conflict that was, essentially, an uncensored war. However, a more contemporary historian, Robert A. Rutland, also believed that the Southern press was one of the freest of all times. He wrote that Southern publishers in the Civil War "retained a wartime freedom of expression that has no modern parallel." Even Civil War historian Mark Neely, who found that the Confederacy profoundly repressed the civil liberties of its individual citizens, was forced to admit in the last pages of his book on the subject that the single exception was the Southern press, which remained essentially free to publish what it would.[50] Censorship was a reality in the Confederacy, but it was not harsh, and its only objective was to protect the military as it fought the war, an objective with which even the most passionate press libertarians would be hard-pressed to disagree.

PRODUCING AND DELIVERING A CONFEDERATE NEWSPAPER

Even before the Civil War began, producing a daily or a weekly newspaper was not an easy task. To be a successful newspaper editor, according to the *Carolina Spartan* of Spartanburg, South Carolina, one needed "the constitution of a horse, obstinancy of a mule, impudence of a beggar and entire resignation to the most confounded of all earthly treadmills; he must be a moving target for everybody to shout at, and is expected to know everything, and to assist busybodies, to pry into the business of his neighbors."[51] Without the sort of gritty perseverence of which the *Spartan* spoke, an editor's chances were not great of successfully guiding his newspaper through the war period.

Early in the war, newspapermen had fewer problems with the actual manufacture of newspapers. A circulation boom kept profits up even though advertising dollars declined as Northern clients pulled their ads from Southern newspapers and Southern businesses closed when their owners and employees went off to fight. That circulation boom, though, was both good and bad. The problem of getting subscribers to pay up was perennial, and with more subscribers, the problem expanded. By the end of the first year of the Civil War, the *Charleston Mercury*'s subscribers owed the newspaper $17,000 in subscription dues. Its advertisers were not doing much better; they owed the newspaper $20,000. Many newspapers, as a result, went to a cash system that required subscribers to pay in advance. Toward the end of the war, as cash became truly scarce in the South and inflation soared at unbelievably high levels, editors would accept just about anything of value in payment for subscriptions. The *Hillsborough Recorder* (Hillsborough, N.C.) announced a subscription price increase in January 1864 but added that the editor would be willing to barter subscriptions for $1 plus "wood, corn, wheat or flour, or butter, eggs, or potatoes, or any article of the kind used in a family." The *Sandersville Central Georgian* had been accepting produce for subscriptions since 1862.[52]

Once the shooting started, demands on editors and their staffs escalated. Editors faced disruptions, dislocations, shortages, and soaring labor and materials costs, printer strikes, and loss of manpower to the army.[53] One of the more vexing shortages was labor. Nearly three-quarters of the South's printers did military service. This rate of volunteerism by printers was not uncommon among white Southern men. In South Carolina, for example, 44,000 men out of a voting population of 68,000 volunteered for the army in the first eighteen months of the war. By 1864, nearly half the men who had worked as printers at Southern newspapers in 1860 were dead. Many of those who still lived were disabled by injury or disease that resulted from their military service. Given that it took about three printers to support the work of one editor, even the loss of a single printer could have a profound effect on the production capacity of a newspaper. Of course, the number of printers needed declined as the other shortages—raw materials, advertisers, subscribers, and news—forced newspapers to cut the number of pages they printed daily and as more and more newspapers went out of business.[54]

With increased demand for news, many newspapers became essentially twenty-four-hour operations as they added evening editions for their city subscribers and bi-weekly or triweekly editions for their country readers. When the *Augusta Evening Dispatch* suspended publication in June 1861, the *Chronicle and Sentinel* was quick to add an evening edition to attract the *Dispatch*'s readers. The new edition would be delivered by carrier every day for a price of 15¢ per week. The *Chronicle and Sentinel* editors promised to provide "the latest news by telegraph, express and mail" that came in as late as 1:30 P.M. The paper's morning edition had a closeout time of 1:00 A.M. so that it could make the morning departures of the mail trains on the South Carolina Railroad and the Athens and Washington Railroad. Papers that went out on those trains would be in the hands of distant subscribers that same day. The next month, the *Chronicle and Sentinel* announced plans to add a triweekly edition as soon as 100 people indicated their interest. The new paper would carry sixteen columns of news.[55]

Local distribution of newspapers was less of a problem than was dissemination to country or out-of-town subscribers. Carriers delivered newspapers to local sub-scribers, and as long as the regular carriers serviced their well-known routes, there were few problems. However, whenever a carrier was not available or one became sick, or when a new carrier was learning a new route, apologies for mistakes were com-mon features in newspaper columns.[56]

Out-of-town deliveries were more vulnerable to the vissicitudes of war. The *Albany Patriot* (Albany, Ga.) complained in the fall of 1864 about how few copies of the *Macon Telegraph and Confederate* were reaching its town. The Albany paper wanted to know "how it is that so few copies of Tuesday's and Wednesday's editions have reached this post office when the subscription list numbers over a hundred. We have not received a copy since Sunday." The *Patriot* speculated that the problem lay in the *Telegraph and Confederate* mail room. More likely, however, the root of the problem was the destruction of the railroads and the disruption of mail service by Union General William T. Sherman's men as they marched through Georgia on their way to the sea.[57]

Production of the South's dailies, and many of the more important weeklies, was accomplished with the aid of steam presses. The *Charleston Mercury* bought a new cylinder press before the war that could print 4,000 sheets per hour. The purchase was made because the paper's existing equipment was not sufficient to keep up with increased demand for subscriptions. The paper lost that press, though, in 1865 when it was moved to Columbia for safekeeping. The staff expected Union General William T. Sherman to strike Charleston in his campaign through the Carolinas. In-stead, Sherman's forces attacked Columbia, and the *Mercury*'s press was destroyed in the conflagration there. The *Selma Reporter* (Selma, Ala.) came up with a truly in-novative printing solution when demand for its morning and evening editions out-stripped the ability of its hand press to meet demand. The paper had extended its deadline for news so as to include the latest dispatches, but that gave the press room less time to actually produce the newspaper, especially since the press run had gone up to meet reader demand for more copies. The demands on the printing staff were so great that they often could not meet them, and the paper frequently appeared too late to make the mail trains. With no press manufacturers in the South, and little money, the situation could have been hopeless had the clever staff at the *Reporter* not devised an amazing solution. The *Reporter*'s staff figured out a way to attach a steam engine to its hand press. The article about this innovation did not describe how the newspaper staff accomplished this engineering feat, but it did note, "The introduction of steam power to the printing business in Selma is an event worthy of more than passing notice." However, since the paper's staff had "neither time or disposition to blow about it," the workers decided to "let our engine do the *puffing*."[58]

Obtaining supplies and spare parts was a constant problem for Confederate newspapers. Printing equipment and other supplies came mostly from the North or from Europe, which caused problems for the blockade-bound newspapers of the Confederacy. Spare parts, new presses, and even new fonts of type had to be smuggled in on blockade runners. A type foundry did operate for a short time in Richmond, Virginia, and it supplied spare parts for printing presses, but the organization went out of business fairly quickly.[59] Obtaining an adequate supply of newsprint and ink also became a great trial. Of the more than 300 paper manufacturing plants in the United States in 1860, fewer than thirty were located in the South, and some of those were not in business during parts of the war.[60] The papermill at Bath, South Carolina, burned in April 1863 and was out of business until the fall of 1864. Other papermills were plagued by strikes and destruction by enemy armies, especially those around Atlanta.[61]

Some Southern newspapers resorted to manufacturing their own ink and decreased their number of pages from four pages daily to two to deal with the paper shortage. Others printed only enough copies for subscribers and gave up on newsstand or street sales. Still others not only went to two pages but also reduced their page size. In September 1861, the *Charleston Courier*, for example, reduced its page size from eight to seven columns, or from 30×44 inches to 18×36 inches. The paper's size would shrink even more as the war continued. Other newspapers went to smaller typefaces for body copy or even printed on other kinds of paper. The Vicksburg papers, for example, were well known for printing on wallpaper during the siege of that city in 1863, but other newspapers made that same choice. The *Augusta Chronicle and Sentinel* in the fall of 1863 noted that it was receiving other newspapers in a multitude of colors. The recent *New Orleans Delta*, for example, had come in a shade of bright orange, and a Mississippi newspaper had arrived in a brilliant vermillion, a sort of rosy red color. Other newspapers, the *Chronicle and Sentinel* noted, were clothed in "sober brown," probably brown wrapping paper. The *Chronicle and Sentinel* itself got into hot water a little later in the war when rumors began circulating around the state that it was hording newsprint in order to resell it at extortionist prices. The editor hotly denounced this claim as a lie and speculated that whoever was spreading the rumor had started it to harm his paper's reputation with the papermills so there would be more paper available for others to purchase.[62]

Southern editors showed innovative thinking and entrepreneurship when dealing with their ink shortage. Before the Civil War, ink had cost between 25¢ and 50¢ a pound. By 1863, the price had risen to anywhere from 75¢ to $2 a pound. To avoid the price increases, as well as to have a regular supply, several newspapers started manufacturing and selling printing ink. The homemade ink was made out of oil and lamp soot or even ordinary shoe-blacking. The *Charleston Mercury* and the *Augusta Chronicle and Sentinel* were among the newspapers that went into ink manufacturing. The *Mercury* opened the Charleston Printing Inks Work on 4 May 1863. The paper was proud of the quality of its ink. The copy in an ad for the new manufacturer assured readers that "The clear print of THE MERCURY, notwithstanding the disadvantages of worn type, inferior paper, &c., ought to be sufficient recommendations of the ink."[63]

THE CONFEDERATE PEOPLE AND THEIR PRESS: EFFECTS OF THE CIVIL WAR

Sometimes war is necessary, but even then, it is not good for newspapers nor for the people who make them and read them. The American Civil War took a terrible toll on Southern newspapers and the Southern people. Nearly half of the newspapers in the South folded during the war, and some 258,000 Southerners died. Yet the South's journalists kept the news coming, and the Confederate army kept up its fight far longer than it should have. Both the soldiers at the front and the people back home relied on newspapers to bring them the latest news. Those newspapers that continued to publish did the best they could, given their circumstances. The news those newspapers offered may not have always been entirely accurate—it rarely has been in any war, at least with regard to the initial accounts of battles—and the papers may not have always arrived with the freshest news, but at least some kind of news did arrive. What happened once the news did arrive is difficult to assess. What was the value for citizens of far-flung Houston, Texas, or Tampa, Florida, to find out about the fighting in Virginia two weeks after it had happened? Was some news better than no news? And what was the effect of finding out another two weeks later that earlier reports of a great Southern victory were just wild exaggeration or wishful thinking on the part of the correspondent? How did the content of Confederate newspapers influence the morale of the people back home? It is easier to raise these questions than it is to answer them.

The problems with news accuracy and diffusion were not significantly different from what they have been in most American wars. The first reports of battles are often wrong; even military leaders themselves have not always known immediately who won or who lost a particular fight. Many in both the South and the North initially thought Confederate General Robert E. Lee's troops had won at Gettysburg, but they were wrong. Without a doubt, accurate news has greater value than inaccurate news, especially when that inaccurate news has to be corrected later to indicate not a victory but a defeat. Civilian morale, an important component of all wars, can tolerate only so much tossing about before it plummets to unfathomable depths. Some historians have blamed the press for the sagging Confederate morale in 1864 and 1865. They point out that the constant editorial criticism of Jefferson Davis must have had an ill effect on public confidence in the Confederate government and its ability to bring the war to a successful conclusion. People who lived through the war implicated newspapers even earlier for lagging civilian morale. Before the war was even a year old, some Southerners were already concerned about the adverse effect of newspapers on readers. South Carolina civil servant Benjamin F. Arthur wrote in a letter:

> The time was in South Carolina when newspapers *informed* [emphasis his] and educated the public mind. They were once conducted and contributed to by the best intellects in the country—but that time has past—and they have degenerated into the

merest trash—conducted in many cases, by men of no attachments and less character. They have become a perfect nuisance and a newspaper reputation is getting to be regarded, rather an equivocal sort of fame.[64]

Those people who read newspapers like the *Charleston Mercury*, the *Augusta Chronicle and Sentinel*, and the *Raleigh Standard* would have been exposed over and over again to articles that cast doubt on Davis's leadership and wisdom. Even the newspapers that were hypercritical of the Confederate government rarely complained about the Southern military, but when they did, army commanders were quick to respond. After a reporter for the *Mobile Advertiser and Register* criticized General Lee in December 1864, Lee retorted that he had come to believe the Confederacy had made its greatest mistake at the outset of the war; it had put all its good generals to work editing newspapers and the bad ones to work commanding the armies in the field.[65]

There were other papers, though, that never lost faith, that believed up to and beyond Appomattox that the South could still pull off a victory if only the people would get behind the cause. These newspapers were culpable for raising the hopes of Confederate citizens beyond what was reasonable or realistic, given the military and economic state of the Confederacy. Newspapers were not the only factor in the waxing and waning of Confederate civilian morale. Confederate military performance on the battlefield or the preacher's sermon on Sunday or even something as common as a neighborly discussion over the fence all had their effects on civilian morale.

The wartime experience of the Southern press was not all that different from the experience of the Southern people. Some kept the faith; some lost it. Some stuggled and fought for the entire four years and were still standing when the war ended. Some died along the way. Those newspapers that were still publishing in April 1865 were shadows of what they had been in 1860, but they were still making the effort to serve their communities, using the resources they had available. Historian Phillip Knightley concluded that newspaper coverage of the Civil War was not very good and that it was particularly bad on the Southern side because of the lack of professional correspondents and other resources. Knightley was right about the lack of resources, but he was looking at the glass as half empty. The alternative view, the one this author advocates, looks at the glass as half full. That the South's journalists kept publishing at all under the circumstances they faced—no paper, no ink, few printers, invading armies—was an amazing accomplishment and a valuable lesson in how the press can function in adversity.

A NOTE ON NEWSPAPER SELECTION CRITERIA AND THE ORGANIZATION OF THIS PART

The quotation from the Charlotte, North Carolina, *Western Democrat* that begins this work is almost prescient in its observation that anyone with a complete file of Confederate newspapers has the best history of the Civil War that could ever be written, at least of events from the Southern point of view. Unfortunately, however, full runs of few Confederate newspapers exist, and in some cases, no issues remain at all. The situation is much better than it was even thirty years ago when J. Culter Andrews published the only history of the Southern press ever written. Since then, various state projects have tracked down and microfilmed many newspapers, but their diligence cannot ferret out what has been destroyed over the years by invading armies, flames, and floods. In many instances, newspapers may exist, but they have not been microfilmed, and they are held only in distant archives to which the researcher cannot travel. For the most part, the newspapers represented in this work were either available at nearby archives, could be obtained by interlibrary loan, or were purchased. Most of the newspapers come from South Carolina, North Carolina, Virginia, Georgia, Tennessee, Alabama, and Louisiana. Newspapers from Texas, Arkansas, Mississippi, and Florida were virtually impossible to obtain, or nonexistent, and so are underrepresented in this collection of articles. The contents are compiled from a range of newspapers from small-town weeklies and dailies to the South's versions of "metropolitan" newspapers to give readers a broad, cross-sectional view of the Confederate press.

Newspaper mortality rates were high in the nineteenth century even under the best circumstances. The average newspaper lasted only a few years before it folded. This trend was exacerbated in the Confederacy. Not only did Southern newspapers face the usual economic and business problems, they also faced invading hordes of enemy soldiers who relished in destroying newsrooms and presses and tossing type out in the street for horses, wagons, and people to grind down into the dirt. A good number of Southern newspapers made it through the entire war; a few others began publication during the war; but many, many others died or were forced to publish in occupied territories. Consequently, readers will note that some newspaper voices were quite loud in 1860 or 1861 but gone entirely by 1862 or later. The *New Orleans Picayune* was a good example. It was the closest thing the South had to a metropolitan newspaper in 1860, and though it continued to publish throughout the war—in fact, is still in publication today under the title *Times-Picayune*—its home city fell into Union hands in April 1862. The *Picayune* continued to publish, but it walked a narrow line proscribed by the Union military governors. At that point, it was no longer a Confederate newspaper, and thus its content fell outside the parameters of this work. Other newspapers, including the *Memphis Appeal*, the *Knoxville Register*, and the *Chattanooga Rebel*, left their home cities and took up publishing elsewhere rather than submit to Union domination. Their voices were heard throughout the war, especially the *Appeal*'s since, in 1863 and 1864, it was a major Southern newspaper publishing a day or less from the western front.

The authors of the articles were all primarily professional journalists, either newspapers editors or paid war correspondents. There are a few exceptions. For example, a common source of war news for Southern newspapers was local soldiers who would write letters for their hometown newspapers. Sometimes, the letters would have been sent to family members who shared them with the newspapers. In all instances, the original spellings, punctuation, and so on, that appeared in the newspapers have been retained.

A final word on organization: This work is organized in chronological fashion, beginning with the 1860 presidential election and the secession crisis. The chapters on the war years, with the exception of the first year of the war, have been divided into two main sections, the Western Theater and the Eastern Theater. The Western Theater, of course, covered the Trans-Mississippi, Mississippi, Tennessee, Georgia, South Carolina, and North Carolina. The Eastern Theater focuses primarily on the action in Virginia and Lee's two attempts at invading the North. The sole exception to the chronological order of this work is the final chapter, which focuses on the Confederate homefront. The Civil War brought enormous changes for women and blacks, and a work that purports to deal with the Southern experience during that conflict cannot in good conscience avoid dealing with the homefront.

NOTES

1. According to a plaque at Fort Sumter National Monument in Charleston's harbor, Ruffin's shot was actually the second one fired that morning. The first shot, though, was a signal shot and thus not aimed nor intended directly at Fort Sumter. Consequently, it is correct to give the wiley old newspaper editor credit for firing the first shot, at the fort itself.

2. Michael F. Holt, *The Political Crisis of the 1850s* (New York: W. W. Norton, 1978), 220.

3. This finding is based on a database created by the author of the Southern press manuscript of 189 newspaper owners, publishers, and editors in North Carolina, South Carolina, and Georgia. The author collected the names of the editors from the newspapers themselves and/or several reference books, then consulted the 1860 U.S. Manuscript Census (White Schedule and Slave Schedule) for entries for each newsman. Reference materials included: Winifred Gregory (Ed.), *American Newspapers, 1821–1936: A Union List of Files Available in the United States and Canada* (New York: H. W. Wilson, 1937); Rabun Lee Brantley, *Georgia Journalism of the Civil War Period* (Nashville, Tenn.: George Peabody College for Teachers, 1929); John Hammond Moore (Ed. and Comp.), *South Carolina Newspapers* (Columbia: University of South Carolina Press, 1988); Kenneth W. Rawlings, "Statistics and Cross-Sections of the Georgia Press to 1870," *Georgia Historical Quarterly* 23 (March 1939): 177–179; Mary Westcott and Allene Ramage, "A Checklist of United States Newspapers (and Weeklies before 1900) in the General Library," *Biographical Contributions of the Duke University Libraries* (1932, 1936, 1937), Part I. Alabama–Georgia, Part II. Idaho–Massachusetts, Part IV. North Carolina, Part V. North Dakota–Vermont; H. G. Jones and Julius H. Avant (Eds.), *Union List of North Carolina Newspapers, 1751–1900* (Raleigh, N.C.: State Department of Archives and History, 1963); University of North Carolina library online catalog at http://www.lib.unc.edu; World Cat online database.

4. Augusta *Chronicle and Sentinel* (Augusta, Ga.), 27 April 1861.

5. *Charleston Mercury*, 18 April 1861.

6. Cornelia Phillips Spencer, *The Last Ninety Days of the War in North Carolina* (New York: Watchman Publishing, 1866; reprint, Wilmington, N.C.: Broadfoot Publishing, 1993), 244.

7. John Nerone, *The Culture of the Press in the Early Republic: Cincinnati, 1793–1848* (New York: Garland, 1989); L. Edward Carter, "The Revolution in Journalism during the Civil War," *Lincoln Herald* 73 (Winter 1971): 238. There are historians who would argue that the press was not particularly influential, especially due to the South's lack of literacy. See Drew Gilpin Faust, *The Creation of Confederate Nationalism* (Baton Rouge: Louisiana State University Press, 1989).

8. *Athens Southern Watchman* (Athens, Ga.), 2 November 1864.

9. Alexis de Tocqueville, *Democracy in America*, ed. and abrid. Richard D. Heffner (New York: Mentor, 1956), 93.

10. Based on figures compiled from the table of Newspapers and Periodicals in the United States in 1860, *Statistics of the United States, (Including Mortality, Property, etc.,) in 1860; Compiled from the Original Returns and Being the Final Exhibit of the Eighth Census, under the direction of the Secretary of the Interior* (Washington, D.C.: Government Printing Office, 1866), 321–322.

11. The Confederate States of America consisted of Virginia, North Carolina, South Carolina, Georgia, Florida, Alabama, Tennessee, Mississippi, Louisiana, Arkansas, and Texas.

12. *Statistics of the United States, (Including Mortality, Property, etc.,) in 1860*, l. The statistics regarding Southern and slave populations are based on calculations made from state population totals on pages 8, 17, 53, 73, 194, 270, 358, 359, 451, 486, 518, and 597 of the above-referenced book.

13. Ibid., 342, 346–348, 508.

14. Nerone, *The Culture of the Press in the Early Republic*, 42–43.

15. Ibid.

16. George C. Rable, *The Confederate Republic: A Revolution against Politics* (Chapel Hill: University of North Carolina Press, 1994).

17. Thomas Cooper DeLeon, *Four Years in Rebel Capitals* (Mobile, Ala.: Gossip Press, 1890), 289; Gerald J. Baldasty, *The Commercialization of the News in the Nineteenth Century* (Madison: University of Wisconsin Press, 1992), 44; Hazel Dicken-Garcia, *Journalistic Standards in Nineteenth-Century America* (Madison: University of Wisconsin Press, 1989), 52–54; Nathan Lande, *Dispatches from the Front: News Accounts of America's Wars from 1776–1991* (New York: Henry Holt & Co., 1995), x.

18. Patricia G. McNeely, *Fighting Words: The History of Media in South Carolina* (Columbia: South Carolina Press Association, 1998), 30; *Anderson Intelligencer* (Anderson, S.C.), 2 February 1865; *Abbeville Press* (Abbeville, S.C.), 2 October 1863.

19. William E. Huntzicker, *The Popular Press, 1833–1865* (Westport, Conn.: Greenwood Press, 1994), 139; Edwin Emery, *The Press and America: An Interpretative History of the Mass Media* (Englewood Cliffs, N.J.: Prentice Hall, 1972), 251; T. Conn Bryan, *Confederate Georgia* (Athens: University of Georgia Press, 1953), 208; J. Cutler Andrews, *The South Reports the Civil War* (Princeton, N.J.: Princeton University Press, 1970), 57.

20. Andrews, *The South Reports the Civil War*, 54, 441, 445–446, 460. For a listing of many of the South's war correspondents, see 548–551.

21. *Charleston Courier*, dispatch dated 17 October 1861.

22. Joseph S. Mathews, *Reporting the Wars* (Minneapolis: The University of Minnesota Press, 1957), 93; Henry Prentice Miller, "The Life and Works of William Tappan Thompson" (Ph.D. diss., University of Chicago, 1942), 33; Andrews, *The South Reports the Civil War*, 18, 21, 516–517; J. Ford Risley, "Georgia's Civil War Newspapers: Partisan, Sanguine, Enterprising" (Ph.D. diss., University of Florida, 1996), 2.

23. *Journal of the Confederate Congress*, vol. 4 (Washington, D.C.: Government Printing Office, 1904), 207; *Proceedings of the Second Confederate Congress, First Session and Second Session in Part*, ed. Frank Vandiver (*Southern Historical Society Papers*, New Series–No. 13; Whole No. 51, 1958), 100, 136, 234.

24. *Athens Southern Banner* (Athens, Ga.), 30 November 1864.

25. Catherine Patricia Oliver, "Problems of South Carolina Editors Who Reported the War" (Master's thesis, University of South Carolina, 1970), 33–34; *Sandersville Central Georgian*, 8 January 1862.

26. Michelle F. Robertson, "The *Savannah Daily Morning News* of the Civil War Period—A Test of Siebert's Proposition II" (Master's thesis, University of Georgia, 1976), 35–37.

27. David J. Russo, "The Origins of Local News in the U.S. Country Press, 1840s–1870s," *Journalism Monographs* 65 (February 1980): 18, 35–36.

28. August Deitz, *The Confederate States Post-Office Department, Its Stamps and Stationary*, 2nd ed. (Richmond: Deitz Press, 1950), 27; Sidney Kobre, *Foundations of American Journalism* (Tallahassee: Florida State University Press, 1958), 345; Quintus Charles Wilson, "A Study and Evaluation of the Military Censorship in the Civil War" (Master's thesis, University of Minnesota, 1945), 292; *First Annual Meeting of the Press Association* (Montgomery: Memphis Appeal Job Printing Establishment, 1864); *Minutes of the Board of Directors of the Press Association, Oct. 14, 1863 and Jan. 14* (Atlanta, Ga.: Franklin Steam Publishing House, 1864).

29. A. D. Banks to Leroy P. Walker, 4 June 1861, Letters received by the Secretary of War, War Department Collection of Confederate Records Document #1265–1861, Record Group 109, National Archives and Records Administration, Washington, D.C; James M. Mathews (Ed.), *Statutes at Large of the Provisional Government of the Confederate States of America* (Richmond, Va.: A. M. Smith, Printer to Congress, 1864), 106; Andrews, *The South Reports the Civil War*, 528.

30. Dicken-Garcia, *Journalistic Standards in Nineteenth-Century America*, 5.

31. William L. King, *The Newspaper Press of Charleston, S.C.: A Chronological and Biographical History, Embracing a Period of One Hundred and Forty Years* (Charleston, S.C.: Edward Perry Book Press, 1872), 78–79, 189.

32. "Constitution of the Press Association," *The Press Association of the Confederate States*, 1863, 9; *The Press Association of the Confederate States of America* (Griffin, Ga.: Hall & Swayze's Printing House, 1863), 28.

33. Russo, "The Origins of Local News in the U.S. Country Press, 1840s–1870s," 21; Oliver, "Problems of South Carolina Editors Who Reported the War," 36.

34. Andrews, *The South Reports the Civil War*, 527.

35. *Darlington Southerner* (Darlington, S.C.), 7 November 1862; *Augusta Chronicle and Sentinel* (Augusta, Ga.), 29 April 1863 and 27 June 1863.

36. William H. Johnson, "Dr. Robert Wilson Gibbes: Southern Editor and Publisher, 1852–1864" (Master's thesis, University of South Carolina, 1969), 66–67; *Charleston Courier*, 3 March 1858; J. L. Hatch, *Rights of Corporators and Reporters* (Columbia, S.C.: Steam-Power Press of R. W. Gibbes, 1857).

37. A *chinquepin* is a dwarf chestnut tree. Its fruit is also called a chinquepin. Chestnuts are prone to getting worms in the South.

38. Donald L. Shaw, "At the Crossroads: Change and Continuity in American Press News 1820–1860," *Journalism History* 8 (1981): 44; *Augusta Chronicle and Sentinel* (Augusta, Ga.), 15 October 1863.

39. *Augusta Chronicle and Sentinel* (Augusta, Ga.), 26 August 1863; *Charleston Mercury*, 16 July 1861.

40. *Official Record of the Rebellion* (OR), Series I, Vol. 11, pt. 3, 636.

41. Richard Kielbowicz, "The Telegraph, Censorship and Politics at the Outset of the Civil War," *Civil War History* 40 (1995): 96.

42. *Augusta Chronicle and Sentinel* (Augusta, Ga.), 15 October 1863.

43. *Charleston Mercury*, 6 July 1861; OR, Series I, Vol. 11, pt. 3, 636; Wilson, "A Study and Evaluation of Military Censorship," 208.

44. OR, Series I, Vol. 5, 1021; *Army Regulations Adopted for the Use of the Army in the Confederate States (Revised from those of the United States, 1857)* (Richmond, Va.: West and Johnson, Publ., 1861), 21; Andrews, *The South Reports the Civil War*, 162.

45. OR, Series I, Vol. 15, 771–772; Donna Lee Dickerson, *The Course of Tolerance: Freedom of the Press in Nineteenth-Century America* (Westport, Conn.: Greenwood Press, 1990), 195–196; *Proceedings of the First Confederate Congress, Second Session*, Southern Historical Society Papers (New Series–No. 7; Whole No. 45, 1925), 225–227; Robert N. Mathis, "Freedom of the Press in the Confederacy," *The Historian* 37:4 (August 1975), 638; John Paul Jones, "The Confederate Press and the Government," *Americana* (January 1943), 14–15.

46. *Athens Southern Watchman* (Athens, Ga.), 6 December 1864; Debra Reddin van Tuyll, "Journalists First, Rebels Second: An Examination of Editorial Reaction to the President's Proposed Conscription of Newspapermen," in *The Civil War and the Press*, eds. David B. Sachsman, S. Kittrell Rushing, and Debra Reddin van Tuyll (New Brunswick, N.J.: Transaction Publishers, 2000), 437–450.

47. *Raleigh Progress*, quoted in the *Augusta Chronicle and Sentinel* (Augusta, Ga.), 23 November 1864.

48. *Proceedings of the Second Congress of the Confederate States of America, Second Session*, New Series–No. 13; Whole No. 51, 285–286.

49. Wilfred Buck Yearns, *The Confederate Congress* (Athens: University of Georgia Press, 1960), 90; N. W. Stephenson, "The Question of Arming the Slaves," *American Historical Review* 18 (October 1912–July 1913): 295–308.

50. Louis Turner Griffith and John Erwin Talmadge, *Georgia Journalism, 1763–1950* (Athens: University of Georgia Press, 1951), 89; Robert A. Rutland, *The Newsmongers: Journalism in the Life of the Nation, 1690–1972* (New York: Dial Press, 1973), 209; Mark Neely, *Southern Rights: Political Prisoners and the Myth of Confederate Constitutionalism* (Charlottesville: University of Virginia Press, 1999).

51. Quoted in John Calhoun Ellen, Jr., "Political Newspapers in the Piedmont Carolinas in the 1850s" (Ph.D. diss., University of South Carolina, 1958), 119.

52. Rutland, *The Newsmongers: Journalism in the Life of the Nation, 1690–1972*, 196; Andrews, *The South Reports the Civil War*, 47; Oliver, "Problems of South Carolina Editors Who Reported the War," 54, 64; Nerone, *The Culture of the Press in the Early Republic*, 47; *Sandersville Central Georgian*, 8 January 1862.

53. Cal M. Logue, Eugene F. Miller, and Christopher J. Scoll, "The Press under Pressure: How Georgia's Newspapers Responded to Civil War Constraints," *American Journalism* 15, no. 1 (Winter 1998): 14–18.

54. *Report of the Historian of the Confederate Records of the General Assembly of South Carolina* (Columbia, S.C.: The State Co., 1898), 5; Debra Reddin van Tuyll, "Rendering the Invisible, Visible: The Wartime Experiences of Confederate Printers" (paper presented at the annual conference of the American Journalism Historians Association, Billings, Mont., 2–4 October 2003); Andrews, *The South Reports the Civil War*, 43; Oliver, "Problems of South Carolina Editors Who Reported the War," 44–45.

55. *Augusta Chronicle and Sentinel* (Augusta, Ga.), 14 January 1863; 7 June 1861; 16 June 1861; 3 July 1861.

56. *Augusta Chronicle and Sentinel* (Augusta, Ga.), 14 January 1864; *Atlanta Southern Confederacy* (Atlanta, Ga.), 14 December 1864.

57. *Albany Patriot* (Albany, Ga.), 9 December 1864; Richard L. Kielbowicz, *News in the Mail: The Press, Post Office and Public Information, 1700–1860s* (Westport, Conn.: Greenwood Press, 1989), 1–2.

58. *Rome True Flag* (Rome, Ga.), 21 September 1861; *Athens Southern Banner* (Athens, Ga.), 12 February 1862; Ernest C. Hynds, *Antebellum Athens and Clark County, Georgia* (Athens: University of Georgia Press, 1974), 97; *Greensborough Patriot* (Greensborough, N.C.), 3 January 1861; *Live Giraffe* (Raleigh, N.C.), 5 February 1859; Rev. R. H. Whitaker, *Whitaker's Remininscences* (Raleigh, N.C.: Edwards and Broughton, 1905), 432; Johnson, "Dr. Robert Wilson Gibbes: Southern Editor and Publisher, 1852–1864," 115; *Charleston Mercury*, 18 February 1861; McNeely, *Fighting Words*, 31; *Selma Reporter* (Selma, Ala.), 5 December 1862.

59. *Charleston Evening News*, 20 July 1861.

60. Lyman Horace Weeks, *A History of Paper Manufacturing in the United States, 1690–1916* (New York: Lockwood Trade Journal Co., 1916); Nancy Telfair, *A History of Columbus, Ga., 1828–1928* (Columbus, Ga.: Historical Publishing Co., 1929), 119.

61. *Constitutionalist* (Augusta, Ga.), 9 November 1864; *Columbus Enquirer* (Columbus, Ga.), 15 November 1864; Arney Robinson Childs, *The Private Journal of Henry William Ravenel* (Columbia: University of South Carolina Press, 1947), 201.

62. *Charleston Courier*, 13 February 1864; Spencer, *The Last Ninety Days of the War in North*

Carolina, 245; Herbert Ravenel Sass, *Outspoken: 150 Years of the News and Courier* (Columbia: University of South Carolina Press, 1953), 32–33; Henry Malone, "Atlanta Journalism during the Confederacy," *Georgia Historical Quarterly* (September 1953): 216; *Augusta Chronicle and Sentinel* (Augusta, Ga.), 22 October 1863.

63. Andrews, *The South Reports the Civil War*, 43; Robert Neal Elliott, Jr. *The Raleigh Register, 1799–1863* (Chapel Hill: University of North Carolina Press, 1955), 107; Oliver, "Problems of South Carolina Editors Who Reported the War," 48; Earl L. Bell and Kenneth C. Crabbe, *The Augusta Chronicle: Indomitable Voice of Dixie, 1785–1960* (Athens: University of Georgia Press, 1960), 50.

64. Benjamin F. Arthur to "My Dear Sir," 23 October 1861, Benjamin F. Arthur Collection, South Caroliniana Library, University of South Carolina, Columbia.

65. *Macon Telegraph and Confederate*, 2 December 1864.

27

THE 1860 PRESIDENTIAL ELECTION
AND SECESSION

More than 600,000 men died during the American Civil War, and the Southern region of the country was so badly devastated—both physically and psychologically—that nearly 150 years later the effects of that conflict are still apparent. There is one legacy of secession, however, that is so profound, yet so subtle, that no one even thinks about it today: the change in the form of the verb *to be* that is used to refer to the United States of America. Prior to 1860, references to the United States often took the form: "The United States *are* . . ." After the war, usage became: "The United States *is* . . ." That shift in verbs denotes in the most succinct way possible that the South's secession from the Union in 1860 did more that lead to the bloodiest war in American history. It resolved, once and for all, questions that had never truly been answered before regarding the fundamental nature of the American Union. That debate had centered on the meaning of the Tenth Amendment and what the Framers had meant when they wrote, "The powers not delegated to the United States by the Constitution, nor prohibited by it to the States, are reserved to the States respectively, or to the people." If the states had the power to choose to enter the American Union, did they or did they not have to power to leave it when they desired? That question had been particularly important during the antebellum period when the South and the North fought over nullification, expansion of slavery into the territories, and fugitive slave laws.

Slavery was at the heart of most of the antebellum period's major political debates, and it was at the heart of the growing distance between the South and the North. While only about 25 percent of Southerners could afford to own at least one slave, it was an institution that shaped the region's culture and politics. Their regular exposure to slavery made white Southerners particularly jealous of their individual liberties. One had only to look out the back door, or across the fields to their wealthier, slave-owning neighbors, to see that the price of lost liberty was subservience. One had only to listen to the speeches of political icons like South Carolina's John

C. Calhoun to learn that the American Union was dear—but not so dear as personal liberty. Indeed, for white Southerners of all social classes, individual liberty was the one common characteristic they shared, the basis of their equality. Even if you were a dirt poor farmer with less than 20 acres of land to your name, you were, in all the important ways, the equal of the planter who owned 2,000 acres and fifty slaves, because you were a free man.

Given this mind-set, it becomes easier to understand the origins of the radical conservativism of the antebellum Southerner and the Southern response to the major issues of the period, beginning with the conflict over the admission of Missouri to the Union. While the nation debated whether to allow slaves to be imported into Missouri after it achieved statehood, many Southerners saw the subtext of the debate as whether the North would be allowed to interfere with Southern property rights. The Missouri Compromise of 1820 more or less settled the issue for the next thirty years. Any new states above the 36th parallel would be admitted as free states; any new states below that latitude would come in as slave states. That did not mean, though, an end to sectional tensions. Conflict over a proposed tariff, the growing extreme states' rights stand of many Southerners, and Northerners' moral indignation over slavery kept the tensions simmering.

In 1850 and 1854, though, the issue of the westward expansion of slavery was raised again. In 1850, the issue was what to do with territory gained in the Mexican-American War. The debate was fueled by the expanding western population brought about by the California gold rush. Antislavery forces favored a proposal made in the Wilmot Proviso to exclude slavery from all the lands acquired by the treaty that ended the Mexican war. Southerners were outraged even though the Proviso never became law. Such a decision would preclude them from exercising their liberty to move their property (i.e., slaves) about the United States as they saw fit. Stephen A. Douglas, Henry Clay, and Daniel Webster were instrumental in putting together a bill that averted secession, at least temporarily, by satisfying both the North and the South on the issue. The bill called for California to be admitted as a free state and the territories of New Mexico and Utah to be left to decide the issue for themselves. The slave trade would be prohibited in Washington, D.C., but the South would get the more stringent fugitive slave law for which it had been clamoring.

In 1854, the issue was what to do about organizing territories west of Iowa and Missouri. To satisfy Southerners, Stephen A. Douglas, chair of the Senate Committee on Territories, proposed legislation to create two new territories, Kansas and Nebraska, rather than a single one. Douglas proposed in his bill to allow residents of the territories to decide whether to come into the Union as slave or free states, a direct violation of the Missouri Compromise since both Kansas and Nebraska were north of the 36th parallel. Antislavery proponents were outraged, but the bill made it through Congress, and the president signed it. The result was anything but a peaceful outcome. Because the decision on whether to allow slavery was left to the people, both pro- and antislavery advocates streamed into Kansas to help citizens "better understand" which way to vote on the issue. The most violent result was "bleeding Kansas," a mini–civil war of sorts within the newly organized territory; the most significant result was the formation of the Republican Party by those who opposed the Kansas and Nebraska Acts.

The presidential election of 1860 was the final straw for many Southerners, especially those of fire-eating bent. They believed that if the citizens of the North were willing to elect a sectional candidate who favored abolition, then the Union was so perverted that there was no saving it. Clearly, many Southerners believed, there could be no question that Yankees and Republicans were willing to crush Southern liberty. Thus, it was time to break free, declare Southern independence, and create a new country that would more closely guard individual liberties and adhere to the requirements of the Constitution.

The fire-eaters' objections to Lincoln overlooked two important facts, though. First, Lincoln did not oppose slavery himself. True enough, his party had an abolitionist plank, but he had no inclination to do anything affirmative to implement it. Further, the president had no power to pass legislation. If slavery was to be ended in the United States, it would require the election of a Republican Congress as well as a Republican president. Those Southerners who opposed secession, or who were more cautious about what it would take to justify so rash an act, made these arguments, but secession fever swept over the South, fanned by the inflammatory rhetoric of fire-eaters such as Robert B. Rhett, South Carolina politician and owner of the *Charleston Mercury*.

Lincoln was elected on 6 November, and within six weeks, South Carolina had seceded from the Union. Within only a few weeks, six other states followed South Carolina out of the Union and then on to Montgomery, Alabama, for a convention to form the Confederate States of America. Four more Southern states would follow by or just after the capitulation of Fort Sumter. The stage was set for the bloodiest conflict in American history.

GEORGE KENDALL OR FRANCIS LUMSDEN: STATES MOVING TOWARD SECESSION IF LINCOLN ELECTED

With the 6 November election virtually upon them, Southern threats of secession became widespread and more frantic. In Mississippi, Governor John J. Pettus announced that should Lincoln be elected president, he would immediately call a special legislative session to address secession. There was little question how Mississippi's legislators would vote on the issue. Alabama's governor, Andrew Barry Moore, was also preparing to call a special legislative session that would see to the protection, that is, secession, of his state. Other Southern states, including Texas and South Carolina, likewise, were moving toward secession, though the Lone Start state's governor, the venerable Sam Houston, had vowed to resist any move toward disunion. Houston would be disappointed by his constituents' decision in February to secede from the United States. After a brief and failed attempt to reestablish the Republic of Texas, Houston resigned his governorship in March. The Mr. Yancey quoted in this story was William Lowndes Yancey, an Alabama politician and avowed fire-eating secessionist.

New Orleans Picayune, 3 November 1860

STATES MOVING

The Governor of Mississippi has announced that the same wire which brings the news of the election of Lincoln to the Presidency, shall carry through the State his call of a special meeting of the Legislature to devise measures for protection, if need be, out of the Union. He avows himself for disunion, in that contingent at all hazards.

Alabama provided last winter, by an act of the Legislature, for an election by the people of delegates to a Southern convention in case a Republican candidate should be elected President of the United States. It is stated that the Governor of the State will at once issue a proclamation for the election on the receipt of the news of Lincoln's success.

Texas took the same initiatory steps by Legislative action

before the inauguration of Gov. Houston. His conservative views will stand between the people and any rash and precipitate action.

South Carolina, it is well known, is prepared to join, if not lead, any action, however radical, against the Union, should the national party of the North triumph. Gov. Gist refuses to be a candidate for Senator of the United States Senate, as he will not serve in Congress with a Republican President.

These movements are earnest and decided the danger to the South from them is imminent. In certain sections of the States the excitement has grown to be almost beyond control. Yet, strange as it may seem, the making up of such an issue on the result simply of the Presidential contest is disapproved, and by no one of them more decidedly than by Mr. Yancey himself. At Montgomery, Alabama in the month of May last, in a public speech, he said:

> I say with all deference to my colleagues that no more inferior issue could be tendered to the South upon which we should dissolve the Union than the loss of an election. If in the contest of 1860 for the Presidency Mr. Seward should receive the legal number of votes necessary to elect him according to the terms of the constitution and the law, gentlemen say that then will be the time to dissolve the Union. If that is made the cause of disunion, I say to them I

will go with them, but I will feel that I am going in the wake of an inferior issue—that there was a banner over me that is not of the kind I would wish. When I am asked to raise the flag of revolution against the constitution, I am asked to do an unconstitutional thing, according to the constitution as it now exists. I am asked to put myself in the position of a rebel, of a traitor—in a position where, if the Government should succeed and put me down in the revolution, I and my friends can be arraigned before the Supreme Court of the United States, which would be the creature of Mr. Seward, as he has given notice in the Senate, and there sentenced to be hanged for violating the constitution and laws of my country. And if I should be asked why sentence should not be passed on me, I could not then, as I can now in reference to past issues, I could not say then even to the bloody judges who would sit upon the bench, my hands are guiltless of wrong against the constitution of my country, and I appeal to an enlightened posterity, to the judgment of the world, to vindicate my name and memory when, [unreadable] country shall have taken her place once more as equal among the nations of the earth.

This opinion, so strongly stated and based upon the most hopeful view of the act by those despairing of justice in the Union, is commended to all who now are so ready to join in applause of a movement that cannot fail to awake the credit, derange the business, and destroy for years the prosperity of the entire South.

GEORGE KENDALL OR FRANCIS LUMSDEN: EDITORIAL—WHAT IS THE TRUE ISSUE IN THIS ELECTION?

In this lengthy editorial, the New Orleans paper reviewed the political controversies that had paved the way to the 1860 presidential election becoming essentially a national referendum on the questions of slavery and secession. "What is the True Issue?" the paper asked. The true issue was slavery.

New Orleans Picayune, 4 November 1860

WHAT IS THE TRUE ISSUE?

We are on the eve of a most important event. The result of the election just at hand may be fraught with momentous consequences. A determination is openly proclaimed in many quarters not to abide by the decision of a majority, if it secure a sectional triumph; and a great nation, blessed beyond all others in its basket and its store, but unfortunately torn by hostile and contending factions, seems on the very verge of revolution.

The gravity of the occasion suggests the inquiry, what is the extent of the wrongs suffered, that so arouse the fears and passions of men as to obliterate the influence of patriotism, and outweigh every consideration of public and private interest? What cause have men of the South to appeal to the god of battles for justice? On what issue is the determination made up to seek safety in a disruption of the government which has only shown an almost unlimited capacity for good?

Those who now strive to excite a tempest of popular passion, declare the election of the chief of a sectional party sufficient cause for resistance; but as if conscious of the weakness of such an issue before a people reverencing constitutional forms of action, and taught the duty of yielding to the voice of a majority, they triumphantly ask, in the manner of a most positive assertion, has not the constitution been often violated? Has not outrage followed on the heels of outrage, and forbearance but encouraged aggression, until honor and manliness, and safety, are only to be maintained by resistance? Aroused to jealousy by the fact that the free States, if united in sentiment, can control the majority of members, in the House of Representatives and the Senate, and have in their power, the distribution of the spoils of office and the direction of the policy of the government—excited beyond measure by the aggressive tendency of this Northern sectional party, that even now exults in the prospect of victory, and proclaims its irreconcilable hostility to slavery, they look back on the closed issues of the past, and all the bleeding wounds, cicatrized by time, open afresh. They seem to see but one continued series of assaults and weak defenses; one perpetual chain of concessions to be followed by those still more vital to the rights of the States, and these united in one bill of complaint are presented to the people, as an irresistible argument to stir them up to immediate and concerted resistance.

But can men of the South revive the strifes of the past to render the present issue with the North more strong? Is our cause of complaint so serious? Have the slave States been constantly suffering wrong, while possessing themselves in patience, always yielding yet never satisfying the grasping demands of the free States? Let us appeal to facts for a decision.

From the adoption of the constitution to the election of Martin Van Buren—from 1789 to 1851—a period of sixty-two years, a Southern man occupied the honored post of Chief Executive of the nation, with the exception of the single term of each of the two Adams, from Massachusetts.

During the period—that of nearly two generations—two thirds of the foreign missions and the more important of the domestic offices were enjoyed by Southern men.

From 1841 to 1860, but two Presidents have been elected—Harrison and Fillmore—who were not emphatically the choice of the South, and really nominated and elected by the South. Of the six Presidents since 1841, three were Southern men.

It was the boast of Southern statesmen as late as ten years ago that the South had dictated the domestic policy of the nation. The purchase of the Louisiana Territory was at the instigation of the South.

The annexation of Texas was conceived by Southern minds and achieved by Southern votes.

The war of 1812 from which the country emerged with so much glory, was voted and sustained by the South.

The war with Mexico, which added an empire in extent to the territory of the Republic, is due to the policy of men of the South, thus extending our Southern boundaries from the western limits of Texas to the Pacific ocean. Of all this has the South reason to complain?

But our position is scarcely less improved in three series of years in regard to the question of slavery. If, under the operation of the laws of climate and production, slavery has been extinguished in that little patch of states denominated New England, in New York, Pennsylvania, and New Jersey, the purchase of the Territory of Louisiana has given us Louisiana, Arkansas and Missouri as slave States—a region of country much larger than that from which State sovereignty has eradicated human bondage.

The annexation of Texas in 1845 devoted to slavery a territory equal to all New England, New York and New Jersey, and the acquisition of New Mexico by conquest, in which slavery has been established by territorial law, carries the in-

stitution two degrees above the line of the Missouri Compromise. Can we complain that the territorial limits of slavery have been circumscribed, or go back to this history of its extension to strengthen the catalogues of our grievances?

But, it is said, the perpetual agitation of this question in and out of Congress, has driven the South to unjust concessions, every one of which should have been made the cause of resistance to the Federal Government and that each as it followed the other in the order of succession increased the intolerance and aggressions of the free North. The Missouri Compromise was the first in order. If it was wrong the South has to blame only itself; for it came from a representative of a slave State, and was supported by the almost unanimous vote of Southern delegates in both Houses of Congress. It was ratified again and again by the popular vote of the slave States until it came to be regarded to have almost as binding a character as the constitution itself.

The next great struggle on the question of slavery resulted in the compromise bill of 1850. There again the South gave birth to the act, and it was sustained not only by the Southern vote in Congress, but was ratified by the people themselves. Georgia and Mississippi and South Carolina made the issue of resistance against it, and the people with majorities unprecedented in any political contest sustained the work of the noble patriots of that gloomy day. The South is then precluded by its own action from reopening the issues then settled and making them living questions at this time. Right or wrong, they belong to the dead past. The golden era of peace and general accord followed, until the elements of essential strife were again let loose from their sealed cavern by the repeal of the Missouri Compromise and the Kansas and Nebraska bill.

Whether the South originated this act or not, it united in almost solid phalanx to sustain it, while the North was almost alone in opposition to the measure.

This reopened the agitations happily set at rest, and again plunged the country into an excitement which has resulted in the birth of a party that now stands avowedly sectional, openly aggressive, and by its doctrines, insults and defies the South. But it has to make a forward step to present a tangible issue that can be met only be a revolution. Its principles are dangerous if an attempt be made to put them in practice. No man with a Southern heart will defend its fanatical fury, or excuse its menacing attitude towards those States coequal with the free commonwealths. But can we look back upon the history of the past and find serious reason to complain, except it be of our own blindness and folly? Can we hope to strengthen the issue now proposed by accumulating with it the series of acts, or any one of them, alluded to in this brief sketch?

The very agitation of which we complain has in one respect accrued to our benefit. It has evolved the true principles on which the institution of slavery is based. It has convinced all Southern men of the moral right, the civil, social and political benefit of slavery. It has done more; it has modified the opinion of a large number of men in the free States, on this subject, and is gradually changing the opinion of the world—bringing it to regard slavery with more liberality.

The number of slaves has increased in a remarkable ration, and to-day is stronger on the whole frontier line of the free States than it was ten, nay five years ago.

These notes of history cannot be denied, and when we meet the crisis created by the ballot of the nation about to be cast, let it be remembered that we have no cause to resist, except the unconstitutional, the weak, the untenable one of having lost our choice for the President of the Republic. The movement of demagogues and politicians to make this election, if adverse to the South, an opportunity for secession—which we have previously shown is but a word to mask the idea of revolution—is full of imminent peril to the South, not to the Union as we have been supposed to have asserted. Upon an issue so weak to go into a contest which involves all the consequences of treason, the South must fail, for she can-

not hope for accord among the citizens of any one State. The time may come when disunion with all its consequences, must be chosen, but a failure now precludes future confidence in leaders or hope in resistance.

Let every Southern man feel it to be a duty he owes not simply to his country, but to his family and himself to vote in the coming election so that he shall in no manner countenance the idea that his State or his parish is in favor of resisting the decision of the ballot. The home perils which a contrary course involve are of the most terrible character. Nations die a terrible death, just in proportion to their strength and vitality. If it be the destiny of the Union now to perish, none can estimate the throes of agony, the terrible scenes of distress, which will precede it. If the fires of civil war be kindled—and kindled they must be by any formidable movement in hostility to the Federal Government—they will burn until all is consumed that is perishable, and the land become a waste over which shall brood the silence of another and hopeless desolation.

S. B. CRAFTON: EDITORIAL—LINCOLN'S ELECTION MAKES OUTLOOK GLOOMY FOR UNION

Like many other Southerners, even on the eve of the 1860 presidential election, the editor of the weekly Sandersville Central Georgian *took the position of Stephen A. Douglas in the following untitled editorial: Election of a Republican president in and of itself did not justify secession. Before secession could be justified, the editor declared, Lincoln would have to take some overt action that directly threatened the South or its "peculiar institution"—slavery. The editor realized, however, that he was likely in the minority and that the result of the previous day's election would be civil war.*

Sandersville Central Georgian, 7 November 1860

Never, since we have been attempting to publish a newspaper, have we taken up our pen with such feelings as crowd our mind this morning. Ere this shall reach many of our readers, we fear the doom of our beloved country will be sealed. We have but little hope of the success of either of the three national candidates. In an exchange paper this morning, we see a statement, said to have been made by Hon. H. V. Johnson, on his return from a northern tour, "that Pennsylvania and New York are irretrievably lost, and that the latter will give a majority for Lincoln of 50,000." If this be true, our last hope is gone. We have never before seen our people look so gloomy on the eve of an election. All seem to realize that tomorrow (we write on Monday) is to be decided the fate of the greatest nation the world has ever known, and to be anxiously looking to the result. If Lincoln be elected, and a dissolution of the Union of these United States takes place, farewell to our heretofore prosperous and happy country. We have no

idea that a peaceable secession can be effected; but the bayonet will, we very much fear, be resorted to; the beat "to arms!" so long silent in our land, will again reverberate over hill and dale. Hostile armies will be marching to and fro over the fertile fields of our beloved South, to meet an opposing force from the North. Can it be so? Can it be so? God forbid it.

While we, individually, confess that the thought of submitting to be ruled over by an executive elected upon principles directly opposed to the interests of the South, and without the assistance of southern votes, yet we are not prepared to say we are for dissolution before some overt act has been committed by that executive. This is a matter of the greatest moments to the American people, and should be well considered before any decisive steps are taken. May the God of nations guide our people right through these troubled times!

AN ANONYMOUS REPORT: FORM AND MANNER OF SOUTH CAROLINA SECESSION ORDINANCE

On 20 December, the telegraph wires buzzed with the news of South Carolina's secession from the Union and reaction to it. Dispatches about the South Carolina decision came in throughout the day, but by 4:00 P.M. the Picayune's *correspondent in South Carolina sent the full text of the Secession Ordinance. Other correspondents quickly sent in reaction stories. Meanwhile, in Washington, D.C., political leaders worked feverishly to reach a compromise that would keep the Union intact, or at the very least, prevent civil war.*

New Orleans Picayune, *21 December 1860*

FURTHER FROM SOUTH CAROLINA
FORM AND MANNER OF SECESSION
Repeal of the Ordinance of 1788

CHARLESTON, Dec. 20, 4 P.M.—The following ordinance passed the convention to day without a dissenting voice, and will be ratified at twelve o'clock to morrow, with becoming solemnity:

"An ordinance to dissolve the union between the State of South Carolina and other States united with her, under a compact entitled 'Constitution of the United States of America.'

"We, the people of the State of South Carolina, in convention assembled, do declare and ordain, and it is hereby declared and ordained, that the ordinance adopted by us in the convention of the 23rd of May, in the year of our Lord 1788, whereby the constitution of the United States of America was ratified, together with all acts and parts of acts of the General Assembly of the State ratifying amendments, said constitution is hereby repealed, and the union now existing between South Carolina and other states, under the name and title of the United States of America, is hereby dissolved."

ROBERT BARNWELL RHETT, JR.: REJOICING AT SOUTH CAROLINA'S DECISION TO SECEDE

South Carolinians rejoiced at the decision of their state convention to remove the Palmetto state from the Union. The conservative revolution had begun, and finally, the South was to be safe from the tyranny of the North. At this point, no one really expected that the South's bid for independence would result in war, much less the blood of so many being spilled.

Charleston Mercury, *21 December 1860*

The 20th Day of December.

Inscribed among the calenders of the world—memorable in time to come—the 20th day of December, in the year of our Lord 1860, has become an epoch in the history of the human race. A great Confederate Republic, overwrought with arrogant and tyrannous oppressions, has fallen from its high estate amongst the nations of the earth.—Conservative liberty has been vindicated. Mobocratic license has been stricken down. Order has conquered, yet liberty has survived. Right has raised his banner aloft, and bidden defiance to Might. The problem of self-government under the check-balance of slavery, has secured itself from threatened destruction.

South Carolina has resumed her entire sovereign powers, and, unshackled, has become one of the nations of the earth.

On yesterday, the 20th of December, 1860, just before one o'clock, p.m., the Ordinance of secession was presented by the Committee on Ordinance, to the Convention of the people of South Carolina. Precisely at seven minutes after one o'clock,

the vote was taken upon the Ordinance—each man's name being called in order. As name by name fell upon the ear of the silent assembly, the brief sound was echoed back, without one solitary exception in that whole grave body—Aye!

At 1:15 o'clock, p.m.—the last name was called, the Ordinance of Secession was announced to have been passed, and the last fetter had fallen from the limbs of a brave, but too long oppressed people.

The Convention sat with closed doors. But upon the announcement outside, and upon the MERCURY bulletin board, that South Carolina was no longer a member of the Federal Union, loud shouts of joy rent the air. The enthusiasm was unsurpassed. Old men went shouting down the streets. Cannon were fired, and bright triumph was depicted on every countenance.

But before the Great Seal of the State was affixed to the Ordinance of Secession, and the names of the Delegates to the Convention were signed, it was proposed that this ceremony should be postponed until 7 o'clock that evening; when the Convention should reassemble and move in procession from the St. Andrew's Hall, where they then sat, to the great Secession Hall; and that there, before the assembled citizens of the State, the Great Seal of the State should be set, and each signature made. The proposition was favorably received.

At 6½ o'clock p.m., the Convention reassembled at St. Andrew's Hall. At 6¾ o'clock p.m., they formed in procession and moved forward in silence to Secession Hall.

The building was filled to overflowing, and they were received by some three thousand people in the Hall.

The Convention was called to order. The scene was one profoundly grand and impressive. There were a people assembled through their highest representatives—men most of them upon whose heads the snows of sixty winters had been shed—patriarchs in age—the dignitaries of the land—the High Priests of the Church of Christ—reverend statesmen—and the wise judges of the law. In the midst of deep silence, an old man, with bowed form, and hair as white as snow, the Rev. Dr. BACHMAN, advanced forward, with upraised hands, in prayer to Almighty God, for His blessing and favor in this great act of his people, about to be consummated. The whole assembly at once rose to its feet, and with hats off, listened to the touching and eloquent appeal to the All Wise Dispenser of events. At the close of the prayer the President advanced with the consecrated parchment upon which was inscribed the decision of the State, with the Great Seal attached. Slowly and solemnly it was read unto the last word—when men could contain themselves no longer, and a shout that shook the very building, reverberating, long-continued, rose to Heaven, and ceased only with the loss of breath. In proud, grave silence, the Convention itself waited the end with beating hearts.

The President then requested the Delegates (by previous decision) to step forward as they were called in the alphabetical order of the Districts which they represented, and sign the Ordinance. Two hours were occupied in this solemn ceremony—the crowd waiting patiently the end. As the delegation from St. Phillip's and St. Michael's came forward, again, the hall was filled with applause. And as the Hon. R. B. RHETT advanced to the parchment, the shouts became deafening, long-continued, until he had seated himself, signed and retired. It was a proud and worthy tribute, gracefully paid, and appreciated. The same special compliment was paid to our Ex-Governor GIST, from the Union.

At the close of the signatures the President, advancing to the front of the platform, announced that the Seal of the State had been set, the signatures of the Convention put to the Ordinance, and he thereby proclaimed the State of South Carolina a separate, independent nationality.

To describe the enthusiasm with which this announcement was greeted, is beyond the power of the pen. The high, burning, bursting heart alone can realize it. A mighty voice of great thoughts and great emotions spoke from the mighty throat of one people as a unit.

The State of South Carolina has recorded herself before the universe. In reverence before God, fearless of man, unawed by power, unterrified by clamor, she has cut the Gordian knot of colonial dependence upon the North—cast her fortune upon her right, and her own right arm, and stands ready to uphold alike her independence and her dignity before the world. Prescribing to none, she will be dictated to by none willing for peace, she is ready for war. Deprecating blood, she is willing to shed it. Valuing her liberties, she will maintain them. Neither swerved by frowns of foes, nor swayed by timorous solicitations of friends, she will pursue her direct path.

JOHN HARVEY: SOUTHERN CONSTITUTIONAL ARGUMENT FOR SECESSION

Southerners believed in the strict construction of the Constitution, that is, that the original meaning of the organic law of the United States should be followed in all circumstances. To remain true to their constitutional values, Confederates had to carefully craft their legal justification for secession carefully. The Alabama Beacon *offered its readers a constitutional argument for secession that was both common and typical in the following untitled article.*

Alabama Beacon, 18 January 1861 (Greensboro, Ala.)

Has a State the right to secede? It is a very unfair way of stating the question so far as the proposed action of the States of the South at this time is concerned. The fair way would be— Has she such a right when the Government which is the creature of the States—made by them—becomes subversive of the purposes for which it was made, and instead of promoting the happiness, security and welfare of her people, becomes

destructive of them all? Her participation in the Federal Union was certainly by the free and voluntary act of her people as a State. By this act of her as a free and independent State a portion of the allegiance due to her by her citizens was transferred to the General Government. As to all the rights of a free and independent State which were not delegated to the General Government, the people, the political organization called States, it is manifest that there could not be reserved rights, if the Federal Government, to which they had not been delegated, and over which it had no control, had the rightful power to pronounce whether there was a palpable, deliberate and dangerous assumption of powers not granted, or in other words, whether it had itself become subversive of the purposes for which it was created. This would be to make its construction of its own powers or pretended powers, and not the Constitution, the law of the land. And whereas these rights not delegated were reserved to the people and the States, this doctrine would involve the absurdity of these very rights being at the same time conferred on General Government (it choosing to claim them,) if it has the right to decide if there is or is not a palpable infringement of them. The State, as to all rights not delegated, is sovereign, and being sovereign, can have no superior to pass upon the question for her, but of necessity must decide for herself, or otherwise any infringement of them is without remedy. Now, having the right to pronounce when these reserved rights are endangered by the Government, she has, as a necessary corollary, the right and duty to decide how they must be vindicated, defended and secured. Consolidation is tyranny in this, that it abstracts from the free State whose rights are infringed or endangered, the right to vindicate, secure and defend them, and places that right in the hands of the very dominant majority of the people of the United States by whose sanction their rights have been invaded. This is not the Government our fathers made. They did not obliterate the existence of the States as free and independent sovereignties over their reserved rights. There several times was the attempt made to confer by the Constitution the right to coerce a State, and every time it failed.

Our Union has intended to be cemented by fraternal regard, and its indissolubility was intended to be secured by mutual interest and reciprocal good will; but failing these, each State was a free and sovereign political community when her rights or happiness were endangered, to pronounce on the occurrence of such fact, and to decide the mode and manner of redress. The President in his late annual message to Congress has denied the right of a State to secede, because such admission would render the Government "a rope of sand."—We would most respectfully reply that the process of disintegration is more sure to follow the denial than the admission of the right of a State to secede when the Government becomes subversive of the purposes for which it was formed. Had this right been unanimously considered and admitted, instead of the doctrine that in some places obtains that a dominant majority of the whole people have the right to decide when they shall have themselves been guilty of subverting the Constitution, the present critical condition of affairs would not now exist. Legislation would necessarily be more conciliatory in its enactments, and the attempt to ride rough shod over the security, rights and sensibilities of the different States would have been less frequently made. All Governments derive their *just* powers from the consent of the Governed, and people are always slow to change the form of Government to which they are accustomed; nor need the President, or any one else, apprehend that the right of secession would be exercised for light and transient causes, any more than they need to apprehend that human life would be insecure because any one may commit a homicide when necessary to protect his own life.

TIBER: CORRESPONDENT PREDICTS THE COMING OF WAR

As the seceded states were electing delegates to send to a convention in Montgomery, the Picayune's *Washington correspondent wrote a letter to his paper that the destruction of the Union had already been accomplished. Bitter hostility was already growing between the sections, though a number of politicians, including Senator Jefferson Davis of Mississippi, were working diligently to find a compromise. Tiber, the correspondent, had picked up the prediction that, within six months, Northern and Southern armies would be meeting on the battlefield. Almost exactly six months from the date of this letter, Confederate and Union armies met in the first major battle of the war, First Manassas.*

New Orleans Picayune, 1 February 1861

LETTER FROM WASHINGTON

[Special Correspondence of the *Picayune*.]
WASHINGTON, Jan. 23, 1861.

It may be doubted whether, even at the South, the public are aware of the fact that the Union is entirely and hopelessly destroyed and the Government on the eve of dissolution. Many have gone into the secession movement without intending that it should lead to a perpetual and total separation of

the North from the South, and perhaps to several distant and separate and sovereign confederacies. Several of the Senators from Southern States who have just withdrawn from their seats, have, in their speeches, proposed reconstruction of the Government after the Southern States shall have seceded. To call a convention of all the Southern States in March, and prepare a new constitution of the government, or a reconstruction of the Union, admitting into it only preferred States, and on terms which the convention should propose, is the process relied upon for a reconstruction of the Government. The difficulties of this project are probably not estimated. Restorations are impopular and impracticable. To heal breeches once made in a government is very difficult. The Union broken by one line, would be soon broken by many lines. It would be difficult to find any one Northern State that would agree to reconstruction upon any plan which the South would present. The Southern States in convention would not, probably, themselves agree upon a plan of reconstruction.

There will arise, and in fact have already arisen, cases of bitter and deadly hostility between the two sections, that will place reconstruction out of the question. It will be thought of after the completion of the secession programme. Measures of mutual defence and offence will occupy all minds. Mr. Jefferson Davis throws out the idea in his speech that by means of a convention of the Southern States, and a simultaneous convention of the Northern States, a league, if not a reunion could be brought about. Here is another impracticable notion. What one state would agree to another would reject, and the very principle upon which the South proceeds is that no State can be bound by any compact longer than she chooses to be.

I have seen but few men, north or south, who comprehend the entire extent and meaning of the present revolution. We shall have in ninety days a fresh, vigorous and united Southern confederacy, and a grieving and jaded and feeble Northern confederacy—the remnant of the present Union.

It is annoying that scarcely a man in New York sees this.

When the New Yorkers come here they open their eyes a little, but still say that there is nothing in the Southern movement but a little bluster. I know one or two Republican members, however, who understand the whole matter, and freely declare the opinion that in six months from this time there will be two organized Governments; that real estate in the city of New York will have fallen to one-half of its present value, and that there will be hostile armies in the field of a hundred thousand men on either side, Northern and Southern.

There is no more doubt that Virginia will secede in the latter part of February than that Louisiana will secede, and all the Southern border States except Delaware, will follow the lead of Virginia. Secession is easy and it is possible. But it leads to a new state of things, the exact bearing of which cannot be well foreseen. But it never will lead to a restoration of the Union.

The prospect of Mr. Crittenden's plan of adjustment, with Mr. Bigler's amendment, is thought by some to be improving, but it may be well doubted whether Lincoln himself could, if here, persuade and considerable number of Republican members to go for it.

The committee of five members of the House, who have had under consideration the President's message concerning the revenue laws, &c., will not report in favor of blockading the ports of the seceding States. They will report a bill that will, however, effectually destroy the trade to and from ports where revenue laws cannot be enforced.

TIBER.

GEORGE KENDALL OR FRANCIS LUMSDEN: ACCOUNT OF MONTGOMERY CONVENTION

The Southern Convention met in Montgomery in early February and within days had written a Constitution for a new nation and elected a president and vice president. The biggest issue on most Southern minds at that point was not the possibility of war. Most still thought that a remote possibility at best. Rather, the issue was whether European powers, especially France and England, would recognize the Confederacy as a sovereign nation.

New Orleans Picayune, 5 February 1861

THE MONTGOMERY CONVENTION

The southern Congress, at Montgomery commences its sessions with six States represented by a number of delegates from each, corresponding to the number of its representation, for Senators and Representatives, in Congress of the old Government. The proportion was a mere matter of discretion, for we suppose that the States will vote as units, each having one vote. Inequalities in representation were matters of compromise, under the constitution of the United States, and cease when the States resume their independence, as all sovereignties are *ex vi termini*—equals. The present number of the body, forty-three, viz: from South Carolina, 8; Georgia, 10;

Florida, 3; Alabama, 9; Louisiana, 6; and Mississippi, 7.

The number is sufficiently large to supply working men on the important committees, and yet not large enough to encourage the popular vice of long speaking. The signers to the constitution of the United States were only 38 in number, but the convention which framed it was a little larger.

The number of States being even, and the number of several of the delegations also being even, the chances are multiplied for *tie* votes on questions in regard to which differences of opinion may arise. Let us hope that these occasions will be few, and that entire harmony may prevail in their deliberations and conclusion.

Before they are many days in session there will be another member present. Texas will appear there, with her four delegates, as the seventh State.

The peaceable assembling of such a body to settle the terms of a new union and a new government for a circle of equal republics is a great epoch in the history of American institutions and principles. The grand idea of the American Revolution was the right of a people to establish their own forms of government and choose their own rulers; the grand idea of the constitution of the United States was the union of political communities under one common agency for external affairs, but with the internal capacity for each to maintain its own rights, liberties and institutions against invasion from any quarter. The recent acts of the Southern people and States have rigidly conformed to both ideas. They have pronounced that the late Government of the United States was destructive of the objects for which it was established, and asserted their right to abolish the same as respects themselves, and to erect another which shall better secure their happiness and safety. They pay homage at the same time to the federative principle, and immediately propose to substitute for the old Union, which they have thrown off as an oppression, one which shall more perfectly "establish justice, insure domestic tranquility, provide for the common defence, and secure the blessings of liberty to ourselves and our posterity."

It is a hypochondriac delusion, which seems to have seized on the minds of many of our countrymen, to despond over these results, as proofs of the utter failure of American institutions, and the final condemnation of the federative principle. There is a good deal to create profound regret and serious uneasiness in the rupture of old associations, and the downfall of a government to which we had been long devoted and from which we had hoped for so much. But, when its character was radically altered, and the government itself was the bane of the most cherished rights, and to reform or abolish it the best homage to those institutions, the effective instrument for accomplishing it was sought in the independent State governments. The dignity, power and success of the movement is the highest vindication of the vigor and value of State sovereignties for the protection of liberty.

A great revolution has been effected by the power of public opinion, freely expressed through the ballot boxes, of seven organized and orderly communities, and perfected through all the legitimate forms of established authority. In what other country, in what other times or under what other form or principle of government, could such a movement have originated and been carried through, to the final solemn announcement of the common will of seven States, without tumult, disorder or blood? How triumphantly does this fact support the theory of the wisest founders of our institutions, that however necessary a common government may be for the exigencies of commerce and war, the bulwark of our liberties and of the happiness and security of every citizen, is to be looked for in the watchful care of the States.

The federative principle is going through a severe test, but its virtue has carried us thus far to the point of a total emancipation from one system, which was tried and has failed us, to the free liberty of forming another, with all the lights of experience and the advantage of a model which leaves little to the province of speculation and experiment. The old constitution was good enough for us all, if it could have been adapted to obvious changes of circumstances, and so defined as to accomplish its own clearly defined intents. We want nothing better than it can be made to be, with few new provisions and adaptations, and the capacity to include within its scope such other States as may be willing to come into a new confederation on terms of equality.

A form of government, permanent or provisional, for the seceded States, is now the matter of urgency. In the adjustments—peaceful or otherwise—with the governments from which they have been parted, a common agency is indispensable. If we are to be opposed, we must have common counsel and common measures for defence. If the separation is to be peaceful we need the machinery for joint negotiation with the North. More especially we need, as soon as possible, a common agency for intercourse with foreign governments.

We do not doubt the readiness of all the principal governments in the world to recognize a Southern Confederacy, provisional or otherwise, as soon as formed and set in motion. It is consistent with the uniform practice of modern times, and has grown into the force of public law, that governments *de facto* are acknowledged for all purposes of trade immediately, in spite of all paper proclamations of the intention to reclaim them, thrown out by the authorities they repudiate. To a regular formed Southern Confederacy, with even eight or nine States, England and France will concede at once the fact of independence.

The same promptness cannot reasonably be looked for in receiving at once seven or eight new States as sovereigns *de facto*.

The complex relations which existed between the States and the General Government of the Union are very indistinctly comprehended, even by well informed statesmen of Europe. The ordinary idea of us which obtains even in Cabinets, and has regulated public action towards us, is that the Federal Government is a consolidated one, with the same supreme authority over the States as the European central governments have over their provinces. These false notions have pervaded most of the views which have been drawn forth on the Continent, and even in England, by the news of our dissensions. Few but close students appreciate the really distinct character of our States, or the full grown organization and perfect rights which they bear with them out of the Union. It would take a long period, and many and precarious negotiations to settle the recognition of the separate independence of so many states, and arrange commercial treaties for them with all the maritime powers.

But the concurrence of seven or eight in one organic act, constituting a common executive authority for intercourse with foreign nations, would be of such significance and dignity as to require and receive immediate recognition. It would be the demonstration of a joint purpose and a completed fact, so large, comprehensive, orderly and powerful, that there is not a government in existence that could consistently decline, and few, if any, that would not cheerfully hasten to accept the new government. They would see the grand result, even if they could not understand the vitalizing federative idea, which could so speedily aggregate the assimilating parts of a disseevered confederacy into a new, vigorous and harmonious whole.

This task is in the hands of the convention at Montgomery. May they be inspired with the wisdom to do their work, so as to command the whole support of their constituents, and establish the blessings of peace and good government forever.

GEORGE KENDALL OR FRANCIS LUMSDEN: BORDER STATE CONFERENCES SEEK COMPROMISE

Many Americans, both Northern and Southern, wanted to find some way to maintain the Union and avert civil war. Peace commissioners traveled from Montgomery to Washington, and even the Border States met to see if they could find a compromise. The Border States met at the same time as the seceded states were meeting in Montgomery to arrange their new national government. The Southerners were more successful in their work than the Border States.

New Orleans Picayune, 6 February 1861

THE BORDER STATE CONFERENCES

At the same moment when the Southern seceding States are uniting in convention at Montgomery to create a new government for a new Union, the border States are holding another convention at Washington City for the purpose of restoring, if possible, the old order of things.

This convention was invited by the Legislature of Virginia, in order, as expressed in the preamble to the resolutions which contain the proposal, "to make a final effort to restore the Union and the constitution to the spirit in which they were established by the Fathers of the Republic."

The invitation has brought together a representation highly respectable in the character and public influence of the delegates appointed from the border slave States, and from a considerable number of Northern border States. Virginia, Delaware, Maryland and Kentucky are powerfully represented. Ohio and New Jersey have sent delegations, and we believe Pennsylvania and New York, North Carolina and Tennessee. Illinois refused, and so we think did Indiana. States that are not represented directly will doubtless be consulted through their leading citizens whom the alarming state of public affairs will have brought together at Washington. There will be no want of outside and inside effort to find a basis for conciliation upon which it may be hoped that a new Union, including all the States may be constructed.

The preservation of the Union, by any of the forms of the present constitution is so plainly impossible that the first and fundamental idea of any convention which looks to a further association of these thirty-four states under one government must be that the old constitution is suspended in fact as to six of the States, and that its powers can never be renewed over them but by the result of negotiations commenced and concluded with them as independent States. They have taken positions from which it is impossible to retreat if they desired it. The dissolution of the relation of each with the Federal authorities had constituted each, by her own theory of right, an integer State, no longer competent to take part in the deliberations of the adhering States on questions of charge in the government she has thrown off. If they desire to make changes to meet her views, it must be done without her, and whatever they do cannot be presented for her concurrence as one of themselves, but for her acceptance as an independent State, free to negotiate, and as free to reject as to accept. This is the position of all the seceded States, now seven in number. They have left themselves no longer the capacity to vote as States in the Union, on any proposition for amending the constitution. Whatever is done that way in the way of conciliation, must be done without them, and submitted to them afterwards, as the original constitution was submitted to the original thirteen. Each State will be competent to accede to the amended constitution as absolutely as if it were an entirely new instrument, and as absolutely free to decline it, and remain independent.

If it were otherwise, and it be conceded by the seceding States that they can vote on proffered charges, under the forms of the constitution as when they were members of the Union, the corresponding obligation would follow, to submit to the adverse decision of the tribunal to which they had consented. To amend the constitution required three-fourths of the thirty-four States—now Kansas is admitted; that is to say, twenty-six States. Nine States could defeat any amendment. It follows that if the seceding States, which have left the Government because eighteen States have pronounced against them—which eighteen has since become nineteen—on a matter of life and death to them, should consent to refer the same questions to a tribunal in which nineteen can foreclose the chance against them, by refusing to vote for the amendment, and *nine* can defeat any proposition they please, it would be equivalent to an agreement to surrender themselves to the judgment of nine of the Abolition States, with the pledge, necessarily implied, to acquiesce in their verdict.

Acts of secession have given formal notice that seven of the States will have no part whatever in proceedings which carry their case before such a tribunal, and which give, by implication, a right to expect that they will submit to such a verdict. They are out of the reach of being outvoted by the Abolition States and there is no way of dealing with them but by negotiating with them separately or conjointly as individual States, who may perhaps be willing to confer upon a fair plan for a reconstructed Union, and perhaps not.

The adhering States do not, however, agree in considering these seven States as actually out of the Union; but persist in shaping their measures—as if they were to be retained by some measure either of compulsion or concession. In the Border State Convention, a difference of opinion on this head will be developed very soon. Some of the States there will hold that a State may rightfully secede, and several, including all the Southern delegations, will be resolute in asserting that there shall be no attempt to assert Federal supremacy by force. These differences may obstruct the action of the convention in *limine*, and prevent them from considering any plan for conciliation at all.

But these considerations waved or overcome, the real difficulties commence.

They are manifold. They may not agree on what shall be proposed. Congress may not consent to pass them by a two-thirds vote for the action of the State Legislatures. Three-fourths of the State Legislatures may not agree to them; and if they should, the seceding States may refuse to accept them as satisfactory and prefer to remain separated.

If the other form be tried, of calling a convention by the demands of three-fourths of the States to consider the border State plan, three-fourths of the Legislatures may not concur; a general convention, if called, may fail to agree; or, if agreeing, the plan may still be rejected by the seceding States, each of whom can act for itself.

These difficulties are made insuperable by the fact that seven of the States, which were interested, while in the Union, in amending the form of government so that they could remain, are out of it, and can take no part in the deliberations, or no action, while the theory of the adhering States, through their representatives in Congress, is that these seven States must be counted in determining the result. In all movements for amending the constitution, thirty-four States

are still reckoned as parts of the Union, and for constitutional amendments, twenty-six are necessary in order to make three-fourths.

The secession of seven States leaves only twenty-seven to deliberate and to act, and of these nineteen are non-slaveholding and eight slaveholding. On the Federal theory that the Union is not and cannot be dissolved but by the assent of a general convention, every proposition for amendment must obtain the concurrence of twenty-six States, and the whole number of States which can act being but twenty-seven, it is obvious that the vote of any two of the twenty-seven will defeat any proposition whatever. Kansas and Vermont can overrule the other twenty-five and thus settle all chance for restoration of harmony among thirty-four by shutting out the possibility of even a submission of terms for adjustment of any kind by the subsisting government, even to the adhering States.

A chance for settlement which depends entirely on the all but unanimous support through all its stages, of the Black Republican States, is too remote a vision of credulous hope or unsubstantial figment of the imagination to be the basis of any acts by the Southern people either compromising their rights or their powers and modes for protecting them.

Who ever has seen any where the signs that eighteen Black Republican States will accede to such terms as will be satisfactory to the eight adhering Southern States, or tolerated by the even seceding States, must have faith in a propitious close of these border State propositions, within the frame of the old constitution, and he would have the further faith that the same converted majority will deal with secessionism as a conceded fact and submit their propositions to free negotiation. That would be to concede at last what is denied at the outset—the right of independent action. Why, then, should it not be acknowledged at once, and dealt with as a basis for all attempts at conciliation, that the Union is dissolved *pro tanto*, and that the adhering states should take all steps needful for their own [*unreadable*] acting, to negotiate fairly upon the grounds of re-union, or the terms for separation.

If conducted in that spirit, the border conference may result in good by presenting the ultimata of concessions in regard to the disputed questions on both sides, and preparing the way for either a fair presentation of a basis for reconstruction, or the general abandonment of the effort as hopeless, with peaceful agreement for each section to pursue its happiness in its own way.

In any other point of view, the Border Convention will prove a total failure in its [*unreadable*] design, for conciliation, although we cannot doubt that it will be of service in preparing the public mind for acquiescing in the necessities which it shall show to be beyond the control of the wisest and most moderate men in the nation.

GEORGE KENDALL OR FRANCIS LUMSDEN: JEFFERSON DAVIS AND ALEXANDER STEPHENS CHOSEN AS PRESIDENT AND VICE PRESIDENT OF CONFEDERACY

The new Confederate nation was established within days of the convening of the delegates in Montgomery. Members wrote a provisional Constitution, and they elected a president and vice president to lead their new country. Initial thoughts were that the presidency should go to Robert Toombs of Georgia, but his fondness for strong drink led many convention delegates to reconsider. Instead of Toombs, the Southern Congress chose Jefferson Davis, a Mississippi senator in the old Union, to be their leader. For his second, they chose Alexander H. Stephens, a well-known and -respected politician from Georgia.

New Orleans Picayune, 10 February 1861

DAVIS AND STEPHENS

The Southern movement for a new Union and a new Government is going on with a quiet force that is as wonderful as it will prove to.

The Congress [*unreadable*] has done the two things necessary to [*unreadable*] organization and the [*unreadable*] cannot be disarranged. [*Unreadable*] essential things settled are the formulation of a Provisional Government and the appointment of Executive officers for the new Confederation.

The main and gratifying fact, which disperses a great chance of misrepresentation and misapprehension is that the constitution of the United States is the model for the new frame or government. It was the work of wise men and true patriots. The alterations of empire and the change of society and time, have rendered some revision necessary, to adapt it to the wants and necessities of the day and this people. We have full trust that such changes will be made in due time, and are content that, for the present, the provisional authority of the new confederacy shall rest on the basis of fundamental truths and enlightened patriotism, which were ever the foundations of that structure which folly and fanaticism have overthrown.

It is telegraphed that the new constitution is changed from the last—in that it establishes entire free trade. We apprehend there is some misapprehension in this. It may be that free trade will be the policy of the new Government and that it is favored by the convention, but it is not likely that a question so purely a matter of legislation, and which concerns so many and diverse interests, and controverted doctrines, would be definitely decided in a provisional constitution.

The convention has also selected a President and Vice President for the Provisional Government. They are Jefferson Davis of Mississippi, for President, and Alexander H. Stephens, of Georgia for Vice President.

The selections are altogether good, both in respect to personal fitness, and in regard to great questions of policy, internal and external.

Jefferson Davis is a statesman, a scholar and a soldier. He was [*unreadable*] in military life, served early in the regular army of the United States in the [*unreadable*] 1st Infantry [*unreadable*] of the Dragoons and as adjutant in the last regiment. Twenty five years ago he resigned from the army and devoted himself to civil occupations [*unreadable*].

TIBER: FATE OF FORT SUMTER AND THE COMING OF WAR

The debate over whether secession would be peaceful or whether it would result in war consumed politicians and citizens alike in both the South and the North. Southerners sent commissioners to Washington to try to persuade the Lincoln government to agree to peaceful secession. The main issue was Fort Sumter. Would Lincoln honor the Southern demand that his forces be removed from the fort in the Charleston harbor, or would he not? Lincoln hoped to find a compromise position—resupply the fort without reinforcing it with more soldiers—but Southern patience would ultimately run out.

New Orleans Picayune, 31 March 1861

LETTER FROM WASHINGTON

[Special Correspondence of the Picayune.]
WASHINGTON, March 23.

The Cabinet conference of yesterday continued from 10 o'clock till a late hour in the evening. It is believed that the subject before it was one that involved the highest issues known to civilization, to wit: those of peace or war.

Probably the subject of consideration was Mr. Seward's answer to the Montgomery commissioner, all three of whom are now here. His answer was not to be made so early as this. But circumstances may render it necessary for the administration to hasten a development of their policy.

Last evening, as I happen to know, and as I telegraphed you, Mr. Seward sent a verbal message to the Montgomery commissioners, to the effect that the Federal Executive Government contemplated a pacific solution of the present difficulties; that no reinforcements would be sent to Fort Pickens, and that Fort Sumter would be forthwith evacuated.

There was a reason for this pacific demonstration. It was in the position of the border States, and particularly of Virginia. If the administration is to be led by Seward, then Virginia must be conciliated so far as it may be in the power of the Lincoln Government to conciliate that great and influential State.

A large majority of the Virginia Convention was elected by Union men. But with the Lincoln inaugural, and with the extraordinary efforts made by radical Republicans and immediate Secessionists to induce the belief that the Lincoln government is for war, there has been a great change of opinion in the Virginia convention. It is believed that a majority in that body is now inclined to immediate secession.

Within a few days past, Mr. R. E. Scott and other prominent Union members of the convention, informed their friends here that secession could no longer be checked, unless the Lincoln administration would show their determination to pursue a pacific policy.

I have reason to believe that response was authorized to be made to those members of the convention, and that it was of a satisfactory character.

The Administration will be obliged, therefore, if it would conciliate the border States, to show their hands very soon.

Before Senator Hunter left this city for Virginia last week he expressed his belief that Virginia would secede in thirty days. Verily, the advices from Richmond look very much like it.

But if the Lincoln Government take a decided and open course in favor of pacific measures, the Virginia Convention will adopt a plan of conciliation, and will lay it before a convention of the border Southern States, by which it will be, no doubt, adopted. The Northern States will then have an opportunity to adopt or reject the proposition. Some of them will agree to it. Pennsylvania and New Jersey will lose no time to accept it. This movement will give us peace.

There is another solution which Virginia politicians contemplate, to wit: the secession of all the States not yet seceded, and their union with the Confederate States. It is not to be doubted that when a common centre shall be established, States will gravitate to it.

A strong hostility to the pacific policy of Mr. Seward and of Gen. Cameron is manifested by the radical Republicans, and especially by some of those in the Senate. I learn, too, from men whose intelligence is to be respected, and who just come from the North and West, that the minds of the people are obstinately bent upon war.

TIBER.

SPECIAL REPORT TO THE *PICAYUNE*: CONFEDERATE CABINET AWAITS WASHINGTON'S RESPONSE TO ITS PEACE COMMISSIONERS

As the following extract from the Picayune's *Montgomery correspondent indicated, the Lincoln cabinet was not the only political body consumed by the issue of war and what the response to the Southern commissioners would be. Davis's cabinet was waiting. The irony of this story is that it ran on 12 April, the day Gen. P.G.T. Beauregard received orders to begin shelling Fort Sumter. To lighten the letter a bit, the reporter included a report of a duel between a Montgomery editor and a navy clerk who believed he had been wronged by something the editor had written.*

New Orleans Picayune, 12 April 1861

LETTER FROM MONTGOMERY

[Special Correspondence of the *Picayune*.]
MONTGOMERY, April 8, 1861.

Eds. Pic.—There is evidently something serious contemplated by the Cabinet here, as it has been in session most of the

day and in telegraphic communication with our Commissioners at Washington. It is supposed they have demanded a distinct answer from Mr. Lincoln, and named an hour beyond which it would not be receivable. The murmurs of the people were making themselves heard, and the warlike demonstrations at

Washington demanded instant attention from the Administration here. Still, if the Federal ships-of-war make no attempts to reinforce at Pensacola, the Confederate States will not yet begin the war.

The affair of honor referred to in a late letter has come off at Pensacola between Mr. Banks, editor of the Confederation, of this city, and Mr. T. P. Moses, a clerk in the Navy Department, who had received a month's leave of absence. The parties exchanged shots, both being unhurt, although the ball from Mr. Banks's pistol passed through the lapel of Mr. Moses's coat. The difficulty was amicably adjusted without a second fire.

FURTHER READINGS

Channing, Steven. *Crisis of Fear: Secession in South Carolina*. New York: W. W. Norton, 1970.

Davis, William C. *"A Government of Our Own": The Making of the Confederacy*. Baton Rouge: Louisiana State University Press, 1994.

Freehling, William W. *Road to Disunion*. New York: Oxford University Press, 1990.

Nevins, Allan. *Ordeal of the Union*. 2 vols. New York: Scribner, 1947.

Phillips, Ulrich Bonnel. *Course of the South to Secession*. 1939. New York: Hill and Wang, 1964.

Potter, David M. *The Impending Crisis, 1848–1861*. New York: Harper and Row, 1976.

Rable, George C. *The Confederate Republic: A Revolution against Politics*. Chapel Hill: University of North Carolina Press, 1994.

Reynolds, Donald E. *Editors Make War: Southern Newspapers in the Secession Crisis*. Nashville, Tenn.: Vanderbilt University Press, 1970.

REPORTING THE WAR, 1861

The Eastern Theater dominated the war-related news in most Confederate newspapers during 1861 since that was where both of the year's major engagements occurred. Like the troops in the field, the reporters who covered these two battles were green. Many had never experienced military combat, much less tried to piece together a coherent story out of chaotically violent clashes, the significance and results of which sometimes even eluded the commanding generals. Confederate war correspondents, like most Southern soldiers, had come from jobs and professions other than the military. In fact, the entire concept of war correspondence was somewhat new. Certainly, previous wars had been reported, both in America and elsewhere, but generally the reports were based on news that circulated back from the front by chance rather than on information intentionally gathered and crafted into a story by a journalist. William H. Russell of the *London Times* had served as the first modern war correspondent only a few years earlier when England had fought against Russia in the Crimea.

The lack of war reporting experience, though, did not stop reporters—both Confederate and Yankee—from flocking to Charleston in March and April 1861. If there was to be a war, and most Southerners certainly hoped secession could be accomplished peacefully, there was no question that it would begin in Charleston. Charleston became the focal point for two reasons. First, it was one of only two federal installations that had not been seized by the Southern states as they seceded from the Union. The other was Fort Pickens at Pensacola. The second reason was that South Carolinians were fiercely protective of their honor and their state's sovereignty. The presence of a federal garrison on South Carolina soil was offensive to both of those sentiments. And so all American eyes turned to the fort in Charleston Harbor, and they and their newspapers both debated whether the Union government would, and should, resupply the garrison there or yield to Southern demands for its withdrawal. Everything hinged on what newly elected President Abraham

Lincoln would do after he was inaugurated on 4 March, for it was pretty clear that current President James Buchanan would take no meaningful action before he left office. Both American presidents were in a tough spot. If they resupplied the fort, then they would be accused of provoking a civil war. If they did nothing, Northerners might lose interest in the secession debate and come to accept the idea of the South as a separate entity.

Twenty-five days after being inaugurated, and nearly that many days of debating the issue with his cabinet, Lincoln made up his mind: Fort Sumter would be resupplied with provisions, but it would not be reinforced with additional soldiers. That was as narrow a compromise as he could devise. As he had promised to do when the Confederate government sent peace commissioners earlier in March, Lincoln sent word to South Carolina that supplies were coming for the garrison at Fort Sumter.

Any newspaper that could afford to send a correspondent to Charleston wanted to have someone on the ground there when the first shot was fired. Some newspapers, including Savannah's two dailies, sent not just ordinary correspondents but their editors in chief. James R. Sneed, of the *Savannah Republican*, and William Tappan Thompson, of the *Savannah Daily Morning News*, got news early on 12 April that the fighting at Fort Sumter had begun, and they traveled together on the 1:00 Savannah-Charleston train to be on hand for whatever happened next.

Around midnight on 12 April, Confederate General Pierre Gustave Toutant Beauregard had sent emissaries to give the Sumter garrison one last opportunity to evacuate the fort. Major Robert Anderson, in command of the federal garrison, declined. At 4:30 that morning, Beauregard offered former U.S. Congressman Roger Pryor the honor of lighting the fuse that would be the first shot of the Civil War. When the politician protested that he could not start the war, Beauregard made the offer to a 67-year-old journalist-turned-Confederate-private, Edmund Ruffin. Ruffin had no qualms. He took the string, pulled the lanyard, and the fighting began. Before the bombardment ended with the garrison's surrender, more than 4,000 shots would be hurled at the fort. The American Civil War had begun.

The day after Major Anderson surrendered Fort Sumter, President Lincoln issued a proclamation that declared the seven seceded states to be in insurrection, but worse, in terms of escalating the conflict, he also called for 75,000 volunteers to put down the rebellion. Lincoln got more than he asked for: Some 100,000 men stepped forward.

From April to mid-July, the United States and the Confederate States worked to build, arm, and train their military forces. From a practical point of view, to win the war, all the South needed to do was, well, nothing—unless the federal army invaded. The South had only to fight a defensive war. From the Northern perspective, though, the issue was far more complex. To win the war, the North would have to conquer the South physically. When the Confederacy moved its capital to Richmond, it simplified the North's military strategy. The Southern capital was no more than 100 miles from the seat of federal power in Washington, D.C. The Southern move also guaranteed that the primary theater of operations for the war would be Virginia. Southern men and boys, many of whom had never been outside their home states, went marching off to war in far, far away Virginia.

Through the early summer, small units of Confederate and Union troops met from time to time in small skirmishes in Virginia, but the second major engagement of 1861 occurred in mid-July 1861. The First Battle of Manassas occurred on the banks of a creek, Bull Run, near the Virginia village from which it took its name. The largest army ever assembled on American soil, 35,000 men under General Irvin McDowell, advanced from Alexandria toward the Confederate lines at Manassas.

While First Manassas resulted in a Confederate victory, the advantage swayed back and forth throughout the day. Who would come away victorious was not a certain thing at virtually any point during the fighting. The Southern troops were just as panicky and raw as the Northern troops, so much so that even though they routed the federal army, the Confederate army was too disorganized to follow up on its victory. There has been much criticism over the years of the Confederate officers for not ordering their army to pursue the federals all the way back to Washington. That order was not issued because it could not have been carried out.

After Manassas, both armies in the East retired to their camps to nurse their wounded, bury their dead, and learn something more about being soldiers. Small skirmishes and battles punctuated the fall, but leaders on both sides were engaged in the business of building armies and planning campaigns for 1862.

In the West, operations focused on Kentucky, which at first was neutral but later declared for the Union. Both Confederate and Union armies invaded Kentucky, but neither truly capitalized on its advances.

THE BUILDUP

South Carolina had taken the first direct step toward civil war when it seceded on 20 December 1860. The Northern states parried that move on 26 December 1860 when the garrison on Sullivan Island's Fort Moultrie, commanded by Major Robert Anderson, moved to the more easily defended Fort Sumter. Anderson's force consisted of two artillery units with a total of slightly more than eighty officers and men. South Carolinians immediately looked to the defense of their most important city and considered what Anderson's move meant. The touchstone issue was whether the U.S. government would withdraw Anderson's forces from a facility the Southerners believed rightly belonged to them, or whether some attempt would be made to resupply the garrison at Sumter so that it could retain possession of the island fort. Rumors flew between Charleston and Washington. One dispatch claimed to have it on good authority that there would be no attempt to resupply, the next that resupply awaited only Lincoln's inauguration. The rhetoric war had begun, and the *Charleston Mercury* was one of the leading "generals."

ROBERT BARNWELL RHETT, JR.: MOVE OF FEDERAL TROOPS TO FORT SUMTER MAY ENCOURAGE PROGRESS OF SOUTHERN SECESSION

The sudden movement in late December of the federal garrison at Fort Moultrie to another, more easily defended coastal fortification, Fort Sumter, was hailed by the trigger-happy in South Carolina, including the fire-eating Charleston Mercury. *The* Mercury, *along with many other Southerners, predicted the unexpected move by Major Robert Anderson and his troops would shock other Southern states into seceding as well. The paper held out hope, though, for a bloodless transition to Southern independence.*

Charleston Mercury, 31 December 1860

THE PROGRESS OF SECESSION

The last week has been full of stirring incidents in the progress of that great movement, which is now working out the deliverance and liberty of the South. Our Commissioners have appeared in Washington. The Custom House, the United States Arsenal, Fort Moultrie and Castle Pinckney are in our possession. On Morris' Island, and on Sullivan's Island, our engineers are busy throwing up earth works, with a view to the Harbor and Fort Sumter. The sudden abandonment of Fort Moultrie by the United States troops, and the occupation by them of Fort Sumter, has filled our people with military enthusiasm. The threatening aspect of the Black Republican party—the resignation of his office by the Secretary of War in Washington, and the confusion and excitement which bankruptcy of the Government and the conflict between the two sections of the Union occasion at the Federal Metropolis, augers well for our cause. The Government stands paralyzed. If it dares to send the Federal troops, now in Fortress Monroe, or the Norfolk Navy Yard, to Charleston, Virginia will rise up and seize the fortresses of the United States within her territory; and before this week is out, every military post on Southern ground will be in possession of the State authorities of the Southern States. They will all see that the issue of force is made by the Federal Government; and that the fate of our Southern State must be the fate of all. The coercive power of the Federal Government, so long vaunted as adequate to suppress the secession of a State, is rapidly proving itself to be, what it has long been supposed and said to be—a wretched humbug—a scarecrow—a dirty bundle of red rags and old clothes. We said it ten years ago, and again a few months since, that secession could not and would not be put down by the Federal Government. Even General JACKSON, in all the plenitude of his popularity, felt the inadequacy of military force to perpetuate the Union; and whilst putting forth his Proclamation and Force Bill with one hand, he was under great apprehension and most busy with the other hand in getting up a Tariff in the House of Representatives, which he afterwards said was far better for the South in its concessions, than the Compromise Tariff of 1833, made by Mr. CLAY. That still greater humbug, of the eighteen millions of freemen, north of the Ohio and MASON and DIXON'S line, who are to rush down upon the South in true Tartarie style, is also rapidly changing its frowns into grimace. Before long, we fear, we will be the tender object of their distorted smiles and grim affections; and by the aid of our frontier Southern States, they will put forth their meek endeavors to win us back to their paternal embraces.

The interest in the proceedings of South Carolina in the great drama of secession, will probably end with this week. Other actors are coming upon the stage. Other States will secede from the Union. Other ports are to be blockaded; other forts are to turn their guns upon the people, or be seized. The spirit of the South is rising to meet the great emergency her safety and honor requires; and as State after State withdraws from the Union, the fixed attention which our little State drew upon herself will be turned to the grand aggregation of free and independent Southern States seeking, in a common assemblage, those new means of preserving their liberties and institutions which their separate organization renders necessary. South Carolina will lose her attractions with the return of the garrison from Fort Sumter to Fort Moultrie, and the quiet triumph of her secession, in the control of her destinies, will be a thing of course.

TIBER: REPORT ON CRITTENDEN COMPROMISE PROPOSALS

President Lincoln was inaugurated on 4 March 1860 and began immediately to form his government. A great frustration to the Washington correspondent of the New Orleans Picayune *was the fact that the U.S. president had given little attention at all to the Southern rebellion, not even, apparently, discussing the matter with his party's representatives in the Senate. The correspondent mistakenly believed, as did many Southerners, that Lincoln would let the region secede in peace. The Crittenden resolution mentioned in the following story was an attempt by U.S. Senator John J. Crittenden to find a compromise to the secession crisis. Crittenden proposed a series of constitutional amendments to address Southern concerns that gained widespread popular favor but failed to garner sufficient Republican support to make it through Congress. Only one provision that Crittenden proposed gained enough support to be approved by Congress. It was an amendment to forbid federal interference with slavery in the states.*

New Orleans Picayune, 2 April 1861

LETTER FROM WASHINGTON

[Special Correspondence of the *Picayune*.]
WASHINGTON, March 26, 1861

The President and his Cabinet have been so closely engaged in making appointments that they have given no attention as yet to the revolution, nor even expressed or formed an opinion in regard to it. They have had the Senate here three weeks and have not communicated to a single member of the body their intended policy, if they have any, in regard to the dismemberment of the Union. When the Republican Senators are questioned on the subject, they say they have no information about it. But a number of them have, in recent debates, expressed the belief that the seceded States would return to their allegiance to Federal Union! Upon this vain hope Mr. Lincoln's Administration is to depend for its success. Therefore, it is quite certain that they will be necessarily led, whether they desired it or not, to a pacific policy. I have no doubt that they will abandon Fort Pickens as they have done Fort Sumter, and resort to no such absurd measures as the Republican press proposes for the collection of revenue.

Thus they will leave the Confederated States to consolidate their power without hindrance. The States which may be inclined to secession will be certain, therefore, to be able to carry out the measure without molestation from the Federal Government.

Secretary Chase thinks that he will be able to collect revenue enough to carry on the Government till next December, and he wants no extra session. The whole Cabinet, and Mr. Lincoln himself, are averse to an extra session, because it will distract and divide the Republican party. Every step of the Republicans as a party plays into the hands of the secessionists. Coercion is not thought of, and could not be adopted without special laws of Congress, and Lincoln will not call them for that purpose. Besides this, the Republicans have adopted a protective and prohibitory tariff at the very time when the Government of the confederated States were preparing to offer the country a free trade tariff, one that ensured diversion of foreign trade from the North to the South, and generously gave up their revenue to the new Confederation of the South.

By the same measure, too, they have furnished inducements to foreign Governments speedily to recognize the Confederate States, and establish commercial treaties with them, appointing Counsels, &c. Never was mother country more indulgent than this to a revolted colony; never was any Government so liberal to those seeking its dismemberment and destruction.

The Virginia Convention will not adopt any act of secession at present. They will recommend to the Border States the holding of a national convention at Frankfort, and that body will, upon their consultation, determine upon the course to be pursued with reference to the reorganization of the Government, and their own position in it. If they remain with the North, they must have constitutional guarantees from the North for their rights, and they will be content with nothing less than the Crittenden resolutions.

The Northern people, or at least the people of most of the Northern States, will concede this or anything else to the border States if it will keep them in the Union; but there is no way in which the people can reach the question, as the State authorities will not give them an opportunity to vote upon it. This being the case, the border States, one after another, and not long after the present year, will probably secede and apply for admission into the Confederate States. Mr. Breckinridge is decidedly of the opinion that this will be the result. The North will repel them, and the South wants them. Mr. Breckinridge declared in his speech in the Senate, to-day, that even Kentucky would withdraw and go into the Southern confederation if the North did not speedily take measures for securing to the South absolute equality in the Territories.

The next question is, how many of the free States will apply for admission into the same Confederacy? Anti-slavery is not a ruling principle in Pennsylvania and New Jersey, and those two states will come in at an early day. Should peace be preserved, the free States on the Ohio will come in.

Mr. Seward will soon lay before the several States the amendment to the constitution which was submitted by Congress at the recent session to the State Legislatures for adoption. It merely provides that the Federal Government shall not in any way interfere with slavery in the States. It will be a part of the constitution when it shall be adopted by twenty six States. It will do nothing towards removing the discontents of the South.

There was a time in December last when the adoption of the Crittenden propositions would have held in the Union every State except South Carolina. It is not so now.

Though the Lincoln government will preserve peace, till the regular session of Congress next December, yet it may not be in their power to do it long after that body shall assemble. When Virginia and Maryland shall move in concert towards secession, we shall have the real crisis of peace or war. Then this Government must recognize disunion and make treaties of peace, &c., with the Confederate States, or war may ensue. In this case it will be hard to tell where the blows will fall thickest and heaviest, but it appears to me that Maryland and this District will be the Flanders of the war.

TIBER.

ROBERT BARNWELL RHETT, JR.: LINCOLN'S DECISION TO RESUPPLY FORT SUMTER IS DECLARATION OF WAR

The same day the Mercury *ran the latest telegraphic dispatches from Washington, it carried an editorial that updated speculation regarding the dispatch of a Lincoln representative to Charleston to meet with South Carolina's Governor Francis Pickens. The messenger had brought word that supplies were on the way for Fort Sumter. That, in the* Mercury's *opinion, was a declaration of war.*

Charleston Mercury, 9 April 1861

WAR DECLARED

Our authorities yesterday evening received notice from LINCOLN'S Government, through a special messenger from Washington, that an effort would be made to supply Fort Sumter with provisions, and that, if this were permitted, no attempt would be made to reinforce it with men! This message comes simultaneously with a fleet, which we understand is now off our bar waiting for daylight and tide to make the effort threatened.

We have partially submitted to the insolent military domination of a handful of men in our bay for over three months after the declaration of our independence of the United States. The object of that self-humiliation has been to avoid the effusion of blood, while such preparation was made as to render it causeless and useless. It seems we have been unable, by discretion, forbearance and preparation, to effect the desired object; and that now the issue of battle is to be forced upon us. The gage is thrown down, and we accept the challenge. We will meet the invader, and the God of Battles must decide the issue between the hostile hirelings of Abolition hate and Northern tyranny, and the people of South Carolina defending their freedom and their homes. We hope such a blow will be struck in behalf of the South, that Sumter and Charleston harbor will be remembered at the North as long as they exist as a people.

THE WAR BEGINS

Lincoln's decision to resupply Fort Sumter put the Confederate government in a tight spot. If the South allowed the resupply, it would be an implicit admission that the facilities still belonged to the American government and that the Secession movement was only hypothetical. If the South tried to stop the resupply, it would have to take the first military action, and it would be setting off a civil war. Robert Toombs, the Confederate secretary of state, tried to dissuade Davis from stopping the resupply. He feared such an action would be tantamount to suicide. Many more Southerners, though, were demanding action be taken in the Charleston Harbor, and so the order came from Montgomery for General Beauregard to demand the immediate evacuation of Fort Sumter by Major Anderson and his garrison.

Three of South Carolina's leading men, Col. James Chesnut, Capt. Stephen D. Lee, and Lt. Col. A. R. Chilsom, were appointed to carry the surrender demand to Anderson. Anderson, a Kentuckian married to a Georgian, declined to surrender. He did, though, tell the three South Carolinians that his garrison would be starved out within a few days if they were not battered into submission sooner. Anderson was hoping with those words to keep the South from taking a precipitous action that would have irreversible results. Beauregard telegraphed Confederate Secretary of War Leroy P. Walker for instructions. Should he try to wait out Anderson? The secretary instructed Beauregard to obtain a precise evacuation date from Anderson. This time, four men sailed across Charleston Harbor shortly past midnight on 12 April under a white flag of truce.

Anderson told these men that he would withdraw no later than 15 April unless he was resupplied or received other instructions from his government. Anderson was unaware that supply ships lay just outside Charleston Harbor with plans to enter the harbor the next morning. The South's representatives, led by former U.S. Congressman Roger Pryor, demanded immediate surrender and assured Anderson that firing would begin on Fort Sumter within an hour if he chose not to capitulate the fort. At 4:30 A.M. on 12 April, Beauregard readied his batteries. He offered the first shot to Pryor, a vociferous fire-eater himself, but the former congressman did not have the stomach to actually fire the shot that would begin a civil war. The second man offered the opportunity had no such qualms. Edmund Ruffin, a 67-year-old fire-eating journalist from Virginia, stepped up to the cannon and let loose the first of more than 4,000 rounds that would be slung at the fort in Charleston Harbor during the two days and nights of the bombardment. Pryor, though reluctant to fire the first shot, did preside over the surrender of Fort Sumter.

YOUR CORRESPONDENT: REPORT OF FIGHTING AT FORT SUMTER—START OF WAR LIKELY

The Picayune*'s correspondent at the Confederate capital knew when he sealed the envelope on his 11 April dispatch that it would not reach his paper's readers in time to appear before the fighting began at Fort Sumter. He was right. The dispatch predicted war would begin on 12 April, but because of the lag in the mail, the article did not reach New Orleans until the 15 or 16 April. The story ran in the 16 April edition, four days after* Picayune *readers had received the first telegraphic reports of the fighting in Charleston Harbor.*

New Orleans Picayune, 16 April 1861

LETTER FROM MONTGOMERY

[Special Correspondence of the *Picayune*.]
MONTGOMERY, April 11, 1861

Eds. Picayune—I advised you to day, by telegraph that President Davis had demanded the possession of Fort Sumter, and allowed Major Anderson til 12 o'clock noon to surrender it, so that the likelihood is, ere this letter reaches you that the Confederate flag will float over that far-famed stronghold.

The Washington Artillery, of Augusta, Georgia, with six pieces, is expected to arrive this evening, *en route*, to Pensacola, their services having been accepted by the Secretary of War. The Oglethorpe Infantry, of the same place, left Montgomery this morning. They are the last of the first requisition on the State of Georgia.

I am informed on reliable authority that our Commissioners left Washington to day.

It is stated that the second Alabama Regiment, Col. Tennent Somars, have tendered their services to the Governor of Alabama to participate in the attack of Fort Pickens.

People here are delighted that the uncertainty is at an end, and that we are now entirely justified in driving the invaders from our soil. No one [*unreadable*] a particle of doubt as to the result, and the only regret is that President Lincoln does not head the expedition.

The only arrival at the hotel from the West, are Messrs. John B. Martin, L. M. Cormack and Col. Henry Wheaton, all from Mississippi.. F. Blish and lady and C. W. Alexander, from Louisiana, and F. S. Randel from Texas.

YOUR CORRESPONDENT.

BY TELEGRAPH: SOUTH CAROLINIANS OPEN FIRE ON FORT SUMTER

News of the firing on Fort Sumter did not reach New Orleans in time for the morning edition of the Picayune, *but the telegraphic dispatches did arrive in time for the afternoon edition. Most of the news from Charleston would have to wait until the next day to run, but the* Picayune *editors did find space for the wire flashes and one short editorial.*

New Orleans Picayune, 12 April 1861

IMPORTANT FROM CHARLESTON
FIRE OPENED ON FORT SUMTER!

[By the American Line.]

MONTGOMERY, April 12.—The Secretary of War (L. Pope Walker) informs me that fire was opened on Fort Sumter this morning, at half past 4 o'clock, by Gen. Beauregard. [Signed]

D. G. DUNCAN.

The above dispatch was transmitted to us, as also to other journals of the city, about half past nine o'clock this morning. It was also transmitted, in the same form, to Mayor Monroe. We have assurances, moreover, from the telegraph office, that it is authentic and may be implicitly relied upon, and therefore we give it publicity.

We may, also, remark here, and to account for the absence of further information on the subject, direct from our correspondent at Charleston, that it is understood that the telegraph lines leading from that city have passed under the control of the military authorities.

We also understand that prudence in the transmission of intelligence North and West concerning the military operations of the Confederate States, has been enjoined upon the proper office in this city.

Since writing the above we have received the following from the agent of the Associated Press:

MONTGOMERY, April 12.—The Secretary of War says Gen. Beauregard opened fire on Fort Sumter this morning at half past four o'clock.

AN ANONYMOUS REPORT: FORT SUMTER SURRENDERS

The day after the bombardment of Fort Sumter began, the telegraph brought word of the garrison's surrender. Their white flag was soon replaced by the Confederate national flag, the Stars and Bars. People throughout the South received the news of the surrender with great gladness.

New Orleans Picayune, 13 April 1861

TELEGRAPHED TO THE NEW ORLEANS PICAYUNE
LATEST FROM CHARLESTON
PARTICULARS OF THE SURRENDER
THE CONFEDERATE FLAG WAVING
OVER FORT SUMTER

Blockade of the Port of Charleston

[By the American Line.]

CHARLESTON, April 13—2 P.M.—Major Anderson has hauled down the United States flag from Fort Sumter and run up the white flag.

The fort has been burning for several hours, from the effect of the bombshells. Two explosions have also been produced by the shells thrown from our batteries.

Maj. Anderson ceased his firing sometime since. The fire of all our batteries has been continued till the present time.

Upon the raising of the white flag the firing ceased, and two aids were sent by Gen. Beauregard to Fort Sumter.

[Second Dispatch.]

CHARLESTON, April 13, 4 P.M.—The flag of the Confederate States of America now floats over Fort Sumter.

The port of Charleston has been blockaded by the U.S. ships of war which recently arrived in the offing of the harbor.

Rejoicing at Montgomery

MONTGOMERY, April 13—The above dispatches were addressed to the Secretary of War, by Gov. Pickens, of South Carolina. They were read by a clerk of the War Department in front of the executive building, and in the presence of President Davis and the Cabinet.

Seven guns were fired, and one for General Beauregard, and another for the Confederate States.

There is great rejoicing among our people.

Great Rejoicing in Mobile

MOBILE, April 13—The news of the surrender of Fort Sumter to the Confederate army was received with immense cheering. Crowds congregate about the streets to discuss the important intelligence.

The Confederate and Palmetto flags are unfurled to the breeze.

Cannon are firing, bells ringing, and the enthusiasm knows no bounds.

Savannah Republican
15 April 1863

For 32 hours, Confederate ordnance bombarded Fort Sumter. Miraculously, the fifty tons of cannon balls slung at the fort, powered by eight tons of powder, killed no one.

Providence, *Savannah Republican* Editor James R. Sneed concluded, had declared that Americans should not spill the blood of their countrymen. The fight was fought. For that day.

The Battle of Charleston

(EDITORIAL CORRESPONDENCE.)
SEAT-OF-WAR
CHARLESTON, April 13th, 1861.

Greek has met Grrek [*sic*], and we have had the "tug of war." That "DIES IRÆ" so long feared and deprecated, and which all hoped would never come to pass, when Americans should meet Americans in deadly strife, has at last arrived. In all respects one of the most remarkable battles on record, has been fought in the harbor of this city; and as it was our privilege to be an eye witness to its dreadful progress, or at least by far the most interesting portion of it, we propose to briefly sketch the event, as we, in company with thousands, saw it at a distance.

Fort Sumter is an immense and powerful fortification built up in Charleston harbor, about four miles from the city and on the south side of the channel. It is entirely surrounded by water. To this stronghold, it is already well known to our readers, Maj. Anderson, accompanied by his small band of Federal troops, retired from Fort Moultrie, late in December last, and soon after the secession of South Carolina from the Union. The number of his effective men, no one, to this day, has been able to ascertain. It has been variously estimated at from 60 to 90. The work of being incompletely armed, it is said that most of his guns have been mounted by himself, on carriages constructed of boards and such other loose materials as he found in the fortification, and bits of timber which he would capture while floating down the bay. The number of guns he secured in placing the battery in this way is also unknown. His position, however, was very strong, both from the peculiar construction of the work and its isolation. His ordnance, too, was of large calibre and of the most destructive patterns. Here we have, imperfectly sketched, one of the parties to the conflict.

The opposing army was composed, almost exclusively of South Carolinians, the General in command, and a few staff volunteers, we believe, being the only exceptions. They were also posted in fortifications around the harbor, most of which are of recent construction.

Fort Moultrie, the leading work, stands on Sullivan's Island about a mile, or a little more, north, slightly east of Fort Sumter. It was originally a formidable point, but has been greatly strengthened and secured by tiers of sand bags along the whole line of parapet on the water side. It was commanded by Major S. R. Ripley, an experienced officer, formerly of the U.S. Army.

Fort Johnson is situated on the opposite side of the Bay, and about one and a quarter miles south-west of Fort Sumter. It is an old fortification and of moderate size and strength, commanded during the engagement by Capt. George S. James.

The Morris Island battery is about twelve hundred yards south-east of Sumter, on a point of land looking out toward the bar. It is a remarkable work, an impromptu one, and wholly original in its construction. It is the invention of a Mr. Stephens, of this city, and its chief peculiarity consists of slanting sides and roof built of railroad iron and in such a position that shot which strikes it glance overhead. It did wonders in the engagement, and fully met the highest expectations of the inventor. It was commanded by Maj. P. F. Stephens, commandant of the Charleston Citadel Academy. A shot or shell from its batteries never failed of its mark.

The Floating Battery, another peculiar structure, was moored in the cove at the north western end of Sullivan's Island, and commanded by Lieutenant John Randolph Hamilton. It also did effective work, and thus disappointed the expectations of croakers.

There was also a Howitzer Battery on Sullivan's Island, a little west of Moultrie, commanded by Capt. Hallonquist, and a battery cast of Moultrie, looking out upon the bar, together with several other smaller works at various points on the harbor. Castle Pinckney, owing to its distance, was not in the engagement.

I have not heard the precise number of guns in these various batteries, but they were all well armed, and garrisoned by a force of some nine thousand men, all under the command of General Beauregard of the Confederate Army.

Such are the parties of the contest, and the reader, if he has followed us, will comprehend their respective positions.

On Thursday last, the 11th instant, General Beauregard despatched several members of his staff to Fort Sumter, with orders to demand the immediate evacuation of the work. The reply of Major Anderson was, that duty to his Government and to his honor as a soldier required that he should decline a compliance with the demand. At this time three U.S. vessels of war were at anchor off the bar, in full view, laden, it is understood, with troops and provisions.

Nothing now remained but to enforce the evacuation by a resort to hostilities. Soon after day light, Friday morning, the contest was opened by two guns, fired in quick succession, from the battery at Fort Johnson. The sound was caught up by the other batteries, and in a few minutes a shower of iron hail poured in upon Sumter from nearly every point of the compass. Two hours and a quarter elapsed before Major Anderson returned the fire. All things ready, he finally opened his ports and turned his guns on Fort Moultrie and the Morris' island battery, but chiefly on the former, nearly every ball taking effect. The engagement then became general, and the rapidity and accuracy with which Major Anderson returned the fire throughout the day, is highly complimented by the officers of the opposing army. Some express the greatest admiration for his gallantry. The firing was kept up with but little intermission throughout the entire day, and though a fierce storm of rain was falling during a good portion of the time, it did not cool the ardor of the combatants. Towards night the firing almost ceased, but soon after dark the battle was resumed, and kept up steadily throughout the night. Thousands were collected on the Charleston Battery to witness the display. We will not attempt to describe that which baffles description. The scene was grand almost beyond conception.

Saturday dawned a bright and lovely day, but the flags of each of the belligerent were still flying in stately defiance, and the deep mouthed cannon continued to belch forth their fiery thunder. Major Anderson's men, though, were evidently wearied by the fatigues of the past twenty-four hours, as they returned the fire on the enemy only at long intervals. About eight o'clock a smoke was seen issuing from the southern side of his fort, showing evidently that a shell or hot shot had taken effect in the woodwork of the interior. It attracted no great attention at first, but the smoke continued to rise, until in the course of some two hours an explosion of gunpowder, yet not loud enough for a magazine, proved that the fort was on fire, and Anderson was blowing up his quarters to arrest the flames. A second explosion, but all to no effect. In a few moments his entire barracks were on fire and the entire fort wrapped in flames and smoke. Thousands were collected on the Battery to witness the conflagration, and the greatest excitement was manifested in every countenance.

And now for an incident of heroism that will go down to the last syllable of recorded time.

In the midst of this disaster, when almost suffocated, it is supposed, with heat and smoke, Anderson's men were at their guns fighting with desperation, and pouring the iron instruments of death into the works of his assailants. The fact is spoken of with the greatest admiration by everybody here; and I am credibly informed that so great was the impression made by this act of intrepidity in his terrible extremity on the garrison at Morris' island, that at every report of his guns they would pull off their hats and unanimously give him three hearty cheers. They then shook their fists at the Government war vessels, four of which were now quietly at anchor in the offing, for not flying to the rescue of their gallant countrymen!

In the course of an hour Major Anderson succeeded in reducing the flames, or rather, we should say, they went out for want of fuel, it being understood that the officers' quarters are entirely destroyed. Exhausted with labor, and finding all chance of reinforcement hopeless, Major Anderson, about ten o'clock, hung out a white flag from the parapet, his flag staff having previously been felled by a ball from Fort Moultrie, and immediately was silent and the war at an end. Boats went over immediately from Moultrie and Morris' Island, and it [*missing words.*] The terms are not yet arranged, though it is believed he will be allowed to come out with his side arms, and embark for New York in one of the Government steamers now lying off the bar. Throughout the long and tiresome engagement, the South Carolina troops—to whom, with their gallant commander Beauregard, all the honor of this great victory is due—conducted themselves with perfect order, the greatest enthusiasm, and with a courage that proved they were invincible. Though the odds were on their side, considering the strength of the fortification they had to subdue, nearly everybody considering the undertaking a hopeless one, they have won golden honors, and worthy of Palmetto fame. They have proved to Lincoln that the South is invincible.

And now for the most remarkable circumstance of the most remarkable, and we may add, unnatural struggle. The battle lasted thirty-two hours with hardly an intermission, some fifty odd tons of cannon balls were exchanged between the belligerent, some eight tons of powder burnt; the weapons used the most destructive known to modern warfare and in skillful hands, and yet *on neither side was there solitary life lost.* We may almost say, in the language of Lincoln, that "nobody is hurt"! We are credibly informed that not one is seriously wounded, and but a very few slightly. The forts though, especially Sumter and Moultrie, are greatly damaged.— There is nothing like this in the annals of the world, and verily it seems that Providence had interposed and resolved that Americans *should not* shed a brother's blood.

An account of the condition of the fortifications in another letter.

S.

GEORGE KENDALL OR FRANCIS LUMSDEN: ACCOUNT OF FALL OF FORT SUMTER

The failure of the U.S. government to turn over Fort Sumter peacefully to the Confederates was something of an epiphany for the New Orleans Picayune. *The paper had been strongly Unionist in its editorial stance since before the November presidential election. After the bombardment of Fort Sumter, though, the paper, like many other Southerners, had a change of heart. If Lincoln was going to use coercion to keep the Union together, then resistance was imperative. The United States had finally completely turned its back on the concepts of self-government and political liberty. A break was not only necessary; it was the only possible principled response.*

New Orleans Picayune, 14 April 1861

FALL OF FORT SUMTER

The flag of the Confederate States floats at least over Fort Sumter. The contest was an unequal one, and ought never to have been permitted by the Federal authorities. They should openly, with proper force, and in due time, have succored the brave soldier to whom they had committed the perilous trust, or they should have withdrawn the slender garrison all together, yielding to imperious necessity, or frankly and honestly avowed a conciliatory and pacific policy. They did nothing manfully or honestly. They halted between two courses, either of which might be sustained as at least direct and open, and temporized and equivocated, protested against violence and plotted in secret for a coup-de-main.

They used honeyed words of persuasion to lull the vigilance of the South, and talked glibly of moderation and conciliation in order to gull their own partisans so as to carry them through an election and to draw out capitalists into a loan. They were all the time contriving an underground plot, through mean tools and by the most perfidious practices, upon the trusting loyalty of the Southern people for a sudden breach of all those engagements, expressed and implied, in their good faith, and the seizure, by stealth, of the advantages they had covenanted to abstain from. If the commissioners and the Government of the Confederate States, have been lulled into false security by these tricks and had been suddenly surprised in finding a Federal force entrenched impregnably in the heart of the South, they could have excused themselves in the court of honor for having confided in the truthfulness and openness of an American Executive and his Cabinet.

But there were wary soldiers, and were not to be put off their guard, even when the world might have so indulged them, for being unsuspicious of so vile a treachery as this Lincoln scheming upon the success of violated promises and broken words of honor. A sense of high duty and great responsibility saved them from the evil consequences of having put trust in Black Republican honesty. It was, therefore, with a sense of scorn for the meanness of the attempt that they turned at once upon the baffled conspirators, and struck at once a decisive blow, invigorated by the contempt of a chivalrous spirit for whatever is paltry and false.

The fall of Fort Sumter is the first incident in the conflict which Northern folly has driven on so relentlessly to overpower the rights of self-government, and the most elementary principles of political liberty in the States of the South, and it will be remembered, not so much for the achievement itself—a wide step in the march towards Southern independence—as by the illustration which it furnishes of the energy, directness and force, with which the men of the Southern States have met this issue when it came to them, and the sinnosities and peddling manœuverings, and frauds, and suspicions by which the Cabinet to whom Lincolnism has given the custody of the honor of the once glorious Union, approached their object.

We are no longer of that people, but we remember what they were in the days when it was a pride and a glory to rally under the same old flag. We are very slow to believe that they are the degenerate race which it would show them to be if they were not ashamed of the hands into which the bastion of Washington has fallen, to be so dishonored. If there be not a wide-spread disquietude so exhibited among them at the miserable figure which their Cabinet makes in its abortive practices about Fort Sumter, as to overthrow the party of its personal supporters, for some more respectable dynasty of rulers, it will give additional cause to the Southern States for having escaped from such associations. It was said in derision of a Pagan superstition, What must the people be where the monkey is a God? It is scarcely too much to paraphrase the saying by asking, what must the people be, in this day, of whom Lincoln, and Seward, and Greeley, are the leaders and prophets?

AN ANONYMOUS REPORT: WAR PROCLAMATION BY LINCOLN

Union response to the firing on Fort Sumter was swift and decisive. President Lincoln called for 75,000 men to volunteer for three months' service in the Union army. Public opinion formed just as quickly, according to the telegraphic dispatch from the New Orleans Picayune's *Washington correspondent: Throughout the North, the sentiment was to support the Lincoln government in putting down the rebellion. Men from throughout that region had begun volunteering for military service, even before Lincoln's proclamation. In the Border States like Maryland, though, feelings were more mixed.*

New Orleans Picayune, 15 April 1861

TELEGRAPHED TO THE NEW ORLEANS PICAYUNE
HIGHLY IMPORTANT FROM WASHINGTON
WAR PROCLAMATION BY LINCOLN
75,000 MEN CALLED FOR

An Extra Session of Congress Called
The City in a Blaze of Excitement

[By the Southwestern and American Lines.]

WASHINGTON, April 14.—This city of Washington is in a perfect uproar of excitement over the proclamation issued by Lincoln, calling for the militia of the several States, and convening the Federal Congress for the 4th of July. Thirty thousand men have already been tendered. The city is strongly guarded at every point. The cavalry is on the road, and the military inside. More troops have been ordered.

Lincoln's Proclamation

The following is Lincoln's proclamation:—

"*Whereas*, the laws of the United States have been and are now opposed in several States by combinations too powerful to be suppressed in the ordinary way,

"I therefore call forth the militia of the several States of the Union to the aggregate of seventy-five thousand, to suppress said combinations and execute the laws.

"I appeal to all loyal citizens to facilitate and aid this effort to maintain the laws and the integrity of the national Union, and the perpetuity of popular governments, and redress wrongs that have been long endured.

"The first service assigned to the forces will be to repossess the forts, places and property that have been seized from the Union.

"The utmost care will be taken consistent with the object to avoid devastation and destruction or interference with the property of peaceful citizens in any part of the country, and I hereby command persons composing the aforesaid combinations to disperse within twenty days from this date.

"I hereby convene both Houses of Congress for the 4th of July next to determine upon measures which the public safety and interest demand.
[Signed]

"Abraham Lincoln."

By W. H. Seward, Sec'y of State.

Reception of the War News
The Feeling in Baltimore

BALTIMORE, April 14.—The fall of Fort Sumter has caused a feeling of gladness here, inasmuch as it is looked upon as a triumph over Lincoln.

As the inauguration of civil war, it has caused feelings of sorrow.

The Union sentiment here is unchanged, but the excitement is intense.

The News in Detroit

DETROIT, April 14.—The war news has produced a profound sensation. There is a unanimous sentiment to sustain the Government.

The News in Chicago

CHICAGO, April 14.—The feeling here is similar to that in Detroit.

The News at Erie, Pa.

ERIE, PA., April 14.—The people here sympathize greatly with the Federal Government. All our volunteer companies offer their services to the Governor to-morrow.

Lincoln's Reply to the Virginia Commissioners

WASHINGTON, April 14.—President Lincoln, in replying to the Virginia Commissioners, says if, as it appears, an unprovoked assault has been made on Fort Sumter, he holds himself at liberty to repossess like seized places, and to the best of his ability, repel force by force. It will perhaps cause the mails to be withdrawn from the seceded States. He shall collect imports by armed invasion, but may land forces to relieve the forts on the border country.

The War Feeling North
Offer of Troops from Ohio

COLUMBUS, April 15.—Adjutant General Carrington has ordered the military laws to be carried into effect providing 6,000 regular militia and a reserve of not less than 35,000 men subject to immediate transfer into the regular force.

The people, irrespective of party, are offering their services.

Lincoln Demands Aid from New York

ALBANY, April 15.—It is rumored that Gov. Morgan has received dispatches from Lincoln asking aid.

Lincoln's reply to the Virginia Commissioners has dissatisfied the Republicans and Democrats.

The Seventh and Sixty-ninth regiments have volunteered their services for the defence of Washington.

Rejoicing at Richmond

RICHMOND, April 15.—The news of the surrender of Fort Sumter was received with demonstrations of joy. A Southern flag was hoisted Saturday night on the capitol, which was subsequently removed by the guard.

Excitement East

BUFFALO, April 15.—Numerous Eastern cities are intensely excited. The military are volunteering their services for the support of the Government. A general determination is manifested to support the Government.

Volunteers from Indiana

INDIANAPOLIS, April 15.—Gov. Morton possesses information from all parts of Indiana that volunteer companies are forming everywhere.

Thirty thousand men can be relied on to defend the national flag.

MADISON, Indiana, April 15.—Several military companies are in the act of being formed for immediate service.

A Union meeting was held Saturday night, at which resolutions were passed to maintain the Government.

Extra Session Illinois Legislature

CHICAGO, April 15.—The Governor of this State has convened the Legislature for the 24th inst.

One Hundred Thousand Men from Pennsylvania

PHILADELPHIA, April 15.—Gov. Curtin has gone to Washington to say that Pennsylvania can send 100,000 men to defend the National capital.

ANONYMOUS REPORT: MAJOR ANDERSON PERMITTED TO DEPART FORT SUMTER

Major Anderson and his men were allowed to surrender with dignity. Confederate Senator Louis T. Wigfall of Texas accepted Anderson's sword but returned it to him. The Union troops were permitted a fifty-gun salute to the fallen U.S. colors, a salute that resulted in the only death at the fort. An ember from one of the guns landed on a powder keg, killing Union Private Daniel Hough and wounding five others. Hough did not merit mention in the dispatch that described the surrender.

New Orleans Picayune, 16 April 1861

FURTHER FROM CHARLESTON

Major Anderson Permitted to Depart
Reception of the News of Montgomery

[By the Southwestern and American Lines.]

MONTGOMERY, April 14.—It is stated by authority of the Secretary of War, Hon. L. Pope Walker, that Major Anderson and his men are permitted to depart unmolested.

Ex-United States Senator Wigfall, of Texas, received Major Anderson's sword at Fort Sumter as aide-de-camp of Gen. Beauregard.

All the force of the Confederate Government is to concentrated at Fort Pickens.

Twenty regiments are offered by Tennessee for our service.

The Confederate Congress on assembling will declare war if the Government at Washington blockades the ports in the Confederate States.

Seven hundred National volunteers at Washington refuse to observe under Lincoln and denounce him.

An offer has been made to the Treasury Department to take the whole Confederate loan of fifteen millions at par, by parties in New Orleans.

Secretary Toombs has received a dispatch from Hon. J. C. Breckinridge and Gov. Magoffin, of Kentucky, stating that greatly excited sympathizers are entirely with the South. Seven thousand men of the Border States are under arms, and have offered to move at a moment's notice.

In reply to a message asking what was the feeling in Montgomery, President Davis says, rough and curt: "Fort Sumter is ours and nobody is hurt. With mortar, paixhan, and petard, we tender old Abe our Beauregard."

When Major Anderson's quarters were burning, Gen. Beauregard sent offers of assistance, before the white flag was run up. Hon. L. T. Wigfall, of Texas, received the sword, and returned it to Major Anderson.

The fleet was still in sight off the Charleston harbor to day.

FIRST BATTLE OF MANASSAS

At the end of the day, the Confederate army was able to claim a victory on the battleground beside Bull Run, near Manassas, Virginia, but it performed only slightly better than its Union oponents. Union General Irvin McDowell had some 35,000 men against Confederate General Pierre T. G. Beauregard's 20,000. As the battle opened, McDowell was not aware that Confederate General Joseph E. Johnston had outmaneuvered the federal force at Harper's Ferry and had arrived with about 12,000 men to reinforce Beauregard. Both commanders, though, devised such complicated attacks that their untrained armies of raw recruits had little chance of executing the plans successfully. McDowell tried unsuccessfully to turn the weaker Confederate left, but the Union attack was checked by the arrival of General Thomas J. Jackson and his Virginians. Jackson's troops moved to envelop McDowell's force, which fled from the battlefield in a panic. It was that day that Jackson earned his well-known epithet. When Jackson arrived, the Confederate units under General Barnard Bee were near to breaking and running themselves. Bee rallied his troops by pointing to Jackson and his seemingly fearless Virginians. He urged his panicky soldiers to rally behind Jackson. Bee pointed to the steely-eyed former mathematics professor and yelled to his men, "Younder stands Jackson like a stone wall; let's go to his assistance." The battle raged throughout the day, but finally around 4:30 that afternoon, McDowell saw that his best move would be a retreat. Civilians who had come out from Washington, D.C., and soldiers alike fled in panicked disorder. The Confederate troops, who were in almost as chaotic a state, were unable to pursue the fleeing federals.

AN ANONYMOUS REPORT: REPORT OF CONFEDERATE VICTORY AT MANASSAS

Two days after the first major battle of the Civil War, the Memphis Appeal *proudly announced the Confederate victory. The* Appeal *ran both the telegraphic news dispatch and an editorial about the Southern victory. As in the initial reporting of any battle, the coverage had several inaccuracies. The Union commanding General McDowell was not mortally wounded; he lived until 1885. Also, Jefferson Davis was present at the battle as a spectator, not as a military leader.*

Memphis Appeal, 23 July 1861

BY TELEGRAPH!

THE WAR NEWS!
GREAT BATTLE AT
MANASSAS!

7000 FEDERALISTS
KILLED!

SOUTHERN LOSS 3000!
MCDOWELL, THE FEDERAL COMMANDER
REPORTED MORTALLY WOUNDED!
BEAUREGARD'S HORSE SHOT
UNDER HIM!

[Special to the New Orleans Press.]

RICHMOND, July 21—9 P.M.—The battle commenced near Manassas at 4 o'clock this morning. It became general about 12 M., and continued until 7 P.M., when the federals retired, leaving us in possession of the field.

Sherman's battery was taken.

The battle was terrible with great slaughter on both sides.

NEW ORLEANS, July 22.—A private dispatch to a gentleman in this city states that seven thousand federalists and three thousand Confederates were killed.

Gen. Beauregard had his horse shot under him, and one of the commanders of the New Orleans Washington artillery was killed early in a fight.

A special to the Delta (not yet published) says Beauregard had his horse shot under him while leading Hampton's S. C. Legion, and that General Johnson seized the colors of a wavering regiment and rallied it.

Another private message says that in the Bull's run battle 990 of the enemy were killed and wounded, and 60 Confederates.

It is reported that Gen. McDowell is mortally wounded.

NEW ORLEANS, July 22.—Dispatches from Richmond to-day say, that the reports of the killed and wounded last night were so unreliable, in the confusion following the victory at Manassas, that no mention was made of them, fearful of giving causeless pain to anxious hearts.

General Beauregard and staff are safe—though Beauregard's horse was shot under him;

General Jos. E. Johnson commands the left where the enemy made their fiercest attack. The right wing was commanded by Beauregard.

President Davis reached the field at noon, and took command of the center. When the left was most severely pressed, the center disengaged a portion of the enemy's force.

No other reliable reports have been received but are hourly expected.

It is stated the enemy was commanded by Generals Scott, Patterson and McDowell, and it is reported the latter was severely wounded.

BENJAMIN F. DILL OR JOHN McCLANAHAN: GREAT VICTORY AT MANASSAS

As great battles and great victories have gone historically, First Manassas was not much of a battle. Two untrained armies, both manned with terrified though determined soldiers, met on a creek bank, fought, killed, and died, then disintegrated into such a chaotic state that one fled and the other could not capitalize on the advantages it had gained. Still, First Manassas was vitally important to the Southern cause, for it seemed to prove the boast of many Confederates that a single soldier from the South could whip three Yankees with one arm tied behind his back. The Southern press certainly treated the battle as a major victory, as the following article from the Memphis Appeal *indicated.*

Memphis Appeal, 23 July 1861

GREAT VICTORY AT MANASSAS

Our dispatches this morning, both from northern and southern sources—Washington and Richmond—give us what we deem to be a reliable account of the great battle of the present campaign, fought with terrible slaughter and desecration at Manassas on the day of the 21st instant, and resulting in the disastrous defeat of the enemy. The details, so far as received, show it to be the grandest conflict that ever transpired upon the American continent, and besides Soiferino, in which not less than 320,000 men were engaged, unequaled, perhaps, in its importance, its splendor, the desperate ferocity with which it was waged, and the probable number of killed and wounded, by any battle of the present century. Though no mention is made of the exact number of forces on each side, there could scarcely have been less, we think, than from eight to ninety thousand federalists, and from eighty to sixty thousand Southrons, who participated immediately and remotely in the contest. The presence of SCOTT and DAVIS upon the occasion, the throwing of Johnson's forces down to the scene of the engagement from Winchester for the purpose of re-enforcement, and also the withdrawal of Patterson's command from Martinsburg on the part of the enemy, together with the daring personal exposure of officers on both sides, furnish us the most unmistakable evidence of the vast importance that was attached to the result by the combatants. The victory on the part of the South is evidently complete, and the route of the enemy scarcely less overwhelming than that which lost BONAPARTE the day at Waterloo. We can scarcely estimate the probably moral effect of this success of our arms upon the North, but have every reason to believe that it will cast a damper upon their energy, which will detract somewhat from the gusto they have so far exhibited for volunteering. It would not, perhaps, be going too far to surmise that it will be the battle of the present war, and will virtually break the backbone of the Washington government. Of such fearful contests it was that Mr. WEBSTER spoke, when he, many years ago, truthfully asserted that "battles have been fought that *fixed the fate of nations.*"

JOHN R. THOMPSON: REJOICING OVER VICTORY AT MANASSAS TEMPERED BY WAIT FOR WORD ABOUT LOVED ONES

News of the Confederate victory was received with tremendous joy in the capital city. The Memphis Appeal *correspondent, Dixie, John R. Thompson, described the reaction to the news about Manassas in a pair of letters that ran together and detailed both the jubilation of the citizens and the apprehension of mothers, sisters, and wives who awaited news of loved ones who were on the battlefield.*

Memphis Appeal, 28 July 1861

FROM THE SEAT OF WAR IN VIRGINIA

[From our Special Correspondent.]

The Battle of Manassas—Reception of the News in Richmond—General Rejoicing—Meeting of the Confederate Congress—Resolutions Adopted—Meeting of Citizens—The Wounded, etc.

RICHMOND, July 22, 1861.

The excitement which pervaded our city and the appearance presented by its streets last night can be adequately communicated to your readers by no words of description of mine. The hot, weary Sabbath had drawn toward its listless close, before the crowds of anxious and expectant citizens, assembled at every corner, had received positive intelligence of a great battle raging on the border. Then ensued three hours of terrible suspense, during which the offices of the newspapers and the telegraph were besieged by thousands, in vain asking for news of the result. At last, after a full moon had risen high in the heavens, the glad announcement was made to the throng in front of the Spotswood house, in a dispatch from President Davis, that we had gained a "glorious but dear-bought victory," and that the enemy were in full flight, closely pursued by our forces. Instantly, the shouts of the multitude were taken up and re-echoed from hill to hill, giving the glad tidings to the entire population. Until long past midnight there was a continuous stream of people of both sexes, flowing through the principal thoroughfares, while at almost every turn the stroller met some well-equipped company in full ranks marching rapidly toward the depot of the Central railway. There was gratulation and rejoicing over the triumph of our arms, but it was tempered with solicitude for relatives in the fight. Here were mothers, wives, sisters, moving in every direction to learn if by chance there were any messages from the dear brother, the fond husband, the darling son; for the "victory," said the President, had been "dearly bought" and this was a presage of desolation to many hearts. And so wore away the calm, midsummer night, with the round white moon shining down upon steeple and roof, and, alas, upon heaps of dead on that Manassas plain, adding a more ghostly pallor to the stark faces of brethren slain by each other's hands.

A pouring rain ushered in the morning, and has continued to descend all day like a deluge, but this has not prevented eager crowds from gathering upon the streets at the usual news marts, to hear further from the great battle of yesterday. At an early hour another regiment (in addition to the five or six sent off last night by the Central railroad) left town in the cars on the Fredericksburg line, to be switched off to the Central at the Junction, twenty-five miles distant from Richmond. The men marched steadily to the train, through the driving storm, their oil skin caps shedding streams of water upon the pavements as they passed along. They seemed to care for little but to keep their powder dry.

Towards noon, continuous files of reekling umbrellas led through all the wet avenues of the square toward the capitol, where the Confederate Congress was to assemble punctually at that hour. The hour had scarcely sounded from the neighboring bell house when the body was called to order by the Hon. Howell Cobb. A solemn gravity was manifest throughout the hall. The galleries and privileged seats were filled with an excited but decorous audience. Directly after the usual opening exercises, a dispatch was ready from President Davis, (which you have received at the time of this writing,) announcing the total rout of the enemy, the capture of guns, prisoners and colors, and the hot pursuit of the flying columns by our dragoons. Mr. Memminger, the Secretary of the Treasury, then rose and offered appropriate and feeling resolutions, which were adopted unanimously, and congress accordingly adjourned. The third of the series had reference to a call, in the newspapers of the morning, by the mayor of the city for a meeting of the citizens, at 5 o'clock P.M., at the base of the Washington monument, in the Capital Square, to adopt measures of succor and relief to the wounded, and provide for the proper burial of the dead. The inclemency of the weather preventing a meeting in the open air, it was held at the hour appointed in the court room of the Hustings court in the city hall. The mayor, Joseph May, Esq., presided. Resolutions, expressions of the sympathy of the entire community, were passed, and efficient acting committees were named, one of twenty-five to proceed immediately to the camp of Gen. Beauregard, at Manassas, with the view of accomplishing the speedy and comfortable removal of the wounded to this city; another to provide hospital and private lodgings for their reception, and nurses to attend them, and a third to raise a proper fund to defray the expenses attending these arrangements. Gallant fellows! The fairest and tenderest hands in Virginia shall minister, with affectionate assiduity to their wants while stretched upon the bed of sickness and suffering; shall twine the [unreadable] for the graves of such as languish away in death, and bind the laurel, fadeless for all time, around the brows of the survivors.

The streets have been filled with rumors, during the afternoon, of the progress of the pursuing cavalry along the road to Alexandria, some alleging that Beauregard already entered the place and was pushing toward Washington. There seems to sufficient ground of confidence for this report, as the enemy had thrown up strong entrenchments near the town, commanding the road, and the day has been eminently unfavorable for military operations. Indeed, the storm with which it commenced, so far from abating, has increased in severity, and now, at nightfall, continues with a volume of water which threatens an inundation of our rivers, and a blustering east wind, which promises small comfort during the night for the blockading vessels of Abraham Lincoln, in Chesapeake bay and Hampton Roads. If the wreck of half a dozen of them were the only damage done by the blow, we should be well content and hail the east wind as a valuable ally.

DIXIE.

Return of President Davis—Arrival of the Wounded from Manassas—Funeral Honors to the Illustrious Dead—A Traitor Prisoner—The Battle of Scary Creek in Kanawha County—the dinner Party (which Didn't Come off) of Senator Wilson—Resignation of Mr. Toombs—Congressional Tributes to the Lamented Gen. Bartow

RICHMOND, July 24, 1861.

There was a scene of much interest and excitement at the depot of the Central railroad last evening. Several thousand persons had gathered there to await the arrival of the evening train from Manassas which should bring fuller intelligence of the battle than the telegraph had been able to supply. There were the committees appointed for the reception of the wounded soldiers, together with a large number of relatives and friends of these brave but unfortunate fellows; there was a special guard of honor to escort the remains of the lamented Gens. Bartow and Bee and Col. Johnson to the capitol where they should remain during the night; there was a large military guard of another kind to march off to jail the prisoners taken in the great engagement, and then there was that miscellaneous multitude, made up of all classes from the respectable citizen to the street loafer, which can be so readily assembled at the hour of dusk in any city upon an extraordinary occasion. The crowd was at length found to be so dense in and around the depot, obstructing the tracks and impeding the convenient approach of the ambulances, that it was absolutely necessary to detail sentries to clear a space and thus prevent a dangerous confusion upon the coming of the train.

At the expected hour, the whistle was heard, and a few minutes afterward the locomotive with its long line of cars, arrived at the depot. In a moment it was known that President Davis was among the passengers, on his return to the seat of government, and a wild about of welcome went up that might have been heard throughout the city. In response to the earnest call of the crowd, the President addressed them in a short speech, marked by his usual modesty and good taste, congratulating them on the victory. [At a later hour of the evening, in acknowledgment of the call of an immense throng at the Spotswood House, where the Hon. Mr. Chesnut of South Carolina, also spoke, the President made a longer address, paying an eloquent tribute to the lofty courage and high military genius of Johnston and Beauregard, and bidding his listeners render their humble thanks to heaven for the glorious success which had crowned our arms.] The enthusiasm elicited by the speech of the President from the platform of the car was succeeded by a universal feeling of sadness and sympathy, as the wounded soldiers were lifted into the ambulances. Some of the poor fellows were dreadfully mutilated and seemed to suffer greatly, but there were no murmurs, while many others, whose arms had been almost shot away or whose faces bore frightful contusions, leaped into the wagons with the *elan* of fresh triumph. I am happy to say, with reference to the wounded, that the arrangements for their treatment are already perfected—few will be taken to the hospitals, as the citizens of

Richmond, on all hands, have opened their houses to them, esteeming it at once a privilege and a duty to minister to the wants of those suffering in such a cause.

About an hour after the arrival of the train with the President and the wounded, came another with six hundred and seventy-five prisoners of war, and still later the funeral train, bringing the bodies of the lamented officers, high in rank, who fell on the field.

Among the prisoners was one who has fairly earned his title to lasting infamy, a certain Captain Edward C. Carrington, at present district-attorney for the District of Columbia. This man is nearly related to some of the best families of Virginia and South Carolina, being a nephew of the Hon. John S. Preston. He was born in Virginia, educated at the expense of the Commonwealth, at the Virginia military institute, and for several years practiced law in this city. If anything could add to the heinousness of his ingratitude toward his native State— a trait of character which he shares with his illustrious companion in arms, Gen. Winfield Scott—it would be the fact that he went out to the Manassas field with the full knowledge that he should meet a uncle and two brothers, fighting on the side of Virginia. What will be done with this miscreant is a matter of doubt, though certainly his case differs widely from that of the ordinary prisoners of war.

To the solemn strains of funeral music, the bodies of the honored dead were borne from the depot to the capitol, where they remained till this afternoon, when the mournful procession was again formed, and the sad dirge again taken up, and the coffins, conveyed through crowded but silent and mournful streets to the train, which was in readiness to bear them South. All the flags upon the public buildings were at half-mast.

We have full accounts to-day of the brilliant victory, of which you have already heard, gained over the federal troops in Kanawha county by a small force, composed entirely of Virginians. The fight took place at the mouth of Scary creek, or Scary run, a small tributary of the Kanawha river. On the afternoon of the 17th instant a body of federalists, 1200 strong, under command of Col. Norton, commander-in-chief of the expedition sent out against Brigadier General Wise, attacked the Virginia troops under Capt. George S. Patton, and were routed, with the loss of 330 killed and many more wounded—not less than seven officers falling into our hands as prisoners—three colonels, one lieut. Colonel, two captains and a lieutenant. We had but 950 men in all, and not more than 400 of these were engaged at any one time, and while the enemy were well supplied with rifled cannon we had but two small smooth bore pieces. And yet they gave way before Capt. Patton's dashing charge, and signalized the place of combat by making a *scary run* of it into an entrenched camp two miles distant from the scene. Our loss in this encounter was three killed and less than a dozen wounded. Among the latter I regret to have to mention the brave Capt. Patton, who received a bullit [sic] in the right breast and shoulder. The officers taken were Col. Norton, Col. Villiers, Col. Woodruff, Lieut. Col. Neff, Captains Hard and Austin and Lieut. Brown.

The news of the defeat at Manassas carried consternation into Washington and Baltimore, as all the arrangements had been made to celebrate the splendid victory of Gen. McDowell. At Centreville, our pursuing cavalry found a large dinner table set out and supplied with twenty baskets of Moet, (green seal) where Senator Henry Wilson of Massachusetts, was to have entertained a select party of congressional friends at dinner, in honor of the triumph of "our arms" in Virginia. The senator proposed to conduct the champagne while Gen. McDowell was conducting the campaign, and found, in his hasty retreat over the hills of Fairfax, that this side of the Potomac was not a champagne country. Among the other abandoned contents of the uneaten banquet were discovered bills of fare, printed in French, for the dinner Mc-Dowell was to give in Richmond on his arrival here. There is little doubt that the sensation preachers of the north had prepared their sensation sermons to be delivered on receipt of the grateful news; the *Te Deum* had probably been rehearsed by the "antiphonal choir" of Trinity, and the star-spangled banner gracefully disposed upon the altar cloth. Let me commend to these divines, one and all, from the Rev. Henry Ward Beecher to the Rev. Stephen H. Tyng, to preach next Sunday from this text, which they will find recorded in II Samuel, 1:25—"How are the mighty fallen in the midst of battle! Oh, Jonathan, thou was slain in thine high places!"

Mr. Toombs has resigned his seat in the cabinet, with the intention of going into the field as a brigadier-general. There is, of course, a good deal of speculation concerning his successor as Secretary of State, but the general expectation is that it will be the Hon. R.M.T. Hunter of Virginia. It is said that John M. Daniel, of the *Examiner*, was yesterday chosen public printer in executive session, and that he declined the appointment.

Congress was to-day engaged only in paying appropriate honors to the memory of a late member, the lamented General F. S. Bartow. The customary resolutions were offered by the Hon. T.R.R. Cobb, who delivered a most impressive eulogy upon the deceased, and tributes were also paid by Messrs. B. H. Hill, Chesnut and James M. Mason. The remarks of the latter were full of eloquence and pathos.

Roger A. Pryor appeared in his seat for the first time to-day.

DIXIE.

BENJAMIN F. DILL OR JOHN McCLANAHAN: CONSEQUENCES OF MANASSAS—MUCH WORK STILL TO BE DONE

Despite its jubilation over the victory at Manassas, the Memphis Appeal's *editors, at least temporarily, put on their Cassandra costume to remind Southerners that one battlefield victory did not signify an end to the war. The paper cautioned Southerners not to believe their work was over or that it would be easy. First Manassas may have been a "brilliant achievement," but there would still be consequences to pay, and they would not all be so pleasant or as sweet as celebrating a victory.*

Memphis Appeal, 30 July 1861

THE MORAL OF MANASSAS

There is a danger we fear that the Southern mind, intoxicated with its exultations over the recent great victory of our arms at Manassas, may overestimate the present advantage as well as the ultimate consequences of that brilliant achievement.

Certainly there can be no difference of opinion as to its having proved a God-send to the cause of southern independence, and true constitutional liberty. It has greatly strengthened the confidence of our people in the ability of their government to maintain itself even at the point of the bayonet, against the marauding legions of Hessian soldiery who have been precipitated by the enemy upon our sacred soil. It has impaired the energies of the "old wreck" of the federal government, and has so far annihilated the confidence of its subjects in the final success of its boasted scheme of subjugation, as to work the most serious detriment to the national credit—which, according to the recent acknowledgment of a congressman, has already failed. It has given a *prestige* to the young republic of the South, just emerging, like Venus, in all the perfection of her beauty, from the foaming sea of political confusion, which will put to naught the vaunting assertion of northern superiority, and perhaps, decide the question of foreign recognition which now trembles in the hesitating balance held by the hands of European powers. In addition to these there may be even other, though less important results flowing from it.

But to suppose that our independence is an accomplished fact, without other like desperate struggles, is a palpable absurdity, the entertainment of which will prove a delusion and a snare. It is true that the forces of the enemy, outnumbering our own more than two to one, were utterly routed, and driven into a retreat styled by themselves both disgraceful and cowardly. But the defeat is not such as to turn the reckless politicians, who manage this movement, from the attempted execution of their direful purpose. Their pride has been sorely wounded, and their passion of revenge stimulated to the performance of new deeds of infamy. At any sacrifice of life or of the people's money, they will rally their routed forces and attempt with still greater desperation to retrieve their lost fortunes. Relying upon the brute force of mere numbers, the enemy are evidently determined to risk other engagements, perhaps of greater magnitude, if for nothing else than the gratification of their malignity, or the palliation of their disgrace now so manifest to the eyes of foreign powers. The vast preparations that are now being made, and the great caution taken in the efficient organization of the army for the future, with the unceremonious dismissal of incompetents, are but a few of the indications to foreshadow their increased, yet fruitless determination.

It may be that the half million men voted for Mr. LINCOLN by his obsequious parliament may not all be obtained, and certainly it is that the five hundred millions of money will come in very tardily, and at great sacrifices on the part of the government, if at all. But it is quite as evident that men and money will be secured for the prosecution of this atrocious war, even though the one be obtained by drafting, and the other by direct taxation and forced loans. We may expect, and must be prepared to encounter, an army of at least four hundred thousand men, who will be gathered at various points upon the borders of our Confederacy, seeking to force an entrance with the bayonet in less than ninety days. Our preparations for the vast campaign, unequalled by any of modern times, and scarcely overshadowed by BONAPARTE'S into Russia, must be commensurate with its magnitude and the importance of confronting it with successful resistance.

The population of the eleven States, comprising the Confederate Government, according to the census of 1860, is just 5,581,649. A levy of ten per cent. Of this amount, which has always been regarded as not only practicable but extremely light for military purposes, would give us an army of five hundred and fifty-eight thousand men. Leaving out the disaffected portions of the country, where recruiting might prove somewhat difficult, we may safely calculate on raising 400,000 men with the greatest facility, for it is estimated that we have more than 200,000 armed and equipped in the field. The Confederate Government should at once exercise its energies in this work. While we can readily whip the enemy in an open field and fair fight, where they do not outnumber us in a proportion greater than three to two, we must not place ourselves in such a condition as to render the result the least doubtful. To make assurance doubly sure, it is our bounden duty to meet the invaders man for man, and by the adoption of a vigorous and aggressive policy make this war a brief one. An eye for an eye and a tooth for a tooth is the maxim that should guide us through this revolution.

But to resume. The point which we most desire to impress upon the minds of the people is the necessity of being prepared yet for the worst. No delusive hope need be entertained for a solitary moment that a peace has been conquered by the result at Manassas. It is only the entering wedge to such a consummation. We may still with propriety advise with PATRICK HENRY, when he eloquently exclaimed, "WE MUST FIGHT! I REPEAT IT, SIRS, WE MUST FIGHT!"

PETER W. ALEXANDER: DESCRIPTION OF MANASSAS BATTLEFIELD

By the time the Civil War began, it had been at least half a century since any Americans had seen actual military action on their home soil. As a result, one of the jobs of war correspondents was to ensure Americans knew something of the carnage of war, to make the fighting real. In this article, Peter W. Alexander, a former Savannah lawyer and politician who would become one of the South's greatest war correspondents, painted a word picture of the horrors of the battlefield at First Manassas.

Savannah Republican, 19 August 1861

ARMY CORRESPONDENCE OF THE SAVANNAH REPUBLICAN

The Battle Field by sunlight—Burying the Dead—Singular postures after Death—The Old Woman on the Hill—Who took Sherman's Battery and reasons of discrepancies with regard to it—The Enemy's Launching Ground—What they left behind them—Manassas in History, &c., &c.
RICHMOND, VA., Aug. 12, 1861.

I promised to give you some account of the battlefield of Manassas as seen by moonlight and by sunlight. The first part

of the promise has been redeemed—the latter, much to my regret, remains to be performed. It is anything but an inviting theme. One soon becomes accustomed to the presence of the dead and the dying—to headless bodies, torn and trembling limbs, and the cries and struggles of the wounded. His blood once up, he may even become indifferent to danger—to the dread shock of battle, "the clash of resounding arms," the leaden hurricane sweeping and crashing among the broken bones and mangled bodies of the contending hosts. The battlefield is not without its sublimity as well as its terror. The long line of glittering bayonets, the roll of a thousand drums, the wheeling and rushing of squadrons, the huge columns of dust and smoke that shoot up like great pyramids from the plains below, the incessant roar of artillery and musketry, the great balls and shells that rush screaming through the air like winged devils escaped from the regions of the damned—there is something in all this to stir the blood, to inspire the heart, nerve the arm, and to make one desire to end his life amid the mighty din and uproar. But when the conflict is over and the blood has resumed its accustomed flow, there is something repulsive, at least to me, in the sight of a battle-field.

It commenced to rain early on Monday morning—the day after the battle—and continued to pour down in torrents all day and night. Tuesday the sun came out, and it was very hot, as it was on Wednesday, when I made my second visit to the field. All of our wounded that could be found, were cared for on Sunday night, though many of them were exposed to the drenching rain on Monday, their tents not having arrived. This was no disadvantage, however, as the rain served to keep down fever and prevent mortification. On Monday our dead were buried or boxed up and sent home for internment, and many of the enemy's wounded were brought in and attended to. All day Tuesday was devoted to burying the dead on the other side, and yet the work had not been half finished when I arrived on the field Wednesday morning. So intolerable was the stench arising from the dead, and especially from the horses, that our men had been compelled to suspend their humane labors. I did hear that some of the prisoners we had taken, were subsequently sent out to finish the work, which they did, though reluctantly.

It was sad sight—the battle field, that day. The enemy's dead still lay scattered in every direction, and the silent vultures had begun to circle above them. They were well clad, and were larger and stouter men than ours. Nearly all of them were lying upon their backs, some of them with their legs and arms stretched out to the utmost. Many had their feel drawn up somewhat, while their arms, from the elbows, were raised, and the hands rather closed, after the fashion of boxers. It was a singular and yet prevailing attitude. Most of them had sandy or red hair, and I have observed that this is the predominant color among our own soldiers. Those who were not killed instantly had almost invariably torn open their shirt collars and loosened their clothing about the waist. There was another mark in addition to this, by which we could tell whether their death was sudden or lingering. It was the color of the face. If the body had time to become cool and quiet before death, the corpse was pale, though not so much so as those who die from disease. Those who were killed instantly, however, and while heated and excited, were purple and black in the face. In such cases, the blood being in full circulation, there was not time for it to return to the heart before the body had ceased all its functions. At least, I suppose such is the explanation, and a physician confirms me in it.

Such of the poor wretches as had been buried were placed in long ditches or trenches, some times twenty or thirty in the same trench. Of course, it was impossible to procure coffins or boxes for them. They were laid away in the same attitude in which they were found, and in which their bodies and limbs had become stiff and rigid—one with his arms and legs stretched out—another bent nearly double—a third with his hands raised, as described above. One poor fellow had died with his arm clasped around a small tree, and others with their hands clasped tightly about their muskets, or such twigs or roots as were in their reach. One was found with his Bible open upon his breast. Some had their hands crossed and the whole body composed after the manner of a corpse. A few were found upon whom there was not the least wound or mark. Whether they had died from sun stroke, or from exhaustion, or simple fright, it were impossible to say, though probably it was from the first cause.

Thus dying and thus buried, their dust will soon commingle, and to mortal vision become one indistinguishable mass. Whether it shall be blown about this pendent globe by the winds of heaven, or scattered by the wheels of Time in its remorseless sweep to that goal to which everything is hurrying, or whether it shall continue to repose quietly where it now sleeps, it is not for us to determine. We only know that this dust shall be gathered together on the morning of the resurrection, and that the spirits which animated it in this life will be summoned before the judgment seat to give an account of the deeds done in the body, among which will be their wicked invasion of Southern homes and altars. Having performed the duty required of us by humanity, we may well leave the rest to that dreaded Judge whose protecting kindness has been around us and over us in all our troubles.

I was glad to see that most of our own dead had been buried upon the battle ground—many of them where they had fallen. In some instances, those belonging to the same company or regiment were gathered up and buried near each other, each little hillock being marked by a board or stone with the name of the hero cut upon it. What more fitting cemetery could be found for the gallant dead than the field which has been sanctified by their precious blood and rendered forever immortal by their deeds of valor! I can sympathize with the tender sentiment that would gather up the honored ashes of its loved ones and transport them for interment in the old family burying-ground in the far South; and yet I can but admire that stern patriotism—if it must be thus called—which would prefer the torn and bloody plains of Manassas to the proudest mausoleum below the sun.

And the heroes who fell upon those plains—who would exchange their lot in this life and that which is to come, for that of the beastly tyrant who would crush us beneath his heel! To me, there has always seemed to be a species of religion in the feeling which prompts a man to forsake father and mother, wife and child, and go forth in defense of the liberties of his country. He who falls in such a case, never falls too soon. The blood thus spilt, one may hope will not be an unacceptable sacrifice before the lord of hosts, the friend of the weak, the avenger of the wronged and oppressed. We may not claim that the spirits of the fallen brave are caught up in chariots of fire, and borne to realms where there shall be no more drawing of the sword and no more oppression; and yet, we may be allowed to indulge the belief that it is no sin in the sight of Heaven for a man to defend the graves of this ancestors and the sanctity of his hearth stone, even to lay down his life in so holy a cause.

You have undoubtedly seen frequent allusions to the house of an aged woman—Mrs. Judith Henry—which occupied nearly the centre of the battlefield, and which was completely riddled by the balls of the contending armies. A son and an ancient maiden daughter, some 50 years old, were with their mother, who was almost bed ridden and got about with great difficulty. It is said that they moved her to a neighboring gully but she would not remain, and that they next placed her in the cellar, and then up stairs, or wherever her fancy would dictate.—Meanwhile, balls and shells continued to tear through the house, and whistle around and above her. Disturbed and restless, like an evil spirit as she was, she insisted upon crawling and groping about amidst the iron hail "that beat upon that house," and finally placed herself upon her own bed, where she was soon shot in three different places and killed. But I do not refer to the incident so much for the purpose of describing the house or manner of her death as to correct an error which has been set afloat by some of the newspapers, as to the character of this old woman. She is represented to have been an extremely exemplary person, of great age (85) and piety. This may be so; but her neighbors, who ought to know her well, tell me that she and her household were Tories, and were in frequent communication with the enemy. If this be true, and I have no doubt of it, then she only received her just deserts, first in the fiery ordeal through which she passed, and then in the terrible doom which ended her life.

It was within a few paces of this house that Col. Bartow fell, and it was here that the great struggle occurred over Sherman's favorite battery. The fighting was furious, and the battle raged and roared around the house, and the hill upon which it stood, until the ground was literally covered with the dead and wounded. It was Sherman's battery, though it was commanded by Capt. Ricketts—Sherman being in command of a regiment—and hence the confusion in the accounts given by correspondents and letter writers. When the battery was finally taken, every horse and man about it had been killed or wounded, or had fled. No particular regiment is entitled to the exclusive credit of capturing it. Our forces, composed of the 7th and 8th Georgia Regiments, the 4th Virginia, Hampton's Legion, and, I think, the 4th Alabama Regiment, all moved upon it about the same time, and in the form of a crescent, and they all reached it about the same time. Lieut. Paxton, of Virginia, who was bearing the flag of the 7th Georgia Regiment, at the time, and Col. Gartrell and other Georgians, insist that it was only the

standard that was planted upon the battery, and that Eli W. Hoyle, of the Atlanta Confederate Volunteers, was the first man to mount the battery. While I have no doubt of the correctness of this account, I entertain as little doubt that the honor of the capture should be equally shared by all the regiments named above.

Not the least interesting part of the battlefield to me was a body of thick woods, three-fourths of a mile in the rear of this battery, and skirting the road by which the enemy had approached from Sudley's Ford. A large body of his forces had evidently halted here long enough to consult their haversacks. It was a "hasty plate of soup," however, if one may judge from the immense quantities of bread and other eatables left scattered upon the ground. Among other things, I found castors, mustard boxes, pickle jars, pieces of fine glass ware, ale and brandy bottles, several numbers of the N. Y. Tribune, various illustrated papers, political and religious tracts, and several pieces of flute music. The officers had evidently been having a good lunch, preparatory to the grand dinner they were to take at Manassas. A little further on, I saw a mosquito net, which some boastful warrior, mindful of his rest, was doubtless taking along to be used in the swamps and lagoons of the South.

In the corner of a fence, and covered over with leaves, I found two splendid Collin's axes, with leather coverings, or holsters, for the blades. A large number of axes were captured—a part, perhaps, of the 7,000 that were sent over from Washington some six weeks ago, by Gen. Scott, to hew a way to Richmond for his grand army. The fences throughout the battle field were torn down in order to enable the men and horses to move with facility. The horses of the enemy were large and fine, and our sharp shooters were very successful in picking them off. The ground around the batteries, where the horses were, for the most part, killed, was torn and rent into gullies by bursting shells and plunging balls from the Confederate guns. Some of the horses had been disemboweled, while others had their heads and limbs carried away.

But enough. When the future historian comes to the chapter devoted to the battle of Manassas,* he will say, if he tells the truth that our soldiers were well handled by the officers, and that the infantry, the cavalry, and the artillery, were manoeuvered skillfully and successfully. He will say, also, and with emphasis, that the day was carried, and the victory won, by the unflagging pluck and dogged courage of our men. Many of these men were young, and, as it were, just from the breast of their mothers, and yet, neither Caesar's legions, nor the Old Guard of Napoleon, nor the Grenadiers of Frederick the Great, ever fought better, or charged more gallantly, or retired more doggedly. All honor, then, now and hereafter, to the last syllable of recorded time, to the heroes of Manassas!

P.W.A.

*Pronounced as if spelt Manasseh.

AFTER MANASSAS

The months immediately following Manassas were spent in small skirmishes and caring for the wounded. Hospital policies and facilities and providing adequate provisions for the soldiers were the pressing issues of the day. Throughout the remainder of the summer and into the fall, Johnston, who had been given command of what would become the Army of the Potomac, was berated by Southern newspapers for inactivity. Why had the pursuit of the Union troops to Washington been stopped? Southern journalists demanded. If only Confederate commanders had followed up on the brilliant success at Manassas and moved immediately on the Northern capital, the war would be over, they argued. Their arguments, though, were not borne out by the facts. At the end of the day at Manassas, the Confederate troops were as confused and disorganized as those of the Union. True enough, Jackson had argued strongly with Davis that pursuit should occur, but given the condition of the Southern troops, it clearly was not possible. Like the North, the Southern troops needed time to pull themselves together. In the meantime, McClellan, who had been given command of the federal armies in Virginia, and Johnston were biding their time. Citizens of both nations began to realize that this was not to be a short, three-months-long war but something much longer and much bloodier. Weapons and other materials were being stockpiled throughout both the North and the South. Through the fall, the few skirmishes fought resulted in what can best be described as a military stalemate. Neither side gained any advantage over the other.

JOAN: ARMY HOSPITALS—WHAT LOUISIANA IS DOING FOR ITS WOUNDED SOLDIERS

One of the few female correspondents for a Southern newspaper during the Civil War worked for the Charleston Courier. *She signed her dispatches only as Joan. One of Joan's primary interests was the military hospitals. Not only did she volunteer for nursing duties in the Richmond hospitals, but she was a keen observer of how the various states and the Confederate government were providing care for their sick and injured soldiers. In this letter, Joan described what the state of Louisiana was doing for its soldiers. Ever the intrepid reporter, Joan let her employers know that she was working on getting a passport so she could move closer to the front and report from nearer the center of action. Joan did not add that she had an ulterior motive for wanting to get to the front: a son who was serving near Fairfax, Virginia, in a South Carolina unit.*

Charleston Courier, 5 September 1861

OUR VIRGINIA CORRESPONDENCE FROM RICHMOND

Correspondence of the Courier

Richmond, August 31, 1861.

My letter had scarcely left my hands on yesterday, when I heard that the Yankee invaders had dared to pollute the soil of Carolina with their foul presence, but they need not unpack their trunks, for we can tell them they will soon get orders to leave. The news of one victory in Western Virginia, in which Colonel Tyler was defeated, came almost simultaneously with the other, and causes great rejoicing, but we cannot console ourselves for having our brave men taken prisoners, that we hold five to one of the enemy in our hands; our men are worth fifty of theirs. We cannot expect our course always to be upward and onward, we must expect some reverses, and if this will teach us to keep our powder at hand, as well as dry, it may prove a salutary lesson to us.

The Committee here from Louisiana to provide a hospital for their sick, have rented for that purpose, as long as the war shall continue, the Baptist College buildings—large commodious brick buildings situated in a very healthy locality, entirely out of the city. They were built to accommodate a hundred students, and have fine buildings on the premises where two resident physicians will be located with their families. They are to be repainted and put in most beautiful order, and elegantly furnished. Louisiana is not only thoughtful of her soldiers in the field, but of their families at home. In New Orleans they have a free market for the families of volunteers. The citizens and planters supply it,—some sending flour, others sugar, meats, vegetables and supplies of every kind,—these are given out in moderate quantities to every applicant.

A friend just from Culpeper was giving me some statistics to-day of the sick in the hospitals, the provision made for their comfort, &c. He said they were using the churches, the school houses, the court house and the jail and had erected beside long ranges of temporary buildings, rudely constructed, but with plenty of windows in them and plank floors. He says the sick might be made much more comfortable than they are if the surgeons would only allow them to go to private houses, which they will not do, for reasons best known to themselves, for no one else can define them. The people come after them for miles around, but they are seldom allowed to go. One gentleman, living near a hospital in Louisa, I think he said, has opened his house to all who were convalescent to come and eat their regular meals as long as they choose. Forty-five sat down to dinner with him that day. One company, who left Manassas a few days since to go forward, had ninety-six members, and only fourteen of the number were able to march.

The proprietors of the Daily News, in New York, have put themselves under the care of the police. A force of four hundred was detailed, ready to serve at short notice. The editor, Mr. Wood, in a card to his subscribers, over his own name, with fearless independence condemns the high-handed usurpation which has suppressed his issues, and in tomes proudly defiant declares he will denounce the war at the risk of his property, personal liberty and life. Would there were more such noble spirits. The office of the Journal of Commerce, too, is guarded.

The protest of the Day Book against the tyranny which is putting down freedom of speech, is bolder and more uncompromising even that the News. He denounces the Administration in bitter terms, and openly charges it with trying to rivet the chains of slavery on millions of white people.

In locations in Pennsylvania where newspaper offices have been mobbed, the spirit of the people is aroused, and men are protesting against it in unmeasured terms. In a regiment forming in Winchester county fifty have resigned out of about a hundred and sixty names registered, in consequence of the attack on the Jeffersonian. The materials of the office were perfectly demolished, and afterwards it was closed by the Marshal. He probably feared that the sympathy of the people would furnish the editor with means to go on again. This would have shown too plainly that the mob was not the

voice of the people. The excitement was so great that a collision was feared, and a large patrol called out armed with rides and muskets.

These signs of the times are fraught with the deepest interest. The leaven is working which is to overthrow the United States Government even at home, and it needs no prophet's eye to see that they are on the very brink of a precipice awful to contemplate. Thank God they cannot draw us in. They have before them the prospect, nay they have now entered upon a reign of terror, which if it is not addressed ere it culminates threatens to tell a tale of suffering which will, only find a parallel in the record of the French revolution—to engulph [sic] the rights of men, to darken their homes with crime. Its result will be to stain their hearthstones with blood, to quench the light of truth, to overthrow every liberty which is dear to freemen, to prostitute the pulpit to unholy ends, to enclose the whole country in moral darkness, which can only be dissipated by fire and sword, which will deluge the earth with human gore, and make it fetid with human sacrifices, and then when the end comes, as it must eventually, who can tell whether it will open under the genius of free institutions or subject to a depots way.

"My soul enter not thou into their secret." To us they are and must ever be foreigners and strangers. We may deplore their calamities as we would those of any other member of the common race, if they do not forfeit all claims to our sympathy by their inhumanity to us and ours. We may grieve over the sufferings of those who have been dear to us in the past; we may sorrow in the name of a common humanity over free institutions so trampled on and constitutional liberty so recklessly set aside, but we have otherwise than this no common interest in the result. Our future paths diverge; they may live under such rule as suits them best. We have chosen the Constitution and Government of our fathers, and under its grateful shade will ever abide. It has borne the test of many a year, and proved itself equal to many a trying test. The great charter of our rights and bulwark of our liberties, it is our nation's pride. God forbid that it should ever have to be snatched again, at the point of the sword, from a people over-riding its authority and setting aside its provisions. Let us learn a lesson from the past, and guard with jealous care the slightest encroachment upon its statutes.

I hear many an incident which leads me to think that there must soon be a loud clash of arms. I await the tidings with the deepest solicitude. It may be that they will blot out the light of my life, and leave me to find my pilgrimage in darkness and alone, yet I do not begrudge my treasures to my country. She is welcome to them, though I do not think what the future would be to me without them. Sometimes I fear that we may be repulsed and defeated in our next movement. We have had so many successes, and my heart almost forgets to beat in the intensity of its prayer that this may not be so; if it should be we must not be discouraged. We *know* that we must ultimately succeed, and should we lose ground we must, with fresh courage, try again.

I have a slight prospect of being able to get nearer to the scene of action. If the efforts now making to get a passport for me succeed I shall go forward on Monday.

                                                                    JOAN

FELIX G. DE FONTAINE: MILITARY RUMORS IN RICHMOND; SOUTH CAROLINA NEEDS TO PROVIDE FOR ITS WOUNDED SOLDIERS

Personne, the nom de guerre used by Felix Gregory de Fontaine, was a correspondent for the Charleston Courier. *Personne became one of the two most famous Southern war correspondents for his reporting from Virginia and, later in the war, from the Western Theater. Personne's writing was enlivened by his mischievous sense of humor, as in this piece when he comments on the frequency of weddings occurring that summer in Richmond. He might have signed his letter, "Yours, in single blessedness," but he, too, would walk down the aisle before the end of the war, and his walk would lead Personne to hang up his nineteenth-century equivalent of a flak jacket and settle into the more staid existence of newspaper editor and publisher in Columbia, the Palmetto State's capital. In this article, Personne notes the prevalence of rumors in Richmond, of the anticipation with which Confederates awaited the army's next move on Washington. Unfortunately, the Confederate army, commanded by General Joseph Johnston, was not able to capitalize on the advantage it gained as a result of the First Battle of Manassas. Personne also took up the topic of providing for South Carolina's wounded and dead soldiers. He reminds readers of the need to establish a state hospital, suggesting Richmond as the logical location, and of the need to provide for the state's soldiers as winter comes on.*

Charleston Courier, 7 September 1861

OUR VIRGINIA CORRESPONDENCE FROM RICHMOND

Correspondence of the Courier

Richmond, Va., September 4, 1861.

Now up, now down; to-day before the golden gate of anticipation; to-morrow in the Slough of Despond, alternately exultant and melancholy, jubilant and bilious, hopeful and doleful, effervescent and stale, "everything by starts and nothing long"—such has been the city of Richmond for the last week or ten days. Rumor has been the ruling god and men have worshipped at the shrine of the deity, until they are no longer able to live without the daily pablum upon which they have been feasted to repletion. The slightest suspicious incident excites the acutest apprehensions. Are the cars detained over one train—a battle is in progress. Are orders received from BEAUREGARD to forward troops or munitions of war—instantly the whole town is in a *furor*. "Hostilities are certainly about to commence—Arlington is to be attacked, and Washington taken immediately; the Potomac has been crossed by JOHNSTON and he is in full march through Maryland." The street corners are therefore thronged, the innocent bulletin boards are encompassed with a cloud of witnesses; the corridors of the Hotels fairly perspire with their loquacious contents, and the telegraph is surrounded frequently until late at night by curious inquirers after the "latest news from Manassas." There is always a moral certainty that a battle is going on. Men seem to feel it in their bones, and you can no more reason them out of their obstinacy than instill into a mule a knowledge of didactic poetry.

This has been the condition of the public mind, especially since Saturday last. I am free to confess that many events have occurred which tend to foster these impressions, but there are no well defined reasons why an attack is ready to be made at this time. While it may be true that a large portion of the army have moved forward further than ever before, that the lighting of the lamps in the city of Washington may be seen from our camps, that preparations are being made on an extensive scale for an advance upon the capital, that our troops have been greatly reinforced at various points, that Johnston is quietly preparing to cross the Potomac, that several days rations have been ordered for a certain time in the future, that the greatest secrecy is manifest in regard to the various details of army operations—while all this may be true, they are but a repetition of the scenes, which, for two or three or more weeks, preceded the battle of Manassas.

For one, therefore, I am not at present prepared to cast my faith with those who believe in immediate hostilities. They may at any moment, however, be sprung upon us. The two armies are so near that, should an encounter take place between one or more of the advanced brigades, the whole force may become engaged and a general battle be precipitated. In fact, I rather imagine that such a result would be desirable, for we should then be saved the terrible sacrifice of life, which must result from the storming of Arlington Heights. We can certainly hope for no more of those disastrous stampedes, at the tail end of which we once might have marched into Washington. McClellan learned his lesson too well not to leave substantial reserves at all pregnable points, where our victorious troops are likely to enter, whether on the North of Washington or in the rear. The coming struggle, therefore, will be of a desperate character. That of Manassas will be child's play to it, and in the rich blood poured out to attain the object will be a sacrifice greater than any which the South has yet been called upon to bear. I am reasoning upon the supposition that we are to attack Arlington Heights, and carry by storm its four hundred heavy guns. Of course, should a strategic [missing text] and ask permission to lie even upon the floor, that they may receive something of the attention of a home; but nine-tenths of the houses are already occupied, and there is no room for more.

Something ought to be done for these men, and quickly. Manassas affords no accommodations; Culpeper, Orange, and other places along the route are overflowing; and Richmond, as a central place, convenient to the rail road and all the means of transportation, is properly the best location for a general South Carolina Hospital. Let there be, in addition, a committee of two or three energetic men to attend to the forwarding home of such dead as may be desired by friends. Scores of poor fellows have lain for hours in the depots, unclaimed, until sent to the Potter's Field; and I have no doubt that the end of the war will show a long list of many brothers, husbands, and parents, who, for the want of proper care on the part of friends, will go down to oblivion with graves unmarked by name or date and unwatered by a solitary sympathizing fear. Let the people of South Carolina take care of their dead, as well as their living. With some such well-organized plan, every volunteer from our State may be made to feel that in time of adversity as well as in prosperity he has friends in Richmond who will be all to him that any man can wish.

Thus far I have seen comparatively few South Carolinians in any other than comfortable circumstances, but in the event of another battle, and with the approach of winter, hundreds will require that nursing and medical attention which can only be had in a well regulated hospital. In a few days, health permitting, I shall be at Manassas, when I shall investigate this subject further, and make such other comments as my interest in it and the necessity may suggest.

In one respect at least, whatever it may be in others, Richmond is just now, by no means a profitable place for a residence. Everything of a domestic character commands the highest price. Cotton, linen, flannel, calico, and similar fabrics, are two, three and four times their usual value, and not easy to be had at that; while articles for male use, such as boots, clothing, shirting, &c., are equally beyond the reach of ordinary purses. For articles of luxury, such as fruity, ice, loaf sugar, &c., the holders make no faces at charging the most exorbitant prices.

There are a class of traders here mean enough to crack nuts for a cripple and throw him the shells. A few are Virginians—whom, I suppose, belong to the S.F.V.'s or "Second" Families of Virginia, but the majority are a hybrid kind of Yankees, whose scruples of asking any price are few and far between. One of these, the other day, charged fifty cents to a poor ague—shivering volunteer for a glass of lemonade; another charges a sick man twenty-five cents for a pound of ice; while of peaches, pears, jellies, and such articles as would be relished by convalescents, are held at figures that make patriotism blush for shame that Shylocks can be found in such a crisis to speculate over the misfortunes of those who are fighting their battles. One or two of the city papers have been bold enough to publicly condemn these miserly miscreants, but in some communities they would be walked out of their stores and into the army, neck and heels, without ado.

Many of the wealthier residents have left the city on their usual summer jaunts to the springs. Marriage and giving in marriage continue unabated, the misfortunes of this character being on a more extensive scale this year than has ever been known before. In these cases the honey moon is either very brief or postponed for a more convenient season; but, as I remarked above, the expenses of domestic life are of a character that may well deter the boldest from dotting and carrying one to the grand sum total of humanity.

Yours, in single blessedness,

PERSONNE.

PETER W. ALEXANDER: CAMP LIFE IN VIRGINIA

In another letter on 1 October, the Savannah Republican's *Virginia correspondent, Peter W. Alexander, described what life in the army camps was like for Georgia soldiers. Most of the fighting occurring in late September was skirmishing near Washington. Manassas had been fought and won two months previously, and the prevailing sentiment of Confederate military leaders was that the South's armies should be concentrated in Virginia until the spring when a new campaign could be launched. Such a strategy made for monotonous life for the South's soldiers and caused many, including Alexander, to become impatient with so cautious a strategy. The volunteers were ready for action, he told his readers. Later in the story, Alexander, ever a defender and always a stalwart advocate of the Confederate soldier, complained about inefficiencies in the Commissary and the Quartermaster departments, two problems that plagued the army in Virginia for much of the war.*

Savannah Republican, 1 October 1861

ARMY CORRESPONDENCE OF THE SAVANNAH REPUBLICAN

Army of the Potomac

Near Fairfax, September 25th, 1861

The campaign still "drags its slow length long." In the morning we rise at the tap of the drum. Next follows breakfast, for which we have appetites sharpened by refreshing sleep and the cool morning air. Then comes the usual drill and yesterday's papers, which are read with avidity and then passed from one to another. After this comes dinner; then guard mounting and dress parade; then supper; then short social visits; then tattoo and roll-call and then to bed. Such is our daily round of life.

"Only this, and nothing more."

The monotony is varied occasionally by the receipt of a batch of papers and letters from "home, sweet home;" or by startling camp rumors that Alexandria has been burnt, or McClellan shot; or that the long-looked-for order has been issued to unleash our columns and let them on to Washington. These rumors do no harm. They occupy the mind for the time and tend to divert the thoughts of the soldier from the dull, leaden routine of camp life, so dispiriting and benumbing in its effects on the eager and enthusiastic volunteer. What a shout will rend the skies when the order is given—"forward, march!" The sick will arise with renewed health and buckle on their knapsacks. The lame and the [*unreadable*] will take up their beds and walk. The great military virtue, Patience, will then give place to Activity. The heart will swell, the eye grow brighter, and the step more elastic, and life and vigor and confidence will be diffused throughout our now moody lines.

Does not an involuntary "God bless the brave boys!" rise to your lips when you remember how much they have endured in sickness, in labor, in privations, in marching and countermarching, *in standing still in front of the enemy*, and then with what frantic eagerness they long to go forward! Everything else will be forgotten in the wild delirium of joy with which the line of march will be taken up. The follies of petty annoyances, of the martinets set above them, the incompetence and short comings of the Commissariat and Quartermaster's departments, the stupidity and criminal ignorance of the Medical bureau—all will be forgiven and forgotten. Lovely and heroic Maryland now writhes and screams in the arms of a brutal ravisher, and they only ask permission to clear the Potomac at a bound and set her free from the despot's embrace.

One who has not been in camp cannot appreciate the effect which an inactive, hesitating policy produces upon the volunteer. His nature is active and aggressive. Any change, any duty, however laborious, is gladly welcomed, so it but vary the dull monotony of the camp. The First Regiment, Georgia Regulars, was ordered to Munson's Hill last week on five days' duty and though they were permitted to carry only their blankets and rations, and had a march of 15 miles before them, they sent up cheer after cheer as they fell into line. The Second Regiment of Georgia Volunteers, who followed a few days after, and other regiments ordered upon the same duty, made similar demonstrations. Anything for a change.

Many interesting incidents are related by those who have returned from Mason's and Munson's Hills. The enemy, they say, has displayed great industry in throwing up defensive works. These works cover a line of several miles along the Potomac in front of Alexandria and Washington. To reach the river in either direction, our troops must turn the works on the right or left, or carry them by storm. As far as the eye can reach, every hill and strategic point seems to be covered by batteries or works of some kind. Look where one may, the enemy appears to be as busy as beavers, throwing up breastworks, digging entrenchments, felling the forests, and hoisting guns into position. Gen. McClellan has made good use of the precious time which Johnston and Beauregard have given.

The picket lines are separated by a space of only three or four hundred yards. Standing on Munson's Hill, the opposing pickets may be seen for a mile or more, patiently walking their beaten rounds and watching each other. There is a growing disposition on both sides to discontinue the practice of firing upon another, and it is only when a new regiment is assigned to duty that there is a departure from the rule. The Yankees are inclined to be very courteous and sociable. They are ready at all times to respond to a white flag and meet our men half way. Sometimes the officers advance under a flag of truce (generally a white handkerchief) and spend an hour together, discussing the news or the prospects of the respective armies. They exchange tobacco or cigars during these interviews and now and then you may hear the clinking of tin-cups when there is anything to drink. The parties separate with many expressions of distinguished personal considerations, and in some instances the Yankees have invited our officers to go over and take a game of whist or a glass of wine with them—a politeness, however, which they have declined thus far. It is said that orders have been issued within the last few days, to stop this intercourse lest some leaky picket might let drop something that would be of service to the enemy.

Every morning when the weather is favorable, Professor Lowe may be seen to ascend in his balloon from Arlington Heights. It is reported, but with what truth I cannot say, that the Professor is sometimes accompanied by Federal officers, who go up to make reconnaissances of our forces and positions. The balloon ascends some seven or eight hundred feet, and remains up about forty minutes. Occasionally it descends, and then ascends again after communicating the result of the aeronaut's first observations to those below. It is believed that the enemy is fully informed in regard to our advanced positions.

Our brigade has been without sugar for some days, owing to stupid mismanagement in the Commissariat department. We procured a small supply for our mess at Fairfax, at 25 cts. per pound, but not until we had fully tested the virtues of coffee without cream or sugar. There is an abundant supply of sugar and rice in the Southern States, and with the least possible system and energy on the part of the Commissary General, the soldier need never be without either. A similar inefficiency and lack of judgment characterize the Quartermaster's department. A simple advertisement in half a dozen papers in North Carolina, Tennessee and Georgia would have secured wagons enough by this time for the transportation of 300,000 men. Every railway and wagon in the Confederacy is at the disposal of the War Office. Why then is the army still without adequate means of transportation?

I infer from an editorial paragraph in the *Republican*, that some one now in Savannah, connected with the Regiment of Georgia Regulars, has taken exception to a remark in a former letter of mine, in which I spoke of the regular service and the regulations adopted by the War Department for its government. I do not know who the fault-finder is—a deprivation to which I feel reconciled by his want of discrimination. You did me no more than justice, Mr. Editor, when you expressed the belief that my remark was intended to apply to the regular service as it existed in the United States previous to the dismemberment of the Union. The rules in force in the old Federal Army for the government of regular troops, have been adopted in the army of the Confederate States for the government of Volunteers; and it is against this policy I complain. The soldier in the old army enlisted for pay. The volunteers in the Confederate service enlisted to defend his hearthstone and the graves of his ancestors. The regular, if physically capable, was received, whatever his character and antecedents might have been. In our volunteer companies, however, I have known men to be rejected on account of their social position.

The Georgia Regulars are encamped within sight of my tent. I have many friends in the regiment, officers and privates, and I know them well. It is considered the best drilled regiment in the service, and will give a good account of itself on the day of battle. But I have been accustomed to regard them as regulars only in name, and as being neither better nor worse than other regiments from Georgia. The men enlisted for three years. Many other regiments enlisted for three years also, and some for the war, whether it lasted for three years, or three times three.

I can only ask the complainant in his case, to come on to Virginia. If he should lose his blanket on the way, I will share mine with him. If his shoes should be worn out, he shall have one of mine, or both if he insist upon it. We are all brothers in this struggle—a struggle in which all sensitiveness and ungenerous suspicions should be banished forever.

P.W.A.

JAMES R. SNEED: SUPPLIES FOR SOLDIERS IN VIRGINIA—OUTRAGEOUS MISMANAGEMENT

The Savannah Republican *took up the cause put forward by Peter Alexander: inefficiencies in the Quartermaster corps. Supplies and mail were not reaching military units quickly enough, the paper contended. It called for reforms in the Quartermaster corps and encouraged the Southern press as a group to editorialize on the issue until reforms had occurred.*

Savannah Republican, 16 October 1861

SUPPLIES FOR THE SOLDIERS IN VIRGINIA—OUTRAGEOUS MISMANAGEMENT

Notwithstanding an arrangement was definitely made for the Quartermaster at Richmond to pay all freights, the sending of an agent to Richmond to receive and forward, and a contract with railroad superintendents to carry all packages promptly with the above understanding, we are reliably informed that not a package sent from this place to our soldiers in Virginia since the 7th September, had reached its destination on the 5th of October. This is positively shameful, and the railroad officials north of Augusta and Charleston, with whom the fault lies, should be held to a strict account for their criminal neglect. Winter clothing and supplies of every kind, intended for our brave volunteers, have thus been allowed to lie neglected by the way side, and as a consequence, our troops to suffer for the absolute comforts and necessities of life.

Now, the Government, too, is at fault in this matter. It has called these men into the field to fight its battles, and it is *its* duty to see that they are comfortably provided for. Much *more* [emphasis his] is it incumbent on the authorities, when the people come forward and by liberal gratuitous contributions save the Government from such expense, to at least see that they are safely conveyed to their destination. This is all the people ask, and yet it seems they are unable to obtain even that little. Our soldiers are made to suffer from the grossest negligence on their part.

We hope the Press of the South will take this matter in hand, and ring it in thunder tones in the ears of the Government at Richmond.

No longer than yesterday, we tried to forward a supply of winter clothing to Richmond and Camp Bartow, but were told there was no security whatever for its reaching its destination for a month to come, if ever. Will the country stand such treatment?

We are satisfied that parties in this city are without blame. They have promptly sent forward everything entrusted to them, with firm contracts on the part of others that they should be forwarded with promptness and despatch. If it has not been done, it is no fault of theirs.

P.S.—Since writing the foregoing, we have received the despatch from Richmond attempting to apologize for the delay. Only think of *"several hundred car loads"* of contributions for the soldiers blocked up for weeks on the various railways of the South! The "destruction of bridges" is all gammon. It has been caused by the criminal neglect and indifference of the railroad officials, and we only regret there is no legal way by which a summary punishment can be visited upon them.

JOAN: CORRESPONDENT'S LAST LETTER FROM VIRGINIA

Joan's final dispatch was a polemic of Confederate nationalism. She decried the loss on 7 November of Port Royal, South Carolina, but she took comfort in the loyalty of the slaves she encountered in Virginia. She was a true Confederate partisan. Unfortunately, there was no further word from Joan after this dispatch. It is unknown whether her son was killed and so she returned home to Charleston, or what fate befell her. With the end of her letters to the Courier, *the South lost a correspondent who had a true love of her country and a knack for writing letters that would stir the faint-hearted.*

Charleston Courier, 19 November 1861

OUR VIRGINIA CORRESPONDENCE FROM RICHMOND

Correspondence of the Courier

Richmond, November 13, 1861.

Deeply as we regret that the Yankees have seized a harbor on our coast none are surprised at it; it would have been a matter of surprise if they had not. We must congratulate ourselves that while they have with their vast armament secured a precarious foothold, they have not taken any prisoners or inflicted upon us any serious injury. It will not take them long to find out that they are in an enemy's country, and if they hold these Sea Islands it must be by keeping a large force there, which will perhaps do as little damage there as any where else. It will keep some of their fleet busy to bring them provisions and forage which will prevent their doing mischief elsewhere; for they will not be able even to steal what they want in this line. They may attempt with great peril to themselves to ravage neighboring plantations, but when they find the crops they are in search of burned, they will feel themselves poorly repaid for the dangerous venture. It is hard on those who have had to apply the torch to their own dwellings, but the negros will feel it more than the masters. Most of the proprietors have other houses to go to, but the negros are left houseless; but if they are turned out without a shelter their masters have been living this way for months. Five hundred thousand gentlemen are living in tents within our borders, sleeping on the ground, in climes many of them less genial than Carolina, and wearing coarse clothing and submitting to coarser fare. I would be glad if I could thus comfort those who I know are grieving less for themselves than their people who are driven from their homes; and as I write I have before me one valued friend, a venerable patriarch, who I know felt no such sorrow in applying the torch to his dwelling and his abundant crops on Hilton Head, perhaps to his splendid orange orchards, as he did in burning the houses of his servants.

But we are in a common struggle, and no doubt the negros will bear their share of the common suffering cheerfully. They do so here and are as eager for our success as any of us. One said to me at Manassas, an old and petted nurse, as she stood with the rest of us watching the regiment of North Carolina cavalry as they passed on up to Centreville, "Do you think the Yankees can whip us when we have so many soldiers, and all the time acoming here." She grieved very much over the sufferings of "our children," as she called her master's sons who were in the army, and thought it hard that boys who had such a luxurious home must live out of doors in tents almost within sight of it. I told her they were more favored than many of our sons, for they could come to it when drenched with rains and find dry clothing, and receive from it many a delicacy. A Mississippian was telling me of a boy of his who had runaway and joined the Yankees, and had managed to get back to him. Said he had seen all he wanted to of Yankees; one of the Generals took him to wait on him, and to use his own expression, "he expected me to work myself to death. I couldn't stand it." He was proud and happy to return to his old position of servitude. A gentleman who left Manassas yesterday morning tells me that a skirmish occurred above Fairfax Monday Morning, between three Virginia, a Maryland and, a Tennessee Regiment on our side, and eight Federal regiment, which resulted in our driving them back without any loss on our side. We took eight prisoners.

The papers of yesterday announced as telegraphed from Augusta, that the black flag had been displayed at Charleston, Savannah, and all along the coast. I have heard several speak of it who admired the spirit it displayed, but I do not share in it. It would make a useless sacrifice of human life. Our enemies have shown again and again that they are inferior to us in courage; they yield very gracefully as prisoners. Indeed many of the prisoners have not hesitated to say that they were glad when they were captured because they would have no more fighting to do. We are abundantly able to overcome them, and it is an [unreadable] to us to keep the prisoners, our privateers must seize enough of their provisions to feed them with, or our army gain it from their own granaries. They boast of their large number of prisoners; say they have three hundred in Columbus, Ohio. Is it any honor to them to secure prisoners, when the way they do it is to surround a man's house with a large body of soldiers, under the cover of darkness, and drag him from his bed and lead him, with pinioned arms, to a prison? Me thinks even a coward ought to blush to own that they took prisoners in this way; yet they have no others but the ones they took at Hatteras.

We have one comfort in giving up the sand fortifications at Port Royal, beside not having left any prisoners in the enemy's hands, there was no treachery there. Our hero soldiers made a noble defense against the fearful odds. It is a glory to them that they fired their fifteen or twenty guns against the hundreds brought against them; but if our enemy's cannon are superior to ours they know very well that they themselves are not superior to us. Let us bide our time. When they land on our shores and attempt to march against us with their muskets, we can show them, as we have repeatedly before, on which side the valor lies.

The Senator to be chosen from Oregon, to fill the vacancy occasioned by Col. BAKER's death, will, it is said, be a man with secession proclivities.

The prevailing opinion here, with regard to FREMONT, is that LINCOLN dare not depose him, lest he should get up a party in the West which would eventually take the Western States out of the Union. He is, no doubt, the ablest General they have, and if he is unprincipled and fond of filling his own pocket, and those of his friends, he cannot excel the other officers in the United States government in his peculations. He has many friends in the West, and with his talents and overweening ambition, it would be strange if he did not give them some trouble either way, whether restrained or dismissed.

JOAN.

FURTHER READINGS

Davis, William C. *Brother against Brother: The War Begins.* Alexandria, Va.: Time-Life Books, 1983.

Detzer, David. *Allegiance: Fort Sumter, Charleston and the Beginning of the Civil War.* New York: Harcourt, 2001.

Freeman, Douglas Southall. *Lee's Lieutenants: A Study in Command.* Vol. 1. New York: Scribner's Sons, 1942–1944.

Klein, Maury. *Days of Defiance: Sumter, Secession and the Coming of the Civil War.* New York: Knopf, 1997.

Reasoner, James. *Manassas.* Nashville, Tenn.: Cumberland House, 1999.

Symonds, Craig L. *Joseph E. Johnston: A Civil War Biography.* New York: Norton, 1992.

Top left: Self-promotional advertisement for the *Southern Banner* of Athens, Georgia, featuring its steam press. Most of the South's larger newspapers, dailies, and important weeklies like the *Southern Banner*, printed with steam presses. Small town or village newspapers were still likely to use the older hand presses. (*Southern Banner*)

Top right: *Charleston Mercury* owner Robert B. Rhett owned this home in Beaufort, South Carolina. Rhett was one of the leading fire-eaters who compelled secession, despite the reluctance of many Southerners to break up the Union. He became a bitter opponent of Jefferson Davis during the war because of the president's advocacy of measures that would lead to a more centralized government and fewer freedoms for Confederate citizens. (Courtesy of the Library of Congress)

Far right: Self-promotional advertisement from the *Augusta Constitutionalist.* Newspapers used self promotions to let potential readers know about their content and their politics. Note that the *Constitutionalist* advertised its commercial (i.e., business) and telegraphic news sections. A change in the Southern political system is reflected in the *Constitutionalist*'s statement on its politics. Rather than claiming to support a particular political party, as most newspapers did before 1861, the *Constitutionalist* merely claims to be "thoroughly Southern" in its political stance. This was because the Confederacy had no political parties. Southern delegates meeting in Montgomery, Alabama, in February 1861, made the decision to abandon political parties in a quest for Confederate unity. (*Augusta Constitutionalist*)

Near right: Self-promotional advertisement from the *North Carolina Argus* of Raleigh. This ad addresses subscribers of the *Argus*'s "country paper." Most dailies also published weekly, bi-weekly, and/or tri-weekly editions that were available by mail to people living in small villages or on farms and plantations outside the larger cities. Note that the *Argus* advertised its war news. This was a change from the antebellum period when most Southern newspapers focused mostly on political commentary. However, with the coming of the war, readers wanted news — about what was happening on the battlefields where their loved ones were fighting. (*North Carolina Argus*)

Support your
COUNTY PAPER.
$1.50
For the ensuing Year, is all that is asked
For the
"ARGUS"
—IN ADVANCE—
It contains
THE LATEST NEWS,
OF THE PROGRESS OF THE
WAR,
Up to the hour of going to press,
And all other matters of interest to the general Reader.

WHO WOULD BE WITHOUT
THE NEWS?

We design making the Argus more of a family paper than we have been enabled to do heretofore. There is no question likely to arise to disturb the harmony existing among us. We have confidence in our President, in our Generals, in our soldiers, in our people. We have confidence in God. So long as we have *this* confidence, we are invincible. We shall give the news—the *news* first, and then fill up with matter interesting, instructive, profitable. Come and subscribe; and stop borrowing your neighbor's paper.

THE
CONSTITUTIONALIST
IS ONE OF THE
BEST PAPERS
PUBLISHED IN THE SOUTH.

IN ITS
COMMERCIAL & NEWS
DEPARTMENT
No labor is spared to give the EARLIEST and most ACCURATE intelligence from ALL QUARTERS. Its

TELEGRAPH COLUMN
Is filled with AMPLE and RELIABLE information of occurrences at all Political and Commercial centres. In

POLITICS,
The CONSTITUTIONALIST is
THOROUGHLY SOUTHERN,
And adheres, under our new Government, to its old principles of
State Rights and Strict Construction.

It advocates the Admission, into the Confederacy only, of those States which recognize
PROPERTY IN SLAVES as a part of their Social System.

TERMS:
DAILY CONSTITUTIONALIST....$20 00
TRI-WEEKLY   " 12 00
WEEKLY   " 4 00

JAS. GARDNER, Proprietor

BOOK & JOB
PRINTING
NEATLY EXECUTED
AT THIS OFFICE
AUGUSTA, GA.

Major Robert Anderson's garrison occupied Fort Moultrie in 1860, but moved to Fort Sumter in early 1861 because Anderson believed it would be safer there. Southerners saw the move as a threat of war. (Courtesy of the Library of Congress)

The interior of Fort Sumter. Built to protect Charleston from foreign naval attack, it was virtually defenseless against the heavy guns of neighboring forts. (Courtesy of the Library of Congress)

Fort Marion near Saint Augustine enabled the Confederacy to defend itself (to some degree) from seaborn attacks by the Union navy. Except for the early contest for the fortifications near Pensacola, there was little Civil War action in Florida. (Courtesy of the Library of Congress)

Near right: Delegates from the seceded states formed the Confederate States of America and in February 1861 chose Jefferson Davis, the U.S. Senator from Mississippi, to become the Confederate president. (Courtesy of the Library of Congress)

Far right: Antebellum newspapers advertised their editorial endorsements within their mastheads. This endorsement is from the *Dallas Herald*, a paper that supported John C. Breckinridge, the Southern Democratic candidate in the 1860 presidential election. Four men ran for president that year: a Republican, Abraham Lincoln; two Democrats, Beckinridge, the candidate of the Southern wing of the Democratic party, and Stephen A. Douglas, the candidate of the Northern wing of the Democratic party; and John Bell, the candidate of the Constitutional Unionist party. Lincoln was not on the ballots of the Southern states. Lincoln won only a plurality among the popular vote. He received 1,866,452 votes to the 2,815,617 cast for the other three candidates. However, he did receive a substantial majority in the Electoral College where the vote was 180 for Lincoln and 123 combined for the three challengers. (*Dallas Herald*, 31 October, 1860)

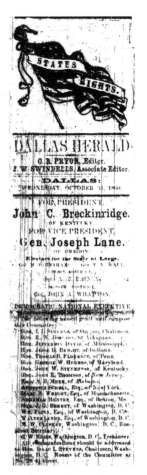

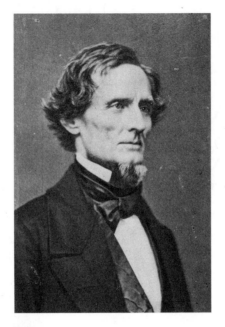

Above: The first major battle of the Civil War occurred near this creek, Bull Run, in July 1861. The Union army named the engagement after the creek, calling it the Battle of Bull Run. A second battle occurred at virtually the same place the following summer. The Confederacy's practice was to name battles after the nearest town, and so in the South, the two fights became known as the First and Second Battles of Manassas. (Courtesy of the Library of Congress)

Above right: Virginia slaves used the opportunity of the Second Battle of Manassas to escape to freedom. In this picture, they are shown fording the Rappahannock. (Courtesy of the Library of Congress)

Left: Confederate winter quarters at Centreville, Virginia. While Civil War armies could and did fight in the winter months, logistical problems discouraged it. (Courtesy of the Library of Congress)

Far left: This self-promotional graphic from the *Atlanta Southern Confederacy* represented a different approach to enticing subscribers. Most newspaper self-promotions were text-based. The *Confederacy* was experimenting with something new: advertising that was more visual than verbal. (*Atlanta Southern Confederacy*)

Near left: This graphic was promoting subscriptions to the weekly edition of the *Atlanta Southern Confederacy*. Like most dailies, the paper produced a weekly edition for readers in the countryside. Many newspapers experienced growth in subscriptions during the Civil War but had trouble collecting subscription fees from their readers. (*Southern Confederacy*)

The nameplate for the *Memphis Daily Appeal*. The banner, without any ornamentation, was more modern looking.

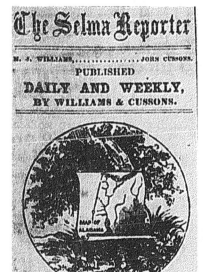

Above left: Masthead logo for the *Selma Reporter* of Selma, Alabama. The masthead typically ran on the second page of a newspaper, just above the editorials and included the name of the editor and, often, the publisher. The *Selma Reporter* included a graphic of a partially unrolled map of Alabama.

Above middle: This is another standing headline graphic used to help readers find the telegraphic news in the *Richmond Enquirer*. The *Enquirer's* graphic featured a representation of the Confederate Stars and Bars, the first national flag of the Confederacy. It is apparent from the number of stars on the flag — eight — that this graphic was created early in the war, before the secession of Arkansas (May 6), North Carolina (May 20), and Tennessee (June 8). (*Richmond Enquirer*)

Right: To drum up advertising to replace what was lost from the North after secession, William H. Barnes of Atlanta established the European and Confederate States Advertising Agency. The agency's intent was to acquire European advertising for Confederate newspapers and place advertisements for Confederate businesses in European papers. Today, it is unknown how succesful this enterprise was, or how long it lasted. (*Atlanta Southern Confederacy*)

Top left: Confederate women at home in Virginia. Women took up many jobs during the war that were closed off to them before. They worked in factories, ran plantations, and even helped produce newspapers by working in composing rooms. At least three Southern women served as Confederate war correspondents, but their names have not been preserved for history. (Courtesy of the Library of Congress)

Top right: Captured Confederate fortifications at Manassas. This seemingly unimportant place was the site of two major battles. (Courtesy of the Library of Congress)

Bottom left: Captured Confederate soldiers in Culpeper, Virginia. Early in the war, prisoners of war were generally exchanged or paroled shortly after battles. However, after the middle of 1863, this system broke down, and both the Union and the Confederacy had to find ways to deal with long-term prisoners. (Courtesy of the Library of Congress)

Middle left: A view of Sharpsburg, Maryland. The battle fought here in 1862 was the single bloodiest day of the war. (Courtesy of the Library of Congress)

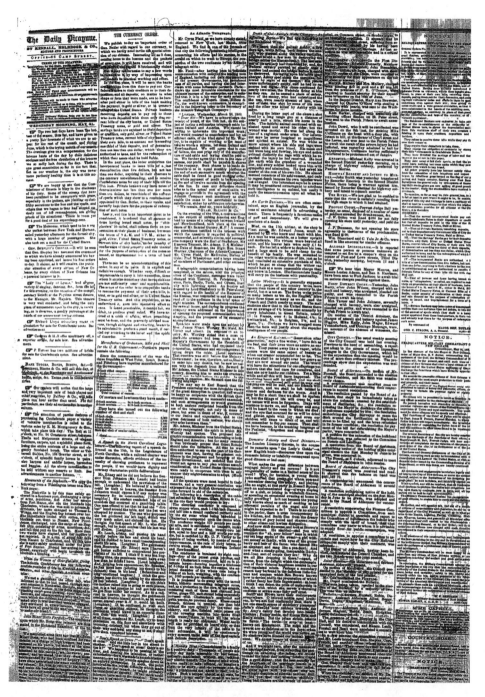

A page from the 21 May 1862 *New Orleans Picayune* shortly after the city fell to the Union. Note that the paper did not use a banner. This saved space since paper supplies were difficult to acquire. Many newspapers, including the *Picayune*, switched from a four-or-more page format to two pages and reduced the size of their pages in order to save paper.

Top left: Confederate prisoners of war at Gettysburg. Never again would the Confederacy launch a major invasion of the North. (Courtesy of the Library of Congress)

Top right: Confederate soldiers killed on July 1, 1863, at Gettysburg. Lee's Confederates were initially successful on the first day of the battle, but they could not capitalize on their early success. (Courtesy of National Archives)

Bottom right: The battlefield at Cold Harbor, Virginia. Grant lost about 7,000 men in the first hour of this battle, compounding the already staggering casualties his assault on Richmond had cost in the spring of 1864. In the month-long campaign for Richmond that began with the Battle of the Wilderness in early May, Grant lost some 55,000 men. (Courtesy of the Library of Congress)

Bottom left: Confederate prisoners of war at Chattanooga. The second loss of Chattanooga was one of the Confederacy's most embarrassing moments, and it opened the door for Sherman's assault on Atlanta and his March to the Sea. (Courtesy of the Library of Congress)

Middle left: The summit of Lookout Mountain, near Chattanooga. Because of the steep cliffs leading to the summit, Confederate guns were virtually useless to repel the Union assault; they could not be aimed at a sharp enough angle to shoot at the advancing Federal troops. (Courtesy of the Library of Congress)

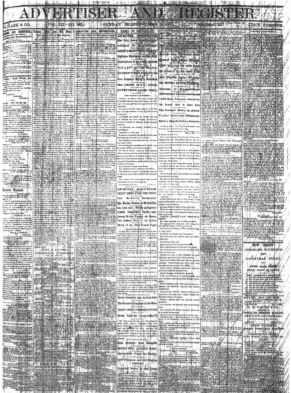

Above: A view of one of Atlanta's main thoroughfares, White Hall Street. By saving Lincoln's administration, the loss of Atlanta sealed the Confederacy's doom. (Courtesy of the Library of Congress)

Top right: The front page of the *Mobile Advertiser and Register,* 8 May 1864. By this time, newspapers were running news on their front pages. This was a change from the prewar practice of putting news on the inside pages and devoting the front page to advertising.

Above: Refugees at the Atlanta train depot, fleeing Sherman's occupation. Once Sherman decided to abandon the city in the fall of 1864, he ordered the remaining civilians to evacuate the city. (Courtesy of the Library of Congress)

Bottom left: Sherman's shelling of Atlanta left the train depot in rubble. The campaign began in early May 1864. Its purpose was to reach Atlanta and stop the flow of resources from the Deep South to the Confederate troops in Virginia. Sherman understood that the Southern fight for independence would not end until the Union had won a devastating victory, and so he embarked upon a campaign of "total war," intending to break up the flow of resources and to demoralize the Southern population. After Atlanta fell in early September, Sherman's troops rested for a few weeks before moving out on his infamous March to the Sea and an even more destructive march through the Carolinas. (Courtesy of the Library of Congress)

Top left: An Atlanta slave market. According to historian Peter Kolchin, in 1860 about one-quarter of Southern slaves lived with resident masters in small holdings of between one and nine slaves. About half lived in mid-sized holdings of ten to forty nine slaves, and the final quarter lived in large holdings of fifty or more slaves. About three-quarters of the slaves in the South worked as field hands, and the other quarter were trained for a variety of jobs, including mill work, blacksmithing, cooking, and nursing the sick and injured. Sometimes slaves even worked as overseers of other slaves. (Courtesy of the Library of Congress)

Top right: The *Atlanta Intelligencer* office on White Hall Street. The *Intelligencer* office was located next to the railroad depot, which made it very easy for the newspaper to get the latest news as each train arrived in town. (Courtesy of the Library of Congress)

Middle right: View of Nashville from the steps of the Tennessee capitol building. The city's early loss was a major blow for the Confederacy and Isham Harris, leader of the Confederate faction in Tennessee. (Courtesy of the Library of Congress)

Bottom right: Fort McAllister guarded the Southern approach to Savannah and represented the last obstacle Union General William T. Sherman had to conquer to be successful in his march through Georgia. The fort's worn out guns were no match for the Union forces that assaulted it on the afternoon of 13 December 1864. The contest for the fort was reduced to hand-to-hand combat, but the bastion fell after only ten or fifteen minutes of fighting. (Courtesy of the Library of Congress)

Left: Confederate works at Petersburg. Artillery proved inadequate to destroy well-built field fortifications. (Courtesy of the Library of Congress)

Above: The siege of Petersburg was one of the most dramatic actions of the war. From June 1864 until April 1865, the Union army ringed Virginia's second largest city to keep supplies from reaching Lee's Confederates. This soldier is one of many Southerners who died in the frequent skirmishes at Petersburg during the nine-month siege. (Courtesy of the Library of Congress)

Confederate encampment at Petersburg, Virginia. The nine-month-long struggle for Virginia's second largest city, with both sides heavily dug in, resembled the trench warfare of World War I. Petersburg was strategically important because it was home to a bullet manufacturer and because it was a railroad hub that connected many different parts of the Confederacy. (Courtesy of the Library of Congress)

Top left: Many of the majestic homes along Charleston's Battery were destroyed by shelling during the siege of the city that began in April 1863. (Courtesy of the Library of Congress)

Top right: Meeting Street, a main thoroughfare in Charleston, was also destroyed by shelling during the siege that began in April 1863. (Courtesy of the Library of Congress)

Bottom right: The Circular Church was destroyed in the siege of Charleston. (Courtesy of the Library of Congress)

Top: A view of Richmond. When a city fell, first its defenders would destroy as much as possible to keep it from the enemy, then looters would help themselves, and then the invaders would destroy what they wished. (Courtesy of the Library of Congress)

Middle left: The Confederate capitol building in Richmond, Virginia. This is where the Confederate Congress met during its sessions. Because of the proximity of Richmond to Washington, D.C., its conquest became a top objective for the Union army. (Courtesy of the Library of Congress)

Above and right: Ruined papermill in Richmond, Virginia. When the Civil War began, the South had only a handful of papermills and relied on European and Northern imports to supply its needs for paper. Paper shortages bedeviled Confederate newspapers from almost the beginning of the conflict. The mill was destroyed in the final Union assault on the Confederate capital in early April 1865. (Courtesy of the Library of Congress)

Civilians gather at Appomattox following Lee's surrender. The surrender agreement was negotiated at the home of Wilmer McLean. McLean had moved to Appomattox after his home near Manassas, Virginia, was converted into a Confederate hospital and headquarters following the First Battle of Manassas. (Courtesy of the Library of Congress)

Confederate General Robert E. Lee (*right*) surrendered to Grant at the McLean house near Appomattox, Virginia (*above*). (Courtesy of the Library of Congress)

29

REPORTING THE WAR, 1862

The dawn of 1862 found the Confederate armies in winter camp, warmed by their military successes of 1861 but still somewhat tentative and green. The coming year would temper the enthusiasm for war among many and in some points even nourish an embryonic Confederate peace movement. On the homefront, a permanent president, vice president, and Congress presided over Confederate policy, and one of its major, and most controversial, actions of the year would be to adopt legislation allowing for the draft of Confederate citizens. The conscription law was unpopular, for it represented an unwarranted expansion of government power and infringed upon cherished individual liberties.

Congress had no choice, though. The enthusiastic volunteers who had stepped forward in such large numbers the previous spring had dried up, but the Southern army's need for manpower had not. While many were optimistic about the performance of the Confederate army in 1861 and the prospects for Southern independence, 1862 would be not produce an easy victory. True, there would be some battlefield success for the South, but there were many defeats as well, including Sharpsburg, the bloodiest single day of the entire war.

On the military front, 1862 can best be summarized as a year of maneuver. The Union sought victory in Virginia by outflanking Confederate defenses by sea and by advancing on Richmond from Yorktown. In the West, Union forces advanced deep into the Confederacy. The Confederacy attempted to turn the tide by invading Kentucky and outflanking the Union through an invasion of Maryland via the Shenandoah Valley. The year also saw the rise of two generals, both of whom would become legends: Ulysses S. Grant for the Union and Robert E. Lee for the Confederacy. Both generals were capable of spectacular campaigns, and both had penchants for trying to destroy their enemy through decisive battles.

In the West, by February, Grant had successfully defeated Confederate forces at two Tennessee forts that were important in the defense of the Mississippi River:

Forts Donelson and Henry. Nashville would follow later that month. In April, Confederate fortunes would change somewhat after Shiloh, yet within only a few weeks, the Confederate army would be pushed back to Chattanooga, and the Union would retain control of western Tennessee.

In the meantime, in Virginia, General George B. McClellan was conducting a sweep by sea to the Yorktown Peninsula, but his failure to advance quickly enough would give Confederate General Joseph E. Johnston time enough to move to protect the capital. Each time the Yankees advanced in the campaign, the Confederates managed to push them back, but at considerable cost in killed and wounded on both sides. The two armies fought the inconclusive Battle of Seven Pines/Fair Oaks in late May, during which Johnston was twice wounded. On 1 June, Davis named one of his military advisers to the command of the Confederate army outside Richmond: Robert E. Lee. Lee would prove to be a skilled military tactician, and he would quickly earn the devotion of both his soldiers and the Confederate citizenry.

Lee immediately launched a series of vigorous attacks that became known as the Seven Days Battles. He forced McClellan to withdraw to the James River. Lee also dispatched General Thomas J. "Stonewall" Jackson to the Shenandoah Valley with orders to distract Union forces so they could not reinforce McClellan. Jackson succeeded beyond anyone's expectations in taking pressure off the harassed Confederate capital and the army protecting it.

By late spring in the West, Union forces threatened both New Orleans and Memphis, and both cities would fall by summer. Confederate generals Braxton Bragg and Kirby Smith staged an ill-considered invasion of Kentucky in early fall, intended to "liberate" that dark and bloody land from control of the North. Though the invasion caught the Union army by surprise, it would ultimately fail. After an inconclusive engagement at Perryville, Bragg withdrew to Chattanooga. Bragg also hoped to fill the ranks of his armies with grateful Kentuckians, but few from the Blue Grass state joined up.

In the meantime, Union forces around Washington, D.C., were formed into a separate army and ordered to attack southward under John Pope. Lee, secure in his belief that McClellan would not attack again, moved north. McClellan's forces were withdrawn from the James River and shipped back to Washington; in the meantime, however, Lee decisively defeated Pope at the Second Battle of Manassas in August. The victory at Second Manassas gave Lee the advantage he needed to invade Maryland. As Lee's army began moving north, McClellan's marched to head off the Confederates. The Union force had significant advantage over Lee as a result of either carelessness or deliberate treachery among the Southern ranks. In Frederick, Maryland, McClellan's advance guard found a copy of Lee's orders that outlined Confederate plans of attack.

On 17 September, the two armies met at Antietam Creek, near Sharpsburg, Maryland. The ensuing battle was in the bloodiest one-day engagement of the entire Civil War. Though the Union carried the day, it failed either to destroy Lee or to prevent him from escaping back into Virginia, again mostly due to McClellan's slow pursuit. As a direct result of McClellan's tardiness in following Lee, Lincoln relieved him of command of the Army of the Potomac. Lincoln's choice for a new commanding general, Ambrose E. Burnside, refused the position. Burnside, a man with remarkable self-knowledge and apparent humility, realized he was not the person to command an important army. Lincoln, however, appointed Burnside to that position anyway on 7 November.

Burnside initially did well in his new position. He planned to move his army to Fredericksburg in a move that would outflank Lee, but his efforts were curtailed by a series of mishaps that forced his army to wait on the far side of the Rappahannock River for pontoon bridges to arrive. This gave Lee enough time to entrench his army before Burnside crossed the river and tried to implement his original plan. The outcome was a major victory for the Confederates; Lee's army inflicted some 12,000 casualties on the Army of the Potomac. Burnside, after a revolt by several of his officers, was relieved of command in January 1863.

The last day of 1862 was marked by renewed action in the Western Theater. Bragg had begun to move northward from Chattanooga with the intention of driving the federals out of Tennessee. Both Bragg and Rosecrans attacked near Murfreesboro, each intending to envelop the other's right flank. Initially, Bragg was successful, but he blundered in his use of his reinforcements, which allowed William S. Rosecrans to take the initiative. Bragg was forced to retreat on 2 January. The victory was important to the federals, whose morale was waning after the recent defeat at Fredericksburg.

After a year of maneuvering, when 1862 ended, the advantage lay with the Union, though who would ultimately win the war was not yet a settled matter. The war in Virginia was essentially where it had been in January; in the West, Union forces had captured the Confederacy's most important port and secured most of Tennessee. However, 1862 had brought a significant change to the nature of the war being waged. After the Battle of Sharpsburg, Lincoln had announced the Emancipation Proclamation, to become effective 1 January 1863. Confederate President Jefferson Davis was furious. Lincoln's proclamation was clever, for it only freed the slaves in the states that had seceded. Slave owners in the states still in the Union retained ownership of their property. With the stroke of his pen, Lincoln changed the cause of the war and ensured that the Confederacy could never receive recognition as a sovereign state from the European powers it was courting and from whom it hoped to receive aid. Politically, countries such as England and France could not offer recognition to a country at war to protect the institution of slavery. The conflict had escalated into one of total war. Given the Confederacy's inferior economic situation, smaller population, and smaller army, it was an open question whether the South's slave-based economy and culture would survive.

THE WESTERN THEATER

Henry-Donelson Campaign

In September 1861, Kentucky had ended its neutrality with the announcement that it intended to remain within the Union. Confederate General Leonidas Polk invaded immediately to secure the Mississippi. His troops occupied Columbus, an important transportation center on the river where steamboats and railroads met up, and a smaller river port near the Kentucky-Tennessee border, Hickman. Polk's men spent the fall busily fortifying Columbus, which would come to be known as "The Gibraltar of the West," and booby-trapping the river in a variety of ways, including stringing an anchor across the river, rigged with torpedoes that would explode on impact. Polk further fortified the area by building Fort Henry on the Tennessee and Fort Donelson on the Cumberland. Grant countered Polk's movement into Kentucky by occupying Paducah and Smithland. Paducah, situated at the confluence of the Tennessee and Ohio rivers, was the major city in western Kentucky. Smithland, though smaller, was also important since it was at the confluence of the Tennessee and Cumberland rivers. In February, Grant combined his 15,000 men with Navy Flag Officer Andrew Foote's gunboats to take on both of the Confederacy's newly constructed forts. Fort Henry fell on 6 February as the result of overwhelming fire from the Union gunboats. Next, Grant turned toward Fort Donelson, which was garrisoned by 15,000 men under Major General John B. Floyd and his lieutenants, Major Generals Gideon Pillow and Simon Bolivar Buckner. The fort was able to repulse the first gunboat attack on 14 February, and the next day, the Confederate forces almost broke through the Union troops that had encircled the fort. The garrison at Fort Donelson held out for three days against a heavy Union bombardment. Finally, the four Confederate commanders on hand at the fort, Floyd, Pillow, Buckner, and cavalry commander Nathan Bedford Forrest, met at an inn near Dover, Kentucky, to decide what to do. Neither Floyd nor Pillow were willing to surrender, and they turned the command over to the Buckner, who accepted the responsibility. Forrest, in disgust, managed to escape with his cavalry before the surrender. Floyd and Pillow also escaped, though their failure to live up to their responsibilities essentially ended both their careers. President Davis cashiered Floyd, and Pillow was suspended for a time. Even when he returned to the army, he was never again given a significant command. Union losses in the campaign were 2,832. The Confederacy's, including prisoners, were 16,623.

BENJAMIN F. DILL OR JOHN McCLANAHAN: REPORT OF FALL OF FORT HENRY

The first of the two river fortifications to fall was Fort Henry. Five Union gunboats bombarded the fort for an hour and a half, but despite returning fire at a goodly pace, the Confederates could not hold out past 2:00 P.M. Fort Henry commander, Brigadier General Lloyd Tilghman, sent most of his men to Fort Donelson before surrendering his remaining garrison of twelve officers and sixty-six men. The victory was accomplished entirely by Foote's naval forces; heavy rains had prevented Grant's land forces from reaching Fort Henry.

Memphis Appeal, 7 February 1862

FORT HENRY FALLEN!

We are forced this morning, as we seriously apprehended, to chronicle the fall of Fort Henry. The enemy attacked the position on yesterday about half past eleven o'clock A.M., with five gunboats, and after a bombardment of an hour and a half, and the disabling of one or two of their boats, compelled a surrender. They then proceeded up the Tennessee river and burned the railroad bridge over that stream.

Our dispatch states that the fate of General TILGHMAN'S command, who were stationed at the fort, is unknown, and it is possible that they may have made good their escape to Fort Donelson, which is on the west bank of the Cumberland river, only twelve miles distant.

We are enabled to state from our own knowledge that the amount of stores and ammunition taken was small. The fort was located on the East bank of the Tennessee river, twenty miles below the railroad bridge, and was purely an earthwork defense, though of considerable magnitude. It was surrounded by a deep ditch and strengthened by rifle pits in the rear.

Only a small portion of Gen. Tilghman's command (probably some 500 men) were stationed immediately in the Fort, the remainder being within supporting distance.

The armament of the fort was very inferior, consisting of fourteen guns of the following description: One 12-pounder, not properly mounted and rendered unserviceable after being fired twice last Tuesday. One 32 pounder, rifled, the only one that could compete in range with the ten inch guns of the enemy. The other were 42 and 23 pounders.

Only four of our guns were in position so as to properly range with the ascending boats.

Submarine batteries were planted below on the east side of the island, and were being laid in the west channel on the day of the enemy's approach, but our plans were disturbed before fully perfected.

BENJAMIN F. DILL OR JOHN McCLANAHAN: SERIOUS CONSEQUENCES OF LOSS OF CUMBERLAND FORTS

The Appeal *was profoundly dismayed by the fall of the forts on the Cumberland River near Nashville and correctly saw dark and gloomy portents in their capture by Union forces. For one thing, the loss of the forts brought into greater light the lack of a Confederate navy capable of contesting control of important waterways. Indeed, Confederate Secretary of the Navy Stephen R. Mallory took considerable blame for not having a navy to counter the federal gunboats.*

Memphis Appeal, 18 February 1862

THE DARK DAYS OF THE REPUBLIC

The fall of Fort Donelson on Saturday last, the evacuation at Bowling Green and the unexplained agreement to surrender Nashville on yesterday, have forcibly engendered the conviction in the public mind that Gen. SIDNEY JOHNSTON has been out generaled by BUELL in the progress of army operations in Kentucky. We have no disposition to harshly judge him in this matter, but the fact is too palpable for denial that some of his blunders have at least temporarily transferred the war from Kentucky to Tennessee soil.

In the events of the last few days we witness disasters which will arouse the spirit of our people throughout the whole Confederacy. There is nothing, it is true, in the surrender of a city or the fall of a fort, to discourage or alarm us. Such things have happened before without [unreadable] the harbingers of subjugation or of [unreadable] disaster to a nation struggling bravely for its freedom. The price of liberty is blood, and if we would obtain the boon, we must pay the price. We cannot expect to achieve our independence without undergoing at least some of the hardships and incurring some of the misfortunes and obstacles that befell our forefathers in the dark days of the American Revolution. The colonies passed through the fiery ordeal of defeat after defeat, and were baptized with continual disasters, without allowing a cowardly despair to seize upon their hearts.

When the Britains captured Charleston and Savannah, and routed the Continental forces at Camden, South Carolina, there was no thought of surrender; nor even yet when defeat overtook the American army at Bunker Hill, and General WASHINGTON was compelled to evacuate New York and make a precipitate retreat, leaving the snow stained with the blood of his bare-footed and fugitive soldiers.

These disasters only nerved a brave and invincible people to renewed determination. The dark hour of trial was upon them, but they saw the light of victory peering through the clouds in the distance. Shall we be less brave, resolute or self-sacrificing than they? Have we less hope than they? On the contrary we have more to gain by victory—more to lose by defeat. Now is the time to test the metal of the true and loyal patriots, and to expose the base treason of the hypocrite and the time server. We have not the shadow of a doubt of the final result in this conflict even yet. Defeats may protract the war, but can subjugate us never! never!! never!!!

"Rise fellow-men, our country still remains,
By that dread name we wave the sword on high,
And swear for her to live—with her to die."

Shiloh and Northern Mississippi

Grant and Foote had won a significant victory in Kentucky with their capture of Forts Henry and Donelson. Not only had they captured Nashville; they had laid open the Tennessee heartland, as well as Alabama and Mississippi, to the Union forces. Further, if the Union army could capture Corinth, it would control the railroad and essentially secure the capitulation of Memphis. If Memphis fell, the federals would control a significant portion of the Mississippi River.

Capitalizing on his advantage would require swift action by Grant, though. Grant planned to follow Johnston to Corinth, but orders from his commanding general, Henry Halleck, stopped his advance; Grant was to wait near Savannah, Tennessee, until General Don Carlos Buell could catch up with him. Grant bivouacked at Pittsburg Landing on the west bank of the Tennessee, only 20 miles from the Confederate stronghold near Corinth. Grant's headquarters were set up next to a log church, Shiloh Chapel. *Shiloh* is a Hebrew word that means "place of peace," which is what Grant expected to find there. The Union general did not expect his Confederate foes to leave Corinth, and so he was lax in putting up defenses for the camp. He dug no entrenchments, sent out no pickets, nor any cavalry patrols.

Johnston realized that his only chance of stopping Grant's army was to attack before he could be reinforced by Buell. For once, the Confederates had the superior force, though only barely: Johnston's Army of Mississippi had 44,000 men to Grant's 42,000. Those odds would change dramatically, though, once Buell's army reached Grant's.

Johnston planned a surprise attack for dawn on 6 April, over Beauregard's objections. Johnston's army was supposed to reach Pittsburg Landing in a single day, but heavy rains slowed the march so that it took three days. The army had not advanced quietly, even taking occasional shots at game to supplement army rations. Beauregard was convinced the element of surprise had been lost, and the attack would be expected. Johnston, however, refused to turn back.

Skirmishers met early on the morning of 6 April about three-quarters of a mile from Shiloh church, but somehow, even fighting that nearby, did not alert the main body of Union troops to the Confederate advance. The Confederate main body overwhelmed the federal skirmishers and crashed in on the Union encampment that was largely unaware of the advance. In some places along the battle lines, the Confederates streamed into the Union camps without any difficulty.

Confederate victory seemed certain for the first twelve hours. The inexperienced Union troops panicked, and many soldiers desperately sought hiding places rather than their weapons. The Confederate attack, though, did not work out exactly as Johnston had planned. A little-known Union general, William T. Sherman, stepped forward to rally and regroup the troops and put up a fight. Among the Confederate high command, there was confusion about whether they were to push Grant's force back to Pittsburg Landing or away from it. In the desperate fighting, Confederate units became intermingled, making control of the Southern forces almost impossible. To make matters worse, in the early afternoon, Johnston was wounded in the leg. At first, he ignored the wound but admitted it was serious when an aid noticed that his right boot was filled with blood. The bullet had severed Johnston's femoral artery, and he was forced to retire from the field. Johnston would die from a wound that would not have been fatal, had he sought care for it sooner.

Beauregard took command of the Confederate troops and pushed the attack forward. By dark, the Southerners held virtually the entire battlefield. The federals retained only the landing itself, and Beauregard chose not to follow through with an attack there. His troops were exhausted, disorganized, and out of ammunition; they could not have carried out an attack successfully. Besides, the Confederate general, unaware that Buell had arrived with 25,000 fresh troops, believed the Yankees were whipped. Beauregard telegraphed the news of a glorious Confederate victory to Richmond.

Grant proved otherwise the next morning with an attack at dawn. He pushed the Confederates back to Corinth. Casualties totaled nearly 24,000 for the two armies combined, with each side losing nearly 2,000 men killed and 8,000 wounded. Shiloh was the bloodiest battle of the war to that time. It was also the battle that made it possible for the Union to split the Confederacy in two. Actually accomplishing that would take more than a year, but the groundwork had been laid. Perhaps if Johnston's and Beauregard's forces had been able to secure that area of Tennessee, they could have retained Memphis and greater control of the Mississippi, but that was not to be.

ROBERT ETTE: REPORTS OF BATTLE OF SHILOH

A Memphis Appeal *correspondent covered the Confederate victory at Shiloh, first sending back a short telegraphic account, then following up with a longer letter. The correspondent's telegraph was sent at the height of the second day's fighting, and did not make it back to Memphis in time for publication in the evening edition of 7 April. Instead, it had to wait and run the morning of 8 April, the same edition in which the longer letter about the first day's battle ran. The correspondent Ette's first telegraph, which appeared on 8 April, along with his later and more detailed letter, follow. Ette's energetic reporting resulted in a finely detailed story that laid out the events of the battle as a crowning Southern achievement, accomplished by brave troops and the most skilled generals.*

Memphis Appeal, 8, 10 April 1862

BY TELEGRAPH
THE BATTLE OF SHILOAH!
THE SECOND DAY'S CONTEST!

[Special to the Memphis Appeal]

BATTLE FIELD, April 7—2 p.m.—We slept last night in the enemy's camp.

Immense spoils and two thousand prisoners in our hands.

The enemy, reinforced by a division seven thousand strong, from below, engaged us again this morning at sunrise. The battle was desperate all the morning, our center and left being engaged.

The enemy was driven back at ten o'clock, but renewed the attack with great vigor, and fresh troops probably from Buell's column.

The battle is raging now, and the fire terrific.

Loss in number very heavy.

Gens. Bowen and Clark are wounded, and Gen. Cheatham has been injured in the shoulder. Col. Blythe, of Miss., is killed.

Sanford's Mississippi battery was captured by the enemy, except one gun.

Our troops are behaving nobly.

ETTE.

THE BATTLE OF SHILOAH!

[Special Correspondence of the Memphis Appeal]
SHILOAH, April 7, 1862

The great battle is over, and the question now stands about what are the results for both peoples engaged?

On Saturday, the 5th inst., preparations were [*unreadable*] on our side to attack the enemy. It was known then that the Federals were on this side of the river with a force of not less than 40,000 men, and it was also known that Buell was coming rapidly toward the Tennessee river, with the intention of reinforcing them, and thus oppose us again with superior numbers. Every [*unreadable*] of sound policy pointed to an immediate attack on our part, in order to prevent this junction, and consequently the attack was determined upon and made by us.

To enable you to understand well the circumstances that attended the great battle of Sunday, I will give you a brief outline of the ground upon which the fighting took place, and its location as regards the Tennessee river and Corinth.

The position occupied by the enemy was at a point called Shiloah, which is composed of an old church and a farm house, distant three and a half miles from the river at Pittsburg landing. Pittsburg landing is the place where most all the Federals landed, and where they kept their reserve in men, guns, and stores of all description, under protection of their gunboats and in sight of their transports.

Their camps extended from the river out to [*unreadable*] and beyond, being almost an uninterrupted line of camps for a distance of five miles.

Our forces had been moving since last Thursday from Corinth and the neighborhood, and marched to within two miles of Shiloah, over very bad roads running through a hilly country, very thinly inhabited and frequently interrupted by streams, branches and swamp bottoms, rendering the transportation by wagon a work undertaken with the greatest difficulty.

However, on Saturday night our troops laid upon their arms almost in sight of the enemy, and about twenty miles from Corinth, confident of a victory and fully aware of the importance of their mission.

On Saturday morning at daybreak the attack commenced.

The plan of the battle, which we understood as due to the genius of Gen. Beauregard, is the strongest one known in military science. It was composed of three parallel lines having its center and two flanks. The reserve was attached to the [unreadable] line, and the artillery laced in position between the front and center. Gen. Hardee commanded the front line, Gen. Bragg the second, and Gen. Polk the third. Gens. Johnston and Beauregard remaining with the reserve. Gen. Bragg also had command of the artillery, Gen. Trudeau acting under him.

Thus, we moved on at daybreak upon the Federals, and as the artillery opened on a line of [unreadable], the firing became terrific. The Federals fought with great valor, but nothing could [unreadable] the impetuosity of our brave Southern Troops.

At a charge at half-past eight o'clock in the morning by three regiments under Brigadier Gen. Gladden, the enemy lost four batteries. The 1st Louisiana regulars took one, the 21st Alabama took two, and Col. Blythe's Mississippi regiment took one. Our loss was very heavy, very heavy indeed. Col. Blythe was there, at the head of his regiment. The Federals engaged were commanded by Gen. Prentiss, and we have it from himself since that his troops suffered terribly.

A short time afterwards, one of their camps was in our possession; and so the fight went on, [unreadable] desperate, without mercy or rest for the whole day, every inch of ground being disputed and won by superior bravery.

At half-past two o'clock P.M., Gen. Albert Sydney Johnston fell, while leading a charge, struck by a ball and a piece of shell. Gen. Cheatham was wounded by a musket shot in the shoulder. Gen. Bowen was shot in the neck and in the side.

At 4 o'clock the enemy were in full retreat towards the river, our whole force closing upon them. Gen. Prentiss was then captured by some staff officers from Polk's command, and brought to Gen. Beauregard. Flag after flag was sent to headquarters, fresh trophies from the enemy. Squads of prisoners were brought [unreadable], and presently a whole brigade, captured by Gen. Bragg's command, moved slowly to the rear. At dark the enemy was driven to the river, finding refuge on their transports under protection of the gunboats. The firing was yet [unreadable] and incessant. Darkness was fast approaching, and all that the enemy possessed on this side of the river was ours; all their camps, ammunition, stores, the best part of eighteen batteries of artillery, one of

their generals, and seven regiments captured. The enemy himself was fast disappearing and crossing over to the other side of the river. Nothing more remained to be done, and our troops came back from the pursuit weary, hungry, and worn out from the fatigue of a 11 hours fight, but victorious. We came back to the Federal encampments and prepared for a night's rest. Fine tents, fine clothing, any quantity of forage and provision were the prey of our soldiers, and added to their comfort. A storm was preparing in the clouds; claps of thunder, mixed with the distant reports of cannonade kept by the gunboats and thus closed Sunday. More anon.

ETTE.

CORINTH, APRIL 8, 1862

I arrived last night from the battle-field and although worn out with fatigue, will try to give you an account of yesterday's fight.

On Sunday night we retired to rest victorious, and never was a victory more gloriously won than the battle of Shiloah. The enemy's plans were broken, their forces slain or disabled on the battle field, and what had escaped destruction were either prisoners or disorganized. After night came, the clouds, accumulating all day by the heavy [unreadable], broke out, and rain poured out upon us in torrents. Many of our troops were then returning homeward from the pursuit, and this added no little to the fatigue and discomfort of a day's fighting. The enemy's gunboats, in the meantime, were keeping up a constant firing into the woods, and to me it became evident that, should they receive reinforcements, they would renew the attack next morning. We knew of a Federal division, 7000 strong, which was encamped eight miles below, at Cramp's Landing, and arrangements were made by our [unreadable] to capture it if possible, and any way, be ready for another fight should it be forced upon us. Early in the morning our pickets were driven in, and while a large portion of our men were yet plundering tents and loading themselves down with all kinds of Federal property, the fight commenced in front of our center. A line of battle was already adopted, and battery after battery brought to bear upon the enemy. From the manner in which the Federals fought, it became evident that fresh troops were now arriving, and it would require the greatest energy to repel them. The fight once engaged became more furious and desperate than that of the day before. The Federals had a disaster to avenge, while we had a victory to maintain. Breckinridge's division had to fall back, and lost some artillery, but shortly afterwards advanced again, and recovered the ground and guns. Driven from the center, the enemy concentrated their fire upon the left, and from there were repulsed also.

It was then 11 o'clock A.M. We had maintained our position against superior numbers and fresh troops. The battle had been most murderous, but the enemy was retreating again, and cheer after cheer went forth from the ranks of our troops as a salute to a new victory, when suddenly we came to a stop. New batteries were found erected in front of us and volley after volley fired from a new line of opponents, clearly indicating that a new enemy was upon us. Buell had arrived with 30,000 fresh troops, and another battle had to be fought. The contest was unequal, and at once steps were taken for a retreat. Train after train, with wounded, stores and ammunition, was sent to the rear; squads of soldiery set to keep the road in passable condition over miry ices; the cavalry set to destroy the Federal property remaining in their camps, yet in our possession, and the remnant of our broken down regiments brought to face the enemy to stop his advance—so the battle went on until dark.

Sanford's Mississippi battery was captured by the enemy, except one gun. They were ordered to retreat, but thought they had time to unlimber on the way and give the enemy a few rounds to check their advance, and protect the retreat of two regiments of infantry, then falling back. They did so, effected their object, but lost some horses, and finally the battery, save one gun.

Bankhead's battery, in Breckinridge's brigade, was captured by the enemy and retaken by us.

The enemy's fire was concentrated on the left.

Gens. Bragg, Hardee, Ruggles, Polk and Beauregard himself, shared all the perils of the fight, but nature, if not courage, was giving way. Broken fragments of regiments could only be found, and yet the enemy was held at bay. Stragglers were found on every road leading to Corinth loaded down with Federal plunder and anxious to save their trophies. They could have been counted by the thousands; and while enough praise cannot be bestowed upon our troops engaged during the last two memorable days, enough reprobation cannot be given to the selfish cowards that prevented us from adding a new victory to the glorious one of yesterday, by their anxiety to secure a few spoils. Yet when darkness came upon the field, then enemy retreated to what camps they had recovered on the right and we occupied their camps in the center and on the left, holding them at bay with a handful of men and a few batteries. Arrangements for a retreat were completed, the enemy too much injured to pursue. Night favoring our movements, strong batteries placed in position to protect them, and all our enemies present on the field to organize and superintend, we retraced our steps to Corinth, where we arrived last night. A short time afterward, Gen. Beauregard and staff came in also, to organize new plans and prepare new victories, and we learn since that the whole army is ordered to fall back to Corinth. It is coming in today. The men are wearied but ready to fight, and are confident of the ultimate success of our cause.

What our losses may be, is not yet known. In wounded it is very heavy; in killed very small in proportion. This is easily accounted for when it is remembered that the battle took place over a broken country, very likely wooded, and where bayonet charges are almost impossible and that for two days it was mostly a fight of artillery and musketry at long range. As to other bases, such as guns, wagons, stores, etc., it will be very trifling, as we had time to secure enough of the enemy's property to compensate for the loss of any of our own.

In a military point of view, the result is not likely to turn against us. The only thing that saved the Federal army from total destruction on Sunday, was their proximity to their gunboats and transports. Should they attempt to attack us here, twenty four miles over such a country and such roads, we could not wish for a better chance to retrieve all our past losses at que blow.

I do not send you any list of the killed and wounded, as it is impossible yet to hear correct reports, and it would be cruel, as well as foolish, to create false alarms. As to incidents, it does hardly look well to mention what few came to your correspondent's notice, while there are so many that will come to light gradually, the principal heroes of which now sleep in a soldier's grave. Yet, I will mention a few at random, with the above restriction.

When Gen. Prentiss was taken prisoner he expressed a great desire to see Gen. Beauregard, and was brought before him on the battlefield. I was there, standing near the general, and witnessed the interview. Gen. Prentiss addressed Gen. Beauregard, and told him that he considered him the best general in our army. You are mistaken, said Beauregard; I know in our army better generals than I am, and among those I will cite Sidney Johnston, whom we have unfortunately lost to-day. Prentiss was surprised to see in Gen. Beauregard a man of small stature, and so easy in manners. He admitted our victory to be as great as Manassas, and our troops to have fought desperately. His battle flag was captured by the 9th Mississippi regiment; I saw it brought this morning to headquarters. Presently three more flags were brought to Beauregard at Shiloah. One of his aids brought in a little quail that had been so frightened by the cannonade that it laid on the ground without trying to escape capture. This will be my living trophy of the battle, remarked the general.

At six o'clock General Bragg came in from the pursuit. I have swept the enemy clear into the river, said he. They are retiring on their transports under protection of the gunboats. Their shelling is furious. Then shaking hands with Gov. Harris, he remarked: Governor, your State is restored to you. Gen. Beauregard then ordered to cease the pursuit.

This morning I saw a private pass with a federal flag. It was the regiment's colors of the 15th Illinois, captured by Private John Williams of Company C, 18th Mississippi regiment, now orderly of Gen. Garner. The 1st Louisiana infantry, in the charge upon the enemy's camp, took a whole section of artillery and three regimental colors. Col. Adams was wounded, and they lost twenty-three officers, killed and wounded, including all the captains save one. A whole brigade of Federals was captured by Gen. Bragg. The prisoners in our hands must amount to over three thousand.

I have just been over the battlefield to hunt for a friend of mine. I find many lost. I met a company in the 3d Kentucky, composed of Paducah friends. How much they have suffered. Capt. Somes, slightly wounded; Geo. Allen, struck by a ball in the foot. How sad is the morrow of a battle.

A train is coming; I must close this.

ETTE.

Northern Mississippi after Shiloh

Less than a month after the Battle of Shiloh, the Confederate and Union armies prepared to meet again, this time near the northern Mississippi town of Corinth. Or so it appeared. Samuel Chester Reid, Jr., Sparta of the *Appeal*, was on hand to report on the buildup, but little did he—or anyone else—know that the Confederates were preparing for a phantom action. General Beauregard realized his troops were hugely outnumbered by the federals, and so he planned what military men would call a "strategic withdrawal." On 29 May, Beauregard withdrew to Tupelo, before the Union army had a chance to force him into battle. At about that same time, Halleck split his force, sent Buell to threaten Chattanooga, and left Grant to defend northern Mississippi in a series of smallish battles that summer as Confederate Generals Price and Van Dorn attempted to unite forces against Grant. Beauregard's speech, which was a prelude to many smaller skirmishes rather than a major battle, was so rousing that Reid himself got caught up in the martial feeling and filed this story, which had the effect of leading Confederate readers to believe a great battle was pending in northern Mississippi, at the same time the fighting in the Peninsula of Virginia was heating up and the Confederate capital came close to falling to the enemy.

HENRY TIMROD: ARMY AT CORINTH—SITUATION IN NORTHERN MISSISSIPPI

With Beauregard's army settled in at Corinth, the Charleston Mercury, *one of the South's best-known newspapers with strong fire-eating tendencies, sent a correspondent to Mississippi to find out what was going on there. Henry Timrod, a Charleston poet and journalist who would become the Confederacy's poet laureate, had no experience as a war correspondent, as he acknowledged in the following article, and even if he had, he wrote in this story, he would not have been able to say much about the military situation due to censorship regulations imposed on reporters with the Southern army. He instead tried to paint a picture for the* Mercury's *readers of what northern Mississippi was like while addressing in a very general way the military situation.*

Charleston Mercury, 7 May 1862

THE CRISIS AT CORINTH

(FROM OUR SPECIAL CORRESPONDENT.)
CORINTH, MISS., April 27.

By a long and circuitous route, and after many tedious delays, I arrived at Corinth early last Thursday morning. But for the fact that I accompanied the Tenth Regiment of South Carolina Volunteers in trains specially appropriated to them, I might have been still upon the road. Such is the deficiency of transportation, and such the crowd pressing forward to this place, that many persons, not less eager than myself to reach the great centre of attraction, have found it as yet impossible to do so. At almost every station I met individuals who had been waiting for days, in the vain hope of getting on.

Worn out with fatigue, dazed by the bustle of the camp and the novelty of my position, I have not been able up to the present date to glean any publishable information of much interest. The enemy, very strongly reinforced, is at Hamburg, on the western side of the Tennessee River. Such, however, is the state of the roads that it is thought he cannot make an advance in less than a week. That he will make an advance as soon as practical, there seems to be no reasonable doubt. But whether, in that event, Beauregard will meet him half way, or await an assault within the lines about Corinth, I have heard too many contrary opinions to justify me in predicting. Our position here is so strong a one (being so protected, it is said, to the right and left by morasses as to compel the foe to attack in front) that the latter course would seem to be the part of prudence. Still the great moral advantage of being the attacking party, may induce Beauregard to assume the offensive. This Delphic putting of the case will, I trust, prove eminently satisfactory to your readers.

Take whatever shape events may, I think I may venture to assert, without ambiguity, that the great battle which is to decide the issue in the West, is very near at hand. Somewhere between Corinth and the Tennessee River our cause, for a time is to be lost or won!

> "Tell thy name, thou trembling field,
> Field of Death! where'er thou be
> Groan thou with our victory!"

Alas, even if I could procure, by means natural or supernatural, an answer to this invocation, I would not be permitted at present to reveal it.

Corinth is really "quite a place!" I expected to see in it an insignificant railway station, with a hut or two, and a shop and postoffice in one. I found it, on the contrary, presenting the appearance of a large village suddenly arrested on its way to become a considerable town. There is a hotel, there are churches, several streets lined with shops (where, however, there is now little to be purchased), and many good private dwellings. But the hotel and the churches have been turned into hospitals, most of the inhabitants have gone away, and the village has been converted into a busy and populous camp.

I passed the first two days after my arrival outside of the town, and thus had an opportunity of observing the nature of the country around it. Even my inexperienced judgment may venture to pronounce that country very badly adapted to the movements of armies. It is made up of a succession of low densely wooded hills and swampy bottoms; it is intersected with innumerable creeks, while the soil is a tenacious clay that retains moisture for a long time. I found the summit of the hills scarcely less muddy than the ravines between them.

Reports of skirmishing are rife. On Thursday there was severe skirmishing between our pickets and those of the enemy near Monterey. Yesterday a body of Confederate cavalry encountered a superior force in the vicinity of Tuscumbia, killed twenty, and captured forty prisoners. A vague rumor, which I have not been able to trace to any authentic source, has just reached me, that the enemy is advancing, in spite of the bad condition of the road. If this be so, you may hear of a battle very shortly indeed.

KAPPA.

SAMUEL CHESTER REID, JR.: LETTER FROM CORINTH—BEAUREGARD'S ROUSING SPEECH TO HIS TROOPS

Samuel Chester Reid, Jr., Sparta of the Appeal, *wrote a rousing review of an address Beauregard made to his troops during their occupation of Corinth. The speech clearly convinced the reporter that complete Confederate victory could not be far off if the South succeeded in the Peninsula Campaign, then ongoing in Virginia, and if Beauregard's men could defeat Grant's at Corinth.*

Memphis Appeal, 6 May 1862

LETTER FROM CORINTH

[Special Correspondence of the Memphis Appeal.]
CORINTH, Saturday, May 3, 1862.

I send you by telegraph to-day the address of General Beauregard to our combined army. It should meet an ardent response from every patriotic heart. Its bold, soldier-like declaration tells us that on the event of the coming battle hangs the fate of the valley of the Mississippi. Already have our people evinced a heroism and devotion of country, unparalleled in the history of revolutionary struggles since the world began. Nothing in the history of Greece or Rome can compare with our struggles on the battle-field, the sacrifices and offerings of our people with their life-blood and property, nor with the high-souled patriotism, toil and devotion of our women, who have shown themselves more than Spartan mothers, and who, from the commencement of the war by the abolition barbarians of the North, have exhibited an unceasing endurance without a murmur, while they have strained to make every exertion in aid of our glorious cause. History will not fail to record their noble deeds of humanity, nor their self-sacrificing martyrdom.

There can be neither retreat, defeat, or surrender in the coming great to our arms, and the glorious deeds of valor which our braves shall exhibit on the battle-field of Corinth, will live for all ages. Let every man therefore go forth to battle as if on his single arm depended the achievement of our liberty and independence. Let them think what we are to achieve by victory, and what we are to lose by—but I will not write the word, as I feel confident no other fate than a glorious success can attend our arms.

As you are told by our noble general, we shall meet the foe in this coming conflict on terms of greater equality than we have ever met the infidels before. Let our people then be strong of heart, full of hope, and not lacking in that high and moral courage which a sincere and abiding faith in the will of the omnipotent Deity cannot fail to inspire, however He may shape and direct our destiny. With the names of Price, Beauregard, Bragg, Polk, Hardee, Breckinridge, Ruggles, Vader, Cheatham, Clark, Chalmers, Manney, Jordon, Preston, and a host of heroic braves, we cannot fail of success, and if there be any truth in the oracles of old the God of battles will surely not desert us. But whatever be our fate, let our people hope on, hope ever, for there can be no despair in the hearts of our patriotic braves who have determined to be free. It is therefore but a question of time. The northern abolition infidels cannot hold out thirty days longer if victory crown our arms at Yorktown and Corinth. Their case is a thousand times more desperate than our own, with a frightful debt engulphing and sapping the very marrow of their resources for support, and still increasing at the rate of over four millions a day, it is utterly impossible for them to hold out, and defeat to them, gives us back New Orleans, the Mississippi, Tennessee, Kentucky, Missouri, and all our conquered territory. Let us look forward, then, to the bright and cheering prospects of the future, for this summer shall see our troops in Kentucky, if not across the Ohio, and our gallant boys revelling in the halls of Porkopolis!

The weather continues fine. The enemy is repairing the roads as he advances, in order to insure a speedy and safe "back track," which he will undoubtedly have the pleasure of making. They are making every preparation, with hospital boats at Savannah and Pittsburg, for their wounded, and everything denotes the extent and anticipated slaughter of the great struggle.

A freight train has just come in and reports having run into a train coming up before them, last night at Pocahontas, killing two men and wounding two others.

No movements of the enemy to-day whatever.

SPARTA.

Fall of New Orleans

New Orleans was the South's most important city, and its capitulation in April 1862 was a crushing blow to the Confederacy's morale, transportation, and economy. The U.S. Department of the Navy chose 60-year-old David G. Farragut to command the fleet near New Orleans. Farragut was a wise choice. Not only had he been reared in New Orleans; he literally had a lifetime's worth of military experience. Farragut had served in the U.S. Navy since 1810 when, at the age of nine, he received a midshipman's commission. Farragut had seen battle action in the War of 1812 and the Mexican-American War.

The defenses of New Orleans were formidable. Just a few miles beyond the mouth of the Mississippi sat heavily armed Forts Jackson and St. Philip. Farther upstream, only a few miles from the city, were two batteries, Chalmette and McGee. Unfortunately, the Confederates had been overly optimistic about the ability of the batteries to protect the city and had removed their heaviest guns. The weapons were installed on gunboats in Lake Pontchartrain. Beyond the batteries, Confederate Commodore George N. Hollins commanded a flotilla of six vessels, nicknamed the "Mosquito Fleet."

Hollins had virtually the same lifelong military experience as Farragut, who was two years younger than the Confederate navy man. Hollins, like Farragut, entered the navy as little more than a boy. At age fifteen, he received his midshipman's commission and was placed aboard the USS *President* under naval legend Stephen Decatur. Despite his experience, Hollins's lightly armed gunboats were no match for the Union navy vessels that had slipped past the forts to the south of New Orleans.

As Farragut's ships steamed up the Mississippi, the Confederate officer in charge of the defense of the city, Major General Mansfield Lovell, decided to abandon the city rather than risk the damage that would occur, should he put up a fight. Farragut arrived at New Orleans on 25 April and demanded the surrender of the city. On 1 May, U.S. Army General Benjamin Butler took control.

The loss of New Orleans had profound consequences for the Confederacy and for the military leaders involved. The blow to Confederate morale from the capitulation of New Orleans was tremendous, and one more blow had been struck for Union control of the Mississippi.

BY TELEGRAPH: ACCOUNT OF BOMBARDMENT OF FORT JACKSON

The fall of New Orleans began when a Northern gunboat fleet slipped past Fort Jackson and proceeded up the Mississippi River toward this most important Southern port city. Heavy fighting had occurred for several days previously. The following series of telegraphed dispatches from the Memphis Appeal *described the bombardment of Fort Jackson. The first dispatch, datelined New Orleans and signed "D," may have been written by Durant Da Ponte, a correspondent for the* New Orleans Daily Delta *who had covered the 1860 convention of Southern states in Montgomery.*

Memphis Appeal, 27 April 1862

BOMBARDMENT OF FORT JACKSON!

[Special to the Memphis Appeal]

NEW ORLEANS, April 23.—General Duncan reports that the bombardment of Fort Jackson is still progressing furiously.

Several of the Federal boats have been sunk by the guns of the fort.

The casualties in the fort are few, and its defenders are gallant, hopeful and earnest.

The attacking Federal fleet consists of twenty-one mortar boats and thirty-six other vessels.

D.

Later from Fort Jackson

[Special to the Memphis Appeal]

NEW ORLEANS, April 23, P.M.—Gen. Duncan reports to-day that the bombardment of Fort Jackson was continued by the enemy all night, and is still progressing.

He has no further casualties to report, and says that Providence is protecting the garrison, who are confident of ultimate success, and regret the doubts of their fellow citizens. Their fortitude is great, and the cause in which they are engaged commendable, and not the least idea of capitulation is entertained. The best guns of the fort continue in good working order, and the discipline of the troops is excellent.

Over 20,000 shells have been thrown by the enemy, thousands of which fell in the fort. Our enemies must soon become exhausted. If not, we can continue the contest as long as they can.

The Fight at Fort Jackson

NEW ORLEANS, April 23.—The following is a copy of an official dispatch from Major-Gen. Lovell:

"To Brigadier-Gen. Duncan, commanding at Fort Jackson: Say to the officers and men of your command that their heroic fortitude in enduring one of the most terrific bombardments ever known to have occurred, and the courage and skill with which they have crushed the enemy whenever he has dared to come from under cover, attacks the admiration of all, and will be recorded in history as a splendid example for patriots and soldiers.

"Anxious by confident families and friends are watching them with firm reliance, based upon the gallant exhibition thus far made of their indomitable courage and great military skill. The enemy will try your powers of endurance, but we believe, with no better success than he has already experienced.

[Signed]

"M. LOVELL, Maj. Gen. Com."

Gen Duncan's reply to Maj. Gen. Lovell is as follows:

"GENERAL: I have to report this morning the same state of things existing. The bombardment is still going on furiously. They keep it up continuously, by reliefs of their divisions.

"One of their gunboats, painted gray, came above the point this morning, but was struck and retired.

"We are hopeful, in good spirits, and very much in earnest.

"I cannot speak in too high praise of all the officers and men, nor have I any further casualties to report.

"Let the people have faith and fortitude, and we will not disgrace them.

[Signed]

*J. K. Duncan,
Brigadier-General."*

Bombardment of Fort Jackson

NEW ORLEANS, April 23.—The following dispatch was received from Fort Jackson to day:

"We have had a heavy and continued bombardment all night, which is still progressing. No other casualties have occurred, except two men slightly wounded. God is certainly protecting us. We are still cheerful, and have an abiding faith in our ultimate success. We are making repairs the best we can. Our best guns are still in working order. The most of them have been disabled at times. Twenty-five thousand thirteen-inch shells have been fired by the enemy, thousands of which have fallen in the fort. They must soon exhaust themselves; if not, we can stand it as long as they can."

[Signed]

J. K. Duncan.
Brigadier-General Commanding.

GEORGE KENDALL OR FRANCIS LUMSDEN: NEW ORLEANS MUST ENDURE YANKEE OCCUPATION

After many days of heavy fighting between the Union naval forces and the Confederate land forces, New Orleans finally surrendered. The Picayune *tried to offer some encouragement to demoralized city residents. The historic city had been saved but now had to endure the yoke of Union oppression.*

New Orleans Picayune, 27 April 1862

THE DUTY OF THE HOUR

We have great satisfaction in reading the several proclamations of Mayor Monroe, addressed to the people of this city, with reference to the duty devolving upon them, at the present solemn and critical exigency. Truly, as he says in that, which has also the [*unreadable*] of the Committee of Safety, through its President, one of our best and most prominent citizens, the circumstances, sad and melancholy as they are, in which we are now placed, require on our part the exercise of the utmost wisdom and forbearance.

We have devoted freely of our men, our substance, and our exertions, to the defence of our beloved city, and have nothing wherewith to reproach ourselves, in the way of dereliction or neglect of duty, to accomplish that object. We have not succeeded. A superior force, availing itself of facilities of approach we had not the power to resist, and of an arm in which we were not capable of competing with it, has accomplished its purpose, and stands before our city, dictating to us terms of surrender.

It now devolves upon us to meet the exigency with dignity—not with craven submissiveness on the one hand, nor, as the Mayor says, with indecent alacrity on the other; but with calm and reliant hope for the moment which we may confidently trust is not remote when our brethren and countrymen will achieve our deliverance.

Meantime, we have domestic interests, near and dear to us, to guard and defend. The preservation of the peace, quiet and good order of our city, is now the paramount duty of every citizen. The Mayor tells the invader that he has a gallant people, a people sensitive of all that can affect their dignity and self-respect, over which to exercise the government he now, we trust but temporarily, can assert. Let us verify, by our example, the character our Chief Magistrate has not unjustly claimed for us. He promises to discharge all the duties imposed upon him by his office, with religious fidelity. Be it ours to sustain him, and the other authorities of our city, in that good work. Let us not, by rash acts of violence, though these may be the dictates of offended pride and deep sense of injury, give the enemy warrant for aspersions he has not been backward, in time past, in throwing upon us; nor furnish him a pretext for inflicting wanton and irreparable injury upon the city.

The strict and full performance of these high and holy duties is not by any means inconsistent with those feelings which, though temporarily defeated, we have, as men and freemen, a right to entertain; nor with that dignity which the soul conscious of rectitude may maintain, even in the midst of disaster.

We have now pressing upon us, with more stringency than ever, many relative obligations, the sacredness of which every good citizen will be free to admit. "The poor ye have ever with you," said One, whose precepts were uttered for our guidance. It is ours to consider more than ever, and in every way possible, their imperative wants. Bakeries, and groceries, and markets, and provision stores, should be kept open, during the day, and thus articles necessary for subsistence be made and kept easy of access and procurement. This is no time to practice extortion, or to haggle about prices. The exorbitant profit upon the sale of articles of prime necessity, wrung from the scantily supplied purse of a fellow citizen, is now more than ever a robbery. We trust that every such instance will meet, at the hands of the community, with the execration it so justly merits.

Battle of Corinth

Northern Mississippi remained relatively free of military engagements through the summer of 1862, but that changed in the fall. In late September, Union General William S. Rosecrans met Confederate forces under General Sterling Price near Iuka, Mississippi. Rosecrans drove the Confederates southwest of Iuka, where Price later met up with his colleague, General Earl Van Dorn. The two decided to combine their forces and march north toward Pocahontas, Tennessee. They hoped to convince Rosecrans they were planning to attack Bolivar, Tennessee. Their real plan was to attack Corinth before Rosecrans could assemble his widely disbursed troops.

Rosecrans was indeed confused by the Confederates' movements, but he was certain of the fortifications he had built in and around Corinth. He doubted the Confederates would move against a city so heavily defended, and he was uncertain whether they would move against the other cities. He expected Van Dorn and Price to try to draw him out of Corinth and into battle in open country.

Van Dorn attacked Corinth on the morning of 3 October. The Confederates met with some success the first day, though their effort was slowed by intense heat and lack of water for the soldiers. Around 3:00 P.M., the Southern soldiers were poised to capture the city when the federals retreated behind their batteries. Van Dorn's instinct was to pursue, but Price knew that his men were exhausted. He persuaded Van Dorn to wait until the next morning to press the attack. That night, both Rosecrans and Van Dorn repositioned their troops.

The next morning's fighting began with an artillery duel that soon turned into hand-to-hand and house-to-house combat inside Corinth itself. The heaviest fighting took place near the Tishomingo Hotel. The Confederates were finally forced to retreat. The second day of the battle was over by 1:00 P.M. Total losses included 315 killed, 1,812 wounded, and 232 prisoners for the federals and 1,423 killed, 5,692 wounded, and 2,268 prisoners for the Confederates.

The battles at Iuka and Corinth were the last major Confederate offensives in northern Mississippi, and the Union victories in those engagements allowed Grant to focus his attention on Vicksburg. Further, the defeats at Corinth and Antietam convinced Confederate politicians that they would not be receiving recognition as an independent country and aid from Europe.

ALBERT J. STREET: ACCOUNT OF BATTLE AT CORINTH

News of the Battle of Corinth was gathered at Tupelo, Mississippi, and telegraphed back to newspapers. This story, written on 6 October with information obtained from a courier, was fairly accurate in its description of the fighting in Corinth. The one piece of information that was completely inaccurate was the estimate of the size of Rosecrans's force. Rather than the 40,000 men General Price's son estimated, Rosecrans had only about 23,000 men at Corinth, though he did receive some reinforcements from Grant. The correspondent who wrote this dispatch may have been having a little fun with the selection of his nom de guerre. N'Importe is French for "It is not important."

Mobile Advertiser and Register, 7 October 1862

NEWS BY TELEGRAPH
SPECIAL DESPATCH
THE BATTLE AT CORINTH

Force of the Enemy Forty Thousand

[FROM OUR SPECIAL CORRESPONDENT.]

TUPELO, Oct. 6, 9 P.M.—There is nothing reliable from Corinth since General Van Dorn's despatch.

A courier arrived to day says that on the 4th our troops drove the enemy from and occupied their entrenchments, but were afterwards forced to fall back from town.

Heavy cannonading was heard yesterday from points above here. A thousand contradictory rumors are afloat. The fight must have been most bloody. A courier is hourly expected from the scene of conflict.

Brig. Gen. Ed. Price, an exchanged prisoner, son of Gen. Sterling Price, arrived to-day from Memphis, which place he left on the 1st. He represents the enemy 40,000 strong, with 70 pieces of artillery, strongly posted at Corinth.

They were fully posted as to our movements, and anticipated an attack from Van Dorn and Price. Sherman, at Memphis, knew their exact whereabouts.

Late Northern papers have been received.—Two-thirds of the press are opposed to Lincoln's abolition proclamation.

N'IMPORTE.

CLINT: ACCOUNT OF RECENT FIGHTING IN MISSISSIPPI

While Lee's army in Virginia was regrouping after its retreat from Maryland, the Confederate army in the West was fighting Union forces near Corinth. Following the Battle of Corinth, on 5 October, Van Dorn's forces were ambushed at the Hatchie River, and heavy fighting followed. While the federals regrouped, the Confederate force retreated to Holly Springs. The campaign accomplished little, other than more men killed and wounded, as the Mobile *paper's correspondent hints in his letter about the aftermath of the Battle of Corinth.*

Mobile Advertiser and Register, 14 October 1862

Letter from Jackson, Miss.
THE AFFAIR AT CORINTH

From our Special Correspondent
JACKSON, Oct. 10, 1862.

The news from Corinth and North Mississippi, while in a great measure unsatisfactory, has caused much alarm and anxiety, and set our people to work with a will that means business. The failure on the part of our army to capture and secure all that it set out to accomplish, as well as its retreat upon Ripley and Holly Springs, while it caused depression, has had its effect of arousing all to action of the most determined nature. Crimination and recriminations are freely indulged in, and there is much disposition to censure our officers, and some are particularly severe upon Gens. Van Dorn, Lovell and Pillow, although the latter General was not in the battle, and Gen. Lovell acted most gallantly, all accounts agreeing that he was brave and even reckless as to personal safety, for if what is said about him is true, he courted every post of danger. Gens. Van Dorn and Price are also said to have acted with courage and gallantry. The troops are said to have behaved as well as the troops on any field, but with all this the Confederates were defeated. In plain English we have fought an important battle and lost it, and all the fault-finding, scolding and abuse that may be resorted to will not mend matters a particle. We must "prick our flints and try again." From the manner in which Gen. Baggies, Gov. Pettus, Gens. Tilghman and Tapper have gone to work, and the efficiency of their action with the means at their action with the means at their command, affords great hopes that notwithstanding the boasted force of [unreadable] in West Tennessee, they will be essentially met and repulsed, although some evacuations may have to take place.

It is said that the Federals were thoroughly posted as to the movements of our army. There is no doubt of that fact, and they will continue to be so, just so long as martial law is not in existence in the entire Valley of the Mississippi. The abolishment of martial law was most unfortunate, and the results will continue to be injurious until it is again thoroughly endorsed. The [unreadable] does not affect this section of the country only, but it affords a natural ground through which Federal spies have undisputed passage to any portion of the Confederacy. Mobile is now a menaced point and with Pensacola on the west and the Gulf on the south, but little can be done by the authorities that the Federals will not be perfectly acquainted with, and to-day they know more about the defences of Mobile than two-thirds of its citizens. Prostitutes are used by the Federals as spies, and they work with diligence and effectiveness. They fly over the roads and lurk for a day or so about the towns and cities, and then disappear. All hail from Memphis. With the dangers that now surround your city, allow me to say that you cannot be too [*unreadable*], watchful and careful.

As the army has fallen back to Holly Springs, the Mobile and Ohio road is endangered, but to what extent I am unable to say. The enemy will hardly venture so far from its base of operations as to attack Columbus. I think his first object will be to secure the Mississippi Valley and river.

CLINT.

Battle of Perryville, Kentucky

Braxton Bragg's invasion of Kentucky started off well enough. Bragg advanced from Chattanooga and his subordinate General Edmund Kirby Smith from Knoxville. The Confederate forces won easy victories at Richmond and Munfordville. Smith's army captured Lexington and Frankfort and threatened Cincinnati, Ohio. At that point, Bragg occupied most of Kentucky, but Bragg's movement to Bardstown after the Battle of Munfordville allowed Union General Don Carlos Buell to reach Louisville uncontested, where he received 25,000 reinforcements and then quickly moved against the Confederates.

As Buell advanced on Bardstown, Bragg's forces withdrew through Springfield and Perryville to a location where some water was available. That summer and fall, Kentucky had experienced a drought, and the Southern soldiers had been suffering from the heat, dust, and lack of good water.

On 7 October, a large Union force advanced toward Perryville. Bragg ordered his subordinates Major General William J. Hardee and Polk to Perryville, where they were to defeat the Union force. On 8 October, the Confederates withstood an all-day attack by 39,000 federals. Bragg had not at first been aware that he faced a force larger than a corps. When he realized the size of the Union force, he withdrew to Harrodsburg and then through the Cumberland Gap back into Tennessee. This was the largest battle fought on Kentucky soil during the Civil War, and it was the bluegrass state's last invasion.

JOHN FORSYTH: ACCOUNT OF BATTLE OF PERRYVILLE

Also in the West, General Braxton Bragg's invasion of Kentucky was halted in what was described as a "pitched battle" at Perryville, southwest of Lexington. A portion of Bragg's army met a portion of General Don Carlos Buell's force in the only major battle to occur in Kentucky. Bragg's invasion of Kentucky had started out well enough with victories in smaller battles near Richmond and Munford, followed by the capture of Lexington and Frankfort by Bragg's lieutenant, General Edmund Kirby Smith. Both Bragg and Buell misread the situation. Bragg did not realize the size of the force his army faced, and only part of Buell's troops took part in the battle. An "acoustic shadow" kept the general from hearing the sound of the engagement. He received word of the fighting late in the afternoon and sent reinforcements. The battle ended with darkness. Losses on both sides were about equal. John Forsyth, editor of the Mobile Advertiser and Register *and a staunch Bragg supporter, was with the Confederate army on its invasion of Kentucky, and he filed an eyewitness account of the Battle of Perryville. Forsyth inaccurately described the outcome of the fight at Perryville as a Confederate victory.*

Mobile Advertiser and Register, 18 October 1862

NEWS BY TELEGRAPH
SPECIAL DESPATCHES
FROM GEN. BRAGG'S HEADQUARTERS
PARTICULARS OF BATTLE OF PERRYVILLE
Battle of Frankfort

[From Our Special Correspondent.]

HARRODSBURG, Oct. 10, via KNOXVILLE, Oct. 17.–Gen. Bragg's first Kentucky pitched battle was fought on Wednesday, the 8th instant, at Perryville, ten miles from this place. The enemy had been following us in force from Bardstown, and they also threatened Frankfort. Gen. Withers' division was sent forward to support Kirby Smith, while the divisions of Cheatham, Beckner and Anderson were countermarched to give battle to the foe in the rear.

Our lines of battle on the right and left of the turnpike, and commanding the only accessible route, opened with artillery at 6 o'clock A.M.—Gen. Bragg and his staff reached the ground about 7 o'clock, and at 10 o'clock the dispositions for the fight were complete. Our right awaited the attack in force, Cheatham and Buckner being posted to meet it.

At 3 o'clock P.M. they advanced in splendid line, with Gen. Bragg's orders to push along the whole line to close quarters. For one hour and a half the enemy maintained his ground bravely in the face of a murderous fire of artillery and musketry. Our troops fought like heroes until the enemy began to falter, when with a shout our boys moved forward and drove them three or four miles, entirely off the field. Meantime an attempt on our left had been repulsed. We captured 500 or 600 prisoners and 21 pieces of artillery, but for want of horses only eight pieces were brought off. The returns of our casualties are not all in, but they are estimated at 1,500. I have opened a list of those ascertained so far.

With one more division the enemy would have been destroyed. Night put an end to the pursuit. The enemy's loss is believed to be more than double our own. Among them is Gen. Jas. Jackson, certain, and Gen. Crittenden reported. Buell was present commanding, and we have prisoners from five different divisions, from which we estimate the enemy's force to have been at least 80,000. We fought only 12,000 strong. Our army is in the highest spirits.

At Frankfort the matter was soon ended. The enemy, under M'Cook, fled before Kirby Smith, and Withers cut off his rear, capturing 700 prisoners and fourteen wagons.

Another battle is at hand. Bragg's depots being menaced, he at once withdrew his army to protect them. At daylight next morning the enemy sent a flag of truce for permission to bury their dead. In the afternoon fight there was not even a Yankee surgeon on the field, and the wounded were all left. Our wounded were removed during the night after the battle.

Gen. Polk had a narrow escape. At Dusk he left his staff and rode up to stop the fire of a Confederate regiment, as he thought, upon our own troops. Seizing the Colonel by the shoulder he demanded, "Why are you firing on your friends." The Colonel said that he did not know that he was. "Who are you?" said Polk. "The Colonel of the 23d Indiana," was the reply. The General again shook him roughly and ordered him to cease firing, and before the Yankee found out who he was, he put spurs to his horse and got away.

Gen. Bragg says he has got the best troops in the world. Two thousand Kentuckians have taken up arms, and more are organizing. Gen. McCrown's army has arrived here. Among our killed are Lieut. Col. Patterson, of the 11th Tennessee regiment; Lieut.-Col. Evans, of the Texas Rangers; Major W. Pricer, Commissary; Capts. Cartwright, of Georgia, and Wm. S. May of Gen. Claiborne's staff.

J. F.

EASTERN THEATER

Peninsula Campaign

The North's first sustained attempt to capture Richmond was supposed to have begun in February. President Lincoln, frustrated with General McClellan's procrastination and failure to explain his plans for waging war against the Confederates, ordered his commander to lead the Army of the Potomac toward the Confederate capital and to begin a campaign by 22 February. Lincoln even gave the general a plan of battle: Move directly overland from a base in Washington, D.C., through Manassas and on to Richmond. McClellan offered an alternative proposal. He preferred to move his troops by water, via the Potomac and Rappahannock rivers, to Urbana, Virginia, just opposite Richmond. McClellan argued that this plan offered the shortest feasible land route to the Confederate capital. Lincoln capitulated, but multiple delays prevented the campaign from beginning immediately. Finally, in the latter half of March, though, the Union army was ready to begin its campaign for Richmond. McClellan set out from Alexandria with his army on barges—130,000 troops, 15,000 horses, 1,100 wagons, and forty-four artillery batteries sailed down the Potomac, past the mouths of the Rappahannock and York rivers, and on to the Virginia Peninsula. By 5 April, the Union army was on land and only 75 miles from Richmond.

Confederate General John B. Magruder was waiting for the Union legions with an entrenched force about a tenth the size of McClellan's. Magruder's job was to hold the Union troops at bay until reinforcements could reach him, and so the general devised one of the most brilliant deceptions of the war. If he could trick the Union forces into believing they were facing a much larger Confederate force, then perhaps they would be less aggressive in their forward movements. Magruder's plan was simple: He would march the troops he had in circles in front of a gap in the Confederate defenses. The trick worked, and the Union army became convinced that Magruder was being reinforced by thousands of troops and that a major siege would be needed to rout the Confederates. Magruder's pantomime slowed the Union advance for a month and bought time for reinforcements to arrive.

After a failed attempt to capture Yorktown on the same day his forces landed (5 April), McClellan's forces sat outside the village for a full month and built artillery batteries. Finally, on 4 May, McClellan was ready to take on Magruder. But Magruder was gone. He had given McClellan the slip and pulled his vastly inferior force out of Yorktown under cover of darkness. McClellan telegraphed Union Secretary of War Edwin Stanton of his brilliant success in capturing Yorktown. McClellan also requested more troops. He was convinced Confederate General Joseph E. Johnston stood between him and Richmond with perhaps a force even larger than his own. McClellan was overly cautious by nature, but he was also getting bad information from Pinkerton detectives who had been hired to gather intelligence for the Union. The Pinkertons were giving McClellan's estimates of a Confederate force two, three, even four times its actual size. In reality, Johnston was certainly in position to try to defend the Confederate capital, but his fighting force was only about half that of McClellan's—some 42,000 against 85,000. Still, McClellan was on the peninsula and slowly but steadily moving toward Richmond.

The Union advance on Richmond began in earnest on 8 May but immediately and literally bogged down. Spring rains had turned the roads in the region into mud holes that could swallow up men, horses, and even wagons. Still, within two weeks, McClellan was within 7 miles of Richmond. Rather than advancing and pressing his advantage, though, McClellan dug in and began arguing with Washington for reinforcements. His force at that point outnumbered the Confederates defending Richmond by some 40,000 men. The capture of Richmond seemed eminent, until the rain started up again.

Most of the time, the Chickahominy River was little more than a stream that flowed into the James River. Generally speaking, it was easily passible. When heavy rains came, though, if the river flooded even to only 2 feet above normal, it would overflow the whole area. From 20 May to 25 May, McClellan moved three corps across the river to demonstrate against Richmond. He kept three corps on the north side of the river in reserve. Then, on 27 May, it started to rain. And it continued to rain until, on 31 May, the Chickahominy was impassible.

On 31 May, Johnston attacked two of McClellan's corps outside Richmond in what would come to be known as the Battle of Seven Pines (Fair Oaks). His attack was successful early on, but the Union lines held, and Johnston was forced to withdraw. Johnston was severely wounded in the battle, so much so, in fact, that he had to be relieved of command. Johnston's hiatus from the army opened the door of command for a man who would become a legend: Robert E. Lee. The Union, though, suffered the greatest casualty of the day. After the Battle of Seven Pines, McClellan lost his nerve. He was immobilized for three weeks.

Lee realized that a prolonged siege of Richmond would result in a Union victory due to McClellan's superior numbers. He understood that he had to go on the offensive immediately and push McClellan as far back as he could, and he knew he had to do so before the Union force's large artillery could be brought up to the front. To improve the numerical odds a bit, Lee recalled Stonewall Jackson's forces from the Shenandoah Valley. On 25 June, Lee and his lieutenants agreed on a pincer movement against McClellan to begin at 3:00 A.M. the next morning.

On 25 June, Confederate forces launched the Seven Days Battles with an attack on Union forces near Mechanicsville. The day ended inconclusively, but McClellan withdrew to Gaines's Mill. Lee pursued, and the fighting was renewed there on 27 June. Lee attacked with 65,000 men and pushed McClellan back near Malvern Hill. Again, Lee pursued the retreating federals. On 1 July, the two armies met again outside Malvern Hill. Confederates smashed into the Union lines, but they held. The obvious victory at Malvern Hill was heartening, and McClellan's men were ready to fight their way back toward Richmond. One officer, Philip Kearny, argued that a retreat and the failure to take Richmond could only be explained by cowardice or treason. McClellan was not so bold. He believed his first responsibility was to ensure his army's safety, and so he ordered a retreat to Harrison's Landing and the protection offered by the Union gunboats on the James River.

The performance of the Confederate army in the Peninsula Campaign and its concluding Seven Days Battles was both brilliant and inept. Magruder's diversions bought the time needed to gather the Confederate army's strength and to build defenses around Richmond, but the offensive campaign Lee waged after taking over what he named the Army of Northern Virginia was marred by miscommunications and tardiness of some units. Still, even though each of its attacks were repulsed during the Seven Days Battles, with the single exception of Gaines's Mill, the Confederacy had secured Richmond—at least for the time being—at the cost 19,000 men. The Union's loss in men was less, 15,000, but the cost in territory and morale was considerable.

DR. GEORGE W. BAGBY: BATTLE OF SEVEN PINES

The Battle of Seven Pines occurred across two days, 31 May to 1 June. Johnston, taking advantage of the division of the Union army and the impassible Chickahominy River, attacked McClellan's left. Johnston had planned a double envelopment, but poor staff work resulted in a series of ineffective frontal attacks that were repulsed once federal reinforcements finally made it across the swollen river. Johnston was seriously wounded in this engagement in which the Union lost 5,000 men to the Confederacy's 6,100.

Charleston Mercury, 9 June 1862

BATTLE OF THE SEVEN PINES

(FROM OUR OWN CORRESPONDENT.)

RICHMOND, Friday, June 6.

McCLELLAN claims a victory at the battles of "Seven Pines." Of course, everything short of a total rout is a victory to him. Night and the delay of one corps saved him from that destruction which even he, unbounded liar as he is, would have been compelled to confess. The fighting of our men is beyond all praise. Mr. DAVIS, who loses no occasion of informing the world of his proximity to a battle, has announced his admiration of the gallantry of our men. It was never exceeded. The South Carolinians who were engaged, covered themselves with glory. Among the troops whose conduct in the battle is spoken of in the highest terms of praise, are Col. Jenkins' Regiment of Sharpshooters; the 5th South Carolina Regiment, Col. Giles, who fell in the thickest of the fight; the 6th South Carolina Regiment, Col Bratton; Mattison's Battalion, S.C.V., and the Hampton Legion. Jenkins' brigade swept steadily and gloriously over all obstacles. The Legion, in attempting to storm a strong work of the enemy, encountered a murderous fire, and was finally repulsed; but the list of casualties tells a tale of heroism. The marvel is that in such a country the men could fight at all. Had the attack been made a day or two earlier, not a live Yankee would have been left this side of the swamp. But Johnston, worried by the newspapers, the President and Gen. Lee, declared he would not fight until he got ready. Hence the article in the Enquirer, asserting, very gratuitously, that there was perfect accord among our high officials.

Another golden opportunity was lost when 20,000 Yankees advanced to Hanover C.H., and Branch was left to his small discretion to attack them with a part of a brigade, to whose assistance, when overpowered, he refused to call reinforcements, though they were within a short distance. It is strange that a flank commanding two important railroads, possessing the advantages of an easy passage across the swamp, and the only firm, dry fighting ground in the neighborhood, should have been left to the most incompetent commanders in the whole army. Doubtless the Circumlocution Office, in its hesitation about confirming A. P. Hill's appointment as Major General, is not wholly guiltless in this matter.

An intelligent negro, who, with others, assisted in burying the Yankee dead, puts down their loss in killed alone at 2000—a surprising statement, for the highest number of dead Yankees seen by any of those who have been over the field, as given to me, is 200, and all agree that our loss in wounded exceeded theirs considerably. But the negro's story may be true, for I hear that the Texan brigade took no prisoners whatever, and other brigades may have followed that example of mercy to our own people by retribution, which the brutality of Wool, Hunter and Butler fully justifies. Our own loss will not fall far short of the number given in my letter two days ago. The killed may not amount to 500, but the wounded may be estimated by the official report of the casualties in Rode's brigade, which went in with 2500 and lost 1,092. It is true this brigade bore much of the brunt of the fight; but there were twelve or fifteen brigades engaged, and I have yet to hear of more than three or four regiments which did not suffer heavily.

The fight failed, it is said, of its legitimate results because the corps that was to have led off early in the morning did not. After waiting two hours Longstreet led off. The enemy were advertised and had full time to prepare. Whiting who was to have gone round, could just hold his own.

As it is, the only profit derived from the victory is the lesson of blood conveyed to the invader. "On to Richmond" is going to be no holiday work. The foe may reach these walls, but, if he does, he will come in ghastly plight. Could we get him out of the swamps and forests upon an open firm field, I should not fear the result. But we will have to fight him again on much the same ground, for we cannot permit him to perfect his trenches. Already he has had too much time. But our army is in better trim than before. Our artillery, cavalry, infantry, all are now in their proper position, with pickets, scouts and videttes posted and distributed as they never were before. The skies all still hang with thick clouds, but ere this letter reaches you the fateful day will, in all probability, have come and gone.

The river is said to be higher this morning than ever before, except on a single occasion—the water belongs six feet above the tops of the obstructions, to which no serious damage is yet reported. So great, indeed, is the freshet, that it is asserted that the Monitor is coming up to Richmond by way of the Petersburg Railroad. Let her come, say the people, and bombard as much as she pleases. If the city falls, our property is all confiscated. So what difference does it make? Better, a thousand-fold, destruction than Yankee possession. I am glad to see this feeling so rife among our people.

Dr. Cullen tells me that, at the time our men stormed the redoubts in the face of a terrible cannonade—the only instance of the kind that has occurred during the war—our own twenty-four pounders were up to their muzzles in mud. The Yankees were taught that, if Richmond falls at all, it will fall into the hands of those who love death most sincerely. They need their miniature bombs not against our caissons, for we had none there, but against our men. One poor fellow is now lying in Seabrook's Warehouse with his face literally blown out—the little bomb having exploded after it entered his mouth.

Capt. Elliott, of the Whig, is raising a battalion for special service in defence of the city—the Common Council offering twenty dollars a month bounty to each man who enlists for six months. Better organize a battalion, nay a brigade, for service in the hospitals. We do not need soldiers so much as nurses.

Nothing from Jackson to-day, nor from the lines around the city. Military operations are impossible in the present state of the roads, which are likely to remain as bad as they can be, judging from the watery skies which overhang us.

I take this method of answering two despatches sent me from Columbia, by Messrs. Guerry and McLees. They were handed, yesterday, by mistake, to my father, who made many enquiries in regard to L. P. Guerry and the dead of Mattison's battalion, but could learn nothing of either. The wounded from South Carolina are not all sent to the C. S. Hospital in Manchester, but are scattered among various private and public hospitals. The same may be said of the wounded of other States. Hence the difficulty of ascertaining with certainty the facts in regard to individuals in particular corps. There should be, and doubtless soon will be, a Central Depot of Information, to which persons can repair with the assurance of getting a reliable answer. Not an unreliable answer obtained after visiting twenty or more hospitals, two of which (Camp Winder and Chimborazo) are cities of sick, holding several thousand. The distance between Chimborazo and Winder is two miles in a direct line, and the Alms House Hospital, the next largest, is a mile to the right of this line, going west. Hence the difficulty of obtaining information.

HERMES.

Seven Days' Battle

No reporters were permitted to be with the Confederate army during the Seven Days' Battle, and so reporting of the fighting in front of Richmond depended on telegraphic reports sent in from the front and information obtained from wounded soldiers who were brought to hospitals in the capital city for treatment. News of the fighting filtered out in bits and pieces, and some newspapers found it necessary to piece together accounts of the battle from wire reports and stories in exchange newspapers. The *Richmond Examiner* did have a representative present during much of the fighting. Editor John M. Daniel, who was an aide to A. P. Hill. Daniel, though, was wounded during the fighting.

DR. GEORGE W. BAGBY: ACCOUNT OF FIGHTING DURING SEVEN DAYS BATTLES

The Charleston Mercury, *like most other Southern newspapers, had to find some way to cover the Seven Days Battles other than eyewitness accounts by correspondents present during the fighting. Its reliable Richmond correspondent, Hermes, better known as George W. Babgy, collected news from dispatches sent to the Confederate War Department and forwarded it to the* Mercury's *editors by telegraph and letter. In this series of telegraphs, Hermes described the Battle of Mechanicsville and the early skirmishing that was preliminary to it.*

Charleston Mercury, 27 June 1862

NEWS BY TELEGRAPH
IMPORTANT NEWS FROM RICHMOND
THE GREAT BATTLE BEGUN YESTERDAY
AFTERNOON, ON THE LEFT WING

RICHMOND, June 26.—The difficulty of obtaining information from the lines is illustrated by the indefinite accounts given by the city papers this morning, of the fight which took place on the Williamsburg road yesterday.

It now appears certain that the 1st Louisiana regiment was engaged for some time with two brigades of the enemy, who had driven in our pickets about 8 a.m. Regardless of the heavy odds brought against them, the Louisiana advanced rapidly upon the foe, shouting, as their battle-cry, "BUTLER! BUTLER!" The Yankees in front immediately gave way before the impetuous advance of our men, and would have been driven from the field, but for the support they received from a heavy crossfire directed against us by several additional regiments of the enemy, which were ambuscaded in the woods.

The 1st Louisiana was afterwards reinforced by other regiments of Gen. WRIGHT'S brigade, and the fight was continued during the day until the Yankees were dislodged from the woods and driven back to their camp.

In the afternoon RANSOM'S and MAHONE'S brigades were engaged, and aided in driving the enemy back. Col. SHIVERS and Major NELLIGAN, of the 1st Louisiana, were both wounded in the arm. Lieuts. GILMORE and MURPHY, of the Montgomery Guards (of New Orleans), were both killed. The total Confederate loss is estimated at about 200 killed and wounded. The enemy's loss was heavy.

Later

Up to one o'clock today only occasional cannonading could be heard along the lines. The general expectation of a great battle today has not been realized.

The Latest

Nine o'clock, p.m. The battle which is to decide the fate of Richmond, was begun this afternoon, on the left wing of the Confederate army. For three hours the firing in the direction of Mechanicsville has been rapid and continuous. The cannonading can be heard distinctly in the city, and crowds have gathered on the hills north of the city, whence the bursting of the shells is occasionally visible.

At eight o'clock the firing was still progressing furiously. It is not probable that any particulars will be received from the battlefield until morning.

There was no fighting of importance on the centre or right today. A general engagement tomorrow is considered inevitable.

CHARLESTON MERCURY: SUMMARY OF RECENT BATTLES BEFORE RICHMOND

When original stories by a newspaper's own correspondents were hard to come by, editors would turn to exchange newspapers for news. Postal laws allowed newspapers to send copies to other newspapers for free, and the custom of the time allowed journalists to borrow freely from one another, so long as proper credit was given to the paper that originated the story. The following summary story of the recent campaigning in Virginia, for example, was taken from the Charleston Mercury, *but it first appeared in the* Richmond Dispatch *some days earlier.*

Charleston Mercury, 3 July 1862

THE GREAT BATTLE OF RICHMOND
DETAILS OF THE ENGAGEMENTS
THE BATTLE OF BEAVER DAM CREEK
CAPTURE OF ELLYSON'S MILLS
THE STORMING OF GAINES' MILLS, &c., &c., &c.

Owing to the total exclusion of the practised correspondents of the press from the lines of the Army of Richmond, the details of the recent terrible battles in front of that city, as we find them in our Virginia exchanges, are exceedingly vague and unsatisfactory. As the narrative given by the *Dispatch*, of Monday, seems to be more full and connected than the accounts contained in the other papers, we transfer it to our columns, interlarding it here and there with interesting extracts from other sources:

FRIDAY MORNING
AND SATURDAY MORNING—THE FIGHT AT
BEAVER DAM CREEK

When Gen. A. P. Hill had steadily driven the enemy from Meadow Bridge, and had taken up the line of march towards Mechanicsville and the road, evening had far advanced, and it was supposed that a halt would take place. Gen. Ripley, however, with the 44th and 48th Georgia, and 2d and 3d North Carolina, made an attack upon the Yankee fortifications at Ellyson's Mills, in which the 44th Georgia and 3d North Carolina suffered extremely, and did not succeed in taking them, owing to the impracticable nature of the ground. Operations were then suspended on our side, but the enemy kept up a deafening roar of artillery till late in the night. Longstreet's forces had meanwhile crossed, and marched parallel with the Chickahominy. The brigades of Gens. Featherstone and Pryor were in advance, and proceeding some distance, halted for the night. About midnight, Featherstone received orders to change his position, and to occupy a skirt of woods near Beaver Dam Creek, and facing the Federal batteries. He did so, and the men were scarcely asleep when, twilight approaching, the enemy discovered the bivouac, and immediately commenced to shell it vigorously. The men, thus unceremoniously aroused, seized their muskets and fell in, and Gen. Featherstone, just arrived from headquarters, led them to storm the position—mounting ten guns, and supported by two or three brigades. Sharp fighting now commenced on all sides, when Gen. Pryor sent for assistance, when Wilcox soon came upon the ground. To cover the infantry attack, and draw off the artillery fire, the 3d Richmond Howitzers, some pieces of the Donaldsonville and the Thomas Artillery moved up and played upon the enemy's position magnificently. Having engaged the enemy for a long time, and finding it impossible to cross the creek without a bridge, one was constructed by some of the 19th Mississippi and 14th Louisiana, under fire, when the whole force advanced and closed up with the enemy, driving them in great confusion from the field.

The attack of our men on this position was impetuous and daring, but the loss was great, for the foe was so screened by their position it was impossible to get at them properly.

THE FIGHT AT ELLYSON'S MILLS

While Featherstone, Pryor and Wilcox were thus successfully engaging the enemy on the right of our advance, Gen. Maxcy Gregg and his brigade were also hard at work, and successfully stormed the strong position of Ellyson's Mills, and took up the line of march on the left. They did not advance on the Mills by the road, as had been done on Friday evening by Ripley, but simply made a feint in that direction, crossed the main body higher up the creek, took the redoubts and rifle pits on flank, carried them with the bayonet, pushed through the camps, and followed the road towards Gaines' Mills, whither the enemy were retiring.

AT GAINES' MILLS

From prisoners captured at both positions—who proved to be of the Valley army—it was ascertained that we might expect stout resistance at Gaines' Mills, since three or four whole divisions were strongly encamped there—McClellan commanding in person, with Major Generals McCall, Porter, Sedgewick, and others—their estimated force being not less than thirty-odd thousand men. As our three columns moved by parallel lines, we followed and conversed with prisoners, who informed us that their loss, on Friday, at Meadow Bridge, Mechanicsville and Ellyson's Mills, had been fearful, and the whole night had been occupied in burial. The Federals carry off all their dead and wounded as fast as shot, and we only discover those who fall and are left at the actual moment of retreat. This information we believe to be correct.

The heads of our three columns having reached Walker Hogan's farm, north bank of the Chickahominy, about nine miles northeast of Richmond, all came to a halt, and Gens. Lee and Longstreet took up quarters in the house and made dispositions for a further advance towards Gaines' Mills, distant about one mile through the woods. Featherstone's brigade having suffered much in the morning, Wilcox led, being followed by Pryor, and Featherstone in reserve. The composition of Wilcox's command is mostly Alabamians; Pryor has the 14th Louisiana, St. Paul's battalion, 3d Virginia, and one other regiment; Featherstone has the 19th and 12th Mississippi, and 2d Mississippi battalion.

CHARACTER OF THE GROUND

Emerging from the woods, the road leads to the left and then to the right round Gaines' house, when the whole country, for the area of some two miles, is an open, unbroken succession of undulating hills. Standing at the north door of Gaines' house, the whole country to the right, for the distance of one mile, is a gradual slope towards a creek, through which the main road runs up an open hill and then winds to the right. In front, to the left, are orchards and gullies, running gradually to a deep creek. Directly in front, for the distance of a mile, the ground is almost table land, suddenly dipping to the deep creek mentioned above, being faced by a timber covered hill fronting all the table land. Beyond this timber covered hill, the country is again open, and a perfect plateau, a farm house and outhouses occupying the centre, the main road mentioned winding to the right and through all the Federal camps. To the left and rear of the second mentioned farm, a road comes in upon the flat lands, joining the main road mentioned. Thus, to recapitulate, except the deep creek and timber covered hill beyond it, the whole country,

as seen from the north door of Gaines' house, is unbroken, open, undulating, and table land, the right forming a descent to the wood covered creek, the left being dips and gullies, with dense timber still farther to the left; the front being for the most part table land. These particulars of the position are as correct, perhaps, as can be mentioned; but, without a map it will always be difficult to understand the topography of this hard fought and victorious field of Gaines' Mills.

But to the southeast of Gaines' house is a large tract of timber, commanding all advances upon the main road, and in this McClellan and McCall had posted a strong body of skirmishers, with artillery, to annoy our flank and rear when advancing on their camps on the high grounds, if we did so by the main road or over the table lands to the north.

STORMING ENTRENCHMENTS

It is now being 3 p.m., and the head of our column in view of the Federal camps, Gen. Pryor was sent forward with his brigade to drive away the heavy mass of skirmishers posted to our rear to annoy the advance. This being accomplished with great success, and with little loss to us, Pryor returned and awaited orders. Meanwhile the Federals, from their camps and several positions on the high grounds, swept the whole face of the country with their numerous artillery, which would have annihilated our entire force if not screened in the dips of the land and in gullies to our left. Advancing cautiously but rapidly in the skirt of woods and in the dips to the left, Wilcox and Pryor deployed their men into line of battle—Featherstone being in the rear—and suddenly appearing on the plateau facing the timber-covered hill, rushed down into the wide gully, crossed it, clambered over all the felled timber, stormed the timber breastworks beyond it, and began the ascent of the hill, under a terrific fire of sharpshooters, and an incessant discharge of grape and canister, from pieces posted on the brow of the hill, and from batteries in their camps to the right on the high flat lands. Such a position was never stormed before. In descending into the deep creek, the infantry and artillery fire that assailed the three brigades was most terrific. Twenty-six pieces were thundering at them, and a perfect hailstorm of lead fell thick and fast around them. One of Wilcox's regiments wavered, down the General rushed, furiously sword in hand, and threatened to behead the first man that hesitated. Pryor steadily advanced, but slowly; and by the time that the three brigades had stormed the position, passed up the hill through timber, and over felled trees, Featherstone was far in advance. Quickly the Federals withdrew their pieces, and took up a fresh position to assail the three brigades advancing in perfect line of battle from the woods and upon the plateau. Officers had no horses, all were shot— Brigadiers marched on foot, sword in hand—regiments were commanded by Captains, and companies by Sergeants, yet onward they rushed, with yells and colors flying, and backward, still backward fell the Federals, their men tumbling every moment in scores. But what a sight met the eyes of these three gallant brigades! In front stood Federal camps, stretching to the northeast for miles! Drawn up in line of battle were more than three full divisions, commanded by McCall, Porter, Sedgewick, &c.,—banners darkened the air—artillery vomited forth incessant volleys of grape, canister and shell—heavy masses were moving on our left through the woods to flank us! Yet onward came Wilcox to the right, Pryor to the left, and Featherstone in the centre—one grand, matchless line of battle—almost consumed by exploits of the day—yet onward they advanced to the heart of the Federal position, and when the enemy had fairly succeeded in almost flanking us on the left, great commotion is heard in the woods!—volleys upon volleys are heard in rapid succession, which are recognized and cheered by our men. "It is Jackson!" they shout, "on the right and rear!" Yes, two or three brigades of Jackson's army have flanked the enemy, and are getting in the rear! Now the fighting was bitter and terrific. Worked up to madness, Wilcox, Featherstone and Pryor dash forward at a run, and drive the enemy with irresistible fury—to our left emerge Hood's Texan brigade, Whiting's comes after, and Pender follows! The line is now complete, and "forward" rings from one end of the line to the other, and the Yankees, over 30,000 strong, begin to retreat! Wheeling their artillery from the front, the Federals turn part of it to break our left, and save their retreat. The very earth shakes at the roar! Not one piece of ours has yet opened! All has been done with the bullet and bayonet, and onward press our troops through camps upon camps, capturing guns, stores, arms, clothing, &c. Yet, like bloodhounds on the trail, the six brigades sweep everything before them, presenting an unbroken, solid front, and, closing in upon the enemy, keep up an incessant succession of volleys upon their confused masses, and unerringly slaughtering them by hundreds and thousands!

"STONEWALL" AT WORK

But "where is Jackson?" ask all. He has travelled fast, and is heading the retreating foe, and as night closes in, all in anxiety for intelligence from him. 'Tis now about 7 p.m., and just as the rout of the enemy is complete—just as the last volleys are sounding in the enemy's rear, the distant and rapid discharges of cannon tell that Jackson has fallen upon the retreating column, broken it, and captured 3000 prisoners! Far in the night, his insatiable troops land upon the enemy, and for miles upon miles are dead, wounded, prisoners, wagons, cannon, &c., scattered in inextricable confusion upon the road. Thus, for four hours, did our inferior force, unaided by a single piece of artillery, withstand over thirty thousand of the enemy, assisted by twenty-six pieces of artillery!

In total, we captured many prisoners, and thirty pieces of artillery up to 5 p.m., Friday, and in the battle of Gaines' Mills, captured 26 field pieces, 15,000 stand of arms, 6 stand of colors, three Generals (Reynolds, Sanders and Rankin), and over 4000 prisoners, including dozens of officers of every grade from Colonel to Lieutenants of the line.

THE FEDERAL FORCE

Every arm of the service was well represented in the Federal line—cavalry were there in force, and, when our men emerged from the woods, attempted to charge, but the three brigades on the right, and Jackson's three brigades on the left, closed up ranks and poured such deadly volleys upon the horsemen, that they left the ground in confusion and entirely for their infantry to decide the day. McCall's, Porter's and Sedgewicke's "crack" divisions melted away before our advance, however; and, had the fight lasted one half hour longer, not one whole regiment would have survived it. McClellan, prisoners say, repeatedly was present, and directed movements, but, when the three brigades to our left emerged from the woods, such confusion and havoc ensued, that he gave orders to retreat, slipped off his horse, and escaped as best he could. Some say that he was severely wounded, and many officers (prisoners) believe the report that he was on the field is undoubtedly true; for everything had been previously prepared for a grand fight at Gaines' Mills—McClellan even promising to capture our whole force, should we attempt to storm his camps.

CHARGES AND REPULSES

Much has been said of repeated "charges" made, and "repulses." Wild imaginations have concocted many such foolish reports. There was but one "charge," and from the moment the word of command was given—"fix bayonets: forward!" our advance was never stopped despite the awful reception which met it. It is true that one or two regiments became confused in passing over the deep ditch, abattis, and timber earth work—it is also true that several slipped from the ranks and ran to the rear, but in many cases these were wounded men; but the total number of "stragglers" would not amount to more than one hundred. This is strictly true, and redounds to our immortal honor. These facts are true of Wilcox's, Pryor's, and Featherstone's brigades, who formed our right, and we are positive that from the composition of Whiting's, Hood's, and Pender's brigades, who flanked the enemy and formed our left, they never could be made to falter, for Whiting had the 11th, 16th and 2d Mississippi, and two other regiments, unknown to us—Hood had four Texan and one Georgia regiment, and the material of Pender's command was equally as good as any, and greatly distinguished itself. These were the troops mostly engaged and that suffered most. It is gross injustice in any to talk of our troops making "three charges," "repulses," &c., &c. Our troops received the command but once, and if Satan and all his host had confronted them, instead of mortal Yankees, the result would have been the same. There were no repulses.

AT GARNETT'S FARM

About eleven o'clock Saturday, Capt. Moody's battery opened fire upon the entrenchments of the enemy, located just beyond Garnett's Farm. The battery fired some ten or fifteen minutes, and meanwhile a body of infantry, consisting of the 7th and 8th Georgia regiments, moved up under cover of the fire from the field pieces. The 8th, in advance, charged across a ravine and up a hill, beyond which the Yankee entrenchments lay. They gained the first line of works and took possession of them; but, it is proper to state, this was unoccupied at the time by the Yankees. The fire of the enemy was murderous, and as soon as our men reached the brow of the hill, rapid volleys of grape, canister, and musketry were poured into them. It was found almost impossible to proceed farther, but the attempt would have been made, had not orders been received to fall back, which was done in good order, still under fire.

The loss in the 7th is reported at seventy odd men killed, wounded and missing. In the 8th, upwards of eighty. Col. Lamar, of the 8th, was severely wounded in the groin, and fell into the hands of the enemy. Lieut. Col. Towers was captured, but uninjured. The Yankees were completely hidden behind their works, and did not suffer much apparently. We took a captain, lieutenant, and some five or six privates, the Yankee picket force at the point. Later a flag of truce was granted to take away our dead and wounded, but a conference with Col. Lamar was refused. The Federal surgeons, however, did not think his wound a fatal one, and, therefore, would not allow him to be taken away.

THE YORK RIVER RAILROAD OCCUPIED

General Lee pushed his advance until 10 o'clock Saturday night, and at 11 was in occupancy of the York River Railroad, the enemy's principal line of communication. This in effect pierces the enemy's centre, and separates their forces on the north side of the Chickahominy from those on the south side. The Confederate forces occupied the enemy's position at the White House, on the Pamunkey, but all the stores of the enemy at that point were destroyed by them in their retreat.

THE EVENTS OF SUNDAY. MCCLELLAN ELUDES US AND RETREATS TOWARDS JAMES RIVER

About 1 a.m. Sunday morning, our pickets down the Nine Mile Road were fiercely attacked by the enemy, and a severe and lively fight ensued. The enemy was easily driven back with loss, many prisoners falling in our hands. Many of the Federals threw down their arms and surrendered voluntarily. Sunday morning, about six or seven o'clock, another fierce picket fight occurred. Gen. Griffith's Mississippi brigade moved down, and pursued them past their fortifications, which were found for the most part deserted. It thus became a matter of fact that the enemy were in full flight.

Pursuit was instantly made, and several fights ensued. All their camps—wagons, commissary and quartermaster camps, also—were totally destroyed. Immense piles of stores were blazing at the moment of our visit, the Mississippians pursuing over the red ashes of the camps and stores. Land explosions were heard during the afternoon, caused by the destruction of

vast quantities of ammunition. Dense columns of smoke darkened the sky. The railroad Merrimac was far in advance of our men, and was vigorously shelling the enemy at every turn.

It is supposed that McClellan's movement is to reach his gunboats, and effect his escape by the James river. Sixty transports are reported to be lying in the stream about fifteen miles below this city; but McClellan must have been a wiser and more provident commander than we are willing to believe, if he has prepared transportation in advance for this avenue of escape.

> Sunday at about noon our troops advanced in the direction of the works, which were found deserted.

THE PURSUIT

At a late hour Sunday evening our advancing columns had not come up with him and were harassing him. The enemy could not have been more than twelve hours in advance, and we are assured that the roads taken by our pursuing columns, and the disposition of our forces between him and the river, will cut off his retreat, and enable us to complete our victory by demoralizing his whole command or capturing a large portion of it. In any event, however, it is mortifying that the enemy has eluded us when we had him in a critical situation, all the advantages of which it will be impossible to renew.

It is impossible to ascertain the precise manner in which McClellan managed to elude our guard.

Six miles from Richmond, on the York River Road, the enemy were in force on Saturday night. During the night our pickets heard them busily at work hammering, sawing, &c. The rumble of cannon carriages was also constantly audible. Sunday about noon our troops advanced in the direction of the works, which were found deserted. Their entrenchments were found to be formidable and elaborate. That immediately across the railroad, at the six mile post, which had been supposed to be a light earth work, designed to sweep the railroad, turned out to be an immense embrasured fortification, extending for hundreds of yards on either side of the track, and capable of protecting ten thousand men. Within this work were found great quantities of fixed ammunition, which had apparently been prepared for removal, and then deserted. All the cannon, as at other entrenchments, had been carried off. McClellan doubtless imagines that if he can keep his guns from falling into our hands it may furnish him with grounds for a future boast. He will claim to have "retreated in good order, carrying off all his guns." These guns he will probably find it convenient to cast into the James River or the Chickahominy.

After passing this battery, our forces cautiously pushed their way down the railroad and to the right, in the direction of the Seven Pines. At three o'clock a dense column of smoke was seen to issue from the woods two miles in advance of the battery and half a mile to the right of the railroad. The smoke was found to proceed from a perfect mountain of the enemy's commissary stores, which they had fired and deserted. The pile was at least thirty feet high, with a base sixty feet in breadth, consisting of sugar, coffee and bacon, butter, prepared meat, vegetables, &c. The fire had so far enveloped the heap as to destroy the value of its contents. The field and woods around this spot was covered with every description of clothing and camp equipage. Blue greatcoats lined the earth like leaves in Valambross. No indication was wanting that the enemy had left this encampment in haste and disorder.

THE LOSSES ON BOTH SIDES

We have been at great pains to ascertain the number of our wounded in the engagements commenced last Thursday evening, and continued almost uninterruptedly since, and are glad to announce that it has fallen far short of our fears and expectations. At five o'clock yesterday evening all of our wounded had been removed from the field, either to the roadside hospitals or to this city. Two thousand have been received at the city hospitals, and gentlemen who have been on the different battlefields, engaged in the removal of the wounded since the beginning of the first fight, inform us there are at most not more than from four to five hundred in the roadside or field hospitals.

Of the number of our killed we have no means of making an estimate, but it will be seen that our wounded fall short of those of the Seven Pines by several hundred.

With regard to the enemy's losses, the estimates vary from 15,000 to 20,000 killed, wounded and missing. Five thousand prisoners had been taken up to Sunday noon, and the Yankee loss in killed and wounded, at the least calculation, was 10,000.

THE BOOTY

The cannon and arms captured in this battle were numerous and of very superior workmanship. The 26 pieces were the most beautiful we have ever seen, while immense piles of guns could be seen on every hand—many scarcely having the manufacturer's "finish" even tarnished. The enemy seemed quite willing to throw them away on the slightest pretext, dozens being found with loads still undischarged. The number of small arms captured, we understand, was not less than 15,000, of every calibre and every make. The field pieces taken are principally Napoleon, Parrot and Blakely (English) guns. We have captured large quantities of army wagons, tents, equipments, shoes.

Money was found quite abundantly among the slain. Some men, in interring the dead, often searched the pockets, etc., one man finding not less than $150 in gold; another fished out of some old clothes not less than $500; another $1000 in Federal notes. Watches, both gold and silver, were found among the spoils, one lucky individual having not less than six chronometers ticking in his pocket at one time. As a general thing, more money was found upon the dead on the field than on any other of which we have heard.

Clothing in abundance was scattered about, and immense piles of new uniforms were found untouched. Our men seemed to take great delight in assuming Federal officers' uniforms, and strutted about serio-comically, much to the amusement of dusty, powder-begrimmed youths, who sat lolling and smoking in the shade. Every conceivable article of clothing was found in these divisional camps, and came quite apropos to our needy soldiery, scores of whom took a cool bath, and changed old for new underclothing, many articles being of costly material, and quite unique.

The amount of ammunition found was considerable, and proved of very superior quality and manufacture. The exact amount captured we have not yet ascertained, but immense piles of boxes were scattered through the camps.

INCIDENTS

The Federal flag made by the Yankees to float over our Capitol was captured by Major Bloomfield, of General Magruder's staff, in the Federal camps, and was exhibited, with great applause, to our troops. It is an immense piece of work, fully twenty feet long, having thirteen stripes and thirty-two stars thereon. We understand McClellan received it as a present from the ladies of the [*unreadable*] of Boston, and promised to plant it on the [*unreadable*] "last ditch" to which the rebels should be run, and afterwards would elevate it, with all military honors, on our Capitol at Richmond.

An armistice of two days, it is reported, was asked by McClellan to bury the dead, &c., but Gen. Lee, it is said, replied, "There is no time now to think of the dead. The only proposition I can receive from Gen. McClellan is for an unconditional surrender."

All the vessels of the enemy, which have for some weeks past been anchored near Verina, six miles below Drury's Bluff, departed on Sunday. It is not known whether they went down the river for the purpose of bringing up reinforcements, or to be in convenient distance to take on the retreating army of McClellan.

The field presented the most remarkable and singular appearance, being thickly dotted with red breeched Zouaves. The water was plenty and good, and our trains following the army were put in fine condition transporting provisions to our men. The destruction of horses was terrible. One shot is said to have killed no less than sixteen in a single battery.

A large number of the quarters of the Yankee officers on the Chickahominy, which are now in possession of our brave men, were filled with the choicest edibles, brandies, whisky, wines, &c., all of which were, of course, confiscated.

The Pennsylvania Eleventh (Reserves) and the Fourth New Jersey were taken entire, every commissioned officer, colonels, majors, captains, lieutenants, surgeons and assistant surgeons falling into our hands. Beyond these two regiments the prisoners were mostly United States regulars, with a slight sprinkling of blue Connecticut Yankees. When the Eleventh Pennsylvania marched into town their rear was brought up by six negro men and a boy about fifteen. Five of the men wore Yankee uniform pants, while the boy was decked out in full Union uniform. The negros were the property of Mrs. Watts and other citizens of Hanover, who had run off from their owners.

The regiment of Bucktail Rifles, of Fremont's command, whose watchword was, "We never Surrender!" adorned the streets yesterday, with their bucktail plumes, on their way to the Confederate States prison. Nearly every one of them was either killed or captured.

The Federal wounded were collected together and formed a very large field hospital. The courtyard of a farmhouse was selected and scores could be seen reclining on the grass and expert surgeons operating with much skill and zeal. By mutual agreement surgeons are not considered prisoners of war, hence at the close of the late battle, many Federal surgeons remained behind and their services seemed very much appreciated by the men. As many as could be were conveyed to town and attended to, good conveyance being furnished, and much care manifested for their welfare.

G. B. CUTHBERT: LATEST REPORTS FROM RICHMOND—LEE DRIVES McCLELLAN FROM CITY

The Charleston paper's Richmond correspondent joyfully reported on the repulse of McClellan from Richmond. The story illustrates how difficult it was to obtain news when correspondents were not with armies. All sorts of rumors were floating around Richmond, and none could be confirmed, but the news of Lee's rout of McClellan was reported with great joy.

Charleston Mercury, 7 July 1862

NEWS BY TELEGRAPH
THE END OF THE GREAT BATTLE—LATEST REPORTS FROM RICHMOND

RICHMOND, Friday, July 4.—Owing to the remoteness of the fugitive Yankee army, it is very difficult now to obtain information of the situation of affairs. Various rumors are afloat, but none of them can be traced to trustworthy sources. It is only certain that the Grand Army of McCLELLAN has been completely routed, and that, whilst a portion of his force may have escaped in their transports, a large number will be captured. Our victory is complete. Captain FRANK RAVENAL, of Gen. RIPLEY'S Staff, fell while leading a regiment in the thickest of the fight.

Second Despatch.) Night. It is not definitely known where the enemy now is. It is supposed that some have crossed the river, that some have gone down the river in transports, and that the bulk of the army is trying to fall back to Yorktown. JACKSON and LONGSTREET are hunting them up. More fighting may take place. Active movements are going forward on our part. Hopes are still entertained of capturing a large portion of McCLELLAN'S army.

RICHMOND, July 4. To the Editor of the Mercury: The following is a list of the killed and wounded of the Palmetto Guard in the battles before Richmond:

Killed: J. H. Royal. Slightly Wounded: Lt. T. S. Brownfield, M. Prendergast, E. L. Tillinghast, J. E. Dubart, M. Brailsford, R. G. Shoolbred, J. E. Millar.

G. B. CUTHBERT,
Capt. Palmetto Guard, 2d Regt. S.C.V.

Shenandoah Valley

Stonewall Jackson, General Thomas J. Jackson, was Robert E. Lee's only rival for the devotion, affection, and trust of the Confederate people. He gained that devotion in large part as a result of the campaign he conducted in the Shenandoah Valley in May and June 1862. Jackson had one job to accomplish in the Valley: He was to stop any Union advance up the Valley and joining McClellan's forces advancing up the Virginia peninsula toward Richmond. Jackson accomplished his objective beyond what anyone could have anticipated or hoped for. With fewer than 18,000 men, Jackson successfully held back some 70,000 Union soldiers and led the federal military authorities to change their whole approach to the fighting in Virginia.

On 1 May, Jackson was at Swift Run Gap. He faced two advancing armies: General Nathaniel P. Banks was coming up the Valley, and General John C. Frémont was advancing from West Virginia with about 15,000 men. Jackson divided his army, leaving about 8,000 men with Brigadier General Richard S. Ewell to meet Banks, while he took the remainder of his force and moved toward McDowell. There, on 8 May, he met Frémont's advanced guard and threw them back. Frémont halted. For the next two weeks, Jackson quickly marched his troops through the Valley. On 23 May, Jackson's men attacked and routed the federal garrison at Front Royal and began their move on Banks's rear. Banks retired to Winchester. On 25 May, Jackson's men threw Banks out of Winchester and drove his army all the way across the Potomac River. Jackson captured 2,000 Union soldiers and 10,000 stands of small arms. Banks lost 1,500 men, killed and wounded, to the Confederacy's 400. Jackson once again had caught the attention of Washington war leaders, and they, once again, readjusted their strategy and the deployment of federal troops.

Hoping to catch Jackson between Winchester and Harper's Ferry, Union armies under Frémont and James Shields tried to squeeze the Confederates from both the east and the west. Frémont's 15,000 men marched east from their position southwest of Winchester, and Shields, with 10,000 men from McDowell's command, marched west, capturing Front Royal as he came. An additional 10,000 Union soldiers followed close behind Shields. Jackson avoided the trap. He marched his 15,000 men, 2,000 prisoners, and a double column of wagons up the Valley toward Harrisonburg. On 8 June, Ewell's men repulsed an attack from Frémont at Cross Keys. A day later, Jackson's force attacked Shields at Port Republic. The double victories cleared the Shenandoah Valley of Union forces and brought the campaign to an end.

Clearing the Valley of Union forces was only one of the tangible outcomes of Jackson's campaign. He cost the Union army more than 5,000 casualties, and he captured 9,000 small arms, while losing only a few more than 3,000 of his own troops. His campaign kept thousands of federal soldiers from reinforcing McClellan's almost-successful advance on Richmond, and Union soldiers came to have a dreadful fear of having Jackson in their rear. The campaign also produced a number of less tangible, though valuable, results. For example, Jackson's troops came to see him as a military mastermind. Their morale and esprit de corps skyrocketed. To serve in Jackson's "foot cavalry," as his men referred to themselves, was to be among the elite Confederate forces.

Real-time reporting of the Shenandoah Valley Campaign was limited. Jackson, by nature rather taciturn, was not friendly with reporters, and he had none with him on this campaign. What news did trickle out of the Valley came from telegraphic operators and local newspapers who could get information from soldiers or send a reporter out to observe what was happening.

DR. GEORGE W. BAGBY: NEWS OF McCLELLAN'S ADVANCE ON RICHMOND, JACKSON'S OPERATIONS IN SHENANDOAH VALLEY

George W. Bagby, Hermes of the Charleston Mercury, *provided an update on Jackson's progress in the Shenandoah Valley, based on a telegraph the general himself had sent back to Richmond. The story went under the heading "The Siege of the Capital" because its initial paragraph also updated readers on McClellan's advance on Richmond, the advance Jackson's efforts in the Shenandoah Valley were intended to retard.*

Charleston Mercury, 29 May 1862

THE SIEGE OF THE CAPITAL

(FROM OUR OWN CORRESPONDENT.)

RICHMOND, Monday, May 26.

If Theophilus Thistle, the successful thistlesifter, in sifting a sieve full of unsifted thistles, thrust three thousand thistles into the thick of his thumb, then must Theophilus Thistle have been the Richmond correspondent of THE CHARLESTON MERCURY on Saturday last, endeavoring to sift the truth out of a city full of unsifted rumors, reports and "reliables" in regard to the skirmishes of that day. The nearest approach to the truth seems to be this: There were two engagements—one of artillery at Mechanicsville (a blacksmith's shop and a dilapidated tavern are dignified with that name), and another of infantry at the New Bridge, on the Meadow Bridge road, which crosses the Chickahominy a mile and a half or two miles above Mechanicsville. In both of these engagements we were worsted—owing to the inferiority of our forces. Gen. Johnston refused to send reinforcements, his aim being, as many to suppose, to draw the enemy over, or to gain time for the completion of certain arrangements by which troops can be rapidly concentrated upon the field of the great battle. General Johnston is too acute to suppose that McClellan, the Cautious, will cross the swamp in force. He will occupy the bridges, while he pushes his men to the head of the Swamp, in the direction of the junction of the Central and Fredericksburg Roads, and there, I feel pretty sure, the great battle will take place. Anderson has already fallen back to the Junction, some of Stuart's cavalry went forward on Saturday, and yesterday a heavy column of infantry marched after them. The rest of the army was engaged in cooking four days' provisions, and this morning the wagons are bringing all the baggage into town. The Petersburg Road is held subject to orders for the transportation exclusively of troops. It is plain, therefore, that the battle is to be no child's play, and that it will take place neither to-day nor to-morrow, as many imagine, but whenever the disposition of the scattered forces can be arranged to the satisfaction of the Generals.

A friend has just this moment come in to tell me of Jackson's

despatch to Gen. Lee, about the taking of 2000 prisoners at Winchester, 2000 more at Front Royal, all the baggage, etc., and still pursuing. This may alter the programme to some extent. It sends Shields and McDowell back to Washington, unless there are forces there of which we know nothing—only 3000 were there at last accounts—but McClellan must fight all the same. It will never do for him to go back to Washington again, or even to Fortress Monroe. He must fight where he is, against men inspired by the memories of Williamsburg and the recent victories of Jackson. An acquaintance, who rode through our lines, on the Chickahominy, yesterday, says he was told by Gen. Howell Cobb that the men were much exasperated by Johnston's positive order for them to withdraw from the infantry fight of the day before—our cavalry having just come up to charge the enemy and rout him, as they would almost certainly have done. With this temper, among our soldiers, it is not unreasonable to expect excellent results from the great battle.

It seems Ewell did join Jackson last Thursday, as I stated, and both were engaged in the affair at Winchester. Some doubt was entertained about yesterday's telegram concerning the Front Royal engagement, except by those who knew that Jackson had written to Hon. Mr. Boteler to come on, that the time had come when, according to promise made a month or more ago, he would take him home to his house in Jefferson county, not far from Harper's Ferry.

Rather a strange Sunday spectacle was witnessed yesterday, to wit: a party of a dozen young men, armed with very long muskets, very small cartridge boxes and very large haversacks, going out to hunt Yankees. They returned without any game. Not a syllable from Corinth since Thursday last—strange! We are preparing to raise a balloon on Church Hill. As both armies are now bivouacing in the dense woods, this ballooning business does little good except when columns are in motion. If these are moved at night, balloons are of no use except to detect wagon trains. The Examiner has a good article against the defensive policy. The Enquirer says that Yankees are hanging guerillas, and calls for retaliation.

HERMES.

AN ANONYMOUS REPORT: ACHIEVEMENTS OF STONEWALL JACKSON IN SHENANDOAH VALLEY CAMPAIGN

The following story, copied from the Richmond Whig, *offered a summary of Jackson's Valley campaign, with particular focus on the later battles. The story only slightly exaggerated Jackson's accomplishments. Because of the lack of information about the campaign, reconstructed narratives such as this one were the most common form of reportage about Jackson's work in the Shenandoah Valley.*

Charleston Mercury, 18 June 1862

THE ACHIEVEMENTS OF STONEWALL JACKSON—THE CAMPAIGN IN THE VALLEY—BATTLES OF CROSS KEYS AND LEWISTON

In the following article, a writer in the Richmond Whig gives some interesting particulars of the glorious campaign of General Stonewall JACKSON in the Valley of Virginia.

In reviewing the operations of General Jackson for the last three months, it will be found that he has probably accomplished more, in that brief period, with the means at his command, than ever was achieved by any other General of ancient or modern times. I believe that his campaign during the Spring will compare favorably even with the almost incredible achievements of Napoleon in his celebrated campaign in Italy. With a handful of citizen soldiers, but partially drilled, and poorly armed and equipped, he has, in little more than sixty days, marched over five hundred miles, fought about twelve battles—five of which were pitched battles—defeated four Generals—routed four armies—captured millions of dollars worth of stores, &c., and killed, wounded and secured as prisoners, almost as many of the enemy as he had soldiers under his command. These are startling assertions, but they are literally true. Explore the pages of history, and see whether they afford the record of more brilliant successes.

In the latter part of March, Jackson was at Winchester, with about three or four thousand men. Being pressed by a superior force, he was compelled to fall back before the hosts of Gen. Banks. Slowly and in good order he retired up the Valley, contesting every inch of ground. At Kernstown he turned upon his pursuer, and for two successive days gave him battle. And here permit me to remark, that the recent occupation of the lower Valley by our forces has enabled us to gather facts in regard to those battles which add new lustre to the glories of those fights. It is now ascertained that Jackson's force at Kernstown was not much over 2500, whilst that of the enemy was 12,000. Of the enemy, 860 were buried in Winchester and on the battlefield, many others were sent home for interment, and 1500 were wounded, whilst our loss in killed and wounded was less than 500. The 84th Pennsylvania Regiment went into the battle with 800 men and came out with 300.

Having taught the enemy this severe lesson, Jackson continued his progress up the Valley, holding the whole army of the enemy in check until he could obtain reinforcements. Arriving at Harrisonburg, with his men wearied and exhausted by continual marching and skirmishing, Jackson left the main Valley road and turned off eastward on the Swift Run Gap road. His object was to cross the Shenandoah river, and, having placed this strong defence between him and the enemy, to lie quiet, to give his men a chance to rest—to watch the movements of the enemy, and, to wait reinforcements. Here he was joined by Gen. Ewell, but their united force was not sufficient to meet the enemy in the open field. It must be remembered, too, that at this time Staunton and the upper part of the Valley were threatened by a large force from the West, under Milroy. Gen. Johnson, with about 3500 men, was the only obstacle to the advance of Milroy. Being thus with a command of less than 20,000 men, including Johnson's, and threatened by Banks, with an estimated force of 35,000, on the one side, and Milroy, with six or eight thousand, on the other, he was obliged to accomplish by stratagem what he could not effect in the open field. To this end, he moved across the Blue Ridge, as if with the view of uniting with the forces of Gen. Jos. E. Johnston. He took care, however, to leave Ewell's forces concealed in the gorges of the mountains, near Swift Run, and Ashby's cavalry to picket the country closely, so as to cut off all information from the enemy as to his true purposes. The maneuver effectually deceived Banks, and he forthwith telegraphed to Washington that Jackson had evacuated the Valley and fled to Gordonsville! In a day or two Jackson turned up at Staunton, and, hastening to join General Ed. Johnson, he fell upon Milroy, at McDowell, and routed him, and pursued him to Franklin, in Pendleton county.

In the meantime, Banks, supposing that Jackson was east of the Ridge, weakened his force, by sending Shields with 10,000 men to join McDowell, and another detachment to reinforce Milroy. Jackson having thus cleared his left flank, by dispersing Milroy's forces, hastened by the nearest route towards Harrisonburg, where he could act in conjunction with Ewell. Ewell came out of his hiding place, and, while a portion of the conjoint forces marched down the Valley turnpike towards Strasburg, to which place the greater portion of Banks' army had fallen back, the residue crossed, the Massanutten Mountain, and hurried down the banks of the Shenandoah to Front Royal, where they attacked and captured the forces stationed at that point. The sound of the cannon gave Banks the first intimation of the proximity of an enemy, and he immediately commenced his precipitate flight to Winchester. An effort was made to intercept him near Newton, but the attempt was only partially successful. The swift-footed Banks had passed the junction of the road, with a part of his army, before the wearied forces of Jackson could come up with them. He pierced Banks' column, however, and drove a portion of it southward up the road, while the main body fled towards Winchester. A running fight of eight or ten miles ensued, Banks flying and Jackson pursuing. Near Winchester the enemy made a stand, but the invincible columns of Jackson bore down upon them with irresistible power, and they broke and fled ingloriously, and were pursued through the streets of Winchester and on to Martinsburg and Harper's Ferry; where the demoralized elements of the once powerful army of Banks sought refuge in Maryland. At Winchester, and Martinsburg, and Front Royal, stores, estimated at from three to five millions of dollars, were taken and near 3000 prisoners. Encumbered with his spoil, and embarrassed by his prisoners, on the very borders of an Enemy's country, Jackson found himself in a critical position. He remained only long enough to secure the booty, which was of the highest importance to our army, and having sent that in wagons up the Valley, he followed to protect his trains and put his prisoners in a place of security.

We all recollect the sensation which these daring achievements created throughout the country. Lincoln was thrown into a paroxysm of fright, and telegrams were despatched throughout the North calling for the whole militia force of the country to protect the United States Capital, which it was feared Jackson might seize at an early day.

When the authorities at Washington recovered from their panic, they were overwhelmed with shame and confusion, and immediately set to work to avenge the wound that had been inflicted on their national honor. It was ascertained that Jackson had but a small force—that he was encumbered with immense trains and vast numbers of prisoners, and that he would have to march 120 miles before he could reach a point of safety. The whole Northern press teemed with threats and promises of the speedy annihilation of Jackson and his daring followers. Three armies—one from the North, under Dix—one from the West, under Fremont and Milroy, and one from the East, under Shields—were immediately set in motion to intercept him, and it was even said, by some of the Northern journals, that Jackson had fallen into the trap that had been set for him.

The reader will observe the position of the parties— Jackson's forces were scattered from the Potomac to Winchester, Dix came by railway from Baltimore, Fremont was west of the North Mountain, at Franklin, in Pendleton, and Shields was east of the Blue Ridge, near Warrenton. The plan was for Fremont and Shields to push forward and unite their forces at Strasburg, and cut off Jackson's retreat up the Valley, while Dix would press him in the rear. The eagle eye of Jackson saw the danger at a glance. By a forced march of over 100 miles in three days, he won the race for Strasburg but, so close was the struggle, that, as he passed the proposed point of union, his rear guard was compelled to fight the advanced columns of the enemy.

Then commenced another retreat and running fight up the Valley, Jackson contesting the advance of the enemy so as to secure his trains and prisoners. When he had accomplished this object, learning that the enemy had divided his overwhelming force into two columns, one of which, under Shields, was advancing east of the Shenandoah river, and the other, under Fremont, up the main Valley turnpike, with a view to unite in the upper part of the Valley, Jackson again turned off at Harrisonburg, having previously caused Ashby to burn the bridge over the Shenandoah, near Swift Run Gap, and went to Port Republic, a small village situated at the point where the North and South rivers come together and form the Shenandoah. There was a bridge over the North River at Port Republic, which was the only means of crossing the stream, which was swollen by recent rains. Jackson occupied the ground near both ends of this bridge, and thus had it in his power to elect which column he would fight, as the two were separated by an impassable river. On Sunday, he determined to attacked Fremont first, and accordingly, leaving a sufficient force to guard the bridge, he marched about five miles to the Cross Keys to meet Fremont, and after a terrible conflict of many hours he succeeded in repulsing Fremont with great loss. He then returned to the bridge, and after passing over it to the Port Republic side, burnt it, so as to prevent Fremont, in case he should be reinforced and rally, from coming to the rescue of Shields. The result vindicated his sagacity, for Fremont on Monday was reinforced and did rally, and advanced with an overwhelming force to renew the conflict with Jackson. But, when he reached the bank of the river, he fount that Jackson had passed over and destroyed the bridge, and that an impassable stream was between them. Fremont was thus compelled to be an unwilling witness of the conflict between Jackson and Shields, for, as soon as the bridge had been effectually destroyed and his rear thus secured, Jackson advanced upon Shields, who was encamped at Lewiston, the estate of Gen. Samuel H. Lewis, about two miles north of Port Republic. Shields was aware of his approach, and made every preparation to receive him. The attack was made about sunrise on Monday, 9th June, and lasted until about 10 or 11 o'clock, when the forces of Shields broke and fled in utter confusion and dismay. The rout was complete. The slaughter was great, and the pursuit continued until a late hour of the day. About 1000 prisoners were taken, and six pieces of artillery. The whole road was strewed with knapsacks, arms, blankets, etc. Those who witnessed it think that the rout was as complete as that inflicted on Banks. The loss of the enemy in the two battles of Cross Keys and Lewiston, in killed, wounded and missing, is estimated at near 6000, while ours does not exceed 600. It seems almost incredible, but it is nevertheless, true.

These two battles are among the most brilliant, if not the most brilliant, of the war. They are the crowning glory of Jackson and his gallant associates. No! I recall that. Not the crowning glory, for I believe still brighter wreaths are destined to encircle their brows if this unhallowed war shall continue.

Thus it will be seen that Jackson and his army, in one month, have routed Milroy, annihilated Banks, discomfited Fremont and overthrown Shields! Was there ever such a series of victories won by an inferior force by dauntless courage and consummate generalship?

With 50,000 fresh troops under Jackson, Lincoln would be compelled to raise the siege of Richmond and look to the security of his own Capital.

Fremont still remains on the hills opposite Port Republic. He is reported to have, about 20,000 men. Shields had 9000, and Jackson encountered him with about the same number.

What the next move will be, it would be impossible for me to say, even if I knew. But Jackson keeps his own counsels. He speaks by deeds, and not by words. Suffice it to say, he will strike at the right time, and in the right place. Whatever courage, skill, industry and patriotism can accomplish, he will be sure to effect.

Second Manassas

Strategically, Lee came out of the Peninsula Campaign in a strong position. True, his smaller army had taken many more casualties than McClellan's, but the sacrifice of lives had kept the federals out of the Confederate capital. McClellan entrenched his command at Harrison's Landing and asked for reinforcements, suggesting to Lincoln's government that he faced a foe of some 200,000 or more. An exasperated Union president had enough of McClellan's procrastination. Lincoln relieved McClellan of the command of all Virginia forces, though the Union commander retained command of a portion of the army in Virginia. Lincoln appointed General John Pope to take command of a new force to be called the Army of Virginia, which had been pieced together from the commands of McDowell, Frémont, and Banks. Pope was a fairly competent commander, but he was not a nice man, and his treatment of the people of Virginia sufficiently angered Lee that the Confederate general developed a personal grudge against his opponent. Not only did Pope mistreat Southerners, whom he considered to be traitors; he was also obnoxious to his own soldiers. Lincoln made one other significant change to the Union command structure: On 11 July, he recalled Halleck from the West to become the Union's general-in-chief.

Lee found the movements of the Union army in the summer of 1862 to be disconcerting. Curious about what exactly was happening, he sent Jackson to observe Pope. On 9 August, Jackson and Pope's commands met at Cedar Mountain, near Culpeper. The engagement was small, but it would have dire consequences for Pope. By nightfall on 9 August, Jackson had driven the Union forces back to Culpeper before withdrawing across the Rapidan.

Soon Lee learned that McClellan's portion of the Union army was moving once again toward the Peninsula, and he knew he would have to try to crush Pope before McClellan could arrive. Lee realized that if McClellan's forces met up with Pope's, the Union armies together would total 150,000 against his own army of 55,000. Lee's strategy violated a basic stratagem of war: Never separate an army in the presence of the enemy, but that was exactly what Lee did. He sent half of his forces with Major General James Longstreet across the Rappahannock to occupy Pope. The other half, he sent with Stonewall Jackson to the northwest with order to make a surprise attack on the rear of Pope's army. They planned a joint strike somewhere near Manassas.

In the meantime, a quick raid by some of Pope's men on the Confederate cavalry captured J.E.B. Stuart's fancy plumed hat, his scarlet-lined cape, and his adjutant. Outraged, Stuart planned a retaliatory raid of his own. On 22 August, Stuart overran Pope's headquarters and made off with the payroll cash, Pope's personal baggage, which included the Union general's dress uniform, 300 prisoners, and important papers that outlined Union plans.

Not long afterward, Jackson's force fell on Pope's. After marching 54 miles in two days of hot August weather, Jackson's men cut Pope's rail and communications lines and looted and burned the Union supply depot at Manassas. Pope turned to follow

Jackson, but he had taken up a hidden defensive position just west of the First Manassas battlefield. On 28 August, Jackson's men clashed with Union soldiers near Groveton. The fighting was ferocious, and it alerted Pope to Jackson's location. Pope ordered his forces to concentrate near Groveton to destroy Jackson once and for all in what would be the two-day-long Second Battle of Manassas.

PETER W. ALEXANDER: ACCOUNT OF SECOND BATTLE OF MANASSAS

As Pope concentrated his forces near Groveton, Lee and Longstreet were advancing to reinforce Jackson. Pope refused to believe Longstreet's command was near, and on 30 August he attacked Jackson, only to be hit in his flank by Longstreet. Pope's army was forced back across Bull Run toward the defenses of Washington in a decisive defeat. The Union withdrawal was in good order. Lee pursued, and in the Battle of Chantilly on 31 August, during a blinding rainstorm, Jackson's assault was checked by Union General Philip Kearny, who was killed in hand-to-hand fighting. Lee made no further advances. Confederate losses in the campaign were 9,197 to the Union's more than 16,000. The Savannah Republican's famous correspondent, Peter W. Alexander, was on hand for the fighting at Second Manassas and filed the following summary story. Three days after the battle, Pope was relieved of his command and sent to fight the Sioux in Minnesota. McClellan was again in command of the Army of the Potomac. Lee's victory had been decisive and provided a much-needed boost for Confederate morale.

Savannah Republican, 9 September 1862

**ARMY CORRESPONDENCE
OF THE SAVANNAH REPUBLICAN**

**Battle of Manassas No. Two
Revised and Improved Edition**

*Another Brilliant Victory—Enemy Routed at all Points—
Heavy Loss—Bartow and Bee Avenged—McClellan and Halleck on the Field*

BATTLE FIELD OF MANASSAS, Aug. 31st.

Another great battle has been fought on the bloody Plains of Manassas, and once more has Heaven crowned our banners with the laurel of victory. The conflict opened Friday afternoon, and last night not a Federal soldier remained on the south side of Bull run, except the prisoners we had taken and those who sleep the sleep that shall know no waking until the great day of Judgment. The people of the Confederate States—those at home no less than the invincible heroes in the field, and the friends of justice and the lovers of liberty everywhere—assuredly have cause for rejoicing and thanksgiving. Never since Adam was planted in the garden of Eden, did a holier cause engage the hearts and arms of any nation; and never did any people establish more clearly their right to be freemen.

I did not arrive in time to witness the battle of Friday, the 29th. Leaving Gordonsville at 9 o'clock that day, on a freight train, I reached Rapidan Station, the present terminus of the railroad, at noon. There I took horse, forded the river; struck for the Rappahannock—forded that river also—to Warrenton

at one o'clock yesterday—rested my horse, and then took the turnpike for the battle-field, fourteen miles distant, where I arrived in one hour and fifteen minutes, and just in time to witness, for the second time, the triumph of Confederate arms on these ever memorable plains.

I cannot undertake to give the number of men engaged on either side. It is not probably, however, that the enemy had more than 75,000 troops on the field. Our own forces were considerably less, a large part of the army not having arrived in time to participate in the fight. Longstreet's *corps d'armee* held the right, A. P. Hill's and Anderson's (late Huger's) division the centre, and Jackson's veterans the left. Jackson was the first to reach to plains below the Blue Ridge; Hill came next, and then Longstreet, who entered at Thoroughfare Gap. The enemy occupied the Gap with a full division, and seemed disposed to dispute the passage of our troops; but Toombs' and Anderson's Georgia brigades, which led the corps, made a bold dash and soon drove them away with but little loss. That was on Thursday, the 28th. Jackson had brought the enemy to bay between Gainesville and Groveton, two miles from the old battle field, on the Warrenton turnpike. Knowing this, Longstreet pressed forward, and succeeded in getting into position on the right of the turnpike, in time to hold that part of our lines while Jackson engaged the enemy on the left.

It should be stated that Longstreet played the enemy a clever trick before he left the south bank of the Rappahannock.

Jackson and Hill having moved around by Sperryville above, he made feints at several fords on the Rappahannock as if he would cross over, and thus drew the attention of the enemy to those points, whilst he put his forces in motion and marched rapidly to the northward and around to Gainesville. So successful was the manoeuvre that a late northern paper now before me congratulates its readers upon the brilliant victory achieved by the Federals in driving us away from the fords.

The enemy advanced to the attack on Friday. He was probably aware of Jackson's comparative weakness. He soon discovered, however, that heavy Confederate column (Longstreet's) had got into position on the right, and immediately commenced a retrograde movement. The battle, which was hotly contested for a time, in which the artillery took a prominent part, continued through the afternoon and resulted in the repulse of the enemy along the entire line. Jackson's forces were chiefly engaged and behaved with their usual gallantry. The scene of the conflict was just in front of Gainesville and on the left of the Warrenton turnpike as you look towards Washington.

The enemy were driven back to the edge of the old battle field of Manassas. The Confederates slept upon the field; and there awaited a renewal of the attack on yesterday. They were not disappointed, for the enemy again advanced against our left at 2 o'clock P.M., and engaged Jackson first. By three the engagement became general, and the battle was joined. Gen. Lee was in command, having come to the front some days ago. But a word of explanation in regard to the field and the position of the combatants.

The Warrenton and Alexandria Turnpike runs nearly eastward, and the road from Sudley ford on Bull Run to Manassas Junction north and South. These highways intersect each other in the centre of the old battle ground. Advancing down the turnpike our forces faced to the east and in the direction of Washington, while the enemy faced to the west, but not exactly towards Richmond. The line of battle, about three miles in length, extended across the turnpike almost at right angles and nearly parallel with and just west of Sudley road. The battle of Manassas was to be fought over, and the point to be decided was, whether we should advance upon Washington or the enemy upon Richmond. This was the issue, and this the battle ground.

We learn from prisoners that Halleck, McClelland and Pope were present. McClelland had brought up his old United States Regulars, eighteen regiments, under Fitz John Porter, Heintzman's division, and other corps of his James river army. It was evident that the enemy were confident of victory. They were aware of Jackson's weakness, and of the fact that not more than half of our army had come up; and by precipitating the battle, they hoped to avenge their shameful defeat on the same ground a little more than one year ago. Indeed, we hear that McDowell, the most civilized officer in the Federal service and the commander at Manassas last year,

made an urgent appeal to his troops to wipe out the disgrace which then befell their arms, and never to leave the field but as conquerors.

As I have already stated, the enemy opened the battle by an attack upon our left. A heavy column, with a full complement of artillery, was launched against Jackson's veterans, but there, as elsewhere, they encountered a "Stonewall" as immovable as the Blue Ridge. The onslaught would have been fearful to any other but Confederate troops struggling for the dearest rights known to man. The attack was repulsed, however, and the enemy forced to retire. In the meantime a heavy force was moved up against A. P. Hill and Anderson in the centre, and Longstreet's splendid corps on the right. The attack upon the centre was not characterized by much vigor, but on the right it was made by McClellan's Regulars, and was furious. After the first movement against the left was repulsed, Jackson found but little difficulty in advancing his lines. The infantry were very reluctant to engage the stern chieftain again, and their artillery alone resisted him with spirit. But on the right the conflict raged with great violence for more than an hour before we had made any impression upon the [unreadable] ranks of the Regulars. When they did yield, it was slowly and in perfect order. It could hardly be called a retreat; we pushed them, as it were, from one elevation to another gradually following them up and firmly holding the ground they had been forced to abandon.

In this way the contest continued until near sunset, the retrograde movement of the enemy growing more rapid and less orderly as the battle proceeded. Jackson pressed forward vigorously on the left; Hill and Anderson did the same in the centre; and as the foe retired faster in that part of the field than on the right, our line finally assumed somewhat the form of a crescent.

Jackson at length bent his line around to the Sudley road, near the church of that name, and about the same time the centre and right reached the old battle ground. Then followed as splendid fighting on the part of the Confederates as the world ever saw. As the fact broke upon them that they again stood upon that glorious field, and that the enemy sought a renewal of the decision rendered there one year ago, they swept on as if they were born onward by the fiat of fate. The eye grew brighter, the arm waxed stronger, and catching the inspiration of the place, and of the children of glory who sleep upon its hills, they sent up shout after shout, that rose high above the mighty din and uproar, and sounded in the ear of the already retreating foe like a sentence of judgment.

About the same time Gen. Toombs, who had been absent under orders, reached the field at the top of his horse's speed. His appearance was greeted with the cheers of ten thousand Georgians in Longstreet's corps. The shouts were caught up along the valley and over the hills as his splendid form swept across the field in the direction of his brigade. He found it at length, and led it immediately forward in the thickest of the fight. Dashing down the hill not far from where Bee and Bartow fell, he got within forty paces of a Federal brigade, which saluted him and his men with a terrific fire. The men called to him to dismount, as otherwise he would certainly be killed. His only reply, uttered in trumpeted tones was: "President Davis can create generals; God only makes the soldier—ON!"

Finally our entire line crossed the Sudley road, and swept past the stone house at the intersection of the roads, the Henry and Lews houses on the right, on towards Bull Run. But the enemy managed his artillery with great skill and judgment. His firing was superb, and I must admit, superior to our own. His batteries were posted at commanding points, and enabled him to cover the retreat of his infantry by delaying our advance. Night, too, came to his rescue, and to Nature and not his own arms, was he indebted for his escape from utter destruction. The pursuit was kept up until darkness prevented further effort, and the order to halt was given.

The enemy escaped across Bull Run during the night, and morning found him in a hurried retreat, for the second time over the same road and from the same battle field, back to Washington. Thus the issue has been decided for a second time in our favor, and the judgment of July, 1861, stands affirmed before the world. The battle of Manassas has been fought over, and a gracious God and our own right arms have given us the victory.

Gen. Stuart advanced to Centreville and beyond this morning, but saw nothing of the enemy, except stragglers who were waiting to be taken.

It is too early to enter into details, either as the part performed by individuals or the extent of the victory. Gen. Drayton was not entirely successful in bringing his excellent brigade into action in time, but otherwise, the battle was a complete success. Every officer and man from Gen. Lee down to the humblest private, with exceptions too unimportant to justify particular notice, performed his whole duty. But our triumph however, has been purchased at the cost of much precious blood. Our loss has been heavy; not less, I fear, than six or seven thousand. The casualties of the enemy, including killed, wounded, and probably fifteen hundred or two thousand prisoners, will not fall much short of ten or twelve thousand men. Among the slain on the part of the Federals, is Gen. McDowell, Col. Webster of Massachusetts, and many other officers, at least such is the report of prisoners. On our side we have to lament the death of Gen. Ewell,* who was wounded yesterday and died this morning. Gens. Mahone and Jenkins were wounded—not dangerously; whilst a number of field officers were killed, including Col. Means, (formerly Governor) of South Carolina and Col. Wilson of the Seventh Georgia. Gen. Pryor was captured, but soon effected his escape.

Among our captures, are several thousand stand of small arms, thrown away by the flying foe, some eighteen or twenty pieces of artillery, many wagons, a large amount of stores and other valuable property. It is reported that Stuart destroyed 17,000 pairs of shoes, by a sudden descent upon Manassas Junction on Friday, and that Jackson destroyed several railway trains loaded with provisions after filling his own wagons the day before.

The strategy of the enemy was clever, and deserves attention. He had attacked Jackson on Friday, and was repulsed. He renewed the attack yesterday, and thus sought to create the belief that his chief object was to turn our left. Having, as he supposed, produced this impression upon Gen. Lee, he suddenly precipitated upon our right a very heavy force, including the old United States Regulars and other picked troops, under Fitz John Porter and Heintzleman. His object doubtless was to turn our right, throw us back against the Blue Ridge, keep open his communications by Alexandria and Orange railway, and with Fredericksburg and his gunboats to the south, and cut us off from the base of our supplies. The conception was excellent, but the execution was faulty.

Bee, Bartow, and others who fell on this field last year have been amply revenged. The shaft erected over the spot where Bartow perished has been removed by vandals, but the ground around the place is marked by the Federal dead. The Henry house, which was riddled by the artillery shot of the enemy last year, and where its aged owner, Mrs. Henry, was killed, has also been removed piecemeal by the enemy, and probably sold as relics but before its very doors, and within its demolished walls, sleep to day the miserable myrmidons of the North.

Batteries were planted and captured yesterday where they were planted and captured last year. The pine thicket where the Fourth Alabama and Eighth Georgia suffered so terribly in the first battle, is now strewn with the slain of the invader. We charged through the same woods yesterday, though from a different point, where Kirby Smith, the Blucher of the day, entered the fight before. These are remarkable coincidences; and they extend even to my own experience. In the road way where I relieved a wounded Irishman from Wisconsin late at night last year, I to-day found another Irishman crying for succor. As I rendered it to the first, so I gave it to the second.

Is not the hand of God in all this? Who but He brought us again face to face with our enemies upon these crimsoned plains, and gave us victory? When before did the same people ever fight two separate battles upon the same ground, within so short a period? For the second time the God of Battles has spoken by the mouth of our cannon and told the North to let us go unto ourselves. Will that ill starred people require Him to repeal the command after the manner of Pharaoh and the purblind Egyptians? We shall see.

P.W.A.

*In a subsequent letter, our correspondent corrects this statement and reports Gen. Ewell doing well.—Edr.

Sharpsburg Campaign

In early September 1862, Lee decided upon a movement that would change the complexion of the war. He would, with the approval of President Davis, lead his ragtag and exhausted army of 55,000 men on an invasion of the North. He would cross the Potomac near Leesburg, Virginia, and move northward into Pennsylvania. Lee and Davis hoped the invasion would bring the desperately needed recognition by England and France that would be a prelude to aid for the Southern struggle for independence. Lee and Davis also hoped that a northward invasion would win over the Border States and inflict a killing blow on Northern morale. Lee's ill-clad, ill-shod, ill-fed army massed at Frederick, Maryland. From there, he could use the Catoctin Mountains as a screen for his troops. McClellan followed from Washington.

McClellan's advanced guard reached Frederick on 12 September, only shortly after Lee's had pulled out, and in time to benefit from a devastating mistake by one of Lee's subcommanders. Confederate General Daniel Harvey Hill had received a duplicate set of Lee's orders regarding the advance into Maryland and had discarded it—scholars disagree on whether accidentally or intentionally. McClellan's force occupied the campground Lee's had abandoned, and there Union Private W. B. Mitchell of the 27th Indiana found the document wrapped around three cigars. Mitchell is said to have retained the cigars, but he passed the orders on to his superiors. McClellan had Lee's plan laid out before him. Since he knew where the Confederates were headed, he would be able to pursue them without the normal delays for reconnaissance—except, what if the supposedly lost order was some sort of elaborate Confederate trick? The Southerners were known for such tactics, after all.

Nevertheless, McClellan pursued Lee and caught up with him on South Mountain, between Frederick and a tiny Maryland village to the west called Sharpsburg. Lee fought a delaying action at the 14 September Battle of South Mountain, one that gave him time to entrench his forces outside Sharpsburg. That same day, Jackson captured the 10,000-man garrison at Harper's Ferry, which freed his force to hurry back to Sharpsburg and reinforce Lee's troops. Lee's defenses at Sharpsburg were entrenched in a bend of the Potomac River between Sharpsburg and Antietam Creek. The creek and the ridges surrounding it provided strong natural defenses for the Confederates.

McClellan planned a three-pronged attack. He intended to attack both of Lee's flanks first, then his center. The planned assault, though, degenerated into separate and disjointed attacks. By midday, the fighting had shifted to the center along a sunken road now called "Bloody Lane." Lee had no more reserves, but the federal offensive had ground to a halt, and the action shifted to Longstreet's sector. The Union corps under Major General Ambrose E. Burnside tried for two desperate hours to take the bridge Longstreet defended. When Burnside finally broke through the Confederate line, he was repulsed by a surprise counterattack from A. P. Hill's 3,000 men who had just made an exhausting 17-mile march from Harper's Ferry. Hill's men drove Burnside across the creek and ended the bloodiest single day of the entire Civil War. Casualties of the two armies together totaled more than 26,000 men, 12,400 for the Union and 13,700 for the Confederacy. Lee's men withdrew back into Virginia, unmolested. It would be nearly a month before McClellan would follow Lee back across the Potomac.

With fewer than 50,000 men, Lee had stopped the Union 70,000 troops who had taken part in the battle—McClellan's entire force numbered some 90,000, but he had held 20,000 men in reserve all day. Tactically, Sharpsburg was a Confederate victory. Strategically, since it halted Lee's northward invasion, it was a major Union victory, which Lincoln used as the opportunity to issue his Preliminary Emancipation Proclamation, the announcement that as of 1 January 1863, all slaves in the seceded states would be emancipated.

PETER W. ALEXANDER: ACCOUNT OF LEE'S RETREAT FROM SHARPSBURG (ANTIETAM)

Lee led his Army of Northern Virginia across the Potomac in September 1862 to meet General McClellan's troops in one of the bloodiest battles of the Civil War. The two armies clashed in the picturesque town of Sharpsburg, just a handful of miles from the steep banks of the Potomac. The Savannah Republican's correspondent, Peter W. Alexander, was on hand for the battle and the silent, nighttime retreat, the subject of this story, which was filed once Lee's defeated army had recrossed the Potomac. Like many Confederates, Alexander had supported the move into Maryland, but that, he wrote, was before he saw the condition of Lee's army. At least a fifth of the men had no shoes. Many wore ragged clothing. None had sufficient food. In the aftermath of the bloodbath at Sharpsburg, Alexander admitted to his Confederate readers that the move had been a mistake. Not only had the army been defeated; the political costs in Maryland had been tremendous. Confederates still hoped to convince Marylanders to secede. A victory at Sharpsburg might have accomplished that. Failure did not. Alexander's dispatch of 25 September ran with another he had written on 20 September and posted from Winchester, Virginia, where he had sought medical treatment for an illness.

Savannah Republican, 1 October 1862

ARMY CORRESPONDENCE
OF THE SAVANNAH REPUBLICAN

SMITHFIELD, VA., Sept. 19th, 1862.

The Confederate army has returned to Virginia. Whether Gen. Lee took this step from a military necessity, or for some strategic purpose, or because he had accomplished the object of his movement into Maryland—the capture of Harper's Ferry—I am unable to say. The order was issued late last evening, and by the time it was quite dark, the wagons, artillery and troops began to move. All the wounded that were in condition to be moved, had been taken across the river. Those whose wounds were very severe [*unreadable*], unfortunately, had to be left behind and fell into the hands of the enemy. Some of the wounded had never been removed from the field, having fallen on a part of the ground still held by the enemy. Many of the dead were buried yesterday, and some were transferred to this bank of the river.

It was not quite three miles to the Potomac, and our wagon trains extended from Sharpsburg over to the Virginia side. There were only two roads by which we could proceed, one of which was taken by the troops and the other by the artillery and wagons. Our lines came up within a short distance of the enemy's yet so silently and adroitly was the movement conducted, that McClellan was not aware of it until the next

morning. It had rained in the afternoon, and the roads were muddy below, while the heavens were covered with a light fog above, both of which facilitated the enterprise.

We had crossed into Maryland by the bright and early morning sun; we returned in silence and at the dead hour of night. The columns wound their way over the hills and along the valleys like some huge, indistinct monster. The trees and overhanging cliffs, and the majestic Blue Ridge loomed up in dim but enlarged and fantastic proportions, and made one feel as if he were in some strange and weird land of grotesque forms, visible only in the hour of dreams.

Whatever was the motive to the movement, it must be regarded as one of the most successful and extraordinary exploits in the history of any country, and stamps the man that ordered and executed it as one of the greatest military leaders in our time and generation. With the exception of the wounded and a few wagons that got turned over in the darkness, not a single man or wagon, nor a single piece of artillery was lost. Longstreet's corps, being nearest the ford, led the way, followed by D. H. Hill's and Jackson's in order of their names. The crossing was accomplished by half-past six this morning, and soon thereafter the enemy's artillery opened a harmless fire from the opposite heights. The bird had flown, however, and his rage was impotent.

There was formerly a splendid stone bridge at Sheperdstown where the army crossed, but the enemy destroyed it last year. The ford was three-fourths of a mile below the bridge, and this made it necessary to pass down the river bank that distance, and then up it on the other side by a narrow road blasted out of the rocky precipice. The troops managed to work their way out from the river along some of the gorges that broke through the cliff, and a few wagons and artillery escaped in the same way. Thus, you perceive, the character of the Virginia side was almost as unfavorable as it could be to the safety of the movement. It is an exceedingly difficult undertaking at any time to transfer an army across a wide stream, but it is especially so under circumstances as surrounded Gen. Lee.

I am frank to say I was in favor of the movement into Maryland. I am equally ready to admit that, under the circumstances I now think it was a mistake. This conviction gradually forced itself upon my mind after I came up with the army and saw the miserable condition in which it was. A fifth of the troops are barefooted; half of them are in rags, and the whole of them insufficiently supplied with food. Men in this condition cannot be relied on to the same extent as when they are properly clothed and subsisted. The best soldiers, under such circumstances, will straggle both on the march and in battle. Since we crossed into Maryland, and even before, they frequently had to march all day, and far into the night for three or four days together, without food of any kind, except such apples and green corn as they could obtain along the way. Our supply of food was limited at best, and the base of our operations so distant, the intervening country so barren by reason of the spoilation perpetrated by Pope and his myrmidons, and our transportation so limited, that is was quite impossible to subsist the army as it should be. The difficulty of passing Confederate money in Maryland was another fruitful source of trouble.

The political effect upon Maryland of our retrograde movement must be highly injurious. We shall doubtless lose ground among the people, and it may be we shall have to make up our minds to loose [sic] the State itself. It should be the direst necessity, however, that would compel us to abandon Maryland. The waters of the Chesapeake are indispensable to the Confederate States as a naval power, as well as for our security and defense.

Gen. Toombs received a painful, though not serious wound in the hand last night, just as the army was about to move. He was mounted and at the head of his division, with his aids around him, when six or eight mounted men approached slowly along his line to where his horse was standing. They were asked who they were, and remaining silent, Capt. Troup commenced to draw upon them; whereupon they said, "don't shoot; we are Massachusetts men." Gen. Toombs was about drawing his pistol from the holsters when Capt. T. fired upon

them. They immediately returned fire, and then wheeling their horses, disappeared in the darkness. Lieut. Robt. Grant received a slight flesh wound in the arm also. The men were doubtless lost, and the affair may have contributed somewhat to the deception practiced upon McClellan by Gen. Lee in withdrawing his army across the river.

WINCHESTER, VA., Sept. 20th

I came on to this place for medical treatment, being quite unwell, and to be where there are some mail facilities for getting off letters.

Intelligence has just been received that Jackson engaged a brigade of the enemy last evening at the Shepherdstown ford. Concealing his own forces, he permitted the enemy's artillery to get into the river and many of his troops to reach the Virginia side, when he set his men upon them and had another Leesburg affair of it. He killed a large number of them and captured a good many, and one report says several pieces of artillery. Those who escaped our fire fled in dismay back into Maryland.

There is a report in circulation that we have re-crossed the river at Williamsport, but it is probably untrue. After Jackson's affair at the ford, he took up his position four miles this side the river. There a large number of our wounded who had been transferred to Shepherdstown, have fallen into the hands of the enemy. We hear they have been paroled. The enemy has also thrown forward scouting parties as far as Middleburg, Upperville and Paris on the eastern side of the Blue Ridge.

Nothing further has transpired in regard to the proposition reported to have been made by Gen. Lee to the Federal government, and alluded to in a former letter of mine. I am credibly informed that such a proposition as that described was certainly made, and under circumstances that encouraged the hope of its acceptance. Recent events, however, may have given a different turn to the affair.

I have just heard of an instance of gallantry in the late battle that deserves to be put on the record. The Floridians always fight well, but the Fifth Florida behaved with distinguished courage and intrepidity at Sharpsburg. The hero in this case was a private—Ben Flowers—of that regiment. He was wounded five different times and in as many different places; yet he continued to shoot away as fearlessly as ever, until he had received the fifth wound, which disabled one of his hands, so that he could not load his piece. He is doing very well; as soon as he is well enough, he says he shall be after the Yankees again.

Maj. Phillip Tracy of the 6th Georgia, wounded in the leg, has since died. He was wounded at Richmond, and only rejoined his regiment the evening before the battle. He had not quite recovered his strength, and the amputation to which his limb was necessarily subjected proved fatal.

P.W.A.

PETER W. ALEXANDER: OUR ARMY, ITS GREAT DEEDS, ITS TRIALS, ITS SUFFERINGS, AND ITS PERILS IN THE FUTURE

Alexander dropped out of the march from Maryland due to exhaustion, exposure, and hunger, but he took the opportunity to continue his campaign to bring the condition of the soldiers in Lee's army to the attention of the Confederates back home. This letter in particular would begin a campaign back home in Georgia to raise money for shoes and other necessities for the state's soldiers in Virginia. Alexander also took on those who criticized infantrymen for straggling in the retreat back into Virginia. In his view, lagging behind was perfectly understandable and justified. The story is perhaps the best example of advocacy journalism of the Confederate press.

Savannah Republican, 3 October 1862

**ARMY CORRESPONDENCE
OF THE SAVANNAH REPUBLICAN**

Our Army, Its Great Deeds, Its Trials,
Its Sufferings, and its Perils in the
Future.
WINCHESTER, VA., Sept. 26, 1862.

My condition is such as to render it impossible for me to rejoin the army at the present. I was not prepared for the hardships, exposures and fastings the army has encountered since it left the Rappahannock, and like many a seasoned campaigner, have had to "fall out by the way." Indeed, I can recall no parallel instance in history, except Napoleon's disastrous retreat from Moscow, where an army has ever done more marching and fighting, under such great disadvantages, than Gen. Lee's has done since it left the banks of the James river. It proceeded directly to the line of the Rappahannock, and moving out from that river, it fought its way to the Potomac, crossed that stream and moved on to Fredericktown and Hagerstown, had a heavy engagement at Boonsboro' Gap, and another at Crampton Gap below, fought the greatest pitched battle of the war at Sharpsburg, and then recrossed the Potomac back into Virginia. During all this time, covering the full space of a month, the troops rested but four days! And let it always be remembered to their honor, that of the men who performed this wonderful feat, one-fifth of them were barefooted, one-half of them in rags, and the whole of them famished. The country from the Rappahannock to the Potomac had been visited by the enemy with fire and sword, and our transportation was insufficient to keep the army supplied from so distant a base as Gordonsville; and when the provision trains would overtake the army, so pressing were the exigencies of their position, the men seldom had time to cook. Their difficulties were increased by the fact that their cooking utensils, in many cases, had been left behind, as well as everything else that would impede their movements. It was not unusual to see a company of starving men have a barrel of flower distributed to them, which it was utterly impossible for them to convert into bread with the means and the time

allowed to them. They could not procure even a piece of plank or a corn or flour sack, upon which to work up their dough.

Do you wonder, then, that there should have been stragglers from the army. That brave and true men should have fallen out of line from sheer exhaustion, or in their efforts to obtain a mouthful to eat along the roadside? Or that many seasoned veterans, the conquerors in the valley, at Richmond and Manassas, should have succumbed to disease and been forced back to the hospital? I look to hear a great outcry raised against the stragglers. Already lazy cavalry men and dainty staff officers and quartermasters, who are mounted and can forage the country for something to eat, are condemning the weary private, who, notwithstanding his body may be covered with dust and perspiration, and his feet with stone bruises, is expected to trudge along under his knapsack and cartridge box, on an empty stomach, and never to turn aside for a morsel of food to sustain his sinking limbs. Out upon such monstrous injustice! That there has been unnecessary stragglers, is readily admitted; but in a large majority of cases, the men have only to point to their bleeding feet, tattered garments and gaunt frames for an answer to the unjust charge.

No army on this continent has ever accomplished as much or suffered as much as the army of Northern Virginia within the last three months. At no period during the first Revolutionary war—not even at Valley Forge—did our forefathers in arms encounter greater hardships, or endure them more uncomplainingly.

But great as have been the trials to which the army has been subjected, they are hardly worthy to be named in comparison with the sufferings in store for this winter, unless the people of the Confederate States, everywhere and in whatever circumstances, come to its immediate relief.

The men must have clothing and shoes this winter. They must have something to cover themselves with when sleeping, and to protect themselves from the driving sleet and snow storms when on duty. This must be done, though our friends at home should have to wear cotton and sit by the fire. The army in Virginia stands guard this day, as it will stand guard this winter, over every hearthstone throughout the South. The ragged sentinel who may pace his weary rounds this winter on the bleak spurs of the Blue Ridge, or along the frozen valleys of the Shenandoah and Rappahannock, will also be your sentinels, my friend, at home. It will be for you and your household that he encounters the wrath of the tempest and the dangers of the night. He suffers and toils and fights for you, too, brave, true hearted women of the South.— Will you not clothe his nakedness then? Will you not put shoes and stockings on his feet? Is it not enough that he has written down his patriotism in crimson characters along that battle road from the Rappahannock to the Potomac? And must his bleeding feet also impress their mark of fidelity upon the snows of the coming winter? I know what your answer will be. God has spoken through the women of the South, and they are his bold oracles in this day of trial and tribulation.

It is not necessary to counsel violent measures; but it is not expected that any person will be permitted to accumulate leather and cloth for purposes of speculation. The necessities of the army rise up like a mountain and cannon, and will not be overlooked. It was hoped at one time, that we might obtain winter supplies in Maryland. This hope was born after the army left Richmond, and has now miserably perished. The Government is unable to furnish the supplies; for they are not to be had in the country. If it had exercised a little foresight last spring and summer, when vessels were running the blockade, and cargoes of calico, linen and other articles of like importance, a partial supply at least of hats, blankets, shoes and woolen goods might have been obtained from England. But foresight is a quality of mind that is seldom put in practice in these days.

But whatever may be done by the people, *should be done immediately*. Not one moment can be lost that will not be marked, as by the second hand of a watch, with the pangs of a sufferer. Already the hills and valleys in this high latitude have been visited by frost, and the nights are uncomfortably cool to the man who sleeps upon the ground. Come up, then, men and women of the South, to this sacred duty. Let nothing stand between you and the performance of it. Neither pride, nor pleasure, nor personal ease and comfort, should withhold your hands from the holy work. The supply of leather and wool, we all know, is limited; but do what you can, and all you can, and as soon as you can. If you cannot send woolen socks, send half woolen or cotton socks; and so with under clothing, coats and pants. And if blankets are not to be had, then substitute comforts made of dyed ossaburgs stuffed with cotton. Anything that will keep off the cold will be acceptable. Even the speculator and extortioner might forego their gains for a season and unite in this religious duty. If they neither clothe the naked, nor feed the hungry, who are fighting for *their* freedom and for *their* houses and property, what right have they to expect anything but eternal damnation, both from god and man?

If the Army of Virginia could march through the South just as it is—ragged and almost barefooted and hatless—many of the men limping along and not quite well of their wounds or sickness, yet cheerful and not willing to abandon their places in the ranks—their clothes riddled with balls and their banners covered with the smoke and dust of battle, and shot into tatters, many of them inscribed with "Williamsburg," "Seven Pines," "Gaines' Mill," "Garnett's Farm," "Front Royal," "McDowel," "Cedar Run," and other victorious fields—if this army of veterans, thus clad and shod, with tattered uniforms and banners, could march from Richmond to Mississippi, it would produce a sensation that has no parallel in history since Peter the Hermit led his swelling hosts across Europe to the rescue of the Holy Sepulchre.

I do not write to create alarm, or to produce a sensation, but to arouse the people to a sense of the true condition of the army. I have yet to learn that anything is to be gained by suppressing the truth, and [*unreadable*].

There is nothing new from the [*unreadable*]. It is reported that Jackson crossed the river at Williamsport a few days ago to repair a road, which he might have occasion to use, and then returned. I see nothing, however, to change the opinion heretofore expressed, yet now the heavy work of the campaign is over, unless McClelland should seek us on the south side of the river. This, some believe, public opinion at the North will compel [*unreadable*]. It may be so, though I doubt it.

I had made arrangements to procure full official lists of the casualties in the Georgia, Alabama and Florida regiments as well as the account of the performances of the troops from those States, and regret that sickness should have prevented me from carrying them out.

P.W.A.

JAMES R. SNEED AND GEORGE W. RANDOLPH: CLOTHING FOR THE SOLDIERS

Savannah Republican correspondent Peter W. Alexander had marched from Virginia to Maryland with Lee's Army of Northern Virginia. He was as familiar with the condition of the men as he would have been had he been a soldier himself. Alexander was also a much respected and beloved war correspondent—the Walter Cronkite or Dan Rather of his day—whose stories were picked up through newspaper exchanges and run in papers throughout the Confederacy. For that reason, when Alexander wrote a series of passionate articles about the needs of Georgia soldiers for the coming winter, the people of the South responded generously. Alexander's stories were among the first, though not the last, examples of advocacy journalism in the Confederate press.

Alexander's claims in stories published on 1 and 3 October that Georgia soldiers were shoeless and in rags apparently evoked considerable disbelief among Savannah residents. Surely the Confederate government would not let its valiant soldiers be reduced to such a state with the onset of winter only weeks away. To answer the questions definitively, the editor of the Republican *wrote to the Confederate secretary of war, and he published the answer he received so as to dispel the public disbelief and to restore the credibility of his Virginia correspondent.*

Savannah Republican, 22 October 1862

CLOTHING FOR THE SOLDIERS—DESPATCH FROM THE SECRETARY OF WAR

As our correspondent's testimony regarding the suffering in the army had been questioned, and a statement given to the public, on the assurance of army officers, that the government was abundantly supplied with shoes, clothing, and other necessaries and comforts for the army, which would be distributed at the proper time, and that private individuals were making unnecessary sacrifices under a mistaken view of the case, we determined, if possible, to satisfy both the public and ourselves on the subject. We, accordingly, addressed a note of enquiry to the Secretary of War, who promptly replied by telegraph as follows:

RICHMOND, Oct. 21.

    J. R. Sneed:

      We desire all the assistance in supplying shoes, blankets and clothing that can be furnished.

                    GEO. W. RANDOLPH,
                         Secretary of War

That settles the question; and now let all the people go to work. Shoes, socks, drawers, vests, neck ties, indeed clothing of every description should be made up as fast as possible and forwarded to the army.

Parties in the state can entrust all packages to the Georgia Hospital and Relief Association, at Augusta.

PETER W. ALEXANDER: WHAT THE GOVERNMENT HAS DONE AND IS DOING FOR SICK, WOUNDED AND DESTITUTE SOLDIERS

Alexander continued his advocacy on behalf of Georgia's soldiers by critiquing the hospital facilities for the state's soldiers in Virginia. Several states set up their own hospitals in Virginia to care for their own soldiers, but even so, medical care was at best rudimentary and haphazard.

Savannah Republican, 22 October 1862

ARMY CORRESPONDENCE OF THE SAVANNAH REPUBLICAN

What the Government has done and is doing
for the Sick, Wounded, and
destitute Soldiers.

WINCHESTER, VA., Oct. 12th, 1862

In my letter of yesterday, I endeavored to anew what may be accomplished by the intelligent and well-directed effort of one State in the matter of providing for its wounded soldiers and relieving its sick and destitute. The State referred to was Georgia, and the agency through which its charity and benefactions distributed was the Georgia Relief and Hospital Association. It was shown that the State, in addition to large individual contributions of money, clothing, medicines and stores, had appropriated the sum of $200,000 for the relief of

the sick and wounded; that the Association had established four large hospitals in Richmond, that these hospitals were provided with surgeons, matrons, nurses and chaplains; that an ample supply of furniture, bed-sacks, sheets, towels, bandages, splints and medicines had been procured; that a large store room had been rented, where clothing was kept for gratuitous distribution among the troops from Georgia and the very needy from other States, where extra baggage and express freight might be stored free of charge; and that the Association had in its employ a number of agents, active and zealous agents, who, upon the occurrence of a battle, repaired immediately to the scene of action, carrying with them a supply of medicine, bed sacks, sheets, towels, bandages, clothing &c., collected up the wounded from their State, and rendered every assistance, moral and physical, it was in their power to bestow. It was shown also, that these agents were industrious and energetic men, full of sympathy and good feeling, who did not wait for the sick and destitute to come to them, but went out in search of the sufferers, got them into as comfortable quarters as possible, put beds of straw under their weary limbs, furnished them with a change of clothing, and nursed them like brothers—as they are.

To-day I proposed to show what the Government is doing for the sick and wounded under the same circumstances—not with a view of finding fault, but to indicate the defects in the system it has adopted, to the end that they may be corrected.

It is customary after a battle has been fought, to collected the wounded together in temporary hospitals or send them to the rear. At Richmond, they were placed in the hospitals in that city; after the second battle of Manassas they were sent back to Warrenton and other towns in the vicinity, and at Sharpsburg they were sent across the river to Sheperdstown and thence to this place and Staunton. The regimental surgeons dress the wound, and set or amputate the limb, as the case may be, before the patient passes from their hands to the rear. Some of these operators perform their work skillfully and conscientiously; others do it hurriedly or ignorantly; whilst a few do it in a manner that can only be properly characterized as brutal. I have known cases of amputations when the lapping part of the flesh was sewed together over the bone so stupidly that the thread would disengage itself and the bone be exposed in less than twenty-four hours. The object of many of the field surgeons seems to be to get through their work, in some sort of fashion, as soon as possible, and turn their subjects over to the hospital surgeons. While engaged at the amputation table, many of them feel it to be their duty, every time they administer brandy to the patient, to take a drink themselves. This part of their work is performed with great unction and conscientiousness. In a majority of instances, however, I am glad to say the field surgeons do quite as well as could be expected of young men who have had but little practical experience in the art of surgery. In cases of ordinary sickness they have but little to do, inasmuch as the Government has been able to furnish them with but few medicines, and they have consequently but little to administer.

But it is when the wounded man falls into the hands of the hospital surgeons that his greatest sufferings begin. I do not mean such surgeons as those in the Richmond hospitals, which are located in a large city under the eye of the Government, and are provided for with careful matrons and nurses and an ample supply of hospital stores; the circumstances surrounding these officers, if nothing else, would constrain them to perform their duties. But I allude to the surgeons in those hospitals which are improvised in the rear of the army, as at this place and Warrenton, and who being of but little value at Richmond and other central points, are sent to the country. Shall I daguerreotype two of these surgeons for you? Sam Weller would call them "Sawbones," and perhaps that is a more appropriate term for them than surgeons.

Nearly two weeks after the battle of Sharpsburg, two young gentlemen, or irreproachable moustaches, were introduced into my room at a hotel in this place by the landlady, who informed me that they would be my room-mates for the present. It appeared from their conversation that they had just arrived from Richmond—that they had been acting in the capacity of assistant surgeons there for nearly a year, and that they had been despatched to Winchester to assist in taking care of the wounded in the battle of Sharpsburg. Two questions of much magnitude occupied their attention for half an hour or more—to wit: 1st, whether they should report to the surgeon of the post in person or by note; 2d, whether, in the event they reported in person, they should "dress up" or go as they were. They finally decided to dress first and then send up their report in writing. The consideration which brought them to this conclusion arose from the fact that they were without paper, and the idea of going into the street to purchase a supply in their present plight, could not be entertained for a moment. Nearly two hours were devoted to their toilet. After washing and scrubbing ever so long, their hair and moustaches had to be carefully cleaned and oiled, their uniforms, covered all over with gold lace, neatly dusted, and their boots duly polished. One of them put on a ruffled calico shirt with a large diamond pin and immense gold studs, a pair of white linen pantaloons, and a handsome black cloth coat made up in the extreme military style. He first thought he would wear a pair of gaiter shoes, but on consulting "Jim" (his companion) it was finally agreed that boots would become the set of his pants better. So he put on the boots.

Having finished their elaborate toilets and started out of the room, the following laconic dialogue ensued.

Boots.—I say, Jim, don't you think we had better take a drop before going out?

Jim.—Yes, I *do* think we had. I feel rather shaky after last night's affair.

They courteously inquired after a moment's hesitation, whether I would not join them; but I was suffering at the time from fever consequent upon a chill, and a still fiercer lever of indignation that such stupid creatures should be sent here to attend the wounded, and I declined to participate. They returned to the room after an hour's absence, complained that they had to walk so far through the heat and dust to get a little paper, prepared their note to the Chief Surgeon of the post, and sent it up to him in due form. The Chief Surgeon, who is represented to be a man of industry and energy, replied promptly, ordering them to a certain hospital, which they proceeded to take charge of the next morning—nearly twenty-four hours after their arrival in town!

You are ready to inquire, of what use can such dainty gentry be in a dirty hospital filled with stern sufferers—men with broken bones and ghastly wounds, whose bodies are covered with filthy rags and alive with vermin—with nothing to lie upon but a little straw, and the air they breathe poisoned by exhalations from the festering wounds and feverish bodies around them? The answer is, they are of no use whatever. If ever so skilled in their profession, the neatness of their toilet and the delicacy of their noses would totally disqualify them for such work as this. A hospital at best is not a desirable place to abide in; but when filthy and filled with vermin, and crammed with sick and wounded men, whose wounds are seldom dressed and whose necessities require them to submit to the most disgusting practices, they fall but little, if any, short of purgatory. The buildings selected for hospitals, instead of being in a quiet, pleasant locality, are almost invariably located in the most noisy, dusty and dirty part of town. It was so at Corinth, and it is so in Winchester. In the former place, they were located immediately around the depot, where the cars were running day and night, and where the wagons from the camps were constantly arriving and departing, whilst the houses in the rest of the town, which the owners had been required to vacate, were occupied by Generals and their [*unreadable*] staff officers.

There are several hundred sick and wounded men here; and yet, if I am correctly informed, the Surgeons did not bring with them a single cot, bedsack, sheet, or towel, or solitary change of clothing for the wounded! Some of the men are now lying on a scant supply of straw, with a foul blanket over them, who are otherwise as naked as when they first came into the world! The little clothing they had was torn off when their wounds were dressed, and it was impossible to recover their knapsacks after they were wounded. But for a few cots in the York hospital, (which is very well kept,) said to have been left there by our enemy, the condition of such of the wounded who could not get into private houses is as deplorable as it can be.

The Surgeons were late in arriving here, and were equally slow, as you have seen, in reporting after they had arrived. The agents of the Georgia Relief and Hospital Association reached Warrenton with their supplies nearly a week in advance of the Surgeons sent up from Richmond. The same is true as to this place. In less than twenty-four hours after their arrival here (the time required for some of the government surgeons to arrange their toilets and report for duty) they have visited every hospital in the town, gathered up many of the wounded from their State, dressed their wounds, furnished them with a change of clothing, and gone to work to secure separate hospital buildings for their accommodation. Why cannot the government Surgeons show equal activity and humanity?

One thing has impressed me more painfully than all others connected with the army. It is the little concern which the government, its officers and surgeons show for the preservation of the lives of their troops. A great parade is made over a single piece of artillery captured from the enemy; and yet what is such a trophy compared with the life of an able-bodied man, even when considered as to its military value! We have none too many men in the South that we should adopt a system so disregardful of life. The whole country is interested in the life and health of every man in it, and if some of the energy displayed in forcing feeble and unhealthy conscripts into the service, were shown in taking care of the sick and wounded, the army would be all the better for it. A planter who would take as little care of the health of his slaves as the government does of its soldiers, would soon have none to care for, while he would be driven out of the community by his indignant neighbors.

P.W.A.

Fredericksburg Campaign

Lee's men withdrew back into Virginia after the September campaign to Sharpsburg, but McClellan's forces did not follow until directly ordered to do so by President Lincoln in early October. McClellan moved out to Warrenton, where he found himself between Longstreet's forces at Culpeper and Jackson's in the Valley. When McClellan refused to go any farther, Lincoln removed the general and gave command of the Army of the Potomac to Burnside. Burnside was not so hesitant to follow the Confederates, and he devised a plan that called for an advance toward Fredericksburg on the Rappahannock. Burnside massed his army on the northeast bank, and Lee, Longstreet, and Jackson gathered their forces on the other side of the river.

Burnside planned an attack on Richmond via Fredericksburg, but his advance was halted when the pontoons needed to build bridges across the Rappahannock failed to arrive. The delay gave Lee time to reinforce and cost Burnside the element of surprise on which he had counted. Finally, though, on 25 November, the pontoons arrived, and Burnside began building bridges.

His men began crossing the Rappahannock before dawn on 11 December. Engineers had spanned about half of the river's width when Confederates under Mississippi

General William Barksdale's men began firing on them. Burnside ordered his artillery to begin firing at Barksdale's Mississippi Brigade, but the troops were not phased by the heavy weapons. They continued to pick off Burnside's men on the bridge.

Burnside's men did get across the Rappahannock by the evening of 11 December, but it was late morning on 13 December before the battle began. Jackson's men, in combination with Stuart's artillery, threw back the Union troops. By evening, Jackson's position was intact, and the Union army held only the river line. To the north, the federals met devastating artillery and small-arms fire from Longstreet's corps on Marye's Heights. Fourteen successive Union charges were repulsed by Confederate fire. Burnside's forces withdrew on 15 December. The Union loss at the Battle of Fredericksburg was 12,653 to the Confederate loss of only 4,201. This was Lee's most lopsided victory of the war.

PETER W. ALEXANDER: ACCOUNTS OF BATTLE AT FREDERICKSBURG

The Battle of Fredericksburg was a key victory for Robert E. Lee. The Republican's *Peter W. Alexander covered the battle, at least initially, from Richmond by collecting information from the War Department and from eyewitnesses. The following two stories are his accounts, one based on an eyewitness account and the other, written the following day, from a broader array of sources. The second letter in this set was actually written on the day the battle commenced, and the first letter was written the next day. However, the mails from Virginia were so disrupted by the fighting there that the first day's letter arrived later than the second—hence the reversed publication dates.*

Savannah Republican, 24, 23 December 1862

**ARMY CORRESPONDENCE
OF THE SAVANNAH REPUBLICAN**

The Battle of Thursday

The irregularity of the mails has rendered very uncertain the receipt of our correspondence from the seat of war. A letter, just received, and written on the day of the great battle of Fredericksburg, contains an interesting account of the fight of Thursday when the enemy attempted to cross and immediately thereafter. We append that portion of it, omitting the commencement, which refers to the probably intentions of the enemy, which have been fully realized:—[EDS.
RICHMOND, DEC. 13th, 1862. . . .

I am indebted to an intelligent friend in the army for the following account of the fight on Thursday. He says the enemy attempted to lay pontoon bridges across the river at four places—two at Fredericksburg, one above the town, and one about a mile and a half below. The Florida brigade, in Anderson's division, repulsed them at the upper ford, and Barksdale's brigade, of McLaws' division, repulsed them three times at the town, each time with heavy loss. At the mouth of Harrison's creek below they were also driven back by the

18th Mississippi, 16th Georgia, and 15th South Carolina, Col. Dessausaure commanding. These regiments belong to McLaws' division also.

About 2 p.m. the enemy concentrated thirty-seven pieces of artillery upon the centre of the town, firing 100 shells every four minutes, and in the midst of this storm they effected a landing, but not without great loss. Barksdale's Mississippians stood manfully to their guns through this heavy bombardment, the crushing timbers and crumbling ruins of brick and mortar, for more than an hour, and stoutly contested the landing. They were finally compelled to retire, however, from their exposed position, and allow the enemy to land. They withdrew back three streets, formed anew, and again charged the heavy masses of the enemy that came pouring into the town, and drove them back across the river, inflicting a severe loss upon them. No troops could have behaved better, and they and their commander were richly entitled to the thanks which Gen. McLaws bestowed upon them for their gallant behavior.

Barksdale's loss was severe, including Capt. Clark of the 13th Miss., killed, and Capt. Green and Thurmond of the 17th and 21st Mississippi seriously wounded.

The Mississippians were relieved by Gen. T.R.R. Cobb's brigade, who held the town until night, when they were ordered to retire to the base of the hills on this side of the town.—the 16th Georgia had several wounded by shells as they lay guarding the lower bridge. Among the wounded brought down last night, I notice the names of W. J. Herring of the 14th Georgia, R. N. Robinson of the 16th Georgia, Corporal J. McCade, J. Craft, Thos. Migell, J. Fielding, J. W. Harper, W. F. Swails and H. Lewis of the 8th Florida; M. Duncan of 1st South Carolina; Lieut. T. A. Diall of the 2nd South Carolina, and W. E. Parker of the 15th South Carolina.

The city was fired in a number of places. Many of the inhabitants had been forced by the bad weather to return, and the suffering among the women and children was very great. The letter before me says "the town is a mass of ruins." The citizens are crowded into the farm houses in the vicinity of town, and in tents through the woods and fields. These tents are made of blankets, sheets, counterpanes, &c., and afford but a frail shelter to feeble women and children against the inclement weather. The enemy have not only got possession of their homes but of their furniture, provisions and clothing. The fugitives brought away but little except what they had on their backs.

Let the people of Savannah remember Fredericksburg and New Orleans, and neither remain in the city and submit to the enemy nor flee and leave all to the spoiler; but having removed the non-combatants, let them stand their ground, defend their homes, and save all—anyhow, their honor.

LATER

Eight p.m.—Heavy skirmishing continued throughout the day yesterday, resulting in a reported loss on our part of about 130 killed and wounded. The same species of warfare was kept up to-day, but with what results I am unable to say. The enemy directed their attention to the woods this side of the town, which they subjected to a heavy fire of shells. Occasionally the pickets and skirmishers took part, when a pretty sharp fire was maintained on both sides. The enemy doubtless desire to get possession of the heights on the south side with a view either to their own protection or an early advance.

The impression in unofficial circles was that the battle would be fought to-morrow, Sunday. Brig. Gen. Randolph, late Secretary at War, reported for duty after his withdrawal from the Department of War, and the President having failed to assign him to duty, he determined to throw up his commission and return to the practice of law.

P.W.A.

ARMY CORRESPONDENCE
OF THE SAVANNAH REPUBLICAN

RICHMOND, Dec. 14th.

A great battle was fought on the Rappahannock yesterday, and the Confederate arms were again victorious. The fight commenced at 9 o'clock in the morning and continued until six in the evening. Nothing was known of the battle here until late that night, after my letter of yesterday evening had been posted. The War Office has taken complete possession of the telegraph, and one can hardly order a bushel of salt by the wires without first getting permission from the authorities. This will explain why you have received nothing from me of late by telegraph, and why you may not in the future.

The enemy made the attack, moving first against our right wing, and as the fog lifted from the valley, it extended along the entire line to our extreme left. The conflict raged without intermission until night set in, and resulted in the complete repulse of the enemy at all points. Our success was not so decisive as to preclude the idea of renewal of the battle today. Indeed, in his description to the War Office, Gen. Lee expresses the opinion that the fighting would be resumed at daybreak this morning. If so, Burnside has greater confidence in his troops than McClellan had at Sharpsburg, where he declined to return to the attack, notwithstanding his vast superiority in numbers.

We have to mourn the loss of many brave officers—among whom are Brig. Gens. T.R.R. Cobb, of Georgia, and Maxcy Gregg, of South Carolina. Though they had not many opportunities to display their qualities for command, these gentlemen were conspicuous for skill, courage and gallantry. Bartow and Bee fell side by side at the first battle of Manassas, and now Cobb and Gregg lock arms in death. For the second time the bloody marriage of South Carolina and Georgia has been celebrated upon the field of battle and to the harsh music of artillery.

Doubtless many gallant officers of the line and hundreds of brave men in the ranks have also been slain or wounded. The enemy had decidedly the advantage in numbers, and the lists of casualties, when they come to be published, will carry grief to many a stricken home in the Confederacy. General Hampton's expedition to Dumfries may have the effect to create a diversion in favor of General Lee. He captured some twenty wagons, and fifty or sixty prisoners, whom he brought back to the Rappahannock. Whilst at Dumfries, he ascertained that Seigel's corps was expected to arrive there from Fairfax C. H. Today. Dumfries is about midway between Alexandria and Fredericksburg, or thirty miles by land from either place. In the present condition of the roads in that quarter, it would require two days' hard marching to bring Seigel to the south bank of the Rappahannock—too late to participate in the fight before Wednesday, unless he proceeded by water; and even then he could not get into position much, if any sooner. Possibly Burnside may await his arrival before renewing the attack.

The late battle at Kinston, N.C., was a glorious affair. The enemy made the attack with fifteen thousand men and nine gunboats, and was repulsed with heavy loss by Gen. Evans, whose force did not exceed one-fifth of the adversary's. There can be no impropriety in making this statement, since it will be some days before this letter can reach you, and since reinforcements have already been sent to the hero of Leesburg.

LATER

12 *m.*—A telegram has just been received at the War Office from Gen. Lee, dated at half-past eleven this morning, in which he says the battle had not been renewed up to that hour. It is thought here that Burnside will not return to the attack. A few hours will decide.

I hope to be able to go up to the Army tomorrow morning. A passport was granted to the correspondent of the London Times, and why should one be refused to the correspondent of the Savannah Republican? Is it because the one is an Englishman and the other a Confederate?

STILL LATER

8 *p.m.*—Passengers who left the Army at 1 *p.m.* to day, say the fighting was renewed this morning, and continued up to the time they left. Despatches to the War Office, on the contrary, speak of heavy skirmishing, especially this afternoon, but say nothing of any general engagement. I have just been to see the body of Gen. Cobb, which was brought down this evening and will be sent south by to-morrow morning's train. His brigade is posted behind a stone wall at the base of the hill, this side of Fredericksburg, and but a short distance from the town. Our batteries were placed on the elevations just behind and above the brigade, and fired over them. When the enemy charged upon Cobb's position, he reserved his fire until they got within one hundred yards, when his men poured into their ranks a fire which seemed literally to sweep them from the earth. The enemy retired, and having reformed their broken lines and been heavily reinforced,

they returned to the charge at a double quick. The Georgians again reserved their fire until they had come within easy range, when they gave them another volley like the first and with the same result. A third charge was finally made, this time in still greater force, out in this instance as in the first and second, the enemy were driven back with tremendous loss. Persons who participated in the fight say that 1,000 dead Yankees were left on the field in front of Cobb's position. Gen. Cobb himself displayed great courage and judgment. His mother was born in the town of Fredericksburg, and he acted as if he were fighting to rescue her birth place from the clutches of a hated foe. His men were protected behind the stone fence, and he and Gen. Cool, of North Carolina, were standing behind a house, from which point they could conveniently issue their orders. A shell passed through this house, and fragments of it struck both of them. Gen. Cobb was hit on the thigh, which was terribly mangled, about two o'clock and died at four. It is reported that Gen. Cook is also dead. A piece of the same shell struck Capt. Brewster, of the 24th Georgia, a most gallant officer, in the leg, and inflicted a severe, but not mortal wound.

It is feared that Capt. Lord King, son of the Hon. T. Butler King and aid to Gen. McLaws, was killed. He is missing, and a telegram to his father says his spurs had been found on the field near a pair of shoes. He had on cavalry boots, and the presumption is that he was wounded, and that some vandal relieved him of them and left his old shoes behind. Capt. K. was brave to a fault, and has always conducted himself in battle with great gallantly and fearlessness.

I hear that Lt. Col. Cook, of Phillips' Legion, was also killed. The 15th Georgia and Phillips' Legion composed a part of Cobb's brigade.

P.W.A.

AN ANONYMOUS REPORT: BATTLE OF FREDERICKSBURG—ANOTHER CONFEDERATE VICTORY

The Richmond Examiner *was able to offer its readers a report on Fredericksburg sooner than most Southern newspapers. Within two days, the paper's correspondent had supplied a summary of the fighting along the Rappahannock.*

Richmond Examiner, 15 December 1862

THE BATTLE OF FREDERICKSBURG— ANOTHER CONFEDERATE VICTORY

HAMILTON'S CROSSING,
December 14th, 1862.

Of the battle yesterday you have from other sources learned the main result, the driving in of the enemy's light batteries, and the repulse of his infantry. I will supply such particulars as came under my observation. But before doing

so, I must endeavor to give you an idea of the positions occupied by the hostile forces at the beginning of the action.

From Fredericksburg the Rappahannock flows nearly due east. The valley of the river, lying mostly on the south side, is a mile in width near the town and widening as you go down stream. At Hamilton's crossing on the railroad the valley is three miles across. From Hamilton's crossing to Fredericksburg the railroad and the old Richmond stage road, both running parallel with the river, skirt this valley. South of the railroad, beginning near the town and running to a point at Hamilton's crossing, and also parallel with the river, is a range of hills covered with dense oak forest fringed on its northern border by pine thickets.—Our forces occupied the whole length of this forest. Longstreet's corps occupied the highlands above, opposite, and for a mile below the town. Jackson's corps rested on Longstreet's right and extended away to the eastward, the extreme right under A. P. Hill crossing the railroad at Hamilton's crossing, and stretching into the valley towards the river. Our front was about six miles in length. Most of the batteries of both corps were posted in the skirts of the forest, along the line of the railroad, the seven batteries of Colonel Lindsay Walker's regiment and Stewart's horse artillery, being stationed in the valley, between the railroad at Hamilton's crossing and the river. The enemy's forces occupied the valley north of the railroad from Fredericksburg to within half a mile of our extreme right. His light batteries were posted over the southern extremity of the valley, at from a quarter of a mile to a mile from the railroad, while the hills on the northern banks of the river from Falmouth to Fitzhugh's farm, five miles below Fredericksburg, were studded at intervals of half a mile with his batteries of heavy guns.

The opinion had prevailed on the night before that the enemy was to attack our lines on yesterday morning, but when the day broke without the sound of guns being [unreadable] he had deferred his advance until this morning.

The sun rose clear, but a dim fog shrouded the valley, limiting the vision to a short half-mile. The enemy was supposed to be within a mile of the railroad at Hamilton's crossing, but there were no indications of his presence.

At half-past eight, A.M., General Lee, attended by his staff, rode slowly along the front of our lines, from west to east, and halted in the valley a mile to the east of Hamilton's crossing, and half a mile in the rear of our batteries on the extreme right. At nine o'clock a column of our troops, which proved to be Ewell's division, Gen. Early commanding, advanced up the valley from the direction of Port Royal, and defiled into the woods to the left of Hamilton's crossing.— The men were marching at a very leisurely pace, with a careless swinging gait; but there was that in the quiet dignity of their demeanor, which told that each, though undaunted, was conscious that the next hour might be one of stern battle and death.—Scarcely had the rear of this division disappeared in the woods, when directly in their front the artillery of the Old Stonewall brigade, Woodis, Braxton's and three other batteries opened a brisk fire on the enemy's batteries north of the railroad. At this time, owing to the fog, few of the enemy's infantry were visible. After events proved that they were lying close to the south bank of the river. The cannonading soon became general along the front of both armies. In ten minutes from the time of firing their first gun, the Danville battery, Captain Woodis, had lost fifteen men killed and wounded, a number of horses, and had two guns disabled.

The enemy's battery, eight hundred yards distant had the exact range from the first fire. In the beginning of the action the loss of the other batteries of Taliafero's division were also quite heavy. Our men fired with great precision, their shells bursting in front or directly above the opposing batteries. In the course of an hour the artillery fight had become so general that it was almost impossible for an observer to distinguish what particular battery of the enemy was engaging the attention of any given battery of ours, and vice versa. Scarcely a battery that had been unmasked on either side but was exposed to a direct and enfilading fire. The roar of cannon along a line of six miles was tremendous. Their air was resonant with the savage music of shells and solid shot. The white smoke wreaths of exploding shells were everywhere visible among the trees of the forest, which hid our forces in the valley and away beyond the river in Scafford.—Lines of ambulances could be seen bearing off the wounded of both armies, but there was nothing by which to judge that the advantage rested with either side.

At noon the fog had cleared away, but there was a thick haze in the atmosphere.—About this time the enemy infantry moved forward from the river towards our batteries on the hills. As they pressed forward across the Valley, Stewart's horse artillery from our extreme right opened upon them a destructive enfilading fire of round shot. This fire, which annoyed them sorely, was kept up in spite of six batteries which were directed against the horse artillery as soon as it was unmasked. By one o'clock the Yankee columns had crossed the Valley and entered the woods south of the railroad. The batteries on both sides slackened their fire, and musketry at first scattering, but quickly increasing to a crash and roar, sounded through the woods. Dense volumes of smoke rose above the trees and, as volley succeeded volley, sometimes so rapidly as to blend into a prolonged and continuous roar. A. P. Hill's division sustained the first shock of battle.—The rest of Jackson's corps were in different lines of reserves. D. H. Hill's division was drawn up in J. L. Marye's field, under a long hill, in rear of our lines of battle. Here they remained during most of the day, being moved from time to time to the right or left, as the exigencies of battle dictated. Shortly after the infantry fight began, a brigade of this division was moved at a double-quick a mile and a half to the right, and posted in a dense clump of pines in supporting distance of Stewart's horse artillery. In ten minutes they were brought back to their original position. The celerity of this movement would be incredible to anyone who had not witnessed it. To an observer the sight was singular and exciting. A long black line shoots from the position of the reserves, crosses the railroad at Hamilton's station, skims across the Valley, and in a few moments is lost in the pines nearly two miles away. After scarcely a breathing spell, the same line emerges from the pines, retraces its steps into its original position. As this brigade resumed its position in reserve, the fire of musketry directly in its front slackened. A few crackling shots were heard to our left, along Longstreet's division, and then a succession of volleys, which were kept up at intervals during the remainder of this evening. The musketry fire on our right was [unreadable], and the battle raged with increased fury. Our batteries along our whole front again re-opened, and Colonel Walker's artillery regiment, composed of Latham's, Letcher's, Braxton's, Pegram's, Crenshaw's, Johnson's, McIntosh's batteries, stationed in the open low grounds to the east of the railroad at Hamilton's station, moved forward several hundred yards in the direction of Fredericksburg. Hill and Early's troops had driven the enemy from the woods and across the railroad in the direction of their pontoon bridges near Deep Run. Our men pursued them a mile and a half across the bottom land, and fell back only when they had gotten under the shelter of their batteries. Our troops then retired to the mouth side of the railroad. Again the enemy rallied and returned to renew the contest, but were again, about five o'clock, P.M., driven back. All the batteries of Jackson's corps were at this time in full play, and in the approaching twilight the blaze of guns and the quick flash of shells were more distinctly visible. The move along the valley was at once splendid [missing words].

The result of the fight on our right wing may be summed up briefly. We drove the enemy back, killing three to one, and at night held the ground occupied by the enemy's batteries in the morning. The enemy had twenty thousand men engaged on this wing; while altogether, from first to last, we had not more than ten thousand in the line of fire.

Longsteet's victory was even more complete.

He drove the enemy into the streets of Fredericksburg, killing at least five to one. At dusk the firing ceased simultaneously on both sides.

It being as yet impossible to ascertain with accuracy the casualties on our side, I forbear to attempt a list.

Our wounded have all been removed from the field. The most severely hurt are receiving treatment in the field hospitals, whilst those slightly wounded are being sent down the railroads. The battle was renewed on our left at sunrise this morning, and soon became general. The battle field is pretty much the same as that of yesterday. No particulars have yet transpired. I hear but one of our generals having been struck yesterday, General Maxcy Gregg, of South Carolina, who is said to be mortally wounded.

FURTHER READINGS

Bannister, Don. *Long Day at Shiloh.* New York: Knopf, 1981.

Capers, Gerald Mortimer. *Occupied City: New Orleans under the Federals, 1862–1865.* Lexington: University of Kentucky Press, 1965.

Connelly, Thomas Lawrence. *Autumn of Glory: The Army of Tennessee, 1862–1865.* Baton Rouge: Louisiana State University Press, 1971.

Cozzens, Peter. *The Darkest Days of the War: The Battles of Iuka & Corinth.* Chapel Hill: University of North Carolina Press, 1997.

Daniel, Larry J. *Shiloh: The Battle That Changed the Civil War.* New York: Simon & Schuster, 1997.

Gallagher, Gary W. *The Antietam Campaign.* Chapel Hill: University of North Carolina Press, 1999.

———. *The Fredericksburg Campaign: Decision on the Rappahannock.* Chapel Hill: University of North Carolina Press, 1995.

———. *The Richmond Campaign of 1862: The Peninsula and the Seven Days.* Chapel Hill: University of North Carolina Press, 2000.

Hearn, Chester G. *When the Devil Came Down to Dixie: Ben Butler in New Orleans.* Baton Rouge: Louisiana State University Press, 1997.

Hess, Earl J. *Banners to the Breeze: The Kentucky Campaign, Corinth, and Stones River.* Lincoln: University of Nebraska Press, 2000.

Ivy, Dick. *Peninsula Campaign in York.* Yorktown, Va.: York County Historical Committee, 1992.

Martin, David G. *The Shiloh Campaign, March–April, 1862.* New York: Fairfax Press, 1987.

McDonough, James L. *War in Kentucky: From Shiloh to Perryville.* Knoxville: University of Tennessee Press, 1994.

McPherson, James M. *Crossroads of Freedom: Antietam.* Oxford: Oxford University Press, 2002.

Newton, Steven Harvey. *The Battle of Seven Pines, May 31–June 1, 1862*. Lynchburg, Va.: H. E. Howard, 1993.

O'Reilly, Francis Augustin. *The Fredericksburg Campaign: Winter War on the Rappahannock*. Baton Rouge: Louisiana State University Press, 2003.

Rable, George C. *Fredericksburg! Fredericksburg!* Chapel Hill: University of North Carolina Press, 2002.

Street, James. *The Struggle for Tennessee: Tupelo to Stones River*. Alexandria, Va.: Time-Life Books, 1985.

Tucker, Spencer. *Unconditional Surrender: The Capture of Forts Henry and Donelson*. Abilene, Tex.: McWhiney Foundation Press, 2001.

Wheeler, Richard. *Lee's Terrible Swift Sword: From Antietam to Chancellorsville: An Eyewitness History*. New York: HarperCollins, 1992.

30

REPORTING THE WAR, 1863

The war's middle year contained a contradiction of dialectical proportions. On the one hand, the Confederacy won two of its biggest battlefield victories in 1863. On the other hand, the chance that the Confederacy could win the war with decisive victories in the field was crushed. Two factors explain this apparent contradiction. First, the Confederacy's weaker economic and manpower base was beginning to undermine its military strength. Although the Southerners were still managing by 1863 to produce all the material they basically needed to wage war, they could not overcome the disabilities imposed by their much smaller industrial economy, weaker currency, and smaller free population, which was a quarter of the North's. Further, desertion rates were increasing, and the Confederate peace movement was gaining strength at an alarming rate in places like Georgia and, in particular, North Carolina.

There was another, more subtle reason why the Confederacy's battlefield victories had not spelled victory in the war; winning Civil War battles did not lead to destruction of the enemy force. Certainly on more than one occasion an army had left the battlefield in complete disorder, First Manassas (Bull Run) being the most famous example, but rarely did the attackers gain a permanent advantage from this. Victory without pursuit has limited results, and pursuit was rare. The victors were often as exhausted and disorganized as the defeated, and the armies were not hardened professional soldiers. They were citizen armies composed mostly of volunteers who had not known what they were getting into or conscriptees who did not necessarily want to be on the battlefield. This was one of the reasons why Emory Upton advocated professional soldiering after the war, arguing that the inefficiencies of amateur armies led to longer wars and greater bloodshed. And there were certain limitations to pursuit. For example, the increasing range of muskets and cannon made closing in on an enemy a hazardous occupation. The artillery of a retreating army could punish careless pursuers. The terrain in North America, especially the ubiquitousness of trees, complicated large-scale maneuvers, nor could armies carelessly rush away from their rail lines. It is not for nothing that the most famous Confederate campaign of maneuver, the Shenandoah Valley Campaign of 1862, had been conducted by exceedingly small forces that did not need the support of long supply lines.

The net result of the war's middle year was that the Confederacy could only win the war if it could exhaust the Union army, but earlier in the year, the situation appeared quite different. The year had opened in the West with the end of the Battle of Murfreesboro (Stones River), where Braxton Bragg had attempted to destroy William T. Rosecrans's Union force. The Union victory was rather narrow but significant since it sealed the doom of Confederate Tennessee. The Eastern Theater was more promising. Ambrose E. Burnside, considered the least competent of the Army of the Potomac's commanders, decided to make a January attack across the Rappahannock but failed when torrential downpours mired his army in the muck—hence the famous nickname "Mud March." The march was such a disaster that it cost Burnside his command. He was succeeded by Joseph T. Hooker, who energetically reorganized and reinvigorated the crestfallen army and in April launched an attack across the Rappahannock near Chancellorsville. Hooker caught Lee completely by surprise and was in position to block the Confederates from Richmond. He hesitated, however, and gave Lee the opportunity to take the initiative and counterattack. After several days of fighting, the Yankees retreated, having lost about 17,000 soldiers. Lee had lost 13,000 men, including the famed Thomas "Stonewall" Jackson, a devastating blow to the Confederate army.

Yet this victory could not compensate for the Confederacy's deteriorating position in the West. Union forces had advanced north and south through the Mississippi delta until Vicksburg remained the sole Confederate fortress on the river. If lost, the trans-Mississippi Confederacy, Louisiana, Texas, Missouri, and Arkansas, would be completely isolated. Grant's first attempts to capture the city were unsuccessful. He then crossed the river south of Vicksburg, abandoning his supply lines and working only with what his army could carry. This confused John C. Pemberton, the commander at Vicksburg. At this point, fate, in the person of Jefferson Davis, intervened on the side of the Union. Davis bypassed theater commander Joseph E. Johnston and ordered Pemberton to hold Vicksburg. Johnston ordered Pemberton to avoid being trapped in Vicksburg, but confused by contradicting orders, the commander chose to make his stand in the city's substantial fortifications. Grant moved north, trapped Pemberton in Vicksburg, and sent William T. Sherman to block all potential relief efforts by Johnston.

The disaster at Vicksburg may have helped Lee make a decision. Lee knew that the Confederacy could only prevail if it inflicted a decisive defeat on the Union, and the Confederate commander decided to go on the offensive—for the second and last time. His Army of Northern Virginia moved through Maryland into southeastern Pennsylvania. Many things were in his favor. The Confederate army had never been stronger, morale was high, he had the advantage of surprise, and the Union had yet another command crisis. George Gordon Meade replaced Hooker as commander of the Army of the Potomac only 48 hours before the two armies collided at Gettysburg. On 1 July 1863, one of Lee's three corps overran the town but failed to dislodge arriving Union divisions from the high ground to the south. On 2 July, Lee attempted to turn Meade's left flank and nearly succeeded. On 3 July, Lee made a desperate attempt ("Pickett's Charge") to break the Union center. Its failure ended the battle; and the day after, Lee began his withdrawal. Losses were immense; Confederate casualties totaled 28,000, Union casualties, 23,000. Meade followed cautiously.

The Confederate war effort in the Western Theater was collapsing. The same day Lee began his withdrawal from Maryland, 4 July, Vicksburg surrendered to Grant. Before too much longer in Tennessee, Rosecrans would outmaneuver Bragg and force the Confederate commander to yield Chattanooga. Confederate hopes would be revived briefly, though, when Rosecrans committed a near-fatal error. Believing that Bragg was defeated, Rosecrans advanced carelessly into northern Georgia and was surprised and defeated at Chickamauga. The Union army came close to destruction. Bragg's failure to maintain reserves deprived the Confederacy of a major chance to turn the tide. The Union army was forced to withdraw to Chattanooga, but in November, Union troops swept the Confederates off the mountains, and the road into the Deep South now lay open.

The campaigning in the closing months of 1863 in the East was indecisive. Meade approached Lee's defenses cautiously. Lee, who had sent part of his army to help Bragg, twice moved north to attack Meade but was easily parried and forced to withdraw behind the Rapidan River.

WESTERN THEATER

Battle of Murfreesboro/Stones River

The first battle of 1863 was actually the last battle of 1862. The fighting started on 31 December 1862 but did not conclude until 2 January 1863. Of all the battles fought during the Civil War, this one had the most poignant beginning, a beginning that reiterated the heartrending nature of a civil war.

The night before the battle began, soldiers in the two armies huddled around fires, trying to stay warm. Everyone in both camps knew what the icy dawn would bring: more bloody fighting. Both Confederate General Braxton Bragg and Union Major General William S. Rosecrans were intending to attack on New Year's Eve morning. To cheer the men and hearten them for the impending battle, a military band fired the first salvos of the Battle of Murfreesboro. The musicians began to play songs from back home, songs from better times. The band from the other camp quickly returned fire with its own musical contribution. Through the evening, the Confederate and Union bands competed with favorites like "Dixie" or "The Bonnie Blue Flag" or "Hail Columbia." Then something truly remarkable happened. One of the bands began to play "Home Sweet Home," a song well known and loved in both the North and the South. The men in both camps began to sing. When the singing was over, the men settled down for what sleep they could get on that cold winter eve of what would be one of the bloodiest battles of the war.[1]

Rosecrans and Bragg had been skirmishing since the end of October, but now both were ready to take the offensive. Rosecrans never got the chance, though. He was concentrating on pulling his own offensive together when he was caught unaware by Bragg's attack. Confederate soldiers streamed out from among the black cedars and smashed into the Union right, where Major General Alexander McCook's soldiers were still at breakfast. The attack was devastating; McCook could only watch as his men were driven back nearly 3 miles.

Bragg's advantage did not last long, however. Rosecrans immediately began establishing lines along the Nashville turnpike and a nearby rail line so as to protect his sources of supplies. The Confederates concentrated on the federal center where Major General George H. Thomas was in command. This was a miscalculation by Bragg. Had he concentrated instead on the Union left flank, there was every possibility that he could have cut the federal army off from its Nashville base. Confederate soldiers charged Thomas's position over and over through a dense cedar forest that came to be called "Hell's Half-Acre" for the desperate fighting there that day. Despite the repeated attacks, Thomas's men were able to hold their position and protect the vital transportation routes. Despite the success of the day, that night Rosecrans considered retreating to Nashville. Instead, he elected to say and continue the fight.

The fighting did not resume until 2 January, when Rosecrans sent a force across Stones River and occupied a position from which it could enfilade the Confederate right. *Enfilade* is a military term that means to shoot down the ranks of the enemy's lines rather than head-on. Enfilade firing is devastating to the victim; it produces many casualties. Bragg sent Breckinridge across Stones River to drive the Union force from their position, a task his men managed to accomplish but on which they could not capitalize due to heavy firing from enemy artillery. Breckinridge lost a third of his men to the relentless fire. The federals reoccupied their previous position, and on 3 January, Rosecrans received reinforcements from Nashville. Bragg was forced to retreat to Tullahoma, Tennessee. Total casualties for the battle were more than 23,000. Tactically and strategically, the battle was a victory for the North. Rosecrans's army was now in a position to threaten the Confederate rail center at Chattanooga.

JOSEPH CLISBY: SUMMARY OF VICTORY AT MURFREESBORO

The Macon Telegraph *published a summary of the Battle of Murfreesboro that was most likely written by the editor, Joseph Clisby, and based on telegraphic accounts. It provides more details and analysis than the first telegraphic report did. As always, the lack of information limited what the newspaper could convey to its readers.*

Macon Telegraph, 2 January 1863

THE VICTORY AT MURFREESBORO'

We hope to get fuller accounts before going to press, but the facts already before us indicate a signal over throw of Rosecrans and his grand army. The fight began at nine o'clock on Tuesday, the 30th, with an artillery duel, but from 12 o'clock to night-fall there was an active engagement of infantry on our left. The fight, however, was but partial, and the enemy made the attack. On Wednesday morning, at half past five, our troops commenced a general assault, and a battle of almost unparalleled spirit and obstinacy raged between the combatants for more than eleven hours, during which the enemy's right was driven back upon Stone Run, a distance of

seven miles from his original line of battle, and his left wing was only able to hold its position. At night, as we have good reason to believe, our enemy encamped four miles in advance of their line the previous morning. Four thousand prisoners, and thirty-one pieces of cannon, are among the trophies of the fight. During the night of the 30th, two million dollars worth of stores, including five days rations, were destroyed by our troops in a raid upon the enemy's rear.—The loss of such an amount of provisions, the enemy being already short and on half rations, must very seriously embarrass his retreat.

All the facts must be considered as amounting, at least, to a fatal frustration of the enemy's campaign in that direction, and completes the story along the whole frontier. In Virginia at Fredericksburg—in North Carolina at Kinston—in Tennessee at Murfreesboro—in Mississippi at Tallahatchie and Vicksburg, the enemy's advance has been severely checked and repulsed, and his little raid of 2000 cavalry a day or two ago upon the East Tennessee Railroad, is as yet the only point where he has not been terribly foiled, and the only thing he can yet show, besides death and disaster, as the fruit of his enormous preparations to crush the South. The repulse has been complete and universal. Choosing, at his leisure, his points of assault and preparing out of his abundant resources a force for each which he boasted would be overwhelming, he has been everywhere driven back, with horrible slaughter, torn, bleeding, discomfited and despondent. The movement on Murfreesboro, was an effort to pierce our centre. If he could have discomfited Bragg's army, penetrated the mountains through Chattanooga, occupied the line of railway and threatened Georgia on the North, he would have carried out his designs in that quarter. The movement upon Goldsboro' was intended to cut off the other railway line, and if both had been successful, he would have severed the Confederacy in two for all practical purposes.

Then to have secured possession of the Mississippi by the capture of Vicksburg—to penetrate the Alabama by taking possession of Mobile—to take Charleston—and lastly, if Burnside could have crossed the Rappahannock and invested Richmond on the North, while the Yankee force at Suffolk marched up and attacked it on the South—the city being in the meanwhile isolated from supplies and reinforcements by cutting off all her railway communications, he would have accomplished probably all the plans of the winter's campaign, and would perhaps have held onto fatal toils.

But so far, every link in this extensive plan of operations has [unreadable]. Every thing attempted has miscarried.

Every fold of the second [unreadable] has been cut before it could fairly be tightened. The enemy has been completely frustrated and baffled in the very flush of his strength and the fullest vigor of his enterprise.

Now, what must be the moral affect of such considerations and reflections of these upon the people of the North the reader can judge for himself. One thing is certain, there has been nothing in the annals of war like the total and sweeping frustration. We have had great success—but they have been isolated triumphs, and often shorn, to some extent, of the effect by contemporaneous defeats of something which could be represented as a defeat. But here is a grand, total, sweeping, ignominious repulse along the whole frontier of the war for a distance of two thousand miles. If this fails to satisfy our enemies that subjugation is impossible—that the war is but a waste of time and money, what will? If it does not put an estoppel upon the complaints against men, and show the North that the difficulty lies not in their Cabinet or their Generals, but in the impossibility of their enterprise, what will?

Rosecrans is perhaps their brightest and best man, and he, no doubt, fought Bragg with great advantage of numbers, but it did not avail. The miscarriage is too universal to be charged to accident of imbecility—it must be traced to the fact that they are attempting an impossible achievement.

Honor to Bragg, as well as his glorious host, for this splendid achievement. He has vindicated his reputation and won back public confidence which had been partially alienated from him by the attacks of the press, and particularly the venomous pens of army correspondents. The judgment of the President and of General Johnston, who left him at so critical a moment to marshal the grand battle, is triumphantly vindicated, and it will be some time before the complains of Bragg's weakness and inefficiency will be openly removed.

Seige of Charleston Harbor and the Assault on Fort Wagner

On 7 April, Union Rear Admiral Samuel F. du Pont attacked Charleston Harbor with nine ironclads. He was decisively repulsed in what was the prelude to a lengthy bombardment that smashed much of Charleston to little more than rubble. The bombardment would begin in earnest come July when Rear Admiral John A. Dahlgren succeeded du Pont. The seige and bombardment would continue throughout much of the remainder of the war.

The naval bombardment was supported by land troops under Major General Quincy A. Gillmore, whose primary target was Fort Wagner. Gillmore made several attempts to capture Fort Wagner with considerable losses. Capturing Fort Wagner was the key to possession of Morris Island, a 400-acre barrier island on the south side of Charleston Harbor. With possession of Morris Island, federal forces could subdue Fort Sumter, which would allow the Union fleet to compel the city's surrender. An attack on the fort in July was led by Boston abolitionist Robert Gould Shaw and his black regiment, the 54th Massachusetts, made famous by the movie *Glory*. The Union was denied Fort Wagner, though, until 6 September when finally the Confederates were forced to evacuate. One of the interesting aspects of the coverage by the Southern press of the attack on Fort Wagner was the failure to mention the use of black troops. The bombardment of Charleston continued on through the fall and early winter, but the city's other fortifications held out.

PETER W. ALEXANDER: UNION ATTACK ON CHARLESTON REPULSED

With no fighting expected in Virginia until May, Peter W. Alexander traveled to Charleston in March to see what would come of the naval engagement that seemed to be brewing. Alexander was on hand to witness the Union's attack on Charleston, which was repulsed by the Confederates. As soon after the battle as he could, Alexander telegraphed the following story to Savannah. He followed that initial story later with a longer letter about the initial battle in the harbor. That story also ran on 10 April.

Savannah Republican, 10 April 1863

TELEGRAPHIC
THE ATTACK ON CHARLESTON
THE KEOKUK AND IRONSIDES DISABLED
THE ENEMY RETIRE

Renewal of Fight Expected To-Day

[Special to Savannah Republican]

CHARLESTON, Apr. 7—The ball opened at 3 o'clock this afternoon. The enemy commenced the engagement with five turreted vessels and the Ironsides.—Their fire was directly chiefly against Fort Sumter.—The engagement lasted until half past five o'clock, when the enemy retired. The Keokuk, with a double turret, was disabled, and the Ironside is believed to be disabled. Steam was seen issuing from the sides of the Ironsides. The monitors were hit frequently and their smoke stacks perforated.

The first on both sides was terrific but deliberate. Fort Sumter, in the harbor, Fort Moultrie, Battery Bee, and Battery Beauregard on Sullivan's Island, and Fort Wagner and the battery at Cummings Point on Morris Island, participated on our side. One gun was dismounted in Sumter, but will be replaced to-night. One drummer boy killed and five men wounded. There were no casualties on Sullivan's Island, except for a man who broke his arm in falling from the flag staff of Fort Moultrie, which had been shot away.

The Confederates remain in high spirits.

Gen. Rieley, in command of all the works, behaved handsomely.

There were no movements on land. The fight will probably be renewed tomorrow.

P. W. A.

ARMY CORRESPONDENCE OF THE
SAVANNAH REPUBLICAN
THE BATTLE OF CHARLESTON

CHARLESTON, April 7.

The day of trial and blood to Charleston has at last arrived, and the blow so long impending over this goodly city, like the sword of Damocles, has at length fallen. It has taken no one by surprise however, and especially the military authorities. Gen. Beauregard had received information some days ago, from a source and by means which must for present be nameless, that the attack would probably be made to-day, and to-day it has been made. Having already sent you a full statement of the affair by telegraph, there is but little left me to add.

It was observed at half past two p.m. That the Federal fleet, which had been lying off the bar since Sunday afternoon, was approaching in hostile array. Eight turreted ironclads and the famous iron covered war steamer Ironsides were put in motion and advanced to the assault by what is known as "Ship Channel." Gen. Beauregard, whose headquarters are in the city, was promptly notified of the movement by telegraph from Fort Sumter. It may be stated that there are wires running from all the Forts and batteries in and around the harbor to the city, and that the telegraph communication is frequent and expeditious between the forts and batteries, as well as with Charleston.

The Ironsides and five of the monitors participated in the engagement. Fort Moultrie was the first to open fire, at five minutes past three o'clock. The double turreted Keokuk—the most formidable vessel of the Federal armada quickly responded. Fort Sumter took up the tale, and poured a broadside into the assailing squadron, and she was followed in turn by Fort Beauregard and Battery Been, on Sullivan's Island, and Fort Wagner and Cummins' Point Battery on Morris Island. In a few minutes the battle became general and the cannonading terrific. The iron clads had entered the outer circle of fire, and from every fort and battery by which the outer harbor is girded they were assailed with great ardor and coolness. The conduct of the enemy was equally spirited, and his fire deliberate and well directed. The principal attack was directed against Sumter, though all the forts and batteries came in for a share of the enemy's attention. But one shot, so far as I could see, passed over Sumter. The Ironsides threw monster shells, which burst over and around the fort with great precision, and the wonder is that the loss of life was so little.

The Keokuk led the attack, and took the post of danger and of honor. And dearly did she pay for the distinction, as will be seen in the sequel. About forty-five minutes after the engagement commenced, a shot from Fort Wagner took effect in the stern of the Ironsides. It is believed she was also penetrated in the side, as steam could be distinctly seen issuing from her side next to the city. She soon withdrew out of range of our guns, and for the remainder of the time was a silent spectator of the conflict. This was a great triumph, as she was manifestly looked to, to test the strength of Fort Sumter. About five o'clock the Keokuk, also, withdrew, evidently badly injured. The others followed soon and by half-past five the entire fleet had retired, and when last seen was rounding Morris Island to the southward.

The practice of our gunners, after they got the range, was excellent. The enemy's vessels, (which were sunk by pumping in water until the decks were nearly level with the water,) were frequently struck, and nearly all their smoke stacks were perforated. This too, notwithstanding they kept shifting their positions. Occasionally they would steam up within 1,000 yards of Sumter, but for the greater part of the time they maintained the fight at a distance of 1,500 to 2,000 yards.—Late in the evening the Ironsides and three monitors were seen moving off slowly around Morris Island, as if they might be going to Port Royal for repairs.

The casualties on our side were slight, considering the nature of the conflict and the monster projectiles used by the enemy. In Fort Sumter, a drummer boy and five men were wounded, two of the men and the boy seriously. One 10-inch Columbiad was dismounted, and one 8-inch bursted. The former will be remounted to-night. The Fort was struck 34 times,

and the flag had a hole shot through it. No casualties occurred on Sullivan's Island, except the shooting away of the flag-staff and the accidental fall of a man who was trying to replace it, and from which he died soon afterwards. On Morris Island (at Fort Wagner,) six men were wounded by the accidental explosion of an ammunition chest, two of whom have since died. Two others are badly injured and will probably die before morning.

Gen. Ripley, said to be one of the best artillery officers in the world, was in command of all the harbor defences, and is entitled to all the honors of the occasion. Col. Butler was in command of Fort Moultrie, Col. Rhett of Fort Sumter, Lieut. Col. Simpkins of Battery Bee, Capt. Sitgraves of Fort Beauregard, Major Huger of Fort Wagner, and Lieut. Lesense, with a detachment from Sumter, of the Battery on Cummings Point—all under the superior direction of Gen. Ripley, and all of whom conducted themselves with great gallantry.

The conflict was witnessed by thousands of spectators from the Battery promenade and the house tops. Among the vast throng there assembled I did not encounter one who expressed any doubt as to the result. It was a magnificent spectacle. The white puffs of smoke issuing from the port holes of their ironclads with a tongue of fire in the centre, the solemn watch kept up by these huge monsters as they wheeled past the forts, the fantastic festoons of smoke that garlanded the heads of the forts and slowly floated off to the north, the bursting of 15 inch shells in mid-air and the deep booming the titanic guns engaged in the conflict, the appearance of the Confederate rams Chicora and Palmetto State steaming energetically up and down their chosen fighting position, the silent city, and the breathless multitude who crowded its housetops and promenade, made up a spectacle at once grand and imposing.

But it is long after midnight, and I must cease.

P.W.A.

AN ANONYMOUS REPORT: ACCOUNT OF UNSUCCESSFUL UNION ATTACK ON BATTERY WAGNER, MORRIS' ISLAND

The attack on Battery Wagner was just another skirmish on an island in the Charleston Harbor, but it is one that lives on in modern memory, thanks to the movie Glory. *As* Glory *depicted, this was a battle where black Union troops played an important combat role. While the Union attack was unsuccessful, it was important because of the use of black soldiers, a fact not mentioned in the* Savannah Republican's *story.*

Savannah Republican, 12 July 1863

FROM CHARLESTON
ATTACK ON BATTERY WAGNER, MORRIS' ISLAND

Saturday morning, about daylight, the 7th Connecticut Volunteers and the 76th Pennsylvania Volunteers, under the command of Brig. Gen. Strong, attempted to carry by storm Battery Wagner, on Morris' Island, near Charleston, S.C. The enemy were met by the 18th Battalion Georgia Volunteers, Major Wm. S. Bassinger; 12th Battalion Georgia Volunteers, Lieut. Col. Capers; a battalion of the 1st Volunteer Regiment of Georgia, Col. Chars. H. Olmstead; and several companies of South Carolina Regulars. The battle raged furiously for about four hours, the enemy being quickly repulsed in every advance.

An official despatch states that the enemy's loss in killed was 95; the beach was strewn with their dead. One hundred and thirty prisoners were taken. These advanced within a short distance of our breastworks, and knowing that retreat was impossible, a large number lay flat on their faces before the works during the fight, and when it was over the precious scoundrels drew from their pockets white flags and surrendered.

Five Yankee officers were captured and five killed.

On the third or forth round of the enemy, Capt. Claus Werner, of the German Volunteers, 1st Volunteer Regiment of Georgia, was instantly killed by a minnie ball taking effect on the left breast and passing through the body.

In the 18th Battalion Georgia Volunteers, Major W. S. Bassinger, the following are the casualties: Killed—Edward Postwell, in the 19th year of his age, a native of Savannah; Julian Alexander Santina, in the 19th year of his age, a native of Savannah; B. Mulloy and James Bryan. Wounded—Lieut. Frederick Tupper, minnie ball passing across the breast; Jessee Osmond, in the wrist; Bernard Maguire, in shoulder. All of the 18th Battalion Georgia Volunteers who were killed in the action were shot in the head.

The body of Capt. Werner, accompanied by Mr. M. Meyer, of Charleston, Capt. D. Werner, brother of deceased, and Mr. A. Seydel, of the German Volunteers, reached this city yesterday morning for interment.

We are permitted by a friend to make the following extract from a letter received by him dated Charleston July 11:

"The enemy made their lodgment on the Southern portion of Morris' Island. Our troops suffered severely yesterday, over 300 casualties occurring. We have to regret the loss of Capt. Cheves of the Engineers and Capt. Haskell. Fort Wagner is now our Southern base of operations on Morris' Island. It is situated about the middle of that island, and where it is so narrow that it is more the character of an isthmus. This point the enemy endeavored to carry at daybreak this morning, with a force of about 2,000 men under Brig. Gen. Strong. Our men allowed them to approach very close and then poured destructive volleys into them. The repulse was highly successful. Ninety five dead bodies at the close of the fight strewed the ground in the vicinity of the intrenchments. One hundred and thirty-five prisoners and many wounded were brought into the city. Gen. Ripley estimates the loss of the enemy at five hundred put *hors du combat*. Four monitors have been pegging away at Fort Wagner, but without doing much damage, Fort Wagner constantly replying to them. From the fact of one monitor having retired this afternoon, it is believed she must have been damaged."

FORT WAGNER, MORRIS' ISLAND
July 11, 1863

MR. EDITOR:—We were attacked this morning at daylight by a brigade of the enemy, which was repulsed with the loss of between fifty and two hundred killed and wounded, and about one hundred prisoners.

Our own loss is very slight. In the 1st Regiment, Capt. Werner, of Co. I, was killed and Private Hancock slightly wounded in the hand. The Guards (18th Battalion) have lost five killed and three wounded. Major Bassenger will send list. The 12th Battalion lost one killed and two wounded.

CHARLES H. OLMSTEAD.
Col. 1St Vol. Reg't Ga.

OFFICIAL DESPATCH

CHARLESTON, July 11, 9:45 a.m.—The enemy attacked, in force, Battery Wagner on Morris' Island at daylight this morning but was quickly repulsed with 95 killed, many wounded and 130 prisoners. Only 5 men killed on our side.

All quiet on James Island.

JAMES R. SNEED: ACCOUNT OF RECENT FIGHTING IN CHARLESTON HARBOR

Once the spring campaign began in Virginia, Alexander returned to his usual post. The Republican *editor, James R. Sneed, went to Charleston, reporting on the siege of the harbor. Sneed cast the fighting as having mixed results for the Confederates. He noted that the Union army had achieved a foothold on Morris Island with the capture of the lower battery, but he cast the previous day's fighting at Battery Wagner as a Southern victory with 400 enemy soldiers killed and an estimated 1,000 wounded.*

Savannah Republican, 13 July 1863

EDITORIAL CORRESPONDENCE
CHARLESTON, Sunday Night,
July 12th, 1863

I have but a few minutes to write, but will devote them to the readers of the Republican, as all eyes are now anxiously turned to this city and all hearts yearning for its safety.

The siege of Charleston has regularly begun. The enemy hope to take it by gradual approaches, and they have at least gained encouragement from their first success—the capture of the lower battery on Morris' Island, thus giving them a foothold, and enabling them to set out hopefully on their tedious work. This disaster is attributable to bad engineering, for which somebody should be held responsible. The lower battery was a shackling affair, and our men left it only when the carriages of their guns had been shattered to pieces.

The battle yesterday morning claims a place among the bloodiest and most destructive of the war, at least so far as the enemy are concerned. Our loss was trifling—only one or two killed and some half-dozen wounded. The first account gave no adequate idea of the slaughter of the Yankees, it having been on evidences immediately in front of the battery. A subsequent reconnaissance exposed over four hundred dead bodies, which were buried by our men. To this add the usual proportion of wounded—five to one—and the casualties become awful. That proportion in this case, however, is too large. The fight was at close quarters, and it is believed that a majority of those who were struck were killed. An officer of high rank gave me to-day his opinion that at least one thousand of the enemy were put hors du combat in the action. In addition to the killed on the field, the surgeon of the hospital where their wounded are now laying informs me that eight died last night, and in all probability as many more will pass to their long account before morning.

Willing to do justice to a brave foe, it may be added that a more daring and gallant assault has not been made on either side since the commencement of the war. The enemy numbered fifteen hundred, according to the best authority at hand. They landed on the lower end of the island, and double quicked it up to the very mouths of our guns, coming in along our pickets, though not surprising the garrison. The advancing column got within forty yards of Battery Wagner before a gun was fired. Gen. Stromm (who commanded the assailants, and was, by the way, Beast Butler's Adjutant at New Orleans,) then cried out in a voice distinctly heard at the fort: "Now's your time boys, go in and take them," and in they went sure enough, some twenty five of them having actually scaled our works and got inside, where they were either killed or captured. The murderous fire poured into them by our artillery and infantry literally mowed down their ranks, but on they pressed until success became hopeless and the dead were piled up under their feet, when they retired.

The whole of to-day, until sundown, has been spent in a continuous artillery duel between the ships and Battery Wagner. There were three monitors, the Atlanta among them (her maiden effort on the Yankee side) and three or four heavy mortar boats. The signal corps report no casualties on our side. From some cause unknown to me, a great battle is expected to-morrow.

A supply boat that was lying on the west side of Morris' Island had a shot put through her belly, and was otherwise injured.

Lieutenant Tupper, whom I called to see this afternoon, is severely wounded, a ball having struck him in the breast, breaking two ribs and passing out at the shoulder. He is not quite easy, and doing the best possible in the hands of a good physician, and the kindest of friends. The other wounded are doing well, most of their injuries being slight.

J.R.S.

Vicksburg

While Grant's campaign to capture Vicksburg is generally dated from May 1863, the Union general had had his eye on the important Mississippi port since the previous fall. On 13 November 1862, Grant started his campaign for Vicksburg by moving south of Grand Junction, Tennessee. Grant sent Major General William T. Sherman with 40,000 men, supported by Rear Admiral David D. Porter, in an amphibious assault on Vicksburg. Raids by the Confederate cavalry under Nathan Bedford Forrest menaced Grant's advance, and an attack on the Union supply depot at Holly Springs, Mississippi, forcing Grant to back off from his objective of capturing Vicksburg.

Meanwhile, Sherman and Porter continued with their raid on Vicksburg. Sherman attempted an assault on Chickasaw Bluffs north of Vicksburg, but after a three-day fight against nearly 14,000 of Pemberton's veteran soldiers, the Union troops were forced to withdraw. Confederates retained control of the Mississippi from Vicksburg to Baton Rouge, but Grant was determined to change that, even if he had failed on his first try.

The Confederates taught Grant a valuable lesson with their attack on Holly Springs. An overland operation supported by a long communications line was impractical. Through the winter and early spring of 1863, Grant probed Vicksburg's defenses to learn more about the best approach for capturing the city and to give the rainy season time to pass.

Naval forces worked closely with Grant's operations to reconnoiter the city. Admiral Porter assigned the *Queen of the West* and the *Indianola* to play cat and mouse with the Vicksburg batteries. The two boats were to make daring runs past the batteries, and they were also to disrupt Confederate river traffic between Vicksburg and Port Hudson. While they accomplished their objectives for awhile, the Confederates captured the *Queen of the West* and destroyed the *Indianola*. From the South, Admiral Farragut fought his way up the Mississippi, though only two of his vessels, his flagship and one other, managed to get past Confederate defenses.

While Grant was slowly tightening his grip on the city, Pemberton was busily trying to figure out what he should do. His situation was made worse by two things. First, he was essentially without intelligence-gathering capabilities. His commanding general, Joseph E. Johnston, had ordered most of his cavalry away to join the Army of Tennessee, and so Pemberton was essentially blind regarding Grant's movements. Pemberton's second problem was that he was receiving contradictory orders from his superiors. On the one hand, President Davis was telling Pemberton to hang on to Vicksburg at all costs. Johnston, who was by far more competent to make intelligent military decisions than his commander-in-chief, ordered Pemberton not to get his army trapped in Vicksburg. Pemberton chose to follow Davis's orders.

Through April, the two generals maneuvered, planned, and positioned their armies. Pemberton's were strung out along the east bank of the Mississippi for about 50 miles. Grant's men were on the west bank. Grant's army marched to Hard Times, Louisiana, south of Vicksburg and waited for Porter. At the same time, Porter's gunboats and transports had begun a series of daring night actions to get past the batteries at Vicksburg and join up with the remainder of Grant's force at Hard Times. On 30 April, Porter ferried Grant's army from Hard Times south to Bruinsburg and the east bank of the Mississippi. On 1 May, Grant's army rebuffed a small Confederate force that tried to stop the Union army's inland advance in the Battle of Port Gibson.

Grant turned to arranging his forces for their assault on Vicksburg. He divided his 41,000 men into three columns. He gave Major General John McClernand orders to advance to the left, along the river. Sherman was the take the center, and his third subcommander, Major General James B. McPherson, would move forward on the right.

On 12 May, Grant met the first Confederate resistance near Raymond, about 14 miles southwest of Jackson. Confederate Brigadier General John Gregg's 5,000 men confronted McPherson's advance guard. Gregg's men held off McPherson's superior force for six hours before being forced to retreat. This gave Grant the opportunity to separate the two Confederate forces near Jackson. He sent McPherson to destroy the railroad at Clinton, and he sent Sherman through Raymond toward Jackson. McClernand was to support the other two corps and be ready to defend an attack by Pemberton from the west. The Union forces were successful at cutting both the rail and telegraph lines, thereby slowing Confederate communications.

On 13 May, Johnston arrived in Jackson, planning to meet up with Pemberton's force and take on Grant head first, but that would not happen. With Grant's force between Vicksburg and Jackson, the plan was impossible. That same day, however, Pemberton advanced out of Vicksburg toward Jackson. He was trying to find Grant's lines of communications, but they had been abandoned. Johnston saw a chance, with Pemberton's army in the field, to strike at Grant's divided forces, and he sent three

couriers—three to ensure that the message got through—to order Pemberton to attack the federal column near Clinton. Grant had sent Sherman to occupy Jackson,
Mississippi's capital, after Johnston abandoned it. The remainder of Grant's force
turned to take on Pemberton's 22,000 men east of the Big Black River.

Johnston's new plan to use his force in combination with Pemberton's did not
work for two reasons. First, Pemberton and his subordinates had decided not to follow Johnston's orders to consolidate the two armies against Grant. Second, Johnston
was the victim of treachery. The already desperate Confederate situation was made
worse when one of the couriers Johnston had sent to Pemberton turned out to be a
secret Northern sympathizer and carried the message to Grant. With the Confederate plans laid out in front of him, Grant immediately moved against Pemberton.

Pemberton showed great ineptitude in the battle that began on 16 May. The two
forces met at Champion's Hill, and rather than choosing to defend the high bluffs
that bordered the west side of the river crossing, Pemberton chose to make his stand
on level ground east of the river. It may have been that Pemberton believed he
could stop Grant if the Union army attacked his main positions from the level
ground, but that is not what Grant did. The night before, Sherman's men had
crossed the river on pontoon bridges and positioned themselves to the north of
Pemberton. At dawn, the federals advanced and outflanked Pemberton. When the
Confederate lines collapsed, their general had no choice but to order a general retreat back to Vicksburg.

In 19 days, Grant had marched some 200 miles while living off the land. He had
defeated numerically superior detachments of the enemy in five different engagements and several skirmishes, and he had inflicted 8,000 casualties on the Confederates compared with his own 4,400. And now he had his opponent locked up tight in
a fortified city with few escape routes.

Again, Johnston ordered Pemberton to consolidate forces with his. Again Pemberton met with his subordinates, and again, they all agreed to disobey their commander's order. They and their 30,000 men would make a stand at Vicksburg, which
Pemberton considered to be the most important place in the Confederacy at that
moment. The terrain around the city did favor its defenders. The Confederates had
more than 100 artillery guns in place around the city. There was, perhaps, a chance
Pemberton and his men could hold on to the city, yet the importance of Vicksburg
as a stronghold had been diminished considerably by Porter's continued flaunting of
his ability to get past the city's river defenses. With the Union navy both to the
north and south of Vicksburg, steamboats would no longer be bringing cargo to the
city's railhead. The last link to the trans-Mississippi had been immobilized.

Grant was uneasy with the idea of an extended siege of the city, and so he tried
twice to take it in direct assaults on 19 and 22 May. Pemberton's men repulsed both
attempts and inflicted 3,000 casualties that day. Given no choice but to lay siege to
the city, Grant set his engineers to digging trenches and preparing other defenses.
Foreshadowing the next year's Battle of the Crater, Grant's men also dug trenches
under Confederate positions and filled them with black powder so as to blow gaps in
Southern defenses. Porter's gunboats and Grant's army, though short on artillery
pieces, shelled the city relentlessly from middle May until its capitulation on 4 July.
Civilians and defenders alike moved into the caves of the high bluffs along the river
to escape the bombardment. Newspapers continued to print through the siege, but

they were forced to use wallpaper or brown wrapping paper. Food supplies ran low, and citizens and soldiers alike were reduced to eating mules and rats.

Finally, on 3 July, after a forty-six-day siege, Pemberton realized that his men could stand no more. At 10:00 A.M., he arranged to meet with Grant. To Pemberton's request for terms, Grant demanded unconditional surrender, but Pemberton outfoxed the Union general. He lied. He told Grant he would not surrender unconditionally; he said the city had enough food to hold out indefinitely. The terms agreed to allowed Pemberton's men to be paroled until they could be exchanged for Union prisoners of war. On Independence Day, Pemberton surrendered. Grant's men celebrated the national holiday in high style. The army marched into the city with its band playing and its flags flying. On the river, the gunboats fired their guns in jubilation. Citizens accepted food from the occupying Union army, but Independence Day would not be celebrated again in Vicksburg until the mid-twentieth century.

Grant had solidified his reputation as a military leader and laid the foundation for his rapid advance to the rank of lieutenant general and commander of all Union armies. Pemberton earned the undying enmity of Southerners everywhere.

AN ANONYMOUS REPORT: MILITARY SITUATION AT VICKSBURG

It all came down to numbers and supplies. Once Johnston finished building his army, he managed to have a force of more than 30,000 men, considerably larger than the Confederate officer who wrote the following letter estimated, yet much smaller than Grant's force. Then there was the matter of supplies. Grant had unharrassed, well-protected supply and communications lines. Johnston's was vunerable. It was long and getting longer with each move closer to Vicksburg. The writer, who may have been the paper's assistant editor Henry Cleveland, tried hard to find an optimistic way to tell his readers back home, but clearly he was on the edge of despair.

Augusta Constitutionalist, 8 July 1863 (Augusta, Ga.)

OUR ARMY CORRESPONDENCE

From Mississippi

The Siege of Vicksburg—Condition of the Opposing Armies—Strength of Grant's Position—Johnston's Resources for Dislodging him—Deductions

From a letter to this paper, written by an intelligent correspondent—an officer in Gen. Johnston's army we make the following extract, which will be found deeply interesting:

ED. CONSTI.

I wish I had some good news to give you. I have not. People away from here expect a great deal, and I am satisfied a great deal too much from Gen. Johnston. There is no room for generalship in this case. Physical obstructions, such as Johnston will have to overcome, will quell and oppress the genius of any man. Grant has entrenched himself around Vicksburg as strongly as Pemberton has in it. The hills are in many places nearly perpendicular, with but little room on their tops, and high enough to permit a very small party to prevent the ascent of as many men as can be got to them. This almost interminable succession of steep hills and deep valleys for miles and miles around Grant's camp has been fortified with all the skill that the devilish ingenuity of these rascals could secure. The hills are crowned with heavy guns, and every gorge is ready to belch forth destruction. He has devastated the country all around him, for 20 to 80 miles, leaving nothing that could contribute to the support of an army advancing on him, and has obstructed all the roads leading towards him in every possible way for many miles. You will perceive that it would be no easy job for Johnston to get to him. Besides, Grant has from 70 to 80,000 men, Johnston not half so many. (I am afraid to commit to paper the strength of this army.) Grant's communications are open, his facilities for receiving stores, supplies and reinforcements are unbounded, while Johnston has to work hard to buy every mouthful his army eats, and then is obliged to hunt it many miles—sometimes 40 or 50, and the farther he goes towards Vicksburg, the farther he must wagon his supplies.

Now with these facts before you, work out the problem. If Grant, with all the men and all the means he wants or asks for can't take Pemberton in Vicksburg, with 18 or 15,000 men, how is Johnston, with only all the men he can get, to destroy or subdue Grant in a fortified camp equally strong, with 80,000 men to defend it. This is the proposition; work it out; put "QE.D.", at the end and send it to me, for I would like mightly to see it.

In all this I do not undervalue nor underrate the elements at Gen. Johnston's command, nor his great ability. His army, (I will state *entre nous*) not as high as 80,000 fighting men, is composed of the very best fighting stock on the continent, and if Johnston could only get Grant into the field would maul a much larger force "till they should think the very devil himself had come from hell." They are anxious to fight, and have every confidence in the General and will do what men can do—yet this is not enough to overcome the immense disadvantages under which he labors.

I do not write this to discourage you, for I know no more of Gen. Johnston's plans than you do, perhaps not so much. I hope that he will be let alone, however, and not driven by taunts and innuendoes, and abuse to sacrifice an army which is confessedly the only barrier that at present protects, in any considerable degree, the States of Mississippi, Alabama and Georgia.

AN ANONYMOUS REPORT: EDITORIAL—WHO IS RESPONSIBLE FOR FALL OF VICKSBURG?

Once the truth began to come out about the actual state of affairs in Vicksburg, journalists began asking questions about the apparent deception that had convinced Confederates that the key city on the Mississippi River could hold out. The Savannah Republican *lashed out with a vitriolic editorial that demanded in an untitled commentary that whomever was responsible be found and, the implication was, punished.*

Savannah Republican, 9 July 1863

VICKSBURG.—There is a heavy weight of responsibility resting on somebody's shoulders for the regular and systematic lying that has been put upon the public regarding the ability of this place to hold out. The western Press, in the very vicinity of the unfortunate city, has been quite as badly imposed on as anybody else. We have forty times read reports, coming from Pemberton himself, that supplies were abundant, and the garrison could "hold out indefinitely." About ten days ago the public was assured, on unquestionable authority, that Kirby Smith had driven 800 beeves across the Mississippi into Vicksburg.

This deception was kept up until the very eve of the surrender on account of starvation. The place fell on the 5th, and just think of such an assurance as the following appearing in the Jackson Mississippian of the 3d:

SUPPLIES FOR VICKSBURG.—Our people need have no apprehension about Vicksburg's being starved out, as we are informed upon very good authority, that there is on hand an abundant supply—and long before it is exhausted our army outside will open a way for the transmission of stores. We might mention the extent of our provisions there, but for prudential reasons refrain. This much we may say, however: If Vicksburg does not fall until her heroic garrison is "starved out," it will be many a long sultry month before the Yankee thieves will realize their dreams of capture.

Within forty eight hours after this assurance was printed, Vicksburg was in the hands of the enemy and the Mississippian "packing up to leave."

Verily the road to truth is difficult in the West. Bad news is about the only true thing we have heard from them since the commencement of the war.

Tullahouma, Chickamauga, and Chattanooga Campaigns

For six months after the Battle of Murfreesboro, Bragg's army sat at Tullahouma, Tennessee. They were a hard six months for Bragg's men. They stayed busy building defensive lines, but they had become demoralized by inactivity, hunger, and infighting among their superiors. Through most of that spring, Bragg's army had never had more than a three-day's supply of rations and had been forced to scavenge the countryside to supplement the shipments they received from Atlanta. Even more devastating to morale, though, was the infighting among the Army of Tennessee's officers. Bragg's subordinates had lost confidence in the general's ability to lead the army, and they had not merely gossiped and griped among themselves. Their public grumbling became so pronounced that at the end of January President Davis sent Joseph Johnston to Tullahouma to try to resolve the situation.

Rosecrans seemingly was content to leave Bragg be through that spring, for he made no move to menace the Confederate position, even though the two armies were no more than 30 miles apart. By June the Union's supreme commander, Henry Halleck, was tired of waiting, and he threatened to fire Rosecrans if he did not do something. Rosecrans responded with the well-planned, well-conducted maneuver he had spent the last six months preparing. With an army twice the size of Bragg's and sound intelligence as to the Army of Tennessee's location, Rosecrans had little difficulty forcing Bragg to retreat to Chattanooga just two days before Pemberton surrendered Vicksburg and Lee began his "strategic withdrawal" from Gettysburg.

Rosecrans's and Bragg's armies spent a month regrouping before beginning the sly cat-and-mouse game that would culminate in Bragg's greatest victory at Chickamauga, Georgia, in mid-September. Bragg spent most of that month rebuilding his force, and by the time Rosecrans attacked on 16 August, Bragg's Army of Tennessee was as ready as it was going to be. The offensive that began that day would squeeze Bragg out of Chattanooga and into north Georgia. Through early September, the two armies fought skirmishes, but finally, on 18 September, they faced one another across West Chickamauga Creek for a major battle that would give Bragg an important victory.

On the night of 18 September, Brag received reinforcements in the form of Longstreet's Virginia veterans. Their presence brought the Army of Tennessee to a total force of 70,000. Bragg spent the night reorganizing his army into two wings and deployed them for battle. Due to a miscommunication, though, the attack did not begin when it was supposed to. Frustrated, Bragg ordered all his divisions into action, and a day of piecemeal attacks began. That night, the federals withdrew back into Chattanooga, and Bragg did not pursue. Losses in the Battle of Chickamauga were huge, each side losing more than a quarter of the men with which it stared the fight. Federal casualties were 1,657 killed, 9,756 wounded, and 4,757 missing. The Confederates lost 2,312 killed, 14,674 wounded, and 1,486 missing. Bragg had routed Rosecrans, and he followed that success up by laying siege to Chattanooga.

In the midst of the siege, on 17 October, General Ulysses S. Grant was made overall Union commander in the West. Grant immediately started out for Chattanooga, and one of his first actions along the way was to replace Rosecrans with Thomas as commander of the Army of the Cumberland. Grant arrived at Chattanooga by mule train on 23 October and immediately set about reviving the flagging morale of the troops there. On 27 October, he took a portion of Thomas's army on pontoon boats and slipped past Confederate positions on Lookout Mountain to open a gap in the line that blockaded the city. Hooker's two corps marched through the line with supplies to relieve the city. Meanwhile, Grant sent word to the newly appointed commander of the Army of the Tennessee, William T. Sherman, to bring his men to Chattanooga. A fight was brewing.

Grant had resolved the Union leadership crisis in Chattanooga when he fired Rosecrans, but the Confederate problem remained. Bickering and infighting still plagued Bragg's Army of Tennessee. Two of Bragg's subcommanders, Nathan Bedford Forrest and James Longstreet, had been allowed to leave his command after they openly and publicly questioned his abilities. The situation among the army's high command was so bad that in October Jefferson Davis himself traveled to the Chattanooga area to try to resolve the problem. The president made the incredible decision to leave Bragg in charge but reshuffled the officer corps and told the army's officers they were responsible for getting along with Bragg.

By 15 November, the Union and Confederate armies at Chattanooga were poised for a major battle. Grant was ready to fight his way out of Bragg's siege, and Bragg was so confident in his positions on the mountaintops surrounding Chattanooga that even as a battle was brewing he sent Longstreet to lay siege to Knoxville. Bragg's plan was to reclaim all of eastern Tennessee for the Confederacy, but it did not quite work out that way because of events in Chattanooga.

Grant's plan to relieve Chattanooga called for a two-prong attack on Confederate forces entrenched along Missionary Ridge and Lookout Mountain. To keep Bragg from reinforcing his flanks, Grant planned an assault by Thomas on a hill between Chattanooga and Missionary Ridge and then a feint toward the Confederate entrenchments at the impregnable center of the ridge. Sherman moved up from the north side of the ridge. Hooker was to take two corps and set out for Lookout Mountain. On 24 November, Hooker fought and won what came to be called the "battle above the clouds" because of the low cloud ceiling that day. Sherman, on the other hand, had terrible luck in the campaign. Not only did inaccurate intelligence result in his men attacking the wrong hill; but he missed the boat that was supposed to carry him to a conference with Grant. Confederate troops under Irishman Patrick Cleburne put up stiff resistance and repulsed Sherman. The Union commander was forced to go on the defensive when he was supposed to be leading the offensive.

On 25 November, Grant put Thomas and Sherman into action. Thomas was to move up to the rifle pits at the base of Missionary Ridge, or if that did not work, move to the left and aid Sherman's advance. Sherman's advance was no more successful that day than it had been the day before, but the fighting was fierce enough that Bragg had to shift reserves from the center on Missionary Ridge to the fighting going on to the north. Meanwhile, Grant and Thomas were watching Thomas's men cautiously move forward toward the rifle pits at the base of Missionary Ridge and anxiously awaiting Hooker's return from Lookout Mountain to aid in the assault on the ridge.

Meanwhile, the attack on Missionary Ridge was taking on a life of its own. Word did not spread to all Thomas's lieutenants that the troops were supposed to stop at the base of the ridge. The fighting at the base of the mountain was so hellish that some of the Union troops attacked up the steep ridge just to get away from the carnage. Others followed, and as the blue line of troops dashed up the ridge, the gray one broke and fled. While Grant was muttering that there would be hell to pay if the attack ended in ruin, Bragg was watching in disbelief as his troops broke and ran. Cleburne's troops had to fight a rear guard defense to keep the entire Confederate army from being destroyed in its retreat to Dalton, Georgia. With the Confederates forced back into north Georgia, it was time for Grant to send aid to Burnside in Knoxville. By 6 December, the Confederates had been completely swept out of Tennessee. Casualties in the Chattanooga fighting totaled just over 12,000 for the two sides. The Union lost 349 killed, 4,722 wounded, and 349 missing. The Confederates lost 361 killed, 2,160 wounded, and 4,146 missing.

ISHAM G. HARRIS AND OTHERS: ACCOUNT OF BATTLE OF CHICKAMAUGA

Telegraphic reports like this one filed by Tennessee Gov. Isham G. Harris, of the Confederate victory at Chickamauga were received and read with great rejoicing in the Confederacy. Finally, after the crushing military defeats suffered earlier in the year, there was good news from the Southern military. In the first day of fighting at the Battle of Chickamauga, Bragg had routed the enemy, driven them from the field. But the battle was not yet decisive; there was more fighting to be done. The author of several of these reports was Isham G. Harris, Confederate governor of Tennessee. With virtually his entire state in Union hands, Harris spent most of the war with the Army of Tennessee.

Memphis Appeal, 22 September 1863

TELEGRAPHIC
BATTLE OF CHICKAMAUGA

The Enemy Driven from
His Positions
Casualties among General Officers

Special to the Memphis Appeal.]

BATTLEFIELD OF CHICKAMAUGA., Sunday, 8 P.M., September 20—After two days' hard fighting we have succeeded in driving the enemy from his positions. The engagement is not yet decisive.

The casualties are heavy on both sides, but those of the enemy are evidently much larger than ours.

Gen. Preston Smith was killed last night, about half past seven o'clock, when gallantly leading his brigade, within a few yards of the enemy's lines. Gen. Deshler was also killed.

Gens. John C. Brown, Hood, Gregg, Dan. Adams and Helm, are wounded.

The Federal General Little was killed.

We have captured about 2500 prisoners, and about twenty-five or thirty pieces of artillery.

Troops never fought better than ours. They are in high spirits, and ready to meet the enemy again tomorrow.

ISHAM G. HARRIS.

LATER—OUR VICTORY COMPLETE!
THE ENEMY ABANDONS HIS
KILLED AND WOUNDED!
FIVE THOUSAND PRISONERS AND
FIFTY-SIX CANNON CAPTURED!

Special to the Memphis Appeal.]

CHICKAMAUGA BATTLE FIELD, September 21, 11 A.M.—The enemy retired from our front under cover of last night, leaving his killed and wounded on the field.

Our victory is complete.

We have captured a large number of small arms. Thirty-six pieces of artillery have already been brought in, and twenty additional pieces are reported. About five thousand prisoners are reported captured.

Our army is in fine spirits and eager for a vigorous pursuit.

I have no additional particulars to report. We met the whole force of Rosecrans' army.

ISHAM G. HARRIS.

FROM THE EXTREME FRONT
THE ENEMY IN FULL RETREAT—
OUR CAVALRY IN
HOT PURSUIT

Special to the Memphis Appeal.]

NEAR CHATTANOOGA, Sept. 21, via RINGGOLD. Our victory is complete. The enemy has been routed and is now in full retreat.

Gen. Forrest is now attacking their rear with great vigor, and our forces are pressing on.

The loss is not as large as at either Shiloh or Murfreesboro.

Gens. Preston Smith and Helm were killed, and Gens. Brown and Adams wounded.

Capt. Donelson, Major Richmond, Lieut. Webber, and Capt. McConica were killed. Major Davis is wounded.

M. C. GALLAWAY.

Another Report—From Our Own
Correspondent

Special to the Memphis Appeal.]

DALTON, Sept. 21—No cannonading is heard in front this morning.

Gen. Preston Smith, of Memphis, and Capt. Donelson, (son of A. J. Donelson) and Capt. King, of his staff, were killed yesterday.

The enemy fell back along his entire line, and his right was within eight miles of Chattanooga yesterday.

Our loss is estimated at about four thousand killed, wounded and missing. The enemy's loss is much heavier.

We have taken three thousand prisoners, thirty-five pieces of artillery yesterday, and twelve pieces on Saturday.

Gen. Hood lost a leg, which was amputated above the knee yesterday.

It is thought Rosecrans has crossed the river.

VERITAS.

CPA REPORTERS: REPORTS FROM CHICKAMAUGA BATTLEFIELD

The Confederate Press Association reporters provided an important service for newspapers that did not have the resources to field war correspondents or those that wanted additional stories to flesh out their coverage. This story, datelined Atlanta, was most likely pulled together at CPA headquarters in that city by the press service's superintendent, John S. Thrasher.

Memphis Appeal, 22 September 1863

**FURTHER FROM THE
BATTLE-FIELD
PRESS ASSOCIATION REPORTS**

ATLANTA, September 22—Advices from the battle-field come in scantily, but sufficient has been received to show that a great success has been achieved in the three days' fighting. The main, if not the entire force of Rosecrans was engaged, and not only driven back from all his positions, but is greatly demoralized and forced to destroy large quantities of stores and baggage. Their resistance is stubborn, but the fight still goes on. Our troops are flushed with victory and eager in the fray, and there is every confidence that the foe will be driven from his present stand in Mission ridge, about six or eight miles from Chattanooga.

The fight yesterday was a most spirited one. Longstreet and Hill attacked the enemy's center at daylight and, after a desperate resistance, the enemy were driven from their positions with a loss of from four to six thousand prisoners and forty two pieces of artillery.

Our latest accounts from the field are yesterday at noon, when the enemy had made a stand at Mission ridge, and the battle would probably be continued.

Our loss in general officers is very great. Brigadier Gen. Helm, of Kentucky, was killed while leading a charge. Gen. Hood's wound is reported to be a mortal one. Brigadier-Generals Adams and John C. Brown are severely wounded. Major Richmond, of Gen. Polk's staff, was killed.

The battle began about three miles west of the east Chickamauga. The enemy was soon driven across Peavine creek, and formed his main line of battle nearly at right angles with that creek and across the road from Chattanooga, whence Rosecrans received his supplies. On this line the enemy had two lines of temporary defenses formed of felled timber, but was gallantly driven from them by our troops, and

it is still asserted that we hold the road to Chattanooga. The Yankees have been driven in all, as we are led to believe from the best accounts we can obtain, about twelve miles to his present position on Mission ridge. He has been defeated on ground of his own choosing, and we are credibly informed that Rosecrans was there with the main force of his army.

No reliable accounts of the extent of our losses or of the injury inflicted on the enemy, can yet be obtained. But few of the wounded from Saturday's fight have reached here, and none of those of the two succeeding days.

Preparations have been made at Marietta and in this city to receive the wounded, and a relief committee, with supplies and hospital appliances, left here this morning for the front.

Every one who comes from the scene of action represents the spirit of the army to be of the most confident and exhilarating character, and it is confidently hoped that Rosecrans has met his utter defeat. The field of Sunday's fight was thickly wooded, like that of Chancellorsville, which Gen. Lee called the battle of the wilderness, and afforded no play or artillery, in consequence of which most of the wounds received by our men on that day were slight, and a very small proportion of our loss is killed. We learn that Hood's division, and the Yankees who fought them, both took to the trees during the engagement, and fought in Indian style, when Benning's brigade, which supported the Texas brigade of Hood's division, made a charge, and drove the Yankees from their skulking holes.

We learn that Generals Wafford and Waithall are unhurt, and that Gen. Benning was again in the saddle after his wound in the breast was dressed. There is also hope of Gen. Hood's recovery. Gen. Presdon died yesterday at 11 o'clock.

Rosecrans has been driven back to the vicinity of the West Chickamauga, an Indian name which means "The Stream of Death."

FELIX G. DE FONTAINE: NEWS OF UNION ACTIVITY AT CHATTANOOGA

In November 1863, the federal army that occupied Chattanooga began to move out. Its objective was to push Bragg's Confederates further away from the Tennessee River town and deeper into Georgia. This movement was necessary to secure supply lines that were threatened by Confederate proximity to the rail lines. Felix Gregory de Fontaine, one of the South's two top war correspondents, had taken on correspondence work for a second newspaper, the Memphis Appeal, *by this time. He wrote for that paper under the name Quel qu'un. De Fontaine was better known as the* Charleston Courier's *Personne. Both names essentially translate from French as "Someone" or "A Person." Quel qu'un noted the initial movement of the federal army that would, later in the month, culminate in the Battle of Lookout Mountain and Bragg's retreat into Georgia.*

Memphis Appeal, 2 November 1863

OUR ARMY CORRESPONDENCE

Special Correspondence of the Memphis Appeal.]
ARMY OF TENNESSEE,
Wednesday, October 28, 1863.

From various manifestations now in progress of development the enemy has at last aroused himself for another struggle. Yesterday we were treated to the first act of the drama.

You will remember that in a former letter I described the successful manner in which our sharpshooters on the other side of Lookout mountain, and some eight or nine miles distant from Chattanooga had blocked up one of the important roads by which the Federals received their supplies. We have also been in the habit of picketing with a comparatively small force along the bank of Tennessee in that locality, principally to watch the movements of the enemy. Annoyed by this presence of Confederate troops, the Federal commander on Monday night, by means of some fifty boats suddenly crossed the river, drove in our thin line, and obtained a foothold on this side. Gen. Law promptly advanced a regiment, when a brisk skirmish ensued which resulted in temporarily checking their movements. Subsequently the enemy threw over troops until according to the statement of prisoners, they numbered between five and six thousand or more than two brigades. Under these circumstances our little command was forced back, with a loss of some fifteen or twenty killed and wounded. The Federals therefore commenced to fortify and to day scouts report a line of intrenchments on the heights occupied. The ground along the back of the river for two or three miles is of an elevated character, which of course, gives an antagonist an admirable position for defense.

During the affair, Moccasin battery, at the base of Lookout Mountain, was busy with his "thunder tongues," and for three or four hours in the morning, the shelling was, at times, incessant. Several of our guns replied, and it is believed, not without effect. Much of the Yankee ammunition was expended in firing at Craven's house on Lookout mountain and the road which runs across the height in front—a favorite mark of the battery; but only three or four of our men were wounded. Among these I may mention the names of Col. Oates, of the 15th Alabama, who received a painful flesh wound in the thigh; Capt. Hagood, of the 1st South Carolina, contusion in leg; and Corporal Rabe of the Palmetto sharpshooters, South Carolina volunteers, flesh wound in leg, behind the knee.

The occupants of Craven's house are mostly female, and although the place has been persistently shelled since the Federals opened fire, and from ten or fifteen projectiles have passed through the premises, the ladies have determined not to budge an inch; and you know the couplet:

> When a woman will, she will, depend on't,
> And when she won't, she won't, and that's the end on't.

In this case "she won't." Yesterday while the shelling was heaviest and our men were "skedaddling" across the line of fire as industriously as their locomotive apparatus would [*unreadable*], the ladies were coolly preparing for dinner. One of the surgeons who was in the house, says that while he was there a fragment penetrated one of the rooms. Without being in the least disconcerted, the Tennessee matron spoke up in a tone very much like that in which she would reprove a servant for breaking china plate, "Eliza go in there and see what's damaged this time."

Think of that, ye weak legged, faint hearted owners of corduroy and Confederate rags, who dodge like "dancing jimmies" every time you hear the shriek of a shell, and take pattern after this brave, undemoralized, impregnable, bomb proof western mother, and don't get "frightened before you're hurt."

On Monday morning about 2 o'clock "Moccasin" opened on our picket lines and some of the camps on the left. Only one man was slightly injured. Several, however, had narrow escapes from death. A captain in one of the Arkansas regiments, who had quietly lain in his blankets listening to the explosion of the shells, at last concluded to get up. As he left the tent a fragment entered and penetrating the knapsack on which his head had rested, tore it to pieces.

The principal commotion was caused among the negroes. Which way to retreat they didn't know, and making the best of their situation, they concealed themselves behind trees and stumps, but which made the most noise, the shells or the negroes, it was difficult to tell. At each diabolical missile that came screaming through the air, you would hear the exclamations issuing from between chattering teeth, "Heyar she comes; hear she comes—get out de way boys—look out all you tree tousand dollar negroes—aint she got a noisy tail," etc., etc. The next morning one of the venerable body servants of the old school, a genuine family mentor among the negroes, was asked what he thought of the demonstration. The old gentleman actually grew blue again as he answered—"Well, I tell you massa, I tink de debbil's in dem balls, and de ole he debbil what frows 'em ober head is wus'u all. If dats de way de Yankees make lub to do colored people, dis chile don't recognize 'em, shuah."

Speaking of negroes, I am told when Kershaw's fine brigade of South Carolinians was moving into the battle of Chickamauga, an old fellow came out from his hut, with eyes distended and hair almost erect in his fright at the sounds of battle, and raising both hands in the most imploring attitude exclaimed: "Gorry 'mity gemmen, gorry mity, what's de use oh shooten one anudder in dis way—why don't you step and argy awhile."

There was a world of good sense in the suggestion of the sable individual, but unfortunately the time to "argue" has past, and naked strength of arm alone must now decide the contest.

But I have branched widely off from my starting point. In addition to the demonstration of the enemy from the rear of Chattanooga, another column, consisting of infantry, artillery and cavalry, is now moving up the valley on the opposite side of Lookout mountain, and to effect a junction with the army at Chattanooga. It is understood that the force crossed at Bridgeport, but in what numbers it is not known. Their object can only be surmised; but unquestionably, it is a well defined attempt on the part of the Federals, to possess themselves of the railroad running between Bridgeport and Chattanooga. If successful, the movement will relieve their wagon trains, and enable them to obtain supplies with both regularity and abundance. To acquire full possession of the road, Lookout mountain is indispensable to the Yankees, but I doubt whether, rather than risk a battle to obtain this situation, they will not be satisfied with a railroad up to a point where the line of transportation by wagons to Chattanooga will be only ten or fifteen miles in length. You will recall the fact predicted in a former letter, that if the enemy made any demonstration, it would be on our left, and have for its object the possession of the railroad.

It is becoming more and more patent every day that the enemy cannot maintain their hold upon Chattanooga during the winter without an improvement in their commissariat, and this can only be had by dispensing with the long and troublesome route by which supplies are brought to their camps. Only yesterday a Federal officer under flag of truce admitted that they were short of forage, and every day our men along the lines are asked by the Yankees to sell them rations or exchange them for blankets. These facts are proof positive that the Federal army are in a critical strait. Hence the movement in question. Further evidence has been furnished me while writing this letter. A scout just in states that a small squad of Yankees went to a house in which there were only females, cocked their guns at the inmates and threatened to blow their brains out if they did not give them something to eat. Afterward they made one of the ladies stand guard at the garden while they killed the hogs on the premises, and stole everything of value they could lay their hands upon. On leaving, one of the wretches remarked that they "had been fighting for the Union, but *now they were fighting for something to eat.*"

It is not proper to refer to army movements within our lines or to the probabilities connected with this extraordinary venture of the enemy, but the public may rest assured that our generals are fully alive to the emergency, and our men in fine spirits for battle.

QUEL QU'UN.

P.S. Daylight, Thursday, 29th.—The body of the enemy seen passing down yesterday, consisted of two corps. A demonstration was made by Hood's division, under command of General Jenkins, of South Carolina, about two o'clock this morning, when an engagement resulted, which continued until near daylight. Jenkins' brigade of Carolinians, Col. Bratton commanding, was sent across Lookout creek, to be left for the purpose of getting among the wagon trains and stragglers, while Law, Robertson, and Benning were aligned on a crest of hills, partially commanding the approach to Bratton's rear, yet on a line occupied by several thousand of the enemy, about two miles above. Bratton, on moving to the left, and engaging, suddenly found himself confronted by an entire corps; but nevertheless, having a full brigade, one of the largest in the army—he promptly gave battle, and was driving the Federals steadily back. The enemy above, however, now moved from their position, in the neighborhood of Brown's ferry, which is in the rear of Chattanooga, and while their artillery was playing on Law, Robertson and Benning, passed around the front of the latter commands, others engaging at the same time, and endeavored to penetrate the gap between their left and Bratton. The movement was made by from five to seven thousand men; but Jenkins, at a glance, discovering the object, checkmated the attempt by ordering Bratton to fall back, and with the rest of the division, to recross the creek, which was done in good order.

Our losses are severe. Col. Kilpatrick, of the 1st South Carolina, a gallant officer, who fired the first shot at the first battle of Manassas, was killed.

This is all the news of the affair I can send you at this hour.

QUEL QU'UN.

SAMUEL CHESTER REID, JR.: REPORTS OF FIGHTING AT LOOKOUT MOUNTAIN

The Battle of Lookout Mountain began on 24 November. The federals pushed the Confederates away from Chattanooga and Lookout Mountain, deeper into Georgia, just as planned. The following dispatch is reprinted from the Atlanta Intelligencer *and written by another famous war correspondent, Samuel*

Chester Reid, Jr., who signed his dispatches "290." The story details some of the fighting, including one of the preliminary skirmishes before the main battle began. The correspondent was right in surmising the enemy's objective was to take Lookout, and indeed he was also right about the federals being concerned about Longstreet's movement on Knoxville.

Memphis Appeal, 26 November 1863

[FROM THE ARMY EDITION]

The Very Latest from the Front

Special Correspondence Atlanta Intelligencer.]

CHICKAMAUGA, November 24, 5 P.M. —As the telegraph line is not working on Missionary ridge, I had to ride down to this point, in the rain, to send off my dispatch of this afternoon.

The demonstrations of the enemy in our front, yesterday was, on their first appearance, not considered serious. By one o'clock P.M. their first line was seen to move forward, they having two lines of reserves in the rear. Our pickets were soon driven in, and at two P.M. they attacked our right and center, drove our men from their rifle pits, when the firing became very heavy on our right. A. J. Vaughan's, Dois', [*unreadable*] and Anderson's brigade becoming warmly engaged, and severely punishing the enemy.

The enemy's batteries at the same time opened briskly. Our men fell back to their intrenchments, and the enemy succeeded in taking two cedar hills on our right center, one of which they last night fortified, placing a battery on it. As night closed in all further operations ceased. Our loss did not exceed 200 killed and wounded in the skirmish. Wm. H. Martin, Isaiah Sanders, 9th Mississippi battalion, sharpshooters; Charles Williamson, Wm. Rains, R. B. Stone, Henry Epps, Arnette Shields, 29th Tennessee; Jos. Lawrence, J. W. Lawrence, J. W. Hill, 11th Tennessee, of A. J. Vaughan's—late Preston's—brigade, were slightly wounded.

This morning the enemy opened at 8 o'clock from the Cedar hill, shelling us for about an hour, but doing no damage. They then opened upon Cheatham's forces in Lookout valley from the batteries over the river, and kept up a heavy cannonading for two hours, when at noon they made an assault with infantry, endeavoring to force our position in order to take Lookout. The musketry firing was very heavy for two hours. At 2 P.M. , the rain increasing, fire ceased. At 2 1/2 P.M. It was again renewed, the enemy also making an attack on our right, having crossed a column over the Tennessee, with a small steamer, at the mouth of the Chickamauga. The firing has continued very heavy up to this time. Our troops still hold their positions, but no result is known.

It is evident the enemy's design is to carry Lookout if possible, as well as to gain the railroad on the Chickamauga side, in order to cut our line to Cleveland. There is no doubt the enemy is aware of our movement on Knoxville, and it may be that he is trying to prevent us reinforcing Longstreet, in order to save Burnside.

No general engagement of all our forces has yet taken place, but there is no telling when it may. It is supposed, however, that the enemy is not in condition to make a general attack. Things wear a curious aspect, and it is as yet impossible to tell what may be the result.

In haste,

290.

AN ANONYMOUS REPORT: ROUT OF BRAGG'S FORCES

The Appeal *was particularly concerned about the news from the front when Bragg admitted to having been routed and forced to retire in disorder. As the newspaper understood, when a proud general like Bragg made such a statement, his army was in major trouble.*

Memphis Appeal, 26 November 1863

FROM THE FRONT

The news from the front is anything but encouraging. The mere falling back of our army to Chickamauga, would not in itself be greatly discouraging provided it had done so in tact, but that the left was forced by assault and pressure and retired in considerable disorder, is a strong admission to come from Gen. BRAGG, and betokens a greater disaster than is revealed in his official dispatch. Our losses will probably not be known until they reach us through Federal sources. Whatever they may be however,

let not the country be discouraged by this temporary reverse.

If the news from Knoxville be true, LONGSTREET has done his work nobly and effectually, and this success will compensate us for our failure in front.

In addition to the intelligence contained in our telegraphic column, we learn that night before last Tuner's station and the wagon train of Gen. M. J. WRIGHT, were burned up by a raiding party of the enemy, which crossed the river near the mouth of Chickamauga creek.

BENJAMIN F. DILL OR JOHN McCLANAHAN: CONSEQUENCES OF DEFEAT AT LOOKOUT MOUNTAIN

The Confederate defeat at Lookout Mountain was devastating. The Memphis Appeal *offered grudging admiration for Bragg's admission that the day was indeed lost, rather than making unseemly excuses. Nevertheless, the paper was absolutely right: Such an ignominious loss was serious beyond question. Bragg, a favorite of President Davis's, was not yet relieved of command of the Army of Tennessee, though there was much clamoring for it. The author of this editorial was correct in his assessment of the utility of Longstreet's army to Bragg.*

Memphis Appeal, 1 December 1863

THE DUTY OF THE HOUR

It is unwise to make light of a defeat, and equally unwise to overstate it. For the first time, as we have said elsewhere, a large Confederate army has been driven from a powerful position and compelled to abandon it altogether. Whether this was done by dint of bravery or by maneuvering and the sudden precipitation of large numbers upon a comparatively weak point, we are as yet without the means of knowing. The probabilities are in favor of the latter supposition, although General Bragg, with a candor which all must admire, and which other Southern generals would do well to imitate, admits that his "left center" was "carried." It will appear, we apprehend, that this center had been weakened in order to prevent the extreme left from being flanked, a danger which all generals take care to guard against, and none are more afraid of than Gen. Bragg.

To have been whipped out of a chosen and naturally strong position is a serious thing to a Southern army. It is an inadequate consolation to know that this happened when fifteen thousand State troops of Georgia had been permitted to return to their homes for agricultural purposes, and when probably as many more under Longstreet had been sent on to what will prove to be a bloodless and hazardous attempt against Knoxville. But when it became known that Sherman, with twenty thousand men, had joined Grant, ought not every man to have been called? Nay, ought they to have been sent beyond the reach of speedy recall?

What is done is done. We can bear the disaster, and another like it, but not many more. If Longstreet be cut off from Bragg, as he doubtless is, the trouble is mightily complicated, for Grant will press his advantages, and, if possible, destroy first the one and then the other. All is clear now to the dullest observation. It was quite clear to military minds from the moment it was known that Bragg has divided his army in the face of an able general who was being rapidly reinforced. Grant seized the occasion which Bragg gratuitously made for him—that is all.

However, Bragg is back upon the field of his great victory. His loss, we know not; the morale of his army, we know not. Admit that the one is heavy, the other bad; admit, too, that there is no help to come from Longstreet. Take the case in its worst aspect, and prepare for it. This is the duty of the president, the duty of Georgia, the duty of all. Georgia will surely do her duty; she has never failed to do it. Will the president do his! We trust he will, we may say we believe he will, for we have observed it ever requires the worst to come to the worst before the pressure that insures prompt action begins to tell on the firm, stern temper of the Executive.

Much has been said about General Bragg, and the hour may come when it will be proper to say much more. But there is no time for quarrelling now. First, make ready to repel Grant and Thomas, both able men; and then we may think of preferring charges. If the army cannot be made to resist the talents of Grant and Thomas without a change of commanders, in Heaven's name let it be done, and that without delay. But until it is done, let us give all possible encouragement to the gallant army at Chickamauga—back them up, support them, strengthen them, cheer them with all that busy hands and grateful voices can accomplish. By hook or by crook, we must beat back the invader. We have done it before, and, by God's help, we will surely do it again. Let us lend every energy to that end.

EASTERN THEATER

Chancellorsville and the Second Battle of Fredericksburg

Chancellorsville, Virginia, was not so much a town as a tavern and a house at a five-way crossroads in a densely wooded region north of Fredericksburg, but it would be the site of one of Robert E. Lee's and Stonewall Jackson's greatest triumphs. They faced Joe Hooker who, since his elevation to the command of the Army of the

Potomac the previous January, had been working to rebuild his force after its ignominious rout at Fredericksburg. Hooker had ensured that his 130,000 men were well
supplied with the best food, best uniforms, and best munitions that Uncle Sam's
money could buy. Along with the new equipment, Hooker had drilled his men daily
into what he considered to be the best fighting force in the world. Hooker showed
aptitude in another vital military area as well: He was a competent spy master and
gatherer of intelligence. His sound use of a variety of information sources, including
Union sympathizers, Confederate deserters, and intercepted messages, had allowed
Hooker to discover not only where the weaknesses lay in Lee's lines around Fredericksburg and along the Rappahannock but the size of the Confederate force as well.
Hooker used his intelligence to devise a plan that initially tricked Lee and allowed
Union forces to steal a march on the Confederate left flank.

Lee faced the challenge of Hooker's well-thought-out strategy with an ill-prepared,
ill-nourished, ill-deployed army. His 60,000 men spanned a 25-mile stretch of the
banks on the Fredericksburg side of the Rappahannock River. The winter had been
hard on the Confederate army, but by some miracle, their morale had not yet flagged.
Lee's soldiers suffered from the cold as well as lack of rations and supplies. They had
subsisted on a daily ration of a few ounces of cornmeal and bacon, frequently rancid.
In addition to fighting with a force of emaciated, sometimes shoeless men, Lee had
diminished his strength when he sent Longstreet's corps, his largest, toward Suffolk
in order to gather provisions that would ease the lack of supplies and rations.

Hooker's strategy was two-pronged. Hooker planned to force 40,000 men, commanded by Major General John Sedgwick, across the Rappahannock at Fredericksburg while he forded the river farther to the northwest with 73,000 men. His men
would march through The Wilderness to encircle Lee's left, while Major General
George Stoneman's cavalry was to sweep south and cut off Lee's communications
with Richmond. While Lee may not have known the details of Hooker's strategy, he
was aware of the Union army's movements, thanks to the work of his own cavalry
under Major General J.E.B. Stuart.

Unfortunately for Hooker, while his strategy worked, the follow-up failed. Hooker
set his plan in motion in mid-April. Almost immediately, Stoneman's cavalry ran
into trouble from rain and muddy roads. Stoneman did manage to get behind Lee's
lines, but Stuart's cavalry effectively screened Lee's left flank. The Union cavalry-
men rode through the woods for a week without having any effect on Lee at all. Finally, on 29 April, Hooker was able to push through Stuart's cavalry screen. While
his men were fending off cavalry attack in the dense woods of The Wilderness, Sedgwick was building pontoon bridges across the Rappahannock in front of Jackson's
position south of Fredericksburg. At first, Lee was uncertain how to proceed in his
attack on Hooker, but on 30 April, the Union general stopped his force to consolidate his position; his advance units had met stiffer resistance than expected, and he
needed to revise his plan. Hooker's hesitation, though, cost him the initiative.
Strong drink may also have been involved in Hooker's hesitation.

Prisoners captured by Stuart's force, as well as intelligence from the cavalry patrols
themselves, helped Lee determine that Hooker was maneuvering north toward
Chancellorsville and that Sedgewick's crossing at Fredericksburg was just a rouse.
Lee left Major General Jubal Early with 10,000 men to defend Fredericksburg and
then moved rapidly west to meet Hooker near Chancellorsville. The first contact

between the two armies was on 1 May. Despite his tremendous advantage in numbers, Hooker halted and went on the defensive.

At 4:00 A.M. on 2 May, Lee sent Jackson with 26,000 men to envelop Hooker's force, while Lee, with 17,000 men, held the front. After marching his men for 20 miles through the heat of the day, Jackson's force fell on Hooker's. The Confederates were positioned along a 2-mile-long attack formation, and as the daylight began to fade, Jackson ordered his lieutenants to begin the attack. The Union force had already called it quits for the day; some of Hooker's men were preparing their suppers when a mass of screaming Rebels burst through the woods and scattered the men. Jackson's men completely demoralized the right wing of Hooker's army before their assault was through. Jackson's advance was halted by heavier Union fire and the loss of cohesion in the darkening woods. They had one final objective to accomplish, though, before they could call their day's work complete: They were to cut Hooker off from his communications line at the Rappahannock. Jackson rode ahead with his staff to reconnoiter in person.

At about 9:00 P.M., disaster struck the Confederate cause. Jackson and his party rode past a position held by troops from the 18th North Carolina. In the darkness and confusion of the postbattle period, the Confederate soldiers made a mistake. They believed the men riding past were Union cavalry. They aimed their muskets, and they fired. Jackson and several of his staff officers were wounded. The general was hit in three places, and one of the bullets had shattered his left arm. Early word was that the doctors expected a full, though lengthy, recovery. But the worst happened: Jackson developed pneumonia, and within days, he succumbed to it. The great Stonewall was dead.

The Confederate attacks resumed on 3 May with Stuart temporarily in command of Jackson's corps. Union resistance slowed the Southern assault near Chancellorsville, and in Fredericksburg, Sedgwick's force drove Early's force from Marye's Heights. Lee left Stuart to face Hooker at Chancellorsville and hurried east to meet Sedgwick on 4 May at Salem Church. That engagement produced mixed results. The next day, Hooker, against the advice of his subordinates, ordered his army to retreat across the Rappahannock. He had the numbers to carry the day, but the Union general had lost the will to fight.

Total casualties for the Union reached more than 16,700. For the South, losses totaled more than 12,750, plus one irreplaceable soldier: Stonewall Jackson.

AN ANONYMOUS REPORT: NEWS OF ADVANCE OF HOOKER'S ARMY

On 29 April, Hooker's army was crossing the Rappahannock at fords above Fredericksburg. The crossing had begun the day before and would not be completed until 1 May. As Hooker's 70,000 men completed their crossing, they moved through The Wilderness into an area with clearings near the home of the Chancellor family, a place today referred to as Chancellorsville. Lee's 47,000-man Army of the Potomac would move out the next day to meet the Union forces in a fight that would become known as the Battle of Chancellorsville.

Richmond Examiner, 1 May 1863

FROM FREDERICKSBURG

[FROM OUR OWN CORRESPONDENT.]

FREDERICKSBURG, April 29th, 1863, 11 P.M.—This morning about five o'clock a courier dashed into the town with the startling exciting intelligence that the enemy were crossing the Rappahannock in this vicinity. Immediately the Episcopal church bell, the ring of which had been previously agreed upon as a signal, sounded the alarm, and the streets presented a busy spectacle of military preparation, and women and children leaving the scene of danger.

Your correspondent reached the advanced line of our pickets about seven o'clock, and found at that early hour, their pontoon bridge at the mouth of Deep Run, on the Mansfield estate, completed, and several regiments of the enemy already across. The troops stationed near report that our regiment on duty at that point was surprised about three o'clock in the morning, by a party of the enemy, who effected the passage of the river in boats. One hundred of the surprised are reported to be prisoners, an exaggeration it is to be hoped. There was no contest at this bridge after sunrise, excepting an occasional cannon shot early in the morning. Four or five other bridges, however, are said to be constructed, or in course of construction, within a space of a mile and a half from that at Mansfield which, by the way, is about that distance from Fredericksburg. Desultory discharges, both of cannon and musketry, have been occurring at those points during the day.

On reaching this side of the river the enemy threw out skirmishers at once, who met no disputants of their advance to the road leading to Hamilton's Crossing, where they established their line of pickets, and retired.

The upper bridge alone, and operations there only, were visible to your correspondent. The Yankees continued to cross there until two o'clock, P.M., infantry, artillery, and wagons. They swarmed irregularly over the field and bluffs of which they had taken possession, seeming not even to have fallen into ranks. About five, P.M., a light rain commenced, when they pitched their tents, and seemed to be making themselves at home.

All throughout the day, their balloons were in the air to a great height, and the opposite banks of the river, as far as the eye could reach, was blue with their crowded columns.

Singular to say, notwithstanding the close proximity of Fredericksburg to those exciting occurrences, the batteries in direct front of the city were not manned throughout the day; the pickets have been lulling quietly on the banks of the river, within short rifle range, of each other; and, excepting a few more spectators than customary, the line has been non-pulsing [unreadable]. A pontoon train is stated to have [unreadable] opposite the lower wharf, and [unreadable] behind the hill. If this be true, tomorrow will be another eventful day in the experience of the [unreadable] town.

It is utterly impossible to estimate, with any accuracy, the number of the enemy who have crossed the river. The force encamped this evening at the upper crossing, did not exceed five thousand. The opposite bank was still covered with infantry, and an immense force of artillery. A general engagement cannot be avoided to-morrow, unless they retire to-night.

ROBERT E. LEE/AN ANONYMOUS REPORT: COMMANDING GENERAL'S REPORT ON BATTLE OF CHANCELLORSVILLE; STONEWALL JACKSON WOUNDED

Lee made his victory over Hooker at Chancellorsville and Fredericksburg sound easy in his terse telegraph to President Davis regarding the victory. This article, though, placed less emphasis on the victory and more on Stonewall Jackson's wound from which, at the point this article was written, he was expected to recover.

Richmond Examiner, 6 May 1863

FROM FREDERICKSBURG—THREE VICTORIES IN ONE DAY—THE YANKEE ARMY
DRIVEN NORTH OF THE RAPPAHANNOCK—GENERAL JACKSON SHOT BY HIS OWN
TROOPS IN THE NIGHT—HIS WOUNDS.

The following dispatch was received from Geuineas last night:

HEADQUARTERS, 10 o'clock, A.M., May 5, 1863.

To HIS EXCELLENCY PRESIDENT DAVIS:

At the close of the battle of Chancellorsville, on Sunday, the enemy was reported advancing from Fredericksburg in our rear. General McLaws was sent back to arrest his progress, and repulsed him handsomely that afternoon. Learning that this force consisted of two corps, under General Sedgewick, I determined to attack it, and marched back yesterday with General Anderson, and uniting with McLaws and Early in the afternoon, succeeded, by the blessing of Heaven, in driving General Sedgewick over the river. We have reoccupied Fredericksburg, and no enemy remains south of the Rappahannock, in its vicinity.
(Signed,)

ROBERT E. LEE, General

From this it will be seen that our armies were thrice victorious on the same day. Hooker was beaten.

In addition to the above, our information as to the particulars of the three great battles mentioned therein amounts to next to nothing. We have heard of no casualties with sufficient certainty to feel authorized to publish them.

Some pleasurable excitement was produced here yesterday by the announcement that a telegram had been received from General Lee, stating that Hooker and his staff had been captured. The only foundation for this story, it turned out, was that the operator at Guinea's informed the operator here that such a report was in circulation at the former place.

A telegram on yesterday morning announced the fact that General Jackson's arm had been amputated, and that he was doing well. Mrs. Jackson, who is at present in the city, has been informed by a letter of the melancholy circumstances under which the General received his wounds.

The following are the facts of the most unhappy affair, as detailed in that letter: At midnight on Saturday night, his men being drawn up in line of battle, a body of troops was seen a short distance in advance of our line. It being doubtful whether they were friends or enemies, General Jackson and staff rode forward to ascertain. Whilst he was engaged in reconnoitering, his men being unaware of his movement, mistook himself and staff for enemies and fired a volley into them, instantly killing one of his staff and severely wounding General Jackson and Major Crutchfield. One bullet passed through the General's right hand, whilst another stuck his left arm below the elbow and, ranging upward, shattered the bone near the shoulder. He instantly fell to the ground. His brother-in-law, who was with him, laid down beside him to ascertain the character of his wounds. In a moment the unknown troops in front, who proved to be the enemy, advanced and captured two other staff officers who were standing over the General without noticing him. Soon after, four of our men placed him on a stretcher, and were bearing him to the rear, when they were all shot down. The injury to his right hand is severe, one of the bones having been shot away, but it is believed he will ultimately recover its use.

AN ANONYMOUS REPORT: ACCOUNT OF BATTLE OF CHANCELLORSVILLE

The Battle of Chancellorsville was a bloody, terrible fight that left the Confederate army exhausted, despite its victory over a hugely superior force. Luck was on the side of the Confederates; a shell struck the house that was serving as Hooker's headquarters. The Union general was struck on the head by falling debris and temporarily disabled. The next day, though, he lost his nerve and ordered a retreat. The following Richmond Examiner *article is an overview of the three days' fighting that had taken place near Chancellorsville.*

Richmond Examiner, *11 May 1863*

FROM FREDERICKSBURG

All is once again quiet along the lines of the Rappahannock. Our army has resumed the position occupied by it previous to the advance of Hooker, and is enjoying the rest made so necessary by the terrible labors and privations of the past week. The extent of the suffering of our troops during the three days battle is almost impossible to realize. From letters written at Chancellorsville, last Monday, we learn that Jackson's command were sixty hours under arms without food and without sleep, and that the first food there obtained by them was from the knapsacks thrown away by the enemy in their flight. Both the Central and Fredericksburg roads being now in full operation the army is abundantly supplied with food for man and beast.

THE BATTLE OF CHANCELLORS

Of the grand result of this memorable battle the whole country has been informed through the official dispatches of General Lee, while many of the details have found publicity through the labors of the press. Yet much remains untold. Persons who were participants in the battles are constantly arriving in the city, each of whom adds something to the general stock of information on the subject.—From their accounts we collate some items of interest. During the battle the large brick tavern on the Orange plank road which, with its out-houses, constituted Chancellorsville, and which was occupied by the Yankees as a hospital, was accidentally set on fire by our shells, and, with all its inmates, five or six hundred in number, was consumed. Among those who lost their lives by this catastrophe, was Brigadier General Seth Williams of Maine, who was Adjutant General, first to McClellan and afterwards to Burnside, and lastly to Hooker, and who is said to have been, before the war, a warm personal friend of General Lee.—Such was the exigency of the hour, the battle being at its fiercest, that none could be spared from the ranks to save the poor wounded wretches from the most horrible of deaths—being roasted alive. As the flames approached them, and they became aware of their situation, their frantic screams were distinctly heard above the roar of battle that raged around them. Subsequently to this, another conflagration, even more appalling occurred. The woods on a portion of the battle field, where laid intermingled the dead and wounded of both armies, took fire, and many, whose wounds prevented their moving, were burnt to death. It is said by some that Hooker had the woods fired to prevent our pursuit of his shattered divisions, but this story is too horrible to be believed even of a Yankee. For the credit of human nature, we are unwilling to believe that a General, even though a Yankee, would consign his own countrymen, who had been disabled in his ranks, to the most excruciating of deaths.

The number of their dead we have heard estimated by a member of General Lee's staff at five thousand. When five thousand men of an army are killed outright the wounded cannot be less than twenty-five thousand—five wounded to one killed being less than the usual proportion. But putting it at that, Hooker's loss in the battle cannot be under forty thousand.

The number of rifles and muskets on the battle field taken from the prisoners is estimated at between thirty and forty thousand. A railroad man tells us it will take the Fredericksburg road two days to haul them to Richmond.

The prisoners continue to arrive in this city daily, the officers in the (ladies') cars and the privates afoot. As these prisoners arrived at Guinea's, we are informed the army suttlers bought up their "greenbacks" with avidity, giving them three dollars Confederate money for one dollar in United States. Many of the Yankees were heard to remark that this did not look much as if we expected to be ultimately successful in our struggle for independence, else we would not, upon the heels of what we claimed to be a great victory, be so ready to give three of our dollars for one of theirs. The moral effect of this sort of traffic is certainly very bad, but there is no help for it, as Congress has refused to pass a law forbidding it.

YANKEE GENERALS KILLED

We have it upon "rumor," which we do not always believe, that six Yankee brigadiers were killed at Chancellorsville, viz: Dan Sickles, Barry, Chief of Artillery; Ruger; Birney; Seth Williams, Chief of Staff; and Howard.

A gentleman who was in the fight at Marye's Hill, speaks of it as the most desperate battle of the war. The Confederate Artillery drove the Yankees back three times, but were overpowered by numbers. The ground near their guns was literally covered with dead Yankees. On Monday when the Yankees were driven from the hill, and while retreating across the river, it is said the First Howitzers of Richmond, fired three hundred rounds into their ranks while in a crowded condition trying to get across the river, causing great slaughter.

JOHN M. DANIEL: DEATH OF STONEWALL JACKSON

Technically, Chancellorsville was a victory for the Confederates, but the Southern cause suffered one of its most devastating losses as a result of that battle: the death of Stonewall Jackson. Jackson died of pneumonia several days after being wounded in the battle. Jackson's death was lamented throughout the South, for he was truly a hero of the people. The former mathematics professor at Virginia Military Institute was known for his bravery in combat, his skill in military tactics, and his religious faith.

Richmond Examiner, 11 May 1863

DEATH OF STONEWALL JACKSON

The hero of the war, that great genius, that noble patriot, the support and hope of this country, is no more. He died yesterday at three o'clock in the afternoon. The immediate cause of his death was pneumonia, against which his constitution, shaken by the sore wounds received in the glorious victory at Chancellors, was unable to struggle. This announcement will draw many a tear in the South, and many a shout of malignant exultation in the North.—Whatever difference of opinion may have existed among the semi-intelligent, the instinct of the people was fixed in the belief, that this silent Virginian was one of the first men, living or dead. In the popular estimate we most sincerely concur. There was the stuff of CROMWELL in JACKSON. HANNIBAL might have been proud of his campaign in the Valley, and the shades of the mightiest warriors should rise to welcome his stern ghost.

Gettysburg Campaign

Lee's decisive victory at Chancellorsville emboldened him to make another attempt to invade the North. Lee spent a month after Chancellorsville reorganizing his army into three infantry corps consisting of three divisions each. Lee named three corps commanders. He retained Longstreet and elevated Ewell and Hill to new positions. Stuart commanded the cavalry. Then, on 3 June, his reorganization complete, Lee's Army of Northern Virginia pulled out from Fredericksburg and marched up the Shenandoah Valley toward western Maryland and ultimately Pennsylvania.

The first engagement of the campaign occurred on 9 June when 12,000 Union cavalry under Major General Alfred Pleasanton surprised Stuart's 10,000-man cavalry near Brandy Station, Virginia. Stuart's horsemen fought the federals to a standstill in the largest purely cavalry battle of the war. This cavalry engagement was Hooker's first warning that Lee was on the move.

Ewell's corps was the first of Lee's 76,000 cohort to make it across the Potomac. On 13 and 14 June, Ewell's men smashed through the Union garrison at Winchester, crossed the Potomac into western Maryland, and then southern Pennsylvania. By late June, though, Ewell and the remaining two corps were deployed in an arc that spanned from Chambersburg northeast toward Harrisburg, the Pennsylvania capital, and then southeast toward York. At the center of the arc was the small college town of Gettysburg.

Hooker at first had not anticipated that Lee was making a major movement, but on 13 June, he began moving his 115,000 Army of the Potomac north to stay between Lee and Washington. The Union army missed repeated opportunities to strike the stretched-out Confederates. Hooker, after reaching Frederick, Maryland, devised a plan to envelop Lee and submitted it to his superior, Halleck, on 27 June. Halleck overruled the plan, and Hooker, in a huff, offered his resignation, which was accepted before dawn on 28 June. That day, Major General George C. Meade was named commander of the Army of the Potomac, its fifth in 10 months.

Within two days, Meade's cavalry and Lee's infantry met in an unexpected clash that led to the greatest battle of the war. On 1 July, the three-day Battle of Gettysburg began when Hill's corps opposed two Union corps under Joseph I. Reynolds and Oliver O. Howard, north and northwest of Gettysburg. Hill outflanked the Union right, but Union troops rallied south of Gettysburg on Cemetery Hill and Culp's Hill, while the Confederates held Seminary Ridge and Gettysburg itself. That night, the rest of Meade's army marched into position along Cemetery Ridge.

Lee's plan for 2 July was to use Longstreet's corps to envelop the Union left. Longstreet objected. He argued instead that, given the strength of the Union position on Cemetery Hill, a flanking move to force a retreat would be a better strategy. Lee disagreed and ordered Longstreet to go on the offensive the next morning.

Longstreet's advance was delayed until the next afternoon, but it succeeded in driving one Union corps back from a peach orchard, and he almost succeeded in turning the Union left. One of Meade's engineers kept that from happening, though, by diverting an infantry brigade and artillery battery to a knob called Little Round Top. This was a key position, and it saved the Union left. The Union army ended up firmly anchored along the ridge from Round Top to Culp's Hill.

Having been repulsed on both Union flanks, Lee decided to attack the Union center on 3 July. He launched ten brigades, supported by tremendous artillery bombardment, in an assault that is now known as "Pickett's Charge." Facing heavy Union bombardment that blew huge holes in their lines, more than 15,000 men pressed forward for half a mile. The Confederates that reached Union lines broke through briefly but were thrown back by Meade's reserves. Only half the men who started out on that charge survived, and they retreated back to Seminary Ridge. Lee, fully aware of the disaster he had ordered, waited for a counterattack, but it never came. Casualties for the two sides were eerily similar. Union casualties for the three days of battle included 3,155 killed, 14,529 wounded, and 5,365 missing. Confederate losses included 3,903 killed, 18,735 wounded, and 5,425 missing.

Given that he had lost 28,000 men in the three-day battle, Lee decided to retreat. His army pulled out on 4 July. Its train of wagons carrying the wounded stretched for 19 miles. Meade followed, but cautiously. The only fighting that occurred was during several Union cavalry raids on the Confederate wagon train. The Army of Northern Virginia crossed over a flood-swollen Potomac at the little village of Williamsport, Maryland. Lee's men were back in Virginia, and there they would remain for the duration of the war. Their leader would tender his resignation out of frustration with his inability to destroy the enemy's army, but President Davis refused to let Lee quit. The well-seasoned Confederate commander spent the remainder of 1863 directing a series of thrusts and parries with Meade's army, but all in all, the Army of Northern Virginia spent the months immediately following Gettysburg essentially in stalemate with the Army of the Potomac.

JAMES R. SNEED: FIRST REPORTS OF BATTLE AT GETTYSBURG

When news of Gettysburg first circulated, Confederates believed they had won a great victory and that Lee's retreat across the Potomac back into Virginia was nothing more than a strategic withdrawal. This article is a good example of the relish with which news of the supposed Confederate victory was received, close on the heels of the capitulation of Vicksburg.

Savannah Republican, 7 July 1863

THE NEWS

We publish this afternoon the most glorious news of the war, it being little less than the total annihilation of the much boasted Yankee Army of the Potomac—"the finest army on the planet," as the vain glorious boaster triumphantly styled it. Lee, it appears, after a battle on Wednesday and desultory fighting on Thursday, collected all his forces in Pennsylvania near the town of Gettysburg, a fight ensued on Sunday, and by one of the most brilliant movements on record, the enemy were surrounded and nearly their entire army either killed, wounded or captured. *Forty thousand prisoners* are said to be now on their way to Richmond.

Such an achievement has no parallel in history, whether as regards the brilliancy of the fight, the number of prisoners taken, or the probable results of the victory. The Yankee army of the Potomac is either in our hands or *hors du combat*, and thus opens up to us the way to Washington. We hope ere this Lee's cannon have thundered at the gates of the Federal city, or, what is more likely, that he has quietly occupied it after an inglorious flight on the part of its defenders.

A late number of the New York Daily news stated that "the army of Hooker had dwindled down to 50,000 men." Make a liberal allowance for reinforcements—say 10,000—and then take out 40,000 prisoners, and how much of the famous Army of the Potomac remains?

In all this our noble army of Virginia have won a fame that belongs to none other in the history of the world. They have shed a lustre upon the Confederate name, and their services will be embalmed in the grateful memories of their countrymen. In Lee, Napoleon, Wellington, Eugene have found their peer, if not a star of still greater magnitude, before the splendor of whose rays the world shall bow in admiration and awe.

We are told that the prisoners taken at Gettysburg refused to be paroled, and are now on their way to Richmond. The object on the part of the wily Yankees is evident; they simply wish to embarrass and clog our movements in the midst of victory by throwing the great incumbrance upon us to be guarded, fed and cared for. There is a remedy for such tricks, and we hope Gen. Lee will apply it—*take no more of the miscreants!*

PETER W. ALEXANDER: ACCOUNT OF FIGHTING AT GETTYSBURG

As soon as Alexander got to a place equipped with a working telegraph, he sent word back to Savannah of the outcome at Gettysburg. The dispatch is long for a telegraph but quite brief when compared to a typical story sent via a letter. Alexander's dispatch actually sounded rather upbeat and cheerful about the outcome. Like many Confederates, he did not realize the significance of the outcome at Gettysburg.

Savannah Republican, 14 July 1863

THE GETTYSBURG FIGHT IN RELIABLE SHAPE
YANKEE LOSS 25,000

Heavy Loss in Confederate Officers

[From our Special Army Correspondence]

GETTYSBURGH, July 5, via Winchester and Staunton. The most desperate battle of the war has been fought here. It commenced on the evening of July 1st, between portions of Ewell's and Lee's commands, and heavy Federal forces under Gen. Reynolds. We drove the enemy back the first day and killed Gens. Reynolds and Paul, and captured three thousand prisoners. The Baltimore papers admit to a loss in this preliminary battle of ten thousand killed, wounded and prisoners. On the 2nd of July both armies concentrated at 4 o'clock. McLaws and Hood, of Longstreet's corps, held the right, attacked and drove the enemy a mile and a half. Hill attacked the centre and Ewell the left. Our success on the left and center was unequal to that on the right wing.

The enemy occupied a range of hills stronger than Malvern Hill.

McLaws and Hood's division took 1,000 prisoners and several [unreadable] and flags, inflicted a terrible loss on the foe and suffered heavily themselves.

On the [unreadable] the battle was resumed. In the afternoon the enemy was driven from several positions, but not dislodged entirely from his strong position when night came.

All was quiet on the 4th. We could not provoke an attack from the enemy. During the night the enemy retreated towards Washington. No pursuit was made.

The loss was heavy on both sides. The following is a list of Confederate casualties:

Killed—Gens. Gannett and Kemper, and Col. Hartman and Williams, of Virginia; Gen. Barksdale, Col. Carter, and Captain Stump, nephew of President Davis, of Mississippi; Col. Desks, of S.C.; Colonel Jack Jones, Wilson, Harris, Wich, and Warden; Lieut. Cols. Caswell, [unreadable], and Mounger, Major [unreadable]; Lieut. Wood, and Captains Hark and Redding of Georgia.

The following were wounded: Major Gens. Hood, Trimble, Pinkett, and [unreadable]. Brig. Gens. Hampton, Semmes, Anderson, Armistead, Robinson, Jenkins, and Jones; Cols. Griffin, Horner, Fiske and Sayers, of Miss.; Col. Kennedy, and Majors McLeod and Miller of S.C.; Cols. Forney, Pinckard and Saunders, Major Fielcher, and Captains King and Smith of Ala.; Cols. Jack Brown, Towers, Little, Anthony; Majors Davidson, Jones and Read; Capts. Frisbee, Carlen, Butler and Lieut. Cowper of Georgia.

The following are wounded and missing: Lt. Col. Harris, Major [unreadable], Capt. George S. Jones, Lieuts. [Unreadable], Cummings, Grannts, R. Campbell, A. A. Freeman of Georgia.

Our total loss, twelve thousand—that of the enemy, twenty-five thousand, including six thousand prisoners.

On the 5th of July, Gen. Lee moved towards Hagerstown, as the enemy had retired. The movement was made to reopen his communications and for other reasons not proper to mention, though satisfactory.

P.W.A.

PETER W. ALEXANDER: REFLECTIONS ON FIGHTING IN 1863

Chancellorsville. Vicksburg. Gettysburg. Battery Wagner. The year 1863 was marked by escalating battlefield violence. Both the North and the South had realized this was not going to be a quick and dirty little conflict. It was all-out war for the Union, if you were a Yankee, and if you were a Confederate, it was a war for independence. With this letter to the Savannah Republican, *the paper's main battlefield reporter, Peter W. Alexander, took a moment to reflect on the bloody events thus far in 1863. He also, toward the end of the article, explained a planned addition to the Confederate army: an engineering corps that was to be organized and staffed.*

Savannah Republican, 11 September 1863

ARMY CORRESPONDENCE
OF THE SAVANNAH REPUBLICAN

ARMY OF NORTHERN VIRGINIA,
September 4, 1863

Spring and Summer have come and gone, and Autumn, with her glowing fingers, is now painting the skies and fields in those gorgeous hues produced only by her skillful hand. We have entered upon the ninth month of 1863, and three acts of the bloody tragedy have passed in review. The first was played at Chancellorsville; the scenery, a sterile soil and a dark wilderness; but the light of victory, reflected back from the Southern Cross, proclaimed the conqueror. The scene shifts, and the second act is ushered in among the rugged hills of Gettysburg. Blood flows in torrents and the slain lay in heaps, but Triumph, unable to decide in favor of either party, turns to Fortune, who warns us to return to our own soil, and fight the battle there.

Form the Potomac we pass to the Father of Waters—to Vicksburg and Port Hudson—where the third act is performed, and where Fortune, less kind than she was wont to be places the crown of victory upon the standard of our enemies. From the great river we step to the sea, and, as the curtain rolls up to the lurid sky, the fourth act opens, and Charleston, and Sumter, and Wagner rise to view. When the curtain, all torn and bloody, and soiled from the terrible conflicts ascends again, it will be upon the fifth and final act of this horrid tragedy of 1863. It may be upon the Rappahannock, and it may be upon the Tennessee.—If here, then the actors are ready; they have studied their parts, they have learned them well and are ready, with the assistance of that kind Prompter who stands above the clouds, to play them through to the bitter end.

Meanwhile, the army is not idle here. The interval between the acts is not left wholly unemployed. Fresh supplies of ammunition have been obtained; newer and better arms have been distributed where any were needed; clothing and shoes have been supplied; the men are exercising and drilling; the animals are resting and improving, and the whole army is preparing for other struggles and other triumphs. Not the least important subjects which now engages the attention of the chiefs, relates to the organization of a corps of engineers. This necessary adjunct of an army should have been provided at the beginning of the war, but better late than never. The corps is intended to embrace pioneers, pontonniers, sappers and miners, as well as engineers proper.

The duties of the engineer are important, and often laborious. If it be necessary for the traveller to be informed beforehand of the roads over which he is to pass, the streams he is to cross, the mountains he is to scale, the defiles he is to thread, and the robbers he is to encounter; how much more important is it that the commander of an army and his chief officers, upon whom depend the safety of their troops, the welfare and honor of their country, and the success of the campaign, should possess the same information? This information cannot be had without the aid of engineers, a part of whose business it is to thoroughly reconnoitre and map the whole country occupied, or expected to be occupied by either army.

This duty is usually performed by a party detailed by the chief of the Engineer Bureau. It should be done early, and the maps deposited in the office of the chief of the bureau in Richmond, where copies are prepared and sent to the department, corps, and division commanders in the field. These maps are on a sufficiently large scale to show accurately the roads, streams, cleared and uncleared land, elevations and depressions of ground, fords, bridges, [*unreadable*]. Particular care is taken to show not only the direction but also the condition of roads, which are classified and each class shown by a different line or mark. It is necessary that all neighborhood and private ways, as well as private roads, should be laid down, as frequently a proper knowledge of roads will enable a General to save much marching by sending his train on one road and his troops by another, thus making the march more rapidly and with less fatigue to his troops. The maps should also go sufficiently into details to enable the General to know where he may encamp his troops on a march. Leaving out of consideration the question of attack and defence, camps on a march should always, if possible, be located convenient to wood and water.

This duty, as above stated, belongs to the party specially detailed by the chief of the bureau; but the engineer acting with the army in the field should take every opportunity of proving the accuracy of the maps, acquiring through their assistance a thorough knowledge of the country. It is his duty, after the line of battle is established, to lay out all works for the strengthening of the line; and it is the duty of the engineer troops, with the aid of such details as are necessary, to construct such works under the superintendence of the officers of the corps. It is also the duty of the engineer, when the line of battle has been established, to acquaint himself most thoroughly with every rod of ground in the neighborhood, both in rear of the line and in front as far as it is safe to reconnoitre. He should know not only where the strong and weak points of his own line are, but also those of the enemy. His knowledge should be such that he could inform his general of the country to be passed over, either in an advance or a retreat; and roads, forts, bridges, &c., should be prepared for both as far as practicable.

As has already been stated, an engineer corps for the field is now being raised. Its organization will be the same as that of the regiment, with a Colonel, Lieut. Colonel, Major, company officers and men. Perhaps it would be more proper to speak of the men as engineer troops. Officers have been detailed to go home to raise volunteers for this inviting service. Among others, Capt. John Bradford, of Florida, an excellent officer, has gone South to raise a company. I would commend him and the service in which he is engaged, to the public generally and especially to all persons within the conscriptage.

P.W.A.

NOTE

1. See the homepage of the Army of the Cumberland at http://www.atoc.net/Murfreesboro.html.

FURTHER READINGS

Burton, E. Milby. *The Siege of Charleston, 1861–1865*. Columbia: University of South Carolina Press, 1970.

Carter, Samuel. *The Final Fortress: The Campaign for Vicksburg, 1862–1863*. New York: St. Martin's Press, 1980.

Catton, Bruce. *Glory Road: The Bloody Road from Fredericksburg to Gettysburg*. Garden City, N.Y.: Doubleday, 1952.

Doubleday, Abner. *Chancellorsville and Gettysburg*. New York: C. Scribner's Sons, 1882.

Dowdey, Clifford. *Death of a Nation: The Story of Lee and His Men at Gettysburg*. New York: Knopf, 1958.

Jones, Archer. *Confederate Strategy from Shiloh to Vicksburg*. Baton Rouge: Louisiana State University Press, 1961.

Martin, David G. *The Vicksburg Campaign April 1862–July 1863*. New York: Gallery Books, 1994.

Rawley, James A. *Turning Points of the Civil War*. Lincoln: University of Nebraska Press, 1966.

Reasoner, James. *Chancellorsville*. Nashville, Tenn.: Cumberland House, 2000.

———. *Chickamauga*. Nashville, Tenn.: Cumberland House, 2002.

———. *Vicksburg*. Nashville, Tenn.: Cumberland House, 2001.

Woodworth, Steven E. *No Band of Brothers: Problems in the Rebel High Command*. Columbia: University of Missouri Press, 1999.

———. *Six Armies in Tennessee: The Chickamauga and Chattanooga Campaigns*. Lincoln: University of Nebraska Press, 1998.

———. *This Grand Spectacle: The Battle of Chattanooga*. Abilene, Tex.: McWhiney Foundation Press, 1999.

31

REPORTING THE WAR, 1864

A slight glimmer of hope remained for the Confederacy in 1864. The Union was, after all, no closer to Richmond than it had been in 1861, and Virginia geography so favored its Southern defenders that the Union had little to show for its gargantuan casualty lists. The situation in the West, though, told the rest of the story. Tennessee remained solidly in Union hands, Sherman and Grant having successfully rolled the Confederates out of the eastern part of the state the previous fall. The South's chances of destroying a Union army in a great decisive battle were shrinking as rapidly as the ranks of the Confederate army. Fewer men were available, and more were deserting. Dissent and dissatisfaction with the war effort would reach a fever pitch before 1864 was out.

The Union war effort was dominated by two generals who had spent most of the war together: Grant, now overall commander as well as effective commander in the East, and Sherman in the West. More modern in their thinking than most of their contemporaries, they sought to attack the Confederacy's capacity to make war, although in different ways. Sherman would attack rebel morale, while Grant decided to grind Lee's army down. The Confederate army, not Richmond, was his real target. In a famously terse order, Grant told his subordinate Meade: "Wherever Lee goes, there you will go also." In May, the Union soldiers set off south again.

Although Grant finally brought strategic clarity to the Union's war effort, his operational perspective was soon found wanting. Constantly underestimating Lee and overestimating Confederate losses, the series of battles Grant waged in May and June of 1864 nearly destroyed the Union army rather than its target. The Battles of The Wilderness, Spotsylvania Courthouse, the North Anna, and Cold Harbor cost him 60,000 men, about 10,000 a week, decimated his best veteran regiments, demoralized many men at a time that enlistments were about to expire, and left Lee undestroyed and Richmond uncaptured. At Cold Harbor, Grant had suffered one of the worst Union defeats of the war, yet it brought him no closer to Richmond than

McClellan had been. To be sure, Grant finally stopped his battering-ram attacks and slipped to the southeast and invested Petersburg, thereby cutting Richmond off from much of the Confederacy. But this brilliant move did little in the short run to make up for his massive casualties—and raised the specter of a Democratic victory in the fall presidential election. Lincoln's opponent, his former chief general, George McClellan, represented a party that was committed to a negotiated peace. Attacking and laying siege to Petersburg would not dissuade people from voting for the Democrats, possibly giving the Confederacy the proverbial eleventh-hour reprieve.

All hopes, both Southern and Northern, hinged on what happened in the West. If the Union could capture Atlanta, Lincoln's reelection would be assured. If the South could stop the assault on its important transportation center, Southern longing for independence had a chance of becoming reality. Northerners and Southerners alike watched the campaign in north Georgia with trepidation. Sherman's advance toward Atlanta progressed slowly at first. His opponent, the wily Johnston, severely punished the Yankees' one attempt to break through, at Kennesaw Mountain in late June. As the battle lines closed in on Atlanta, however, fate, in the person of Jefferson Davis, intervened. Worried about the future of Atlanta, and failing to get clear answers from Johnston on his plans, Davis appointed the aggressive John B. Hood in his place. Hood promptly launched several attacks from the Atlanta fortifications, all of which failed and culminated in his forced withdrawal from the city. On 2 September 1864, Sherman entered Atlanta, probably saving the Lincoln administration in the process.

Grant could now continue his lengthy siege operations at Petersburg, weakening Lee by attacks and stretching the lines to the west, forcing the Confederate front to become thinner and thinner. Although there were occasional disasters, such as the Battle of the Crater on 30 July, which cost the Union nearly 4,000 men to the Confederates' 1,200, the siege forced the Confederate army to sit still, depriving Lee of his vaunted skills at maneuvering an army. The chance for a decisive Confederate battlefield victory had disappeared, because the traditional battlefield had disappeared.

Sherman, however, was concerned that the South might continue the war indefinitely, especially through irregular operations. He resolved to convince the South that its victory was an impossibility. He would do it by waging a total war to end the conflict. In this the Union general was immensely helped by a speech Davis gave in Macon in late September. Speaking to a crowd of refugees who had come to Macon when they fled Atlanta, the president revealed the manpower problems that plagued the Confederate army. The president estimated that somewhere around a third of the soldiers were missing from their positions. Sherman realized that he had virtually no serious opposition. A handful of Confederate cavalry under the controversial General Joseph Wheeler and a few thousand Georgia militiamen and Confederate regulars were all that stood between him and the Atlantic Ocean. The majority of the Confederacy's troops were in Virginia, and the western army against which he had fought so long for possession of Atlanta was off in Tennessee. Come mid-December, Hood's ill-considered plan to draw Sherman away from Atlanta by invading Tennessee would result in the almost total destruction of the Army of Tennessee near Nashville. Thus, Sherman was emboldened to embark on his infamous March to the Sea, burning public buildings along the way and living off the land. Sherman's army captured Savannah on 22 December, prompting the general to send Lincoln the most famous telegraph of the war, the one in which he flamboyantly presented Savannah to Lincoln as a Christmas present. The vulnerability of the Southern interior lands, and the impotence of the Confederate government, had been decisively demonstrated. The plantation economy collapsed as huge numbers of slaves abandoned their bondage.

WESTERN THEATER

Atlanta Campaign

Union General William T. Sherman was reputed to be crazy, but what he truly was, was clever. After the hard fighting at Chattanooga late in 1863, Sherman had several months to survey the situation of the South and to think about his next step in winning a war that had been just as long and bloody as he had predicted it would be back in 1861. The key, he realized, was Atlanta. So long as Lee could get supplies for his Army of Northern Virginia, he could keep up at least some semblance of a fighting force. Georgia was where most of those supplies were produced, and Atlanta was the rail center from which they were shipped. That meant Atlanta had to fall. Sherman, with the blessing of his commanding officer, Ulysses S. Grant, set about building up his army. By spring, Sherman had nearly 100,000 men under his command, and he was ready to begin his campaign for Atlanta through territory with which he was imminently familiar. Early in his army career, Sherman had been stationed in Marietta, a small town to the northwest of Atlanta, and he had thoroughly reconnoitered north Georgia then.

Opposing Sherman was one of the Confederacy's most stalwart and reliable generals, Joseph E. Johnston. Johnston, who had been sent to resolve the hopeless situation at Vicksburg in the summer of 1863, once again got the job of keeping a vastly superior force from capturing a vital Southern city. Johnston had been named commander of the 60,000-man Army of Tennessee after its previous leader, Braxton Bragg, resigned in humiliation over the loss of Chattanooga. Johnston was exactly the right man for the job. He was a master of defensive strategy, almost prescient at knowing when to withdraw and where to put up the mightiest fight. But there was a bad side to Johnston's selection, too: Davis hated him. The president blamed Johnston, not Pemberton, for the loss of Vicksburg, and he was willing to listen to just about any criticism of his least favorite general.

In early May, Sherman's army moved out from Chattanooga. Through May, Johnston skillfully fought Sherman in a series of delaying positions at Dalton, Resaca, and Cassville. Sherman, equally skillfully, outmaneuvered Johnston each time the two forces met. In late May, Sherman began a drive due south and swept past Johnston's position near Allatoona. Johnston withdrew to Marietta to meet Sherman face-to-face in the Battle of Kennesaw Mountain. Through June, the two commanders toyed with one another in small engagements and maneuvers. In late June, the impatient and impetuous Sherman decided he had had enough of small probing movements that bought little ground. It was time to get serious and destroy the Army of Tennessee in one huge, decisive battle. Sherman ordered a direct assault on the Confederate entrenchments on Kennesaw Mountain. The attack began at 8:00 A.M. on 27 June with a Union artillery barrage. Sherman sent McPherson to attack the Confederate positions on the south side of the mountain, Thomas was to support McPherson, and Schofield was to create a diversion with a feint to the south. Almost immediately, Sherman's plans got derailed. The feint did not work, and McPherson's men, though initially successful, were pinned down by heavy Confederate fire. Thomas's men advanced, with bayonets only initially, to within 15 yards of the Confederate line, but after a three-hour fight, they, too, were forced to withdraw. The battle for Sherman was a disaster. He lost 3,000 men to the Confederacy's 800.

Sherman rested his demoralized men for a week before once again moving against Johnston. This time, the Union general's plan was to turn Johnston's left and sweep past him into Marietta. Informed by his scouts of Sherman's movements, Johnston chose to abandon Marietta and take up a strong entrenched position north of the Chattahoochee River.

On 9 July, Sherman's men bypassed Johnston to cross the Chattahoochee, the last natural barrier between the Union army and Atlanta. Two days later, Sherman sent McPherson east to Decatur and Stone Mountain to cut the railroad lines between Atlanta and Augusta, which eliminated the possibility of Johnston receiving reinforcements by rail from Virginia. Johnston was watching the Union army carefully and noted a gap between Thomas's and Schofield's lines. He saw an opening there for a successful attack, but Johnston was waiting for the federals to get closer before attacking. He never got the chance to go on the offensive, though. Jefferson Davis chose that precise moment to fire Johnston. It was one of the worst decisions the president made in the entire war. The ungrateful president had failed to note that his general had waged a remarkable defensive campaign through the early summer. For 2.5 months, Johnston had managed to hold Sherman's advance to an average of 1 mile per day, and the Confederate general had suffered few losses in the campaign. Nevertheless, on 17 July, Johnston was summarily relieved, and his impulsive subordinate, John B. Hood, was elevated to the rank of general and given the command of the Army of Tennessee.

Hood, who had a reputation for being a battlefield brawler, immediately went on the offensive. On 20 July, he ordered an attack intended to push entrenched Thomas's Union infantrymen away from the banks of Peachtree Creek and back toward the Chattahoochee. Hood's orders prior to the attack confused his men about where they were to advance, but he went on with the attack anyway. Hood caught Thomas by surprise but was repulsed nevertheless. Both forces in the Battle of Peachtree Creek had about 20,000 men each. Union losses were 1,600 to the Confederacy's 2,500.

Even before the fighting died down from Peachtree Creek, Sherman was pulling together his forces for an assault on the prize itself: Atlanta. Hood believed he had an opportunity to go on the offensive against McPherson. He positioned Stewart's corps and the Georgia militia in a defensive ring around Atlanta and sent Hardee's troops on an all-night forced march to the east in an attempt to get behind the Northern lines. Wheeler's cavalry also moved east to destroy federal wagons near the town of Decatur. McPherson had anticipated that the Confederates would make exactly this move and had repositioned his forces to repulse the attack. The day ended at least indecisively, if not in outright disaster, for the Confederates.

Despite consecutive successes, Sherman realized he did not have the manpower to besiege Atlanta, but his objective was not so much possession of the Gate City as destroying its function as a transportation center. He could accomplish his objective with fewer resources, in either men or supplies, by focusing on destruction of the last two open railroads into Atlanta. Sherman sent Major General Oliver O. Howard west to destroy the Macon and Western and the Atlanta and West Point lines. He sent his cavalry raiding to the south. Hood learned of Howard's movement and sent two corps to oppose him in the Battle of Ezra Church on 28 July. The Confederates were repulsed, with losses of some 4,300 men to the federal loss of 632. The cavalry raids had less success.

Sherman's 6,000 cavalry, commanded by Hugh Judson Kilpatrick, had two jobs. The first was to cut the railroad, and the second was to liberate Union prisoners at Andersonville. The cavalry worked for nearly a month to accomplish those objectives but failed and lost some 2,000 men on 4 August when Major General George Stoneman was surrounded and forced to surrender.

Sherman was becoming more frustrated with his inability to cut the rail lines and looked for other alternatives. Atlanta's defenses were far too strong for a direct attack, and he had already rejected the idea of a siege. The only option was to shell Atlanta into submission, and so on 9 August, Sherman began an intense bombardment of the city. His artillerymen responded by slinging more than 5,000 shells into the city that day alone. The bombardment continued for two weeks until, finally, on 25 August, it just stopped. The first thought was that Sherman had given up and moved off, but soon word reached Hood of a new federal advance. Sherman left one corps to guard his communications lines and took his remaining three armies forward in a wheeling movement toward the rail lines south of Atlanta. The movement was so successful that it forced Hood to abandon Atlanta.

On 1 September, Sherman's determination paid off. The last rail line into Atlanta was cut. Hardee had managed to hold his position until after nightfall on 1 September, but he could not do anything more. Hood ordered warehouses of Confederate supplies to be put to the torch rather than allow them to fall into Union hands. After midnight, a huge explosion announced the end of an ammunition train Hood had been unable to get away from the city. Sherman heard the explosion 15 miles away in Jonesboro, and he knew then that Atlanta was his.

WAVERLY: STATE OF GENERAL JOHNSTON'S ARMY

In early May, federal General William T. Sherman made the first move in a campaign that would take him through the heartland of the remaining unoccupied Confederate states. The Army of Tennessee, now under command of Joseph E. Johnston, cleverly parried each Union advance and slowed Sherman's force to a snail's pace. The effort would not be sufficient to repulse Sherman, but the Army of Tennessee made him pay dearly for each step toward Atlanta. This was one of the better covered campaigns since reporters from several newspapers were with Johnston, and the Atlanta and Augusta papers, as well as the Confederate Press Association, could easily send reporters to the front from time to time. Waverly, the Memphis Appeal's *correspondent with Johnston's army, sent a pair of dispatches that described the initial advance of Sherman's troops. The* Appeal *had been published in Atlanta since the previous summer. In his first dispatch, Waverly dealt primarily with military matters. He discussed the morale of the Confederate troops and early skirmishes but inaccurately estimated the federal army had some 60,000 men. In truth, Sherman's force at that point was closer to 100,000. Waverly's second dispatch, begun on a quiet Sunday morning, is almost lyrical in its description of Dalton that morning and his anticipation of whether he would hear church bells first or cannon fire that would signal the beginning of the day's engagement. The fight for Atlanta was long and bitter, and Waverly and the other correspondents with Johnston would do their best to tell Confederate citizens what was happening in northern Georgia, but by the end of May, strict censorship by the military would curtail—though not stop—the reporting.*

Memphis Appeal, 9 May 1864

GENERAL JOHNSTON'S ARMY
Letter No. 1
Special Correspondence of the Memphis Appeal
In the Field, May 6, 1864

To-Day

The ball opened at 8 o'clock this morning. The enemy advanced, one division in force, toward Sulcker's gap, four miles above Dalton, on our left, and were handsomely repulsed. The skirmish lay along Stewart's line. The firing was regular for several hours, but not particularly heavy. Small arms were only used by sharp-shooters. Considerable damage was done. Loss trifling on our side.

The Prospect

Every one anticipates a great battle to morrow. The outside indications certainly favor this idea. Couriers are dashing hither and thither, guns are booming now and then, and reports of the most exagerated description go from lip to lip. I do not look for a fight quite so soon, although it is highly probable that they will attack our left to-morrow. Hitherto our right has been regarded as the point of investment, but the scene has shifted.

The Tennessee Troops

Your heart would swell with pride if you could see the noble Tennessee boys, who compose so large a part of this army. Led by the most skillful and vallant commanders, they are especially cheered by the presence of their governor. He is here, and he never fails to be, when a fight is on hand. Just out of West Tennessee, where he passed through Forrest's late campaign, Gov. Harris breathes the air of home to the troops. He appears among them constantly, delivers the most encouraging addresses, and is met with expressions of enthusiastic welcome.

The Force of the Enemy

I know that you want to know something of Sherman's force. Wiser heads estimate it at not over sixty thousand. Kilpatrick's cavalry will not exceed a tenth part of that number. As to our force it is sufficient to say that no one here is frightened.

The Result

Keep up the liveliest heart imaginable in the rear. There is no sort of danger. You never saw such pluck in all your born days. Especially do not believe the monstrous rumors in circulation among the speculators.

WAVERLY.

AFFAIRS IN FRONT
Letter No II

Special Correspondence of the Appeal.]
DALTON, Sunday Morning, May 7, 1864.
The Sabbath Day Near the Enemy—What is the Prospect?—The Struggle for Position—News from Middle Tennessee—The Guns Open, etc.

I take out my watch. The time is just five minutes to 8 o'clock, and the morning is as bright and clear as ever a Sunday in the peaceful days of yore. The birds are bob-o-linking in the leafy trees; the sunny greet, that dances in the wind, is moving with them. The troops slept on their arms last night, but Dalton has very little semblance of war. I think I shall hear the bells presently, and have once or twice oddly fancied that it was most time for Sunday school. Any one of these quiet moments, which steal around me as I write, may be broken into a thousand fragments by the loud report of cannon echoing among the hills and glens. The first gun will call me hence, and so I will hasten to jot you a few random notes before I am disturbed.

The Impending Battle

So the fight has not yet opened. As I wrote you, the wager of battle is not determined. The handkerchief, whose fall is to signal the two armies to combat, still flutters in the air. It may drop today—it may not touch the ground for a week to come. This looks like "an opinion as [*unreadable*] opinion," but it is quite logical. You see both sides are maneuvering for positions. Johnston is so apt at their species of strategy that he befogs Sherman, who shifts from right to left and from left to right, and then masses on the center, like the shuttle of a loom, with this difference, that he isn't weaving much cloth. How far the Virginia news will effect his plans I cannot say, but if there is not a battle of some sort tomorrow (Monday) I shall be very much surprised.

The Mountains of Tennessee

I have had a conversation with one of our scouts lately out of Middle Tennessee. Stokes' (Yankee) cavalry are operating in the mountains with a free hand. One of their latest atrocities was the murder of young Marchbanks, a son of the eminent jurist. Captain Marchbanks was organizing a company in White county, not many miles above his own home. He was pursued, made captive, taken to the woods, tied to a tree and shot. His mother was then sent for and arrived before the body was buried. Stokes is riding the horse of the poor young man, and boasts of his infamous deed of blood. Arthur Mercer, a nephew of Maj. L. D. Mercer, was recently killed in a rancounter with Col. Thomas B. Murray. My informant tells me that the entire mountain country is in a terrible partisan state, and that the return of the Confederates which is expected from week to week, will be a blessing and relief.

Writing in Front

You must not expect these letters of mine to be very carefully prepared or elaborate. If one is [*unreadable*], he has little time left him to be picturesque. Besides, when you have ridden for half a day over rock and hill, through the sun and the dust, and at last reach a place of shade and rest, you are not in a very rhetorical humor. I will give you facts, hints of the goings-on in these parts, stray gleams of suggestive interest. You must fill in my mere outlines with "tines of deeper hue." You must not be afraid of my skeletons. I shall not be sensational, I promise you.

The Guns

Boom! boom! boom! There they go! Just as I had written the last line above, the roll of a cannon broke upon the air. What is it? A general engagement? I don't know. An attack? Perhaps so. I will go and see.

WAVERLY.

WAVERLY: STATE OF MORALE IN ATLANTA

Atlanta was hunkering down for the coming fight. Whitehall, one of the main streets in the town, was a shadow of its former self, Waverly reported after a quick visit. Where flags and ladies used to grace the street, now ordinance jammed the thoroughfare. The ladies were all home packing in case they had to flee. The change in public confidence from two weeks previous was dramatic, the reporter wrote. Waverly used his letter to assure his readers that they were safe and that the Army of Tennessee would carry the day.

Memphis Appeal, 25 May 1864

OUR ARMY CORRESPONDENCE

Letter from "Waverly."]
All Quiet in Front—A Run to Atlanta—The Perturbation of its Inhabitants—A Causeless Alarm—the Prospects upon the Outer Wall—Chattahoochee or Etowah—Reveille, etc., etc.
ATLANTA, Wednesday, May 23.

Everything is very quiet along the line in front, and your correspondent has sought the gay metropolis for a bit of recreation.

Gay, did I say? Pardon me, I would scarce recognize its changed, tumultuous aspect. The sunny side of Whitehall, which erst did gliston [*sic*] with stars and bars, and petticoats, seems to be in a peripatetic condition, blockaded with guards and jammed with bales and boxes of merchandize. Surely you are not expecting a visit from Sherman, or any other distinguished foreigner? Why, I found half a dozen ladies of my acquaintance packing their preserves in bandboxes and their bonnets in butter kegs, out of down-right confusion, they said; four old gentlemen locked themselves in their patent safes, (for safe keeping, I suppose) where they will have to be dug out with pike and mattock, as they drew the keys and keyholes in after them; and even one of my canine friends, partaking of the general disquiet, and having perused the ferocious proclamation of Marshal Jones, had found a dry well and was stocking it with provisions for a siege, when I assured him with tears in my eyes that there is not the least danger in the world! Odds, tremors and quakes, are ye going insane!

But let's be serious, I frankly confess my surprise. To a cool, unagitated mind the scenes transpiring from hour to hour in the streets of Atlanta are very diverting. Why what a panic you have wrought here in this vestibule of the Empire State. I have passed the morning upon Whitehall street watching the ebb and flow of popular feeling and taking notes upon the versatile physiognomy of the town. It is magical, the change. But two weeks are gone, and confidence stood like a pillar of fire before every shop and at every corner; now the very signs are creeping in doors and the street crossings disclose the most eager multitudes of tradesmen, dealing exclusively in rumors, speculations upon reports, extortioners of mischief out of each idle story that flies on the great, national, antigalvanin, non-conductive grape-vine battery! The operators thereof, to my thinking, would find a deal better work behind a dozen batters of a different description that I know of, and as for those who betray so much simplicity as to believe all they hear, they would be happier, and just as healthy, at the front!

Aye, the front. It is not such a very ugly place as you might suppose. There are lads as cheerful as crickets and sing along from morning till night, even though they be rivalled by the shells. The front is a jolly place, and cooler than Atlanta. Come, let us seek its shades of green, its pleasant nooks and coves, its river views, its drums and fifes and flags! The blue sky above us, the blue coats before us, around us the blue fields of grass and grain, we have only to prime our piece and prove our self one, two, or three of a hundred thousand patriots. Listen! Do you not hear the shrill whistle of the iron horse? He scaneth the battle from afar and snorteth for the fray. But hark, there is another sound! It is the cheer of the troops who are going to the front. They too are eager for the fight. Will you join them? Will you step forth from your very shrine to the field which is to decide whether it shall be yours forever or that of an alien master! To the front, to the front! At least to the trenches with musket, with bayonet, with conscious right and resolution! We shall carry the day, never fear it. We shall whip back the foe. There is a handful of us who have undertaken the job, and we are bound to finish it. General Johnston says so, and also that inner spirit which prompts men to do, defy and dare. Hurrah for the front! Hurrah for the line, be it Etowah or Chattahoochee! And three times three hurrahs for the victory we are going to win! We shall make the old, dry woodlands ring with rifle and cannon and we shall strew the sands with Yankee bones. Of all these races since John Gilpin, not excepting the "Camp town Races," the race back to Middle Tennessee will be the hottest, the speediest, aye, and the bloodiest!

WAVERLY.

SPECIAL: CONFEDERATE PREPARATIONS AT KENNESAW MOUNTAIN

Nearly six weeks into the spring offensive in north Georgia, the scene of action began to settle on Kennesaw Mountain, near Marietta. This was the largest engagement fought north of Atlanta, and it was a tactical success for the Confederates, though the Union forces were not stopped for long. This story described the preparations and expectations for the battle. The author, Special, regularly submitted articles to the Appeal.

Memphis Appeal, 21 June 1864

FROM THE FRONT

MARIETTA, JUNE 20, 1864.

I have just returned from a circuit of our lines, and have only time to write you a hurried letter.

Last night our lines were withdrawn to Kennesaw mountain, for reasons which have not, as yet, transpired; and heavy skirmishing has been going on since 8 o'clock this morning along the entire line.

CAPTAIN MATTHEWS: ACCOUNT OF TRUCE TO BURY DEAD AT KENNESAW MOUNTAIN

Periodically, the fighting would be stopped so that the dead could be buried. Here, Harvey, another of the Memphis Appeal's *correspondents with Johnston's army, wrote about such a truce that was arranged three days after the Battle of Kennesaw Mountain. The burial parties turned the lull in battle into a social meeting of the Union and Confederate soldiers. Harvey was a soldier correspondent for the newspaper. All that is known about his identity is that he was a Captain Matthews, though the* Athens Southern Watchman *of 10 August 1864 reported that Captain Matthews lost a leg in the Battle of Atlanta on 22 July.*

Memphis Appeal, 1 July 1864

FROM THE FRONT

Special Correspondence of the Memphis Appeal.]
IN THE FIELD, NEAR MARIETTA,
June 30, 1864.

The last of the Yankee dead in front of Cleburn and Cheatham were buried yesterday under flag of truce. I visited those divisions this morning and endeavored from the different statements and opinions expressed by officers and men, to form an estimate of the Yankee loss. In front of Gen. Cheatham, the lowest calculation I heard made was one thousand Yankees killed, while Cleburne's command claims to have slain fifteen hundred. The killed then may be safely put down at two thousand. Owing to the short range and unerring aim of our men, the proportion of the wounded cannot be so great as usual. Some think it amounted to six or eight thousand, but I will offer no guess.

During the truce a number of officers and men from both sides met midway and mingled freely in friendly conversation. Among others Generals Hindman and Cheatham, the latter in his shirt sleeves. His easy pleasant manner pleasing the Yanks, one of them familiarly elbowed the general in the side, saying, "I think you are a good reb. Give me a drink old fel." Where upon the general politely passed over his canteen of water. "Do you know who you are talking to," inquired one of our men. "No," said the Yank, "but he is a good rebel I am certain." "Well, that is General Cheatham." Blue coat looked profound astonishment, but in a few minutes a crowd of Yankees, surrounded the two generals, gazing eagerly and presenting their pocket books for autographs, which were given.

The Yankees manifested one of their leading characteristics on every available occasion, their propensity to trade. They would sell watches, knives, stirrups, canteens, or anything they had. Tobacco was their great object, they complained of great scarcity of the article. When we sent out the flag of truce, a Yank called out, "What do you want, are you coming over to trade?" "No," replied the colonel, "I am coming to make some arrangements about burying your dead." D—m the dead, I thought you wanted to sell some tobacco for coffee.

About three o'clock this morning, the enemy believing, it is supposed, that we were evacuating our works, came out of their works and advanced cautiously upon ours, our boys though fatigued by constant vigilance, were wide awake and opened a terrible fire upon the enemy, who hastily discharged a volley or two without effect, and hastened under cover of their works. A heavy fire of musketry was kept up by both sides from their works near half an hour. One of our batteries also fired regularly. The light afforded by the flash of the guns and bursting of shells, enabled our men to see the enemy's lines distinctly until they fell back. Our loss was only one or two wounded as far as known. The enemy's unknown, as in the thick darkness that succeeded the firing, they were enabled to carry off all their dead and wounded.

Colonel Jones, of the 33d Tennessee, was killed this morning behind the works. A minie struck a limb of a tree several feet above and outside the works, glancing downwards it passed through the colonel's head, killing him instantly.

Quite a pleasant shower fell this evening, which was much needed and very refreshing.

There is a rumor afloat that Major General Stewart is to be the commander of Polk's corps. Among the numerous distinguished officers suggested for that high command, few, perhaps, combine more eminent qualifications, than this modest, unassuming Christian general.

HARVEY.

TELEGRAPH AND FELIX G. DE FONTAINE: REPORTS OF FIGHTING AROUND ATLANTA

For 2.5 months, Joseph E. Johnston waged a remarkably effective defensive and delaying campaign through north Georgia against a vastly larger Union army. On 17 July, after crossing the Chattahoochee River, an ungrateful President Davis summarily removed Johnston from the command of the Army of Tennessee. He replaced him with the impulsive, perhaps even reckless, John Bell Hood. Hood was the youngest man to achieve a four-star generalship on either side in the Civil War. A Kentucky native, Hood had been Johnston's key corps commander during the campaign for Atlanta, but he had a different strategy for dealing with the larger Union army: head-on assaults. The more aggressive approach won the approval of the Mobile Advertiser and Register, *but it lost Atlanta for the Confederacy. Once General Hood took over command of the Army of Tennessee, the nature of the campaign for Atlanta changed tremendously. As so many Southerners had hoped, he went on the offensive. The following is a telegraphic account of fighting near Griffin, which is south of Atlanta. The companion article to this telegraphic dispatch was written by Felix G. de Fontaine. In the early part of the war, de Fontaine was a correspondent, mostly in Virginia, for the* Charleston Courier. *Earlier in 1864, he had purchased the* South Carolinian *in Columbia from Dr. Robert W. Gibbes, but he left his editorial duties to his trustworthy second, Henry Timrod, and returned to the field as a correspondent for the Atlanta Campaign.*

Mobile Advertiser and Register, 31 July 1864

FURTHER OF THE FIGHT AT ATLANTA
GENS. STUART AND LORING SLIGHTLY WOUNDED
OUR OTHER GENERALS UNHURT

The Raid upon the Railroad

Punishment of the Raiders

Yankee Foragers Come to Grief
Two Negro Regiments Wh'pped
Two White Regiments to be Heard From

GRIFFIN, July 30—A citizen who arrived here late last night, from Atlanta, states that the fight on Friday was fierce and sanguinary. Our troops fought with great gallantry, carrying two lines of the enemy's entrenchments, but now hold their original position.

General Stewart and General Loring are both slightly wounded. Generals Waithall and [*unreadable*] reported killed, were not hurt. Stewart's is a flesh wound in the head. Loring's a ball that passed round his ribs, not entering the cavity.

Gens. Stewart and Loring started down the road on the morning train yesterday, but hearing of the enemy on the road the train turned back and escaped.

The raid, supposed to be under Col. Brownlow, captured Fayetteville yesterday morning, and burnt a lot of wagons. They are supposed to be about seventy-five.

They struck the railroad near Lovejoy's and tore up about a mile and a half of the track, at intervals extending five miles, turned the depot, and destroyed and carried off four miles of telegraph wire.

Before the arrival of their tools for the more effective destruction of the road, our cavalry under Gen. Jackson attacked and drove them off, killing eleven and wounding seventeen. The raiders fled towards Atlanta. The road is being repaired.

A small body of raiders is reported at Jackson, Bolts county this morning, making in the direction of the railroad. Our forces are after them.

Severe Fighting around Atlanta

[Correspondence of the Savannah Republican]
BEHIND THE CHATTAHOOCHEE
July 20, 1860

The movements of this morning have been in a measure significant of the events bout to follow. At daylight the enemy commenced pressing our cavalry on the right, now covering the Augusta and Atlanta railroad, several miles of which they destroyed. Heavy skirmishing ensued, during which the enemy planted a battery within range of the city and three shells in the vicinity of one of our hospitals, no more than 500 yards from the heart of the town. Gen. Wheeler, observing this diabolic act, promptly ran a battery into position, and after half a dozen well directed shells, drove the Yankees from their temporary foothold.

At just twelve o'clock a gathering of Gen. Hood's own military household in front of headquarters announced still another in the chain of mysterious events. But I had not long to wait for the unraveling of the web. The noble Texan, arrayed in full uniform, leaning on his crutch and stick, was standing in the doorway, his manner calm, his eyes flashing, with a strange indescribable light, which gleams in them only in the hour of battle. His first observation as he took my hand was, "Mr. ———, at one I attack the enemy. He has pressed our lines until he is within a short distance of Atlanta, and I must fight or evacuate. I am going to fight. The odds are against us, but I have the issue with the God of battles." We parted, and Gen. Hood, with his staff, Gen. Lovell, Gen. Mackail and escort then proceeded to the lines. I have remained at headquarters to write these hurried words anticipatory of the battle.

The moments are slipping by, as anxious moments always do, tediously and yet not without a sensation of heart agony that is utterly depressing. One hour more and the mettle of an army opposed by double its numbers, fighting behind breastworks, with diabolic incentive, the spires of Atlanta in view, and its booty in prospect, will be undergoing an ordeal by fire. One hour more and hundreds of dead friends, whose merry laugh you have answered around their camp fires, may be wallering in their blood at these strange hillsides or gone forever to their hong homes. One hour more and thousands will become widows and orphans, and weary heart cries will ascend to Heaven over the new sacrifice which the [*unreadable*] struggle demands; while brave men, borne together, will linger for a time under the knife and saw of the surgeons, and then perhaps return to their homes maimed for life.

We read of war and its glories, and enthusiasm pervades our nature at every recital of a heroic act, but when this dreadful reality confronts us, bounded only by the space of an hour or a moment, there is something within us which involuntarily recoils at the repetition of those scores of suffering and death which, however beneficial in their results to the country, such a fearful price for the good attained, that we remember them only with a shudder. How much more so under circumstances like the present, when the very existence of an army hangs in the balance.

Night, July 20.—A [*unreadable*], or rather an engagement has taken place, and the fitful splashes of musketry along the line denote that it has ended without [*unreadable*] results. I am too weary to enter much into details, and probably it would not be prudent to do so first, because of the incompleteness of the affair, and secondly, the liability of capture while the letter is *en route* to Macon, being fear that the enemy will strike our only remaining line of communication tonight. The following, therefore, is only a simple outline of the afternoon's work.

The object of Gen. Hood in planning the attack was of two fold, namely to withdraw if possible from the enemy's left to centre and right a portion of the forces with which he had been so persistently pressing our right, and to defeat and cut up one of its wings.

By examining the map and recalling the preceding description of the situation of Sherman's forces, you will observe that a portion of the latter extended from near the junction of the Chattahoochee and Peachtree Creek in an easterly direction. Into the [unreadable] it was believed that by a proper combination of our forces, we could drive the right of Sherman's army, and affect the object in view. Stewart's corps held our left, Hardee the centre. The attack by these two bodies was nearly simultaneous. The advance commenced about 2 o'clock. Leaving the breastworks, our men slowly but confidently pushed their way towards the front. Skirmishing began almost immediately. Strange to say, a part of the enemy's line was discovered to be also advancing. Our army charged with [unreadable], and drove it back in disorder.

One, two, and in some instances three lines of incipient or temporary breastworks were mounted and left behind, and the battle in our favor appeared to go on swimmingly. Suddenly Stewart was brought to a stand still. In his front was the main line of Yankee entrenchments and a redoubt manned by a battery. Gathering fresh strength, however, one of his brigades plunged against this work and it yielded. A heavy enfilading fire from a park of artillery on the right drove them back. The Federals reoccupied the redoubt. Our men advanced a second time and again captured it, but by the same terrible fire poured upon them from the distant artillery, were compelled to abandon the prise. Meanwhile Hardee had also reached the continuation of the same line. His men fighting bravely had overcome every obstacle thus far and were prepared to dash yet further out and drive the enemy into the creek. But here, the judgment of the commander and the gallantry of the troops were at variance. Gen. Hardee deemed it imprudent to risk the lives of his men in achieving an object which threatened to cost so much. A halt was ordered, and in brief, no further efforts were made to accomplish the end of the expedition.

Of course disappointment prevails throughout the army at the result, for the troops engaged—each one [unreadable] the dash and gallantry of the other—were satisfied of their ability to go on. No blame can, therefore, attach to any one for the negative victory plainly won, and the only regret expressed among the men is that the officers in command were, as they believe, in the present instance, over prudent in putting probabilities against what seemed a certainty.

Our losses in the affair will doubtless not fall short of a thousand [unreadable] in the corps of Gen. Steward [unreadable] captured are two or three stands or colors, and some two or three hundred prisoners. Hooker's corps is represented by [unreadable] badly crippled.

The death of Maj. W. Preston, son of Brig. Gen. John S. Preston, of Columbia, and the dangerous wound of Brig. Gen. C. B. Stevens, of S.C., commanding a Georgia brigade of Walker's division, have been reported by telegraph. The former was one of the most prominent officers in the army, and a universal favorite having filled offices of the highest trust and, in the mall, demonstrated himself with honor and courage. He was killed by a shell while giving orders to his men.

Gen. Stevens has likewise won for himself an enviable reputation for gallantry on every field of battle in which he has been engaged. He was shot while leading his men, the ball entering behind the right ear and lodging in the brain, from which it has not up to this writing been removed. His horse was killed at the same moment, and two men who went to his relief were wounded. One may judge the severity of the enemy's fire from these statements. Gen. S. will probably be sent to Macon to-morrow, and if possible from that point homewards.

While the fight I have recorded was in progress on the left, Wheeler's cavalry successfully held the enemy's infantry in check on our right. With—small brigades he contested the ground with two corps—Dodge's and Logan's—and after twelve or fourteen hours' hard fighting has prevented them from obtaining any advantage. Cannonading has been constant along the lines all day.

The enemy are evidently endeavoring to maneuver Hood out of Atlanta, but there is quite as much probability that within thirty-six hours, Sherman will be maneuvering to get away from him.

F. G. de F.

CONFEDERATE: REPORT ON THE DEFENSE OF ATLANTA

The Columbus Sun's *correspondent, Confederate, sent back a letter that described firsthand the fighting around Atlanta as Sherman's forces desperately tried to cut the rail lines into the city. The story makes it clear that not only are the city's military installations the targets of Sherman's artillery barrage, so is the civilian population. In the face of the Union onslaught, the writer's defiant spirit was remarkable, opening the question as to whether the letter was consciously written to boost morale or whether the writer truly believed the Confederate army might actually be able to keep up the defense of Atlanta and perhaps eventually drive off Sherman. Confederate's comment about the Georgia militia hinted at a long-standing argument between President Davis and Governor Joseph E. Brown over who contolled state troops and how they should be used.*

Columbus Sun, 9 August 1864 (Columbus, Ga.)

CORRESPONDENCE OF THE DAILY SUN
LETTER FROM "CONFEDERATE"

ATLANTA, Aug. 5th, 1864.

The enemy for two days have been constantly shelling the city, from the battery on the Marietta road. Three persons were killed [*unreadable*] before last. Mr. Warner and daughter ten years old killed in bed, the latter being cut in two and died instantly; the former had both his legs cut from his body, lived some hours.—The third person killed was a young lady whose name I have been unable to learn.

Such disposition has been made of our forces, as is believed will in future, prevent the recurrence of the raids which have lately disgraced the country and army and done much serious damage to our lines of communication. Squads of the raiders continue to be picked up through the country and brought in. The capture of the great raider, Stoneman, is a serious loss to the enemy.

The militia continue to arrive by every train. Let them come. They should have been at the front long ago. Among other familiar faces, I notice that of your Mr. DeWolf. He commands a squad of the unterrified. Gen. Toombs appears very active in the discharge of his duties with the militia. Gen. Smith told me yesterday that he believed they would fight as well as any other troops we have. I hope so.

The enemy continues to try and make headway to his right, towards the Atlanta and West Point Railroad. East Point, where the A & W. P. Railroad intersects the Macon Road, is no doubt the point they aim at. A bloody battle will come off before they reach it.

I was pained to notice, while passing through the soldiers cemetery in this place a few days since, the little pains taken in burying the soldiers who have died in the hospitals and been killed in the engagements near here, and the neglect in not having the graves properly marked. I noticed many that had only a rough piece of board, that will decay or fall down in a few months, with the name of the deceased, written on it with a pencil, or a small piece of paper, and in many instances has already been washed off by the rain and gone.—There is no excuse for this and it should not be. At Marietta, the grave of every soldier is plainly marked.

The mails are now sent to us from Griffin.

CONFEDERATE.

AN ANONYMOUS REPORT: FALL OF ATLANTA

Even the journalists still at Atlanta were cut off once the city fell. No information was getting in, and little was getting out. Rumors were circulating in Macon that Hood had evacuated Atlanta the previous day, as indeed he had, but there was no way at the time to verify the information since the rail lines into the city had been cut. The information about the fall of Atlanta is buried in the story, not because the Mercury's editors did not recognize the important part of the story but because news practice of the day was to add dispatches to the bottom of the telegraphic news already typeset.

Charleston Mercury, 5 September 1864

TELEGRAPHIC
FALL OF ATLANTA

MACON, September 3.—Parties from the front report that our losses on Wednesday did not exceed six hundred.

On Thursday the enemy made four assaults on our lines in heavy column. They were each time repulsed with great slaughter. They then concentrated their strength on GOWAN'S front, and, breaking our lines there, the retreat of our forces became necessary—which was effected on Thursday night.

Prisoners report only four Yankee corps engaged—three menacing Atlanta and guarding communications. No reliable information has been received regarding yesterday's operations or the position of HOOD.

During the last two days the city has been full of the wildest rumors, and owing to operations on the line of railroad the communication with the press reported at Atlanta is impracticable. The result of the action on Thursday was that our forces, oppressed with overwhelming numbers, fell back to Lovejoy Station, and, S. D. LEE, by orders of HOOD, fell back towards Atlanta, leaving the railroad in possession of the enemy. It is now ascertained that six corps of SHERMAN'S troops were thrown upon the railroad. Only HARDEE'S and LEE'S corps confronted them.

The loss on both sides is large, but as the Yankees on Thursday attacked our entrenchments, it is supposed they suffered much heavier than we. No reliable details can be obtained.

The report is current in this city, that HOOD evacuated Atlanta yesterday morning, but there is no positive information of his movements. A collision occurred yesterday on the Macon road near Barnesville, killing twenty persons and smashing up the train badly.

EVACUATION OF ATLANTA

MACON, September 4.—All doubts about the fall of Atlanta are ended. It was evacuated by our forces on Thursday night, and occupied by the enemy at 11 o'clock on Friday morning. General HOOD blew up his supplies of ordnance, burned his commissary stores, and drew off on the McDonough Road, leaving nothing in Atlanta but bloodstained ruins.

Yesterday our whole army was concentrated at Lovejoy's Station, on the Macon and Western Railroad. The enemy is reported to be retreating from that point towards Atlanta.

In the fight at Jonesboro on Thursday, Gen. GOWAN, together with the 6th and part of the 2d Arkansas Regiments, were captured. We lost six pieces of artillery, and captured six.

GEN. HOOD'S OFFICIAL ACCOUNT

RICHMOND, September 4.—The following official despatch from Gen. HOOD, dated September 3, has been received at the War Office:

"On the evening of the 30th ult., the enemy made a lodgment across Flint River, near Jonesboro'. We attacked them there on the evening of the 31st, with two corps, but failed to dislodge them. This made it necessary to abandon Atlanta, which was done on the night of the 1st instant. On the evening of the 1st that portion of our lines held by HARDEE'S corps, near Jonesboro', was assaulted by a superior force of the enemy and, being outflanked, was compelled to withdraw during the night, with the loss of eight pieces of artillery. Prisoners taken report the enemy's loss to have been very severe."

AN ANONYMOUS REPORT: EVACUATION OF ATLANTA

The Charleston Mercury *picked up an article from the* Augusta Chronicle and Sentinel's *Atlanta correspondent that described the situation there. The correspondent, writing from Decatur, another railroad town to the east of Atlanta, was able to confirm Hood's evacuation of Atlanta and how supplies there were destroyed so as not to fall into the hands of the Yankees. The correspondent described in the following story the rush to get anything of military value out of the city or distributed to citizens or destroyed, before Hood's army moved out south to McDonough. As bad for the Confederate cause as the loss of Atlanta was, the conclusion of the story hints at an even more pressing problem: desertions and dissatisfaction among the South's soldiers.*

Charleston Mercury, 7 September 1864

THE EVACUATION OF ATLANTA

(Correspondence Augusta Chronicle.)
NEAR DECATUR, FRIDAY MORNING, Sept. 2.

The occurrences of Wednesday last have ended in what I intimated in my last might be the fortunes of the day—the evacuation of the Gate City, and the removal of the forces left in its trenches to a point where they could be united with those who have been acting independently under Gen. Hardee, for the last few days.

Early on the morning of the 1st it was officially ascertained that the disaster on Wednesday evening was fully as serious as first reported and that the forces of the enemy on the Macon road consisted of five full corps of infantry, with a large force of cavalry. It was also known that a large force was south of the Chattahoochee, in the vicinity of the railroad bridge. Both of these were threatening the city, and as it would have been folly to attempt to resist both, an evacuation was promptly determined upon, while the forces of Generals Hardee and Lee should make an attempt to reach a point where they would be joined by those that might be withdrawn from the city.

The removal of all the supplies and ammunition that the transportation facilities of the army would permit, commenced early Thursday, and was continued throughout the day. Large quantities of provisions were also distributed to the people, and at nightfall all on hand stored in the Georgia railroad warehouse, and cars on the track. Throughout the day, also, the several bodies of troops, as they were withdrawn from the defences and filed through the city, were permitted access to the public stores.

The rolling stock of the railroads, consisting of about one hundred cars and six engines, was concentrated near the rolling mill before dark, and by that hour all the troops had passed through, with the exception of the rear guard, left to prevent straggling. And here I would mention a fact creditable to the State troops. Their withdrawal was accomplished in good order, and without confusion or straggling. The regulars acted differently. The order was for the troops to mass in the vicinity of McDonough, and the wagon trains and all moved out in that direction. Previous to my leaving the telegraph office was also closed, and at dark the evacuation was completed, with the exception of the detailed guard before mentioned.

Of course great excitement prevailed throughout the day, but a moderate degree of good order obtained. A few licentious citizens and soldiers embraced the occasion to display the wickedness of their natures, but the great mass of both classes acted with the greatest decorum. The citizens who had suffered from the malice of the enemy during the bombardments, looked on sorrowingly, and indulged in conjectures as to what would be their fate when once in the enemy's power; while the troops filed through the streets, with a steady tread it is true, but nevertheless with sorrow depicted on their weather beaten countenances.

As to the scenes that followed through the night I can only report second handed. The order was to burn only government property left behind, but this would necessarily involve the destruction of the Georgia depot, the rolling stock in the city, and the rolling mill. A gentleman who left the city early this morning informs me the depot was fired about 11 o'clock, and the cars, &c., an hour or two later. The explosion consequent upon the firing of the ordnance train took place about two o'clock this morning, and was heard and felt to a great distance. There are various reports as to the burning of other property, but from the best information I can gather, no instance of great outlawry occurred.

Whether the Yankees yet occupy Atlanta I cannot say, but presume the telegraph will inform you ere this reaches you. I only know that there was nothing to prevent their making an entry, as the evacuation was complete. Many citizens came out, but thousands remained—some because they could not get away, but many from choice. At daybreak this morning the enemy had not made their appearance in the city, but there was nothing to prevent their doing it at any moment.

I hear many reports of desertions by wholesale, and of dissatisfaction and straggling. Some of this is inevitable, but it is to be hoped it has not prevailed to the extent reported. It must be admitted that the discipline of the army has not been so favorable during the last thirty days as previously; why it has been so is palpable. The police regulations of the camp have been much less stringently enforced and it is to be feared that the undue license allowed has resulted deplorably in this emergency.

DR. GEORGE W. BAGBY: GENERAL HOOD MARCHES NORTH FROM ATLANTA

After the fall of Atlanta, Hood retired to western Georgia and eastern Alabama to threaten Sherman's communications lines. His objective was to force Sherman to withdraw from Atlanta, and at first, Sherman did give chase to the Confederate troops. But then the Union general abandoned the pursuit. With Hood continuing on into Tennessee, and anticipating that Sherman was fast behind him, opportunities were opening up in Georgia for a grand movement that would demonstrate just how vulnerable the Confederacy's few remaining states were. Sherman returned to Atlanta to concentrate on planning his march through Georgia. The fact that Hood's army had moved away from Atlanta came as a surprise to many Confederates, including the Charleston paper.

Charleston Mercury, 6 October 1864

LETTER FROM RICHMOND

(CORRESPONDENCE OF THE MERCURY.)
RICHMOND, Wednesday, September 28.

Yesterday we were startled to hear that HOOD's whole army was at Rome. Some said only two corps were there—others that 16,000 men had been sent to East Tennessee, etc., but it is generally agreed that the army has changed its base square around SHERMAN's rear. All concede that it is a "make or break" movement, and yet all like it; for, say they, "we are tired of fooling."

The fight between Early's and Sheridan's cavalry, at Brown's Gap, has been magnified into a general engagement. Not so. The Gap is a powerful position, and Early (or Longstreet) is in better condition to hold it than Fisher's Hill. People from Staunton say our cavalry ran through the town as if the devil were at their heels. Signs are brighter in the valley, and we are more cheerful.

Last night it was confidently predicted that the Secretary of War had revoked all details, and that the order would be published this morning but it does not appear in the papers. It will come, though. Of course there will be revisions of the revocations, for many men must remain detailed. Nothing more has been said within the past day or two about calling out the Virginia reserves.

Persons who were around the War Department say nothing is known there about Lieut. Gen. Forrest, or Beauregard, as commander of the Army of Tennessee, or Longstreet as commander of the Valley army. Fact is, we in Richmond are behind the times.

Mr. Benjamin, in reply to a letter of a returned prisoner, states that arrangements have been made to furnish our prisoners at the North with clothing and rations.—They need both surely. Even the officers on Johnson's Island are half starved of late, as I learn from one lately released.

Butler, the absconding clerk, got nothing from the Treasury except what he drew on Knox's checks. So far, the examination of the Treasurer (Elmore's) accounts reveal nothing wrong. This comes from trustworthy officials in that Department. Hot weather has set in again.

HERMES.

March to the Sea

Union General William T. Sherman had an abiding affection for the South, and that was why he decided he had to devastate it. His successful campaign to take the rail center at Atlanta had already accomplished two of his and Grant's goals: one, to cut off Lee's supplies from the South, and two, to ensure Lincoln's reelection. The next objective was to win the war, and that meant destroying the seemingly unflagging Confederate will to win. Accomplishing that objective meant waging war not only against the Confederate military but also against the South's civilians, a concept known among military historians as "total war." Sherman knew that the only way to get the South to stop fighting a war that, in large measure, had been lost since 1863 was to bring the region to its knees. That meant fire and devastation.

Bringing Georgia to its knees, and with it the rest of the Confederacy, had certain risks. Sherman's supply line ran 400 miles back to Nashville, and stringing it out even further was impossible. However, in late September, Jefferson Davis unknowingly handed Sherman the answer to his problem. Davis traveled to Macon, Georgia, to console the evacuees there from Atlanta. He assured the assembled crowd that the Confederacy could be saved if all the deserters from the army returned and if those not serving stepped up to defend their country. If the Confederacy's manpower problem could be solved, then there was still a chance to attain Southern independence, the president assured the evacuees. Davis's remarks were widely reported in newspapers.

In mid-November, Sherman sent Thomas and his Army of the Cumberland back to Nashville and Chattanooga before cutting his supply lines and marching east from Atlanta toward the sea with 60,000 men, 2,500 wagons, and 600 ambulances laden with supplies. His men would be living off the land. Whatever they could take would be what they would eat. With virtually no opposition, Sherman sent two columns of men, one northwest and one southwest, to cut a 50-mile-wide by 300-mile-long swath of scorched earth to Savannah. His intent was "to make Georgia howl," and that is exactly what he accomplished. His men devastated crops and burned government property; but, in fairness to the general, it must be admitted that so long as civilians stayed with their property, his men might take all their food and valuables, but their houses were not put to the torch. Sherman scrupulously ignored Hood's efforts to distract him with his invasion of Tennessee, which was effectively put to an end in the Battles of Franklin and Nashville.

Confederate Generals Beauregard and Hardee worked feverishly to prepare defenses for Savannah and Charleston. Hardee's 1,500 men abandoned Savannah after the fall of Fort McAllister at the mouth of the Ogeechee River, some 15 miles from Savannah, on 13 December. Savannah fell to Sherman on 21 December without a shot being fired. He would take formal possession of the city on 22 December.

OBSERVER: ACCOUNT OF BATTLE OF GRISWOLDVILLE

The Constitutionalist's *regular correspondent filed a story about the Battle of Griswoldville. As was common, the reporter filed a story that included the best information available at the time but that was not entirely accurate. For example, he estimated Sherman's force to be 25,000 to 30,000. That was true, so far as the number of Union infantry men moving toward Macon was concerned. But there were another 30,000 taking a more northerly path through Madison, Georgia, also moving relentlessly toward the sea. The writer was correct in his assessment that Sherman had to be stopped in Georgia if there was to be any chance of stopping the Union war machine.*

Augusta Constitutionalist, 30 November 1864 (Augusta, Ga.)

SPECIAL CORRESPONDENCE OF THE CONSTITUTIONALIST

From the Front

Battle of Griswoldville—Sherman's course and forces—Depredations of the enemy—Occupation of Sandersville—Conway's men—A gallant scout

SPARTA, Nov. 27th, 9 P.M.

Mr. Editor: We have information from men belonging to Furguson's division of cavalry of the fight at Griswoldville on Tuesday. A feint was made on Macon on Sunday afternoon by some of Kilpatrick's cavalry, but Wheeler's forces were put in line of battle up and down Walnut creek, and after some heavy skirmishing, the enemy fell back to Griswoldville, where he constructed breastworks of fence rails. On Tuesday Wheeler attacked them again, but failed to drive them until our infantry came up (composed mainly of militia.) The enemy gave way, and we followed them about three miles.— Our loss was about four hundred in killed, wounded and missing. The enemy's much heavier.—Our informant, who was in the fight, says we took two hundred and fifty prisoners in one batch, and others were taken, he knows not how many. The enemy fell back towards Gordon and Milledgeville, and destroyed the road as he went. A man who was taken prisoner while helping to repair the road, on Wednesday, says he counted fifty-one dead Confederates on the field, among whom was the brave Col. Redding, of the militia. The Yankees, as usual, tried to claim the victory.

From statements made to this prisoner, we had a fight with them at Bear creek, above Griffin, where they diverged and went down through Butts, Jasper and Jones. The central forces probably passed through Monticello, Willsboro, and on to Milledgeville. They occupied that place from Sunday evening till Friday morning. Their infantry and artillery made but little stay. They left Thursday morning, and General Furguson's cavalry drove out the rear guard of cavalry on Friday morning. Is it possible that forty thousand troops, cavalry and infantry, with a wagon train of eight miles long, could have passed through a narrow bridge in twenty-four hours? We think not; but our military men must decide. Prisoners brought to this place claim sixty thousand, but admit

only four corps. We think the evidence thickens, that Sherman's army does not exceed twenty-five or thirty thousand. Shall we let them escape and make a base at Savannah or Hilton Head? If we do, Charleston and Wilmington falls, and Grant and Sherman's forces united, will necessitate the evacuation of Richmond.

While in Milledgeville, Sherman made his headquarters in the Executive mansion. Our informant saw, and was catechised by Gen. Jeff. Davis and Kilpatrick. The State House was not burned, but much mutilated. The Penitentiary, Arsenal, &c., were burned. The magazine was blown up by the rear guard as they left the city Friday 10, A.M. We heard the double report, and thought them signal guns. The bridge was also burned, but Gen. Furguson had constructed pontoons for his wagons to cross.

From the best authority, General Kilpatrick commanded the left wing of the enemy, which passed along the county line road, from Milledgeville to Shoals of Ogeechee, where they camped on Friday night. They spread out some six or eight miles on either hand, pilfering and burning as they went. Seven miles below this place a ruffian presented a pistol to the breast of a lady, demanding her gold and silver. She told him she had none and called upon an officer in the crowd for protection. Without specially granting it, he informed her rather egotistically that he was General Kilpatrick and permitted his men to go on and pilfer and abuse as much as they pleased. They burned the gin houses of a number of our largest planters, with hundreds of bales of cotton. Among them, Judge Thomas', Col. Turner's, the Sasnetts, Dr. Green's, the Dickinson's &c. They burned no cribs or dwelling houses, and we have no reliable information of the destruction of a single mill or factory in the country, though they passed by a number.—They took nearly all the horses and mules in the country, whether hid or not, for they scoured the swamps, killed some hogs and most of the poultry. The productive interest of the country has suffered seriously— irreparably, we fear. All the young negro men and some women they captured where they were not run off. Many of these have returned, and are still coming back as they can escape.

Our escaped prisoners said that Gen. Howard's corps went down the river from Milledgeville to take the Oconee bridge. It was he, probably, that Gen. Wayne repulsed. Whether he returned to Milledgeville or crossed on pontoons below, we are not apprised. Gen. Sherman, with artillery and infantry, went to Sandersville. His van arrived there Saturday at noon, being on the road two days and a half from Milledgeville, according to escaped negroes. At this rate it will take him about seven days to reach Millen from Sandersville, and seventeen days to reach Savannah—plenty of time for all the forces of the Carolinas and Georgia, with Dick Taylor from the West, to surround, flank and destroy him. I believe it to be of more importance to accomplish this than to hold Richmond. But I have every confidence in our authorities.

Several of our scouts overtook twenty wagons guarded by only twenty-five men. With a small reinforcement they could have captured the whole party. Now is the time for our boys to strike, if they wish to win glory and serve their country.—The enemy must be greatly demoralized; they are living on the fat of land, having plenty of liquor to drink, and many of them carrying their concubines with them. How can such an army fight? Besides, a few heavy battles would expend all their ammunition. Oh, for Wade Hampton's bugle blast to strike them with consternation on their left wing, and wrest from them the plunder of more that a dozen counties.

One good, quick stroke would retard and demoralize them. Charge! Hampton, charge!

On! Taylor, on!
And strike with all thy cavalry.

But we must come down to prose again—painful prose—and bring to the bar of public opinion some recreant scouts, commanded by one Conway. We could not get the Captain to the front when the enemy threatened our town. He sent several of his men with Captain Culver, of this county, and he retired with his company three miles on the safe side to camp. A gallant Kentuckian—Charles Manier—who was cut off from his regiment, the Fourth Kentucky Cavalry, went with him, and they were met by a large force and had to fly. Manier's horse gave out, but he would not surrender. He fired his rifle and repeater, killed one of their horses, and then drew the butt of his gun on his approaching antagonist, who shot him dead, took a Bible from his pocket, containing his name and regiment, and laid it over his heart. He told the lady at whose gate he fell to bury him decently; he was sorry he had to kill him, for he was a brave fellow. Not so, Conway. That night some of his men broke open Purvent's store and stole several hundred dollars worth of goods. They robbed a merchant in Linton of a large sum of money, flourished their five hundred dollar bills, and left Sparta without paying their tavern bill. We are informed that this has been their history during the war. We cannot vouch for this, but we state facts, and hope our authorities will arrest and punish them as they deserve.

OBSERVER.

AN ANONYMOUS REPORT: EFFECTS OF SHERMAN'S MARCH THROUGH GEORGIA

The Mississippian, of Jackson, was another of the Confederacy's displaced newspapers. It had fled to Selma, Alabama, after the fall of its home city in the summer of 1863. Like most Southern newspapers, it watched in appalled amazement as Sherman burned his way through Georgia, but the paper noted that Sherman's raid had one powerful, important, and useful effect: Its cruelty had stamped out any latent "Reconstructionism" that Southerners might have been harboring in their hearts. Antiwar Southerners had been referred to as "Reconstructionists" from the beginning of the war, and while the cruelty of Sherman's raid through Georgia, and later South Carolina, steeled many for continued resistance, other Southerners saw the destruction as evidence to back up their argument that the Confederacy should sue for peace on just about any terms.

The Mississippian, 11 December 1864

THE EFFECT OF SHERMAN'S MARCH

Sherman in his march through Georgia destroyed many things—dwellings, corncribs, agricultural implements, gin houses, clothing of women and children, and in short all that tends to make life comfortable was ruthlessly given to the flames. Cattle, horses, hogs, sheep and goats were destroyed. Nothing was spared but life. Thank God, amidst the universal ruin, one thing was extirpated, root and branch, which amply compensates for all other loss. A thing noxious, rank and un-

clean. A thing that like a foul and venomous toad, leered on the graves of our slain and made light of their blood. A thing that spat on the hallowed mound of the dead and croaked dishonor to the living. This foul abortion—this political Caliban—this spawn of cowardice and treason, was Reconstruction.

Wherever the hostile tread of Sherman's legions passed, all hopes and desires of reconstruction were trampled out of existence. The logic of the bayonet and the rhetoric of the incendiary convinced the most "conservative" that nothing remained to the people of the South but triumph or degradation which would make life intolerable. But the light of his burning dwelling reflected on the pale and frightened faces of his wife and children, and the "conservative" saw the true object of the war, and the real points of the issue. The flame which consumed the labor of a lifetime purified the political atmosphere and kindled in the heart of the sufferer the fires of patriotism. There lives no man who can see his rooftree burned, his lands devastated, his property stolen, his wife and children turned penniless on the world, without resolving on revenge.

But a greater wrong than those enumerated has been perpetrated by the hounds that follow the footsteps of Sherman. Women, pure and spotless, have been violated. The people of Georgia have had the bitterest cup of misery placed to their lips, and been made to drain it to the dregs. They have felt

—the [*unreadable*] wrong,
    The unutterable shame
That turns the coward's heart to steel,
    The sluggard's blood to flame.

They have suffered what can never be forgotten or forgiven. To affiliate with those who have perpetrated these enormities would be worse than dishonorable—it would be base and infamous. It would not only be an acknowledgment that the heroic dead who have fallen upon an hundred battlefields in defence of their country's independence were rebels and traitors, but it would be giving assent to the violation of our household goods.

But we have no fear of this thing. As we said before, Sherman has effectually crushed out any desire for reconstruction which may have been lurking in the heart of some of our people, who have never before been scarred with the fire of Yankee invasion. It has been the experience of this war that wherever the foot of the invader pollutes the soil, such outrages upon civilization and humanity have been committed, and that an undying and unquenchable hate is born in the hearts of the people. The ashes of desolated homesteads are "vocal without noise," and plead with an irresistible, though silent eloquence, for revenge.

From the blackened track which marks the route of Sherman, there comes no cry for reconstruction and submission, but rather a shout, like the sound of many waters, for independence and revenge. And so, with a full appreciation of the ruin which has overtaken some of our worthiest and best, and with the warmest sympathy for their desolation, we cannot, in view of the purification of the State from all taint of reconstruction, help ejaculating, thank God! We have experienced the baptism of fire, and have come for the purified. Thank God!

RICHARD ORME, JR. OR SR.: ATLANTA AFTER SHERMAN'S OCCUPATION

Two weeks after Sherman's troops swept through the Georgia capital, life there was returning to normal. Refugees from the city were returning, often to find their homes destroyed or property stolen. Those who stayed with their property were less likely to suffer at the hands of the federals. Perhaps the greatest offense perpetrated by the Union troops was the trashing of the Georgia state house. Sherman's soldiers scattered state papers all around the capitol and held a mock legislative session at which they repealed Georgia's ordinance of secession.

Milledgeville Confederate Union, 12 December 1864 (Milledgeville, Ga.)

OUR CITY

It has been two weeks since the Yankee Army left us, (today Friday) but the mournful relics of their presence are fresh as when they swarmed in our streets, and crowded our residences and public squares. Many of our citizens who left the city at the approach of the enemy have returned, and familiar faces meet us at every step; but a stillness almost Sabbath like pervades our business streets, and the blackened, sightless walls of the Penitentiary, Arsenal Magazine and Depot remind us constantly of the presence of the vandal hordes of Sherman. It is due to Sherman to say that most of the outrages committed by his men were perpetrated in private residences where the owners, both male and female, had left the premises. Where our citizens remained in their houses night and day, we hear of but few acts of diabolism such as were committed in unoccupied buildings. The attention of the enemy was principal directed to poultry, stock, provisions of all kinds, hogs, harness, money and valuables. Negroes were treated very bad by their professed friends and liberators. They were robbed of money, clothing, blankets—everything stealable. Indeed our negroes have cause to remember the enemy quite as feelingly as their masters and mistresses. Many left us and followed the Yankee army. Some have returned and more will follow in the same direction; but the loss of negroes in the section overrun by Sherman must be very great. It is a little remarkable that those negroes left who were least expected to leave, and in most cases they were idle and vicious characters. It is a little singular, too, that those negroes who took up with the Yankees were universally known to be most free, before the Yankees came. Negroes who had been managed as they should be, were content to stay with their masters, but those who had been permitted to do as they pleased were the first to run away. Our streets and public squares are filled with private papers and public documents. Even private correspondence of a nature the most sacred, is blown to and fro by the wind and subject to the rude criticism of the most vulgar and illiterate. The State House for many days has been knee deep in papers. The building is much defaced. The windows on the side towards the magazine are all broken, and the plastering injured. The fencing around the square is broken down and many of the young trees in the square ruined, the bark being bit off by the horses tied to them. Our churches were not respected. They, too, bear the impress of the unhallowed footstep of the foul invader. But bad as it is with us, we are truly thankful it is no worse. But few ladies or children were insulted or even molested in their houses. It might have been expected to be much worse, from the known character of Sherman's Army. No occupied residences were destroyed. Many feared that the city would be burnt and were greatly relieved when assured that it would not be.—In a few weeks our public offices will be put in repair and the business appertaining to them be progressing as though Sherman had never been in a thousand miles of Milledgeville.

HENRY LYNDEN FLASH: SHERMAN'S CAMPAIGN AGAINST SAVANNAH

The key to Savannah was the earthworks fortification on the Ogeechee River to its south, Fort McAllister. Though the garrison at the fort put up a fight, its worn-out cannons and men were no match for Sherman's army. The fort fell easily, and the gates to Savannah were opened. The federal fleet waited off the coast to support Sherman's efforts to capture the town. The Telegraph *editor still held out hope, but it was a clearly unrealistic hope. Once Sherman captured Savannah, he had accomplished more than the capture of "a very pleasant city." He had proven the Union army's ability to force its will upon the people of the Confederacy. He had proven Union domination.*

Macon Telegraph and Confederate, 20 December 1864

SHERMAN'S CAMPAIGN DEVELOPING

The fall of Fort McAllister, at the mouth of the Ogeechee, is certainly a very serious loss, for thereby Sherman's army can be co-operated with by the fleet in any attempt that General may make to capture the city. Without that co-operation his chances of success are very small; with it the chances are that he will succeed, and the principal seaport of Georgia will be in the enemy's possession.

But should Sherman, contrary to our hopes and belief capture the city, what then? He simply captures a very pleasant city, but one which has been of but little value to us in a maritime point of view. By its possession he may be enabled to send raiding parties into the interior, but by no means to a sufficient extent to do any great deal of harm. The danger most to be apprehended is, that he will make it the base for inland operations against Charleston, and a campaign against Augusta.

Sherman's necessities compelled him to make a rapid march through Georgia, and the policy of his government demanded that it should be marked by wide-spread desolation. Our people laughed at the idea of his marching through Georgia—but he has done it. It was predicted he would be fought, delayed, whipped and starved before he reached the coast. But he wisely avoided battle, and has reached the coast without serious hindrance or loss. The capture of Fort McAllister with its garrison, forming a very important part of the defences of the city, more than compensates for his losses, while it diminishes the chances of failure in his operations against it.

We regard it as impolitic and unwise to lull our people into a false security in reference to the safety of Savannah. We have believed all along that Sherman could take the city if co-operated with by the fleet. We now believe it to be in his power to take it, and that the minds of the public should be prepared for the disaster, and to meet the consequences.

Having secured Savannah what will he do? Will he remain idle? He will in all probability commence operations against Charleston on the land side, or proceed against Augusta. The defenses of the former city we doubt not are fully equal to any demands that may be made upon them, for that city has been regarded as much coveted by the Federals, and has always been looked upon as in more danger than Savannah or Augusta—hence her defences have been made more complete and substantial.

Augusta is in our opinion, too far inland, to be successfully approached. It could hardly be reduced without a co-operating gunboat fleet—and the shallowness of the river, together with the frequent bluffs on its sides, affording the best situations for batteries, will probably prevent that co-operation. Besides this Sherman would be compelled to leave a large garrison at Savannah while ours would be released; thus he would be weakened while we would be strengthened.

But suppose he should capture Augusta also and thus sever the Confederacy on this line—cutting communications between the States north of the Savannah river and those South of it. What then?

We are by no means ruined, while the more he divides and scatters his forces, the more liable he is to be whipped in detail. It is impossible for the enemy to garrison every place he captures, and as soon as he evacuates, we re-enter and repossess them. This was illustrated by Sherman being compelled to withdraw all his garrisons from Atlanta to Chattanooga, to make up an army for this expedition, whereby he lost thirty days, territory it had taken months of time, millions of money, and tens of thousands of lives to gain. As it was with Northern Georgia, so it will be with Eastern Georgia, except where the enemy has the support of his gunboats.

As with Northern Georgia, so it is now quite clear it will be with East Tennessee. That country is fast slipping from Federal clutches. We may soon expect to hear of the evacuation of both Chattanooga and Knoxville for with Hood and Breckinridge where they are, the enemy can hardly hold them.

These two points evacuated, the country is then ours, and in better condition for us than when we lost it, for thanks to the rapaciousness of the enemy, Southern feeling has been intensified and Union feeling materially weakened if not destroyed.

But more and better still, communication between Richmond, and the States South and West of the Savannah will be again re-established, and the darling project of the yankee President, of dividing the Confederacy east and west successfully defeated.

The enemy has the numbers and can flank us, avoid fighting as he desires, take our important cities and burn them, over run and devastate our lands, and destroy our farming implements. Yet this is neither conquest or subjugation; and so long as the people remain as firm and united as they have been and are now, there is no fear of their being either conquered or subjugated. We may be exterminated, but subjugated—never! Let Sherman, then do his worst; and let the people prepare to do, dare and suffer more than ever, and they will surely, in the end, defeat the machinations of our merciless foe and have their efforts crowned with a glorious success.

HENRY LYNDEN FLASH: FALL OF SAVANNAH

The Macon newspaper took three days off for Christmas in 1864, and when it began publication again after the holiday, the editor observed that, in the absence of real news, all sorts of crazy rumors had begun flying around the town. One piece of news, though, was not so crazy. Savannah had indeed fallen. Of course, Hood had also been whipped and a good number of his men captured, but for Georgia, the big news was Savannah.

Macon Telegraph and Confederate, 28 December 1864

THE SITUATION

Since the telegraphic lines have been down, and during the suspension of the city papers, the city has been, as we expected it would be, filled with all kinds of rumors. During this time the President has died—Hood has been whipped and killed, and most of his army captured—Richmond has been evacuated, and Hardee's force driven out of Savannah with a loss of double his force.

But the fog has cleared away somewhat now, and we are enabled to announce that the greatest misfortune we have experienced is the loss of Savannah, (an event the people has been prepared for for several days,) which was evacuated by Gen. Hardee, who is now at Hardeeville, S.C., about twenty-eight miles from Savannah on the railroad to Charleston, with his army intact and in good spirits and fighting trim. The enemy, it is presumed, occupy Savannah.

From Richmond we hear nothing, but as long as General Lee and his invincible army confronts the enemy before that city, no misgivings are felt, whether we hear from there or not.

The latest reliable news we hear from Tennessee is contained in special dispatches to the Mobile Advertiser & Register, from Senatobia, which indicate anything but a defeat or a retreat.

This dispatch states that Gen. Lyon, with 2,500 men, (the dispatch says 25,000, but that is evidently a mistake,) had crossed the Cumberland between Nashville and Clarksville, and was marching on Hopkinsville, Ky.; that Gen. Breckinridge was at Sparta, which is at the western base of the mountains, and about one hundred miles east of Nashville, and endeavoring to form a junction with Gen. Hood, and that our troops had torn up a long stretch of the road to Chattanooga.

Except the loss of Savannah, there is yet nothing positively known that should be in the least discouraging; and that is a much less serious loss than it seems to be. Our garrison is relieved, in excellent health and fighting condition, to be added to our effective force; while the enemy must detach a garrison for its defence, weakening his aggressive power to that extent.

Hood's Invasion of Tennessee

Reinforced by Forrest's cavalry, Hood's 54,000 men crossed the Tennessee River on 14 November and quickly moved toward Nashville. Thomas dispatched Major General John M. Schofield with two corps and Wheeler's cavalry, in all about 32,000 men, to meet the invasion and to delay it. The forces skirmished at Columbia, Tennessee, and at Spring Hill before meeting on 30 November in a major battle at Franklin.

Hood, though he had lost a leg and an arm at Chickamauga and Gettysburg, respectively, was young and impetuous. Despite the counsel of older generals, Hood decided on a frontal assault against the dug-in federals at Franklin. The bad decision was compounded by the fact that about a third of Hood's force was not present, including most of his artillery. Casualties were tremendous. Nearly 7,000 of the 38,000-man Confederate force were lost to the Union's 2,300 out of 32,000. The Confederates also lost twelve generals in that battle, six killed, five wounded, and one captured. More than sixty of a hundred regimental commanders were killed or wounded. There was no doubt that Hood's frontal attack was an unmitigated disaster. Having accomplished his delaying mission, Schofield returned to Nashville that night.

Although his force had been reduced to less than half the size of Thomas's, Hood proceeded toward Nashville, one of the most heavily fortified cities in the United States. Hood reached Nashville on 2 December, but Thomas, ever methodical, was in no hurry to engage him; the Union general was trying to get his army, made up largely of new recruits, trained for what lay ahead.

The Confederate line outside Nashville was stretched disastrously thin, especially after Hood sent Forrest off with most of the cavalry and two brigades of infantry to attack Murfreesboro. That left Hood with fewer than 20,000 men to meet Thomas's attack, which began on 15 December. The Union force easily shattered Hood's exposed left flank. The next day, Hood tried to continue the fight, but Thomas enveloped both his flanks. Wilson's cavalry managed to get behind the Confederate lines and deliver the final blow. The Union managed to inflict losses of around 6,000, compared with their own of just more than 3,000, and to reduce Hood's army to fleeing rabble.

HENRY LYNDEN FLASH: HOOD'S CAMPAIGN IN TENNESSEE

The Montgomery Mail *was one of the few newspapers that had a correspondent assigned to cover Hood's movements in Tennessee. As the Army of Tennessee crept closer to its first major battle on its foolhardy expedition to draw Sherman's main force away from Atlanta, the reporter was stationed in the rear, in northern Alabama in the hamlet of Tuscumbia where he could pick up what little news made its way from the front. The* Macon Telegraph and Confederate *properly attributed the story to the* Mail, *a small irony since the editor of the* Telegraph, *Henry Lynden Flash, a poet and former cavalry officer, constantly berated other Southern newspapers for taking stories from his newspaper without attribution.*

Macon Telegraph and Confederate, 18 November 1864

THE FRONT

[Special Army Correspondence of the Mail.]
TUSCUMBIA, ALA., Nov. 6, 1864

I am afraid that I will find it a very difficult matter to keep you posted in regard to the doings of this army. We are kept so much in the dark in regard to army movements that we know nothing of them until it is too late to be called news. I hardly know what to think of the prospect of going to Middle Tennessee. Sometimes it looks quite flattering, and then again becomes gloomy. I am pretty well convinced, however, that "grand movements," quite in keeping with those we have just accomplished are yet on the [unreadable]. Large quantities of "hard tack" and bacon are being brought to Tuscumbia, the transportation already quite limited, being again reduced—the usual precursors to a move.

Sherman was on yesterday reported with his forces lying between Decatur and Huntsville. Today I was told he was moving in the direction of Pulaski.

Well, let him move. We can move him back through Middle Tennessee as we did out of Georgia.

The Mobile Tribune has private information from Tuscumbia to the 4th inst.:

Our scouts reported that 15,000 of the enemy had arrived at Decatur, and were evidently following up our forces. On the 2nd inst. we shelled them at that place. There were then only three thousand there, and we could have captured it easily, but that was not in the programme. We captured thirty or forty prisoners, and killed and wounded from three to four hundred. Our loss in killed and wounded was about one hundred. We have Florence fortified. The Yankee cavalry is very numerous on the other side, but exhibit no desire to dispute the passage of the modern Rubicon.

Sherman's troops are scattered as follows: the 1st corps, Gen. Osterhaus, is at Atlanta, 15,000 are at Chattanooga, and 5,000 at Bridgeport. There are also some at Stevenson, but how many was not ascertained.

Gen. Hood has been quite unwell for two or three days, but is now all right again. Beauregard is here, but Hood is in command of the army.

HENRY LYNDEN FLASH: ACCOUNT OF BATTLE OF FRANKLIN

From Columbia, Hood's army moved on to Franklin, where it fought a fierce battle that cost Hood more than one-third of his force, including dozens of regimental commanders. The Macon Telegraph and Confederate *picked up this story from the* Chattanooga Rebel. *It is an interview with an officer from Hood's army. The story vastly overestimates federal losses in the battle but otherwise accurately captures the carnage of the day.*

Macon Telegraph and Confederate, 16 December 1864

THE BATTLE OF FRANKLIN

From an officer who left Hood's army on the 1st December, the Rebel gets full and intelligible accounts of the recent severe and bloody fight at Franklin, Tennessee. It appears that the enemy, after being driven out of Columbia evacuated Murfreesboro, and uniting all their forces, took up position on the high cliffs south of Franklin. Gen. Hood pursued them closely in their retreat, and when they formed line of battle on a series of hills below Franklin, he flanked them out of their position. They then fell back to their fortifications on the edge of town, where they formed a strong line of battle. Immediate dispositions were made to assault their works, which was done in front, chiefly by Cheatham's corps, with spirit and vigor, the various commanders leading their columns, the bands playing and men huzzaing.

Stewart's corps was on the right, and Cheatham, aided by some of Lee's corps, formed the centre and left. The remainder of Lee's corps had been detached to create a diversion. Forrest's cavalry defended our right and left flanks. The enemy opened a very severe and destructive fire upon our assaulting line, and it was in this charge the heavy loss of general officers occurred. The irresistible bravery of our men carried everything before them. The lines were occupied by troops, several of our Generals, among them the heroic Cleburne, being shot on the breastworks. This attack was made at five P.M. Despite the terrible losses, the army entered the enemy's lines in the highest spirits, with bands playing and flags waving. It was then discovered that the enemy had a second line, where they had rallied. There they were quickly assaulted by our men, and a severe and close fight ensued, wherein the combatants were separated by a ditch and breastworks.

It soon became a hand to hand fight, which was continued into the night, until the enemy gave way and retired to the third line. The fight was again resumed on this line and kept up until 2 o'clock in the morning, when an escaped prisoner informed our commander that the enemy had evacuated this line and retired to Nashville. Our army then occupied this line, and early the next day pushed on towards Nashville,

Reporting the War, 1864 473

and on the first of December, when our informant left, the rear corps was at Brentwood, eight miles from Nashville. This would bring our front to the fortifications of Nashville. Our informant heard heavy firing in the direction of Nashville, and many rumors that the city had been taken. These we fear are premature. The enemy, it was understood, was commanded by Gen. Schofield, and he and General Wagner were reported to be among the killed.

The loss of the enemy could not be ascertained, as they had removed most of their dead. Our loss was heavy, between two and four hundred. The distressing mortality among our Generals is confirmed. There were five killed—Cleburn, Strahl, Granberry, Cist and John C. Carter. There were five Generals wounded: Quarles, not mortally as first reported. Brown, slightly, Johnston, and the names of the other two were not remembered by our informant, General Gordon was captured. A large amount of stores were captured, especially at Columbia. Recruits are joining Hood's army in numbers more than sufficient to supply all the losses, and the army is in high spirits. General Pillow arrived at his plantation in time to capture large stores.

The Clarion has private intelligence from Hood's army which represents that the fighting at Harpeth Creek, near Franklin on the 30th, was desperate in the extreme, and our losses great in proportion. A magnificent victory was won, but at great sacrifice. Our forces charged three lines of breastworks, and drove the enemy from every position they occupied; and at one place they had to cut a hedge before they could get to the enemy's works, being at the same time exposed to the fire of the batteries which were located behind it. The loss in Stewart's corps was large. Report says it was nearly decimated.

Gen. Loring's division lost 700 men; and the 15th Mississippi lost 79 out of 220 men taken into the fight. The loss in line and company officers was lamentably great, and altogether our casualties number from six to eight thousand. The enemy's loss in killed and wounded was very heavy—over four thousand—while we captured over six thousand prisoners.

JOHN BELL HOOD: COMMANDING GENERAL'S REPORT ON BATTLE OF FRANKLIN

John Bell Hood took nearly two weeks to send word to Richmond of his ignominious defeat at Nashville. His official report painted a very different picture of the results than actually occurred. He claimed to have inflicted heavy losses on the enemy while sustaining few casualties himself. He reported his troops retreated "rapidly" when, in truth, they fled in disorder.

Macon Telegraph and Confederate, 10 January 1865

OFFICIAL FROM GEN. HOOD

RICHMOND, Jan. 8.

Gen. Hood reports from Spring Hill, December 27, that on the morning of the 15th, in front of Nashville, the enemy attacked both flanks of his army. They were repulsed on the right with heavy loss, but towards evening they drove in the infantry outpost on the left flank.

Early on the morning of the 16th the enemy made a general attack on our entire line. All their assaults were repulsed with heavy loss until half-past 3 P.M., when a position of our line to the left of centre suddenly gave way, which caused our lines to give way at all points, our troops retreating rapidly. Fifty pieces of artillery and several ordnance wagons were lost by us that day. Our loss in killed and wounded heretofore was small, in prisoners not ascertained.

Major Gen. Ed. Johnson, Brigadier Generals L. E. Smith, and H. R. Jackson were captured.

EASTERN THEATER

Wilderness–Spotsylvania–Cold Harbor Campaign

Union General Ulysses S. Grant was named commander of the Union army in March 1864. His first action was to begin a campaign to destroy the Confederate army. Three years of bloody war had abundantly proven to the Yankee general that the Southerners would never give up, even though, arguably, their last chance of winning had died with the fall of Vicksburg and the defeat at Gettysburg the previous summer. Total destruction was all that would serve to end the conflict. To accomplish this scheme, Grant had sent his favorite general, William T. Sherman, to Georgia to take on the Confederacy's Army of Tennessee under the wily Joseph E. Johnston. Grant himself, in concert with George Meade's Army of the Potomac, would handle Robert E. Lee's Army of Northern Virginia.

Grant's plan for his and Meade's armies took into account the complexities of the situation in Virginia. No Union army had yet been able to force Lee away from Richmond. The Army of Northern Virginia doggedly and skillfully defended the Confederate capital. That had to change. Grant decided that he would take Lee on wherever he could find him and dislocate the Southern army from Richmond. Grant's plan called for the 105,000 infantrymen in Meade's army to march into the dense thickets of the Virginia wilderness and engage the Army of Northern Virginia wherever it was. Grant put two smaller forces in the field under Major General Franz Sigel and Major General Benjamin Butler. Sigel was to move south toward the Shenandoah Valley to cut Lee's supply lines, while Butler moved toward the James River to cut off Lee's support.

Lee faced an army nearly twice the size of his own. Including cavalry, Grant had nearly 118,000 men he could put in the field against Lee's 61,000. But Lee had some advantages, despite the overwhelming numbers. For one thing, Lee defended interior lines and familiar ground. He also had established key defenses along the Rapidan and Rappahannock Rivers that would dramatically limit Grant's freedom of movement. Grant also faced tactical disadvantages by fighting in The Wilderness. For one thing, command and control of his forces would be complicated by the lack of visibility. Further, maneuvering à large force, as well as artillery and cavalry, through the dense thicket would not be easy. Nevertheless, on 4 May, Grant's force moved out of its winter camps and crossed the Rapidan. Informed by scouts of Grant's move, Lee's troops left their encampments and headed east toward the engagement that would begin the next day.

On 5 May, the armies met in two separate and indecisive engagements between units confused by and entangled in The Wilderness's thickets. The battlefield itself erupted into a conflagration, compounding the terror and bewilderment of the troops. The battlefield became a firey, smokey nightmare. Tall pines blazed as giant pillars of fire. Dense smoke obscured visibility, and the fighting disintegrated into hand-to-hand combat by men blindly stabbing at one another with their bayonets or beating each other with the butts of their guns.

On the second day of the Battle of The Wilderness, Grant set about exploiting a gap in the Confederate lines between Ewell's and Hill's corps. Frontal assaults throughout the day achieved little, and by the end of the day, neither side had achieved a tactical victory, despite major casualties. Lee's biggest loss that day, though, was his subordinate Longstreet, who was wounded at almost the same location where Stonewall Jackson had been fatally shot by his own men the previous year.

Following the battle, Grant wired Lincoln that the offensive would continue no matter what. He dispatched a corps southeast to guard a rail junction at Spotsylvania Court House. Lee, almost smelling Grant's move, rushed a covering force to Spotsylvania that arrived before the Union advance units. The stage was set for another confrontation on a new battlefield.

The terrain around Spotsylvania was more conducive to maneuvering, and for five days, from 8 May through 12 May, the two armies struggled with a series of small engagements. Lee used the time to build up his position into a V-shape that came to be called the Bloody Angle. When Grant's grand assault came on 12 May, the Confederates were in a strong enough position to repulse the attack. In some places during the contest, the fighting would have to stop long enough to clear the dead, in some places five deep, from the trenches so the living could continue the carnage. In other places, the combatants had to fire their guns from their hips because the enemy was too close for them to put their guns to their shoulders. The fighting did not end in the horror at Spotsylvania. For six days, Grant searched for Lee's flanks but was thwarted by Lee's masterful shifting of his reserves. Confederate losses for the twelve-day period referred to as the Battle of Spotsylvania totaled 12,000. The Union losses were around 18,000. After eleven days of continuous fighting, Grant moved east toward Fredericksburg, then south toward Richmond, once again trying to find a way into the Confederate capital.

Grant probed the Confederate position but found it too strong for a major attack before sidestepping Lee's right flank and crossing the Pamunkey River. Lee rapidly shifted positions to interpose his army between the federals and the Confederate capital. Again, Grant probed to find Lee's right flank, and this time he located it near Cold Harbor, Virginia.

Cold Harbor proved to be a huge mistake for Grant. He believed Lee's lines were overextended, but he was not sure where the weakness was. The Union general ordered a frontal assault on the entrenched Confederates, figuring such an attack would find the weakness. Grant's miscalculation cost the Union army staggering casualties, for a delay in the arrival of a Union corps—it had gotten lost along the way—gave Lee the time to shore up his position with reinforcements. Grant's assault was pushed back by confident veteran soldiers in well-fortified positions, supported by a strong artillery corps. The Confederate fire was so thick, most of the advancing Union troops did not get anywhere near the Southern lines. Within half an hour, most of the Union troops had turned and were headed back to their lines. First reports of the battle were sufficiently misleading that Grant ordered the fighting to continue. His on-the-spot commanders, though, were so stunned by the carnage that those orders never got carried out. Grant lost nearly 7,000 men in less than an hour of fighting to the Confederate's loss of only about 1,500. Small skirmishes continued for several days, and on 12 July, the Army of the Potomac pulled out, headed for Petersburg.

Lee had inflicted nearly 60,000 Union casualties in just over a month and had stopped the federal advance on Richmond. Grant and his commanders were bitterly criticized for the bloody summer campaign in Virginia, and for Cold Harbor in particular, but the general argued that he was applying pressure Lee could not withstand. Grant's men were traumatized by their experiences and wary of their general's penchant for bloody assaults. At Petersburg, few attacks would be made, as both armies settled into trenches around the rail center where they would spend the next nine months.

JOHN R. THOMPSON: START OF WILDERNESS CAMPAIGN; POLITICAL NEWS FROM RICHMOND

The people of Richmond knew the spring fighting had begun in Richmond when the ambulances were summoned to the front. The action that was starting was The Wilderness Campaign. The war was not the only news, as the Richmond correspondent for the Appeal, Dixie, *John R. Thompson, also included in his letter. Politics were dragging on in Richmond as the Confederate congressmen debated monetary policy and sparred with one another over their support for Southern peace movements.*

Memphis Appeal, 10 May 1864

LETTER FROM RICHMOND

Special Correspondence of the Memphis Appeal.]
RICHMOND, MAY 5, 1864.

The ambulance committee has been ordered to the front and left town this afternoon by a special train. We all know in Richmond what this means. A sudden and violent depression of the barometer at sea does not more surely indicate a storm than the departure of the ambulance committee indicates a battle. The Yankees are in force on this side of the Rapidan and are endeavoring to turn the right flank of Gen. Lee's army. There will probably be much maneuvering for position for several days and then the great shock of arms. There is a feverish excitement here, as is natural, but no sort of apprehension as to the result. What we hear of Grant's army does not inspire apprehension. It is not the well appointed and well disciplined host that came under McClellan two years ago to "drive the revels to the wall." It is probably not so large nor so hopeful as the column that moved on to their destruction under fighting Joe Hooker at Chancellorsville. There are some disaffected brigades in it. Large reinforcements have no doubt arrived during the last week from Washington, brought from Tennessee and Charleston, or new levies, but they are composed in great part of negroes or foreigners, excellent materials for demoralization and [*unreadable*] should Grant be repulsed. But the proof of the material will be in the fighting. A week will probably show what sort of army Grant leads to the attack. Yankee gunboats are ascending James river to-day, probably for the purpose of creating a diversion in concert with the Federal force in the Peninsula. Preparations to meet and repel any hostile movement in this quarter have been fully made, and as for the river, the gunboats will probably come no higher than City Point. They have a salutary fear of torpedoes, and they have no idea at all of coming within range of Drewry's Bluff.

Northern papers as late as the 3rd have been received here. The news is unimportant. The military critics are still demonstrating the inevitable capture of Richmond with mathematical certainty. The committee charged with investigating the Fort Pillow "Massacer" [*sic*] have returned to Washington and made their report. It is a very lively report. The half had not been told of the "rebel" barbarities. Gen. Forrest, according to this committee, is such a man as might be the result of a combination of all the Yankee ruffians, Butler, Turchin, McNiell, Mitroy, Spears, [*unreadable*] and the lamented Ulric Dahlgren in one person. Men were not merely murdered in Fort Pillow in cold blood. They were nailed to boards. They were roasted. They were buried alive. Fortunately, Europeans will know exactly how much of this to believe—that is to say, they will believe nothing of it.

The Emperor Maximillian sailed from Civita Vecchia for Havana on the 20th of April, and if he had a favorable voyage he should be in Havana at this moment. News had not been received from the other side of the Atlantic of the passage of Winter Davis' resolutions on the Monroe doctrine. Of course, Maximillian will hear nothing of the recent successes of the Juarez party and of the flight of Vidaturri from Montgomery until he reaches Cuba. He will hear at the same time of the cordial fraternization of the Yankees and the adherents of Juarez at Matamoros, of Cortina's reception in Brownsville, etc., etc., all of which we may reasonably suppose, will not prove disadvantageous to the success of General Preston, who will repair to Mexico immediately after the new Emperor shall have arrived at the capital.

Congress has done very little yet. Both houses have changed their places of session to the halls of the Virginia Senate and House of Representatives, respectively, where they have more light and space. In the House, yesterday, on motion of Col. Swann, of Tennessee, the matter of placing the five dollar bills on the footing of the new currency, received its quietus by an overwhelming vote. Some sensation was created when Mr. J. F. Leach, of North Carolina, in making a personal explanation of his political status—what the French call a *profession du foi*—acknowledged, in reply to a question addressed to him by Mr. Staples, of Virginia, that he was for peace on any terms short of subjugation. This Mr. Leach must not be confounded with Mr. J. M. Leach, his colleague, who was said in advance of his arrival here, to be a Union man, but who declared that he stood exactly on the same platform as did Vice-President Stephens, Gov. Brown of Georgia, and Gov. Vance, of his own State. The House to-day drew for seats, and having accomplished this, a spirited debate arose between Messrs. Foote and Conrad upon the subject of secret sessions. Mr. Foot moving so to amend the old rule as to make a majority of two thirds necessary to keep the doors closed.

In the Senate a discussion took place on the matter of an early adjournment in which Messrs. Johnson of Arkansas, Orr of South Carolina, and Wigfall parted pale. The latter gentleman spoke somewhat at length on what he conceived Congress had to do—he depreciated hastily legislation—believed in the doctrine of "Fesitua Lente"—alluded to the bill, laid over from the last session, for limiting the term of office of members of the Cabinet—and declared himself ready to defend the privilege of the writ of habeas corpus, avowing that when the matter came up he would be prepared to show that Vice-President Stephens did not understand the Constitution he had sworn to support. The Senate passed a bill to prevent the detention of members of Congress while traveling by provost marshals, requiring passports to be furnished them which all Confederate officers should be bound to respect. Messrs. Orr and Wigfall spoke from opposite points of view on this bill, Mr. Orr giving it as his opinion that

there was no power whatever in the Executive to authorize the military commandants to enforce military law anywhere in the Confederate States outside of the camps and military posts, while Mr. Wigfall sustained the enforcement of the most stringent regulations, and said the public had no business to travel in times like these. There was also a rambling debate on the Senate on the question of reference to the military committee of a vote of thanks to Gen. Forrest, before voting on which the Senate went into executive session.

The ink was hardly dry on my last letter, in which I spoke of the clouds giving us no rain, when a storm of great violence burn over the city, blowing down chimneys, unroofing houses, carrying off a considerable portion of the Petersburg railroad bridge, and doing other damage. There was heavy lightning and a vivid fall of rain. Since this storm the weather has been bright and cool.

DIXIE.

BENJAMIN F. DILL OR JOHN McCLANAHAN: THE WAR CAN BE WON

By the spring of 1864, the Confederate military position was dire in both the Eastern and Western fronts. Through the coming summer, Sherman would begin to push Johnston's Army of the Tennessee south toward Atlanta. Johnston had been given command of the Army of Tennessee after Bragg was forced to resign following his abysmal performance the previous fall at Chattanooga. In Virginia that May, Lee's army was driven back in The Wilderness Campaign and defeated at Spotsylvania. Civilian morale was beginning to plummet, but newspapers were striving to put a good face on the Confederate situation. Indeed, many Confederates, journalists and otherwise, believed—and some historians would agree with them—that it was still possible in the spring of 1864 for the South to defeat the North and win its independence.

Memphis Appeal, 14 May 1864

THE DAY AND THE HOUR

In the two great struggles now going on at Richmond and Dalton, all must feel that we are now in the most critical period we have passed through since the commencement of the war. In every respect except numbers, we certainly have the enemy at a disadvantage, we being the resisting and they the assaulting. We are moreover, doing battle on our own soil and in defense of our homes and property and family altars, while our foe is fighting only for plunder and his monthly pay. It is true the pride of character of the Northern people, as well as their future welfare, is involved in the issue of this great contest, and hence the gigantic efforts now being made by them to overcome and wear out the armies of Generals LEE and JOHNSTON. Success will give them a temporary respite or exemption from the calamities and disasters which defeat would speedily precipitate upon them. To postpone this evil day they are now mastering all their forces and concentrating all their energies, and to resist them successfully, will require

all the resources that we can bring to bear. If necessary, it is the duty of the States, with their militia and reserved forces, to come to the help of the Confederacy. Now is the day and now the hour to make short work of the war. By partial success over the enemy at Dalton, it may be prolonged indefinitely, whereas, by a decisive triumph, it will be brought to a speedy termination. From GRANT'S tactics, it would seem that he is disposed to carry out the original policy of the Federal authorities, and is determined to make the contest short and sharp. But this is a game which we can play at more successfully than he, if we will but summon all our energies and throw them into the contest. We can stand defeat and live to fight again, but he cannot. In this we have an immense advantage over the foe, but we hope such a thing as defeat will be thought of neither by the people nor the troops in the field. Every consideration of weal to the country should prompt us to adopt the policy of the enemy and make the contest short and sharp, by a triumphant victory over him.

With the success that has crowned our arms in the West, we now have it in our power, by similar success in the pending conflict, to put an end to the war, and once more bless the country with peace and prosperity. The Confederate authorities, we know are straining all their energies to effect this desirable result; and we trust the States will be equally as resolute and energetic in their co-operation with the Confederate Government. Now is the accepted time for us to finish up our work. We have the enemy away from his gunboats and a long distance from his base of supplies, where we have always wanted to get him, in order that we might strike him a fatal and decisive blow. Let us all then, both people and army, both Confederate and State authorities, summon all our energies, muster all our resources, and crown the triumphs of the spring campaign with victories at Richmond and Dalton, and the war is at an end.

PETER W. ALEXANDER: BATTLE OF THE WILDERNESS

This exchange story by the Savannah Republican's *Peter W. Alexander chronicled the early May Battle of The Wilderness as a victory for the Confederates. Alexander was showing his Confederate partisanism; the outcome of the two-day battle was more indecisive than Alexander indicated. However, the Confederate army's spirits were high at the end of the battle and fully expected to have the Army of the Potomac on the run back to Washington before long.*

Selma Reporter, 1 June 1864 (Selma, Ala.)

BATTLE OF THE WILDERNESS
LETTER FROM P.W.A.

ARMY OF NORTHERN VIRGINIA, Battlefield, May 7, 1864.

Again it becomes my grateful task to chronicle another victory. While it can not be regarded in its military aspects as a decisive battle, since the enemy was neither routed nor driven back across the Rapidan; yet, when we consider the circumstances under which it was fought, the elaborate preparation made by the enemy, the large arm of veteran troops with which he advanced, and the common consent with which both sides had come to regard the present campaign as probably the last act of the bloody drama which has convulsed the North American continent for the last three years, we cannot but look upon it as one of the most important battles of the whole war. The boasted leader of the Federal army chose his own time and place to deliver battle; he made the attack and was repulsed with heavy [unreadable]; his combinations were penetrated and defeated, and his whole movement checkmated, at least for present. These are results of great consequence, and for them the country should be grateful to the Giver of all victory, and to the brave army by whose valor they have been achieved. But let us take up the narrative at the beginning and bring it down to the present time, and thus see what was done and how it was done.

Arriving at Gordonsville Wednesday, the 4th instant, at 1 o'clock and learning that Grant had crossed the Rapidan below at Germana and Ely's Fords, and was endeavoring to turn Lee's right flank, I took horse and pushed on to the point to which both armies seemed to be approaching. The moment Gen. Lee ascertained that Grant had really cut loose from his base at Culpepper, Hill's and Ewell's corps were withdrawn from their positions on the Rapidan and ordered to advance upon the enemy's line of march, the former taking the plank road and the latter the turnpike, both leading from Orange Courthouse [sic] to Fredericksburg. Longstreet, who was in the vicinity of Gordonsville, ready to move upon any point, was ordered to march down the Carthaplu road. The main body of Grant's army crossed at Germana Ford, and took the road loading from thence in the direction of Bowling Green and Richmond, and known in the neighborhood as Brock's Road, by which name I shall speak of it hereafter. The first object at which he aimed, doubtless, was to reach the point where that road intersects with the Orange and Fredericksburg plank road and turnpike. These highways run nearly parallel to each other, the distance between them varying from one to three miles and more. There is an unfinished railroad which also runs nearly parallel to the other two roads, and extends from Orange Court house [sic] to Fredericksburg. The turnpike lies on the north side or next to the river, the railroad on the south side, and the plank road between the two. These roads do not cross Brock's Road, along which Grant was moving, at right angles, but diagonally, the distance between the points where they cut Brock's Road being as follows: between the railway bed and the plank road about five hundred yards, and between the plank road and turnpike nearly four miles. The enemy's line of battle extended along Brock's road from the unfinished railroad across the plank road to the turnpike, and was consequently about four miles in length. Chancellorsville is four miles below, on the plank road, and Fredericksburg about fifteen miles. The surrounding country is very appropriately called the Wilderness, the people being ignorant, the soil destitute of fertility, the supply of water scant, the ground broken and covered with dense and almost impenetrable growth of stunted bushes, pines and blackjacks. It is a blighted region adjoining the district known as the "poisoned fields of Orange," and producing but little for the subsistence of either man or beast. So thick are the woods in some places that it is impossible to distinguish a man, even in the absence of verdure, at a distance of fifty paces. The reader can readily imagine that it would be difficult to select more unfavorable ground for a battle between two great armies. It only remains to be added that the battle was fought near the western boundary of Spotsylvania county, the line of battle being nearly at right angles to a straight line drawn from Fredericksburg through Chancellorsville to Orange Courthouse.

If the reader will keep these points clearly in his mind, and will place a good map before him, he will find but little difficulty in forming a satisfactory conception of the battle.

As has already been stated, Ewell moved down the turnpike, which is on the left and nearest to the river, and Hill down the plank road. Stuart passed still further to the South, and marched down the Catherpin road, so as to throw his cavalry in front of the head of Grant's army and retard its march. His troopers did their duty well, especially Rosser's brigade of Hampton's division, and forced the Federal cavalry, which was marching up the road by which he was advancing, back, into Brock's Road with considerable loss in men and horses, indeed, Grant had thrown his cavalry on the turnpike, plank road and Catherpin road, in the vain hope that he might be able to interpose a screen between himself and the Confederates, and thus both protect and conceal his movements. But Lee was not slow to penetrate his designs, and immediately sprung upon his flank like a tiger upon the side of an ox. Ewell and Hill pushed rapidly down the turnpike and plank roads, encountered and drove in the cavalry and infantry supports, which had been thrown forward to block up those highways and compelled the whole army to halt and defend itself. Stuart in the meantime had reached Brock's road, in front of the enemy, and thus opposed another obstacle to his further advance. It is not known that Grant especially directed to give battle here, but he saw the danger of his position and immediately formed into line of battle and advanced nearly two miles to meet the threatened attack. This, it will be seen hereafter, was all that saved him from a most disastrous defeat, since it gave him time to send his trains to the rear and throw up strong entrenchments parallel with and in front of the road by which he had been marching, and behind which he might rally his troops in the event they were beaten back. This was Thursday, the 5th, one year and one day after the great battle of Chancellorsville.

It was about 4 in the afternoon when the two armies encountered each other. Grant attacked heavily and repeatedly along the whole line, and especially on our right, which he showed a disposition to turn, and thus place him between Lee's army and Richmond; but in every instance he was repulsed with heavy loss. He was persistent, however, in his efforts to break our lines, and continued his assaults until night. His last advance against Hill's front was made just before dark, and was handsomely repulsed by Wilcox's and Heath's division. His final attack upon Ewell was made after night, against that part of the line held by Edward Johnson's division. Here, too, he was beaten back, leaving many dead and wounded on the ground. During these operations, Ewell captured 2,000 prisoners, nearly all of whom were taken by Gordon's Georgia brigade and Hays' Louisiana, both of whom behaved with distinguished gallantry.

Longstreet had not yet reached the ground. Leaving Gordonsville at 4 o'clock Wednesday afternoon, he marched fifteen miles that night. The next day he drove the Catharpin (this is correct spelling) road (so called from a run which it crosses) seventeen miles, his orders being to strike Brock's road at a point south of the unfinished railroad. He halted during the afternoon within eight miles of the battle-field; but owing to the peculiar condition of the atmosphere and the density of the forest, he could not hear the guns of Hill and Ewell, and was not aware the battle had commenced until the receipt of a dispatch from Gen. Lee, at midnight, ordering him to come over to the plank road to the [unreadable] of Hill. Hill's corps was put in motion immediately, and reached the field Friday morning soon after sunrise. Hill's troops were aware of the approach of Longstreet's corps, and that it would take their place in the line. They had had a hard fight the previous evening and rested but little that night, and when the head of McLaws' division (now commanded by that medal soldier, Brig. Gen. Kershaw,) came in sight, they relaxed somewhat their vigilance, and were preparing to withdraw, when they were attacked in front with great fury by a very heavy force. Under these untoward circumstances, Wilcox's and Heath's divisions, which had done so well the evening before, were thrown into confusion and gave way, just as Kershaw double quicked it to the front in columns. The latter succeeded in throwing three regiments of his old brigade, commanded by Col. Hinnegan, into line, while Wilcox's and Heath's men were falling back over his troops, and with this small but heroic band, he confronted the heavy masses of the enemy; now flushed with the hope of an easy victory and pressing rapidly forward. These regiments suffered severely, but they maintained their ground until the remainder of the division could be got into some sort of line under the terrible fire to which it was exposed. Gen. Lee witnessed the unfortunate and [unreadable] confusion and withdrawal of the divisions of Wilcox and Heath, in both of which he had reposed so much confidence, and which had behaved so handsomely on former occasions, and tears rushed to his eyes. He at once placed himself at the head of Gregg's Texas brigade, Field's division, formerly Hood's, and prepared to lead in person. The heroes of the Lone Star, who had made the circuit of the Confederacy under Longstreet, remonstrated against such an unnecessary exposure of his life—a life so important and precious to the Confederacy and to all friends of liberty throughout the world. He replied that he must win this battle at every hazard—that he must whip the fight. The Texans, who had not yet moved from their tracks, answered that they could whip the fight without his leading them, and would do it. In the meantime, appeals were made by several officers to Longstreet, as the only person who could probably dissuade Gen. Lee from taking so rash a proceeding. He went immediately to Gen. Lee and begged him to restrain himself, and not to think of exposing himself and the cause which he held so much at heart to such terrible chances. The Texans, too, finally gave him [*unreadable*] and, in the most respectful and affectionate manner, that they would obey any order he might give, provided he remained behind, but that they would not budge an inch if he led them. Gen. Lee was at length prevailed upon to desist from, the hazardous undertaking, and right glorious did the heroic Texans redeem their pledge.

Kershaw has, by the unanimous voice of the army, won his spurs and Major General's commission. He has ever proved himself equal to the occasion, however critical, but yesterday he displayed a degree of skill, energy and intrepidity that elicited the admiration of all who witnessed or have heard of his performances. When he and Fields, another officer who behaved with great judgment and gallantry, at length got into position under these difficult circumstances, with their old leader, Longstreet, to guide and direct them, it would have done you good to have seen how they and their officers and men pressed forward with shouts that rent the skies, and finally repulsed the immense numbers that crowded upon them with terrible slaughter. They saved the day, which for nearly two hours trembled in doubt, and were at length enabled to assume the offensive. It was evidently Grant's object to turn our right wing, and if he had succeeded, it is impossible to say what might not have been the results.

On the left we were equally successful. An attempt was made to pierce that part of Ewell's line which was held by Pegram's brigade, but it was signally defeated. You will regret to hear that Gen. Pegram was severely wounded, and that Brig. Gen. Jones of Virginia and Stafford of Louisiana, were killed the evening before. With this exception, the left wing was not required to take any further part in the heavy fighting of the day, the enemy's almost exclusive attention being given to our right.

About 11 o'clock Longstreet was ordered to move upon the enemy's left flank, and if possible dislodge him from the railroad cut and the plank road, and drive him back upon Brock's Road. The brigades selected for this movement were G. T. Anderson's and Jenkins', of Fields' division; Mahone's and Davis' of R. H. Anderson's division, and Wofford's and perhaps two other, of Kershaw's divisions. Anderson's division, but lately arrived, having been left at Orange Courthouse to guard against any demonstration upon our rear. The flank movement was completely successful; the enemy was taken by surprise and driven back from the railroad cut across the plank road with heavy loss, a portion of his troops

retreating rapidly down the plankroad to Brock's road. Mahone's Virginia brigade, of Anderson's division, ran over the 4th United States infantry, a regiment which boasted that it had never been broken before. The plank road being clear, Longstreet advanced down it at the head of Jenkins' brigade, and had hardly gone a half of a mile when he was fired upon by Mahone's brigade, which was drawn up in the dense woods parallel to the road, and not more than seventy-five paces from it. Mahone was waiting there to catch such of the enemy as might have been cut off up the road, and when Jenkins' brigade arrived opposite him, his men, being unable to distinguish one man from another through the woods, very naturally concluded it was a body of the enemy retiring, and opened fire upon their friends, killing eight or ten and wounding several others. Capt. Daby, of Kershaw's staff, was killed instantly; the intrepid Gen. Jenkins, of South Carolina, received a mortal wound on the head, from which he died in a few hours afterwards, and Gen. Longstreet was shot in the neck. The ball struck him in front of the right of the larynx, passing under the skin and carrying away a part of the spine of the scapula and coming out behind the right shoulder. The wound is severe, but is not considered mortal. The only damage apprehended being from secondary hemorrhage. Should he survive ten or twelve days and the [*unreadable*] artery not become involved, it is the opinion of Dr. Cullen, his medical director, that he will be able to return to the field in a few weeks. He has lost temporary use of his right arm—what surgeons call the conical plexus of nerves being injured. He was carried to the rear this morning, and was doing remarkably well when he left. Gen. Lee called to see him just before he was moved, and when he bade him farewell and came out of the tent where his great lieutenant lay, his eyes were filled with tears. It is a remarkable co-incidence that Jackson received his death wound just twelve months ago, only four miles from the spot where his companion in arms fell, and just after he had completed a successful flank movement, and under almost precisely the same circumstances. Heaven grant that Lee may not lose his left arm now, as he lost his right arm then!

Gen. Longstreet had just been congratulated by Gen. Lee, Gen. Kershaw and others, upon the complete success of his attack upon the flank of the enemy, and he was sweeping down the plank road to pluck the rich fruits of his victory, then almost within his grasp, when he was struck down by his own friends. The delay of an hour which ensued gave the enemy time to escape back behind his entrenchments on the Brock's Road. The commander of the corps then devolved upon Maj. Gen. Fields, and today it was turned over to Maj. Gen. Anderson, of Hill's corps, who has been reporting to Longstreet after his arrival, and who formerly belonged to the corps.

The enemy had thus been repulsed along our whole line, and left many dead and wounded in our hands. In many places, his dead appeared to be five or six times as multitudinous as our own. Our loss was not so heavy as at first reported, and will not exceed 5,000, of whom not more than 600 were killed. Most of the wounds were comparatively slight, owing to the protection afforded by the trees and brushes. The enemy's loss cannot be much less than 15,000 inclusive of prisoners. The unfavorable character of the ground and the thick chaparral prevented both sides from using artillery, only a few guns being put in position. Among all the killed, no [unreadable] or braver knight ever fell to defense of the liberties of his country than the gallant and accomplished Col. Nance, of South Carolina; and no harder fighter or more perfect gentleman ever received a wound on the field of battle than General Benning of Georgia. The one has gone to the rest of the true soldier—let us pray that the other may long be spared to the country he has served with so much modesty and courage.

At half past four o'clock, General Lee determined to feel the enemy and ascertain his position on Brock's road. On the right, where I had my position, the brigades of Kershaw, Humphreys and Wofford, of Kershaw's division, Anderson, Jenkins, Gregg and Law of Field's division, and Mahone's, of Anderson's division, moved forward in the form of the letter V, with the sharp point towards the enemy. G. T. Anderson, known in the corps as "Tiger Anderson," formed the apex of the line, and succeeded in reaching the enemy's entrenchments, two of his men falling within the work. On the left, Ewell was equally successful. The result of the attack or reconnaissance was the discovery that Grant had been driven back a mile and a half; that he had thrown up a strong line of entrenchment in front of Brock's road, and that his left wing rested upon a deep cut in the railroad, along which he had posted a force that effectually protected it. His position is, therefore, a strong one, being rendered the more so by the dense woods through which his line runs. Lee's position is equally satisfactory.

Last night, Gordon, of Early's division, threw his brigade around an exposed point in the enemy's lines and took Brig. Gens. Seymore, of Ocean Pond memory, and Shaler, and about 500 prisoner. Seymore admits that Grant has been whipped and that the Federal army will continue to be whipped until their ports are closed and the troops reduced to "parched corn and beans like the rebels." He says Grant drinks too much liquor, and that the war, on the part of the North, is conducted as if it were a matter of frolic and contract.

Our lines were withdrawn a few hundred yards last night and from the enemy's immediate front, for the purpose of improving their position. Not understanding exactly what the movement meant, Grant advanced with heavy force this morning, at half past 10 o'clock, but so soon discovered where the Confederate troops were. He was driven back with ease, and now, at sunset, is cowering behind his entrenchments in the Wilderness. His troops have not done as well as they did under McClellan, Burnside or even Hooker. The Confederates, on the contrary, never fought better. Gen. Lee had caused it to be circulated among them some days ago

that they must not think of defeat as possible—it was a thing not to be even dreamed of. Nobly have his invincible legions responded to the call of their great chief. Oh, that we may ever have such a leader and such an army!

P.W.A.

ARMY OF NORTHERN VIRGINIA, Spotsylvania C.H., MAY 10, 1864.

We have had more bloody work to-day, and again, as at the Wilderness, our losses are miraculously small. It has been a singular battle, not only in its results, but especially in regard to the manner in which it was delivered by the Federal commander. The greater part of the forenoon was consumed by him in an attempt to make Gen. Lee develope [sic] his plans and positions. Artillery was used freely, and skirmishers and sharpshooters were pushed forward along the lines, and vigorous efforts made to provoke Lee to unmask his batteries and show his hand. At length Grant seemed to grow weary of this kind of work, and ordered an assault to be made. The infantry came up to the work in handsome style, and yet they seemed to have no stomach for the fight; for three separate assaults upon Anderson's corps (late Longstreet's) they were repulsed by his skirmishers and sharpshooters alone. The result was not dissimilar in front of Ewell. The heavy masses of the enemy were pushed back with the ease with which one puts a drunken man away from him. The Confederates fought behind field work thrown up hurriedly, and they appear to relish the fun amazingly. The last assault made upon Anderson's position was late in the afternoon, and was headed by a regiment of the old United States army. The enemy succeeded, after a hard struggle, in gaining a salient angle, occupied, I am told, by Gregg's Texan brigade; but of all who cleared the entrenchments, not one lived to return—they were either killed or taken. They met with a temporary success also in front of Rhodes' division, Ewell's corps, where they captured a portion, if not all, of the guns belonging to the 3d Company, Richmond Howitzers, of Gen. Alexander's artillery command. The guns were soon recovered, however, and the assailants beaten off with heavy loss. Toward noon, it was ascertained that the enemy were moving upon our left and center with cavalry and infantry. Early was sent off with Heth's division to drive them off and repossess us of the bridge over the Po, one of the branches of the Mattapony. He accomplished the object of his mission in his own gallant manner. Heath's men were glad of an opportunity to prove to all that the temporary confusion into which they were thrown at the Wilderness was the result of accident rather than a lack of spirit. The enemy were well punished, and driven entirely from that part of the field. I have spoken of our casualties to-day as miraculously small. They are less than 1,000; and including the loss resulting from the heavy skirmishing yesterday, they will not exceed 1,200. The enemy's loss, on the contrary, since our arrival here, is estimated as high as 15,000, and at the Wilderness, as high as 30,000, including prisoners. These figures are probably too large, though they reflect the opinion which obtains in high official circles here. The calculation rests upon the number of the enemy whom we have buried—2,700—and the 4,000 prisoners who fell into our hands. It is proper to add that papers have been captured since the battle of the Wilderness which admit the loss there of 20,000. These papers contain a confession also that Grant was beaten badly on his right, (our left,) where Ewell commanded, and that Gorman, in his night attack, inflicted heavy losses, but they claim he was successful on his left, (our right). The first is true, but the latter is not. Our victory was complete on every part of he field.

It is reported that Grant, just before opening the battle this morning, issued an order in which he announced to his troops that Butler had taken Petersburg, and was then investing Richmond, with every prospect of reducing it at an early day; also, that Johnston had been defeated at Dalton, leaving his dead and wounded in the hands of Sherman. We have not heard from Dalton for some days, but we know that the order utters a falsehood when it claims that Butler has occupied Petersburg and invested Richmond. The courage of Grant's army, however, like that of the man in the play, is oozing out at their fingers' ends, and it requires to be stimulated.

PETER W. ALEXANDER: ACCOUNT OF BATTLE OF COLD HARBOR

With 100,000 men, Grant was confident he could split Lee's overextended lines with little difficulty. Grant miscalculated, though. The frontal attack the Union general ordered at Cold Harbor ended up being one of the biggest mistakes of his career. Grant's army faced staggering casualties in the nine-day battle—more than 13,000 total, including more than 7,000 in less than an hour on 3 June. Grant's mistake gave Lee his last clear victory of the war. In this pair of dispatches that ran together, the Mobile paper's correspondent, A., better known as the Savannah Republican's *correspondent P.W.A., described the fighting and also a trick Grant tried to use to keep from admitting defeat.*

Mobile Advertiser and Register, 16 June 1864

OUR ARMY CORRESPONDENCE
LETTER FROM GENERAL LEE'S ARMY

[FROM OUR SPECIAL CORRESPONDENT.]
ARMY OF NORTHERN VIRGINIA.
Battlefield of Cold Harbor, June 6, 1864.

My last letter [*unreadable*] the 3d. Inst., 4 P.M., and concluded with an intimation that the enemy, though badly beaten in the bloody battle of that morning, was probably preparing to make an assault at night. The assault was made that night, soon after dark, against that part of the line held by Gens. Breckinridge and Finnegan, as they were preparing to establish their skirmish lines. The enemy was soon repulsed with heavy loss. Immediately afterwards an attack was made upon Gen. [unreadable] front, with like result.— These assaults were repeated on the nights of the 4th and 5th, and repulsed as often as made.

The assault last night was intended to cover another movement to the right, in the direction of James river. It was suggested to this correspondent some days ago, Gen. Grant was aiming for James river, and probably the south side of it, his object being to throw his army between Richmond and the South. This is now the prevailing opinion in the army of Northern Virginia, and in high official quarters in the capital. Should he stop on the north side of the river, near City Point, he might easily throw a number of pontoon bridges across at that point, (which you will see by an inspection of the map, is on the north side of the mouth of the Appomattox) or across to

Bermuda Hundreds, which is between the two rivers, and at the point of their confluences. With his army strongly intrenched on the north side of the James, his bridges protected by his monitors, and a foothold already gained by Butler between the rivers, he would be able to rush a raiding party across the river any dark night, and out the Petersburg and Weldon railroad, and probably the Richmond and Danville road also. Should he throw his army behind the Appomattox and across the Petersburg and Weldon road, with his left extending well up towards the Danville road, he might annoy us a great deal if he did nothing more, while Gen. Lee would find it exceedingly difficult, if not impossible, to dislodge him. The chief objection to this late course is the danger to which his communications would be exposed by our artillerists and sharpshooters posted along the north bank of the James. Possibly he would endeavor to guard against this danger by drawing a portion of his supplies from Norfolk by the Petersburg and Norfolk railway.

But will he be able to reach James river? If he continues to move down the north side of the Chickahominy, he probably will be; but should he attempt to cross the stream, and march directly across to the James, he will never reach his destination. But suppose he does reach the James, and establish himself on the banks of the stream or the Appomattox, what then—will he be able to carry Richmond by assault? He will not; his object will be to starve us out. Will he be able to do this? The future alone can give a satisfactory answer to this inquiry. If, however, one may be permitted to venture an opinion so far in advance, I should say that under the leadership of Lee and Beauregard, with the guidance of Heaven, which has never forsaken us except for our own good, the enemy will be able to reduce the capital neither by battle nor starvation.

As already stated, the enemy commenced to move last night. It was observed this morning that he had disappeared in front of our left wing, and the probability is that he is repeating the movement by which, like the crab, he has been advancing sideways since he left the Wilderness. In addition to the assault last night, Grant made a further effort to conceal this movement by sending a communication to Gen. Lee proposing that hereafter, when the enemies are not actually engaged, either side may send out parties to bury its dead and remove its wounded. Gen Lee replied in [unreadable] terms, stating, however, that he preferred the custom common among military men, viz: when the commander of either side desired to succor his wounded and bury his dead, he should send in a flag of truce and ask permission to do so, and that the party sent upon the field to attend to the human duty, should carry white flags. To this Grant sent a rejoinder this morning, affecting to understand that Gen. Lee had agreed to his proposition, and adding that he would send out a force to look after his wounded and dead to-day between 12 and 3 o'clock, and that they should be accompanied by flags of the kind suggested by Gen. Lee. To this *smart* attempt Gen. Lee replied, informing him that he had misunderstood

his former communication—that he meant to indicate the usual custom of a flag of truce as the proper mode of accomplishing his object as stated in his first dispatch, and notifying him that if he sent forward a burial party without conforming to the usage and first obtaining permission to do so, he would cause it to be warned off.

I am not informed whether any further communication has been received from Gen. Grant. His object was transparent enough. He desired to conceal his movement last night, to bury his dead and succor his wounded before leaving, and to avoid the confession of defeat implied by his asking permission to perform this human duty.—His dead and wounded still remain in front of our entrenchments, exposed to the rain and sun, the one poisoning the air by their stench, the other vexing it by their cries for help. The poor creatures—the wounded—may be seen appealing to their friends by waving their handkerchiefs or beckoning them with their pale hands. Grant left many of his dead and wounded uncared for at the Wilderness and Spotsylvania Courthouse, and he will be guilty of the same barbarity here, unless he smother his pride and obtain Gen. Lee's leave to attend to them. I endeavored today to obtain an official statement of our casualties on the 3d, but did not succeed. I learned enough, however, to venture to say that they do not exceed 1,000, and that in all the engagements, skirmishes and picketing that have occurred since we left Hanover Junction, they do not exceed 2,000. The loss of the enemy is probably ten times as great—say 20,000.

A.

Siege of Petersburg

After Cold Harbor, Grant immediately moved against the railroads south of Petersburg. He hoped to isolate Lee from his southern supply route. Grant's men dug in around Petersburg and conducted a number of spectacular sorties in the many months of the siege as they tried to encircle Richmond and Petersburg. The operation lasted much of 1864 and on almost to the surrender at Appomattox in April 1865.

Petersburg was a valuable Confederate asset not only because it was a rail center but also because it was home to a bullet manufacturer. The Confederates had fortified the city in 1862 as a precaution, but it was never really threatened until the spring of 1864. Twice that spring, the city nearly fell, but the resolute and outnumbered Confederates managed to hold on. The danger increased after mid-June when Grant shifted the Army of the Potomac across the James River to attack Petersburg.

P.G.T. Beauregard, commander of the Confederate forces at Petersburg, worked diligently to obtain reinforcements for the two brigades he had at Petersburg and to dig trenches to repel the federal attack in mid-June. Beauregard managed to repulse that early assault, though he lost some of the city's permanent defenses and was pushed back to a second line of trenches. On 18 June, Grant made almost his last head-on attack on a Confederate position in Virginia but was again denied Petersburg. The remainder of the campaign, he relied on grand flanking maneuvers, and the first one came on 22 June at Ream's Station. The Union infantry under Generals

D. B. Birney and H. G. Wright attacked from the Jerusalem Plank Road toward Globe Tavern on the Weldon Railroad. They were supported by a cavalry raid on Burke's station 15 miles to the west. The Union infantry was thrown back by Confederate General A. P. Hill's counterattack, and their colleagues on horseback were very nearly captured.

To distract Lee's attention from his army's attempt to cross the James, Grant sent Sheridan to threaten Lynchburg in mid-June. Lee responded by ordering cavalry commander Jubal Early to engage Sheridan's forces. Early's operation would transmogrify into a raid across the Potomac and into Maryland and Pennsylvania. Sweeping Major General Lew Wallace's 6,000 out of his way at the Monocacy, Early reached the outskirts of a terrified Washington, D.C., on 11 July. In August, Grant would send Sheridan back to the Shenandoah Valley to deal with Early and to lay waste to Virginia. Sheridan's men carried out their orders with alacrity. Through the fall, Sheridan systematically desolated the beautiful valley, and neither Early nor Confederate guerrillas could do anything to stop him.

While Sheridan and Early were pursuing one another through the Shenandoah Valley, Grant and Lee squared off at Petersburg and Richmond. Lee, a master at maneuver, was tied down defending Richmond and its communications center at Petersburg. He had been able to protect Richmond through the war by keeping the enemy far away from the Confederate capital, but Grant denied Lee the opportunity to play to his strength by constricting his position with a tactical, rather than a physical, siege. Petersburg was never surrounded by the enemy, but Grant's defensive positions at Bermuda Hundred, along the lower Appomattox and east of Petersburg, made up essentially a dug-in camp from which he could launch operations against Richmond or Petersburg. Lee had enough freedom of movement to assault Grant's communications and to counterattack Grant's offensives. Essentially, though, the two armies were spinning their wheels in place.

One of the great tragedies of the war occurred during the siege at Petersburg when Grant ordered a massive trench dug under the Confederate works. The trench was to be filled with explosives that would be set off in order to blow a hole, literally, in the Confederate defensive lines. When the 4 tons of gunpowder exploded on 30 July, the attackers were almost as surprised as the defenders. Burnside's corps was supposed to attack through the crater, but they stalled there due to a lack of clear orders from their leaders. They became sitting ducks for Confederate artillery and small arms fire that succeeded in sealing the breach in the Petersburg defenses. The Union lost nearly 4,000 men in the fiasco. Total Union casualties for the siege, including the eight offensives Grant launched during it, reached more than 61,000, not quite double the Confederacy's estimated loss of some 38,000 men.

AN ANONYMOUS REPORT: BATTLE OF THE CRATER

The Battle of the Crater was the most spectacular engagement that occurred during the long siege of Petersburg. Grant's idea was to blow a hole in the Confederate line and then spring forward in an assault. Once the mine blew, though, confusion reigned, and thousands of Union soldiers were killed in the relentless Confederate fire.

Macon Telegraph, 3 August 1864

FROM PETERSBURG

Fighting on Saturday
Our Casualties
1100 Prisoners Captured
20 Colors Taken

PETERSBURG, August 2.—Our loss in Saturday's affair foot up twelve hundred. Three hundred were killed and wounded and three hundred prisoners from Elliot's South Carolina brigade. Mahone losses 450 killed and wounded. The mine was spring on Bashrod Johnson's front.

On yesterday evening Burnside sent in a flag of truce asking permission to bury his dead. The communication was returned with the endorsement that an application from the commanding general of the army would be entertained. Meade then sent in a flag and permission was granted and the hours from five to nine named. This period was diligently occupied and over 700 were buried.

The Yankee officers said their loss in wounded was three thousand.

There is great complaint against Burnside for his failure.

Our captures of battle flags reached 20 and prisoners 1100.

Yankee prisoners say that Grant is organizing a grand raid on the Weldon railroad.

General Elliott is improving. Nothing of importance to day.

DR. GEORGE W. BAGBY: NEWS FROM PETERSBURG

In mid-September, Hermes traveled to Petersburg to see firsthand how the siege there was progressing. George W. Bagby, Hermes's real name, was clearly irritated to find so many men detailed as teamsters rather than serving as soldiers. It was one more piece of evidence, he believed, that proved the Richmond government was doing a bad job of running the country and the military. By this point, for many Confederates, it took little evidence to support accusations of incompetence on behalf of the Richmond government. Discontent and distrust of the Davis administration, and the president himself, were growing throughout the Confederacy. The recent loss of Atlanta and the inaction in Virginia were exasperating the situation.

Charleston Mercury, 16 September 1864

LETTER FROM RICHMOND

(CORRESPONDENCE OF THE MERCURY.)
RICHMOND, Monday, September 12.

On my return from Petersburg yesterday, everybody wanted to know if the city had been, or was going to be evacuated. Whether General LEE and staff had been captured, etc. In Petersburg, everybody wanted to know if Mobile had been captured. The Yankee pickets had said so, etc. So we go with our Sunday rumors.

I saw enough of the enemy's works, and talked enough with our officers, to be thoroughly convinced of the importance of filling up the ranks at once. At the same time I saw white teamsters enough to make a division. Why do not Messrs. Davis, Seddon and Lee enforce the laws, instead of complaining and appealing to the people? And why will the people continually bedevil the authorities, civil and military, until they are fairly worried into granting details which they know to be wrong?

I am glad to hear that General Butler, of your State, has been made Major General of cavalry. Unacquainted personally, I have, nevertheless, ample testimony from men in his army of the service to assure me of his competency for the important post he now fills. Perhaps, if he were in place of Lomax, we should get better accounts from the Valley.

Beast Butler's letter to Ould puts a quietus on the question of exchange. There will be none until we acknowledge the equality of the negro, or win fresh victories. The Beast is ingenious in his sophistry; but the world knows the North is afraid to let us have back our 30,000 veterans. That is the whole secret.

The official organ is rather complimentary this morning on the Chicago Convention, which it professes to regard as the inauguration of a States Rights Conservative party. A good General sent two months ago to Atlanta would have saved this useless bit of flattery. McClellan is defunct—his Convention a farce.

Gilman & Co., of Scotland, had £35,000 worth of tobacco burnt in Manchester last Friday night. It was carried there to be out of the way of the general tobacco conflagration which the citizens threaten in case the Yankees ever get to this place.

Seward's "right of succession" doctrine, promulgated in his late Auburn speech, lets the Republican cat out of the bag. It is a monarchy they are aiming at, as we long ago suspected, Seward is a little too hasty in his announcement; it will recoil heavily on his party—after the next Confederate victory—not till then.

Much cooler; fall like.

HERMES

DR. GEORGE W. BAGBY: ACCOUNT OF FIGHTING IN SHENANDOAH VALLEY

Early had sent back word of his operations in the Shenandoah Valley to the Confederate War Department, but facts were sketchy about the recent engagement with Sheridan. While the story did not name the battle described, it was most likely the Third Battle of Winchester (Battle of Opequon). Early, with 19,000 men, met Sheridan's 41,000 head-on near Winchester. Initially, it appeared that the Confederates were making headway, but the Union cavalry, personally led by Sheridan, turned Early's left and threw the Confederate force back to Fisher's Hill. Union and Confederate losses for the day were both around 5,000.

Charleston Mercury, 27 September 1864

LETTER FROM RICHMOND

(CORRESPONDENCE OF THE MERCURY.)
RICHMOND, Wednesday, September 21.

General EARLY'S despatch throws little light on our late reverse in the Valley. It is probable the enemy, taking advantage of the departure of a division, succeeded in getting in his rear—our inferior force of not too well commanded cavalry offering scarcely any opposition.

Rhodes is a great loss to the service. His fall will be deplored by the whole country. He was the brightest ornament of Alabama, and the pride of his native State, Virginia.

The President left this city yesterday on the Southern train, and the "Reliable Gentlemen" is much excited in consequence. One version is, that the President has gone to Macon, in order to foil Sherman's efforts to inveigle Governor Brown and others into a peace conference at Atlanta. Most likely his visit has reference solely to army matters.

We have pleasant rumors about events forthcoming in a certain vicinity, but do not place much faith in them. We have heard such rumors too often.

Today everybody is required to go up and register name, occupation, etc., for the benefit of the Conscript officers, who are beginning to show new energy. A very material increase of the army is expected.

How it happens that the exchange of officers and of sick and wounded (at odd and uncertain times) is allowed by the enemy, is quite a puzzle to us all; in fact the freaks of the foe in this matter are entirely unaccountable. It is to be hoped that most of the prisoners who arrived today came from Fort Delaware, the horrors of which, as detailed to me by persons lately released from there, beggar all description. Our men suffer from hunger so intensely that they actually fish up the kitchen garbage thrown into the sink, and eat it.

Dark and cloudy—the equinoctial gales coming on.

HERMES.

JOHN M. DANIEL: FALL CAMPAIGN IN RICHMOND

An exchange editorial from the Richmond Examiner *looked at the situation facing the Confederacy in late September. Its editors were confident that the South would win its independence. Somehow the editors had convinced themselves that the Union would never again be as careless with the lives of its troops as its commanding general had been in the previous year. Richmond was the key, the paper argued, and one that Grant would never attain. In fact, the* Mercury's *editors were confident Grant's reputation would sink into insignificance compared with Sherman's. This article was typical of the sorts of morale-building content most of the South's remaining newspapers were running in the fall of 1864. There is little doubt that editors had convinced themselves of the veracity of their words, though in truth the* Mercury *was more accurate than its editors knew when it predicted that the war was drawing to a close, though with a much different outcome than it predicted.*

Richmond Examiner, reprinted in the Charleston Mercury, 28 September 1864

THE FALL CAMPAIGN IN VIRGINIA

(From the Richmond Examiner.)

The final struggle for the possession of Richmond and of Virginia is now near. This war draws to a close. If Richmond is held by the South till the first of November, it will be ours forevermore; for the North will never throw another huge army into the abyss where so many lie; and the war will conclude, beyond a doubt, with the independence of the Southern States. Events have made this city—in itself insignificant—the keystone of the arch. Probably the last immense effort for its destruction which the enemy is now about to make would not be attempted had not Atlanta fallen from the hands of Hood. But Sherman's triumph compels Grant to match it, or sink into insignificance.

According to their well settled custom, the enemy proclaims the intention. Grant himself, in a public speech made during his late journey, has notified his country that whereas "Sherman had scotched the tail in Georgia, he was on his way to crush the head of the rebellion in Virginia." What is of more importance, he has brought up the James fifty-five thousand new troops. It is true that they will hardly do more than make up the depletion of the last two months. It is also true that they are troops of the very meanest descriptions—the substitutes, the crimped levies, the refuse of the Yankee army. But they are not brought here now, in mass, except to be employed immediately. The blow must be struck within the next three weeks, or it cannot be struck at all. Even success would be useless for the election, unless obtained in the coming month.

But it is useless to enumerate the proofs of the proposition which no intelligent observer can treat as doubtful, that the final struggle for Virginia is about to be made below Petersburg; and perhaps, too, in the Valley. Only one fear clouds the reflecting mind. It is not the fear that our generals will be found unequal to their duty, or that our armies are insufficient. It is a fear arising from memories of the past conduct of our central military authority on every crisis. Just when the scale trembles, just when the tiger is about to spring, just when the enemy's columns are about to emerge from the mist, that has hitherto been found their chosen moment to disintegrate our own force, and to attempt insignificant conquest a hundred miles away. Longstreet was sent to threaten Knoxville, while Grant was about to bound on Lookout Mountain; an army was distinguishing itself before "Little Washington" while Butler was landing at Bermuda Hundred; Breckinridge was ordered out of the Valley, while Hunter was entering it. Recollections like these crowd upon the mind and painfully oppress it now. This species of strategy, so often occurring, is the sole fear of the army and the country at this moment. But surely at this time at least, we tremble before shadows. Some personages in history have been styled worse than the untaught, because they were unteachable, but their existence may be doubted. By such stern lessons as the Confederate authorities have received, they must have learned at least this much—that troops must be concentrated in a country at stake, not sent out of it.

FURTHER READINGS

Cavanaugh, Michael Arthur. *The Petersburg Campaign: The Battle of the Crater "The Horrid Pit," June 25–August 6, 1864.* Lynchburg, Va.: H. E. Howard, 1989.

Davis, Stephen. *Atlanta Will Fall: Sherman, Joe Johnston, and the Yankee Heavy Battalions.* Wilmington, Del.: Scholarly Resources, 2001.

Frassanito, William A. *Grant and Lee: The Virginia Campaigns, 1864–1865.* New York: Scribner, 1983.

Glatthaar, Joseph T. *The March to the Sea and Beyond: Sherman's Troops in the Savannah and Carolinas Campaigns.* New York: New York University Press, 1985.

Grimsley, Mark. *And Keep Moving On: The Virginia Campaign, May–June 1864.* Lincoln: University of Nebraska Press, 2002.

Groom, Winston. *Shrouds of Glory: From Atlanta to Nashville—the Last Great Campaign of the Civil War.* New York: Atlantic Monthly Press, 1995.

McDonough, James L. *"War So Terrible": Sherman and Atlanta.* New York: Norton, 1987.

Miles, Jim. *Fields of Glory: A History and Tour Guide of the Atlanta Campaign.* Nashville, Tenn.: Rutledge Hill Press, 1989.

Pleasants, Henry. *Inferno at Petersburg.* Philadelphia: Chilton Book Co., Book Division, 1961.

Reasoner, James. *Shenandoah.* Nashville, Tenn.: Cumberland House, 2002.

Rhea, Gordon C. *To the North Anna River: Grant and Lee, May 13–25, 1864.* Baton Rouge: Louisiana State University Press, 2000.

Scaife, William R. *Hood's Campaign for Tennessee.* Atlanta, Ga.: W. R. Scaife, 1986.

Sommers, Richard J. *Richmond Redeemed: The Siege at Petersburg.* Garden City, N.Y.: Doubleday, 1981.

Wheeler, Richard. *On Fields of Fury: From the Wilderness to the Crater, an Eyewitness History.* New York: HarperCollins, 1991.

32

REPORTING THE WAR, 1865

In a conventional warfare sense, the Confederacy was doomed. Its Army of Northern Virginia was waging a protracted defense of Petersburg, and its resources were dwindling. Far more important, however, was the fact that the southern end of the Confederacy had no defense left. No significant force existed to even slow down William T. Sherman's marauding army. Small forces under Joseph Wheeler and Joseph Johnston could do little more than harass and shadow Sherman's immense force. The Confederate army's manpower situation was so dire in 1865 that Congress debated and passed a bill that would allow slaves to serve in combat positions in return for their freedom at the end of their service. This was an extraordinary step for the Confederacy, one that spoke to the basic premise of its revolution against the American government.

The Confederacy could have waged war in an irregular style, and the capacity for such warfare existed. Cavalry raiders such as the plumed and red-caped Colonel John S. Mosby, paramilitary cutthroats such as William Quantrill, and the formation of the Ku Klux Klan after the war demonstrated that there were white Southerners capable of guerrilla actions. Such tactics on a large scale were somewhat futile, however. Guerrilla war could not protect Southern society. As Sherman rolled through the Deep South, the slave system unraveled as he went. The war against the Union could be continued through unconventional means; the war for the Confederacy could not. Nor could such a war be fought according to the ideals and self-image of the leading Confederates, who saw themselves as gentlemen planters. Sherman's methods were also motivated by a desire to discourage any thought of continuing the war by other means.

Casualties and desertion inspired the belated decision to enlist slaves. There were no illusions about what this meant: Emancipation, for those who fought, and a widely altered social conception of the capabilities of black men. So in the closing months of the war the Confederacy offered to sacrifice part of the labor system it was defending on the altar of military victory. However, the congressional action authorizing the recruitment of slaves into combat units did not occur until March, too late to allow blacks to actually take up arms in defense of the Confederacy and in order to win their freedom.

The Confederacy also appointed Robert E. Lee its supreme military commander in February. Until then, the Confederate army had only theater military commanders who reported to the War Department and Jefferson Davis. Coordinated military command had always been difficult due to the Confederacy's poor communications and logistics. By 1865, the appointment of Lee as supreme commander was mostly a gesture since only one command retained enough troops to make a difference, but it was a decision that had a powerful and positive effect on lagging civilian morale. Lee did attempt to use his power as chief military leader to order a link with Johnston in North Carolina, but it was too late.

After months of engagements along the siege lines at Petersburg, the Confederate army was forced to withdraw from the city in early April. Richmond fell almost immediately. The Union army mercilessly pursued Lee until his remaining 30,000 men were forced to surrender at Appomattox on 9 April. Five days later, Joe Johnston surrendered near Durham Station, North Carolina. Sherman and Johnston arranged such lenient surrender terms for Johnston's that charges of treason were leveled against the Union general. In the flush of victory, these accusations were soon forgotten (not by the fiery-tempered Sherman, however).

There were no more major actions after Appomattox, although minor skirmishes continued. The last fight, a Confederate victory, occurred in Texas. Jefferson Davis was captured near Washington, Georgia, following an arduous flight from Richmond through the Carolinas. The Confederate archives and treasury were traveling with him, and the fact that the treasury gold has never been found has led many to speculate that it is buried somewhere in or near the picturesque little town. Davis was imprisoned at Fort Monroe, Virginia, where, early in his incarceration, he was forced to endure shackles and forbidden to communicate with anyone or to have visitors. His fate, though, was less final than Abraham Lincoln's. The Union president was assassinated on 14 April. This would make the postwar era far more contentious and inconclusive than it might otherwise have been.

WESTERN THEATER

Carolinas Campaign

Sherman's army spent Christmas and New Year's in Savannah, then rested there for about a month before moving out on the final stage of its march of terror through the South. Sherman knew, and had told at least one Georgia woman, that the restraint his men had shown in Georgia would evaporate when they hit the South Carolina state line. He indicated there would be little he could do to control the men once they arrived in the state that was the first to secede, but he also showed little inclination to do so. Sherman had set out on his March to the Sea to "make Georgia howl," but he knew his men intended to bring arrogant South Carolina to its knees.

Sherman's plan was to sweep through the two Carolinas, inflicting as much devastation as possible along the way, and then meet up with Grant in Virginia for the final and total destruction of Lee's Army of Northern Virginia. Lee surrendered before Sherman could reach Grant, but that was the only part of the plan that Sherman's army did not complete. South Carolinians and North Carolinians alike were terrified by the news that Sherman's men were on the move again.

When Sherman's force headed out on 1 February, all eyes were on Charleston. South Carolina Governor Andrew Magrath was frantic to protect his beloved home city. His repeated shrill demands to Richmond for additional troops to repel the invaders asked for far more than the Confederacy had to give. Magrath became so desperate that he negotiated with Governor Zebulon Vance of North Carolina and Governor Joseph E. Brown of Georgia for a "mutual protection pact" that sounded to some like an attempt to repudiate the Confederate government.

Sherman's first target was not Charleston, as Magrath had expected. It was the state capital, Columbia. Johnston, commanding a tiny force at that point, had also expected Sherman to march on Charleston and perhaps Augusta, the site of the Confederacy's only gunpowder manufacturing plant. Each of those cities had been garrisoned with about 10,000 troops. Columbia, though, was essentially undefended and would be "easy pickin's" for the Union army.

The march from Savannah to Columbia was punctuated with small cavalry raids by Major General Hugh Judson Kilpatrick's horsemen. Sherman's cavalry struck at the small towns of Aiken and Lexington and specifically targeted the home of South Carolina writer and journalist William Gilmore Simms. They destroyed his home in order to destroy his library, one of the largest and finest collections of books in the state of South Carolina.

Sherman's men arrived at Columbia on 17 February and before he left, the city had been essentially destroyed. Nearly a third of the city burned to the ground, including the new statehouse. The fire started when locals set bales of cotton on fire to keep them from falling into enemy hands, but it quickly raged out of control with the aid of Sherman's men and gale-force winds. An investigation of the fire after the war found that Sherman himself had not ordered the conflagration and had taken steps to bring it under control, but his enthusiastic soldiers were slow to obey their officers' orders to cease and desist. The ruin of Columbia significantly contributed to Sherman's reputation for ruthlessness toward Southern civilians. The day Sherman captured Columbia, Hardee abandoned Charleston and set out toward North Carolina, where he was to combine forces with Johnston. Sherman rushed to cut off the concentration of the Confederate troops.

Union General John A. Schofield was already operating in North Carolina with the objective of combining his army with Sherman's. Along the way, his army captured Wilmington, North Carolina, on 22 February, the Confederacy's last open port. The Confederate garrisons from Augusta and Charleston abandoned those positions and headed toward North Carolina, too, so as to block Sherman's route toward Grant.

On 15 March, Sherman reached the vicinity of Fayetteville, North Carolina, just south of Raleigh, his next target. Johnston was in a desperate situation. He had too few men to contend with Sherman's 60,000-man legion, but he hoped to defeat at least a portion of the Union army before it could concentrate with Schofield's. Johnston attacked Sherman's advance units near Bentonville on 19 March and was initially successful, but he was unable to hold on to his gains. Sherman's force smashed

Johnston's left, and on 23 March, the Confederates withdrew to Goldsboro where the troops from Augusta and Charleston were rendezvousing.

A by-product of Sherman's march through Georgia and the Carolinas was a much smaller and weaker Confederate press. During his occupation of Atlanta, the newspapers there all either fled or shut down permanently. Several were back in operation within a few weeks but not all. Of the two Savannah newspapers, one closed down and the other was taken over by a Yankee journalist traveling with Sherman's army. The Southern press's voice was becoming fainter.

AN ANONYMOUS REPORT: OPPOSING SHERMAN IN SOUTH CAROLINA

Sherman had been on his move through South Carolina for slightly more than two weeks when an Augusta newspaper picked up this piece from the Edgefield Advertiser, *a newspaper located in a community just across the Savannah River in South Carolina. News was slow to come in about Sherman's movements, though that did not stop newspapers from speculating about the Union army's whereabouts. This story described the feint Kilpatrick's cavalry made on the Edgefield County town of Aiken. Though the fighting there has been referred to as the Battle of Aiken, it was a relatively minor engagement. However, any news of Sherman's whereabouts and doings was welcomed by readers. The* Advertiser *made an important point in its editorial. Up to that point in the war, the people of the South Carolina homefront, beyond Charleston, had been relatively unscathed by the fighting.*

Augusta Constitutionalist, 18 February 1865 (Augusta, Ga.)

FROM THE ADVERTISER
TROUBLOUS TIMES IN EDGEFIELD

During the war, we people of Edgefield have had, compared to the hundreds of other places in the Confederacy, a very calm and pleasant walk on the highway of life. And our walk is still comparatively calm and pleasant. How long will it remain so, God only knows? Lately however, we have been wandering in wet and slippery roads, in bad times and wintry weather. For four days, our whole population was in hourly expectation of being pounced upon by a pack of howling, ravenous, blood thirsty wolves—of being at any moment, night or day, gnashed, gnawed, crashed and gobbled up, in the most merciless and ferocious manner. Women imagined all sorts of battle, murder and sudden death. Children had "Raw Head and Bloody bones" ever before their eyes. Men of large property were green and yellow and grinned with horrible agony. But let us narrate facts. Early on Thursday morning last, it was announced among us that a large and formidable body of Yankee cavalry, under Kilpatrick, had entered Aiken during the previous night. Refugees and straggling soldiers, passing through from below, confirmed this rumor, and added that Kilpatrick was passing on to Graniteville and Vaucluse and would no doubt devastate the whole country. The supporting force of Edgefield district being in camp near the village, our vigilant and energetic enrolling officer, Lieutenant Moses, immediately chose from that body a number of brave

and well mounted men and departed with them towards Aiken, intending to establish a line of couriers between that place and Edgefield; this he did, and to him and them the community is not a little indebted.

About noon on Thursday, some half dozen soldiers from Wheeler's command, in charge of 150 or 200 broken down cavalry horses, entered our town—horses and all. On the approach of the Yankees, they had quitted a recruiting camp on the South Carolina Railroad, and were taking their horses up the country. They reported no Yankees in Aiken, but a large force twelve miles below. These bare and bony *chevaux de battle* were the Yankees that had entered Aiken the night before!

By nightfall on Thursday, our courier brought us reliable intelligence that none of the enemy had entered Aiken; and that a considerable body of Wheeler's cavalry was between that point and the enemy. In the meantime, our people, though for the most part calm and collected, were busy setting their houses in order for the reception of the foe; or rather in turning them topsy turvy. Provisions, furniture, clothing, were sent off and lodged in safe places; silver, jewelry, glass, china &.,&., were consigned to the safe and silent bosom of earth. Oh that we possessed half the gold and silver now hid in Edgefield soil! We would snap our fingers scornfully at Potosi, Golconda, and Ophir.

Friday was comparatively a quiet day, the couriers bringing

news from time to time that Wheeler was successfully holding the enemy at bay some miles below Aiken. In the course of Friday night, however, a courier brought tidings that the Yankees had entered Aiken and burned it. Refugees and stragglers again confirmed the report, and many strange and horrible items of information. This report was premature; the enemy did not enter Aiken until Saturday. Nor did they burn it, or any part of it.

Excitement in Edgefield was now high and wild, and continued so until Saturday night, when it was ascertained for certainty that the enemy had been driven out of Aiken and pushed back some miles down the railroad. During the day the enemy had dashed into Aiken, and Wheeler's cavalry had engaged them fiercely in the very streets of the town, whipped them back and finally compelled them to retire discomfited. On this day, Sunday, Wheeler shipped them in three or four different fights in and around Aiken. General Wheeler may have a great many worthless men in his command, evidently has, but after this, let us cease to talk about his troops not fighting.

On Sunday, according to the report of our couriers, the enemy retired from the railroad and made off eastwardly towards Orangeburg. Gen. Wheeler had followed them, going to Merritt's bridge, which leads across the Edisto from Barnwell into Lexington. This bridge is thirteen miles from Aiken, and twenty-three from Edgefield.—The Yankee force operating lately below Aiken was a part of Kilpatrick's cavalry; it is said they have a large infantry support. For two days past, we have been tranquil and free from war's wild alarms. We know not how long this tranquillity will last. Perhaps but few days. God grant it forever. Wonder if the earth is giving up its treasures!

DR. NAGLE: SHERMAN'S ADVANCE INTO NORTH CAROLINA

Sherman was on the move. He had passed through Columbia, and all eyes were turning to Charlotte, North Carolina, anticipated to be his target. Once again, though, Sherman surprised the Southerners and moved out instead toward the North Carolina capital. He would meet light, ineffectual resistance. The Dr. Nagle mentioned in the following story was a reporter for the Confederate Press Association.

Augusta Constitutionalist, 23 February 1865 (Augusta, Ga.)

[Dr. Nagle, of the Press Association, has favored us with the following interesting items:

Sherman's force consists of about 50,000 men of all arms. He is evidently advancing on Charlotte, effectually destroying the Railroad and everything else, along a wide track. Apparently, his intention is to reach Greenesboro, and destroy the Danville Road, avoiding castles and fortified places.

Columbia was occupied by the enemy for a short time.

Troops are being well armed and equipped as they arrive here.

The wagon train of the Army of Tennessee is arriving and will rendezvous at Washington, Ga. Parties going to Columbia and Richmond pass through Augusta.

General D. H. Hill has been relieved from the command of this military district. Gen. B. D. Fry succeeds to the command of the District of Georgia, in addition to his present duty as Commandant of Post. Much satisfaction is expressed by the people at the appointment.

The most extravagant prices ever paid in this country for goods occurred at auction yesterday in this city.

AN ANONYMOUS REPORT: EVACUATION OF CHARLESTON

With all the usual means of disseminating news breaking down, Southern newspapers in 1865 were much slower than usual in reporting important events. This story, written as the result of an interview with a railroad employee, was the first news in Augusta of the fall of Charleston. Without the usual sources available, it was impossible to verify the story, but any news, by this point, was better than no news.

Augusta Constitutionalist, 25 February 1865 (Augusta, Ga.)

AUTHENTIC FROM CHARLESTON
THE EVACUATION—TERRIBLE CALAMITY
THREE HUNDRED WOMEN AND CHILDREN
KILLED

We have at length what we conceive to be authentic intelligence of the fall of Charleston. It were worse than useless to bemoan over this event, though it will cause poignant sorrow in the hearts of thousands. Not only those whose homes were in the beautiful "city by the sea," will lament the giving up of the place to the enemy; who for four years have vainly thundered at its portals; but there are myriads of sympathizing hearts throughout Christendom who must mourn the military necessity that has yielded to our vandal foe the seat of so much elegance, refinement, hospitality and true chivalry. Fallen though Charleston be, her name will live in history, and her heroic defence be chronicled on the brightest pages of that record which transmits to posterity the matchless deeds of this revolution.

The evacuation was successfully completed on Thursday, the 16th of February, between the hours of twelve and one o'clock. Our troops left on the cars of the North Eastern railway going in the direction of Kingstree.

In addition to the fall of the city, of itself sorrowful in the extreme, we have to record one of the most horrible calamities that ever befell any population. The Depot of the South Carolina Railroad company between Mary and Ann streets was filled with stores of the Commissary, Quartermaster and Ordnance Department. Upon the departure of our forces such supplies as could not be removed were allowed to the indigent citizens, and the building was thrown open for them. While crowded with women and children some fixed ammunition was exploded, destroying the house and causing the death of three hundred persons. The sight was a most pitiable one an beggars description.

The flames immediately spread with the greatest rapidity, and it is feared that a large portion of the city must have been destroyed. The fire was in progress when the Federal troops landed, and they immediately tendered assistance and protection to the firemen engaged in staying the conflagration.

The explosion is supposed to have been purely accidental, some boys having been seen engaged in amusing themselves with shells. It was certainly not caused by any military order.

There is now no enemy between this city and Charleston, the line of the South Carolina Railroad being occupied at no point.

We are indebted to Captain Disher of the South Carolina Railroad for the above interesting items. He left Johnson's Turn Out yesterday, where he conversed with one of General Young's scouts who had just arrived from Ridgeville.

The story circulated of an alleged Yankee Indignity to the British Consul and flag, is without foundation. England has no commercial representative in Savannah at present. Mr. Molyneux, the Consul, died in Paris some months ago, and Mr. Fullerton, the Vice Consul, was ordered out of the country by the President about a year ago, for insolent interference with the conscript law.

Fifty three officers, including Gen. G. P. Harrison, a private citizen of much worth, captured by Sherman, have arrived at Washington from Savannah, and were committed to the Old Capitol.

J. W. Morrel and Isaac Cohen, leading merchants of the city, have died.

No order for the banishment of the families of Confederate officers had been executed at last accounts, though the policy was still under discussion.

WILLIAM W. HOLDEN: UNION ADVANCE ON WILMINGTON

The next important Southern city to fall after Charleston was Wilmington, the Confederacy's last open port. Lee had earlier predicted that if Wilmington fell, he would not be able to maintain his army, and after the fall of Fort Fisher in January, it would only be a matter of time before the vastly stronger Union combined naval and land force would capture the coastal city. The loss of the city received little coverage throughout the Confederacy because virtually no newspaper had a correspondent on the scene. All relied on telegraphic or exchange coverage, which was constructed from interviews with people who had escaped from the city. Even then, few details were available.

Raleigh Weekly Standard, 1 March 1865

FROM WILMINGTON

The Goldsborough *Journal* of the 24th contains some information from Wilmington, most probably furnished by the Editor of the Wilmington *Journal* who was in that town. We shall get no more papers from Wilmington soon. It is believed that Hagood's brigade, with the exception of the 7th battalion, was captured by the enemy. Our troops retreated across the northeast branch of the Cape Fear, at what is known as Big Bridge Ferry. They were pursued by the enemy, and some skirmishing took place. The *Journal* complains that the authorities were too silent in relation to the approach of the enemy and the probabilities of the capture of the town. "About the sacking of the town of Wilmington," says that paper, "we believe very little of it, indeed almost nothing. All citizens were out as a guard for private residences, especially those in which ladies resided. Of course there will be suffering, but all those who are compelled to stay in Wilmington ought not to be denounced. They are there, and physically and pecuniarily they are unable to leave. There are good and true men and women among them.

Gen. Schofield is probably in force no further north of Wilmington than Northeast River, some fifteen miles, at which point the exchange of prisoners is going on. We fear that a considerable portion of our forces fell into the hands of the enemy. We have no idea of the number of our troops in that quarter. Those mainly engaged with the enemy were of Hoke's division. We notice a conjecture in the *Confederate* of Monday morning, that Schofield "will try next the Fayetteville route, or attempt to effect a junction with Sherman."

DR. NAGLE: GENERAL JOHNSTON'S BATTLE NEAR BENTONVILLE; OCCUPIED SAVANNAH

One of the last major battles in the Western Theater occurred near Bentonville, North Carolina. It was the largest battle ever fought in North Carolina and the only serious attempt General Joseph E. Johnston's men would mount to stem Sherman's march through the Carolinas. Johnston's 20,000 men did their best to halt Sherman's advance toward Goldsboro but were forced to evacuate by torch light on 21 March. The great slaughter of 5,000 enemy soldiers referred to in the story actually equaled 1,500 killed, wounded, and missing Union soldiers over the two-day battle. The Confederate army, on the other hand, lost nearly 2,500 men in the Battle of Bentonville. With news about the battle so scarce, the author of this story, a reporter for the Confederate Press Association, turned to a second topic: the state of affairs in occupied Savannah.

Augusta Constitutionalist, 23 March 1865 (Augusta, Ga.)

GEN. JOHNSTONS' BATTLE

[DR. NAGLE'S DISPATCH.]

AUGUSTA, March 23.

General Johnston attacked the army under the immediate command of Sherman near Bentonville, Sunday morning, the 19th, and at nightfall had killed, wounded and captured five thousand. Our loss about five hundred. The battle was renewed on Monday morning and was progressing at 4 P.M., Monday. Results not known but good.

By special request of General Joseph E. Johnston, Surgeon A. J. Foard is placed on his staff as Medical Director of the Army. By orders received from the War Department on the 20th instant, he is relieved from duty as Medical Inspector of the hospitals and armies in Georgia, Alabama and Mississippi and assigned to duty with General Johnston in the field.

General S. D. Lee left Augusta on the 17th, Address Army of Tennessee.

Ladies who left Savannah on the 16th instant, report that the city is garrisoned entirely by negro troops, officered by white fellows. Their pickets are very insolent and strict.

The Yankees were very anxious to learn the result of Sherman's operations. Many fears were entertained that he had received serious opposition from General Johnston. They eagerly seek news from Augusta and other points in the Confederacy, but do not permit anything to be brought out.

Scouting parties, composed of negroes, hunt our scouts in the vicinity of that city with dogs. They capture all the able bodied negroes they find on the plantations in their route, and place them in the Yankee army.

Northern journals declare that Andy Johnston was immured in the asylum for insanity near Silver Springs by a cabal with Preston King and Blair to manage the matter.

They look on his accession to the second position in the Executive Administration of National affairs as disgraceful and an insult to the people.

A competent board of medical examiners pronounced him to be laboring under temporary aberration of mind—insanity caused by beastly intoxications, requiring his confinement.

It is expected the opposition faction will manage his overthrow, despite the influence and interference of his friends with his patron Seward at the head.

On Sunday evening the 19th, scouts from Chalk Bluff, twenty miles down the river from this city, reported to General Fry that they heard heavy and rapid discharges of artillery during the evening as though a hard battle was occurring somewhere northeast. On Monday noon the telegraph announced the battle of Bentonville.

The firing was heard a distance of more than two hundred miles.

Yankees are concentrating a force at Corinth, Miss., and Pittsburg Landing on Tennessee River.

REFUGEE: EVACUATION OF FAYETTEVILLE

As Sherman's invading troops neared Fayetteville, North Carolina, the town's newspaper, the Observer, *continued to publish. The* Observer's *legendary editor, E. J. Hale, had been one of North Carolina's political king-makers for decades, and he showed his characteristic aplomb by continuing to print and distribute copies of his paper—free to Confederate soldiers—even as the enemy threat loomed nearer and nearer. Eventually, though, Hale was forced to flee, along with the rest of the Fayetteville citizens, and his newspaper office was wrecked by the conquering Union army. The source of the information, the* Biblical Recorder, *was the state's Southern Baptist newspaper.*

Charlotte Western Democrat, 28 March 1865

THE EVACUATION OF FAYETTEVILLE

The following interesting account of the evacuation of Fayetteville is taken from the Biblical Recorder:

When Gen. Sherman started on his raid from Savannah, it was generally believed in military circles that he would follow the course of the railroad from Columbia to Charlotte. Preparations were made to check him before he reached the latter place. On arriving at Chester he turned his column to the right, captured Camden, and moved on the main road to Cheraw. Gen. Hardee was compelled to evacuate the town and retreat to Rockingham. He was then ordered by General Johnston to fall back upon Fayetteville. On reaching the vicinity, on Wednesday the 8th, he took a position six miles from town, where he was reinforced by the command of Lieut. General Hampton. It was believed that a stand would be made and the place defended. It did seem that the splendid arsenal, the seven cotton and three oil factories, &c., made it a place of sufficient importance to the government to make a more determined defence. On Thursday the artillery and trains began to cross the river. Then it was announced that Gen. Johnston had left, and all hope of defence abandoned. Thursday was a gloomy day. The weather was inclement; the people sad; the soldiers disappointed. The citizens began to secrete their provisions, plate, jewelry, &c. The ladies had provisions cooked for the soldiers, and the citizens who were likely to be molested began to prepare to leave.

Friday was fast day. In the morning it rained heavily. The church bells called the people to the house of prayer, but few obeyed the call. About noon the clouds passed away, and the sun shone as brightly and the evening was as calm as if the sound of war had never been heard in the land. Late in the afternoon it was announced that the infantry were entrenching, and this led many to believe that the town was not lost. The wish was father to the thought. To those conversant with military movements it indicated an immediate retreat. About sunset nearly five hundred prisoners, captured in the morning, were brought in and hurried to the front. As the shades of darkness began to cover the old town, the quartermaster and ordnance wagons moved towards the river and the infantry began to pass to the front. Those of us who intended leaving were assured that we could not remain till morning; and we retired to our homes and partook of our evening repast with feelings that are not easily described. Loved ones separated; fathers embraced their children; husbands and wives parted— but I must stop. The grief of such partings is too sacred for the public eye. On hurrying to the streets, I found them thronged with soldiers. It took me three hours to cross the bridge, just one mile from my residence. On crossing we repaired to the house of a friend, and sought a few hour's repose.

Saturday morning, we returned to the river. Soldiers and citizens were hurrying across. The enemy had entered the town, and been driven back in confusion. The cavalry on the outposts were drawn in and a line formed for the defence of the bridge. The troops crossed in a very orderly, quiet manner. Just before the last detachment of cavalry crossed, the steamers and flats in the river were fired. These well known favorites floated from their moorings as the flames shot up towards the heavens. The enemy, in force, entered the town and commenced firing upon the rear of our retreating column.

The confusion among the citizens was, of course, intense. In a few moments the streets were cleared, and the troops engaged in a spirited fight at long range. Just as soon as the last detachment crossed, the bridge was fired. In a few moments it was enveloped in flames and fell with a crash that resembled the roar of artillery. A 32-pounder was posted in front of the bridge, so as to command a portion of Hay street, and all that portion of it which passes through what is called Campbellton. The street was in a few moments crowded with mounted men. The roar of the flames that were consuming the bridge, boats and old ware houses, the exultant cheers of the invaders, the screams of excited females, the hallooing of thoughtless boys, all broke upon the stillness of a lovely morning. The enemy rush in triumph towards the bridge, heedless of danger, when a solid shot, from a 32-pounder, strikes the head of their column and passes through it. Then, after a momentary pause, the column closes, and on they come. The next moment a shell is thrown into their midst; the shell explodes; there is confusion; another and another, and the street is deserted. Gen. Hampton then discovered that they were endeavoring to reach a [*unreadable*] to the left of the bridge. To do this they had to pass over an open field. The gun was moved to a point which commanded the field, and a few well directed shots completed the evacuation. Scarcely a man was cut off, and no stores were lost.

E. J. Hale, the *veteran* editor of the Observer, had just finished working off the usual issue of his paper on Thursday. Having a good supply of paper on hand, he put his press to work on Friday and supplied the troops with the Observer gratis.

The citizens, up to the night of the evacuation, continued to receive Confederate money. The ladies were as indefatigable as ever in ministering to the wants of the soldiers. They have the proud satisfaction of knowing that the troops will never forget them. They are a noble people.

REFUGEE.

EASTERN THEATER

Petersburg to Appomattox

While Union forces were finishing off the Confederacy in the Deep South, in Virginia, Grant concentrated on keeping Lee pinned down between Petersburg and Richmond. Through the winter and early spring 1865, Grant tightened his grasp on Petersburg by driving deeper and deeper into Dinwiddie County. Grant was able to accomplish this in spite of diverting several brigades to North Carolina to assist with the assaults on Fort Fisher and Wilmington. Lee put up the best fight he could. In late March, Confederate troops under John B. Gordon launched a surprise attack. Lee hoped the attack would allow his army to slip out of Grant's grasp, but it only succeeded in making matters worse for the Confederates. The Southerners were able to conquer the position they were attacking, but they were pushed back again in a four-hour battle.

Grant began his final offensive on 29 March with an attack near the Dinwiddie county seat. He caught Lee by surprise and was able to mass sixteen divisions against the seven Southern divisions protecting Lee's communications line into Petersburg. The Southerners, under George Pickett and Fitzhugh Lee, counterattacked and drove the Union cavalry back to Dinwiddie Courthouse, but the Confederate forces were routed the next day near Five Forks.

On 2 April Grant achieved a decisive victory at Petersburg. Union infantry spearheads broke through Lee's thin lines. Only Gordon's force at Petersburg was able to hold its position, but he was virtually encircled by Union troops. Lee had only one choice: Evacuate Petersburg and Richmond and get his army to North Carolina, where he could join forces with Johnston. Lee sent Longstreet to Petersburg to reinforce Gordon long enough to buy additional time to evacuate Richmond, and he sent word to Davis that it was time to flee.

Davis was at church that Sunday morning when Lee's telegraph arrived. He rose and quietly left to go to his office. Davis had been expecting Lee to abandon Petersburg, had known the general could not hold out forever, but the speed with which the city had fallen caught him by surprise. Davis telegraphed Lee, asking if it was possible for the general to stall the Union army longer, so as to facilitate the evacuation of Richmond. Lee's answer was a terse no. He had given Davis all the time he could. That night, Davis and his cabinet were on a train to Danville, a town to the southwest of Richmond and right on the Virginia/North Carolina border. Davis paused in Danville, fully expecting Lee to arrive to protect the town and the government.

Lee had no hope of making it to Danville, though. The better supplied, equipped, and fed Union army was moving faster than Lee could, which made it impossible for him to make for North Carolina and join up with Johnston south of Danville. Instead, Grant was pushing Lee due west, toward a river and a small place that shared a name: Appomattox. By 8 April, the Union army blocked Lee's way west as well. Breckinridge, by then the Confederate secretary of war, reported to Davis that Lee's situation was close to hopeless. That night, a young officer who had slipped through the Union lines made it to Danville and reported to Davis and his cabinet that surrender was imminent. On 9 April, Lee and Grant met around midday at Appomattox in the home of Wilmer McLean, who had fled Manassas in 1861 to get away from the fighting.

The surrender of Lee has been the inspiration for many myths, including the one about the great Confederate general proffering his sword to Grant, and the Union general's refusal. That myth sprang up almost spontaneously at the moment, for it was reported as truth in Confederate newspapers. The surrender was not without its poignant moments, though. On 12 April, Gordon was leading the Confederate soldiers to surrender their arms when a Union general, Joshua Chamberlain, ordered his men to salute the ragtag, exhausted Southerners. Gordon, touched by the gesture, had his men return the honor.

The surrender at Appomattox was, for all intents and purposes, the end of the Civil War. It would be many weeks before word spread to the far reaches of the Confederacy that the war was over, and it would be a year before Andrew Johnson issued a proclamation declaring the hostilities over. In that year, much happened to reconcile the sections and much happened to push them further apart, particularly Lincoln's assassination on 14 April. Three days later, Johnston and Sherman began negotiating an armistice in North Carolina, but the terms were considered too generous, and the U.S. Congress rejected the arrangement. Johnston finally surrendered on 26 April.

LARKIN: LETTER FROM RICHMOND

Robert E. Lee was among the supporters of the bill to draft slaves into the Confederate army. His support was imminently practical. Lee, somehow, was supposed to keep Richmond out of the hands of the Union army and take back all the territory captured elsewhere in the South. But Lee was hemmed in at Petersburg, and he did not have enough men in the field to break his way through, just as there had not been enough men in Georgia and the Carolinas to subdue Sherman. To compound Lee's problems, citizen morale was flagging in the wake of all the many reverses of the Confederate cause in 1864. Further, a Tennessee representative, Henry S. Foote, had thrown up his hands in frustration with the Davis government's willingness to stomp on individual rights or to end the war. Foote left Congress and traveled to the North, hoping to work out peace terms himself. The Union secretary of state rebuffed Foote's advances.

Augusta Constitutionalist, 5 January 1865 (Augusta, Ga.)

Letter from Richmond.
RICHMOND, Dec. 29th, 1864.

"Sherman's army will be decimated;" and "Savannah will be held to the last extremity," had deluded our people to a full confidence in the false assurances of (what now appears) almost a shameless military censor. The fall of Savannah was totally unexpected, and created a gloom and despondency I have never before witnessed in the Capitol. Hardeville will never claim her own until she has a full receipt for all the military leaders who amuse themselves by feeding our people with false hopes only to be crushed, and grind their heroic spirits to dust. This may be military "strategy," or "secrecy," or "necessity," but it is not what is due to, or expected by, a brave people.

The heavy raiding column of the enemy in Southwestern Virginia seems to have accomplished all it was sent out for, and has returned to East Tennessee. They succeeded in destroying a large amount of the rolling stock, and some fifty miles of the Virginia & Tennessee railroad, the Wythe county lead mines and the [unreadable] works—the latter, I hear was almost totally destroyed. Many and horrible were outrages perpetrated upon the citizens of the county through which they massed. Neither age nor sex could claim immunity at the hands of the dastardly scoundrels.

The currency bill has passed the House by a decided vote, and is now under discussion in the Senate, where it will, it is thought, be passed without much opposition, after going through the "regular channels."

We are again assured that Wilmington is "safe." The attack on Fort Fisher has commenced in dead earnest, and all eyes are turned in that direction. We hope the great efforts, we know the Government is making to hold this important seaport, may be successful. Great confidence is felt here of the result.

The gallant partizan, Colonel John Singleton Mosby, has again been badly wounded, though it is reported not to be dangerous.

True to his threat, Hon. H. S. Foote, of Tennessee, has not been in his seat since Monday.

LARKIN.

AN ANONYMOUS REPORT: BATTLE IN FRONT OF PETERSBURG

For months, both the Union and the Confederate armies had been entrenched around Petersburg. Both sides were expecting decisive results in 1865, and in late March, both sides began making the initial moves in a short-lived campaign that did indeed lead to a decisive result—Lee's surrender on 9 April at Appomattox.

Augusta Constitutionalist, 28 March 1865 (Augusta, Ga.)

BATTLE IN FRONT OF PETERSBURG

PETERSBURG, March 26.

About 4 o'clock this morning General Lee attacked the enemy on our left in the vicinity of the Appomattox, assaulting and capturing two lines of works, and one or more heavy forts.

Our men advanced well into action, but the enemy massed his artillery so heavily in the neighborhood of the forts, and was enabled to pour such a terrible enfilading fire through our ranks that it was deemed best to withdraw.

The captured works were therefore abandoned, and our troops reoccupied their original position.

Gens. Gordon's and Bushrod Johnson's divisions were the troops engaged on our side.

Our loss was several hundred. Five hundred prisoners were captured from the enemy, among them Gen. McLaughlin, and a number of officers.

The Yankee General Warren is reported killed.

On our side Brigadier General Terry was wounded. Many pieces of artillery and mortars are captured. The latter were abandoned, and some of the former brought off.

The attack was a surprise to the enemy.

Their lines were swept for a distance of five hundred yards right and left. The enemy made two efforts to recover the captured works which were handsomely repulsed. It was found, however, that enclosed works in the rear, commanding the enemies main line could only be taken at a great sacrifice, and the troops were withdrawn to their original position.

AN ANONYMOUS REPORT: SHERIDAN'S RAID IN SHENANDOAH VALLEY

The following story, reprinted from the Richmond Sentinel, *detailed Sheridan's operations in the Shenandoah Valley. In his raids, Sheridan destroyed all railroads and rolling stock he could find, while occasionally fighting small engagements with Confederate troops. The engagement at Waynesboro described in this story allowed Sheridan to crush what was left of Early's army.*

Augusta Constitutionalist, 31 March 1865 (Augusta, Ga.)

[From the Richmond Sentinel.]

SHERIDAN'S RAID

From the reports published by the enemy and the accounts which have gained publicity in our own papers, we make up the following memorandum of Sheridan's cavalry expedition:

Sheridan's force consists of the 1st cavalry division, General Merritt; the 3d cavalry division, General Custar, and one brigade of the 2d cavalry division, commanded by Colonel Caphart. Four pieces of artillery accompanied the expedition. The whole numbered five to six thousand men.

General Sheridan broke camp on the 27th. He moved very rapidly, reaching Staunton, as is alleged, on the third day.

The next morning, (March 2d,) Sheridan pushed for Waynesboro, Custar's division in the advance. Near Waynesboro, Custar encountered Early's small force, and speedily dispersed it. The Yankee accounts claim the capture of eighty-seven officers and one thousand one hundred and sixty-five privates, seven cannon and one hundred wagons, ambulances, &c. General Early escaped. The Yankees claim to have captured his staff; also a railroad train, laden with stores, artillery, &c.

The next day (Friday, the 3d inst.,) Sheridan entered Charlottesville about two p.m., without opposition. The mayor and civil authorities met him outside and surrendered the town, receiving a promise of protection. General Merritt's headquarters were at Mrs. B. H. Shackleford's; General Sheridan's at Mrs. E. Cole's. The supplies of citizens were seized, and the thieving around town was universal. The factories in reach were destroyed. On Monday morning, the 5th, they evacuated Charlottesville, leaving in four columns, carrying off many negroes with them. A detail of their subsequent operations is, for the present, contraband.

AN ANONYMOUS REPORT: REPORT OF FIGHTING AROUND PETERSBURG

The Appomattox Campaign, Lee's last, officially began on 29 March when Grant's army moved to cut the Southside Railroad, Petersburg's major supply line. The following story describes some of the early action in the campaign that led up to the first decisive battle of the campaign at Five Forks on 1 April.

Augusta Constitutionalist, 1 April 1865 (Augusta, Ga.)

FROM PETERSBURG

RICHMOND, March 30.

The Petersburg Express of this morning says:

Last night at 11 o'clock the enemy opened on our lines near the Appomattox with a fearful artillery fire, while a simultaneous movement made on the part of their infantry.

The troops of Gen. Gordon repulsed the troops with coolness.

Up to 12 o'clock the fighting was continued with great rigor and fierceness.

The enemy in all made five separate assaults—all of them being repulsed.

The enemy's loss must have been immense.—They came in swarms, supposed to be several lines, and we are informed that the slaughter was fearful.

The gallantry of our troops was displayed in the most gratifying manner. Their conduct is the theme of universal praise. During the entire fight, which lasted two hours, not a man was seen coming to the rear.

P.S.—An officer just from the front says the enemy charged up within ten feet of the muzzles of our guns, and were literally mowed down. Our loss unprecedentedly small.

LATER FROM PETERSBURG

RICHMOND, March 30.

Passengers from Petersburg say that the reports of the fight last night are greatly exaggerated. The enemy made demonstrations on a portion of General Gordon's lines, and were repulsed.

The cannonading was very heavy, and distinctly heard here.

AN ANONYMOUS REPORT: NEWS OF UNION BREAKTHROUGH AT PETERSBURG

Grant's army had begun moving in late March, and by 1 April, it was poised for the final assault on the beleaguered Petersburg. The attack came on 2 April. Lee was able to hold off Grant all through the day, but that night he began the evacuation of his forces from Richmond and Petersburg toward Amelia Courthouse.

Richmond Examiner, 3 April 1865

THE WAR NEWS

The decisive battle of the war in Virginia, as far as concerns the fate of Richmond, is believed to have been fought yesterday. On Friday and Saturday there had been preliminary skirmishing of a determined character on the Petersburg lines, but not until daylight yesterday morning did the storm of battle burst with all its fury. At that hour General Grant made a general attack upon General Lee. The front of battle was many miles in extent, stretching from Appomattox east of Petersburg, south of that city, and thence westward to the Southside railroad. General Lee's lines were penetrated in several places, and all attempts to recover the lost ground were unsuccessful.

This is believed to decide the fate of Richmond. It is not for us to write any particulars as to the future.

AN ANONYMOUS REPORT: LATEST FROM LEE'S ARMY

Readers were anxious for the latest news from Virginia, and miraculously, the telegraph lines continued to reach the lower South. The news, though, was not encouraging, despite this writer's feeble attempt to offer some ray of hope by mentioning Northern casualties and the supposed fear in the North about the prospects of war with a foreign nation. Nevertheless, Lee was still on the run, fighting was heavy, and prospects for the South were growing dimmer daily.

Augusta Constitutionalist, 11 April 1865 (Augusta, Ga.)

LATEST FROM LEE'S ARMY
HEAVY FIGHTING

DANVILLE, April 9.

General Lee has moved to the vicinity of Farmville, followed by Grant, fighting daily.

There was heavy fighting on Thursday. No particulars.

The enemy have established hospitals at the Junction, where there is a large number of their wounded. Their loss was very heavy in the late fights.

They are not approaching this way on the line of the Richmond and Danville Railroad.

Communication being still open to Keysville.

A wounded soldier who escaped from the enemy says they are very uneasy about a foreign war.

It is reported that a courier from the army brings a New York Herald which says, the Emperor Napoleon recognized this Government on the 5th of March.

LATER FROM DANVILLE

DANVILLE, 9th.

A column of cavalry is reported at Henry C.H. Thirty eight miles from here, probably Stoneman's.

A slight skirmish took place near there Saturday without results.

A column of the enemy is reported near Lynchburg.

Persons coming out from Richmond confirm the burning and say the enemy treated the blacks very harshly.

AN ANONYMOUS REPORT: EVACUATION OF RICHMOND

Lee's army was no longer able to protect Richmond. His soldiers evacuated, the Confederate government fled, and citizens were left to fend for themselves as best they could. Davis and his government evacuated on 2 April, hoping to reestablish the Confederate cause in the trans-Mississippi. They took with them the treasury and as many government papers as they could carry. Many citizens did not have the luxury of escape; they had nowhere to go. The Richmond mayor and his staff met a small party of Union officers around 5:30 A.M. on 3 April with a flag of truce. Later that morning, U.S. flags were raised over city hall and the state capitol. The fleeing Confederate army had set fires that decimated a huge section of the city.

Augusta Constitutionalist, 14 April 1865 (Augusta, Ga.)

THE EVACUATION OF RICHMOND

The Danville (Va.) Register of Wednesday, April 6th, states that persons who left the capital Sunday night and Monday morning, represent that the scene which followed the evacuation of the city by our troops, beggars all description. To preserve order and protect the property of the citizens who unavoidably remained there, as far as could be done, the 19th Virginia militia under Colonel Evans, was placed on police duty in the city, to await the coming of the enemy; but accounts state they failed to render any aid or protection to the people whatever. On Sunday night a mob of the lower classes of the city, composed, it is said, mostly of the foreign element, visited a number of the largest store houses of the city and robbed them of their contents.

It is affirmed that Main street was pillaged and then burned, and that some of the milling establishments were also committed to the flames. We have no doubt that a considerable portion of that brave city has been laid in ashes, and a number of its people insulted, outraged, robbed and massacred. How painful the thought that the place should be given over to rapine and plunder even before the public enemy entered its limits! But the fact only proves that the people of Richmond have had secret enemies in their own midst scarcely less savage and even more treacherous and vindictive than the open foe.

We are told that the people banded together, during the violent proceeding of the mob, and resisted them with force, a street fight ensuing in which several persons were killed.

No intelligence has reached us of the enemy's troops occupying the city. The last trains on the Danville railroad which came out of the place left Monday morning, and passengers upon them had heard nothing from the enemy. The greater portion of Grant's army was transferred to the southside of James river some days ago, only the command of Gen Ord, which is composed mostly if not entirely of negro troops, being left on the north side. This command will enter and occupy the city. Some of our people who are acquainted with the character of Gen. Ord, think they have reason to hope that his treatment of the unfortunate people of Richmond will not be so hard and cruel and inhuman, as that which has fallen upon the heads of our fellow citizens in some other captured cities.

All the specie and other valuables belonging to the banks in Richmond was removed from the city on Sunday, and have been carried to places of safety.

A considerable amount of goods purchased by the State, for distribution to the people, we regret to learn, had to be left behind. Also the archives remained in the city, but we perceive no motive the enemy can have in destroying them, as they will, no doubt, endeavor to occupy the city permanently and establish a State Government at Richmond under the Federal Union.

The newspapers of Richmond, we suppose, all fell into the hands of the enemy. The evacuation of the city was so sudden and unexpected—scarcely any one being prepared for it—that no time was left for the removal of so cumbrous an establishment as a city newspaper office. In a few days we may expect to hear that the Enquirer or the Whig or the Examiner is issued as a Yankee paper.

All the rolling stock of the Richmond and Danville railroad, in running order was saved, on the retreat from Richmond. A few old cars, not in a movable condition were left at Manchester. No trains were captured by the enemy near the Junction, as was at one time reported; and indeed we do not believe that any body of Yankees had struck the road, at any point up to yesterday evening.

The Secretary of War, the Quartermaster General, Commissary general, and a number of other officers of the Government left Richmond on horseback, and will probably arrive at this place to-morrow.

Should General Lee establish his lines east of the Junction, we suppose the State Legislature will be convened at Lynchburg.

CARTOUCHE: TERRIBLE BATTLE OF PETERSBURG

The Constitutionalist *took from its exchanges with the* Danville Register *another story of the fall of Richmond, this one written by the Virginia newspaper's correspondent as he fled the Confederate capital on the last train out. The writer's story was told with great excitement and sadness. The Confederacy's hopes had all died. The cause was lost.*

Augusta Constitutionalist, 19 April 1865 (Augusta, Ga.)

FROM THE DANVILLE REGISTER
TERRIBLE BATTLE OF PETERSBURG, 2D OF APRIL

ON CARS TO DANVILLE,
April 3d, 1865.

Richmond is fallen—Petersburg captured—our noble army defeated! Sad day. Secretly and silently, Grant moved a heavy force from north of the river, on Saturday, the 1st of April, the fight commenced, but on Sunday the decisive battle was fought. The enemy's line of battle extended from the banks of the Appomattox, east of Petersburg, thence westward to the Southside railroad. The Confederate lines were penetrated at several points and the unity of the army destroyed. Loss on both sides very heavy; the precise amount not ascertained at this early date. It is said that General A. P. Hill was killed and Fitzhugh Lee mortally wounded. Lane's N.C. Brigade is cut to pieces and captured. General Longstreet came up with reinforcements, but was utterly unable to restore the order of battle. General Gordon drove the enemy back and succeeded in regaining his lost positions, except that of Rive's salient; Gordon is regarded as the hero of the day.

On the reception of this news, all Richmond was in the greatest consternation. Every truck, dray or other carriage that was in the city was placed in immediate requisition on Sunday afternoon. Main street was covered with vehicles taking out beds, chairs and other furniture from the city. People running in every direction with anxious countenances enquiring the news. Greatest activity prevailed in Government offices; heads of departments, packing up records and shipping by rail. The President and other high officials left at 8 P.M., on a special train. At night a lawless mob commenced breaking open stores, restaurants, banking houses, and this morning the sidewalks were covered with the debris of the gutted establishments. As I hurried down Main street at an early hour this morning, on my way from the hotel to the depot, I noticed particularly the houses of Powhatan Weiseger and Genet; they were turned upside down. The loss of the latter was estimated at $500,000.

A little after midnight the city was terribly concussed by the explosion of the magazines of ironclads Virginia, (Commodore Semmes' flag ship,) the Richmond, Fredericksburg and Torpedo, and of the wooden ships Raleigh, Hampton and Nansemond. After daybreak the Patrick Henry, (used as a school ship) and the Schrapnel were destroyed. The shock was so severe that the panes of glass were shivered in the Spotswood Hotel. There were no bridges burnt over James river at the hour of our leaving (8 A.M.) save that of the Petersburg and Richmond railroad. The burning of that costly structure was one of the most magnificent sights that I ever beheld.

As the cars rolled off, we were told that Mayo's bridge was burnt. The crackling flames and falling timbers of Haxall's immense buildings, other contiguous houses, reports of bursting ordnance, explosion of bombs at the Laboratory and Arsenal, the devoted city enveloped in thick wreaths of pitchy smoke; (its localities identified only by the thickest smoke of more recent explosions, or the fiery tongues of the leaping flames,) presented a sight, the like of which, may I never see again. The quartermaster's establishment at the basin, commissary's quarters, the Gallego Mills and Haxall's tobacco warehouses and lots, with whole acres of tobacco, the shipping at Rookett's, and perhaps immense amounts of other property beyond the reach of my vision, were all on fire about the hour of sunrise.

From the stand point of your correspondent, south of the James, the unfortunate metropolis seemed to be one vast funeral pyre.

At 3 P.M., on Sunday afternoon, the Legislature was called together; no quorum appearing, it adjourned to meet at some other place.

The Dispatch is the only paper on to-day that I have seen; do not know whether any other is out, as the second class militia were all out yesterday and last night.

This is written on the last train leaving Richmond. No rolling stock that can be moved is left behind. Two detached locomotives follow this train. Admiral Semmes and all the personnel of the navy have just entered the cars. We are now six miles of Burkville (junction) and hear that a body of Yankees are there pressing us. An artillery officer, our latest arrival from Richmond, crossed the James in a canoe, says the enemy entered the city, and an officer (supposed Yankee general) was addressing a crowd from the Washington monument.

I have seen the last of Richmond—poor, unhappy Richmond. Heaven save her the fate of Columbia.

CARTOUCHE.

AN ANONYMOUS REPORT: CAPITULATION OF LEE'S ARMY

A few days after announcing Lee's capitulation, the Constitutionalist *ran a full article on the surrender at Appomattox. The story is prepared from information taken from the* South Carolinian, *then in publication at Charlotte. The section of the story that dealt with Lee's proffer of his sword and Grant's refusal is, according to modern historians, merely apocryphal. Articles such as the following one were indeed the stuff of which legends were made.*

Augusta Constitutionalist, 23 April 1865 (Augusta, Ga.)

CAPITULATION OF LEE'S ARMY

General Lee a Prisoner of War
Sad Details

From the Carolinian we make a summary of the sad intelligence below. Prior to the eventful Sunday of capitulation, and from the evacuation of Richmond and Petersburg, our army suffered from retreat and disasters, and was sorely pressed from overwhelming odds, but still fought bravely, until completely surrounded:

Sunday, April 10th—A bright, clear, beautiful day, but it opened gloomily. Our army had reached Appomattox Court House, on the road to Lynchburg. Thomas, with his army, had arrived before us and effected a junction with Grant; cavalry, infantry and artillery completely surrounded our little command. We had from five to eight thousand prisoners, and only eight thousand effective men with muskets, all told. The supply of ammunition was nearly exhausted. In this emergency General Lee determined to cut his way through. Orders were given for a grand charge, and our troops massed accordingly.

General Grimes' division led the charge, followed successively by two others. The engagement commenced shortly after sunrise, and was continued until our men had broke through the Federal lines, driven them nearly a mile and a half and captured several pieces of artillery, and some hundreds of prisoners. The old spirit of fight was unsubdued. Meanwhile a heavy force of cavalry threatened our flanks. For some reason General Lee issued orders to the troops to cease firing and withdraw.

Subsequently an officer, said to be Gen. Custar of the Yankee cavalry, entered our lines with a flag of truce. Whether his appearance was in response to a request from General Lee, or he was the bearer of a formal demand for the surrender initiated by Gen'l Grant, we are not informed. At this time, our army was in line of battle on or near the Appomattox road, the skirmishers thrown out, while 250 yards from these, over an emanence, was a large body of federal cavalry.

Soon after the return of Gen. Custar to his lines, Gen. Grant, accompanied by his staff, rode to the headquarters of Gen. Lee, which were under an apple tree near the road. The interview is described as exceedingly impressive. After the salutatory formalities, which were doubtless brief and business-like, General Lee tendered his sword to Grant in token of surrender. That officer, however, with a courtesy for which we must accord him due respect, declined to receive it, or receiving it declined to retain it, and accompanied its return with substantially the following remarks:

"General Lee keep that sword. You have won it by your gallantry. You have not been whipped, but overpowered and I cannot receive it as a token of surrender from so brave a man."

The reply of Gen. Lee we do not know. But Grant and himself are said to have been deeply affected by the occasion and to have shed tears. The scene occurred between ten and eleven o'clock A.M., when the sad event became known to the army, officers and men gave way to their emotions and some among the veterans wept like children. A considerable number swore that they would never surrender and made their way to the woods. Generals Gary of South Carolina and Rosser of Virginia, with a few followers, cut their way out and escaped. But the bulk of the army, the men who for four years have done battle so nobly for the cause, together with leaders like Longstreet, Gordon, Kershaw and others whose names are forever distinguished, were obliged to accept the proffered terms.

These were—capitulation with all the honors of war—officers to retain their side arms and personal property and the men their baggage. Each one was there upon paroled and allowed to go his way.

During Sunday and Monday a large number of Federal soldiers and officers visited our camps and looked curiously on our commands, but there was nothing like exultation, no shouting for joy and no word uttered that could add to the mortification already sustained. On the contrary every symptom of respect was manifested, and the southern army was praised for the noble and brave manner in which it had defended our cause.

The force of the Yankee army is estimated at 200,000. Our own, at the time of surrender, embraced not more than 8,800 effective infantry and 2,000 cavalry, but it is said that the total number paroled was about 23,000 of all arms and conditions.

All the Federals spoke of General Lee in unbounded praise. The remark was frequently made "he would receive as many cheers in going down our lines as Gen. Grant himself."

It is understood that Gens. Lee, Longstreet and other officers are now on parole in the city of Richmond.

The following is a true copy of General Lee's address to his army, issued after the surrender to General Grant at Appomattox C.H., on Sunday April 9th, 1865.

HEADQUARTERS ARMY NORTHERN VA.

April 10, 1865.

GENERAL ORDERS,

No. 9

After four years of arduous service marked by unsurpassed

courage and fortitude, the Army of Northern Virginia has been compelled to yield to overwhelming numbers and resources.

I need not tell the brave survivors of so many hard fought battles who have remained steadfast to the last, that I have consented to this result from no distrust of them. But feeling that valor and devotion could accomplish nothing that could compensate for the loss that would have attended the continuance of the contest I determined to avoid the useless sacrifice of those whose past service have endeared them to their countrymen.

By the terms of the agreement officers and men can return to their homes and remain until exchanged. You will take with you the satisfaction that proceeds from the consciousness of duty faithfully performed, and I earnestly pray that a merciful God will extend to you his blessing and protection.

With unceasing admiration of your constancy and devotion to your country and a grateful remembrance of your kind and generous consideration for myself, I bid you an affectionate farewell.

R. E. LEE, General.

Below is a special order embracing Gen. Grant's order for the passage of paroled soldiers to their homes and also the form of pass given them.

HEADQR'S ARMY OF N.V.

April 10, 1865

Special Order

No. ————.

All officers and men of the Confederate service paroled at Appomattox C. H. Va., who, to reach their homes are compelled to pass through the lines of the Union armies, will be allowed to do so, and to pass free on all Government transports and military railroads.

By command of Lt. Gen. Grant.,
E.S. Parker,
Lt. Col. A.A.G.

By command of
R. E. LEE
C. L. Venable, A.A.G.

[Form of pass.]

APPOMATTOX, C. H., VA.,
April 10th, 1865.

The bearer ———— of Co ———— right ———— of ————, a paroled prisoner of the Army of Northern Virginia, has permission to go to his home and there remain undisturbed.

Lastly is the form of the parole of honor signed by commanding officers of divisions &c., in behalf of the men of their command. This is taken from a copy of one signed by General Fitz Hugh Lee.

I, the undersigned, commanding officer of ———— do for the within named prisoners of war belonging to the army of Northern Virginia, who have been this day surrendered by Gen. R. E. Lee, C.S.A., commanding said armies, to Lieut. Gen. U. S. Grant, commanding the armies of the United States, hereby give my solemn parole of honor that the within named shall not hereafter serve in the armies of the Confederate States or in any military capacity whatever against the United States of America, or render aid to the enemies of the latter, until properly exchanged in such manner as shall be mutually approved by the respective authorities.

Done at Appomattox Court House, Va., this 9th day of April 1865.

AN ANONYMOUS REPORT: DEATH OF LINCOLN REPORTED

The assassination of President Abraham Lincoln sent shock waves through people of both the South and the North. For the first time in the history of the nation, a chief executive's life had been taken by a disgruntled citizen. The assassination of Lincoln by a Southerner, John Wilkes Booth, further enflamed passions of Northerners who were already demanding that the South be punished for its rebellion.

Augusta Chronicle and Sentinel, 27 April 1865 (Augusta, Ga.)

THE DEATH OF LINCOLN

DeQuincy in that strange essay "Murder considered as one of the Five Arts," has collected a multitude of instances not unlike the tragedy at Ford's Theatre, which resulted in the death of the President of the United States. As we anticipated, it has aroused a tempest of indignation throughout the North, but the more sober journalists are disposed to regard it as the act of a half crazy fanatic; while none, we believe, have been so reckless as to charge the Confederate authorities with complicity in this design.

Assassination for political ends has rarely occurred amongst civilized nations. The assassination of Caesar by Brutus and his fellow-conspirators, was an ill-advised affair; and as is well known, proved the overthrow of the Senatorial party and paved the way to the Imperial rule of Augustus. The murder of Henry Fourth was prompted solely by religious fanaticism and was so far successful in its aims that next to the St. Bartholomew massacre it did more than any single event to root out the reformed religion from France.

The assassination of William of Orange at Delft was likewise the offspring, in part, of religious fanaticism and it inflicted a stunning blow on the rising Dutch Republic. Fortunately, however, it came too late to be of any material service to the Spanish cause.

The assassination of Abraham Lincoln is the first example of the kind that has occurred in American history. John Wilkes Booth, the individual accused of the deed, is the third son of J. B. Booth, an actor of some celebrity in the past generation, who resided for many years in the vicinity of Baltimore, is about thirty years of age, a professional actor of reputation—and altogether, fine looking, if not prepossessing in appearance. He is represented by the Northern papers as a fierce secessionist and personally hostile to Lincoln, having frequently given vent to his feelings during the war. His trial, which we suppose will be conducted according to the form of law, will doubtless rank with the *cause celebres* of all countries.

ANDREW JOHNSON: PRESIDENT JOHNSON'S AMNESTY PROCLAMATION

The fighting in the Civil War ended with the surrender of Lee's army at Appomattox and Johnston's army in North Carolina, but the political machinations were only beginning. Many in the North favored harsh punishment for the Southern states they believed had been in rebellion for the previous four years. President Andrew Johnson, though, favored a more magnanimous ending and offered liberal terms of amnesty to the South's former combatants. This was one of his early missteps—from the perspective of the Northern Congress—that would eventually lead to an attempt to impeach Johnson.

Augusta Chronicle and Sentinel, 3 June 1865 (Augusta, Ga.)

PRESIDENT JOHNSON'S AMNESTY PROCLAMATION

Through the kindness of an official stationed at Atlanta, the Intelligencer of that city has been favored with the perusal of the Chattanooga Gazette of May 30. From it is taken the following important telegraphic report containing the President's Amnesty Proclamation. We hope soon to lay before our readers the Proclamation itself in all its details. What we present below embraces only the Oath to be administered and the exceptions prescribed in this amnesty.

THE OATH

I do solemnly swear or affirm in the presence of Almighty God that I will henceforth faithfully defend the Constitution of the United States and the union of the States, and will abide and faithfully support all laws and proclamations which have been made during the existing rebellion with references to the emancipation of slaves. So help me God.

PERSONS EXCEPTED

All who have been civil, diplomatic or otherwise, domestic or foreign agents of the pretended Confederate States.

All who left Judicial stations under the United States to aid the rebellion.

All Military and Naval Officers above the rank of Colonel in the Army, and Lieutenant in the Navy.

All who left seats in the Congress of the United States.

All who resigned or tendered the resignation of their commissions in the Army and Navy of the United States.

All engaged any way in treating otherwise than lawfully as prisoners of war persons forced (found) in the United States service.

All Military and Naval Officers who were educated in the United States.

All the pretended Governors in the insurrectionary States.

All who left their homes within the Federal lines and passed into the rebel lines to aid the rebellion.

All who have engaged in the destruction of the commerce on the high seas, and all who have made raids from Canada or engaged in destroying commerce on land and rivers.

All who at the time when they seek to obtain benefit hereof by taking the oath and remain in military, naval or civil confinement, or under bond of military or naval authorities as agents of the United States, prisoners of war, or persons detained for offenses of any kind whether before or after conviction.

FURTHER READINGS

Davis, William C. *The Last Days of the Confederate Government*. New York: Harcourt, 2001.

Fonvielle, Chris Eugene. *The Wilmington Campaign: Last Rays of Departing Hope*. Campbell, Calif.: Savas, 1997.

Hitchcock, Henry. *Marching with Sherman: Passages from the Letters and Campaign Diaries of Henry Hitchcock, Major and Assistant Adjutant General of Volunteers, November 1864–May 1865*. New Haven, Conn.: Yale University Press, 1927.

Korn, Jerry. *Pursuit to Appomattox: The Last Battles*. Alexandria, Va.: Time-Life Books, 1987.

Marvel, William. *A Place Called Appomattox*. Chapel Hill: University of North Carolina Press, 2000.

Rawl, Miriam Freeman. *From the Ashes of Ruin*. Columbia, S.C.: Summerhouse Press, 1999.

Simms, William Gilmore. *Sack and Destruction of the City of Columbia, S.C.* Columbia, S.C.: Power Press of Daily Phoenix, 1865.

Trudeau, Noah Andre. *The Last Citadel: Petersburg, Virginia, June 1864–April 1865*. Boston, Mass.: Little, Brown, 1991.

Winik, Jay. *April 1865: The Month That Saved America*. New York: HarperCollins, 2001.

THE CONFEDERATE HOME FRONT: WOMEN AND SLAVES, SACRIFICE AND VALOR

Women fought the Civil War, just as men did. Their battles and their battlefields were different, and their weapons were as well, but without the contributions of women, the Confederate army and the Confederate cause would have been severely disabled. Women sacrificed food, money, companionship, clothing, and leisure so as to provide for their families, both those members at home and those at the front. They raised money, sewed garments and flags, and cared for ill and injured soldiers in hospitals or even in their private homes. Some women were even forced to go so far as to take jobs outside their homes. While this was not necessarily anything new for lower-class women, it certainly was for women of the upper social echelons. Further, lower-class women, in particular, replaced men as essential labor in factories and on farms, and upper-class women, many for the first time ever, were left on their own to manage hearth, home, fields, and slaves without the support and protection of a man.

Women of all classes also faced shortages and deprivations, particularly as the war became more and more protracted. Some women, even of the middle to upper classes, were forced to buy secondhand clothing. When soldiers came through, either the enemy's or the Confederacy's, women were often left with little. Lower-class women, especially, faced tough times with food shortages, no money, and no man to do the heavy physical labor around the farm. In some Southern cities, including Richmond, Virginia, and Columbus, Georgia, women of the lower classes would become so desperate to feed their children later in the war that they resorted to rioting to call attention to their plight. In Richmond in 1863, more than 1,000 women rampaged through the streets and looted shops. Women and their children suffered especially from the South's wartime economic problems and the high prices speculators charged for necessary goods.

Many upper-class Southern women were strong supporters of secession and war, at least initially. Women of the lower classes were almost immediately forced to contend with the realities of life without a male provider or head of household. For women who had been brought up expecting male protection as their due, coping on their own was demanding.

Because of their strong support for the war and the fact that they were used to a type of rarified treatment as due their gender, women were more likely than men to challenge the Yankees with taunts and jeers. In occupied New Orleans, women were so rude and so provocative to General Benjamin Butler's troops that he was finally compelled to issue an order that proclaimed any woman arrested for her conduct toward Union soldiers would be treated as a prostitute. "Woman of the town" was the term Butler used, but his implication was clear. Southerners were so appalled by his order that they nicknamed the general "Beast Butler," an epithet that followed him throughout the war in the Southern press.

Slaves and free blacks were also denizens of the home front during the Civil War, and their experiences were documented, too, in Southern newspapers, though not to the same level as that of women. Early in the war, newspapers often carried articles about loyal slaves who stood with their white masters in their support for the war for Southern independence. Even free blacks were depicted as supporting the war effort through donations of money or flags to Confederate combat forces in which they would not have been allowed to serve, even had they wanted to. As the war progressed, though, and the availability of Southern manpower declined, blacks, usually slaves, were mustered into the army to serve as teamsters, cooks, or officers' valets. In late 1864, the shortage of men became so acute that Jefferson Davis asked, and Congress seriously considered, drafting slaves into the Confederate army with the promise of emancipation for military service.

J.C.C. FEATHERSTONE OR JAMES A. HOYT: "THE WHEEL OF LIFE"—SIX ARTICLES ON NINETEENTH-CENTURY SOCIAL THOUGHT AND VALUES

The following six articles appeared as a unit in the third column on page 1 of the 1 November 1860 edition of the Anderson Intelligencer *of Anderson, South Carolina, and are representative of the types of "improving" articles that many Southern newspapers carried during the antebellum and Confederate periods. These articles were intended primarily for female readers and, in some cases, to be used as material to assist mothers as they taught their children to read. To twenty-first-century readers, the articles provide helpful insight into the "mind" of Southerners and into nineteenth-century Southern values. The article headed "The Advantages of Necessity" is particularly useful in explaining the thinking that allowed Southerners to own slaves and to proscribe a more restrictive lifestyle for women in the region. Southerners accepted the idea that all people are born to a particular station of life, what they termed a "sphere." Women and slaves lived in the private sphere behind the fence gate because of their alleged inherent inferiorities to white men. Men were considered to live in the public sphere due to their various involvements and entanglements with the world outside the home.*

Slaves were considered family members, just like children were, though they had none of the rights and privileges of white children. Southerners believed slaves were born into bondage because that was where God decreed they should be. Such ideas are abhorrent today but were as commonplace and accepted in the nineteenth century as our more enlightened twenty-first-century notions that women should be paid the same as men for the same work and that people of all races are entitled to the same civil rights.

Anderson Intelligencer, 1 November 1860 (Anderson, S.C.)

THE WHEEL OF LIFE.—Man is the most destructive of beings. He pursues the great leviathan within the polar circle to light his home. He ransacks the sea and land in every latitude; he slays and plunders with unsparing hand. He enslaves the horse, camel, and elephant, he robs and slaughters the ox, the sheep, the swine, the bee, the beaver, and the worm; the fowls do not escape him, and he levies taxes on everything taxable. In this manner he gathers his food and his raiment, the balsam of his diseases, and the fuel that cheers his hearth. Despite the ravages of diseases, and violent and natural deaths he increases in number, every season opens to him as bountiful a supply as before. In civilized life he is often a prey to numberless accidents, to the beasts of the fields, and the monsters of the deep. If he escape these, at the last he becomes food for worms. Man eats his mutton, and the lion eats man. One law encircles, directs and confines all created beings—each within its proper sphere. The evil that befalls one, the other cannot escape—disease and death are the lot of all.

THE ADVANTAGES OF NECESSITY.—If every man were wise and virtuous, capable to discern the best use of time, and resolute to practice it, it might be granted, we think, without hesitation, that total liberty would be a blessing; and that it would be desirable to be left at large to the exercise of religious and social duties, without the interruption of importunate avocations.

But since felicity is relative, and that which is the means of happiness to one man may be to another the cause of misery, we are to consider, what state is best adapted to human nature in its present degeneracy and frailty. And, surely, to the far greater number it is highly expedient, that they should by some settled scheme of duties, be rescued from the tyranny of caprice; that they should be driven on by necessity through the paths of life, with their attention confined to a stated task, that they may be less at leisure to deviate into mischief at the call of folly.

PLEASURE OF CONTENTMENT.—I have a rich neighbor who is always so busy that he has no leisure to laugh; the whole business of his life is to get money, and more money. He is still drudging on, saying that Solomon says, "The diligent hand maketh rich." And it is true, indeed; but he considers not that it is not in the power of riches to make a man happy, for it was wisely said by a man of great observation, "that there be as many miseries beyond riches as on this side of them." We see but the outside of the rich man's happiness; few consider him to be like the silk-worm, that, when she seems to play, it is at the very same time spinning her own bowels, and consuming herself. And this many rich men do—loading themselves with corroding cares, to keep what they have already to. Let us, therefore, be thankful for health and competence, and above all, for a quiet conscience.

JUDGE NOT RASHLY.—Alas! how unreasonable as well as unjust a thing it is for any to censure the infirmities of another, when we see that even good men are not able to dive through the mystery of their own! Be assured there can be but little honesty, without thinking as well as possible of others, and there can be no safety without thinking humbly and distrustfully of ourselves.

THE BEST MEDICINE.—Good, wholesome food, and temperance, with pure, cold water to drink, and bathe in, with fresh air, plenty of exercise, and a clear conscience, are said to do more to restore or preserve health, and prolong life, than every doctor and medicine in the universe.

OUR COMMON INDEBTEDNESS.—Of those whom Providence has qualified to make any additions to human knowledge, the number is extremely small; and what can be added by each single mind, even of this superior class, is very little. The greater part of mankind must owe far the larger part of it, to the information of others.

D. A. HOBBIE OR B. H. THRASHER: EDITORIAL—THE PLACE OF WOMEN

The place of women in nineteenth-century America was the home. They lived within the fence gate, and their role was to care for the household. With this limited role, though, came a sort of veneration that is strikingly odd, compared to more modern ways of thinking. Women were vessels of purity and domesticity, and those were considered high callings, worthy of great honor. However, as this editorial from an Alabama newspaper indicated, men also well understood that women had reserves of strength that could carry them through hard times.

Troy Southern Advertiser, 4 January 1861 (Troy, Ala.)

WOMAN.—Place her among flowers, foster her as a tender plant, and she is a thing of fancy, waywardness, and sometimes folly—annoyed by a dew drop fretted by the touch of a butterfly's wing, and ready to faint at the rustle of a beetle; the zephyr are too rough, the showers too heavy, and she is overpowered by the perfume of a rosebud.—But let real calamity come—rouse her affection—enkindle the fires of her heart, and mark her then; how her heart strengthens itself—how strong is her purpose. Place her in the heat of battle—give her a child, a bird—any thing she loves or pities, to protect—and see her, as in a relative instance, raising her white arms as a shield, as her own blood crimsons her upturned forehead, praying for life to protect the helpless.

Transplant her in the dark places of earth—awaken her energies to action, and her breath becomes a healing—her presence a blessing. She disputes, inch by inch, the stride of the stacking pestilence, when men, the strong and brave, shrinks away pale and afrighted. Misfortune haunts her not; she wears away a life of silent endurance, and goes forward with less timidity than to her bridal. In prosperity she is a bud of odors, waiting but for the winds of adversity to scatter them abroad—pure gold, valuable, but untried in the furnace. In short, woman is a miracle—a [unreadable] the centre from which radiates the great charm of existence.

C. E. HAYNES: SOUTHERN WOMEN AS NURSES

Armies from throughout the new Confederate States of America began massing in Virginia after the shelling of Fort Sumter and Lincoln's immediate call for 75,000 volunteers to put down the Southern rebellion. Southerners and Northerners alike knew it was only a matter of time until their armies clashed. Nurses would be necessary once the conflict escalated to outright war, and with so many men under arms, that role would likely fall to women. Already in the North, according to the Cahaba Gazette, *women were volunteering to nurse sick and wounded soldiers, just as the most famous military nurse of the day, Florence Nightingale, had during Britain's Crimean War. The paper suspected that Southern women would be called on to fulfill the same role—and would be up to the task—despite their more delicate upbringing. This article offers an excellent view of how women were viewed in the Old South and just how much the war would change their place in that society. The reference to Pensacola at the very end of the article calls attention to the city's importance as a port and the recent confrontation there over another coastal installation, Fort Pickens.*

Cahaba Gazette, 31 May 1861 (Cahaba, Ala.)

NURSES

The ever famous FLORENCE NIGHTINGALE did much to alleviate the sufferings of her sick and wounded countrymen, and set an example to her sex which will be followed by them in all countries. We see that great numbers of Northern women have volunteered as nurses to the Northern troops. Southern women are more delicately nurtured than those of the North, and have not been at all accustomed to being brought into rude or disagreeable contact with the sterner sex. We will not say that they have more real virtue than the women of the North, but they have been taught to be more reserved in their intercourse with men.

But stern times have come upon us, and our women must prepare themselves to perform stern and disagreeable duties. Like angels of mercy, they must visit our brave defenders and nurse them in their sickness and in their wounds, and must smooth their dying pillows. It needs not prompting from us to remind them of their duty. They will perform it, God bless them, willingly.

It is with pleasure we copy the following from a late number of the Montgomery Advertiser:

Some time ago a letter was sent from Columbus, Georgia to President Davis, written by a patriotic lady, offering her services and those of several young ladies as nurses during the war. The President expressed much gratification at the offer, and spoke in commendable terms of the ladies of Columbus. It seems they are still active in good work for the soldiers. The Enquirer contains the following:

The Ladies of Columbus held meetings on Tuesday and Wednesday morning, and organized a "Soldiers' Friend Society," the object of which is to perform Woman's part in the service of their country in time of war.—The officers elected are Mrs. A. Chappell, President; Mrs. Robt. Carter, Vice President; Mrs. J. A. Urquhart, Secretary; and Mrs. Richard Patton, Treasurer.

In addition to this we will state that a letter has been received from Dr. THOMAS LENOIR (son of Maj. JAMES M. LENOIR), who belongs to Col. WITHERS' Regiment, in which he says he was left near Norfolk, with 30 or 40 sick under his charge, and that the ladies of the neighborhood—rich and poor, young and old—came to his assistance and tenderly nursed the brave men who had come from Alabama to defend Virginia from invasion.

The ladies who read our paper, we know, will be ready to go to the place where their services may be needed, and in such numbers as will be necessary. If our own friends and neighbors at Pensacola should get into a fight, or if disease should spread among them, they should first be attended to.

JOHN HARVEY: HOW SOUTHERN WOMEN SUPPORT THE CONFEDERATE WAR EFFORT

Women were prevented by their gender and by rigid social roles in the nineteenth-century South from participating directly in the Civil War. However, they played vital supporting roles, particularly as nurses and caregivers for sick and wounded soldiers, seamstresses who made clothing and knitted socks for the men at the front, and as fund-raisers who gathered money and goods for the Southern armies. This article recognizes the efforts of local women—especially those from the country—in gathering winter clothes for soldiers serving in the Virginia mountains.

Alabama Beacon, 2 August 1861 (Greensboro, Ala.)

RESPONDING TO THE CALL.—The ladies of this section are responding promptly, and in a most patriotic spirit to the call made upon them for clothing for the soldiers. Mr. Carson has already received quite a number of articles sent in from the country, which will be forwarded at an early day.

As the nights will soon be getting cool in the mountainous regions of Virginia, the soldiers should be supplied with woolen clothing—especially drawers and undershirts—as early as possible, certainly by the first of September. Flannel shirts, made to fit loosely, and good woolen socks, also made large—(no sock, or shoe, that fits closely, is suitable to march in)—are essential to the health and comfort of the soldier.

JOAN: FEMALE CORRESPONDENT DESCRIBES WOMEN'S WAR WORK

Women's contributions to the Confederate cause were often overlooked by male correspondents and editors who might be likely to publish brief articles thanking women for their contributions but who were not always aware of the work that went into knitting twelve pairs of socks or sewing uniforms. Joan, a correspondent for the Charleston Courier *in Virginia, was familiar with women's work, and in this story, she painted a clear picture for her readers that at first seems to be a color piece about life in Richmond. The article took a bend, though, to touch on the work by Richmond women to tend to the needs of the South's soldiers. One of the more interesting stories to which Joan gives only a brief mention is that of Major General John C. Frémont, commander of the Union's Western Department, which included Missouri. Frémont shocked the nation, and caused big headaches for President Lincoln, when he issued his own Emancipation Proclamation in Missouri. He also declared martial law in that state and threatened to court-martial any man found armed in the Union-controlled areas of Missouri. The article is remarkable, too, because it was written by a woman. Because Southern women lived in the private sphere, few ever wrote for publication. That Joan was willing to do so is an indication of how, even early in the war, women's roles were already changing.*

Charleston Courier, 7 September 1861

CORRESPONDENCE OF THE COURIER

Richmond, September 3, 1861.

Every interest of life in Richmond is secondary to military considerations. If you pass a cabinet warehouse, you see nothing exposed for sale but camp bedstands, camp stools, cots for hospitals and the like, while the exposition of wares at the tinners is confined almost wholly to tin cups and pans, coffee pots and canteens. Tent makers establishments are numerous. If you go to a shoe store and asked to be measured for a pair of gaiters, they will tell you they take none but Government; or to a saddler's establishment, and ask even the small favor to have a handle repaired on your traveling bag, you meet with the same reply. You cannot get a piece of goods woven at a factory in the State for private use; they are under contract to manufacture alone for the Government, while a statement of operations at the Armory at this place, together with the Military Institute at Lexington, says that since the 1st of April they have issued 61,954 arms and 186 pieces of cannon; have re-bored 200 pieces of artillery, mounted them on good carriages, and carefully prepared the accompanying caissons, and mounted 40 brass field pieces. Military trappings are exposed in about every third shop window, and signs informing you of the whereabouts of military tailors are frequent—though I should suppose they would hardly find much to do, so diligent are the ladies with their needles. Hundreds of ladies have been sewing every day since last April—many of them from eight o'clock in the morning until dark, and when the work was hurrying, have had their dinners sent to them. Some among them, unused to such toilsome service, have had their health seriously impaired by it. Very many have ignored in a great [unreadable] all social and domestic ties to devote themselves to this labor of love. Each church has its own organization, and officers wanting clothing made for their men no matter of what description, can always get it done by applying to the rooms. Then when you remember that almost every man's house is thrown open to the sick, and that ladies are continually passing about in their carriages laden with delicacies for the sick at the hospitals, and edibles for the haversacks of the departing soldiers, you will realize something of the all-absorbing interest felt in those who are defending our rights.

The New York Times has a very gloomy article upon the war. It says the people are giving millions of dollars and hundreds of thousands of men, but the country reaps no benefit from the gift, and they look to the War Department as being responsible for the "disheartening disappointment." The peace feeling at the North is increasing, and has so alarmed Lincoln that he has issued another royal edict, declaring that the Administration regards all Peace Conventions as in the highest degree treasonable, and all advocates of peace as traitors, and prescribing the Conventions advertised to be held in Maryland and Kentucky on the 10th inst. It is possible that before that time Maryland will be beyond his jurisdiction, and Kentucky—will she stand such dictation? Fremont's abolition proclamation may well be received by them with amazement; they can see their own doom foreshadowed in it if they stand paralyzed much longer. East Tennessee is gracefully yielding in the matter of allegiance to her State, and the loud mouthed demagogues who were so anxious to see her kneeling at Lincoln's feet are now foremost among those who oppose his rule. The protestations of those who go only with the tide are valuable to us merely as indications of which way the tide is running. Fremont has over reached himself. Had his proclamation been a little more

moderate, he might possibly have retained a party about him. If he would like to know how many will sustain him in it let him count the number of Yankee hirelings by whom he is surrounded, and he can tell to a man, for well we know that no Southerner living can ever stoop low enough to have such a yoke fastened around his neck. If he has any in his ranks who claim to be Southerners let him watch them well; they do but bide their time. It is said one company of "Fremont Body Guards," numbering eighty well mounted cavalry, deserted in a body and made tracks for Gen. Pillow's quarters, and that desertions are constantly occurring.

A New York correspondent of a Philadelphia paper is distressed at the Secession sympathy manifested in New York. He says "I am not sure that an army of Confederates invading New York would not find a good amount of their own colors waiting for them. There is a dreadful state of sentiment here; of this there is no doubt." And another states that two hundred men in Belfast, Maine, have received muskets from Boston and armed themselves, declaring they will resist any attempt made to collect war taxes, or to draft any of their men. It is the leaven of interest working which is stirring up the peace feeling. There are, too, hundreds of thousands of people who know as confidently as we do that there is no question about our ultimate success, who would be as ready perhaps as any to prosecute the war, if they thought there was any possibility of their being able to accomplish their aims, but convinced of the fruitlessness of them would fain desire ere they are driven more deeply into the vortex of ruin.

The Washington Cabinet seem very anxious to devise some plan by which they may be able to retain the benefits of the telegraph themselves, and at the same time deprive us of them. They will hardly succeed, though it seems Kentucky has consented to a censorship. Seward has made a very convenient errand to New York. We do not hear that Lincoln and Scott have followed suit, but it is more than likely they have. The atmosphere of Washington is perhaps too heavily charged with electricity to please them.

It seems the Union gun which has been held up to us as such a formidable monster, one which was to prove so efficient in our subjugation, signally fails in its execution, not only requiring a great many men but a great deal of time to load and fire it, but it cannot throw a projectile either with directness or precision, nor is the range satisfactory.

It seems the people of Quincy, Ill., are getting excited upon the subject of an attack. They may well expect retaliation from us, for their encroachments. Even Christian forbearance does not demand of us always to sit with folded hands, and tamely take their insults. We should not have submitted as quietly as we have, had we not known our power; it will not be long now before they will be made to know it. Our President, when he was a member of the Washington Congress, in his closing speech before them, exhibited to them in glowing colors the advantages we would have over them in a conflict. The day is not far distant when they will appreciate his logic.

Some fifty Yankee prisoners came in last night, many of them wounded. All we heard about their capture was, that they were taken on the Potomac, in a skirmish. The prisoners in the city have been allowed to go to market, under a guard, and purchase such supplies as they choose to pay for; but I understand orders have been given to put a stop to it. I do not know why. The guard now does the marketing for them.

JOAN.

SOUTHRON: TRIBUTE TO THE WOMEN OF THE SOUTH

As the Civil War moved into its second year, the demands on Southern women became greater. Not only did they give their husbands, sons, and fathers to the army, they also contributed their labor in sewing or nursing sick soldiers and their household supplies to keep the soldiers fed. This story, which ran in the Christmas Day edition, served as a tribute to the South's women and their contributions but also as a recognition of the power—informal though it be—of women. The mention of "Roman matrons" and of the "mothers of '76" was typical of the day. Southerners identified with the Roman republic, and they esteemed the War of Independence and its leaders as the great cause of great Americans. In reality, women were not always so patriotic nor so patient with the new roles in which they were cast as a result of the war. Many women, for example, wrote to the Confederate government to send their men home because they were having trouble accomplishing their agricultural work or supervising their slaves without a strong male presence. Still, though overly romanticized and showing little real understanding of what the life of a typical woman was like, the article is a nice tribute to those women who were making sacrifices for the war.

Troy Southern Advertiser, 25 December 1861 (Troy, Ala.)

THE WOMEN OF THE SOUTH

Woman, in all ages of the world, has been the ruling spirit; from the time when Mother Eve decoyed Adam to taste of the forbidden fruit, til the present time, woman, exerting her power over man, has wielded the destinies of the world.

Man may for a time resist her power, but woman's influence is felt throughout the whole civilized world. It is to our mothers and our sisters that we all owe what little of goodness, politeness or generosity we may possess; and peculiarly is this true of the women of the present age. The Roman matrons had justly been celebrated for their devotion to their country; and the Spartan mother, who told her son to return with his shield, or on it, will be remembered by all posterity. To the memory of Josaphine, of Madame Roland, of Charlotte Corday, and many other noble women of the perilous times of the French Revolution, be many a line inscribed.

Our mothers of '76 will always be remembered by their sons with pride, that they are the descendants of such women; but to the brave Southern women of '61, it has been reserved to excel in devotion to the cause of liberty, love of their country, and in the predominance of those virtues which should characterize a soldier's wife or mother. We read of women, who, in the revolutionary times, when our forefathers gained the liberty which we have inherited, repulsed the insolent British soldiery when they attempted to insult or plunder, and we have read of some who fought for their country, but where is an example equal to that of the brave and noble lady, who replied when asked if she really desired her husband to go to war, "I do not like to be separated from him. It will be a terrible trial; but some must go; and between submission to the North and a separation from my husband, it is easy to choose. I cannot go and fight, but I can stay and take his place on the plantation while he is gone. Let him go and do his duty, and I will stay and do mine."

And there are thousands of just such women all over the Confederacy. Their language is, "If we cannot fight, we can stay at home and take care of our husbands' crops, and take the places of our brothers." Young ladies, who a year ago, were not esteemed of any use, but to pore over embroidery or while away their time at the piano, are now engaged in knitting socks, making uniforms, or sewing on underclothing for our brave volunteers. Ladies, who not long since thought it a disgrace to work, are now engaged in teaching school, or take the places of their brothers behind the counter.

Such is the character of our Southern women; and with such mothers and sisters to encourage us in our brave work what need we fear? As I have frequently heard it observed, before the hordes of the North could conquer us, the very women and children would meet the invaders of their peaceful homes, and drive them from their hearth stones. No! the South can never be conquered. We are fighting for our homes, for our loved ones, and while one spark of Southern blood flows through the veins of the free people, submit we will never,

SOUTHRON.

AN ANONYMOUS REPORT: ACCOUNT OF SOUTHERN WOMEN OUTWITTING YANKEES

Confederate newspapers published many articles celebrating the accomplishments of Southern women during the war, particularly when those accomplishments involved outwitting Union forces. This story, taken from the Richmond Dispatch, *purports to have a Northern source and tells an amusing story about a pro-Southern woman who fled Washington, D.C., for Richmond. The story served a double purpose—it was amusing and entertaining, but also such stories about the supposedly weak and frail woman outsmarting the Union soldier served the purpose of building Confederate morale; for certainly if a Southern woman could best a Yankee soldier in repartee, it would be a small matter for a Southern man to do the same thing on the battlefield.*

Richmond Dispatch, reprinted in the Savannah Republican, 5 March 1863

SOUTHERN WOMEN.—On the occasion of the recent departure of women for the South, from Washington, some remarkable developments took place. A Yankee correspondent says:

One lady had seven pairs of gaiters, five pairs of boots, five pairs of morocco slippers, three pairs of dancing slippers of white kid, four pairs of India rubber overshoes, and a pair of the longest legged cavalry boots, with double soles, studded with good spikes, heels tapped with shoes of iron, and tops splendidly ornamented with an abundance of patch work of waxed ends on a ground work of patent leather.

"How about these, madam?" said the officer, as he quietly insinuated the cavalry boots into her astonished gaze. "If you will put them on and wear them on your trip to Richmond, you can take them, but they can go with you under no other circumstances."

"Done—I'll do it," said the heroine, and grasping the heavy leather in her hands, she retired behind the friendly crinoline of a group of sympathizers, and planting her pretty feet—gaiters and all—into the depths of that monstrous foot harness, returned, and awkwardly displayed them, double-cased, to the gaping eyes of the this time astonished official. He kept his word. The boots went to somebody in the Confederate army, or they may have been an intended Christmas present for Gen. Stuart. These secesh women do such things.

Richmond Dispatch.

ANONYMOUS REPORT: USEFUL ADVICE FOR WOMEN—A SUBSTITUTE FOR BREAD

Newspapers would not add women's pages for more than half a century, but they were already carrying news of interest to women. Often during the Civil War, the stories would offer advice on how to stretch staples or what could substitute for what. This became particularly useful information as shortages and speculation on prices placed many kinds of goods out of the reach of many women. The following article on bread originally appeared in the Edgefield Advertiser *in South Carolina.*

Edgefield Advertiser, reprinted in the Savannah Republican, 20 March 1863

A SUBSTITUTE FOR BREAD.—Now that meat is hard to get about our villages and towns, we recommend lie-hominy as a good substitute, at least as a change. The simple plan of preparing it is follows: To a gallon of shelled corn add a half gallon of good ashes. Boil together until the husk begins to come off the corn. Then rub briskly to clear the grain completely of husk. Wash the corn clear and boil it for ten or twelve hours, adding water from time to time to keep it from burning. It is then ready, and has only to be warmed over for use as it is needed. It is perhaps better fried. This is said to be more wholesome than big hominy, and it is as good diet as corn bread, if not better. It is easy to prepare, and saves the toll. Most housekeepers know how to make it; but a few may not be informed on this important subject; and we pen this paragraph for their benefit.—

Edgefield Advertiser.

JAMES R. SNEED: CAREER OF A FEMALE VOLUNTEER

While most women contented themselves with aiding the war effort through traditional women's work, a handful shouldered arms and took to the battlefield. Mrs. Laura J. Williams volunteered after being deserted by her Yankee husband at the beginning of the war. Other women also were documented as serving in both the Union and the Confederate armies. For lower-class women, one of the inducements for joining up was the pay. With their husbands away, and the Confederate government often unable to pay the salaries promised to soldiers, uneducated women of the under classes had few legal ways of earning money.

Savannah Republican, 29 June 1863

CAREER OF A FEMALE VOLUNTEER

Among the registered enemies of the United States government who have been recently sent across the lines from New Orleans, there is now in Jackson, Mississippi, a lady whose adventures place her in the ranks of the Molly Pitchers of the present revolution. At the breaking out of the war Mrs. Laura J. Williams was a resident of Arkansas. Like most of the women of the South, her whole soul was enlisted in the struggle for independence. Her husband was a Northern man by birth and education, and a strong Union man. After Arkansas seceded from the Union he went to Connecticut, he said, to see his relations and settle up some business. Mrs. Williams suspected his purpose and finally she received information that he had joined the Yankee army. The Jackson Mississippian gives the rest of her history:

She disguised herself in a Confederate uniform, and adopting the name of "Henry Benford," she proceeded to Texas, where she raised and equipped an independent company, and went to Virginia with it as 1st Lieutenant. She was in the battle of Leesburg and several skirmishes; but finally her sex having been discovered by the surgeon of the regiment—the 5th Texas Volunteers, to which the company had been attached—she returned to her home in Arkansas. After remaining there a short time she proceeded to Corinth, and was in the battle of Shiloh, where she displayed great coolness and courage. She saw her father on the field, but, of course, he did not recognize her and she did not make herself known to him. In the second day's fighting she was wounded in the head and was ordered to the rear. She wrote to her father, and then came on down to Grenada where she waited for some time, but never saw or heard from him.

She then visited New Orleans, was taken sick, and while sick the city was captured. On recovery she retired to the coast, where she employed herself carrying communications and assisting parties to run the blockade with drugs and cloth for uniforms. She was informed on by a negro and arrested and brought before Gen. Butler. She made her appearance before Gen. B. in a Southern homespun dress. She refused to take the oath—told him she gloried in being a rebel—had fought side by side with Southern *men* for Southern rights, and if she ever lived to see "Dixie" she would do it again. Butler denounced her as the most incorrigible she-rebel he had ever met with. By order of the Beast she was placed in confinement where she remained three months. Some time after her release, she was arrested for carrying on "contraband correspondence," and kept in a dungeon fourteen days on bread and water, at the expiration of which time she was placed in the State Prison as a dangerous enemy. Her husband, it so happened, was a Lieutenant in the 13th Conn. Regiment, and on duty as provost guard in the city. He accidentally found her out and asked if she wanted to see him. She sent word she never wanted to see him so long as he wore the Yankee uniform. But he forced himself upon her, tried to persuade her to take the oath, and get a release, when he said he would resign and take her to his relations in Connecticut. She indignantly spurned his proposition, and he left her to her fate. When Gen. Banks assumed command he released a great many prisoners, but kept her in confinement until the 17th of May last when she was sent across the lines to Meadesville with the registered enemies.

An article was recently published in the New York World in relation to the part Mrs. Williams has played in this war, but the above is, we are assured, a true account of her remarkable career. We understand she has attached herself to the medical staff of a brigade new in this city, and will render all the assistance in her power to the wounded in the approaching struggle for possession of the great Valley of the Mississippi.

JAMES R. SNEED: GEORGIA WOMEN RIOT AGAINST SHORTAGES

As prices soared, speculators preyed on civilians at home; as shortages grew worse, some Confederate women decided to take matters into their own hands. Bread riots occurred in several Southern cities, including the capital at Richmond. The women were frustrated at their inability to find food at affordable prices for their families and for the lack of government aid to the families of soldiers in the field. Large cities were not the only locales for these protests; hinterland towns were not immune to female unrest, either. The shortages could be accounted for in part by the impressment of goods for use by the military. The story below mentions the problem Georgia had had in 1861 with overpriced salt and is a reference to the shortage of salt experienced throughout the South during the war. Salt was an essential item for preserving meat, but because of the military demand for it, it was in short supply. Georgia Governor Joseph E. Brown, quite a Populist, had used state resources to acquire salt that could be distributed to poorer families at reasonable prices.

Savannah Republican, 13 April 1863

AMAZONIANS.—On Thursday and Friday last, feeble outbreaks of females armed with pistols and bowie knives, headed by a few vagabonds, were made in Augusta, Milledgeville and Columbus, in this State, for the purpose of helping themselves to merchandize at what they considered fair prices—all of which were promptly suppressed by the proper authorities.

The Columbus Sun, alluding to the affair in that city, says:

This is some of the legitimate fruits of what Gov. Brown is pleased to call "impressments" for the benefit of the *people*! It began in this state with that functionary, two years ago, in Atlanta, or other markets in Georgia, where salt was selling at ten and twelve dollars per sack, and has culminated in just such riots and lawless outbreaks as we witnessed in Columbus this morning.

AN ANONYMOUS REPORT: PATRIOTIC FEMALES MAINTAIN TELEGRAPH COMMUNICATION IN GEORGIA

Women did not limit their contributions to the war to merely nursing and sewing for the soldiers. Some undertook very practical, but very dangerous, chores, as did Mrs. Blackman and Miss Carrie Simms who did their best to ensure that the Confederate army in north Georgia did not lose its telegraphic communications, despite the efforts of Yankee raiders.

Memphis Appeal, 14 May 1864

PATRIOTIC FEMALES.—A correspondent of the APPEAL, a few days since, stated that when the party of Yankee raiders cut the telegraph wires between Resaca and Tilton, that two ladies, whose names he did not learn, united the wires, on the retreat of the foe. The *Intelligencer*, of yesterday, gives the following version of the occurrence, with the names of the noble women: "A portion of the enemy succeeded in getting to the railroad at Green's station, three miles above Resaca, and immediately set fire to the wood shed and cut the telegraph wire. Being apprehensive, no doubt, that they were risking their lives, they did not remain very long to enjoy the mischief they supposed they had done. As soon as they left, Mrs. Blackman and Miss Carrie Simms, daughters of Col. Henry L. Sims, who are living near, carried water and extinguished the burning wood shed, and then attempted to mend the telegraphic wire. Their strength was not sufficient to accomplish this feat; but still they continued their efforts until Capt. Clerk of our forces, came up, when, with his assistance, these patriotic ladies succeeded in drawing up and uniting the wires."

D. A. HOBBIE OR B. H. THRASHER: STORY OF YANKEES OUTWITTED BY A SLAVE

The following untitled tale is no doubt apocryphal and was probably meant as a joke on abolitionists. However, it had a second theme that was also important: the clever slave who bested a bunch of not-so-bright Yankees. Such stories were intended to play to Southern feelings of superiority over Northerners, but it is placed here because it reflects contemporary attitudes about blacks as well. After all, many Southerners believed, if a slave could outwit a Yankee, there could be no question that the Confederate army would easily whip the North's, should the Yankees be so stupid as to begin a war over secession.

Troy Southern Advertiser, 4 January 1861 (Troy, Ala.)

A short time ago, a widow lady living near the northern line of Missouri, sent her negro man with a load of wheat to a mill in Iowa, to have it manufactured into flour.—The mill was much crowded on his arrival there, and the prospect was that he would have to wait several days for "his turn."— While waiting, some of the "freedom shriekers" in that latitude got around the darkie and proposed aiding him in securing his freedom. The negro seemed to be struck with the idea but did not have any money to pay his expenses.

"Well," said they, "sell your mules."

"Dont know bout dat, missus couldn't get'long widout dem," said Cuff.

"Well, then," rejoined they, "you can sell the wagon, that will bring the money."

"Well, I believe, missus needs the wagon, too," answered the black, "but if I had de wheat ground, I could sell de flour, dat wud fetch de money."

"Oh, well," said the negro equalists, "we will swap you flour for your wheat to accommodate you."

So the trade was made. The wheat was exchanged for the proper portion of flour and the colored man was loaded all ready to drive off and sell his flower. But when he was about ready to start, he said, "Massa I's binstudyin bout freedom, but I don't believe missus can spare the flour either," and drove off with a grin, displaying two rows of ivory, much to the mortification of the negro-loving Iowains.

JAMES R. SNEED: DEDICATION OF FIRST AFRICAN BAPTIST CHURCH OF SAVANNAH

Religion was an important part of life for both Southern whites and blacks. The completion and dedication of a newly completed church for a black Baptist congregation was a significant community event that would be attended by representatives of all classes. Civic and religious activities of blacks, both free and slaves, got more coverage in the Confederate press than might be supposed.

Savannah Republican, 4 May 1861

FIRST AFRICAN BAPTIST CHURCH

The new and tasteful house of worship just finished by this congregation on Franklin Square, will be dedicated on Sabbath next, with appropriate exercises. To avoid interfering with the regular morning services of other congregations, some of whom wish to attend, the services will commence at 12 o'clock in the following order:

1st, Anthem by the Choir.
2d, prayer by Rev. D. G. Daniell.
3d, Reading Scriptures and Hymn by Rev. D. O. Tibeau.
4th, Sermon by Rev. S. Landrum.
5th, Dedicatory Prayer by Rev. S. G. Daniel, of Albany, Ga.
6th, Doxology and Benediction.

The building is of brick and contains a lecture room in the basement, and a main audience room above, with galleries on the sides and end. The audience will seat, comfortably, 700 persons. The house is neatly finished, plastered and painted. The pulpit is white and pews oaked, and the aisles covered with oil cloth. The house is provided with a good organ, which will be played on the occasion by a young lady of this city.

The cost of the building is a little over $10,000; about $1,500 still unpaid.

The Trustee, masters of the servants, citizens generally, and Baptists especially, are invited to attend the dedication, and to contribute to the payment of the debt.

JAMES R. SNEED: OUR FREE COLORED POPULATION

Free persons of color were in a difficult position when the Civil War broke out. There was considerable pressure for all Southerners, white and black, to fall in line and support the Confederate war effort. A number of free blacks did volunteer to aid the military, and it is an open question as to whether they did so out of Southern patriotism or because they believed they must in order to protect themselves and their families.

Savannah Republican, 11 June 1861

OUR FREE COLORED POPULATION

It is gratifying to witness the public spirit that rules among this class of our community. Not content to be idle spectators of the military operations progressing for the defense of the State against invasion, they have nobly come forward and offered their services, as will appear from the following written tender addressed to General Lawton:

TO BRIGADIER GEN. LAWTON,
Com. Military District.

The undersigned free men of color, residing in the city of Savannah, and county of Chatham, fully impressed with the feeling of duty we owe to the State of Georgia, as inhabitants thereof, which has for so long a period, extended to ourselves and families its protection, and has been to us the source of many benefits,

Beg leave respectfully, in this the hour of danger, to tender to yourself our services, to be employed in the defence of the State, at any place or point, at any time, or for any length of time, and in any service for which you may consider us best fitted, and in which we can contribute to the public good.

Signed by fifty-five free men of color.

The Commanding General promptly accepted their proposition, and yesterday fifty-five able bodied men embarked on board the steamer *Ida*, for the military works below the city. Their services are entirely voluntary without any stipulation for pay, and many more were ready to go, but as they constitute an important branch of our fire department, is was thought best not to spare them from the city.

Such bearing on the part of our colored population is worthy of all praise, and our authorities will doubtless see to it that they lose nothing by their devotion to their State and country.

D. A. HOBBIE OR B. H. THRASHER: MAINTAINING CONTROL OF SLAVES WHILE THE MEN ARE AWAY AT WAR

Despite the bravado about the loyalty of their slaves, there was much anxiety among Southerners regarding the bondsmen. A major concern was that so many men were away, serving in the army. That left women in charge of slaves, often large numbers of them, and the women themselves felt inadequate to meet the demands of motivating and disciplining their slaves. This editorial put those concerns into words.

Troy Southern Advertiser, 31 July 1861 (Troy, Ala.)

LOOK OUT.—It is very important at the present time for our citizens to keep a sharp watch over the slaves of the country. There is no knowing what is brewing among them. Almost every one knows something of the difficulty that is going on and has vague ideas as to the cause of it. Some no doubt suppose that old Abe is really coming South, having heard white men speaking in a jesting manner about his threatened visit to Richmond and Montgomery. And now men leaving our own part of the country and every one speaking of the battles that are being fought, the negroes may shape their dark imaginations into a belief that Lincoln is really advancing to Montgomery. There can be nothing wrong with taking care now that the country is being depopulated by men volunteering for the war. The absence of

men, will cause some negroes to feel a degree of importance, independence and restlessness, which they would not otherwise possess.—The negro who has always been obedient in the presence of his master, may in his absence become the most turbulent and disobedient. Add to this the knowledge of the negro—(for they are close observers of the movements and diligence of white men) that a careful watch of superintendence is not kept over them, and the probability of disobedience and turbulence is increased. Whereas if they discover that a sharp look out is kept over them they will be afraid to attempt or do many things they otherwise would do. We would not become alarmists but we wish to call the attention of our people to this thing so that due care may be taken of it.—A patrol, simply the knowledge of one's existence has a great influence on the slave, to keep him in his place. In some parts of the country, not even these are in existence. Every man should strictly

superintend his own premises during the present time. A little neglect might be the cause of much trouble. Let our citizens then look out.

HENRY CLEVELAND: TREATMENT OF SLAVES AND FREE BLACKS—MAY DAY PARTY FOR BLACK "ELITES"

An Augusta newspaper gave considerable space to the story of a May Day party for the "elite" of the local black society. It did so not because its editors believed the story deserved such coverage in and of itself but to use the story as an illustration of how slaves and free blacks were treated in the South. The party story ran only a few months after Lincoln's Emancipation Proclamation, and the paper specifically mentioned the Union president, saying it wished the Yankee administration could only see how closely Southern slaves resembled in dress and manners the "wage slaves" of the North. There was one major difference between the South's black slaves and the "wage slaves" of the North: One was free, and the other was not.

Augusta Constitutionalist, 3 May 1863 (Augusta, Ga.)

SABLE CORONATION

The "Americans of African descent" in our city had quite a novel and *recherche* entertainment on Friday night, at which the elite portion of our "colored siety" was out in full leather. The festival consisted of the coronation of a May Queen, a supper, and a dancing party. The affair was gotten up by permission from the authorities, with city officers in attendance. Every thing was done up *a la mode*. The addresses were rehearsed, and the queen wore her honors with a degree of taste and majesty that would have illustrated the court of the Queen of Dahoumey in her palmiest days. The court costumes were unexceptional—the muslins and tarles tons ethereal—the white kids immaculate—the wreaths gorgeous and of a redolence rivalling the native frangipane. The table groaned beneath a wealth of cakes and condiments that would tempt an epicure, and the wines—yes the wines—were pronounced by a testing committee of "buckra's" present, to be fragrant with the "boquet" of purity and age.

The dance was equally *au fad*; none of your Ethiopian fandangos, but such a combination of square dances and round dances, and squeezing dances, (we are ignorant of the technical

names) as would have met the admiration of Professor Nimbleheels, the dancing master.

But enough, perhaps some may say, too much, of this festival of the colored people. We allude to it to show the way in which the "poor slave" wears his chains in these days of scarcity and suffering. We wish Lincoln and his Cabinet could have looked on that happy throng, that they might have compared them with the deluded beings they are dragging from happy homes to the squalid want and degradation of a quasi freedom. Aye, that he might have compared them in dress and manners, or elasticity of spirit, with the working classes who cringe and fawn beneath his despotic rule.

The admission fee to this festival was $5, and woe to the darkey whose finances were not equal to the crisis. While we regard the frequent recurrence of negro balls in our city as mischievous, we see no objection to allowing them to hold occasional holiday festivals. They have always been the favorite pastimes of the slave, from the grotesque fandangos of the Gold Coast, to the diablerie of the "Dios de Reyes" in the West Indies. They are about the only people on this continent whose spirits are not bowed down with care or suffering, and who may with propriety and taste indulge in frivolous amusement.

RUTH RAYMOND: CONVERSATIONS WITH MY FEMALE FRIENDS—THE LIKELY CONSEQUENCES OF THE WAR FOR SOUTHERN WOMEN

The following is a truly amazing article for two reasons. First, it is one of only a handful of bylined articles located in any Confederate newspaper; second, it was written by a woman. Further, Ruth Raymond, the author, accurately predicted what the outcome of the Civil War would be for Southern women: an entirely new way of life where privilege and special status due to one's gender gave way to the realities of earning a living.

Darlington Southerner, 28 October 1864 (Darlington, S.C.)

CONVERSATIONS WITH MY FEMALE FRIENDS
BY RUTH RAYMOND
AN HONORABLE INDEPENDENCE

There is one fact, which sooner or later, our Southern women must look boldly in the face—and that is how they can best gain *an honorable independence.*—Hitherto, as a class, they have depended on the exertions of their male relatives, or looked to matrimony as a source of support. Many a woman sooner than exert herself in her own maintenance has married a man for whom she cared about as much as she did for the Emperor of China, nay, even whom she positively loathed. No wonder when matrimony is only a thing of convenience, and people rush into it utterly regardless of affection or congeniality, that we hear of so many unhappy matches, so much strife and selfishness, so little of the genuine sunshine of love. Better, far better is it for a woman to live a single life of honorable independence, supporting herself by her own exertions than thus to perjure herself by a loveless marriage; looking upon man not as a companion and friend, but as a disagreeable appendage to the purse strings, something which in taking the purse has to be taken with it. This is a degrading view certainly for women to take of the most sacred of all human connections.

The immense slaughter of our male population caused by this terrible war, has thrown many women on their own resources for a living. In the future, the women of the South must preponderate greatly over the males. Where will husbands be found for one third of them? The hope of marrying for a living, then, will be utterly cut off. The inroads of the enemy, too, upon our lands, and the immense destruction and capture of property, has deprived many a Southern woman of a comfortable home and support, and thrown her upon the cold charities of the world. Many a luxurious Southern girl, who dressed in velvet and diamonds, lived in a costly mansion, and was waited upon by liveried servants, now finds herself suddenly shorn of these bright possessions, and with the stern necessity of doing that from which her very soul recoils—gaining her own livelihood. But exiled royalty has had to do the same; and the struggle of the French Revolution threw the future of Queen of Holland, the beautiful Hortense into a milliners shop. With the prospect then before them of gaining their own living, the question naturally occurs how can the women of the South best meet the emergency before them? The one great idea now appears to be to rush into the "note department" in Columbia, where the work is light, and the pay good.—But as the services of *all* needy Southern women are not required in this charitable institution, many must necessarily be excluded. The times do not admit of new boarding-houses being opened, nothing then remains but teaching. The avenues of business for a woman, especially at

the South, are very few. At the North they have their female physicians, a class rapidly increasing, and much patronized by their own sex; female clerks are numerous, female writers, who gain support by their literary labors, and painters, who dare to compete in this field of labor with their brother artists. The School of Design, too, has by its instructions afforded women a pleasant means of subsistence. The women of the South are greatly restricted in their means of support. Perhaps the most common and the most useful is that of teaching. This opens a wide sphere of usefulness; and though I cannot see with a friend, who has been engaged many years in this honorable employment, "the poetry of teaching," it is not, at all events, the worse prose. There was a time—and I fervently pray that this time has forever past, when we thought that unless our young ladies were sent to the North to be educated, or we obtained Northern teachers for them, that they were not properly instructed. So well aware are the Yankees themselves of this fact, a fact disgraceful to the South, that they have never ceased to exultingly remind us of it. Now, why was this? Not that as a people we have not as much brains as those of the North, not that we have not sufficient intellectual force and training to fit us for good teachers, but because our Southern women refused to come before the world in this capacity. Sooner would they be a clog on some unwilling male relative, than thus shake off the iron shackles of dependence. They would rather sell themselves to some unworthy or unloved suitor than live a true, honest life of independence.

But our people are at fault here too. Whilst they encouraged Northern adventures, whilst they freely gave up their children to be influenced by Yankee teachers, home merit, home industry, was entirely overlooked, ignored, despised.—Whilst the Yankee teacher could count her pupils by the fifties, the Southern lady counted hers by the fives. Of course, discouraged, disappointed, she retired from the field, leaving it to her exultant rival; and her example proved a beacon-light to others. I say that I earnestly pray that the time for this prejudice has forever past, and that Southern people are prepared to recognize Southern talent, and encourage Southern industry.—If not, then we must make up our minds to continue in the future what we have been in the past, mere vessels and dependents of the North, looking to them for our goods, our literature, our education. There is no reason why we should not, indeed, there is every reason why we should, educate our own children. Let our women come out nobly and independently, and educate the youth of the land. Let all who feel themselves fitted for this work, and whose circumstances require an exertion on their part, exert their talents in this useful field. Let the women of the South be so educated, that it will be needless to encourage Yankee teachers. Let every exertion be made to educate thoroughly the girls of the present day, so that we may have properly qualified female teachers of our own—women, who whilst they are occupying an honorable and useful position, can yet be gaining a respectable livelyhood, an agreeable independence.

FURTHER READINGS

Bailey, Anne J., and Joslyn, Mauriel. *Valor and Lace: The Roles of Confederate Women, 1861–1865.* Murfreesboro, Tenn.: Southern Heritage Press, 1996.

Berlin, Ira. *Free at Last: A Documentary History of Slavery, Freedom, and the Civil War.* New York: New Press, 1992.

Blair, William Alan. *Virginia's Private War: Feeding Body and Soul in the Confederacy, 1861–1865.* New York: Oxford University Press, 1998.

Campbell, Edward D. C., and Rice, Kym S. (Eds.). *A Woman's War: Southern Women, Civil War, and the Confederate Legacy.* Richmond, Charlottesville: Museum of the Confederacy, University Press of Virginia, 1996.

Durden, Robert Franklin. *The Gray and the Black: The Confederate Debate on Emancipation.* Baton Rouge: Louisiana State University Press, 1972.

Faust, Drew Gilpin. *Mothers of Invention: Women of the Slaveholding South in the American Civil War.* Chapel Hill: University of North Carolina Press, 1996.

Jordan, Winthrop D. *Tumult and Silence at Second Creek: An Inquiry into a Civil War Slave Conspiracy.* Baton Rouge: Louisiana State University Press, 1993.

Leonard, Elizabeth D. *All the Daring of the Soldier: Women of the Civil War Armies.* New York: W. W. Norton, 1999.

McCline, John. *Slavery in the Clover Bottoms: John McCline's Narrative of His Life during Slavery and the Civil War.* Knoxville: University of Tennessee Press, 1998.

Moore, John Hammond. *Southern Homefront, 1861–1865.* Columbia, S.C.: Summerhouse Press, 1998.

Ransom, Roger L. *Conflict and Compromise: The Political Economy of Slavery, Emancipation, and the American Civil War.* New York: Cambridge University Press, 1989.

Vorenberg, Michael. *Final Freedom: The Civil War, the Abolition of Slavery, and the Thirteenth Amendment.* New York: Cambridge University Press, 2001.

Whites, Lee Ann. *Civil War as a Crisis in Gender: Augusta, Georgia, 1860–1890.* Athens: University of Georgia Press, 1995.

SELECTED BIBLIOGRAPHY

BOOKS

Abbott, A. O. *Prison Life in the South: At Richmond, Macon, Savannah, Charleston, Columbia, Charlotte, Raleigh, Goldsborough, and Andersonville, during the Years 1864 and 1865.* New York: Harper & Bros., 1865.

Alexander, Edward Porter. *Fighting for the Confederacy: The Personal Recollections of General Edward Porter Alexander.* Chapel Hill: University of North Carolina Press, 1989.

Alexander, Thomas B., and Beringer, Richard E. *The Anatomy of the Confederate Congress: A Study of the Influences of Member Characteristics on Legislative Voting Behavior, 1861–1865.* Nashville, Tenn.: Vanderbilt University Press, 1972.

Andrews, J. Culter. *The South Reports the Civil War.* Princeton, N.J.: Princeton University Press, 1970.

Ash, Stephen V. *When the Yankees Came: Conflict and Chaos in the Occupied South, 1861–1865.* Chapel Hill: University of North Carolina Press, 1995.

Bailey, Anne J. *The Chessboard of War: Sherman and Hood in the Autumn Campaigns of 1864.* Lincoln: University of Nebraska Press, 2000.

———. *War and Ruin: William T. Sherman and the Savannah Campaign.* Wilmington, Del.: Scholarly Resources, 2003.

Bell, Earl L., and Crabbe, Kenneth C. *The Augusta Chronicle: Indomitable Voice of Dixie, 1785–1960.* Athens: University of Georgia Press, 1960.

Berringer, Richard E.; Hattaway, Herman; Jones, Archer; and Still, William N., Jr. *The Elements of Confederate Defeat: Nationalism, War Aims and Religion.* Athens: University of Georgia Press, 1988.

———. *Why the South Lost the Civil War.* Athens: University of Georgia Press, 1986.

Black, Robert C., III. *The Railroads of the Confederacy.* Chapel Hill: University of North Carolina Press, 1952.

Bridges, Peter. *Pen of Fire: John Moncure Daniel.* Kent, Ohio: Kent State University Press, 2002.

Cardozo, John N. *Reminiscences of Charleston.* Charleston, S.C.: Joseph Walker, Agt., Stationer and Printer, 1866.

Carpenter, Jesse T. *The South as a Conscious Minority, 1789–1861.* Columbia: University of South Carolina Press, 1990.

Carter, Hodding. *Their Words Were Bullets: The Southern Press in War, Reconstruction and Peace.* Mercer University Lamar Memorial Lectures No. 12. Athens: University of Georgia Press, 1969.

Carter, Samuel. *The Final Fortress: The Campaign for Vicksburg, 1862–1863.* New York: St. Martin's Press, 1980.

Clark, Thomas D. *The Southern Country Editor.* Columbia: University of South Carolina Press, 1991.

Cooper, William C. *Jefferson Davis: American.* New York: Knopf, 2000.

Cozzens, Peter. *The Shipwreck of Their Hopes: The Battles for Chattanooga.* Urbana: University of Illinois Press, 1994.

———. *This Terrible Sound: The Battle of Chickamauga.* Urbana: University of Illinois Press, 1992.

Daniel, Larry J. *Soldiering in the Army of Tennessee: A Portrait of Life in a Confederate Army.* Chapel Hill: University of North Carolina Press, 1991.

Davis, Stephen. *Atlanta Will Fall: Sherman, Joe Johnston, and the Yankee Heavy Battalions.* Wilmington, Del.: Scholarly Resources, 2001.

Davis, William C. *Brother against Brother: The War Begins.* Alexandria, Va.: Time-Life Books, 1983.

———. *First Blood: Fort Sumter to Bull Run.* Alexandria, Va.: Time-Life Books, 1983.

———. *"A Government of Our Own": The Making of the Confederacy.* Baton Rouge: Louisiana State University Press, 1994.

———. *An Honorable Defeat: The Last Days of the Confederate Government.* New York: Harcourt, 2001.

———. *Look Away: A History of the Confederate States of America.* New York: Free Press, 2002.

———. *The Union That Shaped the Confederacy: Robert Toombs and Alexander H. Stephens.* Lawrence: University of Kansas Press, 2001.

DeLeon, Thomas Cooper. *Four Years in Rebel Capitals.* Mobile, Ala.: Gossip Press, 1890.

Durden, Robert F. *The Self-Inflicted Wound: Southern Politics in the 19th Century.* Lexington: University of Kentucky Press, 1985.

East, Charles. *Sarah Morgan: The Civil War Diary of a Southern Woman.* New York: Simon & Schuster, 1991.

Eaton, Clement. *A History of the Southern Confederacy.* New York: Macmillan, 1956.

———. *Jefferson Davis.* New York: Free Press, 1977.

Elkins, Stanley M. *Slavery: A Problem in American Institutional Life.* 3rd ed. Chicago: University of Chicago Press, 1976.

Elliott, Robert Neal, Jr. *The Raleigh Register, 1799–1863.* Chapel Hill: University of North Carolina Press, 1955.

Escott, Paul D. *After Secession: Jefferson Davis and the Failure of Confederate Nationalism.* Baton Rouge: Louisiana State University Press, 1978.

Faust, Drew Gilpin. *The Creation of Confederate Nationalism.* Baton Rouge: Louisiana State University Press, 1989.

Gallagher, Gary. *The American Civil War: The War in the East, 1861–May 1863.* Oxford, United Kingdom: Osprey, 2001.

———. *The Confederate War: How Popular Will, Nationalism and Military Strategy Could Not Stave Off Defeat.* Cambridge: Harvard University Press, 1997.

———. *Lee and His Army in Confederate History.* Chapel Hill: University of North Carolina Press, 1997.

———. *The Myth of the Lost Cause and Civil War History.* Bloomington: Indiana University Press, 2001.

————. *The Wilderness Campaign*. Chapel Hill: University of North Carolina Press, 1997.

Genovese, Eugene D. *The Political Economy of Slavery: Studies in the Economy and Society of the Slave South*. New York: Pantheon Books, 1965.

Gibson, John M. Gibso. *Those 163 Days: A Southern Account of Sherman's March from Atlanta to Raleigh*. New York: Coward-McCann, 1961.

Greene, A. Wilson. *Breaking the Backbone of the Rebellion: The Final Battles of the Petersburg Campaign*. Mason City, Iowa: Sawas, 2000.

Griffith, Louis Turner, and Talmadge, John Erwin. *Georgia Journalism, 1763–1950*. Athens: University of Georgia Press, 1951.

Grimsley, Mark. *The Hard Hand of War: Union Military Policy toward Southern Civilians, 1861–1865*. New York: Cambridge University Press, 1995.

Grimsley, Mark, and Rogers, Clifford J. *Civilians in the Path of War*. Lincoln: University of Nebraska Press, 2002.

Grimsley, Mark, and Simpson, Brooks D. *The Collapse of the Confederacy*. Lincoln: University of Nebraska Press, 2001.

Hattaway, Herman, and Beringer, Richard E. *Jefferson Davis, Confederate President*. Lawrence: University Press of Kansas, 2002.

Hennessy, John J. *Return to Bull Run: The Campaign and Battle of Second Manassas*. New York: Simon & Schuster, 1993.

Hess, Earl J. *Banners to the Breeze: The Kentucky Campaign, Corinth, and Stones River*. Lincoln: University of Nebraska Press, 2000.

Huntzicker, William E. *The Popular Press, 1833–1865*. Westport, Conn.: Greenwood Press, 1994.

Jones, Charles Colcock. *The Siege of Savannah in December 1864, and the Confederate Operations in Georgia and the Third Military District of South Carolina during General Sherman's March from Atlanta to the Sea*. Albany, N.Y.: J. Munsell, 1874.

King, William L. *The Newspaper Press of Charleston, S.C.: A Chronological and Biographical History, Embracing a Period of One Hundred and Forty Years*. Charleston, S.C.: Edward Perry Book Press, 1872.

McDonough, James L. *Chattanooga—A Death Grip on the Confederacy*. Knoxville: University of Tennessee Press, 1984.

————. *Five Tragic Hours: The Battle of Franklin*. Knoxville: University of Tennessee Press, 1983.

————. *Shiloh, in Hell before Night*. Knoxville: University of Tennessee Press, 1977.

————. *Stones River—Bloody Winter in Tennessee*. Knoxville: University of Tennessee Press, 1980.

McPherson, James M., and Cooper, William J. *Writing the Civil War: The Quest to Understand*. Columbia: University of South Carolina Press, 1998.

Mohr, Clarence L. *On the Threshold of Freedom: Masters and Slaves in Civil War Georgia*. Athens: University of Georgia Press, 1986.

Moore, Albert B. *Conscription and Conflict in the Confederacy*. New York: Macmillan, 1924.

Moore, John Hammond. *Southern Homefront, 1861–1865*. Columbia, S.C.: Summerhouse Press, 1998.

Neely, Mark. *Southern Rights: Political Prisoners and the Myth of Confederate Constitutionalism*. Charlottesville: University of Virginia Press, 1999.

Osthaus, Carl R. *Partisans of the Southern Press: Editorial Spokesmen of the Nineteenth Century*. Lexington: University of Kentucky Press, 1994.

Putnam, Sallie Brock. *Richmond during the War: Four Years of Personal Observations*. Introduction by Virginia Scharff. Lincoln: University of Nebraska Press, 1996.

Rable, George C. *Civil Wars: Women and the Crisis of Southern Nationalism*. Urbana: University of Illinois Press, 1989.

————. *The Confederate Republic: A Revolution against Politics*. Chapel Hill: University of North Carolina Press, 1994.

Ramsdell, Charles V. *Behind the Lines in the Southern Confederacy*. Baton Rouge: Louisiana State University Press, 1944.

Reasoner, James. *Savannah*. Nashville, Tenn.: Cumberland House, 2003.

Reynolds, Donald E. *Editors Make War: Southern Newspapers in the Secession Crisis*. Nashville, Tenn.: Vanderbilt University Press, 1970.

————. *Southern Newspapers in the Secession Crisis*. Nashville, Tenn.: Vanderbilt University Press, 1966.

Rhea, Gordon C. *Cold Harbor: Grant and Lee, May 26–June 3, 1864*. Baton Rouge: Louisiana State University Press, 2002.

Ringold, Mary Spencer. *The Role of the State Legislatures in the Confederacy*. Athens: University of Georgia Press, 1966.

Robinson, William M., Jr. *Justice in Grey: A History of the Judicial System of the Confederate States of America*. Cambridge: Harvard University Press, 1968.

Sachsman, David B.; Rushing, S. Kittrell; and van Tuyll, Debra Reddin (Eds.). *The Civil War and the Press*. New Brunswick, N.J.: Transaction Publishers, 2000.

Sass, Herbert Ravenel. *Outspoken: 150 Years of the News and Courier*. Columbia: University of South Carolina Press, 1953.

Smith, Culver H. *The Press, Politics and Patronage: The American Government's Use of Newspapers, 1789–1875*. Athens: University of Georgia Press, 1977.

Soley, James Russell. *The Blockade and the Cruisers*. New York: C. Scribner's, 1883.

Spencer, Cornelia Phillips. *The Last Ninety Days of the War in North Carolina*. New York: Watchman Publishing, 1866; reprint, Wilmington, N.C.: Broadfoot Publishing, 1993.

Tatum, Georgia Lee. *Disloyalty in the Confederacy*. Chapel Hill: University of North Carolina Press, 1934.

Turner, George Edgar. *Victory Rode the Rails: The Strategic Place of Railroads in the Civil War*. Indianapolis, Ind.: Bobbs-Merrill, 1953.

Wagner, Margaret E., and Gallagher, Gary. *The Library of Congress Civil War Desk Reference*. New York: Simon & Schuster, 2002.

Wheeler, Richard. *On Fields of Fury: From the Wilderness to the Crater, an Eyewitness History*. New York: HarperCollins, 1991.

White, Laura. *Robert Barnwell Rhett: Father of Secession*. Gloucester, Mass.: Peter Smith, 1965.

Woodward, C. Vann. *Mary Chesnut's Civil War*. New Haven, Conn.: Yale University Press, 1983.

Woodworth, Steven E. *Cultures in Conflict—The American Civil War*. Westport, Conn.: Greenwood Press, 2000.

THE SOUTHERN PRESS

Abbeville Press (Abbeville, S.C.)

Alabama Beacon (Greensboro, Ala.)

Albany Patriot (Albany, Ga.)

Anderson Intelligencer (Anderson, S.C.)

Athens Southern Banner (Athens, Ga.)

Athens Southern Watchman (Athens, Ga.)

Atlanta Intelligencer

Atlanta Southern Confederacy (Atlanta, Ga.)

Augusta Chronicle and Sentinel (Augusta, Ga.)

Augusta Constitutionalist (Augusta, Ga.)

Augusta Evening Dispatch
Cahaba Gazette (Cahaba, Ala.)
Carolina Spartan
Central Georgian (Sandersville, Ga.)
Charleston Courier
Charleston Evening News
Charleston Mercury
Charlotte Western Democrat
Chattanooga Rebel
Columbia South Carolinian
Columbus Enquirer (Columbus, Ga.)
Columbus Sun (Columbus, Ga.)
Daily Morning News (Savannah, Ga.)
Darlington Southerner (Darlington, S.C.)
Edgefield Advertiser (Edgefield, S.C.)
Greensborough Patriot (Greensborough, N.C.)
Greenville Southern Enterprise (Greenville, S.C.)
Hillsborough Recorder (Hillsborough, N.C.)
Live Giraffe (Raleigh, N.C.)
Macon Telegraph and Confederate
Memphis Appeal
Milledgeville Confederate Union (Milledgeville, Ga.)
The Mississippian
Mobile Advertiser and Register
Montgomery Mail (Montgomery, Tenn.)
New Orleans Delta
New Orleans Picayune
New York Herald
New York Times
Raleigh Standard
Raleigh Weekly Standard
Richmond Dispatch
Richmond Examiner
Richmond Sentinel
Richmond Whig
Rome True Flag (Rome, Ga.)
Sandersville Central Georgian
Savannah Daily Morning News
Savannah Republican
Selma Reporter (Selma, Ala.)
Troy Southern Advertiser (Troy, Ala.)
Western Democrat (Charlotte, N.C.)

WEB SITES

The American Civil War Home Page. http://sunsite.utk.edu/civil-war. U.S. Civil War Center. http://www.cwc.lsu.edu.
The Avalon Project at Yale Law School: Confederate States of America Documents. http://www.yale.edu/lawweb/avalon/csa/csapage.htm.
The Civil War Home Page. http://www.civil-war.net.

Civil War Maps. http://memory.loc.gov/ammem/gmdhtml/cwmhtml/cwmhome.html.

Civil War Women: Primary Sources on the Internet. http://scriptorium.lib.duke.edu/women/cwdocs.html.

The History Place: The U.S. Civil War, 1861–1865. http://www.historyplace.com/civilwar.

Journal of the Congress of the Confederate States of America, 1861–1865. http://www.yale.edu/lawweb/avalon/csa/csapage.htm.

Selected Civil War Photographs. http://memory.loc.gov/ammem/cwphtml/cwphome.html.

The Valley of the Shadow. http://valley.vcdh.virginia.edu.